# Complete Solutions Manual

# Precalculus
## Functions and Graphs

### TWELFTH EDITION

## Earl W Swokowski
late of Marquette University

## Jeffery A Cole
Anoka-Ramsey Community College

Prepared by

## Jeffery A Cole
Anoka-Ramsey Community College

## BROOKS/COLE
CENGAGE Learning™

Australia • Brazil • Japan • Korea • Mexico • Singapore • Spain • United Kingdom • United States

# Preface

This manual contains solutions/answers to all exercises in the text *Precalculus: Functions and Graphs, Twelfth Edition*, by Earl W. Swokowski and Jeffery A. Cole. A *Student's Solutions Manual* is also available; it contains solutions for the odd-numbered exercises in each section and for the Discussion Exercises, as well as solutions for all the exercises in the Review Sections and for the Chapter Tests.

For most problems, a reasonably detailed solution is included. It is my hope that by merely browsing through the solutions, professors will save time in determining appropriate assignments for their particular class.

I appreciate feedback concerning errors, solution correctness or style, and manual style— comments from professors using previous editions have greatly strengthened the ancillary package as well as the text. Any comments may be sent directly to me at the address below, at jeff.cole@anokaramsey.edu, or in care of the publisher: Brooks/Cole|Cengage Learning, 20 Davis Drive, Belmont, CA 94002-3098.

I would like to thank: Marv Riedesel and Mary Johnson for accuracy checking of the new exercises; Andrew Bulman-Fleming, for manuscript preparation; Brian Morris and the late George Morris, of Scientific Illustrators, for creating the mathematically precise art package; and Cynthia Ashton, of Cengage Learning, for checking the manuscript. I dedicate this book to my children, Becky and Brad.

Jeffery A. Cole

Anoka-Ramsey Community College

11200 Mississippi Blvd. NW

Coon Rapids, MN 55433

# Table of Contents

# Table of Contents

# Table of Contents

# To the Instructor

In the chapter review sections, the solutions are abbreviated since more detailed solutions were given in chapter sections. In easier groups of exercises, representative solutions are shown. When appropriate, only the answer is listed.

All figures have been plotted using computer software, offering a high degree of precision. The calculator graphs are from various TI screens. When possible, we tried to make each piece of art with the same scale to show a realistic and consistent graph.

This manual was done using $\mathbb{EXP}$: *The Scientific Word Processor*.

The following <u>notations</u> are used in the manual.

*Note:* Notes to the instructor/student pertaining to hints on instruction or conventions to follow.

| | |
|---|---|
| { } | { comments to the reader are in braces } |
| LS | { Left Side of an equation } |
| RS | { Right Side of an equation } |
| $\Rightarrow$ | { implies, next equation, logically follows } |
| $\Leftrightarrow$ | { if and only if, is equivalent to } |
| $\bullet$ | { bullet, used to separate problem statement from solution or explanation } |
| $\star$ | { used to identify the answer to the problem } |
| $\S$ | { *section* references } |
| $\forall$ | { For all, i.e., $\forall x$ means "for all $x$". } |
| $\mathbb{R} - \{a\}$ | { The set of all real numbers except $a$. } |
| $\therefore$ | { therefore } |
| QI–QIV | { quadrants I, II, III, IV } |

# To the Instructor

In the chapter reviews sections, the solutions are abbreviated since more detailed solutions were given in chapter sections. In easier groups of exercises, representative solutions are shown. When appropriate, only the answer is listed.

All figures have been plotted using computer software, offering a high degree of precision. The calculator graphs are from various TI screens. When possible, we tried to make each piece of art with the same scale to show a realistic and consistent graph.

This manual was done using LATEX Scientific Word Processor.

The following notations are used in the manual.

Note: Notes to the instructor/student pertaining to hints on instruction or conventions to follow.

| | |
|---|---|
| { } | { comments to the reader are in braces } |
| LS | { Left Side of an equation } |
| RS | { Right Side of an equation } |
| ⇒ | { implies, next equation logically follows } |
| ⇔ | { if and only if, is equivalent to } |
| • | { bullet, used to separate problem statement from solution or explanation } |
| ★ | { used to identify the answer to the problem } |
| | { section references } |
| ∀x | { For all x, "∀" means "for all x" } |
| R − {a} | { The set of all real numbers except a } |
| ∴ | { therefore } |
| QI–QIV | { Quadrants I, II, III, IV } |

## 1.1 Exercises

1. (a) Since $x$ and $y$ have opposite signs, the product $xy$ is negative.

   (b) Since $x^2 > 0$ and $y > 0$, the product $x^2 y$ is positive.

   (c) Since $x < 0$ {$x$ is negative} and $y > 0$ {$y$ is positive}, the quotient $\dfrac{x}{y}$ is negative.

   Thus, $\dfrac{x}{y} + x$ is the sum of two negatives, which is negative.

   (d) Since $y > 0$ and $x < 0$, $y - x > 0$.

2. (a) Since $x$ and $y$ have opposite signs, the quotient $\dfrac{x}{y}$ is negative.

   (b) Since $x < 0$ and $y^2 > 0$, the product $xy^2$ is negative.

   (c) Since $x - y < 0$ and $xy < 0$, $\dfrac{x - y}{xy} > 0$.      (d) Since $y > 0$ and $y - x > 0$, $y(y - x) > 0$.

3. (a) Since $-7$ is to the left of $-4$ on a coordinate line, $-7\boxed{<}-4$.

   (b) Using a calculator, we see that $\frac{\pi}{2} \approx 1.57$. Hence, $\frac{\pi}{2}\boxed{>}1.5$. (c) $\sqrt{225}\boxed{=}15$ **Note:** $\sqrt{225} \neq \pm 15$

4. (a) Since $-3$ is to the right of $-6$ on a coordinate line, $-3\boxed{>}-6$.

   (b) Using a calculator, we see that $\frac{\pi}{4} \approx 0.79$. Hence, $\frac{\pi}{4}\boxed{<}0.8$. (c) $\sqrt{289}\boxed{=}17$ **Note:** $\sqrt{289} \neq \pm 17$

5. (a) Since $\frac{1}{11} = 0.\overline{09} = 0.0909\ldots$, $\frac{1}{11}\boxed{>}0.09$.      (b) Since $\frac{2}{3} = 0.\overline{6} = 0.6666\ldots$, $\frac{2}{3}\boxed{>}0.666$.

   (c) Since $\frac{22}{7} = 3.\overline{142857}$ and $\pi \approx 3.141593$, $\frac{22}{7}\boxed{>}\pi$.

6. (a) Since $\frac{1}{7} = 0.\overline{142857}$, $\frac{1}{7}\boxed{<}0.143$.      (b) Since $\frac{5}{6} = 0.8\overline{3} = 0.8333\ldots$, $\frac{5}{6}\boxed{>}0.833$.

   (c) Since $\sqrt{2} \approx 1.414$, $\sqrt{2}\boxed{>}1.4$.

7. (a) "$x$ is negative" is equivalent to $x < 0$. We symbolize this by writing "$x$ is negative $\Leftrightarrow x < 0$."

   (b) $y$ is nonnegative $\Leftrightarrow y \geq 0$      (c) $q$ is less than or equal to $\pi \Leftrightarrow q \leq \pi$

   (d) $d$ is between 4 and 2 $\Leftrightarrow 2 < d < 4$      (e) $t$ is not less than 5 $\Leftrightarrow t \geq 5$

   (f) The negative of $z$ is not greater than 3 $\Leftrightarrow -z \leq 3$

   (g) The quotient of $p$ and $q$ is at most 7 $\Leftrightarrow \dfrac{p}{q} \leq 7$      (h) The reciprocal of $w$ is at least 9 $\Leftrightarrow \dfrac{1}{w} \geq 9$

   (i) The absolute value of $x$ is greater than 7 $\Leftrightarrow |x| > 7$

**Note:** An informal definition of absolute value that may be helpful is

$$|something| = \begin{cases} itself & \text{if } itself \text{ is positive or zero} \\ -(itself) & \text{if } itself \text{ is negative} \end{cases}$$

8. (a) $b$ is positive $\Leftrightarrow b > 0$      (b) $s$ is nonpositive $\Leftrightarrow s \leq 0$

   (c) $w$ is greater than or equal to $-4 \Leftrightarrow w \geq -4$

(d) $c$ is between $\frac{1}{5}$ and $\frac{1}{3}$ $\Leftrightarrow$ $\frac{1}{5} < c < \frac{1}{3}$　　　　(e) $p$ is not greater than $-2$ $\Leftrightarrow$ $p \leq -2$

(f) The negative of $m$ is not less than $-2$ $\Leftrightarrow$ $-m \geq -2$

(g) The quotient of $r$ and $s$ is at least $\frac{1}{5}$ $\Leftrightarrow$ $\frac{r}{s} \geq \frac{1}{5}$　　　(h) The reciprocal of $f$ is at most $14$ $\Leftrightarrow$ $\frac{1}{f} \leq 14$

(i) The absolute value of $x$ is less than $4$ $\Leftrightarrow$ $|x| < 4$

$\boxed{9}$ (a) $|-3 - 4| = |-7| = -(-7)\ \{\text{since}\ -7 < 0\} = 7$

(b) $|-5| - |2| = -(-5) - 2 = 5 - 2 = 3$　　　(c) $|7| + |-4| = 7 + [-(-4)] = 7 + 4 = 11$

$\boxed{10}$ (a) $|-11 + 1| = |-10| = -(-10)\ \{\text{since}\ -10 < 0\} = 10$

(b) $|6| - |-3| = 6 - [-(-3)] = 6 - 3 = 3$　　　(c) $|8| + |-9| = 8 + [-(-9)] = 8 + 9 = 17$

$\boxed{11}$ (a) $(-5)|3 - 6| = (-5)|-3| = (-5)[-(-3)] = (-5)(3) = -15$

(b) $|-6|/(-2) = -(-6)/(-2) = 6/(-2) = -3$　　　(c) $|-7| + |4| = -(-7) + 4 = 7 + 4 = 11$

$\boxed{12}$ (a) $(4)|6 - 7| = (4)|-1| = (4)[-(-1)] = (4)(1) = 4$

(b) $5/|-2| = 5/[-(-2)] = 5/2$　　　(c) $|-1| + |-9| = -(-1) + [-(-9)] = 1 + 9 = 10$

$\boxed{13}$ (a) Since $(4 - \pi)$ is positive, $|4 - \pi| = 4 - \pi$.

(b) Since $(\pi - 4)$ is negative, $|\pi - 4| = -(\pi - 4) = 4 - \pi$.

(c) Since $\left(\sqrt{2} - 1.5\right)$ is negative, $\left|\sqrt{2} - 1.5\right| = -\left(\sqrt{2} - 1.5\right) = 1.5 - \sqrt{2}$.

$\boxed{14}$ (a) Since $\left(\sqrt{3} - 1.7\right)$ is positive, $\left|\sqrt{3} - 1.7\right| = \sqrt{3} - 1.7$.

(b) Since $\left(1.7 - \sqrt{3}\right)$ is negative, $\left|1.7 - \sqrt{3}\right| = -\left(1.7 - \sqrt{3}\right) = \sqrt{3} - 1.7$.

(c) $\left|\frac{1}{5} - \frac{1}{3}\right| = \left|\frac{3}{15} - \frac{5}{15}\right| = \left|-\frac{2}{15}\right| = -\left(-\frac{2}{15}\right) = \frac{2}{15}$

$\boxed{15}$ (a) $d(A, B) = |7 - 3| = |4| = 4$　　　(b) $d(B, C) = |-5 - 7| = |-12| = 12$

(c) $d(C, B) = d(B, C) = 12$　　　(d) $d(A, C) = |-5 - 3| = |-8| = 8$

$\boxed{16}$ (a) $d(A, B) = |-2 - (-6)| = |4| = 4$　　　(b) $d(B, C) = |4 - (-2)| = |6| = 6$

(c) $d(C, B) = d(B, C) = 6$　　　(d) $d(A, C) = |4 - (-6)| = |10| = 10$

$\boxed{17}$ (a) $d(A, B) = |1 - (-9)| = |10| = 10$　　　(b) $d(B, C) = |10 - 1| = |9| = 9$

(c) $d(C, B) = d(B, C) = 9$　　　(d) $d(A, C) = |10 - (-9)| = |19| = 19$

$\boxed{18}$ (a) $d(A, B) = |-4 - 8| = |-12| = 12$　　　(b) $d(B, C) = |-1 - (-4)| = |3| = 3$

(c) $d(C, B) = d(B, C) = 3$　　　(d) $d(A, C) = |-1 - 8| = |-9| = 9$

**Note:** Because $|a| = |-a|$, the answers to Exercises 19–24 could have a different form. For example, $|-3 - x| \geq 8$ is equivalent to $|x + 3| \geq 8$.

$\boxed{19}$ $A = x$ and $B = 7$, so $d(A, B) = |7 - x|$. Thus, "$d(A, B)$ is less than $2$" can be written as $|7 - x| < 2$.

$\boxed{20}$ $d(A, B) = \left|-\sqrt{2} - x\right|$ $\Rightarrow$ $\left|-\sqrt{2} - x\right| > 1$

$\boxed{21}$ $d(A, B) = |-3 - x|$ $\Rightarrow$ $|-3 - x| \geq 8$　　　$\boxed{22}$ $d(A, B) = |4 - x|$ $\Rightarrow$ $|4 - x| \leq 5$

**23** $d(A, B) = |x - 4| \Rightarrow |x - 4| \le 3$      **24** $d(A, B) = |x - (-2)| = |x + 2| \Rightarrow |x + 2| \ge 4$

*Note:* In Exercises 25–32, you may want to substitute a permissible value for the variable to first test if the expression inside the absolute value symbol is positive or negative.

**25** Pick an arbitrary value for $x$ that is less than $-3$, say $-5$.

Since $3 + (-5) = -2$ is negative, we conclude that if $x < -3$, then $3 + x$ is negative.

Hence, $|3 + x| = -(3 + x) = -x - 3$.

**26** If $x > 5$, then $5 - x < 0$, and $|5 - x| = -(5 - x) = x - 5$.

**27** If $x < 2$, then $2 - x > 0$, and $|2 - x| = 2 - x$.

**28** If $x \ge -7$, then $7 + x \ge 0$, and $|7 + x| = 7 + x$.

**29** If $a < b$, then $a - b < 0$, and $|a - b| = -(a - b) = b - a$.

**30** If $a > b$, then $a - b > 0$, and $|a - b| = a - b$.

**31** Since $x^2 + 4 > 0$ for every $x$, $|x^2 + 4| = x^2 + 4$.

**32** Since $-x^2 - 1 < 0$ for every $x$, $|-x^2 - 1| = -(-x^2 - 1) = x^2 + 1$.

**33** LS $= \dfrac{ab + ac}{a} = \dfrac{ab}{a} + \dfrac{ac}{a} = b + c \boxed{\ne}$ RS (which is $b + ac$).

**34** LS $= \dfrac{ab + ac}{a} = \dfrac{ab}{a} + \dfrac{ac}{a} = b + c \boxed{=}$ RS.

**35** LS $= \dfrac{b + c}{a} = \dfrac{b}{a} + \dfrac{c}{a} \boxed{=}$ RS.

**36** LS $= \dfrac{a + c}{b + d} = \dfrac{a}{b + d} + \dfrac{c}{b + d} \boxed{\ne}$ RS $\left(\text{which is } \dfrac{a}{b} + \dfrac{c}{d}\right)$.

**37** LS $= (a \div b) \div c = \dfrac{a}{b} \cdot \dfrac{1}{c} = \dfrac{a}{bc}$. RS $= a \div (b \div c) = a \div \dfrac{b}{c} = a \cdot \dfrac{c}{b} = \dfrac{ac}{b}$. LS $\boxed{\ne}$ RS

**38** LS $= (a - b) - c = a - b - c$. RS $= a - (b - c) = a - b + c$. LS $\boxed{\ne}$ RS

**39** LS $= \dfrac{a - b}{b - a} = \dfrac{-(b - a)}{b - a} = -1 \boxed{=}$ RS.

**40** LS $= -(a + b) = -a - b \boxed{\ne}$ RS (which is $-a + b$).

**41** (a) On the TI-83/4 Plus, the absolute value function is choice 1 under MATH, NUM.

Enter abs(3.2^2-$\sqrt{}$(4.27)). $\left|3.2^2 - \sqrt{4.27}\right| \approx 8.1736$

     (b) $\sqrt{(15.6 - 1.5)^2 + (4.3 - 5.4)^2} \approx 14.1428$

**42** (a) $\dfrac{3.42 - 1.29}{5.83 + 2.64} \approx 0.2515$      (b) $\pi^3 \approx 31.0063$

**43** (a) $\dfrac{1.2 \times 10^3}{3.1 \times 10^2 + 1.52 \times 10^3} \approx 0.6557 = 6.557 \times 10^{-1}$

*Note:* For the TI-83/4 Plus, use 1.2E3/(3.1E2 + 1.52E3), where E is obtained by pressing $\boxed{\text{2nd}}$ $\boxed{\text{EE}}$.

     (b) $(1.23 \times 10^{-4}) + \sqrt{4.5 \times 10^3} \approx 67.08 = 6.708 \times 10^1$

**44** (a) $\sqrt{|3.45 - 1.2 \times 10^4| + 10^5} \approx 334.7 = 3.347 \times 10^2$

(b) $(1.79 \times 10^2) \times (9.84 \times 10^3) = 1{,}761{,}360 \approx 1.761 \times 10^6$

**45** Construct a right triangle with sides of lengths $\sqrt{2}$ and 1. The hypotenuse will have length $\sqrt{\left(\sqrt{2}\right)^2 + 1^2} = \sqrt{3}$.

Next construct a right triangle with sides of lengths $\sqrt{3}$ and $\sqrt{2}$. The hypotenuse will have length $\sqrt{\left(\sqrt{3}\right)^2 + \left(\sqrt{2}\right)^2} = \sqrt{5}$.

**46** Use $C = 2\pi r$ with $r = 1, 2$, and 10 to obtain $2\pi$, $4\pi$, and $20\pi$ units from the origin.

**47** The large rectangle has area $= \text{width} \times \text{length} = a(b + c)$. The sum of the areas of the two small rectangles is $ab + ac$. Since the areas are the same, we have $a(b + c) = ab + ac$.

**48** $x_1 = \dfrac{3}{2}$ and $n = 2 \;\Rightarrow\; x_2 = \dfrac{1}{2}\left(x_1 + \dfrac{n}{x_1}\right) = \dfrac{1}{2}\left(\dfrac{3}{2} + \dfrac{2}{\frac{3}{2}}\right) = \dfrac{1}{2}\left(\dfrac{3}{2} + \dfrac{4}{3}\right) = \dfrac{1}{2}\left(\dfrac{17}{6}\right) = \dfrac{17}{12}$.

$$x_3 = \dfrac{1}{2}\left(x_2 + \dfrac{2}{x_2}\right) = \dfrac{1}{2}\left(\dfrac{17}{12} + \dfrac{2}{\frac{17}{12}}\right) = \dfrac{1}{2}\left(\dfrac{17}{12} + \dfrac{24}{17}\right) = \dfrac{1}{2}\left(\dfrac{577}{204}\right) = \dfrac{577}{408}$$

**49** (a) Since the decimal point is 5 places to the right of the first nonzero digit, $427{,}000 = 4.27 \times 10^5$.

(b) Since the decimal point is 8 places to the left of the first nonzero digit, $0.000\,000\,093 = 9.3 \times 10^{-8}$.

(c) Since the decimal point is 8 places to the right of the first nonzero digit, $810{,}000{,}000 = 8.1 \times 10^8$.

**50** (a) $85{,}200 = 8.52 \times 10^4$                        (b) $0.000\,005\,4 = 5.4 \times 10^{-6}$

(c) $24{,}900{,}000 = 2.49 \times 10^7$

**51** (a) Moving the decimal point 5 places to the right, we have $8.3 \times 10^5 = 830{,}000$.

(b) Moving the decimal point 12 places to the left, we have $2.9 \times 10^{-12} = 0.000\,000\,000\,002\,9$.

(c) Moving the decimal point 8 places to the right, we have $5.64 \times 10^8 = 564{,}000{,}000$.

**52** (a) $2.3 \times 10^7 = 23{,}000{,}000$                        (b) $7.01 \times 10^{-9} = 0.000\,000\,007\,01$

(c) $1.25 \times 10^{10} = 12{,}500{,}000{,}000$

**53** Since the decimal point is 24 places to the left of the first nonzero digit,

$$0.000\,000\,000\,000\,000\,000\,000\,001\,7 = 1.7 \times 10^{-24}.$$

**54** $9.1 \times 10^{-31} = 0.000\,000\,000\,000\,000\,000\,000\,000\,000\,000\,91$

**55** It is helpful to write the units of any fraction, and then "cancel" those units to determine the units of the final answer. $\dfrac{186{,}000 \text{ miles}}{\text{second}} \cdot \dfrac{60 \text{ seconds}}{1 \text{ minute}} \cdot \dfrac{60 \text{ minutes}}{1 \text{ hour}} \cdot \dfrac{24 \text{ hours}}{1 \text{ day}} \cdot \dfrac{365 \text{ days}}{1 \text{ year}} \cdot 1 \text{ year} \approx 5.87 \times 10^{12} \text{ mi}$

**56** (a) 100 billion $= 100{,}000{,}000{,}000 = 1 \times 10^{11}$

(b) $d \approx (100{,}000 \text{ yr})\left(5.87 \times 10^{12}\,\dfrac{\text{mi}}{\text{yr}}\right) = 5.87 \times 10^{17} \text{ mi}$

**57** $\dfrac{\dfrac{1.01 \text{ grams}}{\text{mole}}}{\dfrac{6.02 \times 10^{23} \text{ atoms}}{\text{mole}}} \cdot 1 \text{ atom} = \dfrac{1.01 \text{ grams}}{6.02 \times 10^{23}} \approx 0.1678 \times 10^{-23} \text{ g} = 1.678 \times 10^{-24} \text{ g}$

**58** $(2.5 \text{ million})(0.00035\%) = (2.5 \times 10^6)(3.5 \times 10^{-6}) = 8.75 \approx 9 \text{ halibut}$

**59** $\dfrac{24 \text{ frames}}{\text{second}} \cdot \dfrac{60 \text{ seconds}}{1 \text{ minute}} \cdot \dfrac{60 \text{ minutes}}{1 \text{ hour}} \cdot 48 \text{ hours} = 4.1472 \times 10^6 \text{ frames}$

**60** $\dfrac{2 \times 10^{11} \text{ calculations}}{\text{second}} \cdot \dfrac{60 \text{ seconds}}{1 \text{ minute}} \cdot \dfrac{60 \text{ minutes}}{1 \text{ hour}} \cdot \dfrac{24 \text{ hours}}{1 \text{ day}} \cdot 60 \text{ days} = 1.0368 \times 10^{18} \text{ calculations}$

**61** (a) $1 \text{ ft}^2 = 144 \text{ in}^2$, so the force on one square foot of a wall is $144 \text{ in}^2 \times 1.4 \text{ lb/in}^2 = 201.6 \text{ lb}$.

(b) The area of the wall is $40 \times 8 = 320 \text{ ft}^2$, or $320 \text{ ft}^2 \times 144 \text{ in}^2/\text{ft}^2 = 46{,}080 \text{ in}^2$.

The total force is $46{,}080 \text{ in}^2 \times 1.4 \text{ lb/in}^2 = 64{,}512 \text{ lb}$.

Converting to tons, we have $64{,}512 \text{ lb}/(2000 \text{ lb/ton}) = 32.256 \text{ tons}$.

**62** (a) We start with 400 adults, 150 yearlings, and 200 calves {total = 750}

Number of Adults = surviving adults + surviving yearlings
$$= (0.90)(400) + (0.80)(150) = \underline{480}$$

Number of Yearlings = surviving calves
$$= (0.75)(200) = \underline{150}$$

Number of Calves = number of female adults
$$= (0.50)(480) = \underline{240}$$

(b) 75% of last spring's calves equal the number of this year's yearlings (150), so the number of calves is $\underline{200}$.

The number of calves is equal to the number of adult females and this is one-half of the number of adults,

so the number of adults is $\underline{400}$.

90% of these (360) are part of the 400 adults this year. The other 40 adults represent

80% of last year's yearlings, so the number of yearlings is $\underline{50}$.

## 1.2 Exercises

**1** $\left(-\dfrac{2}{3}\right)^4 = \left(-\dfrac{2}{3}\right) \cdot \left(-\dfrac{2}{3}\right) \cdot \left(-\dfrac{2}{3}\right) \cdot \left(-\dfrac{2}{3}\right) = \dfrac{16}{81}$

**Note:** Do not confuse $(-x)^4$ and $-x^4$ since $(-x)^4 = x^4$ and $-x^4$ is the negative of $x^4$.

**2** $(-3)^3 = -27 = \dfrac{-27}{1}$

**3** $\dfrac{2^{-3}}{3^{-2}} = \dfrac{3^2}{2^3} = \dfrac{9}{8}$

**Note:** Remember that negative exponents don't necessarily give negative results—that is, $2^{-3} = \dfrac{1}{2^3} = \dfrac{1}{8}$, not $-\dfrac{1}{8}$.

**4** $\dfrac{2^0 + 0^2}{2 + 0} = \dfrac{1 + 0}{2} = \dfrac{1}{2}$

**5** $-2^4 + 3^{-1} = -16 + \dfrac{1}{3} = -\dfrac{48}{3} + \dfrac{1}{3} = -\dfrac{47}{3}$

**6** $\left(-\dfrac{3}{2}\right)^4 - 2^{-4} = \dfrac{81}{16} - \dfrac{1}{16} = \dfrac{80}{16} = \dfrac{5}{1}$

**7** $9^{5/2} = \left(\sqrt{9}\right)^5 = 3^5 = \dfrac{243}{1}$

**8** $16^{-3/4} = 1/16^{3/4} = 1/\left(\sqrt[4]{16}\right)^3 = 1/2^3 = \dfrac{1}{8}$

**9** $(-0.008)^{2/3} = \left(\sqrt[3]{-0.008}\right)^2 = (-0.2)^2 = 0.04 = \dfrac{4}{100} = \dfrac{1}{25}$

**10** $(0.008)^{-2/3} = 1/(0.008)^{2/3} = 1/\left(\sqrt[3]{0.008}\right)^2 = 1/(0.2)^2 = 1/(0.04) = \dfrac{25}{1}$

**11** $\left(\dfrac{1}{2}x^4\right)(16x^5) = \left(\dfrac{1}{2} \cdot 16\right)x^{4+5} = 8x^9$

**12** $(-3x^{-2})(4x^4) = (-3 \cdot 4)x^{-2+4} = -12x^2$

**13**   A common mistake is to write $x^3x^2 = x^6$, and another is to write $(x^2)^3 = x^5$.
The following solution illustrates the proper use of the exponent rules.

$$\frac{(2x^3)(3x^2)}{(x^2)^3} = \frac{(2 \cdot 3)x^{3+2}}{x^{2 \cdot 3}} = \frac{6x^5}{x^6} = 6x^{5-6} = 6x^{-1} = \frac{6}{x}$$

**14**   $\dfrac{(2x^2)^3 y^2}{4x^4 y^2} = \dfrac{8x^6}{4x^4} = 2x^2$

**15**   $\left(\frac{1}{6}a^5\right)\left(-3a^2\right)\left(4a^7\right) = \frac{1}{6} \cdot (-3) \cdot 4 \cdot a^{5+2+7} = -2a^{14}$

**16**   $(-4b^3)\left(\frac{1}{6}b^2\right)(-9b^4) = (-4) \cdot \frac{1}{6} \cdot (-9) \cdot b^{3+2+4} = 6b^9$

**17**   $\dfrac{(6x^3)^2}{(2x^2)^3} \cdot (3x^2)^0 = \dfrac{6^2 x^{3 \cdot 2}}{2^3 x^{2 \cdot 3}} \cdot 1$ {an expression raised to the zero power is equal to 1} $= \dfrac{36x^6}{8x^6} = \dfrac{36}{8} = \dfrac{9}{2}$

**18**   $\dfrac{(3y^3)(2y^2)^2}{(y^4)^3} \cdot (5y^3)^0 = \dfrac{(3y^3)(4y^4)}{y^{12}} \cdot 1 = \dfrac{12y^7}{y^{12}} = \dfrac{12}{y^5}$

**19**   $(3u^7 v^3)(4u^4 v^{-5}) = 12u^{7+4}v^{3+(-5)} = 12u^{11}v^{-2} = \dfrac{12u^{11}}{v^2}$

**20**   $(x^2 y z^3)(-2x z^2)(x^3 y^{-2}) = -2x^{2+1+3}y^{1-2}z^{3+2} = -2x^6 y^{-1} z^5 = \dfrac{-2x^6 z^5}{y}$

**21**   $(8x^4 y^{-3})\left(\frac{1}{2}x^{-5}y^2\right) = 4x^{4-5}y^{-3+2} = 4x^{-1}y^{-1} = \dfrac{4}{xy}$

**22**   $\left(\dfrac{4a^2 b}{a^3 b^2}\right)\left(\dfrac{5a^2 b}{2b^4}\right) = \dfrac{20a^{2+2}b^{1+1}}{2a^3 b^{2+4}} = \dfrac{20a^4 b^2}{2a^3 b^6} = \dfrac{10a^{4-3}b^{2-6}}{1} = \dfrac{10a}{b^4}$

**23**   $\left(\dfrac{1}{3}x^4 y^{-3}\right)^{-2} = \left(\dfrac{1}{3}\right)^{-2}(x^4)^{-2}(y^{-3})^{-2} = \left(\dfrac{3}{1}\right)^2 x^{-8}y^6 = 3^2 x^{-8}y^6 = \dfrac{9y^6}{x^8}$

**24**   $(-2xy^2)^5\left(\dfrac{x^7}{8y^3}\right) = (-32x^5 y^{10})\left(\dfrac{x^7}{8y^3}\right) = -4x^{12}y^7$

**25**   $(3y^3)^4 (4y^2)^{-3} = 3^4 y^{12} \cdot 4^{-3} y^{-6} = 81y^6 \cdot \dfrac{1}{4^3} = \dfrac{81}{64}y^6$

**26**   $(-3a^2 b^{-5})^3 = -27a^6 b^{-15} = -\dfrac{27a^6}{b^{15}}$

**27**   $(-2r^4 s^{-3})^{-2} = (-2)^{-2}r^{-8}s^6 = \dfrac{s^6}{(-2)^2 r^8} = \dfrac{s^6}{4r^8}$

**28**   $(2x^2 y^{-5})(6x^{-3}y)\left(\frac{1}{3}x^{-1}y^3\right) = 4x^{-2}y^{-1} = \dfrac{4}{x^2 y}$

**29**   $(5x^2 y^{-3})(4x^{-5}y^4) = 20x^{2-5}y^{-3+4} = 20x^{-3}y^1 = \dfrac{20y}{x^3}$

**30**   $(-2r^2 s)^5 (3r^{-1}s^3)^2 = (-32r^{10}s^5)(9r^{-2}s^6) = -288r^8 s^{11}$

**31**   $\left(\dfrac{3x^5 y^4 z}{x^0 y^{-3}z}\right)^2$ {remember that $x^0 = 1$, cancel $z$} $= \dfrac{9x^{10}y^8}{y^{-6}} = 9x^{10}y^{8-(-6)} = 9x^{10}y^{14}$

**32**   $(4a^2 b)^4 \left(\dfrac{-a^3}{2b}\right)^2 = (256a^8 b^4)\left(\dfrac{a^6}{4b^2}\right) = 64a^{14}b^2$

**33**   $(-5a^{3/2})(2a^{1/2}) = -5 \cdot 2a^{(3/2)+(1/2)} = -10a^{4/2} = 8a^2$

**34** $(-6x^{7/5})(2x^{8/5}) = -6 \cdot 2x^{(7/5)+(8/5)} = -12x^{15/5} = -12x^3$

**35** $(3x^{5/6})(8x^{2/3}) = 3 \cdot 8x^{(5/6)+(4/6)} = 24x^{9/6} = 24x^{3/2}$

**36** $(8r)^{1/3}(2r^{1/2}) = (2r^{1/3})(2r^{1/2}) = 4r^{(2/6)+(3/6)} = 4r^{5/6}$

**37** $(27a^6)^{-2/3} = 27^{-2/3}a^{-12/3} = \dfrac{a^{-4}}{27^{2/3}} = \dfrac{1}{\left(\sqrt[3]{27}\right)^2 a^4} = \dfrac{1}{3^2 \, a^4} = \dfrac{1}{9a^4}$

**38** $(25z^4)^{-3/2} = 25^{-3/2}z^{-12/2} = \dfrac{z^{-6}}{25^{3/2}} = \dfrac{1}{\left(\sqrt{25}\right)^3 z^6} = \dfrac{1}{5^3 \, z^6} = \dfrac{1}{125z^6}$

**39** $(8x^{-2/3})x^{1/6} = 8x^{(-4/6)+(1/6)} = 8x^{-3/6} = \dfrac{8}{x^{1/2}}$     **40** $(3x^{1/2})(-2x^{5/2}) = -6x^{(1/2)+(5/2)} = -6x^3$

**41** $\left(\dfrac{-8x^3}{y^{-6}}\right)^{2/3} = \dfrac{(-8)^{2/3}(x^3)^{2/3}}{(y^{-6})^{2/3}} = \dfrac{\left(\sqrt[3]{-8}\right)^2 x^{(3)(2/3)}}{y^{(-6)(2/3)}} = \dfrac{(-2)^2 x^2}{y^{-4}} = \dfrac{4x^2}{y^{-4}} = 4x^2y^4$

**42** $\left(\dfrac{-y^{3/2}}{y^{-1/3}}\right)^3 = \dfrac{-y^{9/2}}{y^{-1}} = -y^{11/2}$

**43** $\left(\dfrac{x^6}{16y^{-4}}\right)^{-1/2} = \dfrac{x^{-3}}{16^{-1/2}y^2} = \dfrac{16^{1/2}}{x^3y^2} = \dfrac{4}{x^3y^2}$     **44** $\left(\dfrac{c^{-4}}{81d^8}\right)^{3/4} = \dfrac{c^{-3}}{\left(\sqrt[4]{81}\right)^3 d^6} = \dfrac{c^{-3}}{3^3d^6} = \dfrac{1}{27c^3d^6}$

**45** $\dfrac{(x^6y^3)^{-1/3}}{(x^4y^2)^{-1/2}} = \dfrac{(x^6)^{-1/3}(y^3)^{-1/3}}{(x^4)^{-1/2}(y^2)^{-1/2}} = \dfrac{x^{-2}y^{-1}}{x^{-2}y^{-1}} = 1$     **46** $a^{4/3}a^{-3/2}a^{1/6} = a^{(8/6)-(9/6)+(1/6)} = a^{0/6} = a^0 = 1$

**47** $\sqrt[4]{x^4 + y} = (x^4 + y)^{1/4}$     **48** $\sqrt[3]{x^3 + y^2} = (x^3 + y^2)^{1/3}$

**49** $\sqrt[3]{(a+b)^2} = \left[(a+b)^2\right]^{1/3} = (a+b)^{2/3}$     **50** $\sqrt{a + \sqrt{b}} = (a + b^{1/2})^{1/2}$

**51** $\sqrt{x^2 + y^2} = (x^2 + y^2)^{1/2}$    **Note:** $\sqrt{x^2 + y^2} \ne x + y$    **52** $\sqrt[3]{r^3 - s^3} = (r^3 - s^3)^{1/3}$

**53** (a) $4x^{3/2} = 4x^1x^{1/2} = 4x\sqrt{x}$ (b) $(4x)^{3/2} = (4x)^1(4x)^{1/2} = (4x)^1 4^{1/2}x^{1/2} = 4x \cdot 2 \cdot x^{1/2} = 8x\sqrt{x}$

**54** (a) $4 + x^{3/2} = 4 + x^1x^{1/2} = 4 + x\sqrt{x}$ (b) $(4 + x)^{3/2} = (4 + x)^1(4 + x)^{1/2} = (4 + x)\sqrt{4 + x}$

**55** (a) $8 - y^{1/3} = 8 - \sqrt[3]{y}$                (b) $(8 - y)^{1/3} = \sqrt[3]{8 - y}$

**56** (a) $64y^{1/3} = 64\sqrt[3]{y}$                  (b) $(64y)^{1/3} = 64^{1/3}y^{1/3} = 4\sqrt[3]{y}$

**57** $\sqrt{81} = \sqrt{9^2} = 9$                 **58** $\sqrt[3]{-216} = \sqrt[3]{(-6)^3} = -6$

**59** $\sqrt[5]{-64} = \sqrt[5]{-32}\sqrt[5]{2} = \sqrt[5]{(-2)^5}\sqrt[5]{2} = -2\sqrt[5]{2}$     **60** $\sqrt[4]{512} = \sqrt[4]{256}\sqrt[4]{2} = \sqrt[4]{4^4}\sqrt[4]{2} = 4\sqrt[4]{2}$

**61** In the denominator, you would like to have $\sqrt[3]{2^3}$. How do you get it? Multiply by $\sqrt[3]{2^2}$, or, equivalently, $\sqrt[3]{4}$. Of course, we have to multiply the numerator by the same value so that we don't change the value of the given fraction.

$$\frac{1}{\sqrt[3]{2}} = \frac{1}{\sqrt[3]{2}} \cdot \frac{\sqrt[3]{4}}{\sqrt[3]{4}} = \frac{\sqrt[3]{4}}{\sqrt[3]{2 \cdot 4}} = \frac{\sqrt[3]{4}}{\sqrt[3]{8}} = \frac{\sqrt[3]{4}}{2} = \frac{1}{2}\sqrt[3]{4}$$

**62** $\sqrt{\dfrac{1}{5}} = \dfrac{\sqrt{1}}{\sqrt{5}} = \dfrac{1}{\sqrt{5}} \cdot \dfrac{\sqrt{5}}{\sqrt{5}} = \dfrac{1}{5}\sqrt{5}$

**63** $\sqrt{9x^{-4}y^6} = \left(9x^{-4}y^6\right)^{1/2} = 9^{1/2}\left(x^{-4}\right)^{1/2}\left(y^6\right)^{1/2} = 3x^{-2}y^3 = \dfrac{3y^3}{x^2}$

**64** $\sqrt{16a^8b^{-2}} = 4a^4b^{-1} = \dfrac{4a^4}{b}$

**65** $\sqrt[3]{8a^6b^{-3}} = 2a^2b^{-1} = \dfrac{2a^2}{b}$              **66** $\sqrt[4]{81r^5s^8} = \sqrt[4]{3^4r^4s^8}\,\sqrt[4]{r} = 3rs^2\sqrt[4]{r}$

**Note:** For exercises similar to numbers 67–74, pick a multiplier that will make all of the exponents of the terms in the denominator a multiple of the index.

**67** The index is 2. Choose the multiplier to be $\sqrt{2y}$ so that the denominator contains only terms with even exponents.

$\sqrt{\dfrac{3x}{2y^3}} = \sqrt{\dfrac{3x}{2y^3}} \cdot \dfrac{\sqrt{2y}}{\sqrt{2y}} = \dfrac{\sqrt{6xy}}{\sqrt{4y^4}} = \dfrac{\sqrt{6xy}}{2y^2}$, or $\dfrac{1}{2y^2}\sqrt{6xy}$

**68** $\sqrt{\dfrac{1}{3x^3y}} = \sqrt{\dfrac{1}{3x^3y}} \cdot \dfrac{\sqrt{3xy}}{\sqrt{3xy}} = \dfrac{\sqrt{3xy}}{\sqrt{9x^4y^2}} = \dfrac{1}{3x^2y}\sqrt{3xy}$

**69** The index is 3. Choose the multiplier to be $\sqrt[3]{3x^2}$ so that the denominator contains only terms with exponents that are multiples of 3.

$\sqrt[3]{\dfrac{2x^4y^4}{9x}} = \sqrt[3]{\dfrac{2x^4y^4}{9x}} \cdot \dfrac{\sqrt[3]{3x^2}}{\sqrt[3]{3x^2}} = \dfrac{\sqrt[3]{6x^6y^4}}{\sqrt[3]{27x^3}} = \dfrac{\sqrt[3]{x^6y^3}\,\sqrt[3]{6y}}{3x} = \dfrac{x^2y\,\sqrt[3]{6y}}{3x} = \dfrac{xy}{3}\sqrt[3]{6y}$

**70** $\sqrt[3]{\dfrac{3x^2y^5}{4x}} = \sqrt[3]{\dfrac{3x^2y^5}{4x}} \cdot \dfrac{\sqrt[3]{2x^2}}{\sqrt[3]{2x^2}} = \dfrac{\sqrt[3]{6x^4y^5}}{\sqrt[3]{8x^3}} = \dfrac{\sqrt[3]{x^3y^3}\,\sqrt[3]{6xy^2}}{2x} = \dfrac{xy\,\sqrt[3]{6xy^2}}{2x} = \dfrac{y}{2}\sqrt[3]{6xy^2}$

**71** The index is 4. Choose the multiplier to be $\sqrt[4]{3x^2}$ so that the denominator contains only terms with exponents that are multiples of 4.

$\sqrt[4]{\dfrac{5x^8y^3}{27x^2}} = \sqrt[4]{\dfrac{5x^8y^3}{27x^2}} \cdot \dfrac{\sqrt[4]{3x^2}}{\sqrt[4]{3x^2}} = \dfrac{\sqrt[4]{15x^{10}y^3}}{\sqrt[4]{81x^4}} = \dfrac{\sqrt[4]{x^8}\,\sqrt[4]{15x^2y^3}}{3x} = \dfrac{x^2\,\sqrt[4]{15x^2y^3}}{3x} = \dfrac{x}{3}\sqrt[4]{15x^2y^3}$

**72** $\sqrt[4]{\dfrac{x^7y^{12}}{125x}} = \sqrt[4]{\dfrac{x^7y^{12}}{125x}} \cdot \dfrac{\sqrt[4]{5x^3}}{\sqrt[4]{5x^3}} = \dfrac{\sqrt[4]{5x^{10}y^{12}}}{\sqrt[4]{625x^4}} = \dfrac{\sqrt[4]{x^8y^{12}}\,\sqrt[4]{5x^2}}{5x} = \dfrac{x^2y^3\,\sqrt[4]{5x^2}}{5x} = \dfrac{xy^3}{5}\sqrt[4]{5x^2}$

**73** The index is 5. Choose the multiplier to be $\sqrt[5]{4x^2}$ so that the denominator contains only terms with exponents that are multiples of 5.

$\sqrt[5]{\dfrac{5x^7y^2}{8x^3}} = \sqrt[5]{\dfrac{5x^7y^2}{8x^3}} \cdot \dfrac{\sqrt[5]{4x^2}}{\sqrt[5]{4x^2}} = \dfrac{\sqrt[5]{20x^9y^2}}{\sqrt[5]{32x^5}} = \dfrac{\sqrt[5]{x^5}\,\sqrt[5]{20x^4y^2}}{2x} = \dfrac{x\,\sqrt[5]{20x^4y^2}}{2x} = \dfrac{1}{2}\sqrt[5]{20x^4y^2}$

**74** $\sqrt[5]{\dfrac{3x^{11}y^3}{9x^2}} = \sqrt[5]{\dfrac{3x^{11}y^3}{9x^2}} \cdot \dfrac{\sqrt[5]{27x^3}}{\sqrt[5]{27x^3}} = \dfrac{\sqrt[5]{81x^{14}y^3}}{\sqrt[5]{243x^5}} = \dfrac{\sqrt[5]{x^{10}}\,\sqrt[5]{81x^4y^3}}{3x} = \dfrac{x^2\,\sqrt[5]{81x^4y^3}}{3x} = \dfrac{x}{3}\sqrt[5]{81x^4y^3}$

**75** $\sqrt[4]{\left(5x^5y^{-2}\right)^4} = 5x^5y^{-2} = \dfrac{5x^5}{y^2}$        **76** $\sqrt[6]{\left(7u^{-3}v^4\right)^6} = 7u^{-3}v^4 = \dfrac{7v^4}{u^3}$

**77** $\sqrt[5]{\dfrac{8x^3}{y^4}}\,\sqrt[5]{\dfrac{4x^4}{y^2}} = \sqrt[5]{\dfrac{8x^3}{y^4}}\,\sqrt[5]{\dfrac{4x^4}{y^2}} \cdot \dfrac{\sqrt[5]{y^4}}{\sqrt[5]{y^4}} = \dfrac{\sqrt[5]{32x^5}\,\sqrt[5]{x^2y^4}}{\sqrt[5]{y^{10}}} = \dfrac{\sqrt[5]{32x^5}\,\sqrt[5]{x^2y^4}}{y^2} = \dfrac{2x}{y^2}\sqrt[5]{x^2y^4}$

**78** $\sqrt{5xy^7}\,\sqrt{15x^3y^3} = \sqrt{25x^4y^{10}}\,\sqrt{3} = 5x^2y^5\sqrt{3}$

**79** $\sqrt[3]{3t^4v^2}\sqrt[3]{-9t^{-1}v^4} = \sqrt[3]{-27t^3v^6} = -3tv^2$      **80** $\sqrt[3]{(2r-s)^3} = 2r-s$

**81** $\sqrt{x^6y^4} = \sqrt{(x^3)^2(y^2)^2} = \sqrt{(x^3)^2}\sqrt{(y^2)^2} = |x^3||y^2| = |x^3|y^2$ since $y^2$ is always nonnegative.

                                           **Note:** $|x^3|$ could be written as $x^2|x|$.

**82** $\sqrt{x^4y^{10}} = \sqrt{(x^2)^2(y^5)^2} = |x^2||y^5| = x^2|y^5|$

**83** $\sqrt[4]{x^8(y-3)^{12}} = \sqrt[4]{(x^2)^4((y-3)^3)^4} = |x^2||(y-3)^3| = x^2|(y-3)^3|$, or $x^2(y-3)^2|(y-3)|$

**84** $\sqrt[4]{(x+2)^{12}y^4} = \sqrt[4]{((x+2)^3)^4y^4} = |(x+2)^3||y|$, or $(x+2)^2|(x+2)y|$

**85** $(a^r)^2 = a^{2r} \boxed{\neq} a^{(r^2)}$ since $2r \neq r^2$ for all values of $r$; for example, let $r = 1$.

**86** Squaring the right side gives us $(a+1)^2 = a^2 + 2a + 1$. Squaring the left side gives us $a^2 + 1$.

  $a^2 + 2a + 1 \boxed{\neq} a^2 + 1$ for all values of $a$; for example, let $a = 1$.

**87** $(ab)^{xy} = a^{xy}b^{xy} \boxed{\neq} a^xb^y$ for all values of $x$ and $y$; for example, let $x = 1$ and $y = 2$.

**88** $\sqrt{a^r} = (a^r)^{1/2} = (a^{1/2})^r \boxed{=} (\sqrt{a})^r$      **89** $\sqrt[n]{\dfrac{1}{c}} = \left(\dfrac{1}{c}\right)^{1/n} = \dfrac{1^{1/n}}{c^{1/n}} \boxed{=} \dfrac{1}{\sqrt[n]{c}}$

**90** $\dfrac{1}{a^k} = a^{-k} \boxed{\neq} a^{1/k}$ since $-k \neq 1/k$ for all values of $k$; for example, let $k = 1$.

**91** (a) $(-3)^{2/5} = [(-3)^2]^{1/5} = 9^{1/5} \approx 1.5518$      (b) $(-7)^{4/3} = [(-7)^4]^{1/3} = 2401^{1/3} \approx 13.3905$

**92** (a) $(-1.2)^{3/7} = [(-1.2)^3]^{1/7} = (-1.728)^{1/7} \approx -1.0813$

  (b) $(-5.08)^{7/3} = [(-5.08)^7]^{1/3} \approx (-87,306.38)^{1/3} \approx -44.3624$

**93** (a) $\sqrt{\pi + 1} \approx 2.0351$      (b) $\sqrt[3]{17.1} + 5^{1/4} \approx 4.0717$

**94** (a) $(2.6 - 1.3)^{-2} \approx 0.5917$      (b) $5^{\sqrt{7}} \approx 70.6807$

**95** $\$200(1.04)^{180} \approx \$232,825.78$

**96** $h = 1454\,\text{ft} \Rightarrow d = 1.2\sqrt{h} = 1.2\sqrt{1454} \approx 45.8\,\text{mi}$

**97** $W = 230\,\text{kg} \Rightarrow L = 0.46\sqrt[3]{W} = 0.46\sqrt[3]{230} \approx 2.82\,\text{m}$

**98** $L = 25\,\text{ft} \Rightarrow W = 0.0016L^{2.43} = 0.0016(25)^{2.43} \approx 3.99\,\text{tons}$

**99** $b = 75$ and $w = 180 \Rightarrow W = \dfrac{w}{\sqrt[3]{b-35}} = \dfrac{180}{\sqrt[3]{75-35}} \approx 52.6$.

  $b = 120$ and $w = 250 \Rightarrow W = \dfrac{w}{\sqrt[3]{b-35}} = \dfrac{250}{\sqrt[3]{120-35}} \approx 56.9$.

  It is interesting to note that the 75-kg lifter can lift 2.4 times his/her body weight and the 120-kg lifter can lift approximately 2.08 times his/her body weight, but the formula ranks the 120-kg lifter as the superior lifter.

**100** (a) $h = 72\,\text{in.}$ and $w = 175\,\text{lb} \Rightarrow S = (0.1091)w^{0.425}h^{0.725} = (0.1091)(175)^{0.425}(72)^{0.725} \approx 21.76\,\text{ft}^2$.

  (b) $h = 66\,\text{in.} \Rightarrow S_1 = (0.1091)w^{0.425}(66)^{0.725}$. A 10% increase in weight would be represented by $1.1w$ and thus $S_2 = (0.1091)(1.1w)^{0.425}(66)^{0.725}$. $S_2/S_1 = (1.1)^{0.425} \approx 1.04$, which represents a 4% increase in $S$.

**101** $W = 0.1166h^{1.7}$

| Height | 64 | 65 | 66 | 67 | 68 | 69 | 70 | 71 |
|--------|-----|-----|-----|-----|-----|-----|-----|-----|
| Weight | 137 | 141 | 145 | 148 | 152 | 156 | 160 | 164 |
| Height | 72 | 73 | 74 | 75 | 76 | 77 | 78 | 79 |
| Weight | 168 | 172 | 176 | 180 | 184 | 188 | 192 | 196 |

**102** $W = 0.1049h^{1.7}$

| Height | 60 | 61 | 62 | 63 | 64 | 65 | 66 | 67 |
|--------|-----|-----|-----|-----|-----|-----|-----|-----|
| Weight | 111 | 114 | 117 | 120 | 123 | 127 | 130 | 133 |
| Height | 68 | 69 | 70 | 71 | 72 | 73 | 74 | 75 |
| Weight | 137 | 140 | 144 | 147 | 151 | 154 | 158 | 162 |

## 1.3 Exercises

**1**   $(2u + 3)(u - 4) + 4u(u - 2) = (2u^2 - 5u - 12) + (4u^2 - 8u) = 6u^2 - 13u - 12$

**2**   $(3u - 1)(u + 2) + 7u(u + 1) = (3u^2 + 5u - 2) + (7u^2 + 7u) = 10u^2 + 12u - 2$

**3**   $\dfrac{8x^2y^3 - 6x^3y}{2x^2y} = \dfrac{8x^2y^3}{2x^2y} - \dfrac{6x^3y}{2x^2y} = 4y^2 - 3x$

**4**   $\dfrac{6x^2yz^3 - xy^2z}{xyz} = \dfrac{6x^2yz^3}{xyz} - \dfrac{xy^2z}{xyz} = 6xz^2 - y$

**5**   We recognize this product as the difference of two squares.

$$(2x + 7y)(2x - 7y) = (2x)^2 - (7y)^2 = 4x^2 - 49y^2$$

**6**   $(5x + 3y)(5x - 3y) = (5x)^2 - (3y)^2 = 25x^2 - 9y^2$

**7**   $(3x + 2y)^2 = (3x)^2 + 2(3x)(2y) + (2y)^2 = 9x^2 + 12xy + 4y^2$

**8**   $(5x - 4y)^2 = (5x)^2 - 2(5x)(4y) + (4y)^2 = 25x^2 - 40xy + 16y^2$

**9**   $\left(\sqrt{x} + \sqrt{y}\right)\left(\sqrt{x} - \sqrt{y}\right) = \left(\sqrt{x}\right)^2 - \left(\sqrt{y}\right)^2 = x - y$

**10**   $\left(\sqrt{x} + \sqrt{y}\right)^2\left(\sqrt{x} - \sqrt{y}\right)^2 = \left[\left(\sqrt{x} + \sqrt{y}\right)\left(\sqrt{x} - \sqrt{y}\right)\right]^2 = (x - y)^2 = x^2 - 2xy + y^2$

**11**   Use Product Formula (3) on page 30 of the text.

$$(x - 2y)^3 = (x)^3 - 3(x)^2(2y) + 3(x)(2y)^2 - (2y)^3 = x^3 - 6x^2y + 12xy^2 - 8y^3$$

**12**   $(x + 3y)^3 = (x)^3 + 3(x)^2(3y) + 3(x)(3y)^2 + (3y)^3 = x^3 + 9x^2y + 27xy^2 + 27y^3$

**13**   We recognize $8x^2 - 17x - 21$ as a trinomial that may be able to be factored into the product of two binomials. Using trial and error, we obtain $8x^2 - 17x - 21 = (8x + 7)(x - 3)$. If you are interested in a sure-fire method for factoring trinomials, see Example 6 on page 48 of the text.

**14**   Using trial and error, we obtain $7x^2 + 10x - 8 = (7x - 4)(x + 2)$.

**15**   The factors for $x^2 + 4x + 5$ would have to be of the form $\left(x + \_\_\right)$ and $\left(x + \_\_\right)$.
The factors of 5 are 1 and 5, but their sum is 6 (*not* 4). Thus, $x^2 + 4x + 5$ is irreducible.

**16**   $3x^2 - 4x + 2$ is irreducible.

**17**   $36x^2 - 60x + 25 = (6x - 5)(6x - 5) = (6x - 5)^2$      **18**   $9x^2 + 24x + 16 = (3x + 4)(3x + 4) = (3x + 4)^2$

**19** $x^4 - 4x^2 = x^2(x^2 - 4) = x^2(x^2 - 2^2) = x^2(x+2)(x-2)$

**20** $x^3 - 16x = x(x^2 - 16) = x(x^2 - 4^2) = x(x+4)(x-4)$

**21** We recognize $8x^3 - y^6$ as the difference of two cubes.

$$8x^3 - y^6 = (2x)^3 - (y^2)^3 = (2x - y^2)\left[(2x)^2 + (2x)(y^2) + (y^2)^2\right]$$
$$= (2x - y^2)(4x^2 + 2xy^2 + y^4)$$

**22** $x^6 - 27y^3 = (x^2)^3 - (3y)^3 = (x^2 - 3y)\left[(x^2)^2 + (x^2)(3y) + (3y)^2\right] = (x^2 - 3y)(x^4 + 3x^2y + 9y^2)$

**23** We recognize $343x^3 + y^9$ as the sum of two cubes.

$$343x^3 + y^9 = (7x)^3 + (y^3)^3 = (7x + y^3)\left[(7x)^2 - (7x)(y^3) + (y^3)^2\right]$$
$$= (7x + y^3)(49x^2 - 7xy^3 + y^6)$$

**24** $x^3 + 64 = (x)^3 + (4)^3 = (x+4)\left[(x)^2 - (x)(4) + (4)^2\right] = (x+4)(x^2 - 4x + 16)$

**25** $\begin{aligned}
3x^3 + 3x^2 - 27x - 27 &= 3(x^3 + x^2 - 9x - 9) &&\{\text{gcf} = 3\} \\
&= 3[x^2(x+1) - 9(x+1)] &&\{\text{factor by grouping}\} \\
&= 3(x^2 - 9)(x+1) &&\{\text{factor out } (x+1)\} \\
&= 3(x+3)(x-3)(x+1) &&\{\text{difference of two squares}\}
\end{aligned}$

**26** $\begin{aligned}
5x^3 + 10x^2 - 20x - 40 &= 5(x^3 + 2x^2 - 4x - 8) = 5[x^2(x+2) - 4(x+2)] \\
&= 5(x^2 - 4)(x+2) = 5(x+2)(x-2)(x+2) = 5(x+2)^2(x-2)
\end{aligned}$

**27** We could treat $a^6 - b^6$ as the difference of two squares or the difference of two cubes. Factoring $a^6 - b^6$ as the difference of two squares and then factoring as the sum and difference of two cubes leads to the following:

$$a^6 - b^6 = (a^3)^2 - (b^3)^2 = (a^3 + b^3)(a^3 - b^3)$$
$$= (a+b)(a-b)(a^2 - ab + b^2)(a^2 + ab + b^2)$$

**28** $x^8 - 16 = (x^4)^2 - 4^2 = (x^4 + 4)(x^4 - 4) = (x^4 + 4)(x^2 + 2)(x^2 - 2)$

**29** We might first try to factor $x^2 + 4x + 4 - 9y^2$ by grouping since it has more than 3 terms, but this would prove to be unsuccessful. Instead, we will group the terms containing $x$ and the constant term together, and then proceed as in Example 2(c).

$$x^2 + 4x + 4 - 9y^2 = (x+2)^2 - (3y)^2 = (x+2+3y)(x+2-3y)$$

**30** $x^2 - 4y^2 - 6x + 9 = (x^2 - 6x + 9) - 4y^2 = (x-3)^2 - (2y)^2 = (x-3+2y)(x-3-2y)$

**31** $\dfrac{y^2 - 25}{y^3 - 125} = \dfrac{(y+5)(y-5)}{(y-5)(y^2 + 5y + 25)} = \dfrac{y+5}{y^2 + 5y + 25}$

**32** $\dfrac{12 + r - r^2}{r^3 + 3r^2} = \dfrac{(3+r)(4-r)}{r^2(r+3)} = \dfrac{4-r}{r^2}$

**33** $\begin{aligned}
\dfrac{9x^2 - 4}{3x^2 - 5x + 2} \cdot \dfrac{9x^4 - 6x^3 + 4x^2}{27x^4 + 8x} &= \dfrac{(3x+2)(3x-2)}{(3x-2)(x-1)} \cdot \dfrac{x^2(9x^2 - 6x + 4)}{x(27x^3 + 8)} \\
&= \dfrac{(3x+2)(3x-2)x^2(9x^2 - 6x + 4)}{(3x-2)(x-1)x(3x+2)(9x^2 - 6x + 4)} = \dfrac{x}{x-1}
\end{aligned}$

**34** $\dfrac{5a^2 + 12a + 4}{a^4 - 16} \div \dfrac{25a^2 + 20a + 4}{a^2 - 2a} = \dfrac{(5a+2)(a+2)}{(a^2 + 4)(a+2)(a-2)} \cdot \dfrac{a(a-2)}{(5a+2)(5a+2)} = \dfrac{a}{(a^2 + 4)(5a+2)}$

**35** $\dfrac{4}{3s+1} - \dfrac{11}{(3s+1)^2} = \dfrac{4(3s+1)}{(3s+1)^2} - \dfrac{11}{(3s+1)^2} = \dfrac{12s+4-11}{(3s+1)^2} = \dfrac{12s-7}{(3s+1)^2}$

**36** $\dfrac{4}{(5s-2)^2} + \dfrac{s}{5s-2} = \dfrac{4}{(5s-2)^2} + \dfrac{s(5s-2)}{(5s-2)^2} = \dfrac{4+5s^2-2s}{(5s-2)^2} = \dfrac{5s^2-2s+4}{(5s-2)^2}$

**37** $\dfrac{2}{x} + \dfrac{3x+1}{x^2} - \dfrac{x-2}{x^3} = \dfrac{2x^2}{x^3} + \dfrac{(3x+1)x}{x^3} - \dfrac{(x-2)}{x^3} = \dfrac{2x^2+3x^2+x-x+2}{x^3} = \dfrac{5x^2+2}{x^3}$

**38** $\dfrac{5}{x} - \dfrac{2x-1}{x^2} + \dfrac{x+7}{x^3} = \dfrac{5x^2}{x^3} - \dfrac{(2x-1)x}{x^3} + \dfrac{x+7}{x^3} = \dfrac{5x^2-2x^2+x+x+7}{x^3} = \dfrac{3x^2+2x+7}{x^3}$

**39** $\dfrac{3t}{t+2} + \dfrac{5t}{t-2} - \dfrac{40}{t^2-4} = \dfrac{3t}{t+2} + \dfrac{5t}{t-2} - \dfrac{40}{(t+2)(t-2)}$

$$= \dfrac{3t(t-2)}{(t+2)(t-2)} + \dfrac{5t(t+2)}{(t+2)(t-2)} - \dfrac{40}{(t+2)(t-2)}$$

$$= \dfrac{3t^2-6t+5t^2+10t-40}{(t+2)(t-2)}$$

$$= \dfrac{8t^2+4t-40}{(t+2)(t-2)} = \dfrac{4(2t^2+t-10)}{(t+2)(t-2)} = \dfrac{4(2t+5)(t-2)}{(t+2)(t-2)} = \dfrac{4(2t+5)}{t+2}$$

**40** $\dfrac{t}{t+3} + \dfrac{4t}{t-3} - \dfrac{18}{t^2-9} = \dfrac{t(t-3)+4t(t+3)-18}{t^2-9} = \dfrac{5t^2+9t-18}{t^2-9} = \dfrac{(5t-6)(t+3)}{(t+3)(t-3)} = \dfrac{5t-6}{t-3}$

**41** $\dfrac{4x}{3x-4} + \dfrac{8}{3x^2-4x} + \dfrac{2}{x} = \dfrac{4x(x)+8+2(3x-4)}{x(3x-4)} = \dfrac{4x^2+6x}{x(3x-4)} = \dfrac{2x(2x+3)}{x(3x-4)} = \dfrac{2(2x+3)}{3x-4}$

**42** $\dfrac{12x}{2x+1} - \dfrac{3}{2x^2+x} + \dfrac{5}{x} = \dfrac{12x(x)-3+5(2x+1)}{x(2x+1)} = \dfrac{12x^2+10x+2}{x(2x+1)} = \dfrac{2(6x^2+5x+1)}{x(2x+1)}$

$$= \dfrac{2(2x+1)(3x+1)}{x(2x+1)} = \dfrac{2(3x+1)}{x}$$

**43** $\dfrac{2x}{x+2} - \dfrac{8}{x^2+2x} + \dfrac{3}{x} = \dfrac{2x(x)-8+3(x+2)}{x(x+2)} = \dfrac{2x^2+3x-2}{x(x+2)} = \dfrac{(2x-1)(x+2)}{x(x+2)} = \dfrac{2x-1}{x}$

**44** $\dfrac{5x}{2x+3} - \dfrac{6}{2x^2+3x} + \dfrac{2}{x} = \dfrac{5x(x)-6+2(2x+3)}{x(2x+3)} = \dfrac{5x^2+4x}{x(2x+3)} = \dfrac{x(5x+4)}{x(2x+3)} = \dfrac{5x+4}{2x+3}$

**45** $3 + \dfrac{5}{u} + \dfrac{2u}{3u+1} = \dfrac{3u(3u+1)+5(3u+1)+2u(u)}{u(3u+1)}$    {common denominator}

$$= \dfrac{9u^2+3u+15u+5+2u^2}{u(3u+1)}$$    {multiply terms}

$$= \dfrac{11u^2+18u+5}{u(3u+1)}$$    {add like terms}

**46** $6 + \dfrac{2}{u} - \dfrac{3u}{u+5} = \dfrac{6u(u+5)+2(u+5)-3u(u)}{u(u+5)} = \dfrac{3u^2+32u+10}{u(u+5)}$

**47** $\dfrac{2x+1}{x^2+4x+4} - \dfrac{6x}{x^2-4} + \dfrac{3}{x-2} = \dfrac{2x+1}{(x+2)^2} - \dfrac{6x}{(x+2)(x-2)} + \dfrac{3}{x-2}$

$$= \dfrac{(2x+1)(x-2)-6x(x+2)+3(x^2+4x+4)}{(x+2)^2(x-2)}$$

$$= \dfrac{2x^2-3x-2-6x^2-12x+3x^2+12x+12}{(x+2)^2(x-2)}$$

$$= \dfrac{-x^2-3x+10}{(x+2)^2(x-2)} = -\dfrac{x^2+3x-10}{(x+2)^2(x-2)} = -\dfrac{(x+5)(x-2)}{(x+2)^2(x-2)} = -\dfrac{x+5}{(x+2)^2}$$

**48** $\dfrac{4x+12}{x^2+6x+9} + \dfrac{5x}{x^2-9} + \dfrac{7}{x-3} = \dfrac{4}{x+3} + \dfrac{5x}{x^2-9} + \dfrac{7}{x-3} = \dfrac{4(x-3)+5x+7(x+3)}{x^2-9} = \dfrac{16x+9}{x^2-9}$

**49** The lcd of the entire expression is $ab$. Thus, we will multiply both the numerator and denominator by $ab$.

$$\dfrac{\dfrac{b}{a} - \dfrac{a}{b}}{\dfrac{1}{a} - \dfrac{1}{b}} = \dfrac{\left(\dfrac{b}{a} - \dfrac{a}{b}\right)\cdot ab}{\left(\dfrac{1}{a} - \dfrac{1}{b}\right)\cdot ab} = \dfrac{b^2 - a^2}{b-a} = \dfrac{(b+a)(b-a)}{b-a} = a+b$$

**50** The lcd of the entire expression is $x^2y^2$. Thus, we will multiply both the numerator and denominator by $x^2y^2$.

$$\dfrac{\dfrac{x}{y^2} - \dfrac{y}{x^2}}{\dfrac{1}{y^2} - \dfrac{1}{x^2}} = \dfrac{\left(\dfrac{x}{y^2} - \dfrac{y}{x^2}\right)\cdot x^2y^2}{\left(\dfrac{1}{y^2} - \dfrac{1}{x^2}\right)\cdot x^2y^2} = \dfrac{x^3 - y^3}{x^2 - y^2} = \dfrac{(x-y)(x^2+xy+y^2)}{(x+y)(x-y)} = \dfrac{x^2+xy+y^2}{x+y}$$

**51** The lcd of the entire expression is $xy$. Thus, we will multiply both the numerator and denominator by $xy$.

$$\dfrac{y^{-1}+x^{-1}}{(xy)^{-1}} = \dfrac{\dfrac{1}{y}+\dfrac{1}{x}}{\dfrac{1}{xy}} = \dfrac{\left(\dfrac{1}{y}+\dfrac{1}{x}\right)\cdot xy}{\left(\dfrac{1}{xy}\right)\cdot xy} = \dfrac{x+y}{1} = x+y$$

**52** $\dfrac{y^{-2}-x^{-2}}{y^{-2}+x^{-2}} = \dfrac{\dfrac{1}{y^2}-\dfrac{1}{x^2}}{\dfrac{1}{y^2}+\dfrac{1}{x^2}} = \dfrac{\left(\dfrac{1}{y^2}-\dfrac{1}{x^2}\right)\cdot x^2y^2}{\left(\dfrac{1}{y^2}+\dfrac{1}{x^2}\right)\cdot x^2y^2} = \dfrac{x^2-y^2}{x^2+y^2}$

**53** $\dfrac{\dfrac{r}{s}+\dfrac{s}{r}}{\dfrac{r^2}{s^2}-\dfrac{s^2}{r^2}} = \dfrac{\left(\dfrac{r}{s}+\dfrac{s}{r}\right)\cdot r^2s^2}{\left(\dfrac{r^2}{s^2}-\dfrac{s^2}{r^2}\right)\cdot r^2s^2} = \dfrac{r^3s+rs^3}{r^4-s^4} = \dfrac{rs(r^2+s^2)}{(r^2+s^2)(r^2-s^2)} = \dfrac{rs}{r^2-s^2}$

**54** $\dfrac{\dfrac{2}{w}-\dfrac{4}{2w+1}}{\dfrac{5}{w}+\dfrac{8}{2w+1}} = \dfrac{\dfrac{2(2w+1)-4w}{w(2w+1)}}{\dfrac{5(2w+1)+8w}{w(2w+1)}} = \dfrac{4w+2-4w}{10w+5+8w} = \dfrac{2}{18w+5}$

**55** $\dfrac{(x+h)^2 - 3(x+h) - (x^2-3x)}{h} = \dfrac{x^2+2xh+h^2-3x-3h-x^2+3x}{h}$

$\qquad\qquad = \dfrac{2xh+h^2-3h}{h} = \dfrac{h(2x+h-3)}{h} = 2x+h-3$

**56** $\dfrac{(x+h)^3 + 5(x+h) - (x^3+5x)}{h} = \dfrac{x^3+3x^2h+3xh^2+h^3+5x+5h-x^3-5x}{h}$

$\qquad\qquad = \dfrac{3x^2h+3xh^2+h^3+5h}{h}$

$\qquad\qquad = \dfrac{h(3x^2+3xh+h^2+5)}{h} = 3x^2+3xh+h^2+5$

**57** $\dfrac{\dfrac{5}{x-1}-\dfrac{5}{a-1}}{x-a} = \dfrac{\dfrac{5(a-1)-5(x-1)}{(x-1)(a-1)}}{x-a} = \dfrac{5a-5x}{(x-1)(a-1)(x-a)} = \dfrac{5(a-x)}{(x-1)(a-1)(x-a)}$

$\qquad\qquad\qquad\qquad\qquad = -\dfrac{5}{(x-1)(a-1)}$

**58** $\dfrac{\dfrac{x+2}{x}-\dfrac{a+2}{a}}{x-a}=\dfrac{\dfrac{a(x+2)-x(a+2)}{ax}}{x-a}=\dfrac{2a-2x}{ax(x-a)}=\dfrac{2(a-x)}{ax(x-a)}=-\dfrac{2}{ax}$

**59** $\dfrac{\dfrac{1}{(x+h)^3}-\dfrac{1}{x^3}}{h}=\dfrac{\dfrac{x^3-(x+h)^3}{(x+h)^3x^3}}{h}$

$\qquad=\dfrac{x^3-(x+h)^3}{hx^3(x+h)^3}=\dfrac{[x-(x+h)]\left[x^2+x(x+h)+(x+h)^2\right]}{hx^3(x+h)^3}$ {difference of two cubes}

$\qquad=\dfrac{-h[x^2+x^2+xh+x^2+2xh+h^2]}{hx^3(x+h)^3}=\dfrac{-h(3x^2+3xh+h^2)}{hx^3(x+h)^3}=-\dfrac{3x^2+3xh+h^2}{x^3(x+h)^3}$

**60** $\dfrac{\dfrac{1}{x+h}-\dfrac{1}{x}}{h}=\dfrac{\dfrac{x-(x+h)}{(x+h)x}}{h}=\dfrac{-h}{hx(x+h)}=\dfrac{-1}{x(x+h)}$

**61** The conjugate of $\sqrt{t}-5$ is $\sqrt{t}+5$. Multiply the numerator and the denominator by the conjugate of the denominator. This will eliminate the radical in the denominator.

$$\frac{\sqrt{t}+5}{\sqrt{t}-5}=\frac{\sqrt{t}+5}{\sqrt{t}-5}\cdot\frac{\sqrt{t}+5}{\sqrt{t}+5}=\frac{\left(\sqrt{t}\right)^2+2\cdot5\sqrt{t}+5^2}{\left(\sqrt{t}\right)^2-5^2}=\frac{t+10\sqrt{t}+25}{t-25}$$

**62** $\dfrac{16x^2-y^2}{2\sqrt{x}-\sqrt{y}}=\dfrac{16x^2-y^2}{2\sqrt{x}-\sqrt{y}}\cdot\dfrac{2\sqrt{x}+\sqrt{y}}{2\sqrt{x}+\sqrt{y}}=\dfrac{(4x+y)(4x-y)\left(2\sqrt{x}+\sqrt{y}\right)}{4x-y}=(4x+y)\left(2\sqrt{x}+\sqrt{y}\right)$

**63** We must recognize $\sqrt[3]{a}-\sqrt[3]{b}$ as the first factor of the product formula for the difference of two cubes, $x^3-y^3=(x-y)(x^2+xy+y^2)$. The second factor is then

$$\left(\sqrt[3]{a}\right)^2+\left(\sqrt[3]{a}\right)\left(\sqrt[3]{b}\right)+\left(\sqrt[3]{b}\right)^2=\sqrt[3]{a^2}+\sqrt[3]{ab}+\sqrt[3]{b^2}.$$

$$\frac{1}{\sqrt[3]{a}-\sqrt[3]{b}}=\frac{1}{\sqrt[3]{a}-\sqrt[3]{b}}\cdot\frac{\sqrt[3]{a^2}+\sqrt[3]{ab}+\sqrt[3]{b^2}}{\sqrt[3]{a^2}+\sqrt[3]{ab}+\sqrt[3]{b^2}}=\frac{\sqrt[3]{a^2}+\sqrt[3]{ab}+\sqrt[3]{b^2}}{a-b}$$

**64** $\dfrac{1}{\sqrt[3]{x}+\sqrt[3]{y}}=\dfrac{1}{\sqrt[3]{x}+\sqrt[3]{y}}\cdot\dfrac{\sqrt[3]{x^2}-\sqrt[3]{xy}+\sqrt[3]{y^2}}{\sqrt[3]{x^2}-\sqrt[3]{xy}+\sqrt[3]{y^2}}=\dfrac{\sqrt[3]{x^2}-\sqrt[3]{xy}+\sqrt[3]{y^2}}{x+y}$

**65** $\dfrac{\sqrt{a}-\sqrt{b}}{a^2-b^2}=\dfrac{\sqrt{a}-\sqrt{b}}{a^2-b^2}\cdot\dfrac{\sqrt{a}+\sqrt{b}}{\sqrt{a}+\sqrt{b}}=\dfrac{a-b}{(a+b)(a-b)\left(\sqrt{a}+\sqrt{b}\right)}=\dfrac{1}{(a+b)\left(\sqrt{a}+\sqrt{b}\right)}$

**66** $\dfrac{\sqrt{b}+\sqrt{c}}{b^2-c^2}=\dfrac{\sqrt{b}+\sqrt{c}}{b^2-c^2}\cdot\dfrac{\sqrt{b}-\sqrt{c}}{\sqrt{b}-\sqrt{c}}=\dfrac{b-c}{(b+c)(b-c)\left(\sqrt{b}-\sqrt{c}\right)}=\dfrac{1}{(b+c)\left(\sqrt{b}-\sqrt{c}\right)}$

**67** $\dfrac{\sqrt{2(x+h)+1}-\sqrt{2x+1}}{h}=\dfrac{\sqrt{2(x+h)+1}-\sqrt{2x+1}}{h}\cdot\dfrac{\sqrt{2(x+h)+1}+\sqrt{2x+1}}{\sqrt{2(x+h)+1}+\sqrt{2x+1}}$

$\qquad=\dfrac{(2x+2h+1)-(2x+1)}{h\left(\sqrt{2(x+h)+1}+\sqrt{2x+1}\right)}$

$\qquad=\dfrac{2h}{h\left(\sqrt{2(x+h)+1}+\sqrt{2x+1}\right)}=\dfrac{2}{\sqrt{2(x+h)+1}+\sqrt{2x+1}}$

**68** $\dfrac{\sqrt{x} - \sqrt{x+h}}{h\sqrt{x}\sqrt{x+h}} = \dfrac{\sqrt{x} - \sqrt{x+h}}{h\sqrt{x}\sqrt{x+h}} \cdot \dfrac{\sqrt{x} + \sqrt{x+h}}{\sqrt{x} + \sqrt{x+h}} = \dfrac{x - (x+h)}{h\sqrt{x}\sqrt{x+h}\left(\sqrt{x} + \sqrt{x+h}\right)}$

$$= \dfrac{-h}{h\sqrt{x}\sqrt{x+h}\left(\sqrt{x} + \sqrt{x+h}\right)} = \dfrac{-1}{\sqrt{x}\sqrt{x+h}\left(\sqrt{x} + \sqrt{x+h}\right)}$$

**69** $\dfrac{3x^2 - x + 7}{x^{2/3}} = \dfrac{3x^2}{x^{2/3}} - \dfrac{x}{x^{2/3}} + \dfrac{7}{x^{2/3}} = 3x^{4/3} - x^{1/3} + 7x^{-2/3}$

**70** $\dfrac{x^2 + 4x - 6}{\sqrt{x}} = \dfrac{x^2}{\sqrt{x}} + \dfrac{4x}{\sqrt{x}} - \dfrac{6}{\sqrt{x}} = x^{3/2} + 4x^{1/2} - 6x^{-1/2}$

**71** $\dfrac{\left(x^2 + 2\right)^2}{x^5} = \dfrac{x^4 + 4x^2 + 4}{x^5} = \dfrac{x^4}{x^5} + \dfrac{4x^2}{x^5} + \dfrac{4}{x^5} = x^{-1} + 4x^{-3} + 4x^{-5}$

**72** $\dfrac{\left(\sqrt{x} - 3\right)^2}{x^3} = \dfrac{x - 6\sqrt{x} + 9}{x^3} = \dfrac{x}{x^3} - \dfrac{6\sqrt{x}}{x^3} + \dfrac{9}{x^3} = x^{-2} - 6x^{-5/2} + 9x^{-3}$

**Note:** You may wish to demonstrate the three techniques shown in Example 7 with one of these simpler expressions in 73–76.

**Note:** Exercises 73–90 are worked using the factoring concept given as the third method of simplification in Example 7.

**73** The smallest exponent that appears on the variable $x$ is $-3$.

$$x^{-3} + x^2 \text{ \{factor out } x^{-3}\} = x^{-3}\left(1 + x^{2-(-3)}\right) = x^{-3}\left(1 + x^5\right) = \dfrac{1 + x^5}{x^3}$$

**74** $x^{-5} - x$ {factor out $x^{-5}$} $= x^{-5}\left(1 - x^{1-(-5)}\right) = x^{-5}(1 - x^6) = \dfrac{1 - x^6}{x^5}$

**75** $x^{-1/2} - x^{3/2}$ {factor out $x^{-1/2}$} $= x^{-1/2}\left(1 - x^{3/2-(-1/2)}\right) = x^{-1/2}(1 - x^2) = \dfrac{1 - x^2}{x^{1/2}}$

**76** $x^{-2/3} + x^{7/3}$ {factor out $x^{-2/3}$} $= x^{-2/3}\left(1 + x^{7/3-(-2/3)}\right) = x^{-2/3}(1 + x^3) = \dfrac{1 + x^3}{x^{2/3}}$

**77** $\left(2x^2 - 3x + 1\right)(4)(3x + 2)^3(3) + (3x + 2)^4(4x - 3)$

$= (3x + 2)^3\left[12\left(2x^2 - 3x + 1\right) + (3x + 2)(4x - 3)\right]$ {factor out the gcf of $(3x + 2)^3$}

$= (3x + 2)^3\left(24x^2 - 36x + 12 + 12x^2 - x - 6\right)$

$= (3x + 2)^3\left(36x^2 - 37x + 6\right)$

**78** $(6x - 5)^3(2)\left(x^2 + 4\right)(2x) + \left(x^2 + 4\right)^2(3)(6x - 5)^2(6) = 2(6x - 5)^2\left(x^2 + 4\right)\left[2x(6x - 5) + 9\left(x^2 + 4\right)\right]$

$$= 2(6x - 5)^2\left(x^2 + 4\right)\left(12x^2 - 10x + 9x^2 + 36\right)$$

$$= 2\left(x^2 + 4\right)(6x - 5)^2\left(21x^2 - 10x + 36\right)$$

**79** The smallest exponent that appears on the factor $(x^2 - 4)$ is $-\frac{1}{2}$ and the smallest exponent that appears on the factor $(2x + 1)$ is 2. Thus, we will factor out $(x^2 - 4)^{-1/2}(2x + 1)^2$.

$\left(x^2 - 4\right)^{1/2}(3)(2x + 1)^2(2) + (2x + 1)^3\left(\tfrac{1}{2}\right)\left(x^2 - 4\right)^{-1/2}(2x) = \left(x^2 - 4\right)^{-1/2}(2x + 1)^2\left[6\left(x^2 - 4\right) + x(2x + 1)\right]$

If you are unsure of this factoring, it is easy to visually check at this stage by merely multiplying the expression— that is, we mentally add the exponents on the factor $(x^2 - 4)$, $-\frac{1}{2}$ and 1, and we get $\frac{1}{2}$, which is the exponent we started with.

Proceeding: $\left(x^2 - 4\right)^{-1/2}(2x + 1)^2\left[6\left(x^2 - 4\right) + x(2x + 1)\right] = \left(x^2 - 4\right)^{-1/2}(2x + 1)^2\left(6x^2 - 24 + 2x^2 + x\right)$

$$= \dfrac{(2x + 1)^2\left(8x^2 + x - 24\right)}{\left(x^2 - 4\right)^{1/2}}$$

**80** $(3x+2)^{1/3}(2)(4x-5)(4) + (4x-5)^2\left(\frac{1}{3}\right)(3x+2)^{-2/3}(3) = (3x+2)^{-2/3}(4x-5)[8(3x+2)+(4x-5)]$

$$= \frac{(4x-5)(28x+11)}{(3x+2)^{2/3}}$$

**81** $(3x+1)^6\left(\frac{1}{2}\right)(2x-5)^{-1/2}(2) + (2x-5)^{1/2}(6)(3x+1)^5(3)$

$= (3x+1)^5(2x-5)^{-1/2}[(3x+1)+18(2x-5)]$    $\left\{\text{factor out } (3x+1)^5(2x-5)^{-1/2}\right\}$

$= \dfrac{(3x+1)^5(3x+1+36x-90)}{(2x-5)^{1/2}} = \dfrac{(3x+1)^5(39x-89)}{(2x-5)^{1/2}}$

**82** $(x^2+9)^4\left(-\frac{1}{3}\right)(x+6)^{-4/3} + (x+6)^{-1/3}(4)(x^2+9)^3(2x)$

$= \left(\frac{1}{3}\right)(x^2+9)^3(x+6)^{-4/3}\left[-(x^2+9)+24x(x+6)\right] = \dfrac{(x^2+9)^3(23x^2+144x-9)}{3(x+6)^{4/3}}$

**83** $\dfrac{(6x+1)^3(27x^2+2)-(9x^3+2x)(3)(6x+1)^2(6)}{(6x+1)^6} = \dfrac{(6x+1)^2[(6x+1)(27x^2+2)-18(9x^3+2x)]}{(6x+1)^6}$

$$= \frac{(6x+1)^2(162x^3+27x^2+12x+2-162x^3-36x)}{(6x+1)^6}$$

$$= \frac{27x^2-24x+2}{(6x+1)^4}$$

**84** $\dfrac{(x^2-1)^4(2x)-x^2(4)(x^2-1)^3(2x)}{(x^2-1)^8} = \dfrac{(2x)(x^2-1)^3[(x^2-1)-4x^2]}{(x^2-1)^8} = \dfrac{2x(-3x^2-1)}{(x^2-1)^5} = \dfrac{-2x(3x^2+1)}{(x^2-1)^5}$

**85** $\dfrac{(x^2+2)^3(2x)-x^2(3)(x^2+2)^2(2x)}{\left[(x^2+2)^3\right]^2} = \dfrac{(x^2+2)^2(2x)\left[(x^2+2)^1-x^2(3)\right]}{(x^2+2)^6} =$

$$\frac{2x(x^2+2-3x^2)}{(x^2+2)^4} = \frac{2x(2-2x^2)}{(x^2+2)^4} = \frac{4x(1-x^2)}{(x^2+2)^4}$$

**86** $\dfrac{(x^2-5)^4(3x^2)-x^3(4)(x^2-5)^3(2x)}{\left[(x^2-5)^4\right]^2} = \dfrac{(x^2-5)^3(x^2)\left[(x^2-5)^1(3)-(x)(4)(2x)\right]}{(x^2-5)^8} =$

$$\frac{x^2(3x^2-15-8x^2)}{(x^2-5)^5} = \frac{x^2(-5x^2-15)}{(x^2-5)^5} = -\frac{5x^2(x^2+3)}{(x^2-5)^5}$$

**87** $\dfrac{(x^2+4)^{1/3}(3)-(3x)\left(\frac{1}{3}\right)(x^2+4)^{-2/3}(2x)}{\left[(x^2+4)^{1/3}\right]^2} = \dfrac{(x^2+4)^{-2/3}[3(x^2+4)-2x^2]}{(x^2+4)^{2/3}} = \dfrac{3x^2+12-2x^2}{(x^2+4)^{4/3}} = \dfrac{x^2+12}{(x^2+4)^{4/3}}$

**88** $\dfrac{(1-x^2)^{1/2}(2x)-x^2\left(\frac{1}{2}\right)(1-x^2)^{-1/2}(-2x)}{\left[(1-x^2)^{1/2}\right]^2} = \dfrac{x(1-x^2)^{-1/2}[2(1-x^2)+x^2]}{(1-x^2)^1} = \dfrac{x(2-2x^2+x^2)}{(1-x^2)^{3/2}} = \dfrac{x(2-x^2)}{(1-x^2)^{3/2}}$

**89** $\dfrac{(4x^2+9)^{1/2}(2)-(2x+3)\left(\frac{1}{2}\right)(4x^2+9)^{-1/2}(8x)}{\left[(4x^2+9)^{1/2}\right]^2} = \dfrac{(4x^2+9)^{-1/2}[2(4x^2+9)-4x(2x+3)]}{(4x^2+9)^1}$

$$= \frac{8x^2+18-8x^2-12x}{(4x^2+9)^{3/2}} = \frac{18-12x}{(4x^2+9)^{3/2}} = \frac{6(3-2x)}{(4x^2+9)^{3/2}}$$

**90** $\dfrac{(3x+2)^{1/2}\left(\frac{1}{3}\right)(2x+3)^{-2/3}(2) - (2x+3)^{1/3}\left(\frac{1}{2}\right)(3x+2)^{-1/2}(3)}{\left[(3x+2)^{1/2}\right]^2}$

$= \dfrac{\left(\frac{1}{3}\right)\left(\frac{1}{2}\right)(3x+2)^{-1/2}(2x+3)^{-2/3}[4(3x+2)-9(2x+3)]}{(3x+2)^1}$

$= \dfrac{\left(\frac{1}{6}\right)(12x+8-18x-27)}{(3x+2)^{3/2}(2x+3)^{2/3}} = \dfrac{\left(\frac{1}{6}\right)(-6x-19)}{(3x+2)^{3/2}(2x+3)^{2/3}} = -\dfrac{6x+19}{6(3x+2)^{3/2}(2x+3)^{2/3}}$

**91** Table $Y_1 = \dfrac{113x^3 + 280x^2 - 150x}{22x^3 + 77x^2 - 100x - 350}$ and $Y_2 = \dfrac{3x}{2x+7} + \dfrac{4x^2}{1.1x^2 - 5}$.

| $x$ | $Y_1$ | $Y_2$ |
|---|---|---|
| 1 | −0.6923 | −0.6923 |
| 2 | −26.12 | −26.12 |
| 3 | 8.0392 | 8.0392 |
| 4 | 5.8794 | 5.8794 |
| 5 | 5.3268 | 5.3268 |

The values for $Y_1$ and $Y_2$ agree. Therefore, the two expressions might be equal.

**92** Table $Y_1 = \dfrac{20x^2 + 41x + 31}{10x^3 + 10x^2}$ and $Y_2 = \dfrac{1}{x} + \dfrac{1}{x+1} + \dfrac{3.2}{x^2}$.

| $x$ | $Y_1$ | $Y_2$ |
|---|---|---|
| 1 | 4.6 | 4.7 |
| 2 | 1.6083 | 1.6333 |
| 3 | 0.92778 | 0.93889 |
| 4 | 0.64375 | 0.65 |
| 5 | 0.49067 | 0.49467 |

The values for $Y_1$ and $Y_2$ do not agree. Therefore, the two expressions are not equal.

**93** In the second figure, the dimensions of area I are $(x)$ and $(x-y)$. The area of I is $(x-y)x$, and the area of II is $(x-y)y$. The area $A = x^2 - y^2$ {in the first figure}
$= \underline{(x-y)x + (x-y)y}$ {in the second figure}
$= \underline{(x-y)(x+y)}$. {in the third figure}

**94** Volume of I is $x^2(x-y)$, volume of II is $xy(x-y)$, and volume of III is $y^2(x-y)$.
$$V = \underline{x^3 - y^3} = x^2(x-y) + xy(x-y) + y^2(x-y) = \underline{(x-y)(x^2 + xy + y^2)}.$$

**95** (a) For the 25-year-old female, use
$C_f = 66.5 + 13.8w + 5h - 6.8y$ with $w = 59$, $h = 163$, and $y = 25$.
$C_f = 66.5 + 13.8(59) + 5(163) - 6.8(25) = 1525.7$ calories

For the 55-year-old male, use
$C_m = 655 + 9.6w + 1.9h - 4.7y$ with $w = 75$, $h = 178$, and $y = 55$.
$C_m = 655 + 9.6(75) + 1.9(178) - 4.7(55) = 1454.7$ calories

(b) As people age they require fewer calories. The coefficients of $w$ and $h$ are positive because large people require more calories.

## 1.4 Exercises

1  $4x - 3 = -5x + 6 \Rightarrow 4x + 5x = 6 + 3 \Rightarrow 9x = 9 \Rightarrow x = 1$

2  $5x - 4 = 2(x - 2) \Rightarrow 5x - 4 = 2x - 4 \Rightarrow 3x = 0 \Rightarrow x = 0$

3  $(3x - 2)^2 = (x - 5)(9x + 4) \Rightarrow 9x^2 - 12x + 4 = 9x^2 - 41x - 20 \Rightarrow 29x = -24 \Rightarrow x = -\frac{24}{29}$

4  $(x + 5)^2 + 3 = (x - 2)^2 \Rightarrow x^2 + 10x + 25 + 3 = x^2 - 4x + 4 \Rightarrow 14x = -24 \Rightarrow x = -\frac{12}{7}$

5  $\left[\dfrac{3x + 1}{6x - 2} = \dfrac{2x + 5}{4x - 13}\right] \cdot (6x - 2)(4x - 13) \Rightarrow (3x + 1)(4x - 13) = (2x + 5)(6x - 2) \Rightarrow$

   $12x^2 - 35x - 13 = 12x^2 + 26x - 10 \Rightarrow -3 = 61x \Rightarrow x = -\frac{3}{61}$ $\left\{\text{note that } x \neq \frac{1}{3}, \frac{13}{4}\right\}$

6  $\left[\dfrac{7x + 2}{14x - 3} = \dfrac{x - 8}{2x + 3}\right] \cdot (14x - 3)(2x + 3) \Rightarrow (7x + 2)(2x + 3) = (x - 8)(14x - 3) \Rightarrow$

   $14x^2 + 25x + 6 = 14x^2 - 115x + 24 \Rightarrow 140x = 18 \Rightarrow x = \frac{9}{70}$

7  $\left[\dfrac{4}{x + 2} + \dfrac{1}{x - 2} = \dfrac{5x - 6}{x^2 - 4}\right] \cdot (x + 2)(x - 2) \Rightarrow 4(x - 2) + 1(x + 2) = 5x - 6 \Rightarrow$

   $4x - 8 + x + 2 = 5x - 6 \Rightarrow 5x - 6 = 5x - 6$ {or $0 = 0$}, indicating an identity. The solution is $\mathbb{R} - \{\pm 2\}$.

8  $\left[\dfrac{2}{2x + 5} + \dfrac{3}{2x - 5} = \dfrac{10x + 5}{4x^2 - 25}\right] \cdot (2x + 5)(2x - 5) \Rightarrow 2(2x - 5) + 3(2x + 5) = 10x + 5 \Rightarrow$

   $4x - 10 + 6x + 15 = 10x + 5 \Rightarrow 10x + 5 = 10x + 5$ {or $0 = 0$}, indicating an identity.

   The solution is $\mathbb{R} - \left\{\pm\frac{5}{2}\right\}$.

9  $\left[\dfrac{5}{2x + 3} + \dfrac{4}{2x - 3} = \dfrac{14x + 3}{4x^2 - 9}\right] \cdot (2x + 3)(2x - 3) \Rightarrow 5(2x - 3) + 4(2x + 3) = 14x + 3 \Rightarrow$

   $10x - 15 + 8x + 12 = 14x + 3 \Rightarrow 18x - 3 = 14x + 3 \Rightarrow 4x = 6 \Rightarrow$

   $x = \frac{3}{2}$, which is not in the domain of the given expressions. **No solution**

10  $\left[\dfrac{-3}{x + 4} + \dfrac{7}{x - 4} = \dfrac{-5x + 4}{x^2 - 16}\right] \cdot (x + 4)(x - 4) \Rightarrow -3(x - 4) + 7(x + 4) = -5x + 4 \Rightarrow$

   $-3x + 12 + 7x + 28 = -5x + 4 \Rightarrow 4x + 40 = -5x + 4 \Rightarrow 9x = -36 \Rightarrow$

   $x = -4$, which is not in the domain of the given expressions. **No solution**

11  Divide both sides by a nonzero constant whenever possible. In this case, 5 divides evenly into both sides.

   $75x^2 + 35x - 10 = 0$ {divide by 5} $\Rightarrow 15x^2 + 7x - 2 = 0$ {factor} $\Rightarrow$

   $(3x + 2)(5x - 1) = 0$ {zero factor theorem} $\Rightarrow x = -\frac{2}{3}, \frac{1}{5}$

12  $48x^2 + 12x - 90 = 0$ {divide by 6} $\Rightarrow 8x^2 + 2x - 15 = 0 \Rightarrow (2x + 3)(4x - 5) = 0 \Rightarrow x = -\frac{3}{2}, \frac{5}{4}$

13  Here, the lcd is $x(x + 3)$ and we need to remember that $x \neq 0, -3$.

   $\left[\dfrac{x}{x + 3} + \dfrac{1}{x} - 4 = \dfrac{9}{x^2 + 3x}\right] \cdot x(x + 3) \Rightarrow x(x) + 1(x + 3) - 4(x^2 + 3x) = 9 \Rightarrow$

   $x^2 + x + 3 - 4x^2 - 12x = 9 \Rightarrow 0 = 3x^2 + 11x + 6 \Rightarrow (3x + 2)(x + 3) = 0 \Rightarrow$

   $x = -\frac{2}{3}$ {$-3$ is not in the domain of the given expressions}

**14** $\left[\dfrac{3x}{x-2}+\dfrac{1}{x+2}=\dfrac{-4}{x^2-4}\right]\cdot(x+2)(x-2) \;\Rightarrow\; 3x(x+2)+1(x-2)=-4 \;\Rightarrow\;$
$3x^2+6x+x-2=-4 \;\Rightarrow\; 3x^2+7x+2=0 \;\Rightarrow\; (3x+1)(x+2)=0 \;\Rightarrow\;$
$$x=-\tfrac{1}{3}\ \{-2\text{ is not in the domain of the given expressions}\}$$

**15** $25x^2=9 \;\Rightarrow\; x^2=\dfrac{9}{25} \;\Rightarrow\; x=\pm\sqrt{\dfrac{9}{25}} \;\Rightarrow\; x=\pm\dfrac{3}{5}$

**16** $64x^2=49 \;\Rightarrow\; x^2=\dfrac{49}{64} \;\Rightarrow\; x=\pm\sqrt{\dfrac{49}{64}} \;\Rightarrow\; x=\pm\dfrac{7}{8}$

**17** $(x-3)^2=17 \;\Rightarrow\; x-3=\pm\sqrt{17} \;\Rightarrow\; x=3\pm\sqrt{17}$

**18** $(x+5)^2=29 \;\Rightarrow\; x+5=\pm\sqrt{29} \;\Rightarrow\; x=-5\pm\sqrt{29}$

**19** $x^2+6x+3=0 \;\Rightarrow\; x=\dfrac{-6\pm\sqrt{36-12}}{2(1)}=\dfrac{-6\pm\sqrt{24}}{2}=\dfrac{-6\pm2\sqrt{6}}{2}=-3\pm\sqrt{6}$

**20** $x^2-4x-2=0 \;\Rightarrow\; x=\dfrac{4\pm\sqrt{16+8}}{2(1)}=\dfrac{4\pm\sqrt{24}}{2}=\dfrac{4\pm2\sqrt{6}}{2}=2\pm\sqrt{6}$

**21** The *expression* is $x^2+x-30$. The associated quadratic *equation* is $x^2+x-30=0$.

Using the quadratic formula, $x=\dfrac{-b\pm\sqrt{b^2-4ac}}{2a}$, to solve for $x$ with $a=1$, $b=1$, and $c=-30$ gives us:

$$x=\dfrac{-1\pm\sqrt{1^2-4(1)(-30)}}{2(1)}=\dfrac{-1\pm\sqrt{1+120}}{2}=\dfrac{-1\pm\sqrt{121}}{2}=\dfrac{-1\pm11}{2}=\dfrac{10}{2},\dfrac{-12}{2}=5,-6$$

Write the equation as a product of linear factors: $[x-(5)]\,[x-(-6)]=0$

Now simplify: $(x-5)(x+6)=0$

So the final factored form of $x^2+x-30$ is $(x-5)(x+6)$.

**22** $x^2-11x=0\ \{a=1,\,b=-11,\,c=0\}$, so $x=\dfrac{11\pm\sqrt{121-0}}{2}=\dfrac{11\pm11}{2}=11,0$.

Thus, $x^2-11x=(x-11)(x-0)=x(x-11)$.

**23** $12x^2-16x-3=0\ \{a=12,\,b=-16,\,c=-3\}$, so $x=\dfrac{16\pm\sqrt{256+144}}{24}=\dfrac{16\pm20}{24}=\dfrac{3}{2},-\dfrac{1}{6}$.

Write the equation as a product of linear factors: $\left[x-\left(\tfrac{3}{2}\right)\right]\left[x-\left(-\tfrac{1}{6}\right)\right]=0$

Now multiply the first factor by 2 and the second factor by 6. $(2x-3)(6x+1)=0$

So the final factored form of $12x^2-16x-3$ is $(2x-3)(6x+1)$.

**24** $15x^2+34x-16=0\ \{a=15,\,b=34,\,c=-16\}$, so $x=\dfrac{-34\pm\sqrt{1156+960}}{30}=\dfrac{-34\pm46}{30}=\dfrac{2}{5},-\dfrac{8}{3}$.

Thus, $15x^2+34x-16=5\left[x-\left(\tfrac{2}{5}\right)\right]\cdot3\left[x-\left(-\tfrac{8}{3}\right)\right]=(5x-2)(3x+8)$.

**25** We must first isolate the absolute value term before proceeding.

$|3x-2|+3=7 \;\Rightarrow\; |3x-2|=4 \;\Rightarrow\; 3x-2=4 \text{ or } 3x-2=-4 \;\Rightarrow\;$
$$3x=6 \text{ or } 3x=-2 \;\Rightarrow\; x=2 \text{ or } x=-\tfrac{2}{3}$$

**26** $2|5x+2|-1=5 \;\Rightarrow\; 2|5x+2|=6 \;\Rightarrow\; |5x+2|=3 \;\Rightarrow\;$
$$5x+2=3 \text{ or } 5x+2=-3 \;\Rightarrow\; 5x=1 \text{ or } 5x=-5 \;\Rightarrow\; x=\tfrac{1}{5} \text{ or } x=-1$$

**27** $3|x+1|-5=-11 \;\Rightarrow\; 3|x+1|=-6 \;\Rightarrow\; |x+1|=-2$.

Since the absolute value of an expression is nonnegative, $|x+1|=-2$ has no solution.

**28** $|x - 3| + 6 = 6 \Rightarrow |x - 3| = 0$. Since the absolute value of an expression can only

equal 0 if the expression itself is 0, $|x - 3| = 0 \Rightarrow x - 3 = 0 \Rightarrow x = 3$.

**29** Since there are four terms, we first try factoring by grouping.

$9x^3 - 18x^2 - 4x + 8 = 0 \Rightarrow 9x^2(x - 2) - 4(x - 2) = 0 \Rightarrow$

$(9x^2 - 4)(x - 2) = 0 \Rightarrow x^2 = \frac{4}{9}$ or $x = 2 \Rightarrow x = \pm\frac{2}{3}, 2$

**30** Notice that we can factor an $x$ out of each term, and then factor by grouping.

$4x^4 + 10x^3 = 6x^2 + 15x \Rightarrow 4x^4 + 10x^3 - 6x^2 - 15x = 0 \Rightarrow x(4x^3 + 10x^2 - 6x - 15) = 0 \Rightarrow$

$x\left[2x^2(2x + 5) - 3(2x + 5)\right] = 0 \Rightarrow x(2x^2 - 3)(2x + 5) = 0 \Rightarrow$

$x = 0$ or $x^2 = \frac{3}{2}$ or $x = -\frac{5}{2} \Rightarrow x = 0, \pm\frac{1}{2}\sqrt{6}, -\frac{5}{2}$

***Note:*** $x^2 = \frac{3}{2} \Rightarrow x = \pm\sqrt{\frac{3}{2}} = \pm\frac{\sqrt{3}}{\sqrt{2}} \cdot \frac{\sqrt{2}}{\sqrt{2}} = \pm\frac{\sqrt{6}}{2} = \pm\frac{1}{2}\sqrt{6}$.

There are several ways to write this answer—your professor may have a preference.

**31** $y^{3/2} = 5y \Rightarrow y^{3/2} - 5y = 0 \Rightarrow y(y^{1/2} - 5) = 0 \Rightarrow y = 0$ or $y^{1/2} = 5$.

$y^{1/2} = 5 \Rightarrow \left(y^{1/2}\right)^2 = 5^2 \Rightarrow y = 25$. The solutions are $y = 0$ and $y = 25$.

***Note:*** The following guidelines may be helpful when solving radical equations.

### Guidelines for Solving a Radical Equation

(1)   Isolate the radical. If we cannot get the radical isolated on one side of the equals sign because there is more than one radical, then we will split up the radical terms as evenly as possible on each side of the equals sign. For example, if there are two radicals, we put one on each side; if there are three radicals, we put two on one side and one on the other.

(2)   Raise both sides to the same power as the root index. ***Note:*** Remember here that

$$\boxed{\left(a + b\sqrt{n}\right)^2 = a^2 + 2ab\sqrt{n} + b^2n}$$

and that $\left(a + b\sqrt{n}\right)^2$ is **not** $a^2 + b^2n$.

(3)   If your equation contains no radicals, proceed to part (4). If there are still radicals in the equation, go back to part (1).

(4)   Solve the resulting equation.

(5)   Check the answers found in part (4) in the original equation to determine the valid solutions.

     ***Note:*** You may check the solutions in any equivalent equation of the original equation, that is, an equation which occurs prior to raising both sides to a power. Also, extraneous real number solutions are introduced when raising both sides to an even power. Hence, all solutions *must* be checked in this case. Checking solutions when raising each side to an odd power is up to the individual professor.

**32** $y^{4/3} = -4y \Rightarrow y^{4/3} + 4y = 0 \Rightarrow y(y^{1/3} + 4) = 0 \Rightarrow y = 0$ or $y^{1/3} = -4$.

$y^{1/3} = -4 \Rightarrow \left(y^{1/3}\right)^3 = (-4)^3 \Rightarrow y = -64. \; y = 0, -64$

**33** $\sqrt{7 - 5x} = 8 \Rightarrow \left(\sqrt{7 - 5x}\right)^2 = 8^2 \Rightarrow 7 - 5x = 64 \Rightarrow -57 = 5x \Rightarrow x = -\frac{57}{5}$

**34** $\sqrt{3 - x} - x = 3 \Rightarrow \left(\sqrt{3 - x}\right)^2 = (x + 3)^2 \Rightarrow 3 - x = x^2 + 6x + 9 \Rightarrow x^2 + 7x + 6 = 0 \Rightarrow$

$(x + 1)(x + 6) = 0 \Rightarrow x = -1$ and $-6$ is an extraneous solution.

**35** $x = 3 + \sqrt{5x - 9} \;\Rightarrow\; x - 3 = \sqrt{5x - 9} \;\Rightarrow\; x^2 - 6x + 9 = 5x - 9 \;\Rightarrow$
$$x^2 - 11x + 18 = 0 \;\Rightarrow\; (x - 2)(x - 9) = 0 \;\Rightarrow\; x = 9 \text{ and } 2 \text{ is an extraneous solution.}$$

**36** $x + \sqrt{5x + 19} = -1 \;\Rightarrow\; \sqrt{5x + 19} = -x - 1 \;\Rightarrow\; 5x + 19 = x^2 + 2x + 1 \;\Rightarrow$
$$x^2 - 3x - 18 = 0 \;\Rightarrow\; (x - 6)(x + 3) = 0 \;\Rightarrow\; x = -3, 6.$$

**Check** $x = -3$: LS $= -3 + 2 = -1 =$ RS $\;\Rightarrow\; x = -3$ is a solution.

**Check** $x = 6$: LS $= 6 + 7 = 13 \neq$ RS $\;\Rightarrow\; x = 6$ is an extraneous solution.

**Note:** Substitution could be used instead of factoring for the following exercises.

**37** We recognize this equation as a quadratic equation in $y^2$ and apply the quadratic formula, solving for $y^2$, *not y*.

$5y^4 - 7y^2 + 1.5 = 0 \;\Rightarrow\; y^2 = \dfrac{7 \pm \sqrt{19}}{10} \cdot \dfrac{10}{10} = \dfrac{70 \pm 10\sqrt{19}}{100} \;\Rightarrow\; y = \pm\dfrac{1}{10}\sqrt{70 \pm 10\sqrt{19}}$

Alternatively, let $u = y^2$ and solve $5u^2 - 7u + 1.5 = 0$.

**38** $3y^4 - 5y^2 + 1.5 = 0 \;\Rightarrow\; y^2 = \dfrac{5 \pm \sqrt{7}}{6} \cdot \dfrac{6}{6} = \dfrac{30 \pm 6\sqrt{7}}{36} \;\Rightarrow\; y = \pm\dfrac{1}{6}\sqrt{30 \pm 6\sqrt{7}}$

**39** $36x^{-4} - 13x^{-2} + 1 = 0 \;\Rightarrow\; (4x^{-2} - 1)(9x^{-2} - 1) = 0 \;\Rightarrow\; x^{-2} = \tfrac{1}{4}, \tfrac{1}{9} \;\Rightarrow\; x^2 = 4, 9 \;\Rightarrow\; x = \pm 2, \pm 3$

Alternatively, let $u = x^{-2}$ and solve $36u^2 - 13u + 1 = 0$.

**40** $x^{-2} - 2x^{-1} - 35 = 0 \;\Rightarrow\; (x^{-1} - 7)(x^{-1} + 5) = 0 \;\Rightarrow\; x^{-1} = 7, -5 \;\Rightarrow\; x = \tfrac{1}{7}, -\tfrac{1}{5}$

**41** $3x^{2/3} + 4x^{1/3} - 4 = 0 \;\Rightarrow\; (3x^{1/3} - 2)(x^{1/3} + 2) = 0 \;\Rightarrow$
$$\sqrt[3]{x} = \tfrac{2}{3}, -2 \;\Rightarrow\; x = \left(\tfrac{2}{3}\right)^3, (-2)^3 \;\Rightarrow\; x = \tfrac{8}{27}, -8$$

Alternatively, let $u = x^{1/3}$ and solve $3u^2 + 4u - 4 = 0$.

**42** $2y^{1/3} - 3y^{1/6} + 1 = 0 \;\Rightarrow\; (2y^{1/6} - 1)(y^{1/6} - 1) = 0 \;\Rightarrow\; \sqrt[6]{y} = \tfrac{1}{2}, 1 \;\Rightarrow\; y = \tfrac{1}{64}, 1$

**43** See the illustrations and discussion on text page 51 for help on solving equations by raising both sides to a reciprocal power. Note that if $x^{m/n}$ is in the given equation and $m$ is even, we have to use the $\pm$ symbol for the solutions. Here are a few more examples:

| Equation | Solution |
| --- | --- |
| $x^{1/2} = 4$ | $\left(x^{1/2}\right)^{2/1} = 4^{2/1} \;\Rightarrow\; x = 16$ |
| $x^{-1/2} = 5$ | $\left(x^{-1/2}\right)^{-2/1} = 5^{-2/1} \;\Rightarrow\; x = \tfrac{1}{25}$ |
| $x^{3/4} = 8$ | $\left(x^{3/4}\right)^{4/3} = 8^{4/3} \;\Rightarrow\; x = 16$ |
| $x^{4/3} = 81$ | $\left(x^{4/3}\right)^{3/4} = 81^{3/4} \;\Rightarrow\; x = \pm 27 \{ \pm \text{ since 4 is even}\}$ |

(a) $x^{5/3} = 32 \;\Rightarrow\; \left(x^{5/3}\right)^{3/5} = (32)^{3/5} \;\Rightarrow\; x = \left(\sqrt[5]{32}\right)^3 = 2^3 = 8$

(b) $x^{4/3} = 16 \;\Rightarrow\; \left(x^{4/3}\right)^{3/4} = \pm(16)^{3/4} \;\Rightarrow\; x = \pm\left(\sqrt[4]{16}\right)^3 = \pm 2^3 = \pm 8$

(c) $x^{2/3} = -64 \;\Rightarrow\; \left(x^{2/3}\right)^{3/2} = \pm(-64)^{3/2} \;\Rightarrow\; x = \pm\left(\sqrt{-64}\right)^3$, which are not real numbers.

**No real solutions**

(d) $x^{3/4} = 125 \;\Rightarrow\; \left(x^{3/4}\right)^{4/3} = (125)^{4/3} \;\Rightarrow\; x = \left(\sqrt[3]{125}\right)^4 = 5^4 = 625$

(e) $x^{3/2} = -27 \;\Rightarrow\; \left(x^{3/2}\right)^{2/3} = (-27)^{2/3} \;\Rightarrow\; x = \left(\sqrt[3]{-27}\right)^2 = (-3)^2 = 9$,

which is an extraneous solution. **No real solutions**

**44** (a) $x^{3/5} = -27 \Rightarrow \left(x^{3/5}\right)^{5/3} = (-27)^{5/3} \Rightarrow x = \left(\sqrt[3]{-27}\right)^5 = (-3)^5 = -243$

    (b) $x^{2/3} = 25 \Rightarrow \left(x^{2/3}\right)^{3/2} = \pm(25)^{3/2} \Rightarrow x = \pm\left(\sqrt{25}\right)^3 = \pm 5^3 = \pm 125$

    (c) $x^{4/3} = -49 \Rightarrow \left(x^{4/3}\right)^{3/4} = \pm(-49)^{3/4} \Rightarrow x = \pm\left(\sqrt[4]{-49}\right)^3$, which are not real numbers.

**No real solutions**

    (d) $x^{3/2} = 64 \Rightarrow \left(x^{3/2}\right)^{2/3} = (64)^{2/3} \Rightarrow x = \left(\sqrt[3]{64}\right)^2 = 4^2 = 16$

    (e) $x^{3/4} = -8 \Rightarrow \left(x^{3/4}\right)^{4/3} = (-8)^{4/3} \Rightarrow x = \left(\sqrt[3]{-8}\right)^4 = (-2)^4 = 16$, which is an extraneous solution.

**No real solutions**

**45** (a) For this exercise, we must recognize the equation as a quadratic in $x$, that is,

$$Ax^2 + Bx + C = 0$$

where $A$ is the coefficient of $x^2$, $B$ is the coefficient of $x$, and $C$ is the collection of all terms that do not contain $x^2$ or $x$.

$4x^2 - 4xy + 1 - y^2 = 0 \Rightarrow (4)x^2 + (-4y)x + (1 - y^2) = 0 \Rightarrow$

$$x = \frac{4y \pm \sqrt{16y^2 - 16(1 - y^2)}}{2(4)} = \frac{4y \pm \sqrt{16\left[y^2 - (1 - y^2)\right]}}{2(4)} = \frac{4y \pm 4\sqrt{2y^2 - 1}}{2(4)} = \frac{y \pm \sqrt{2y^2 - 1}}{2}$$

    (b) Similar to part (a), we must now recognize the equation as a quadratic equation in $y$.

$4x^2 - 4xy + 1 - y^2 = 0 \Rightarrow (-1)y^2 + (-4x)y + (4x^2 + 1) = 0 \Rightarrow$

$$y = \frac{4x \pm \sqrt{16x^2 + 4(4x^2 + 1)}}{2(-1)} = \frac{4x \pm \sqrt{4\left[4x^2 + (4x^2 + 1)\right]}}{-2} = \frac{4x \pm 2\sqrt{8x^2 + 1}}{-2} = -2x \pm \sqrt{8x^2 + 1}$$

**46** (a) $2x^2 - xy = 3y^2 + 1 \Rightarrow (2)x^2 + (-y)x + (-3y^2 - 1) = 0 \Rightarrow$

$$x = \frac{y \pm \sqrt{y^2 - 8(-3y^2 - 1)}}{2(2)} = \frac{y \pm \sqrt{25y^2 + 8}}{4}$$

    (b) $2x^2 - xy = 3y^2 + 1 \Rightarrow (-3)y^2 + (-x)y + (2x^2 - 1) = 0 \Rightarrow$

$$y = \frac{x \pm \sqrt{x^2 + 12(2x^2 - 1)}}{2(-3)} = \frac{x \pm \sqrt{25x^2 - 12}}{-6}$$

**47** (a) $x = \dfrac{-4{,}500{,}000 \pm \sqrt{4{,}500{,}000^2 - 4(1)(-0.96)}}{2} \approx 0$ and $-4{,}500{,}000$

    (b) $x = \dfrac{-b \pm \sqrt{b^2 - 4ac}}{2a} \cdot \dfrac{-b \mp \sqrt{b^2 - 4ac}}{-b \mp \sqrt{b^2 - 4ac}} = \dfrac{b^2 - (b^2 - 4ac)}{2a\left(-b \mp \sqrt{b^2 - 4ac}\right)}$

$$= \frac{4ac}{2a\left(-b \mp \sqrt{b^2 - 4ac}\right)} = \frac{2c}{-b \mp \sqrt{b^2 - 4ac}}$$

The root near zero was obtained in part (a) using the plus sign. In the second formula, it corresponds to the minus sign. $x = \dfrac{2(-0.96)}{-4{,}500{,}000 - \sqrt{4{,}500{,}000^2 - 4(1)(-0.96)}} \approx 2.13 \times 10^{-7}$

**48** (a) $x = \dfrac{73{,}000{,}000 \pm \sqrt{(-73{,}000{,}000)^2 - 4(1)(2.01)}}{2} \approx 73{,}000{,}000$ and $0$

    (b) The root near zero was obtained in part (a) using the minus sign. In the second formula, it corresponds to the plus sign. $x = \dfrac{2(2.01)}{73{,}000{,}000 + \sqrt{(-73{,}000{,}000)^2 - 4(1)(2.01)}} \approx 2.75 \times 10^{-8}$

$\boxed{49}$ $EK + L = D - TK$ {given equation, solve for $K$}

$\quad\quad EK + TK = D - L$ {get $K$-terms on one side, everything else on the other}

$\quad\quad K(E + T) = D - L$ {factor out $K$}

$\quad\quad\quad K = \dfrac{D - L}{E + T}$ {divide by $(E + T)$ to solve for $K$}

$\boxed{50}$ $CD + C = PC + R \;\Rightarrow\; CD + C - PC = R \;\Rightarrow\; C(D + 1 - P) = R \;\Rightarrow\; C = \dfrac{R}{D + 1 - P}$

$\boxed{51}$ $N = \dfrac{Q + 1}{Q} \;\Rightarrow\; NQ = Q + 1 \;\Rightarrow\; NQ - Q = 1 \;\Rightarrow\; Q(N - 1) = 1 \;\Rightarrow\; Q = \dfrac{1}{N - 1}$

$\boxed{52}$ $\beta = \dfrac{\alpha}{1 - \alpha} \;\Rightarrow\; \beta(1 - \alpha) = \alpha \;\Rightarrow\; \beta - \beta\alpha = \alpha \;\Rightarrow\; \beta = \alpha + \beta\alpha \;\Rightarrow\; \beta = \alpha(1 + \beta) \;\Rightarrow\; \alpha = \dfrac{\beta}{1 + \beta}$

$\boxed{53}$ $A = P + Prt \;\Rightarrow\; A - P = Prt \;\Rightarrow\; r = \dfrac{A - P}{Pt}$

$\boxed{54}$ $s = \dfrac{1}{2}gt^2 + v_0 t \;\Rightarrow\; 2s = gt^2 + 2v_0 t \;\Rightarrow\; 2s - gt^2 = 2v_0 t \;\Rightarrow\; v_0 = \dfrac{2s - gt^2}{2t}$

$\boxed{55}$

$\quad\quad\quad S = \dfrac{p}{q + p(1 - q)}$ {given equation, solve for $q$}

$\quad\quad S[q + p(1 - q)] = p$ {eliminate the fraction}

$\quad\quad Sq + Sp(1 - q) = p$ {multiply terms}

$\quad\quad Sq + Sp - Spq = p$ {multiply terms}

$\quad\quad Sq - Spq = p - Sp$ {isolate terms containing $q$}

$\quad\quad Sq(1 - p) = p(1 - S)$ {factor our $Sq$}

$\quad\quad\quad q = \dfrac{p(1 - S)}{S(1 - p)}$ {divide by $S(1 - p)$ to solve for $q$}

$\boxed{56}$ $S = 2(lw + hw + hl) \;\Rightarrow\; S = 2lw + 2hw + 2hl \;\Rightarrow\; S - 2lw = 2h(w + l) \;\Rightarrow\; h = \dfrac{S - 2lw}{2(w + l)}$

$\boxed{57}$ $\dfrac{1}{f} = \dfrac{1}{p} + \dfrac{1}{q}$ {multiply by the lcd, $fpq$} $\;\Rightarrow$

$\quad\quad\quad\quad pq = fq + fp \;\Rightarrow\; pq - fq = fp \;\Rightarrow\; q(p - f) = fp \;\Rightarrow\; q = \dfrac{fp}{p - f}$

$\boxed{58}$ $\dfrac{1}{R} = \dfrac{1}{R_1} + \dfrac{1}{R_2} + \dfrac{1}{R_3}$ {multiply by the lcd, $RR_1R_2R_3$} $\;\Rightarrow\; R_1R_2R_3 = RR_2R_3 + RR_1R_3 + RR_1R_2 \;\Rightarrow$

$\quad R_1R_2R_3 - RR_2R_3 - RR_1R_2 = RR_1R_3 \;\Rightarrow\; R_2(R_1R_3 - RR_3 - RR_1) = RR_1R_3 \;\Rightarrow$

$\quad\quad\quad\quad\quad\quad\quad\quad\quad\quad\quad\quad\quad\quad\quad R_2 = \dfrac{RR_1R_3}{R_1R_3 - RR_3 - RR_1}$

$\boxed{59}$ $K = \dfrac{1}{2}mv^2 \;\Rightarrow\; v^2 = \dfrac{2K}{m} \;\Rightarrow\; v = \pm\sqrt{\dfrac{2K}{m}} \;\Rightarrow\; v = \sqrt{\dfrac{2K}{m}}$ since $v > 0$.

$\boxed{60}$ $F = g\dfrac{mM}{d^2} \;\Rightarrow\; d^2 = \dfrac{gmM}{F} \;\Rightarrow\; d = \pm\sqrt{\dfrac{gmM}{F}} \;\Rightarrow\; d = \sqrt{\dfrac{gmM}{F}}$ since $d > 0$.

$\boxed{61}$ $A = 2\pi r(r + h) \;\Rightarrow\; A = 2\pi r^2 + 2\pi rh \;\Rightarrow\; (2\pi)r^2 + (2\pi h)r - A = 0$ {a quadratic equation in $r$} $\;\Rightarrow$

$\quad\quad r = \dfrac{-(2\pi h) \pm \sqrt{(2\pi h)^2 - 4(2\pi)(-A)}}{2(2\pi)} = \dfrac{-2\pi h \pm \sqrt{4\pi^2 h^2 + 8\pi A}}{2(2\pi)}$

$\quad\quad\quad\quad = \dfrac{-2\pi h \pm 2\sqrt{\pi^2 h^2 + 2\pi A}}{2(2\pi)} = \dfrac{-\pi h \pm \sqrt{\pi^2 h^2 + 2\pi A}}{2\pi}$

Since $r > 0$, we must use the plus sign, and $r = \dfrac{-\pi h + \sqrt{\pi^2 h^2 + 2\pi A}}{2\pi}$.

**62** $s = \frac{1}{2}gt^2 + v_0 t \;\Rightarrow\; \left(\frac{1}{2}g\right)t^2 + (v_0)t - s = 0 \;\Rightarrow\; t = \dfrac{-v_0 \pm \sqrt{v_0^2 + 2gs}}{g}.$

Since $t > 0$, we must use the plus sign, and $t = \dfrac{-v_0 + \sqrt{v_0^2 + 2gs}}{g}.$

**63** $d = \frac{1}{2}\sqrt{4R^2 - C^2} \;\Rightarrow\; 2d = \sqrt{4R^2 - C^2} \;\Rightarrow\; 4d^2 = 4R^2 - C^2 \;\Rightarrow\; C^2 = 4R^2 - 4d^2 \;\Rightarrow$

$\qquad C^2 = 4(R^2 - d^2) \;\Rightarrow\; C = \pm 2\sqrt{R^2 - d^2} \;\Rightarrow\; C = 2\sqrt{R^2 - d^2}$ since $C > 0$

**64** $S = \pi r \sqrt{r^2 + h^2} \;\Rightarrow\; \dfrac{S}{\pi r} = \sqrt{r^2 + h^2} \;\Rightarrow\; \left(\dfrac{S}{\pi r}\right)^2 = \left(\sqrt{r^2 + h^2}\right)^2 \;\Rightarrow\; \dfrac{S^2}{\pi^2 r^2} = r^2 + h^2 \;\Rightarrow$

$\dfrac{S^2}{\pi^2 r^2} - r^2 = h^2 \;\Rightarrow\; \dfrac{S^2}{\pi^2 r^2} - \dfrac{\pi^2 r^4}{\pi^2 r^2} = h^2 \;\Rightarrow\; h^2 = \dfrac{1}{\pi^2 r^2}\left(S^2 - \pi^2 r^4\right) \;\Rightarrow\; h = \pm \dfrac{1}{\pi r}\sqrt{S^2 - \pi^2 r^4} \;\Rightarrow$

$\qquad\qquad h = \dfrac{1}{\pi r}\sqrt{S^2 - \pi^2 r^4}$ since $h > 0$

**65** Let $x$ denote the number of months needed to recover the cost of the insulation. The savings in one month is 10% of \$200 = \$20, so the savings in $x$ months is $20x$. $\qquad 20x = 2400 \;\Rightarrow\; x = 120$ months (or 10 yr).

**66** Let $x$ denote the amount (in millions) invested in bonds.

$x(0.06) + (800 - x)(0.05) = 42 \;\Rightarrow\; 0.06x + 40 - 0.05x = 42 \;\Rightarrow\; 0.01x = 2 \;\Rightarrow\; x = 200.$

The arena should be financed by selling \$200 million in bonds and borrowing \$600 million.

**67** (a) They will meet when the sum of their distances is 224. Let $t$ denote the desired number of seconds.

Using distance = rate × time, we have $1.5t + 2t = 224 \;\Rightarrow\; 3.5t = 224 \;\Rightarrow\; t = 64$ sec.

(b) The children will have walked $64(1.5) = 96$ m and $64(2) = 128$ m, respectively.

**68** Let $l$ denote the length of the side parallel to the river bank. $P = 2w + l$

(a) $l = 2w \;\Rightarrow\; P = 2w + 2w = 4w.\ 4w = 180 \;\Rightarrow\; w = 45$ ft and $A = (45)(90) = 4050$ ft$^2$.

(b) $l = \frac{1}{2}w \;\Rightarrow\; P = 2w + \frac{1}{2}w = \frac{5}{2}w.\ \frac{5}{2}w = 180 \;\Rightarrow\; w = 72$ ft and $A = (72)(36) = 2592$ ft$^2$.

(c) $l = w \;\Rightarrow\; P = 2w + w = 3w.\ 3w = 180 \;\Rightarrow\; w = 60$ ft and $A = (60)(60) = 3600$ ft$^2$.

**69** Let $x$ denote the distance to the target. We know the total time involved and need a formula for time. Solving $d = rt$ for $t$ gives us $t = d/r$.

Time$_{\text{to target}}$ + Time$_{\text{from target}}$ = Time$_{\text{total}} \;\Rightarrow\; \dfrac{x}{3300} + \dfrac{x}{1100} = 1.5$ {multiply by the lcd, 3300} $\Rightarrow$

$\qquad\qquad x + 3x = 1.5(3300) \;\Rightarrow\; 4x = 4950 \;\Rightarrow\; x = 1237.5$ ft.

**70** Let $x$ denote the miles in one direction. A 6-minute-mile pace is equivalent to a rate of $\frac{1}{6}$ mile/min. Solving $d = rt$ for $t$ gives us $t = d/r$. Minutes$_{\text{north}}$ + Minutes$_{\text{south}}$ = Minutes$_{\text{total}} \;\Rightarrow\; \dfrac{x}{1/6} + \dfrac{x}{1/7} = 47 \;\Rightarrow$

$\qquad\qquad 6x + 7x = 47 \;\Rightarrow\; x = \frac{47}{13}.$ The total distance is $2 \cdot \frac{47}{13} = \frac{94}{13}$, or $7\frac{3}{13}$ mi.

**71** Let $b_2$ denote the larger base. $A = \frac{1}{2}(b_1 + b_2)h \;\Rightarrow\; 5 = \frac{1}{2}(3 + b_2)(1) \;\Rightarrow\; 10 = 3 + b_2 \;\Rightarrow\; b_2 = 7$ ft.

**72** Let $h_1$ denote the height of the cylinder. $V = \frac{2}{3}\pi r^3 + \pi r^2 h_1 = 11{,}250\pi$ and $r = 15 \;\Rightarrow$

$\qquad 2250\pi + 225\pi h_1 = 11{,}250\pi \;\Rightarrow\; 225\pi h_1 = 9000\pi \;\Rightarrow\; h_1 = 40.$ The total height is 40 ft + 15 ft = 55 ft.

**73** (a) $T = T_0 - \left(\frac{5.5}{1000}\right)h \;\bullet\; h = 5280$ ft and $T_0 = 70°$F $\;\Rightarrow\; T = 70 - \left(\frac{5.5}{1000}\right)5280 = 40.96°$F.

(b) $T = 32°$F $\;\Rightarrow\; 32 = 70 - \left(\frac{5.5}{1000}\right)h \;\Rightarrow\; \left(\frac{5.5}{1000}\right)h = 38 \;\Rightarrow\; h = 38\left(\frac{1000}{5.5}\right) \approx 6909$ ft.

**74** (a) $h = 227(T - D)$ • $T = 70°F$ and $D = 55°F$ $\Rightarrow$ $h = 227(70 - 55) = 3405$ ft.

(b) $h = 3500$ ft and $D = 65°F$ $\Rightarrow$ $3500 = 227(T - 65)$ $\Rightarrow$ $T = \frac{3500}{227} + 65 \approx 80.4°F$

**75** $T = B - \left(\frac{3}{1000}\right)h$ • $B = 55°F$ and $h = 10,000 - 4000 = 6000$ ft $\Rightarrow$ $T = 55 - \left(\frac{3}{1000}\right)(6000) = 37°F$.

**76** (a) $h = 65 + 3.14x$ • $x = 30$ cm $\Rightarrow$ $h = 65 + 3.14(30) = 159.2$ cm.

(b) $h = 73.6 + 3.0x$ • $x = 34$ $\Rightarrow$ $h = 73.6 + 3(34) = 175.6$ cm. The height of the skeleton has decreased by $175.6 - 174 = 1.6$ cm due to aging after age 30. $\frac{1.6}{0.06} \approx 27$ years. The male was approximately $30 + 27 = 57$ years old at death.

**77** (a) $v = 55$ $\Rightarrow$ $d = v + (v^2/20) = 55 + (55^2/20) = 206.25$ ft

(b) $d = 120$ $\Rightarrow$ $120 = v + (v^2/20)$ $\Rightarrow$ $2400 = 20v + v^2$ $\Rightarrow$ $v^2 + 20v - 2400 = 0$ $\Rightarrow$
$$(v + 60)(v - 40) = 0 \quad \Rightarrow \quad v = 40 \text{ mi/hr}$$

**78** (a) $T = 98$ $\Rightarrow$ $h = 1000(100 - T) + 580(100 - T)^2 = 1000(2) + 580(2)^2 = 4320$ m.

(b) If $x = 100 - T$ and $h = 8840$, then $8840 = 1000x + 580x^2$ $\Rightarrow$
$$29x^2 + 50x - 442 = 0 \quad \Rightarrow \quad x = \frac{-50 \pm \sqrt{2500 + 51,272}}{2(29)} = \frac{-25 \pm \sqrt{13,443}}{29} \approx -4.86, 3.14.$$
$x = -4.86$ $\Rightarrow$ $T = 100 - x = 104.86°C$, which is outside the allowable range of $T$.
$x = 3.14$ $\Rightarrow$ $T = 100 - x = 96.86°C$ for $95 \le T \le 100$.

**79** (a) The northbound plane travels $\frac{1}{2} \cdot 200 = 100$ miles from 2 P.M. to 2:30 P.M., so the distances of the northbound and eastbound planes are $100 + 200t$ and $400t$, respectively. Using the Pythagorean theorem,
$$d = \sqrt{(100 + 200t)^2 + (400t)^2} = \sqrt{100^2(1 + 2t)^2 + 100^2(4t)^2} = \sqrt{100^2\left[(1 + 2t)^2 + (4t)^2\right]}$$
$$= 100\sqrt{1 + 4t + 4t^2 + 16t^2} = 100\sqrt{20t^2 + 4t + 1}.$$

(b) $d = 500$ $\Rightarrow$ $500 = 100\sqrt{20t^2 + 4t + 1}$ $\Rightarrow$ $5 = \sqrt{20t^2 + 4t + 1}$ $\Rightarrow$ $5^2 = 20t^2 + 4t + 1$ $\Rightarrow$
$20t^2 + 4t - 24 = 0$ $\Rightarrow$ $5t^2 + t - 6 = 0$ $\Rightarrow$ $(5t + 6)(t - 1) = 0$ $\Rightarrow$
$$t = 1 \text{ hour after 2:30 P.M., or 3:30 P.M.}$$

**80** Let $t$ denote the number of seconds the rock falls, so that $4 - t$ is the number of seconds for the sound to travel.
$\text{Distance}_{down} = \text{Distance}_{up}$ $\Rightarrow$ $16t^2 = 1100(4 - t)$ $\{d = rt\}$ $\Rightarrow$ $4t^2 = 275(4 - t)$ $\Rightarrow$
$4t^2 + 275t - 1100 = 0$ $\Rightarrow$ $t = \frac{-275 \pm \sqrt{93,225}}{2(4)} = \frac{-275 + 5\sqrt{3729}}{8} \approx 3.79$.
$$\text{The height is } 16t^2 \approx 229.94, \text{ or 230 ft.}$$

**81** Let $x$ denote the number of $10 reductions in price.
Revenue = (unit price) $\times$ (# of units) $\Rightarrow$ $7000 = (300 - 10x)(15 + 2x)$ $\Rightarrow$
$7000 = 10(30 - x)(15 + 2x)$ $\Rightarrow$ $700 = -2x^2 + 45x + 450$ $\Rightarrow$ $2x^2 - 45x + 250 = 0$ $\Rightarrow$
$(2x - 25)(x - 10) = 0$ $\Rightarrow$ $x = 10$ or $12.5$.
$$\text{The selling price is } \$300 - \$10(10) = \$200, \text{ or } \$300 - \$10(12.5) = \$175.$$

**82** The total surface area is the sum of the surface area of the cylinder and that of the top and bottom.
$S = 2\pi rh + 2\pi r^2$ and $h = 4$ $\Rightarrow$ $10\pi = 8\pi r + 2\pi r^2$ {divide by $2\pi$} $\Rightarrow$ $5 = 4r + r^2$ $\Rightarrow$
$r^2 + 4r - 5 = 0$ $\Rightarrow$ $(r + 5)(r - 1) = 0$ $\Rightarrow$ $r = 1$, and the diameter is 2 ft.

**83** (a)   $\text{Area}_{\text{capsule}} = \text{Area}_{\text{sphere}}$ {the two ends are hemispheres} $+ \text{Area}_{\text{cylinder}}$

$$= 4\pi r^2 + 2\pi rh = 4\pi\left(\tfrac{1}{4}\right)^2 + 2\pi\left(\tfrac{1}{4}\right)\left(2 - \tfrac{1}{2}\right) = \tfrac{\pi}{4} + \tfrac{3\pi}{4} = \pi \text{ cm}^2.$$

$\text{Area}_{\text{tablet}} = \text{Area}_{\text{top and bottom}} + \text{Area}_{\text{cylinder}} = 2\pi r^2 + 2\pi r\left(\tfrac{1}{2}\right) = 2\pi r^2 + \pi r.$

Equating the two surface areas yields $2\pi r^2 + \pi r = \pi \;\Rightarrow$

$$2r^2 + r - 1 = 0 \;\Rightarrow\; (2r - 1)(r + 1) = 0 \;\Rightarrow\; r = \tfrac{1}{2}, \text{ and the diameter is 1 cm.}$$

(b)   $\text{Volume}_{\text{capsule}} = \text{Volume}_{\text{sphere}} + \text{Volume}_{\text{cylinder}}$

$$= \tfrac{4}{3}\pi r^3 + \pi r^2 h = \tfrac{4}{3}\pi\left(\tfrac{1}{4}\right)^3 + \pi\left(\tfrac{1}{4}\right)^2\tfrac{3}{2} = \tfrac{\pi}{48} + \tfrac{3\pi}{32} = \tfrac{11\pi}{96} \approx 0.360 \text{ cm}^3.$$

$\text{Volume}_{\text{tablet}} = \text{Volume}_{\text{cylinder}} = \pi r^2 h = \pi\left(\tfrac{1}{2}\right)^2\tfrac{1}{2} = \tfrac{\pi}{8} \approx 0.393 \text{ cm}^3.$

**84** $P = 15{,}700 S^{5/2} RD \;\Rightarrow\; S^{5/2} = \dfrac{P}{15{,}700 RD} \;\Rightarrow$

$$S = \left(\frac{P}{15{,}700 RD}\right)^{2/5} = \left[\frac{380}{(15{,}700)(0.113/2)(2)}\right]^{2/5} \approx 0.54$$

**85** From the Pythagorean theorem, $d^2 + h^2 = L^2$. Since $d$ is to be 25% of $L$, we have

$d = \tfrac{1}{4}L$, so $\left(\tfrac{1}{4}L\right)^2 + h^2 = L^2 \;\Rightarrow\; h^2 = L^2 - \left(\tfrac{1}{4}L\right)^2 \;\Rightarrow\; h^2 = 1L^2 - \tfrac{1}{16}L^2 \;\Rightarrow$

$h^2 = \tfrac{15}{16}L^2 \;\Rightarrow\; h = \sqrt{\tfrac{15}{16}L^2}$ {since $h > 0$} $= \tfrac{\sqrt{15}}{4}L \approx 0.97L$. Thus, $h \approx 97\%L$.

**86** $T = 0.25 P^{1/4}/\sqrt{v} \;\Rightarrow\; P^{1/4} = 4T\sqrt{v} \;\Rightarrow\; P = (4T)^4 v^2 = 4^4 3^4 5^2 = 518{,}400$

**87** $\text{Cost}_{\text{underwater}} + \text{Cost}_{\text{overland}} = \text{Cost}_{\text{total}} \;\Rightarrow\; 7500 \cdot (\text{underwater miles}) + 6000 \cdot (\text{overland miles}) = 35{,}000 \;\Rightarrow$

$7500\sqrt{x^2 + 1} + 6000(5 - x) = 35{,}000 \;\Rightarrow\; 7500\sqrt{x^2 + 1} + 30{,}000 - 6000x = 35{,}000 \;\Rightarrow$

$7500\sqrt{x^2 + 1} = 6000x + 5{,}000 \;\Rightarrow\; 15\sqrt{x^2 + 1} = 12x + 10$ {divide by 500} $\;\Rightarrow$

$225(x^2 + 1) = 144x^2 + 240x + 100 \;\Rightarrow\; 225x^2 + 225 = 144x^2 + 240x + 100 \;\Rightarrow$

$81x^2 - 240x + 125 = 0 \;\Rightarrow\; x = \dfrac{240 \pm \sqrt{17{,}100}}{162} = \dfrac{6 \cdot 40 \pm \sqrt{900 \cdot 19}}{6 \cdot 27} = \dfrac{6 \cdot 40 \pm 30\sqrt{19}}{6 \cdot 27} = \dfrac{40 \pm 5\sqrt{19}}{27} \approx$

$2.2887, 0.6743$ mi. There are two possible routes.

**88** The $y$-value decreases 1.2 units for each 1 unit increase in the $x$-value. The data are best described by equation (1), $y = -1.2x + 2$.

**89** The $y$-values are increasing rapidly and can best be described by equation (4), $y = x^3 - x^2 + x - 10$.

**90** (a) Let $Y_1 = T_1 = -1.09L + 96.01$ and $Y_2 = T_2 = -0.011L^2 - 0.126L + 81.45$. Table each equation and compare them to the actual temperatures.

| $x$ (L) | 85 | 75 | 65 | 55 | 45 | 35 | 25 | 15 | 5 |
|---|---|---|---|---|---|---|---|---|---|
| $Y_1$ | 3.36 | 14.26 | 25.16 | 36.06 | 46.96 | 57.86 | 68.76 | 75.66 | 90.56 |
| $Y_2$ | $-8.74$ | 10.13 | 26.79 | 41.25 | 53.51 | 63.57 | 71.43 | 77.09 | 80.55 |
| S. Hem. | $-5$ | 10 | 27 | 42 | 53 | 65 | 75 | 78 | 79 |

Comparing $Y_1$ ($T_1$) with $Y_2$ ($T_2$), we can see that the linear equation $T_1$ is not as accurate as the quadratic equation $T_2$.

(b) $L = 50 \;\Rightarrow\; T_2 = -0.011(50)^2 - 0.126(50) + 81.45 = 47.65°\text{F}.$

**91** (a) Let $Y_1 = D_1 = 6.096L + 685.7$ and $Y_2 = D_2 = 0.00178L^3 - 0.072L^2 + 4.37L + 719.$

Table each equation and compare them to the actual values.

| $x\ (L)$ | 0 | 10 | 20 | 30 | 40 | 50 | 60 |
|----------|----|----|----|----|----|----|----|
| $Y_1$ | 686 | 747 | 808 | 869 | 930 | 991 | 1051 |
| $Y_2$ | 719 | 757 | 792 | 833 | 893 | 980 | 1106 |
| Summer | 720 | 755 | 792 | 836 | 892 | 978 | 1107 |

Comparing $Y_1\ (D_1)$ with $Y_2\ (D_2)$,

we see that the linear equation $D_1$ is not as accurate as the cubic equation $D_2$.

(b) $L = 35 \implies D_2 = 0.00178(35)^3 - 0.072(35)^2 + 4.37(35) + 719 \approx 860$ min.

## 1.5 Exercises

$\boxed{1}$ $(5 - 2i) + (-3 + 6i) = [5 + (-3)] + (-2 + 6)i = 2 + 4i$

$\boxed{2}$ $(-5 + 4i) + (3 + 9i) = (-5 + 3) + (4 + 9)i = -2 + 13i$

$\boxed{3}$ $(7 - 8i) - (-5 - 3i) = (7 + 5) + (-8 + 3)i = 12 - 5i$

$\boxed{4}$ $(-3 + 8i) - (2 + 3i) = (-3 - 2) + (8 - 3)i = -5 + 5i$

$\boxed{5}$ $(3 + 5i)(2 - 7i) = (3 + 5i)2 + (3 + 5i)(-7i)$  {distributive property}

$\qquad = 6 + 10i - 21i - 35i^2$  {multiply terms}

$\qquad = 6 - 11i - 35(-1)$  {combine $i$-terms, $i^2 = -1$}

$\qquad = 6 - 11i + 35$

$\qquad = 41 - 11i$

$\boxed{6}$ $(-2 + 3i)(8 - i) = (-16 - 3i^2) + (2 + 24)i = (-16 + 3) + 26i = -13 + 26i$

$\boxed{7}$ $(4 - 3i)(2 + 7i) = (8 - 21i^2) + (28 - 6)i = (8 + 21) + 22i = 29 + 22i$

$\boxed{8}$ $(8 + 2i)(7 - 3i) = (56 - 6i^2) + (-24 + 14)i = (56 + 6) - 10i = 62 - 10i$

$\boxed{9}$ Use the *special product formula* for $(x - y)^2$ on the inside front cover of the text.

$\qquad (5 - 2i)^2 = 5^2 - 2(5)(2i) + (2i)^2 = 25 - 20i + 4i^2 = (25 - 4) - 20i = 21 - 20i$

$\boxed{10}$ $(6 + 7i)^2 = 6^2 + 2(6)(7i) + (7i)^2 = (36 - 49) + 84i = -13 + 84i$

$\boxed{11}$ $i(3 + 4i)^2 = i\left[3^2 + 2(3)(4i) + (4i)^2\right] = i\left[(9 - 16) + 24i\right] = i(-7 + 24i) = -24 - 7i$

$\boxed{12}$ $i(2 - 7i)^2 = i\left[2^2 + 2(2)(-7i) + (-7i)^2\right] = i\left[(4 - 49) - 28i\right] = i(-45 - 28i) = 28 - 45i$

$\boxed{13}$ $(3 + 4i)(3 - 4i)$  {note that this difference of squares … }

$\qquad = 3^2 - (4i)^2 = 9 - (-16) = \{\dots$ becomes a "sum of squares"$\}\ 9 + 16 = 25$

$\boxed{14}$ $(4 + 7i)(4 - 7i) = 4^2 - (7i)^2 = 16 - (-49) = 16 + 49 = 65$

$\boxed{15}$ (a) Since $i^k = 1$ if $k$ is a multiple of 4, we will write $i^{43}$ as $i^{40}i^3$, knowing that $i^{40}$ will reduce to 1.

$\qquad i^{43} = i^{40}i^3 = \left(i^4\right)^{10}(-i) = 1^{10}(-i) = -i$

(b) As in Example 3(e), choose $b = 20$. $i^{-20} \cdot i^{20} = i^0 = 1$.

$\boxed{16}$ (a) $i^{68} = \left(i^4\right)^{17} = 1^{17} = 1$

(b) As in Example 3(e), choose $b = 36$. $i^{-33} \cdot i^{36} = i^3 = -i$.

**17** (a) Since $i^k = 1$ if $k$ is a multiple of 4, we will write $i^{73}$ as $i^{72}i^1$, knowing that $i^{72}$ will reduce to 1.

$$i^{73} = i^{72}i = \left(i^4\right)^{18}i = 1^{18}i = i$$

(b) As in Example 3(e), choose $b = 48$. $i^{-46} \cdot i^{48} = i^2 = -1$.

**18** (a) $i^{66} = i^{64}i^2 = \left(i^4\right)^{16}(-1) = 1^{16}(-1) = -1$

(b) As in Example 3(e), choose $b = 56$. $i^{-55} \cdot i^{56} = i^1 = i$.

**19** Multiply both the numerator and the denominator by the conjugate of the denominator to eliminate all $i$'s in the denominator. The new denominator is the sum of the squares of the coefficients—in this case, $2^2$ and $4^2$.

$$\frac{3}{2+4i} \cdot \frac{2-4i}{2-4i} = \frac{3(2-4i)}{4-(-16)} = \frac{6-12i}{20} = \frac{6}{20} - \frac{12}{20}i = \frac{3}{10} - \frac{3}{5}i$$

**20** $\dfrac{5}{3-7i} \cdot \dfrac{3+7i}{3+7i} = \dfrac{5(3+7i)}{9-(-49)} = \dfrac{15+35i}{58} = \dfrac{15}{58} + \dfrac{35}{58}i$

**21** Multiply both the numerator and the denominator by the conjugate of the denominator to eliminate all $i$'s in the denominator. The new denominator is the sum of the squares of the coefficients—in this case, $6^2$ and $2^2$.

$$\frac{1-7i}{6-2i} \cdot \frac{6+2i}{6+2i} = \frac{(6+14)+(2-42)i}{36-(-4)} = \frac{20-40i}{40} = \frac{20}{40} - \frac{40}{40}i = \frac{1}{2} - i$$

**22** $\dfrac{2+9i}{-3-i} \cdot \dfrac{-3+i}{-3+i} = \dfrac{(-6-9)+(2-27)i}{9-(-1)} = \dfrac{-15-25i}{10} = -\dfrac{3}{2} - \dfrac{5}{2}i$

**23** $\dfrac{-4+6i}{2+7i} \cdot \dfrac{2-7i}{2-7i} = \dfrac{(-8+42)+(28+12)i}{4-(-49)} = \dfrac{34+40i}{53} = \dfrac{34}{53} + \dfrac{40}{53}i$

**24** $\dfrac{-3-2i}{5+2i} \cdot \dfrac{5-2i}{5-2i} = \dfrac{(-15-4)+(6-10)i}{25-(-4)} = \dfrac{-19-4i}{29} = -\dfrac{19}{29} - \dfrac{4}{29}i$

**25** Multiplying the denominator by $i$ will eliminate the $i$'s in the denominator.

$$\frac{4-2i}{-7i} = \frac{4-2i}{-7i} \cdot \frac{i}{i} = \frac{4i-2i^2}{-7i^2} = \frac{2+4i}{7} = \frac{2}{7} + \frac{4}{7}i$$

**26** $\dfrac{-2+6i}{3i} = \dfrac{-2+6i}{3i} \cdot \dfrac{-i}{-i} = \dfrac{2i-6i^2}{-3i^2} = \dfrac{6+2i}{3} = 2 + \dfrac{2}{3}i$

**27** Use the *special product formula* for $(x+y)^3$ on the inside front cover of the text.

$$(2+5i)^3 = (2)^3 + 3(2)^2(5i) + 3(2)(5i)^2 + (5i)^3$$
$$= 8 + 60i + 6\left(25i^2\right) + 125i^3$$
$$= \left(8 + 150i^2\right) + \left(60i + 125i^3\right) = (8-150) + (60-125)i = -142 - 65i$$

**28** $(3-2i)^3 = (3)^3 + 3(3)^2(-2i) + 3(3)(-2i)^2 + (-2i)^3 = 27 - 54i + 9\left(4i^2\right) - 8i^3$
$$= \left(27 + 36i^2\right) + \left(-54i - 8i^3\right) = (27-36) + (-54+8)i = -9 - 46i$$

**29** A common mistake is to multiply $\sqrt{-4}\,\sqrt{-16}$ and obtain $\sqrt{64}$, or 8.

The correct procedure is $\sqrt{-4}\,\sqrt{-16} = \sqrt{4}\,i \cdot \sqrt{16}\,i = (2i)(4i) = 8i^2 = -8$.

$$\left(2 - \sqrt{-4}\right)\left(3 - \sqrt{-16}\right) = (2-2i)(3-4i) = (6-8) + (-6i-8i) = -2 - 14i$$

**30** $\left(-3 + \sqrt{-25}\right)\left(8 - \sqrt{-36}\right) = (-3+5i)(8-6i) = (-24+30) + (40i+18i) = 6 + 58i$

**31** $\dfrac{4 + \sqrt{-81}}{2 - \sqrt{-9}} = \dfrac{4 + 9i}{2 - 3i} \cdot \dfrac{2 + 3i}{2 + 3i} = \dfrac{(8 - 27) + (12 + 18)i}{4 - (-9)} = \dfrac{-19 + 30i}{13} = -\dfrac{19}{13} + \dfrac{30}{13}i$

**32** $\dfrac{5 - \sqrt{-121}}{1 + \sqrt{-25}} = \dfrac{5 - 11i}{1 + 5i} \cdot \dfrac{1 - 5i}{1 - 5i} = \dfrac{(5 - 55) + (-25 - 11)i}{1 - (-25)} = \dfrac{-50 - 36i}{26} = -\dfrac{25}{13} - \dfrac{18}{13}i$

**33** $\dfrac{\sqrt{-36}\,\sqrt{-49}}{\sqrt{-16}} = \dfrac{(6i)(7i)}{4i} = \dfrac{42i^2}{4i} = \dfrac{-21}{2i} = \dfrac{-21}{2i} \cdot \dfrac{-i}{-i} = \dfrac{21i}{-2i^2} = \dfrac{21i}{2} = \dfrac{21}{2}i$

**34** $\dfrac{\sqrt{-25}}{\sqrt{-16}\,\sqrt{-81}} = \dfrac{5i}{(4i)(9i)} = \dfrac{5i}{36i^2} = \dfrac{5i}{-36} = -\dfrac{5}{36}i$

**35** We need to equate the real parts and the imaginary parts on each side of " = ".

$4 + (x + 2y)i = x + 2i \;\Rightarrow\; 4 = x \text{ and } x + 2y = 2 \;\Rightarrow$

$x = 4 \text{ and } 4 + 2y = 2 \;\Rightarrow\; 2y = -2 \;\Rightarrow\; y = -1, \text{ so } x = 4 \text{ and } y = -1.$

**36** $(x - y) + 3i = 4 + yi \;\Rightarrow\; 3 = y \text{ and } x - y = 4 \;\Rightarrow\; x - 3 = 4 \;\Rightarrow\; x = 7, y = 3$

**37** $(2x - y) - 16i = 10 + 4yi \;\Rightarrow\; 2x - y = 10 \text{ and } -16 = 4y \;\Rightarrow\; y = -4 \text{ and } 2x - (-4) = 10 \;\Rightarrow$

$2x + 4 = 10 \;\Rightarrow\; 2x = 6 \;\Rightarrow\; x = 3, \text{ so } x = 3 \text{ and } y = -4.$

**38** $8 + (3x + y)i = 2x - 4i \;\Rightarrow\; 2x = 8 \text{ and } 3x + y = -4 \;\Rightarrow\; x = 4 \text{ and } 12 + y = -4 \;\Rightarrow\; x = 4, y = -16$

**39** $x^2 - 6x + 13 = 0 \;\Rightarrow\; x = \dfrac{-(-6) \pm \sqrt{(-6)^2 - 4(1)(13)}}{2(1)} = \dfrac{6 \pm \sqrt{36 - 52}}{2} = \dfrac{6 \pm \sqrt{-16}}{2} = \dfrac{6 \pm 4i}{2} = 3 \pm 2i$

**40** $x^2 - 2x + 26 = 0 \;\Rightarrow$

$x = \dfrac{-(-2) \pm \sqrt{(-2)^2 - 4(1)(26)}}{2(1)} = \dfrac{2 \pm \sqrt{4 - 104}}{2} = \dfrac{2 \pm \sqrt{-100}}{2} = \dfrac{2 \pm 10i}{2} = 1 \pm 5i$

**41** $x^2 + 12x + 37 = 0 \;\Rightarrow$

$x = \dfrac{-12 \pm \sqrt{(-12)^2 - 4(1)(37)}}{2(1)} = \dfrac{-12 \pm \sqrt{144 - 148}}{2} = \dfrac{-12 \pm \sqrt{-4}}{2} = \dfrac{-12 \pm 2i}{2} = -6 \pm i$

**42** $x^2 + 8x + 17 = 0 \;\Rightarrow\; x = \dfrac{-8 \pm \sqrt{64 - 68}}{2(1)} = \dfrac{-8 \pm \sqrt{-4}}{2} = \dfrac{-8 \pm 2i}{2} = -4 \pm i$

**43** $x^2 - 5x + 20 = 0 \;\Rightarrow\; x = \dfrac{-(-5) \pm \sqrt{(-5)^2 - 4(1)(20)}}{2(1)} = \dfrac{5 \pm \sqrt{25 - 80}}{2} = \dfrac{5 \pm \sqrt{-55}}{2} = \dfrac{5}{2} \pm \dfrac{1}{2}\sqrt{55}\,i$

**44** $x^2 + 3x + 6 = 0 \;\Rightarrow\; x = \dfrac{-3 \pm \sqrt{9 - 24}}{2(1)} = \dfrac{-3 \pm \sqrt{-15}}{2} = -\dfrac{3}{2} \pm \dfrac{1}{2}\sqrt{15}\,i$

**45** $4x^2 + x + 3 = 0 \;\Rightarrow\; x = \dfrac{-1 \pm \sqrt{1^2 - 4(4)(3)}}{2(4)} = \dfrac{-1 \pm \sqrt{1 - 48}}{8} = \dfrac{-1 \pm \sqrt{-47}}{8} = -\dfrac{1}{8} \pm \dfrac{1}{8}\sqrt{47}\,i$

**46** $-3x^2 + x - 5 = 0 \;\Rightarrow\; x = \dfrac{-1 \pm \sqrt{1^2 - 4(-3)(-5)}}{2(-3)} = \dfrac{-1 \pm \sqrt{1 - 60}}{-6} = \dfrac{1}{6} \pm \dfrac{1}{6}\sqrt{59}\,i$

**47** Solving $x^3 = -64$ by taking the cube root of both sides would only give us the solution $x = -4$, so we need to factor $x^3 + 64$ as the sum of cubes. $x^3 + 64 = 0 \;\Rightarrow\; (x + 4)(x^2 - 4x + 16) = 0 \;\Rightarrow$

$x = -4 \text{ or } x = \dfrac{4 \pm \sqrt{16 - 64}}{2} = \dfrac{4 \pm 4\sqrt{3}\,i}{2}.$ The three solutions are $-4, 2 \pm 2\sqrt{3}\,i.$

**48** $x^3 - 27 = 0 \Rightarrow (x-3)(x^2 + 3x + 9) = 0 \Rightarrow$

$$x = 3 \text{ or } x = \frac{-3 \pm \sqrt{9-36}}{2} = \frac{-3 \pm 3\sqrt{3}\,i}{2}. \text{ The three solutions are } 3, -\frac{3}{2} \pm \frac{3}{2}\sqrt{3}\,i.$$

**49** $27x^3 = (x+5)^3 \Rightarrow (3x)^3 - (x+5)^3 = 0 \Rightarrow$

{difference of cubes} $[3x - (x+5)]\left[(3x)^2 + 3x(x+5) + (x+5)^2\right] = 0 \Rightarrow$

$(3x - x - 5)(9x^2 + 3x^2 + 15x + x^2 + 10x + 25) = 0 \Rightarrow$

$(2x-5)(13x^2 + 25x + 25) = 0 \Rightarrow x = \frac{5}{2} \text{ or } x = \frac{-25 \pm \sqrt{625 - 1300}}{2(13)} = \frac{-25 \pm 15\sqrt{3}\,i}{26}.$

$$\text{The three solutions are } \tfrac{5}{2}, -\tfrac{25}{26} \pm \tfrac{15}{26}\sqrt{3}\,i.$$

**50** $16x^4 = (x-4)^4 \Rightarrow (4x^2)^2 - \left[(x-4)^2\right]^2 = 0 \Rightarrow$ {difference of squares}

$\left[4x^2 + (x-4)^2\right]\left[4x^2 - (x-4)^2\right] = 0 \Rightarrow (5x^2 - 8x + 16)(3x^2 + 8x - 16) = 0 \Rightarrow$

$5x^2 - 8x + 16 = 0 \text{ or } 3x^2 + 8x - 16 = (x+4)(3x-4) = 0.$

$5x^2 - 8x + 16 = 0 \Rightarrow x = \frac{8 \pm \sqrt{64 - 320}}{10} = \frac{8 \pm 16i}{10} = \frac{4 \pm 8i}{5}. \text{ The four solutions are } -4, \frac{4}{3}, \frac{4}{5} \pm \frac{8}{5}i.$

**51** $x^4 = 625 \Rightarrow x^4 - 625 = 0 \Rightarrow (x^2 - 25)(x^2 + 25) = 0 \Rightarrow$

$$x^2 = 25, -25 \Rightarrow x = \pm\sqrt{25}, \pm\sqrt{-25} \Rightarrow x = \pm 5, \pm 5i$$

**52** $x^4 = 81 \Rightarrow x^4 - 81 = 0 \Rightarrow (x^2 - 9)(x^2 + 9) = 0 \Rightarrow$

$$x^2 = 9, -9 \Rightarrow x = \pm\sqrt{9}, \pm\sqrt{-9} \Rightarrow x = \pm 3, \pm 3i$$

**53** $4x^4 + 25x^2 + 36 = 0 \Rightarrow (x^2 + 4)(4x^2 + 9) = 0 \Rightarrow$

$$x^2 = -4, -\frac{9}{4} \Rightarrow x = \pm\sqrt{-4}, \pm\sqrt{-\frac{9}{4}} \Rightarrow x = \pm 2i, \pm\frac{3}{2}i$$

**54** $27x^4 + 21x^2 + 4 = 0 \Rightarrow (9x^2 + 4)(3x^2 + 1) = 0 \Rightarrow$

$$x^2 = -\frac{4}{9}, -\frac{1}{3} \Rightarrow x = \pm\sqrt{-\frac{4}{9}}, \pm\sqrt{-\frac{1}{3}} \Rightarrow x = \pm\frac{2}{3}i, \pm\frac{1}{3}\sqrt{3}\,i$$

**55** $x^3 + 3x^2 + 4x = 0 \Rightarrow x(x^2 + 3x + 4) = 0 \Rightarrow$

$$x = 0 \text{ or } x = \frac{-3 \pm \sqrt{9-16}}{2} = \frac{-3 \pm \sqrt{7}\,i}{2}. \text{ The three solutions are } 0, -\frac{3}{2} \pm \frac{1}{2}\sqrt{7}\,i.$$

**56** $8x^3 - 12x^2 + 2x - 3 = 0 \Rightarrow 4x^2(2x-3) + 1(2x-3) = 0 \Rightarrow (4x^2 + 1)(2x-3) = 0 \Rightarrow$

$$x^2 = -\frac{1}{4} \text{ or } x = \frac{3}{2} \Rightarrow x = \pm\sqrt{-\frac{1}{4}} \text{ or } x = \frac{3}{2} \Rightarrow x = \frac{3}{2}, \pm\frac{1}{2}i$$

**Note:** In Exercises 57–62: Let $z = a + bi$ and $w = c + di$.

**57** $\overline{z + w} = \overline{(a + bi) + (c + di)}$     {definition of $z$ and $w$}

$= \overline{(a + c) + (b + d)i}$     {write in complex number form}

$= (a + c) - (b + d)i$     {definition of conjugate}

$= (a - bi) + (c - di)$     {rearrange terms (*)}

$= \overline{z} + \overline{w}$     {definition of conjugates of $z$ and $w$}

(*) We are really looking ahead to the terms we want to obtain, $\overline{z}$ and $\overline{w}$.

**58** $\overline{z - w} = \overline{(a + bi) - (c + di)} = \overline{(a - c) + (b - d)i} = (a - c) - (b - d)i = (a - bi) - (c - di) = \overline{z} - \overline{w}.$

**59** $\overline{z \cdot w} = \overline{(a + bi) \cdot (c + di)} = \overline{(ac - bd) + (ad + bc)i}$

$= (ac - bd) - (ad + bc)i = ac - adi - bd - bci = a(c - di) - bi(c - di) = (a - bi) \cdot (c - di) = \overline{z} \cdot \overline{w}$

**60** $\overline{\left(\dfrac{z}{w}\right)} = \overline{\left(\dfrac{a+bi}{c+di}\right)} = \overline{\left(\dfrac{a+bi}{c+di} \cdot \dfrac{c-di}{c-di}\right)} = \overline{\left(\dfrac{(ac+bd)+(bc-ad)i}{c^2+d^2}\right)} = \overline{\left(\dfrac{ac+bd}{c^2+d^2} + \dfrac{bc-ad}{c^2+d^2}i\right)}$

$= \dfrac{ac+bd}{c^2+d^2} - \dfrac{bc-ad}{c^2+d^2}i = \dfrac{(ac+bd)+(ad-bc)i}{c^2+d^2} = \dfrac{a-bi}{c-di} \cdot \dfrac{c+di}{c+di} = \dfrac{a-bi}{c-di} = \dfrac{\overline{(a+bi)}}{\overline{(c+di)}} = \dfrac{\overline{z}}{\overline{w}}$

**61** **(1)** If $\overline{z} = z$, then $a - bi = a + bi$ and hence $-bi = bi$, or $2bi = 0$. Thus, $b = 0$ and $z = a$ is real.

**(2)** Conversely, if $z$ is real, then $b = 0$ and hence $\overline{z} = \overline{a + 0i} = a - 0i = a + 0i = z$.

Thus, by **(1)** and **(2)**, $\overline{z} = z$ if and only if $z$ is real.

**62** $\overline{z^2} = \overline{(a+bi)^2} = \overline{a^2 + 2abi - b^2} = \overline{(a^2 - b^2) + 2abi} = (a^2 - b^2) - 2abi = a^2 - 2abi - b^2 = (a - bi)^2 = (\overline{z})^2$

## 1.6 Exercises

**Note:** Brackets, "[" and "]", are used with $\le$ or $\ge$ and indicate that the endpoint of the interval is part of the solution.

Parentheses, "(" and ")", are used with $<$ or $>$ and indicate that the endpoint is *not* part of the solution.

**1** $x < -2 \Leftrightarrow (-\infty, -2)$

**2** $x \ge 4 \Leftrightarrow [4, \infty)$

**3** $5 > x \ge -2 \Leftrightarrow -2 \le x < 5 \Leftrightarrow [-2, 5)$

**4** $3 \le x \le 7 \Leftrightarrow [3, 7]$

**5** $(-5, 4] \Leftrightarrow -5 < x \le 4$

**6** $(-6, \infty) \Leftrightarrow x > -6$

**7** $2x + 5 < 3x - 7 \Rightarrow -x < -12 \Rightarrow x > 12 \text{ \{change inequality\}} \Leftrightarrow (12, \infty)$

**8** $x - 6 > 5x + 3 \Rightarrow -4x > 9 \Rightarrow x < -\frac{9}{4} \text{ \{change inequality\}} \Leftrightarrow \left(-\infty, -\frac{9}{4}\right)$

**9** $\left[3 \le \dfrac{2x - 9}{5} < 7\right] \cdot 5 \text{ \{multiply by the lcd, 5\}} \Rightarrow 15 \le 2x - 9 < 35 \Rightarrow$

$24 \le 2x < 44 \text{ \{add 9 to all three parts\}} \Rightarrow 12 \le x < 22 \text{ \{divide all three parts by 2\}} \Leftrightarrow$

$[12, 22) \text{ \{equivalent interval notation\}}$

**10** $\left[-2 < \dfrac{4x + 1}{3} \le 0\right] \cdot 3 \Rightarrow -6 < 4x + 1 \le 0 \Rightarrow -7 < 4x \le -1 \Rightarrow -\frac{7}{4} < x \le -\frac{1}{4} \Leftrightarrow \left(-\frac{7}{4}, -\frac{1}{4}\right]$

**11** By the law of signs, a quotient is positive if the sign of the numerator and the sign of the denominator are the same.

Since the numerator is positive, $\dfrac{4}{3x + 2} > 0 \Rightarrow 3x + 2 > 0 \Rightarrow x > -\frac{2}{3} \Leftrightarrow \left(-\frac{2}{3}, \infty\right)$.

The expression is never equal to 0 since the numerator is never 0. Thus, the solution of $\dfrac{4}{3x + 2} \ge 0$ is $\left(-\frac{2}{3}, \infty\right)$.

**12** $\dfrac{3}{2x + 5} \le 0 \Rightarrow 2x + 5 < 0 \text{ \{denominator must be negative\}} \Rightarrow 2x < -5 \Rightarrow x < -\frac{5}{2} \Leftrightarrow \left(-\infty, -\frac{5}{2}\right)$

**13** $\dfrac{-7}{4 - 3x} > 0 \Rightarrow 4 - 3x < 0 \text{ \{denominator must also be negative\}} \Rightarrow$

$4 < 3x \Rightarrow 3x > 4 \Rightarrow x > \frac{4}{3} \Leftrightarrow \left(\frac{4}{3}, \infty\right)$

**14** $\dfrac{-3}{2 - x} < 0 \Rightarrow 2 - x > 0 \Rightarrow 2 > x \Rightarrow x < 2 \Leftrightarrow (-\infty, 2)$

**15** $(1 - x)^2 > 0 \; \forall x \text{ except } 1$. Thus, $\dfrac{5}{(1 - x)^2} > 0$ has solution $\mathbb{R} - \{1\}$.

**16** $x^2 + 4 > 0 \ \forall x$. Hence, $\dfrac{3}{x^2 + 4} > 0 \ \forall x$, and $\dfrac{3}{x^2 + 4} < 0$ has no solution.

**17** $|x + 3| < 0.01 \ \Rightarrow \ -0.01 < x + 3 < 0.01 \ \Rightarrow \ -3.01 < x < -2.99 \ \Leftrightarrow \ (-3.01, -2.99)$

**18** $|x - 4| \le 0.03 \ \Rightarrow \ -0.03 \le x - 4 \le 0.03 \ \Rightarrow \ 3.97 \le x \le 4.03 \ \Leftrightarrow \ [3.97, 4.03]$

**19** $|3x - 7| \ge 5 \ \Rightarrow \ 3x - 7 \ge 5 \text{ or } 3x - 7 \le -5 \ \Rightarrow \ 3x \ge 12 \text{ or } 3x \le 2 \ \Rightarrow$

$$x \ge 4 \text{ or } x \le \tfrac{2}{3} \ \Leftrightarrow \ \left(-\infty, \tfrac{2}{3}\right] \cup [4, \infty)$$

**20** $2|-11 - 7x| - 2 > 10 \ \Rightarrow \ 2|-11 - 7x| > 12 \ \Rightarrow \ |-11 - 7x| > 6 \ \Rightarrow$

$-11 - 7x > 6 \text{ or } -11 - 7x < -6 \ \Rightarrow \ -7x > 17 \text{ or } -7x < 5 \ \Rightarrow$

$$x < -\tfrac{17}{7} \text{ or } x > -\tfrac{5}{7} \ \Leftrightarrow \ \left(-\infty, -\tfrac{17}{7}\right) \cup \left(-\tfrac{5}{7}, \infty\right)$$

**21** Since $|7x + 2| \ge 0 \ \forall x$, $|7x + 2| > -2$ has solution $(-\infty, \infty)$.

**22** Since $|6x - 5| \ge 0 \ \forall x$, $|6x - 5| \le -2$ has no solution.

**23** $|3x - 9| > 0 \ \forall x$ except when $3x - 9 = 0$, or $x = 3$. The solution is $(-\infty, 3) \cup (3, \infty)$.

**24** $|5x + 2| = 0$ if $x = -\tfrac{2}{5}$, but is never less than 0. Thus, $|5x + 2| \le 0$ has solution $x = -\tfrac{2}{5}$.

**25** $-2 < |x| < 4 \ \Rightarrow \ -2 < |x| \ and \ |x| < 4$. Since $-2$ is always less than $|x|$ {because $|x| \ge 0$},

we only need to consider $|x| < 4$. $|x| < 4 \ \Rightarrow \ -4 < x < 4 \ \Leftrightarrow \ (-4, 4)$

**26** $1 < |x| < 5 \ \Rightarrow \ 1 < x < 5 \ or \ 1 < -x < 5 \ \Rightarrow \ 1 < x < 5 \text{ or } -1 > x > -5 \ \Rightarrow$

$$1 < x < 5 \text{ or } -5 < x < -1 \ \Leftrightarrow \ (-5, -1) \cup (1, 5)$$

**27** $(3x + 1)(5 - 10x) > 0$ • See the sign chart for details concerning the signs of the individual factors and the resulting sign. The given inequality has solutions in the interval $\left(-\tfrac{1}{3}, \tfrac{1}{2}\right)$, which corresponds to the positive values for the **Resulting sign**.

| Interval | $\left(-\infty, -\tfrac{1}{3}\right)$ | $\left(-\tfrac{1}{3}, \tfrac{1}{2}\right)$ | $\left(\tfrac{1}{2}, \infty\right)$ |
|---|---|---|---|
| Sign of $5 - 10x$ | + | + | − |
| Sign of $3x + 1$ | − | + | + |
| **Resulting sign** | − | + | − |

**28** $(x + 2)(x - 1)(4 - x) \le 0$ • From the chart, we see the product is negative for $x \in (-2, 1) \cup (4, \infty)$. Since we want to also include the values that make the product equal to zero $\{-2, 1, \text{ and } 4\}$, the solution is $[-2, 1] \cup [4, \infty)$.

| Interval | $(-\infty, -2)$ | $(-2, 1)$ | $(1, 4)$ | $(4, \infty)$ |
|---|---|---|---|---|
| Sign of $4 - x$ | + | + | + | − |
| Sign of $x - 1$ | − | − | + | + |
| Sign of $x + 2$ | − | + | + | + |
| **Resulting sign** | + | − | + | − |

**29** $x^2 - x - 6 < 0 \ \Rightarrow \ (x - 3)(x + 2) < 0$      ★ $(-2, 3)$

| Interval | $(-\infty, -2)$ | $(-2, 3)$ | $(3, \infty)$ |
|---|---|---|---|
| Sign of $x - 3$ | − | − | + |
| Sign of $x + 2$ | − | + | + |
| **Resulting sign** | + | − | + |

**30** $x^2 + 4x + 3 \geq 0 \Rightarrow (x+1)(x+3) \geq 0$       $\bigstar (-\infty, -3] \cup [-1, \infty)$

| Interval | $(-\infty, -3)$ | $(-3, -1)$ | $(-1, \infty)$ |
|---|---|---|---|
| Sign of $x + 1$ | − | − | + |
| Sign of $x + 3$ | − | + | + |
| **Resulting sign** | + | − | + |

**31** $x(2x+3) \geq 5 \Rightarrow 2x^2 + 3x - 5 \geq 0 \Rightarrow (2x+5)(x-1) \geq 0$    $\bigstar \left(-\infty, -\frac{5}{2}\right] \cup [1, \infty)$

| Interval | $\left(-\infty, -\frac{5}{2}\right)$ | $\left(-\frac{5}{2}, 1\right)$ | $(1, \infty)$ |
|---|---|---|---|
| Sign of $x - 1$ | − | − | + |
| Sign of $2x + 5$ | − | + | + |
| **Resulting sign** | + | − | + |

**32** $8x - 15 > x^2 \Rightarrow x^2 - 8x + 15 < 0 \Rightarrow (x-3)(x-5) < 0$      $\bigstar (3, 5)$

| Interval | $(-\infty, 3)$ | $(3, 5)$ | $(5, \infty)$ |
|---|---|---|---|
| Sign of $x - 5$ | − | − | + |
| Sign of $x - 3$ | − | + | + |
| **Resulting sign** | + | − | + |

**Note:** Solving $x^2 < a^2$ or $x^2 > a^2$ for $a > 0$ may be achieved using factoring, that is, $x^2 - a^2 < 0 \Rightarrow (x+a)(x-a) < 0 \Rightarrow -a < x < a$; or by taking the square root of each side, that is, $\sqrt{x^2} < \sqrt{a^2} \Rightarrow |x| < a \Rightarrow -a < x < a$. The most common mistake is forgetting that $\sqrt{x^2} = |x|$.

**33** $25x^2 - 16 < 0 \Rightarrow x^2 < \frac{16}{25} \Rightarrow |x| < \frac{4}{5} \Rightarrow -\frac{4}{5} < x < \frac{4}{5} \Leftrightarrow \left(-\frac{4}{5}, \frac{4}{5}\right)$

**34** $25x^2 - 16x < 0 \Rightarrow x(25x - 16) < 0$      $\bigstar \left(0, \frac{16}{25}\right)$

| Interval | $(-\infty, 0)$ | $\left(0, \frac{16}{25}\right)$ | $\left(\frac{16}{25}, \infty\right)$ |
|---|---|---|---|
| Sign of $25x - 16$ | − | − | + |
| Sign of $x$ | − | + | + |
| **Resulting sign** | + | − | + |

**35** $\dfrac{x^2(x+2)}{(x+2)(x+1)} \leq 0 \Rightarrow \dfrac{x^2}{x+1} \leq 0$ {we will exclude $x = -2$ since it makes the original expression undefined} $\Rightarrow \dfrac{1}{x+1} \leq 0$ {we can divide by $x^2$ since $x^2 \geq 0$ and we will include $x = 0$ since it makes $x^2$ equal to zero and we want all solutions less than *or equal to* zero} $\Rightarrow x + 1 < 0$ {the fraction cannot equal zero and $x + 1$ must be negative so that the fraction is negative} $\Rightarrow x < -1$    $\bigstar (-\infty, -2) \cup (-2, -1) \cup \{0\}$

**36** $\dfrac{(x^2+1)(x-3)}{x^2 - 9} \geq 0 \Rightarrow \dfrac{x-3}{(x+3)(x-3)} \geq 0$ {$x^2 + 1 > 0$} $\Rightarrow \dfrac{1}{x+3} \geq 0$ {exclude 3} $\Rightarrow$ $x + 3 > 0$ {exclude −3} $\Rightarrow x > -3$      $\bigstar (-3, 3) \cup (3, \infty)$

**37** $\dfrac{x^2 - x}{x^2 + 2x} \leq 0 \Rightarrow \dfrac{x(x-1)}{x(x+2)} \leq 0 \Rightarrow \dfrac{x-1}{x+2} \leq 0$ {we will exclude $x = 0$ from the solution} $\bigstar (-2, 0) \cup (0, 1]$

| Interval | $(-\infty, -2)$ | $(-2, 1)$ | $(1, \infty)$ |
|---|---|---|---|
| Sign of $x - 1$ | − | − | + |
| Sign of $x + 2$ | − | + | + |
| **Resulting sign** | + | − | + |

**38** $\dfrac{(x+3)^2(2-x)}{(x+4)(x^2-4)} \le 0 \ \Rightarrow \ \dfrac{2-x}{(x+4)(x+2)(x-2)} \le 0$ {include $-3$} $\ \Rightarrow \ \dfrac{1}{(x+4)(x+2)} \ge 0$ {cancel, change inequality, exclude 2}

$\bigstar \ (-\infty, -4) \cup \{-3\} \cup (-2, 2) \cup (2, \infty)$

| Interval | $(-\infty, -4)$ | $(-4, -2)$ | $(-2, \infty)$ |
|---|---|---|---|
| Sign of $x + 2$ | $-$ | $-$ | $+$ |
| Sign of $x + 4$ | $-$ | $+$ | $+$ |
| **Resulting sign** | $+$ | $-$ | $+$ |

**39** $\dfrac{x-2}{x^2-3x-10} \ge 0 \ \Rightarrow \ \dfrac{x-2}{(x-5)(x+2)} \ge 0$ {$x = 2$ is a solution since it makes the fraction equal to zero, $x = 5$ and $x = -2$ are excluded since these values make the fraction undefined}

$\bigstar \ [-2, 2) \cup (5, \infty)$

| Interval | $(-\infty, -2)$ | $(-2, 2)$ | $(2, 5)$ | $(5, \infty)$ |
|---|---|---|---|---|
| Sign of $x - 5$ | $-$ | $-$ | $-$ | $+$ |
| Sign of $x - 2$ | $-$ | $-$ | $+$ | $+$ |
| Sign of $x + 2$ | $-$ | $+$ | $+$ | $+$ |
| **Resulting sign** | $-$ | $+$ | $-$ | $+$ |

**40** $\dfrac{x+6}{x^2-7x+12} \le 0 \ \Rightarrow \ \dfrac{x+6}{(x-3)(x-4)} \le 0$

$\bigstar \ (-\infty, -6] \cup (3, 4)$

| Interval | $(-\infty, -6)$ | $(-6, 3)$ | $(3, 4)$ | $(4, \infty)$ |
|---|---|---|---|---|
| Sign of $x - 4$ | $-$ | $-$ | $-$ | $+$ |
| Sign of $x - 3$ | $-$ | $-$ | $+$ | $+$ |
| Sign of $x + 6$ | $-$ | $+$ | $+$ | $+$ |
| **Resulting sign** | $-$ | $+$ | $-$ | $+$ |

**41** $\dfrac{-3x}{x^2-9} > 0 \ \Rightarrow \ \dfrac{x}{(x+3)(x-3)} < 0$ {divide by $-3$}

$\bigstar \ (-\infty, -3) \cup (0, 3)$

| Interval | $(-\infty, -3)$ | $(-3, 0)$ | $(0, 3)$ | $(3, \infty)$ |
|---|---|---|---|---|
| Sign of $x - 3$ | $-$ | $-$ | $-$ | $+$ |
| Sign of $x$ | $-$ | $-$ | $+$ | $+$ |
| Sign of $x + 3$ | $-$ | $+$ | $+$ | $+$ |
| **Resulting sign** | $-$ | $+$ | $-$ | $+$ |

**42** $\dfrac{5x}{16-x^2} < 0 \ \Rightarrow \ \dfrac{x}{(4+x)(4-x)} < 0$ {divide by 5}

$\bigstar \ (-4, 0) \cup (4, \infty)$

| Interval | $(-\infty, -4)$ | $(-4, 0)$ | $(0, 4)$ | $(4, \infty)$ |
|---|---|---|---|---|
| Sign of $4 - x$ | $+$ | $+$ | $+$ | $-$ |
| Sign of $x$ | $-$ | $-$ | $+$ | $+$ |
| Sign of $4 + x$ | $-$ | $+$ | $+$ | $+$ |
| **Resulting sign** | $+$ | $-$ | $+$ | $-$ |

**43** $\dfrac{x+1}{2x-3} > 2 \ \Rightarrow \ \dfrac{x+1}{2x-3} - 2 > 0 \ \Rightarrow \ \dfrac{x+1-2(2x-3)}{2x-3} > 0 \ \Rightarrow \ \dfrac{x+1-4x+6}{2x-3} > 0 \ \Rightarrow$

$\dfrac{-3x+7}{2x-3} > 0$. From the sign chart, the solution is $\left(\frac{3}{2}, \frac{7}{3}\right)$. Note that you should *not* multiply by the factor $2x - 3$ as we did with rational *equations* because $2x - 3$ may be positive or negative, and multiplying by it would require solving two inequalities. This method of solution tends to be more difficult than the sign chart method.

| Interval | $\left(-\infty, \frac{3}{2}\right)$ | $\left(\frac{3}{2}, \frac{7}{3}\right)$ | $\left(\frac{7}{3}, \infty\right)$ |
|---|---|---|---|
| Sign of $-3x + 7$ | $+$ | $+$ | $-$ |
| Sign of $2x - 3$ | $-$ | $+$ | $+$ |
| **Resulting sign** | $-$ | $+$ | $-$ |

**44** $\dfrac{x-2}{3x+5} \le 4 \;\Rightarrow\; \dfrac{x-2-4(3x+5)}{3x+5} \le 0 \;\Rightarrow\; \dfrac{-11x-22}{3x+5} \le 0$ ★ $(-\infty, -2] \cup \left(-\frac{5}{3}, \infty\right)$

| Interval | $(-\infty, -2)$ | $\left(-2, -\frac{5}{3}\right)$ | $\left(-\frac{5}{3}, \infty\right)$ |
|---|---|---|---|
| Sign of $3x+5$ | $-$ | $-$ | $+$ |
| Sign of $-11x-22$ | $+$ | $-$ | $-$ |
| **Resulting sign** | $-$ | $+$ | $-$ |

**45** $\dfrac{1}{x-2} \ge \dfrac{3}{x+1} \;\Rightarrow\; \dfrac{1}{x-2} - \dfrac{3}{x+1} \ge 0 \;\Rightarrow\; \dfrac{1(x+1) - 3(x-2)}{(x-2)(x+1)} \ge 0 \;\Rightarrow$

$\dfrac{x+1-3x+6}{(x-2)(x+1)} \ge 0 \;\Rightarrow\; \dfrac{-2x+7}{(x-2)(x+1)} \ge 0$ ★ $(-\infty, -1) \cup \left(2, \frac{7}{2}\right]$

| Interval | $(-\infty, -1)$ | $(-1, 2)$ | $\left(2, \frac{7}{2}\right)$ | $\left(\frac{7}{2}, \infty\right)$ |
|---|---|---|---|---|
| Sign of $-2x+7$ | $+$ | $+$ | $+$ | $-$ |
| Sign of $x-2$ | $-$ | $-$ | $+$ | $+$ |
| Sign of $x+1$ | $-$ | $+$ | $+$ | $+$ |
| **Resulting sign** | $+$ | $-$ | $+$ | $-$ |

**46** $\dfrac{2}{2x+3} \le \dfrac{2}{x-5} \;\Rightarrow\; \dfrac{2(x-5) - 2(2x+3)}{(2x+3)(x-5)} \le 0 \;\Rightarrow\; \dfrac{-2x-16}{(2x+3)(x-5)} \le 0$ ★ $\left[-8, -\frac{3}{2}\right) \cup (5, \infty)$

| Interval | $(-\infty, -8)$ | $\left(-8, -\frac{3}{2}\right)$ | $\left(-\frac{3}{2}, 5\right)$ | $(5, \infty)$ |
|---|---|---|---|---|
| Sign of $x-5$ | $-$ | $-$ | $-$ | $+$ |
| Sign of $2x+3$ | $-$ | $-$ | $+$ | $+$ |
| Sign of $-2x-16$ | $+$ | $-$ | $-$ | $-$ |
| **Resulting sign** | $+$ | $-$ | $+$ | $-$ |

**47** $\dfrac{x}{3x-5} \le \dfrac{2}{x-1} \;\Rightarrow\; \dfrac{x}{3x-5} - \dfrac{2}{x-1} \le 0 \;\Rightarrow\; \dfrac{x(x-1) - 2(3x-5)}{(3x-5)(x-1)} \le 0 \;\Rightarrow$

$\dfrac{x^2-x-6x+10}{(3x-5)(x-1)} \le 0 \;\Rightarrow\; \dfrac{x^2-7x+10}{(3x-5)(x-1)} \le 0 \;\Rightarrow\; \dfrac{(x-2)(x-5)}{(3x-5)(x-1)} \le 0$ ★ $\left(1, \frac{5}{3}\right) \cup [2, 5]$

| Interval | $(-\infty, 1)$ | $\left(1, \frac{5}{3}\right)$ | $\left(\frac{5}{3}, 2\right)$ | $(2, 5)$ | $(5, \infty)$ |
|---|---|---|---|---|---|
| Sign of $x-5$ | $-$ | $-$ | $-$ | $-$ | $+$ |
| Sign of $x-2$ | $-$ | $-$ | $-$ | $+$ | $+$ |
| Sign of $3x-5$ | $-$ | $-$ | $+$ | $+$ | $+$ |
| Sign of $x-1$ | $-$ | $+$ | $+$ | $+$ | $+$ |
| **Resulting sign** | $+$ | $-$ | $+$ | $-$ | $+$ |

**48** $\dfrac{x}{2x-1} \ge \dfrac{3}{x+2} \;\Rightarrow\; \dfrac{x}{2x-1} - \dfrac{3}{x+2} \ge 0 \;\Rightarrow\; \dfrac{x(x+2) - 3(2x-1)}{(2x-1)(x+2)} \ge 0 \;\Rightarrow$

$\dfrac{x^2+2x-6x+3}{(2x-1)(x+2)} \ge 0 \;\Rightarrow\; \dfrac{x^2-4x+3}{(2x-1)(x+2)} \ge 0 \;\Rightarrow\; \dfrac{(x-1)(x-3)}{(2x-1)(x+2)} \ge 0$. ★ $(-\infty, -2) \cup \left(\frac{1}{2}, 1\right] \cup [3, \infty)$

| Interval | $(-\infty, -2)$ | $\left(-2, \frac{1}{2}\right)$ | $\left(\frac{1}{2}, 1\right)$ | $(1, 3)$ | $(3, \infty)$ |
|---|---|---|---|---|---|
| Sign of $x-3$ | $-$ | $-$ | $-$ | $-$ | $+$ |
| Sign of $x-1$ | $-$ | $-$ | $-$ | $+$ | $+$ |
| Sign of $2x-1$ | $-$ | $-$ | $+$ | $+$ | $+$ |
| Sign of $x+2$ | $-$ | $+$ | $+$ | $+$ | $+$ |
| **Resulting sign** | $+$ | $-$ | $+$ | $-$ | $+$ |

**49** $x^3 > x \implies x^3 - x > 0 \implies x(x^2 - 1) > 0 \implies x(x+1)(x-1) > 0$ ⭐ $(-1, 0) \cup (1, \infty)$

| Interval | $(-\infty, -1)$ | $(-1, 0)$ | $(0, 1)$ | $(1, \infty)$ |
|---|---|---|---|---|
| Sign of $x - 1$ | − | − | − | + |
| Sign of $x$ | − | − | + | + |
| Sign of $x + 1$ | − | + | + | + |
| **Resulting sign** | − | + | − | + |

**50** $x^4 \geq x^2 \implies x^4 - x^2 \geq 0 \implies x^2(x^2 - 1) \geq 0 \implies x^2(x+1)(x-1) \geq 0$. Since $x^2 \geq 0$, $x^2$ does not need to be included in the sign chart, but 0 must be included in the answer because of the equality.

⭐ $(-\infty, -1] \cup \{0\} \cup [1, \infty)$

| Interval | $(-\infty, -1)$ | $(-1, 1)$ | $(1, \infty)$ |
|---|---|---|---|
| Sign of $x - 1$ | − | − | + |
| Sign of $x + 1$ | − | + | + |
| **Resulting sign** | + | − | + |

**51** (a) $|x + 5| = 3 \implies x + 5 = 3$ or $x + 5 = -3 \implies x = -2$ or $x = -8$.

(b) $|x + 5| < 3$ has solutions between the values found in part (a), that is, $(-8, -2)$.

(c) The solutions of $|x + 5| > 3$ are the portions of the real line that are not in

parts (a) and (b), that is, $(-\infty, -8) \cup (-2, \infty)$.

**52** (a) $|x - 4| < 3 \implies -3 < x - 4 < 3 \implies 1 < x < 7 \iff (1, 7)$.

(b) $|x - 4| = 3$ has solutions at the endpoints of the interval in part (a); that is, at $x = 1$ and $x = 7$.

(c) As in Exercise 51(c), $|x - 4| > 3$ has solutions in $(-\infty, 1) \cup (7, \infty)$.

**53** We could think of this statement as "the difference between $w$ and 141 is at most 2." In symbols, we have $|w - 141| \leq 2$. Intuitively, we know that this inequality must describe the weights from 139 to 143.

**54** "$r$ must be within 0.01 centimeter of 1 centimeter" is written as $|r - 1| \leq 0.01$.

**55** $M = \dfrac{f}{f - p}$ • We want to know what condition will assure us that an object's image is at least 3 times as large as the object, or, equivalently, when $M \geq 3$. $M \geq 3$ { and $f = 6$} $\implies \dfrac{6}{6 - p} \geq 3 \implies 6 \geq 18 - 3p$ {since $6 - p > 0$, we can multiply by $6 - p$ and not change the direction of the inequality} $\implies 3p \geq 12 \implies p \geq 4$, but $p < 6$ since $p < f$. Thus, $4 \leq p < 6$.

**56** $c = \dfrac{3.5t}{t + 1}$ • $c > 1.5 \implies \dfrac{3.5t}{t + 1} > 1.5 \implies \{t + 1 > 0\}\ 3.5t > 1.5t + 1.5 \implies 2t > \dfrac{3}{2} \implies t > \dfrac{3}{4}$ hr

**57** Let $x$ denote the number of years before $A$ becomes more economical than $B$.

The costs are the initial costs plus the yearly costs times the number of years.

$\text{Cost}_A < \text{Cost}_B \implies 100{,}000 + 8000x < 80{,}000 + 11{,}000x \implies 20{,}000 < 3000x \implies x > \frac{20}{3}$, or $6\frac{2}{3}$ yr.

**58** Let $t$ denote the time in years from the present. $\text{Cost}_B < \text{Cost}_A \implies$

$\text{Purchase}_B + \text{Insurance}_B + \text{Gas}_B < \text{Purchase}_A + \text{Insurance}_A + \text{Gas}_A \implies$

$24{,}000 + 1200t + \dfrac{15{,}000}{50} \cdot 3t < 20{,}000 + 1000t + \dfrac{15{,}000}{30} \cdot 3t \implies$

$24{,}000 + 2100t < 20{,}000 + 2500t \implies 4000 < 400t \implies t > 10$ yr.

**59** $s > 9 \Rightarrow -16t^2 + 24t + 1 > 9 \Rightarrow -16t^2 + 24t - 8 > 0 \Rightarrow 2t^2 - 3t + 1 < 0$ {divide by $-8$} $\Rightarrow$

$(2t - 1)(t - 1) < 0$ {use a sign chart} $\Rightarrow \frac{1}{2} < t < 1$.

The dog is more than 9 ft off the ground for $1 - \frac{1}{2} = \frac{1}{2}$ sec.

**60** $s \geq 1536 \Rightarrow -16t^2 + 320t \geq 1536 \Rightarrow -16t^2 + 320t - 1536 \geq 0 \Rightarrow$

$t^2 - 20t + 96 \leq 0$ {divide by $-16$} $\Rightarrow (t - 8)(t - 12) \leq 0$ {use a sign chart} $\Leftrightarrow 8 \leq t \leq 12$

**61** $d < 75 \Rightarrow v + \frac{1}{20}v^2 < 75$ {multiply by 20} $\Rightarrow 20v + v^2 < 1500 \Rightarrow v^2 + 20v - 1500 < 0 \Rightarrow$

$(v + 50)(v - 30) < 0$ {use a sign chart} $\Rightarrow -50 < v < 30 \Rightarrow 0 \leq v < 30$ {since $v \geq 0$}

**62** $M \geq 45 \Rightarrow -\frac{1}{30}v^2 + \frac{5}{2}v \geq 45$ {multiply by $-30$} $\Rightarrow v^2 - 75v \leq -1350 \Rightarrow$

$v^2 - 75v + 1350 \leq 0 \Rightarrow (v - 30)(v - 45) \leq 0$ {use a sign chart} $\Leftrightarrow 30 \leq v \leq 45$

**63** (a) 5 ft 9 in = 69 in. In a 40 year period, a person's height will decrease by $40 \times 0.024 = 0.96$ in $\approx 1$ in. The person will be approximately one inch shorter, or 5 ft 8 in. at age 70.

(b) 5 ft 6 in = 66 in. In 20 years, a person's height $(h = 66)$ will change by $0.024 \times 20 = 0.48$ in. Thus, $66 - 0.48 \leq h \leq 66 + 0.48 \Rightarrow 65.52 \leq h \leq 66.48$.

**64** $7500 \leq W \leq 10{,}000 \Rightarrow 7500 \leq 0.00334V^2S \leq 10{,}000 \Rightarrow 7500 \leq 0.00334(210)V^2 \leq 10{,}000 \Rightarrow$

$\dfrac{7500}{0.7014} \leq V^2 \leq \dfrac{10{,}000}{0.7014} \Rightarrow \sqrt{\dfrac{7500}{0.7014}} \leq V \leq \sqrt{\dfrac{10{,}000}{0.7014}} \Rightarrow 103.4 \leq V \leq 119.4$ {in ft/sec}. To convert

ft/sec to mi/hr, multiply by $\dfrac{60}{88}$ or $\dfrac{15}{22}$, which are reduced forms of $\dfrac{1 \text{ foot}}{1 \text{ second}} \times \dfrac{3600 \text{ seconds}}{1 \text{ hour}} \times \dfrac{1 \text{ mile}}{5280 \text{ feet}}$. Using

the approximations in ft/sec, we get $103.4 \leq V \leq 119.4$ {in ft/sec} $\Rightarrow 70.5 \leq V \leq 81.4$ {in mi/hr}.

**65** The numerator is equal to zero when $x = 2, 3$ and the denominator is equal to zero when $x = \pm 1$. From the table,

the expression $Y_1 = \dfrac{(2 - x)(3x - 9)}{(1 - x)(x + 1)}$ is positive when $x \in [-2, -1) \cup (1, 2) \cup (3, 3.5]$. See the table on the left.

| $x$ | $Y_1$ | $x$ | $Y_1$ |
|------|--------|------|--------|
| $-2.0$ | 20 | 1.0 | ERROR |
| $-1.5$ | 37.8 | 1.5 | 1.8 |
| $-1.0$ | ERROR | 2.0 | 0 |
| $-0.5$ | $-35$ | 2.5 | $-0.1429$ |
| 0.0 | $-18$ | 3.0 | 0 |
| 0.5 | $-15$ | 3.5 | 0.2 |

| $x$ | $Y_1$ | $x$ | $Y_1$ |
|------|--------|------|--------|
| $-3.5$ | 30.938 | 1.0 | 36 |
| $-3.0$ | 0 | 1.5 | 19.688 |
| $-2.5$ | $-7.313$ | 2.0 | 0 |
| $-2.0$ | 0 | 2.5 | $-18.56$ |
| $-1.5$ | 14.438 | 3.0 | $-30$ |
| $-1.0$ | 30 | 3.5 | $-26.81$ |
| $-0.5$ | 42.188 | 4.0 | 0 |
| 0.0 | 48 | 4.5 | 60.938 |
| 0.5 | 45.938 | 5.0 | 168 |

**66** By using a table it can be shown that the expression is equal to zero when $x = -3, -2, 2, 4$.

The expression $Y_1 = x^4 - x^3 - 16x^2 + 4x + 48$ is negative when $x \in (-3, -2) \cup (2, 4)$. See the table on the right.

## Chapter 1 Review Exercises

**1** If $x \leq -3$, then $x + 3 \leq 0$, and $|x + 3| = -(x + 3) = -x - 3$.

**2** If $2 < x < 3$, then $x - 2 > 0$ {$x - 2$ is positive} and $x - 3 < 0$ {$x - 3$ is negative}. Thus, $(x - 2)(x - 3) < 0$ {positive times negative is negative}, and since the absolute value of an expression that is negative is the negative of the expression, $|(x - 2)(x - 3)| = -(x - 2)(x - 3)$, or, equivalently, $(2 - x)(x - 3)$.

**3** $\left(\dfrac{a^{2/3}b^{3/2}}{a^2 b}\right)^6 = \dfrac{a^4 b^9}{a^{12} b^6} = \dfrac{b^3}{a^8}$
   
**4** $(-2p^2 q)^3 \left(\dfrac{p}{4q^2}\right)^2 = (-8p^6 q^3)\left(\dfrac{p^2}{16q^4}\right) = -\dfrac{p^8}{2q}$

**5** $\left(\dfrac{xy^{-1}}{\sqrt{z}}\right)^4 \div \left(\dfrac{x^{1/3}y^2}{z}\right)^3 = \dfrac{x^4 y^{-4}}{z^2} \cdot \dfrac{z^3}{xy^6} = \dfrac{x^3 z}{y^{10}}$
   
**6** $\left(\dfrac{-64x^3}{z^6 y^9}\right)^{2/3} = \dfrac{\left(\sqrt[3]{-64}\right)^2 x^2}{z^4 y^6} = \dfrac{16x^2}{z^4 y^6}$

**7** $\left[\left(a^{2/3}b^{-2}\right)^3\right]^{-1} = (a^2 b^{-6})^{-1} = a^{-2}b^6 = \dfrac{b^6}{a^2}$
   
**8** $x^{-2} - y^{-1} = \dfrac{1}{x^2} - \dfrac{1}{y} = \dfrac{y - x^2}{x^2 y}$

**9** $\sqrt[3]{27x^5 y^3 z^4} = \sqrt[3]{27x^3 y^3 z^3}\sqrt[3]{x^2 z} = 3xyz\sqrt[3]{x^2 z}$

**10** $\sqrt[4]{(-4a^3 b^2 c)^2} = \sqrt[4]{16a^6 b^4 c^2} = \sqrt[4]{2^4 a^4 b^4}\sqrt[4]{a^2 c^2} = 2ab\sqrt[4]{(ac)^2} = 2ab\sqrt{ac}$

**11** $\dfrac{1}{\sqrt{t}}\left(\dfrac{1}{\sqrt{t}} - 1\right) = \dfrac{1}{\sqrt{t}}\left(\dfrac{1}{\sqrt{t}} - \dfrac{\sqrt{t}}{\sqrt{t}}\right) = \dfrac{1}{\sqrt{t}}\left(\dfrac{1 - \sqrt{t}}{\sqrt{t}}\right) = \dfrac{1 - \sqrt{t}}{t}$
   
**12** $\sqrt{\sqrt[3]{(c^3 d^6)^4}} = \sqrt[6]{c^{12} d^{24}} = c^2 d^4$

**13** $\dfrac{\sqrt{12x^4 y}}{\sqrt{3x^2 y^7}} = \sqrt{\dfrac{12x^4 y}{3x^2 y^7}} = \sqrt{\dfrac{4x^2}{y^6}} = \dfrac{2x}{y^3}$
   
**14** $\dfrac{3 + \sqrt{x}}{3 - \sqrt{x}} = \dfrac{3 + \sqrt{x}}{3 - \sqrt{x}} \cdot \dfrac{3 + \sqrt{x}}{3 + \sqrt{x}} = \dfrac{x + 6\sqrt{x} + 9}{9 - x}$

**15** $(3x^3 - 4x^2 + x - 6) + (x^4 - 2x^3 + 3x^2 + 5) = x^4 + x^3 - x^2 + x - 1$

**16** $(x + 4)(x + 3) - (2x - 3)(x - 5) = (x^2 + 7x + 12) - (2x^2 - 13x + 15) = -x^2 + 20x - 3$

**17** $(3a - 5b)(4a + 7b) = 12a^2 + 21ab - 20ab - 35b^2 = 12a^2 + ab - 35b^2$

**18** $(4r^2 - 3s)^2 = (4r^2)^2 - 2(4r^2)(3s) + (3s)^2 = 16r^4 - 24r^2 s + 9s^2$

**19** $(13a^2 + 5b)(13a^2 - 5b) = (13a^2)^2 - (5b)^2 = 169a^4 - 25b^2$

**20** $(2a + b)^3 = (2a)^3 + 3(2a)^2(b) + 3(2a)(b)^2 + (b)^3 = 8a^3 + 12a^2 b + 6ab^2 + b^3$

**21** $(3x + 2y)^2(3x - 2y)^2 = [(3x + 2y)(3x - 2y)]^2 = (9x^2 - 4y^2)^2 = 81x^4 - 72x^2 y^2 + 16y^4$

**22** $(a + b + c + d)^2 = a^2 + b^2 + c^2 + d^2 + 2(ab + ac + ad + bc + bd + cd)$

**23** $60xw + 50w = 10w(6x + 5)$

**24** $16a^4 + 24a^2 b^2 + 9b^4 = (4a^2 + 3b^2)(4a^2 + 3b^2) = (4a^2 + 3b^2)^2$

**25** $8x^3 + 64y^3 = 8(x^3 + 8y^3) = 8\left[(x)^3 + (2y)^3\right] = 8(x + 2y)(x^2 - 2xy + 4y^2)$

**26** $u^3 v^4 - u^6 v = u^3 v(v^3 - u^3) = u^3 v(v - u)(v^2 + uv + u^2)$

**27** $p^8 - q^8 = (p^4)^2 - (q^4)^2 = (p^4 + q^4)(p^4 - q^4) = (p^4 + q^4)(p^2 + q^2)(p^2 - q^2)$
$$= (p^4 + q^4)(p^2 + q^2)(p + q)(p - q)$$

**28** $x^4 - 12x^3 + 36x^2 = x^2(x^2 - 12x + 36) = x^2(x - 6)(x - 6) = x^2(x - 6)^2$

**29** $x^2 - 49y^2 - 14x + 49 = (x^2 - 14x + 49) - 49y^2 = (x - 7)^2 - (7y)^2 = (x - 7 + 7y)(x - 7 - 7y)$

**30** $x^5 - 4x^3 + 8x^2 - 32 = x^3(x^2 - 4) + 8(x^2 - 4) = (x^3 + 8)(x^2 - 4)$
$$= \left[(x + 2)(x^2 - 2x + 4)\right]\left[(x + 2)(x - 2)\right] = (x - 2)(x + 2)^2(x^2 - 2x + 4)$$

**31** $\dfrac{6}{4x-5} - \dfrac{15}{10x+1} = \dfrac{6(10x+1) - 15(4x-5)}{(4x-5)(10x+1)} = \dfrac{60x+6 - 60x+75}{(4x-5)(10x+1)} = \dfrac{81}{(4x-5)(10x+1)}$

**32** $\dfrac{7}{x+2} + \dfrac{3x}{(x+2)^2} - \dfrac{5}{x} = \dfrac{7(x)(x+2) + 3x(x) - 5(x+2)^2}{x(x+2)^2} = \dfrac{7x^2 + 14x + 3x^2 - 5x^2 - 20x - 20}{x(x+2)^2} =$

$$\dfrac{5x^2 - 6x - 20}{x(x+2)^2}$$

**33** $\dfrac{x + x^{-2}}{1 + x^{-2}} = \dfrac{x + \dfrac{1}{x^2}}{1 + \dfrac{1}{x^2}} = \dfrac{\left(x + \dfrac{1}{x^2}\right) \cdot x^2}{\left(1 + \dfrac{1}{x^2}\right) \cdot x^2} = \dfrac{x^3 + 1}{x^2 + 1}$. We could factor the numerator,

but since it doesn't lead to a reduction of the fraction, we leave it in this form.

**34** $(a^{-1} + b^{-1})^{-1} = \left(\dfrac{1}{a} + \dfrac{1}{b}\right)^{-1} = \left(\dfrac{b+a}{ab}\right)^{-1} = \left(\dfrac{ab}{a+b}\right)^{1} = \dfrac{ab}{a+b}$

**35** $\dfrac{\dfrac{x}{x+2} - \dfrac{4}{x+2}}{x - 3 - \dfrac{6}{x+2}} = \dfrac{\dfrac{x-4}{x+2}}{\dfrac{(x-3)(x+2) - 6}{x+2}} = \dfrac{x-4}{(x^2 - x - 6) - 6} = \dfrac{x-4}{x^2 - x - 12} = \dfrac{x-4}{(x+3)(x-4)} = \dfrac{1}{x+3}$

**36** $\dfrac{(4 - x^2)\left(\frac{1}{3}\right)(6x+1)^{-2/3}(6) - (6x+1)^{1/3}(-2x)}{(4 - x^2)^2} = \dfrac{2(6x+1)^{-2/3}[(4 - x^2) + x(6x+1)]}{(4 - x^2)^2}$

$$= \dfrac{2(4 - x^2 + 6x^2 + x)}{(6x+1)^{2/3}(4 - x^2)^2} = \dfrac{2(5x^2 + x + 4)}{(6x+1)^{2/3}(4 - x^2)^2}$$

**37** $\left[\dfrac{3x+1}{5x+7} = \dfrac{6x+11}{10x-3}\right] \cdot (5x+7)(10x-3) \Rightarrow (3x+1)(10x-3) = (6x+11)(5x+7) \Rightarrow$

$$30x^2 + x - 3 = 30x^2 + 97x + 77 \Rightarrow -96x = 80 \Rightarrow x = -\tfrac{5}{6}$$

**38** $2x^2 + 7x - 15 = 0 \Rightarrow (x+5)(2x-3) = 0 \Rightarrow x = -5, \tfrac{3}{2}$

**39** $x(3x+4) = 2 \Rightarrow 3x^2 + 4x - 2 = 0 \Rightarrow x = \dfrac{-4 \pm \sqrt{16+24}}{6} = \dfrac{-4 \pm 2\sqrt{10}}{6} = -\dfrac{2}{3} \pm \dfrac{1}{3}\sqrt{10}$

**40** $4x^4 - 37x^2 + 75 = 0 \Rightarrow (4x^2 - 25)(x^2 - 3) \Rightarrow x^2 = \tfrac{25}{4}, 3 \Rightarrow x = \pm\tfrac{5}{2}, \pm\sqrt{3}$

**41** $20x^3 + 8x^2 - 55x - 22 = 0 \Rightarrow 4x^2(5x+2) - 11(5x+2) = 0 \Rightarrow$

$$(4x^2 - 11)(5x+2) = 0 \Rightarrow x^2 = \tfrac{11}{4} \text{ or } x = -\tfrac{2}{5} \Rightarrow x = \pm\tfrac{1}{2}\sqrt{11}, -\tfrac{2}{5}$$

**42** $|4x - 1| = 7 \Rightarrow 4x - 1 = 7 \text{ or } 4x - 1 = -7 \Rightarrow 4x = 8 \text{ or } 4x = -6 \Rightarrow x = 2 \text{ or } x = -\tfrac{3}{2}$

**43** $2|2x+1| + 1 = 15 \Rightarrow 2|2x+1| = 14 \Rightarrow |2x+1| = 7 \Rightarrow$

$$2x + 1 = 7 \text{ or } 2x + 1 = -7 \Rightarrow 2x = 6 \text{ or } 2x = -8 \Rightarrow x = 3 \text{ or } x = -4$$

**44** $\left[\dfrac{1}{x} + 6 = \dfrac{5}{\sqrt{x}}\right] \cdot x \Rightarrow 1 + 6x = 5\sqrt{x} \Rightarrow$

$6x - 5\sqrt{x} + 1 = 0$ {factoring or substituting would be appropriate} $\Rightarrow$

$$(2\sqrt{x} - 1)(3\sqrt{x} - 1) = 0 \Rightarrow \sqrt{x} = \tfrac{1}{2}, \tfrac{1}{3} \Rightarrow x = \left(\tfrac{1}{2}\right)^2, \left(\tfrac{1}{3}\right)^2 \Rightarrow x = \tfrac{1}{4}, \tfrac{1}{9}$$

**Check** $x = \tfrac{1}{4}$: LS $= 4 + 6 = 10$; RS $= 5/\tfrac{1}{2} = 10 \Rightarrow x = \tfrac{1}{4}$ is a solution.

**Check** $x = \tfrac{1}{9}$: LS $= 9 + 6 = 15$; RS $= 5/\tfrac{1}{3} = 15 \Rightarrow x = \tfrac{1}{9}$ is a solution.

**45** $\sqrt{7x+2} + x = 6 \Rightarrow \left(\sqrt{7x+2}\right)^2 = (6 - x)^2 \Rightarrow 7x + 2 = 36 - 12x + x^2 \Rightarrow$

$$x^2 - 19x + 34 = 0 \Rightarrow (x - 2)(x - 17) = 0 \Rightarrow x = 2 \text{ and } 17 \text{ is an extraneous solution.}$$

**46** $\sqrt{3x+1} - \sqrt{x+4} = 1 \Rightarrow \sqrt{3x+1} = 1 + \sqrt{x+4} \Rightarrow (\sqrt{3x+1})^2 = (1 + \sqrt{x+4})^2 \Rightarrow$

$3x+1 = 1 + 2\sqrt{x+4} + x + 4 \Rightarrow 2\sqrt{x+4} = 2x - 4 \Rightarrow \sqrt{x+4} = x - 2 \Rightarrow$

$(\sqrt{x+4})^2 = (x-2)^2 \Rightarrow x+4 = x^2 - 4x + 4 \Rightarrow x^2 - 5x = 0 \Rightarrow x(x-5) = 0 \Rightarrow x = 0, 5.$

**Check** $x = 0$: LS $= 1 - 2 = -1 \neq$ RS $\Rightarrow x = 0$ is an extraneous solution.

**Check** $x = 5$: LS $= 4 - 3 = 1 =$ RS $\Rightarrow x = 5$ is a solution.

**47** $10 - 7x < 4 + 8x \Rightarrow -15x < -6 \Rightarrow x > \frac{2}{5} \Leftrightarrow (\frac{2}{5}, \infty)$

**48** $\left[ -\frac{1}{2} < \frac{2x+3}{5} < \frac{3}{2} \right] \cdot 10 \Rightarrow -5 < 4x + 6 < 15 \Rightarrow -11 < 4x < 9 \Rightarrow -\frac{11}{4} < x < \frac{9}{4} \Leftrightarrow (-\frac{11}{4}, \frac{9}{4})$

**49** $\dfrac{7}{10x+3} < 0 \Rightarrow 10x + 3 < 0 \text{ \{since } 7 > 0\} \Rightarrow x < -\frac{3}{10} \Leftrightarrow (-\infty, -\frac{3}{10})$

**50** $|4x+7| < 21 \Rightarrow -21 < 4x + 7 < 21 \Rightarrow -28 < 4x < 14 \Rightarrow -7 < x < \frac{7}{2} \Leftrightarrow (-7, \frac{7}{2})$

**51** $2|3-x| + 1 > 5 \Rightarrow 2|3-x| > 4 \Rightarrow |3-x| > 2 \Rightarrow 3 - x > 2 \text{ or } 3 - x < -2 \Rightarrow$

$1 > x \text{ or } 5 < x \Rightarrow x < 1 \text{ or } x > 5 \Leftrightarrow (-\infty, 1) \cup (5, \infty)$

**52** $|16 - 3x| \geq 5 \Rightarrow 16 - 3x \geq 5 \text{ or } 16 - 3x \leq -5 \Rightarrow -3x \geq -11 \text{ or } -3x \leq -21 \Rightarrow$

$x \leq \frac{11}{3} \text{ or } x \geq 7 \Leftrightarrow (-\infty, \frac{11}{3}] \cup [7, \infty)$

**53** $10x^2 + 11x > 6 \Rightarrow 10x^2 + 11x - 6 > 0 \Rightarrow (2x+3)(5x-2) > 0 \qquad \star (-\infty, -\frac{3}{2}) \cup (\frac{2}{5}, \infty)$

| Interval | $(-\infty, -\frac{3}{2})$ | $(-\frac{3}{2}, \frac{2}{5})$ | $(\frac{2}{5}, \infty)$ |
|---|---|---|---|
| Sign of $5x - 2$ | $-$ | $-$ | $+$ |
| Sign of $2x + 3$ | $-$ | $+$ | $+$ |
| **Resulting sign** | $+$ | $-$ | $+$ |

**54** $x(x-3) \leq 18 \Rightarrow x^2 - 3x - 18 \leq 0 \Rightarrow (x-6)(x+3) \leq 0 \qquad \star [-3, 6]$

| Interval | $(-\infty, -3)$ | $(-3, 6)$ | $(6, \infty)$ |
|---|---|---|---|
| Sign of $x - 6$ | $-$ | $-$ | $+$ |
| Sign of $x + 3$ | $-$ | $+$ | $+$ |
| **Resulting sign** | $+$ | $-$ | $+$ |

**55** $\dfrac{x^2(3-x)}{x+2} \leq 0 \Rightarrow \dfrac{3-x}{x+2} \leq 0 \text{ \{} x^2 \geq 0, \text{ include } 0\} \qquad \star (-\infty, -2) \cup \{0\} \cup [3, \infty)$

| Interval | $(-\infty, -2)$ | $(-2, 3)$ | $(3, \infty)$ |
|---|---|---|---|
| Sign of $3 - x$ | $+$ | $+$ | $-$ |
| Sign of $x + 2$ | $-$ | $+$ | $+$ |
| **Resulting sign** | $-$ | $+$ | $-$ |

**56** $\dfrac{x^2 - x - 2}{x^2 + 4x + 3} \leq 0 \Rightarrow \dfrac{(x-2)(x+1)}{(x+1)(x+3)} \leq 0 \Rightarrow \dfrac{x-2}{x+3} \leq 0 \text{ \{exclude } -1\} \qquad \star (-3, -1) \cup (-1, 2]$

| Interval | $(-\infty, -3)$ | $(-3, 2)$ | $(2, \infty)$ |
|---|---|---|---|
| Sign of $x - 2$ | $-$ | $-$ | $+$ |
| Sign of $x + 3$ | $-$ | $+$ | $+$ |
| **Resulting sign** | $+$ | $-$ | $+$ |

**57** $\dfrac{3}{2x+3} < \dfrac{1}{x-2}$ $\Rightarrow$ $\dfrac{3}{2x+3} - \dfrac{1}{x-2} < 0$ $\Rightarrow$ $\dfrac{3(x-2) - 1(2x+3)}{(2x+3)(x-2)} < 0$ $\Rightarrow$

$\dfrac{3x - 6 - 2x - 3}{(2x+3)(x-2)} < 0$ $\Rightarrow$ $\dfrac{x-9}{(2x+3)(x-2)} < 0$ ★ $\left(-\infty, -\frac{3}{2}\right) \cup (2,9)$

| Interval | $\left(-\infty, -\frac{3}{2}\right)$ | $\left(-\frac{3}{2}, 2\right)$ | $(2,9)$ | $(9,\infty)$ |
|---|---|---|---|---|
| Sign of $x-9$ | − | − | − | + |
| Sign of $x-2$ | − | − | + | + |
| Sign of $2x+3$ | − | + | + | + |
| **Resulting sign** | − | + | − | + |

**58** $\dfrac{x+2}{x^2-25} \le 0$ $\Rightarrow$ $\dfrac{x+2}{(x+5)(x-5)} \le 0$ ★ $(-\infty, -5) \cup [-2, 5)$

| Interval | $(-\infty, -5)$ | $(-5, -2)$ | $(-2, 5)$ | $(5, \infty)$ |
|---|---|---|---|---|
| Sign of $x-5$ | − | − | − | + |
| Sign of $x+2$ | − | − | + | + |
| Sign of $x+5$ | − | + | + | + |
| **Resulting sign** | − | + | − | + |

**59** $x^3 > x^2$ $\Rightarrow$ $x^2(x-1) > 0$ $\{x^2 \ge 0\}$ $\Rightarrow$ $x - 1 > 0$ $\Rightarrow$ $x > 1$ $\Leftrightarrow$ $(1, \infty)$

**60** $(x^2 - x)(x^2 - 5x + 6) < 0$ $\Rightarrow$ $x(x-1)(x-2)(x-3) < 0$ ★ $(0,1) \cup (2,3)$

| Interval | $(-\infty, 0)$ | $(0,1)$ | $(1,2)$ | $(2,3)$ | $(3,\infty)$ |
|---|---|---|---|---|---|
| Sign of $x-3$ | − | − | − | − | + |
| Sign of $x-2$ | − | − | − | + | + |
| Sign of $x-1$ | − | − | + | + | + |
| Sign of $x$ | − | + | + | + | + |
| **Resulting sign** | + | − | + | − | + |

**61** $P + N = \dfrac{C+2}{C}$ $\Rightarrow$ $C(P+N) = C + 2$ $\Rightarrow$ $CP + CN = C + 2$ $\Rightarrow$

$CP + CN - C = 2$ $\Rightarrow$ $C(P + N - 1) = 2$ $\Rightarrow$ $C = \dfrac{2}{P+N-1}$

**62** $A = B\sqrt[3]{\dfrac{C}{D}} - E$ $\Rightarrow$ $A + E = B\sqrt[3]{\dfrac{C}{D}}$ $\Rightarrow$ $\dfrac{A+E}{B} = \sqrt[3]{\dfrac{C}{D}}$ $\Rightarrow$ $\left(\dfrac{A+E}{B}\right)^3 = \dfrac{C}{D}$ $\Rightarrow$

$D \cdot \dfrac{(A+E)^3}{B^3} = C$ $\Rightarrow$ $D(A+E)^3 = C \cdot B^3$ $\Rightarrow$ $D = \dfrac{CB^3}{(A+E)^3}$

**63** $F = \dfrac{\pi P R^4}{8VL}$ $\Rightarrow$ $R^4 = \dfrac{8FVL}{\pi P}$ $\Rightarrow$ $R = \pm\sqrt[4]{\dfrac{8FVL}{\pi P}}$ $\Rightarrow$ $R = \sqrt[4]{\dfrac{8FVL}{\pi P}}$ since $R > 0$

**64** $V = \frac{1}{3}\pi h(r^2 + R^2 + rR)$ $\Rightarrow$ $3V = \pi h(r^2 + R^2 + rR)$ $\Rightarrow$ $(\pi h)r^2 + (\pi h R)r + (\pi h R^2 - 3V) = 0$ $\Rightarrow$

$r = \dfrac{-(\pi h R) \pm \sqrt{(\pi h R)^2 - 4(\pi h)(\pi h R^2 - 3V)}}{2(\pi h)} = \dfrac{-\pi h R \pm \sqrt{12\pi h V - 3\pi^2 h^2 R^2}}{2\pi h}$.

Since $r > 0$, we must use the plus sign, and $r = \dfrac{-\pi h R + \sqrt{12\pi h V - 3\pi^2 h^2 R^2}}{2\pi h}$.

**65** $(5 + 8i)^2 = 5^2 + 2(5)(8i) + (8i)^2 = (25 - 64) + 80i = -39 + 80i$

**66** $\dfrac{1}{9 - \sqrt{-4}} = \dfrac{1}{9 - 2i} = \dfrac{1}{9 - 2i} \cdot \dfrac{9 + 2i}{9 + 2i} = \dfrac{9 + 2i}{81 + 4} = \dfrac{9}{85} + \dfrac{2}{85}i$

**67** $\dfrac{6-3i}{2+7i} = \dfrac{6-3i}{2+7i} \cdot \dfrac{2-7i}{2-7i} = \dfrac{(12-21)+(-42-6)i}{4+49} = -\dfrac{9}{53} - \dfrac{48}{53}i$

**68** $\dfrac{24-8i}{4i} = \dfrac{4(6-2i)}{4i} = \dfrac{6-2i}{i} \cdot \dfrac{-i}{-i} = \dfrac{-6i+2i^2}{-i^2} = \dfrac{-2-6i}{1} = -2-6i$

**69** Let $P$ denote the principal that will be invested, and $r$ the yield rate of the stock fund.

Income$_{stocks}$ − 28% federal tax − 7% state tax = Income$_{bonds}$ $\Rightarrow$

$(Pr) - 0.28(Pr) - 0.07(Pr) = 0.07186P$ {divide by $P$} $\Rightarrow$ $1r - 0.28r - 0.07r = 0.07186$ $\Rightarrow$

$\qquad\qquad 0.65r = 0.07186 \Rightarrow r = \frac{0.07186}{0.65} \Rightarrow r \approx 0.11055$, or, 11.055%.

**70** Let $x$ denote the number of cm$^3$ of gold. Grams$_{gold}$ + Grams$_{silver}$ = Grams$_{total}$ $\Rightarrow$

$x(19.3) + (5-x)(10.5) = 80 \Rightarrow 19.3x + 52.5 - 10.5x = 80 \Rightarrow 8.8x = 27.5 \Rightarrow x = 3.125$.

$\qquad\qquad$ The number of grams of gold is $19.3x = 60.3125 \approx 60.3$.

**71** Let $x$ denote the number of ounces of the vegetable portion, $10 - x$ the number of ounces of meat.

Protein$_{vegetable}$ + Protein$_{meat}$ = Protein$_{total}$ $\Rightarrow$ $\frac{1}{2}(x) + 1(10-x) = 7 \Rightarrow \frac{1}{2}x + 10 - x = 7 \Rightarrow$

$\qquad\qquad -\frac{1}{2}x = -3 \Rightarrow x = 6$. Use 6 oz of vegetables and 4 oz of meat.

**72** Let $x$ denote the number of gallons of 20% solution, $120 - x$ the number of gallons of 50% solution.

$20(x) + 50(120-x) = 30(120)$ {all in %} $\Rightarrow$ $20x + 6000 - 50x = 3600 \Rightarrow 2400 = 30x \Rightarrow x = 80$.

$\qquad\qquad$ Use 80 gal of the 20% solution and 40 gal of the 50% solution.

**73** Let $x =$ the amount of copper they have to mix with 140 kg of zinc to make brass.

Copper$_{amount\ put\ in}$ = Copper$_{amount\ in\ final\ product}$ $\Rightarrow$

$\qquad\qquad x = 0.65(x+140) \Rightarrow x = 0.65x + 91 \Rightarrow 0.35x = 91 \Rightarrow x = \frac{91}{0.35} = 260$ kg

**74** Let $x$ denote the number of hours needed to fill an empty bin.

Using the hourly rates, $\left[\dfrac{1}{2} - \dfrac{1}{5} = \dfrac{1}{x}\right] \cdot 10x \Rightarrow 5x - 2x = 10 \Rightarrow 3x = 10 \Rightarrow$

$\qquad\qquad x = \frac{10}{3}$ hr. Since the bin was half-full at the start, $\frac{1}{2}x = \frac{1}{2} \cdot \frac{10}{3} = \frac{5}{3}$ hr, or, 1 hr 40 min.

**75** (a) The eastbound car has distance $20t$ and the southbound car has distance $(-2 + 50t)$.

$\qquad d^2 = (20t)^2 + (-2+50t)^2 \Rightarrow d^2 = 400t^2 + 4 - 200t + 2500t^2 \Rightarrow d = \sqrt{2900t^2 - 200t + 4}$

(b) $104 = \sqrt{2900t^2 - 200t + 4} \Rightarrow 10{,}816 = 2900t^2 - 200t + 4 \Rightarrow 2900t^2 - 200t - 10{,}812 = 0 \Rightarrow$

$\quad 725t^2 - 50t - 2703 = 0$ {divide by 4} $\Rightarrow$

$\qquad\qquad t = \dfrac{50 \pm \sqrt{7{,}841{,}200}}{1450}$ {$t > 0$} $= \dfrac{5 + 2\sqrt{19{,}603}}{145} \approx 1.97$, or approximately 11:58 A.M.

**76** Let $l$ and $w$ denote the length and width, respectively. $3l + 6w = 270 \Rightarrow 6w = 270 - 3l \Rightarrow w = 45 - \frac{1}{2}l$.

The total area is to be $10 \cdot 100 = 1000$ ft$^2$. Area $= lw \Rightarrow 1000 = l\left(45 - \frac{1}{2}l\right) \Rightarrow 1000 = 45l - \frac{1}{2}l^2 \Rightarrow$

$l^2 - 90l + 2000 = 0 \Rightarrow (l-40)(l-50) = 0 \Rightarrow l = 40, 50$ and $w = 25, 20$.

$\qquad\qquad$ There are two arrangements: 40 ft × 25 ft and 50 ft × 20 ft.

**77** Let $x$ denote the length of one side of an end.

(a) $V = lwh \Rightarrow 48 = 6 \cdot x \cdot x \Rightarrow x^2 = 8 \Rightarrow x = 2\sqrt{2}$ ft

(b) $S = lw + 2wh + 2lh \Rightarrow 44 = 6x + 2(x^2) + 2(6x) \Rightarrow 44 = 2x^2 + 18x \Rightarrow$

$\qquad\qquad x^2 + 9x - 22 = 0 \Rightarrow (x+11)(x-2) = 0 \Rightarrow x = 2$ ft

[78] $pv = 200 \Rightarrow v = \dfrac{200}{p}.$ $25 \le v \le 50 \Rightarrow 25 \le \dfrac{200}{p} \le 50 \Rightarrow \dfrac{1}{25} \ge \dfrac{p}{200} \ge \dfrac{1}{50} \Rightarrow 8 \ge p \ge 4 \Rightarrow$
$$4 \le p \le 8$$

[79] Let $x$ denote the amount of yearly business. $\text{Pay}_B > \text{Pay}_A \Rightarrow \$40{,}000 + 0.20x > \$50{,}000 + 0.10x \Rightarrow$
$$0.10x > \$10{,}000 \Rightarrow x > \$100{,}000$$

[80] $v > 1100 \Rightarrow 1087\sqrt{\dfrac{T}{273}} > 1100 \Rightarrow \sqrt{\dfrac{T}{273}} > \dfrac{1100}{1087} \Rightarrow \dfrac{T}{273} > \dfrac{1100^2}{1087^2} \Rightarrow T > \dfrac{273 \cdot 1100^2}{1087^2} \Rightarrow$
$$T > 279.57 \text{ K}$$

[81] Let $x$ denote the number of trees *over* 24. Then $24 + x$ represents the total number of trees planted per acre, and $600 - 12x$ represents the number of apples per tree.

$$\textbf{Total apples} = (\text{number of trees})(\text{number of apples per tree})$$
$$= (24 + x)(600 - 12x) = -12x^2 + 312x + 14{,}400$$

Apples $\ge 16{,}416 \Rightarrow -12x^2 + 312x + 14{,}400 \ge 16{,}416 \Rightarrow -12x^2 + 312x - 2016 \ge 0 \Rightarrow$
$x^2 - 26x + 168 \le 0 \Rightarrow (x - 12)(x - 14) \le 0 \Rightarrow 12 \le x \le 14 \Rightarrow 36 \le 24 + x \le 38$

Hence, 36 to 38 trees per acre should be planted.

[82] Let $x$ denote the number of \$25 increases in rent. Then the number of occupied apartments is $218 - 5x$ and the rent per apartment is $940 + 25x$.

$$\textbf{Total income} = (\text{number of occupied apartments})(\text{rent per apartment})$$
$$= (218 - 5x)(940 + 25x) = -125x^2 + 750x + 204{,}920$$

Income $\ge 205{,}920 \Rightarrow -125x^2 + 750x + 204{,}920 \ge 205{,}920 \Rightarrow -125x^2 + 750x - 1000 \ge 0 \Rightarrow$
$x^2 - 6x + 8 \le 0 \Rightarrow (x - 2)(x - 4) \le 0 \Rightarrow 2 \le x \le 4 \Rightarrow 990 \le 940 + 25x \le 1040$

Hence, the rent charged should be \$990 to \$1040.

[83] The $y$-values are increasing slowly and can best be described by equation (3), $y = 3\sqrt{x - 0.5}$.

## Chapter 1 Discussion Exercises

[1] $\dfrac{\$1 \text{ in cash back}}{100 \text{ points}} \times \dfrac{1 \text{ point}}{\$10 \text{ charged}} = \dfrac{\$1 \text{ in cash back}}{\$1000 \text{ charged}} = 0.001$, or 0.1%.

[2] Squaring the right side gives us $(a + b)^2 = a^2 + 2ab + b^2$. Squaring the left side gives us $a^2 + b^2$. Now $a^2 + 2ab + b^2$ will equal $a^2 + b^2$ only if $2ab = 0$. The expression $2ab$ equals zero only if either $a = 0$ or $b = 0$.

[3] We first need to determine the term that needs to be added and subtracted. Since $25 = 5^2$, it makes sense to add and subtract $2 \cdot 5x = 10x$. Then we will obtain the square of a binomial—i.e.,
$(x^2 + 10x + 25) - 10x = (x + 5)^2 - 10x$. We can now factor this expression as the difference of two squares,
$$(x + 5)^2 - 10x = (x + 5)^2 - \left(\sqrt{10x}\right)^2 = \left(x + 5 + \sqrt{10x}\right)\left(x + 5 - \sqrt{10x}\right).$$

[4] The expression $\dfrac{1}{x + 1}$ can be evaluated at $x = 1$, whereas the expression $\dfrac{x - 1}{x^2 - 1}$ is undefined at $x = 1$.

$\boxed{5}$ Try $\dfrac{3x^2 - 4x + 7}{8x^2 + 9x - 100}$ with $x = 10^3$, $10^4$, and $10^5$. You get approximately 0.374, 0.3749, and 0.37499. The numbers seem to be getting closer to 0.375, which is the decimal representation for $\frac{3}{8}$, which is the ratio of the coefficients of the $x^2$ terms. In general, the quotients of this form get close to the ratio of leading coefficients as $x$ gets larger.

$\boxed{6}$ $\dfrac{3x^2 - 5x - 2}{x^2 - 4} = \dfrac{(3x + 1)(x - 2)}{(x + 2)(x - 2)} = \dfrac{3x + 1}{x + 2}$. Evaluating the original expression and the simplified expression with any $x \neq \pm 2$ gives us the same value. This evaluation does not prove that the expressions are equal for any value of $x$ other than the one selected. The simplification proves that the expressions are equal for all values of $x$ except $x = 2$.

$\boxed{7}$ Follow the algebraic simplification given.

| | |
|---|---|
| 1) Write down his/her age. | Denote the age by $x$. |
| 2) Multiply it by 2. | $2x$ |
| 3) Add 5. | $2x + 5$ |
| 4) Multiply this sum by 50. | $50(2x + 5) = 100x + 250$ |
| 5) Subtract 365. | $(100x + 250) - 365 = 100x - 115$ |
| 6) Add his/her height (in inches). | $100x - 115 + y$, where $y$ is the height |
| 7) Add 115. | $100x - 115 + y + 115 = 100x + y$ |

As a specific example, suppose the age is 21 and the height is 68. The number obtained by following the steps is $100x + y = 2168$ and we can see that the first two digits of the result equal the age and the last two digits equal the height.

$\boxed{8}$ $V_{\text{out}} = I_{\text{in}}\left(-\dfrac{RXi}{R - Xi}\right) = \dfrac{V_{\text{in}}}{Z_{\text{in}}}\left(-\dfrac{RXi}{R - Xi}\right)$ {definition of $I_{\text{in}}$}

$= \dfrac{V_{\text{in}}}{\dfrac{R^2 - X^2 - 3RXi}{R - Xi}}\left(-\dfrac{RXi}{R - Xi}\right)$ {definition of $Z_{\text{in}}$}

$= \dfrac{V_{\text{in}}(R - Xi)}{R^2 - X^2 - 3RXi}\left(-\dfrac{RXi}{R - Xi}\right)$

$= -\dfrac{RXi}{R^2 - X^2 - 3RXi}(V_{\text{in}})$

$= -\dfrac{RRi}{R^2 - R^2 - 3RRi}(V_{\text{in}})$ {let $X = R$}

$= -\dfrac{R^2 i}{-3R^2 i}(V_{\text{in}}) = \frac{1}{3}V_{\text{in}}$

$\boxed{9}$ We need to solve the equation $x^2 - xy + y^2 = 0$ for $x$.

Use the quadratic formula with $a = 1$, $b = -y$, and $c = y^2$.

$x = \dfrac{-(-y) \pm \sqrt{(-y)^2 - 4(1)(y^2)}}{2(1)} = \dfrac{y \pm \sqrt{y^2 - 4y^2}}{2} = \dfrac{y \pm \sqrt{-3y^2}}{2} = \dfrac{y \pm |y|\sqrt{3}\,i}{2}$.

Since this equation has imaginary solutions, $x^2 - xy + y^2$ is not factorable over the reals.

A similar argument holds for $x^2 + xy + y^2$.

$\boxed{10}$ The solutions are $x_1 = \dfrac{-b + \sqrt{b^2 - 4ac}}{2a}$ and $x_2 = \dfrac{-b - \sqrt{b^2 - 4ac}}{2a}$.

The average is $\dfrac{x_1 + x_2}{2} = \dfrac{-2b/2a}{2} = -\dfrac{b}{2a}$. Suppose you solve the equation $-x^2 + 4x + 7 = 0$ and obtain the solutions $x_1 \approx -1.32$ and $x_2 \approx 5.32$. Averaging these numbers gives us the value 2, which we can easily see is equal to $-b/(2a)$.

**11** (a) $\dfrac{1}{\dfrac{a+bi}{c+di}} = \dfrac{c+di}{a+bi} \cdot \dfrac{a-bi}{a-bi} = \dfrac{ac+bd+(ad-bc)i}{a^2+b^2} = \dfrac{ac+bd}{a^2+b^2} + \dfrac{ad-bc}{a^2+b^2}\, i = p+qi$

(b) Yes, try an example such as $\frac{3}{4}$. Let $a = 3$, $b = 0$, $c = 4$, and $d = 0$. Then, from part (a),

$$p+qi = \tfrac{12}{9} + \tfrac{0}{9}i = \tfrac{12}{9} = \tfrac{4}{3}, \text{ which is the multiplicative inverse of } \tfrac{3}{4}.$$

(c) $a$ and $b$ cannot both be 0 because then the denominator would be 0.

**12** Since we don't know the value of $x$, we don't know the sign of $x - 2$, and hence we are unsure of whether or not to reverse the direction of the inequality sign.

**13** *Hint*: Try these examples to help you get to the general solution.

(1) $x^2 + 1 \geq 0$ {In this case, $a > 0$, $D = -4 < 0$, and by examining a sign chart with $x^2 + 1$ as the only factor,

we see that the solution is $x \in \mathbb{R}$.}

(2) $x^2 - 2x - 3 \geq 0$

(3) $-x^2 - 4 \geq 0$

(4) $-x^2 - 2x - 1 \geq 0$

(5) $-x^2 + 2x + 3 \geq 0$

General solutions categorized by $a$ and $D$:

(1) $a > 0$, $D \leq 0$: solution is $x \in \mathbb{R}$

(2) $a > 0$, $D > 0$: let $x_1 = \dfrac{-b - \sqrt{D}}{2a}$ and $x_2 = \dfrac{-b + \sqrt{D}}{2a}$ $\Rightarrow$ solution is $(-\infty, x_1] \cup [x_2, \infty)$

(3) $a < 0$, $D < 0$: no solution

(4) $a < 0$, $D = 0$: solution is $x = -\dfrac{b}{2a}$

(5) $a < 0$, $D > 0$: solution is $[x_1, x_2]$

**14** (a) This problem is solved in three steps.

(i) First, we must determine the height of the cloud base using the formula in Exercise 74 in Section 1.4, $h = 227(T - D) = 227(80 - 68) = 2724$ ft.

(ii) Next, we must determine the temperature $T$ at the cloud base. From (i), the height of the cloud base is $h = 2724$ and $T = T_0 - \frac{5.5}{1000}h = 80 - \frac{5.5}{1000} \cdot 2724 = 65.018°$F.

(iii) Finally, we must solve the equation $T = B - \frac{3}{1000}h$ for $h$, when $T = 32°$F and $B = 65.018°$F.

$$32 = 65.018 - \tfrac{3}{1000}h \quad \Rightarrow \quad h = (65.018 - 32)\tfrac{1000}{3} = 11{,}006 \text{ ft.}$$

(b) Following the procedure in part (a) and changing a few variable names, we obtain the following:

(i) $H = 227(G - D) = 227G - 227D$

(ii) $T = T_0 - \frac{5.5}{1000}h \Rightarrow B = G - \frac{11}{2000}H \Rightarrow B = G - \frac{11}{2000}(227G - 227D) \Rightarrow$
$B = G - \frac{2497}{2000}G + \frac{2497}{2000}D = \frac{2497}{2000}D - \frac{497}{2000}G$

(iii) $h = (B - 32)\frac{1000}{3} \Rightarrow h = \left(\frac{2497}{2000}D - \frac{497}{2000}G - 32\right)\frac{1000}{3} \Rightarrow h = \frac{2497}{6}D - \frac{497}{6}G - \frac{32{,}000}{3} \Rightarrow$
$h = \frac{2497}{6}D - \frac{497}{6}G - \frac{64{,}000}{6} \Rightarrow h = \frac{1}{6}(2497D - 497G - 64{,}000)$

**15** The first equation, $\sqrt{2x-3} + \sqrt{x+5} = 0$, is a sum of square roots that is equal to 0. The only way this could be true is if both radicals are actually equal to 0. It is easy to see that $\sqrt{x+5}$ is equal to 0 only if $x = -5$, but $-5$ will not make $\sqrt{2x-3}$ equal to 0, so there is no reason to try to solve the first equation.

On the other hand, the second equation, $\sqrt[3]{2x-3} + \sqrt[3]{x+5} = 0$, can be written as $\sqrt[3]{2x-3} = -\sqrt[3]{x+5}$. This just says that one cube root is equal to the negative of another cube root, which could happen since a cube root can be negative. Solving this equation gives us $2x-3 = -(x+5) \;\Rightarrow\; 3x = -2 \;\Rightarrow\; x = -\frac{2}{3}$.

**16** $\sqrt{x} = cx - 2/c \;\Rightarrow\; c\sqrt{x} = c^2 x - 2 \;\Rightarrow\; c^2 x = c^4 x^2 - 4c^2 x + 4 \;\Rightarrow\; 0 = c^4 x^2 - 5c^2 x + 4 \;\Rightarrow$
$0 = (c^2 x - 1)(c^2 x - 4) \;\Rightarrow\; x_{1,2} = \dfrac{1}{c^2}, \dfrac{4}{c^2}$.

**Check** $x_1 = \dfrac{1}{c^2} = \dfrac{1}{(2 \times 10^{500})^2} = \dfrac{1}{4 \times 10^{1000}}$.

$\text{LS} = \sqrt{x_1} = \dfrac{1}{2 \times 10^{500}}$

$\text{RS} = cx_1 - \dfrac{2}{c} = \dfrac{2 \times 10^{500}}{4 \times 10^{1000}} - \dfrac{2}{2 \times 10^{500}} = \dfrac{1}{2 \times 10^{500}} - \dfrac{2}{2 \times 10^{500}} = -\dfrac{1}{2 \times 10^{500}}$

**Check** $x_2 = \dfrac{4}{c^2} = \dfrac{4}{(2 \times 10^{500})^2} = \dfrac{4}{4 \times 10^{1000}} = \dfrac{1}{10^{1000}}$.

$\text{LS} = \sqrt{x_2} = \dfrac{1}{10^{500}}$

$\text{RS} = cx_2 - \dfrac{2}{c} = \dfrac{2 \times 10^{500}}{10^{1000}} - \dfrac{2}{2 \times 10^{500}} = \dfrac{2}{10^{500}} - \dfrac{1}{10^{500}} = \dfrac{1}{10^{500}}$

So $x_2$ is a valid solution. The right side of the original equation, $cx - 2/c$, must be nonnegative since it is equal to a square root. Note that the right side equals a negative number when $x = x_1$.

**17** (a) $S = 975$, $A = 599$, and $x = 1.83 \;\Rightarrow\;$ winning percentage $= \dfrac{S^x}{S^x + A^x} \approx 0.709\,206$. Since they played 154 games $(110 + 44)$, the number of wins using the estimated winning percentage would be $0.709(154) \approx 109$. Hence, the Pythagorean win-loss record of the 1927 Yankees is 109–45 (only one game off their actual record).

(b) The actual winning percentage is $\frac{110}{154} \approx 0.714\,286$. For an estimate of $x$, we'll assign $\dfrac{975^x}{975^x + 599^x}$ to $Y_1$ and look at a table of values of $x$ starting with $x = 1.80$ and incrementing by 0.01. From the table, we see that $x = 1.88$ corresponds to $Y_1 \approx 0.714\,204$, which is the closest value to the actual winning percentage. Thus, the value of $x$ is 1.88.

**18** 1 gallon $\approx 0.13368$ ft$^3$ is a conversion factor that would help.

The volume of the tank is 10,000 gallons $\approx 1336.8$ ft$^3$. Use $V = \frac{4}{3}\pi r^3$ to determine the radius.

$1336.8 = \dfrac{4}{3}\pi r^3 \;\Rightarrow\; r^3 = \dfrac{1002.6}{\pi} \;\Rightarrow\; r \approx 6.83375$ ft. Then use $S = 4\pi r^2$ to find the surface area.

$$S = 4\pi(6.83375)^2 \approx 586.85 \text{ ft}^2.$$

## Chapter 1 Test

**1** $y^{99}$ is negative since it is a negative number raised to an odd power. $y - x$ is negative since it is a negative number made even more negative by subtracting a positive number. The quotient of two negatives is a *positive* number.

**2** The quotient of $x$ and $y$ is not greater than 5 $\;\Leftrightarrow\; \dfrac{x}{y} \le 5$.

**3** Since $-x^2 - 3 < 0$ for every $x$ (it doesn't matter that $x$ is negative), $|-x^2 - 3| = -(-x^2 - 3) = x^2 + 3$.

**4** Using distance = rate × time, we get $t = \dfrac{d}{r} = \dfrac{91{,}500{,}000 \text{ miles}}{186{,}000 \text{ miles per second}} \approx 492$ seconds.

**5** $\dfrac{x^2 y^{-3}}{z}\left(\dfrac{3x^0}{zy^2}\right)^{-2} = \dfrac{x^2}{y^3 z}\left(\dfrac{zy^2}{3x^0}\right)^2 = \dfrac{x^2}{y^3 z} \cdot \dfrac{z^2 y^4}{3^2} = \dfrac{x^2 y z}{9}$

**6** $x^{-2/3} x^{3/4} = x^{-8/12} x^{9/12} = x^{(-8/12)+(9/12)} = x^{1/12} = \sqrt[12]{x}$

**7** $\sqrt[3]{\dfrac{x^2 y}{3}} = \dfrac{\sqrt[3]{x^2 y}}{\sqrt[3]{3}} \cdot \dfrac{\sqrt[3]{xy^2}}{\sqrt[3]{xy^2}} = \dfrac{\sqrt[3]{x^3 y^3}}{\sqrt[3]{3xy^2}} = \dfrac{xy}{\sqrt[3]{3xy^2}}$

**8** $\begin{aligned}(x+2)(x^2 - 3x + 5) &= x(x^2) + x(-3x) + x(5) + 2(x^2) + 2(-3x) + 2(5) \\ &= x^3 - 3x^2 + 5x + 2x^2 - 6x + 10 \\ &= x^3 - x^2 - x + 10\end{aligned}$

**9** The leading term of $2x^2(2x+3)^4$ will be determined by multiplying $2x^2$ times $(2x)^4$. The " + 3" will affect other terms, but not the leading term. Hence, $2x^2(2x)^4 = 2x^2(16x^4) = 32x^6$.

**10** By trial and error, $2x^2 + 7x - 15 = (2x - 3)(x + 5)$.

**11** $3x^3 - 27x = 3x(x^2 - 9) = 3x(x + 3)(x - 3)$

**12** Recognizing this polynomial as a sum of cubes, we get
$$64x^3 + 1 = (4x)^3 + 1^3 = (4x + 1)[(4x)^2 - (4x)(1) + 1^2] = (4x + 1)(16x^2 - 4x + 1).$$

**13** We must recognize that $(\sqrt[3]{x})^3 = x$, and then factor as we would any other difference of cubes.
$$x - 5 = (\sqrt[3]{x})^3 - (\sqrt[3]{5})^3 = (\sqrt[3]{x} - \sqrt[3]{5})[(\sqrt[3]{x})^2 + (\sqrt[3]{x})(\sqrt[3]{5}) + (\sqrt[3]{5})^2] = (\sqrt[3]{x} - \sqrt[3]{5})(\sqrt[3]{x^2} + \sqrt[3]{5x} + \sqrt[3]{25})$$

**14** Factor by grouping. $2x^2 + 4x - 3xy - 6y = 2x(x + 2) - 3y(x + 2) = (2x - 3y)(x + 2)$

**15** Recognizing this polynomial as a difference of cubes, we get
$$x^{93} - 1 = (x^{31})^3 - 1^3 = (x^{31} - 1)[(x^{31})^2 + (x^{31})(1) + 1^2] = (x^{31} - 1)(x^{62} + x^{31} + 1).$$

**16** $\begin{aligned}\dfrac{3x}{x-2} + \dfrac{5}{x} - \dfrac{12}{x^2 - 2x} &= \dfrac{3x(x) + 5(x - 2) - 12}{x(x - 2)} = \dfrac{3x^2 + 5x - 10 - 12}{x(x - 2)} \\ &= \dfrac{3x^2 + 5x - 22}{x(x - 2)} = \dfrac{(3x + 11)(x - 2)}{x(x - 2)} = \dfrac{3x + 11}{x}\end{aligned}$

**17** Multiply numerator and denominator by $xy$.
$$\dfrac{\dfrac{x^2}{y} - \dfrac{y^2}{x}}{\dfrac{x}{y} + 1 + \dfrac{y}{x}} = \dfrac{\left(\dfrac{x^2}{y} - \dfrac{y^2}{x}\right) \cdot xy}{\left(\dfrac{x}{y} + 1 + \dfrac{y}{x}\right) \cdot xy} = \dfrac{x^3 - y^3}{x^2 + xy + y^2} = \dfrac{(x - y)(x^2 + xy + y^2)}{x^2 + xy + y^2} = x - y$$

**18** $\begin{aligned}\dfrac{(x+h)^2 + 7(x+h) - (x^2 + 7x)}{h} &= \dfrac{x^2 + 2xh + h^2 + 7x + 7h - x^2 - 7x}{h} = \dfrac{2xh + h^2 + 7h}{h} \\ &= \dfrac{h(2x + h + 7)}{h} = 2x + h + 7\end{aligned}$

**19** $\begin{aligned}\dfrac{6h^2}{\sqrt{x+h} - \sqrt{x}} &= \dfrac{6h^2}{\sqrt{x+h} - \sqrt{x}} \cdot \dfrac{\sqrt{x+h} + \sqrt{x}}{\sqrt{x+h} + \sqrt{x}} = \dfrac{6h^2(\sqrt{x+h} + \sqrt{x})}{(x+h) - x} = \dfrac{6h^2(\sqrt{x+h} + \sqrt{x})}{h} \\ &= 6h(\sqrt{x+h} + \sqrt{x})\end{aligned}$

**20** $(x+2)^3(4)(x-3)^3 + (x-3)^4(3)(x+2)^2 = (x+2)^2(x-3)^3[4(x+2)+3(x-3)]$
$$= (x+2)^2(x-3)^3(4x+8+3x-9) = (x+2)^2(x-3)^3(7x-1)$$

**21** $\dfrac{(x^2-3)^2(2x) - x^2(2)(x^2-3)(2x)}{[(x^2-3)^2]^2} = \dfrac{(x^2-3)(2x)[(x^2-3)-2x^2]}{(x^2-3)^4} = \dfrac{2x(-3-x^2)}{(x^2-3)^3}$

**22** $\left[\dfrac{5x}{x-3} + \dfrac{7}{x} = \dfrac{45}{x^2-3x}\right] \cdot x(x-3) \Rightarrow 5x^2 + 7(x-3) = 45 \Rightarrow 5x^2 + 7x - 66 = 0 \Rightarrow$

$(5x+22)(x-3) = 0 \Rightarrow x = -\frac{22}{5}, 3$. But $x$ cannot equal 3 since it would make denominators in the original

equation equal to 0, so $x = -\frac{22}{5}$.

**23** $A = \dfrac{3B}{2B-5} \Rightarrow A(2B-5) = 3B \Rightarrow 2AB - 5A = 3B \Rightarrow 2AB - 3B = 5A \Rightarrow$
$$B(2A-3) = 5A \Rightarrow B = \dfrac{5A}{2A-3}$$

**24** Let $x$ denote the original value of the stock. Then $x + 0.2x$ is the value after the first year and $x + 0.3(x + 0.2x)$ is
the value after the next year, so an equation that describes the problem is $x + 0.3(x + 0.2x) = 2720$. Solving gives
us $x + 0.3(x + 0.2x) = 2720 \Rightarrow x + 0.3x + 0.06x = 2720 \Rightarrow 1.36x = 2720 \Rightarrow x = \frac{2720}{1.36} = 2000$.

The original value was $2000.

**25** $3x^2 + \sqrt{60}xy + 5y^2 = 0 \Rightarrow 3x^2 + \left(\sqrt{60}y\right)x + 5y^2 = 0 \Rightarrow$
$$x = \dfrac{-\sqrt{60}y \pm \sqrt{\left(\sqrt{60}y\right)^2 - 4(3)(5y^2)}}{2(3)} = \dfrac{-\sqrt{4}\sqrt{15}y \pm \sqrt{60y^2 - 60y^2}}{2(3)} = \dfrac{-2\sqrt{15}y \pm 0}{2(3)} = \dfrac{-\sqrt{15}y}{3}$$

**26** $(x-y+z)^2 = 9 \Rightarrow x-y+z = \pm 3 \Rightarrow x = y - z \pm 3$

**27** $h = 1584 \Rightarrow -16t^2 + 320t = 1584 \Rightarrow -16t^2 + 320t - 1584 = 0 \Rightarrow$
$t^2 - 20t + 99 = 0$ {divide by $-16$} $\Rightarrow (t-9)(t-11) = 0 \Rightarrow t = 9$ or $11$.

Thus, the object is 1584 feet above the ground after 9 seconds and after 11 seconds.

**28** $i^{4x+3} = \left(i^{4x}\right)(i^3) = \left(i^4\right)^x(i^3) = (1)^x(-i) = (1)(-i) = -i = 0 - i$, so $a = 0$ and $b = -1$.

**29** $x^3 - 64 = 0 \Rightarrow (x-4)(x^2+4x+16) = 0 \Rightarrow x = 4$ or $x^2 + 4x + 16 = 0$.

By the quadratic formula, $x = \dfrac{-4 \pm \sqrt{4^2 - 4(1)(16)}}{2(1)} = \dfrac{-4 \pm \sqrt{16-64}}{2} = \dfrac{-4 \pm \sqrt{-48}}{2}$    ★ $4, -2 \pm 2\sqrt{3}i$
$$= \dfrac{-4 \pm \sqrt{16}\sqrt{-3}}{2} = \dfrac{-4 \pm 4\sqrt{3}i}{2} = -2 \pm 2\sqrt{3}i.$$

**30** $A = B\sqrt{x^2+r^2} \Rightarrow \dfrac{A}{B} = \sqrt{x^2+r^2} \Rightarrow \left(\dfrac{A}{B}\right)^2 = x^2 + r^2 \Rightarrow \dfrac{A^2}{B^2} - r^2 = x^2 \Rightarrow$
$$x^2 = \dfrac{1}{B^2}(A^2 - B^2r^2) \Rightarrow x = \pm \dfrac{1}{B}\sqrt{A^2 - B^2r^2}$$

**31** $3x^{32}(x+2)^{65}(x-5)^{13}(x^{2/3}-4) = 0 \Rightarrow x^{32} = 0$ or $(x+2)^{65} = 0$ or $(x-5)^{13} = 0$ or $x^{2/3} - 4 = 0 \Rightarrow$
$x = 0$ or $x = -2$ or $x = 5$ or $x^{2/3} = 4$. Now $x^{2/3} = 4 \Rightarrow \left(x^{2/3}\right)^{3/2} = \pm(4)^{3/2} \Rightarrow$
$x = \pm\left(\sqrt{4}\right)^3 = \pm 2^3 = \pm 8$. Thus, the solutions of the equation are $0, -2, 5$, and $\pm 8$.

**32** $20{,}000 = \frac{4}{3}\pi r_1^3 \Rightarrow r_1^3 = 15{,}000/\pi \Rightarrow r_1 = \sqrt[3]{15{,}000/\pi}$.

Similarly, $25{,}000 = \frac{4}{3}\pi r_2^3 \Rightarrow r_2 = \sqrt[3]{18{,}750/\pi}$. The radius increased $(r_2 - r_1)/r_1 \approx 0.077$, or about 7.7%.

**33** Plan A pays out $3300 per month for 10 years before plan B starts, so its total payout is $(10)(12)(3300) + 3300x$, where $x$ is the number of months that plan B has paid out. Plan B's total payout is $4200x$.

Plan B $\geq$ Plan A $\Rightarrow$ $4200x \geq 396{,}000 + 3300x$ $\Rightarrow$ $900x \geq 396{,}000$ $\Rightarrow$ $x \geq 440$.

It will take plan B 440 months (36 years, 8 months) to have a total payout at least as large as plan A.

**34** $-\frac{1}{4}|3 - 2x| + 6 \geq 2$ $\Rightarrow$ $-\frac{1}{4}|3 - 2x| \geq -4$ $\Rightarrow$ $|3 - 2x| \leq 16$ $\Rightarrow$ $-16 \leq 3 - 2x \leq 16$ $\Rightarrow$ $-19 \leq -2x \leq 13$ $\Rightarrow$ $\frac{19}{2} \geq x \geq -\frac{13}{2}$. The solution in interval notation is $\left[-\frac{13}{2}, \frac{19}{2}\right]$.

**35** $x(2x + 1) \geq 3$ $\Rightarrow$ $2x^2 + x - 3 \geq 0$ $\Rightarrow$ $(2x + 3)(x - 1) \geq 0$ $\Rightarrow$ the solution is $\left(-\infty, -\frac{3}{2}\right] \cup [1, \infty)$.

**36** $\dfrac{(x + 1)^2(x - 7)}{(7 - x)(x - 4)} \leq 0$ $\Rightarrow$ $\dfrac{x - 7}{(7 - x)(x - 4)} \leq 0$ {include $-1$} $\Rightarrow$

$\dfrac{1}{x - 4} \geq 0$ {cancel, change inequality, exclude 7} $\Rightarrow$ $x - 4 > 0$ {exclude 4} $\Rightarrow$ $x > 4$ $\Rightarrow$

the solution is $\{-1\} \cup (4, 7) \cup (7, \infty)$.

**37** $\dfrac{2}{x - 3} \leq \dfrac{2}{x + 1}$ $\Rightarrow$ $\dfrac{2}{x - 3} - \dfrac{2}{x + 1} \leq 0$ $\Rightarrow$ $\dfrac{2(x + 1) - 2(x - 3)}{(x - 3)(x + 1)} \leq 0$ $\Rightarrow$

$\dfrac{2x + 2 - 2x + 6}{(x - 3)(x + 1)} \leq 0$ $\Rightarrow$ $\dfrac{8}{(x - 3)(x + 1)} \leq 0$ $\Rightarrow$ $(x - 3)(x + 1) < 0$     $\bigstar$ $(-1, 3)$

| Interval | $(-\infty, -1)$ | $(-1, 3)$ | $(3, \infty)$ |
|---|---|---|---|
| Sign of $x - 3$ | $-$ | $-$ | $+$ |
| Sign of $x + 1$ | $-$ | $+$ | $+$ |
| **Resulting sign** | $+$ | $-$ | $+$ |

**38** Let $L$ and $W$ denote the length and width of the rectangle. Then $L + W = 14$, so $L = 14 - W$ and the area is $A = LW = (14 - W)W$. Since $A \geq 45$, we have $(14 - W)W \geq 45$ $\Rightarrow$ $-W^2 + 14W \geq 45$ $\Rightarrow$ $-W^2 + 14W - 45 \geq 0$ $\Rightarrow$ $W^2 - 14W + 45 \leq 0$ $\Rightarrow$ $(W - 5)(W - 9) \leq 0$.

| Interval | $(-\infty, 5)$ | $(5, 9)$ | $(9, \infty)$ |
|---|---|---|---|
| Sign of $W - 5$ | $-$ | $+$ | $+$ |
| Sign of $W - 9$ | $-$ | $-$ | $+$ |
| **Resulting sign** | $+$ | $-$ | $+$ |

From the sign chart, we see that the inequality is satisfied for $5 \leq W \leq 9$. Of course, once the width passes 7, it becomes the length, but that's not the point of the problem.

# Chapter 2: Functions and Graphs

## 2.1 Exercises

**1** The points $A(5, -2)$, $B(-5, -2)$, $C(5, 2)$, $D(-5, 2)$, $E(3, 0)$, and $F(0, 3)$ are plotted in the figure.

**2** The points $A(-3, 1)$, $B(3, 1)$, $C(-2, -3)$, $D(0, 3)$, and $E(2, -3)$, as well as $\overline{AB}$, $\overline{BC}$, $\overline{CD}$, $\overline{DE}$, $\overline{EA}$, are plotted in the figure.

**3** The points $A(0, 0)$, $B(1, 1)$, $C(3, 3)$, $D(-1, -1)$, and $E(-2, -2)$ are plotted in the figure. The set of all points of the form $(a, a)$ is the line bisecting quadrants I and III.

**4** The points $A(0, 0)$, $B(1, -1)$, $C(3, -3)$, $D(-1, 1)$, and $E(-3, 3)$ are plotted in the figure. The set of all points of the form $(a, -a)$ is the line bisecting quadrants II and IV.

**5** The points are $A(3, 3)$, $B(-3, 3)$, $C(-3, -3)$, $D(3, -3)$, $E(1, 0)$, and $F(0, 3)$.

**6** The points are $A(0, 4)$, $B(-4, 0)$, $C(0, -4)$, $D(4, 0)$, $E(2, 2)$, and $F(-2, -2)$.

**7** (a) $x = -2$ is the line parallel to the $y$-axis that intersects the $x$-axis at $(-2, 0)$.

  (b) $y = 5$ is the line parallel to the $x$-axis that intersects the $y$-axis at $(0, 5)$.

  (c) $x \geq 0$ {$x$ is zero or positive} is the set of all points to the right of and on the $y$-axis.

  (d) $xy > 0$ {$x$ and $y$ have the same sign, that is, either both are positive or both are negative} is the set of all points in quadrants I and III.

  (e) $y < 0$ {$y$ is negative} is the set of all points below the $x$-axis.

  (f) $x = 0$ is the set of all points on the $y$-axis.

**8** (a) $y = -2$ is the line parallel to the $x$-axis that intersects the $y$-axis at $(0, -2)$.

  (b) $x = 4$ is the line parallel to the $y$-axis that intersects the $x$-axis at $(4, 0)$.

(c) $x/y < 0$ is the set of all points in quadrants II and IV {$x$ and $y$ have opposite signs}.

(d) $xy = 0$ is the set of all points on the $x$-axis or $y$-axis.

(e) $y > 1$ is the set of all points above the line parallel to the $x$-axis which intersects the $y$-axis at $(0, 1)$.

(f) $y = 0$ is the set of all points on the $x$-axis.

**9** (a) $A(4, -3), B(6, 2) \Rightarrow d(A, B) = \sqrt{(6 - 4)^2 + [2 - (-3)]^2} = \sqrt{4 + 25} = \sqrt{29}$

     (b) $A(4, -3), B(6, 2) \Rightarrow M_{AB} = \left( \dfrac{4 + 6}{2}, \dfrac{-3 + 2}{2} \right) = \left( 5, -\dfrac{1}{2} \right)$

**10** (a) $A(-2, -5), B(4, 6) \Rightarrow d(A, B) = \sqrt{[4 - (-2)]^2 + [6 - (-5)]^2} = \sqrt{36 + 121} = \sqrt{157}$

     (b) $A(-2, -5), B(4, 6) \Rightarrow M_{AB} = \left( \dfrac{-2 + 4}{2}, \dfrac{-5 + 6}{2} \right) = \left( 1, \dfrac{1}{2} \right)$

**11** (a) $A(-7, 0), B(-2, -4) \Rightarrow d(A, B) = \sqrt{[-2 - (-7)]^2 + (-4 - 0)^2} = \sqrt{25 + 16} = \sqrt{41}$

     (b) $A(-7, 0), B(-2, -4) \Rightarrow M_{AB} = \left( \dfrac{-7 + (-2)}{2}, \dfrac{0 + (-4)}{2} \right) = \left( -\dfrac{9}{2}, -2 \right)$

**12** (a) $A(5, 2), B(5, -2) \Rightarrow d(A, B) = \sqrt{(5 - 5)^2 + (-2 - 2)^2} = \sqrt{0 + 16} = 4$

     (b) $A(5, 2), B(5, -2) \Rightarrow M_{AB} = \left( \dfrac{5 + 5}{2}, \dfrac{2 + (-2)}{2} \right) = (5, 0)$

**13** (a) $A(7, -3), B(3, -3) \Rightarrow d(A, B) = \sqrt{(3 - 7)^2 + [-3 - (-3)]^2} = \sqrt{16 + 0} = 4$

     (b) $A(7, -3), B(3, -3) \Rightarrow M_{AB} = \left( \dfrac{7 + 3}{2}, \dfrac{-3 + (-3)}{2} \right) = (5, -3)$

**14** (a) $A(-4, 7), B(0, -8) \Rightarrow d(A, B) = \sqrt{[0 - (-4)]^2 + (-8 - 7)^2} = \sqrt{16 + 225} = \sqrt{241}$

     (b) $A(-4, 7), B(0, -8) \Rightarrow M_{AB} = \left( \dfrac{-4 + 0}{2}, \dfrac{7 + (-8)}{2} \right) = \left( -2, -\dfrac{1}{2} \right)$

**15** The points are $A(6, 3)$, $B(1, -2)$, and $C(-3, 2)$. We need to show that the sides satisfy the Pythagorean theorem. Finding the distances, we have $d(A, B) = \sqrt{50}$, $d(B, C) = \sqrt{32}$, and $d(A, C) = \sqrt{82}$. Since $d(A, C)$ is the largest of the three values, it must be the hypotenuse, hence, we need to check if $d(A, C)^2 = d(A, B)^2 + d(B, C)^2$. Since $\left( \sqrt{82} \right)^2 = \left( \sqrt{50} \right)^2 + \left( \sqrt{32} \right)^2$, we know that $\triangle ABC$ is a right triangle. The area of a triangle is given by $A = \frac{1}{2}(\text{base})(\text{height})$. We can use $d(B, C)$ for the base and $d(A, B)$ for the height. Hence, area $= \frac{1}{2}bh = \frac{1}{2} \left( \sqrt{32} \right) \left( \sqrt{50} \right) = \frac{1}{2} \left( 4\sqrt{2} \right) \left( 5\sqrt{2} \right) = \frac{1}{2}(20)(2) = 20$.

**16** The points are $A(-6, 3)$, $B(3, -5)$, and $C(-1, 5)$.

Show that $d(A, B)^2 = d(A, C)^2 + d(B, C)^2$; that is, $\left( \sqrt{145} \right)^2 = \left( \sqrt{29} \right)^2 + \left( \sqrt{116} \right)^2$.

Area $= \frac{1}{2}bh = \frac{1}{2} \cdot d(A, C) \cdot d(B, C) = \frac{1}{2} \left( \sqrt{29} \right) \left( \sqrt{116} \right) = \frac{1}{2} \left( \sqrt{29} \right) \left( 2\sqrt{29} \right) = 29$.

**17** The points are $A(-4, 2)$, $B(1, 4)$, $C(3, -1)$, and $C(-2, -3)$. We need to show that all four sides are the same length. Checking, we find that $d(A, B) = d(B, C) = d(C, D) = d(D, A) = \sqrt{29}$. This guarantees that we have a rhombus {a parallelogram with 4 equal sides}. Thus, we also need to show that adjacent sides meet at right angles. This can be done by showing that two adjacent sides and a diagonal form a right triangle. Using $\triangle ABC$, we see that $d(A, C) = \sqrt{58}$ and hence $d(A, C)^2 = d(A, B)^2 + d(B, C)^2$. We conclude that $ABCD$ is a square.

**18** The points are $A(-4, -1)$, $B(0, -2)$, $C(6, 1)$, and $C(2, 2)$.

Show that $d(A, D) = d(B, C) = \sqrt{45}$ and $d(A, B) = d(C, D) = \sqrt{17}$.

**19** Let $B = (x, y)$. $A(-3, 8)$ $\Rightarrow$ $M_{AB} = \left(\dfrac{-3 + x}{2}, \dfrac{8 + y}{2}\right)$.

Since $M_{AB} = C(5, -10)$, we must have $\dfrac{-3 + x}{2} = 5$ and $\dfrac{8 + y}{2} = -10$ $\Rightarrow$

$-3 + x = 2(5)$ and $8 + y = 2(-10)$ $\Rightarrow$ $x = 13$ and $y = -28$. Thus, $B = (13, -28)$.

**20** If $Q$ is the midpoint of segment $AB$, then the midpoint of $QB$ is the point that is three-fourths of the way from $A(5, -8)$ to $B(-6, 2)$.

$Q = M_{AB} = \left(\dfrac{5 + (-6)}{2}, \dfrac{-8 + 2}{2}\right) = \left(-\dfrac{1}{2}, -3\right)$. $M_{QB} = \left(\dfrac{(-1/2) + (-6)}{2}, \dfrac{-3 + 2}{2}\right) = \left(-\dfrac{13}{4}, -\dfrac{1}{2}\right)$.

**21** The perpendicular bisector of $AB$ is the line that passes through the midpoint of segment $AB$ and intersects segment $AB$ at a right angle. The points on the perpendicular bisector are all equidistant from $A$ and $B$. Thus, we need to show that $d(A, C) = d(B, C)$, where $A = (-4, -3)$, $B = (6, 1)$, and $C = (3, -6)$. Since each of these distances is $\sqrt{58}$, we conclude that $C$ is on the perpendicular bisector of $AB$.

**22** Show that $d(A, C) = d(B, C) = \sqrt{125}$, where $A = (-3, 2)$, $B = (5, -4)$, and $C = (7, 7)$.

**23** The points are $A(-4, -3)$, $B(6, 1)$, and $P(x, y)$. We must have $d(A, P) = d(B, P)$.

$\sqrt{(x + 4)^2 + (y + 3)^2} = \sqrt{(x - 6)^2 + (y - 1)^2}$ $\Rightarrow$

$x^2 + 8x + 16 + y^2 + 6y + 9 = x^2 - 12x + 36 + y^2 - 2y + 1$ {square both sides} $\Rightarrow$

$8x + 6y + 25 = -12x - 2y + 37$ $\Rightarrow$ $20x + 8y = 12$ $\Rightarrow$ $5x + 2y = 3$

**24** The points are $A(-3, 2)$, $B(5, -4)$, and $P(x, y)$. We must have $d(A, P) = d(B, P)$.

$\sqrt{(x + 3)^2 + (y - 2)^2} = \sqrt{(x - 5)^2 + (y + 4)^2}$ $\Rightarrow$

$x^2 + 6x + 9 + y^2 - 4y + 4 = x^2 - 10x + 25 + y^2 + 8y + 16$ {square both sides} $\Rightarrow$

$6x - 4y + 13 = -10x + 8y + 41$ $\Rightarrow$ $16x - 12y = 28$ $\Rightarrow$ $4x - 3y = 7$

**25** Let $O(0, 0)$ represent the origin. Applying the distance formula with $O$ and $P(x, y)$, we have

$d(O, P) = 5$ $\Rightarrow$ $\sqrt{(x - 0)^2 + (y - 0)^2} = 5$ $\Rightarrow$ $\sqrt{x^2 + y^2} = 5$.

This formula represents a circle of radius 5 with center at the origin.

**26** $d(C, P) = r$ $\Rightarrow$ $\sqrt{(x - h)^2 + (y - k)^2} = r$. This formula represents a circle of radius $r$ and center $(h, k)$.

**27** Let $Q(0, y)$ be an arbitrary point on the $y$-axis. Applying the distance formula with $Q$ and $P(5, 3)$, we have

$6 = d(P, Q)$ $\Rightarrow$ $6 = \sqrt{(0 - 5)^2 + (y - 3)^2}$ $\Rightarrow$ $36 = 25 + y^2 - 6y + 9$ $\Rightarrow$

$y^2 - 6y - 2 = 0$ $\Rightarrow$ $y = 3 \pm \sqrt{11}$. The points are $\left(0, 3 + \sqrt{11}\right)$ and $\left(0, 3 - \sqrt{11}\right)$.

**28** Let $Q(x, 0)$ be an arbitrary point on the $x$-axis. Applying the distance formula with $Q$ and $P(-2, 4)$, we have

$5 = d(P, Q)$ $\Rightarrow$ $5$ $\Rightarrow$ $\sqrt{(x + 2)^2 + (0 - 4)^2}$ $\Rightarrow$ $25 = x^2 + 4x + 4 + 16$ $\Rightarrow$

$x^2 + 4x - 5 = 0$ $\Rightarrow$ $(x + 5)(x - 1) = 0$ $\Rightarrow$ $x = -5, 1$. The points are $(1, 0)$ and $(-5, 0)$.

**29** $d = 5$ with points $(2a, a)$ and $(1, 3)$ $\Rightarrow$ $5 = \sqrt{(2a - 1)^2 + (a - 3)^2}$ $\Rightarrow$

$25 = 4a^2 - 4a + 1 + a^2 - 6a + 9$ $\Rightarrow$ $5a^2 - 10a - 15 = 0$ $\Rightarrow$ $a^2 - 2a - 3 = 0$ $\Rightarrow$

$(a-3)(a+1)=0 \Rightarrow a=3,-1.$

Since the $y$-coordinate is negative in the third quadrant, $a=-1$, and $(2a,a)=(-2,-1)$.

[30] $d=3$ with points $(a,a)$ and $(-2,1) \Rightarrow 3=\sqrt{(a+2)^2+(a-1)^2} \Rightarrow$

$9=a^2+4a+4+a^2-2a+1 \Rightarrow 0=2a^2+2a-4 \Rightarrow a^2+a-2=0 \Rightarrow (a+2)(a-1)=0 \Rightarrow$

$a=-2,1.$ The points are $(-2,-2)$ and $(1,1)$.

[31] With $P(a,3)$ and $Q(5,2a)$, we get $d(P,Q)>\sqrt{26} \Rightarrow \sqrt{(5-a)^2+(2a-3)^2}>\sqrt{26} \Rightarrow$

$25-10a+a^2+4a^2-12a+9>26 \Rightarrow 5a^2-22a+8>0 \Rightarrow (5a-2)(a-4)>0.$

| Interval | $(-\infty,\frac{2}{5})$ | $(\frac{2}{5},4)$ | $(4,\infty)$ |
| --- | --- | --- | --- |
| Sign of $5a-2$ | − | + | + |
| Sign of $a-4$ | − | − | + |
| **Resulting sign** | + | − | + |

From the sign chart, we see that $a<\frac{2}{5}$ or $a>4$ will assure us that $d(P,Q)>\sqrt{26}$.

[32] $A(-2,0),\ B(2,0),\ P(x,y)$ • $d(A,P)+d(B,P)=5 \Rightarrow \sqrt{(x+2)^2+y^2}+\sqrt{(x-2)^2+y^2}=5 \Rightarrow$

$\sqrt{x^2+4x+4+y^2}=5-\sqrt{x^2-4x+4+y^2} \Rightarrow$

$x^2+4x+4+y^2=25-10\sqrt{x^2-4x+4+y^2}+x^2-4x+4+y^2 \Rightarrow$

$10\sqrt{x^2-4x+4+y^2}=25-8x \Rightarrow 100(x^2-4x+4+y^2)=625-400x+64x^2 \Rightarrow$

$100x^2-400x+400+100y^2=625-400x+64x^2 \Rightarrow 36x^2+100y^2=225$

[33] Let $M$ be the midpoint of the hypotenuse. Then $M=\left(\frac{1}{2}a,\frac{1}{2}b\right)$. Since $A=(a,0)$, we have

$$d(A,M)=\sqrt{\left(a-\tfrac{1}{2}a\right)^2+\left(0-\tfrac{1}{2}b\right)^2}=\sqrt{\left(\tfrac{1}{2}a\right)^2+\left(-\tfrac{1}{2}b\right)^2}=\sqrt{\tfrac{1}{4}a^2+\tfrac{1}{4}b^2}=\sqrt{\tfrac{1}{4}(a^2+b^2)}=\tfrac{1}{2}\sqrt{a^2+b^2}$$

In a similar fashion, show that $d(B,M)=d(O,M)=\frac{1}{2}\sqrt{a^2+b^2}$.

[34] Let $D(a,b+c)$ be the fourth vertex as shown in the figure. We need to show

that the midpoint of $OD$ is the same as the midpoint of $AC$.

$M_{OD}=\left(\dfrac{0+a}{2},\dfrac{0+b+c}{2}\right)=\left(\dfrac{a}{2},\dfrac{b+c}{2}\right)$ and

$M_{CA}=\left(\dfrac{0+a}{2},\dfrac{c+b}{2}\right)=\left(\dfrac{a}{2},\dfrac{b+c}{2}\right)$.

[35] Plot the points $A(-5,-3.5),\ B(-2,2),\ C(1,0.5),\ D(4,1),$ and $E(7,2.5)$.

[−10, 10] by [−10, 10]

*Figure 35*

[−12, 12] by [−8, 8]

*Figure 36*

[36] Plot the points $A(-10,4),\ B(-7,-1.1),\ C(0,-6),\ D(3,-5.1),$ and $E(9,2.1)$.

[37] (a) Plot $(1984, 87{,}073),\ (1993, 98{,}736),\ (2003, 113{,}126),$ and $(2009, 119{,}296)$.

(b) The number of U.S. households with a computer is increasing each year.

[1982, 2012] by [80E3, 120E3, 10E3] {80E3 = 80 × 10³}                [1895, 2005, 10] by [0, 3000, 1000]

*Figure 37*                                          *Figure 38*

**38** (a)  Plot (1900, 2226), (1920, 2042), (1940, 1878), (1960, 1763), (1980, 1745), and (2000, 1480).

(b)  Find the midpoint of (1920, 2042) and (1940, 1878). $\left(\dfrac{1920 + 1940}{2}, \dfrac{2042 + 1878}{2}\right) = (1930, 1960)$.

The midpoint formula predicts 1960 daily newspapers published in the year 1930 compared to the actual value of 1942 daily newspapers.

## 2.2 Exercises

**1**  As in Example 1, we expect the graph of $y = 2x - 3$ to be a line.
Creating a table of values similar to those in the text, we have:

| $x$ | $-2$ | $-1$ | $0$ | $1$ | $2$ |
|-----|------|------|-----|-----|-----|
| $y$ | $-7$ | $-5$ | $-3$ | $-1$ | $1$ |

By plotting these points and connecting them, we obtain the figure.

To find the $x$-intercept, let $y = 0$ in $y = 2x - 3$, and solve for $x$ to get 1.5.

To find the $y$-intercept, let $x = 0$ in $y = 2x - 3$, and solve for $y$ to get $-3$.

*Figure 1*                                          *Figure 2*

**2**  $y = 4x + 2$ • $y = 0$ gives the $x$-intercept $-\frac{1}{2}$; $x = 0$ gives the $y$-intercept 2

**3**  $y = -x + 2$ • $x$-intercept: $y = 0 \;\Rightarrow\; 0 = -x + 2 \;\Rightarrow\; x = 2$
$y$-intercept: $x = 0 \;\Rightarrow\; y = -0 + 2 = 2$

*Figure 3*                                          *Figure 4*

**4**  $y = -2x - 3$ • $x$-intercept: $y = 0 \;\Rightarrow\; x = -1.5$; $y$-intercept: $x = 0 \;\Rightarrow\; y = -3$

**5** $y = -2x^2$ • Multiplying the $y$-values of $y = x^2$ by $-2$ gives us all negative $y$-values for $y = -2x^2$. The vertex of the parabola is at $(0,0)$, so its $x$-intercept is 0 and its $y$-intercept is 0.

Figure 5

Figure 6

**6** $y = \frac{1}{3}x^2$ • $x$-intercept 0; $y$-intercept 0

**7** $y = 2x^2 - 1$ • $x$-intercepts: $y = 0 \Rightarrow 0 = 2x^2 - 1 \Rightarrow 1 = 2x^2 \Rightarrow x^2 = \frac{1}{2} \Rightarrow x = \pm\sqrt{\frac{1}{2}}$, which can be written as $\pm\frac{1}{\sqrt{2}}$ or $\pm\frac{\sqrt{2}}{2}$ or $\pm\frac{1}{2}\sqrt{2}$; $y$-intercept: $x = 0 \Rightarrow y = -1$

Since we can substitute $-x$ for $x$ in the equation and obtain an equivalent equation, we know the graph is symmetric with respect to the $y$-axis. We will make use of this fact when constructing our table. As in Example 2, we obtain a parabola.

| $x$ | $\pm2$ | $\pm\frac{3}{2}$ | $\pm1$ | $\pm\frac{1}{2}$ | 0 |
|---|---|---|---|---|---|
| $y$ | 7 | $\frac{7}{2}$ | 1 | $-\frac{1}{2}$ | $-1$ |

Figure 7

Figure 8

**8** $y = -x^2 + 2$ • $x$-intercepts: $y = 0 \Rightarrow x^2 = 2 \Rightarrow x = \pm\sqrt{2}$; $y$-intercept 2

**9** $x = \frac{1}{4}y^2$ • This graph is similar to the one in Example 5—multiplying by $\frac{1}{4}$ narrows the parabola $x = y^2$. The $x$-intercept is 0 and the $y$-intercept is 0.

Figure 9

Figure 10

**10** $x = -2y^2$ • $x$-intercept 0; $y$-intercept 0

**11** $x = -y^2 + 5$ • x-intercept: $y = 0$ ⇒ $x = 5$;

y-intercepts: $x = 0$ ⇒ $0 = -y^2 + 5$ ⇒ $y^2 = 5$ ⇒ $y = \pm\sqrt{5}$

Since we can substitute $-y$ for $y$ in the equation and obtain an equivalent equation, we know the graph is symmetric with respect to the x-axis. We will make use of this fact when constructing our table. As in Example 5, we obtain a parabola.

| $x$ | −11 | −4 | 1 | 4 | 5 |
|---|---|---|---|---|---|
| $y$ | ±4 | ±3 | ±2 | ±1 | 0 |

Figure 11                                                            Figure 12

**12** $x = 2y^2 - 4$ • x-intercept −4; y-intercepts: $x = 0$ ⇒ $y^2 = 4$ ⇒ $y = \pm\sqrt{2}$

**13** $y = -\frac{1}{4}x^3$ • The graph is similar to the graph of $y = \frac{1}{4}x^3$ in Example 6. The negative has the effect of "flipping" the graph about the x-axis. The x-intercept is 0 and the y-intercept is 0.

Figure 13                                                            Figure 14

**14** $y = \frac{1}{2}x^3$ • x-intercept 0; y-intercept 0

**15** $y = x^3 - 8$ • x-intercept: $y = 0$ ⇒ $0 = x^3 - 8$ ⇒ $x^3 = 8$ ⇒ $x = \sqrt[3]{8} = 2$;

y-intercept: $x = 0$ ⇒ $y = -8$

The effect of the −8 is to shift the graph of $y = x^3$ down 8 units.

| $x$ | −2 | −1 | 0 | 1 | 2 |
|---|---|---|---|---|---|
| $y$ | −16 | −9 | −8 | −7 | 0 |

Figure 15                                                            Figure 16

**16** $y = -x^3 + 1$ • x-intercept: $y = 0$ ⇒ $x^3 = 1$ ⇒ $x = \sqrt[3]{1} = 1$; y-intercept 1

**17** $y = \sqrt{x}$ • $x$-intercept 0; $y$-intercept 0. This is the top half of the parabola $x = y^2$. An equation of the bottom half is $y = -\sqrt{x}$.

*Figure 17*

*Figure 18*

**18** $y = \sqrt{-x}$ • The negative has the effect of "flipping" the graph of $y = \sqrt{x}$ about the $y$-axis. The $x$-intercept is 0 and the $y$-intercept is 0.

**19** $y = \sqrt{x} - 4$ • $x$-intercept: $y = 0 \ \Rightarrow \ 0 = \sqrt{x} - 4 \ \Rightarrow \ 4 = \sqrt{x} \ \Rightarrow \ x = 16$ (not on graph)
  $y$-intercept: $x = 0 \ \Rightarrow \ y = -4$

| $x$ | 0 | 1 | 4 | 9 | 16 |
|---|---|---|---|---|---|
| $y$ | −4 | −3 | −2 | −1 | 0 |

*Figure 19*

*Figure 20*

**20** $y = \sqrt{x - 4}$ • $x$-intercept 4; $y$-intercept: None

**21** You may be able to do this exercise mentally. For example (using Exercise 1 with $y = 2x - 3$), we see that substituting $-x$ for $x$ gives us $y = -2x - 3$; substituting $-y$ for $y$ gives us $-y = 2x - 3$ or, equivalently, $y = -2x + 3$; and substituting $-x$ for $x$ and $-y$ for $y$ gives us $-y = -2x - 3$ or, equivalently, $y = 2x + 3$. None of the resulting equations are equivalent to the original equation, so there is no symmetry with respect to the $y$-axis, $x$-axis, or the origin.

(a) The graphs of the equations in Exercises 5 and 7 are symmetric with respect to the $y$-axis.

(b) The graphs of the equations in Exercises 9 and 11 are symmetric with respect to the $x$-axis.

(c) The graph of the equation in Exercise 13 is symmetric with respect to the origin.

**22** (a) 6, 8        (b) 10, 12        (c) 14

**23** (a) As $x \to -1^-$, $f(x) \to \underline{2}$     (b) As $x \to 2^+$, $f(x) \to \underline{1}$     (c) As $x \to 3$, $f(x) \to \underline{4}$

(d) As $x \to \infty$, $f(x) \to \underline{\infty}$     (e) As $x \to -\infty$, $f(x) \to \underline{-\infty}$

**24** (a) As $x \to 2^-$, $f(x) \to \underline{3}$      (b) As $x \to -1^+$, $f(x) \to \underline{-3}$      (c) As $x \to 0$, $f(x) \to \underline{-1}$

    (d) As $x \to \infty$, $f(x) \to \underline{-\infty}$      (e) As $x \to -\infty$, $f(x) \to \underline{\infty}$

**25** $x^2 + y^2 = 11$  $\Leftrightarrow$  $(x-0)^2 + (y-0)^2 = \left(\sqrt{11}\right)^2$ is a circle of radius $\sqrt{11}$ with center at the origin.

*Figure 25*

*Figure 26*

**26** $x^2 + y^2 = 5$  $\Leftrightarrow$  $(x-0)^2 + (y-0)^2 = \left(\sqrt{5}\right)^2$ is a circle of radius $\sqrt{5}$ with center at the origin.

**27** $(x+3)^2 + (y-2)^2 = 9$ is a circle of radius $r = \sqrt{9} = 3$ with center $C(-3, 2)$. To determine the center from the given equation, it may help to ask yourself "What values makes the expressions $(x+3)$ and $(y-2)$ equal to zero?" The answers are $-3$ and $2$.

*Figure 27*

*Figure 28*

**28** $(x-3)^2 + (y+2)^2 = 4$ is a circle of radius $r = \sqrt{4} = 2$ with center $C(3, -2)$.

**29** $(x+3)^2 + y^2 = 16$ is a circle of radius $r = \sqrt{16} = 4$ with center $C(-3, 0)$.

*Figure 29*

*Figure 30*

**30** $x^2 + (y-2)^2 = 25$ is a circle of radius $r = \sqrt{25} = 5$ with center $C(0, 2)$.

**31** $4x^2 + 4y^2 = 1 \Rightarrow x^2 + y^2 = \frac{1}{4}$ is a circle of radius $r = \sqrt{\frac{1}{4}} = \frac{1}{2}$ with center $C(0,0)$.

*Figure 31*

*Figure 32*

**32** $9x^2 + 9y^2 = 4 \Rightarrow x^2 + y^2 = \frac{4}{9}$ is a circle of radius $r = \sqrt{\frac{4}{9}} = \frac{2}{3}$ with center $C(0,0)$.

**33** As in Example 9, $y = -\sqrt{16 - x^2}$ is the lower half of the circle $x^2 + y^2 = 16$.

*Figure 33*

*Figure 34*

**34** $y = \sqrt{4 - x^2}$ is the upper half of the circle $x^2 + y^2 = 4$.

**35** $x = \sqrt{9 - y^2}$ is the right half of the circle $x^2 + y^2 = 9$.

*Figure 35*

*Figure 36*

**36** $x = -\sqrt{25 - y^2}$ is the left half of the circle $x^2 + y^2 = 25$.

**37** Center $C(2, -3)$, radius 5 • $(x - 2)^2 + [y - (-3)]^2 = 5^2 \Leftrightarrow (x - 2)^2 + (y + 3)^2 = 25$

**38** Center $C(-5, 1)$, radius 3 • $[x - (-5)]^2 + (y - 1)^2 = 3^2 \Leftrightarrow (x + 5)^2 + (y - 1)^2 = 9$

**39** Center $C\left(\frac{1}{4}, 0\right)$, radius $\sqrt{5}$ • $\left(x - \frac{1}{4}\right)^2 + (y - 0)^2 = \left(\sqrt{5}\right)^2 \Leftrightarrow \left(x - \frac{1}{4}\right)^2 + y^2 = 5$

**40** Center $C\left(\frac{3}{4}, -\frac{2}{3}\right)$, radius $3\sqrt{2}$ • $\left(x - \frac{3}{4}\right)^2 + \left[y - \left(-\frac{2}{3}\right)\right]^2 = \left(3\sqrt{2}\right)^2 \Leftrightarrow \left(x - \frac{3}{4}\right)^2 + \left(y + \frac{2}{3}\right)^2 = 18$

**41** An equation of a circle with center $C(-4, 6)$ is $(x + 4)^2 + (y - 6)^2 = r^2$.

Since the circle passes through $P(3, 1)$, we know that $x = 3$ and $y = 1$ is one solution of the general equation.

Letting $x = 3$ and $y = 1$ yields $7^2 + (-5)^2 = r^2 \Rightarrow r^2 = 74$. An equation is $(x + 4)^2 + (y - 6)^2 = 74$.

**42** An equation of a circle with center at the origin is $x^2 + y^2 = r^2$.

Letting $x = 4$ and $y = -7$ yields $4^2 + (-7)^2 = r^2 \Rightarrow r^2 = 65$. $x^2 + y^2 = 65$

**43** "Tangent to the $y$-axis" means that the circle will intersect the $y$-axis at exactly one point. The distance from the center $C(-3, 6)$ to this point of tangency is 3 units—this is the length of the radius of the circle.

An equation is $(x + 3)^2 + (y - 6)^2 = 9$.

**44** The circle is tangent to the $x$-axis and has center $C(4, -3)$.

Its radius, 3, is the distance from the $x$-axis to the $y$-value of the center. An equation is $(x - 4)^2 + (y + 3)^2 = 9$.

**45** Since the radius is 2 and $C(h, k)$ is in QII, $h = -2$ and $k = 2$. An equation is $(x + 2)^2 + (y - 2)^2 = 4$.

**46** Since the radius is 3 and $C(h, k)$ is in QIV, $h = 3$ and $k = -3$. An equation is $(x - 3)^2 + (y + 3)^2 = 9$.

**47** The center of the circle is the midpoint $M$ of $A(4, -3)$ and $B(-2, 7)$. $M_{AB} = (1, 2)$. The radius of the circle is

$\frac{1}{2} \cdot d(A, B) = \frac{1}{2}\sqrt{[4 - (-2)]^2 + (-3 - 7)^2} = \frac{1}{2}\sqrt{36 + 100} = \frac{1}{2}\sqrt{136} = \frac{1}{2}\sqrt{4 \cdot 34} = \sqrt{34}$.

An equation is $(x - 1)^2 + (y - 2)^2 = 34$.

Alternatively, once we know the center, $(1, 2)$, we also know that the equation has the form $(x - 1)^2 + (y - 2)^2 = r^2$. Now substitute 4 for $x$ and $-3$ for $y$ to obtain

$3^2 + (-5)^2 = r^2 \Rightarrow 9 + 25 = r^2$, or $r^2 = 34$.

**48** As in the solution to Exercise 47, $M_{AB} = (-1, 4)$ and $r = \frac{1}{2} \cdot d(A, B) = \frac{1}{2}\sqrt{80} = \sqrt{20}$.

An equation is $(x + 1)^2 + (y - 4)^2 = 20$.

**49** $x^2 + y^2 - 4x + 6y - 36 = 0$ {complete the square on $x$ and $y$} $\Rightarrow$

$x^2 - 4x + \underline{4} + y^2 + 6y + \underline{9} = 36 + \underline{4} + \underline{9} \Rightarrow (x - 2)^2 + (y + 3)^2 = 49$.

This is a circle with center $C(2, -3)$ and radius $r = 7$.

**50** $x^2 + y^2 + 8x - 10y + 37 = 0 \Rightarrow x^2 + 8x + \underline{16} + y^2 - 10y + \underline{25} = -37 + \underline{16} + \underline{25} \Rightarrow$

$(x + 4)^2 + (y - 5)^2 = 4$. $C(-4, 5)$; $r = 2$

**51** $x^2 + y^2 + 4y - 7 = 0$ {complete the square on $x$ and $y$} $\Rightarrow x^2 + y^2 + 4y + \underline{4} = 7 + \underline{4} \Rightarrow$

$x^2 + (y + 2)^2 = 11$. This is a circle with center $C(0, -2)$ and radius $r = \sqrt{11}$.

**52** $x^2 + y^2 - 10x + 18 = 0 \Rightarrow x^2 - 10x + \underline{25} + y^2 = -18 + \underline{25} \Rightarrow (x - 5)^2 + y^2 = 7$. $C(5, 0)$; $r = \sqrt{7}$

**53** $2x^2 + 2y^2 - 12x + 4y - 15 = 0$ {add 15 to both sides and divide by 2} $\Rightarrow$

$x^2 + y^2 - 6x + 2y = \frac{15}{2}$ {complete the square on $x$ and $y$} $\Rightarrow$

$x^2 - 6x + \underline{9} + y^2 + 2y + \underline{1} = \frac{15}{2} + \underline{9} + \underline{1} \Rightarrow (x - 3)^2 + (y + 1)^2 = \frac{35}{2}$.

This is a circle with center $C(3, -1)$ and radius $r = \frac{1}{2}\sqrt{70}$.

**54** $4x^2 + 4y^2 + 16x + 24y + 31 = 0 \Rightarrow x^2 + y^2 + 4x + 6y = -31 \Rightarrow$

$x^2 + 4x + \underline{4} + y^2 + 6y + \underline{9} = -\frac{31}{4} + \underline{4} + \underline{9} \Rightarrow (x + 2)^2 + (y + 3)^2 = \frac{21}{4}$. $C(-2, -3)$; $r = \frac{1}{2}\sqrt{21}$

**55** $x^2 + y^2 + 4x - 2y + 5 = 0 \Rightarrow x^2 + 4x + \underline{4} + y^2 - 2y + \underline{1} = -5 + \underline{4} + \underline{1} \Rightarrow$

$(x + 2)^2 + (y - 1)^2 = 0$. $C(-2, 1)$; $r = 0$ (a point)

**56** $x^2 + y^2 - 6x - 4y + 13 = 0 \Rightarrow x^2 - 6x + \underline{9} + y^2 - 4y + \underline{4} = -13 + \underline{9} + \underline{4} \Rightarrow$

$(x - 3)^2 + (y - 2)^2 = 0$. $C(3, 2)$; $r = 0$ (a point)

**57** $x^2 + y^2 - 2x - 8y + 21 = 0 \;\Rightarrow\; x^2 - 2x + \underline{1} + y^2 - 8y + \underline{16} = -21 + \underline{1} + \underline{16} \;\Rightarrow$
$(x - 1)^2 + (y - 4)^2 = -4.$ This is not a circle since $r^2$ cannot equal $-4$.

**58** $x^2 + y^2 + 4x + 6y + 16 = 0 \;\Rightarrow\; x^2 + 4x + \underline{4} + y^2 + 6y + \underline{9} = -16 + \underline{4} + \underline{9} \;\Rightarrow$
$(x + 2)^2 + (y + 3)^2 = -3.$ This is not a circle since $r^2$ cannot equal $-3$.

**59** To obtain equations for the upper and lower halves, we solve the given equation for $y$ in terms of $x$.
$x^2 + y^2 = 25 \;\Rightarrow\; y^2 = 25 - x^2 \;\Rightarrow\; y = \pm\sqrt{25 - x^2}.$
The upper half is $y = \sqrt{25 - x^2}$ and the lower half is $y = -\sqrt{25 - x^2}$.
To obtain equations for the right and left halves, we solve the given equation for $x$ in terms of $y$.
$x^2 + y^2 = 25 \;\Rightarrow\; x^2 = 25 - y^2 \;\Rightarrow\; x = \pm\sqrt{25 - y^2}.$
The right half is $x = \sqrt{25 - y^2}$ and the left half is $x = -\sqrt{25 - y^2}$.

**60** $(x + 3)^2 + y^2 = 64 \;\Rightarrow\; y^2 = 64 - (x + 3)^2 \;\Rightarrow\; y = \pm\sqrt{64 - (x + 3)^2}.$
$(x + 3)^2 + y^2 = 64 \;\Rightarrow\; (x + 3)^2 = 64 - y^2 \;\Rightarrow\; x + 3 = \pm\sqrt{64 - y^2} \;\Rightarrow\; x = -3 \pm \sqrt{64 - y^2}.$

**61** To obtain equations for the upper and lower halves, we solve the given equation for $y$ in terms of $x$.
$(x - 2)^2 + (y + 1)^2 = 49 \;\Rightarrow\; (y + 1)^2 = 49 - (x - 2)^2 \;\Rightarrow\; y + 1 = \pm\sqrt{49 - (x - 2)^2} \;\Rightarrow$
$y = -1 \pm \sqrt{49 - (x - 2)^2}.$
The upper half is $y = -1 + \sqrt{49 - (x - 2)^2}$ and the lower half is $y = -1 - \sqrt{49 - (x - 2)^2}$.
To obtain equations for the right and left halves, we solve the given equation for $x$ in terms of $y$.
$(x - 2)^2 + (y + 1)^2 = 49 \;\Rightarrow\; (x - 2)^2 = 49 - (y + 1)^2 \;\Rightarrow\; x - 2 = \pm\sqrt{49 - (y + 1)^2} \;\Rightarrow$
$x = 2 \pm \sqrt{49 - (y + 1)^2}.$ The right half is $x = 2 + \sqrt{49 - (y + 1)^2}$ and the left half is $x = 2 - \sqrt{49 - (y + 1)^2}$.

**62** $(x - 3)^2 + (y - 5)^2 = 4 \;\Rightarrow\; (y - 5)^2 = 4 - (x - 3)^2 \;\Rightarrow\; y - 5 = \pm\sqrt{4 - (x - 3)^2} \;\Rightarrow$
$y = 5 \pm \sqrt{4 - (x - 3)^2}.$
$(x - 3)^2 + (y - 5)^2 = 4 \;\Rightarrow\; (x - 3)^2 = 4 - (y - 5)^2 \;\Rightarrow\; x - 3 = \pm\sqrt{4 - (y - 5)^2} \;\Rightarrow$
$x = 3 \pm \sqrt{4 - (y - 5)^2}.$

**63** From the figure, we see that the diameter {look at the $x$-values of the rightmost and leftmost points} of the circle is
$1 - (-7) = 8$ units, so the radius is $\frac{1}{2}(8) = 4$. The center $(h, k)$ is at the average of the extreme values; that is,
$h = \dfrac{-7 + 1}{2} = -3$, and similarly, $k = \dfrac{-2 + 6}{2} = 2$. Using the standard form of an equation of a circle,
$(x - h)^2 + (y - k)^2 = r^2$, we have $[x - (-3)]^2 + (y - 2)^2 = 4^2$, or $(x + 3)^2 + (y - 2)^2 = 4^2$ {or use 16}.

**64** diameter $= 4 - (-2) = 6$; radius $= \frac{1}{2}(6) = 3$; $h = \dfrac{-2 + 4}{2} = 1$ and $k = \dfrac{-5 + 1}{2} = -2$
An equation is $(x - 1)^2 + [y - (-2)]^2 = 3^2$, or $(x - 1)^2 + (y + 2)^2 = 3^2$ {or use 9}.

**65** The figure shows the lower semicircle of a circle centered at the origin having radius 4. The circle has equation
$x^2 + y^2 = 4^2$. We want the lower semicircle, so we must have *negative* $y$-values, indicating that we should solve
for $y$ and use the negative sign. $x^2 + y^2 = 4^2 \;\Rightarrow\; y^2 = 4^2 - x^2 \;\Rightarrow\; y = \pm\sqrt{4^2 - x^2}$, so $y = -\sqrt{4^2 - x^2}$ is
the desired equation.

**66** $x^2 + y^2 = 3^2 \;\Rightarrow\; x^2 = 3^2 - y^2 \;\Rightarrow\; x = \pm\sqrt{3^2 - y^2}$, so $x = -\sqrt{3^2 - y^2}$ is the desired equation since we
want *negative* $x$-values.

**67** We need to determine if the distance from $P$ to $C$ is *less than* $r$, *greater than* $r$, or *equal to* $r$ and hence, $P$ will be *inside* the circle, *outside* the circle, or *on* the circle, respectively.

(a) $P(2,3), C(4,6) \Rightarrow d(P,C) = \sqrt{4+9} = \sqrt{13} < r \{r=4\} \Rightarrow P$ is *inside* $C$.

(b) $P(4,2), C(1,-2) \Rightarrow d(P,C) = \sqrt{9+16} = 5 = r \{r=5\} \Rightarrow P$ is *on* $C$.

(c) $P(-3,5), C(2,1) \Rightarrow d(P,C) = \sqrt{25+16} = \sqrt{41} > r \{r=6\} \Rightarrow P$ is *outside* $C$.

**68** (a) $P(3,8), C(-2,-4) \Rightarrow d(P,C) = \sqrt{25+144} = 13 = r \{r=13\} \Rightarrow P$ is *on* $C$.

(b) $P(-2,5), C(3,7) \Rightarrow d(P,C) = \sqrt{25+4} = \sqrt{29} < r \{r=6\} \Rightarrow P$ is *inside* $C$.

(c) $P(1,-2), C(6,-7) \Rightarrow d(P,C) = \sqrt{25+25} = \sqrt{50} > r \{r=7\} \Rightarrow P$ is *outside* $C$.

**69** (a) To find the $x$-intercepts of $x^2 + y^2 - 4x - 6y + 4 = 0$, let $y = 0$ and solve the resulting equation for $x$.
$$x^2 - 4x + 4 = 0 \Rightarrow (x-2)^2 = 0 \Rightarrow x - 2 = 0 \Rightarrow x = 2.$$

(b) To find the $y$-intercepts of $x^2 + y^2 - 4x - 6y + 4 = 0$, let $x = 0$ and solve the resulting equation for $y$.
$$y^2 - 6y + 4 = 0 \Rightarrow y = \frac{6 \pm \sqrt{36-16}}{2} = \frac{6 \pm 2\sqrt{5}}{2} = 3 \pm \sqrt{5}.$$

**70** (a) $x^2 + y^2 - 10x + 4y + 13 = 0 \bullet y = 0 \Rightarrow x^2 - 10x + 13 = 0 \Rightarrow x = \frac{10 \pm \sqrt{100-52}}{2} = 5 \pm 2\sqrt{3}$

(b) $x^2 + y^2 - 10x + 4y + 13 = 0 \bullet x = 0 \Rightarrow y^2 + 4y + 13 = 0 \Rightarrow y = \frac{-4 \pm \sqrt{16-52}}{2}.$

The negative discriminant implies that there are no real solutions to the equation and hence, no $y$-intercepts.

**71** $x^2 + y^2 + 4x - 6y + 4 = 0 \Leftrightarrow (x+2)^2 + (y-3)^2 = 9$. This is a circle with center $C(-2,3)$ and radius 3. The circle we want has the same center, $C(-2,3)$, and radius that is equal to the distance from $C$ to $P(2,6)$.
$$d(P,C) = \sqrt{16+9} = 5, \text{ so an equation is } (x+2)^2 + (y-3)^2 = 25.$$

**72** By the Pythagorean theorem, the two stations are $d = \sqrt{100^2 + 80^2} \approx 128.06$ miles apart. The sum of their radii, $80 + 50 = 130$, is greater than $d$, indicating that the circles representing their broadcast ranges do overlap.

**73** The equation of circle $C_2$ is $(x-h)^2 + (y-2)^2 = 2^2$. If we draw a line from the origin to the center of $C_2$, we form a right triangle with hypotenuse $5 - 2 \{C_2 \text{ radius} - C_1 \text{ radius}\} = 3$ and sides of length 2 and $h$. Thus, $h^2 + 2^2 = 3^2 \Rightarrow h = \sqrt{5}$.

**74** The equation of circle $C_2$ is $(x-h)^2 + (y-3)^2 = 2^2$. If we draw a line from the origin to the center of $C_2$, we form a right triangle with hypotenuse $5 + 2 \{C_2 \text{ radius} + C_1 \text{ radius}\} = 7$ and sides of length 3 and $h$. Thus, $h^2 + 3^2 = 7^2 \Rightarrow h = \sqrt{40}$.

**75** The graph of $y_1$ is *below* the graph of $y_2$ to the left of $x = -3$ and to the right of $x = 2$. Writing the $x$-values in interval notation gives us $(-\infty, -3) \cup (2, \infty)$.

Note that the $y$-values play no role in writing the answer in interval notation.

**76** $y_1 < y_2$ between $x = -8$ and $x = 8$, so the interval is $(-8, 8)$.

**77** $y_1 < y_2$ between $x = -1$ and $x = 1$, excluding $x = 0$ since $y_1 = y_2$ at that value, so the interval is $(-1, 0) \cup (0, 1)$.

**78** $y_1 < y_2$ to the left of $x = -8$, between $x = -1$ and $x = 1$, and to the right of $x = 8$, so the interval notation is $(-\infty, -8) \cup (-1, 1) \cup (8, \infty)$.

**79** The viewing rectangles significantly affect the shape of the circle. The second viewing rectangle results in a graph that most looks like a circle.

**(1)** $[-2, 2]$ by $[-2, 2]$

**(2)** $[-3, 3]$ by $[-2, 2]$

**(3)** $[-2, 2]$ by $[-5, 5]$

**(4)** $[-5, 5]$ by $[-2, 2]$

**80** (a)  From the graph, there are two $x$–intercepts and two $y$–intercepts.

(b)  Using the free–moving cursor, one can conclude that $|x| + |y| < 5$ is true whenever the point $(x, y)$ is located inside the diamond shape.

**81** Assign $x^3 - \frac{9}{10}x^2 - \frac{43}{25}x + \frac{24}{25}$ to $Y_1$. After trying a standard viewing rectangle, we see that the $x$-intercepts are near the origin and we choose the viewing rectangle $[-6, 6]$ by $[-4, 4]$. This is simply one choice, not necessarily the best choice. For most graphing calculator exercises, we have selected viewing rectangles that are in a $3:2$ proportion (horizontal : vertical) to maintain a true proportion. From the graph, there are three $x$-intercepts. Use a root feature to determine that they are $-1.2$, $0.5$, and $1.6$.

$[-6, 6]$ by $[-4, 4]$

*Figure 81*

$[-6, 6]$ by $[-4, 4]$

*Figure 82*

**82** From the graph, there are four $x$-intercepts. They are approximately $-1.8$, $-0.7$, $0.3$ and $1.35$.

**83** Make the assignments $Y_1 = x^3 + x$, $Y_2 = \sqrt{1 - x^2}$, and $Y_3 = -Y_2$. From the graph, there are two points of intersection. They are approximately $(0.6, 0.8)$ and $(-0.6, -0.8)$.

*Figure 83*

*Figure 84*

**84** Make the assignments $Y_1 = 3x^4 - \frac{3}{2}$, $Y_2 = \sqrt{1 - x^2}$, and $Y_3 = -Y_2$. From the graph, there are four points of intersection. They are approximately $(\pm 0.9, 0.4)$ and $(\pm 0.7, -0.7)$.

**85** Depending on the type of graphing utility used, you may need to solve for $y$ first.

$x^2 + (y - 1)^2 = 1 \Rightarrow y = 1 \pm \sqrt{1 - x^2}$; $(x - \frac{5}{4})^2 + y^2 = 1 \Rightarrow y = \pm\sqrt{1 - (x - \frac{5}{4})^2}$.

Make the assignments $Y_1 = \sqrt{1 - x^2}$, $Y_2 = 1 + Y_1$, $Y_3 = 1 - Y_1$, $Y_4 = \sqrt{1 - (x - \frac{5}{4})^2}$, and $Y_5 = -Y_4$.

Be sure to "turn off" $Y_1$ before graphing. From the graph, there are two points of intersection.

They are approximately $(0.999, 0.968)$ and $(0.251, 0.032)$.

*Figure 85*

*Figure 86*

**86** $(x + 1)^2 + (y - 1)^2 = \frac{1}{4} \Rightarrow y = 1 \pm \sqrt{\frac{1}{4} - (x + 1)^2}$; $(x + \frac{1}{2})^2 + (y - \frac{1}{2})^2 = 1 \Rightarrow$

$y = \frac{1}{2} \pm \sqrt{1 - (x + \frac{1}{2})^2}$. From the graph, there are two points of intersection.

They are approximately $(-0.79, 1.46)$ and $(-1.46, 0.79)$.

**87** The cars are initially 4 miles apart. The distance between them decreases to 0 when they meet on the highway after 2 minutes. Then, the distance between them starts to increase until it is 4 miles after a total of 4 minutes.

*Figure 87*

*Figure 88*

**88** At noon on Sunday the pool is empty since when $x = 0$, $A = 0$. It is then filled with water, until at noon on Wednesday ($x = 3$), it contains 18,000 gallons. It is then drained until at noon on Saturday ($x = 6$), it is empty again.

**89** (a) $v = 1087\sqrt{\dfrac{T + 273}{273}}$ • $T = 20°C \Rightarrow v = 1087\sqrt{\dfrac{20 + 273}{273}} \approx 1126$ ft/sec.

(b) *Algebraically:* $v = 1000 \Rightarrow 1000 = 1087\sqrt{\dfrac{T+273}{273}} \Rightarrow \sqrt{\dfrac{T+273}{273}} = \dfrac{1000}{1087} \Rightarrow$

$\dfrac{T+273}{273} = \dfrac{1000^2}{1087^2} \Rightarrow T + 273 = \dfrac{273 \cdot 1000^2}{1087^2} \Rightarrow T = \dfrac{273 \cdot 1000^2}{1087^2} - 273 \approx -42°\text{C}.$

*Graphically:* Graph $Y_1 = 1087\sqrt{(T+273)/273}$ and $Y_2 = 1000$.

At the point of their intersection, $T \approx -42°\text{C}$.

[−50, 50, 10] by [900, 1200, 100]

*Figure 89*

[14, 16] by [95, 105]

*Figure 90*

**90** The horizontal lines ($y = 99$ and $y = 101$) intersect the graph of $A = \left(\sqrt{3}/4\right)s^2$ at $s \approx 15.12, 15.27$.

Thus, if $15.12 \le s \le 15.27$, then $99 \le A \le 101$.

## 2.3 Exercises

**1** $A(-3, 2), B(5, -4) \Rightarrow m_{AB} = \dfrac{y_2 - y_1}{x_2 - x_1} = \dfrac{(-4) - 2}{5 - (-3)} = \dfrac{-6}{8} = -\dfrac{3}{4}$

*Figure 1*

*Figure 2*

**2** $A(4, -1), B(-6, -3) \Rightarrow m_{AB} = \dfrac{y_2 - y_1}{x_2 - x_1} = \dfrac{-3 - (-1)}{-6 - 4} = \dfrac{-2}{-10} = \dfrac{1}{5}$

**3** $A(3, 4), B(-6, 4) \Rightarrow m_{AB} = \dfrac{y_2 - y_1}{x_2 - x_1} = \dfrac{4 - 4}{-6 - 3} = \dfrac{0}{-9} = 0$ {horizontal line}

*Figure 3*

*Figure 4*

**4** $A(4, -3), B(4, 2) \Rightarrow m_{AB} = \dfrac{y_2 - y_1}{x_2 - x_1} = \dfrac{2 - (-3)}{4 - 4} = \dfrac{5}{0} \Rightarrow m$ is undefined {vertical line}

**5** $A(-3,2), B(-3,5) \Rightarrow m_{AB} = \dfrac{y_2 - y_1}{x_2 - x_1} = \dfrac{5-2}{-3-(-3)} = \dfrac{3}{0} \Rightarrow m$ is undefined {vertical line}

*Figure 5*

*Figure 6*

**6** $A(4,-2), B(-3,-2) \Rightarrow m_{AB} = \dfrac{y_2 - y_1}{x_2 - x_1} = \dfrac{-2-(-2)}{-3-4} = \dfrac{0}{-7} = 0$ {horizontal line}

**7** To show that the polygon is a parallelogram, we must show that the slopes of opposite sides are equal.

$$A(-2,1), B(6,3), C(4,0), D(-4,-2) \Rightarrow m_{AB} = \tfrac{1}{4} = m_{DC} \text{ and } m_{DA} = \tfrac{3}{2} = m_{CB}.$$

**8** To show that the polygon is a trapezoid, we must show that the slopes of one pair of opposite sides are equal.

$$A(0,3), B(3,-1), C(-2,-6), D(-8,2) \Rightarrow m_{AB} = -\tfrac{4}{3} = m_{CD}.$$

**9** To show that the polygon is a rectangle, we must show that the slopes of opposite sides are equal (parallel lines) and the slopes of two adjacent sides are negative reciprocals (perpendicular lines).

$$A(6,15), B(11,12), C(-1,-8), D(-6,-5) \Rightarrow m_{DA} = \tfrac{5}{3} = m_{CB} \text{ and } m_{AB} = -\tfrac{3}{5} = m_{DC}.$$

**10** To show that the polygon is a right triangle, we must show that the slopes of two adjacent sides are negative reciprocals (perpendicular lines).          $A(1,4), B(6,-4), C(-15,-6) \Rightarrow m_{AB} = -\tfrac{8}{5} \text{ and } m_{AC} = \tfrac{5}{8}.$

**11** $A(-1,-3)$ is 5 units to the left and 5 units down from $B(4,2)$. The fourth vertex $D$ will have the same relative position from $C(-7,5)$, that is, 5 units to the left and 5 units down from $C$. Its coordinates are $(-7-5, 5-5) = (-12, 0)$.

**12** Let $E = M_{AB} = \left(\dfrac{x_1 + x_2}{2}, \dfrac{y_1 + y_2}{2}\right)$, $F = M_{BC} = \left(\dfrac{x_2 + x_3}{2}, \dfrac{y_2 + y_3}{2}\right)$, $G = M_{CD} = \left(\dfrac{x_3 + x_4}{2}, \dfrac{y_3 + y_4}{2}\right)$, and $H = M_{AD} = \left(\dfrac{x_1 + x_4}{2}, \dfrac{y_1 + y_4}{2}\right)$. The slopes of opposite sides are equal (or lines are vertical).

$$m_{EF} = m_{GH} = \dfrac{y_3 - y_1}{x_3 - x_1} \text{ and } m_{FG} = m_{EH} = \dfrac{y_4 - y_2}{x_4 - x_2}.$$

**13** $m = 3, -2, \tfrac{2}{3}, -\tfrac{1}{4}$ • Lines with equation $y = mx$ pass through the origin. Draw lines through the origin with slopes 3 {rise = 3, run = 1}, $-2$ {rise = $-2$, run = 1}, $\tfrac{2}{3}$ {rise = 2, run = 3}, and $-\tfrac{1}{4}$ {rise = $-1$, run = 4}. A negative "rise" can be thought of as a "drop."

*Figure 13*

*Figure 14*

**14** $m = 5, -3, \tfrac{1}{2}, -\tfrac{1}{3}$ •

**15** Draw lines through the point $P(3, 1)$ with slopes $\frac{1}{2}$ {rise $= 1$, run $= 2$}, $-1$ {rise $= -1$, run $= 1$}, and $-\frac{1}{5}$ {rise $= -1$, run $= 5$}.

*Figure 15*

*Figure 16*

**16** $P(-2, 4)$; $m = 1, -2, -\frac{1}{2}$ •

**17** From the figure, the slope of one of the lines is $\frac{\Delta y}{\Delta x} = \frac{5}{4}$, so the slopes are $\pm \frac{5}{4}$.

Using the point-slope form for the equation of a line with slope $m = \pm \frac{5}{4}$ and point $(x_1, y_1) = (2, -3)$ gives us

$$y - (-3) = \pm \tfrac{5}{4}(x - 2), \text{ or } y + 3 = \pm \tfrac{5}{4}(x - 2).$$

**18** $m = \frac{\Delta y}{\Delta x} = \frac{3}{4}$, so the slopes are $\pm \frac{3}{4}$.

Using the point $(x_1, y_1) = (-1, 2)$ gives us $y - 2 = \pm \tfrac{3}{4}[x - (-1)]$, or $y - 2 = \pm \tfrac{3}{4}(x + 1)$.

**19** The line $y = 1x + 3$ has slope 1 and $y$-intercept 3. The line $y = 1x + 1$ has slope 1 and $y$-intercept 1. The line $y = -1x + 1$ has slope $-1$ and $y$-intercept 1. Check your graph for parallel and perpendicular lines.

*Figure 19*

*Figure 20*

**20** $y = -2x - 1$, $y = -2x + 3$, $y = \frac{1}{2}x + 3$ •   Check your graph for parallel and perpendicular lines.

**21** (a) "Parallel to the $y$-axis" implies the equation is of the form $x = k$.

The $x$-value of $A(3, -1)$ is 3, hence $x = 3$ is the equation.

(b) "Perpendicular to the $y$-axis" implies the equation is of the form $y = k$.

The $y$-value of $A(3, -1)$ is $-1$, hence $y = -1$ is the equation.

**22** (a) The line through $A(-4, 2)$ and parallel to the $x$-axis is $y = 2$.

(b) The line through $A(-4, 2)$ and perpendicular to the $x$-axis is $x = -4$.

**23** Using the point-slope form, the equation of the line through $A(5, -3)$ with slope $-4$ is

$$y - (-3) = -4(x - 5) \quad \Rightarrow \quad y + 3 = -4x + 20 \quad \Rightarrow \quad 4x + y = 17.$$

**24** Using the point-slope form, the equation of the line through $A(-1, 4)$ with slope $\frac{2}{5}$ is

$$y - 4 = \tfrac{2}{5}[x - (-1)] \;\;\Rightarrow\;\; 5(y - 4) = 2(x + 1) \;\;\Rightarrow\;\; 5y - 20 = 2x + 2 \;\;\Rightarrow\;\; 2x - 5y = -22.$$

**25** $A(4, 1)$; slope $-\frac{1}{3}$ {use the point-slope form of a line} $\;\Rightarrow$

$$y - 1 = -\tfrac{1}{3}(x - 4) \;\;\Rightarrow\;\; 3(y - 1) = -1(x - 4) \;\;\Rightarrow\;\; 3y - 3 = -x + 4 \;\;\Rightarrow\;\; x + 3y = 7.$$

**26** $A(0, -2)$; slope $5 \;\Rightarrow\;\; y + 2 = 5(x - 0) \;\;\Rightarrow\;\; y + 2 = 5x \;\;\Rightarrow\;\; 5x - y = 2.$

**27** $A(4, -5)$, $B(-3, 6) \;\;\Rightarrow\;\; m_{AB} = -\frac{11}{7}$. By the point-slope form, with $A(4, -5)$, an equation of the line is

$$y + 5 = -\tfrac{11}{7}(x - 4) \;\;\Rightarrow\;\; 7(y + 5) = -11(x - 4) \;\;\Rightarrow\;\; 7y + 35 = -11x + 44 \;\;\Rightarrow\;\; 11x + 7y = 9.$$

**28** $A(-1, 6)$, $B(5, 0) \;\;\Rightarrow\;\; m_{AB} = -1$. $y - 0 = -1(x - 5) \;\;\Rightarrow\;\; y = -x + 5 \;\;\Rightarrow\;\; x + y = 5.$

**29** $5x - 2y = 4 \;\Leftrightarrow\; 5x - 4 = 2y \;\Leftrightarrow\; y = \frac{5}{2}x - 2$. Using the same slope, $\frac{5}{2}$, with $A(3, -1)$, gives us

$$y + 1 = \tfrac{5}{2}(x - 3) \;\;\Rightarrow\;\; 2(y + 1) = 5(x - 3) \;\;\Rightarrow\;\; 2y + 2 = 5x - 15 \;\;\Rightarrow\;\; 5x - 2y = 17.$$

**30** $x + 3y = 1 \;\Leftrightarrow\; 3y = -x + 1 \;\Leftrightarrow\; y = -\frac{1}{3}x + \frac{1}{3}$. Using the same slope, $-\frac{1}{3}$, with $A(-3, 5)$, gives us

$$y - 5 = -\tfrac{1}{3}(x + 3) \;\;\Rightarrow\;\; 3y - 15 = -x - 3 \;\;\Rightarrow\;\; x + 3y = 12.$$

**31** $2x - 5y = 8 \;\Leftrightarrow\; 2x - 8 = 5y \;\Leftrightarrow\; y = \frac{2}{5}x - \frac{8}{5}$. The slope of this line is $\frac{2}{5}$, so we'll use the negative reciprocal, $-\frac{5}{2}$, for the slope of the new line, with $A(7, -3)$.

$$y + 3 = -\tfrac{5}{2}(x - 7) \;\;\Rightarrow\;\; 2(y + 3) = -5(x - 7) \;\;\Rightarrow\;\; 2y + 6 = -5x + 35 \;\;\Rightarrow\;\; 5x + 2y = 29.$$

**32** $3x + 2y = 7 \;\Leftrightarrow\; y = -\frac{3}{2}x + \frac{7}{2}$. Using the negative reciprocal of $-\frac{3}{2}$ for the slope, with $A(5, 4)$,

$$y - 4 = \tfrac{2}{3}(x - 5) \;\;\Rightarrow\;\; 3y - 12 = 2x - 10 \;\;\Rightarrow\;\; 2x - 3y = -2.$$

**33** $A(4, 0)$, $B(0, -3) \;\;\Rightarrow\;\; m_{AB} = \frac{3}{4}$.

Since $B$ *is* the $y$-intercept, we use the slope-intercept form with $b = -3$ to get $y = \frac{3}{4}x - 3$.

**34** $A(-6, 0)$, $B(0, -1) \;\;\Rightarrow\;\; m_{AB} = -\frac{1}{6}$. Using the slope-intercept form with $b = -1$ gives us $y = -\frac{1}{6}x - 1$.

**35** $A(5, 2)$, $B(-1, 4) \;\;\Rightarrow\;\; m_{AB} = -\frac{1}{3}$. By the point-slope form, with $A(5, 2)$, an equation of the line is

$$y - 2 = -\tfrac{1}{3}(x - 5) \;\;\Rightarrow\;\; y = -\tfrac{1}{3}x + \tfrac{5}{3} + 2 \;\;\Rightarrow\;\; y = -\tfrac{1}{3}x + \tfrac{11}{3}.$$

**36** $A(-3, 1)$, $B(2, 7) \;\;\Rightarrow\;\; m_{AB} = \frac{6}{5}$. By the point-slope form, with $A(-3, 1)$, an equation of the line is

$$y - 1 = \tfrac{6}{5}(x + 3) \;\;\Rightarrow\;\; y = \tfrac{6}{5}x + \tfrac{18}{5} + 1 \;\;\Rightarrow\;\; y = \tfrac{6}{5}x + \tfrac{23}{5}.$$

**37** We need the line through the midpoint $M$ of segment $AB$ that is perpendicular to segment $AB$.

$A(3, -1)$, $B(-2, 6) \;\;\Rightarrow\;\; M_{AB} = \left(\frac{1}{2}, \frac{5}{2}\right)$ and $m_{AB} = -\frac{7}{5}$. Use $M_{AB}$ and $m = \frac{5}{7}$ in the point-slope form.

$$y - \tfrac{5}{2} = \tfrac{5}{7}\left(x - \tfrac{1}{2}\right) \;\;\Rightarrow\;\; 7\left(y - \tfrac{5}{2}\right) = 5\left(x - \tfrac{1}{2}\right) \;\;\Rightarrow\;\; 7y - \tfrac{35}{2} = 5x - \tfrac{5}{2} \;\;\Rightarrow\;\; 5x - 7y = -15.$$

**38** $A(4, 2)$, $B(-2, -6) \;\;\Rightarrow\;\; M_{AB} = (1, -2)$ and $m_{AB} = \frac{4}{3}$. Use $M_{AB}$ and $m = -\frac{3}{4}$ in the point-slope form.

$$y + 2 = -\tfrac{3}{4}(x - 1) \;\;\Rightarrow\;\; 4y + 8 = -3x + 3 \;\;\Rightarrow\;\; 3x + 4y = -5.$$

**39** An equation of the line with slope $-1$ through the origin is $y - 0 = -1(x - 0)$, or $y = -x$.

**40** An equation of the line with slope $1$ through the origin is $y - 0 = 1(x - 0)$, or $y = x$.

**41** We can solve the given equation for $y$ to obtain the slope-intercept form, $y = mx + b$.

$$2x = 15 - 3y \;\Rightarrow\; 3y = -2x + 15 \;\Rightarrow\; y = -\tfrac{2}{3}x + 5; \; m = -\tfrac{2}{3}, \, b = 5$$

*Figure 41*

*Figure 42*

**42** $7x = -4y - 8 \;\Rightarrow\; -4y = 7x + 8 \;\Rightarrow\; y = -\tfrac{7}{4}x - 2; \; m = -\tfrac{7}{4}, \, b = -2$

**43** $4x - 3y = 9 \;\Rightarrow\; -3y = -4x + 9 \;\Rightarrow\; y = \tfrac{4}{3}x - 3; \; m = \tfrac{4}{3}, \, b = -3$

*Figure 43*

*Figure 44*

**44** $x - 5y = -15 \;\Rightarrow\; -5y = -x - 15 \;\Rightarrow\; y = \tfrac{1}{5}x + 3; \; m = \tfrac{1}{5}, \, b = 3$

**45** (a) An equation of the horizontal line with $y$-intercept 3 is $y = 3$.

    (b) An equation of the line through the origin with slope $-\tfrac{1}{2}$ is $y = -\tfrac{1}{2}x$.

    (c) An equation of the line with slope $-\tfrac{3}{2}$ and $y$-intercept 1 is $y = -\tfrac{3}{2}x + 1$.

    (d) An equation of the line through $(3, -2)$ with slope $-1$ is $y + 2 = -(x - 3)$.

                          Alternatively, we have a slope of $-1$ and a $y$-intercept of 1, i.e., $y = -x + 1$.

**46** (a) An equation of the vertical line with $x$-intercept $-2$ is $x = -2$.

    (b) An equation of the line through the origin with slope $\tfrac{4}{3}$ is $y = \tfrac{4}{3}x$.

    (c) An equation of the line with slope $\tfrac{1}{3}$ and $y$-intercept $-2$ is $y = \tfrac{1}{3}x - 2$.

    (d) An equation of the line through $(-2, -5)$ with slope 3 is $y + 5 = 3(x + 2)$.

                          Alternatively, we have a slope of 3 and a $y$-intercept of 1, i.e., $y = 3x + 1$.

**47** Since we want to obtain a "1" on the right side of the equation, we will divide by 6.

$$[4x - 2y = 6] \cdot \tfrac{1}{6} \;\Rightarrow\; \frac{4x}{6} - \frac{2y}{6} = \frac{6}{6} \;\Rightarrow\; \frac{2x}{3} - \frac{y}{3} = 1 \;\Rightarrow\; \frac{x}{\frac{3}{2}} + \frac{y}{-3} = 1.$$

                              The $x$-intercept is $\tfrac{3}{2}$ and the $y$-intercept is $-3$.

**48** $[x - 3y = -2] \cdot \dfrac{1}{-2} \;\Rightarrow\; \dfrac{x}{-2} + \dfrac{3y}{2} = 1 \;\Rightarrow\; \dfrac{x}{-2} + \dfrac{y}{\frac{2}{3}} = 1.$ The $x$-intercept is $-2$ and the $y$-intercept is $\tfrac{2}{3}$.

**49** The radius of the circle is the vertical distance from the center of the circle to the line $y = 5$, that is,

$$r = 5 - (-2) = 7. \text{ With } C(3, -2), \text{ an equation is } (x - 3)^2 + (y + 2)^2 = 49.$$

**50** The line through the origin and $P$ is perpendicular to the desired line.

This line has equation $y = \frac{4}{3}x$, so the desired line has slope $-\frac{3}{4}$.

$$\text{With } P(3, 4), \text{ an equation is } y - 4 = -\frac{3}{4}(x - 3) \Rightarrow y = -\frac{3}{4}x + \frac{9}{4} + 4 \Rightarrow y = -\frac{3}{4}x + \frac{25}{4}.$$

**51** $L = 1.53t - 6.7 \bullet L = 28 \Rightarrow 1.53t - 6.7 = 28 \Rightarrow t = \dfrac{28 + 6.7}{1.53} \approx 22.68$, or approximately 23 weeks.

**52** $S = 0.03 + 1.805C \bullet S = 0.35 \Rightarrow 0.03 + 1.805C = 0.35 \Rightarrow C = \dfrac{0.35 - 0.03}{1.805} \approx 0.177.$

**53** (a) $W = 1.70L - 42.8 \bullet L = 40 \Rightarrow W = 1.70(40) - 42.8 = 25.2$ tons

   (b) Error in $L = \pm 2 \Rightarrow$ Error in $W = 1.70(\pm 2) = \pm 3.4$ tons

**54** (a) $L = at + b$ and $L = 24$ when $t = 0 \Rightarrow L = at + 24$.

$$L = 53 \text{ when } t = 7 \Rightarrow 53 = 7a + 24 \Rightarrow a = \frac{29}{7} \text{ and } L = \frac{29}{7}t + 24.$$

   (b) From part (a), the slope is $\frac{29}{7}$ ft/month $= \frac{29}{210}$ ft/day $\approx 1.657$ inches/day.

   (c) $W = at + b$ and $W = 3$ when $t = 0 \Rightarrow W = at + 3$.

$$W = 23 \text{ when } t = 7 \Rightarrow 23 = 7a + 3 \Rightarrow a = \frac{20}{7} \text{ and } W = \frac{20}{7}t + 3.$$

   (d) From part (c), the slope is $\frac{20}{7}$ tons/month $= \frac{2}{21}$ tons/day $\approx 190.476$ pounds/day.

**55** (a) $y = mx = \dfrac{\text{change in } y \text{ from the beginning of the season}}{\text{change in } x \text{ from the beginning of the season}}(x) = \dfrac{5 - 0}{14 - 0}x = \dfrac{5}{14}x.$

   (b) $x = 162 \Rightarrow y = \frac{5}{14}(162) \approx 58.$

**56** (a) $y = mx = \dfrac{\text{change in } y \text{ for the year}}{\text{change in } x \text{ for the year}}(x) = \dfrac{18,000 - 0}{(31 + 28 + 24) - 0}x = \dfrac{18,000}{83}x.$

   (b) $x = 365 \Rightarrow y = \frac{18,000}{83}(365) \approx 79,157.$

**57** (a) Using the slope-intercept form, $W = mt + b = mt + 10.$

$$W = 30 \text{ when } t = 3 \Rightarrow 30 = 3m + 10 \Rightarrow$$
$$m = \frac{20}{3} \text{ and } W = \frac{20}{3}t + 10.$$

   (b) $t = 6 \Rightarrow W = \frac{20}{3}(6) + 10 \Rightarrow W = 50$ lb

   (c) $W = 70 \Rightarrow 70 = \frac{20}{3}t + 10 \Rightarrow 60 = \frac{20}{3}t \Rightarrow$

$$t = 9 \text{ years old}$$

   (d) The graph has endpoints at $(0, 10)$ and $(12, 90)$.

**58** (a) Using the slope-intercept form, $P = mt + b = mt + 8250.$

$$P = 8125 \text{ when } t = 1 \text{ \{after one payment\}} \Rightarrow$$
$$8125 = m + 8250 \Rightarrow m = -125 \text{ and } P = -125t + 8250.$$

   (b) $P = 5000 \Rightarrow -125t + 8250 = 5000 \Rightarrow$

$$-125t = -3250 \Rightarrow t = 26 \text{ months}$$

   (c) $\frac{8250}{125} = 66$ payments. The graph has endpoints at $(0, 8250)$ and $(66, 0).$

**59** Using $(10, 2480)$ and $(25, 2440)$ {since an increase of 15°C lowers $H$ by 40}, we have

$$H - 2440 = \frac{2440 - 2480}{25 - 10}(T - 25) \quad\Rightarrow\quad H - 2440 = \frac{-40}{15}(T - 25) \quad\Rightarrow\quad H - 2440 = -\frac{8}{3}(T - 25) \quad\Rightarrow$$

$$H - \tfrac{7320}{3} = -\tfrac{8}{3}T + \tfrac{200}{3} \quad\Rightarrow\quad H = -\tfrac{8}{3}T + \tfrac{7520}{3}.$$

**60** (a) Using $(1800, 100)$ and $(5000, 40)$, we have $P - 40 = \dfrac{40 - 100}{5000 - 1800}(h - 5000) \quad\Rightarrow$

$$P - 40 = -\tfrac{3}{160}(h - 5000) \quad\Rightarrow\quad P - \tfrac{6400}{160} = -\tfrac{3}{160}h + \tfrac{15{,}000}{160} \quad\Rightarrow\quad P = -\tfrac{3}{160}h + \tfrac{21{,}400}{160} \quad\Rightarrow$$

$$P = -\tfrac{3}{160}h + \tfrac{535}{4} \text{ for } 1800 \le h \le 5000.$$

(b) $h = 2400 \quad\Rightarrow\quad P = -\tfrac{3}{160}(2400) + \tfrac{535}{4} = -\tfrac{180}{4} + \tfrac{535}{4} = \tfrac{355}{4}$, or 88.75%.

**61** (a) Using the slope-intercept form with $m = 0.032$ and $b = 13.5$, we have $T = 0.032t + 13.5$.

(b) $t = 2020 - 1915 = 105 \quad\Rightarrow\quad T = 0.032(105) + 13.5 = 16.86$°C.

**62** (a) Using $(1870, 11.8)$ and $(1969, 13.5)$, we have

$$T - 13.5 = \frac{13.5 - 11.8}{1969 - 1870}(t - 1969), \text{ or } T = \frac{1.7}{99}(t - 1969) + 13.5.$$

(b) $T = 12.5 \quad\Rightarrow\quad 12.5 - 13.5 = \dfrac{1.7}{99}(t - 1969) \quad\Rightarrow\quad -1 = \dfrac{1.7}{99}(t - 1969) \quad\Rightarrow\quad -\dfrac{99}{1.7} = t - 1969 \quad\Rightarrow$

$$t \approx 1910.76, \text{ or during the year 1910.}$$

**63** (a) Expenses $(E) = (\$1000) + (5\% \text{ of } R) + (\$2600) + (50\% \text{ of } R) \quad\Rightarrow$

$$E = 1000 + 0.05R + 2600 + 0.50R \quad\Rightarrow\quad E = 0.55R + 3600.$$

(b) Profit $(P) = $ Revenue $(R) - $ Expenses $(E) \quad\Rightarrow\quad P = R - (0.55R + 3600) \quad\Rightarrow$

$$P = R - 0.55R - 3600 \quad\Rightarrow\quad P = 0.45R - 3600.$$

(c) *Break even* means $P$ would be 0. $P = 0 \quad\Rightarrow\quad 0 = 0.45R - 3600 \quad\Rightarrow$

$$0.45R = 3600 \quad\Rightarrow\quad \tfrac{45}{100}R = 3600 \quad\Rightarrow\quad R = 3600\left(\tfrac{100}{45}\right) = \$8000/\text{month}$$

**64** (a) $a = 100$ gives us $y = \tfrac{25}{6}(t + 1)$ with endpoints $\left(0, \tfrac{25}{6}\right)$ and

$\left(12, \tfrac{325}{6}\right)$, and $y = 8t$ with endpoints $(0, 0)$ and $(12, 96)$.

(b) $\tfrac{1}{24}(t + 1)a = \tfrac{2}{25}ta \quad\Rightarrow\quad \tfrac{1}{24}(t + 1) = \tfrac{2}{25}t \quad\Rightarrow$

$25(t + 1) = 24(2t) \quad\Rightarrow\quad 25t + 25 = 48t \quad\Rightarrow$

$$25 = 23t \quad\Rightarrow\quad t = \tfrac{25}{23} \text{ yr} \approx 13 \text{ months}$$

**65** The targets are on the $x$-axis {which is the line $y = 0$}. To determine if a target is hit, set $y = 0$ and solve for $x$.

(a) $y - 2 = -1(x - 1) \quad\Rightarrow\quad x + y = 3.\; y = 0 \quad\Rightarrow\quad x = 3$ and a creature is hit.

(b) $y - \tfrac{5}{3} = -\tfrac{4}{9}\left(x - \tfrac{3}{2}\right) \quad\Rightarrow\quad 4x + 9y = 21.\; y = 0 \quad\Rightarrow\quad x = 5.25$ and no creature is hit.

**66** (a) $C = F$ and $C = \tfrac{5}{9}(F - 32) \quad\Rightarrow\quad F = \tfrac{5}{9}(F - 32) \quad\Rightarrow\quad 9F = 5F - 160 \quad\Rightarrow\quad 4F = -160 \quad\Rightarrow$

$$F = -40.$$

(b) $F = 2C$ and $C = \tfrac{5}{9}(F - 32) \quad\Rightarrow\quad C = \tfrac{5}{9}(2C - 32) \quad\Rightarrow\quad 9C = 10C - 160 \quad\Rightarrow$

$$C = 160 \text{ and hence, } F = 320.$$

**67** $s = \dfrac{v_2 - v_1}{h_2 - h_1} \quad\Rightarrow\quad 0.07 = \dfrac{v_2 - 22}{185 - 0} \quad\Rightarrow\quad 0.07(185) = v_2 - 22 \quad\Rightarrow\quad v_2 = 22 + 12.95 = 34.95 \text{ mi/hr.}$

**68** From Exercise 67, the average wind shear is $s = \dfrac{v_2 - v_1}{h_2 - h_1}$.

We know $v_1 = 32$ at $h_1 = 20$. We need to find $v_2$ at $h_2 = 200$. $\dfrac{v_1}{v_2} = \left(\dfrac{h_1}{h_2}\right)^P \Rightarrow \dfrac{v_2}{v_1} = \left(\dfrac{h_2}{h_1}\right)^P \Rightarrow$

$$v_2 = v_1 \left(\dfrac{h_2}{h_1}\right)^P = 32\left(\dfrac{200}{20}\right)^{0.13}. \text{ Thus, } s = \dfrac{32(10^{0.13}) - 32}{200 - 20} \approx 0.062 \text{ (mi/hr)/ft.}$$

**69** The slope of $AB$ is $\dfrac{-1.11905 - (-1.3598)}{-0.55 - (-1.3)} = 0.321$. Similarly, the slopes of $BC$ and $CD$ are also 0.321.

Therefore, the four points all lie on the same line. Since the common slope is 0.321, let $a = 0.321$.

$y = 0.321x + b \Rightarrow -1.3598 = 0.321(-1.3) + b \Rightarrow b = -0.9425$.

Thus, the points are linearly related by the equation $y = 0.321x - 0.9425$.

**70** The slopes of $AB$ and $BC$ are both $-0.44$, whereas the slope of $CD$ is approximately $-1.107$.

Thus, the points do not lie on the same line.

**71** $x - 3y = -58 \Leftrightarrow y = (x + 58)/3$ and $3x - y = -70 \Leftrightarrow y = 3x + 70$. Assign $(x + 58)/3$ to $Y_1$ and $3x + 70$ to $Y_2$. Using a standard viewing rectangle, we don't see the lines. Zooming out gives us an indication where the lines intersect and by using an intersect feature, we find that the lines intersect at $(-19, 13)$.

$[-30, 3, 2]$ by $[-2, 20, 2]$

*Figure 71*

$[-12, 12]$ by $[-2, 14]$

*Figure 72*

**72** $x + 10y = 123 \Leftrightarrow y = (-x + 123)/10$ and $2x - y = -6 \Leftrightarrow y = 2x + 6$. Assign $(-x + 123)/10$ to $Y_1$ and $y = 2x + 6$ to $Y_2$. Similarly to Exercise 71, the lines intersect at $(3, 12)$.

**73** From the graph, we can see that the points of intersection are $A(-0.8, -0.6)$, $B(4.8, -3.4)$, and $C(2, 5)$. The lines intersecting at $A$ are perpendicular since they have slopes of 2 and $-\frac{1}{2}$. Since $d(A, B) = \sqrt{39.2}$ and $d(A, C) = \sqrt{39.2}$, the triangle is isosceles. Thus, the polygon is a right isosceles triangle.

$[-15, 15]$ by $[-10, 10]$

*Figure 73*

$[-3, 3]$ by $[-2, 2]$

*Figure 74*

**74** The equations of the lines can be rewritten as $y = \frac{1}{4.2}x + 0.17$, $y = -4.2x - 1.9$, $y = \frac{1}{4.2}x - 1.3$, and $y = -4.2x + 3.5$. From the graph, we can see that the points of intersection are approximately $A(0.75, 0.35)$, $B(1.08, -1.04)$, $C(-0.14, -1.33)$, and $D(-0.47, 0.059)$. The first and third lines are parallel as are the second and fourth lines. In addition, these pairs of lines are perpendicular to each other since their slopes are $-4.2$ and $\frac{1}{4.2}$. Since $d(A, B) \approx 1.43$ and $d(A, D) \approx 1.25$, it is not a square. Thus, the polygon is a rectangle.

**75** The data appear to be linear. Using the two arbitrary points $(0.6, 1.3)$ and $(4.6, 8.5)$, the slope of the line is

$\dfrac{8.5 - 1.3}{4.6 - 0.6} = 1.8$. An equation of the line is $y - 1.3 = 1.8(x - 0.6) \Rightarrow y = 1.8x + 0.22$.

If we find the regression line on a calculator, we get the model $y \approx 1.84589x + 0.21027$.

$[0, 5]$ by $[0, 10]$                                        $[0, 5]$ by $[0, 3.5]$

*Figure 75*                                        *Figure 76*

**76** The data appear to be linear. Using the two arbitrary points $(0.4, 2.88)$ and $(4.4, 0.68)$, the slope of the line is

$\dfrac{0.68 - 2.88}{4.4 - 0.4} = -0.55$. An equation of the line is $y - 2.88 = -0.55(x - 0.4) \Rightarrow y = -0.55x + 3.1$.

If we find the regression line on a calculator, we get the model $y \approx -0.54951x + 3.09621$.

**77** (a) Plot the points with the form (Year, Distance): $(1911, 15.52)$, $(1932, 15.72)$, $(1955, 16.56)$, $(1975, 17.89)$, and $(1995, 18.29)$.

(b) To find a first approximation for the line use the arbitrary points $(1911, 15.52)$ and $(1995, 18.29)$. The resulting line is $D_1 \approx 0.033Y - 47.545$. Adjustments may be made to this equation. If we find the regression line on a calculator, we get the model $D \approx 0.03648Y - 54.47409$.

(c) Using $D_1$ from part (b), when $x = 1985$, $y = 17.96$ (so the distance is 17.96 meters)—almost equal to the actual record of 17.97 meters.

$[1900, 2010, 20]$ by $[15, 20]$                    $[1900, 2010, 20]$ by $[210, 260, 10]$

*Figure 77*                                        *Figure 78*

**78** (b) For an approximation for the line, we'll use the first and last points given; that is, $(1913, 254.4)$ and $(1999, 223.1)$. These points determine the line $T - 254.4 = \dfrac{223.1 - 254.4}{1999 - 1913}(Y - 1913) \Rightarrow$

$T \approx -0.36395Y + 950.643$. The regression line is $y \approx -0.37455x + 970.58262$.

(c) $T = -0.36395(1985) + 950.643 \approx 228.2$ seconds, which is off by 1.9 seconds.

(d) The slope of the line is approximately $-0.4$. This means that *on the average*, the record time for the mile has decreased by 0.4 sec/yr.

## 2.4 Exercises

**1** $f(x) = -x^2 - x - 4 \Rightarrow f(-2) = -4 + 2 - 4 = -6$, $f(0) = -4$, and $f(4) = -16 - 4 - 4 = -24$.

**2** $f(x) = -x^3 - x^2 + 3 \Rightarrow f(-3) = 27 - 9 + 3 = 21$, $f(0) = 3$, and $f(2) = -8 - 4 + 3 = -9$.

**3**  $f(x) = \sqrt{x-2} + 3x \implies f(3) = \sqrt{3-2} + 3(3) = \sqrt{1} + 9 = 1 + 9 = 10.$

Similarly,                   $f(6) = \sqrt{6-2} + 3(6) = \sqrt{4} + 18 = 2 + 18 = 20$

and                          $f(11) = \sqrt{11-2} + 3(11) = \sqrt{9} + 33 = 3 + 33 = 36.$

Note that $f(a)$, with $a < 2$, would be undefined.

**4**  $f(x) = \dfrac{x}{x-3} \implies f(-2) = \dfrac{2}{5}, f(0) = 0,$ and $f(3)$ is undefined.

**5**  (a)  $f(x) = 5x - 2 \implies f(a) = 5(a) - 2 = 5a - 2$   (b)  $f(-a) = 5(-a) - 2 = -5a - 2$

(c)  $-f(a) = -1 \cdot (5a - 2) = -5a + 2$            (d)  $f(a+h) = 5(a+h) - 2 = 5a + 5h - 2$

(e)  $f(a) + f(h) = (5a - 2) + (5h - 2) = 5a + 5h - 4$

(f)  Using parts (d) and (a), $\dfrac{f(a+h) - f(a)}{h} = \dfrac{(5a + 5h - 2) - (5a - 2)}{h} = \dfrac{5h}{h} = 5.$

**6**  (a)  $f(x) = 1 - 4x \implies f(a) = 1 - 4(a) = 1 - 4a$   (b)  $f(-a) = 1 - 4(-a) = 1 + 4a$

(c)  $-f(a) = -1 \cdot (1 - 4a) = 4a - 1$            (d)  $f(a+h) = 1 - 4(a+h) = 1 - 4a - 4h$

(e)  $f(a) + f(h) = (1 - 4a) + (1 - 4h) = 2 - 4a - 4h$

(f)  Using parts (d) and (a), $\dfrac{f(a+h) - f(a)}{h} = \dfrac{(1 - 4a - 4h) - (1 - 4a)}{h} = \dfrac{-4h}{h} = -4.$

**7**  (a)  $f(x) = -x^2 + 3 \implies f(a) = -(a)^2 + 3 = -a^2 + 3$

(b)  $f(-a) = -(-a)^2 + 3 = -a^2 + 3$          (c)  $-f(a) = -1 \cdot (-a^2 + 3) = a^2 - 3$

(d)  $f(a+h) = -(a+h)^2 + 3 = -(a^2 + 2ah + h^2) + 3 = -a^2 - 2ah - h^2 + 3$

(e)  $f(a) + f(h) = (-a^2 + 3) + (-h^2 + 3) = -a^2 - h^2 + 6$

(f)  $\dfrac{f(a+h) - f(a)}{h} = \dfrac{(-a^2 - 2ah - h^2 + 3) - (-a^2 + 3)}{h} = \dfrac{-2ah - h^2}{h} = \dfrac{h(-2a - h)}{h} = -2a - h$

**8**  (a)  $f(x) = 3 - x^2 \implies f(a) = 3 - (a)^2 = 3 - a^2$   (b)  $f(-a) = 3 - (-a)^2 = 3 - a^2$

(c)  $-f(a) = -1 \cdot (3 - a^2) = -3 + a^2$

(d)  $f(a+h) = 3 - (a+h)^2 = 3 - (a^2 + 2ah + h^2) = 3 - a^2 - 2ah - h^2$

(e)  $f(a) + f(h) = (3 - a^2) + (3 - h^2) = 6 - a^2 - h^2$

(f)  $\dfrac{f(a+h) - f(a)}{h} = \dfrac{(3 - a^2 - 2ah - h^2) - (3 - a^2)}{h} = \dfrac{-2ah - h^2}{h} = \dfrac{h(-2a - h)}{h} = -2a - h$

**9**  (a)  $f(x) = x^2 - x + 3 \implies f(a) = (a)^2 - (a) + 3 = a^2 - a + 3$

(b)  $f(-a) = (-a)^2 - (-a) + 3 = a^2 + a + 3$       (c)  $-f(a) = -1 \cdot (a^2 - a + 3) = -a^2 + a - 3$

(d)  $f(a+h) = (a+h)^2 - (a+h) + 3 = a^2 + 2ah + h^2 - a - h + 3$

(e)  $f(a) + f(h) = (a^2 - a + 3) + (h^2 - h + 3) = a^2 + h^2 - a - h + 6$

(f)  $\dfrac{f(a+h) - f(a)}{h} = \dfrac{(a^2 + 2ah + h^2 - a - h + 3) - (a^2 - a + 3)}{h} = \dfrac{2ah + h^2 - h}{h} = \dfrac{h(2a + h - 1)}{h}$
$$= 2a + h - 1$$

**10**  (a)  $f(x) = 2x^2 + 3x - 7 \implies f(a) = 2(a)^2 + 3(a) - 7 = 2a^2 + 3a - 7$

(b)  $f(-a) = 2(-a)^2 + 3(-a) - 7 = 2a^2 - 3a - 7$

(c)  $-f(a) = -1 \cdot (2a^2 + 3a - 7) = -2a^2 - 3a + 7$

(d) $f(a+h) = 2(a+h)^2 + 3(a+h) - 7 = 2(a^2 + 2ah + h^2) + 3a + 3h - 7 =$

$$2a^2 + 4ah + 2h^2 + 3a + 3h - 7$$

(e) $f(a) + f(h) = (2a^2 + 3a - 7) + (2h^2 + 3h - 7) = 2a^2 + 2h^2 + 3a + 3h - 14$

(f) $\dfrac{f(a+h) - f(a)}{h} = \dfrac{(2a^2 + 4ah + 2h^2 + 3a + 3h - 7) - (2a^2 + 3a - 7)}{h}$

$$= \dfrac{4ah + 2h^2 + 3h}{h} = \dfrac{h(4a + 2h + 3)}{h} = 4a + 2h + 3$$

**11** (a) $g(x) = 4x^2 \ \Rightarrow \ g\left(\dfrac{1}{a}\right) = 4\left(\dfrac{1}{a}\right)^2 = 4 \cdot \dfrac{1}{a^2} = \dfrac{4}{a^2}$    (b) $g(a) = 4a^2 \ \Rightarrow \ \dfrac{1}{g(a)} = \dfrac{1}{4a^2}$

(c) $g(\sqrt{a}) = 4(\sqrt{a})^2 = 4a$           (d) $\sqrt{g(a)} = \sqrt{4a^2} = 2|a| = 2a$ since $a > 0$

**12** (a) $g(x) = 2x - 7 \ \Rightarrow \ g\left(\dfrac{1}{a}\right) = 2\left(\dfrac{1}{a}\right) - 7 = \dfrac{2}{a} - 7 = \dfrac{2 - 7a}{a}$    (b) $\dfrac{1}{g(a)} = \dfrac{1}{2(a) - 7} = \dfrac{1}{2a - 7}$

(c) $g(\sqrt{a}) = 2(\sqrt{a}) - 7 = 2\sqrt{a} - 7$        (d) $\sqrt{g(a)} = \sqrt{2a - 7}$

**13** (a) $g(x) = \dfrac{2x}{x^2 + 1} \ \Rightarrow \ g\left(\dfrac{1}{a}\right) = \dfrac{2(1/a)}{(1/a)^2 + 1} = \dfrac{2/a}{1/a^2 + 1} \cdot \dfrac{a^2}{a^2} = \dfrac{2a}{1 + a^2} = \dfrac{2a}{a^2 + 1}$

(b) $\dfrac{1}{g(a)} = \dfrac{1}{\dfrac{2a}{a^2 + 1}} = \dfrac{a^2 + 1}{2a}$          (c) $g(\sqrt{a}) = \dfrac{2\sqrt{a}}{(\sqrt{a})^2 + 1} = \dfrac{2\sqrt{a}}{a + 1}$

(d) $\sqrt{g(a)} = \sqrt{\dfrac{2a}{a^2 + 1}} \cdot \dfrac{\sqrt{a^2 + 1}}{\sqrt{a^2 + 1}} = \dfrac{\sqrt{2a(a^2 + 1)}}{a^2 + 1}$, or, equivalently, $\dfrac{\sqrt{2a^3 + 2a}}{a^2 + 1}$

**14** (a) $g(x) = \dfrac{x^2}{x + 1} \ \Rightarrow \ g\left(\dfrac{1}{a}\right) = \dfrac{\left(\dfrac{1}{a}\right)^2}{\dfrac{1}{a} + 1} = \dfrac{\dfrac{1}{a^2}}{\dfrac{1 + a}{a}} \cdot \dfrac{a^2}{a^2} = \dfrac{1}{a(a + 1)}$    (b) $\dfrac{1}{g(a)} = \dfrac{1}{\dfrac{a^2}{a + 1}} = \dfrac{a + 1}{a^2}$

(c) $g(\sqrt{a}) = \dfrac{(\sqrt{a})^2}{\sqrt{a} + 1} \cdot \dfrac{\sqrt{a} - 1}{\sqrt{a} - 1} = \dfrac{a(\sqrt{a} - 1)}{a - 1}$      (d) $\sqrt{g(a)} = \sqrt{\dfrac{a^2}{a + 1}} \cdot \sqrt{\dfrac{a + 1}{a + 1}} = \dfrac{a\sqrt{a + 1}}{a + 1}$

**15** All vertical lines intersect the graph in at most one point,

so the graph *is* the graph of a function because it passes the Vertical Line Test.

**16** At least one vertical line intersects the graph in more than one point,

so the graph *is not* the graph of a function because it fails the Vertical Line Test.

**17** The domain $D$ is the set of $x$-values; that is, $D = [-4, 1] \cup [2, 4)$. Note that the solid dots on the figure correspond to using brackets {including}, whereas the open dot corresponds to using parentheses {excluding}. The range $R$ is the set of $y$-values; that is, $R = [-3, 3)$.

**18** Domain $D = \{x\text{-values}\} = [-4, 4)$. Range $R = \{y\text{-values}\} = (-3, -1) \cup [1, 3]$.

**19** (a) The domain of a function $f$ is the set of all $x$-values for which the function is defined. In this case, the graph extends from $x = -3$ to $x = 4$. Hence, the domain is $[-3, 4]$.

(b) The range of a function $f$ is the set of all $y$-values that the function takes on. In this case, the graph includes all values from $y = -2$ to $y = 2$. Hence, the range is $[-2, 2]$.

(c) $f(1)$ is the $y$-value of $f$ corresponding to $x = 1$. In this case, $f(1) = 0$.

(d) If we were to draw the horizontal line $y = 1$ on the same coordinate plane, it would intersect the graph at $x = -1, \frac{1}{2}$, and 2. Hence, $f(x) = 1 \Rightarrow x = -1, \frac{1}{2}$, and 2.

(e) The function is above 1 between $x = -1$ and $x = \frac{1}{2}$, and also to the right of $x = 2$. Hence, $f(x) > 1 \Rightarrow x \in \left(-1, \frac{1}{2}\right) \cup (2, 4]$.

**20** (a) $[-5, 7]$　　　　　　　(b) $[-1, 2]$　　　　　　　(c) $f(1) = -1$

(d) $f(x) = 1 \Rightarrow x = -3, -1, 3, 5$　　　　　(e) $f(x) > 1 \Rightarrow x \in (-3, -1) \cup (3, 5)$

**Note:** In Exercises 21–32, we need to make sure that the radicand {the expression under the radical sign} is greater than or equal to zero and that the denominator is not equal to zero.

**21** $f(x) = \sqrt{2x + 7}$ • $2x + 7 \ge 0 \Rightarrow 2x \ge -7 \Rightarrow x \ge -\frac{7}{2} \Leftrightarrow \left[-\frac{7}{2}, \infty\right)$

**22** $f(x) = \sqrt{4 - 3x}$ • $4 - 3x \ge 0 \Rightarrow 4 \ge 3x \Rightarrow x \le \frac{4}{3} \Leftrightarrow \left(-\infty, \frac{4}{3}\right]$

**23** $f(x) = \sqrt{16 - x^2}$ • $16 - x^2 \ge 0 \Rightarrow 16 \ge x^2 \Rightarrow x^2 \le 16 \Rightarrow |x| \le 4 \Rightarrow$
$-4 \le x \le 4$, or $[-4, 4]$ in interval notation.

**24** $f(x) = \sqrt{x^2 - 25}$ • $x^2 - 25 \ge 0 \Rightarrow |x| \ge 5 \Rightarrow x \ge 5$ or $x \le -5 \Leftrightarrow (-\infty, -5] \cup [5, \infty)$

**25** $f(x) = \dfrac{x + 1}{x^3 - 9x}$ • For this function we must have the denominator not equal to 0. The denominator is $x^3 - 9x = x(x^2 - 9) = x(x + 3)(x - 3)$, so $x \ne 0, -3, 3$. The solution is then all real numbers *except* $0, -3, 3$. In interval notation, we have $(-\infty, -3) \cup (-3, 0) \cup (0, 3) \cup (3, \infty)$. We could also denote this solution as $\mathbb{R} - \{\pm 3, 0\}$.

**26** $f(x) = \dfrac{4x}{6x^2 + 13x - 5}$ • $6x^2 + 13x - 5 = 0 \Rightarrow (2x + 5)(3x - 1) = 0 \Rightarrow \mathbb{R} - \left\{-\frac{5}{2}, \frac{1}{3}\right\}$

**27** $f(x) = \dfrac{\sqrt{2x - 5}}{x^2 - 5x + 4}$ • For this function we must have the radicand greater than or equal to 0 *and* the denominator not equal to 0. The radicand is greater than or equal to 0 if $2x - 5 \ge 0$, or, equivalently, $x \ge \frac{5}{2}$. The denominator is $(x - 1)(x - 4)$, so $x \ne 1, 4$. The solution is then all real numbers greater than or equal to $\frac{5}{2}$, excluding 4. In interval notation, we have $\left[\frac{5}{2}, 4\right) \cup (4, \infty)$.

**28** $f(x) = \dfrac{\sqrt{4x - 3}}{x^2 - 4}$ • $x^2 - 4 = 0 \Rightarrow (x + 2)(x - 2) = 0 \Rightarrow x = \pm 2$;
$4x - 3 \ge 0 \Rightarrow x \ge \frac{3}{4}$, so the domain is $\left[\frac{3}{4}, 2\right) \cup (2, \infty)$

**29** $f(x) = \dfrac{x - 4}{\sqrt{x - 2}}$ • For this function we must have $x - 2 > 0 \Rightarrow x > 2$.
Note that " $>$ " must be used since the denominator cannot *equal* 0. In interval notation, we have $(2, \infty)$.

**30** $f(x) = \dfrac{1}{(x - 3)\sqrt{x + 3}}$ • $x + 3 > 0 \Rightarrow x > -3 \{x \ne 3\}$, so the domain is $(-3, 3) \cup (3, \infty)$

**31** $f(x) = \sqrt{x + 3} + \sqrt{3 - x}$ • We must have $x + 3 \ge 0 \Rightarrow x \ge -3$ and $3 - x \ge 0 \Rightarrow x \le 3$.
The domain is the intersection of $x \ge -3$ and $x \le 3$, that is, $[-3, 3]$.

**32** $f(x) = \sqrt{(x - 2)(x - 6)}$ • $(x - 2)(x - 6) \ge 0 \Rightarrow x \le 2$ or $x \ge 6$ {use a sign chart} $\Rightarrow$
$(-\infty, 2] \cup [6, \infty)$

**33** (a) $D = \{x\text{-values}\} = [-5, -3) \cup (-1, 1] \cup (2, 4]$; $R = \{y\text{-values}\} = \{-3\} \cup [-1, 4]$.

     Note that the notation for including the single value $-3$ in $R$ uses braces.

     (b) $f$ **is increasing** on an interval if it goes up as we move from left to right,

                                                    so $f$ is increasing on $[-4, -3) \cup [3, 4]$.

         $f$ **is decreasing** on an interval if it goes down as we move from left to right, so $f$ is decreasing on $[-5, -4] \cup (2, 3]$. Note that the values $x = -4$ and $x = 3$ are in intervals that are listed as increasing and in intervals that are listed as decreasing.

         $f$ **is constant** on an interval if the $y$-values do not change, so $f$ is constant on $(-1, 1]$.

**34** (a) $D = \{x\text{-values}\} = [-5, -3) \cup (-2, -1] \cup 0, 2) \cup (3, 5]$; $R = \{y\text{-values}\} = [-3, 3] \cup \{4\}$

     (b) $f$ **is increasing** on $[-5, -3) \cup (3, 4]$. $f$ **is decreasing** on $[0, 2)$. $f$ **is constant** on $(-2, -1] \cup [4, 5]$.

**35** The graph of the function is increasing on $(-\infty, -3]$ and is decreasing on $[-3, 2]$, so there must be a high point at $x = -3$. Now the graph of the function is increasing on $[2, \infty)$, so there must be a low point at $x = 2$.

Figure 35

Figure 36

**36** The graph of the function is decreasing on $(-\infty, -2]$ and $[1, 4]$, and is increasing on $[-2, 1]$ and $[4, \infty)$.

**37** (a) $f(x) = -2x + 1$ • This is a line with slope $-2$ and $y$-intercept $1$.

     (b) The domain $D$ and the range $R$ are equal to $(-\infty, \infty)$.

     (c) $f$ is decreasing on its entire domain, that is, $(-\infty, \infty)$.

Figure 37

Figure 38

**38** (a) $f(x) = 2x - 1$ • This is a line with slope $2$ and $y$-intercept $-1$.

     (b) $D = (-\infty, \infty)$, $R = (-\infty, \infty)$

     (c) Increasing on $(-\infty, \infty)$

**39** (a) To sketch the graph of $f(x) = 4 - x^2$, we can make use of the symmetry with respect to the $y$-axis.

| $x$ | $\pm 4$ | $\pm 3$ | $\pm 2$ | $\pm 1$ | 0 |
|-----|---------|---------|---------|---------|---|
| $y$ | $-12$   | $-5$    | 0       | 3       | 4 |

(b) Since we can substitute any number for $x$, the domain is all real numbers, that is, $D = \mathbb{R}$. By examining the figure, we see that the values of $y$ are at most 4. Hence, the range of $f$ is all reals less than or equal to 4, that is, $R = (-\infty, 4]$.

(c) A common mistake is to confuse the function values, the $y$'s, with the input values, the $x$'s. We are not interested in the specific $y$-values for determining if the function is increasing, decreasing, or constant. We are only interested if the $y$-values are going up, going down, or staying the same. For the function $f(x) = 4 - x^2$, we say $f$ is increasing on $(-\infty, 0]$ since the $y$-values are getting larger as we move from left to right over the $x$-values from $-\infty$ to 0. Also, $f$ is decreasing on $[0, \infty)$ since the $y$-values are getting smaller as we move from left to right over the $x$-values from 0 to $\infty$. Note that this answer would have been the same if the function was $f(x) = 500 - x^2$, $f(x) = -300 - x^2$, or any function of the form $f(x) = a - x^2$, where $a$ is any real number.

*Figure 39*

*Figure 40*

**40** (b) $D = (-\infty, \infty)$, $R = [-1, \infty)$

(c) Decreasing on $(-\infty, 0]$, increasing on $[0, \infty)$

**41** (a) $f(x) = \sqrt{x - 1}$ • This is half of a parabola opening to the right. It has an $x$-intercept of 1 and no $y$-intercept.

(b) $x - 1 \geq 0 \Rightarrow x \geq 1$, so the domain is $D = [1, \infty)$.
The $y$-values are all positive or zero, so the range is $R = [0, \infty)$.

(c) $f$ is increasing on its entire domain, that is, on $[1, \infty)$.

*Figure 41*

*Figure 42*

**42** (a) $f(x) = x^2 - 1$ • (b) $D = (-\infty, 4]$, $R = [0, \infty)$ (c) Decreasing on $(-\infty, 4]$

**43** (a) $f(x) = -4$  ● This is a horizontal line with $y$-intercept $-4$.

(b) The domain is $D = (-\infty, \infty)$ and the range consists of a single value, so $R = \{-4\}$.

(c) $f$ is constant on its entire domain, that is, $(-\infty, \infty)$.

*Figure 43*

*Figure 44*

**44** (a) $f(x) = 3$  ● (b) $D = (-\infty, \infty)$, $R = \{3\}$　(c) Constant on $(-\infty, \infty)$

**45** (a) We recognize $y = f(x) = -\sqrt{36 - x^2}$ as the lower half of the circle $x^2 + y^2 = 36$.

(b) To find the domain, we solve $36 - x^2 \geq 0$. $36 - x^2 \geq 0 \Rightarrow x^2 \leq 36 \Rightarrow |x| \leq 6 \Rightarrow D = [-6, 6]$. From the figure, we see that the $y$-values vary from $y = -6$ to $y = 0$. Hence, the range $R$ is $[-6, 0]$.

(c) As we move from left to right, for $x = -6$ to $x = 0$, the $y$-values are decreasing. From $x = 0$ to $x = 6$, the $y$-values increase. Hence, $f$ is decreasing on $[-6, 0]$ and increasing on $[0, 6]$.

*Figure 45*

*Figure 46*

**46** (a) $f(x) = \sqrt{16 - x^2}$  ● (b) $D = [-4, 4]$, $R = [0, 4]$　(c) Increasing on $[-4, 0]$, decreasing on $[0, 4]$

**47** $f(x) = x^2 - 6x$, so $f(2) = 2^2 - 6(2) = 4 - 12 = -8$.

$$\frac{f(2+h) - f(2)}{h} = \frac{[(2+h)^2 - 6(2+h)] - (-8)}{h} = \frac{4 + 4h + h^2 - 12 - 6h + 8}{h} = \frac{h - 2h}{h} = \frac{h(h - 2)}{h} = h - 2$$

**48** $f(x) = -2x^2 + 5$, so $f(2) = -2(2)^2 + 5 = -2 \cdot 4 + 5 = -8 + 5 = -3$.

$$\frac{f(2+h) - f(2)}{h} = \frac{[-2(2+h)^2 + 5] - (-3)}{h} = \frac{-2(4 + 4h + h^2) + 5 + 3}{h} = \frac{-8 - 8h - 2h^2 + 8}{h}$$
$$= \frac{-8h - 2h^2}{h} = \frac{h(-8 - 2h)}{h} = -2h - 8$$

**49** $\frac{f(x+h) - f(x)}{h} = \frac{[(x+h)^2 + 5] - [x^2 + 5]}{h} = \frac{(x^2 + 2xh + h^2 + 5) - (x^2 + 5)}{h} = \frac{2xh + h^2}{h} = \frac{h(2x + h)}{h}$
$= 2x + h$

**50** $\dfrac{f(x+h)-f(x)}{h}=\dfrac{\dfrac{1}{(x+h)^2}-\dfrac{1}{x^2}}{h}=\dfrac{\dfrac{x^2-(x+h)^2}{(x+h)^2\,x^2}}{h}=\dfrac{x^2-(x^2+2xh+h^2)}{hx^2(x+h)^2}$

$$=\dfrac{-2xh-h^2}{hx^2(x+h)^2}=-\dfrac{h(2x+h)}{hx^2(x+h)^2}=-\dfrac{2x+h}{x^2(x+h)^2}$$

**51** $\dfrac{f(x)-f(a)}{x-a}=\dfrac{\sqrt{x-3}-\sqrt{a-3}}{x-a}=\dfrac{\sqrt{x-3}-\sqrt{a-3}}{x-a}\cdot\dfrac{\sqrt{x-3}+\sqrt{a-3}}{\sqrt{x-3}+\sqrt{a-3}}$

$$=\dfrac{(x-3)-(a-3)}{(x-a)\left(\sqrt{x-3}+\sqrt{a-3}\right)}=\dfrac{x-a}{(x-a)\left(\sqrt{x-3}+\sqrt{a-3}\right)}=\dfrac{1}{\sqrt{x-3}+\sqrt{a-3}}$$

**52** $\dfrac{f(x)-f(a)}{x-a}=\dfrac{(x^3-2)-(a^3-2)}{x-a}=\dfrac{x^3-a^3}{x-a}=\dfrac{(x-a)(x^2+ax+a^2)}{x-a}=x^2+ax+a^2$

**53** As in Example 7, $a=\dfrac{2-1}{3-(-3)}=\dfrac{1}{6}$ and $f$ has the form $f(x)=\dfrac{1}{6}x+b$.

$f(3)=\dfrac{1}{6}(3)+b=\dfrac{1}{2}+b$. But $f(3)=2$, so $\dfrac{1}{2}+b=2 \;\Rightarrow\; b=\dfrac{3}{2}$, and $f(x)=\dfrac{1}{6}x+\dfrac{3}{2}$.

**54** As in Example 7, $a=\dfrac{-2-7}{4-(-2)}=-\dfrac{9}{6}=-\dfrac{3}{2}$ and $f$ has the form $f(x)=-\dfrac{3}{2}x+b$.

$f(-2)=-\dfrac{3}{2}(-2)+b=3+b$. But $f(-2)=7$, so $3+b=7 \;\Rightarrow\; b=4$, and $f(x)=-\dfrac{3}{2}x+4$.

**Note:** For Exercises 55–64, a good question to consider is, "Given a particular value of $x$, can a unique value of $y$ be found?" If the answer is yes, the value of $y$ (general formula) is given. If not, two ordered pairs satisfying the relation having $x$ in the first position are given.

**55** $3y=x^2+7 \;\Rightarrow\; y=\dfrac{x^2+7}{3}$, which is a function

**56** $x=3y+2 \;\Rightarrow\; x-2=3y \;\Rightarrow\; y=\dfrac{x-2}{3}$, which is a function

**57** $x^2+y^2=4 \;\Rightarrow\; y^2=4-x^2 \;\Rightarrow\; y=\pm\sqrt{4-x^2}$, not a function: $(0,\pm2)$

**58** $y^2-x^2=4 \;\Rightarrow\; y^2=4+x^2 \;\Rightarrow\; y=\pm\sqrt{4+x^2}$, not a function: $(0,\pm2)$

**59** $y=5$ is a function since for any $x$, $(x,5)$ is the only ordered pair in $W$ having $x$ in the first position.

**60** $x=3$ is not a function: $(3,0)$ and $(3,1)$

**61** Any ordered pair with $x$-coordinate 0 satisfies $xy=0$. Two such ordered pairs are $(0,0)$ and $(0,1)$. Not a function

**62** $x+y=0 \;\Rightarrow\; y=-x$, which is a function

**63** $|y|=|x| \;\Rightarrow\; \pm y=\pm x \;\Rightarrow\; y=\pm x$, not a function: $(1,\pm1)$

**64** Many ordered pairs with $x$-coordinate 3 (or any other number) satisfy $y<x$.

Two such ordered pairs are $(3,1)$ and $(3,2)$. Not a function

**65** $V=lwh=(30-x-x)(20-x-x)(x)$
$=(30-2x)(20-2x)(x)=2(15-x)\cdot 2(10-x)(x)=4x(15-x)(10-x)$

**66** $S=2\pi rh+2(2\pi r^2)=2\pi r(10)+4\pi r^2=20\pi r+4\pi r^2=4\pi r(5+r)$

**67** (a)  The formula for the area of a rectangle is $A = lw$ {Area = length × width}.

$$A = 500 \quad \Rightarrow \quad xy = 500 \quad \Rightarrow \quad y = \frac{500}{x}$$

(b)  We need to determine the number of linear feet $(P)$ first.  There are two walls of length $y$, two walls of length $(x - 3)$, and one wall of length $x$, so $P = $ Linear feet of wall $= x + 2(y) + 2(x - 3) = 3x + 2\left(\dfrac{500}{x}\right) - 6$.

The cost $C$ is 100 times $P$, so $C = 100P = 300x + \dfrac{100,000}{x} - 600$.

**68** (a)  $V = lwh \quad \Rightarrow \quad 6 = xy(1.5) \quad \Rightarrow \quad xy = 4 \quad \Rightarrow \quad y = \dfrac{4}{x}$

(b)  Surface area $S = xy + 2(1.5)x + 2(1.5)y = x\left(\dfrac{4}{x}\right) + 3x + 3\left(\dfrac{4}{x}\right) = 4 + 3x + \dfrac{12}{x}$

**69**  The expression $(h - 25)$ represents the number of feet *above* 25 feet.

$S(h) = 6(h - 25) + 100 = 6h - 150 + 100 = 6h - 50.$

**70**  $T(x) = \dfrac{125,000 \text{ BTUs}}{1 \text{ gallon of gas}} \cdot x \text{ gallons} \cdot \dfrac{\$0.342}{1,000,000 \text{ BTU}} = \$0.04275x.$

**71** (a)  Using $(6, 48)$ and $(7, 50.5)$, we have

$y - 48 = \dfrac{50.5 - 48}{7 - 6}(t - 6)$, or $y = 2.5t + 33$.

(b)  The slope represents the yearly increase in height, 2.5 in./yr.

(c)  $t = 10 \quad \Rightarrow \quad y = 2.5(10) + 33 = 58$ in.

**72**  Let $A$ denote the area of the contamination.  $A$ is linearly related to $t$, so $A = at + b$.

$A = 0$ when $t = 0 \quad \Rightarrow \quad b = 0$.  $A = 40,000$ when $t = 40 \quad \Rightarrow \quad a = 1000$.

Thus, $A = 1000t$.  Since the contamination is circular, $A = \pi r^2$.  Hence, $\pi r^2 = 1000t \quad \Rightarrow \quad r = \sqrt{\dfrac{1000t}{\pi}}.$

**73**  The height of the balloon is $2t$.  Using the Pythagorean theorem,

$$d^2 = 100^2 + (2t)^2 = 10,000 + 4t^2 \quad \Rightarrow \quad d = \sqrt{4(2500 + t^2)} \quad \Rightarrow \quad d = 2\sqrt{t^2 + 2500}.$$

**74** (a)  By the Pythagorean theorem, $x^2 + y^2 = 15^2 \quad \Rightarrow \quad y = \sqrt{225 - x^2}$.

(b)  $A = \frac{1}{2}bh = \frac{1}{2}xy = \frac{1}{2}x\sqrt{225 - x^2}$.

The domain of this function is $-15 \le x \le 15$; however, only $0 < x < 15$ will form triangles.

**75** (a)  $CTP$ forms a right angle, so the Pythagorean theorem may be applied.

$(CT)^2 + (PT)^2 = (PC)^2 \quad \Rightarrow \quad r^2 + y^2 = (h + r)^2 \Rightarrow$

$r^2 + y^2 = h^2 + 2hr + r^2 \quad \Rightarrow \quad y^2 = h^2 + 2hr \ \{y > 0\} \quad \Rightarrow \quad y = \sqrt{h^2 + 2hr}$

(b)  $y = \sqrt{(200)^2 + 2(4000)(200)} = \sqrt{(200)^2(1 + 40)} = 200\sqrt{41} \approx 1280.6$ mi

**76** (a)  The dimensions $L$, 50, and $x - 2$ form a right triangle 2 feet off the ground.

Thus, $L^2 = 50^2 + (x - 2)^2 \quad \Rightarrow \quad L = \sqrt{2500 + (x - 2)^2}.$

(b)  $L = 75 \quad \Rightarrow \quad 75^2 = 50^2 + (x - 2)^2 \quad \Rightarrow \quad x - 2 = \pm\sqrt{3125} \quad \Rightarrow \quad x = 25\sqrt{5} + 2 \approx 57.9$ ft

**77** Form a right triangle with the control booth and the beginning of the runway. Let $y$ denote the distance from the control booth to the beginning of the runway and apply the Pythagorean theorem. $y^2 = 300^2 + 20^2 \Rightarrow y^2 = 90,400$. Now form a right triangle, in a different plane, with sides $y$ and $x$ and hypotenuse $d$. Then $d^2 = y^2 + x^2 \Rightarrow d^2 = 90,400 + x^2 \Rightarrow d = \sqrt{90,400 + x^2}$.

**78** $\text{Time}_{\text{total}} = \text{Time}_{\text{rowing}} + \text{Time}_{\text{walking}}$ {use $t = d/r$ and $d(A, P) = 6 - x$} $\Rightarrow$

$$T = \frac{\sqrt{2^2 + (6 - x)^2}}{3} + \frac{x}{5} \Rightarrow T = \frac{\sqrt{x^2 - 12x + 40}}{3} + \frac{x}{5}$$

**79** (b) The maximum $y$-value of 0.75 occurs when $x \approx 0.55$ and the minimum $y$-value of $-0.75$ occurs when $x \approx -0.55$. Therefore, the range of $f$ is approximately $[-0.75, 0.75]$.

(c) $f$ is decreasing on $[-2, -0.55]$ and on $[0.55, 2]$. $f$ is increasing on $[-0.55, 0.55]$.

[−2, 2] by [−2, 2]

*Figure 79*

[−1, 1] by [−1, 1]

*Figure 80*

**80** (b) The maximum $y$-value of 0.5 occurs when $x = -1$ and the minimum $y$-value of $-0.094$ occurs when $x \approx -0.56$. Therefore, the range of $f$ is approximately $[-0.094, 0.5]$.

(c) $f$ is decreasing on $[-1, -0.56]$ and on $[0.12, 0.75]$. $f$ is increasing on $[-0.56, 0.12]$ and on $[0.75, 1]$.

**81** (b) The maximum $y$-value of 1 occurs when $x = 0$ and the minimum $y$-value of $-1.03$ occurs when $x \approx 1.06$. Therefore, the range of $f$ is approximately $[-1.03, 1]$.

(c) $f$ is decreasing on $[0, 1.06]$. $f$ is increasing on $[-0.7, 0]$ and on $[1.06, 1.4]$.

[−0.7, 1.4] by [−1.1, 1]

*Figure 81*

[−4, −4] by [−4, −4]

*Figure 82*

**82** (b) The maximum $y$-value of 1.08 occurs when $x \approx -0.69$ and the minimum $y$-value of $-0.42$ occurs when $x \approx 1.78$. Therefore, the range of $f$ is approximately $[-0.42, 1.08]$.

(c) $f$ is decreasing on $[-0.69, 1.78]$. $f$ is increasing on $[-4, -0.69]$ and on $[1.78, 4]$.

**83** For each of (a)–(e), an assignment to $Y_1$, an appropriate viewing rectangle and the solution(s) are listed.

(a) $Y_1 = (x^5)^{(1/3)} = 32$,
VR: $[-40, 40, 10]$ by $[-40, 40, 10]$, $x = 8$

(b) $Y_1 = (x^4)^{(1/3)} = 16$,
VR: $[-40, 40, 10]$ by $[-40, 40, 10]$, $x = \pm 8$

(c) $Y_1 = (x^2)^{(1/3)} = -64$, VR: $[-40, 40, 10]$ by $[-40, 40, 10]$, no real solutions

(d) $Y_1 = (x^3)^{(1/4)} = 125$, VR: $[0, 800, 100]$ by $[0, 200, 100]$, $x = 625$

(e) $Y_1 = (x^3)^{(1/2)} = -27$, VR: $[-30, 30, 10]$ by $[-30, 30, 10]$, no real solutions

**84** (a) $Y_1 = (x^3)^{(1/5)} = -27$, VR: $[-250, 250, 100]$ by $[-30, 30, 10]$, $x = -243$

(b) $Y_1 = (x^2)^{(1/3)} = 25$, VR: $[-130, 130, 50]$ by $[0, 30, 10]$, $x = \pm 125$

(c) $Y_1 = (x^4)^{(1/3)} = -49$, VR: $[-50, 50, 10]$ by $[-50, 50, 10]$, no real solutions

(d) $Y_1 = (x^3)^{(1/2)} = 64$, VR: $[-5, 30, 5]$ by $[-5, 30, 5]$, $x = 16$

(e) $Y_1 = (x^3)^{(1/4)} = -8$, VR: $[-10, 10,]$ by $[-10, 10]$, no real solutions

**85** (a) There are $95 \times 63 = 5985$ total pixels in the screen.

(b) If a function is graphed in dot mode, only one pixel in each column of pixels on the screen can be darkened. Therefore, there are at most 95 pixels darkened. **Note:** In connected mode this may not be true.

**86** (a) $[0, 75, 10]$ by $[0, 600, 100]$*

(b) The data and plot show that stopping distance is not a linear function of the speed. The distance required to stop a car traveling at 30 mi/hr is 86 ft whereas the distance required to stop a car traveling at 60 mi/hr is 414 ft. $\frac{414}{86} \approx 4.81$ rather than double.

(c) If you double the speed of a car, it requires almost *five times* the stopping distance. If stopping distance were a linear function of speed, doubling the speed would require twice the stopping distance.

**87** (a) First, we must determine an equation of the line that passes through the points $(1993, 16{,}871)$ and $(2000, 20{,}356)$.

$[1990, 2010, 10]$ by $[1\text{E}4, 3\text{E}4, 1\text{E}4]$

$y - 16{,}871 = \frac{20{,}356 - 16{,}871}{2000 - 1993}(x - 1993) = \frac{3485}{7}(x - 1993) \Rightarrow$

$y = \frac{3485}{7}x - \frac{6{,}827{,}508}{7}$. Thus, let $f(x) = \frac{3485}{7}x - \frac{6{,}827{,}508}{7}$ and graph $f$.

(b) The average annual increase in the price paid for a new car is equal to the slope: $\frac{3485}{7} \approx \$497.86$.

(c) Graph $y = \frac{3485}{7}x - \frac{6{,}827{,}508}{7}$ and $y = 25{,}000$ on the same coordinate axes. Their point of intersection is approximately $(2009.33, 25{,}000)$. Thus, according to this model, in the year 2009 the average price paid for a new car will be $\$25{,}000$.

## 2.5 Exercises

**1** Since $f$ is an even function, $f(-x) = f(x)$. From the table, we see that $f(2) = 7$, so $f(-2) = 7$. In general, if $f$ is an even function, and $(a, b)$ is a point on the graph of $f$, then the point $(-a, b)$ is also on the graph.

Since $g$ is an odd function, $g(-x) = -g(x)$. From the table, we see that $g(2) = -6$, so $g(-2) = -(-6) = 6$. In general, if $f$ is an odd function, and $(a, b)$ is a point on the graph of $f$, then the point $(-a, -b)$ is also on the graph.

**2** Since $f$ is an even function, $f(-x) = f(x)$. From the table, we see that $f(3) = -5$, so $f(-3) = -5$.

Since $g$ is an odd function, $g(-x) = -g(x)$. From the table, we see that $g(3) = 6$, so $g(-3) = -6$.

**3** $f(x) = 5x^3 + 2x \Rightarrow f(-x) = 5(-x)^3 + 2(-x) = -5x^3 - 2x$ and

$-f(x) = -1 \cdot f(x) = -(5x^3 + 2x) = -5x^3 - 2x$.

Since $f(-x) = -f(x)$, $f$ is odd and its graph is symmetric with respect to the origin.

    Note that this means if $(a, b)$ is a point on the graph of $f$, then the point $(-a, -b)$ is also on the graph.

**4** $f(x) = |x| - 3 \Rightarrow f(-x) = |-x| - 3 = |x| - 3 = f(x)$, so $f$ is even

**5** $f(x) = 3x^4 - 6x^2 - 5 \Rightarrow f(-x) = 3(-x)^4 - 6(-x)^2 - 5 = 3x^4 - 6x^2 - 5 = f(x)$.

Since $f(-x) = f(x)$, $f$ is even and its graph is symmetric with respect to the $y$-axis.

    Note that this means if $(a, b)$ is a point on the graph of $f$, then the point $(-a, b)$ is also on the graph.

**6** $f(x) = 7x^5 + 2x^3 \Rightarrow f(-x) = 7(-x)^5 + 2(-x)^3 = -7x^5 - 2x^3 = -(7x^5 + 2x^3) = -f(x)$, so $f$ is odd

**7** $f(x) = 8x^3 - 3x^2 \Rightarrow f(-x) = 8(-x)^3 - 3(-x)^2 = -8x^3 - 3x^2$

$-f(x) = -1 \cdot f(x) = -1(8x^3 - 3x^2) = -8x^3 + 3x^2$

               Since $f(-x) \neq f(x)$ and $f(-x) \neq -f(x)$, $f$ is neither even nor odd.

**8** $f(x) = \sqrt[3]{5} \Rightarrow f(-x) = \sqrt[3]{5} = f(x)$, so $f$ is even

**9** $f(x) = \sqrt{x^2 + 4} \Rightarrow f(-x) = \sqrt{(-x)^2 + 4} = \sqrt{x^2 + 4} = f(x)$.

       Since $f(-x) = f(x)$, $f$ is even and its graph is symmetric with respect to the $y$-axis.

**10** $f(x) = 3x^2 + 2x - 4 \Rightarrow f(-x) = 3(-x)^2 + 2(-x) - 4 = 3x^2 - 2x - 4 \neq \pm f(x)$,

                        so $f$ is neither even nor odd

**11** $f(x) = \sqrt[3]{x^3 - x} \Rightarrow$

$f(-x) = \sqrt[3]{(-x)^3 - (-x)} = \sqrt[3]{-x^3 + x} = \sqrt[3]{-1(x^3 - x)} = \sqrt[3]{-1}\sqrt[3]{x^3 - x} = -\sqrt[3]{x^3 - x}$.

$-f(x) = -1 \cdot f(x) = -1 \cdot \sqrt[3]{x^3 - x} = -\sqrt[3]{x^3 - x}$.

       Since $f(-x) = -f(x)$, $f$ is odd and its graph is symmetric with respect to the origin.

**12** $f(x) = x^3 - \dfrac{1}{x} \Rightarrow f(-x) = (-x)^3 - \dfrac{1}{-x} = -x^3 + \dfrac{1}{x} = -\left(x^3 - \dfrac{1}{x}\right) = -f(x)$, so $f$ is odd

**13** $f(x) = |x| + c$, $c = -3, 1, 3$ • Shift $g(x) = |x|$ {in Figure 1 in the text} down 3, up 1, and up 3 units, respectively.

Figure 13

Figure 14

**14** $f(x) = |x - c|$, $c = -3, 1, 3$ • Shift $g(x) = |x|$ left 3, right 1, and right 3 units, respectively.

**15** $f(x) = -x^2 + c$, $c = -4, 2, 4$ • Shift $g(x) = -x^2$ {in Figure 5 in the text} down 4, up 2, up 4, respectively.

Figure 15

Figure 16

**16** $f(x) = 2x^2 - c$, $c = -4, 2, 4$ • Shift $g(x) = 2x^2$ up 4, down 2, down 4, respectively.

**17** $f(x) = 2\sqrt{x} + c$, $c = -3, 0, 2$ • The graph of $y^2 = x$ is shown in Figure 3 in Section 2.2 of the text. The top half of this graph is the graph of the square root function, $h(x) = \sqrt{x}$. The second value of $c$, 0, gives us the graph of $g(x) = 2\sqrt{x}$, which is a vertical stretching of $h$ by a factor of 2. The effect of adding $-3$ and 2 is to vertically shift $g$ down 3 units and up 2 units, respectively.

Figure 17

Figure 18

**18** $f(x) = \sqrt{9 - x^2} + c$, $c = -3, 0, 2$ • Shift $g(x) = \sqrt{9 - x^2}$ down 3, up 2, respectively.

**19** $f(x) = \frac{1}{2}\sqrt{x - c}$, $c = -3, 0, 4$ • The graph of $g(x) = \frac{1}{2}\sqrt{x}$ is a vertical compression of the square root function by a factor of $1/(1/2) = 2$. The effect of subtracting $-3$ and $4$ from $x$ will be to horizontally shift $g$ left 3 units and right 4 units, respectively. If you forget which way to shift the graph, it is helpful to find the domain of the function. For example, if $h(x) = \sqrt{x - 2}$, then $x - 2$ must be nonnegative. $x - 2 \geq 0 \Rightarrow x \geq 2$, which also indicates a shift of 2 units to the right.

*Figure 19*

*Figure 20*

**20** $f(x) = -\frac{1}{2}(x - c)^2$, $c = -3, 0, 4$ • Shift $g(x) = -\frac{1}{2}x^2$ left 3, right 4, respectively.

**21** $f(x) = c\sqrt{4 - x^2}$, $c = -2, 1, 3$ • For $c = 1$, the graph of $g(x) = \sqrt{4 - x^2}$ is the upper half of the circle $x^2 + y^2 = 4$. For $c = -2$, reflect $g$ through the $x$-axis and vertically stretch it by a factor of 2. For $c = 3$, vertically stretch $g$ by a factor of 3.

*Figure 21*

*Figure 22*

**22** $f(x) = (x + c)^3$, $c = -2, 1, 2$ • Shift $g(x) = x^3$ right 2, left 1, and left 2, respectively.

**23** $f(x) = cx^3$, $c = -\frac{1}{3}, 1, 2$ • For $c = 1$, see a graph of the cubing function in Appendix I of the text. For $c = -\frac{1}{3}$, reflect $g(x) = x^3$ through the $x$-axis and vertically compress it by a factor of $1/(1/3) = 3$. For $c = 2$, vertically stretch $g$ by a factor of 2.

*Figure 23*

*Figure 24*

**24** $f(x) = (cx)^3 + 1$, $c = -1, 1, 4$ • For $c = -1$, reflect $g(x) = x^3 + 1$ through the $y$-axis. For $c = 4$, horizontally compress $g$ by a factor of 4 {this could also be considered as a vertical stretch by a factor of $4^3 = 64$}.

**25** $f(x) = \sqrt{cx} - 1$, $c = -1$, $\frac{1}{9}$, $4$ • If $c = 1$, then the graph of $g(x) = \sqrt{x} - 1$ is the graph of the square root function vertically shifted down one unit. For $c = -1$, reflect $g$ through the $y$-axis. For $c = \frac{1}{9}$, horizontally stretch $g$ by a factor $1/(1/9) = 9$ {$x$-intercept changes from 1 to 9}. For $c = 4$, horizontally compress $g$ by a factor 4 {$x$-intercept changes from 1 to $\frac{1}{4}$}.

*Figure 25*

*Figure 26*

**26** $f(x) = -\sqrt{16 - (cx)^2}$, $c = 1$, $\frac{1}{2}$, $4$ • For $c = \frac{1}{2}$, horizontally stretch $g(x) = -\sqrt{16 - x^2}$ by a factor of $1/(1/2) = 2$ {$x$-intercepts change from $\pm 4$ to $\pm 8$}. For $c = 4$, horizontally compress $g$ by a factor of 4 {$x$-intercepts change from $\pm 4$ to $\pm 1$}.

**27** You know that $y = f(x + 2)$ is the graph of $y = f(x)$ shifted to the left 2 units, so the point $P(0, 5)$ would move to the point $(-2, 5)$. The graph of $y = f(x + 2) - 1$ is the graph of $y = f(x + 2)$ shifted down 1 unit, so the point $(-2, 5)$ moves to $(-2, 4)$. Summarizing these steps gives us the following:

$$P(0, 5) \qquad \{x + 2 \quad [\text{subtract 2 from the } x\text{-coordinate}]\} \qquad \rightarrow (-2, 5)$$
$$\{-1 \quad [\text{subtract 1 from the } y\text{-coordinate}]\} \qquad \rightarrow (-2, 4)$$

**28** $y = 2f(x) + 4$ • $P(3, -1)$ $\quad\{\times 2 \quad [\text{multiply the } y\text{-coordinate by 2}]\} \quad \rightarrow (3, -2)$
$\{+4 \quad [\text{add 4 to the } y\text{-coordinate}]\} \quad \rightarrow (3, 2)$

**29** To determine what happens to a point $P$ under this transformation, think of how you would evaluate $y = 2f(x - 4) + 1$ for a particular value of $x$. You would first subtract 4 from $x$ and then put that value into the function, obtaining a corresponding $y$-value. Next, you would multiply that $y$-value by 2 and finally, add 1. Summarizing these steps using the given point $P$, we have the following:

$$P(3, -2) \qquad \{x - 4 \quad [\text{add 4 to the } x\text{-coordinate}]\} \qquad \rightarrow (7, -2)$$
$$\{\times 2 \quad [\text{multiply the } y\text{-coordinate by 2}]\} \qquad \rightarrow (7, -4)$$
$$\{+1 \quad [\text{add 1 to the } y\text{-coordinate}]\} \qquad \rightarrow (7, -3)$$

**30** $y = \frac{1}{2}f(x - 3) + 3$ • $P(-5, 8)$ $\quad\{x - 3 \quad [\text{add 3 to the } x\text{-coordinate}]\} \qquad \rightarrow (-2, 8)$
$\{\times \frac{1}{2} \quad [\text{multiply the } y\text{-coordinate by } \frac{1}{2}]\} \qquad \rightarrow (-2, 4)$
$\{+3 \quad [\text{add 3 to the } y\text{-coordinate}]\} \qquad \rightarrow (-2, 7)$

**31** $y = \frac{1}{3}f(\frac{1}{2}x) - 1$ • $P(4, 9)$ $\quad\{\frac{1}{2}x \quad [\text{multiply the } x\text{-coordinate by 2}]\} \qquad \rightarrow (8, 9)$
$\{\times \frac{1}{3} \quad [\text{multiply the } y\text{-coordinate by } \frac{1}{3}]\} \qquad \rightarrow (8, 3)$
$\{-1 \quad [\text{subtract 1 from the } y\text{-coordinate}]\} \qquad \rightarrow (8, 2)$

**32** $y = -3f(2x) - 5$ • $P(-2, 1)$ $\quad\{2x \quad [\text{divide the } x\text{-coordinate by 2}]\} \qquad \rightarrow (-1, 1)$
$\{\times (-3) \quad [\text{multiply the } y\text{-coordinate by } -3]\} \qquad \rightarrow (-1, -3)$
$\{-5 \quad [\text{subtract 5 from the } y\text{-coordinate}]\} \qquad \rightarrow (-1, -8)$

**33** For $y = f(x - 2) + 3$, the graph of $f$ is shifted 2 units to the right and 3 units up.

**34** For $y = 3f(x - 1)$, the graph of $f$ is shifted 1 unit to the right and stretched vertically by a factor of 3.

**35** For $y = f(-x) - 4$, the graph of $f$ is reflected through the $y$-axis and shifted 4 units down.

**36** For $y = -f(x + 2)$, the graph of $f$ is shifted 2 units to the left and reflected through the $x$-axis.

**37** For $y = -\frac{1}{2}f(x)$, the graph of $f$ is compressed vertically by a factor of 2 and reflected through the $x$-axis.

**38** For $y = f\left(\frac{1}{2}x\right) - 3$, the graph of $f$ is stretched horizontally by a factor of 2 and shifted 3 units down.

**39** For $y = -2f\left(\frac{1}{3}x\right)$, the graph of $f$ is stretched horizontally by a factor of 3, stretched vertically by a factor of 2, and reflected through the $x$-axis.

**40** For $y = \frac{1}{3}|f(x)|$, the part of the graph of $f$ below the $x$-axis is reflected through the $x$-axis and that graph is compressed vertically by a factor of 3.

**41** When graphing the parts in this exercise, it may help to keep track of at least one of the points $(0, 3)$, $(2, 0)$, or $(4, 3)$, on the given graph.

(a) $y = f(x + 3)$  •  shift $f$ left 3 units

(b) $y = f(x - 3)$  •  shift $f$ right 3 units

(c) $y = f(x) + 3$  •  shift $f$ up 3 units

(d) $y = f(x) - 3$  •  shift $f$ down 3 units

(e) $y = -3f(x)$  •  reflect $f$ through the $x$-axis {the effect of the negative sign in front of 3} and vertically stretch it by a factor of 3

(f) $y = -\frac{1}{3}f(x)$  •  reflect $f$ through the $x$-axis {the effect of the negative sign in front of $\frac{1}{3}$} and vertically compress it by a factor of $1/(1/3) = 3$

(g) $y = f\left(-\frac{1}{2}x\right)$ • reflect $f$ through the $y$-axis {the effect of the negative sign inside the parentheses} and horizontally stretch it by a factor of $1/(1/2) = 2$

(h) $y = f(2x)$ • horizontally compress $f$ by a factor of 2

(i) $y = -f(x+2) - 3$ • shift $f$ left 2 units, reflect it through the $x$-axis, and then shift it down 3 units

(j) $y = f(x-2) + 3$ • shift $f$ right 2 units and up 3

(k) $y = |f(x)|$ • since no portion of the graph lies below the $x$-axis, the graph is unchanged

(l) $y = f(|x|)$ • include the reflection of the given graph through the $y$-axis since all points have positive $x$-coordinates

**42** (a) $y = f(x-2)$ • shift $f$ right 2 units

(b) $y = f(x+2)$ • shift $f$ left 2 units

(c) $y = f(x) - 2$ • shift $f$ down 2 units

(d) $y = f(x) + 2$ • shift $f$ up 2 units

(e) $y = -2f(x)$ • reflect $f$ through the $x$-axis and vertically stretch it by a factor of 2

(f) $y = -\frac{1}{2}f(x)$ • reflect $f$ through the $x$-axis and vertically compress it by a factor of $1/(1/2) = 2$

(g) $y = f(-2x)$ • reflect $f$ through the $y$-axis and horizontally compress it by a factor of 2

(h) $y = f\left(\frac{1}{2}x\right)$ • horizontally stretch $f$ by a factor of $1/(1/2) = 2$

(i) $y = -f(x+4) - 2$ • reflect $f$ about the $x$-axis, shift it left 4 units and down 2

(j) $y = f(x-4) + 2$ • shift $f$ right 4 units and up 2

(k)   $y = |f(x)|$   •   reflect the portion of the graph below the $x$-axis through the $x$-axis.

(l)   $y = f(|x|)$   •   include the reflection of the given graph through the $y$-axis since all points have positive $x$-coordinates

**43** (a)   The minimum point on $y = f(x)$ is $(2, -1)$. On the graph labeled (a), the minimum point is $(-7, 0)$. It has been shifted left 9 units and up 1. Hence, $y = f(x + 9) + 1$.

(b)   $f$ is reflected through the $x$-axis   $\Rightarrow$   $y = -f(x)$

(c)   $f$ is reflected through the $x$-axis and shifted left 7 units and down 1   $\Rightarrow$   $y = -f(x + 7) - 1$

**44** (a)   $f$ is shifted left 1 unit and up 1   $\Rightarrow$   $y = f(x + 1) + 1$

(b)   $f$ is reflected through the $x$-axis   $\Rightarrow$   $y = -f(x)$ {or $y = f(-x)$}

(c)   $f$ is reflected through the $x$-axis and shifted right 2 units   $\Rightarrow$   $y = -f(x - 2)$

**45** (a)   $f$ is shifted left 4 units   $\Rightarrow$   $y = f(x + 4)$

(b)   $f$ is shifted up 1 unit   $\Rightarrow$   $y = f(x) + 1$

(c)   $f$ is reflected through the $y$-axis   $\Rightarrow$   $y = f(-x)$

**46** (a)   $f$ is shifted right 2 units and up 2   $\Rightarrow$   $y = f(x - 2) + 2$

(b)   $f$ is reflected through the $x$-axis   $\Rightarrow$   $y = -f(x)$

(c)   $f$ is reflected through the $x$-axis and shifted left 4 units and up 2   $\Rightarrow$   $y = -f(x + 4) + 2$

**47**   $f(x) = \begin{cases} 3 & \text{if } x \le -1 \\ -2 & \text{if } x > -1 \end{cases}$   •   We can think of $f$ as 2 functions: If $x \le -1$, then $y = 3$ {include the point $(-1, 3)$}, and if $x > -1$, then $y = -2$ {exclude the point $(-1, -2)$}.

*Figure 47*

*Figure 48*

**48**   $f(x) = \begin{cases} -1 & \text{if } x \text{ is an integer} \\ -2 & \text{if } x \text{ is not an integer} \end{cases}$   •   Solid dots at every integer. The line $y = -2$ with holes at every integer

**49** $f(x) = \begin{cases} 3 & \text{if } x < -2 \\ -x+1 & \text{if } |x| \le 2 \\ -4 & \text{if } x > 2 \end{cases}$  •

For the second part of the function, we have $|x| \le 2$, or, equivalently, $-2 \le x \le 2$. On this part of the domain, we want to graph $f(x) = -x+1$, a line with slope $-1$ and $y$-intercept $1$. Include both endpoints, $(-2, 3)$ and $(2, -1)$.

*Figure 49*

*Figure 50*

**50** $f(x) = \begin{cases} -2x & \text{if } x < -1 \\ x^2 & \text{if } -1 \le x < 1 \\ -2 & \text{if } x \ge 1 \end{cases}$  •

A line with slope $-2$ and endpoint $(-1, 2)$
A parabola portion with open endpoint $(-1, 1)$ and endpoint $(1, 1)$
A horizontal line with endpoint $(1, -2)$

**51** $f(x) = \begin{cases} x+2 & \text{if } x \le -1 \\ x^3 & \text{if } |x| < 1 \\ -x+3 & \text{if } x \ge 1 \end{cases}$  •

If $x \le -1$, we want the graph of $y = x+2$. To determine the endpoint of this part of the graph, merely substitute $x = -1$ in $y = x+2$, obtaining $y = 1$. If $|x| < 1$, or, equivalently, $-1 < x < 1$, we want the graph of $y = x^3$. We do not include the endpoints $(-1, -1)$ and $(1, 1)$. If $x \ge 1$, we want the graph of $y = -x+3$ and include its endpoint $(1, 2)$.

*Figure 51*

*Figure 52*

**52** $f(x) = \begin{cases} x-3 & \text{if } x \le -2 \\ -x^2 & \text{if } -2 < x < 1 \\ -x+4 & \text{if } x \ge 1 \end{cases}$  •

A line with slope $1$ and endpoint $(-2, -5)$
A parabola portion with open endpoints $(-2, -4)$ and $(1, -1)$
A line with slope $-1$ and endpoint $(1, 3)$

**53** (a) $f(x) = [\![x-3]\!]$  •
shift $g(x) = [\![x]\!]$ right 3 units
{see Figure 10 on page 146
of the text}

(b) $f(x) = [\![x]\!] - 3$  •
shift $g(x) = [\![x]\!]$ down 3 units,
which is the same graph as in
part (a).

(c) $f(x) = 2[\![x]\!]$  •
vertically stretch $g(x) = [\![x]\!]$
by a factor of 2

(d) $f(x) = [\![2x]\!]$  •  horizontally compress $g(x) = [\![x]\!]$ by a factor of 2

Alternatively, we could determine the pattern of "steps" for this function by finding the values of $x$ that make $f(x)$ change from 0 to 1, then from 1 to 2, etc. If $2x = 0$, then $x = 0$, and if $2x = 1$, then $x = \frac{1}{2}$.

Thus, the function will equal 0 from $x = 0$ to $x = \frac{1}{2}$ and then jump to 1 at $x = \frac{1}{2}$. If $2x = 2$, then $x = 1$. The pattern is established: each step will be $\frac{1}{2}$ unit long.

(e) $f(x) = [\![-x]\!]$  •  reflect $g(x) = [\![x]\!]$ through the $y$-axis

**54** (a) $f(x) = [\![x + 2]\!]$  •  shift $g(x) = [\![x]\!]$ left 2 units    (b) $f(x) = [\![x]\!] + 2$  •  shift $g(x) = [\![x]\!]$ up 2 units, which is the same graph as in part (a).

(c) $f(x) = \frac{1}{2}[\![x]\!]$  •  vertically compress $g(x) = [\![x]\!]$ by a factor of $1/(1/2) = 2$    (d) $f(x) = [\![\frac{1}{2}x]\!]$  •  horizontally stretch $g(x) = [\![x]\!]$ by a factor of $1/(1/2) = 2$

(e) $f(x) = -[\![-x]\!]$  •  reflect $g(x) = [\![x]\!]$ through the $y$-axis and through the $x$-axis

**55** (a) As $x \to 1^-$, $f(x) \to \underline{0}$    (b) As $x \to 1^+$, $f(x) \to \underline{2}$      (c) As $x \to -2$, $f(x) \to \underline{1}$

    (d) As $x \to \infty$, $f(x) \to \underline{4}$     (e) As $x \to -\infty$, $f(x) \to \underline{-\infty}$

**56** (a) As $x \to 2^-$, $f(x) \to \underline{3}$    (b) As $x \to 2^+$, $f(x) \to \underline{1}$      (c) As $x \to -1$, $f(x) \to \underline{-2}$

    (d) As $x \to \infty$, $f(x) \to \underline{-\infty}$  (e) As $x \to -\infty$, $f(x) \to \underline{4}$

**57** A question you can ask to help determine if a relationship is a function is "If $x$ is a particular value, can I find a *unique* $y$-value?" In this case, if $x$ was 16, then $16 = y^2 \Rightarrow y = \pm 4$. Since we cannot find a *unique* $y$-value, this is not a function. Graphically, {see Figure 3 in Section 2.2 in the text} given any $x$-value greater than 0, there are two points on the graph and a vertical line intersects the graph in more than one point.

**58** The graph of $x = -|y|$ is not the graph of a function because if $x < 0$,

two different points on the graph have $x$-coordinate $x$.

**59** Reflect each portion of the graph that is below the $x$-axis through the $x$-axis.

*Figure 59*

*Figure 60*

**60** Reflect each portion of the graph that is below the $x$-axis through the $x$-axis.

**61** $y = |4 - x^2|$ • First sketch $y = 4 - x^2$, then reflect the portions of the graph below the $x$-axis through the $x$-axis.

*Figure 61*

*Figure 62*

**62** $y = |x^3 - 1|$ • First sketch $y = x^3 - 1$, then reflect the portions of the graph below the $x$-axis through the $x$-axis.

**63** $y = |\sqrt{x} - 2|$ • First sketch $y = \sqrt{x} - 2$, which is the graph of the square root function shifted down 2 units. Then reflect the portions of the graph below the $x$-axis through the $x$-axis.

Figure 63                                             Figure 64

**64** $y = ||x| - 1|$ • First sketch $y = |x| - 1$, which is the graph of the absolute value function shifted down 1 unit. Then reflect the portions of the graph below the $x$-axis through the $x$-axis.

**65** (a) For $y = -2f(x)$, multiply the $y$-coordinates by $-2$. So the given range, $[-4, 8]$, becomes $[-16, 8]$ {note that we changed the order so that $-16$ appears first—listing the range as $[8, -16]$ is incorrect}. The domain {$x$-coordinates} remains the same.                                         $D = [-2, 6], R = [-16, 8]$

(b) For $y = f\left(\frac{1}{2}x\right)$, multiply the $x$-coordinates by 2. The range {$y$-coordinates} remains the same.
$$D = [-4, 12], R = [-4, 8]$$

(c) For $y = f(x - 3) + 1$, add 3 to the $x$-coordinates and add 1 to the $y$-coordinates.        $D = [1, 9], R = [-3, 9]$

(d) For $y = f(x + 2) - 3$, subtract 2 from the $x$-coordinates and subtract 3 from the $y$-coordinates.
$$D = [-4, 4], R = [-7, 5]$$

(e) For $y = f(-x)$, multiply all $x$-coordinates by $-1$.                                $D = [-6, 2], R = [-4, 8]$

(f) For $y = -f(x)$, multiply all $y$-coordinates by $-1$.                                $D = [-2, 6], R = [-8, 4]$

(g) $y = f(|x|)$ • Graphically, we can reflect all points with positive $x$-coordinates through the $y$-axis, so the domain $[-2, 6]$ becomes $[-6, 6]$. Algebraically, we are replacing $x$ with $|x|$, so $-2 \le x \le 6$ becomes $-2 \le |x| \le 6$, which is equivalent to $|x| \le 6$, or, equivalently, $-6 \le x \le 6$. The range stays the same because of the given assumptions: $f(2) = 8$ and $f(6) = -4$; that is, the full range is taken on for $x \ge 0$. Note that the range could not be determined if $f(-2)$ was equal to 8.                                $D = [-6, 6], R = [-8, 4]$

(h) $y = |f(x)|$ • The points with $y$-coordinates having values from $-4$ to 0 will have values from 0 to 4, so the range will be $[0, 8]$.                                $D = [-2, 6], R = [0, 8]$

**66** (a) For $y = \frac{1}{2}f(x)$, multiply the $y$-coordinates by $\frac{1}{2}$.                                $D = [-6, -2], R = [-5, -2]$

(b) For $y = f(2x)$, multiply the $x$-coordinates by $\frac{1}{2}$.                                $D = [-3, -1], R = [-10, -4]$

(c) For $y = f(x - 2) + 5$, add 2 to the $x$-coordinates and add 5 to the $y$-coordinates.        $D = [-4, 0], R = [-5, 1]$

(d) For $y = f(x + 4) - 1$, subtract 4 from the $x$-coordinates and subtract 1 from the $y$-coordinates.
$$D = [-10, -6], R = [-11, -5]$$

(e) For $y = f(-x)$, negate all $x$-coordinates.

(f) For $y = -f(x)$, negate all $y$-coordinates.

$D = [2, 6], R = [-10, -4]$

$D = [-6, -2], R = [4, 10]$

(g) For $y = f(|x|)$, there is no graph since the domain of $f$ consists of only negative values, $-6$ to $-2$, and $|x|$ is never negative.

(h) For $y = |f(x)|$, the negative $y$-coordinates having values from $-10$ to $-4$ will have values from $4$ to $10$.

$D = [-6, -2], R = [4, 10]$

**67** If $x \le 20,000$, then $T(x) = 0.15x$. If $x > 20,000$, then the tax is 15% of the first 20,000, which is 3000, plus 20% of the amount over 20,000, which is $(x - 20,000)$. We may summarize and simplify as follows:

$$T(x) = \begin{cases} 0.15x & \text{if } 0 \le x \le 20,000 \\ 3000 + 0.20(x - 20,000) & \text{if } x > 20,000 \end{cases} = \begin{cases} 0.15x & \text{if } 0 \le x \le 20,000 \\ 3000 + 0.20x - 4000 & \text{if } x > 20,000 \end{cases}$$
$$= \begin{cases} 0.15x & \text{if } 0 \le x \le 20,000 \\ 0.20 - 1000 & \text{if } x > 20,000 \end{cases}$$

**68** If $0 \le x \le 600,000$, then $T(x) = 0.01x$. If $x > 600,000$, then the tax is 1% of the first 600,000, which is 6000, plus 1.25% of the amount over 600,000.

$$T(x) = \begin{cases} 0.01x & \text{if } 0 \le x \le 600,000 \\ 6000 + 0.0125(x - 600,000) & \text{if } x > 600,000 \end{cases} = \begin{cases} 0.01x & \text{if } 0 \le x \le 600,000 \\ 0.0125x - 1500 & \text{if } x > 600,000 \end{cases}$$

**69** The author receives \$1.20 on the first 10,000 copies, \$1.50 on the next 5000, and \$1.80 on each additional copy.

$$R(x) = \begin{cases} 1.20x & \text{if } 0 \le x \le 10,000 \\ 12,000 + 1.50(x - 10,000) & \text{if } 10,000 < x \le 15,000 \\ 19,500 + 1.80(x - 15,000) & \text{if } x > 15,000 \end{cases} = \begin{cases} 1.20x & \text{if } 0 \le x \le 10,000 \\ 1.50x - 3000 & \text{if } 10,000 < x \le 15,000 \\ 1.80x - 7500 & \text{if } x > 15,000 \end{cases}$$

**70** The cost for 1000 kWh is \$57.70 and the cost for 5000 kWh is $57.70 + 4000(\$0.0532) = \$270.50$.

$$C(x) = \begin{cases} 0.0577x & \text{if } 0 \le x \le 1000 \\ 57.70 + 0.0532(x - 1000) & \text{if } 1000 < x \le 5000 \\ 270.50 + 0.0511(x - 5000) & \text{if } x > 5000 \end{cases} = \begin{cases} 0.0577x & \text{if } 0 \le x \le 1000 \\ 4.50 + 0.0532x & \text{if } 1000 < x \le 5000 \\ 15.00 + 0.0511x & \text{if } x > 5000 \end{cases}$$

**71** Assign ABS$(1.3x + 2.8)$ to $Y_1$ and $1.2x + 5$ to $Y_2$. The viewing rectangle $[-10, 50, 10]$ by $[-10, 50, 10]$ shows intersection points at exactly $-3.12$ and $-22$. The solution of $|1.3x + 2.8| < 1.2x + 5$ is the interval $(-3.12, 22)$.

**72** The solutions of $|0.3x| - 2 = 2.5 - 0.63x^2$ are approximately $\pm 2.45$ {by symmetry}.

The solution of $|0.3x| - 2 > 2.5 - 0.63x^2$ is $(-\infty, -2.45) \cup (2.45, \infty)$.

**73** Assign ABS$(1.2x^2 - 10.8)$ to $Y_1$ and $1.36x + 4.08$ to $Y_2$. The standard viewing rectangle $[-15, 15]$ by $[-10, 10]$ shows intersection points at exactly $-3$ and at approximately $1.87$ and $4.13$.

The solution of $|1.2x^2 - 10.8| > 1.36x + 4.08$ is $(-\infty, -3) \cup (-3, 1.87) \cup (4.13, \infty)$.

**74** The solutions of $\left| \sqrt{16 - x^2} - 3 \right| = 0.12x^2 - 0.3$ are approximately $\pm 3.60, \pm 2.25$ {by symmetry}.

The solution of $\left| \sqrt{16 - x^2} - 3 \right| < 0.12x^2 - 0.3$ is $(-3.60, -2.25) \cup (2.25, 3.60)$.

[75] $f(x) = (0.5x^3 - 4x - 5)$ and $g(x) = (0.5x^3 - 4x - 5) + 4 = f(x) + 4$, so the graph of $g$ can be obtained by shifting the graph of $f$ upward a distance of 4.

[−12, 12] by [−8, 8]

Figure 75

[−12, 12] by [−8, 8]

Figure 76

[76] $f(x) = (0.25x^3 - 2x + 1)$ and $g(x) = (-0.25x^3 + 2x - 1) = -f(x)$, so the graph of $g$ can be obtained reflecting the graph of $f$ through the $x$–axis.

[77] $f(x) = x^2 - 5$ and $g(x) = \left(\frac{1}{2}x\right)^2 - 5 = f\left(\frac{1}{2}x\right)$, so the graph of $g$ can be obtained by stretching the graph of $f$ horizontally by a factor of 2.

[−12, 12] by [−8, 8]

Figure 77

[−12, 12] by [−8, 8]

Figure 78

[78] $f(x) = |x + 2|$ and $g(x) = |(x + 2) - 5| - 3 = f(x - 5) - 3$, so the graph of $g$ can be obtained by shifting the graph of $f$ horizontally to the right a distance of 5 and vertically downward a distance of 3.

[79] $f(x) = x^3 - 5x$ and $g(x) = |x^3 - 5x| = |f(x)|$, so the graph of $g$ is the same as the graph of $f$ if $f$ is nonnegative. If $f(x) < 0$, then the graph of $f$ will be reflected through the $x$–axis.

[−12, 12] by [−8, 8]

Figure 79

[−12, 12] by [−8, 8]

Figure 80

[80] $f(x) = (0.5x^2 - 2x - 5)$ and $g(x) = (0.5x^2 + 2x - 5) = f(-x)$, so the graph of $g$ can be obtained from the graph of $f$ by reflecting the graph of $f$ through the $y$–axis.

[81] (a) Option I gives $C_1 = 4(\$45.00) + \$0.40(500 - 200) = 180.00 + 120.00 = \$300.00$.

Option II gives $C_2 = 4(\$58.75) + \$0.25(500) = 235.00 + 125.00 = \$360.00$.

(b) Let $x$ represent the mileage. The cost function for Option I is the piecewise linear function

$$C_1(x) = \begin{cases} 180.00 & \text{if } 0 \le x \le 200 \\ 180.00 + 0.40(x - 200) & \text{if } x > 200 \end{cases}$$

Option II is the linear function $C_2(x) = 235.00 + 0.25x$ for $x \ge 0$.

(c) Let $C_1 = Y_1$ and $C_2 = Y_2$. Table $Y_1 = 180.00 + 0.40(x - 200)*(x > 200)$ and $Y_2 = 235.00 + 0.25x$

| $x$ | 100 | 200 | 300 | 400 | 500 | 600 | 700 | 800 | 900 | 1000 | 1100 | 1200 |
|---|---|---|---|---|---|---|---|---|---|---|---|---|
| $Y_1$ | 180 | 180 | 220 | 260 | 300 | 340 | 380 | 420 | 460 | 500 | 540 | 580 |
| $Y_2$ | 260 | 285 | 310 | 335 | 360 | 385 | 410 | 435 | 460 | 485 | 510 | 535 |

(d) From the table, we see that the options are equal in cost for $x = 900$ miles. Option I is preferable if $x \in [0, 900)$ and Option II is preferable if $x > 900$.

**82** (a) Since 1 mi $= 5{,}280$ ft and each car requires $(12 + d)$ ft, it follows directly that the bridge can hold $[\![5280/(12 + d)]\!]$ cars. The greatest integer function is necessary since a fraction of a car is not allowed.

(b) Since the bridge is 1 mile long, the car "density" is $\dfrac{5280}{12 + d}$ cars/mi. If each car is moving at $v$ mi/hr, then the flow rate is $F = [\![5280v/(12 + d)]\!]$ cars/hr.

## 2.6 Exercises

**1** Using the standard equation of a parabola with a vertical axis having vertex $V(-3, 1)$, we have $y = a[x - (-3)]^2 + 1$. The coefficient $a$ determines whether the parabola opens upward {if $a$ is positive} or opens downward {if $a$ is negative}. If $|a| > 1$, then the parabola is narrower {steeper} than the graph of $y = x^2$; if $|a| < 1$, then the parabola is wider {flatter} than the graph of $y = x^2$. Simplifying the equation gives us $y = a(x + 3)^2 + 1$.

**2** $V(5, -4) \bullet y = a(x - h)^2 + k \Rightarrow y = a(x - 5)^2 - 4$

**3** $V(0, -2) \bullet$ We can use the standard equation of a parabola with a vertical axis.
$$y = a(x - h)^2 + k \Rightarrow y = a(x - 0)^2 - 2 \Rightarrow y = ax^2 - 2.$$

**4** $V(-7, 0) \bullet y = a(x - h)^2 + k \Rightarrow y = a[x - (-7)]^2 + 0 \Rightarrow y = a(x + 7)^2$

**5** The approach shown here {like Solution 1 in Example 2} requires us to *factor out the leading coefficient*.

$$
\begin{aligned}
f(x) &= -x^2 - 4x - 5 && \{\text{given}\} \\
&= -\left(x^2 + 4x + \underline{\phantom{00}}\right) - 5 + \underline{\phantom{00}} && \{\text{factor out } -1 \text{ from } -x^2 - 4x\} \\
&= -\left(x^2 + 4x + \underline{4}\right) - 5 + \underline{4} && \{\text{complete the square for } x^2 + 4x\} \\
&= -(x + 2)^2 - 1 && \{\text{equivalent equation}\}
\end{aligned}
$$

**6** $f(x) = x^2 - 6x + 11 = x^2 - 6x + \underline{9} + 11 - \underline{9} = (x - 3)^2 + 2$

**7** The approach shown here {like Solution 2 in Example 2} requires us to *divide both sides by the leading coefficient*—remember to multiply both sides by the same coefficient in the end. Either method is fine.

$$
\begin{aligned}
f(x) &= 2x^2 - 16x + 35 && \{\text{given}\} \\
\tfrac{1}{2}f(x) &= \left(x^2 - 8x + \underline{\phantom{00}}\right) + \tfrac{35}{2} - \underline{\phantom{00}} && \{\text{divide the equation by 2}\} \\
&= \left(x^2 - 8x + \underline{16}\right) + \tfrac{35}{2} - \underline{16} && \{\text{complete the square for } x^2 - 8x\} \\
&= (x - 4)^2 + \tfrac{3}{2} && \{\text{equivalent equation}\} \\
2 \cdot \tfrac{1}{2}f(x) &= 2 \cdot \left[(x - 4)^2 + \tfrac{3}{2}\right] && \{\text{multiply the equation by 2}\} \\
f(x) &= 2(x - 4)^2 + 3 && \{\text{the desired standard form}\}
\end{aligned}
$$

**8** $f(x) = 5x^2 + 20x + 14 \ \Rightarrow \ \frac{1}{5}f(x) = x^2 + 4x + \underline{4} + \frac{14}{5} - \underline{4} = (x+2)^2 - \frac{6}{5} \ \Rightarrow$

$$5 \cdot \frac{1}{5}f(x) = 5 \cdot \left[(x+2)^2 - \frac{6}{5}\right] \ \Rightarrow \ f(x) = 5(x+2)^2 - 6$$

**9** $f(x) = -3x^2 - 6x - 5$ {divide by $-3$ and proceed as in Exercise 7} $\ \Rightarrow$

$-\frac{1}{3}f(x) = x^2 + 2x + \underline{1} + \frac{5}{3} - \underline{1} = (x+1)^2 + \frac{2}{3} \ \Rightarrow$

$$-3 \cdot \left(-\frac{1}{3}\right)f(x) = -3 \cdot \left[(x+1)^2 + \frac{2}{3}\right] \ \Rightarrow \ f(x) = -3(x+1)^2 - 2$$

**10** $f(x) = -4x^2 + 16x - 13 \ \Rightarrow \ -\frac{1}{4}f(x) = x^2 - 4x + \underline{4} + \frac{13}{4} - \underline{4} = (x-2)^2 - \frac{3}{4} \ \Rightarrow$

$$-4 \cdot \left(-\frac{1}{4}\right)f(x) = -4 \cdot \left[(x-2)^2 - \frac{3}{4}\right] \ \Rightarrow \ f(x) = -4(x-2)^2 + 3$$

**11** $f(x) = -\frac{3}{4}x^2 + 9x - 34$ {divide by $-\frac{3}{4}$ and proceed as in Exercise 7} $\ \Rightarrow$

$-\frac{4}{3}f(x) = x^2 - 12x + \frac{136}{3} = x^2 - 12x + \underline{36} + \frac{136}{3} - \underline{36} = (x-6)^2 + \frac{28}{3} \ \Rightarrow$

$$\left(-\frac{3}{4}\right)\left(-\frac{4}{3}\right)f(x) = \left(-\frac{3}{4}\right)\left[(x-6)^2 + \frac{28}{3}\right] \ \Rightarrow \ f(x) = -\frac{3}{4}(x-6)^2 - 7$$

**12** $f(x) = \frac{2}{5}x^2 - \frac{12}{5}x + \frac{23}{5} \ \Rightarrow \ \frac{5}{2}f(x) = x^2 - 6x + \frac{23}{2} = x^2 - 6x + \underline{9} + \frac{23}{2} - \underline{9} = (x-3)^2 + \frac{5}{2} \ \Rightarrow$

$$\frac{2}{5} \cdot \frac{5}{2}f(x) = \frac{2}{5} \cdot \left[(x-3)^2 + \frac{5}{2}\right] \ \Rightarrow \ f(x) = \frac{2}{5}(x-3)^2 + 1$$

**13** (a) $x^2 - 6x = 0$ {$a = 1, b = -6, c = 0$} $\ \Rightarrow \ x = \dfrac{6 \pm \sqrt{36 - 0}}{2} = \dfrac{6 \pm 6}{2} = 0, 6$

(b) Using the theorem for locating the vertex of a parabola with $y = x^2 - 6x$ gives us $x$-coordinate $-\dfrac{b}{2a} = -\dfrac{-6}{2(1)} = 3$. The parabola opens upward since $a = 1 > 0$, so there is a minimum value of $y$. To find the minimum, substitute 3 for $x$ in $f(x) = x^2 - 6x$ to get $f(3) = -9$.

Figure 13

Figure 14

**14** (a) $-x^2 - 6x = 0$ {$a = -1, b = -6, c = 0$} $\ \Rightarrow \ x = \dfrac{6 \pm \sqrt{36 - 0}}{-2} = -6, 0$

(b) $f(x) = -x^2 - 6x \ \Rightarrow \ -\dfrac{b}{2a} = -\dfrac{-6}{2(-1)} = -3.$ $f(-3) = 9$ is a maximum since $a < 0$.

**15** (a) $f(x) = -12x^2 + 11x + 15 = 0 \ \Rightarrow \ x = \dfrac{-11 \pm \sqrt{121 + 720}}{-24} = \dfrac{-11 \pm 29}{-24} = -\dfrac{3}{4}, \dfrac{5}{3}$

(b) The $x$-coordinate of the vertex is given by $x = -\dfrac{b}{2a} = -\dfrac{11}{2(-12)} = \dfrac{11}{24}$. Note that this value is easily obtained from part (a). The $y$-coordinate of the vertex is then $f\left(\frac{11}{24}\right) = \frac{841}{48} \approx 17.52$. This is a maximum since $a = -12 < 0$.

Figure 15

Figure 16

**16** (a) $6x^2 + 7x - 24 = 0 \implies x = \dfrac{-7 \pm \sqrt{49 + 576}}{12} = \dfrac{-7 \pm 25}{12} = -\dfrac{8}{3}, \dfrac{3}{2}$

(b) $f(x) = 6x^2 + 7x - 24 \implies -\dfrac{b}{2a} = -\dfrac{7}{2(6)} = -\dfrac{7}{12}$. $f\left(-\dfrac{7}{12}\right) = -\dfrac{625}{24} \approx -26.04$ is a minimum since $a > 0$.

**17** (a) $9x^2 + 24x + 16 = 0 \implies x = \dfrac{-24 \pm \sqrt{576 - 576}}{18} = \dfrac{-24}{18} = -\dfrac{4}{3}$

(b) $f(x) = 9x^2 + 24x + 16 \implies -\dfrac{b}{2a} = -\dfrac{24}{2(9)} = -\dfrac{4}{3}$. $f\left(-\dfrac{4}{3}\right) = 0$ is a minimum since $a > 0$.

Figure 17

Figure 18

**18** (a) $-4x^2 + 4x - 1 = 0 \implies x = \dfrac{-4 \pm \sqrt{16 - 16}}{-8} = \dfrac{-4}{-8} = \dfrac{1}{2}$

(b) $f(x) = -4x^2 + 4x - 1 \implies -\dfrac{b}{2a} = -\dfrac{4}{2(-4)} = \dfrac{1}{2}$. $f\left(\dfrac{1}{2}\right) = 0$ is a maximum since $a < 0$.

**19** (a) $x^2 + 4x + 9 = 0 \implies x = \dfrac{-4 \pm \sqrt{16 - 36}}{2} = \dfrac{-4 \pm \sqrt{-20}}{2} = -2 \pm \sqrt{5}\,i$.

The imaginary part indicates that there are no $x$-intercepts.

(b) $f(x) = x^2 + 4x + 9 \implies -\dfrac{b}{2a} = -\dfrac{4}{2(1)} = -2$. $f(-2) = 5$ is a minimum since $a = 1 > 0$.

Figure 19

Figure 20

**20** (a) $-3x^2 - 6x - 6 = 0 \Rightarrow x = \dfrac{6 \pm \sqrt{36 - 72}}{-6} = \dfrac{6 \pm \sqrt{-36}}{-6} = \dfrac{6 \pm 6i}{-6} = -1 \pm i.$

The imaginary part indicates that there are no $x$-intercepts. See *Figure 20* on the preceding page.

(b) $f(x) = -3x^2 - 6x - 6 \Rightarrow -\dfrac{b}{2a} = -\dfrac{-6}{2(-3)} = -1.$ $f(-1) = -3$ is a maximum since $a < 0$.

**21** (a) $-2x^2 + 16x - 26 = 0 \Rightarrow x = \dfrac{-16 \pm \sqrt{256 - 208}}{-4} = 4 \pm \dfrac{1}{4}\sqrt{48} = 4 \pm \sqrt{3} \approx 5.73, 2.27$

(b) $f(x) = -2x^2 + 16x - 26 \Rightarrow -\dfrac{b}{2a} = -\dfrac{16}{2(-2)} = 4.$ $f(4) = 6$ is a maximum since $a < 0$.

*Figure 21*

*Figure 22*

**22** (a) $2x^2 - 4x - 11 = 0 \Rightarrow x = \dfrac{4 \pm \sqrt{16 + 88}}{4} = 1 \pm \dfrac{1}{2}\sqrt{26} \approx 3.55, -1.55$

(b) $f(x) = 2x^2 - 4x - 11 \Rightarrow -\dfrac{b}{2a} = -\dfrac{-4}{2(2)} = 1.$ $f(1) = -13$ is a minimum since $a > 0$.

**23** $V(4, -1) \Rightarrow y = a(x - 4)^2 - 1.$ Substituting 0 for $x$ and 1 for $y$ gives us

$1 = a(0 - 4)^2 - 1 \Rightarrow 2 = 16a \Rightarrow a = \frac{1}{8}.$ Hence, $y = \frac{1}{8}(x - 4)^2 - 1.$

**24** $V(2, 4) \Rightarrow y = a(x - 2)^2 + 4.$ Substituting 0 for $x$ and 0 for $y$ gives us

$0 = a(0 - 2)^2 + 4 \Rightarrow -4 = 4a \Rightarrow a = -1.$ Hence, $y = -(x - 2)^2 + 4.$

**25** $V(-2, 5) \Rightarrow y = a(x + 2)^2 + 5.$ Substituting 2 for $x$ and 0 for $y$ gives us

$0 = a(2 + 2)^2 + 5 \Rightarrow -5 = 16a \Rightarrow a = -\frac{5}{16}.$ Hence, $y = -\frac{5}{16}(x + 2)^2 + 5.$

**26** $V(-1, -2) \Rightarrow y = a(x + 1)^2 - 2.$ Substituting 2 for $x$ and 3 for $y$ gives us

$3 = a(2 + 1)^2 - 2 \Rightarrow 5 = 9a \Rightarrow a = \frac{5}{9}.$ Hence, $y = \frac{5}{9}(x + 1)^2 - 2.$

**27** From the figure, the $x$-intercepts are $-2$ and $4$, so the equation must have the form

$y = a[x - (-2)](x - 4) = a(x + 2)(x - 4).$ To find the value of $a$, use the point $(2, 4)$.

$4 = a(2 + 2)(2 - 4) \Rightarrow 4 = a(4)(-2) \Rightarrow -8a = 4 \Rightarrow a = -\frac{1}{2},$

so the equation is $y = -\frac{1}{2}(x + 2)(x - 4).$

**28** $y = a(x + 3)(x - 7) \bullet x = 5, y = -4 \Rightarrow -4 = a(8)(-2) \Rightarrow a = \frac{1}{4},$

so the equation is $y = \frac{1}{4}(x + 3)(x - 7).$

**29** $V(0, -2) \Rightarrow (h, k) = (0, -2).$ $x = 3, y = 25 \Rightarrow 25 = a(3 - 0)^2 - 2 \Rightarrow 27 = 9a \Rightarrow a = 3.$

Hence, $y = 3(x - 0)^2 - 2,$ or $y = 3x^2 - 2.$

**30** $V(0, 7) \Rightarrow (h, k) = (0, 7).$ $x = 2, y = -1 \Rightarrow -1 = a(2 - 0)^2 + 7 \Rightarrow -8 = 4a \Rightarrow a = -2.$

Hence, $y = -2(x - 0)^2 + 7,$ or $y = -2x^2 + 7.$

31 $V(3, 1) \Rightarrow y = a(x - 3)^2 + 1$ **(*)**. If the $x$-intercept is 0, then the point $(0, 0)$ is on the parabola. Substituting $x = 0$ and $y = 0$ into **(*)** gives us $0 = a(0 - 3)^2 + 1 \Rightarrow -1 = 9a \Rightarrow a = -\frac{1}{9}$. Hence, $y = -\frac{1}{9}(x - 3)^2 + 1$.

32 $V(4, -7) \Rightarrow y = a(x - 4)^2 - 7$. $x = -4, y = 0 \Rightarrow 0 = a(-4 - 4)^2 - 7 \Rightarrow 7 = 64a \Rightarrow a = \frac{7}{64}$.

Hence, $y = \frac{7}{64}(x - 4)^2 - 7$.

33 Since the $x$-intercepts are $-3$ and 5, the $x$-coordinate of the vertex of the parabola is 1 {the average of the $x$-intercept values}. Since the highest point has $y$-coordinate 4, the vertex is $(1, 4)$.

$V(1, 4) \Rightarrow y = a(x - 1)^2 + 4$. We can use the point $(-3, 0)$ since there is an $x$-intercept of $-3$.

$x = -3, y = 0 \Rightarrow 0 = a(-3 - 1)^2 + 4 \Rightarrow -4 = 16a \Rightarrow a = -\frac{1}{4}$. Hence, $y = -\frac{1}{4}(x - 1)^2 + 4$.

34 Since the $x$-intercepts are 8 and 0, the $x$-coordinate of the vertex of the parabola is 4 {the average of the $x$-intercept values}. Since the lowest point has $y$-coordinate $-48$, the vertex is $(4, -48)$.

$V(4, -48) \Rightarrow y = a(x - 4)^2 - 48$. $x = 0, y = 0 \Rightarrow 0 = a(0 - 4)^2 - 48 \Rightarrow 48 = 16a \Rightarrow a = 3$.

Hence, $y = 3(x - 4)^2 - 48$.

35 Let $d$ denote the distance between the parabola and the line.

$$d = (\text{parabola}) - (\text{line}) = (-2x^2 + 4x + 3) - (x - 2) = -2x^2 + 3x + 5.$$

This relation is quadratic and the $x$-value of its maximum value is $-\dfrac{b}{2a} = -\dfrac{3}{2(-2)} = \dfrac{3}{4}$.

Thus, maximum $d = -2\left(\frac{3}{4}\right)^2 + 3\left(\frac{3}{4}\right) + 5 = \frac{49}{8} = 6.125$. Note that the maximum value *of the parabola* is $f(1) = 5$, which is not the same as the maximum value of the distance $d$.

36 As in Exercise 35, $d = (\text{line}) - (\text{parabola}) = (-x + 3) - (2x^2 + 8x + 4) = -2x^2 - 9x - 1$, and

$$-\frac{b}{2a} = -\frac{-9}{2(-2)} = -\frac{9}{4}. \text{ Thus, maximum } d = -2\left(-\frac{9}{4}\right)^2 - 9\left(-\frac{9}{4}\right) - 1 = \frac{73}{8} = 9.125.$$

**Note:** We may find the vertex of a parabola in the following problems using either:

1) the complete the square method,
2) the formula method, $-b/(2a)$, or
3) the fact that the vertex lies halfway between the $x$-intercepts.

37 For $D(h) = -0.058h^2 + 2.867h - 24.239$, the vertex is located at $h = \dfrac{-b}{2a} = \dfrac{-2.867}{2(-0.058)} \approx 24.72$ km.

Since $a < 0$, this will produce a maximum value.

38 The vertex is located at $h = \dfrac{-b}{2a} = \dfrac{-3.811}{2(-0.078)} \approx 24.43$ km. Since $a < 0$, this will produce a maximum value.

39 Since the $x$-intercepts of $y = cx(21 - x)$ are 0 and 21,

the maximum will occur halfway between them, that is, when the infant weighs 10.5 lb.

40 (a) $M = -\frac{1}{30}v^2 + \frac{5}{2}v$ • $M$ will be a maximum when $v = \dfrac{-b}{2a} = \dfrac{-5/2}{2(-1/30)} = \dfrac{75}{2}$, or 37.5 mi/hr.

(b) $v = \frac{75}{2} \Rightarrow M = -\frac{1}{30}\left(\frac{75}{2}\right)^2 + \frac{5}{2}\left(\frac{75}{2}\right) = -\frac{375}{8} + \frac{375}{4} = \frac{375}{8} = 46.875$ mi/gal.

41 (a) $s(t) = -16t^2 + 144t + 100$ • $s$ will be a maximum when $t = \dfrac{-b}{2a} = \dfrac{-144}{2(-16)} = \dfrac{9}{2}$.

$$s\left(\tfrac{9}{2}\right) = -16\left(\tfrac{9}{2}\right)^2 + 144\left(\tfrac{9}{2}\right) + 100 = -324 + 648 + 100 = 424 \text{ ft}.$$

(b) When $t = 0$, $s(t) = 100$ ft, which is the height of the building.

**42** (a) $s(t) = -16t^2 + v_0 t$  •  $s = 0$ when $t = 12$  $\Rightarrow$  $0 = -16(12)^2 + v_0(12)$  $\Rightarrow$  $v_0 = 192$ ft/sec.

(b) Since the total flight is 12 seconds, the maximum height will occur when $t = 6$.

$$s(6) = -16(6)^2 + 192(6) = 576 \text{ ft.}$$

**43** Let $x$ and $40 - x$ denote the numbers. Their product $P$ is $P = x(40 - x) = -x^2 + 40x$.

$P$ has zeros at 0 and 40 and is a maximum (since $a < 0$) when $x = \dfrac{0 + 40}{2} = 20$.

The product will be a maximum when both numbers are 20.

**44** Let $x$ and $x - 60$ denote the numbers. Their product $P$ is $P = x(x - 60) = x^2 - 60x$.

$P$ has zeros at 0 and 60 and is a minimum (since $a > 0$) when $x = \dfrac{0 + 60}{2} = 30$.

The product will be a minimum for $x = 30$ and $x - 60 = -30$.

**45** (a) The 1000 ft of fence is made up of 3 sides of length $x$ and 4 sides of length $y$.

To express $y$ as a function of $x$, we need to solve $3x + 4y = 1000$ for $y$.

$$3x + 4y = 1000 \quad \Rightarrow \quad 4y = 1000 - 3x \quad \Rightarrow \quad y = 250 - \tfrac{3}{4}x.$$

(b) Using the value of $y$ from part (a), $A = xy = x\left(250 - \tfrac{3}{4}x\right) = -\tfrac{3}{4}x^2 + 250x$.

(c) $A$ will be a maximum when $x = \dfrac{-b}{2a} = \dfrac{-250}{2(-3/4)} = \dfrac{500}{3} = 166\tfrac{2}{3}$ ft.

Using part (a) to find the corresponding value of $y$, $y = 250 - \tfrac{3}{4}\left(\tfrac{500}{3}\right) = 250 - 125 = 125$ ft.

**46** Represent the perimeter of the field by $2y + 4x = 1000$. $A = xy = x(500 - 2x)$.

$A$ has zeros at 0 and 250 and will be a maximum when $x = \dfrac{0 + 250}{2} = 125$ yd. $y = 500 - 2(125) = 250$ yd.

The dimensions should be 125 yd by 250 yd with intermediate fences parallel to the short side.

**47** The parabola has vertex $V\left(\tfrac{9}{2}, 3\right)$. Hence, the equation has the form $y = a\left(x - \tfrac{9}{2}\right)^2 + 3$.

Using the point $(9, 0)$ {or $(0, 0)$}, we have $0 = a\left(9 - \tfrac{9}{2}\right)^2 + 3$  $\Rightarrow$  $a = -\tfrac{4}{27}$.

Thus, the path may be described by $y = -\tfrac{4}{27}\left(x - \tfrac{9}{2}\right)^2 + 3$.

**48** (a) $y = ax^2 + x + c$  •  Since $(0, 15)$ is on the graph, $c = 15$. Substituting $(175, 0)$ for $(x, y)$ yields

$$0 = a(175)^2 + 175 + 15 \quad \Rightarrow \quad a = -\frac{190}{175^2} \text{ and } y = -\frac{190}{175^2}x^2 + x + 15.$$

(b) $y$ will be a maximum when $x = \dfrac{-b}{2a} = \dfrac{-1}{2(-190/175^2)} = \dfrac{175^2}{380} \approx 80.59$.

The corresponding $y$-value is $y = -\dfrac{190}{175^2}\left(\dfrac{175^2}{380}\right)^2 + \dfrac{175^2}{380} + 15 = \dfrac{8405}{152} \approx 55.3$ ft.

**49** (a) Since the vertex is at $(0, 10)$, an equation for the parabola is $y = ax^2 + 10$.

The points $(200, 90)$ and $(-200, 90)$ are on the parabola. Substituting $(200, 90)$ for $(x, y)$ yields

$$90 = a(200)^2 + 10 \quad \Rightarrow \quad 80 = 40{,}000a \quad \Rightarrow \quad a = \tfrac{80}{40{,}000} = \tfrac{1}{500}. \text{ Hence, } y = \tfrac{1}{500}x^2 + 10.$$

(b) The cables are spaced 40 ft apart. Using $y = \tfrac{1}{500}x^2 + 10$ with $x = 40, 80, 120,$ and 160, we get

$y = \tfrac{66}{5}, \tfrac{114}{5}, \tfrac{194}{5}$, and $\tfrac{306}{5}$, respectively. There is one cable of length 10 ft and 2 cables of each of the other lengths. Thus, the total length is $10 + 2\left(\tfrac{66}{5} + \tfrac{114}{5} + \tfrac{194}{5} + \tfrac{306}{5}\right) = 282$ ft.

**50** (a) Substituting $x = 0$ and $m = 0$ into $m = 2ax + b$ yields $b = 0$.

Substituting $x = 800$ and $m = \tfrac{1}{5}$ into $m = 2ax$ yields $a = \tfrac{1}{8000}$, hence, $y = \tfrac{1}{8000}x^2$.

(b) Substitute $x = 800$ into $y = \tfrac{1}{8000}x^2$ to get $y = 80$. Thus, $B = (800, 80)$.

[51] An equation describing the doorway is $y = ax^2 + 9$. Since the doorway is 6 feet wide at the base, $x = 3$ when $y = 0 \Rightarrow 0 = a(3)^2 + 9 \Rightarrow 0 = 9a + 9 \Rightarrow 9a = -9 \Rightarrow a = -1$. Thus, the equation is $y = -x^2 + 9$. To fit an 8 foot high box through the doorway, we must find $x$ when $y = 8$. If $y = 8$, then $8 = -x^2 + 9 \Rightarrow x^2 = 1 \Rightarrow x = \pm 1$. Hence, the box can only be $1 - (-1) = 2$ feet wide.

[52] (a) The maximum height of the baseball occurs at the vertex of the parabola.

The horizontal $(x)$ coordinate of the vertex is $x = -\frac{b}{2a} = -\frac{3/10}{-3/4000} = 200$, so the corresponding

vertical $(y)$ coordinate is $y = -\frac{3}{4000}(200)^2 + \frac{3}{10}(200) + 3 = 33$. The maximum height is 33 feet.

(b) The height of the baseball when $x = 385$ is $y = -\frac{3}{4000}(385)^2 + \frac{3}{10}(385) + 3 \approx 7.33$, which is less than 8, so no, the baseball does not clear an 8-foot fence that is 385 feet from home plate.

[53] Let $x$ denote the number of pairs of shoes that are ordered. If $x < 50$, then the amount $A$ of money that the company makes is $40x$. If $50 \le x \le 600$, then each pair of shoes is discounted $0.04x$, so the price per pair is $40 - 0.04x$, and the amount of money that the company makes is $(40 - 0.04x)x$. In piecewise form, we have

$$A(x) = \begin{cases} 40x & \text{if } x < 50 \\ (40 - 0.04x)x & \text{if } 50 \le x \le 600 \end{cases}$$

The maximum value of the first part of $A$ is $(\$40)(49) = \$1960$. For the second part of $A$, $A = -0.04x^2 + 40x$ has a maximum when $x = \dfrac{-b}{2a} = \dfrac{-40}{2(-0.04)} = 500$ pairs.

$$A(500) = 10{,}000 > 1960, \text{ so } x = 500 \text{ produces a maximum for both parts of } A.$$

[54] Let $x$ denote the number of people in the group. The discount per person is $0.50(x - 30)$. The amount of money taken in by the agency may be expressed as:

$$A(x) = \begin{cases} 60x & \text{if } x \le 30 \\ [60 - 0.50(x - 30)]x & \text{if } 30 < x \le 90 \end{cases}$$

The maximum value of the first part of $A$ is $(\$60)(30) = \$1800$. For the second part of $A$, $A = \left(75 - \frac{1}{2}x\right)x$ has a maximum when $x = 75$ {the $x$-intercepts are 0 and 150}. This value corresponds to each person receiving a discount of $\$22.50$ and hence, paying $\$37.50$ for the tour. $A(75) = 2812.50 > 1800$, so $x = 75$ produces a maximum for both parts of $A$.

[55] (a) Let $y$ denote the number of \$5 decreases in the monthly charge.

$$R(y) = (\text{\# of customers})(\text{monthly charge per customer}) = (8000 + 1000y)(50 - 5y)$$

Now let $x$ denote the monthly charge, which is $50 - 5y$. $x = 50 - 5y \Rightarrow 5y = 50 - x \Rightarrow y = \dfrac{50 - x}{5}$.

$R$ becomes

$$\left[8000 + 1000\left(\frac{50 - x}{5}\right)\right](x) = [8000 + 200(50 - x)](x) = 200x[40 + (50 - x)] = 200x(90 - x).$$

(b) $R$ has $x$-intercepts at 0 and 90, and must have its vertex halfway between them at $x = 45$.

Note that this gives us $y = \dfrac{50 - 45}{5} = 1$, and we have

$8000 + 1000(1) = 9000$ customers for a revenue of

$(9000)(\$45) = \$405{,}000$.

**56** Let $x$ denote the number of $25 increases in rent and $M(x)$ the monthly income. The number of occupied apartments is $218 - 5x$ and the rent per apartment is $940 + 25x$.

$$M(x) = (\text{\# of occupied apartments})(\text{rent per apartment}) = (218 - 5x)(940 + 25x) = 5(218 - 5x)(188 + 5x).$$

The $x$-intercepts of $M$ are $\frac{218}{5}$ and $-\frac{188}{5}$. Hence, the maximum of $M$ will occur when

$$x = \tfrac{1}{2}\left(-\tfrac{188}{5} + \tfrac{218}{5}\right) = \tfrac{1}{2}(6) = 3. \text{ The rent charged should be } \$940 + \$25(3) = \$1015.$$

**57** From the graph of $f(x) = x^2 - x - \frac{1}{4}$ and $y = x^3 - x^{1/3}$, there are three points of intersection. Their coordinates are approximately $(-0.57, 0.64)$, $(0.02, -0.27)$, and $(0.81, -0.41)$.

$[-3, 3]$ by $[-2, 2]$

*Figure 57*

$[-6, 6]$ by $[-4, 4]$

*Figure 58*

**58** From the graph of $f(x) = -x^2 + 0.5x + 0.4$ and $y = x^3 - x^{1/3}$, there are three points of intersection. Their coordinates are approximately $(-1.61, -2.99)$, $(-0.05, 0.37)$, and $(0.98, -0.06)$.

**59** $y = ax^2 + x + 1$ for $a = \frac{1}{4}, \frac{1}{2}, 1, 2,$ and $4$  •  Since $a > 0$, all parabolas open upward. From the graph, we can see that smaller values of $a$ result in the parabola opening wider while larger values of $a$ result in the parabola becoming narrower.

$[-8, 4]$ by $[-1, 7]$

*Figure 59*

$[-6, 6]$ by $[-2, 6]$

*Figure 60*

**60** $y = x^2 + bx + 1$ for $b = 0, \pm 1, \pm 2,$ and $\pm 3$  •  As $|b|$ increases, the graph of each parabola shifts downward. Negative values of $b$ shift the parabola to the right while positive values of $b$ shift the parabola to the left.

**61** (a) Let January correspond to 1, February to 2, . . . , and December to 12.

(b) Let $f(x) = a(x - h)^2 + k$. The vertex appears to occur near $(7, 0.77)$ Thus, $h = 7$ and $k = 0.77$. Using trial and error, a reasonable value for $a$ is 0.17. Thus, let $f(x) = 0.17(x - 7)^2 + 0.77$. {From the TI-83/4 Plus, the quadratic regression equation is $y \approx 0.1676x^2 - 2.1369x + 7.9471$.}

(c) $f(4) \approx 2.3$, compared to the actual value of 2.55 in.

$[0, 13]$ by $[0, 8]$

*Figure 61*

$[1980, 1995]$ by $[5, 15]$

*Figure 62*

**62** (a) Overall, the data decrease slightly and then start to increase, although there is an unexpected decrease in 1987.

(b) Start by choosing a vertex. The lowest data point is $(1984, 7.6)$, so let $h = 1984$ and $k = 7.6$ in the equation $f(x) = a(x - h)^2 + k$. Choosing one more point will determine the parabola.

$f(1993) = 13.3 \implies 13.3 = a(1993 - 1984)^2 + 7.6 \implies a \approx 0.07$.

Let $f(x) = 0.07(x - 1984)^2 + 7.6$. $f$ can be adjusted to give a slightly better fit.

**63** (a) The equation of the line passing through $A(-800, -48)$ and $B(-500, 0)$ is $y = \frac{4}{25}x + 80$.

The equation of the line passing through $D(500, 0)$ and $E(800, -48)$ is $y = -\frac{4}{25}x + 80$.

Let $y = a(x - h)^2 + k$ be the equation of the parabola passing through the points $B(-500, 0)$, $C(0, 40)$, and $D(500, 0)$. The vertex is located at $(0, 40)$ so $y = a(x - 0)^2 + 40$. Since $D(500, 0)$ is on the graph, $0 = a(500 - 0)^2 + 40 \implies a = -\frac{1}{6250}$ and $y = -\frac{1}{6250}x^2 + 40$. Thus, let

$$f(x) = \begin{cases} \frac{4}{25}x + 80 & \text{if } -800 \le x < -500 \\ -\frac{1}{6250}x^2 + 40 & \text{if } -500 \le x \le 500 \\ -\frac{4}{25}x + 80 & \text{if } 500 < x \le 800 \end{cases}$$

(b) Graph the equations: $Y_1 = (4/25 * x + 80)/(x < -500)$,

$Y_2 = (-1/6250 * x\hat{\,}2 + 40)/(x \ge -500 \text{ and } x \le 500)$, $Y_3 = (-4/25 * x + 80)/(x > 500)$

$[-800, 800, 100]$ by $[-100, 200, 100]$      $[-500, 2000, 500]$ by $[0, 800, 100]$

*Figure 63*

*Figure 64*

**64** (a) The equation of the line passing through $A\left(-500, 243\frac{1}{3}\right)$ and $B(0, 110)$ is $y = -\frac{4}{15}x + 110$.

The equation of the line passing through $D(1500, 110)$ and $E\left(2000, 243\frac{1}{3}\right)$ is $y = \frac{4}{15}x - 290$.

Let $y = a(x - h)^2 + k$ be the equation of the parabola passing through the points $B(0, 110)$, $C(750, 10)$, and $D(1500, 110)$. The vertex is located at $(750, 10)$ so $y = a(x - 750)^2 + 10$. Since $D(1500, 110)$ is on the graph, $110 = a(1500 - 750)^2 + 10 \implies a = \frac{1}{5625}$; $y = \frac{1}{5625}(x - 750)^2 + 10$. Thus, let

$$f(x) = \begin{cases} -\frac{4}{15}x + 110 & \text{if } -500 \le x < 0 \\ \frac{1}{5625}(x - 750)^2 + 10 & \text{if } 0 \le x \le 1500 \\ \frac{4}{15}x - 290 & \text{if } 1500 < x \le 2000 \end{cases}$$

(b) Graph the equations: $Y_1 = (-4/15 * x + 110)/(x < 0)$,

$Y_2 = (1/5625 * (x - 750)\hat{\,}2 + 10)/(x \ge 0 \text{ and } x \le 1500)$, $Y_3 = (4/15 * x - 290)/(x > 1500)$

**65** (a) $f$ must have zeros of 0 and 150. Thus, $f(x) = a(x - 0)(x - 150)$.      (b)    $[0, 180, 50]$ by $[0, 120, 50]$

Also, $f$ will have a maximum of 100 occurring at $x = 75$.

(The vertex will be midway between the zeros of $f$.)

$a(75 - 0)(75 - 150) = 100 \implies a = \dfrac{100}{(75)(-75)} = -\dfrac{4}{225}$.

$f(x) = -\frac{4}{225}(x)(x - 150) = -\frac{4}{225}x^2 + \frac{8}{3}x$, so $a = -\frac{4}{225}$ and $b = \frac{8}{3}$.

(c) $y = kax^2 + bx$ for $k = \frac{1}{4}, \frac{1}{2}, 1, 2,$ and 4 • The value of $k$ affects both the distance and the height traveled by the object. The distance and height decrease by a factor of $\frac{1}{k}$ when $k > 1$ and increase by a factor of $\frac{1}{k}$ when $0 < k < 1$.

$[0, 600, 50]$ by $[0, 400, 50]$

## 2.7 Exercises

**1** $f(x) = x + 3, g(x) = x^2$ • $f(3) = 3 + 3 = 6, g(3) = 3^2 = 9$

(a) $(f + g)(3) = f(3) + g(3) = 6 + 9 = 15$

(b) $(f - g)(3) = f(3) - g(3) = 6 - 9 = -3$

(c) $(fg)(3) = f(3) \cdot g(3) = 6 \cdot 9 = 54$

(d) $(f/g)(3) = \dfrac{f(3)}{g(3)} = \dfrac{6}{9} = \dfrac{2}{3}$

**2** $f(x) = -x^2, g(x) = 2x - 1$ • $f(3) = -3^2 = -9, g(3) = 2(3) - 1 = 5$

(a) $(f + g)(3) = f(3) + g(3) = -9 + 5 = -4$

(b) $(f - g)(3) = f(3) - g(3) = -9 - 5 = -14$

(c) $(fg)(3) = f(3) \cdot g(3) = -9 \cdot 5 = -45$

(d) $(f/g)(3) = \dfrac{f(3)}{g(3)} = \dfrac{-9}{5} = -\dfrac{9}{5}$

**3** (a) $(f + g)(x) = f(x) + g(x) = (x^2 + 2) + (2x^2 - 1) = 3x^2 + 1$;

$(f - g)(x) = f(x) - g(x) = (x^2 + 2) - (2x^2 - 1) = 3 - x^2$;

$(fg)(x) = f(x) \cdot g(x) = (x^2 + 2) \cdot (2x^2 - 1) = 2x^4 + 3x^2 - 2$; $\left(\dfrac{f}{g}\right)(x) = \dfrac{f(x)}{g(x)} = \dfrac{x^2 + 2}{2x^2 - 1}$

(b) The domain of $f + g$, $f - g$, and $fg$ is the set of all real numbers, $\mathbb{R}$.

(c) The domain of $f/g$ is the same as in (b), except we must exclude the zeros of $g$.

$2x^2 - 1 = 0 \Rightarrow x^2 = \frac{1}{2} \Rightarrow x = \pm\sqrt{\frac{1}{2}} = \pm\frac{\sqrt{2}}{2}$ or $\pm\frac{1}{2}\sqrt{2}$.

Hence, the domain of $f/g$ is all real numbers except $\pm\frac{1}{2}\sqrt{2}$.

**4** (a) $(f + g)(x) = f(x) + g(x) = (x^2 + x) + (x^2 - 4) = 2x^2 + x - 4$;

$(f - g)(x) = f(x) - g(x) = (x^2 + x) - (x^2 - 4) = x + 4$;

$(fg)(x) = f(x) \cdot g(x) = (x^2 + x) \cdot (x^2 - 4) = x^4 + x^3 - 4x^2 - 4x$; $\left(\dfrac{f}{g}\right)(x) = \dfrac{f(x)}{g(x)} = \dfrac{x^2 + x}{x^2 - 4}$

(b) The domain of $f + g$, $f - g$, and $fg$ is the set of all real numbers, $\mathbb{R}$.

(c) The domain of $f/g$ is all real numbers except $\pm 2$.

**5** (a) $(f + g)(x) = f(x) + g(x) = \sqrt{x + 5} + \sqrt{x + 5} = 2\sqrt{x + 5}$;

$(f - g)(x) = f(x) - g(x) = \sqrt{x + 5} - \sqrt{x + 5} = 0$; $(fg)(x) = f(x) \cdot g(x) = \sqrt{x + 5} \cdot \sqrt{x + 5} = x + 5$;

$\left(\dfrac{f}{g}\right)(x) = \dfrac{f(x)}{g(x)} = \dfrac{\sqrt{x + 5}}{\sqrt{x + 5}} = 1$

(b) The radicand, $x + 5$, must be nonnegative; that is $x + 5 \geq 0 \Rightarrow x \geq -5$.

Thus, the domain of $f + g$, $f - g$, and $fg$ is $[-5, \infty)$.

(c) Now the radicand must be positive {can't have zero in the denominator}. Thus, the domain of $f/g$ is $(-5, \infty)$.

6. (a) $(f+g)(x) = f(x) + g(x) = \sqrt{5-2x} + \sqrt{x+3}$; $(f-g)(x) = f(x) - g(x) = \sqrt{5-2x} - \sqrt{x+3}$;

$(fg)(x) = f(x) \cdot g(x) = \sqrt{5-2x} \cdot \sqrt{x+3} = \sqrt{(5-2x)(x+3)}$;

$\left(\dfrac{f}{g}\right)(x) = \dfrac{f(x)}{g(x)} = \dfrac{\sqrt{5-2x}}{\sqrt{x+3}} = \sqrt{\dfrac{5-2x}{x+3}}$

(b) The radicands must be nonnegative. $5 - 2x \geq 0 \Rightarrow 2x \leq 5 \Rightarrow x \leq \frac{5}{2}$ and $x + 3 \geq 0 \Rightarrow x \geq -3$.

Thus, the domain of $f+g$, $f-g$, and $fg$ is $\left[-3, \frac{5}{2}\right]$.

(c) Now $x + 3$ must be positive {can't have zero in the denominator}. Thus, the domain of $f/g$ is $\left(-3, \frac{5}{2}\right]$.

7. (a) $(f+g)(x) = f(x) + g(x) = \dfrac{2x}{x-4} + \dfrac{x}{x+5} = \dfrac{2x(x+5) + x(x-4)}{(x-4)(x+5)} = \dfrac{3x^2 + 6x}{(x-4)(x+5)}$;

$(f-g)(x) = f(x) - g(x) = \dfrac{2x}{x-4} - \dfrac{x}{x+5} = \dfrac{2x(x+5) - x(x-4)}{(x-4)(x+5)} = \dfrac{x^2 + 14x}{(x-4)(x+5)}$;

$(fg)(x) = f(x) \cdot g(x) = \dfrac{2x}{x-4} \cdot \dfrac{x}{x+5} = \dfrac{2x^2}{(x-4)(x+5)}$; $\left(\dfrac{f}{g}\right)(x) = \dfrac{f(x)}{g(x)} = \dfrac{2x/(x-4)}{x/(x+5)} = \dfrac{2(x+5)}{x-4}$

(b) The domain of $f$ is $\mathbb{R} - \{4\}$ and the domain of $g$ is $\mathbb{R} - \{-5\}$. The intersection of these two domains, $\mathbb{R} - \{-5, 4\}$, is the domain of the three functions.

(c) To determine the domain of the quotient $f/g$, we also exclude any values that make the denominator $g$ equal to zero. Hence, we exclude $x = 0$ and the domain of the quotient is all real numbers except $-5$, $0$, and $4$, that is, $\mathbb{R} - \{-5, 0, 4\}$.

8. (a) $(f+g)(x) = f(x) + g(x) = \dfrac{x}{x-2} + \dfrac{7x}{x+4} = \dfrac{x(x+4) + 7x(x-2)}{(x-2)(x+4)} = \dfrac{8x^2 - 10x}{(x-2)(x+4)}$;

$(f-g)(x) = f(x) - g(x) = \dfrac{x}{x-2} - \dfrac{7x}{x+4} = \dfrac{x(x+4) - 7x(x-2)}{(x-2)(x+4)} = \dfrac{-6x^2 + 18x}{(x-2)(x+4)}$;

$(fg)(x) = f(x) \cdot g(x) = \dfrac{x}{x-2} \cdot \dfrac{7x}{x+4} = \dfrac{7x^2}{(x-2)(x+4)}$; $\left(\dfrac{f}{g}\right)(x) = \dfrac{f(x)}{g(x)} = \dfrac{x/(x-2)}{7x/(x+4)} = \dfrac{x+4}{7(x-2)}$

(b) All real numbers except $-4$ and $2$

(c) All real numbers except $-4$, $0$, and $2$

9. (a) $f(x) = 2x - 1$, $g(x) = -x^2$ • $(f \circ g)(x) = f(g(x)) = f(-x^2) = 2(-x^2) - 1 = -2x^2 - 1$

(b) $(g \circ f)(x) = g(f(x)) = g(2x-1) = -(2x-1)^2 = -(4x^2 - 4x + 1) = -4x^2 + 4x - 1$

(c) $(f \circ f)(x) = f(f(x)) = f(2x-1) = 2(2x-1) - 1 = (4x-2) - 1 = 4x - 3$

(d) $(g \circ g)(x) = g(g(x)) = g(-x^2) = -(-x^2)^2 = -(x^4) = -x^4$

10. (a) $(f \circ g)(x) = f(g(x)) = f(x-2) = 3(x-2)^2 = 3(x^2 - 4x + 4) = 3x^2 - 12x + 12$

(b) $(g \circ f)(x) = g(f(x)) = g(3x^2) = (3x^2) - 2 = 3x^2 - 2$

(c) $(f \circ f)(x) = f(f(x)) = f(3x^2) = 3(3x^2)^2 = 3(9x^4) = 27x^4$

(d) $(g \circ g)(x) = g(g(x)) = g(x-2) = (x-2) - 2 = x - 4$

**Note:** In Exercises 11–34, let $h(x) = (f \circ g)(x) = f(g(x))$ and $k(x) = (g \circ f)(x) = g(f(x))$.

$h(-2)$ and $k(3)$ could be worked two ways, as in Example 3(c) in the text.

11. (a) $h(x) = f(3x+4) = 2(3x+4) - 5 = 6x + 3$ (b) $k(x) = g(2x-5) = 3(2x-5) + 4 = 6x - 11$

(c) Using the result from part (a), $h(-2) = 6(-2) + 3 = -12 + 3 = -9$.

(d) Using the result from part (b), $k(3) = 6(3) - 11 = 18 - 11 = 7$.

**12** (a) $h(x) = f(6x - 3) = 5(6x - 3) + 2 = 30x - 13$ (b) $k(x) = g(5x + 2) = 6(5x + 2) - 3 = 30x + 9$

(c) Using the result from part (a), $h(-2) = 30(-2) - 13 = -60 - 13 = -73$.

(d) Using the result from part (b), $k(3) = 30(3) + 9 = 90 + 9 = 99$.

**13** (a) $h(x) = f(5x) = 3(5x)^2 + 4 = 75x^2 + 4$ (b) $k(x) = g(3x^2 + 4) = 5(3x^2 + 4) = 15x^2 + 20$

(c) $h(-2) = 75(-2)^2 + 4 = 300 + 4 = 304$ (d) $k(3) = 15(3)^2 + 20 = 135 + 20 = 155$

**14** (a) $h(x) = f(4x^2) = 3(4x^2) - 1 = 12x^2 - 1$

(b) $k(x) = g(3x - 1) = 4(3x - 1)^2 = 4(9x^2 - 6x + 1) = 36x^2 - 24x + 4$

(c) $h(-2) = 12(-2)^2 - 1 = 48 - 1 = 47$

(d) $k(3) = 36(3)^2 - 24(3) + 4 = 324 - 72 + 4 = 256$

**15** (a) $h(x) = f(2x - 1) = 2(2x - 1)^2 + 3(2x - 1) - 4 = 8x^2 - 2x - 5$

(b) $k(x) = g(2x^2 + 3x - 4) = 2(2x^2 + 3x - 4) - 1 = 4x^2 + 6x - 9$

(c) $h(-2) = 8(-2)^2 - 2(-2) - 5 = 32 + 4 - 5 = 31$

(d) $k(3) = 4(3)^2 + 6(3) - 9 = 36 + 18 - 9 = 45$

**16** (a) $h(x) = f(3x^2 - x + 2) = 5(3x^2 - x + 2) - 7 = 15x^2 - 5x + 3$

(b) $k(x) = g(5x - 7) = 3(5x - 7)^2 - (5x - 7) + 2 = 75x^2 - 215x + 156$

(c) $h(-2) = 15(-2)^2 - 5(-2) + 3 = 60 + 10 + 3 = 73$

(d) $k(3) = 75(3)^2 - 215(3) + 156 = 675 - 645 + 156 = 186$

**17** (a) $h(x) = f(2x^3 - 5x) = 4(2x^3 - 5x) = 8x^3 - 20x$ (b) $k(x) = g(4x) = 2(4x)^3 - 5(4x) = 128x^3 - 20x$

(c) $h(-2) = 8(-2)^3 - 20(-2) = -64 + 40 = -24$ (d) $k(3) = 128(3)^3 - 20(3) = 3456 - 60 = 3396$

**18** (a) $h(x) = f(3x) = (3x)^3 + 2(3x)^2 = 27x^3 + 18x^2$ (b) $k(x) = g(x^3 + 2x^2) = 3(x^3 + 2x^2) = 3x^3 + 6x^2$

(c) $h(-2) = 27(-2)^3 + 18(-2)^2 = -216 + 72 = -144$ (d) $k(3) = 3(3)^3 + 6(3)^2 = 81 + 54 = 135$

**19** (a) $h(x) = f(-7) = |-7| = 7$ (b) $k(x) = g(|x|) = -7$

(c) $h(-2) = 7$ since $h(\text{any value}) = 7$ (d) $k(3) = -7$ since $k(\text{any value}) = -7$

**20** (a) $h(x) = f(x^2) = -5$ (b) $k(x) = g(-5) = (-5)^2 = 25$

(c) $h(-2) = -5$ since $h(\text{any value}) = -5$ (d) $k(3) = 25$ since $k(\text{any value}) = 25$

**21** (a) $h(x) = f\left(\sqrt{x + 2}\right) = \left(\sqrt{x + 2}\right)^2 - 3\left(\sqrt{x + 2}\right) = x + 2 - 3\sqrt{x + 2}$. The domain of $f \circ g$ is the set of all $x$ in the domain of $g$, $x \geq -2$, such that $g(x)$ is in the domain of $f$. Since the domain of $f$ is $\mathbb{R}$, any value of $g(x)$ is in its domain. Thus, the domain is all $x$ such that $x \geq -2$. Note that *both* $g(x)$ *and* $f(g(x))$ are defined for $x$ in $[-2, \infty)$.

(b) $k(x) = g(x^2 - 3x) = \sqrt{(x^2 - 3x) + 2} = \sqrt{x^2 - 3x + 2}$. The domain of $g \circ f$ is the set of all $x$ in the domain of $f$, $\mathbb{R}$, such that $f(x)$ is in the domain of $g$. Since the domain of $g$ is $x \geq -2$, we must solve $f(x) \geq -2$.

$x^2 - 3x \geq -2 \quad \Rightarrow \quad x^2 - 3x + 2 \geq 0 \quad \Rightarrow \quad (x - 1)(x - 2) \geq 0$

| Interval | $(-\infty, 1)$ | $(1, 2)$ | $(2, \infty)$ |
|---|---|---|---|
| Sign of $x - 2$ | $-$ | $-$ | $+$ |
| Sign of $x - 1$ | $-$ | $+$ | $+$ |
| **Resulting sign** | $+$ | $-$ | $+$ |

From the sign chart, $(x - 1)(x - 2) \geq 0 \Rightarrow x \in (-\infty, 1] \cup [2, \infty)$.

Thus, the domain is all $x$ such that $x \in (-\infty, 1] \cup [2, \infty)$.

Note that *both $f(x)$ and $g(f(x))$* are defined for $x$ in $(-\infty, 1] \cup [2, \infty)$.

**22** (a) $h(x) = f(x^2 + 2x) = \sqrt{(x^2 + 2x) - 15} = \sqrt{x^2 + 2x - 15}$.

Domain of $g = \mathbb{R}$. Domain of $f = [15, \infty)$. $g(x) \geq 15 \Rightarrow x^2 + 2x \geq 15 \Rightarrow x^2 + 2x - 15 \geq 0 \Rightarrow$
$$(x + 5)(x - 3) \geq 0 \Rightarrow x \in (-\infty, -5] \cup [3, \infty).$$

(b) $k(x) = g\left(\sqrt{x - 15}\right) = \left(\sqrt{x - 15}\right)^2 + 2\left(\sqrt{x - 15}\right) = x - 15 + 2\sqrt{x - 15}$.

Domain of $f = [15, \infty)$. Domain of $g = \mathbb{R}$. Since $f(x)$ is always in the domain
of $g$, the domain of $g \circ f$ is the same as the domain of $f$, $[15, \infty)$.

**23** (a) $h(x) = f\left(\sqrt{3x}\right) = \left(\sqrt{3x}\right)^2 - 4 = 3x - 4$. Domain of $g = [0, \infty)$. Domain of $f = \mathbb{R}$.

Since $g(x)$ is always in the domain of $f$, the domain of $f \circ g$ is the same as the domain of $g$, $[0, \infty)$.

Note that *both $g(x)$ and $f(g(x))$* are defined for $x$ in $[0, \infty)$.

(b) $k(x) = g(x^2 - 4) = \sqrt{3(x^2 - 4)} = \sqrt{3x^2 - 12}$. Domain of $f = \mathbb{R}$. Domain of $g = [0, \infty)$.

$f(x) \geq 0 \Rightarrow x^2 - 4 \geq 0 \Rightarrow x^2 \geq 4 \Rightarrow |x| \geq 2 \Rightarrow x \in (-\infty, -2] \cup [2, \infty)$.

Note that *both $f(x)$ and $g(f(x))$* are defined for $x$ in $(-\infty, -2] \cup [2, \infty)$.

**24** (a) $h(x) = f\left(\sqrt{x}\right) = -\left(\sqrt{x}\right)^2 + 1 = -x + 1$. Domain of $g = [0, \infty)$. Domain of $f = \mathbb{R}$.

Since $g(x)$ is always in the domain of $f$, the domain of $f \circ g$ is the same as the domain of $g$, $[0, \infty)$.

(b) $k(x) = g(-x^2 + 1) = \sqrt{-x^2 + 1}$. Domain of $f = \mathbb{R}$. Domain of $g = [0, \infty)$.

$$f(x) \geq 0 \Rightarrow -x^2 + 1 \geq 0 \Rightarrow x^2 \leq 1 \Rightarrow |x| \leq 1 \Rightarrow x \in [-1, 1].$$

**25** (a) $h(x) = f\left(\sqrt{x + 5}\right) = \sqrt{\sqrt{x + 5} - 2}$. Domain of $g = [-5, \infty)$. Domain of $f = [2, \infty)$.

$$g(x) \geq 2 \Rightarrow \sqrt{x + 5} \geq 2 \Rightarrow x + 5 \geq 4 \Rightarrow x \geq -1 \text{ or } x \in [-1, \infty).$$

(b) $k(x) = g\left(\sqrt{x - 2}\right) = \sqrt{\sqrt{x - 2} + 5}$. Domain of $f = [2, \infty)$. Domain of $g = [-5, \infty)$.

$f(x) \geq -5 \Rightarrow \sqrt{x - 2} \geq -5$. This is always true since the result of a square root is nonnegative.

The domain is $[2, \infty)$.

**26** (a) $h(x) = f\left(\sqrt{x + 2}\right) = \sqrt{3 - \sqrt{x + 2}}$. Domain of $g = [-2, \infty)$. Domain of $f = (-\infty, 3]$.

$g(x) \leq 3 \Rightarrow \sqrt{x + 2} \leq 3 \Rightarrow x + 2 \leq 9 \Rightarrow x \leq 7$.

We must remember that $x \geq -2$, hence, $-2 \leq x \leq 7$.

(b) $k(x) = g\left(\sqrt{3 - x}\right) = \sqrt{\sqrt{3 - x} + 2}$. Domain of $f = (-\infty, 3]$. Domain of $g = [-2, \infty)$.

$f(x) \geq -2 \Rightarrow \sqrt{3 - x} \geq -2$. This is always true since the result of a square root is nonnegative.

The domain is $(-\infty, 3]$.

**27** (a) $h(x) = f\left(\sqrt{x^2 - 16}\right) = \sqrt{3 - \sqrt{x^2 - 16}}$. Domain of $g = (-\infty, -4] \cup [4, \infty)$. Domain of $f = (-\infty, 3]$.

$g(x) \le 3 \Rightarrow \sqrt{x^2 - 16} \le 3 \Rightarrow x^2 - 16 \le 9 \Rightarrow x^2 \le 25 \Rightarrow x \in [-5, 5]$.

But $|x| \ge 4$ from the domain of $g$, so the domain of $f \circ g$ is $[-5, -4] \cup [4, 5]$.

(b) $k(x) = g\left(\sqrt{3 - x}\right) = \sqrt{\left(\sqrt{3 - x}\right)^2 - 16} = \sqrt{3 - x - 16} = \sqrt{-x - 13}$. Domain of $f = (-\infty, 3]$.

Domain of $g = (-\infty, -4] \cup [4, \infty)$. $f(x) \ge 4$ {$f(x)$ cannot be less than 0} $\Rightarrow$

$\sqrt{3 - x} \ge 4 \Rightarrow 3 - x \ge 16 \Rightarrow x \le -13$.

**28** (a) $h(x) = f\left(\sqrt[3]{x - 5}\right) = \left(\sqrt[3]{x - 5}\right)^3 + 5 = x - 5 + 5 = x$. Domain of $g = \mathbb{R}$. Domain of $f = \mathbb{R}$.

All values of $g(x)$ are in the domain of $f$. Hence, the domain of $f \circ g$ is $\mathbb{R}$.

(b) $k(x) = g(x^3 + 5) = \sqrt[3]{(x^3 + 5) - 5} = \sqrt[3]{x^3} = x$. Domain of $f = \mathbb{R}$. Domain of $g = \mathbb{R}$.

All values of $f(x)$ are in the domain of $g$. Hence, the domain of $g \circ f$ is $\mathbb{R}$.

**29** (a) $h(x) = f\left(\dfrac{5x - 3}{2}\right) = \dfrac{2\left(\dfrac{5x - 3}{2}\right) + 3}{5} = \dfrac{5x - 3 + 3}{5} = \dfrac{5x}{5} = x$. Domain of $g = \mathbb{R}$. Domain of $f = \mathbb{R}$.

All values of $g(x)$ are in the domain of $f$. Hence, the domain of $f \circ g$ is $\mathbb{R}$.

(b) $k(x) = g\left(\dfrac{2x + 3}{5}\right) = \dfrac{5\left(\dfrac{2x + 3}{5}\right) - 3}{2} = \dfrac{2x + 3 - 3}{2} = \dfrac{2x}{2} = x$. Domain of $f = \mathbb{R}$. Domain of $g = \mathbb{R}$.

All values of $f(x)$ are in the domain of $g$. Hence, the domain of $g \circ f$ is $\mathbb{R}$.

**30** (a) $h(x) = f(x - 1) = \dfrac{1}{(x - 1) - 1} = \dfrac{1}{x - 2}$. Domain of $g = \mathbb{R}$. Domain of $f = \mathbb{R} - \{1\}$.

$g(x) \ne 1 \Rightarrow x - 1 \ne 1 \Rightarrow x \ne 2$. Hence, the domain of $f \circ g$ is $\mathbb{R} - \{2\}$.

(b) $k(x) = g\left(\dfrac{1}{x - 1}\right) = \dfrac{1}{x - 1} - 1 = \dfrac{1 - (x - 1)}{x - 1} = \dfrac{2 - x}{x - 1}$. Domain of $f = \mathbb{R} - \{1\}$. Domain of $g = \mathbb{R}$.

All values of $f(x)$ are in the domain of $g$. The domain of $g \circ f$ is $\mathbb{R} - \{1\}$.

**31** (a) $h(x) = f\left(\dfrac{1}{x^3}\right) = \left(\dfrac{1}{x^3}\right)^2 = \dfrac{1}{x^6}$. Domain of $g = \mathbb{R} - \{0\}$. Domain of $f = \mathbb{R}$.

All values of $g(x)$ are in the domain of $f$. Hence, the domain of $f \circ g$ is $\mathbb{R} - \{0\}$.

(b) $k(x) = g(x^2) = \dfrac{1}{(x^2)^3} = \dfrac{1}{x^6}$. Domain of $f = \mathbb{R}$. Domain of $g = \mathbb{R} - \{0\}$.

All values of $f(x)$ are in the domain of $g$ except for 0. Since $f$ is 0 when $x$ is 0, the domain of $f \circ g$ is $\mathbb{R} - \{0\}$.

**32** (a) $h(x) = f\left(\dfrac{3}{x}\right) = \dfrac{3/x}{(3/x) - 2} \cdot \dfrac{x}{x} = \dfrac{3}{3 - 2x}$. Domain of $g = \mathbb{R} - \{0\}$. Domain of $f = \mathbb{R} - \{2\}$.

$g(x) \ne 2 \Rightarrow \dfrac{3}{x} \ne 2 \Rightarrow x \ne \tfrac{3}{2}$. Hence, the domain of $f \circ g$ is $\mathbb{R} - \left\{0, \tfrac{3}{2}\right\}$.

(b) $k(x) = g\left(\dfrac{x}{x - 2}\right) = \dfrac{3}{x/(x - 2)} = \dfrac{3x - 6}{x}$. Domain of $f = \mathbb{R} - \{2\}$. Domain of $g = \mathbb{R} - \{0\}$.

$f(x) \ne 0 \Rightarrow \dfrac{x}{x - 2} \ne 0 \Rightarrow x \ne 0$. Hence, the domain of $g \circ f$ is $\mathbb{R} - \{0, 2\}$.

**33** (a) $h(x) = f\left(\dfrac{x - 3}{x - 4}\right) = \dfrac{\dfrac{x - 3}{x - 4} - 1}{\dfrac{x - 3}{x - 4} - 2} \cdot \dfrac{x - 4}{x - 4} = \dfrac{x - 3 - 1(x - 4)}{x - 3 - 2(x - 4)} = \dfrac{1}{5 - x}$.

Domain of $g = \mathbb{R} - \{4\}$. Domain of $f = \mathbb{R} - \{2\}$.

$g(x) \ne 2 \Rightarrow \dfrac{x - 3}{x - 4} \ne 2 \Rightarrow x - 3 \ne 2x - 8 \Rightarrow x \ne 5$. The domain is $\mathbb{R} - \{4, 5\}$.

(b) $k(x) = g\left(\dfrac{x-1}{x-2}\right) = \dfrac{\dfrac{x-1}{x-2} - 3}{\dfrac{x-1}{x-2} - 4} \cdot \dfrac{x-2}{x-2} = \dfrac{x-1-3(x-2)}{x-1-4(x-2)} = \dfrac{-2x+5}{-3x+7}$.

Domain of $f = \mathbb{R} - \{2\}$. Domain of $g = \mathbb{R} - \{4\}$.

$f(x) \neq 4 \;\Rightarrow\; \dfrac{x-1}{x-2} \neq 4 \;\Rightarrow\; x-1 \neq 4x-8 \;\Rightarrow\; x \neq \frac{7}{3}$. The domain is $\mathbb{R} - \left\{2, \frac{7}{3}\right\}$.

**34** (a) $h(x) = f\left(\dfrac{x-5}{x+4}\right) = \dfrac{\dfrac{x-5}{x+4} + 2}{\dfrac{x-5}{x+4} - 1} \cdot \dfrac{x+4}{x+4} = \dfrac{x-5+2(x+4)}{x-5-1(x+4)} = \dfrac{3x+3}{-9} = \dfrac{-x-1}{3}$.

Domain of $g = \mathbb{R} - \{-4\}$. Domain of $f = \mathbb{R} - \{1\}$. $g(x) \neq 1 \;\Rightarrow\; \dfrac{x-5}{x+4} \neq 1 \;\Rightarrow\; x-5 \neq x+4$.

This is always true—so no additional values need to be excluded, and thus, the domain is $\mathbb{R} - \{-4\}$.

(b) $k(x) = g\left(\dfrac{x+2}{x-1}\right) = \dfrac{\dfrac{x+2}{x-1} - 5}{\dfrac{x+2}{x-1} + 4} \cdot \dfrac{x-1}{x-1} = \dfrac{x+2-5(x-1)}{x+2+4(x-1)} = \dfrac{-4x+7}{5x-2}$.

Domain of $f = \mathbb{R} - \{1\}$. Domain of $g = \mathbb{R} - \{-4\}$. $f(x) \neq -4 \;\Rightarrow\; \dfrac{x+2}{x-1} \neq -4 \;\Rightarrow$

$x+2 \neq -4x+4 \;\Rightarrow\; x \neq \frac{2}{5}$. The domain is $\mathbb{R} - \left\{\frac{2}{5}, 1\right\}$.

**35** $f(x) = x^2 - 2, \; g(x) = x+3 \; \bullet \; (f \circ g)(x) = f(g(x)) = f(x+3) = (x+3)^2 - 2$.

$\qquad (f \circ g)(x) = 0 \;\Rightarrow\; (x+3)^2 - 2 = 0 \;\Rightarrow\; (x+3)^2 = 2 \;\Rightarrow\; x+3 = \pm\sqrt{2} \;\Rightarrow\; x = -3 \pm \sqrt{2}$

**36** $f(x) = x^2 - x - 2, \; g(x) = 2x - 5 \; \bullet$

$(f \circ g)(x) = f(g(x)) = f(2x-5) = (2x-5)^2 - (2x-5) - 2 = 4x^2 - 22x + 28$.

$\qquad (f \circ g)(x) = 0 \;\Rightarrow\; 4x^2 - 22x + 28 = 0 \;\Rightarrow\; (2x-4)(2x-7) = 0 \;\Rightarrow\; x = 2, \frac{7}{2}$

**37** (a) $(f \circ g)(6) = f(g(6)) = f(8) = 5$        (b) $(g \circ f)(6) = g(f(6)) = g(7) = 6$

(c) $(f \circ f)(6) = f(f(6)) = f(7) = 6$        (d) $(g \circ g)(6) = g(g(6)) = g(8) = 5$

(e) $(f \circ g)(9) = f(g(9)) = f(4)$, but $f(4)$ cannot be determined from the table.

**38** (a) $(T \circ S)(1) = T(S(1)) = T(0) = 2$        (b) $(S \circ T)(1) = S(T(1)) = S(3) = 2$

(c) $(T \circ T)(1) = T(T(1)) = T(3) = 0$        (d) $(S \circ S)(1) = S(S(1)) = S(0) = 1$

(e) $(T \circ S)(4) = T(S(4)) = T(5)$, but $T(5)$ cannot be determined from the table.

**39** $D(t) = \sqrt{400 + t^2}, \; R(x) = 20x \; \bullet \; (D \circ R)(x) = D(R(x)) = D(20x) = \sqrt{400 + (20x)^2} = \sqrt{400 + 400x^2}$

$\qquad\qquad\qquad\qquad\qquad = \sqrt{400(1 + x^2)} = \sqrt{400}\,\sqrt{x^2 + 1} = 20\sqrt{x^2 + 1}$

**40** $S(r) = 4\pi r^2, \; D(t) = 2t + 5 \; \bullet \; (S \circ D)(t) = S(D(t)) = S(2t+5) = 4\pi(2t+5)^2$

**41** We need to examine $(fg)(-x)$—if we obtain $(fg)(x)$, then $fg$ is an even function,

whereas if we obtain $-(fg)(x)$, then $fg$ is an odd function.

$\begin{aligned}
(fg)(-x) &= f(-x)g(-x) \quad &\{\text{definition of the product of two functions}\} \\
&= -f(x)g(x) \quad &\{f \text{ is odd, so } f(-x) = -f(x); \, g \text{ is even, so } g(-x) = g(x)\} \\
&= -(fg)(x) \quad &\{\text{definition of the product of two functions}\}
\end{aligned}$

Since $(fg)(-x) = -(fg)(x)$, $fg$ is an odd function.

**42** If $f$ is even and odd, then $f(-x) = f(x)$ and $f(-x) = -f(x)$.

Thus, $f(x) = -f(x) \Rightarrow 2f(x) = 0 \Rightarrow f(x) = 0$. Hence, $f(x) = 0$ is a function that is both even and odd.

**43** $(\text{ROUND2} \circ \text{SSTAX})(525.00) = \text{ROUND2}(\text{SSTAX}(525.00))$
$$= \text{ROUND2}(0.0765 \cdot 525.00)$$
$$= \text{ROUND2}(40.1625) = 40.16$$

**44** (a) $(\text{CHR} \circ \text{ORD})(\text{``C''}) = \text{CHR}(\text{ORD}(\text{``C''})) = \text{CHR}(67) = \text{``C''}$

(b) $\text{CHR}(\text{ORD}(\text{``A''}) + 3) = \text{CHR}(65 + 3) = \text{CHR}(68) = \text{``D''}$

**45** $r = 5t$ and $A = \pi r^2 \Rightarrow A = \pi(5t)^2 = 25\pi t^2$ ft$^2$.

**46** $V = \dfrac{4}{3}\pi r^3 \Rightarrow r^3 = \dfrac{3V}{4\pi} \Rightarrow r = \sqrt[3]{\dfrac{3V}{4\pi}}$. $V = \dfrac{9}{2}\pi t \Rightarrow r(t) = \sqrt[3]{\dfrac{3(\frac{9}{2}\pi t)}{4\pi}} = \sqrt[3]{\dfrac{27t}{8}} = \dfrac{3}{2}\sqrt[3]{t}$ ft.

**47** The formula for the volume of a cone is $V = \frac{1}{3}\pi r^2 h = \frac{1}{3}\pi r^3$ {since $h = r$} $\Rightarrow$
$$r^3 = \frac{3V}{\pi} \Rightarrow r = \sqrt[3]{\frac{3V}{\pi}}. \quad V = 243\pi t \Rightarrow r = \sqrt[3]{\frac{3 \cdot 243\pi t}{\pi}} = \sqrt[3]{729t} = 9\sqrt[3]{t} \text{ ft.}$$

**48** $x^2 + x^2 = y^2 \Rightarrow y^2 = 2x^2 \Rightarrow y = \sqrt{2}x$. $y^2 + x^2 = d^2 \Rightarrow d^2 = 3x^2 \Rightarrow d(x) = \sqrt{3}x$.

**49** Let $l$ denote the length of the rope. At $t = 0$, $l = 20$. At $t = 1$, $l = 25$.

At time $t$, $l = 20 + 5t$, *not* just $5t$. We have a right triangle with sides $20$, $h$, and $l$. $h^2 + 20^2 = l^2 \Rightarrow$
$$h = \sqrt{(20 + 5t)^2 - 20^2} = \sqrt{25t^2 + 200t} = \sqrt{25(t^2 + 8t)} = 5\sqrt{t^2 + 8t}.$$

**50** The triangle has sides of length $28$, $50$, and $\sqrt{28^2 + 50^2} = \sqrt{3284} = 2\sqrt{821}$.

Let $y = h - 2$. Using similar triangles and the fact that $d = 2t$,
$$\frac{y}{d} = \frac{28}{2\sqrt{821}} \Rightarrow y = \frac{14}{\sqrt{821}}d \Rightarrow h(t) = \frac{28}{\sqrt{821}}t + 2.$$

**51** From Exercise 77 of Section 2.4, $d(x) = \sqrt{90{,}400 + x^2}$. The distance $x$ of the plane

from the control tower is 500 feet plus 150 feet per second, that is, $x(t) = 500 + 150t$. Thus,
$$d(t) = \sqrt{90{,}400 + (500 + 150t)^2} = \sqrt{90{,}400 + 250{,}000 + 150{,}000t + 22{,}500t^2}$$
$$= \sqrt{22{,}500t^2 + 150{,}000t + 340{,}400} = 10\sqrt{225t^2 + 1500t + 3404}$$

**52** Consider the cable to be a right circular cylinder.

$A = 2\pi r h = \pi dh = 1200\pi d$ {$h = 1200$ inches} $\Rightarrow d = \dfrac{A}{1200\pi}$.

$A = -750t$, so $d(t) = $ original value $+$ change $= 4 - \dfrac{750t}{1200\pi} = 4 - \dfrac{5}{8\pi}t$ inches.

**53** $y = (x^2 + 5x)^{1/3}$ • Suppose you were to find the value of $y$ if $x$ was equal to 3. Using a calculator, you might
compute the value of $x^2 + 5x$ first, and then raise that result to the $\frac{1}{3}$ power. Thus, we would choose $y = u^{1/3}$ and
$u = x^2 + 5x$.

**54** For $y = \sqrt[4]{x^4 - 64}$, choose $u = x^4 - 64$ and $y = \sqrt[4]{u}$.

**55** For $y = \dfrac{1}{(x - 3)^6}$, choose $u = x - 3$ and $y = \dfrac{1}{u^6} = u^{-6}$.

**56** For $y = 4 + \sqrt{x^2 + 1}$, choose $u = x^2 + 1$ and $y = 4 + \sqrt{u}$.

**57** For $y = (x^4 - 2x^2 + 5)^5$, choose $u = x^4 - 2x^2 + 5$ and $y = u^5$.

**58** For $y = \dfrac{1}{(x^2 + 3x - 5)^3}$, choose $u = x^2 + 3x - 5$ and $y = \dfrac{1}{u^3} = u^{-3}$.

**59** For $y = \dfrac{\sqrt{x+4} - 2}{\sqrt{x+4} + 2}$, there is not a "simple" choice for $y$ as in previous exercises.

One choice for $u$ is $u = x + 4$. Then $y$ would be $\dfrac{\sqrt{u} - 2}{\sqrt{u} + 2}$.

Another choice for $u$ is $u = \sqrt{x+4}$. Then $y$ would be $\dfrac{u - 2}{u + 2}$.

**60** For $y = \dfrac{\sqrt[3]{x}}{1 + \sqrt[3]{x}}$, choose $u = \sqrt[3]{x}$ and $y = \dfrac{u}{1 + u}$.

**61** $(f \circ g)(x) = f(g(x)) = f(x^3 + 1) = \sqrt{x^3 + 1} - 1$. We will multiply this expression by $\dfrac{\sqrt{x^3 + 1} + 1}{\sqrt{x^3 + 1} + 1}$, treating it

as though it was one factor of a difference of two squares.

$$\left(\sqrt{x^3 + 1} - 1\right) \times \frac{\sqrt{x^3 + 1} + 1}{\sqrt{x^3 + 1} + 1} = \frac{\left(\sqrt{x^3 + 1}\right)^2 - 1^2}{\sqrt{x^3 + 1} + 1} = \frac{x^3}{\sqrt{x^3 + 1} + 1}$$

Thus, $(f \circ g)(0.0001) = f\left(g(10^{-4})\right) \approx \dfrac{(10^{-4})^3}{2} = 5 \times 10^{-13}$.

**62** $f(1.12) \approx 0.321170$, $g(1.12) \approx 0.280105$, $f(5.2) \approx 4.106542$, and $f(f(5.2)) \approx 3.014835$ $\Rightarrow$

$$\frac{(f + g)(1.12) - (f/g)(1.12)}{[(f \circ f)(5.2)]^2} = \frac{[f(1.12) + g(1.12)] - f(1.12)/g(1.12)}{\{f[f(5.2)]\}^2} \approx -0.059997$$

**63** ***Note:*** If we relate this problem to the composite function $g(f(u))$, then $Y_2$ can be considered to be $f$, $Y_1$ {which can be considered to be $u$} is the function of $x$ we are substituting into $f$, and $Y_3$ {which can be considered to be $g$} is accepting $Y_2$'s output values as its input values. Hence, $Y_3$ is a function of a function of a function.

***Note:*** The graphs often do not show the correct endpoints—you need to change the viewing rectangle, or zoom in to actually view them on the screen.

(a) $y = -2f(x)$; $Y_1 = x$, $Y_2 = 3\sqrt{(Y_1 + 2)(6 - Y_1)} - 4$, graph $Y_3 = -2Y_2$ {turn off $Y_1$ and $Y_2$, leaving only $Y_3$ on}; $D = [-2, 6]$, $R = [-16, 8]$

$[-12, 12, 2]$ by $[-16, 8, 2]$

(b) $y = f\left(\tfrac{1}{2}x\right)$; $Y_1 = 0.5x$, graph $Y_2$; $D = [-4, 12]$, $R = [-4, 8]$

$[-12, 12, 2]$ by $[-16, 8, 2]$

(c) $y = f(x - 3) + 1$; $Y_1 = x - 3$, graph $Y_3 = Y_2 + 1$; $D = [1, 9]$, $R = [-3, 9]$

$[-12, 12, 2]$ by $[-6, 10, 2]$

(d) $y = f(x + 2) - 3$; $Y_1 = x + 2$, graph $Y_3 = Y_2 - 3$; $D = [-4, 4]$, $R = [-7, 5]$

$[-12, 12, 2]$ by $[-8, 8, 2]$

(e) $y = f(-x)$; $Y_1 = -x$, graph $Y_2$;

$D = [-6, 2]$, $R = [-4, 8]$

$[-12, 12, 2]$ by $[-8, 8, 2]$

(f) $y = -f(x)$; $Y_1 = x$, graph $Y_3 = -Y_2$;

$D = [-2, 6]$, $R = [-8, 4]$

$[-12, 12, 2]$ by $[-8, 8, 2]$

(g) $y = f(|x|)$; $Y_1 = \text{abs } x$, graph $Y_2$;

$D = [-6, 6]$, $R = [-4, 8]$

$[-12, 12, 2]$ by $[-6, 10, 2]$

(h) $y = |f(x)|$; $Y_1 = x$, graph $Y_3 = \text{abs } Y_2$;

$D = [-2, 6]$, $R = [0, 8]$

$[-4, 8]$ by $[-2, 10]$

**64** (a) $y = \frac{1}{2}f(x)$; $Y_1 = x$, graph $Y_3 = 0.5Y_2$;

$D = [-6, -2]$, $R = [-5, -2]$

$[-10, 6]$ by $[-11, 10]$

(b) $y = f(2x)$; $Y_1 = 2x$, graph $Y_2$;

$D = [-3, -1]$, $R = [-10, -4]$

$[-10, 6]$ by $[-11, 10]$

(c) $y = f(x - 2) + 5$; $Y_1 = x - 2$, graph

$Y_3 = Y_2 + 5$; $D = [-4, 0]$, $R = [-5, 1]$

$[-10, 6]$ by $[-11, 10]$

(d) $y = f(x + 4) - 1$; $Y_1 = x + 4$, graph

$Y_3 = Y_2 - 1$; $D = [-10, -6]$, $R = [-11, -5]$

$[-10, 6]$ by $[-11, 10]$

(e) $y = f(-x)$; $Y_1 = -x$, graph $Y_2$;

$D = [2, 6]$, $R = [-10, -4]$

$[-10, 6]$ by $[-11, 10]$

(f) $y = -f(x)$; $Y_1 = x$, graph $Y_3 = -Y_2$;

$D = [-6, -2]$, $R = [4, 10]$

$[-10, 6]$ by $[-11, 10]$

(g) $y = f(|x|)$; No graph

(h) $y = |f(x)|$; $Y_1 = x$, graph $Y_3 = $ abs $Y_2$; $D = [-6, -2]$, $R = [4, 10]$

$[-10, 6]$ by $[-11, 10]$

## Chapter 2 Review Exercises

1. If $y/x < 0$, then $y$ and $x$ must have opposite signs, and hence, the set consists of all points in quadrants II and IV.

2. The points are $A(3, 1)$, $B(-5, -3)$, and $C(4, -1)$.

   Show that $d(A, B)^2 + d(A, C)^2 = d(B, C)^2$; that is, $\left(\sqrt{80}\right)^2 + \left(\sqrt{5}\right)^2 = \left(\sqrt{85}\right)^2$.

   $$\text{Area} = \tfrac{1}{2}bh = \tfrac{1}{2}\left(\sqrt{80}\right)\left(\sqrt{5}\right) = \tfrac{1}{2}\left(4\sqrt{5}\right)\left(\sqrt{5}\right) = 10.$$

3. (a) $P(-5, 9)$, $Q(-8, -7)$ $\Rightarrow$ $d(P, Q) = \sqrt{[-8 - (-5)]^2 + (-7 - 9)^2} = \sqrt{9 + 256} = \sqrt{265}$.

   (b) $P(-5, 9)$, $Q(-8, -7)$ $\Rightarrow$ $M_{PQ} = \left(\dfrac{-5 + (-8)}{2}, \dfrac{9 + (-7)}{2}\right) = \left(-\dfrac{13}{2}, 1\right)$.

   (c) Let $R = (x, y)$. $Q = M_{PR}$ $\Rightarrow$ $(-8, -7) = \left(\dfrac{-5 + x}{2}, \dfrac{9 + y}{2}\right)$ $\Rightarrow$ $-8 = \dfrac{-5 + x}{2}$ and

   $-7 = \dfrac{9 + y}{2}$ $\Rightarrow$ $-5 + x = -16$ and $9 + y = -14$ $\Rightarrow$ $x = -11$ and $y = -23$ $\Rightarrow$ $R = (-11, -23)$.

4. Let $Q(0, y)$ be an arbitrary point on the $y$-axis.

   $13 = d(P, Q)$ {with $P = (12, 8)$} $\Rightarrow$ $13 = \sqrt{(0 - 12)^2 + (y - 8)^2}$ $\Rightarrow$ $169 = 144 + y^2 - 16y + 64$ $\Rightarrow$

   $y^2 - 16y + 39 = 0$ $\Rightarrow$ $(y - 3)(y - 13) = 0$ $\Rightarrow$ $y = 3, 13$. The points are $(0, 3)$ and $(0, 13)$.

5. With $P(a, 1)$ and $Q(-2, a)$, $d(P, Q) < 3$ $\Rightarrow$ $\sqrt{(-2 - a)^2 + (a - 1)^2} < 3$ $\Rightarrow$

   $4 + 4a + a^2 + a^2 - 2a + 1 < 9$ $\Rightarrow$ $2a^2 + 2a - 4 < 0$ $\Rightarrow$ $a^2 + a - 2 < 0$ $\Rightarrow$ $(a + 2)(a - 1) < 0$.

   | Interval | $(-\infty, -2)$ | $(-2, 1)$ | $(1, \infty)$ |
   |---|---|---|---|
   | Sign of $a + 2$ | $-$ | $+$ | $+$ |
   | Sign of $a - 1$ | $-$ | $-$ | $+$ |
   | **Resulting sign** | $+$ | $-$ | $+$ |

   From the chart, we see that $-2 < a < 1$ will assure us that $d(P, Q) < 3$.

6. The equation of a circle with center $C(7, -4)$ is $(x - 7)^2 + (y + 4)^2 = r^2$.

   Letting $x = -2$ and $y = 5$ yields $(-9)^2 + 9^2 = r^2$ $\Rightarrow$ $r^2 = 162$. An equation is $(x - 7)^2 + (y + 4)^2 = 162$.

7. The center of the circle is the midpoint of $A(8, 10)$ and $B(-2, -14)$, so the center is

   $M_{AB} = \left(\dfrac{8 + (-2)}{2}, \dfrac{10 + (-14)}{2}\right) = (3, -2)$. The radius of the circle is

   $\tfrac{1}{2} \cdot d(A, B) = \tfrac{1}{2}\sqrt{(-2 - 8)^2 + (-14 - 10)^2} = \tfrac{1}{2}\sqrt{100 + 576} = \tfrac{1}{2} \cdot 26 = 13$.

   An equation is $(x - 3)^2 + (y + 2)^2 = 13^2 = 169$.

**8**   We need to solve the equation for $x$. $(x+2)^2 + y^2 = 7 \;\Rightarrow\; (x+2)^2 = 7 - y^2 \;\Rightarrow\; x+2 = \pm\sqrt{7-y^2} \;\Rightarrow\;$
$x = -2 \pm \sqrt{7-y^2}$. Choose the term with the minus sign for the left half. $x = -2 - \sqrt{7-y^2}$

**9**   $C(11,-5), D(-6,8) \;\Rightarrow\; m_{CD} = \dfrac{8-(-5)}{-6-11} = \dfrac{13}{-17} = -\dfrac{13}{17}.$

**10**   Show that the slopes of one pair of opposite sides are equal.
$$A(-3,1),\, B(1,-1),\, C(4,1),\, \text{and } D(3,5) \;\Rightarrow\; m_{AD} = \tfrac{2}{3} = m_{BC}.$$

**11**   (a)   $6x + 2y + 5 = 0 \;\Leftrightarrow\; y = -3x - \tfrac{5}{2}$. Using the same slope, $-3$, with $A\left(\tfrac{1}{2}, -\tfrac{1}{3}\right)$, we have
$$y + \tfrac{1}{3} = -3\left(x - \tfrac{1}{2}\right) \;\Rightarrow\; 6\left(y + \tfrac{1}{3}\right) = -18\left(x - \tfrac{1}{2}\right) \;\Rightarrow\; 6y + 2 = -18x + 9 \;\Rightarrow\; 18x + 6y = 7.$$

(b)   Using the negative reciprocal of $-3$ for the slope,
$$y + \tfrac{1}{3} = \tfrac{1}{3}\left(x - \tfrac{1}{2}\right) \;\Rightarrow\; 6\left(y + \tfrac{1}{3}\right) = 2\left(x - \tfrac{1}{2}\right) \;\Rightarrow\; 6y + 2 = 2x - 1 \;\Rightarrow\; 2x - 6y = 3.$$

**12**   Solving for $y$ gives us: $8x + 3y - 15 = 0 \;\Leftrightarrow\; 3y = -8x + 15 \;\Leftrightarrow\; y = -\tfrac{8}{3}x + 5$

**13**   The radius of the circle is the distance from the line $x = 4$ to the $x$-value of the
center $C(-5,-1); r = 4 - (-5) = 9$. An equation is $(x+5)^2 + (y+1)^2 = 81$.

**14**   $x^2 + y^2 - 4x + 10y + 26 = 0 \;\Rightarrow\; x^2 - 4x + \underline{4} + y^2 + 10y + \underline{25} = -26 + \underline{4} + \underline{25} \;\Rightarrow\;$
$(x-2)^2 + (y+5)^2 = 3 \;\Rightarrow\; C(2,-5)$. We want the equation of the line through $(-3,0)$ and $(2,-5)$.
$$y - 0 = \dfrac{-5-0}{2+3}(x+3) \;\Rightarrow\; y = -1(x+3) \;\Rightarrow\; x + y = -3.$$

**15**   $P(3,-7)$ with $m = 4 \;\Rightarrow\; y + 7 = 4(x-3) \;\Rightarrow\; y + 7 = 4x - 12 \;\Rightarrow\; 4x - y = 19.$

**16**   $A(-1,2)$ and $B(3,-4) \;\Rightarrow\; M_{AB} = (1,-1)$ and $m_{AB} = -\tfrac{3}{2}$. We want the equation of the line through $(1,-1)$
with slope $\tfrac{2}{3}$ {the negative reciprocal of $-\tfrac{3}{2}$}. $y + 1 = \tfrac{2}{3}(x-1) \;\Rightarrow\; 3y + 3 = 2x - 2 \;\Rightarrow\; 2x - 3y = 5.$

**17**   $x^2 + y^2 - 12y + 31 = 0 \;\Rightarrow\; x^2 + y^2 - 12y + \underline{36} = -31 + \underline{36} \;\Rightarrow\; x^2 + (y-6)^2 = 5. \; C(0,6); r = \sqrt{5}$

**18**   $4x^2 + 4y^2 + 24x - 16y + 41 = 0 \;\Rightarrow\; x^2 + y^2 + 6x - 4y + \tfrac{41}{4} = 0 \;\Rightarrow\;$
$x^2 + 6x + \underline{9} + y^2 - 4y + \underline{4} = -\tfrac{41}{4} + \underline{9} + \underline{4} \;\Rightarrow\; (x+3)^2 + (y-2)^2 = \tfrac{11}{4}. \; C(-3,2); r = \tfrac{1}{2}\sqrt{11}$

**19**   (a)   $f(x) = \dfrac{x}{\sqrt{x+3}} \;\Rightarrow\; f(1) = \dfrac{1}{\sqrt{4}} = \dfrac{1}{2}$       (b)   $f(-1) = \dfrac{-1}{\sqrt{-1+3}} = -\dfrac{1}{\sqrt{2}}$

(c)   $f(0) = \dfrac{0}{\sqrt{3}} = 0$       (d)   $f(-x) = \dfrac{-x}{\sqrt{-x+3}} = -\dfrac{x}{\sqrt{3-x}}$

(e)   $-f(x) = -1 \cdot f(x) = -\dfrac{x}{\sqrt{x+3}}$       (f)   $f(x^2) = \dfrac{x^2}{\sqrt{x^2+3}}$

(g)   $[f(x)]^2 = \left(\dfrac{x}{\sqrt{x+3}}\right)^2 = \dfrac{x^2}{x+3}$

**20**   $f(x) = \dfrac{-32(x^2-4)}{(9-x^2)^{5/3}} \;\Rightarrow\; f(4) = \dfrac{(-)(+)}{(-)} = +. \; f(4)$ is positive.

Note that the factor $-32$ always contributes one negative sign to the quotient.

**21** $f(x) = \dfrac{-2(x^2 - 20)(3 - x)}{(6 - x^2)^{4/3}}$ $\Rightarrow$ $f(4) = \dfrac{(-)(-)(-)}{(+)} = (-)$. $f(4)$ is negative.

Note that the factor $-2$ always contributes one negative sign to the quotient and that

the denominator is always positive if $x \neq \pm \sqrt{6}$.

**22** (a) $y = f(x) = \sqrt{3x - 4}$ • $3x - 4 \geq 0$ $\Rightarrow$ $x \geq \frac{4}{3}$; $D = [\frac{4}{3}, \infty)$.

Since $y$ is the result of a square root, $y \geq 0$; $R = [0, \infty)$.

(b) $y = f(x) = \dfrac{1}{(x + 4)^2}$ • $D = $ All real numbers except $-4$.

Since $y$ is the square of the nonzero term $\dfrac{1}{x + 4}$, $y > 0$; $R = (0, \infty)$.

**23** $\dfrac{f(a + h) - f(a)}{h} = \dfrac{[-(a + h)^2 + (a + h) + 5] - [-a^2 + a + 5]}{h}$

$= \dfrac{-a^2 - 2ah - h^2 + a + h + 5 + a^2 - a - 5}{h}$

$= \dfrac{-2ah - h^2 + h}{h} = \dfrac{h(-2a - h + 1)}{h} = -2a - h + 1$

**24** $\dfrac{f(a + h) - f(a)}{h} = \dfrac{\dfrac{1}{a + h + 4} - \dfrac{1}{a + 4}}{h} = \dfrac{\dfrac{(a + 4) - (a + h + 4)}{(a + h + 4)(a + 4)}}{h}$

$= \dfrac{-h}{(a + h + 4)(a + 4)h} = -\dfrac{1}{(a + h + 4)(a + 4)}$

**25** $f(x) = ax + b$ is the desired form. $f(1) = 3$ and $f(4) = 8$ $\Rightarrow$ $a = \text{slope} = \dfrac{8 - 3}{4 - 1} = \dfrac{5}{3}$.

$f(x) = \frac{5}{3}x + b$ $\Rightarrow$ $f(1) = \frac{5}{3} + b$, but $f(1) = 3$, so $\frac{5}{3} + b = 3$, and $b = \frac{4}{3}$. Thus, $f(x) = \frac{5}{3}x + \frac{4}{3}$.

**26** (a) $f(x) = \sqrt[3]{x^3 + 4x}$ $\Rightarrow$ $f(-x) = \sqrt[3]{(-x)^3 + 4(-x)} = \sqrt[3]{-1(x^3 + 4x)} = -\sqrt[3]{x^3 + 4x} = -f(x)$,

so $f$ is odd

(b) $f(x) = \sqrt[3]{\pi x^2 - x^3}$ $\Rightarrow$ $f(-x) = \sqrt[3]{\pi(-x)^2 - (-x)^3} = \sqrt[3]{\pi x^2 + x^3} \neq \pm f(x)$,

so $f$ is neither even nor odd

(c) $f(x) = \sqrt[3]{x^4 - 3x^2 + 5}$ $\Rightarrow$ $f(-x) = \sqrt[3]{(-x)^4 - 3(-x)^2 + 5} = \sqrt[3]{x^4 - 3x^2 + 5} = f(x)$, so $f$ is even

**27** $x + 5 = 0$ $\Leftrightarrow$ $x = -5$, a vertical line; $x$-intercept $-5$; $y$-intercept: None

*Figure 27*

*Figure 28*

**28** $2y - 7 = 0$ $\Leftrightarrow$ $y = \frac{7}{2}$, a horizontal line; $x$-intercept: None; $y$-intercept 3.5

**29** $2y + 5x - 8 = 0 \iff y = -\frac{5}{2}x + 4$, a line with slope $-\frac{5}{2}$ and $y$-intercept 4.

$x$-intercept: $y = 0 \Rightarrow 2(0) + 5x - 8 = 0 \Rightarrow 5x = 8 \Rightarrow x = 1.6$

*Figure 29*

*Figure 30*

**30** $x = 3y + 4 \iff y = \frac{1}{3}x - \frac{4}{3}$, a line with slope $\frac{1}{3}$ and $y$-intercept $-\frac{4}{3}$; $x$-intercept 4

**31** $9y + 2x^2 = 0 \iff y = -\frac{2}{9}x^2$, a parabola opening down; $x$- and $y$-intercept 0

*Figure 31*

*Figure 32*

**32** $3x - 7y^2 = 0 \iff x = \frac{7}{3}y^2$, a parabola opening to the right; $x$- and $y$-intercept 0

**33** $y = \sqrt{1 - x}$ • The radicand must be nonnegative for the radical to be defined. $1 - x \geq 0 \Rightarrow 1 \geq x$, or equivalently, $x \leq 1$.

The domain is $(-\infty, 1]$ and the range is $[0, \infty)$.

$x$-intercept: $y = 0 \Rightarrow 0 = \sqrt{1 - x} \Rightarrow 0 = 1 - x \Rightarrow x = 1$

$y$-intercept: $x = 0 \Rightarrow y = \sqrt{1 - 0} = 1$

*Figure 33*

*Figure 34*

**34** $y = (x - 1)^3$ • shift $y = x^3$ right one unit; $x$-intercept 1; $y$-intercept $-1$

**35** $y^2 = 16 - x^2 \Leftrightarrow x^2 + y^2 = 16$; $x$-intercepts $\pm 4$; $y$-intercepts $\pm 4$

*Figure 35*

*Figure 36*

**36** $x^2 + y^2 + 4x - 16y + 64 = 0 \Rightarrow x^2 + 4x + \underline{4} + y^2 - 16y + \underline{64} = -64 + \underline{4} + \underline{64} \Rightarrow$
$(x+2)^2 + (y-8)^2 = 4$; $C(-2, 8)$, $r = \sqrt{4} = 2$; $x$-intercept: None; $y$-intercept 8

**37** $x^2 + y^2 - 8x = 0 \Leftrightarrow x^2 - 8x + \underline{16} + y^2 = \underline{16} \Leftrightarrow (x-4)^2 + y^2 = 16$. This is a circle with center $C(4, 0)$
and radius $r = \sqrt{16} = 4$. $x$-intercepts: $y = 0 \Rightarrow x^2 - 8x = 0 \Rightarrow x(x-8) = 0 \Rightarrow x = 0$ and 8;
$y$-intercept: 0

*Figure 37*

*Figure 38*

**38** $x = -\sqrt{9 - y^2}$ is the left half of the circle $x^2 + y^2 = 9$; $x$-intercept $-3$; $y$-intercepts $\pm 3$

**39** $y = (x-3)^2 - 2$ is a parabola that opens upward and has vertex $(3, -2)$.
$x$-intercepts: $y = 0 \Rightarrow 0 = (x-3)^2 - 2 \Rightarrow (x-3)^2 = 2 \Rightarrow x - 3 = \pm\sqrt{2} \Rightarrow x = 3 \pm \sqrt{2}$
$y$-intercept: $x = 0 \Rightarrow y = (0-3)^2 - 2 = 9 - 2 = 7$

*Figure 39*

*Figure 40*

**40** $y = -x^2 - 2x + 3 = -(x^2 + 2x + \underline{1}) + 3 + \underline{1} = -(x+1)^2 + 4$; $V(-1, 4)$; $x$-intercepts $-3$ and 1; $y$-intercept 3

**41** The radius of the large circle is 3 and the radius of the small circle is 1. Since the center of the small circle is 4 units

from the origin and lies on the line $y = x$, we must have $x^2 + y^2 = 4^2 \Rightarrow x^2 + x^2 = 16 \Rightarrow 2x^2 = 16 \Rightarrow$

$x^2 = 8 \Rightarrow x = \sqrt{8}$. The center of the small circle is $\left( \sqrt{8}, \sqrt{8} \right)$.

**42** The graph of $y = -f(x-2)$ is the graph of $y = f(x)$ shifted to the right 2 units and reflected through the $x$-axis.

**43** (a) The graph of $f(x) = \dfrac{1-3x}{2} = -\dfrac{3}{2}x + \dfrac{1}{2}$ is a line with slope $-\dfrac{3}{2}$ and $y$-intercept $\dfrac{1}{2}$.

(b) The function is defined for all $x$, so the domain $D$ is the set of all real numbers.

The range is the set of all real numbers, so $D = \mathbb{R}$ and $R = \mathbb{R}$.

(c) The function $f$ is decreasing on $(-\infty, \infty)$.

*Figure 43*

*Figure 44*

**44** $f(x) = 1000$ • (b) $D = \mathbb{R}$; $R = \{1000\}$          (c) Constant on $(-\infty, \infty)$

**45** (a) The graph of $f(x) = |x + 3|$ can be thought of as the graph of $g(x) = |x|$ shifted left 3 units.

(b) The function is defined for all $x$, so the domain $D$ is the set of all real numbers. The range is the set of all

nonnegative numbers, that is, $R = [0, \infty)$.

(c) The function $f$ is decreasing on $(-\infty, -3]$ and is increasing on $[-3, \infty)$.

*Figure 45*

*Figure 46*

**46** $f(x) = -\sqrt{10 - x^2}$ • (b) $D = \left[ -\sqrt{10}, \sqrt{10} \right]$; $R = \left[ -\sqrt{10}, 0 \right]$

(c) Decreasing on $\left[ -\sqrt{10}, 0 \right]$, increasing on $\left[ 0, \sqrt{10} \right]$

**47** (a) $f(x) = 1 - \sqrt{x+1} = -\sqrt{x+1} + 1$ • We can think of this graph as the graph of $y = \sqrt{x}$ shifted left 1 unit, reflected through the $x$-axis, and shifted up 1 unit.

(b) For $f$ to be defined, we must have $x + 1 \geq 0 \Rightarrow x \geq -1$, so $D = [-1, \infty)$. The $y$-values of $f$ are all the values less than or equal to 1, so $R = (-\infty, 1]$.

(c) The function $f$ is decreasing on $[-1, \infty)$.

*Figure 47*

*Figure 48*

**48** $f(x) = \sqrt{2-x}$ • (b) $D = (-\infty, 2]$; $R = [0, \infty)$

(c) Decreasing on $(-\infty, 2]$

**49** (a) $f(x) = 9 - x^2 = -x^2 + 9$ • We can think of this graph as the graph of $y = x^2$ reflected through the $x$-axis and shifted up 9 units.

(b) The function is defined for all $x$, so the domain $D$ is the set of all real numbers. The $y$-values of $f$ are all the values less than or equal to 9, so $R = (-\infty, 9]$.

(c) The function $f$ is increasing on $(-\infty, 0]$ and is decreasing on $[0, \infty)$.

*Figure 49*

*Figure 50*

**50** $f(x) = x^2 + 6x + 16 = x^2 + 6x + 9 + 7 = (x+3)^2 + 7$. The vertex is $(-3, 7)$.

(b) $D = \mathbb{R}$; $R = [7, \infty)$

(c) Decreasing on $(-\infty, -3]$, increasing on $[-3, \infty)$

**51** (a) $f(x) = \begin{cases} x^2 & \text{if } x < 0 \\ 3x & \text{if } 0 \leq x < 2 \\ 6 & \text{if } x \geq 2 \end{cases}$

If $x < 0$, we want the graph of the parabola $y = x^2$. The endpoint of this part of the graph is $(0, 0)$, but it is not included. If $0 \leq x < 2$, we want the graph of $y = 3x$, a line with slope 3 and $y$-intercept 0. Now we do include the endpoint $(0, 0)$, but we don't include the endpoint $(2, 6)$. If $x \geq 2$, we want the graph of the horizontal line $y = 6$ and include its endpoint $(2, 6)$, so there are no open endpoints on the graph of $f$.

(b) The function is defined for all $x$, so the domain $D$ is the set of all real numbers. The $y$-values of $f$ are all the values greater than or equal to 0, so $R = [0, \infty)$.

(c) $f$ is decreasing on $(-\infty, 0]$, increasing on $[0, 2]$, and constant on $[2, \infty)$.

Figure 51

Figure 52

**52** (a) $f(x) = 1 + 2[\![x]\!]$  •  The "2" in front of $[\![x]\!]$ has the effect of doubling all the $y$-values of $g(x) = [\![x]\!]$. The "+1" has the effect of vertically shifting the graph of $h(x) = 2[\![x]\!]$ up 1 unit.

(b) The function is defined for all $x$, so the domain $D$ is the set of all real numbers. The range of $g(x) = [\![x]\!]$ is the set of integers, that is, $\{\ldots, -2, -1, 0, 1, 2, \ldots\}$. The range of $h(x) = 2[\![x]\!]$ is the set of even integers since we are doubling the values of $g$—that is, $\{\ldots, -4, -2, 0, 2, 4, \ldots\}$. Since $f(x) = 1 + h(x)$, the range $R$ of $f$ is $\{\ldots, -3, -1, 1, 3, \ldots\}$.

(c) The function $f$ is constant on intervals such as $[0, 1)$, $[1, 2)$, and $[2, 3)$. In general, $f$ is constant on $[n, n + 1)$, where $n$ is any integer.

**53** (a) $y = \sqrt{x}$  •  This is the square root function, whose graph is a half-parabola.
(b) $y = \sqrt{x + 4}$  •  shift $y = \sqrt{x}$ left 4 units

(c) $y = \sqrt{x} + 4$ • shift $y = \sqrt{x}$ up 4 units

(d) $y = 4\sqrt{x}$ • vertically stretch the graph of $y = \sqrt{x}$ by a factor of 4

(e) $y = \frac{1}{4}\sqrt{x}$ • vertically compress the graph of $y = \sqrt{x}$ by a factor of $1/\frac{1}{4} = 4$

(f) $y = -\sqrt{x}$ • reflect the graph of $y = \sqrt{x}$ through the $x$-axis

**54** (a) $y = f(x - 2)$ • shift $f$ right 2 units

(b) $y = f(x) - 2$ • shift $f$ down 2 units

(c) $y = f(-x)$ • reflect $f$ through the $y$-axis

(d) $y = f(2x)$ • horizontally compress $f$ by a factor of 2

(e) $y = f\left(\frac{1}{2}x\right)$ • horizontally stretch $f$ by a factor of $1/(1/2) = 2$

(f) $y = |f(x)|$ • reflect the portion of the graph below the $x$-axis through the $x$-axis.

(g) $y = f(|x|)$ • include the reflection of all points with positive $x$-coordinates through the $y$-axis— results in the same graph as in part (f).

**55** Using the intercept form of a line with $x$-intercept 5 and $y$-intercept $-2$, an equation of the line is $\dfrac{x}{5} + \dfrac{y}{-2} = 1$.

Multiplying by 10 gives us $\left[\dfrac{x}{5} + \dfrac{y}{-2} = 1\right] \cdot 10$, or, equivalently, $2x - 5y = 10$.

**56** The midpoint of $(-7, 1)$ and $(3, 1)$ is $M(-2, 1)$. This point is 5 units from either of the given points.

An equation of the circle is $(x + 2)^2 + (y - 1)^2 = 5^2 = 25$.

**57** $V(2, -4)$ and $P(-2, 4)$ with $y = a(x - h)^2 + k$ $\Rightarrow$ $4 = a(-2 - 2)^2 - 4$ $\Rightarrow$ $8 = 16a$ $\Rightarrow$ $a = \frac{1}{2}$.

An equation of the parabola is $y = \frac{1}{2}(x - 2)^2 - 4$.

**58** The graph could be made by taking the graph of $y = |x|$, reflecting it through the $x$-axis $\{y = -|x|\}$, then shifting that graph to the right 2 units $\{y = -|x - 2|\}$, and then shifting that graph down 1 unit, resulting in the graph of the equation $y = -|x - 2| - 1$.

**59** $f(x) = 3x^2 - 24x + 46$ $\Rightarrow$ $-\dfrac{b}{2a} = -\dfrac{-24}{2(3)} = 4$. $f(4) = -2$ is a minimum since $a = 3 > 0$.

**60** $f(x) = -2x^2 - 12x - 24$ $\Rightarrow$ $-\dfrac{b}{2a} = -\dfrac{-12}{2(-2)} = -3$. $f(-3) = -6$ is a maximum since $a = -2 < 0$.

**61** $f(x) = -12(x + 4)^2 + 20$ is in the standard form. $f(-4) = 20$ is a maximum since $a = -12 < 0$.

**62** $f(x) = 3(x + 2)(x - 10)$ has $x$-intercepts at $-2$ and 10. The vertex is halfway between them at $x = 4$.

$f(4) = 3 \cdot 6 \cdot (-6) = -108$ is a minimum since $a = 3 > 0$.

**63** $f(x) = -2x^2 + 12x - 14 = -2\left(x^2 - 6x + \underline{\quad}\right) - 14 + \underline{\quad}$ {complete the square}

$= -2\left(x^2 - 6x + \underline{9}\right) - 14 + 18 = -2(x - 3)^2 + 4$.

**64** $V(3, -2)$ $\Rightarrow$ $(h, k) = (3, -2)$ in $y = a(x - h)^2 + k$.

$x = 1, y = -5$ $\Rightarrow$ $-5 = a(1 - 3)^2 - 2$ $\Rightarrow$ $-3 = 4a$ $\Rightarrow$ $a = -\frac{3}{4}$. Hence, $y = -\frac{3}{4}(x - 3)^2 - 2$.

**65** The domain of $f(x) = \sqrt{9 - x^2}$ is $[-3, 3]$. The domain of $g(x) = \sqrt{x}$ is $[0, \infty)$.

(a) The domain of $fg$ is the intersection of those two domains, $[0, 3]$.

(b) The domain of $f/g$ is the same as that of $fg$, excluding any values that make $g$ equal to 0.

$$\text{Thus, the domain of } f/g \text{ is } (0, 3].$$

**66** (a) $f(x) = 8x - 3$ and $g(x) = \sqrt{x - 2}$ $\Rightarrow$ $(f \circ g)(2) = f(g(2)) = f(0) = -3$

(b) $(g \circ f)(2) = g(f(2)) = g(13) = \sqrt{11}$

**67** (a) $f(x) = 2x^2 - 5x + 1$ and $g(x) = 3x + 2$ $\Rightarrow$
$(f \circ g)(x) = f(g(x)) = 2(3x + 2)^2 - 5(3x + 2) + 1 = 2(9x^2 + 12x + 4) - 15x - 10 + 1 = 18x^2 + 9x - 1$

(b) $(g \circ f)(x) = g(f(x)) = 3(2x^2 - 5x + 1) + 2 = 6x^2 - 15x + 3 + 2 = 6x^2 - 15x + 5$

**68** (a) $f(x) = \sqrt{3x + 2}$ and $g(x) = \dfrac{1}{x^2}$ $\Rightarrow$ $(f \circ g)(x) = f(g(x)) = \sqrt{3\left(\dfrac{1}{x^2}\right) + 2} = \sqrt{\dfrac{3 + 2x^2}{x^2}}$

(b) $(g \circ f)(x) = g(f(x)) = \dfrac{1}{\left(\sqrt{3x + 2}\right)^2} = \dfrac{1}{3x + 2}$

**69** (a) $(f \circ g)(x) = f(g(x)) = f\left(\sqrt{x - 3}\right) = \sqrt{25 - \left(\sqrt{x - 3}\right)^2} = \sqrt{25 - (x - 3)} = \sqrt{28 - x}$.
Domain of $g(x) = \sqrt{x - 3} = [3, \infty)$. Domain of $f(x) = \sqrt{25 - x^2} = [-5, 5]$.
$g(x) \le 5$ {$g(x)$ cannot be less than 0} $\Rightarrow$ $\sqrt{x - 3} \le 5$ $\Rightarrow$ $x - 3 \le 25$ $\Rightarrow$ $x \le 28$.
$$[3, \infty) \cap (-\infty, 28] = [3, 28]$$

(b) $(g \circ f)(x) = g(f(x)) = g\left(\sqrt{25 - x^2}\right) = \sqrt{\sqrt{25 - x^2} - 3}$. Domain of $f = [-5, 5]$. Domain of $g = [3, \infty)$.
$f(x) \ge 3$ $\Rightarrow$ $\sqrt{25 - x^2} \ge 3$ $\Rightarrow$ $25 - x^2 \ge 9$ $\Rightarrow$ $x^2 \le 16$ $\Rightarrow$ $x \in [-4, 4]$.

**70** (a) $(f \circ g)(x) = f(g(x)) = f\left(\dfrac{2}{x}\right) = \dfrac{2/x}{3(2/x) + 2} \cdot \dfrac{x}{x} = \dfrac{2}{6 + 2x} = \dfrac{1}{x + 3}$. Domain of $g = \mathbb{R} - \{0\}$.
Domain of $f = \mathbb{R} - \{-\frac{2}{3}\}$. $g(x) \ne -\frac{2}{3}$ $\Rightarrow$ $\dfrac{2}{x} \ne -\dfrac{2}{3}$ $\Rightarrow$ $x \ne -3$.

$$\text{Hence, the domain of } f \circ g \text{ is } \mathbb{R} - \{-3, 0\}.$$

(b) $(g \circ f)(x) = g(f(x)) = g\left(\dfrac{x}{3x + 2}\right) = \dfrac{2}{x/(3x + 2)} = \dfrac{6x + 4}{x}$. Domain of $f = \mathbb{R} - \{-\frac{2}{3}\}$. Domain

of $g = \mathbb{R} - \{0\}$. $f(x) \ne 0$ $\Rightarrow$ $\dfrac{x}{3x + 2} \ne 0$ $\Rightarrow$ $x \ne 0$. Hence, the domain of $g \circ f$ is $\mathbb{R} - \{-\frac{2}{3}, 0\}$.

**71** For $y = \sqrt[3]{x^2 - 5x}$, choose $u = x^2 - 5x$ and $y = \sqrt[3]{u}$.

**72** The slope of the ramp should be between $\frac{1}{12}$ and $\frac{1}{20}$.

If the rise of the ramp is 3 feet, then the run should be between $3 \times 12 = 36$ ft and $3 \times 20 = 60$ ft.

$$\text{The range of the ramp lengths should be from } L = \sqrt{3^2 + 36^2} \approx 36.1 \text{ ft to } L = \sqrt{3^2 + 60^2} \approx 60.1 \text{ ft.}$$

**73** (a) The year 2016 corresponds to $t = 2016 - 1948 = 68$. $d = 181 + 1.065(68) = 253.42 \approx 253$ ft

(b) $d = 265$ $\Rightarrow$ $265 = 181 + 1.065t$ $\Rightarrow$ $84 = 1.065t$ $\Rightarrow$ $t = \frac{84}{1.065} \approx 78.9$ yr,

$$\text{which corresponds to } 79 + 1948 = 2027 \text{ or Olympic year 2028.}$$

**74** (a) $V = at + b$ is the desired form. $V = 179{,}000$ when $t = 0$ $\Rightarrow$ $V = at + 179{,}000$.

$V = 215{,}000$ when $t = 6$ $\Rightarrow$ $215{,}000 = 6a + 179{,}000$ $\Rightarrow$ $a = \frac{36{,}000}{6} = 6000$ and hence,

$$V = 6000t + 179{,}000.$$

(b) $V = 193{,}000$ $\Rightarrow$ $193{,}000 = 6000t + 179{,}000$ $\Rightarrow$ $t = \frac{14{,}000}{6000} = \frac{7}{3}$, or $2\frac{1}{3}$.

**75** (a) $F = aC + b$ is the desired form. $F = 32$ when $C = 0$ $\Rightarrow$ $F = aC + 32$. $F = 212$ when $C = 100$ $\Rightarrow$

$$212 = 100a + 32 \quad \Rightarrow \quad a = \frac{180}{100} = \frac{9}{5} \text{ and hence, } F = \frac{9}{5}C + 32.$$

(b) If $C$ increases $1°$, $F$ increases $\left(\frac{9}{5}\right)°$, or $1.8°$.

**76** (a) $C_1(x) = \left(3.00 \, \dfrac{\text{dollars}}{\text{gallon}}\right) \div \left(20 \, \dfrac{\text{miles}}{\text{gallon}}\right) \cdot x \text{ miles} = \dfrac{3}{20}x$, or $0.15x$.

(b) After the tune-up, the gasoline mileage will be 10% more than 20 mi/gal; that is, 22 mi/gal.

$$C_2(x) = \tfrac{3}{22}x + 120 \approx 0.136x + 120.$$

(c) $C_2 < C_1$ $\Rightarrow$ $\left[\tfrac{3}{22}x + 120 < \tfrac{3}{20}x\right] \cdot 220$ $\Rightarrow$ $30x + 26{,}400 < 33x$ $\Rightarrow$ $3x > 26{,}400$ $\Rightarrow$

$$x > 8800 \text{ miles.}$$

**77** (a) The length across the top of the pen is $3x$ and the length across the bottom is $2y$. These lengths are equal, so

$2y = 3x$ $\Rightarrow$ $y = \tfrac{3}{2}x$, or $y(x) = \tfrac{3}{2}x$.

(b) There are 6 long lengths ($y$) and 9 short lengths ($x$), so the perimeter $P$ is given by $P = 6y + 9x$ and

$C = 10P = 10(6y + 9x) = 10\left[(6 \cdot \tfrac{3}{2}x) + 9x\right] = 10(9x + 9x) = 10(18x) = 180x$. Thus, $C(x) = 180x$.

**78** The distances covered by cars A and B in $t$ seconds are $88t$ and $66t$, respectively. The vertical distance between car A and car B after $t$ seconds is $(20 + 88t) - 66t = 20 + 22t$. Using the Pythagorean theorem, we have

$d(t) = \sqrt{10^2 + (20 + 22t)^2} = \sqrt{100 + 400 + 880t + 484t^2} = 2\sqrt{121t^2 + 220t + 125}$.

**79** Surface area $S = 2(4)(x) + (4)(y) = 8x + 4y$. Cost $C = 2(8x) + 5(4y) = 16x + 20y$.

(a) $C = 400$ $\Rightarrow$ $16x + 20y = 400$ $\Rightarrow$ $20y = -16x + 400$ $\Rightarrow$ $y = -\tfrac{4}{5}x + 20$

(b) $V = lwh = (y)(4)(x) = 4xy = 4x\left(-\tfrac{4}{5}x + 20\right)$

**80** $V = \pi r^2 h$ and $V = 24\pi$ $\Rightarrow$ $h = \dfrac{24}{r^2}$. $S = \pi r^2 + 2\pi rh = \pi r^2 + 2\pi r \cdot \dfrac{24}{r^2} = \pi r^2 + \dfrac{48\pi}{r}$.

$$C = (0.30)(\pi r^2) + (0.10)\left(\frac{48\pi}{r}\right) = \frac{3\pi r^2}{10} + \frac{48\pi}{10r} = \frac{3\pi(r^3 + 16)}{10r}.$$

**81** (a) $V = (10 \text{ ft}^3 \text{ per minute})(t \text{ minutes}) = 10t$

(b) The height and length of the bottom triangular region are in the proportion 6–60, or 1–10, and the length is 10 times the height. When $0 \le h \le 6$, the volume is

$$V = (\text{cross sectional area})(\text{pool width}) = \tfrac{1}{2}bh(40) = \tfrac{1}{2}(10h)(h)(40) = 200h^2 \text{ ft}^3.$$

When $6 < h \le 9$, the triangular region is full and $V = 200(6)^2 + (h - 6)(80)(40) = 7200 + 3200(h - 6)$.

(c) For $0 \le h \le 6$: $10t = 200h^2 \Rightarrow h^2 = \dfrac{10t}{200} \Rightarrow h = \sqrt{\dfrac{t}{20}}$;

$$0 \le h \le 6 \Rightarrow 0 \le \sqrt{\dfrac{t}{20}} \le 6 \Rightarrow 0 \le \dfrac{t}{20} \le 36 \Rightarrow 0 \le t \le 720.$$

For $6 < h \le 9$: $10t = 7200 + 3200(h-6) \Rightarrow h - 6 = \dfrac{10t - 7200}{3200} \Rightarrow h = 6 + \dfrac{t - 720}{320}$;

$$6 < h \le 9 \Rightarrow 6 < 6 + \dfrac{t-720}{320} \le 9 \Rightarrow 0 < \dfrac{t-720}{320} \le 3 \Rightarrow 0 < t - 720 \le 960 \Rightarrow$$

$$720 < t \le 1680.$$

**82** (a) Using similar triangles, $\dfrac{r}{x} = \dfrac{2}{4} \Rightarrow r = \dfrac{1}{2}x$.

(b) $\text{Volume}_{\text{cone}} + \text{Volume}_{\text{cup}} = \text{Volume}_{\text{total}} \Rightarrow \frac{1}{3}\pi r^2 h + \pi r^2 h = 5 \Rightarrow$

$$\tfrac{1}{3}\pi\left(\tfrac{1}{2}x\right)^2(x) + \pi(2)^2(y) = 5 \Rightarrow 4\pi y = 5 - \tfrac{\pi}{12}x^3 \Rightarrow y = \tfrac{5}{4\pi} - \tfrac{1}{48}x^3$$

**83** (a) $\dfrac{y}{b} = \dfrac{y+h}{a} \Rightarrow ay = by + bh \Rightarrow ay - by = bh \Rightarrow y(a-b) = bh \Rightarrow y = \dfrac{bh}{a-b}$

(b) $V = \dfrac{1}{3}\pi a^2(y+h) - \dfrac{1}{3}\pi b^2 y = \dfrac{1}{3}\pi a^2 y + \dfrac{1}{3}\pi a^2 h - \dfrac{1}{3}\pi b^2 y = \dfrac{\pi}{3}\left[(a^2 - b^2)y + a^2 h\right]$

$$= \dfrac{\pi}{3}\left[(a^2 - b^2)\dfrac{bh}{a-b} + a^2 h\right] = \dfrac{\pi}{3}h\left[(a+b)b + a^2\right] = \dfrac{\pi}{3}h(a^2 + ab + b^2)$$

(c) $a = 6, b = 3, V = 600 \Rightarrow 600 = \tfrac{\pi}{3}h(6^2 + 6 \cdot 3 + 3^2) \Rightarrow h = \tfrac{1800}{63\pi} = \tfrac{200}{7\pi} \approx 9.1$ ft

**84** If $0 \le x \le 5000$, then $B(x) = \$3.61(x/1000)$. If $x > 5000$, then the charge is $\$3.61(5000/1000)$ for the first 5000 gallons, which is $\$18.05$, plus $\$4.17/1000$ for the number of gallons over 5000, which is $(x - 5000)$. We may summarize and simplify as follows:

$$B(x) = \begin{cases} 3.61\left(\frac{x}{1000}\right) & \text{if } 0 \le x \le 5000 \\ 3.61(5) + 4.17\left(\frac{x-5000}{1000}\right) & \text{if } x > 5000 \end{cases} = \begin{cases} 0.00361x & \text{if } 0 \le x \le 5000 \\ 18.05 + 0.00417(x - 5000) & \text{if } x > 5000 \end{cases}$$

$$= \begin{cases} 0.00361x & \text{if } 0 \le x \le 5000 \\ 0.00417x - 2.8 & \text{if } x > 5000 \end{cases}$$

**85** The high point of the path occurs halfway through the jump, that is, at $\frac{1}{2}(8.95) = 4.475$ meters from the beginning of the jump. Using the form $y = a(x - h)^2 + k$, we have $y = a(x - 4.475)^2 + 1$. Substituting 0 for $x$ and 0 for $y$ {or equivalently, 8.95 for $x$}, we get $0 = a(0 - 4.475)^2 + 1 \Rightarrow -1 = a(4.475)^2 \Rightarrow$

$$a = -\frac{1}{4.475^2}, \text{ and an equation is } y = -\frac{1}{4.475^2}(x - 4.475)^2 + 1.$$

**86** (a) $P = 24 \Rightarrow 2x + 2y = 24 \Rightarrow y = 12 - x$ (b) $A = xy = x(12 - x)$

(c) $A$ is zero at 0 and 12 and will be a maximum when $x = \dfrac{0 + 12}{2} = 6$.

Thus, the maximum value of $A$ occurs if the rectangle is a square.

**87** Let $t$ denote the time (in hr) after 1:00 P.M. If the starting point for ship B is the origin, then the locations of A and B are $-30 + 15t$ and $-10t$, respectively. Using the Pythagorean theorem,

$$d^2 = (-30 + 15t)^2 + (-10t)^2 = 900 - 900t + 225t^2 + 100t^2 = 325t^2 - 900t + 900.$$

The time at which the distance between the ships is minimal is the same as the time at which the square of the distance between the ships is minimal. Thus, $t = -\dfrac{b}{2a} = -\dfrac{-900}{2(325)} = \dfrac{18}{13}$, or about 2:23 P.M.

**88** Let $r$ denote the radius of the semicircles and $x$ the length of the rectangle. Perimeter = half-mile $\Rightarrow$

$2x + 2\pi r = \frac{1}{2} \Rightarrow x = -\pi r + \frac{1}{4}$. $A = 2rx = 2r\left(-\pi r + \frac{1}{4}\right) = -2\pi r^2 + \frac{1}{2}r$.

The maximum value of $A$ occurs when $r = -\frac{b}{2a} = -\frac{1/2}{2(-2\pi)} = \frac{1}{8\pi}$ mi. $x = -\pi\left(\frac{1}{8\pi}\right) + \frac{1}{4} = \frac{1}{8}$ mi.

**89** (a) $f(t) = -\frac{1}{2}gt^2 + 16t$ • $g = 32 \Rightarrow f(t) = -16t^2 + 16t$.

Solving $f(t) = 0$ gives us $-16t(t - 1) \Rightarrow t = 0, 1$. The player is in the air for 1 second.

(b) $t = -\frac{b}{2a} = -\frac{16}{2(-16)} = \frac{1}{2}$. $f\left(\frac{1}{2}\right) = 4 \Rightarrow$ the player jumps 4 feet high.

(c) $g = \frac{32}{6} \Rightarrow f(t) = -\frac{8}{3}t^2 + 16t$. Solving $f(t) = 0$ yields $t = 0$ or 6.

The player would be in the air for 6 seconds on the moon.

$t = -\frac{b}{2a} = -\frac{16}{2(-8/3)} = 3$. $f(3) = 24 \Rightarrow$ the player jumps 24 feet high.

**90** (a) Solving $-0.016x^2 + 1.6x = \frac{1}{5}x$ for $x$ represents the intersection between the parabola and the line.

$-0.08x^2 + 8x = x$ {multiply by 5} $\Rightarrow 7x - \frac{8}{100}x^2 = 0 \Rightarrow x\left(7 - \frac{8}{100}x\right) = 0 \Rightarrow x = 0, \frac{175}{2}$.

The rocket lands at $\left(\frac{175}{2}, \frac{35}{2}\right) = (87.5, 17.5)$.

(b) The *difference* $d$ between the parabola and the line is to be maximized here.

$d = (-0.016x^2 + 1.6x) - \left(\frac{1}{5}x\right) = -0.016x^2 + 1.4x$. $d$ obtains a maximum when

$x = -\frac{b}{2a} = -\frac{1.4}{2(-0.016)} = 43.75$. The maximum height of the rocket *above the ground* is

$$d = -0.016(43.75)^2 + 1.4(43.75) = 30.625 \text{ units}.$$

## Chapter 2 Discussion Exercises

**1** Graphs of equations of the form $y = x^{p/q}$, where $x \geq 0$, and $p$ and $q$ are positive integers all pass through $(0, 0)$ and $(1, 1)$. If $p/q < 1$, the graph is above $y = x$ for $0 \leq x \leq 1$ and below $y = x$ for $x \geq 1$. The closer $p/q$ is to 1, the closer $y = x^{p/q}$ is to $y = x$. If $p/q > 1$, the graph is below $y = x$ for $0 \leq x \leq 1$ and above $y = x$ for $x \geq 1$.

**2** (a) About the $x$-axis • replace $y$ with $-y$: $-y = \frac{1}{2}x - 3 \Rightarrow g(x) = -\frac{1}{2}x + 3$

(b) About the $y$-axis • replace $x$ with $-x$: $y = \frac{1}{2}(-x) - 3 \Rightarrow g(x) = -\frac{1}{2}x - 3$

(c) About the line $y = 2$ • by examining the graphs of $f(x) = \frac{1}{2}x - 3$ and $y = 2$, we observe that the slope of the reflected line should be $-\frac{1}{2}$ and the $y$-intercept should be 5 units above $y = 2$ (since the $y$-intercept of $f$ is 5 units below 2). Hence, $g(x) = -\frac{1}{2}x + 7$.

(d) About the line $x = 3$ • similar to part (c), the slope of $g$ is $-\frac{1}{2}$. The $x$-intercept of $f$, 6, is 3 units to the right of $x = 3$, so the $x$-intercept of $g$ should be 3 units to the left of $x = 3$. Hence, $g(x) = -\frac{1}{2}x$.

***Note:*** An interesting generalization can be made for problems of the form of those in parts (a)–(d) which would be a worthwhile exploratory exercise in itself. It goes as follows: If the graph of $y = f(x)$ is reflected about the line $y = k$ (or $x = k$), how can you obtain the equation of the new graph? Answer: For $y = k$, replace $y$ with $2k - y$; for $x = k$, replace $x$ with $2k - x$.

3. For the graph of $g(x) = \sqrt{f(x)}$, where $f(x) = ax^2 + bx + c$, consider 2 cases:

**1) $(a > 0)$** If $f$ has 0 or 1 $x$-intercept(s), the domain of $g$ is $\mathbb{R}$ and its range is $[\sqrt{k}, \infty)$, where $k$ is the $y$-value of the vertex of $f$. If $f$ has 2 $x$-intercepts (say $x_1$ and $x_2$ with $x_1 < x_2$), then the domain of $g$ is $(-\infty, x_1] \cup [x_2, \infty)$ and its range is $[0, \infty)$. The general shape is similar to the v-shape of the graph of $y = \sqrt{a}|x|$.

**2) $(a < 0)$** If $f$ has no $x$-intercepts, there is no graph of $g$. If $f$ has 1 $x$-intercept, the graph of $g$ consists of that point. If $f$ has 2 $x$-intercepts, the domain of $g$ is $[x_1, x_2]$ and the range is $\left[0, \sqrt{k}\right]$. The shape of $g$ is that of the top half of an oval.

The main advantage of graphing $g$ as a composition $\left(\text{say } Y_1 = f \text{ and } Y_2 = \sqrt{Y_1} \text{ on a graphing calculator}\right)$ is to observe the relationship between the range of $f$ and the domain of $g$.

4. $f(x) = ax^2 + bx + c \implies$

$$\frac{f(x+h) - f(x)}{h} = \frac{[a(x+h)^2 + b(x+h) + c] - [ax^2 + bx + c]}{h}$$

$$= \frac{ax^2 + 2ahx + ah^2 + bx + bh + c - ax^2 - bx - c}{h}$$

$$= \frac{2ahx + ah^2 + bh}{h} = \frac{h(2ax + ah + b)}{h} = 2ax + ah + b$$

5. The expression $2x + h + 6$ represents the slope of the line between the points $P(x, f(x))$ and $Q(x+h, f(x+h))$. If $h = 0$, then $2x + 6$ represents the slope of the tangent line at the point $P(x, f(x))$.

6. To determine the $x$-coordinate of $R$, we want to start at $x_1$ and go $\dfrac{m}{n}$ of the way to $x_2$.

We could write this as $x_3 = x_1 + \dfrac{m}{n}\Delta x = x_1 + \dfrac{m}{n}(x_2 - x_1) = x_1 + \dfrac{m}{n}x_2 - \dfrac{m}{n}x_1 = \left(1 - \dfrac{m}{n}\right)x_1 + \dfrac{m}{n}x_2$.

Similarly, $y_3 = \left(1 - \dfrac{m}{n}\right)y_1 + \dfrac{m}{n}y_2$.

7. The values of the $x$-intercepts (if they exist) are found using the quadratic formula $x = -\dfrac{b}{2a} \pm \dfrac{\sqrt{b^2 - 4ac}}{2a}$.

Hence, the distance $d$ from the axis of symmetry, $x = -\dfrac{b}{2a}$, to either $x$-intercept is $d = \dfrac{\sqrt{b^2 - 4ac}}{2|a|}$ and

$d^2 = \dfrac{b^2 - 4ac}{4a^2}$. From page 155 of the text, the $y$-coordinate of the vertex is $h = c - \dfrac{b^2}{4a} = \dfrac{4ac - b^2}{4a}$, so

$$\frac{h}{d^2} = \frac{\dfrac{4ac - b^2}{4a}}{\dfrac{b^2 - 4ac}{4a^2}} = \frac{4a^2(4ac - b^2)}{4a(b^2 - 4ac)} = -a.$$

Thus, $h = -ad^2$. Note that this relationship also reveals a connection between the discriminant $D = b^2 - 4ac$ and the $y$-coordinate of the vertex, namely $h = -D/(4a)$.

8. The graph of $y = -[\![-x]\!]$ in the solution to Exercise 56(e) of Section 2.5 illustrates the concept of one of the most common billing methods with the open and closed endpoints reversed from those of the greatest integer function. Starting with $y = -[\![-x]\!]$ and adjusting for jumps every 15 minutes gives us $y = -[\![-x/15]\!]$. Since each quarter-hour charge is \$20, we multiply by 20 to obtain $y = -20[\![-x/15]\!]$. Because of the initial \$40 charge, we must add 40 to obtain the function $f(x) = 40 - 20[\![-x/15]\!]$.

9　$D = 0.0833x^2 - 0.4996x + 3.5491 \Rightarrow 0.0833x^2 - 0.4996x + (3.5491 - D) = 0.$

Solving for $x$ with the quadratic formula yields $x = \dfrac{0.4996 \pm \sqrt{(-0.4996)^2 - 4(0.0833)(3.5491 - D)}}{2(0.0833)}$,

or, equivalently, $x = \dfrac{4996 \pm \sqrt{33{,}320{,}000D - 93{,}295{,}996}}{1666}$.

From the figure (a graph of $D$), we see that $3 \le x \le 15$ corresponds to the right half of the parabola.

Hence, we choose the plus sign in the equation for $x$.

$[-20, 20, 2]$ by $[0, 40, 2]$

Figure 9

$[0.5, 12.5]$ by $[0, 5]$

Figure 10

10　(a)　Let January correspond to 1, February to 2, ..., and December to 12.

　(b)　The data points are (approximately) parabolic on the interval $[1, 6]$ and linear on $[6, 12]$.

　　　Let $f_1(x) = a(x - h)^2 + k$ on $[1, 6]$ and $f_2(x) = mx + b$ on $[6, 12]$. On $[1, 6]$, let the vertex $(h, k) = (1, 0.7)$.

　　　Since $(6, 4)$ is on the graph of $f_1$, $f_1(6) = a(6 - 1)^2 + 0.7 = 4 \Rightarrow a = 0.132$.

　　　Thus, $f_1(x) = 0.132(x - 1)^2 + 0.7$ on $[1, 6]$. Now, let $f_2(x) = mx + b$ pass through the points

　　　$(6, 4)$ and $(12, 0.9)$. An equation of this line is approximately $(y - 4) = -0.517(x - 6)$.

　　　Thus, let $f_2(x) = -0.517x + 7.102$ on $[6, 12]$.

$$f(x) = \begin{cases} 0.132(x - 1)^2 + 0.7 & \text{if } 1 \le x \le 6 \\ -0.517x + 7.102 & \text{if } 6 < x \le 12 \end{cases}$$

　(c)　To plot the piecewise function, let

$$Y_1 = (0.132(x - 1)\text{^}2 + 0.7)/(x \le 6) \quad \text{and} \quad Y_2 = (-0.517x + 7.102)/(x > 6).$$

　　　These assignments use the concept of Boolean division. For example, when $(x \le 6)$ is false, the expression $Y_1$

　　　will be undefined (division by 0) and the calculator will not plot any values.

## Chapter 2 Test

1　To get to $B(1, 2)$ from $A(-3, 4)$, move 4 units right and 2 units down.

Since that represents one-tenth of the distance, 40 units right and 20 units down represents the whole distance to

$$P(x, y) = P(-3 + 40, 4 - 20) = P(37, -16).$$

2　$d(P, Q) > 5 \Rightarrow \sqrt{(6 - 2)^2 + (a - 3)^2} > 5 \Rightarrow 4^2 + a^2 - 6a + 9 > 5^2 \Rightarrow a^2 - 6a > 0 \Rightarrow$

$a(a - 6) > 0 \Rightarrow a < 0$ or $a > 6$. Make a sign chart to establish the final answer.

| Interval | $(-\infty, 0)$ | $(0, 6)$ | $(6, \infty)$ |
|---|---|---|---|
| Sign of $a$ | $-$ | $+$ | $+$ |
| Sign of $a - 6$ | $-$ | $-$ | $+$ |
| **Resulting sign** | $+$ | $-$ | $+$ |

3. The standard equation of the circle with center $(4, 5)$ has the form $(x - 4)^2 + (y - 5)^2 = r^2$. Since an $x$-intercept is 0, a $y$-intercept is 0, so $(0 - 4)^2 + (0 - 5)^2 = r^2 \Rightarrow 16 + 25 = r^2 \Rightarrow 41 = r^2$, and the desired equation is $(x - 4)^2 + (y - 5)^2 = 41$.

4. To go from the center $(4, 5)$ to the origin, it's 5 units down and 4 units left. By symmetry, to get to the other $y$-intercept from the center, move 5 units up and 4 units left to the point $(0, 10)$; and to get to the other $x$-intercept, move 5 units down and 4 units right to the point $(8, 0)$. Another method would be to find the standard equation of the circle, and then substitute 0 for $x$ to find the $y$-intercept and then 0 for $y$ to find the $x$-intercept.

5. The tangent line and the circle pass through the origin. The slope of the line from the origin to the center of the circle is $\frac{5}{4}$. Since the tangent line is perpendicular to that line, it has slope $-\frac{4}{5}$ and equation $y = -\frac{4}{5}x$.

6. $2x - 7y = 3 \Rightarrow -7y = -2x + 3 \Rightarrow y = \frac{2}{7}x - \frac{3}{7}$, so the slope of the given line is $\frac{2}{7}$ and the slope of the desired line is $-\frac{7}{2}$ {the negative reciprocal of $\frac{2}{7}$}. Since the desired line has $x$-intercept 4, its equation is $y - 0 = -\frac{7}{2}(x - 4) \Rightarrow y = -\frac{7}{2}x + 14$.

7. The cost of the pizza plus the toppings is $9 + 0.80x$. Multiply by 1.10 to get the total cost including the tax. Thus, $T(x) = 1.10(9 + 0.80x) \Rightarrow T(x) = 9.9 + 0.88x$, or $T(x) = 0.88x + 9.9$.

8. $f(x) = \dfrac{\sqrt{-x}}{(x + 2)(x - 2)}$ ● The numerator is defined for $x \le 0$. The denominator is defined for all real numbers, but we must exclude $\pm 2$ since the denominator is zero for those values.

Thus, the domain of $f$ is $(-\infty, -2) \cup (-2, 0]$.

9. For $f(x) = x^2 + 5x - 7$:

$$\frac{f(a + h) - f(a)}{h} = \frac{[(a + h)^2 + 5(a + h) - 7] - (a^2 + 5a - 7)}{h}$$
$$= \frac{[a^2 + 2ah + h^2 + 5a + 5h - 7] - (a^2 + 5a - 7)}{h}$$
$$= \frac{2ah + h^2 + 5h}{h} = \frac{h(2a + h + 5)}{h} = 2a + h + 5$$

Based on that answer, a prediction of $2a + h - 7$ seems reasonable for the second function, $f(x) = x^2 - 7x + 5$, since it appears that only the coefficient of $x$ is part of the answer.

10. $V = 2 \times y \times y = 2y^2 \Rightarrow y^2 = V/2 \Rightarrow y = \sqrt{V/2}$. There are four sides of area $2 \times y$ and the top and bottom each have area $y \times y$, so $S(y) = 4(2y) + 2(y^2) \Rightarrow S(V) = 8\sqrt{V/2} + 2(V/2) = V + 8\sqrt{V/2}$ or $V + 4\sqrt{2V}$.

11. Start with the point $P(3, -2)$ on $f$ and find the corresponding point on the graph of $y = 2|f(x - 3)| - 1$.

| | | |
|---|---|---|
| $P(3, -2)$ | $\{x - 3 \text{ [add 3 to the } x\text{-coordinate] }\}$ | $\rightarrow (6, -2)$ |
| | $\{|\text{absolute value}| \text{ [make the } y\text{-coordinate positive] }\}$ | $\rightarrow (6, 2)$ |
| | $\{\times 2 \text{ [multiply the } y\text{-coordinate by 2] }\}$ | $\rightarrow (6, 4)$ |
| | $\{-1 \text{ [subtract 1 from the } y\text{-coordinate] }\}$ | $\rightarrow (6, 3)$ |

12. The salesman makes \$1.20 per cap on the first 1000 caps and \$1.80 on each additional cap.

$$C(x) = \begin{cases} 1.20x & \text{if } 0 \le x \le 1000 \\ 1.20(1000) + 1.80(x - 1000) & \text{if } x > 1000 \end{cases} = \begin{cases} 1.20x & \text{if } 0 \le x \le 1000 \\ 1.80x - 600 & \text{if } x > 1000 \end{cases}$$

**13** The standard equation of a parabola with vertical axis and vertex $V(-2, 1)$ is $y = a(x + 2)^2 + 1$.

If $a < 0$, then the graph will have two $x$-intercepts, so the desired restriction is $a > 0$.

**14** A parabola that has $x$-intercepts $-2$ and $4$ has equation $f(x) = a(x + 2)(x - 4)$.

Since $(3, -15)$ is on the parabola, $-15 = a(3 + 2)(3 - 4)$ $\Rightarrow$ $-15 = -5a$ $\Rightarrow$ $a = 3$.

The vertex has $x$-coordinate that is halfway between the $x$-intercepts, that is, $x = 1$.

The minimum value is of $f(x) = 3(x + 2)(x - 4)$ is $f(1) = 3(1 + 2)(1 - 4) = 3(3)(-3) = -27$.

**15** Let $x$ and $2x - 9$ denote the numbers, so that the product is $p = x(2x - 9)$. The intercepts of the graph of $p$ are $0$ and $\frac{9}{2}$, so the vertex is halfway between them at $x = \frac{9}{4}$, and the minimum value is $\frac{9}{4}[2(\frac{9}{4}) - 9] = \frac{9}{4}(-\frac{9}{2}) = -\frac{81}{8}$.

We could also use $p = 2x^2 - 9x$ and note that $-\frac{b}{2a} = -\frac{-9}{2(2)} = \frac{9}{4}$.

**16** Let $x$ denote the number of people in the group. The cost per person can be represented by $4 - 0.01(x - 100) = 4 - 0.01x + 1 = 5 - 0.01x$. The total cost $T$ of the group is the product of these two expressions, so $T = x(5 - 0.01x)$. The intercepts of the graph of $T$ are $0$ and $500$, so the vertex is at $x = 250$. $T(250) = 250(5 - 2.5) = 625$. The tour is only offered for 100 to 300 people at a time, so we check the endpoints and get $T(100) = 100(5 - 1) = 400$ and $T(300) = 300(5 - 3) = 600$. Thus, the maximum total cost for the group is \$625 when 250 people are in the group and the minimum total cost for the group is \$400 when 100 people are in the group. Note that group sizes from 251 to 300 have a smaller total cost than \$625.

**17** $f(x) = x^2$ and $g(x) = \sqrt{x - 3}$ $\Rightarrow$ $(f \circ g)(x) = f(g(x)) = (\sqrt{x - 3})^2 = x - 3$, which is defined for all reals, but $g$ is defined for only $x \geq 3$, so the domain of $(f \circ g)(x)$ is $[3, \infty)$.

**18** $C = y^2 - 2y + 10$ and $y(t) = 5t$, so $(C \circ y)(t) = C(y(t)) = (5t)^2 - 2(5t) + 10 = 25t^2 - 10t + 10$.

The minimum cost occurs when $t = -\frac{b}{2a} = -\frac{-10}{2(25)} = \frac{1}{5}$.

This cost is $C(\frac{1}{5}) = 25(\frac{1}{25}) - 10(\frac{1}{5}) + 10 = 1 - 2 + 10 = 9$, which represents \$9000.

# Chapter 3: Polynomial and Rational Functions

## *3.1 Exercises*

**1**   $f(x) = 2x^3 + c$   •   The graph of $y = g(x) = 2x^3$ is the graph of $y = x^3$ stretched vertically by a factor of 2.

(a) The effect of the "3" for $c$ is to shift the graph of $g$ *up* 3 units.

(b) The effect of the "$-3$" for $c$ is to shift the graph of $g$ *down* 3 units.

**2**   (a) $f(x) = -2x^3 + c$   •   $c = -2$       (b) $c = 2$

**3**   $f(x) = ax^3 + 2$   •   The "$+2$" will shift each graph up 2 units.

(a) The effect of the "2" for $a$ is to vertically stretch $g(x) = x^3 + 2$ by a factor of 2 and make it appear "steeper."

(b) The effect of the "$\frac{1}{3}$" for $a$ is to vertically compress $g(x) = x^3$ by a factor of $1/(1/3) = 3$, making it appear "flatter." The "$-$" reflects the graph of $h(x) = \frac{1}{3}x^3$ through the $x$-axis.

**4**  (a)   $f(x) = ax^3 - 3$  •  $a = -2$                     (b)   $a = \frac{1}{8}$

**5**   We need to show that there is a sign change between $f(3)$ and $f(4)$ for $f(x) = x^3 - 4x^2 + 3x - 2$.

$$f(3) = 27 - 36 + 9 - 2 = -2 \quad \text{and} \quad f(4) = 64 - 64 + 12 - 2 = 10.$$

Since $f(3) = -2 < 0$ and $f(4) = 10 > 0$, the intermediate value theorem for polynomial functions assures us that $f$ takes on every value between $-2$ and $10$ in the interval $[3, 4]$, namely, $0$.

**6**   $f(x) = 2x^3 + 6x^2 - 3;\, a = -3,\, b = -2$  •  $f(-3) = -3 < 0,\, f(-2) = 5 > 0$

**7**   As in Exercise 5, with $f(x) = -x^4 + 3x^3 - 2x + 1,\, a = 2,\, b = 3$, we have $f(2) = 5 > 0$ and $f(3) = -5 < 0$.

**8**   $f(x) = 2x^4 + 3x - 2;\, a = 0,\, b = 1$  •  $f(0) = -2 < 0,\, f(1) = 3 > 0$

**9**   As in Exercise 5, with $f(x) = x^5 + x^3 - 3x + 1,\, a = -2,\, b = -1$,

                                    we have $f(-2) = -33 < 0$ and $f(-1) = 2 > 0$.

**10**   $f(x) = x^5 - 3x^4 - 9x - 6;\, a = 3,\, b = 4$  •  $f(3) = -33 < 0,\, f(4) = 214 > 0$

**11**  (a)   The graph has $x$-intercepts at $-1, 1$, and $2$—so $(x+1)$, $(x-1)$, and $(x-2)$ are factors in its equation. It is the graph of a cubic. **C**

    (b)   The graph has $x$-intercepts at $-1, 1$, and $2$. It is the graph of a quartic. **D**

    (c)   The graph has $x$-intercepts at $0$ and $2$. It is the graph of a cubic with a negative leading coefficient. **B**

    (d)   The graph has $x$-intercepts at $0$ and $2$. It is the graph of a cubic with a positive leading coefficient. **A**

**12**  (a)   The graph has $x$-intercepts at $-2, -1$, and $1$—so $(x+2)$, $(x+1)$, and $(x-1)$ are factors in its equation. It is the graph of a quartic. **D**

    (b)   The graph has $x$-intercepts at $0$ and $1$. It is the graph of a cubic. **A**

    (c)   The graph has $x$-intercepts at $-2$ and $0$. It is the graph of a cubic with a negative leading coefficient. **B**

    (d)   The graph has $x$-intercepts at $-2, -1$, and $3$. It is the graph of a cubic with a positive leading coefficient. **C**

**13**  (a)   As $x$ gets very large, $y$ (or $f(x)$) gets very large as determined by the dominant term, $3x^5$. Thus, as $x \to \infty$, $f(x) \to \infty$. As $x$ gets very large negative, $y$ (or $f(x)$) gets very large negative as determined by the dominant term, $3x^5$. Thus, as $x \to -\infty$, $f(x) \to -\infty$.

    (b)   As $x \to \infty$, $f(x) \to -\infty$. As $x \to -\infty$, $f(x) \to \infty$.

    (c)   As $x \to \pm\infty$, $f(x) \to \infty$.

    (d)   As $x \to \pm\infty$, $f(x) \to -\infty$.

**14** (a) As $x$ gets very large (positive or negative), $y$ (or $f(x)$) gets very large as determined by the dominant term, $3x^4$. Thus, as $x \to \pm\infty$, $f(x) \to \infty$.

(b) As $x \to \pm\infty$, $f(x) \to -\infty$.

(c) As $x \to \infty$, $f(x) \to \infty$. As $x \to -\infty$, $f(x) \to -\infty$.

(d) As $x \to \infty$, $f(x) \to -\infty$. As $x \to -\infty$, $f(x) \to \infty$,

**15** $f(x) = \frac{1}{4}x^3 - 2 = \frac{1}{4}(x^3 - 8) = \frac{1}{4}(x - 2)(x^2 + 2x + 4)$ • The general shape of the graph is that of $g(x) = x^3$. To find the $x$-intercepts, set $y$ {$f(x)$} equal to 0. This means either $x - 2 = 0$ or $x^2 + 2x + 4 = 0$. $x - 2 = 0 \Rightarrow x = 2$ and $x^2 + 2x + 4 = 0 \Rightarrow x = -1 \pm \sqrt{3}\,i$. The imaginary solutions mean that we have no $x$-intercepts from the factor $x^2 + 2x + 4$ and the only $x$-intercept is 2. To find the $y$-intercept, set $x$ equal to 0. $x = 0 \Rightarrow y = -2$. The graph of $f$ lies above the $x$-axis for all values of $x$ greater than 2, so $f(x) > 0$ if $x > 2$. The graph of $f$ lies below the $x$-axis for all values of $x$ less than 2, so $f(x) < 0$ if $x < 2$.

*Figure 15*

*Figure 16*

**16** $f(x) = -\frac{1}{9}x^3 - 3 = -\frac{1}{9}(x^3 + 27) = -\frac{1}{9}(x + 3)(x^2 - 3x + 9)$ • $f(x) > 0$ if $x < -3$, $f(x) < 0$ if $x > -3$

**17** $f(x) = -\frac{1}{16}x^4 + 1 = -\frac{1}{16}(x^4 - 16) = -\frac{1}{16}(x^2 + 4)(x + 2)(x - 2)$ • The general shape of the graph is that of $g(x) = -x^4$. The $x$-intercepts are $-2$ and $2$. The $y$-intercept is 1. The graph of $f$ lies *above* the $x$-axis for all values of $x$ such that $-2 < x < 2$, so we can write $f(x) > 0$ if $|x| < 2$. The graph of $f$ lies *below* the $x$-axis for all values of $x$ such that $x < -2$ or $x > 2$, so we can write $f(x) < 0$ if $|x| > 2$.

*Figure 17*

*Figure 18*

**18** $f(x) = x^5 + 1 = (x + 1)(x^4 - x^3 + x^2 - x + 1)$ • $f(x) > 0$ if $x > -1$, $f(x) < 0$ if $x < -1$

**19** $f(x) = x^4 - 4x^2 = x^2(x+2)(x-2)$  •  The general shape of the graph is that of $g(x) = x^4$. The $x$-intercepts are $-2, 0$, and $2$. The $y$-intercept is $0$. The graph of $f$ lies *above* the $x$-axis for all values of $x$ such that $x < -2$ or $x > 2$, so we can write $f(x) > 0$ if $|x| > 2$. The graph of $f$ lies *below* the $x$-axis for all values of $x$ such that $-2 < x < 0$ or $0 < x < 2$, so we can write $f(x) < 0$ if $0 < |x| < 2$. Note that $x = 0$ is excluded in the last inequality since $f(x)$ *is equal to* $0$ if $x = 0$.

*Figure 19*

*Figure 20*

**20** $f(x) = 9x - x^3 = x(3+x)(3-x)$  •  $f(x) > 0$ if $x < -3$ or $0 < x < 3$, $f(x) < 0$ if $-3 < x < 0$ or $x > 3$

**21** $f(x) = -x^3 + 2x^2 + 8x = -x(x^2 - 2x - 8) = -x(x+2)(x-4)$  •  The general shape of the graph is that of $g(x) = -x^3$. The $x$-intercepts are $-2, 0$, and $4$. The $y$-intercept is $0$. The graph of $f$ lies *above* the $x$-axis for all values of $x$ such that $x < -2$ or $0 < x < 4$, so $f(x) > 0$ if $x < -2$ or $0 < x < 4$. The graph of $f$ lies *below* the $x$-axis for all values of $x$ such that $-2 < x < 0$ or $x > 4$, so $f(x) < 0$ if $-2 < x < 0$ or $x > 4$.

*Figure 21*

*Figure 22*

**22** $f(x) = x^4 + 3x^3 - 4x^2 = x^2(x^2 + 3x - 4) = x^2(x+4)(x-1)$  •

$f(x) > 0$ if $x < -4$ or $x > 1$, $f(x) < 0$ if $-4 < x < 0$ or $0 < x < 1$

**23** $f(x) = \frac{1}{6}(x+2)(x-3)(x-4)$  •  If we were to multiply the terms of $f$, we would obtain a polynomial of the form $f(x) = \frac{1}{6}x^3 + $ (other terms), so the general shape of the graph is that of $g(x) = x^3$. The $x$-intercepts are $-2, 3$, and $4$. The $y$-intercept is $f(0) = \frac{1}{6}(0+2)(0-3)(0-4) = \frac{1}{6}(2)(-3)(-4) = 4$.

To determine the intervals on which $f(x) > 0$ and $f(x) < 0$, you may want to refer back to the concept of a sign chart. Below is a sign chart for this function. Note how the sign of each region correlates to the sign of $f(x)$.

| Interval | $(-\infty, -2)$ | $(-2, 3)$ | $(3, 4)$ | $(4, \infty)$ |
|---|---|---|---|---|
| Sign of $x - 4$ | $-$ | $-$ | $-$ | $+$ |
| Sign of $x - 3$ | $-$ | $-$ | $+$ | $+$ |
| Sign of $x + 2$ | $-$ | $+$ | $+$ | $+$ |
| **Resulting sign** | $-$ | $+$ | $-$ | $+$ |

The graph of $f$ lies *above* the $x$-axis for all values of $x$ such that $-2 < x < 3$ or $x > 4$, so $f(x) > 0$ if $-2 < x < 3$

or $x > 4$. The graph of $f$ lies *below* the $x$-axis for all values of $x$ such that $x < -2$ or $3 < x < 4$, so $f(x) < 0$ if $x < -2$ or $3 < x < 4$.

*Figure 23*

*Figure 24*

$\boxed{24}$ $f(x) = -\frac{1}{8}(x+4)(x-2)(x-6)$ • $f(x) > 0$ if $x < -4$ or $2 < x < 6$, $f(x) < 0$ if $-4 < x < 2$ or $x > 6$

$\boxed{25}$ $f(x) = x^3 + 2x^2 - 4x - 8$
$= x^2(x+2) - 4(x+2)$ {factor by grouping}
$= (x^2 - 4)(x+2)$ {factor out $(x+2)$}
$= (x+2)(x-2)(x+2)$
$= (x+2)^2(x-2)$.

The general shape of the graph is that of $g(x) = x^3$. The $x$-intercepts are $-2$ and $2$. The $y$-intercept is $-8$.

If an intercept value has a corresponding *linear* factor {a factor with exponent 1}, the graph will go through that intercept—that is, there will be a sign change from positive to negative or negative to positive in the function.

Thus, at $x = 2$ the graph of the function "goes through" the point. If an intercept value has a corresponding quadratic factor [as in the case of $-2$ and $(x+2)^2$], then the function will not change sign. Hence, at $x = -2$ the graph of the function "touches the point and turns around."

The above discussion can be generalized as follows:

1) If an intercept value has a corresponding factor raised to an *odd* power,

then the function *will* change sign at that point.

2) If an intercept value has a corresponding factor raised to an *even* power,

then the function *will not* change sign at that point.

The graph of $f$ lies *above* the $x$-axis for all values of $x$ such that $x > 2$, so $f(x) > 0$ if $x > 2$. The graph of $f$ lies *below* the $x$-axis for all values of $x$ such that $x < -2$ or $-2 < x < 2$, so we write $f(x) < 0$ if $x < -2$ or $|x| < 2$.

*Figure 25*

*Figure 26*

$\boxed{26}$ $f(x) = x^3 - x^2 - x + 1 = x^2(x-1) - 1(x-1) = (x-1)^2(x+1)$ •
$f(x) > 0$ if $|x| < 1$ or $x > 1$, $f(x) < 0$ if $x < -1$

**27** $f(x) = x^4 - 6x^2 + 8 = (x^2 - 2)(x + 2)(x - 2)$ • The general shape of the graph is that of $g(x) = x^4$. The $x$-intercepts are $\pm 2$ and $\pm\sqrt{2}$. The $y$-intercept is 8. The graph of $f$ lies *above* the $x$-axis for all values of $x$ such that $x < -2$ or $-\sqrt{2} < x < \sqrt{2}$ or $x > 2$, so we can write $f(x) > 0$ if $|x| > 2$ or $|x| < \sqrt{2}$. The graph of $f$ lies *below* the $x$-axis for all values of $x$ such that $-2 < x < -\sqrt{2}$ or $\sqrt{2} < x < 2$, so we can write $f(x) < 0$ if $\sqrt{2} < |x| < 2$.

*Figure 27*

*Figure 28*

**28** $f(x) = -x^4 + 12x^2 - 27 = (-x^2 + 3)(x^2 - 9) = -(x^2 - 3)(x + 3)(x - 3)$ •

$$f(x) > 0 \text{ if } \sqrt{3} < |x| < 3, \ f(x) < 0 \text{ if } |x| > 3 \text{ or } |x| < \sqrt{3}$$

**29** $f(x) = x^2(x + 2)(x - 1)^2(x - 2)$ • If we were to multiply the terms of $f$, we would obtain a polynomial of the form $f(x) = x^6 + $ (other terms), so the general shape of the graph is that of $g(x) = x^6$. The $x$-intercepts are $-2, 0, 1,$ and 2. The $y$-intercept is $f(0) = 0$.

The graph of $f$ lies *above* the $x$-axis for all values of $x$ such that $x < -2$ or $x > 2$, so we can write $f(x) > 0$ if $|x| > 2$. The graph of $f$ lies *below* the $x$-axis for all values of $x$ such that $-2 < x < 0$ or $0 < x < 1$ or $1 < x < 2$, so we can write $f(x) < 0$ if $|x| < 2, x \neq 0, x \neq 1$.

*Figure 29*

*Figure 30*

**30** $f(x) = x^3(x + 1)^2(x - 2)(x - 4)$ • $f(x) > 0$ if $0 < x < 2$ or $x > 4$, $f(x) < 0$ if $x < 0, x \neq -1$ or $2 < x < 4$

**31** The sign of $f(x)$ is positive on $(-\infty, -4)$, so the graph of $f$ must be above the $x$-axis on that interval. The sign of $f(x)$ is negative on $(-4, 0)$, so the graph of $f$ must cross the $x$-axis at $x = -4$ and be below the $x$-axis on the interval $(-4, 0)$. The sign of $f(x)$ is negative on $(0, 1)$, so the graph of $f$ must touch the $x$-axis at $x = 0$ and then fall below the $x$-axis on $(0, 1)$.

The sign of $f(x)$ is positive on $(1, 3)$, so the graph of $f$ must cross the $x$-axis at $x = 1$ and be above the $x$-axis on that interval. The sign of $f(x)$ is negative on $(3, \infty)$, so the graph of $f$ must cross the $x$-axis at $x = 3$ and be below the $x$-axis on the interval $(3, \infty)$.

*Figure 31*

*Figure 32*

**32** The graph of $f$ is above the $x$-axis on $(-\infty, -2)$, touching the axis at $x = -3$. The graph is below the $x$-axis on $(-2, 0)$, above the $x$-axis on $(0, 2)$, and below the $x$-axis on $(2, \infty)$.

**33** (a) The graph of $f(x) = (x - a)(x - b)(x - c)$, where $a < 0 < b < c$, must have one negative zero, $a$, and two positive zeros, $b$ and $c$. The general shape is that of a cubic polynomial.

   (b) The $y$-intercept is $f(0) = (-a)(-b)(-c) = -abc$.

   (c) The solution to $f(x) < 0$ is $(-\infty, a) \cup (b, c)$; that is, where the graph of $f$ is below the $x$-axis.

   (d) The solution to $f(x) \geq 0$ is $[a, b] \cup [c, \infty)$; that is, where the graph of $f$ is above or on the $x$-axis.

*Figure 33*

*Figure 34*

**34** (a) The graph of $f(x) = (x - a)^2(x - b)(x - c)$, where $a < b < 0 < c$, must have two negative zeros, $a$ and $b$, and one positive zero, $c$. The general shape is that of a quartic polynomial.

   (b) The $y$-intercept is $f(0) = (-a)^2(-b)(-c) = a^2bc$

   (c) The solution to $f(x) > 0$ is $(-\infty, a) \cup (a, b) \cup (c, \infty)$; that is, where the graph of $f$ is above the $x$-axis.

   (d) The solution to $f(x) \leq 0$ is $\{a\} \cup [b, c]$; that is, where the graph of $f$ is below or on the $x$-axis.

**35** If $f(x)$ is a polynomial such that the coefficient of every odd power of $x$ is 0, then $f(x)$ consists of only even-powered terms. If $n$ is even, then $(-x)^n = x^n$ and hence $f(-x) = f(x)$, which is the condition that must be true for $f$ to be an even function. Thus, $f$ is an even function.

**36** If $n$ is odd, then $(-x)^n = -x^n$ and hence $f(-x) = -f(x)$. Thus, $f$ is an odd function.

**37** If a graph contains the point $(-1, 4)$, then $f(-1) = 4$. For this function, $f(x) = 3x^3 - kx^2 + x - 5k$,

$$f(-1) = 3(-1)^3 - k(-1)^2 + (-1) - 5k = -3 - k - 1 - 5k = -4 - 6k.$$

Thus, $-4 - 6k$ must equal 4. Solving for $k$ yields $-4 - 6k = 4 \Rightarrow k = -\frac{4}{3}$.

**38** $f(x) = kx^3 + x^2 - kx + 2$ •

$$f(2) = 8k + 4 - 2k + 2 \text{ and } f(2) = 12 \Rightarrow 6k + 6 = 12 \Rightarrow 6k = 6 \Rightarrow k = 1.$$

**39** If one zero of $f(x) = x^3 - 2x^2 - 16x + 16k$ is 2, then $f(2) = 0$.

But $f(2) = 16k - 32$, so $16k - 32 = 0 \Rightarrow 16k = 32 \Rightarrow k = 2$. Thus,

$$\begin{aligned} f(x) &= x^3 - 2x^2 - 16x + 32 && \{\text{let } k = 2\} \\ &= x^2(x - 2) - 16(x - 2) && \{\text{factor by grouping}\} \\ &= (x^2 - 16)(x - 2) && \{\text{factor out } (x - 2)\} \\ &= (x + 4)(x - 4)(x - 2) \end{aligned}$$

So the other two zeros of $f$ are $\pm 4$.

**40** $f(x) = x^3 - 3x^2 - kx + 12$ • $f(-2) = 2k - 8$ and $f(-2) = 0 \Rightarrow 2k - 8 = 0 \Rightarrow 2k = 8 \Rightarrow k = 4$.

$f(x) = x^3 - 3x^2 - 4x + 12 = x^2(x - 3) - 4(x - 3) = (x - 3)(x^2 - 4) = (x - 3)(x + 2)(x - 2)$.

The other two zeros are 2 and 3.

**41** $P(x) = \frac{1}{2}(5x^3 - 3x) = \frac{1}{2}x(5x^2 - 3)$. $P(x) = 0 \Rightarrow x = 0$ or

$x^2 = \frac{3}{5} \Leftrightarrow x = \pm\sqrt{\frac{3}{5}} = \pm\sqrt{\frac{3 \cdot 5}{5 \cdot 5}} = \pm\frac{1}{5}\sqrt{15}$.

$P(x) > 0$ on $\left(-\frac{1}{5}\sqrt{15}, 0\right)$ and $\left(\frac{1}{5}\sqrt{15}, \infty\right)$.

$P(x) < 0$ on $\left(-\infty, -\frac{1}{5}\sqrt{15}\right)$ and $\left(0, \frac{1}{5}\sqrt{15}\right)$.

**42** $f(x) = 8x^4 - 8x^2 + 1$ • $x^2 = \dfrac{8 \pm 4\sqrt{2}}{16} = \dfrac{2 \pm \sqrt{2}}{4} \Rightarrow x = \pm\frac{1}{2}\sqrt{2 \pm \sqrt{2}} \approx \pm 0.92, \pm 0.38;$

$$f(x) > 0 \text{ if } |x| < \frac{1}{2}\sqrt{2 - \sqrt{2}} \text{ or } |x| > \frac{1}{2}\sqrt{2 + \sqrt{2}}$$

**43** (a) $V(x) = lwh = (30 - x - x)(20 - x - x)x = x(20 - 2x)(30 - 2x)$.

(b) $V(x) = x(20 - 2x)(30 - 2x) = x(-2)(x - 10)(-2)(x - 15) = 4x(x - 10)(x - 15)$. The $x$-intercepts of $V$ are 0, 10, and 15. $V(x) > 0$ on $(0, 10)$ and $(15, \infty)$. Allowable values for $x$ are in $(0, 10)$.

Figure 43

Figure 44

Figure 45

**44** (a) Since we are disregarding the thickness of the lumber, 4 boards are $y$ feet long and 8 boards are $x$ feet long.

Total length $= 24 \Rightarrow 4y + 8x = 24 \Rightarrow y = 6 - 2x$. $V = x^2y = x^2(6 - 2x) = 6x^2 - 2x^3$.

(b) From part (a), $V = 6x^2 - 2x^3$, or, equivalently, $V = -2x^2(x - 3)$. See Figure 44.

**45** We will work part (b) first.

(b) $T = \frac{1}{20}t(t - 12)(t - 24)$ has the general shape of a cubic polynomial with zeros at $0, 12$, and $24$.

Its sign pattern is negative, positive, negative, positive. See Figure 45.

(a) $T = \frac{1}{20}t(t - 12)(t - 24) = 0 \Rightarrow t = 0, 12, 24$.

$T > 0$ for $0 < t < 12$ {6 A.M. to 6 P.M.}; $T < 0$ for $12 < t < 24$ {6 P.M. to 6 A.M.}.

(c) 12 noon corresponds to $t = 6$, $T(6) = 32.4 > 32°$F and $T(7) = 29.75 < 32°$F.

**46** (a) At the end of the board, $s = 10$. Letting $d = 1$ and $L = 10$ yields $1 = 100c(20) \Rightarrow c = \frac{1}{2000}$.

(b) $s = 6.5 \Rightarrow d = \left(\frac{1}{2000}\right)(6.5)^2\,[3(10) - 6.5] \approx 0.4964 < \frac{1}{2}$.

$s = 6.6 \Rightarrow d = \left(\frac{1}{2000}\right)(6.6)^2\,[3(10) - 6.6] \approx 0.5097 > \frac{1}{2}$.

**47** (a) $N(t) = -t^4 + 21t^2 + 100$

$\quad = -\left(t^4 - 21t^2 - 100\right)$        {factor out $-1$}

$\quad = -\left(t^2 - 25\right)\left(t^2 + 4\right)$      {factor as a quadratic in $t^2$}

$\quad = -(t + 5)(t - 5)\left(t^2 + 4\right)$    {difference of two squares}

$N$ has the general shape of a quartic polynomial reflected through

the $t$-axis. If $t > 0$, then $N(t) > 0$ for $0 < t < 5$.

(b) The population becomes extinct when $N = 0$. This occurs after

5 years.

**48** (a) $R = 0 \Rightarrow -4t^3 + 42t = 0 \Rightarrow -2t(2t^2 - 21) = 0 \Rightarrow t = \frac{1}{2}\sqrt{42}$ {for $t > 0$}.

The population ceases to grow after $\frac{1}{2}\sqrt{42} \approx 3.24$ years.

(b) $R > 0$ if $t$ is in the interval $\left(0, \frac{1}{2}\sqrt{42}\right)$.

**49** (a) $f(x) = 2x^4$, $g(x) = 2x^4 - 5x^2 + 1$, $h(x) = 2x^4 + 5x^2 - 1$, $k(x) = 2x^4 - x^3 + 2x$ •

| $x$ | $f(x)$ | $g(x)$ | $h(x)$ | $k(x)$ |
|---|---|---|---|---|
| $-60$ | 25,920,000 | 25,902,001 | 25,937,999 | 26,135,880 |
| $-40$ | 5,120,000 | 5,112,001 | 5,127,999 | 5,183,920 |
| $-20$ | 320,000 | 318,001 | 321,999 | 327,960 |
| 20 | 320,000 | 318,001 | 321,999 | 312,040 |
| 40 | 5,120,000 | 5,112,001 | 5,127,999 | 5,056,080 |
| 60 | 25,920,000 | 25,902,001 | 25,937,999 | 25,704,120 |

(b) As $|x|$ becomes large, the function values become similar.

(c) The term with the highest power of $x$: $2x^4$.

**50** (a)   $f(x) = -3x^3$, $g(x) = -3x^3 - x^2 + 1$, $h(x) = -3x^3 + x^2 - 1$, $k(x) = -3x^3 - 2x^2 + 2x$ •

$[-2, 2]$ by $[-2, 2]$                          $[-10, 10]$ by $[-10, 10]$

$[-50, 50, 10]$ by $[-5\text{E}3, 5\text{E}3, 1\text{E}3]$         $[-100, 100, 10]$ by $[-5\text{E}5, 5\text{E}5, 1\text{E}5]$

(b)   As the viewing rectangle increases in size, the graphs look alike.

(c)   Their end behavior is similar because their highest degree term is $-3x^3$. This term determines the shape of the graph when $|x|$ is large.

**51** (a)                 $[-9, 9]$ by $[-6, 6]$                                 $[-9, 9]$ by $[-6, 6]$

$[-9, 9]$ by $[-6, 6]$                                     $[-9, 9]$ by $[-6, 6]$

(b) (1) $f(x) = x^3 - x + 1$ •         As $x$ approaches $\infty$, $f(x)$ approaches $\infty$; as $x$ approaches $-\infty$, $f(x)$ approaches $-\infty$

     (2) $f(x) = -x^3 + 4x^2 - 3x - 1$ •        As $x$ approaches $\infty$, $f(x)$ approaches $-\infty$; as $x$ approaches $-\infty$, $f(x)$ approaches $\infty$

     (3) $f(x) = 0.1x^3 - 1$ •         As $x$ approaches $\infty$, $f(x)$ approaches $\infty$; as $x$ approaches $-\infty$, $f(x)$ approaches $-\infty$

     (4) $f(x) = -x^3 + 4x + 2$ •         As $x$ approaches $\infty$, $f(x)$ approaches $-\infty$; as $x$ approaches $-\infty$, $f(x)$ approaches $\infty$

(c)   For the cubic function $f(x) = ax^3 + bx^2 + cx + d$ with $a > 0$, $f(x)$ approaches $\infty$ as $x$ approaches $\infty$ and $f(x)$ approaches $-\infty$ as $x$ approaches $-\infty$. With $a < 0$, $f(x)$ approaches $-\infty$ as $x$ approaches $\infty$ and $f(x)$ approaches $\infty$ as $x$ approaches $-\infty$.

**52** (a)                [−9, 9] by [−6, 6]                              [−9, 9] by [−6, 6]

       [−9, 9] by [−6, 6]                              [−9, 9] by [−6, 6]

(b) (1) $f(x) = -x^4 - 2x^3 + 5x^2 + 6x - 3$  •        As $x \to \pm\infty$, $f(x) \to -\infty$

    (2) $f(x) = x^4 - 2x^3 + 1$  •        As $x \to \pm\infty$, $f(x) \to \infty$

    (3) $f(x) = -\frac{1}{2}x^4 + 2x^2 - x + 1$  •        As $x \to \pm\infty$, $f(x) \to -\infty$

    (4) $f(x) = \frac{1}{5}x^4 - \frac{1}{2}x^3 - \frac{7}{3}x^2 + \frac{7}{2}x + 3$  •        As $x \to \pm\infty$, $f(x) \to \infty$

(c) For the fourth–degree polynomial $f(x) = ax^4 + bx^3 + cx^2 + dx + e$ with $a > 0$, $f(x)$ approaches $\infty$ as $|x|$ approaches $\infty$ and with $a < 0$, $f(x)$ approaches $-\infty$ as $|x|$ approaches $\infty$.

**53** From the graph, $f(x) = x^3 + 0.2x^2 - 2.6x + 1.1$ has three zeros at approximately $-1.89, 0.49$, and $1.20$.

        [−4.5, 4.5] by [−3, 3]                    [−4.5, 4.5] by [−3, 3]

            *Figure 53*                                *Figure 54*

**54** From the graph, $f(x) = -x^4 + 4x - 1$ has two zeros at approximately $0.25$, and $1.49$.

**55** From the graph, $f(x) = x^3 - 3x + 1$ has three zeros at approximately $-1.88, 0.35$, and $1.53$.

        [−4.5, 4.5] by [−3, 3]                    [−4.5, 4.5] by [−3, 3]

            *Figure 55*                                *Figure 56*

**56** From the graph, $f(x) = 2x^3 - 4x^2 - 3x + 1$ has three zeros at approximately $-0.77, 0.26$, and $2.52$.

**57** If $f(x) = x^3 + 5x - 2$ and $k = 1$, then $f(x) > k$ on $(0.56, \infty)$. Use an intersect feature to find the value 0.56.

$[-4.5, 4.5]$ by $[-3, 3]$

Figure 57

$[-4.5, 4.5]$ by $[-2, 4]$

Figure 58

**58** If $f(x) = x^4 - 4x^3 + 3x^2 - 8x + 5$ and $k = 3$, then $f(x) > k$ on $(-\infty, 0.27) \cup (3.73, \infty)$.

**59** If $f(x) = x^4 - 2x^3 + 10x - 26$ and $k = -1$, then $f(x) > k$ on $(-\infty, -2.24) \cup (2.24, \infty)$.

$[-4.5, 4.5]$ by $[-3, 3]$

Figure 59

$[-4.5, 4.5]$ by $[-3, 3]$

Figure 60

**60** If $f(x) = x^5 - 2x^2 + 2$ and $k = -2$, then $f(x) > k$ on $(-1.10, \infty)$.

**61** From the graph, there are three points of intersection.

Their coordinates are approximately $(-1.29, -0.77)$, $(0.085, 2.66)$, and $(1.36, -0.42)$.

$[-4.5, 4.5]$ by $[-2, 4]$

Figure 61

$[-5.5, 5]$ by $[-3, 4]$

Figure 62

**62** From the graph, there are three points of intersection. One is $(-1, 0)$.

The others are approximately $(0.71, 1.72)$ and $(1.87, -1.25)$.

**63** (a) Graph $Y_1 = -0.000\,015(x - 1973)^3 - 0.005(x - 1973)^2 + 0.75(x - 1973) + 23.5$.

　　　The number of Medicare recipients has increased over this time period.

　　(b) Using the points $(1973, 23{,}545{,}363)$ and $(2005, 42{,}394{,}926)$, we get the slope $\frac{42{,}394{,}926 - 23{,}545{,}363}{2005 - 1973} \approx 0.59$, so with the same constant term as in part (a), we can use the linear model $y = 0.59x + 23.5$ for $1970 \le x \le 2010$ and $y$ in millions. The linear model is more realistic since $Y_1$ will decrease and even become negative.

$[1970, 2010, 10]$ by $[20, 45, 5]$

Figure 63

$[0, 40, 10]$ by $[0, 1{,}000{,}000, 100{,}000]$

Figure 64

**64** (a) Graph $Y_1 = f(x) = -0.11x^4 - 46x^3 + 4000x^2 - 76{,}000x + 760{,}000$. The number of preschool children decreased between 1966 and 1976, but since then, it has increased.

(b) $x = 1986 - 1966 = 20 \Rightarrow f(20) \approx 454{,}400$

(c) Graph $Y_1 = f(x)$ and $Y_2 = 500{,}000$. There are two points of intersection at $x \approx 4.38, 21.7$. Thus, there were approximately 500,000 participants during the years 1970 and 1988.

## 3.2 Exercises

**Note for students:** Refer to the illustration on page 194. We will walk through the steps to obtain the quotient and remainder for this example.

(1) Determine the quotient of the first terms of the dividend $(x^4 - 16)$ and the divisor $(x^2 + 3x + 1)$. $\frac{x^4}{x^2} = x^2$—this is the first term of the resulting quotient.

(2) Multiply the result in step (1), $x^2$, by the divisor, $x^2 + 3x + 1$. This product is $x^4 + 3x^3 + x^2$.

(3) Subtract the result in step (2) from the dividend. This result is $-3x^3 - x^2$ (there is no need to worry about the lower degree terms here, namely, $-16$.) A common mistake is to forget to subtract *all* of the terms and obtain (in this case) $3x^3 + x^2$.

(4) Repeat steps (1) through (3) for the remaining dividend until the degree of the remainder is less than the degree of the divisor.

**1** $f(x) = 2x^4 - x^3 - 3x^2 + 7x - 12; \qquad p(x) = x^2 - 3 \bullet$

$$
\begin{array}{r}
2x^2 \phantom{xx} - \phantom{x} x \phantom{x} + \phantom{x} 3 \\
x^2 - 3 \overline{\smash{\big)}\ 2x^4 \phantom{x} - \phantom{x} x^3 \phantom{x} - \phantom{x} 3x^2 \phantom{x} + \phantom{x} 7x \phantom{x} - \phantom{x} 12} \\
2x^4 \phantom{xxxxxx} - \phantom{x} 6x^2 \phantom{xxxxxxxxxxxx} \\
\hline
-x^3 \phantom{x} + \phantom{x} 3x^2 \phantom{x} + \phantom{x} 7x \phantom{xxxxx} \\
-x^2 \phantom{xxxxxx} + \phantom{x} 3x \phantom{xxxxx} \\
\hline
3x^2 \phantom{x} + \phantom{x} 4x \phantom{x} - \phantom{x} 12 \\
3x^2 \phantom{xxxxxx} - \phantom{x} 9 \\
\hline
4x \phantom{x} - \phantom{x} 3
\end{array}
$$

First step: $\dfrac{2x^4}{x^2} = 2x^2$

★ $q(x) = 2x^2 - x + 3; r(x) = 4x - 3$

**2** $f(x) = 3x^4 + 2x^3 - x^2 - x - 6; \qquad p(x) = x^2 + 1 \bullet \qquad \qquad$ ★ $3x^2 + 2x - 4; -3x - 2$

**3** $f(x) = 3x^3 + 2x - 4; \qquad p(x) = 2x^2 + 1 \bullet$

$$
\begin{array}{r}
\tfrac{3}{2}x \phantom{xxxxx} \\
2x^2 + 1 \overline{\smash{\big)}\ 3x^3 \phantom{x} - \phantom{x} 0x^2 \phantom{x} + \phantom{x} 2x \phantom{x} - \phantom{x} 4} \\
3x^3 \phantom{xxxxxx} + \phantom{x} \tfrac{3}{2}x \phantom{xxx} \\
\hline
\tfrac{1}{2}x \phantom{x} - \phantom{x} 4
\end{array}
$$

First step: $\dfrac{3x^3}{2x^2} = \dfrac{3}{2}x$

★ $q(x) = \tfrac{3}{2}x; r(x) = \tfrac{1}{2}x - 4$

**4** $f(x) = 3x^3 - 5x^2 - 4x - 8; \qquad p(x) = 2x^2 + x \bullet \qquad \qquad$ ★ $\tfrac{3}{2}x - \tfrac{13}{4}; -\tfrac{3}{4}x - 8$

$\boxed{5}$ Note that we can't divide $f(x) = 7x + 2$ by $p(x) = 2x^2 - x - 4$ since the degree of the dividend is already less than the degree of the divisor. So the quotient is 0 and the remainder is $7x + 2$.

$\boxed{6}$   $f(x) = -5x^2 + 3;$                          $p(x) = x^3 - 3x + 9$  •                    ★ $0; -5x^2 + 3$

$\boxed{7}$   $f(x) = 10x + 4; p(x) = 2x - 5$  •                          First step: $\dfrac{10x}{2x} = 5$

$$2x - 5 \overline{\smash{\big)}\, 10x + 4}$$
$$\underline{10x - 25}$$
$$29$$

★ $q(x) = 5; r(x) = 29$

$\boxed{8}$   $f(x) = 7x^2 + 3x - 10;$                    $p(x) = x^2 - x + 10$  •                    ★ $7; 10x - 80$

$\boxed{9}$ We wish to find $f(2)$ by using the remainder theorem. Thus, we need to divide $f(x) = 3x^3 - x^2 - 4$ by $x - 2$ using either long division or synthetic division. Using synthetic division, we have

$$\begin{array}{r|rrrr} 2 & 3 & -1 & 0 & -4 \\ & & 6 & 10 & 20 \\ \hline & 3 & 5 & 10 & 16 \end{array}$$

The last number in the third row, 16, is our remainder. Hence, $f(2) = 16$.

$\boxed{10}$ Divide $f(x) = 2x^3 + 4x^2 - 3x - 1$ by $x - 3$ to obtain a remainder of 80.

$\boxed{11}$ We divide by $x + 3$ or $x - (-3)$. Note that we include a 0 for the missing $x^3$ term in $f(x) = x^4 - 6x^2 + 4x - 8$.

$$\begin{array}{r|rrrrr} -3 & 1 & 0 & -6 & 4 & -8 \\ & & -3 & 9 & -9 & 15 \\ \hline & 1 & -3 & 3 & -5 & 7 \end{array}$$

Hence, $f(-3) = 7$.

$\boxed{12}$ Divide $f(x) = x^4 + 3x^2 - 12$ by $x + 2$ to obtain a remainder of 16.

$\boxed{13}$ To show that $x + 3$ is a factor of $f(x) = x^3 + x^2 - 2x + 12$, we must show that $f(-3) = 0$.

$$f(-3) = -27 + 9 + 6 + 12 = 0, \text{ and, hence, } x + 3 \text{ is a factor of } f(x).$$

$\boxed{14}$ Since $f(2) = 0$, $x - 2$ is a factor of $f(x) = x^3 + x^2 - 11x + 10$.

$\boxed{15}$ To show that $x + 2$ is a factor of $f(x) = x^{12} - 4096$, we must show that $f(-2) = 0$.

$$f(-2) = (-2)^{12} - 4096 = 4096 - 4096 = 0, \text{ and, hence, } x + 2 \text{ is a factor of } f(x).$$

$\boxed{16}$ To show that $x + 4$ is a factor of $f(x) = x^5 + 1024$, we must show that $f(-4) = 0$.

$$f(-4) = (-4)^5 + 1024 = -1024 + 1024 = 0, \text{ and, hence, } x + 4 \text{ is a factor of } f(x).$$

$\boxed{17}$ To show that $x - 3$ is a factor of $f(x) = x^4 - 2x^3 + 3x - 36$, we must show that $f(3) = 0$.

$$f(3) = 81 - 54 + 9 - 36 = 0, \text{ and, hence, } x - 3 \text{ is a factor of } f(x).$$

$\boxed{18}$ Since $f(2) = 0$, $x - 2$ is a factor of $f(x) = x^4 - 3x^3 + 5x - 2$.

$\boxed{19}$ $f$ has degree 3 with zeros $-2, 0, 5$  ⇒

$$f(x) = a\,[x - (-2)](x - 0)(x - 5) \quad \{\text{let } a = 1\} \quad = x(x + 2)(x - 5) = x(x^2 - 3x - 10) = x^3 - 3x^2 - 10x$$

$\boxed{20}$ $f$ has degree 3 with zeros $\pm 2, 3$  ⇒

$$f(x) = a(x + 2)(x - 2)(x - 3) \quad \{\text{let } a = 1\} \quad = (x^2 - 4)(x - 3) = x^3 - 3x^2 - 4x + 12$$

**21** $f$ has degree 3 with zeros $\pm 3, 1 \Rightarrow$

$$f(x) = a(x+3)(x-3)(x-1) \quad \{\text{let } a = 1\} \quad = (x^2 - 9)(x-1) = x^3 - x^2 - 9x + 9$$

**22** $f$ has degree 3 with zeros $-3, 0, 4 \Rightarrow$

$$f(x) = a\,[x-(-3)](x-0)(x-4) \quad \{\text{let } a = 1\} \quad = x(x+3)(x-4) = x(x^2 - x - 12) = x^3 - x^2 - 12x$$

**23** $f$ has degree 4 with zeros $-2, \pm 1, 4 \Rightarrow$

$$f(x) = a(x+2)(x+1)(x-1)(x-4) \quad \{\text{let } a = 1\} \quad = (x^2 - 1)(x^2 - 2x - 8) = x^4 - 2x^3 - 9x^2 + 2x + 8$$

**24** $f$ has degree 4 with zeros $-3, 0, 1, 5 \Rightarrow$

$$f(x) = a(x+3)(x)(x-1)(x-5) \quad \{\text{let } a = 1\} \quad = x(x^2 + 2x - 3)(x-5) = x^4 - 3x^3 - 13x^2 + 15x$$

**25** $2x^3 - 3x^2 + 4x - 5; \; x - 2$ •

$$\begin{array}{r|rrrr} 2 & 2 & -3 & 4 & -5 \\ & & 4 & 2 & 12 \\ \hline & 2 & 1 & 6 & 7 \end{array}$$

The synthetic division indicates that the quotient is $2x^2 + x + 6$ and the remainder is 7.

**26** $3x^3 + 10x^2 - 7x + 8; \; x + 4$ •  ★ $3x^2 - 2x + 1; 4$

**27** $x^3 - 8x - 5; \; x + 3$ •

$$\begin{array}{r|rrrr} -3 & 1 & 0 & -8 & -5 \\ & & -3 & 9 & -3 \\ \hline & 1 & -3 & 1 & -8 \end{array}$$

The synthetic division indicates that the quotient is $x^2 - 3x + 1$ and the remainder is $-8$.

**28** $5x^3 - 18x^2 - 15; \; x - 4$ •  ★ $5x^2 + 2x + 8; 17$

**29** $3x^5 + 6x^2 + 7 = \underline{3}\,x^5 + \underline{0}\,x^4 + \underline{0}\,x^3 + \underline{6}\,x^2 + \underline{0}\,x + \underline{7}; \; x + 2$ •

$$\begin{array}{r|rrrrrr} -2 & 3 & 0 & 0 & 6 & 0 & 7 \\ & & -6 & 12 & -24 & 36 & -72 \\ \hline & 3 & -6 & 12 & -18 & 36 & -65 \end{array}$$

The synthetic division indicates that the quotient is $3x^4 - 6x^3 + 12x^2 - 18x + 36$ and the remainder is $-65$.

**30** $-2x^4 + 10x - 3; \; x - 3$ •  ★ $-2x^3 - 6x^2 - 18x - 44; -135$

**31** $4x^4 - 5x^2 + 1; \; x - \frac{1}{2}$ •

$$\begin{array}{r|rrrrr} \frac{1}{2} & 4 & 0 & -5 & 0 & 1 \\ & & 2 & 1 & -2 & -1 \\ \hline & 4 & 2 & -4 & -2 & 0 \end{array}$$

The synthetic division indicates that the quotient is $4x^3 + 2x^2 - 4x - 2$ and the remainder is 0.

**32** $9x^3 - 6x^2 + 3x - 4; \; x - \frac{1}{3}$ •  ★ $9x^2 - 3x + 2; -\frac{10}{3}$

**33** $f(x) = 2x^3 + 3x^2 - 4x + 4; \; c = 3$ •

$$\begin{array}{r|rrrr} 3 & 2 & 3 & -4 & 4 \\ & & 6 & 27 & 69 \\ \hline & 2 & 9 & 23 & 73 \end{array}$$

The synthetic division indicates that $f(3) = 73$.

**34** $f(x) = -x^3 + 4x^2 + x; \; c = -2$ •  ★ $f(-2) = 22$

**35** $f(x) = 0.3x^3 + 0.4x; c = -0.2$ •

$$
\begin{array}{r|rrrr}
-0.2 & 0.3 & 0 & 0.4 & 0 \\
& & -0.06 & 0.012 & -0.0824 \\
\hline
& 0.3 & -0.06 & 0.412 & -0.0824
\end{array}
$$

The remainder is $-0.0824$ and the remainder theorem indicates that this is $f(-0.2)$.

**36** $f(x) = 0.1x^3 + 0.5x; c = 0.3$ •

$$
\begin{array}{r|rrrr}
0.3 & 0.1 & 0 & 0.5 & 0 \\
& & 0.03 & 0.009 & 0.1527 \\
\hline
& 0.1 & 0.03 & 0.509 & 0.1527
\end{array}
$$

The remainder is $0.1527$ and the remainder theorem indicates that this is $f(0.3)$.

**37** $f(x) = 27x^5 + 2x^2 + 1; c = \frac{1}{3}$ •

$$
\begin{array}{r|rrrrrr}
\frac{1}{3} & 27 & 0 & 0 & 2 & 0 & 1 \\
& & 9 & 3 & 1 & 1 & \frac{1}{3} \\
\hline
& 27 & 9 & 3 & 3 & 1 & \frac{4}{3}
\end{array}
$$

The remainder is $\frac{4}{3}$ and the remainder theorem indicates that this is $f\left(\frac{1}{3}\right)$.

**38** $f(x) = 8x^5 - 3x^2 + 7; c = \frac{1}{2}$ •                               ★ $f\left(\frac{1}{2}\right) = \frac{13}{2}$

**39** $f(x) = x^2 + 3x - 5; c = 2 + \sqrt{3}$ •

$$
\begin{array}{r|rrr}
2 + \sqrt{3} & 1 & 3 & -5 \\
& & 2 + \sqrt{3} & 13 + 7\sqrt{3} \\
\hline
& 1 & 5 + \sqrt{3} & 8 + 7\sqrt{3}
\end{array}
$$

The remainder is $8 + 7\sqrt{3}$ and the remainder theorem indicates that this is the value of $f\left(2 + \sqrt{3}\right)$.

**40** $f(x) = x^3 - 3x^2 - 8; c = 1 + \sqrt{2}$ •                    ★ $f\left(1 + \sqrt{2}\right) = -10 - \sqrt{2}$

**41** $-2$ is a zero of $f(x) = 3x^4 + 8x^3 - 2x^2 - 10x + 4$ if we can show that $f(-2) = 0$.

$$
\begin{array}{r|rrrrr}
-2 & 3 & 8 & -2 & -10 & 4 \\
& & -6 & -4 & 12 & -4 \\
\hline
& 3 & 2 & -6 & 2 & 0
\end{array}
$$

Hence, $f(-2) = 0$ and $-2$ is a zero of $f(x)$.

**42** $f(x) = 4x^3 - 9x^2 - 8x - 3; c = 3$ •                             ★ $f(3) = 0$

**43** $\frac{1}{2}$ is a zero of $f(x) = 4x^3 - 6x^2 + 8x - 3$ if we can show that $f\left(\frac{1}{2}\right) = 0$.

$$
\begin{array}{r|rrrr}
\frac{1}{2} & 4 & -6 & 8 & -3 \\
& & 2 & -2 & 3 \\
\hline
& 4 & -4 & 6 & 0
\end{array}
$$

Hence, $f\left(\frac{1}{2}\right) = 0$ and $\frac{1}{2}$ is a zero of $f(x)$.

**44** $f(x) = 27x^4 - 9x^3 + 3x^2 + 6x + 1; c = -\frac{1}{3}$ •               ★ $f\left(-\frac{1}{3}\right) = 0$

**45** $f(x) = kx^3 + x^2 + k^2x + 3k^2 + 11$, so

$$
\begin{aligned}
f(-2) &= k(-2)^3 + (-2)^2 + k^2(-2) + 3k^2 + 11 \\
&= -8k + 4 - 2k^2 + 3k^2 + 11 \\
&= k^2 - 8k + 15
\end{aligned}
$$

The remainder, $k^2 - 8k + 15$, must be zero if $f(x)$ is to be divisible by $x + 2$.

$$
k^2 - 8k + 15 = 0 \;\Rightarrow\; (k - 3)(k - 5) = 0 \;\Rightarrow\; k = 3, 5.
$$

**46** $f(x) = k^2x^3 - 4kx + 3$; $x - 1$ • $f(1) = k^2 - 4k + 3$.

As in the previous exercise, $k^2 - 4k + 3 = 0 \Rightarrow (k-1)(k-3) = 0 \Rightarrow k = 1, 3$.

**47** $x - c$ will not be a factor of $f(x) = 3x^4 + x^2 + 5$ for any real number $c$ if the remainder of dividing $f(x)$ by $x - c$ is not zero for any real number $c$. The remainder is $f(c)$, or $3c^4 + c^2 + 5$. Since $3c^4 + c^2 + 5$ is greater than or equal to 5 for any real number $c$, it is never zero and hence, $x - c$ is never a factor of $f(x)$.

**48** $f(c) = -c^4 - 3c^2 - 2 \le -2 \; \forall c \in \mathbb{R}$; that is, the remainder cannot be zero.

**49** $f(x) = 3x^{100} + 5x^{85} - 4x^{38} + 2x^{17} - 6 \Rightarrow f(-1) = 3 - 5 - 4 - 2 - 6 = -14$.

{change sign on coefficients of odd powers of $x$}

**50** If $f(x) = x^n - y^n$, then $f(y) = y^n - y^n = 0$. Hence, $x - y$ is a factor of $f$.

**51** If $f(x) = x^n - y^n$ and $n$ is even, then $f(-y) = (-y)^n - (y)^n = y^n - y^n = 0$. Hence, $x + y$ is a factor of $x^n - y^n$.

**52** If $f(x) = x^n + y^n$ and $n$ is odd, then $f(-y) = (-y)^n + y^n = -y^n + y^n = 0$. Hence, $x + y$ is a factor of $x^n + y^n$.

**53** (a) The radius of the resulting cylinder is $x$ and the height is $y$, that is, $6 - x$. $V = \pi r^2 h = \pi x^2(6 - x)$

(b) The volume of the cylinder of radius 1 and altitude 5 is $\pi(1)^2 5 = 5\pi$. To determine another value of $x$ which would result in the same volume, we need to solve the equation $5\pi = \pi x^2(6 - x)$. $5\pi = \pi x^2(6 - x) \Rightarrow 5 = 6x^2 - x^3 \Rightarrow x^3 - 6x^2 + 5 = 0$. We know that $x = 1$ is a solution to this equation. Synthetically dividing, we obtain

$$\begin{array}{r|rrrr} 1 & 1 & -6 & 0 & 5 \\ & & 1 & -5 & -5 \\ \hline & 1 & -5 & -5 & 0 \end{array}$$

The quotient is $x^2 - 5x - 5$. Using the quadratic formula, we see that the solutions are $x = \frac{1}{2}\left(5 \pm \sqrt{45}\right)$.

Since $x$ must be positive in the first quadrant, $\frac{1}{2}\left(5 + \sqrt{45}\right) \approx 5.85$ would be an allowable value of $x$.

If $x = \frac{1}{2}\left(5 + \sqrt{45}\right)$, then $y = 6 - x = 6 - \frac{1}{2}\left(5 + \sqrt{45}\right) = \frac{12}{2} - \frac{5}{2} - \frac{1}{2}\sqrt{45} = \frac{1}{2}\left(7 - \sqrt{45}\right)$.

The point $P$ is $P(x, y) = \left(\frac{1}{2}\left(5 + \sqrt{45}\right), \frac{1}{2}\left(7 - \sqrt{45}\right)\right) \approx (5.85, 0.15)$.

**54** The width, depth, and diameter form a right triangle. $w^2 + d^2 = 2^2 \Rightarrow d^2 = 4 - w^2 = \frac{7}{4}$ for $w = \frac{3}{2}$.

$S = kwd^2 = k\left(\frac{3}{2}\right)\left(\frac{7}{4}\right) = \frac{21}{8}k$. Now $\frac{21}{8}k = kw(4 - w^2) \Rightarrow 21 = 8w(4 - w^2) \Rightarrow$

$8w^3 - 32w + 21 = 0 \Rightarrow$ {we know $\frac{3}{2}$ is a zero, so $w - \frac{3}{2}$ is a factor} $\left(w - \frac{3}{2}\right)(8w^2 + 12w - 14) = 0 \Rightarrow$

$w = \frac{3}{2}, \frac{-3 \pm \sqrt{37}}{4}$. Thus, $\frac{\sqrt{37} - 3}{4} \approx 0.77$ would be an allowable value of $w$.

**55** (a) $A = lw = (2x)(y) = 2x(4 - x^2) = 8x - 2x^3$

(b) This solution is similar to the solution in Exercise 53(b).

$A = 6 \Rightarrow 6 = 8x - 2x^3 \Rightarrow x^3 - 4x + 3 = 0 \Rightarrow (x - 1)(x^2 + x - 3) = 0 \Rightarrow$

$x = 1$ or $x^2 + x - 3 = 0$. Solving the second equation, we get $x = \dfrac{-1 \pm \sqrt{13}}{2}$.

The value $\dfrac{\sqrt{13} - 1}{2}$ would be an allowable value of $x$. The base, $2x$, would then be $\sqrt{13} - 1 \approx 2.61$.

**56** (a) Let $\frac{3}{2} - 2r$ denote the length of the right circular cylinder portion of the capsule.

$V_{\text{Total}} = V_{2 \text{ Hemispheres}} + V_{\text{Cylinder}} \Rightarrow$

$V = 2 \cdot \frac{2}{3}\pi r^3 + \pi r^2 h = \frac{4}{3}\pi r^3 + \pi r^2\left(\frac{3}{2} - 2r\right) = \pi r^2\left(\frac{4}{3}r + \frac{3}{2} - 2r\right) = \pi r^2\left(\frac{3}{2} - \frac{2}{3}r\right).$

(b) The tablet has volume $\pi\left(\frac{1}{2}\right)^2 \cdot \frac{1}{3} = \frac{\pi}{12}$. So $\frac{\pi}{12} = \pi r^2\left(\frac{3}{2} - \frac{2}{3}r\right) \Rightarrow 1 = 12r^2\left(\frac{3}{2} - \frac{2}{3}r\right) \Rightarrow$

$8r^3 - 18r^2 + 1 = 0 \Rightarrow (4r - 1)(2r^2 - 4r - 1) = 0 \Rightarrow r = \frac{1}{4}, 1 \pm \frac{1}{2}\sqrt{6}.$

$\frac{1}{4}$ cm is the only allowable solution.

**57** If $f(x) = x^8 - 7.9x^5 - 0.8x^4 + x^3 + 1.2x - 9.81$, then the remainder is $f(0.21) \approx -9.55$.

[−1, 1] by [−20, 0, 2]

[−1, 1] by [−20, 0, 2]

*Figure 57*                                         *Figure 58*

**58** If $f(x) = 3.33x^6 - 2.5x^5 + 6.9x^3 - 4.1x^2 + 1.22x - 6.78$, then the remainder is $f(0.21) \approx -6.64$.

**59** $f(x) = x^3 + k^3x^2 + 2kx - 2k^4; x - 1.6 \bullet f(1.6) = -2k^4 + 2.56k^3 + 3.2k + 4.096.$

Graph $y = -2k^4 + 2.56k^3 + 3.2k + 4.096$ (that is, $y = -2x^4 + 2.56x^3 + 3.2x + 4.096$). From the graph, we see

that $y = 0$ when $k \approx -0.75, 1.96$. Thus, if $k$ assumes either of these values, $f(1.6) = 0$ and $f$ will be divisible by

$x - 1.6$ by the factor theorem.

[−9, 9] by [−3, 9]

[−4.5, 4.5] by [−3, 3]

*Figure 59*                                         *Figure 60*

**60** $f(x) = k^5x^3 - 2.1x^2 + k^3x - 1.2k^2; x + 0.4 \bullet f(-0.4) = -0.064k^5 - 0.4k^3 - 1.2k^2 - 0.336.$

Graph $y = -0.064k^5 - 0.4k^3 - 1.2k^2 - 0.336$. From the graph, we see that $y = 0$ when $k \approx -1.98$.

Thus, if $k$ assumes this value, $f(-0.4) = 0$ and $f$ will be divisible by $x + 0.4$ by the factor theorem.

## 3.3 Exercises

**1** The polynomial is of the form $f(x) = a(x - (-1))(x - 2)(x - 3) = a(x + 1)(x - 2)(x - 3)$.

$f(-2) = a(-1)(-4)(-5) = 80 \Rightarrow -20a = 80 \Rightarrow a = -4.$

Hence, the polynomial is $-4(x + 1)(x - 2)(x - 3)$, or $-4x^3 + 16x^2 - 4x - 24$.

**2** $f(x) = a(x + 5)(x - 2)(x - 4); f(3) = a(8)(1)(-1) = -24 \Rightarrow -8a = -24 \Rightarrow a = 3$

Hence, the polynomial is $3(x + 5)(x - 2)(x - 4)$, or $3x^3 - 3x^2 - 66x + 120$.

**3.** The polynomial is of the form $f(x) = a(x - (-4))(x - 3)(x - 0) = a(x + 4)(x - 3)(x)$.

$f(2) = a(6)(-1)(2) = -36 \Rightarrow -12a = -36 \Rightarrow a = 3$.

Hence, the polynomial is $3x(x + 4)(x - 3)$, or $3x^3 + 3x^2 - 36x$.

**4.** $f(x) = a(x + 3)(x + 2)(x); f(-4) = a(-1)(-2)(-4) = 16 \Rightarrow -8a = 16 \Rightarrow a = -2$

Hence, the polynomial is $-2x(x + 3)(x + 2)$, or $-2x^3 - 10x^2 - 12x$.

**5.** The polynomial is of the form $f(x) = a(x - (-2i))(x - 2i)(x - 3)$.

$f(1) = a(1 + 2i)(1 - 2i)(-2) = 20 \Rightarrow -10a = 20 \Rightarrow a = -2$.

Hence, the polynomial is $-2(x + 2i)(x - 2i)(x - 3) = -2(x^2 + 4)(x - 3)$, or $-2x^3 + 6x^2 - 8x + 24$.

**6.** $f(x) = a(x + 3i)(x - 3i)(x - 4); f(-1) = a(-1 + 3i)(-1 - 3i)(-5) = 50 \Rightarrow -50a = 50 \Rightarrow a = -1$

Hence, the polynomial is $-1(x + 3i)(x - 3i)(x - 4) = -(x^2 + 9)(x - 4)$, or $-x^3 + 4x^2 - 9x + 36$.

**7.** The polynomial is of the form $f(x) = a(x - (-i))(x - i)(x - 0)$.

$f(2) = a(2 + i)(2 - i)(2) = 30 \Rightarrow a(4 + 1)(2) = 30 \Rightarrow 10a = 30 \Rightarrow a = 3$.

Hence, the polynomial is $3(x + i)(x - i)(x) = 3(x^2 + 1)(x)$, or $3x^3 + 3x$.

**8.** The polynomial is of the form $f(x) = a(x - (-4i))(x - 4i)(x - 0)$.

$f(4) = a(4 + 4i)(4 - 4i)(4) = 1 \Rightarrow a(16 + 16)(4) = 1 \Rightarrow 128a = 1 \Rightarrow a = \frac{1}{128}$.

Hence, the polynomial is $\frac{1}{128}(x + 4i)(x - 4i)(x) = \frac{1}{128}(x^2 + 16)(x)$, or $\frac{1}{128}x^3 + \frac{1}{8}x$.

**9.** $f(x) = a(x + 4)^2(x - 3)^2 = (x^2 + x - 12)^2$ {let $a = 1$} $= x^4 + 2x^3 - 23x^2 - 24x + 144$

*Figure 9*

*Figure 10*

**10.** $f(x) = a(x + 5)^2(x - 2)^2 = (x^2 + 3x - 10)^2$ {let $a = 1$} $= x^4 + 6x^3 - 11x^2 - 60x + 100$.

Note that the figure can be obtained by shifting the figure from the previous solution left 1 unit.

**11.** $f(x) = a(x)^3(x - 3)^3$, so $f(2) = a(8)(-1) = -8a$. But $f(2) = -24$, so $-8a = -24$, or, $a = 3$.

$f(x) = 3(x)^3(x^3 - 9x^2 + 27x - 27) = 3x^6 - 27x^5 + 81x^4 - 81x^3$.

*Figure 11*

*Figure 12*

**12** $f(x) = a(x)^3(x+2)^2(x-2)^2$, so $f(-1) = a(-1)(1)(9) = -9a$. But $f(-1) = 27$, so $-9a = 27$, or, $a = -3$.

$$f(x) = -3x^3(x^2-4)^2 = -3x^3(x^4 - 8x^2 + 16) = -3x^7 + 24x^5 - 48x^3. \text{ See Figure 12.}$$

**13** The graph has $x$-intercepts at $-1$, $\frac{3}{2}$, $3$, and $f(0) = \frac{7}{2}$.

$$f(x) = a(x+1)\left(x - \tfrac{3}{2}\right)(x-3); f(0) = a(1)\left(-\tfrac{3}{2}\right)(-3) = \tfrac{7}{2} \;\Rightarrow\; \tfrac{9}{2}a = \tfrac{7}{2} \;\Rightarrow\; a = \tfrac{7}{9}.$$

$$f(x) = \tfrac{7}{9}(x+1)\left(x - \tfrac{3}{2}\right)(x-3).$$

**14** The graph has $x$-intercepts at $0, 1, 3, 5$, and $f(-1) = 4$.

$$f(x) = a(x)(x-1)(x-3)(x-5); f(-1) = a(-1)(-2)(-4)(-6) = 4 \;\Rightarrow\; 48a = 4 \;\Rightarrow\; a = \tfrac{1}{12}.$$

$$f(x) = \tfrac{1}{12}x(x-1)(x-3)(x-5).$$

**15** $3$ is a zero of multiplicity one, $1$ is a zero of multiplicity two, and $f(0) = 3$.

$$f(x) = a(x-1)^2(x-3); f(0) = a(1)(-3) = 3 \;\Rightarrow\; a = -1. \; f(x) = -1(x-1)^2(x-3).$$

**16** $4$ is a zero of multiplicity one, $2$ is a zero of multiplicity two, and $f(1) = -3$.

$$f(x) = a(x-2)^2(x-4); f(1) = a(1)(-3) = -3 \;\Rightarrow\; a = 1. \; f(x) = 1(x-2)^2(x-4).$$

**17** The values of $x$ that make $f(x) = x^2(3x+2)(2x-5)^3$ equal to zero are $0$, $-\frac{2}{3}$, and $\frac{5}{2}$. The exponents associated with these zeros are $2, 1$, and $3$, respectively. Thus, $0$ is a root of multiplicity $2$, $-\frac{2}{3}$ is a root of multiplicity $1$, and $\frac{5}{2}$ is a root of multiplicity $3$.

**18** $f(x) = x(x+1)^4(3x-7)^2$ ★ $-1$ (multiplicity 4); $0$ (multiplicity 1); $\frac{7}{3}$ (multiplicity 2)

**19** $f(x) = 4x^5 + 12x^4 + 9x^3 = x^3(4x^2 + 12x + 9) = x^3(2x+3)^2$, so $0$ is a root of multiplicity $3$ and $-\frac{3}{2}$ is a root of multiplicity $2$.

**20** $f(x) = 16x^5 - 40x^4 + 25x^3 = x^3(16x^2 - 40x + 25) = x^3(4x-5)^2$, so $0$ is a root of multiplicity $3$ and $\frac{5}{4}$ is a root of multiplicity $2$.

**21** $f(x) = (x^2-3)^2 = \left[\left(x+\sqrt{3}\right)\left(x-\sqrt{3}\right)\right]^2 = \left(x+\sqrt{3}\right)^2\left(x-\sqrt{3}\right)^2$, so $\pm\sqrt{3}$ are each roots of multiplicity $2$.

**22** $f(x) = (4x^2-5)^2 = \left[\left(2x+\sqrt{5}\right)\left(2x-\sqrt{5}\right)\right]^2 = \left(2x+\sqrt{5}\right)^2\left(2x-\sqrt{5}\right)^2$, so $\pm\frac{1}{2}\sqrt{5}$ are each roots of multiplicity $2$.

**23** $f(x) = (x^2 + x - 12)^3(x^2-9)^2 = [(x+4)(x-3)]^3[(x+3)(x-3)]^2$

$$= (x+4)^3(x-3)^3(x+3)^2(x-3)^2 = (x+4)^3(x+3)^2(x-3)^5$$

★ $-4$ (multiplicity 3); $-3$ (multiplicity 2); $3$ (multiplicity 5)

**24** $f(x) = (6x^2 + 7x - 5)^4(4x^2-1)^2 = (3x+5)^4(2x-1)^4(2x+1)^2(2x-1)^2$

★ $-\frac{5}{3}$ (multiplicity 4); $-\frac{1}{2}$ (multiplicity 2); $\frac{1}{2}$ (multiplicity 6)

**25** $f(x) = x^4 + 7x^2 - 144 = (x^2+16)(x^2-9) = (x^2+16)(x+3)(x-3)$ ★ $\pm 4i$, $\pm 3$ (each of multiplicity 1)

**26** $f(x) = x^4 + 21x^2 - 100 = (x^2+25)(x^2-4) = (x^2+25)(x+2)(x-2)$ ★ $\pm 5i$, $\pm 2$ (each of multiplicity 1)

**27** $f(x) = x^4 + 5x^3 + 6x^2 - 4x - 8$ • We use synthetic division:

$$-3 \,|\, 1 \quad 7 \quad 13 \quad -3 \quad -18$$
$$\quad\quad\quad -3 \quad -12 \quad -3 \quad 18$$
$$\quad\quad 1 \quad 4 \quad 1 \quad -6 \quad 0 \quad \text{...and again...}$$

$$-3 \,|\, 1 \quad 4 \quad 1 \quad -6$$
$$\quad\quad\quad -3 \quad -3 \quad 6$$
$$\quad\quad 1 \quad 1 \quad -2 \quad 0$$

The remaining polynomial, $x^2 + x - 2$, can be factored as $(x+2)(x-1)$.

Hence, $f(x) = (x+3)^2(x+2)(x-1)$.

**28** $f(x) = x^4 - 9x^3 + 22x^2 - 32$ • *Note:* If the sum of the coefficients of $f(-x)$ is 0, then $-1$ is a zero of $f$.
Since $1 + 9 + 22 - 32 = 0$, first try $-1$, then try 2. $f(x) = (x-4)^2(x-2)(x+1)$.

**29** $f(x) = x^4 + 5x^3 + 6x^2 - 4x - 8$ • We use synthetic division:

$$-2 \,|\, 1 \quad 5 \quad 6 \quad -4 \quad -8$$
$$\quad\quad\quad -2 \quad -6 \quad 0 \quad 8$$
$$\quad\quad 1 \quad 3 \quad 0 \quad -4 \quad 0 \quad \text{...and again...}$$

$$-2 \,|\, 1 \quad 3 \quad 0 \quad -4$$
$$\quad\quad\quad -2 \quad -2 \quad 4$$
$$\quad\quad 1 \quad 1 \quad -2 \quad 0$$

The remaining polynomial, $x^2 + x - 2$, can be factored as $(x+2)(x-1)$. Hence, $f(x) = (x+2)^3(x-1)$.

**30** $f(x) = x^4 - 11x^3 + 36x^2 - 16x - 64$ • Try $-1$, then try 4. $f(x) = (x-4)^3(x+1)$.

**31** *Note:* If the sum of the coefficients of the polynomial is 0, then 1 is a zero of the polynomial.
Synthetically dividing 1 five times, we obtain the remaining polynomial, $x + 1$.
Hence, $f(x) = x^6 - 4x^5 + 5x^4 - 5x^2 + 4x - 1 = (x-1)^5(x+1)$.

**32** $f(x) = x^5 + x^4 - 6x^3 - 14x^2 - 11x - 3$ • Try $-1$ three times. $f(x) = (x+1)^4(x-3)$.

*Note:* For the following exercises, let $f(x)$ denote the polynomial, P, the number of sign changes in $f(x)$, and N, the number of sign changes in $f(-x)$. The types of possible solutions are listed in the order positive, negative, nonreal complex.

**33** $f(x) = 4x^3 - 6x^2 + x - 3$. The sign pattern for coefficients is $+, -, +, -$. Since there are 3 sign changes in $f(x)$, P = 3. $f(-x) = -4x^3 - 6x^2 - x - 3$. *Note:* Simply change the sign of the coefficients of the odd-powered terms of $f(x)$ to find $f(-x)$. The sign pattern for coefficients is $-, -, -, -$. Since there are no sign changes in $f(-x)$, N = 0. If there are 3 positive solutions, then there are no negative or nonreal complex. If there is 1 positive solution, there are no negative and 2 nonreal complex solutions.

**34** $f(x) = 5x^3 - 6x - 4 \Rightarrow P = 1$. $f(-x) = -5x^3 + 6x - 4 \Rightarrow N = 2$. ★ $1, 2, 0$ or $1, 0, 2$

**35** $f(x) = 4x^3 + 2x^2 + 1 \Rightarrow P = 0$. $f(-x) = -4x^3 + 2x^2 + 1 \Rightarrow N = 1$. ★ $0, 1, 2$

**36** $f(x) = 3x^3 - 4x^2 + 3x + 7 \Rightarrow P = 2$. $f(-x) = -3x^3 - 4x^2 - 3x + 7 \Rightarrow N = 1$. ★ $2, 1, 0$ or $0, 1, 2$

**37** $f(x) = 3x^4 + 2x^3 - 4x + 2 \Rightarrow P = 2$. $f(-x) = 3x^4 - 2x^3 + 4x + 2 \Rightarrow N = 2$.
★ $2, 2, 0; 2, 0, 2; 0, 2, 2; 0, 0, 4$

**38** $f(x) = 2x^4 - x^3 + x^2 - 3x + 4 \Rightarrow P = 4$. $f(-x) = 2x^4 + x^3 + x^2 + 3x + 4 \Rightarrow N = 0$.
★ $4, 0, 0; 2, 0, 2; 0, 0, 4$

**39** $f(x) = x^5 + 4x^4 + 3x^3 - 4x + 2 \Rightarrow P = 2$. $f(-x) = -x^5 + 4x^4 - 3x^3 + 4x + 2 \Rightarrow N = 3$.
★ $2, 3, 0; 2, 1, 2; 0, 3, 2; 0, 1, 4$

**40** $f(x) = 2x^6 + 5x^5 + 2x^2 - 3x + 4 \implies P = 2.$ $f(-x) = 2x^6 - 5x^5 + 2x^2 + 3x + 4 \implies N = 2.$

★ $2, 2, 2;\ 2, 0, 4;\ 0, 2, 4;\ 0, 0, 6$

**41** Synthetically dividing 5 into the polynomial yields a bottom row consisting of all nonnegative numbers (see below). Synthetically dividing $-2$ into the polynomial yields a bottom row that alternates in sign (see below).

$$
\begin{array}{r|rrrr}
5 & 1 & -4 & -5 & 7 \\
  &   & 5  & 5  & 0 \\
\hline
  & 1 & 1  & 0  & 7
\end{array}
\qquad
\begin{array}{r|rrrr}
-2 & 1 & -4 & -5 & 7 \\
   &   & -2 & 12 & -14 \\
\hline
   & 1 & -6 & 7  & -7
\end{array}
$$

These results indicate that the upper bound is 5 and the lower bound is $-2$.

From the graph of $f(x) = x^3 - 4x^2 - 5x + 7$, we see that the bounds given by the theorem (5 and $-2$) are indeed the smallest and largest integers that are upper and lower bounds.

**42** From the graph of $f(x) = 2x^3 - 5x^2 + 4x - 8$, we see that the least integer upper bound is 3 and the greatest integer lower bound is 2. According to the first theorem, the greatest *negative* integer lower bound is $-1$ (the first theorem gives no information about a greatest *positive* integer lower bound).

**43** Synthetically dividing 2 into the polynomial yields a bottom row consisting of all nonnegative numbers (see below). Synthetically dividing $-2$ into the polynomial yields a bottom row that alternates in sign (see below).

$$
\begin{array}{r|rrrrr}
2 & 1 & -1 & -2 & 3 & 6 \\
  &   & 2  & 2  & 0 & 6 \\
\hline
  & 1 & 1  & 0  & 3 & 12
\end{array}
\qquad
\begin{array}{r|rrrrr}
-2 & 1 & -1 & -2 & 3 & 6 \\
   &   & -2 & 6  & -8 & 10 \\
\hline
   & 1 & -3 & 4  & -5 & 16
\end{array}
$$

These results indicate that the upper bound is 2 and the lower bound is $-2$.

From the graph of $f(x) = x^4 - x^3 - 2x^2 + 3x + 6$, we see that there are *no* real zeros. Remember, the theorem only gives us upper positive and lower negative bounds for the zeros of a polynomial—it doesn't guarantee that there are any zeros.

**44** Similar to Exercise 41 with $f(x) = 2x^4 - 9x^3 - 8x - 10$, upper bound 5, and lower bound $-1$.

**45** Similar to Exercise 41 with $f(x) = 2x^5 - 13x^3 + 2x - 5$, upper bound 3, and lower bound $-3$.

$$
\begin{array}{r|rrrrrr}
3 & 2 & 0 & -13 & 0 & 2 & -5 \\
  &   & 6 & 18 & 15 & 45 & 141 \\
\hline
  & 2 & 6 & 5 & 15 & 47 & 136
\end{array}
\qquad
\begin{array}{r|rrrrrr}
-3 & 2 & 0 & -13 & 0 & 2 & -5 \\
   &   & -6 & 18 & -15 & 45 & -141 \\
\hline
   & 2 & -6 & 5 & -15 & 47 & -146
\end{array}
$$

**46** Similar to Exercise 42 with $f(x) = 3x^5 + 2x^4 - x^3 - 8x^2 - 7$, upper bound 2, and lower bound $-1$. From the graph of $f$, the lower bound is 1.

**47** The zero at $x = -1$ must be of even multiplicity since the graph does not cross the $x$-axis. Since we want $f$ to have minimal degree, we will let the associated factor be $(x + 1)^2$. The graph goes through the zero at $x = 1$ without "flattening out," so the associated factor is $(x - 1)^1$. Because the graph flattens out at the zero at $x = 2$, we will let its associated factor be $(x - 2)^3$. Thus, $f$ has the form

$$f(x) = a(x + 1)^2(x - 1)(x - 2)^3.$$

Since the $y$-intercept is $(0, -2)$, we have $f(0) = a(1)(-1)(-8) = 8a$ and $f(0) = -2 \implies 8a = -2 \implies a = -\frac{1}{4}$. Hence, $f(x) = -\frac{1}{4}(x + 1)^2(x - 1)(x - 2)^3$.

**48** $f(x) = a(x + 2)(x + 1)(x - 2)^2.$ $f(0) = a(2)(1)(4) = 8a$ and $f(0) = 1 \implies a = \frac{1}{8}.$

**49** (a)  Similar to the discussion in the solution of Exercise 47, we have

$$f(x) = a(x+3)^3(x+1)(x-2)^2.$$

(b)  $a = 1$ and $x = 0$  $\Rightarrow$   $f(0) = 1(0+3)^3(0+1)(0-2)^2 = 1(3)^3(1)(-2)^2 = 108.$

**50** (a)  $f(x) = a(x+2)^3(x-3)^2.$

(b)  $a = -1$ and $x = 0$  $\Rightarrow$   $f(0) = -1(2)^3(-3)^2 = -72.$

**51** From the graph, we see that $f(x) = x^5 - 16.75x^3 + 12.75x^2 + 49.5x - 54$ has zeros of $-4, -2, 1.5,$ and $3$. There is a double root at $1.5$. Since the leading coefficient of $f$ is $1$, we have $f(x) = 1(x+4)(x+2)(x-1.5)^2(x-3).$

$[-5, 5]$ by $[-150, 150, 25]$     $[-5, 5]$ by $[-100, 100, 25]$

*Figure 51*                          *Figure 52*

**52** From the graph, we see that $f(x) = x^5 - 2.5x^4 - 12.75x^3 + 19.625x^2 + 27.625x + 7.5$ has zeros of $-3, -0.5,$ $2.5,$ and $4$. There is a double root at $-0.5$. Since the leading coefficient of $f$ is $1$, we have $f(x) = (x+3)(x+0.5)^2(x-2.5)(x-4).$

**53** Since the zeros are $-2, 1, 2,$ and $3$, the polynomial must have the form

$$f(x) = a(x+2)(x-1)(x-2)(x-3).$$

Now, $f(0) = a(2)(-1)(-2)(-3) = -12a$ and $f(0) = -24$  $\Rightarrow$   $-12a = -24$  $\Rightarrow$   $a = 2.$

Let $f(x) = 2(x+2)(x-1)(x-2)(x-3)$. Since $f$ has been completely determined, we must check the remaining data point(s).  $f(-1) = 2(1)(-2)(-3)(-4) = -48 \neq -52.$

Thus, a fourth-degree polynomial *does not* fit the data points.

**54** $f(x) = a(x)(x+3)(x+1)(x-2)(x-3)$. $f(-2) = a(-2)(1)(-1)(-4)(-5) = 40a$ and $f(-2) = 5$  $\Rightarrow$

$40a = 5$  $\Rightarrow$   $a = \frac{1}{8}$. Let $f(x) = \frac{1}{8}x(x+3)(x+1)(x-2)(x-3)$. $f(1) = \frac{1}{8}(1)(4)(2)(-1)(-2) = 2.$

Thus, a fifth-degree polynomial *does* fit the data points.

**55** Since the zeros are $2, 5.2,$ and $10.1$, the polynomial must have the form

$$f(x) = a(x-2)(x-5.2)(x-10.1).$$

Now, $f(1.1) = a(-33.21) = -49.815$  $\Rightarrow$   $a = 1.5$. Let $f(x) = 1.5(x-2)(x-5.2)(x-10.1)$. Since $f$ has been completely determined, we must check the remaining data points.  $f(3.5) = 25.245$ and $f(6.4) = -29.304.$

Thus, a third-degree polynomial *does* fit the data points.

**56** $f(x) = a(x-1.25)(x-2)(x-6.5)(x-10)$. $f(2.5) = a(18.75) = 56.25$  $\Rightarrow$   $a = 3.$

Let $f(x) = 3(x-1.25)(x-2)(x-6.5)(x-10)$. $f(2.5) = 56.25$ and $f(3) = 128.625.$

However, $f(9) = -406.875 \neq -307.75$. Thus, a fourth-degree polynomial *does not* fit the data points.

**57** The zeros are $0, 5, 19, 24,$ and $f(12) = 10$. $f(t) = a(t)(t-5)(t-19)(t-24);$

$f(12) = a(12)(7)(-7)(-12) = 10$  $\Rightarrow$   $7056a = 10$  $\Rightarrow$   $a = \frac{10}{7056} = \frac{5}{3528}.$

$$f(t) = \frac{5}{3528}t(t-5)(t-19)(t-24)$$

**58** $f(x) = a(x - c_1)(x - c_2)(x - c_3); f(c) = a(c - c_1)(c - c_2)(c - c_3) = 1 \Rightarrow a = \dfrac{1}{(c - c_1)(c - c_2)(c - c_3)}$

$$f(x) = \frac{1}{(c - c_1)(c - c_2)(c - c_3)}(x - c_1)(x - c_2)(x - c_3)$$

**59** The graph of $f$ does not cross the $x$-axis at a zero of even multiplicity, but does cross the $x$-axis at a zero of odd multiplicity. The higher the multiplicity of a zero, the more horizontal the graph of $f$ is near that zero.

$[-3, 3]$ by $[-2, 2]$

*Figure 59*

$[-3, 3]$ by $[-2, 2]$

*Figure 60*

**60** The conclusions from Exercise 59 do not change when there is more than one zero.

**61** From the graph of $f$ there are two zeros. They are $-1.2$ and $1.1$. The zero at $-1.2$ has even multiplicity and the zero at $1.1$ has odd multiplicity. Since $f$ has degree 3, the zero at $-1.2$ must have multiplicity 2 and the zero at $1.1$ has multiplicity 1.

$[-3, 3]$ by $[-3, 1]$

*Figure 61*

$[-3, 3]$ by $[-2, 2]$

*Figure 62*

**62** From the graph of $f$ there are two zeros. They are $-0.75$ and $1.25$. The zero at $-0.75$ has odd multiplicity and the zero at $1.25$ has even multiplicity. Since $f$ has degree 5, there are two possibilities for the multiplicity: $-0.75$ has multiplicity 1 and $1.25$ has multiplicity 4, or $-0.75$ has multiplicity 3 and $1.25$ has multiplicity 2. By careful inspection we can see that the graph of $f$ levels off as it crosses the $x$-axis at $-0.75$. This means that the multiplicity of this zero is greater than 1. (See Exercise 59. Thus, $-0.75$ has multiplicity 3 and $1.25$ has multiplicity 2.

**63** From the graph of $A(t) = -\frac{1}{2400}t^3 + \frac{1}{20}t^2 + \frac{7}{6}t + 340$, we see that $A = 450$ when $t \approx 43.2$. Thus, the carbon dioxide concentration will be 450 in $1980 + 43.2 = 2023.2$, or, during the year 2023.

$[0, 60, 10]$ by $[0, 600, 100]$

Intersection
X=43.162055   Y=450

*Figure 63*

$[0, 60, 10]$ by $[-2, 2]$

*Figure 64*

**64** From the graph of $T(t) = \frac{21}{5,000,000}t^3 - \frac{127}{1,000,000}t^2 + \frac{1293}{50,000}t - 1$, we see that $T = 0$ when $t \approx 37.1$. Thus, the average temperature will have increased by 1°C in $1980 + 37.1 = 2017.1$, or, during the year 2017.

**65** (a) Graphing the data and the functions show that the best fit is $h(x)$.

    (b) Since the temperature changes sign between April and May and between October and November, an average temperature of 0°F occurs when $4 \le x \le 5$ and $10 \le x \le 11$.

    (c) Finding the zeros of $h$ between 1 and 12 gives us $x \approx 4.02, 10.53$.

$[0.5, 12.5]$ by $[-30, 50, 10]$     $[0.5, 12.5]$ by $[-20, 70, 10]$

*Figure 65*          *Figure 66*

**66** (a) Graphing the data and the functions show that the best fit is $h(x)$.

    (b) Since the temperature changes sign between February and March and between November and December, an average temperature of 0°F occurs when $2 \le x \le 3$ and $11 \le x \le 12$.

    (c) Finding the zeros of $h$ between 1 and 12 gives us $x \approx 2.54, 11.42$.

**67** Let $r = 6$ and $k = 0.7$. Graph $Y_1 = \frac{4}{3}k\pi r^3 - \pi x^2 r + \frac{1}{3}\pi x^3 = \frac{604.8\pi}{3} - 6\pi x^2 + \frac{1}{3}\pi x^3$ and determine the positive zeros. There are two zeros located at $x \approx 7.64, 15.47$. Since the sphere floats, it will not sink deeper than twice the radius, which is 12 centimeters. Thus, the pine sphere will sink approximately 7.64 centimeters into the water.

$[-20, 20, 5]$ by $[-800, 800, 100]$     $[-20, 20, 5]$ by $[-1000, 1000, 100]$

*Figure 67*          *Figure 68*

**68** Let $r = 6$ and $k = 0.85$. Graph $Y_1 = \frac{4}{3}k\pi r^3 - \pi x^2 r + \frac{1}{3}\pi x^3 = \frac{734.4\pi}{3} - 6\pi x^2 + \frac{1}{3}\pi x^3$ and determine the positive zeros. There are two zeros located at $x \approx 9.07, 14.51$. Since the sphere floats, it will not sink deeper than twice the radius, which is 12. Thus, the oak sphere will sink approximately 9.07 centimeters into the water. This is slightly deeper than the pine sphere because the density of oak wood is greater than that of pine.

**69** Let $r = 6$ and $k = 1$.

Graph $Y_1 = \frac{4}{3}k\pi r^3 - \pi x^2 r + \frac{1}{3}\pi x^3 = 288\pi - 6\pi x^2 + \frac{1}{3}\pi x^3$ and determine the positive zero. There is a zero at $x = 12$. This means that the entire sphere is just submerged. The sphere has the same density as water and neither sinks nor floats, much like a balloon filled with water.

$[-20, 20, 5]$ by $[-1000, 1000, 100]$

## 3.4 Exercises

**Note:** It is helpful to remember that if $a + bi$ is a zero, then $[x^2 - 2ax + (a^2 + b^2)]$ is the associated quadratic factor for the following exercises. See page 214 (after Example 1) in the text.

[1]   Since $3 + 2i$ is a root, so is $3 - 2i$. As in the preceding note, $a = 3$ and $b = 2$, and hence, $-2a = -6$ and $a^2 + b^2 = 13$. Thus, the polynomial is of the form

$$[x - (3 + 2i)][x - (3 - 2i)] = x^2 - 2(3)x + \underline{(3)^2 + (2)^2} = x^2 - 6x + 13.$$

[2]   $[x - (-4 + 3i)][x - (-4 - 3i)] = x^2 - 2(-4)x + \underline{(-4)^2 + (3)^2} = x^2 + 8x + 25$

[3]   Since 2 is a zero, $x - 2$ is a factor. The associated quadratic factor for $-2 \pm 5i$ is $x^2 - 2(-2)x + \underline{(-2)^2 + (-5)^2}$, or, equivalently, $x^2 + 4x + 29$. Hence, the polynomial is of the form $(x - 2)(x^2 + 4x + 29)$.

[4]   $(x + 3)[x - (1 - 7i)][x - (1 + 7i)] = x^2 - 2(1)x + \underline{(1)^2 + (-7)^2} = (x + 3)(x^2 - 2x + 50)$

[5]   Since $-1$ and 0 are zeros, $x + 1$ and $x$ are factors. The associated quadratic factor for $3 \pm i$ is $x^2 - 2(3)x + \underline{(3)^2 + (1)^2}$, or, equivalently, $x^2 - 6x + 10$. Hence, the polynomial is of the form $(x)(x + 1)(x^2 - 6x + 10)$.

[6]   $x(x - 2)[x - (-2 - i)][x - (-2 + i)] = x^2 - 2(-2)x + \underline{(-2)^2 + (-1)^2} = x(x - 2)(x^2 + 4x + 5)$

[7]   Since $4 + 3i$ is a root, so is $4 - 3i$. The associated quadratic factor for $4 \pm 3i$ is

$$x^2 - 2(4)x + \underline{(4)^2 + (3)^2}, \text{ or, equivalently, } x^2 - 8x + 25.$$

Since $-2 + i$ is a root, so is $-2 - i$. The associated quadratic factor for $-2 \pm i$ is

$$x^2 - 2(-2)x + \underline{(-2)^2 + (1)^2}, \text{ or, equivalently, } x^2 + 4x + 5.$$

Hence, the polynomial is of the form $(x^2 - 8x + 25)(x^2 + 4x + 5)$.

[8]   $[x - (3 + 5i)][x - (3 - 5i)][x - (-1 - i)][x - (-1 + i)] = (x^2 - 6x + 34)(x^2 + 2x + 2)$

[9]   Since 0 is a zero, $x$ is a factor. If $-2i$ is a zero, then $2i$ is a zero. Thus, $(x - 2i)[x - (-2i)] = x^2 - 4i^2 = x^2 + 4$ is the associated factor. The associated quadratic factor for $1 \pm i$ is $x^2 - 2(1)x + \underline{(1)^2 + (-1)^2}$, or, equivalently, $x^2 - 2x + 2$. Hence, the polynomial is of the form $(x)(x^2 + 4)(x^2 - 2x + 2)$.

[10]   $x[x - (3i)][x - (-3i)][x - (4 + i)][x - (4 - i)] = x(x^2 + 9)(x^2 - 8x + 17)$

**Note:** Show that none of the possible rational roots listed satisfy the equation in Exercises 11–16.

[11]   $x^3 + 3x^2 - 4x + 6 = 0$   •   The constant term, 6, has positive integer divisors $1, 2, 3, 6$. The leading coefficient, 1, has integer divisors $\pm 1$. By the theorem on rational zeros of a polynomial, any rational root will be of the form

$$\frac{\text{positive divisors of } 6}{\text{divisors of } 1} = \frac{1, 2, 3, 6}{\pm 1} \longrightarrow \pm 1, \pm 2, \pm 3, \pm 6.$$

Note that this quotient gives us the same possible rational roots as the one on page 216:

$$\frac{\text{factors of } a_0}{\text{factors of } a_n} = \frac{\pm 1, \pm 2, \pm 3, \pm 6}{\pm 1} \longrightarrow \pm 1, \pm 2, \pm 3, \pm 6.$$

Since $\pm 1$ are always potential solutions, they are as good as any other values to begin with. If the coefficients of the polynomial ($x^3 + 3x^2 - 4x + 6$ in this exercise) sum to 0, then 1 is a zero. In this case, the sum is $1 + 3 + (-4) + 6 = 6 \neq 0$. Thus, 1 is eliminated and we will try $-1$. If $f(x)$ is the polynomial, then $-1$ will be a zero if the coefficients of $f(-x)$ sum to 0. In this case, $f(-x) = -x^3 + 3x^2 + 4x + 6$ and the sum of the coefficients is $(-1) + 3 + 4 + 6 = 12 \neq 0$. Thus, $-1$ is not a zero. We now use synthetic division to show that $\pm 2, \pm 3$, and $\pm 6$ are not zeros of $f(x)$, and thus, the equation has no rational root.

[12] For $3x^3 - 4x^2 + 7x + 5 = 0$, $a_0 = 5$ and $a_n = 3$.          $\dfrac{\text{factors of } a_0}{\text{factors of } a_n} = \dfrac{\pm 1, \pm 5}{\pm 1, \pm 3} \longrightarrow \pm 1, \pm\dfrac{1}{3}, \pm 5, \pm\dfrac{5}{3}$

Show that $\pm 1, \pm\frac{1}{3}, \pm 5$, and $\pm\frac{5}{3}$ are not zeros of $f(x) = 3x^3 - 4x^2 + 7x + 5$.

[13] For $5x^4 + 3x^2 - 5 = 0$, $a_0 = -5$ and $a_n = 5$.          $\dfrac{\text{factors of } a_0}{\text{factors of } a_n} = \dfrac{\pm 1, \pm 5}{\pm 1, \pm 5} \longrightarrow \pm 1, \pm\dfrac{1}{5}, \pm 5$

Show that $\pm 1, \pm\frac{1}{5}$, and $\pm 5$ are not zeros of $f(x) = 5x^4 + 3x^2 - 5$.

[14] For $x^4 - 9x + 7 = 0$, $a_0 = 7$ and $a_n = 1$.          $\dfrac{\text{factors of } a_0}{\text{factors of } a_n} = \dfrac{\pm 1, \pm 7}{\pm 1} \longrightarrow \pm 1, \pm 7$

Show that $\pm 1$ and $\pm 7$ are not zeros of $f(x) = x^4 - 9x + 7 = 0$.

[15] For $x^5 - 3x^3 + 4x^2 + x - 2 = 0$, $a_0 = -2$ and $a_n = 1$.          $\dfrac{\text{factors of } a_0}{\text{factors of } a_n} = \dfrac{\pm 1, \pm 2}{\pm 1} \longrightarrow \pm 1, \pm 2$

Show that $\pm 1$ and $\pm 2$ are not zeros of $f(x) = x^5 - 3x^3 + 4x^2 + x - 2$.

[16] For $2x^5 + 3x^3 + 7 = 0$, $a_0 = 7$ and $a_n = 2$.          $\dfrac{\text{factors of } a_0}{\text{factors of } a_n} = \dfrac{\pm 1, \pm 7}{\pm 1, \pm 2} \longrightarrow \pm 1, \pm\dfrac{1}{2}, \pm 7, \pm\dfrac{7}{2}$

Show that $\pm 1, \pm\frac{1}{2}, \pm 7$, and $\pm\frac{7}{2}$ are not zeros of $f(x) = 2x^5 + 3x^3 + 7$.

[17] (a) For $4x^3 - 4x^2 - 11x + 6 = 0$, $a_0 = 6$ and $a_n = 4$.

$\dfrac{\text{factors of } a_0}{\text{factors of } a_n} = \dfrac{\pm 1, \pm 2, \pm 3, \pm 6}{\pm 1, \pm 2, \pm 4} \longrightarrow \pm 1, \pm\dfrac{1}{2}, \pm\dfrac{1}{4}, \pm 2, \pm 3, \pm\dfrac{3}{2}, \pm\dfrac{3}{4}, \pm 6$

(b) Use $-6 \le x \le 6$ and $-1 \le y \le 1$ to see where the graph of $f$ crosses the $x$-axis.

(c) From the graph, we see that the only reasonable choices for rational roots are $\frac{1}{2}, 2$, and $-\frac{3}{2}$. This doesn't prove that they are the zeros, but now we know that these are the only rational zeros that we need to check.

[18] (a) For $8x^3 + 34x^2 + 33x + 9 = 0$, $a_0 = 9$ and $a_n = 8$.

$\dfrac{\text{factors of } a_0}{\text{factors of } a_n} = \dfrac{\pm 1, \pm 3, \pm 9}{\pm 1, \pm 2, \pm 4, \pm 8} \longrightarrow \pm 1, \pm\dfrac{1}{2}, \pm\dfrac{1}{4}, \pm\dfrac{1}{8}, \pm 3, \pm\dfrac{3}{2}, \pm\dfrac{3}{4}, \pm\dfrac{3}{8}, \pm 9, \pm\dfrac{9}{2}, \pm\dfrac{9}{4}, \pm\dfrac{9}{8}$

(b) Use $-9 \le x \le 9$ and $-1 \le y \le 1$ to see where the graph of $f$ crosses the $x$-axis.

(c) From the graph, we see that the only reasonable choices for rational roots are $-\frac{1}{2}, -3, -\frac{3}{4}$, and possibly $-\frac{3}{8}$. Note that we can immediately exclude all positive roots. This doesn't prove that they are the zeros, but now we know that these are the only rational zeros that we need to check.

**19** $x^3 - x^2 - 10x - 8 = 0$ • The constant term, $-8$, has positive integer divisors $1, 2, 4, 8$. The leading coefficient has integer divisors $\pm 1$. Hence, any rational root will be of the form

$$\frac{\text{positive divisors of } -8}{\text{divisors of } 1} = \frac{1, 2, 4, 8}{\pm 1} \longrightarrow \pm 1, \pm 2, \pm 4, \pm 8.$$

We now need to try to find one solution of the equation. Once we have one solution, the resulting polynomial will be a quadratic and then we can use the quadratic formula to find the other 2 solutions. As in the solution to Exercise 11, we will try $\pm 1$ first. After determining that 1 is not a solution, we try $-1$. In this case, $f(-x) = -x^3 - x^2 + 10x - 8$ and the sum of the coefficients is $(-1) + (-1) + 10 + (-8) = 0$. Thus, $-1$ is a zero and we will use synthetic division to find the remaining polynomial.

$$
\begin{array}{r|rrrr}
-1 & 1 & -1 & -10 & -8 \\
   &   & -1 &   2 &  8 \\
\hline
   & 1 & -2 &  -8 &  0
\end{array}
$$

The remaining polynomial is $(x^2 - 2x - 8) = (x - 4)(x + 2)$. Hence, the solutions are $-2, -1$, and $4$.

**20** $x^3 + x^2 - 14x - 24 = 0$ • $\dfrac{1, 2, 3, 4, 6, 8, 12, 24}{\pm 1} \longrightarrow \pm 1, \pm 2, \pm 3, \pm 4, \pm 6, \pm 8, \pm 12, \pm 24$ ★ $-3, -2, 4$

**21** $2x^3 - 3x^2 - 17x + 30 = 0$ • As previously noted, we first check $\pm 1$. Neither of these values are solutions so we list the possible rational roots. The values listed below are obtained by taking quotients of each number in the numerator with $\pm 1$, and then each number in the numerator with $\pm 2$, while discarding any repeat choices.

$$\frac{1, 2, 3, 5, 6, 10, 15, 30}{\pm 1, \pm 2} \longrightarrow \pm 1, \pm 2, \pm 3, \pm 5, \pm 6, \pm 10, \pm 15, \pm 30, \pm \frac{1}{2}, \pm \frac{3}{2}, \pm \frac{5}{2}, \pm \frac{15}{2}$$

Trying 2, we obtain

$$
\begin{array}{r|rrrr}
2 & 2 & -3 & -17 & 30 \\
  &   &  4 &   2 & -30 \\
\hline
  & 2 &  1 & -15 &  0
\end{array}
$$

The remaining polynomial is $(2x^2 + x - 15) = (2x - 5)(x + 3)$. Hence, the solutions are $-3, 2$, and $\frac{5}{2}$.

**22** $12x^3 + 8x^2 - 3x - 2 = 0$ • $\dfrac{\pm 1, \pm 2}{1, 2, 3, 4, 6, 12} \longrightarrow \pm 1, \pm \frac{1}{2}, \pm \frac{1}{3}, \pm \frac{1}{4}, \pm \frac{1}{6}, \pm \frac{1}{12}, \pm 2, \pm \frac{2}{3}$ ★ $-\frac{2}{3}, \pm \frac{1}{2}$

**23** $x^4 + 3x^3 - 30x^2 - 6x + 56 = 0$ • $\dfrac{1, 2, 4, 7, 8, 14, 28, 56}{\pm 1} \longrightarrow \pm 1, \pm 2, \pm 4, \pm 7, \pm 8, \pm 14, \pm 28, \pm 56$

Again, $\pm 1$ are not solutions. Trying 4 and then $-7$ (using a slightly different format) we obtain

$$
\begin{array}{r|rrrrr}
4 & 1 & 3 & -30 & -6 & 56 \\
  &   & 4 &  28 & -8 & -56 \\
\hline
  & 1 & 7 &  -2 & -14 & 0
\end{array}
\qquad
\begin{array}{r|rrrr}
-7 & 1 & 7 & -2 & -14 \\
   &   & -7 &  0 &  14 \\
\hline
   & 1 & 0 & -2 &  0
\end{array}
$$

The remaining polynomial is $x^2 - 2$. Its solutions are $\pm\sqrt{2}$. Hence, the solutions are $-7, \pm\sqrt{2}$, and $4$.

**24** $x^4 - x^3 - 9x^2 + 3x + 18 = 0$ • $\dfrac{1, 2, 3, 6, 9, 18}{\pm 1} \longrightarrow \pm 1, \pm 2, \pm 3, \pm 6, \pm 9, \pm 18$

Again, $\pm 1$ are not solutions. Trying 3 and then $-2$ (using a slightly different format) we obtain

$$
\begin{array}{r|rrrrr}
3 & 1 & -1 & -9 & 3 & 18 \\
  &   &  3 &  6 & -9 & 18 \\
\hline
  & 1 &  2 & -3 & -6 &  0
\end{array}
\qquad
\begin{array}{r|rrrr}
-2 & 1 & 2 & -3 & -6 \\
   &   & -2 &  0 &  6 \\
\hline
   & 1 & 0 & -3 &  0
\end{array}
$$

The remaining polynomial is $x^2 - 3$. Its solutions are $\pm\sqrt{3}$. Hence, the solutions are $-2, \pm\sqrt{3}$, and $3$.

**25** $2x^4 - 9x^3 + 9x^2 + x - 3 = 0$ • To check if 1 is a root, we add the coefficients, $2 - 9 + 9 + 1 - 3$, and get 0, so

1 is a root. $\underline{1\,|\,2\quad -9\quad 9\quad 1\quad -3}$ The division shows that the remaining polynomial is $2x^3 - 7x^2 + 2x + 3$. The

$$\underline{\phantom{xx}\quad 2\quad -7\quad 2\quad 3}$$
$$\phantom{x}2\quad -7\quad 2\quad 3\quad 0$$

sum of the coefficients is again 0, so 1 is a root of multiplicity 2 (at least). $\underline{1\,|\,2\quad -7\quad 2\quad 3}$ This division shows

$$\underline{\phantom{xxxx}\quad 2\quad -5\quad -3}$$
$$\phantom{x}2\quad -5\quad -3\quad 0$$

that the remaining polynomial is $2x^2 - 5x - 3$, which can be factored as $(2x+1)(x-3)$. Hence, the solutions are
1 (multiplicity 2), $-\frac{1}{2}$, and 3.

**26** $3x^5 - 10x^4 - 6x^3 + 24x^2 + 11x - 6 = 0$ • $\dfrac{1, 2, 3, 6}{\pm 1, \pm 3} \longrightarrow \pm 1, \pm 2, \pm 3, \pm 6, \pm\frac{1}{3}, \pm\frac{2}{3}$

$\bigstar$ $-1$ (multiplicity 2), $\frac{1}{3}$, 2, 3

**27** $6x^5 + 19x^4 + x^3 - 6x^2 = 0$ • We first factor out $x^2$, leaving us with the equation $x^2(6x^3 + 19x^2 + x - 6) = 0$.
The $x^2$ factor indicates that the number 0 is a zero of multiplicity two. We can now concentrate on solving the
equation $6x^3 + 19x^2 + x - 6 = 0$.

$$\frac{1, 2, 3, 6}{\pm 1, \pm 2, \pm 3, \pm 6} \longrightarrow \pm 1, \pm 2, \pm 3, \pm 6, \pm\frac{1}{2}, \pm\frac{3}{2}, \pm\frac{1}{3}, \pm\frac{2}{3}, \pm\frac{1}{6}$$

$$\underline{-3\,|\,6\quad 19\quad 1\quad -6}$$
$$\underline{\phantom{xxx}\quad -18\quad -3\quad 6}$$
$$\phantom{x}6\quad 1\quad -2\quad 0$$

$6x^2 + x - 2 = (3x+2)(2x-1)$ $\qquad\qquad\qquad\qquad\qquad\bigstar$ $-3, -\frac{2}{3}, \frac{1}{2}$

**28** $6x^4 + 5x^3 - 17x^2 - 6x = 0$ • $\dfrac{1, 2, 3, 6}{\pm 1, \pm 2, \pm 3, \pm 6} \longrightarrow \pm 1, \pm 2, \pm 3, \pm 6, \pm\frac{1}{2}, \pm\frac{3}{2}, \pm\frac{1}{3}, \pm\frac{2}{3}, \pm\frac{1}{6}$ $\bigstar$ $-2, -\frac{1}{3}, 0, \frac{3}{2}$

**29** $8x^3 + 18x^2 + 45x + 27 = 0$ •
$$\frac{1, 3, 9, 27}{\pm 1, \pm 2, \pm 4, \pm 8} \longrightarrow \pm 1, \pm 3, \pm 9, \pm 27, \pm\frac{1}{2}, \pm\frac{1}{4}, \pm\frac{1}{8}, \pm\frac{3}{2}, \pm\frac{3}{4}, \pm\frac{3}{8}, \pm\frac{9}{2}, \pm\frac{9}{4}, \pm\frac{9}{8}, \pm\frac{27}{2}, \pm\frac{27}{4}, \pm\frac{27}{8}$$
This is a tough one because only $-\frac{3}{4}$ is a solution.

$$\underline{-\tfrac{3}{4}\,|\,8\quad 18\quad 45\quad 27}$$
$$\underline{\phantom{xxxx}\quad -6\quad -9\quad -27}$$
$$\phantom{x}8\quad 12\quad 36\quad 0$$

$8x^2 + 12x + 36 = 0$ {divide by 4} $\Rightarrow$ $2x^2 + 3x + 9 = 0$ $\Rightarrow$

$x = \dfrac{-3 \pm \sqrt{9 - 72}}{4} = -\dfrac{3}{4} \pm \dfrac{1}{4}\sqrt{63}\,i = -\dfrac{3}{4} \pm \dfrac{3}{4}\sqrt{7}\,i$ $\qquad\qquad\bigstar$ $-\frac{3}{4}, -\frac{3}{4} \pm \frac{3}{4}\sqrt{7}\,i$

**30** $3x^3 - x^2 + 11x - 20 = 0$ • $\dfrac{1, 2, 4, 5, 10, 20}{\pm 1, \pm 3} \longrightarrow \pm 1, \pm 2, \pm 4, \pm 5, \pm 10, \pm 20, \pm\frac{1}{3}, \pm\frac{2}{3}, \pm\frac{4}{3}, \pm\frac{5}{3}, \pm\frac{10}{3}, \pm\frac{20}{3}$

$\bigstar$ $\frac{4}{3}, -\frac{1}{2} \pm \frac{1}{2}\sqrt{19}\,i$

**31** $f(x) = 6x^5 - 23x^4 + 24x^3 + x^2 - 12x + 4$ has zeros at $-\frac{2}{3}$, $\frac{1}{2}$, 1 (multiplicity 2), and 2.

Thus, $f(x) = 6\left(x + \frac{2}{3}\right)\left(x - \frac{1}{2}\right)(x-1)^2(x-2) = (3x+2)(2x-1)(x-1)^2(x-2)$.

**32** $f(x) = -6x^5 + 5x^4 + 14x^3 - 8x^2 - 8x + 3$ has zeros at $-1$ (multiplicity 2), $\frac{1}{3}$, 1, and $\frac{3}{2}$.

Thus, $f(x) = -6(x+1)^2\left(x - \frac{1}{3}\right)(x-1)\left(x - \frac{3}{2}\right) = (x+1)^2(3x-1)(1-x)(2x-3)$.

**33** From the graph, we see that $f(x) = 2x^3 - 25.4x^2 + 3.02x + 24.75$ has zeros of approximately $-0.9, 1.1,$ and $12.5$. Since the leading coefficient of $f$ is 2, we have $f(x) = 2(x + 0.9)(x - 1.1)(x - 12.5)$.

$[-5, 15, 5]$ by $[-600, 100, 100]$

**Figure 33**

$[-5, 5]$ by $[-15, 15, 5]$

**Figure 34**

**34** From the graph, we see that $f(x) = 0.5x^3 + 0.65x^2 - 5.365x + 1.5375$ has zeros of approximately $-4.1, 0.3,$ and $2.5$. Since the leading coefficient of $f$ is 0.5, we have $f(x) = 0.5(x + 4.1)(x - 0.3)(x - 2.5)$.

**35** No. If $i$ is a root, then $-i$ is also a root. Hence, the polynomial would have factors $x - 1, x + 1, x - i, x + i$ and therefore would be of degree greater than 3.

**36** The theorem applies only to polynomials with real coefficients whereas the polynomial in question,
$f(x) = x^3 - ix^2 + 2ix + 2$, has nonreal complex coefficients.

**37** Since $n$ is odd and nonreal complex zeros occur in conjugate pairs for polynomials with real coefficients, there must be at least one real zero.

**38** By the theorem on rational zeros, $r$ is of the form $c/d$, where $c$ is a factor of $a_0$ and $d$ is a factor of $a_n$.

Since $a_n$ is 1, its divisors are $\pm 1$. Thus, $r$ will be an integer and a factor of $a_0$.

**39** (a) From Exercise 43 in Section 3.1, the allowable range was $0 < x < 10$ and $V(x) = 4x(x - 10)(x - 15)$.
$V = 1000 \Rightarrow 4x(x - 10)(x - 15) = 1000 \Rightarrow x(x - 10)(x - 15) = 250 \Rightarrow$
$x(x^2 - 25x + 150) - 250 = 0 \Rightarrow x^3 - 25x^2 + 150x - 250 = 0$.

We can show that 5 is a root, so the last equation can be written as $(x - 5)(x^2 - 20x + 50) = 0$. Using the quadratic equation gives us $(x - 5)\left[x - \left(10 - 5\sqrt{2}\right)\right]\left[x - \left(10 + 5\sqrt{2}\right)\right] = 0$. Discard $10 + 5\sqrt{2} \{ > 10\}$.

The dimensions of the box are $x, 20 - 2x,$ and $30 - 2x$. So the two boxes ⟦A⟧ and ⟦B⟧ having volume 1000 in³ have dimensions

⟦A⟧: $5 \times \underline{20 - 2(5)} \times \underline{30 - 2(5)} = 5 \times 10 \times 20$ and ⟦B⟧:
$\left(10 - 5\sqrt{2}\right) \times \underline{20 - 2\left(10 - 5\sqrt{2}\right)} \times \underline{30 - 2\left(10 - 5\sqrt{2}\right)} = \left(10 - 5\sqrt{2}\right) \times \left(10\sqrt{2}\right) \times \left(10 + 10\sqrt{2}\right)$.

(b) The surface area function is $S(x) = (20 - 2x)(30 - 2x) + 2(x)(20 - 2x) + 2(x)(30 - 2x) = -4x^2 + 600$.
$S(5) = 500$ and $S\left(10 - 5\sqrt{2}\right) = 400\sqrt{2} \approx 565.7$, so box ⟦A⟧ has less surface area.

**40** From Exercise 44 in Section 3.1, $V(x) = x^2(6 - 2x)$. $V(x) = 4 \Rightarrow x^3 - 3x^2 + 2 = 0 \Rightarrow$
$(x - 1)(x^2 - 2x - 2) = 0 \Rightarrow \{x > 0\} \ x = 1, 1 + \sqrt{3}$.

**41** (a) Let $x$ denote one of the sides of the triangle and $x + 1$ its hypotenuse.
Using the Pythagorean theorem, the third side $y$ is given by

$$x^2 + y^2 = (x + 1)^2 \Rightarrow y^2 = (x^2 + 2x + 1) - x^2 \Rightarrow y = \sqrt{2x + 1}.$$

Hence, the sides of the triangle are $x, \sqrt{2x + 1},$ and $x + 1$.
$A = \frac{1}{2}bh \Rightarrow 30 = \frac{1}{2}x\sqrt{2x + 1} \Rightarrow 60 = x\sqrt{2x + 1} \Rightarrow 60^2 = x^2(2x + 1) \Rightarrow$
$$3600 = 2x^3 + x^2 \Rightarrow 2x^3 + x^2 - 3600 = 0.$$

(b) There is one sign change in $f(x) = 2x^3 + x^2 - 3600$. By Descartes' rule of signs there is one positive real root. Synthetically dividing 13 into $f$, we obtain

$$\begin{array}{r|rrrr} 13 & 2 & 1 & 0 & -3600 \\ & & 26 & 351 & 4563 \\ \hline & 2 & 27 & 351 & 963 \end{array}$$

The numbers in the third row are nonnegative, so 13 is an upper bound for the zeros of $f$.

(c) $2x^3 + x^2 - 3600 = 0 \Leftrightarrow (x - 12)(2x^2 + 25x + 300) = 0$.

The solutions of $2x^2 + 25x + 300 = 0$ are $x = -\dfrac{25}{4} \pm \dfrac{5}{4}\sqrt{71}\, i$, and hence, $x = 12$ is the only real solution.

The legs of the triangle are 12 ft and 5 ft, and the hypotenuse is 13 ft.

**42** $V(x) = 27\pi \Rightarrow 10\pi x^2 + \frac{4}{3}\pi x^3 = 27\pi \Rightarrow 4x^3 + 30x^2 - 81 = 0 \Rightarrow (2x - 3)(2x^2 + 18x + 27) = 0$.

$x = \frac{3}{2}$ is the only positive solution, so the radius is 1.5 ft.

**43** (a) $\text{Volume}_{\text{total}} = \text{Volume}_{\text{cube}} + \text{Volume}_{\text{roof}}$

$= x^3 + \frac{1}{2}bhx = x^3 + \frac{1}{2}(x)(6 - x)(x) = x^3 + \frac{1}{2}x^2(6 - x)$.

(b) Volume $= 80 \Rightarrow x^3 + \frac{1}{2}x^2(6 - x) = 80 \Rightarrow x^3 + 3x^2 - \frac{1}{2}x^3 = 80 \Rightarrow$

$\frac{1}{2}x^3 + 3x^2 = 80 \Rightarrow x^3 + 6x^2 - 160 = 0 \Rightarrow (x - 4)(x^2 + 10x + 40) = 0$.

The length of the side is 4 ft.

**44** Form a triangle with the center pole and the midpoint of any side. The hypotenuse (call it $y$) is the height of one of the triangular sides with base $x$. $\left(\frac{1}{2}x\right)^2 + (8)^2 = y^2 \Rightarrow y = \sqrt{64 + \frac{1}{4}x^2}$.

$\text{Area}_{\text{total}} = \text{Area}_{\text{base}} + \text{Area}_{4\,\text{sides}} = (\text{side})(\text{side}) + 4\left(\frac{1}{2}\right)(\text{base})(\text{height}) = x^2 + 4\left(\frac{1}{2}\right)(x)\sqrt{64 + \frac{1}{4}x^2} = 384 \Rightarrow$

$2x\sqrt{64 + \frac{1}{4}x^2} = 384 - x^2 \Rightarrow 4x^2\left(64 + \frac{1}{4}x^2\right) = 147{,}456 - 768x^2 + x^4 \Rightarrow$

$256x^2 + x^4 = 147{,}456 - 768x^2 + x^4 \Rightarrow 1024x^2 = 147{,}456 \Rightarrow x^2 = 144 \Rightarrow x = 12$.

**45** $x^5 + 1.1x^4 - 3.21x^3 - 2.835x^2 + 2.7x + 0.62 = -1 \Leftrightarrow x^5 + 1.1x^4 - 3.21x^3 - 2.835x^2 + 2.7x + 1.62 = 0$.

The graph of $y = x^5 + 1.1x^4 - 3.21x^3 - 2.835x^2 + 2.7x + 1.62$ intersects the $x$-axis three times. The zeros at $-1.5$ and $1.2$ have even multiplicity (since the graph is tangent to the $x$-axis at these points) and the zero at $-0.5$ has odd multiplicity (since the graph crosses the $x$-axis at this point). Since the equation has degree 5, the only possibility is that the zeros at $-1.5$ and $1.2$ have multiplicity 2 and the zero at $-0.5$ has multiplicity 1. Thus, the equation has no nonreal solutions.

$[-4.5, 4.5]$ by $[-3, 3]$         $[-4.5, 4.5]$ by $[-3, 3]$

*Figure 45*

*Figure 46*

**46** $x^4 - 0.4x^3 - 2.6x^2 + 1.1x + 3.5 = 2 \Leftrightarrow x^4 - 0.4x^3 - 2.6x^2 + 1.1x + 1.5 = 0$. The graph of $y = x^4 - 0.4x^3 - 2.6x^2 + 1.1x + 1.5$ crosses the $x$-axis twice. There are two real zeros and they have odd multiplicity. By careful inspection we can see that the graph does not level off at either zero. Therefore, the zeros must have multiplicity 1. (See Exercise 59 in Section 3.3.) Since the equation has degree 4, there are two nonreal solutions.

**47** Graph $y = x^4 + 1.4x^3 + 0.44x^2 - 0.56x - 0.96$. From the graph, zeros are located at $-1.2$ and $0.8$.

Using synthetic division, $\dfrac{x^4 + 1.4x^3 + 0.44x^2 - 0.56x - 0.96}{x + 1.2} = x^3 + 0.2x^2 + 0.2x - 0.8$ and

$\dfrac{x^3 + 0.2x^2 + 0.2x - 0.8}{x - 0.8} = x^2 + x + 1$. The zeros of $x^2 + x + 1$ are $-\frac{1}{2} \pm \frac{\sqrt{3}}{2}i$.

Thus, the solutions to the equation are $-1.2, 0.8, -\frac{1}{2} \pm \frac{\sqrt{3}}{2}i$.

$[-4.5, 4.5]$ by $[-3, 3]$          $[-6.5, 7]$ by $[-3, 6]$

*Figure 47*          *Figure 48*

**48** Graph $y = x^5 + 1.1x^4 - 2.62x^3 - 4.72x^2 - 0.2x + 5.44$. From the graph, zeros are located at $-1.7, 1$, and $1.6$.

Using synthetic division, $\dfrac{x^5 + 1.1x^4 - 2.62x^3 - 4.72x^2 - 0.2x + 5.44}{x + 1.7} = x^4 - 0.6x^3 - 1.6x^2 - 2x + 3.2$,

$\dfrac{x^4 - 0.6x^3 - 1.6x^2 - 2x + 3.2}{x - 1} = x^3 + 0.4x^2 - 1.2x - 3.2$, and $\dfrac{x^3 + 0.4x^2 - 1.2x - 3.2}{x - 1.6} = x^2 + 2x + 2$.

The zeros of $x^2 + 2x + 2$ are $-1 \pm i$. Thus, the solutions to the equation are $-1.7, 1, 1.6, -1 \pm i$.

**49** From the graph, we see that $D(h) = 0.4$ when $h \approx 10{,}200$. Thus, the density of the atmosphere is 0.4 kg/m$^3$ at 10,200 m.

$[0, 30{,}000, 2000]$ by $[0, 1.2, 0.2]$          $[0, 1000, 100]$ by $[0, 5]$

*Figure 49*          *Figure 50*

**50** From the graph, we see that $D(h) = 3.7$ when $h \approx 418$. Thus, the density of Earth is 3.7 g/cm$^3$ at 418 m.

(The graphs also intersect at $h \approx -674$ and $h \approx 1394$. However, these values are not in the domain of $D$.)

## 3.5 Exercises

**Note:** We will use the guidelines listed on page 225 of the text. Below is a summary of these guidelines.

Let $f(x) = \dfrac{a_n x^n + a_{n-1} x^{n-1} + \cdots + a_1 x + a_0}{b_k x^k + b_{k-1} x^{k-1} + \cdots + b_1 x + b_0}$, where $a_n \neq 0$ and $b_k \neq 0$.

(1)   Find the $x$-intercepts {the zeros of the numerator}.

(2)   Find the vertical asymptotes {the zeros of the denominator}.

(3)   Find the $y$-intercept {the ratio of constant terms, $a_0 / b_0$}.

(4)   Find the horizontal or oblique asymptote.

    (a)   If $n < k$, then $y = 0$ {the $x$-axis} is the horizontal asymptote.

    (b)   If $n = k$, then $y = a_n / b_k$ {the ratio of leading coefficients} is the horizontal asymptote.

    (c)   If $n > k$, then the asymptote is found by long division. The graph of $f$ is asymptotic to $y = q(x)$, where $q(x)$ is the quotient of the division process.

(5) Find the intersection points of the function and the asymptote found in step 3. This will help us decide *how* the function approaches the asymptote.

(6) Sketch the graph by regions, where the regions are determined by the vertical asymptotes. We may use the sign of a particular function value to help us determine if the function is positive or negative. We will not plot any points since the purpose in this section is to determine the general shape of the graph and understand the general principles involved with asymptotes.

$\boxed{1}$ $f(x) = 4/x$ •

(a) (1) There are no $x$-intercepts since the numerator is never equal to zero.

(2) There is a vertical asymptote at $x = 0$ {the $y$-axis}.

(3) There is no $y$-intercept since the function is undefined for $x = 0$.

(4) The degree of the numerator is 0, which is less than the degree of the denominator, 1, so the horizontal asymptote is $y = 0$ {the $x$-axis}.

(5) Setting the function equal to the value of the asymptote found in step 4 gives us $4/x = 0$, which has no solutions.

(6) There is one vertical asymptote, and it separates the plane into 2 regions. For the region $x < 0$, $f(x) = 4/x < 0$—that is, the $y$-values are negative. This indicates that the graph is under the $y$-axis as in the figure. For the region $x > 0$, $f(x) > 0$, and the graph is above the $x$-axis.

(b) The domain $D$ is the set of all nonzero real numbers—that is, $\mathbb{R} - \{0\}$. The range $R$ is equal to the same set of numbers.

(c) The function is decreasing on $(-\infty, 0)$ and also on $(0, \infty)$.

*Figure 1*

*Figure 2*

$\boxed{2}$ $f(x) = 1/x^2$ • (b) $D$ = all nonzero real numbers; $R = (0, \infty)$

(c) Increasing on $(-\infty, 0)$, decreasing on $(0, \infty)$

$\boxed{3}$ (a) As $x$ gets very large negative, $y$ (or $f(x)$) gets close to the horizontal asymptote, so $y \to -2$.

(b) As $x \to \infty$, $f(x) \to -2$.

(c) As $x$ approaches 3 from the left, $y$ gets very large, so $f(x) \to \infty$.

(d) As $x$ approaches 3 from the right, $y$ gets very large negative, so $f(x) \to -\infty$.

(e) As $x \to 0$, $f(x) \to 0$.

$\boxed{4}$ (a) As $x$ gets very large negative, $y$ (or $f(x)$) gets close to the horizontal asymptote, so $y \to 3$.

(b) As $x \to \infty$, $f(x) \to 3$.

(c) As $x$ approaches $-2$ from the left, $y$ gets very large, so $f(x) \to \infty$.

(d) As $x$ approaches $-2$ from the right, $y$ gets very large negative, so $f(x) \to -\infty$.

(e) As $x \to 0$, $f(x) \to 0$.

**5** (a) $f(x) = \dfrac{2}{x-3}$ • Since the degree of the numerator is less than the degree of the denominator, $y = 0$ is the horizontal asymptote. As $x$ gets very large (positive or negative), $y$ (or $f(x)$) gets close to the horizontal asymptote, so as $x \to \pm\infty$, $f(x) \to 0$.

(b) $f(x) = \dfrac{2x}{x-3}$ • Since the degree of the numerator is equal to the degree of the denominator,

$y = \frac{2}{1} = 2$ (the ratio of leading coefficients) is the horizontal asymptote. Thus, as $x \to \pm\infty$, $f(x) \to 2$.

**6** (a) $f(x) = \dfrac{-3}{x+2}$ • Since the degree of the numerator is less than the degree of the denominator, $y = 0$ is the horizontal asymptote. As $x$ gets very large (positive or negative), $y$ (or $f(x)$) gets close to the horizontal asymptote, so as $x \to \pm\infty$, $f(x) \to 0$.

(b) $f(x) = \dfrac{-3x}{x+2}$ • Since the degree of the numerator is equal to the degree of the denominator,

$y = \frac{-3}{1} = -3$ (the ratio of leading coefficients) is the horizontal asymptote. Thus, as $x \to \pm\infty$, $f(x) \to -3$.

**7** $f(x) = \dfrac{-2(x+5)(x-6)}{(x-3)(x-6)} = \dfrac{-2(x+5)}{(x-3)}$ if $x \neq 6$ • Note that $x - 6$ appears in both the numerator and denominator, so there is a hole at $x = 6$. The $y$-value for the hole can be found by substituting 6 for $x$ in the rest of the function. $\dfrac{-2(6+5)}{(6-3)} = \dfrac{-2(11)}{3} = -\dfrac{22}{3}$, so the hole is at $\left(6, -\frac{22}{3}\right)$. There is one other zero of the denominator, namely 3, so there is a vertical asymptote of $x = 3$. The degrees of the numerator and denominator are the same, namely 2, so the ratio of leading coefficients gives us the value of the horizontal asymptote. In this case, it is $y = \frac{-2}{1} = -2$.

**8** $f(x) = \dfrac{2(x+4)(x+2)}{5(x+2)(x-1)} = \dfrac{2(x+4)}{5(x-1)}$ if $x \neq -2$ • There is a hole at $x = -2$. Its $y$-value is $\dfrac{2(2)}{5(-3)} = -\dfrac{4}{15}$. The vertical asymptote is $x = 1$ and the horizontal asymptote is $y = \frac{2}{5}$.

**9** There is a hole at $x = -2$, so $(x+2)$ must be a factor in both the numerator and denominator. There is a vertical asymptote of $x = 1$, so $(x-1)$ must be a factor in the denominator. There is an $x$-intercept at $-3$, so $(x+3)$ must be a factor in the numerator. The horizontal asymptote is $y = 2$, so the ratio of leading coefficients must be 2. Combining this information gives us this possibility: $f(x) = \dfrac{2(x+3)(x+2)}{(x-1)(x+2)}$

*Figure 9*

*Figure 10*

**10** There is a hole at $x = 4$, so $x - 4$ must be a factor in both the numerator and denominator. There is a vertical asymptote of $x = -1$, so $x + 1$ must be a factor in the denominator. There is an $x$-intercept at 3, so $x - 3$ must be a factor in the numerator. The horizontal asymptote is $y = -2$, so the ratio of leading coefficients must be $-2$. Combining this information gives us this possibility: $f(x) = \dfrac{-2(x-3)(x-4)}{(x+1)(x-4)}$

**11** $f(x) = \dfrac{3}{x-4} = 3\left(\dfrac{1}{x-4}\right)$ • Rather than use the guidelines, we will think of this graph in terms of the shifting and stretching properties presented in Section 3.5. Consider the graph of $g(x) = 1/x$, which is similar to the graph in Exercise 6. Now $h(x) = 1/(x-4)$ is just $g(x-4)$, which shifts the graph of $g$ to the right by 4 units, making $x = 4$ the vertical asymptote. The effect of the 3 in the numerator is to vertically stretch the graph of $h$ by a factor of 3.

*Figure 11*

*Figure 12*

**12** $f(x) = \dfrac{-3}{x+3} = -3\left(\dfrac{1}{x-(-3)}\right)$ • VA of $x = -3$

**13** $f(x) = \dfrac{-3x}{x+2}$ •

(1) Numerator $= 0 \ \Rightarrow \ -3x = 0 \ \Rightarrow \ x = 0$, the *only* $x$-intercept.

(2) Denominator $= 0 \ \Rightarrow \ x + 2 = 0 \ \Rightarrow \ x = -2$, the only vertical asymptote.

(3) $f(0) = \dfrac{0}{2} = 0 \ \Rightarrow \ 0$ is the $y$-intercept. {We already knew this from step 1.}

(4) Degree of numerator $= 1 =$ degree of denominator $\Rightarrow$
$$y = \tfrac{-3}{1} \ \text{\{ratio of leading coefficients\}} = -3 \text{ is the horizontal asymptote.}$$

(5) Function $=$ horizontal asymptote value $\Rightarrow \ f(x) = -3 \ \Rightarrow \ \dfrac{-3x}{x+2} = -3 \ \Rightarrow \ -3x = -3(x+2) \ \Rightarrow$
$-3x = -3x - 6 \ \Rightarrow \ 0 = -6$. This is a contradiction and indicates that there are *no* intersection points on the horizontal asymptote. Remember, the function can not intersect a vertical asymptote, but can intersect the horizontal asymptote.

(6) For the region $x < -2$, there are no $x$-intercepts and the graph must be below the horizontal asymptote $y = -3$. {If it was above $y = -3$, it would have to intersect the $x$-axis at some point, but from (1), we know that 0 is the *only* $x$-intercept.}

For the region $x > -2$, there is an $x$-intercept at 0 and the graph is above the horizontal asymptote. A common mistake is to confuse the $x$-axis with the horizontal asymptote. Remember, as $x \to \infty$ or $x \to -\infty$, $f(x)$ will get close to the horizontal or oblique asymptote, not the $x$-axis {unless the $x$-axis is the horizontal asymptote}.

Figure 13

Figure 14

**14** $f(x) = \dfrac{4x}{2x - 5}$ • VA of $x = \frac{5}{2}$

**15** $f(x) = \dfrac{4x - 1}{2x + 3}$ •

(1) $4x - 1 = 0 \Rightarrow 4x = 1 \Rightarrow x = \frac{1}{4}$, the *only* x-intercept.

(2) $2x + 3 = 0 \Rightarrow 2x = -3 \Rightarrow x = -\frac{3}{2}$, the only vertical asymptote.

(3) $f(0) = \dfrac{-1}{3} = -\dfrac{1}{3} \Rightarrow -\dfrac{1}{3}$ is the y-intercept.

(4) Degree of numerator $= 1 =$ degree of denominator $\Rightarrow$

$\qquad\qquad\qquad y = \frac{4}{2}$ {ratio of leading coefficients} $= 2$ is the horizontal asymptote.

(5) Function $=$ horizontal asymptote value $\Rightarrow f(x) = 2 \Rightarrow \dfrac{4x - 1}{2x + 3} = 2 \Rightarrow 4x - 1 = 2(2x + 3) \Rightarrow$

$4x - 1 = 4x + 6 \Rightarrow -1 = 6$. This is a contradiction and indicates that there are *no* intersection points on the horizontal asymptote. Remember, the function can not intersect a vertical asymptote, but can intersect the horizontal asymptote.

(6) For the region $x < -\frac{3}{2}$, there are no x-intercepts and the graph must be above the horizontal asymptote $y = 2$. {If it was below $y = 2$, it would have to intersect the x-axis at some point, but from (1), we know that $\frac{1}{4}$ is the *only* x-intercept.} As $x$ approaches $-\frac{3}{2}$ from the left, $y$ approaches $\infty$. As $x$ approaches $-\infty$, $y$ approaches $2$ through values larger than 2.

For the region $x > -\frac{3}{2}$, there is a y-intercept at $-\frac{1}{3}$ and an x-intercept at $\frac{1}{4}$, so the graph is below the horizontal asymptote. As $x$ approaches $-\frac{3}{2}$ from the right, $y$ approaches $-\infty$. As $x$ approaches $\infty$, $y$ approaches $2$ through values smaller than 2.

Figure 15

Figure 16

**16** $f(x) = \dfrac{5x + 3}{3x - 7}$ • VA of $x = \frac{7}{3}$

**17** $f(x) = \dfrac{(4x-1)(x-2)}{(2x+3)(x-2)} = \dfrac{4x-1}{2x+3}$ for $x \neq 2$. The reduced function is the same as the function in Exercise 15.

The only difference is that this function has a hole in the graph at $x = 2$. To determine the value of $y$ when $x = 2$, substitute 2 into $\dfrac{4x-1}{2x+3}$ to get $\dfrac{7}{7} = 1$. There is a hole in the graph at $(2, 1)$.

*Figure 17*

*Figure 18*

**18** $f(x) = \dfrac{(5x+3)(x+1)}{(3x-7)(x+1)}$  •  VA of $x = \frac{7}{3}$; hole at $x = -1$

**19** $f(x) = \dfrac{x-2}{x^2 - x - 6} = \dfrac{x-2}{(x+2)(x-3)}$  •

(1) $x - 2 = 0 \Rightarrow x = 2$, the only $x$-intercept

(2) $(x+2)(x-3) = 0 \Rightarrow x = -2$ and $x = 3$, the vertical asymptotes

(3) $f(0) = \dfrac{-2}{-6} = \dfrac{1}{3} \Rightarrow \frac{1}{3}$ is the $y$-intercept

(4) Degree of numerator $= 1 < 2 =$ degree of denominator $\Rightarrow y = 0$ is the horizontal asymptote.

(5) We have already solved $f(x) = 0$ in step 1.

Hence, we know that the function will cross the horizontal asymptote at $(2, 0)$.

(6) For $x < -2$, we have no information and will examine $f(-5)$ {−5 is to the left of −2}. Using the factored form of $f$ and only the signs of the values, we obtain $f(-5) = \dfrac{(-)}{(-)(-)} = \{$some negative number$\} < 0$ since the combination of 3 negative signs will be negative. Hence, the graph will be below the horizontal asymptote.

For $-2 < x < 3$, we have an $x$-intercept at 2 and need to know what the function does on each side of 2. Choosing 0 and 2.5 for test points, we check the sign of $f(0)$ and $f(2.5)$ as above. $f(0) = \dfrac{(-)}{(+)(-)} > 0$ and $f(2.5) = \dfrac{(+)}{(+)(-)} < 0$.

Hence, the function will change signs from positive to negative as it passes through 2.

For $x > 3$, $f(5) = \dfrac{(+)}{(+)(+)} > 0$ and the function is above the horizontal asymptote.

*Figure 19*

*Figure 20*

**Note:** Let $I$ denote the point of intersection between the function and its horizontal or oblique asymptote.

**20** $f(x) = \dfrac{x+1}{x^2 + 2x - 3} = \dfrac{x+1}{(x+3)(x-1)}$; $I = (-1, 0)$

**21** $f(x) = \dfrac{-4}{(x-2)^2}$ • Note that the function is always negative since it is the quotient of a negative and a positive, provided $x \neq 2$. The $y$-intercept is $f(0) = -1$, the vertical asymptote is $x = 2$, and the horizontal asymptote is $y = 0$.

*Figure 21*

*Figure 22*

**22** $f(x) = \dfrac{2}{(x+1)^2}$ •

**23** $f(x) = \dfrac{x-3}{x^2-1} = \dfrac{x-3}{(x+1)(x-1)}$ •

(1) $x - 3 = 0 \;\Rightarrow\; x = 3$, the only $x$-intercept

(2) $(x+1)(x-1) = 0 \;\Rightarrow\; x = -1$ and $x = 1$, the vertical asymptotes

(3) $f(0) = \dfrac{-3}{-1} = 3 \;\Rightarrow\; 3$ is the $y$-intercept

(4) Degree of numerator $= 1 < 2 =$ degree of denominator $\;\Rightarrow\; y = 0$ is the horizontal asymptote.

(5) We have already solved $f(x) = 0$ in step 1.

           Hence, we know that the function will cross the horizontal asymptote at $(3, 0)$.

(6) For $-1 < x < 1$, we have the $y$-intercept at 3. Since the function cannot intersect the $x$-axis {the only $x$-intercept is at 3}, the function remains positive and we have $f(x) \to \infty$ as $x \to 1^-$ and $f(x) \to \infty$ as $x \to -1^+$.

For $x > 1$, we have the $x$-intercept at 3 as a point to work with. The function will change sign at 3 since 3 is a zero of odd multiplicity {1}. If the function was going to merely touch the point $(3, 0)$ and "turn around", 3 would have to be a zero of even multiplicity. Hence, it suffices to find only one sign. We choose 2 as our test point. $f(2) = \dfrac{(-)}{(+)(+)} < 0$. The function values are negative for $1 < x < 3$ and positive for $x > 3$. Remember, eventually $f(x)$ will be extremely close to 0 as $x \to \infty$. Make sure your sketch reflects that fact.

*Figure 23*

*Figure 24*

**24** $f(x) = \dfrac{x+4}{x^2-4} = \dfrac{x+4}{(x+2)(x-2)}; I = (-4, 0)$

[25] $f(x) = \dfrac{2x^2 - 2x - 4}{x^2 + x - 12} = \dfrac{2(x^2 - x - 2)}{(x+4)(x-3)} = \dfrac{2(x+1)(x-2)}{(x+4)(x-3)}$ • As a generalization, you should always factor the

function first. For steps 1–6 of the guidelines, it is convenient to use the original function for steps 3, 4, and 5, and to use the factored form for steps 1, 2, and 6. After this problem, we will concentrate on steps 5 and 6. You should be able to pick up the information for steps 1–4 by merely looking at both forms of the function {except for the oblique asymptote case}.

(1) $2(x+1)(x-2) = 0 \Rightarrow x = -1, 2$; the $x$-intercepts

(2) $(x+4)(x-3) = 0 \Rightarrow x = -4, 3$; the vertical asymptotes

(3) $f(0) = \dfrac{-4}{-12} = \dfrac{1}{3} \Rightarrow \dfrac{1}{3}$ is the $y$-intercept

(4) Degree of numerator $= 2 =$ degree of denominator $\Rightarrow y = \frac{2}{1} = 2$ is the horizontal asymptote.

(5) $\dfrac{2x^2 - 2x - 4}{x^2 + x - 12} = 2 \Rightarrow 2x^2 - 2x - 4 = 2(x^2 + x - 12) \Rightarrow 2x^2 - 2x - 4 = 2x^2 + 2x - 24 \Rightarrow$

$20 = 4x \Rightarrow x = 5$. Hence, the function will intersect the horizontal asymptote *only* at the point $(5, 2)$.

(6) For $x < -4$, there are no $x$-intercepts so the function is above the horizontal asymptote. For $-4 < x < 3$, the function must go through $(-1, 0)$, $(0, \frac{1}{3})$, and $(2, 0)$. It must go "down" by both vertical asymptotes because if it went "up", it would have to cross the horizontal asymptote. But we know this only occurs at the point $(5, 2)$ and not in this region.

For $x > 3$, we know that the graph goes up as we get close to 3 because if it went down, there would have to be an $x$-intercept, but there isn't one. The function goes through $(5, 2)$, but then turns around {before touching the $x$-axis} and gets very close to 2 as $x$ increases.

*Figure 25*

*Figure 26*

[26] $f(x) = \dfrac{-3x^2 - 3x + 6}{x^2 - 9} = \dfrac{-3(x+2)(x-1)}{(x+3)(x-3)}$. $f(x) = -3 \Rightarrow \dfrac{-3x^2 - 3x + 6}{x^2 - 9} = -3 \Rightarrow$

$-3x^2 - 3x + 6 = -3x^2 + 27 \Rightarrow -3x = 21 \Rightarrow x = -7, I = (-7, -3)$.

[27] $f(x) = \dfrac{-x^2 - x + 6}{x^2 + 3x - 4} = \dfrac{-1(x^2 + x - 6)}{(x+4)(x-1)} = \dfrac{-1(x+3)(x-2)}{(x+4)(x-1)}$ •

(5) $\dfrac{-x^2 - x + 6}{x^2 + 3x - 4} = -1 \Rightarrow -x^2 - x + 6 = -x^2 - 3x + 4 \Rightarrow 2x = -2 \Rightarrow x = -1, I = (-1, -1)$

(6) For $x < -4$, the function is below $y = -1$ since there are no $x$-intercepts.

For $-4 < x < 1$, the function passes through $(-3, 0)$, $(-1, -1)$, and $(0, -\frac{3}{2})$. These points are known from finding information in steps 1–5.

For $x > 1$, the function passes through $(2, 0)$ and is always above the horizontal asymptote since it only intersects the horizontal asymptote at $(-1, -1)$.

*Figure 27*

*Figure 28*

**28** $f(x) = \dfrac{x^2 - 3x - 4}{x^2 + x - 6} = \dfrac{(x+1)(x-4)}{(x+3)(x-2)}; I = \left(\frac{1}{2}, 1\right)$

**29** $f(x) = \dfrac{3(x+3)(x-4)}{(x+2)(x-1)} = \dfrac{3(x^2 - x - 12)}{(x+2)(x-1)} = \dfrac{3x^2 - 3x - 36}{x^2 + x - 2}$ •

(5) $\dfrac{3x^2 - 3x - 36}{x^2 + x - 2} = 3 \;\Rightarrow\; 3x^2 - 3x - 36 = 3x^2 + 3x - 6 \;\Rightarrow\; -30 = 6x \;\Rightarrow\; x = -5, I = (-5, 3)$

(6) For $x < -2$, the function passes through $(-3, 0)$ and $(-5, 3)$ and stays above the horizontal asymptote, $y = 3$, as $x \to -\infty$.

For $-2 < x < 1$, we have the $y$-intercept at 18. Since the graph doesn't intersect the horizontal asymptote in this region, the function goes up as it gets close to each vertical asymptote.

For $x > 1$, we have the $x$-intercept 4 and the function stays below the horizontal asymptote.

*Figure 29*

*Figure 30*

**30** $f(x) = \dfrac{2(x+6)(x-4)}{(x+5)(x-2)} = \dfrac{2(x^2 + 2x - 24)}{x^2 + 3x - 10} = \dfrac{2x^2 + 4x - 48}{x^2 + 3x - 10}; I = (-14, 2)$

**31** $f(x) = \dfrac{-2x^2 + 10x - 12}{x^2 + x} = \dfrac{-2(x^2 - 5x + 6)}{(x+1)(x)} = \dfrac{-2(x-2)(x-3)}{(x+1)(x)}$ •

(2) Since $(x+1)(x) = 0 \;\Rightarrow\; x = -1$ and $0$,

we have the $y$-axis as a vertical asymptote, and hence, there is no $y$-intercept.

(5) $\dfrac{-2x^2 + 10x - 12}{x^2 + x} = -2 \;\Rightarrow\; -2x^2 + 10x - 12 = -2x^2 - 2x \;\Rightarrow\; 12x = 12 \;\Rightarrow\; x = 1, I = (1, -2)$

(6) For $-1 < x < 0$, $f\left(-\frac{1}{2}\right) = \dfrac{(-)(-)(-)}{(+)(-)} > 0$ and the function is above the $x$-axis.

For $x > 0$, the function goes through $(1, -2)$, $(2, 0)$, and $(3, 0)$ and gradually gets closer to $y = -3$ as $x \to \infty$.

*Figure 31*

*Figure 32*

**32** $f(x) = \dfrac{2x^2 + 8x + 6}{x^2 - 2x} = \dfrac{2(x^2 + 4x + 3)}{x(x - 2)} = \dfrac{2(x + 3)(x + 1)}{x(x - 2)}; \ I = \left(-\frac{1}{2}, 2\right)$

**33** $f(x) = \dfrac{x - 1}{x^3 - 4x} = \dfrac{x - 1}{(x)(x^2 - 4)} = \dfrac{x - 1}{(x + 2)(x)(x - 2)}$  •

(5) The horizontal asymptote is $y = 0$ {the $x$-axis} and the $x$-intercept is 1, so we know that the function will cross the horizontal asymptote at $(1, 0)$.

(6) For $-2 < x < 0$, $f(-1) = \dfrac{(-)}{(+)(-)(-)} < 0$ and the function is below the $x$-axis.

For $0 < x < 1$, $f\left(\frac{1}{2}\right) = \dfrac{(-)}{(+)(+)(-)} > 0$ and the function is above the $x$-axis.

For $1 < x < 2$, $f\left(\frac{3}{2}\right) = \dfrac{(+)}{(+)(+)(-)} < 0$ and the function is below the $x$-axis.

*Figure 33*

*Figure 34*

**34** $f(x) = \dfrac{x^2 - 2x + 1}{x^3 - 9x} = \dfrac{(x - 1)^2}{(x + 3)(x)(x - 3)}; \ I = (1, 0)$

**35** $f(x) = \dfrac{-3x^2}{x^2 + 1}$  •  $f$ is an even function.

(2) There are no vertical asymptotes since $x^2 + 1 \neq 0$ for any real number.

(5) $\dfrac{-3x^2}{x^2 + 1} = -3 \ \Rightarrow \ -3x^2 = -3x^2 - 3 \ \Rightarrow \ 0 = -3 \ \Rightarrow$

there are no intersection points of the horizontal asymptote and the function.

(6) We have the $x$-intercept at 0 and the function must get close to the horizontal asymptote, $y = -3$, as $x \to \infty$ or $x \to -\infty$.

*Figure 35*

*Figure 36*

**36** $f(x) = \dfrac{x^2 - 4}{x^2 + 1} = \dfrac{(x+2)(x-2)}{x^2 + 1}$; $f$ is an even function

**37** $f(x) = \dfrac{x^2 - x - 6}{x + 1} = \dfrac{(x+2)(x-3)}{x + 1}$ •

(4) We could use long division to find the oblique asymptote, but since the denominator is of the from $x - c$, we will use synthetic division.

$$\begin{array}{r|rrr} -1 & 1 & -1 & -6 \\ & & -1 & 2 \\ \hline & 1 & -2 & -4 \end{array}$$

The third row indicates that $f(x) = x - 2 - \dfrac{4}{x+1}$. The expression $\dfrac{4}{x+1} \to 0$ as $x \to \pm\infty$, so $y = x - 2$ is an oblique asymptote for $f$.

(5) $\dfrac{x^2 - x - 6}{x + 1} = x - 2 \ \Rightarrow \ x^2 - x - 6 = (x-2)(x+1) \ \Rightarrow \ x^2 - x - 6 = x^2 - x - 2 \ \Rightarrow$

$-6 = -2 \ \Rightarrow \ $ there are no intersection points of the oblique asymptote and the function.

(6) For $x < -1$, we have the $x$-intercept at $-2$ and the function is above the oblique asymptote.

For $x > -1$, we have the points $(0, -6)$ and $(3, 0)$ and the function is below the oblique asymptote.

*Figure 37*

*Figure 38*

**38** $f(x) = \dfrac{2x^2 - x - 3}{x - 2} = \dfrac{(x+1)(2x-3)}{x - 2} = 2x + 3 + \dfrac{3}{x - 2}$

**39** $f(x) = \dfrac{8 - x^3}{2x^2} = \dfrac{(2-x)(4 + 2x + x^2)}{2x^2}$ •

(4) By dividing, we can write $f$ in the form $f(x) = -\dfrac{1}{2}x + \dfrac{8}{2x^2}$. The oblique asymptote is $y = -\dfrac{1}{2}x$.

(5) Function = oblique asymptote $\ \Rightarrow \ \dfrac{8 - x^3}{2x^2} = -\dfrac{1}{2}x \ \Rightarrow \ 8 - x^3 = -x^3 \ \Rightarrow \ 8 = 0 \ \Rightarrow$

there are no intersection points of the asymptote and the function.

(6) For $x < 0$, there are no $x$-intercepts, so the function is above the oblique asymptote.

For $x > 0$, we have the $x$-intercept 2, and the function is above the asymptote.

*Figure 39*

*Figure 40*

**40** $f(x) = \dfrac{x^3 + 1}{x^2 - 9} = \dfrac{(x+1)(x^2-x+1)}{(x+3)(x-3)} = x + \dfrac{9x+1}{x^2-9}$

$$f(x) = x \;\Rightarrow\; \frac{x^3+1}{x^2-9} = x \;\Rightarrow\; x^3 + 1 = x^3 - 9x \;\Rightarrow\; x = -\tfrac{1}{9},\; I = \left(-\tfrac{1}{9}, -\tfrac{1}{9}\right).$$

**41** $f(x) = \dfrac{x^4 - x^2 - 5}{x^2 - 2}$     First step: $\dfrac{x^4}{x^2} = x^2$

$$
\begin{array}{r}
x^2 \phantom{xxxxxxx} + 1 \\
x^2 - 2 \;\overline{\big)\; x^4 + 0x^3 - x^2 + 0x - 5} \\
\underline{x^4 \phantom{xxxx} - 2x^2 \phantom{xxxxxxxxxx}} \\
x^2 \phantom{xxxxxxxxxx} \\
\underline{x^2 \phantom{xxxx} - 2 \phantom{xxxx}} \\
- 3
\end{array}
$$

The curvilinear asymptote for $f$ is $y = x^2 + 1$.

**42** $f(x) = \dfrac{x^5 - 3x^3 - x^2 + 1}{x^2 - 3}$

$$
\begin{array}{r}
x^3 \phantom{xxxxxxxxx} - 1 \\
x^2 - 3 \;\overline{\big)\; x^5 + 0x^4 - 3x^3 - x^2 + 0x + 1} \\
\underline{x^5 \phantom{xxxx} - 3x^3 \phantom{xxxxxxxxxxxx}} \\
- x^2 \phantom{xxxxxxxx} \\
\underline{- x^2 \phantom{xxxx} + 3} \\
- 2
\end{array}
$$

The curvilinear asymptote for $f$ is $y = x^3 - 1$.

**43** $f(x) = \dfrac{2x^2 + x - 6}{x^2 + 3x + 2} = \dfrac{(x+2)(2x-3)}{(x+2)(x+1)} = \dfrac{2x-3}{x+1}$ for $x \neq -2$. We must reduce the function first and then *sketch the reduced function*. After sketching the reduced function, we need to remember to put a hole in the graph where the original function was undefined. In this case, the reduced function is $f(x) = \dfrac{2x-3}{x+1}$. We sketch this as we did the other rational functions. To determine the value of $y$ when $x = -2$, substitute $-2$ into $\dfrac{2x-3}{x+1}$ to get 7. There is a hole in the graph at $(-2, 7)$.

*Figure 43*

*Figure 44*

**44** $f(x) = \dfrac{x^2 - x - 6}{x^2 - 2x - 3} = \dfrac{(x+2)(x-3)}{(x+1)(x-3)} = \dfrac{x+2}{x+1}$ for $x \neq 3$; hole at $\left(3, \frac{5}{4}\right)$.

**45** $f(x) = \dfrac{x-1}{1-x^2} = \dfrac{x-1}{(1+x)(1-x)} = \dfrac{-1(1-x)}{(1+x)(1-x)} = \dfrac{-1}{x+1}$ for $x \neq 1$.

Substituting 1 for $x$ in $\dfrac{-1}{x+1}$ gives us a hole in the graph at $\left(1, -\frac{1}{2}\right)$.

*Figure 45*

*Figure 46*

**46** $f(x) = \dfrac{x+2}{x^2-4} = \dfrac{x+2}{(x+2)(x-2)} = \dfrac{1}{x-2}$ for $x \neq -2$; hole at $\left(-2, -\frac{1}{4}\right)$

**47** $f(x) = \dfrac{x^2+x-2}{x+2} = \dfrac{(x+2)(x-1)}{x+2} = x-1$ for $x \neq -2$.

Substituting $-2$ for $x$ in $x-1$ gives us a hole in the graph {a line} at $(-2, -3)$.

*Figure 47*

*Figure 48*

**48** $f(x) = \dfrac{x^3 - 2x^2 - 4x + 8}{x-2} = \dfrac{(x^2-4)(x-2)}{x-2} = x^2 - 4$ for $x \neq 2$; hole at $(2, 0)$

**49** $f(x) = \dfrac{x^2+4x+4}{x^2+3x+2} = \dfrac{(x+2)^2}{(x+1)(x+2)} = \dfrac{x+2}{x+1}$ for $x \neq -2$. Substituting $-2$ for $x$ in $\dfrac{x+2}{x+1}$ gives us 0, so there

is a hole in the graph {on the $x$-axis} at $(-2, 0)$.

*Figure 49*

*Figure 50*

**50** $f(x) = \dfrac{(x^2 + x)(2x - 1)}{(x^2 - 3x + 2)(2x - 1)} = \dfrac{x(x + 1)(2x - 1)}{(x - 1)(x - 2)(2x - 1)} = \dfrac{x(x + 1)}{(x - 1)(x - 2)}$ for $x \neq \frac{1}{2}$.

Note that the hole is on the horizontal asymptote at $\left(\frac{1}{2}, 1\right)$.

**51** The vertical asymptote of $x = 5$ implies that $x - 5$ is a factor in the denominator. Since 2 is an $x$-intercept, $x - 2$ is a factor in the numerator. The ratio of leading coefficients must be $-1$ because the horizontal asymptote is $y = -1$, and hence, we must have a factor of $-1$ in the numerator. Therefore, $f$ has the form

$$f(x) = \frac{-1(x - 2)}{x - 2}, \text{ or equivalently, } f(x) = \frac{2 - x}{x - 5}.$$

**52** $f(x) = \dfrac{a(x - 2)}{x(x + 2)}; \ f(3) = 1$ and $f(3) = \dfrac{a(1)}{3(5)} = \dfrac{a}{15} \ \Rightarrow \ a = 15; \ f(x) = \dfrac{15x - 30}{x^2 + 2x}$

**53** The vertical asymptotes of $x = -3$ and $x = 1$ imply that $x + 3$ and $x - 1$ are factors in the denominator. Since $-1$ is an $x$-intercept, $x + 1$ is a factor in the numerator. The hole at $x = 2$ indicates that $x - 2$ is a factor in the numerator and in the denominator. If we let $a$ denote an arbitrary coefficient, then $f$ has the form

$$f(x) = \frac{a(x + 1)(x - 2)}{(x - 1)(x + 3)(x - 2)}.$$

Note that $y = 0$ is the horizontal asymptote since the degree of the numerator is less than the degree of the denominator. To determine the value of $a$, we use the fact that $f(0) = -2$.

$$f(0) = -2 \text{ and } f(0) = \frac{a(1)}{(-1)(3)} = \frac{a}{-3} \ \Rightarrow \ \frac{a}{-3} = -2 \ \Rightarrow \ a = 6.$$

Therefore, $f$ has the form $f(x) = \dfrac{6(x + 1)(x - 2)}{(x - 1)(x + 3)(x - 2)}$, or equivalently, $\dfrac{6x^2 - 6x - 12}{x^3 - 7x + 6}$.

**54** $f(x) = \dfrac{2(x + 2)(x - 1)x}{(x + 1)(x - 3)x} = \dfrac{2x(x^2 + x - 2)}{x(x^2 - 2x - 3)} = \dfrac{2x^3 + 2x^2 - 4x}{x^3 - 2x^2 - 3x}$

**55** (a) The radius of the outside cylinder is $(r + 0.5)$ ft and its height is $(h + 1)$ ft.

Since the volume is $16\pi$ ft$^3$ and the volume is also $\pi(\text{radius})^2(\text{height})$, we have

$$16\pi = \pi(r + 0.5)^2(h + 1) \ \Rightarrow \ h + 1 = \frac{16\pi}{\pi(r + 0.5)^2} \ \Rightarrow \ h = \frac{16}{(r + 0.5)^2} - 1.$$

(b) Substituting for $h$ from part (a), $V(r) = \pi r^2 h = \pi r^2 \left[ \dfrac{16}{(r + 0.5)^2} - 1 \right]$.

(c)  $r$ and $h$ must both be positive. $h > 0 \Rightarrow \dfrac{16}{(r+0.5)^2} - 1 > 0 \Rightarrow \dfrac{16}{(r+0.5)^2} > 1 \Rightarrow$

$16 > (r+0.5)^2 \Rightarrow (r+0.5)^2 < 16 \Rightarrow \sqrt{(r+0.5)^2} < \sqrt{16} \Rightarrow |r+0.5| < 4 \Rightarrow$

$-4 < r + 0.5 < 4 \Rightarrow -4.5 < r < 3.5.$

The last inequality combined with the fact that $r > 0$ means that the excluded values are $r \le 0$ and $r \ge 3.5$.

**56**  $a = 100$ and $y = ta/(t+12) \Rightarrow y = 100t/(t+12).$

Figure 56

Figure 58

**57**  (a)  Since 5 gallons of water flow into the tank each minute, $V(t) = 50 + 5t.$

Since each additional gallon of water contains 0.1 lb of salt, $A(t) = 5(0.1)t = 0.5t.$

(b) $c(t) = \dfrac{A(t)}{V(t)} = \dfrac{0.5t}{50+5t} \cdot \dfrac{2}{2} = \dfrac{t}{10t+100}$ lb/gal

(c) As $t \to \infty$, $c(t) \to 0.1$ lb. of salt per gal.

**58**  (a)  As $t$ increases, the total number of inches of rain approaches the constant $a$.

(b)  Note that at the start of the storm, $I = 0.25$ and $R = 0$, i.e., the intensity is greater than the accumulation.

**59**  (a)  $R > S \Rightarrow \dfrac{4500S}{S+500} > S \Rightarrow \dfrac{4500S}{S+500} - S > 0 \Rightarrow \dfrac{4500S}{S+500} - \dfrac{S(S+500)}{S+500} > 0 \Rightarrow$

$\dfrac{4500S - S^2 - 500S}{S+500} > 0 \Rightarrow \dfrac{4000S - S^2}{S+500} > 0 \Rightarrow \dfrac{S^2 - 4000S}{S+500} < 0$ {multiply both sides by $-1$ and

reverse the direction of the inequality} $\Rightarrow \dfrac{S(S-4000)}{S+500} < 0$. From the chart, and using the fact that

$S > 0$, we conclude that $R > S$ when $0 < S < 4000$.

| Interval | $(-\infty, -500)$ | $(-500, 0)$ | $(0, 4000)$ | $(4000, \infty)$ |
|---|---|---|---|---|
| Sign of $S - 4000$ | $-$ | $-$ | $-$ | $+$ |
| Sign of $S$ | $-$ | $-$ | $+$ | $+$ |
| Sign of $S + 500$ | $-$ | $+$ | $+$ | $+$ |
| **Resulting sign** | $-$ | $+$ | $-$ | $+$ |

(b)  The greatest possible number of offspring that survive to maturity is 4500, the horizontal asymptote value.

90% of 4500 is 4050. $R = 4050 \Rightarrow 4050 = \dfrac{4500S}{S+500} \Rightarrow 4050S + 2{,}025{,}000 = 4500S \Rightarrow$

$2{,}025{,}000 = 450S \Rightarrow S = 4500.$

(c)  80% of 4500 is 3600. $R = 3600 \Rightarrow 3600 = \dfrac{4500S}{S+500} \Rightarrow 3600S + 1{,}800{,}000 = 4500S \Rightarrow$

$1{,}800{,}000 = 900S \Rightarrow S = 2000.$

(d) A 125% increase $\left\{\dfrac{4500 - 2000}{2000} \times 100\right\}$ in the number $S$ of spawners produces only a 12.5% increase $\left\{\dfrac{4050 - 3600}{3600} \times 100\right\}$ in the number $R$ of offspring surviving to maturity.

**60** (a) $D = \dfrac{5000x}{x^2 + 36}$ • $x = 20 \Rightarrow D \approx 229.4$ and $x = 25 \Rightarrow D = 189.1$; the density decreases

(b) As $x \to \infty$, $D \to 0$. The density gets closer to 0 as the distance from the center increases.

(c) $D > 400 \Rightarrow \dfrac{5000x}{x^2 + 36} > 400 \Rightarrow 5000x > 400(x^2 + 36) \Rightarrow 25x > 2(x^2 + 36) \Rightarrow$
$25x > 2x^2 + 72 \Rightarrow 2x^2 - 25x + 72 < 0 \Rightarrow (2x - 9)(x - 8) < 0 \Rightarrow 4.5 < x < 8$

**61** Assign $20x^2 + 80x + 72$ to $Y_1$, $10x^2 + 40x + 41$ to $Y_2$, and $Y_1/Y_2$ to $Y_3$. Zoom-in around $(-2, -8)$ to confirm that this a low point and that there is not a vertical asymptote of $x = -2$. To determine the vertical asymptotes, graph $Y_2$ only {turn off $Y_3$}, and look for its zeros. If these values are not zeros of the numerator, then they are the values of the vertical asymptotes. No vertical asymptotes in this case.

$[-9, 3]$ by $[-9, 3]$

*Figure 61*

$[-5, 9]$ by $[-1, 13]$

*Figure 62*

**62** Similarly to Exercise 61, there is a high point at $(2, 8)$. No vertical asymptotes.

**63** $f(x) = \dfrac{(x - 1)^2}{(x - 0.999)^2}$ • Note that the standard viewing rectangle gives the horizontal line $y = 1$. The figure was obtained by using Dot mode. If Connected mode is used, the calculator will draw a near-vertical line at $x = 0.999$. An equation of the vertical asymptote is $x = 0.999$.

$[0.7, 1.3, 0.1]$ by $[0.8, 1.2, 0.1]$

*Figure 63*

$[-4, 8]$ by $[-1, 7]$

*Figure 64*

**64** $f(x) = \dfrac{x^2 - 9.01}{x - 3}$ • Note that a standard viewing rectangle gives a line, but we recognize that there is a vertical asymptote at $x = 3$ since $x - 3$ is a factor of the denominator but not of the numerator.

**65** (a) The graph of $g$ is the horizontal line $y = 1$ with holes at $x = 0, \pm 1, \pm 2, \pm 3$.

The TI-85/86 shows a small break in the line to indicate a hole.

(b) The graph of $h$ is the graph of $p$ with holes at $x = 0, \pm 1, \pm 2, \pm 3$.

**66** (a) The graph of $f$ is that of a seventh-degree polynomial with zeros at $x = 0$, $\pm1$, $\pm2$, $\pm3$. Its sign changes at each zero.

(b) The graph of $k$ has vertical asymptotes at $x = 0$, $\pm1$, $\pm2$, $\pm3$. Its sign changes at each asymptote. The values of $k$ are reciprocals of the values of $f$—so as $f$ gets larger, $k$ gets smaller, and vice versa. Try graphing $k$ with a viewing rectangle of $[-4, 4]$ by $[-0.5, 0.5]$.

**67** (a) GPA with additional credits = desired GPA $\Rightarrow$ $\dfrac{48(2.75) + y(4.0)}{48 + y} = x$ $\Rightarrow$ $132 + 4y = 48x + xy$ $\Rightarrow$

$$132 - 48x = xy - 4y \quad \Rightarrow \quad 132 - 48x = y(x - 4) \quad \Rightarrow \quad y = \frac{132 - 48x}{x - 4}$$

(b)

| X | Y1 |
|---|-----|
| 2.8 | 2 |
| 3 | 12 |
| 3.2 | 27 |
| 3.4 | 52 |
| 3.6 | 102 |
| 3.8 | 252 |
| 4 | ERROR |

X=2.8

(c)          [2, 4] by [0, 1000, 100]

(d) The vertical asymptote of the graph is $x = 4$.

(e) Regardless of the number of additional credit hours obtained at 4.0, a cumulative GPA of 4.0 is not attainable.

## 3.6 Exercises

**1** $u$ is directly proportional to $v$ $\Rightarrow$ $u = kv$. If $v = 30$, then $u = 12$ $\Rightarrow$ $12 = k(30)$.

Solving for the constant of proportionality, $k$, we have $12 = 30k$ $\Rightarrow$ $k = \frac{2}{5}$.

**2** $s = kt$ • $18 = k(10)$ $\Rightarrow$ $k = \frac{9}{5}$

**3** $V$ varies directly as the cube of $r$ $\Rightarrow$ $V = kr^3$. If $r = 3$, then $V = 36\pi$ $\Rightarrow$ $36\pi = k(3)^3$.

Solving for the constant of proportionality, $k$, we have $36\pi = 27k$ $\Rightarrow$ $k = \frac{4}{3}\pi$.

**4** $S = kx^2$ • $24 = k(2)^2$ $\Rightarrow$ $k = 6$

**5** $r$ varies directly as $s$ and inversely as $t$ $\Rightarrow$ $r = k\dfrac{s}{t}$. If $s = -2$ and $t = 4$, then $r = 7$ $\Rightarrow$ $7 = \dfrac{k(-2)}{4}$.

Solving for the constant of proportionality, $k$, we have $7 = \dfrac{k(-2)}{4}$ $\Rightarrow$ $k = -14$.

**6** $w = k\dfrac{z}{\sqrt{u}}$ • $6 = \dfrac{k(2)}{3}$ $\Rightarrow$ $k = 9$

**7** $y$ is directly proportional to the square of $x$ and inversely proportional to the cube of $z$ $\Rightarrow$ $y = k\dfrac{x^2}{z^3}$.

Substituting $x = 5$, $z = 3$, and $y = 25$ gives us $25 = \dfrac{k(25)}{27}$.

Solving for the constant of proportionality, $k$, we have $25(27) = 25k$ $\Rightarrow$ $k = 27$.

**8** $y$ is directly proportional to $x$ and inversely proportional to the square of $z$ $\Rightarrow$ $y = k\dfrac{x}{z^2}$.

Substituting $x = 4$, $z = 3$, and $y = 16$ gives us $16 = \dfrac{k(4)}{9}$.

Solving for the constant of proportionality, $k$, we have $16(9) = 4k$ $\Rightarrow$ $k = 36$.

**9** $z$ is directly proportional to the product of the square of $x$ and the cube of $y$ $\Rightarrow$ $z = kx^2y^3$.

Substituting $x = 7$, $y = -2$, and $z = 16$ gives us $16 = k(49)(-8)$.

Solving for the constant of proportionality, $k$, we have $k = -\frac{2}{49}$.

**10** $z$ is directly proportional to the product of $x$ and the cube root of $y$ $\Rightarrow$ $z = kx\sqrt[3]{y}$.

Substituting $x = 2$, $y = 8$, and $z = 12$ gives us $12 = k(2)\sqrt[3]{8} = k(2)(2)$.

Solving for the constant of proportionality, $k$, we have $k = 3$.

**11** $z$ is directly proportional to the product of $x$ and $y$ and inversely proportional to the cube root of $w$ $\Rightarrow$

$z = k\dfrac{xy}{\sqrt[3]{w}}$. Substituting $x = 6$, $y = 4$, $w = 27$, and $z = 16$ gives us $16 = k\dfrac{(6)(4)}{\sqrt[3]{27}} = k\dfrac{24}{3}$.

Solving for the constant of proportionality, $k$, we have $k = 2$.

**12** $r = k\dfrac{sv}{p^3}$  $\bullet$  $40 = \dfrac{k(2)(3)}{125}$ $\Rightarrow$ $k = \dfrac{2500}{3}$

**13** $q$ is inversely proportional to the sum of $x$ and $y$ $\Rightarrow$ $q = \dfrac{k}{x + y}$. Substituting $x = 0.5$, $y = 0.7$, and $q = 1.4$

gives us $1.4 = \dfrac{k}{0.5 + 0.7} = \dfrac{k}{1.2}$. Solving for the constant of proportionality, $k$, we have $k = 1.68$.

**14** $y = k\dfrac{x}{r + s}$  $\bullet$  $2 = \dfrac{k(3)}{5 + 7}$ $\Rightarrow$ $k = 8$

**15** $y$ is directly proportional to the square root of $x$ and inversely proportional to the cube of $z$ $\Rightarrow$ $y = k\dfrac{\sqrt{x}}{z^3}$.

Substituting $x = 9$, $z = 2$, and $y = 5$ gives us $5 = \dfrac{k(3)}{8}$.

Solving for the constant of proportionality, $k$, we have $k = \frac{40}{3}$.

**16** $y = k\dfrac{x^2}{\sqrt{z}}$  $\bullet$  $10 = \dfrac{k(25)}{4}$ $\Rightarrow$ $k = \dfrac{8}{5}$

**17** (a) $P = kd$          (b) $118 = k(2)$ $\Rightarrow$ $k = 59$          (c) $d = 5$ $\Rightarrow$ $P = 59(5) = 295$ lb/ft$^2$

(d) $P = 59d$ is a simple linear relationship. The graph is a line with slope 59 and $y$-intercept 0.

*Figure 17*

*Figure 18*

**18** (a) $F = kx$          (b) $4 = k(0.3)$ $\Rightarrow$ $k = \frac{40}{3}$          (c) $x = 1.5$ $\Rightarrow$ $F = \frac{40}{3}(1.5) = 20$ lb

(d) $F = \frac{40}{3}x$ is a simple linear relationship. The graph is a line with slope $\frac{40}{3}$ and $y$-intercept 0.

**19** (a) $R = k\dfrac{l}{d^2} = \dfrac{kl}{d^2}$      (b) $25 = \dfrac{k(100)}{(0.01)^2} \Rightarrow 25(0.01)^2 = 100k \Rightarrow k = \dfrac{25}{100(10,000)} = \dfrac{1}{40,000}$

(c) $R = \dfrac{kl}{d^2} = \dfrac{(1/40,000)(100)}{d^2} = \dfrac{1}{400d^2}$. The graph of $R$ for $d > 0$ has a vertical asymptote of $d = 0$ and a horizontal asymptote of $R = 0$.

(d) $R = \dfrac{50}{(40,000)(0.015)^2} = \dfrac{50}{9}$ ohms

*Figure 19*

*Figure 20*

**20** (a) $I = \dfrac{k}{d^2}$          (b) $1,000,000 = \dfrac{k}{50^2} \Rightarrow k = 50^2 \times 10^6 = 2.5 \times 10^9$

(c) $I = \dfrac{2.5 \times 10^9}{d^2}$ has a VA of $I = 0$ and a HA of $d = 0$.     (d) $I = \dfrac{2.5 \times 10^9}{5280^2} \approx 89.7$ candlepower

**21** (a) $P = k\sqrt{l}$       (b) $1.5 = k\sqrt{2} \Rightarrow k = \dfrac{3}{4}\sqrt{2}$       (c) $P = \dfrac{3}{4}\sqrt{2}\left(\sqrt{5}\right) = \dfrac{3}{4}\sqrt{10}$ sec

**22** (a) $C = 2\pi r \Leftrightarrow r = \dfrac{C}{2\pi}$. $V = \pi r^2 L = \pi \left(\dfrac{C}{2\pi}\right)^2 L = \dfrac{1}{4\pi}C^2 L$.

(b) $V = \dfrac{1}{4\pi}(22)^2(27) = \dfrac{3267}{\pi} \approx 1039.9$ cm$^3$, or 1040 cm$^3$

**23** (a) $T = kd^{3/2}$                      (b) $365 = k(93)^{3/2} \Rightarrow k = \dfrac{365}{(93)^{3/2}}$

(c) $T = \dfrac{365}{(93)^{3/2}} \cdot (67)^{3/2} \approx 223.2$ days

**24** (a) $R = kv^2$        (b) $150 = k(70)^2 \Rightarrow k = \dfrac{3}{98}$    (c) $R = \dfrac{3}{98}(80)^2 = \dfrac{9600}{49} \approx 195.9$ ft

**25** (a) $V = k\sqrt{L}$             (b) $35 = k\sqrt{50} \Rightarrow k = \dfrac{7}{2}\sqrt{2}$

(c) $V = \dfrac{7}{2}\sqrt{2}\left(\sqrt{162}\right) = \dfrac{7}{2}\sqrt{324} = \dfrac{7}{2}(18) = 63$ mi/hr

**26** (a) $F = k\dfrac{Q_1 Q_2}{d^2} = \dfrac{kQ_1 Q_2}{d^2}$

(b) $F = \dfrac{kQ_1 Q_2}{\left(\frac{1}{4}d\right)^2} = 16\left(\dfrac{kQ_1 Q_2}{d^2}\right)$, the force $F$ is multiplied by 16

**27** (a) $W = kh^3$            (b) $200 = k(6)^3 \Rightarrow k = \dfrac{25}{27}$

(c) 5 feet 6 inches is $\dfrac{11}{2}$ feet. Hence, $W = \dfrac{25}{27}\left(\dfrac{11}{2}\right)^3 \approx 154.1$ lb, or 154 lb.

**28** (a) $V = k\dfrac{nT}{P} = \dfrac{knT}{P}$                (b) $V = \dfrac{k(2n)\left(\frac{1}{2}T\right)}{\left(\frac{1}{2}P\right)} = 2\left(\dfrac{knT}{P}\right)$, i.e., $V$ is doubled.

**29** (a) $F = kPr^4 \implies P = \dfrac{F}{kr^4}$ under normal conditions.

(b) "Normal flow rates triple" means that we will use $3F$ for the flow rate $F$.

"Radius increases by 10%" means that we will use $(r + 10\%r) = 1.1r$ for the radius.

Hence, $3F = kP(1.1r)^4 \implies P = \dfrac{3F}{(1.1)^4 kr^4} \approx 2.05 \left( \dfrac{F}{kr^4} \right)$, or about 2.05 times as hard as normal.

**30** $T = kn \ \bullet \ 10 = k(300) \implies k = \frac{1}{30}; \ 200 = \frac{1}{30}n \implies n = 6000$

**31** $C = \dfrac{kDE}{Vt} \implies D = \left( \dfrac{Ct}{k} \right) \dfrac{V}{E}$, where $\dfrac{Ct}{k}$ is constant. If $V$ is twice its original value and $E$ is 0.8 of its original

value (reduced by 20%), then $D$ becomes $D_1 = \left( \dfrac{Ct}{k} \right) \dfrac{2V}{0.8E}$. Comparing $D_1$ to $D$, we have

$$\dfrac{D_1}{D} = \dfrac{\left( \dfrac{Ct}{k} \right) \dfrac{2V}{0.8E}}{\left( \dfrac{Ct}{k} \right) \dfrac{V}{E}} = \dfrac{2}{0.8} = 2.5 = 250\% \text{ of its original value. Thus, } D \text{ increases by } 250\%.$$

**32** $C = \dfrac{kDE}{Vt}$. $D$ increases to $\frac{13}{10}$ of its original value, $V$ decreases to $\frac{9}{10}$ of its original value, and $t$ increases to $\frac{16}{10}$ of

its original value. $C$ becomes $\dfrac{(13/10)}{(9/10)(16/10)} = \dfrac{65}{72} \approx 90.3\%$ of its original value.

Thus, $C$ decreases by approximately 9.7%.

**33** The square of the distance from the origin to the point $(x, y)$ is $\left( \sqrt{x^2 + y^2} \right)^2 = x^2 + y^2$, so $d = \dfrac{k}{x^2 + y^2}$.

If $(x_1, y_1)$ is the new point that has density $d_1$, then

$$d_1 = \dfrac{k}{x_1^2 + y_1^2} = \dfrac{k}{\left( \frac{1}{3}x \right)^2 + \left( \frac{1}{3}y \right)^2} = \dfrac{k}{\frac{1}{9}x^2 + \frac{1}{9}y^2} = \dfrac{k}{\frac{1}{9}(x^2 + y^2)} = 9 \cdot \dfrac{k}{x^2 + y^2} = 9d.$$

The density $d$ is multiplied by 9.

**34** The distance from the origin to the point $(x, y)$ is $\sqrt{x^2 + y^2}$, so $T = \dfrac{k}{\sqrt{x^2 + y^2}}$.

$$T = 20 \text{ and } P(3, 4) \implies 20 = \dfrac{k}{\sqrt{3^2 + 4^2}} = \dfrac{k}{5} \implies k = 100. \ T = \dfrac{100}{\sqrt{24^2 + 7^2}} = \dfrac{100}{25} = 4°C.$$

**35** We need to examine $y/x$ for the given set of data points.

$\dfrac{y}{x} = \dfrac{0.72}{0.6} = \dfrac{1.44}{1.2} = \dfrac{5.04}{4.2} = \dfrac{8.52}{7.1} = 1.2$.

Thus, $y$ varies directly as $x$ with constant of variation $k = 1.2$, and $y = 1.2x$.

**36** For the data points, $xy = 0.2(-26.5) = 0.4(-13.25) = 0.8(-6.625) = -5.3$.

Thus, $y$ varies inversely as $x$ with constant of variation $k = -5.3$, and $y = -\dfrac{5.3}{x}$.

**37** For the data points, $x^2 y = (0.8)^2(-15.78125) = (1.6)^2(-3.9453125) = (3.2)^2(-0.986328125) = -10.1$.

Thus, $y$ varies inversely as $x^2$ with constant of variation $k = -10.1$, and $y = -\dfrac{10.1}{x^2}$.

**38** For the data points, $\dfrac{y}{x^3} = \dfrac{0.5616}{0.6^3} = \dfrac{4.4928}{1.2^3} = \dfrac{35.9424}{2.4^3} = 2.6$.

Thus, $y$ varies directly as the cube of $x$ with constant of variation $k = 2.6$, and $y = 2.6x^3$.

39 (a) $D = kS^{2.3}$ $\Rightarrow$ $k = \dfrac{D}{S^{2.3}}$. Using the 6 data points:

$$\frac{33}{20^{2.3}} \approx 0.0336; \quad \frac{86}{30^{2.3}} \approx 0.0344; \quad \frac{167}{40^{2.3}} \approx 0.0345;$$

$$\frac{278}{50^{2.3}} \approx 0.0344; \quad \frac{414}{60^{2.3}} \approx 0.0337; \quad \frac{593}{70^{2.3}} \approx 0.0338.$$

Let $k = 0.034$. Thus, $D = 0.034S^{2.3}$.

$[0, 75, 10]$ by $[0, 600, 100]$

(b) Graph the data together with $Y_1 = 0.034x^{2.3}$.

## Chapter 3 Review Exercises

1. To graph $f(x) = (x + 2)^3$, shift $y = x^3$ left 2 units. $f(x) > 0$ if $x > -2$, $f(x) < 0$ if $x < -2$.

*Figure 1*

*Figure 2*

2. To graph $f(x) = x^6 - 32$, shift $y = x^6$ down 32 units. To find the $x$-intercepts, let $y = 0$: $0 = x^6 - 32$ $\Rightarrow$ $32 = x^6$ $\Rightarrow$ $x = \pm\sqrt[6]{32}$. $f(x) > 0$ if $x < -\sqrt[6]{32}$ or $x > \sqrt[6]{32}$, $f(x) < 0$ if $-\sqrt[6]{32} < x < \sqrt[6]{32}$.

3. $f(x) = -\frac{1}{4}(x + 2)(x - 1)^2(x - 3)$ has zeros at $-2, 1$ (multiplicity 2), and 3. The graph of $f$ has the general shape of $y = -x^4$. $f(x) > 0$ if $-2 < x < 1$ or $1 < x < 3$, $f(x) < 0$ if $x < -2$ or $x > 3$.

*Figure 3*

*Figure 4*

4. $f(x) = 2x^2 + x^3 - x^4 = x^2(2 + x - x^2) = -x^2(x - 2)(x + 1)$.

$f(x) > 0$ if $-1 < x < 0$ or $0 < x < 2$, $f(x) < 0$ if $x < -1$ or $x > 2$.

5. $f(x) = x^3 + 2x^2 - 8x = x(x^2 + 2x - 8) = x(x + 4)(x - 2)$. $f$ has zeros at $-4, 0$, and 2. The graph of $f$ has the general shape of $y = x^3$. $f(x) > 0$ if $-4 < x < 0$ or $x > 2$, $f(x) < 0$ if $x < -4$ or $0 < x < 2$.

Figure 5

Figure 6

**6** $f(x) = \frac{1}{15}\left(x^5 - 20x^3 + 64x\right) = \frac{1}{15}x\left(x^4 - 20x^2 + 64\right) = \frac{1}{15}x(x^2 - 4)(x^2 - 16)$

$$= \frac{1}{15}x(x + 2)(x - 2)(x + 4)(x - 4)$$

$f(x) > 0$ if $-4 < x < -2, 0 < x < 2$, or $x > 4$, $f(x) < 0$ if $x < -4, -2 < x < 0$, or $2 < x < 4$.

**7** $f(x) = x^3 - 5x^2 + 7x - 9$ • $f(0) = -9 < 100$ and $f(10) = 561 > 100$. By the intermediate value theorem for polynomial functions, $f$ takes on every value between $-9$ and $561$. Hence, there is at least one real number $a$ in $[0, 10]$ such that $f(a) = 100$.

**8** Let $f(x) = x^5 - 3x^4 - 2x^3 - x + 1$. $f(0) = 1 > 0$ and $f(1) = -4 < 0$. By the intermediate value theorem for polynomial functions, $f$ takes on every value between $-4$ and $1$. Hence, there is at least one real number $a$ in $[0, 1]$ such that $f(a) = 0$.

**9** $f(x) = 3x^5 - 4x^3 + x + 5; p(x) = x^3 - 2x + 7$ •

$$
\begin{array}{r}
3x^2 \qquad\qquad + \quad 2 \\
x^3 - 2x + 7 \overline{\smash{\big)}\; 3x^5 + 0x^4 - 4x^3 + 0x^2 + x + 5} \\
\underline{3x^5 \qquad\quad - 6x^3 + 21x^2} \\
2x^3 - 21x^2 \\
\underline{2x^3 \qquad\quad - 4x + 14} \\
-21x^2 + 5x + 14
\end{array}
$$

First step: $\dfrac{3x^5}{x^3} = 3x^2$

★ $q(x) = 3x^2 + 2; r(x) = -21x^2 + 5x - 9$

**10** $\dfrac{4x^3 - x^2 + 2x - 1}{x^2} = \dfrac{4x^3}{x^2} - \dfrac{x^2}{x^2} + \dfrac{2x - 1}{x^2} = 4x - 1 + \dfrac{2x - 1}{x^2}$ ★ $4x - 1; 2x - 1$

**11** Synthetically dividing $f(x) = -4x^4 + 3x^3 + 20x^2 + 7x - 10$ by $x + 2$, we have

$$
\begin{array}{r|rrrrr}
-2 & -4 & 3 & 20 & 7 & -10 \\
   &    & 8 & -22 & 4 & -22 \\
\hline
   & -4 & 11 & -2 & 11 & -32
\end{array}
$$

By the remainder theorem, $f(-2) = -32$.

**12** If $f(x) = 2x^4 - 5x^3 - 4x^2 + 9$, then $f(3) = 0$ and $x - 3$ is a factor of $f$.

**13** Synthetically dividing $f(x) = 6x^5 - 4x^2 + 8$ by $x + 2$, we have

$$
\begin{array}{r|rrrrrr}
-2 & 6 & 0 & 0 & -4 & 0 & 8 \\
   &   & -12 & 24 & -48 & 104 & -208 \\
\hline
   & 6 & -12 & 24 & -52 & 104 & -200
\end{array}
$$

The synthetic division indicates that the quotient is $6x^4 - 12x^3 + 24x^2 - 52x + 104$ and the remainder is $-200$.

**14** Synthetically dividing $f(x) = 2x^3 + 5x^2 - 2x + 1$ by $x - 3$, we have

$$
\begin{array}{r|rrrr}
3 & 2 & 5 & -2 & 1 \\
  &   & 6 & 33 & 93 \\
\hline
  & 2 & 11 & 31 & 94
\end{array}
$$

The synthetic division indicates that the quotient is $2x^2 + 11x + 31$ and the remainder is 94.

**15** Since $-3 + 5i$ is a zero, so is $-3 - 5i$.

$f(x) = a[x - (-3 + 5i)][x - (-3 - 5i)](x + 1) = a(x^2 + 6x + 34)(x + 1)$.

$f(1) = a(41)(2)$ and $f(1) = 4 \;\Rightarrow\; 82a = 4 \;\Rightarrow\; a = \frac{2}{41}$. Hence, $f(x) = \frac{2}{41}(x^2 + 6x + 34)(x + 1)$.

**16** $f(x) = a[x - (1 - i)][x - (1 + i)](x - 3)(x) = ax(x^2 - 2x + 2)(x - 3)$.

$f(2) = a(2)(2)(-1)$ and $f(2) = -1 \;\Rightarrow\; -4a = -1 \;\Rightarrow\; a = \frac{1}{4}$. Hence, $f(x) = \frac{1}{4}x(x^2 - 2x + 2)(x - 3)$.

**17** $f(x) = x^5(x + 3)^2$　　　　{leading coefficient is 1}

　　　　　　　　　　　　　　　{0 is a zero of multiplicity 5}

　　　　　　　　　　　　　　　{$-3$ is a zero of multiplicity 2}

$\quad = x^5(x^2 + 6x + 9)$

$\quad = x^7 + 6x^6 + 9x^5$

**18** Synthetically dividing $f(x) = x^5 - 4x^4 - 3x^3 + 34x^2 - 52x + 24$ by $x - 2$ three times

gives us $(x - 2)^3(x^2 + 2x - 3)$. Hence, $f(x) = (x - 2)^3(x + 3)(x - 1)$.

**19** $f(x) = (x^2 - 2x + 1)^2(x^2 + 2x - 3) = \left[(x - 1)^2\right]^2(x + 3)(x - 1) = (x + 3)(x - 1)^5$

★ 1 (multiplicity 5); $-3$ (multiplicity 1)

**20** $f(x) = x^6 + 2x^4 + x^2 = x^2(x^4 + 2x^2 + 1) = x^2(x^2 + 1)^2$　　　　★ $0, \pm i$ (all have multiplicity 2)

**21** (a) Let $f(x) = 2x^4 - 4x^3 + 2x^2 - 5x - 7$. Since there are 3 sign changes in $f(x)$ and 1 sign change in $f(-x) = 2x^4 + 4x^3 + 2x^2 + 5x - 7$, there are either 3 positive and 1 negative solution or 1 positive, 1 negative, and 2 nonreal complex solutions.

(b) Upper bound is 3, lower bound is $-1$

**22** (a) Let $f(x) = x^5 - 4x^3 + 6x^2 + x + 4$. Since there are 2 sign changes in $f(x)$ and 3 sign changes in $f(-x)$, there are either 2 positive and 3 negative solutions; 2 positive, 1 negative, and 2 nonreal complex; 3 negative and 2 nonreal complex; or 1 negative and 4 nonreal complex solutions.

(b) Upper bound is 2, lower bound is $-3$

**23** Since there are only even powers, $x^6 + 2x^4 + 3x^2 + 1 \geq 1$ for every real number $x$.

**24** $x^4 + 9x^3 + 31x^2 + 49x + 30 = 0$　•　Use synthetic division to find that $-3$ and $-2$ are solutions. The remaining equation, $x^2 + 4x + 5 = 0$, can be solved by the quadratic formula to give $-2 \pm i$ as the other two solutions.

★ $-3, -2, -2 \pm i$

**25** $16x^3 - 20x^2 - 8x + 3 = 0$ • $\dfrac{\text{positive divisors of 3}}{\text{divisors of 16}} = \dfrac{1, 3}{\pm 1, \pm 2, \pm 4, \pm 8, \pm 16} \longrightarrow$

$\pm 1, \pm 3, \pm\frac{1}{2}, \pm\frac{3}{2}, \pm\frac{1}{4}, \pm\frac{3}{4}, \pm\frac{1}{8}, \pm\frac{3}{8}, \pm\frac{1}{16}, \pm\frac{3}{16}$  After a few attempts, we try $-\frac{1}{2}$.

$$
\begin{array}{r|rrrr}
-\frac{1}{2} & 16 & -20 & -8 & 3 \\
 & & -8 & 14 & -3 \\
\hline
 & 16 & -28 & 6 & 0
\end{array}
$$

Now $16x^2 - 28x + 6 = 0 \;\Rightarrow\; 8x^2 - 14x + 3 = 0 \;\Rightarrow\; (4x - 1)(2x - 3) = 0 \;\Rightarrow\; x = \frac{1}{4}, \frac{3}{2}$.

Thus, the solutions of $16x^3 - 20x^2 - 8x + 3 = 0$ are $x = -\frac{1}{2}, \frac{1}{4}, \frac{3}{2}$.

**26** $x^4 + x^3 - 7x^2 - x + 6 = 0$ • Use synthetic division to find that $-1$ and $1$ are solutions. The remaining equation, $x^2 + x - 6 = 0$, can be factored, $(x + 3)(x - 2) = 0$, so $-3$ and $2$ are the other two solutions.  ★ $-3, 2, \pm 1$

**27** The graph has $x$-intercepts at $-2, 1$, and $3$. The equation must have the form $f(x) = a(x + 2)^m (x - 1)^n (x - 3)^p$, where $m + n + p = 6$ since $f$ is a sixth-degree polynomial. The graph goes through the $x$-axis at $m$ and $p$, so they must be odd, and it doesn't change sign at $n$, so it must be even. Since the graph flattens out at $x = -2$, $m$ must be greater than $p$. The only possibility is $m = 3$, $n = 2$, and $p = 1$, so $f$ has the form

$f(x) = a(x + 2)^3 (x - 1)^2 (x - 3)$. The $y$-intercept is 4, so $f(0) = 4 \;\Rightarrow\; 4 = a(2)^3 (-1)^2 (-3) \;\Rightarrow\;$

$$-24a = 4 \;\Rightarrow\; a = -\tfrac{1}{6}. \text{ Thus, } f(x) = -\tfrac{1}{6}(x + 2)^3 (x - 1)^2 (x - 3).$$

**28** The graph has $x$-intercepts at $-3, 0$, and $3$. The equation must have the form $f(x) = a(x + 3)^2 (x)^2 (x - 3)^2$ since the graph doesn't change sign at any of the intercepts.

$$f(1) = 4 \;\Rightarrow\; 4 = a(4)^2 (1)^2 (-2)^2 \;\Rightarrow\; 64a = 4 \;\Rightarrow\; a = \tfrac{1}{16}.$$

**29** $f(x) = \dfrac{4(x + 2)(x - 1)}{3(x + 2)(x - 5)} = \dfrac{4(x - 1)}{3(x - 5)}$ if $x \ne -2$ • Note that $x + 2$ appears in both the numerator and

denominator, so there is a hole at $x = -2$. The $y$-value for the hole can be found by substituting $-2$ for $x$ in the

rest of the function. $\dfrac{4(-2 - 1)}{3(-2 - 5)} = \dfrac{4(-3)}{3(-7)} = \dfrac{4}{7}$, so the hole is at $\left(-2, \frac{4}{7}\right)$. There is one other zero of the

denominator, namely 5, so there is a vertical asymptote of $x = 5$. The degrees of the numerator and denominator

are the same, namely 2, so the ratio of leading coefficients gives us the value of the horizontal asymptote. In this

case, it is $y = \frac{4}{3}$. There is one other zero of the numerator, namely 1, so there is an $x$-intercept of 1. If we substitute

0 for $x$, we get $\dfrac{4(2)(-1)}{3(2)(-5)} = \dfrac{4}{15}$, the $y$-intercept.

**30** $f(x) = \dfrac{-2}{(x + 1)^2}$ • There is a vertical asymptote of $x = -1$.

Since the numerator is negative and the denominator is positive,

the functions values are negative and so $f$ is always

below the $x$-axis.

Figure 30

**31** $f(x) = \dfrac{1}{(x-1)^3}$ •

*Figure 31*

*Figure 32*

**32** $f(x) = \dfrac{3x^2}{16 - x^2} = \dfrac{3x^2}{(4+x)(4-x)}$. $f(x) = -3 \Rightarrow 3x^2 = 3x^2 - 48 \Rightarrow 0 = -48$, a contradiction $\Rightarrow$ the function does not intersect the horizontal asymptote.

**33** $f(x) = \dfrac{x}{(x+5)(x^2 - 5x + 4)} = \dfrac{x}{(x+5)(x-1)(x-4)}$

*Figure 33*

*Figure 34*

**34** $f(x) = \dfrac{x^3 - 2x^2 - 8x}{-x^2 + 2x} = \dfrac{x(x^2 - 2x - 8)}{x(2-x)} = \dfrac{(x-4)(x+2)}{2-x}$ for $x \neq 0$.

Substituting $x = 0$ into $\dfrac{(x-4)(x+2)}{2-x}$ gives us $-4$. Thus, we have a hole at $(0, -4)$.

By long division, $f(x) = -x + \dfrac{-8x}{-x^2 + 2x}$, so $y = -x$ is an oblique asymptote.

**35** $f(x) = \dfrac{x^2 - 2x + 1}{x^3 - x^2 + x - 1} = \dfrac{(x-1)(x-1)}{x^2(x-1) + 1(x-1)} = \dfrac{(x-1)^2}{(x^2+1)(x-1)} = \dfrac{x-1}{x^2+1}$ for $x \neq 1$; hole at $(1, 0)$

*Figure 35*

*Figure 36*

**36** $f(x) = \dfrac{3x^2 + x - 10}{x^2 + 2x} = \dfrac{(3x-5)(x+2)}{x(x+2)} = \dfrac{3x-5}{x}$ if $x \neq -2$. The horizontal asymptote is $y = 3$.

The $x$-intercept is $\frac{5}{3}$ and there is no $y$-intercept since $x = 0$ is a vertical asymptote.

Substituting $x = -2$ into $\dfrac{3x-5}{x}$ gives us $\dfrac{11}{2}$. Thus, we have a hole at $\left(-2, \dfrac{11}{2}\right)$.

**37** $f(x) = \dfrac{-2x^2 - 8x - 6}{x^2 - 6x + 8} = \dfrac{-2(x^2 + 4x + 3)}{(x-2)(x-4)} = \dfrac{-2(x+1)(x+3)}{(x-2)(x-4)}$. The vertical asymptotes are $x = 2$ and $x = 4$.

The $x$-intercepts are $-3$ and $-1$. $y = -2$ is a horizontal asymptote. $f(x) = -2 \implies$

$-2x^2 - 8x - 6 = -2x^2 + 12x - 16 \implies 10 = 20x \implies x = \frac{1}{2}$, so $I = \left(\frac{1}{2}, -2\right)$.

*Figure 37*

*Figure 38*

**38** $f(x) = \dfrac{x^2 + 2x - 8}{x+3} = \dfrac{(x+4)(x-2)}{x+3} = x - 1 - \dfrac{5}{x+3}$. The vertical asymptote is $x = -3$. The $x$-intercepts

are $-4$ and $2$. $y = x - 1$ is an oblique asymptote.

**39** $f(x) = \dfrac{x^4 - 16}{x^3} = \dfrac{(x^2 + 4)(x+2)(x-2)}{x^3} = x - \dfrac{16}{x^3}$. The $x$-intercepts are $-2$ and $2$. $y = x$ is an oblique

asymptote.

*Figure 39*

*Figure 42*

**40** There is a hole at $x = 2$, so $(x - 2)$ must be a factor in both the numerator and denominator. There is a vertical

asymptote of $x = -3$, so $(x + 3)$ must be a factor in the denominator. There is an $x$-intercept at $5$, so $(x - 5)$ must

be a factor in the numerator. The horizontal asymptote is $y = \frac{3}{2}$, so the ratio of leading coefficients must be $\frac{3}{2}$.

Combining this information gives us this possibility:

$$f(x) = \frac{3(x-5)(x-2)}{2(x+3)(x-2)}, \quad \text{or equivalently,} \quad f(x) = \frac{3x^2 - 21x + 30}{2x^2 + 2x - 12}$$

**41** $y = \dfrac{k\sqrt[3]{x}}{z^2} \quad \bullet \quad 6 = \dfrac{k\sqrt[3]{8}}{3^2} \implies 6 = \dfrac{2k}{9} \implies k = \dfrac{54}{2} = 27$

**42** $y = \dfrac{k}{x^2} \implies 18 = \dfrac{k}{4^2} \implies k = 18 \cdot 16 = 288$, so graph $y = \dfrac{288}{x^2}$ for $x > 0$. See *Figure 42* above.

**43** (a) $y = cx^2(x^2 - 4lx + 6l^2) \quad \bullet \quad l = 10, x = 10,$ and $y = 2 \implies 2 = c(10)^2(10^2 - 4 \cdot 10 \cdot 10 + 6 \cdot 10^2) \implies$

$2 = c(100)(100 - 400 + 600) \implies 2 = c(100)(300) \implies 2 = 30,000c \implies c = \dfrac{1}{15,000}$

(b) $x = 6.1 \implies y \approx 0.9754 < 1$ and $x = 6.2 \implies y \approx 1.0006 > 1$.

**44** (a)  Edge $AB$ has length $2\pi r$ where $r$ is the radius of the cylinder.

$$2\pi r = \sqrt{l^2 - x^2} \quad\Rightarrow\quad r^2 = \frac{1}{4\pi^2}\left(l^2 - x^2\right). \text{ Now } V = \pi r^2 x = \pi\left[\frac{1}{4\pi^2}\left(l^2 - x^2\right)\right](x) = \frac{1}{4\pi}\,x\left(l^2 - x^2\right).$$

(b)  If $x > 0$, $V > 0$ if $l^2 - x^2 > 0$ or $l > x$. Thus, when $0 < x < l$, $V > 0$.

**45**  $T = \frac{1}{20}t(t-12)(t-24)$ and $T = 32 \quad\Rightarrow\quad \frac{1}{20}t(t-12)(t-24) = 32 \quad\Rightarrow\quad t(t^2 - 36t + 288) = 640 \quad\Rightarrow$

$t^3 - 36t^2 + 288t - 640 = 0$. Synthetically dividing $t^3 - 36t^2 + 288t - 640$ by $t - 4$ gives us

$$
\begin{array}{r|rrrr}
4 & 1 & -36 & 288 & -640 \\
  &   & 4   & -128 & 640 \\
\hline
  & 1 & -32 & 160 & 0
\end{array}
$$

Now use the quadratic formula to solve $t^2 - 32t + 160 = 0$ for $t$.

$t = \dfrac{32 \pm \sqrt{32^2 - 4(1)(160)}}{2(1)} = \dfrac{32 \pm \sqrt{384}}{2} = \dfrac{32 \pm 8\sqrt{6}}{2} = 16 \pm 4\sqrt{6}$.  Since $0 \le t \le 24$, $t = 4$ (10:00 A.M.)

and $t = 16 - 4\sqrt{6} \approx 6.2020$ (12:12 P.M.) are the times when the temperature was 32°F.

**46**  $N(t) = -t^4 + 21t^2 + 100$ and $N(t) > 180 \quad\Rightarrow\quad t^4 - 21t^2 + 80 < 0 \quad\Rightarrow\quad (t^2 - 5)(t^2 - 16) < 0$.

The positive values of $t$ satisfying this inequality are in the interval $\left(\sqrt{5}, 4\right)$.

**47** (a)  $S$ is the value that is changing. As $S$ gets large, the value of $R = \dfrac{kS^n}{S^n + a^n}$ will approach the ratio of leading

coefficients, $k/1$. Hence, an equation of the horizontal asymptote is $R = k$.

(b)  $k$ is the maximum rate at which the liver can remove alcohol from the bloodstream.

**48** (a)  $C(x) = \dfrac{0.3x}{101 - x}$

$C(100) = \$30$ million and $C(90) \approx \$2.5$ million.

(b)  Notice the great difference in cost as $x$ approaches 100.

$C(50)$ is only $\$0.29$ million and $C(80)$ is $\$1.14$ million.

**49**  $C = \dfrac{kP_1 P_2}{d^2} \quad\bullet\quad 2000 = \dfrac{k(10{,}000)(5000)}{(25)^2} \quad\Rightarrow\quad k = \dfrac{1}{40}; C = \dfrac{(10{,}000)(15{,}000)}{40(100)^2} = 375$

**50**  $P = kA^2 v^3 \quad\bullet\quad 3000 = k\left[\pi(5)^2\right]^2(20)^3 \quad\Rightarrow\quad k = \dfrac{3}{5000\pi^2}; P = \dfrac{3}{5000\pi^2}\left[\pi(5)^2\right]^2(30)^3 = 10{,}125 \text{ watts}$

## *Chapter 3 Discussion Exercises*

**1**  **For even-degreed polynomials:** the domain is $\mathbb{R}$ and the number of $x$-intercepts ranges from *zero* to the degree of the polynomial; if the leading coefficient is positive, the range is of the form $[c, \infty)$ and the general shape has $y \to \infty$ as $|x| \to \infty$; if the leading coefficient is negative, the range is of the form $(-\infty, c]$ and the general shape has $y \to -\infty$ as $|x| \to \infty$.

**For odd-degreed polynomials:** the domain is $\mathbb{R}$, the range is $\mathbb{R}$, and the number of $x$-intercepts ranges from *one* to the degree of the polynomial; if the leading coefficient is positive, then $y \to \infty$ as $x \to \infty$ and $y \to -\infty$ as $x \to \infty$, if the leading coefficient is negative, then $y \to -\infty$ as $x \to \infty$ and $y \to \infty$ as $x \to -\infty$.

$\boxed{2}$ After trying a few examples, students should come up with the conclusion that complex numbers can be used in the synthetic division process.

$\boxed{3}$ By long division, we obtain the quotient $2x^2 - 7x + 5$ with remainder $-6$. By synthetic division with $k = -\frac{3}{2}$, we obtain a bottom row of $4, -14, 10, -6$. The first three numbers are twice the coefficients of the quotient and the last number is the remainder. For the factor $ax + b$, we can use synthetic division with $k = -b/a$, and obtain $a$ times the quotient and the remainder in the bottom row.

$\boxed{4}$ $f(x) = a(x-1)(x-2)(x-3)$. $f(0) = a(-6) = 6 \Rightarrow a = -1$. $f(-1) = 24 \neq 25 \Rightarrow$ the point cannot be on the polynomial.

$\boxed{5}$ From your previous experience, you know that 2 points specify a first-degree polynomial (a line) and that 3 points specify a second-degree polynomial (a parabola). After working Discussion Exercise 4, you should guess that 4 points specify a third-degree polynomial, so a logical conclusion is that $n + 1$ points specify an $n$-degree polynomial.

$\boxed{6}$ Let us consider the polynomial

$$f(x) = a_n x^n + a_{n-1} x^{n-1} + \cdots + a_1 x + a_0,$$

where each coefficient $a_k$ is a real number and $a_n \neq 0$. If $f(z) = 0$, then

$$a_n z^n + a_{n-1} z^{n-1} + \cdots + a_1 z + a_0 = 0.$$

If two complex numbers are equal, then so are their conjugates. Hence, the conjugate of the left-hand side of the last equation equals the conjugate of the right-hand side; that is,

$$\overline{a_n z^n + a_{n-1} z^{n-1} + \cdots + a_1 z + a_0} = \overline{0} = 0.$$

The fact that $\overline{0} = 0$ follows from $\overline{0} = \overline{0 + 0i} = 0 - 0i = 0$.

If $z$ and $w$ are complex numbers, then it can be shown that $\overline{z + w} = \overline{z} + \overline{w}$. More generally, the conjugate of *any* sum of complex numbers is the sum of the conjugates. Consequently,

$$\overline{a_n z^n} + \overline{a_{n-1} z^{n-1}} + \cdots + \overline{a_1 z} + \overline{a_0} = 0.$$

It can also be shown that $\overline{z \cdot w} = \overline{z} \cdot \overline{w}$, $\overline{z^n} = \overline{z}^n$ for every positive integer $n$, and $\overline{z} = z$ if and only if $z$ is real. Thus, for every $k$,

$$\overline{a_k z^k} = \overline{a_k} \cdot \overline{z^k} = \overline{a_k} \cdot \overline{z}^k = a_k \overline{z}^k,$$

and therefore

$$a_n \overline{z}^n + a_{n-1} \overline{z}^{n-1} + \cdots + a_1 \overline{z} + a_0 = 0.$$

The last equation states that $f(\overline{z}) = 0$, which completes the proof.

$\boxed{7}$ If the common factor is never equal to zero for any real number, then it can be canceled and has no effect on its graph. Such a factor is $x^2 + 1$, and an example of a function is $f(x) = \dfrac{(x^2 + 1)(x - 1)}{(x^2 + 1)(x - 2)}$.

$\boxed{8}$ (a) The horizontal asymptote is $y = \dfrac{a}{c}$. Solving $f(x) = \dfrac{a}{c}$ gives us $\dfrac{ax + b}{cx + d} = \dfrac{a}{c}$ $\Rightarrow$

$acx + bc = acx + ad$ $\Rightarrow$ $bc = ad$ $\Rightarrow$ no solution, and $f$ doesn't cross its horizontal asymptote.

(b) The horizontal asymptote is $y = \dfrac{a}{d}$. Solving $f(x) = \dfrac{a}{d}$ gives us $\dfrac{ax^2 + bx + c}{dx^2 + ex + f} = \dfrac{a}{d}$ $\Rightarrow$

$adx^2 + bdx + cd = adx^2 + aex + af$ $\Rightarrow$ $aex - bdx = cd - af$ $\Rightarrow$ $x = \dfrac{cd - af}{ae - bd}$,

provided the denominator is not zero.

$\boxed{9}$ (a) $B = \dfrac{GW}{29.3 + 53.1E - 22.7C}$ • $G = 3 \cdot 500 = 1500$, $W = 5$, $E = -0.05$, and $C = 0.95$, so

$B = \dfrac{1500(5)}{29.3 + 53.1(-0.05) - 22.7(0.95)} \approx 1476$. This tells us that a bankroll of about \$1476 would allow us to

play 1500 games and be 95% confident that we will survive the 3-hour gambling session.

(b) If we use the same values for $G$, $W$, and $E$, we get $B = \dfrac{7500}{26.645 - 22.7C}$. A graph of $B$ has a vertical

asymptote at $C \approx 1.17$, but that is 117% confident of surviving the 3-hour gambling session. The highest

confidence value for any model like this should be 100, so the formula should have a restricted domain with it.

$\boxed{10}$ Let $x$, $x + 1$, and $x + 2$ denote three consecutive integers. Their product is $x(x + 1)(x + 2) = x^3 + 3x^2 + 2x$.

Now add the second integer to get

$$(x^3 + 3x^2 + 2x) + (x + 1) = x^3 + 3x^2 + 3x + 1.$$

Only $x + 1$ or $x - 1$ could be factors, and it turns out that $x + 1$ is a factor three times. Thus, if you multiply three

consecutive integers together and then add the second integer to that product, you obtain the cube of the second

integer.

$\boxed{11}$ (a) $P$ represents the amount of personal property tax and $S \cdot I$ represents the amount of income tax, so the total tax

paid by the individual is $P + SI$. To get the individual's state tax rate, we'll divide the total tax by the income,

that is, $R(I) = \dfrac{P + SI}{I}$.

(b) As $I$ gets very large, $R$ will approach its horizontal asymptote, which is $S$.

(c) As income gets larger, individuals pay more in taxes, but fixed tax amounts play a smaller role in determining

the overall tax rate.

$\boxed{12}$ (a) $R = \dfrac{25(A + 40C + 2Y + 160T - 200I)}{12A}$ •

$A = 497$, $C = 336$, $Y = 4557$, $T = 49$, and $I = 10$ $\Rightarrow$ $R \approx 121.1$.

(b) We could let $R = 121.5$ and solve the equation for $Y$ to get $Y = 4604$, which is 47 more yards than 4557.

Another approach is to let $Y_1 = \dfrac{25(497 + 40 \cdot 336 + 2 \cdot X + 160 \cdot 49 - 200 \cdot 10)}{12 \cdot 497}$ and table $Y_1$ with

TableStart $= 4557$ and $\Delta$Table $= 1$ and see that $Y_1 = 121.5$ when X $= 4604$.

(c) If he could make one more touchdown pass, then we would have $A = 498$, $C = 337$, $Y = 4557 + X$, $T = 50$,

and $I = 10$ in $R$, where $X$ represents the length of the touchdown pass. Solving or using a table, we need

$X \geq 36$ to get $R \geq 122$.

## Chapter 3 Test

**1** $f(x) = \frac{1}{6}(x+3)(x-2)(x-4) \Rightarrow$
$f(0) = \frac{1}{6}(3)(-2)(-4) = 4$,
so the $y$-intercept is 4.

There are $x$-intercepts at $x = -3$, 2, and 4.

**2** $f$ must have the form $x^a(x-1)^b(x-2)^c$. $b$ must be even since $f$ doesn't change sign at $x = 1$. $a$ and $c$ must be odd since $f$ changes sign at $x = 0$ and $x = 2$, respectively. $a$ must be greater than $c$ since $f$ is flatter at 0 than at 2. Putting this information together, we get a possible equation of $f(x) = x^3(x-1)^2(x-2)^1$. *Note:* The equation used for the figure is $f(x) = 3x^3(x-1)^2(x-2)$.

**3** $f(x) = x^3 + 2x^2 - x - 1$ • $f(0) = -1 < 0$ and $f(2) = 13 > 0$, so there is a number $c$ such that $0 < c < 2$ and $f(c) = 0$.

**4** $f(x) = (x-a)(x-b)^2(x-c)$ • The general shape of $f$ is a quartic polynomial that has negative values between $a$ and $c$ and passes through the point $(b, 0)$ [but does not go through the $x$-axis since the exponent on $b$ is even]. Thus, $f(x) < 0$ for $x$ in $(a, b) \cup (b, c)$.

**5** The population becomes extinct when $N(t) = 0 \Rightarrow -t^4 + 48t^2 + 49 = 0 \Rightarrow t^4 - 48t^2 - 49 = 0 \Rightarrow$
$(t^2 - 49)(t^2 + 1) = 0 \Rightarrow (t+7)(t-7)(t^2+1) = 0 \Rightarrow t = 7$ for $t > 0$, so the population becomes extinct after 7 years.

**6** $f(x) = 2x^3 - 6x + 2$ and $g(x) = 2x^3 + 2x - 30$ • If the range were changed from $-50 \le y \le 10$ to $-2000 \le y \le 2000$, the graphs of $f$ and $g$ would look nearly identical since the leading terms are equal.

**7** $f(x) = x^3 - 3x^2 - 10x + 24$ • Use synthetic division to show that $f(2) = 0$.

**8** $f(x) = a(x-1)(x-2)(x-3)$ • $f(4) = a(4-1)(4-2)(4-3) = a(3)(2)(1) = 6a$, so $6a = b \Rightarrow a = \frac{b}{6}$.

**9** $f(x) = k^2x^4 - kx^3 - 6$ • For $f$ to be divisible by $x - 1$, $f(1)$ must equal 0.
$$f(1) = k^2 - k - 6 = 0 \Rightarrow (k+2)(k-3) = 0 \Rightarrow k = -2 \text{ or } k = 3.$$

**10** $f$ has 3 as a zero of multiplicity 1, $-1$ as a zero of multiplicity 2 •
$f$ must have the form $f(x) = a(x-3)(x+1)^2$.
Since $f$ passes through the point $(2, -27)$, $f(2) = a(2-3)(2+1)^2 = a(-1)(3)^2 = -9a$ and $f(2) = -27$.
$$\text{Thus, } -9a = -27 \Rightarrow a = 3, \text{ and } f(x) = 3(x-3)(x+1)^2.$$

**11** $f$ passes through $(-2, 0), (1, 0)$, and $(3, 0)$ • $f$ must have the form $f(x) = a(x+2)(x-1)(x-3)$.
Since $f$ passes through the point $(0, 3)$, $f(0) = a(2)(-1)(-3) = 6a$ and $f(0) = 3$. Thus, $6a = 3 \Rightarrow a = \frac{1}{2}$, and $f(x) = \frac{1}{2}(x+2)(x-1)(x-3)$. So $f$ is determined and there can only be one value of $b$, that is, $f(4) = \frac{1}{2}(6)(3)(1) = 9$.

**12** Yes, but the polynomial will not have *real* coefficients. $f(x) = x(x-1)(x-i)$

**13** $f(x) = 702x^4 - 57x^3 - 5227x^2 - 163x + 6545$ •

5 is a factor of 6545 and 2 is a factor of 702, so $\frac{5}{2}$ is a possible rational root of $f$.

Factored, $f(x) = (2x - 5)(3x + 7)(9x - 11)(13x + 17)$.

**14** There is only one negative zero and it must be $-1$ since the graph crosses the $x$-axis at $x = -1$. The graph crosses the $x$-axis between 1 and 2, and there are only two possible rational zeros between 1 and 2, $\frac{3}{2}$ and $\frac{6}{5}$. Since that zero is closer to 1 than it is to 2, the second zero must be $\frac{6}{5}$. Similarly, the third zero between 2 and 3 must be $\frac{5}{2}$.

**15** $f(x) = \dfrac{3x^2 + x + 13}{x^2 + 2x + 1}$ • From $f$, we see that the horizontal asymptote is $y = 3$.

$f(x) = 3 \Rightarrow \dfrac{3x^2 + x + 13}{x^2 + 2x + 1} = 3 \Rightarrow 3x^2 + x + 13 = 3x^2 + 6x + 3 \Rightarrow 10 = 5x \Rightarrow x = 2$.

$f(2) = \frac{27}{9} = 3$, so the point of intersection is $(2, 3)$.

**16** $f(x) = \dfrac{3x^2 + x - 2}{3x^2 - 8x + 4} = \dfrac{(3x - 2)(x + 1)}{(3x - 2)(x - 2)} = \dfrac{x + 1}{x - 2}$ for $x \neq \dfrac{2}{3}$.

Substituting $\dfrac{2}{3}$ for $x$ in $\dfrac{x + 1}{x - 2}$ gives us $\dfrac{5/3}{-4/3} = -\dfrac{5}{4}$, so the hole is $\left( \dfrac{2}{3}, -\dfrac{5}{4} \right)$.

**17** The degrees of the numerator and denominator are the same, so the horizontal asymptote value is the ratio of leading coefficients, $\frac{2}{1}$, and the HA is $y = 2$. There is a hole at $x = 3$. Substituting 3 for $x$ in $\dfrac{2(x + 1)}{x - 1}$ gives us $\dfrac{8}{2} = 4$, so the hole is $(3, 4)$. From $y = \dfrac{2(x + 1)}{x - 1}$, we see that there is an $x$-intercept at $-1$ and a VA of $x = 1$. The $y$-intercept is $f(0) = -2$.

**18** The $x$-intercept at 4 means that $x - 4$ is a factor in the numerator. A vertical asymptote of $x = 2$ means that $x - 2$ is factor in the denominator. A horizontal asymptote of $y = -3$ means that the ratio of leading coefficients is $\frac{-3}{1}$. A hole at $x = -1$ means that $x + 1$ is a factor in both the numerator and the denominator. Putting this information together gives us the function $f(x) = \dfrac{-3(x - 4)(x + 1)}{(x - 2)(x + 1)}$.

**19** $z = k\dfrac{x^2}{y}$ • $6 = k\dfrac{3^2}{2} \Rightarrow k = \dfrac{12}{9} = \dfrac{4}{3}$. Thus, $z = \dfrac{4x^2}{3y} = \dfrac{4(6)^2}{3(12)} = 4$.

# Chapter 4: Inverse, Exponential, and Logarithmic Functions

## 4.1 Exercises

**1** (a) $f$ is one-to-one and $f(4) = 5$, so $f^{-1}(5) = 4$.

(b) $g$ is *not* one-to-one since $g(1) = g(5) = 6$, so we cannot find $g^{-1}(6)$. **Not possible**

**Note:** To help determine if you should try to prove the function is one-to-one or look for a counterexample to show that it is not one-to-one, consider the question: "If $y$ was a particular value, could I find a unique $x$?" If the answer is yes, try to prove the function is one-to-one. Also, consider the Horizontal Line Test listed on page 250 in the text.

**2** (a) $f$ is one-to-one and $f(3) = 5$, so $f^{-1}(5) = 3$.

(b) $g$ is *not* one-to-one since $g(2) = g(4) = 6$, so we cannot find $g^{-1}(6)$. **Not possible**

**3** (a) The graph is the graph of a function since it passes the Vertical Line Test.
Since it passes the Horizontal Line Test, it is also one-to-one.

(b) The graph is the graph of a function, but since it doesn't pass the Horizontal Line Test, it is not one-to-one.

(c) The graph is not the graph of a function since it doesn't pass the Vertical Line Test.

**4** (a) The graph is the graph of a function, but since it doesn't pass the Horizontal Line Test, it is not one-to-one.

(b) The graph is the graph of a function since it passes the Vertical Line Test. Since it passes the Horizontal Line Test, it is also one-to-one.

(c) The graph is not the graph of a function since it doesn't pass the Vertical Line Test.

**Note:** For Exercises 5–16, we use the method illustrated in Example 1; however, the Horizontal Line Test or the theorem on increasing and decreasing functions could also be used.

**5** If $y$ was a particular value, say 7, we would have $7 = 2x + 5$. Trying to solve for $x$ would yield $2 = 2x$ $\Rightarrow$ $x = 1$. Since we could find a unique $x$, we will try to prove that the function is one-to-one.
**Proof** Suppose that $f(a) = f(b)$ for some numbers $a$ and $b$ in the domain. This gives us $2a + 5 = 2b + 5$ $\Rightarrow$ $2a = 2b$ $\Rightarrow$ $a = b$. Since $f(a) = f(b)$ implies that $a = b$, we conclude that $f$ is one-to-one.

**6** Suppose $f(a) = f(b)$. $\dfrac{1}{a-2} = \dfrac{1}{b-2}$ $\Rightarrow$ $a - 2 = b - 2$ $\Rightarrow$ $a = b$. $f$ is one-to-one.

**7** If $y$ was a particular value, say 11, we would have $11 = x^2 - 5$. Trying to solve for $x$ would yield $16 = x^2$ $\Rightarrow$ $x = \pm 4$. Since we could not find a *unique* $x$, we will show that two different numbers have the same function value. Using the information already obtained, $f(4) = 11$ and $f(-4) = 11$, but $4 \neq -4$ and hence, $f$ is *not* one-to-one.

**8** For $f(x) = x^2 + 3$, $f(1) = 4 = f(-1)$. $f$ is *not* one-to-one.

**9** Suppose $f(a) = f(b)$ with $a, b \geq 0$. $\sqrt{a} = \sqrt{b}$ $\Rightarrow$ $\left(\sqrt{a}\right)^2 = \left(\sqrt{b}\right)^2$ $\Rightarrow$ $a = b$. $f$ is one-to-one.

**10** Suppose $f(a) = f(b)$. $\sqrt[3]{a} = \sqrt[3]{b} \Rightarrow \left(\sqrt[3]{a}\right)^3 = \left(\sqrt[3]{b}\right)^3 \Rightarrow a = b$. $f$ is one-to-one.

**11** For $f(x) = |x|$, $f(-1) = 1 = f(1)$. $f$ is *not* one-to-one.

**12** For $f(x) = 3$, $f(2) = 3 = f(4)$. $f$ is *not* one-to-one.

**13** For $f(x) = \sqrt{4 - x^2}$, $f(-1) = \sqrt{3} = f(1)$. $f$ is *not* one-to-one.

**14** Suppose $f(a) = f(b)$. $2a^3 - 4 = 2b^3 - 4 \Rightarrow 2a^3 = 2b^3 \Rightarrow a^3 = b^3 \Rightarrow a = b$. $f$ is one-to-one.

**15** Suppose $f(a) = f(b)$. $\dfrac{1}{a} = \dfrac{1}{b} \Rightarrow a = b$. $f$ is one-to-one.

**16** For $f(x) = 1/x^2$, $f(-1) = 1 = f(1)$. $f$ is *not* one-to-one.

**17** (a) On $f$, as $y \to -4$, $x \to -1$; so on $f^{-1}$, as $x \to -4$, $f^{-1}(x) \to -1$.

    (b) On $f$, as $y \to \infty$, $x \to -2^-$; so on $f^{-1}$, as $x \to \infty$, $f^{-1}(x) \to -2^-$ (or simply $-2$).

    (c) On $f$, as $y \to -\infty$, $x \to -2^+$; so on $f^{-1}$, as $x \to -\infty$, $f^{-1}(x) \to -2^+$ (or simply $-2$).

    (d) On $f$, as $y \to 4^+$, $x \to -\infty$; so on $f^{-1}$, as $x \to 4^+$, $f^{-1}(x) \to -\infty$.

    (e) On $f$, as $y \to 4^-$, $x \to \infty$; so on $f^{-1}$, as $x \to 4^-$, $f^{-1}(x) \to \infty$.

**18** (a) On $f$, as $y \to 0$, $x \to 3$; so on $f^{-1}$, as $x \to 0$, $f^{-1}(x) \to 3$.

    (b) On $f$, as $y \to \infty$, $x \to 1^+$; so on $f^{-1}$, as $x \to \infty$, $f^{-1}(x) \to 1^+$ (or simply 1).

    (c) On $f$, as $y \to -\infty$, $x \to 1^-$; so on $f^{-1}$, as $x \to -\infty$, $f^{-1}(x) \to 1^-$ (or simply 1).

    (d) On $f$, as $y \to -2^+$, $x \to \infty$; so on $f^{-1}$, as $x \to -2^+$, $f^{-1}(x) \to \infty$.

    (e) On $f$, as $y \to -2^-$, $x \to -\infty$; so on $f^{-1}$, as $x \to -2^-$, $f^{-1}(x) \to -\infty$.

**Note:**  For Exercises 19–22, we need to show that $f(g(x)) = x = g(f(x))$.

**19** $f(g(x)) = 3\left(\dfrac{x+2}{3}\right) - 2 = x + 2 - 2 = x$. $g(f(x)) = \dfrac{(3x-2)+2}{3} = \dfrac{3x}{3} = x$.

*Figure 19*

*Figure 20*

**20** $f(g(x)) = \left(-\sqrt{x-5}\right)^2 + 5 = x - 5 + 5 = x$.

    $g(f(x)) = -\sqrt{(x^2+5) - 5} = -\sqrt{x^2} = -|x| = -(-x)$ {since $x \le 0$} $= x$.

**21** $f(g(x)) = -\left(\sqrt{3-x}\right)^2 + 3 = -(3-x) + 3 = x.$

$g(f(x)) = \sqrt{3 - (-x^2 + 3)} = \sqrt{x^2} = |x| = x$ {since $x \geq 0$}.

*Figure 21*

*Figure 22*

**22** $f(g(x)) = \left(\sqrt[3]{x+4}\right)^3 - 4 = x + 4 - 4 = x.$  $g(f(x)) = \sqrt[3]{(x^3 - 4) + 4} = \sqrt[3]{x^3} = x.$

**23** $f(x) = -\dfrac{2}{x-1}$ • The domain of $f$ is $\mathbb{R} - \{1\}$. The horizontal asymptote of $f$ is $y = 0$ and the range of $f$ is $\mathbb{R} - \{0\}$, or equivalently, $(-\infty, 0) \cup (0, \infty)$. The domain of $f^{-1}$ is equal to the range of $f$; that is, $\mathbb{R} - \{0\}$. The range of $f^{-1}$ is equal to the domain of $f$; that is, $\mathbb{R} - \{1\}$, or equivalently, $(-\infty, 1) \cup (1, \infty)$.

**24** $f(x) = \dfrac{5}{x+3}$ • Domain of $f^{-1}$ = range of $f = \mathbb{R} - \{0\}$. Range of $f^{-1}$ = domain of $f = \mathbb{R} - \{-3\}$.

★ $(-\infty, 0) \cup (0, \infty); (-\infty, -3) \cup (-3, \infty)$

**25** $f(x) = \dfrac{4x+5}{3x-8}$ • The domain of $f$ is $\mathbb{R} - \{\frac{8}{3}\}$. The horizontal asymptote of $f$ is $y = \frac{4}{3}$ and the range of $f$ is $\mathbb{R} - \{\frac{4}{3}\}$, or equivalently, $(-\infty, \frac{4}{3}) \cup (\frac{4}{3}, \infty)$. The domain of $f^{-1}$ is equal to the range of $f$; that is, $\mathbb{R} - \{\frac{4}{3}\}$. The range of $f^{-1}$ is equal to the domain of $f$; that is, $\mathbb{R} - \{\frac{8}{3}\}$, or equivalently, $(-\infty, \frac{8}{3}) \cup (\frac{8}{3}, \infty)$.

**26** $f(x) = \dfrac{2x-7}{9x+1}$ • Domain of $f^{-1}$ = range of $f = \mathbb{R} - \{\frac{2}{9}\}$. Range of $f^{-1}$ = domain of $f = \mathbb{R} - \{-\frac{1}{9}\}$.

★ $(-\infty, \frac{2}{9}) \cup (\frac{2}{9}, \infty); (-\infty, -\frac{1}{9}) \cup (-\frac{1}{9}, \infty)$

**27** We need to solve for $x$. $y = 3x + 5 \Rightarrow y - 5 = 3x \Rightarrow x = \dfrac{y-5}{3}.$

Now exchange $x$ and $y$. $y = f^{-1}(x) = \dfrac{x-5}{3}$

**28** $f(x) = 7 - 2x \Rightarrow 2x = 7 - y \Rightarrow x = \dfrac{7-y}{2},$ so $y = f^{-1}(x) = \dfrac{7-x}{2}$

**29** $f(x) = \dfrac{3}{2x-5} \Rightarrow y(2x-5) = 3 \Rightarrow 2xy - 5y = 3 \Rightarrow 2xy = 5y + 3 \Rightarrow$

$x = \dfrac{5y+3}{2y},$ so $y = f^{-1}(x) = \dfrac{5x+3}{2x}$

**30** $f(x) = \dfrac{1}{x+3} \Rightarrow xy + 3y = 1 \Rightarrow xy = 1 - 3y \Rightarrow x = \dfrac{1-3y}{y},$ so $y = f^{-1}(x) = \dfrac{1-3x}{x}$

**31** $f(x) = \dfrac{3x+2}{2x-5} \Rightarrow 2xy - 5y = 3x + 2 \Rightarrow 2xy - 3x = 5y + 2 \Rightarrow x(2y-3) = 5y + 2 \Rightarrow$

$x = \dfrac{5y+2}{2y-3},$ so $y = f^{-1}(x) = \dfrac{5x+2}{2x-3}$

**32** $f(x) = \dfrac{4x}{x-2} \Rightarrow xy - 2y = 4x \Rightarrow xy - 4x = 2y \Rightarrow x = \dfrac{2y}{y-4},$ so $y = f^{-1}(x) = \dfrac{2x}{x-4}$

**33** $f(x) = 2 - 3x^2$, $x \leq 0$ $\Rightarrow$ $y + 3x^2 = 2$ $\Rightarrow$

$$x^2 = \frac{2-y}{3} \quad \Rightarrow \quad x = \pm\sqrt{\frac{2-y}{3}} \text{ \{choose minus since } x \leq 0\}, \text{ so } y = f^{-1}(x) = -\sqrt{\frac{2-x}{3}}$$

**34** $f(x) = 5x^2 + 2$, $x \geq 0$ $\Rightarrow$ $y - 2 = 5x^2$ $\Rightarrow$

$$x^2 = \frac{y-2}{5} \quad \Rightarrow \quad x = \pm\sqrt{\frac{y-2}{5}} \text{ \{choose plus since } x \geq 0\}, \text{ so } y = f^{-1}(x) = \sqrt{\frac{x-2}{5}}$$

**35** $f(x) = 2x^3 - 5$ $\Rightarrow$ $y + 5 = 2x^3$ $\Rightarrow$ $\dfrac{y+5}{2} = x^3$ $\Rightarrow$ $x = \sqrt[3]{\dfrac{y+5}{2}}$, so $y = f^{-1}(x) = \sqrt[3]{\dfrac{x+5}{2}}$

**36** $f(x) = -x^3 + 2$ $\Rightarrow$ $x^3 = 2 - y$ $\Rightarrow$ $x = \sqrt[3]{2-y}$, so $y = f^{-1}(x) = \sqrt[3]{2-x}$

**37** $f(x) = \sqrt{3-x}$ $\Rightarrow$ $y^2 = 3 - x$ $\Rightarrow$ $x = 3 - y^2$ {Since $y \geq 0$ for $f$, $x \geq 0$ for $f^{-1}$}, so

$$y = f^{-1}(x) = 3 - x^2, \ x \geq 0$$

**38** $f(x) = \sqrt{x+4}$ $\Rightarrow$ $y^2 = x + 4$ $\Rightarrow$ $x = y^2 - 4$ {Since $y \geq 0$ for $f$, $x \geq 0$ for $f^{-1}$}, so

$$y = f^{-1}(x) = x^2 - 4, \ x \geq 0$$

**39** $f(x) = \sqrt[3]{x} + 1$ $\Rightarrow$ $y - 1 = \sqrt[3]{x}$ $\Rightarrow$ $x = (y-1)^3$, so $y = f^{-1}(x) = (x-1)^3$

**40** $f(x) = \sqrt[3]{x} - 4$ $\Rightarrow$ $y + 4 = \sqrt[3]{x}$ $\Rightarrow$ $x = (y+4)^3$, so $y = f^{-1}(x) = (x+4)^3$

**41** $f(x) = (x^5 - 6)^3$ $\Rightarrow$ $\sqrt[3]{y} = x^5 - 6$ $\Rightarrow$ $x^5 = \sqrt[3]{y} + 6$ $\Rightarrow$ $x = \sqrt[5]{\sqrt[3]{y} + 6}$, so $y = f^{-1}(x) = \sqrt[5]{\sqrt[3]{x} + 6}$

**42** $f(x) = (x^3 + 1)^5$ $\Rightarrow$ $\sqrt[5]{y} = x^3 + 1$ $\Rightarrow$ $x^3 = \sqrt[5]{y} - 1$ $\Rightarrow$ $x = \sqrt[3]{\sqrt[5]{y} - 1}$, so $y = f^{-1}(x) = \sqrt[3]{\sqrt[5]{x} - 1}$

**43** $f(x) = x$ $\Rightarrow$ $y = x$ $\Rightarrow$ $x = y$, so $y = f^{-1}(x) = x$ {note that $f = f^{-1}$}

**44** $f(x) = -x$ $\Rightarrow$ $y = -x$ $\Rightarrow$ $x = -y$, so $y = f^{-1}(x) = -x$ {note that $f = f^{-1}$}

**45** $f(x) = \sqrt{4 - x^2}$, $0 \leq x \leq 2$ $\Rightarrow$ $y^2 = 4 - x^2$ $\Rightarrow$ $x^2 = 4 - y^2$ $\Rightarrow$

$$x = \pm\sqrt{4 - y^2} \text{ \{choose plus since } 0 \leq x \leq 2\}, \text{ so } y = f^{-1}(x) = \sqrt{4 - x^2}, \ 0 \leq x \leq 2 \text{ \{note that } f = f^{-1}\}$$

**46** $f(x) = -\sqrt{9 - x^2}$, $-3 \leq x \leq 0$ $\Rightarrow$ $y^2 = 9 - x^2$ $\Rightarrow$ $x^2 = 9 - y^2$ $\Rightarrow$

$$x = \pm\sqrt{9 - y^2} \text{ \{choose minus since } -3 \leq x \leq 0\}, \text{ so } y = f^{-1}(x) = -\sqrt{9 - x^2}, \ -3 \leq x \leq 0 \text{ \{note that } f = f^{-1}\}$$

**47** $f(x) = x^2 - 6x$, $x \geq 3$ $\Rightarrow$ $y = x^2 - 6x$ $\Rightarrow$ $x^2 - 6x - y = 0$.

This is a quadratic equation in $x$ with $a = 1$, $b = -6$, and $c = -y$. Solving with the quadratic formula gives us

$$x = \frac{-(-6) \pm \sqrt{(-6)^2 - 4(1)(-y)}}{2(1)} = \frac{6 \pm \sqrt{36 + 4y}}{2} = \frac{6 \pm 2\sqrt{9 + y}}{2} = 3 \pm \sqrt{9 + y}.$$

Since $x \geq 3$, we choose the "+" and obtain $y = f^{-1}(x) = 3 + \sqrt{x + 9}$.

**48** $f(x) = x^2 - 4x + 3$, $x \leq 2$ $\Rightarrow$ $y = x^2 - 4x + 3$ $\Rightarrow$ $x^2 - 4x + (3 - y) = 0$ $\Rightarrow$

$$x = \frac{4 \pm \sqrt{16 - 4(1)(3 - y)}}{2} = \frac{4 \pm \sqrt{4 + 4y}}{2} = \frac{4 \pm 4\sqrt{1 + y}}{2} = 2 \pm \sqrt{y + 1}.$$

Since $x \leq 2$, we choose the "−" and obtain $y = f^{-1}(x) = 2 - \sqrt{x + 1}$.

**49** (a) $(g^{-1} \circ f^{-1})(2) = g^{-1}(f^{-1}(2))$

$\qquad\qquad\qquad = g^{-1}(5) \qquad\qquad$ {since $f(5) = 2$}

$\qquad\qquad\qquad = 3 \qquad\qquad\qquad$ {since $g(3) = 5$}

(b) $(g^{-1} \circ h)(3) = g^{-1}(h(3)) = g^{-1}(1) = -1$ {since $g(-1) = 1$}

(c) $\left(h^{-1} \circ f \circ g^{-1}\right)(3) = h^{-1}\left(f\left(g^{-1}(3)\right)\right)$

$\qquad\qquad\qquad = h^{-1}(f(2)) \qquad \{\text{since } g(2) = 3\}$

$\qquad\qquad\qquad = h^{-1}(-1)$

$\qquad\qquad\qquad = 5 \qquad\qquad \{\text{since } -1 = 4 - x \;\Rightarrow\; x = 5\}$

**50** (a) $(g \circ f^{-1})(-1) = g(f^{-1}(-1)) = g(2) = 3$

(b) $(f^{-1} \circ g^{-1})(3) = f^{-1}(g^{-1}(3)) = f^{-1}(2) = 5$

(c) $(h^{-1} \circ g^{-1} \circ f)(6) = h^{-1}(g^{-1}(f(6))) = h^{-1}(g^{-1}(3)) = h^{-1}(2) = 2$ $\{\text{since } 2 = 4 - x \;\Rightarrow\; x = 2\}$

**51** (a) Remember that the domain of $f$ is the range of $f^{-1}$ and that the range of $f$ is the domain of $f^{-1}$.

(b) $D = [-1, 2];\ R = \left[\frac{1}{2}, 4\right]$ \qquad\qquad (c) $D_1 = R = \left[\frac{1}{2}, 4\right];\ R_1 = D = [-1, 2]$

*Figure 51*

*Figure 52*

**52** (b) $D = [1, 10];\ R = [0, 9]$ \qquad\qquad (c) $D_1 = R = [0, 9];\ R_1 = D = [1, 10]$

**53** (b) $D = [-3, 3];\ R = [-2, 2]$ \qquad\qquad (c) $D_1 = R = [-2, 2];\ R_1 = D = [-3, 3]$

*Figure 53*

*Figure 54*

**54** (b) $D = [0, 3];\ R = [-1, 1]$ \qquad\qquad (c) $D_1 = R = [-1, 1];\ R_1 = D = [0, 3]$

**55** (a) Since $f$ is one-to-one, an inverse exists. If $f(x) = ax + b$, then $f^{-1}(x) = \dfrac{x - b}{a}$ for $a \neq 0$.

(b) No, because a constant function is not one-to-one.

**56** (1) If $P(a, b)$ is on the graph of $f$, then $f(a) = b$.

$\qquad$ Also, $f^{-1}(f(a)) = f^{-1}(b)$ or $a = f^{-1}(b)$. So $Q(b, a)$ is on the graph of $f^{-1}$.

(2) $M_{PQ} = \left(\dfrac{a + b}{2}, \dfrac{b + a}{2}\right)$. Since the $x$ and $y$ coordinates are equal, the point is on the line $y = x$.

(3) $m_{PQ} = \dfrac{a - b}{b - a} = -1$ and the slope of the line $y = x$ is 1.

$\qquad$ Since the slopes of the lines are negative reciprocals of each other, the lines are perpendicular.

**57** (a) $f(x) = -x + b \Rightarrow y = -x + b \Rightarrow x = -y + b$, or $f^{-1}(x) = -x + b$.

(b) $f(x) = \dfrac{ax + b}{cx - a}$ for $c \neq 0 \Rightarrow y = \dfrac{ax + b}{cx - a} \Rightarrow cyx - ya = ax + b \Rightarrow$

$$cyx - ax = ay + b \Rightarrow x(cy - a) = ay + b \Rightarrow x = \frac{ay + b}{cy - a}, \text{ or } f^{-1}(x) = \frac{ax + b}{cx - a}.$$

(c) The graph of $f$ is symmetric about the line $y = x$. Thus, $f(x) = f^{-1}(x)$.

**58** (a) $f(x) = x^n$ for $x \geq 0$. • If $n$ is odd, then $y = x^n \Rightarrow x = y^{1/n}$. If $n$ is even, then $y = x^n \Rightarrow$

$$x = \pm y^{1/n} \text{ \{choose plus since } x \geq 0\text{\}}, \text{ or } f^{-1}(x) = x^{1/n}.$$

(b) $f(x) = x^{m/n}$ for $x \geq 0$ and $m$ any positive integer. •

$$y = x^{m/n} \Rightarrow y^n = x^m \Rightarrow x = y^{n/m} \text{ \{for the same reasons as in part (a)\}}.$$

**59** From the figure, we see that $f$ is always increasing. Thus, $f$ is one-to-one.

$[-6, 6]$ by $[-4, 4]$          $[-2, 2]$ by $[-2.5, 0.5]$

*Figure 59*          *Figure 60*

**60** From a graph of $f$, we see that $f$ is both decreasing and increasing near the point $(0, -2)$.
The horizontal line $y = -1.9$ will intersect the graph of $f$ more than once. Thus, $f$ is not one-to-one.

**61** (a) The high point is approximately $(-0.27, 3.31)$ and the low point is $(1.22, -0.20)$.

Thus, $f$ decreases and is one-to-one on $[-0.27, 1.22]$.

(b) The function $g$ is the same as $f$ with a limited domain. The domain of $g^{-1}$ is the same as the range of $g$, that is, $[-0.20, 3.31]$. The range of $g^{-1}$ is the same as the domain of $g$, that is, $[-0.27, 1.22]$.

$[-1, 2]$ by $[-1, 4]$          $[-2, 2]$ by $[-1.33, 1.33]$

*Figure 61*          *Figure 62*

**62** (a) The low point is approximately $(-1.27, -0.88)$ and the high point is $(1.31, 1.14)$.

Thus, $f$ increases and is one-to-one on $[-1.27, 1.31]$.

(b) Domain of $g^{-1}$ is $[-0.88, 1.14]$; range of $g^{-1}$ is $[-1.27, 1.31]$.

**63** The graph of $f$ will be reflected through the line $y = x$. $y = \sqrt[3]{x - 1} \Rightarrow y^3 = x - 1 \Rightarrow x = y^3 + 1 \Rightarrow$
$f^{-1}(x) = x^3 + 1$. Graph $Y_1 = \sqrt[3]{x - 1}$, $Y_2 = x^3 + 1$, and $Y_3 = x$.

[-12, 12] by [-8, 8]

*Figure 63*

[0, 12] by [0, 8]

*Figure 64*

**64** The graph of $f$ will be reflected through the line $y = x$. $y = 2(x-2)^2 + 3 \Rightarrow \dfrac{y-3}{2} = (x-2)^2 \Rightarrow$

$x - 2 = \pm\sqrt{\dfrac{y-3}{2}} \Rightarrow x = 2 \pm\sqrt{\dfrac{y-3}{2}}$. Let $f^{-1}(x) = 2 + \sqrt{\dfrac{x-3}{2}}$ since we must have $f^{-1}(x) \geq 2$.

Graph $Y_1 = \left(2(x-2)^2 + 3\right)/(x \geq 2)$, $Y_2 = 2 + \sqrt{\dfrac{x-3}{2}}$, and $Y_3 = x$.

**65** (a) $V(23) = 35(23) = 805 \ \text{ft}^3/\text{min}$

(b) $V^{-1}(x) = \frac{1}{35}x$. Given an air circulation of $x$ cubic feet per minute, $V^{-1}(x)$ computes the maximum number of people that should be in the restaurant at one time.

(c) $V^{-1}(2350) = \frac{1}{35}(2350) \approx 67.1 \Rightarrow$ the maximum number of people is 67.

**66** (a) [1945, 2005, 10] by [0, 13E3, 1E3]

(b) Use the two arbitrary points $(1950, 2773)$ and $(2000, 12{,}717)$ to determine $f$. $m = \frac{12{,}717 - 2773}{2000 - 1950} = \frac{9944}{50} = 198.88 \Rightarrow$

$y - 12{,}717 = 198.88(x - 2000) = 198.88x - 397{,}760 \Rightarrow$

$f(x) = 198.88x - 385{,}043$

(c) $y = 198.88x - 385{,}043 \Rightarrow \dfrac{y + 385{,}043}{198.88} = x \Rightarrow$

$f^{-1}(x) = \dfrac{x + 385{,}043}{198.88}$. $f^{-1}(x)$ computes the year when $x$ radio stations were on the air.

(d) $f^{-1}(11{,}987) = \frac{11{,}987 + 385{,}043}{198.88} \approx 1996.3$, which is slightly more than 1995.

## 4.2 Exercises

**1** $7^{x+6} = 7^{3x-4} \Rightarrow x + 6 = 3x - 4 \Rightarrow 10 = 2x \Rightarrow x = 5$

**2** $6^{7-x} = 6^{2x+1} \Rightarrow 7 - x = 2x + 1 \Rightarrow 6 = 3x \Rightarrow x = 2$

**3** $3^{2x+3} = 3^{(x^2)} \Rightarrow 2x + 3 = x^2 \Rightarrow x^2 - 2x - 3 = 0 \Rightarrow (x-3)(x+1) = 0 \Rightarrow x = -1, 3$

**4** $9^{(x^2)} = 3^{3x+2} \Rightarrow (3^2)^{(x^2)} = 3^{3x+2} \Rightarrow 3^{(2x^2)} = 3^{3x+2} \Rightarrow 2x^2 = 3x + 2 \Rightarrow 2x^2 - 3x - 2 = 0 \Rightarrow$

$(2x+1)(x-2) = 0 \Rightarrow x = -\frac{1}{2}, 2$

**5** We need to obtain the same base on each side of the equals sign, then we can apply part 2 of the theorem about exponential functions being one-to-one. $2^{-100x} = (0.5)^{x-4} \Rightarrow (2^{-1})^{100x} = \left(\frac{1}{2}\right)^{x-4} \Rightarrow$

$\left(\frac{1}{2}\right)^{100x} = \left(\frac{1}{2}\right)^{x-4} \Rightarrow 100x = x - 4 \Rightarrow 99x = -4 \Rightarrow x = -\frac{4}{99}$

**6** $\left(\frac{1}{2}\right)^{6-x} = 2 \Rightarrow \left(\frac{1}{2}\right)^{6-x} = \left(\frac{1}{2}\right)^{-1} \Rightarrow 6 - x = -1 \Rightarrow x = 7$

**7**   $25^{x-3} = 125^{4-x}$   $\Rightarrow$   $\left(5^2\right)^{x-3} = \left(5^3\right)^{4-x}$   $\Rightarrow$   $5^{2x-6} = 5^{12-3x}$   $\Rightarrow$   $2x - 6 = 12 - 3x$   $\Rightarrow$

$$5x = 18 \quad \Rightarrow \quad x = \tfrac{18}{5}$$

**8**   $27^{x-1} = 9^{2x-3}$   $\Rightarrow$   $\left(3^3\right)^{x-1} = \left(3^2\right)^{2x-3}$   $\Rightarrow$   $3^{3x-3} = 3^{4x-6}$   $\Rightarrow$   $3x - 3 = 4x - 6$   $\Rightarrow$   $x = 3$

**9**   $4^x \cdot \left(\tfrac{1}{2}\right)^{3-2x} = 8 \cdot \left(2^x\right)^2$   $\Rightarrow$   $2^{2x} \cdot \left(2^{-1}\right)^{3-2x} = 2^3 \cdot 2^{2x}$   $\Rightarrow$   $2^{2x-3+2x} = 2^{3+2x}$   $\Rightarrow$   $2^{4x-3} = 2^{2x+3}$   $\Rightarrow$

$$4x - 3 = 2x + 3 \quad \Rightarrow \quad 2x = 6 \quad \Rightarrow \quad x = 3$$

**10**   $9^{2x} \cdot \left(\tfrac{1}{3}\right)^{x+2} = 27 \cdot \left(3^x\right)^{-2}$   $\Rightarrow$   $3^{4x} \cdot \left(3^{-1}\right)^{x+2} = 3^3 \cdot 3^{-2x}$   $\Rightarrow$   $3^{4x-x-2} = 3^{3-2x}$   $\Rightarrow$   $3^{3x-2} = 3^{3-2x}$   $\Rightarrow$

$$3x - 2 = 3 - 2x \quad \Rightarrow \quad 5x = 5 \quad \Rightarrow \quad x = 1$$

**11** (a)   $f(x) = a^x + c$ with $a > 1$   $\bullet$   As $x$ gets very large, $y$ (or $f(x)$) increases without bound, so $y \to \infty$.

     (b)   As $x$ gets very large negative, $a^x$ gets close to 0, so $y$ (or $f(x)$) gets close to the horizontal asymptote, that is, $y \to c$.

**12** (a)   $f(x) = a^{-x} + c$ with $a > 1$   $\bullet$   As $x$ gets very large, $a^{-x}$ gets close to 0, so $y$ (or $f(x)$) gets close to the horizontal asymptote, that is, $y \to c$.

     (b)   As $x$ gets very large negative, $y$ (or $f(x)$) increases without bound, so $y \to \infty$.

**13** (a)   Let $g = f(x) = 2^x$ for reference purposes. The graph of $g$ goes through the points $\left(-1, \tfrac{1}{2}\right)$, $(0, 1)$, and $(1, 2)$.

     (b)   $f(x) = -2^x$   $\bullet$   Reflect $g$ through the $x$-axis since $f$ is just $-1 \cdot 2^x$. Do not confuse this function with $(-2)^x$—remember, the base is positive for exponential functions.

     (c)   $f(x) = 3 \cdot 2^x$   $\bullet$   vertically stretch $g$ by a factor of 3

Figure 13(a)

Figure 13(b)

Figure 13(c)

     (d)   $f(x) = 2^{x+3}$   $\bullet$   shift $g$ left 3 units since $f$ is $g(x + 3)$

     (e)   $f(x) = 2^x + 3$   $\bullet$   shift $g$ up 3 units

     (f)   $f(x) = 2^{x-3}$   $\bullet$   shift $g$ right 3 units since $f$ is $g(x - 3)$

Figure 13(d)

Figure 13(e)

Figure 13(f)

(g)  $f(x) = 2^x - 3$  •  shift $g$ down 3 units

(h)  $f(x) = 2^{-x}$  •  reflect $g$ through the $y$-axis since $f(x)$ is $g(-x)$

*Figure 13(g)*

*Figure 13(h)*

(i)  $f(x) = \left(\frac{1}{2}\right)^x$  •  $\left(\frac{1}{2}\right)^x = (2^{-1})^x = 2^{-x}$, same graph as in part (h)

(j)  $f(x) = 2^{3-x}$  •  $2^{3-x} = 2^{-(x-3)}$, shift $g$ right 3 units and reflect through the line $x = 3$.

   Alternatively, $2^{3-x} = 2^3 2^{-x} = 8\left(\frac{1}{2}\right)^x$, vertically stretch $y = \left(\frac{1}{2}\right)^x$ {the graph in part (i)} by a factor of 8.

*Figure 13(i)*

*Figure 13(j)*

**14** (a)  Let $F = f(x) = \left(\frac{1}{2}\right)^x$. This graph goes through $(-1, 2)$, $(0, 1)$, and $\left(1, \frac{1}{2}\right)$.

(b)  $f(x) = -\left(\frac{1}{2}\right)^x$  •  reflect $F$ through the $x$-axis

(c)  $f(x) = 3 \cdot \left(\frac{1}{2}\right)^x$  •  vertically stretch $F$ by a factor of 3

*Figure 14(a)*

*Figure 14(b)*

*Figure 14(c)*

(d) $f(x) = \left(\frac{1}{2}\right)^{x+3}$ • shift $F$ left 3 units

(e) $f(x) = \left(\frac{1}{2}\right)^{x} + 3$ • shift $F$ up 3 units

(f) $f(x) = \left(\frac{1}{2}\right)^{x-3}$ • shift $F$ right 3 units

Figure 14(d)

Figure 14(e)

Figure 14(f)

(g) $f(x) = \left(\frac{1}{2}\right)^{x} - 3$ • shift $F$ down 3 units

(h) $f(x) = \left(\frac{1}{2}\right)^{-x}$ • reflect $F$ through the $y$-axis

Figure 14(g)

Figure 14(h)

(i) $f(x) = \left(\dfrac{1}{1/2}\right)^{x}$ • $\left(\dfrac{1}{1/2}\right)^{x} = (2)^{x}$, same graph as in part (h) or Exercise 13(a)

(j) $f(x) = \left(\frac{1}{2}\right)^{3-x}$ • Since $\left(\frac{1}{2}\right)^{3-x} = \left(\frac{1}{2}\right)^{-(x-3)}$, we can shift $F$ right 3 units and reflect through the line $x = 3$.

Or, since $\left(\frac{1}{2}\right)^{3-x} = \left(\frac{1}{2}\right)^{3}\left(\frac{1}{2}\right)^{-x} = \frac{1}{8} \cdot 2^{x}$, we can vertically compress $y = 2^{x}$ by a factor of 8.

Figure 14(i)

Figure 14(j)

**15** $f(x) = \left(\frac{2}{5}\right)^{-x} = \left[\left(\frac{2}{5}\right)^{-1}\right]^x = \left(\frac{5}{2}\right)^x$ • goes through $\left(-1, \frac{2}{5}\right)$, $(0, 1)$, and $\left(1, \frac{5}{2}\right)$

*Figure 15*

*Figure 16*

**16** $f(x) = \left(\frac{2}{5}\right)^x$ • goes through $\left(-1, \frac{5}{2}\right)$, $(0, 1)$, and $\left(1, \frac{2}{5}\right)$

**17** $f(x) = 5\left(\frac{1}{2}\right)^x + 3$ • vertically stretch $y = \left(\frac{1}{2}\right)^x$ by a factor of 5 and shift up 3 units

*Figure 17*

*Figure 18*

**18** $f(x) = 8(4)^{-x} - 2$ • vertically stretch $y = \left(\frac{1}{4}\right)^x$ by a factor of 8 and shift down 2 units

**19** $f(x) = -\left(\frac{1}{2}\right)^x + 4$ • reflect $y = \left(\frac{1}{2}\right)^x$ through the $x$-axis and shift up 4 units

*Figure 19*

$y = 9$

*Figure 20*

**20** $f(x) = -3^{-x} + 9 = -\left(\frac{1}{3}\right)^x + 9$ • reflect $y = \left(\frac{1}{3}\right)^x$ through the $x$-axis and shift up 9 units

**21** $f(x) = -\left(\frac{1}{2}\right)^{-x} + 8$ • reflect $y = 2^x$ through the $x$-axis and shift up 8 units

$y = 8$

*Figure 21*

*Figure 22*

**22** $f(x) = -3^x + 9$ • reflect $y = 3^x$ through the $x$-axis and shift up 9 units

**23** $f(x) = 2^{|x|} = \begin{cases} 2^x & \text{if } x \geq 0 \\ 2^{-x} & \text{if } x < 0 \end{cases} = \begin{cases} 2^x & \text{if } x \geq 0 \\ \left(\frac{1}{2}\right)^x & \text{if } x < 0 \end{cases}$

Use the portion of $y = 2^x$ with $x \geq 0$ and reflect it through the $y$-axis since $f$ is even.

Figure 23

Figure 24

**24** $f(x) = 2^{-|x|} = \left(\frac{1}{2}\right)^{|x|}$ ● Use the portion of $y = \left(\frac{1}{2}\right)^x$ with $x \geq 0$ and reflect it through the $y$-axis since $f$ is even.

**Note:** For Exercises 25 and 26, refer to Example 6 in the text for the basic graph of

$$y = a^{-x^2} = (a^{-1})^{x^2} = \left(\frac{1}{a}\right)^{x^2}, \text{ where } a > 1.$$

**25** $f(x) = 3^{1-x^2} = 3^1 3^{-x^2} = 3\left(\frac{1}{3}\right)^{(x^2)}$ ● stretch $y = \left(\frac{1}{3}\right)^{(x^2)}$ by a factor of 3

Figure 25

Figure 26

**26** $f(x) = 2^{-(x+1)^2} = \left(\frac{1}{2}\right)^{(x+1)^2}$ ● shift $y = \left(\frac{1}{2}\right)^{x^2}$ left 1 unit

**27** $f(x) = 3^x + 3^{-x}$ ● Adding the functions $g(x) = 3^x$ and $h(x) = 3^{-x} = \left(\frac{1}{3}\right)^x$ together, we see that the $y$-intercept will be 2. If $x > 0$, $f$ looks like $y = 3^x$ since $3^x$ dominates $3^{-x}$ ($3^{-x}$ gets close to 0 and $3^x$ grows very large). If $x < 0$, $f$ looks like $y = 3^{-x}$ since $3^{-x}$ dominates $3^x$.

Figure 27

Figure 28

**28** $f(x) = 3^x - 3^{-x}$ ● if $x > 0$, $f$ looks like $y = 3^x$ since $0 < 3^{-x} < 1$;

if $x < 0$, $f$ looks like $y = -3^{-x}$ since $0 < 3^x < 1$

**29** The graph has a horizontal asymptote of $y = 0$, so $c = 0$ and the equation has the form $f(x) = ba^x$.
The point $(0, 2)$ is on the graph, so $f(0) = 2 \Rightarrow 2 = ba^0 \Rightarrow 2 = b(1) \Rightarrow 2 = b$, and hence, $f(x) = 2a^x$.
Since the point $P(1, 5)$ is on the graph, $f(1) = 5$. Thus, $5 = 2a^1 \Rightarrow a = \frac{5}{2}$, and the function is $f(x) = 2\left(\frac{5}{2}\right)^x$.

**30** The graph has a horizontal asymptote of $y = 0$, so $c = 0$ and the equation has the form $f(x) = ba^x$. The point
$\left(0, \frac{1}{2}\right)$ is on the graph, so $f(0) = \frac{1}{2} \Rightarrow \frac{1}{2} = ba^0 \Rightarrow \frac{1}{2} = b(1) \Rightarrow \frac{1}{2} = b$, and hence, $f(x) = \frac{1}{2}a^x$. Since
the point $P(-2, 8)$ is on the graph, $f(-2) = 8$. Thus, $8 = \frac{1}{2}a^{-2} \Rightarrow \frac{1}{a^2} = 16 \Rightarrow a^2 = \frac{1}{16} \Rightarrow a = \pm\frac{1}{4}$,
but $a$ must be positive, and the function is $f(x) = \frac{1}{2}\left(\frac{1}{4}\right)^x$.

**31** The graph has a horizontal asymptote of $y = -3$, so $c = -3$ and the equation has the form $f(x) = ba^x - 3$. The
point $(0, -1)$ is on the graph, so $f(0) = -1 \Rightarrow -1 = ba^0 - 3 \Rightarrow -1 = b(1) - 3 \Rightarrow 2 = b$, and hence,
$f(x) = 2a^x - 3$. Since the point $P(-1, 0)$ is on the graph, $f(-1) = 0$. Thus, $0 = 2a^{-1} - 3 \Rightarrow$
$3 = \frac{2}{a} \Rightarrow 3a = 2 \Rightarrow a = \frac{2}{3}$, and the function is $f(x) = 2\left(\frac{2}{3}\right)^x - 3$.

**32** The graph has a horizontal asymptote of $y = 1$, so $c = 1$ and the equation has the form $f(x) = ba^x + 1$. The point
$(0, 5)$ is on the graph, so $f(0) = 5 \Rightarrow 5 = ba^0 + 1 \Rightarrow 4 = b$, and hence, $f(x) = 4a^x + 1$. Since the point
$P(1, 7)$ is on the graph, $f(1) = 7$. Thus, $7 = 4a^1 + 1 \Rightarrow 6 = 4a \Rightarrow a = \frac{3}{2}$, and the function is
$f(x) = 4\left(\frac{3}{2}\right)^x + 1$.

**33** Since the $y$-intercept is 8, we must have $f(0) = 8$. $f(x) = ba^x$, so $f(0) = 8 \Rightarrow 8 = ba^0 \Rightarrow 8 = b(1) \Rightarrow$
$8 = b$, and hence, $f(x) = 8a^x$. Since the point $P(3, 1)$ is on the graph, $f(3) = 1$.
$$\text{Thus, } 1 = 8a^3 \Rightarrow a^3 = \tfrac{1}{8} \Rightarrow a = \tfrac{1}{2}, \text{ and the function is } f(x) = 8\left(\tfrac{1}{2}\right)^x.$$

**34** $f(x) = ba^x$ and $f(0) = 5 \Rightarrow 5 = ba^0 \Rightarrow 5 = b \Rightarrow f(x) = 5a^x$.
$$f(2) = \tfrac{5}{16} \Rightarrow \tfrac{5}{16} = 5a^2 \Rightarrow a^2 = \tfrac{1}{16} \Rightarrow a = \tfrac{1}{4} \, \{a > 0\}. \text{ Thus, } f(x) = 5\left(\tfrac{1}{4}\right)^x.$$

**35** The horizontal asymptote is $y = 32$, so $f(x) = ba^{-x} + c$ has the form $f(x) = ba^{-x} + 32$. The $y$-intercept is 212,
so $f(0) = 212 \Rightarrow 212 = ba^{-0} + 32 \Rightarrow 212 = b(1) + 32 \Rightarrow 180 = b \Rightarrow f(x) = 180a^{-x} + 32$.
The function passes through the point $P(2, 112)$, so $f(2) = 112 \Rightarrow 112 = 180a^{-2} + 32 \Rightarrow$
$80 = 180a^{-2} \Rightarrow 80 = \frac{180}{a^2} \Rightarrow a^2 = \frac{180}{80} \Rightarrow a^2 = \frac{9}{4} \Rightarrow$
$$a = \tfrac{3}{2} \, \{\text{since } a \text{ must be positive, } a = -\tfrac{3}{2} \text{ is not allowed}\} \Rightarrow f(x) = 180(1.5)^{-x} + 32.$$

**36** The horizontal asymptote is $y = 72$, so $f(x) = ba^{-x} + c$ has the form $f(x) = ba^{-x} + 72$.
$f(0) = 425 \Rightarrow 425 = ba^{-0} + 72 \Rightarrow 353 = b$, so $f(x) = 353a^{-x} + 72$. $f(1) = 248.5 \Rightarrow$
$$248.5 = 353a^{-1} + 72 \Rightarrow 176.5 = \tfrac{353}{a} \Rightarrow a = \tfrac{353}{176.5} = 2 \Rightarrow f(x) = 353(2)^{-x} + 72.$$

**37** (a) $N(t) = 100(0.9)^t \Rightarrow N(5) = 100(0.9)^5 \approx 59$ elk

(b) In general, $N(t + 1)$ is the number of elk alive one year after $N(t)$.

So the percentage of elk *alive* after one year is $\dfrac{N(t+1)}{N(t)} = \dfrac{100(0.9)^{t+1}}{100(0.9)^t} = 0.9$; that is, 90% lives, or 10% dies.

**38** (a) $A(t) = 10(0.8)^t \Rightarrow A(8) = 10(0.8)^8 \approx 1.68$ mg

(b) In general, $A(t + 1)$ is the amount in the body one hour after $A(t)$.

So the percentage of the drug still in the body after one hour is
$$\dfrac{A(t+1)}{A(t)} = \dfrac{10(0.8)^{t+1}}{10(0.8)^t} = 0.8; \text{ that is, 80\% remains, or 20\% is eliminated.}$$

**39** (a) $f(t) = 600(3)^{t/2}$ • 8:00 A.M. corresponds to $t = 1$ and $f(1) = 600\sqrt{3} \approx 1039$.

10:00 A.M. corresponds to $t = 3$ and $f(3) = 600\left(3\sqrt{3}\right) = 1800\sqrt{3} \approx 3118$.

11:00 A.M. corresponds to $t = 4$ and $f(4) = 600(9) = 5400$.

(b) The graph of $f$ is an increasing exponential that passes through $(0, 600)$ and the points in part (a).

*Figure 39*

*Figure 40*

**40** (a) 2:00 P.M. corresponds to $t = 1$ and $f(1) = 87.5°$.

3:30 P.M. corresponds to $t = \frac{5}{2}$ and $f\left(\frac{5}{2}\right) = 76.5625 \approx 76.6°$.

4:00 P.M. corresponds to $t = 3$ and $f(3) = 75.78125 \approx 75.8°$.

(b) The endpoints are $(0, 125)$ and $(4, \approx 75.2)$.

**41** (a) $f(t) = 100(2)^{-t/5}$, so $f(5) = 100(2)^{-1} = 50$ mg, $f(10) = 100(2)^{-2} = 25$ mg,

and $f(12.5) = 100(2)^{-2.5} = \frac{100}{4\sqrt{2}} = \frac{25}{2}\sqrt{2} \approx 17.7$ mg.

(b) The endpoints of this decreasing exponential are $(0, 100)$ and $(30, 1.5625)$.

*Figure 41*

*Figure 42*

*Figure 44*

**42** (a) $I(x) = 10(0.4)^x \Rightarrow I(2) = 10(0.4)^2 = 1.6$ calories/cm²/sec

(b) The endpoints are $(0, 10)$ and $(5, 0.1024)$.

**43** A half-life of 1600 years means that when $t = 1600$, the amount remaining, $q(t)$, will be one-half the original amount—that is, $\frac{1}{2}q_0$. $q(t) = \frac{1}{2}q_0$ when $t = 1600 \Rightarrow$

$$\tfrac{1}{2}q_0 = q_0 2^{k(1600)} \Rightarrow 2^{-1} = 2^{1600k} \Rightarrow 1600k = -1 \Rightarrow k = -\tfrac{1}{1600}.$$

**44** See *Figure 44* above. The endpoints of the graph of $q(t) = 10\left(\frac{4}{5}\right)^t$ are $(0, 10)$ and $(10, \approx 1.07)$.

**45** Using $A = P\left(1 + \dfrac{r}{n}\right)^{nt}$, we have $P = 1000$, $r = 0.07$, and $n = 12$.

Consider $A$ to be a function of $t$; that is, $A(t) = 1000\left(1 + \frac{0.07}{12}\right)^{12t}$.

(a) $A\left(\frac{1}{12}\right) \approx \$1005.83$         (b) $A\left(\frac{6}{12}\right) \approx \$1035.51$

(c) $A(1) \approx \$1072.29$                   (d) $A(20) \approx \$4,038.74$

**46** $A = 5000 \Rightarrow 5000 = P\left(1 + \dfrac{0.03}{2}\right)^{2 \cdot 1} \Rightarrow P = \dfrac{5000}{(1.015)^2} \approx \$4853.31$

**47** $C = 25{,}000 \Rightarrow V(t) = 0.78(25{,}000)(0.85)^{t-1} = 19{,}500(0.85)^{t-1}$

    (a) $V(1) = \$19{,}500$      (b) $V(4) \approx \$11{,}975.44$, or $\$11{,}975$      (c) $V(7) \approx \$7354.42$, or $\$7354$

**48** $V = P(1.04)^t$  •  The year 2016 corresponds to $t = 2016 - 1986 = 30$.

    $P = 80{,}000 \Rightarrow V = 80{,}000(1.04)^{30} \approx \$259{,}471.80$, which is $\$259{,}000$ to the nearest $\$1000$.

**49** $t = 2012 - 1626 = 386;\ A = \$24(1 + 0.06/4)^{4 \cdot 386} \approx \$231{,}089{,}639{,}204.11$. That's right—$\$231$ billion!

**50** $P = 500$, $r = 0.24$, and $n = 12 \Rightarrow A = 500\left(1 + \frac{0.24}{12}\right)^{12 \cdot 1} = 500(1.02)^{12} \approx \$634.12$

**51** (a) Examine the pattern formed by the value $y$ in the year $n$.

| Year ($n$) | Value ($y$) |
|---|---|
| 0 | $y_0$ |
| 1 | $(1-a)y_0 = y_1$ |
| 2 | $(1-a)y_1 = (1-a)\left[(1-a)y_0\right] = (1-a)^2 y_0 = y_2$ |
| 3 | $(1-a)y_2 = (1-a)\left[(1-a)^2 y_0\right] = (1-a)^3 y_0 = y_3$ |

    (b) $s = (1-a)^T y_0 \Rightarrow (1-a)^T = s/y_0 \Rightarrow 1 - a = \sqrt[T]{s/y_0} \Rightarrow a = 1 - \sqrt[T]{s/y_0}$

**52** (a) $t = \dfrac{100}{1000} = \dfrac{1}{10}$ millennium and

       $N\left(\frac{1}{10}\right) = N_0(0.805)^{1/10} \approx 0.9785\,N_0$.

       This is a 97.85% retention, or a 2.15% loss.

    (b) The endpoints are $(0, 200)$ and $(5, \approx 67.61)$.

**53** (a) $M = \dfrac{Lrk}{12(k-1)}$ and $k = \left(1 + \dfrac{r}{12}\right)^{12t}$  •  $r = 0.08$, $t = 30$, $L = 250{,}000 \Rightarrow$

                     $k = \left(1 + \dfrac{0.08}{12}\right)^{12 \cdot 30} \approx 10.93573$ and $M = \dfrac{250{,}000(0.08)k}{12(k-1)} \approx \$1834.41$.

    (b) Total interest paid $=$ total of payments $-$ original loan amount

               $= (12 \cdot 30 \text{ payments}) \times \$1834.41 - \$250{,}000 = \$410{,}387.60$

**54** $r = 0.07$, $t = 25$, $M = 1500 \Rightarrow k = \left(1 + \frac{0.07}{12}\right)^{12 \cdot 25} \approx 5.72542$.

               $M = \dfrac{Lrk}{12(k-1)} \Rightarrow L = \dfrac{12M(k-1)}{rk} = \dfrac{12(1500)(k-1)}{(0.07)k} \approx \$212{,}230.36$.

**55** $r = 0.10$, $t = 3$, $M = 500 \Rightarrow k = \left(1 + \frac{0.10}{12}\right)^{12 \cdot 3} \approx 1.34818$.

               $M = \dfrac{Lrk}{12(k-1)} \Rightarrow L = \dfrac{12M(k-1)}{rk} = \dfrac{12(500)(k-1)}{(0.10)k} \approx \$15{,}495.62$.

**56** (a) $r = 0.075$, $t = 2$, $L = 3000 \Rightarrow k = \left(1 + \dfrac{0.075}{12}\right)^{12 \cdot 2} \approx 1.16129$ and $M = \dfrac{3000(0.075)k}{12(k-1)} \approx \$135.00$.

    (b) Total interest paid $=$ total of payments $-$ original loan amount

               $= (12 \cdot 2 \text{ payments}) \times \$135.00 - \$3000 = \$240.00$

**57** (a) $f(x) = 13^{\sqrt{x+1.1}} \Rightarrow f(3) = 13^{\sqrt{3+1.1}} \approx 180.1206$

    (b) $h(x) = (2^x + 2^{-x})^{2x} \Rightarrow h(1.06) = (2^{1.06} + 2^{-1.06})^{2(1.06)} \approx 7.3639$

**58** (a) $f(x) = 2^{\sqrt{1-x}} \;\Rightarrow\; f(0.5) = 2^{\sqrt{1-0.5}} \approx 1.6325$

(b) $h(x) = \dfrac{3^{-x}+5}{3^x-16} \;\Rightarrow\; h(1.4) = \dfrac{3^{-1.4}+5}{3^{1.4}-16} \approx -0.4597$

**59** Part (b) may be interpreted as doubling an investment at 8.5%.

(a) If $y = (1.085)^x$ and $x = 40$, then $y \approx 26.13$.　　(b) If $y = 2$, then $x \approx 8.50$.

$[0,60,5]$ by $[0,40,5]$　　　　$[0,60,5]$ by $[0,40,5]$

*Figure 59*　　　　　　*Figure 60*

**60** Compare the doubling time in part (b) with the result in Exercise 59(b).

(a) If $y = (1.0525)^x$ and $x = 40$, then $y \approx 7.74$.　　(b) If $y = 2$, then $x \approx 13.55$.

**61** First graph $y = 1.4x^2 - 2.2^x - 1$. The $x$-intercepts are the roots of the equation.

Using a zero or root feature, the roots are $x \approx -1.02, 2.14,$ and $3.62$.

$[-10.5, 10.5]$ by $[-7,7]$　　　　$[-10.5, 10.5]$ by $[-7,7]$

*Figure 61*　　　　　　*Figure 62*

**62** First graph $y = 1.21^{3x} + 1.4^{-1.1x} - 2x - 0.5$. The $x$-intercepts are the roots of the equation.

Using a zero or root feature, the roots are $x \approx 0.97$ and $3.41$.

**63** (a) $f$ is not one-to-one since the horizontal line $y = -0.1$ intersects the graph of $f$ more than once.

(b) The only zero of $f$ is $x = 0$.

$[-3,3]$ by $[-2,2]$　　　　$[-4,4]$ by $[-2.7, 2.7]$

*Figure 63*　　　　　　*Figure 64*

**64** (a) On older calculator models, rewrite $f(x) = \pi^{0.6x} - 1.3^{(x^{1.8})}$ as $f(x) = \pi^{0.6x} - 1.3^{(x^{9/5})}$.

$f$ is not one-to-one since the horizontal line $y = 1$ intersects the graph of $f$ more than once.

(b) The zeros of $f$ are $x \approx -3.33, 0,$ and $3.33$.

65 (a) The low points are about $(-3.37, -1.79)$ and $(0.52, 0.71)$. The high point is approximately $(-1.19, 1.94)$.

Thus, $f$ is increasing on $[-3.37, -1.19]$ and $[0.52, 1]$. $f$ is decreasing on $[-4, -3.37]$ and $[-1.19, 0.52]$.

(b) The range of $f$ on $[-4, 1]$ is approximately $[-1.79, 1.94]$.

$[-4, 1]$ by $[-2, 3]$

*Figure 65*

$[-3, 3]$ by $[-2, 2]$

*Figure 66*

66 (a) $f$ is increasing on $[-3, -1]$ and $[1.11, 3]$. $f$ is decreasing on $[-1, 1.11]$.

(b) The range of $f$ on $[-3, 3]$ is approximately $[-0.69, 0.62]$.

67 The figure shows a graph of $N(t) = 1000(0.9)^t$.

By using an intersect feature, we can determine that $N = 500$ when $t \approx 6.58$ yr.

$[0, 10]$ by $[0, 1000, 100]$

*Figure 67*

$[0, 20]$ by $[0, 1, 0.1]$

*Figure 68*

68 From a graph of $B(t) = (0.95)^t$, we determine that $B = 0.5$ when $t \approx 13.51$ yr.

69 Graph $y = 4(0.125)^{(0.25^x)}$. The line $y = k = 4$ is a horizontal asymptote for the Gompertz function.

The maximum number of sales of the product approaches $k$.

$[0, 7.5]$ by $[0, 5]$

*Figure 69*

$[0, 7.5]$ by $[0, 5]$

*Figure 70*

70 Graph $y = \dfrac{1}{0.25 + 0.125(0.625)^x}$. The line $y = 1/k = 4$ is a horizontal asymptote for the logistic function. The maximum number of sales of the product approaches $1/k$.

71 Using an intersect feature, we determine that $A = \dfrac{100\left(1 + \frac{0.05}{12}\right)\left[\left(1 + \frac{0.05}{12}\right)^{12n} - 1\right]}{\frac{0.05}{12}}$ and $A = 100,000$ intersect

when $n \approx 32.8$.

[0, 40, 10] by [0, 200,000, 50,000]                    [0, 40, 10] by [0, 2E5, 5E4]

Figure 71                                    Figure 72

**72** Using an intersect feature, we determine that $A = \dfrac{250\left(1 + \frac{0.09}{12}\right)\left[\left(1 + \frac{0.09}{12}\right)^{12n} - 1\right]}{\frac{0.09}{12}}$ and $A = 100{,}000$ intersect

when $n \approx 15.4$.

**73** (a) Let $x = 0$ correspond to 1910, $x = 20$ to 1930, ..., and $x = 90$ to 2000.

Graph the data together with the functions

$\qquad$ **(1)** $f(x) = 0.786(1.094)^x$ and **(2)** $g(x) = 0.503x^2 - 27.3x + 149.2$.

[−10, 100, 10] by [−200, 2200, 1000]          [−10, 100, 10] by [−200, 2200, 1000]

Figure 73(a)                                 Figure 73(c)

(b) The exponential function $f$ best models the data.

(c) Graph $Y_1 = f(x)$ and $Y_2 = 1000$. The graphs intersect at $x \approx 79$, or in 1989.

**74** (a) Change the date in the table to the number of days after August 12. Graph the data together with the functions

$$f(t) = 653(1.028)^t \quad \text{and} \quad g(t) = 54{,}700e^{-(t-200)^2/7500}.$$

| $t$ (days) | 0 | 28 | 56 | 84 | 112 | 140 | 168 |
|---|---|---|---|---|---|---|---|
| New cases | 506 | 1289 | 3487 | 9597 | 18,817 | 33,835 | 47,191 |

[0, 400, 100] by [0, 6E4, 1E4]               [0, 400, 100] by [0, 6E4, 1E4]

Figure 74(a)                                 Figure 74(b)

(b) The function $g$ models Farr's prediction better than $f$ since the graph of $g$ attains a maximum and then decreases.

(c) The maximum number of new cases occurred 200 days after August 12, which is February 28, 1841. After this date, the number of new cases decreased.

**75** The model is $y = 0.04b^t$, with $t = 0$ corresponding to 1958. The year 2009 corresponds to $t = 2009 - 1958 = 51$, so $0.44 = 0.04b^{51}$ $\Rightarrow$ $\frac{44}{4} = b^{51}$ $\Rightarrow$ $b = \sqrt[51]{11} \approx 1.0481$. The model is $y = 0.04(1.0481)^t$. Using $t = 2020 - 1958 = 62$, we predict the cost of a first-class stamp in 2020 will be $0.04(1.0481)^{62} \approx 0.7363$, or 74¢.

**76** (a) Plot the points with the form (Year − 1967, Cost): $(0, 42)$, $(10, 125)$, $(20, 600)$, $(30, 1200)$, and $(40, 2600)$.

(b) The model is $y = 42b^x$, with $x = 0$ corresponding to 1967. The year 2007 corresponds to $x = 2007 - 1967 = 40$, so $2600 = 42b^{40}$ $\Rightarrow$ $\frac{2600}{42} = b^{40}$ $\Rightarrow$ $b = \sqrt[40]{\frac{2600}{42}} \approx 1.1086$. The model is $y = 42\left(\sqrt[40]{\frac{2600}{42}}\right)^x$.

(c) The year 2002 corresponds to $t = 2002 - 1967 = 35$, so $y = 42\left(\sqrt[40]{\frac{2600}{42}}\right)^{35} \approx 1552.415$. The model predicts the cost of a 30-second commercial in 2002 to be $1,552,415 compared to the actual cost of $1,900,000.

$[-10, 50, 10]$ by $[-500, 3000, 1000]$

*Figure 76*

**77** (a) $t = 1999 - 1974 = 25$ and $r/n$ is 0.0025, so $A = P\left(1 + \dfrac{r}{n}\right)^{nt} = \$353{,}022(1 + 0.0025)^{12 \cdot 25} = \$746{,}648.43$;

the website gives $1,192,971.

(b) Let $r$ denote the annual interest rate. $\$6{,}616{,}585 = \$353{,}022\left(1 + \dfrac{r}{1}\right)^{1 \cdot 25}$ $\Rightarrow$ $\dfrac{6{,}616{,}585}{353{,}022} = (1 + r)^{25}$ $\Rightarrow$ $1 + r = \sqrt[25]{\dfrac{6{,}616{,}585}{353{,}022}}$ $\Rightarrow$ $r = \sqrt[25]{\dfrac{6{,}616{,}585}{353{,}022}} - 1 \approx 0.1244$, so $r$ is about 12.44%.

(c) In part (a), the base is constant and the variable is in the exponent, so this is an *exponential* function.

In part (b), the base is variable and the exponent is constant, so this is a *polynomial* function.

**78** The model is $y = 37.80b^t$, with $t = 0$ corresponding to 1970. The year 2000 corresponds to $t = 2000 - 1970 = 30$, so $168.80 = 37.80b^{30}$ $\Rightarrow$ $\frac{1688}{378} = b^{30}$ $\Rightarrow$ $b = \sqrt[30]{\frac{1688}{378}} \approx 1.0511$. The model is $y = 37.80\left(\sqrt[30]{\frac{1688}{378}}\right)^t$ or $y = 37.80(1.0511)^t$. Using $t = 2020 - 1970 = 50$, we predict the value of the CPI in 2020 will be $37.80\left(\sqrt[30]{\frac{1688}{378}}\right)^{50} \approx 457.75$, or $457.75.

## 4.3 Exercises

**Note:** Examine Figure 1 in this section to reinforce the idea that $y = e^x$ is just a special case of $y = a^x$ with $a > 1$.

**1** (a) $f(x) = e^{-x}$ • reflect $y = e^x$ through the $y$-axis

(b) $f(x) = -e^x$ • reflect $y = e^x$ through the $x$-axis

*Figure 1(a)*

*Figure 1(b)*

**2** (a) $f(x) = e^{2x} = (e^x)^2$ • square the $y$ values of $y = e^x$

(b) $f(x) = 2e^x$ • vertically stretch $y = e^x$ by a factor of 2

*Figure 2(a)*

*Figure 2(b)*

**3** (a) $f(x) = e^{x+4}$ • shift $y = e^x$ left 4 units

(b) $f(x) = e^x + 4$ • shift $y = e^x$ up 4 units

*Figure 3(a)*

*Figure 3(b)*

**4** (a) $f(x) = e^{-2x}$ • reflect $y = e^x$ through the $y$-axis and square the $y$ values

(b) $f(x) = -2e^x$ • reflect $y = e^x$ through the $x$-axis and double the $y$ values

*Figure 4(a)*

*Figure 4(b)*

**5** $A = Pe^{rt}$ • With $P = 1000$, $r = 5\frac{1}{4}$, and $t = 5$, $A = 1000e^{(0.0525)(5)} \approx \$1300.18$.

**6** $A = Pe^{rt}$ • With $P = 100$, $r = 3\frac{1}{2}$, and $t = 10$, $A = 100e^{(0.035)(10)} \approx \$141.91$.

**7** $A = Pe^{rt}$ • $100,000 = Pe^{(0.034)(18)} \Rightarrow P = \dfrac{100,000}{e^{0.612}} \approx \$54,226.53$

**8** $A = Pe^{rt}$ • $15,000 = Pe^{(0.045)(4)} \Rightarrow P = \dfrac{15,000}{e^{0.18}} \approx \$12,529.05$

**9** $4055 = 1000e^{(r)(20)} \Rightarrow e^{20r} = 4.055$. Using a trial and error approach on a scientific calculator or tracing and zooming or an intersect feature on a graphing calculator, we determine that $e^x \approx 4.055$ if $x \approx 1.4$. Thus, $20r = 1.4$ and $r = 0.07$ or 7%.

**10** $890.20 = 400e^{(r)(16)} \Rightarrow e^{16r} = 2.2255$. As in Exercise 9, $e^x = 2.2255$ if $x \approx 0.8$.

Thus, $16r = 0.8$ and $r = 0.05$ or 5%.

**11** $e^{(x^2)} = e^{7x-12} \Rightarrow x^2 = 7x - 12 \Rightarrow x^2 - 7x + 12 = 0 \Rightarrow (x-3)(x-4) = 0 \Rightarrow x = 3, 4$

**12** $e^{3x} = e^{2x-1} \Rightarrow 3x = 2x - 1 \Rightarrow x = -1$

**13** $(e^x + 1)(ex - 1) = 0 \Rightarrow e^x = -1$ {but $e^x > 0$} or $ex = 1 \Rightarrow x = 1/e$

**14** $e^x(x + e) \Rightarrow e^x = 0$ {but $e^x > 0$} or $x + e = 0 \Rightarrow x = -e$

**15** $xe^x + e^x = 0 \Rightarrow e^x(x + 1) = 0 \Rightarrow x = -1$ {Note that $e^x \neq 0$.}

**16** $-x^2e^{-x} + 2xe^{-x} = 0 \Rightarrow xe^{-x}(-x + 2) = 0 \Rightarrow x = 0, 2$ {Note that $e^{-x} \neq 0$.}

**17** $x^3(4e^{4x}) + 3x^2e^{4x} = 0 \Rightarrow x^2e^{4x}(4x + 3) = 0 \Rightarrow x = -\frac{3}{4}, 0$ {Note that $e^{4x} \neq 0$.}

**18** $x^2(2e^{2x}) + 2xe^{2x} + e^{2x} + 2xe^{2x} = 0 \Rightarrow e^{2x}(2x^2 + 4x + 1) = 0 \Rightarrow x = -1 \pm \frac{1}{2}\sqrt{2}$ {Note that $e^{2x} \neq 0$.}

**19** When we multiply $(e^x + e^{-x})$ times $(e^x + e^{-x})$, we get

$e^{x+x} + e^{x+(-x)} + e^{(-x)+x} + e^{(-x)+(-x)} = e^{2x} + e^0 + e^0 + e^{-2x} = e^{2x} + 2 + e^{-2x}$. Using this gives us

$\dfrac{(e^x + e^{-x})(e^x + e^{-x}) - (e^x - e^{-x})(e^x - e^{-x})}{(e^x + e^{-x})^2} = \dfrac{(e^{2x} + 2 + e^{-2x}) - (e^{2x} - 2 + e^{-2x})}{(e^x + e^{-x})^2} = \dfrac{4}{(e^x + e^{-x})^2}$.

**20** $\dfrac{(e^x - e^{-x})^2 - (e^x + e^{-x})^2}{(e^x + e^{-x})^2} = \dfrac{(e^{2x} - 2 + e^{-2x}) - (e^{2x} + 2 + e^{-2x})}{(e^x + e^{-x})^2} = \dfrac{-4}{(e^x + e^{-x})^2}$

**21** $W(t) = W_0e^{kt}$ • $t = 30 \Rightarrow W(30) = 68e^{(0.2)(30)} \approx 27,433$ mg, or 27.43 grams

**22** $W(t) = W_0e^{kt}$ • $W(10) = W_0e^{(0.21)(10)} = 575 \Rightarrow W_0 = \dfrac{575}{e^{2.1}} \approx 70.41$ mg

**23** The year 2020 corresponds to $t = 2020 - 1980 = 40$. Using the law of growth formula, $q = q_0e^{rt}$, with $q_0 = 231$ and $r = 0.0103$, we have $N(t) = 231e^{0.0103t}$. Thus, $N(40) = 231e^{(0.0103)(40)} = 231e^{0.412} \approx 348.8$ million.

**24** The year 2015 corresponds to $t = 2015 - 1985 = 30$. Using the law of growth formula, $q = q_0 e^{rt}$, with $q_0 = 766$ and $r = 0.0182$, we have $N(t) = 766 e^{0.0182t}$. Thus, $N(30) = 766 e^{(0.0182)(30)} = 766 e^{0.546} \approx 1{,}322$ million.

**25** (a) Use the decay formula $q = q_0 e^{rt}$ with initial quantity $q_0$, rate of decay $r = -0.0525$, and time $t = 26.4$ hours. The amount remaining after 26.4 hours is $q_0 e^{-0.0525(26.4)} = q_0 e^{-1.386} \approx 0.25 q_0$, which is 25% of the initial amount.

(b) Since 25% of the initial amount remains after 26.4 hours, 50% remained after one-half that amount of time, or 13.2 hours.

**26** (a) Use the decay formula $q = q_0 e^{rt}$ with initial quantity $q_0$, rate of decay $r = -0.0462$, and time $t = 30$ hours. The amount remaining after 30 hours is $q_0 e^{-0.0462(30)} = q_0 e^{-1.386} \approx 0.25 q_0$, which is 25% of the initial amount.

(b) Since 25% of the initial amount remains after 30 hours, 50% remained after one-half that amount of time, or 15 hours.

**27** $N(t) = N_0 e^{-0.2t} \Rightarrow N(10) = N_0 e^{-2}$. The percentage of the original number still alive after 10 years is $\left( \dfrac{N(10)}{N_0} \right) \times 100 = \left( \dfrac{N_0 e^{-2}}{N_0} \right) \times 100 = 100 e^{-2} \approx 13.5\%$.

**28** (a) $A(t) = A_0 e^{-0.0249t}$ • $A_0 = 35, t = 2 \Rightarrow A(2) = 35 e^{-0.0498} \approx 33.3$ units are available.

(b) $A(t) = 35, t = 2 \Rightarrow 35 = A_0 e^{-0.0498} \Rightarrow A_0 = 35 e^{0.0498} \approx 36.8$ units should be shipped.

**29** $N(t) = 4500 e^{-0.1345t}$ • The year 2015 corresponds to $t = 2015 - 1980 = 35$.
$$N(35) = 4500 e^{(-0.1345 \cdot 35)} \approx 40.6 \approx 41.$$

**30** (a) $f(t) = a\left(1 - b e^{-kt}\right)$ • $f(10) = 200\left(1 - 0.956 e^{-0.18(10)}\right) \approx 168.4$ cm

(b) $f(0) = 8.8$ cm. As $t \to \infty$, $0.956 e^{-0.18t} \to 0$, and $f(t) \to 200$ cm.

**31** (a) $p = 29 e^{-0.000\,034h}$ • $h = 30{,}000 \Rightarrow p = 29 e^{(-0.000\,034)(30{,}000)} = 29 e^{(-1.02)} \approx 10.46$ in.

(b) $h = 40{,}000 \Rightarrow p = 29 e^{(-0.000\,034)(40{,}000)} = 29 e^{(-1.36)} \approx 7.44$ in.

**32** $A = c e^{-0.00495t}$ • Consider $A$ to be a function of $t$ with $c = 50$, so $A(t) = 50 e^{-0.00495t}$.

(a) $A(30) = 50 e^{-0.00495(30)} = 50 e^{-0.1485} \approx 43.10$ mg

(b) $A(180) = 50 e^{-0.00495(180)} = 50 e^{-0.891} \approx 20.51$ mg

(c) $A(365) = 50 e^{-0.00495(365)} = 50 e^{-1.80675} \approx 8.21$ mg

**33** $y = 79.041 + 6.39x - e^{3.261 - 0.993x}$ • $x = 1 \Rightarrow y = 79.041 + 6.39(1) - e^{3.261 - 0.993(1)} \approx 75.77$ cm.
$R = 6.39 + 0.993 e^{3.261 - 0.993x}$ • $x = 1 \Rightarrow R = 6.39 + 0.993 e^{3.261 - 0.993(1)} \approx 15.98$ cm/yr.

**34** (a) As $t$ increases, $e^{-at} \to 0$ and $s \approx \dfrac{v_0}{a}$.    (b) $s \approx \dfrac{v_0}{a} = \dfrac{10}{8 \times 10^5} = 1.25 \times 10^{-5}$ m.

**35** $2020 - 1971 = 49 \Rightarrow t = 49$ years. Using the continuously compounded interest formula with
$$P = 1.60 \text{ and } r = 0.05, \text{ we have } A = 1.60 e^{(0.05)(49)} \approx \$18.54 \text{ per hour.}$$

**36** Let $P$ denote the cost of one acre in 1867. $P = \left( \dfrac{\$7{,}200{,}000}{586{,}400 \text{ mi}^2} \right) \left( \dfrac{1 \text{ mi}^2}{640 \text{ acres}} \right) (1 \text{ acre}) \approx \$0.02$.
$$2020 - 1867 = 153 \Rightarrow t = 153 \text{ years. } A = P e^{(0.03)(153)} = P e^{4.59} \approx \$1.89.$$

**37** (a) $r = 7$, quarterly • Note here that the amount of money invested is not of interest and that we are only concerned with the percent of growth. $\left(1 + \frac{0.07}{4}\right)^{4 \cdot 1} \approx 1.0719$. $(1.0719 - 1) \times 100\% = 7.19\%$

(b) $r = 7$, continuously • $e^{(0.07)(1)} \approx 1.0725$. $(1.0725 - 1) \times 100\% = 7.25\%$. The results indicate that we would receive an extra 0.06% in interest by investing our money in an account that is compounded continuously rather than quarterly. This is only an extra 6 cents on a $100 investment, but $600 extra on a $1,000,000 investment (actually $649.15 if the computations are carried beyond 0.01%).

**38** (a) $r = 12$, quarterly • $\left(1 + \frac{0.12}{4}\right)^{4 \cdot 1} \approx 1.1255$. $(1.1255 - 1) \times 100\% = 12.55\%$

(b) $r = 12$, continuously • $e^{(0.12)(1)} \approx 1.1275$. $(1.1275 - 1) \times 100\% = 12.75\%$

**39** (a) $r = 5$, quarterly • $\left(1 + \frac{0.05}{4}\right)^{4 \cdot 1} \approx 1.0509$. $(1.0509 - 1) \times 100\% = 5.09\%$

(b) $r = 5$, continuously • $e^{(0.05)(1)} \approx 1.0513$. $(1.0513 - 1) \times 100\% = 5.13\%$

**40** (a) $r = 3$, quarterly • $\left(1 + \frac{0.03}{4}\right)^{4 \cdot 1} \approx 1.0303$. $(1.0303 - 1) \times 100\% = 3.03\%$

(b) $r = 3$, continuously • $e^{(0.03)(1)} \approx 1.0305$. $(1.0305 - 1) \times 100\% = 3.05\%$

**41** The graph of $y = e^{1000x}$ nearly coincides with the negative $x$-axis and then increases so fast that it nearly coincides with the positive $y$-axis. To see the graph on a calculator, try "turning off" your axes display.

Figure 41

Figure 42

**42** $y = e^{-1000x}$ • Similar to the previous exercise.

**43** It may be of interest to compare this graph with the graph of $y = (1.085)^x$ in Exercise 59 of Section 4.2. Both are compounding functions with $r = 8.5\%$. Note that $e^{0.085x} = \left(e^{0.085}\right)^x \approx (1.0887)^x > (1.085)^x$ for $x > 0$.

(a) If $y = e^{0.085x}$ and $x = 40$, then $y \approx 29.96$.      (b) If $y = 2$, then $x \approx 8.15$.

$[0, 60, 5]$ by $[0, 40, 5]$          $[0, 60, 5]$ by $[0, 40, 5]$

Figure 43

Figure 44

**44** Compare with Exercise 60 in Section 4.2.

(a) If $y = e^{0.0525x}$ and $x = 40$, then $y \approx 8.17$.      (b) If $y = 2$, then $x \approx 13.20$.

**45** (a) As $x \to \infty$, $e^{-x} \to 0$ and $f$ will resemble $\frac{1}{2}e^x$. As $x \to -\infty$, $e^x \to 0$ and $f$ will resemble $-\frac{1}{2}e^x$.

(b) At $x = 0$, $f(x) = 0$, and $g$ will have a vertical asymptote since $g$ is undefined (division by 0).

As $x \to \infty$, $f(x) \to \infty$, and since the reciprocal of a large positive number is a small positive number, we have $g(x) \to 0$.

As $x \to -\infty$, $f(x) \to -\infty$, and since the reciprocal of a large negative number is a small negative number, we have $g(x) \to 0$.

$[-7.5, 7.5]$ by $[-5, 5]$

*Figure 45(a)*

*Figure 45(b)*

**46** (a) See Example 6 for a graph of $f(x) = \dfrac{e^x + e^{-x}}{2}$.

(b) At $x = 0$, $f(x)$ and $g(x) = 1$. As $x \to \infty$ or $x \to -\infty$, $f(x) \to \infty$ and $g(x) \to 0$.

$[-7.5, 7.5]$ by $[-5, 5]$

*Figure 46(a)*

*Figure 46(b)*

**47** (a) $f(x) = \dfrac{e^x - e^{-x}}{e^x + e^{-x}} = \dfrac{e^x - 1/e^x}{e^x + 1/e^x} \cdot \dfrac{e^x}{e^x} = \dfrac{e^{2x} - 1}{e^{2x} + 1}$. At $x = 0$, $f(x) = 0$. As $x \to \infty$, $f(x) \to 1$ since the numerator and denominator are nearly the same number. As $x \to -\infty$, $f(x) \to \dfrac{0 - 1}{0 + 1} = -1$.

(b) At $x = 0$, we will have a vertical asymptote. As $x \to \infty$, $f(x) \to 1$, and since $g$ is the reciprocal of $f$, $g(x) \to 1$. Similarly, as $x \to -\infty$, $g(x) \to -1$.

$[-4.5, 4.5]$ by $[-3, 3]$

*Figure 47(a)*

*Figure 47(b)*

*Figure 48*

**48** $\sigma = 1$ and $\mu = 0$ $\Rightarrow$ $z = x$. $f(x) = \frac{1}{\sqrt{2\pi}} e^{-x^2/2}$ is an even function with $f(0) = \frac{1}{\sqrt{2\pi}} \approx 0.3989$, $f(\pm 1) = \frac{1}{\sqrt{2\pi e}} \approx 0.2420$, and $f(\pm 2) = \frac{1}{\sqrt{2\pi\, e^2}} \approx 0.0540$.

**49** The approximate coordinates of the points where the graphs of $f$ and $g$ intersect are $(-1.04, -0.92)$, $(2.11, 2.44)$, and $(8.51, 70.42)$. The region near the origin in the first figure is enhanced in the second. Thus, the solutions are $x \approx -1.04, 2.11$, and $8.51$.

$$[-3, 11] \text{ by } [-10, 80, 10]$$

$$[-2.26, 3.34] \text{ by } [-7.14, 8.57, 10]$$

**50** The approximate coordinates of the points where the graphs of $f$ and $g$ intersect are $(-0.93, 0.12)$, $(-0.25, 0.23)$, $(1.36, 1.17)$, and $(7.04, 341.46)$. The region near the origin in the first figure is enhanced in the second. Thus, the solutions of the equation $f(x) = g(x)$ are $x \approx -0.93, -0.25, 1.36$, and $7.04$.

$$[-5, 8] \text{ by } [-50, 400, 50]$$

$$[-1.37, 1.79] \text{ by } [-1.11, 2.06]$$

**51** $f(x) = x + 1$ is a more accurate approximation to $e^x$ near $x = 0$, whereas $g(x) = 1.72x + 1$ is a more accurate approximation to $e^x$ near $x = 1$.

$$[0, 4.5] \text{ by } [0, 3]$$
*Figure 51*

$$[0, 4.5] \text{ by } [0, 3]$$
*Figure 52*

**52** Both approximations are quite accurate for $0 \le x \le \frac{1}{2}$. For $\frac{1}{2} \le x \le 1$, $g$ is a more accurate approximation. (Careful inspection will show that $f$ is a more accurate approximation near $x = 0$.)

**53** From the graph, we see that $f(x) = x^2 e^x - x e^{(x^2)} + 0.1$ has zeros at $x \approx 0.11, 0.79$, and $1.13$.

$$[-2, 2.5] \text{ by } [-1, 2]$$
*Figure 53*

$$[-6, 3] \text{ by } [-3, 3]$$
*Figure 54*

**54** Using a zero feature, we determine that $f(x) = x^3 e^x - x^2 e^{2x} + 1$ has zeros at $x \approx -4.54, -1.71$, and $0.65$.

**55** From the graph, there is a horizontal asymptote of $y \approx 2.71$. $f$ is approaching the value of $e$ asymptotically.

[0, 200, 50] by [0, 8]

*Figure 55*

[0, 200, 50] by [0, 8]

*Figure 56*

**56** From the graph, there is a horizontal asymptote of $y \approx 7.32$.

$f$ is approaching the value of $e^2$ ( $\approx 7.389$) asymptotically.

**57** $Y_1 = e^{-x}$ and $Y_2 = x$ intersect when $x \approx 0.567$.

[−4.5, 4.5] by [−3, 3]

*Figure 57*

[−4.5, 4.5] by [0, 6]

*Figure 58*

**58** $Y_1 = e^{3x}$ and $Y_2 = 5 - 2x$ intersect when $x \approx 0.467$.

**59** $f(x) = xe^x$ is increasing on $[-1, \infty)$ and $f$ is decreasing on $(-\infty, -1]$.

[−5.5, 5] by [−2, 5]

*Figure 59*

[−2, 2.5] by [−1, 2]

*Figure 60*

**60** $f(x) = x^2 e^{-2x}$ is increasing on $[0, 1]$ and $f$ is decreasing on $(-\infty, 0]$ and $[1, \infty)$.

**61** (a)  When $y = 0$ and $z = 0$, the equation becomes $C = \dfrac{2Q}{\pi vab} e^{-h^2/(2b^2)}$.

As $h$ increases, the exponent becomes a larger *negative* value, and hence the concentration $C$ decreases.

(b)  When $z = 0$, the equation becomes $C = \dfrac{2Q}{\pi vab} e^{-y^2/(2a^2)} e^{-h^2/(2b^2)}$.

As $y$ increases, the concentration $C$ decreases.

**62** Graph $C = e^{-(z-100)^2/288} + e^{-(z+100)^2/288}$. From the graph, we see that the concentration of the pollution first increases as the height increases and then decreases. The maximum concentration occurs when $z = 100$ m.

[0, 200, 10] by [0, 1, 0.5]

**63** (a) Choose two arbitrary points that appear to lie on the curve such as $(0, 1.225)$ and $(10{,}000, 0.414)$.

$$f(0) = Ce^0 = C = 1.225 \quad \text{and} \quad f(10{,}000) = 1.225e^{10{,}000k} = 0.414.$$

To solve the last equation, graph $Y_1 = 1.225e^{10{,}000x}$ and $Y_2 = 0.414$. The graph of $Y_1$ increases so rapidly that it nearly "covers" the positive $y$-axis, so a viewing rectangle such as $[-0.001, 0]$ by $[0, 1]$ is needed to see the point of intersection. The graphs intersect at $x \approx -0.0001085$. Thus, $f(x) = 1.225e^{-0.0001085x}$.

(b) $f(3000) \approx 0.885$ {actual = 0.909} and $f(9000) \approx 0.461$ {actual = 0.467}.

$[-1000, 10{,}100, 1000]$ by $[0, 1.5, 0.5]$ $\qquad\qquad$ $[-10, 100, 10]$ by $[-100, 1900, 500]$

Figure 63 $\qquad\qquad\qquad\qquad\qquad\qquad$ Figure 64

**64** (a) Choose two arbitrary points that appear to lie on the curve such as $(0, 0.7)$ and $(90, 1789.1)$. $A(0) = A_0e^0 = A_0 = 0.7$. $A(90) = 0.7e^{90k} = 1789.1$. To solve the last equation for $k$, graph $Y_1 = 0.7e^{90x}$ and $Y_2 = 1789.1$ in the viewing rectangle $[0, 0.15, 0.01]$ by $[0, 1900, 500]$. The graphs intersect at $x \approx 0.087\,179\,37$. Thus, $A(x) = 0.7e^{0.087\,179\,37x}$.

(b) Graph $Y_1 = A(x)$ and $Y_2 = 1000$. The graphs intersect at $x \approx 83.33$. The federal government first spent one trillion dollars in 1993.

## 4.4 Exercises

**Note:** Exercises 1–4 are designed to familiarize the reader with the definition of $\log_a$ in this section. It is very important that you can generalize your understanding of this definition to the following case:

$$\boxed{\log_{\text{base}}(\text{argument}) = \text{exponent} \quad \textit{is equivalent to} \quad (\text{base})^{\text{exponent}} = \text{argument}}$$

Later in this section, you will also want to be able to use the following two special cases with ease:

$$\boxed{\log(\text{argument}) = \text{exponent} \quad \textit{is equivalent to} \quad (10)^{\text{exponent}} = \text{argument}}$$

$$\boxed{\ln(\text{argument}) = \text{exponent} \quad \textit{is equivalent to} \quad (e)^{\text{exponent}} = \text{argument}}$$

**1** (a) In this case, the *base* is 4, the *exponent* is 3, and the *argument* is 64. Thus,

$$4^3 = 64 \quad \text{is equivalent to} \quad \log_4 64 = 3.$$

(b) $4^{-3} = \frac{1}{64} \Leftrightarrow \log_4 \frac{1}{64} = -3$ $\qquad\qquad$ (c) $t^r = s \Leftrightarrow \log_t s = r$

(d) $3^x = 4 - t \Leftrightarrow \log_3(4 - t) = x$

(e) In this case, the *base* is 5, the *exponent* is $7t$, and the *argument* is $\dfrac{a+b}{a}$. Thus,

$$5^{7t} = \frac{a+b}{a} \quad \text{is equivalent to} \quad \log_5 \frac{a+b}{a} = 7t.$$

(f) $(0.7)^t = 5.3 \Leftrightarrow \log_{0.7}(5.3) = t$

**2** (a) $3^5 = 243 \Leftrightarrow \log_3 243 = 5$  (b) $3^{-4} = \frac{1}{81} \Leftrightarrow \log_3 \frac{1}{81} = -4$

(c) $c^p = d \Leftrightarrow \log_c d = p$  (d) $7^x = 100p \Leftrightarrow \log_7(100p) = x$

(e) $3^{-2x} = \frac{P}{F} \Leftrightarrow \log_3 \frac{P}{F} = -2x$  (f) $(0.9)^t = \frac{1}{2} \Leftrightarrow \log_{0.9}\left(\frac{1}{2}\right) = t$

**3** (a) In this case, the *base* is 2, the *argument* is 32, and the *exponent* is 5. Thus,

$$\log_2 32 = 5 \quad \text{is equivalent to} \quad 2^5 = 32.$$

(b) $\log_3 \frac{1}{243} = -5 \Leftrightarrow 3^{-5} = \frac{1}{243}$  (c) $\log_t r = p \Leftrightarrow t^p = r$

(d) $\log_3(x + 2) = 5 \Leftrightarrow 3^5 = (x + 2)$

(e) In this case, the *base* is 2, the *argument* is $m$, and the *exponent* is $3x + 4$. Thus,

$$\log_2 m = 3x + 4 \quad \text{is equivalent to} \quad 2^{3x+4} = m.$$

(f) $\log_b 512 = \frac{3}{2} \Leftrightarrow b^{3/2} = 512$

**4** (a) $\log_3 81 = 4 \Leftrightarrow 3^4 = 81$  (b) $\log_4 \frac{1}{256} = -4 \Leftrightarrow 4^{-4} = \frac{1}{256}$

(c) $\log_v w = q \Leftrightarrow v^q = w$  (d) $\log_6(2x - 1) = 3 \Leftrightarrow 6^3 = 2x - 1$

(e) $\log_4 p = 5 - x \Leftrightarrow 4^{5-x} = p$  (f) $\log_a 343 = \frac{3}{4} \Leftrightarrow a^{3/4} = 343$

**5** $2a^{t/3} = 5 \Leftrightarrow a^{t/3} = \frac{5}{2} \Leftrightarrow t/3 = \log_a \frac{5}{2} \Leftrightarrow t = 3\log_a \frac{5}{2}$

**6** $3a^{4t} = 10 \Leftrightarrow a^{4t} = \frac{10}{3} \Leftrightarrow 4t = \log_a \frac{10}{3} \Leftrightarrow t = \frac{1}{4}\log_a \frac{10}{3}$

**7** In order to solve for $t$, we must isolate the expression containing $t$—in this case, that expression is the exponential $Ca^t$.

$$K = H - Ca^t \Rightarrow Ca^t = H - K \Rightarrow a^t = \frac{H - K}{C} \Rightarrow t = \log_a\left(\frac{H - K}{C}\right)$$

**8** $F = D + Ba^t \Rightarrow Ba^t = F - D \Rightarrow a^t = \frac{F - D}{B} \Rightarrow t = \log_a\left(\frac{F - D}{B}\right)$

**9** In order to solve for $t$, we must isolate the expression containing $t$—in this case, that expression is the exponential $a^{Ct}$. $A = Ba^{Ct} + D \Rightarrow A - D = Ba^{Ct} \Rightarrow$

$$\frac{A - D}{B} = a^{Ct} \Rightarrow Ct = \log_a\left(\frac{A - D}{B}\right) \Rightarrow t = \frac{1}{C}\log_a\left(\frac{A - D}{B}\right).$$

The confusing step to most students in the above solution is $\frac{A - D}{B} = a^{Ct} \Rightarrow Ct = \log_a\left(\frac{A - D}{B}\right)$. This step

is similar to $y = a^x \Rightarrow \log_a y = x$, except $x$ and $y$ are more complicated expressions.

**10** $L = Ma^{t/N} - P \Rightarrow L + P = Ma^{t/N} \Rightarrow$

$$\frac{L + P}{M} = a^{t/N} \Rightarrow \frac{t}{N} = \log_a\left(\frac{L + P}{M}\right) \Rightarrow t = N\log_a\left(\frac{L + P}{M}\right)$$

**11** (a) Changing $10^5 = 100{,}000$ to logarithmic form gives us $\log_{10} 100{,}000 = 5$.

Since this is a common logarithm, we denote it as $\log 100{,}000 = 5$.

(b) $10^{-3} = 0.001 \Leftrightarrow \log 0.001 = -3$  (c) $10^x = y - 3 \Leftrightarrow \log(y - 3) = x$

(d) Changing $e^7 = p$ to logarithmic form gives us $\log_e p = 7$.

Since this is a natural logarithm, we denote it as $\ln p = 7$.

(e) Changing $e^{2t} = 3 - x$ to logarithmic form gives us $\log_e(3 - x) = 2t$.

Since this is a natural logarithm, we denote it as $\ln(3 - x) = 2t$.

$\boxed{12}$ (a) $10^4 = 10,000 \iff \log 10,000 = 4$   (b) $10^{-2} = 0.01 \iff \log 0.01 = -2$

(c) $10^x = 38z \iff \log(38z) = x$   (d) $e^4 = D \iff \ln D = 4$

(e) $e^{0.1t} = x + 2 \iff \ln(x + 2) = 0.1t$

$\boxed{13}$ (a) Remember that $\log x = 50$ is the same as $\log_{10} x = 50$. Changing to exponential form, we have $10^{50} = x$.

(b) $\log x = 20t$ $\{\log_{10} x = 20t\} \iff 10^{20t} = x$

(c) Remember that $\ln x = 0.1$ is the same as $\log_e x = 0.1$. Changing to exponential form, we have $e^{0.1} = x$.

(d) $\ln w = 4 + 3x$ $\{\log_e w = 4 + 3x\} \iff e^{4+3x} = w$

(e) $\ln(z - 2) = \frac{1}{6}$ $\{\log_e(z - 2) = \frac{1}{6}\} \iff e^{1/6} = z - 2$

$\boxed{14}$ (a) $\log x = -8 \iff 10^{-8} = x$   (b) $\log x = y + 4 \iff 10^{y+4} = x$

(c) $\ln x = \frac{1}{2} \iff e^{1/2} = x$   (d) $\ln z = 7 + x \iff e^{7+x} = z$

(e) $\ln(t - 5) = 1.2 \iff e^{1.2} = t - 5$

$\boxed{15}$ (a) $\log_5 1 = 0$ since $5^0 = 1$ $\{\log_a 1 = 0$ for any allowable base $a\}$

(b) $\log_3 3 = 1$ $\{\log_a a = 1$ since $a^1 = a\}$

(c) Remember that you cannot take the logarithm, any base, of a negative number. Hence, $\log_4(-2)$ is undefined.

(d) $\log_7 7^2 = 2$ $\{\log_a a^x = x\}$   (e) $3^{\log_3 8} = 8$ $\{a^{\log_a x} = x\}$

(f) $\log_5 125 = \log_5 5^3 = 3$, as in part (d)

(g) We will change the form of $\frac{1}{16}$ so that it can be written as an exponential expression with the same base as the logarithm—in this case, that base is 4. $\log_4 \frac{1}{16} = \log_4 4^{-2} = -2$

$\boxed{16}$ (a) $\log_8 1 = 0$   (b) $\log_9 9 = 1$

(c) $\log_5 0$ is undefined, not possible   (d) $\log_6 6^7 = 7$

(e) $5^{\log_5 4} = 4$   (f) $\log_3 243 = \log_3 3^5 = 5$

(g) $\log_2 128 = \log_2 2^7 = 7$

$\boxed{17}$ Parts (a)–(d) are direct applications of the properties in the chart on page 290 of the text.

(a) $10^{\log 3} = 3$   (b) $\log 10^5 = 5$

(c) $\log 100 = \log 10^2 = 2$   (d) $\log 0.0001 = \log 10^{-4} = -4$

(e) $10^{1 + \log 3} = 10^1 10^{\log_{10} 3} = 10(3) = 30$

$\boxed{18}$ (a) $10^{\log 7} = 7$   (b) $\log 10^{-6} = -6$

(c) $\log 100,000 = \log 10^5 = 5$   (d) $\log 0.001 = \log 10^{-3} = -3$

(e) $10^{-1 + \log 5} = 10^{-1} 10^{\log_{10} 5} = \frac{1}{10}(5) = \frac{1}{2}$

$\boxed{19}$ (a) $e^{\ln 2} = 2$   (b) $\ln e^{-3} = -3$

For part (c), we use a property of exponents that will enable us to use the property $e^{\ln x} = x$.

(c) $e^{2 + \ln 3} = e^2 e^{\ln 3} = e^2(3) = 3e^2$

$\boxed{20}$ (a) $e^{\ln 8} = 8$   (b) $\ln e^{2/3} = \frac{2}{3}$

(c) $e^{1 + \ln 5} = e^1 e^{\ln 5} = e(5) = 5e$

**21** $\log_4(x+10) = \log_4(8-x) \Rightarrow x+10 = 8-x$ {since the logarithm function is one-to-one} $\Rightarrow$
$2x = -2 \Rightarrow x = -1$. We must check to make sure that all proposed solutions do not make any of the original
expressions undefined. Checking $x = -1$ in the original equation gives us $\log_4(-1+10) = \log_4(8-(-1))$,
which is a true statement, so $x = -1$ is a valid solution.

**22** $\log_3(x+4) = \log_3(1-x) \Rightarrow x+4 = 1-x \Rightarrow 2x = -3 \Rightarrow x = -\frac{3}{2}$

**23** $\log_5(x-2) = \log_5(3x+7) \Rightarrow x-2 = 3x+7 \Rightarrow 2x = -9 \Rightarrow x = -\frac{9}{2}$. The value $x = -\frac{9}{2}$ is
extraneous since it makes either of the original logarithm expressions undefined. Hence, there is no solution.

**24** $\log_7(x-5) = \log_7(6x) \Rightarrow x-5 = 6x \Rightarrow 5x = -5 \Rightarrow x = -1$. $-1$ is extraneous
since it makes either of the given logarithm expressions undefined; no solution.

**25** $\log x^2 = \log(-3x-2) \Rightarrow x^2 = -3x-2 \Rightarrow x^2+3x+2 = 0 \Rightarrow$
$(x+1)(x+2) = 0 \Rightarrow x = -1, -2$. Checking $-1$ and $-2$, we find that both are valid solutions.

**26** $\ln x^2 = \ln(12-x) \Rightarrow x^2 = 12-x \Rightarrow x^2+x-12 = 0 \Rightarrow (x+4)(x-3) = 0 \Rightarrow x = -4, 3$

**27** $\log_3(x-4) = 2 \Rightarrow x-4 = 3^2 \Rightarrow x-4 = 9 \Rightarrow x = 13$

**28** $\log_2(x-5) = 4 \Rightarrow x-5 = 2^4 \Rightarrow x-5 = 16 \Rightarrow x = 21$

**29** $\log_9 x = -\frac{3}{2} \Rightarrow x = 9^{-3/2} = \left(9^{-1/2}\right)^3 = \left(\frac{1}{3}\right)^3 = \frac{1}{27}$

**30** $\log_4 x = -\frac{3}{2} \Rightarrow x = 4^{-3/2} = \left(4^{-1/2}\right)^3 = \left(\frac{1}{2}\right)^3 = \frac{1}{8}$

**31** $\ln x^2 = -2 \Rightarrow x^2 = e^{-2} \Rightarrow x^2 = \frac{1}{e^2} \Rightarrow x = \pm\sqrt{\frac{1}{e^2}} \Rightarrow x = \pm\frac{1}{e}$

**32** $\log x^2 = -4 \Rightarrow x^2 = 10^{-4} \Rightarrow x^2 = \frac{1}{10^4} \Rightarrow x = \pm\sqrt{\frac{1}{10^4}} \Rightarrow x = \pm\frac{1}{10^2} = \pm\frac{1}{100}$

**33** $e^{2\ln x} = 9 \Rightarrow \left(e^{\ln x}\right)^2 = 9 \Rightarrow x^2 = 9 \Rightarrow x = \pm 3$; $-3$ is extraneous

**34** $e^{-\ln x} = 0.2 \Rightarrow \left(e^{\ln x}\right)^{-1} = 0.2 \Rightarrow x^{-1} = 0.2 \Rightarrow \frac{1}{x} = \frac{1}{5} \Rightarrow x = 5$

**35** $e^{x\ln 3} = 27 \Rightarrow \left(e^{\ln 3}\right)^x = 27 \Rightarrow 3^x = 3^3 \Rightarrow x = 3$

**36** $e^{x\ln 2} = 0.25 \Rightarrow \left(e^{\ln 2}\right)^x = \frac{1}{4} \Rightarrow 2^x = 2^{-2} \Rightarrow x = -2$

**37** (a) $f(x) = \log x$ • As $x$ approaches 1, $y$ (or $f(x)$) $\to 0$.

(b) As $x$ approaches 10, $y$ (or $f(x)$) $\to 1$.

(c) As $x$ gets very large, $y$ (or $f(x)$) increases without bound, so $y \to \infty$.

(d) As $x \to 0^+$, $y$ (or $f(x)$) approaches the vertical asymptote (the $y$-axis) through negative values, so $y \to -\infty$.

**38** (a) $f(x) = \ln x$ • As $x$ approaches 1, $y$ (or $f(x)$) $\to 0$.

(b) As $x$ approaches $e$, $y$ (or $f(x)$) $\to 1$.

(c) As $x$ gets very large, $y$ (or $f(x)$) increases without bound, so $y \to \infty$.

(d) As $x \to 0^+$, $y$ (or $f(x)$) approaches the vertical asymptote (the $y$-axis) through negative values, so $y \to -\infty$.

**39** (a)  $f(x) = \log_4 x$  •  This graph has a vertical asymptote of $x = 0$ and goes through $\left(\frac{1}{4}, -1\right)$, $(1, 0)$, and $(4, 1)$. For reference purposes, call this $F(x)$.

(b)  $f(x) = -\log_4 x$  •  reflect $F$ through the $x$-axis

(c)  $f(x) = 2\log_4 x$  •  vertically stretch $F$ by a factor of 2

*Figure 39(a)*

*Figure 39(b)*

*Figure 39(c)*

(d)  $f(x) = \log_4(x + 2)$  •  shift $F$ left 2 units

(e)  $f(x) = (\log_4 x) + 2$  •  shift $F$ up 2 units

(f)  $f(x) = \log_4(x - 2)$  •  shift $F$ right 2 units

*Figure 39(d)*

*Figure 39(e)*

*Figure 39(f)*

(g)  $f(x) = (\log_4 x) - 2$  •  shift $F$ down 2 units

(h)  $f(x) = \log_4|x|$  •  include the reflection of $F$ through the $y$-axis since $x$ may be positive or negative, but $\log_4|x|$ will give the same result

(i)  $f(x) = \log_4(-x)$  •  $x$ must be negative so that $-x$ is positive, reflect $F$ through the $y$-axis

*Figure 39(g)*

*Figure 39(h)*

*Figure 39(i)*

(j)   $f(x) = \log_4(3 - x) = \log_4 [-(x - 3)]$  •  Shift $F$ right 3 units and reflect through the line $x = 3$. It may be helpful to determine the domain of this function. We know that $3 - x$ must be positive for the function to be defined. Thus, $3 - x > 0 \;\Rightarrow\; 3 > x$, or, equivalently, $x < 3$.

(k)   $f(x) = |\log_4 x|$  •  reflect points with negative $y$-coordinates through the $x$-axis

(l)   $f(x) = \log_{1/4} x$  •  reflect the graph of $y = \log_4 x$ about the $x$-axis

*Figure 39(j)*

*Figure 39(k)*

*Figure 39(l)*

**40** The graphs are found in a manner similar to that of Exercise 39.

The graph of $y = \log_5 x$ goes through $\left(\frac{1}{5}, -1\right)$, $(1, 0)$, and $(5, 1)$.

**41** $f(x) = \log(x + 10)$  •  This is the graph of $g(x) = \log x$ shifted 10 units to the left.

There is a vertical asymptote of $x = -10$. $g$ goes through $\left(\frac{1}{10}, -1\right)$, $(1, 0)$, and $(10, 1)$, so $f$ goes through $\left(\frac{1}{10} - 10, -1\right)$, $(1 - 10, 0)$, and $(10 - 10, 1)$, that is, $(-9.9, -1)$, $(-9, 0)$, and $(0, 1)$.

*Figure 41*

*Figure 42*

**42** $f(x) = \log(x + 100)$  •  This is the graph of $g(x) = \log x$ shifted 100 units to the left.

There is a vertical asymptote of $x = -100$.

**43** $f(x) = \ln|x|$  •  This is the graph of $g(x) = \ln x$ and its reflection through the $y$-axis.

There is a vertical asymptote of $x = 0$. The graph of $g$ goes through $\left(\frac{1}{e}, -1\right)$, $(1, 0)$, and $(e, 1)$, so the graph of $f$ goes through $\left(\pm\frac{1}{e}, -1\right)$, $(\pm 1, 0)$, and $(\pm e, 1)$.

*Figure 43*

*Figure 44*

**44** $f(x) = \ln|x-1|$ • This is the graph of $g(x) = \ln|x|$ shifted 1 unit to the right.

There is a vertical asymptote of $x = 1$.

**45** $f(x) = \ln e + x = 1 + x$. This is the graph of a line with slope 1 and $y$-intercept 1.

Figure 45

Figure 46

**46** $f(x) = \ln(e+x)$ • This is the graph of $g(x) = \ln x$ shifted $e$ units to the left.

There is a vertical asymptote of $x = -e$.

**47** The point $(9, 2)$ is on the graph of $f(x) = \log_a x$, so $f(9) = 2 \Rightarrow 2 = \log_a 9 \Rightarrow$
$a^2 = 9 \Rightarrow a = \pm 3$. Since the base $a$ must be positive, $a = 3$.

**48** The point $(8, 3)$ is on the graph of $f(x) = \log_a x$, so $f(8) = 3 \Rightarrow 3 = \log_a 8 \Rightarrow a^3 = 8 \Rightarrow a = 2$.

**49** This is the graph of $F$ reflected through the $x$-axis. $\qquad\qquad \star\ f(x) = -F(x)$

**50** This is the graph of $F$ reflected through the $y$-axis. $\qquad\qquad \star\ f(x) = F(-x)$

**51** This is the graph of $F$ shifted right 2 units. $\qquad\qquad \star\ f(x) = F(x-2)$

**52** This is the graph of $F$ shifted left 3 units. $\qquad\qquad \star\ f(x) = F(x+3)$

**53** This is the graph of $F$ shifted up 1 unit. $\qquad\qquad \star\ f(x) = F(x)+1$

**54** The $y$-coordinates are doubled, so multiply $F$ by 2. $\qquad\qquad \star\ f(x) = 2\,F(x)$

**55** (a) $\log x = 3.6274 \Rightarrow x = 10^{3.6274} \approx 4240.333$, or 4240 to three significant figures

(b) $\log x = 0.9469 \Rightarrow x = 10^{0.9469} \approx 8.849$, or 8.85 to three significant figures

(c) $\log x = -1.6253 \Rightarrow x = 10^{-1.6253} \approx 0.023697$, or 0.0237 to three significant figures

(d) $\ln x = 2.3 \Rightarrow x = e^{2.3} \approx 9.974$, or 9.97 to three significant figures

(e) $\ln x = 0.05 \Rightarrow x = e^{0.05} \approx 1.051$, or 1.05 to three significant figures

(f) $\ln x = -1.6 \Rightarrow x = e^{-1.6} \approx 0.2019$, or 0.202 to three significant figures

**56** (a) $\log x = 1.8965 \Rightarrow x = 10^{1.8965} \approx 78.795$, or 78.8 to three significant figures

(b) $\log x = 4.9680 \Rightarrow x = 10^{4.968} \approx 92{,}896.639$, or 92,900 to three significant figures

(c) $\log x = -2.2118 \Rightarrow x = 10^{-2.2118} \approx 0.00614$ to three significant figures

(d) $\ln x = 3.7 \Rightarrow x = e^{3.7} \approx 40.447$, or 40.4 to three significant figures

(e) $\ln x = 0.95 \Rightarrow x = e^{0.95} \approx 2.5857$, or 2.59 to three significant figures

(f) $\ln x = -5 \Rightarrow x = e^{-5} \approx 0.00674$ to three significant figures

**57** $f(x) = 1000(1.05)^x = 1000e^{x \ln 1.05}$ (see the illustration on page 290 of the text).

This is approximately $1000e^{x(0.0487901642)} \approx 1000e^{0.0488x}$, so the growth rate of $f$ is about 4.88%.

**58** $f(x) = 50(\frac{9}{8})^x = 50e^{x \ln (9/8)}$ (see the illustration on page 290 of the text).

This is approximately $50e^{x(0.117783)} \approx 50e^{0.1178x}$, so the growth rate of $f$ is about 11.78%.

**59** $f(x) = 20(0.97)^x = 20e^{x \ln 0.97}$.

This is approximately $20e^{x(-0.030459)} \approx 20e^{-0.0305x}$, so the decay rate of $f$ is about 3.05% ($-3.05\%$).

**60** $f(x) = 100(\frac{1}{2})^x = 100e^{x \ln(1/2)}$.

This is approximately $100e^{x(-0.693147)} \approx 100e^{-0.6931x}$, so the decay rate of $f$ is about 69.31% ($-69.31\%$).

**61** $q = q_0(2)^{-t/1600} \Rightarrow \dfrac{q}{q_0} = 2^{-t/1600}$ {change to logarithm form} $\Rightarrow$

$-\dfrac{t}{1600} = \log_2\left(\dfrac{q}{q_0}\right)$ {multiply by $-1600$} $\Rightarrow t = -1600 \log_2\left(\dfrac{q}{q_0}\right)$.

**62** $Q = k(2)^{-t/5} \Rightarrow \dfrac{Q}{k} = 2^{-t/5} \Rightarrow -\dfrac{t}{5} = \log_2\left(\dfrac{Q}{k}\right) \Rightarrow t = -5 \log_2\left(\dfrac{Q}{k}\right)$

**63** $I = 20e^{-Rt/L} \Rightarrow \dfrac{I}{20} = e^{-Rt/L} \Rightarrow \ln\left(\dfrac{I}{20}\right) = -\dfrac{Rt}{L} \Rightarrow t = -\dfrac{L}{R} \ln\left(\dfrac{I}{20}\right)$

**64** $Q = Q_0 e^{kt} \Rightarrow \dfrac{Q}{Q_0} = e^{kt} \Rightarrow \ln\left(\dfrac{Q}{Q_0}\right) = kt \Rightarrow t = \dfrac{1}{k} \ln\left(\dfrac{Q}{Q_0}\right)$

**65** $I = 10^a I_0 \Rightarrow R = \log\left(\dfrac{I}{I_0}\right) = \log\left(\dfrac{10^a I_0}{I_0}\right) = \log 10^a = a$.

Hence, for $10^2 I_0$, $10^4 I_0$, and $10^5 I_0$, the answers are: (a) 2   (b) 4   (c) 5

**66** $8 \le R \le 9 \Rightarrow \log 10^8 \le \log\left(\dfrac{I}{I_0}\right) \le \log 10^9 \Rightarrow 10^8 \le \dfrac{I}{I_0} \le 10^9 \Rightarrow 10^8 I_0 \le I \le 10^9 I_0$

**67** We will find a general formula for $\alpha$ first.

$I = 10^a I_0 \Rightarrow \alpha = 10 \log\left(\dfrac{I}{I_0}\right) = 10 \log\left(\dfrac{10^a I_0}{I_0}\right) = 10(\log 10^a) = 10(a) = 10a$.

Hence, for $10^1 I_0$, $10^3 I_0$, and $10^4 I_0$, the answers are: (a) 10   (b) 30   (c) 40

**68** $\alpha = 140 \Rightarrow 140 = 10 \log\left(\dfrac{I}{I_0}\right) \Rightarrow \log\left(\dfrac{I}{I_0}\right) = 14 \Rightarrow \dfrac{I}{I_0} = 10^{14} \Rightarrow I = 10^{14} I_0$.

**69** $N(t) = 231e^{0.0103t}$ • 1980 corresponds to $t = 0$ and $N(0) = 231$ million. We need to find $t$ when $N = 2 \cdot 231$.

$2 \cdot 231 = 231e^{0.0103t} \Rightarrow 2 = e^{0.0103t} \Rightarrow \ln 2 = 0.0103t \Rightarrow t = \dfrac{\ln 2}{0.0103} \Rightarrow t \approx 67.3$,

which corresponds to the year $1980 + 67 = 2047$.

Alternatively, using the doubling time formula on page 292 of the text, $t = (\ln 2)/r = (\ln 2)/0.0103 \approx 67.3$.

**70** $N(t) = 766e^{0.0182t}$ • 1985 corresponds to $t = 0$. $N(t) = 1500 \Rightarrow 1500 = 766e^{0.0182t} \Rightarrow$

$e^{0.0182t} = \frac{1500}{766} \Rightarrow 0.0182t = \ln\left(\frac{1500}{766}\right) \Rightarrow t \approx 36.9$, which corresponds to the year 2021.

**71** (a) $\ln W = \ln 2.4 + (1.84)h$ {change to exponential form} $\Rightarrow W = e^{[\ln 2.4 + (1.84)h]} \Rightarrow$

$W = e^{\ln 2.4} e^{1.84h}$ {since $e^x e^y = e^{x+y}$} $\Rightarrow W = 2.4e^{1.84h}$

(b) $h = 1.5 \Rightarrow W = 2.4e^{(1.84)(1.5)} = 2.4e^{2.76} \approx 37.92$ kg

**72** $A = Pe^{rt}$ • $25{,}000 = 6000e^{0.04t} \Rightarrow \frac{25}{6} = e^{0.04t} \Rightarrow 0.04t = \ln \frac{25}{6} \Rightarrow t = \dfrac{\ln \frac{25}{6}}{0.04} \approx 35.7$ yr

**73** (a) $p(h) = 14.7e^{-0.0000385h}$ • $p(h) = 10$ $\Rightarrow$ $10 = 14.7e^{-0.0000385h}$ $\Rightarrow$ $\frac{10}{14.7} = e^{-0.0000385h}$ $\Rightarrow$

$$\ln\frac{10}{14.7} = -0.0000385h \Rightarrow h = -\frac{1}{0.0000385}\ln\frac{10}{14.7} \approx 10{,}007 \text{ ft.}$$

(b) At sea level, $h = 0$, and $p(0) = 14.7$. Setting $p(h)$ equal to $\frac{1}{2}(14.7)$,

and solving as in part (a), we have $h = -\frac{1}{0.0000385}\ln\frac{1}{2} \approx 18{,}004$ ft.

**74** $\log P = a + \dfrac{b}{c+T}$ $\Rightarrow$ $P(T) = 10^{a+b/(c+T)}$ $\Rightarrow$ $P(T) = 10^a 10^{b/(c+T)}$

**75** (a) $t = 0$ $\Rightarrow$ $W = 2600\left(1 - 0.51e^{-0.075(0)}\right)^3 = 2600(0.49)^3 \approx 305.9$ kg

(b) (1) From the graph, if $W = 1800$, $t$ appears to be about 20.

(2) Solving the equation for $t$, we have $1800 = 2600\left(1 - 0.51e^{-0.075t}\right)^3$ $\Rightarrow$

$\frac{1800}{2600} = \left(1 - 0.51e^{-0.075t}\right)^3$ $\Rightarrow$ $\sqrt[3]{\frac{1800}{2600}} = 1 - 0.51e^{-0.075t}$ $\Rightarrow$ $\frac{51}{100}e^{-0.075t} = 1 - \sqrt[3]{\frac{9}{13}}$ $\Rightarrow$

$e^{-0.075t} = \left(\frac{100}{51}\right)\left(1 - \sqrt[3]{\frac{9}{13}}\right)$ $\Rightarrow$ $-0.075t = \ln\left[\left(\frac{100}{51}\right)\left(1 - \sqrt[3]{\frac{9}{13}}\right)\right]$ $\Rightarrow$

$$t = \frac{\ln\left[\left(\frac{100}{51}\right)\left(1 - \sqrt[3]{\frac{9}{13}}\right)\right]}{-0.075} \approx 19.8 \text{ yr.}$$

**76** The formula for $R$ is not needed. $T = 50$ $\Rightarrow$ $50 = 325\left(e^{0.02t} - 1\right)$ $\Rightarrow$

$$e^{0.02t} - 1 = \frac{2}{13} \Rightarrow e^{0.02t} = \frac{15}{13} \Rightarrow 0.02t = \ln\frac{15}{13} \Rightarrow t = 50\ln\frac{15}{13} \approx 7.16 \text{ yr}$$

**77** $D = ae^{-bx}$ with $a = 5.5$ and $b = 0.10$ • The population density equals 2000 per square mile means that $D = 2$.

$D = 2$ $\Rightarrow$ $5.5e^{-0.1x} = 2$ $\Rightarrow$ $e^{-0.1x} = \frac{2}{5.5}$ $\Rightarrow$ $-0.1x = \ln\frac{4}{11}$ $\Rightarrow$ $x = -10\ln\frac{4}{11}$ mi $\approx 10.1$ mi

**78** (a) $m = 6 - 2.5\log\left(\dfrac{10^{0.4}L_0}{L_0}\right) = 6 - 2.5\log 10^{0.4} = 6 - 2.5(0.4) = 6 - 1 = 5$

(b) $m = 6 - 2.5\log\left(\dfrac{L}{L_0}\right)$ $\Rightarrow$ $\log\left(\dfrac{L}{L_0}\right) = \dfrac{6-m}{2.5}$ $\Rightarrow$ $\dfrac{L}{L_0} = 10^{(6-m)/2.5}$ $\Rightarrow$ $L = L_0\, 10^{(6-m)/2.5}$

**79** $A(t) = A_0 a^{-t}$ • Since the half-life is eight days, $A(t) = \frac{1}{2}A_0$ when $t = 8$.

Thus, $\frac{1}{2}A_0 = A_0 a^{-8}$ $\Rightarrow$ $a^{-8} = \frac{1}{2}$ $\Rightarrow$ $\dfrac{1}{a^8} = \dfrac{1}{2}$ $\Rightarrow$ $a^8 = 2$ $\Rightarrow$ $a = 2^{1/8}$ {take the eighth root} $\approx 1.09$.

**80** $A(t) = A_0 e^{-0.0239t}$ • Since the field is *currently* 2.5 times the safe level $S$, we let $A_0 = 2.5S$ and $A(t) = S$.

$$S = 2.5Se^{-0.0239t} \Rightarrow \frac{1}{2.5} = e^{-0.0239t} \Rightarrow \ln 0.4 = -0.0239t \Rightarrow t = \frac{\ln 0.4}{-0.0239} \approx 38.3 \text{ yr.}$$

**81** (a) $S = 0.05 + 0.86\log P$ • Since $\log P$ is an increasing function, increasing the population increases the

walking speed. Pedestrians have faster average walking speeds in large cities.

(b) $S = 5$ $\Rightarrow$ $5 = 0.05 + 0.86\log P$ $\Rightarrow$ $4.95 = 0.86\log P$ $\Rightarrow$ $\frac{4.95}{0.86} = \log P$ $\Rightarrow$

$$P = 10^{4.95/0.86} \approx 570{,}000$$

**82** (a) $F = 1 - e^{-ct}$ • Larger values of $c$ cause $F$ to increase more rapidly. This indicates that the chip will fail

sooner and be less reliable.

(b) $c = 0.125$ and $F = 35\%$ $\Rightarrow$ $0.35 = 1 - e^{-0.125t}$ $\Rightarrow$ $e^{-0.125t} = 0.65$ $\Rightarrow$

$$-0.125t = \ln 0.65 \Rightarrow t = \frac{\ln 0.65}{-0.125} \approx 3.45 \text{ yr.}$$

**83** (a) $f(x) = \ln(x+1) + e^x$ $\Rightarrow$ $f(2) = \ln(2+1) + e^2 \approx 8.4877$

(b) $g(x) = \dfrac{(\log x)^2 - \log x}{4}$ $\Rightarrow$ $g(3.97) = \dfrac{(\log 3.97)^2 - \log 3.97}{4} \approx -0.0601$

**84** (a) $f(1.95) = \log(2 \times 1.95^2 + 1) - 10^{-1.95} \approx 0.9235$

(b) $g(0.55) = \dfrac{0.55 - 3.4}{\ln 0.55 + 4} \approx -0.8377$

**85** The figure shows a graph of $Y_1 = x \ln x$ and $Y_2 = 1$. By using an intersect feature, we determine that $x \ln x = 1$ when $x \approx 1.763$. Alternatively, we could graph $Y_1 = x \ln x - 1$, and find the zero of that graph.

$[0, 4]$ by $[-1, 1.67]$

*Figure 85*

$[-3, 4.5]$ by $[-1, 4]$

*Figure 86*

**86** Using a root feature, $\ln x + x = 0$ when $x \approx 0.567$.

**87** The domain of $f(x) = 2.2 \log(x + 2)$ is $x > -2$. The domain of $g(x) = \ln x$ is $x > 0$. From the figure, we determine that $f$ intersects $g$ at about 14.90. Thus, $f(x) \geq g(x)$ on approximately $(0, 14.90]$, not $(-2, 14.90]$ since $g$ is not defined if $x \leq 0$. In general, the larger the base of the logarithm, the slower its graph will rise. In this case, we have base 10 and base $e \approx 2.72$, so we know that $g$ will eventually intersect $f$ even if we don't see this intersection in our first window.

$[-2, 16]$ by $[-4, 8]$

*Figure 87*

$[-2, 4]$ by $[-1, 4]$

*Figure 88*

**88** Note that $f(x) = x \ln |x|$ is not defined at $x = 0$. The graph of $f$ intersects the graph of $g(x) = 0.15 e^x$ four times:
$$x \approx -0.94, \; -0.05, \; 1.59, \text{ and } 3.23. \text{ Thus, } f(x) \geq g(x) \text{ on } [-0.94, -0.05] \cup [1.59, 3.23].$$

**89** (a) $R = 2.07 \ln x - 2.04 = 2.07 \ln \dfrac{C}{H} - 2.04 = 2.07 \ln \dfrac{242}{78} - 2.04 \approx 0.3037 \approx 30\%$.

(b) Graph $Y_1 = 2.07 \ln x - 2.04$ and $Y_2 = 0.75$. From the graph, $R \approx 0.75$ when $x = \dfrac{C}{H} \approx 3.85$.

$[3, 5, 0.5]$ by $[0, 1, 0.5]$

*Figure 89*

$[3, 5, 0.5]$ by $[0, 1, 0.5]$

*Figure 90*

**90** (a) $R = 1.36 \ln x - 1.19 = 1.36 \ln \dfrac{C}{H} - 1.19 = 1.36 \ln \dfrac{287}{65} - 1.19 \approx 0.8297 \approx 83\%$.

(b) Graph $Y_1 = 1.36 \ln x - 1.19$ and $Y_2 = 0.75$. From the graph, $R \approx 0.75$ when $x = \dfrac{C}{H} \approx 4.16$.

## 4.5 Exercises

1. (a) $\log_4(xz) = \log_4 x + \log_4 z$         (b) $\log_4(y/x) = \log_4 y - \log_4 x$

   (c) $\log_4 \sqrt[3]{z} = \log_4 z^{1/3} = \frac{1}{3}\log_4 z$

2. (a) $\log_3(xyz) = \log_3(xy) + \log_3 z = \log_3 x + \log_3 y + \log_3 z$

   (b) $\log_3(xz/y) = \log_3(xz) - \log_3 y = \log_3 x + \log_3 z - \log_3 y$

   (c) $\log_3 \sqrt[5]{y} = \log_3 y^{1/5} = \frac{1}{5}\log_3 y$

3. $\log_a \dfrac{x^3 w}{y^2 z^4} = \log_a\left(x^3 w\right) - \log_a\left(y^2 z^4\right) = \left(\log_a x^3 + \log_a w\right) - \left(\log_a y^2 + \log_a z^4\right)$

$$= 3\log_a x + \log_a w - 2\log_a y - 4\log_a z$$

The most common mistake is to not have the minus sign in front of $4\log_a z$.

This error results from not having the parentheses in the correct place.

4. $\log_a \dfrac{y^5 w^2}{x^4 z^3} = \log_a y^5 w^2 - \log_a x^4 z^3 = \log_a y^5 + \log_a w^2 - \left(\log_a x^4 + \log_a z^3\right)$

$$= 5\log_a y + 2\log_a w - 4\log_a x - 3\log_a z$$

5. $\log \dfrac{\sqrt[3]{z}}{x\sqrt{y}} = \log \sqrt[3]{z} - \log\left(x\sqrt{y}\right) = \log z^{1/3} - \left(\log x + \log y^{1/2}\right) = \frac{1}{3}\log z - \log x - \frac{1}{2}\log y$

6. $\log \dfrac{\sqrt{y}}{x^4 \sqrt[3]{z}} = \log \sqrt{y} - \log\left(x^4 \sqrt[3]{z}\right) = \log y^{1/2} - \left(\log x^4 + \log y^{1/3}\right) = \frac{1}{2}\log y - 4\log x - \frac{1}{3}\log z$

7. $\ln \sqrt[4]{\dfrac{x^7}{y^5 z}} = \ln \dfrac{x^{7/4}}{y^{5/4} z^{1/4}} = \ln x^{7/4} - \ln\left(y^{5/4} z^{1/4}\right) = \ln x^{7/4} - \left(\ln y^{5/4} + \ln z^{1/4}\right) = \frac{7}{4}\ln x - \frac{5}{4}\ln y - \frac{1}{4}\ln z$

8. $\ln x \sqrt[3]{\dfrac{y^4}{z^5}} = \ln x + \ln \dfrac{y^{4/3}}{z^{5/3}} = \ln x + \ln y^{4/3} - \ln z^{5/3} = \ln x + \frac{4}{3}\ln y - \frac{5}{3}\ln z$

**Note:** As a generalization for situations similar to Exercises 1–8, if the exponents on the variables are positive, then the sign in front of the individual logarithms will be positive if the variable was originally in the numerator and negative if the variable was originally in the denominator.

9. (a) $\log_3 x + \log_3(5y) = \log_3(x \cdot 5y) = \log_3(5xy)$      (b) $\log_3(2z) - \log_3 x = \log_3(2z/x)$

   (c) $\frac{1}{5}\log_3 y = \log_3 y^{1/5} = \log_3 \sqrt[5]{y}$

10. (a) $\log_4(3z) + \log_4 x = \log_4(3xz)$       (b) $\log_4 x - \log_4(7y) = \log_4\left[x/(7y)\right]$

   (c) $\frac{1}{3}\log_4 w = \log_4 w^{1/3} = \log_4 \sqrt[3]{w}$

11. $2\log_a x - \frac{1}{3}\log_a(x-2) - 5\log_a(2x+3) = \log_a x^2 - \log_a(x-2)^{1/3} - \log_a(2x+3)^5$    {logarithm law 3}

$$= \log_a x^2 - \left[\log_a(x-2)^{1/3} + \log_a(2x+3)^5\right] \quad \text{\{factor out } -1\text{\}}$$

$$= \log_a x^2 - \log_a\left[\sqrt[3]{x-2}\,(2x+3)^5\right] \quad \text{\{logarithm law 1\}}$$

$$= \log_a \frac{x^2}{\sqrt[3]{x-2}\,(2x+3)^5} \quad \text{\{logarithm law 2\}}$$

12. $5\log_a x - \frac{1}{2}\log_a(3x-4) - 3\log_a(5x+1) = \log_a x^5 - \log_a(3x-4)^{1/2} - \log_a(5x+1)^3$

$$= \log_a x^5 - \left[\log_a(3x-4)^{1/2} + \log_a(5x+1)^3\right]$$

$$= \log_a x^5 - \log_a \sqrt{3x-4}\,(5x+1)^3 = \log_a \frac{x^5}{\sqrt{3x-4}\,(5x+1)^3}$$

**13** $\log(x^3y^2) - 2\log x\sqrt[3]{y} - 3\log\left(\dfrac{x}{y}\right) = \log(x^3y^2) - \left[\log\left(x\sqrt[3]{y}\right)^2 + \log\left(\dfrac{x}{y}\right)^3\right]$

$$= \log(x^3y^2) - \left[\log\left(\dfrac{x^2y^{2/3}}{1}\cdot\dfrac{x^3}{y^3}\right)\right] = \log\left(\dfrac{x^3y^2}{1}\right) - \log\left(\dfrac{x^5}{y^{7/3}}\right)$$

$$= \log\left(\dfrac{\frac{x^3y^2}{1}}{\frac{x^5}{y^{7/3}}}\right) = \log\left(\dfrac{x^3y^2}{1}\cdot\dfrac{y^{7/3}}{x^5}\right) = \log\left(\dfrac{y^{2+7/3}}{x^{5-3}}\right) = \log\dfrac{y^{13/3}}{x^2}$$

**14** $2\log\dfrac{y^3}{x} - 3\log y + \dfrac{1}{2}\log x^4y^2 = \log\dfrac{y^6}{x^2} - \log y^3 + \log x^2y^1 = \log\dfrac{(y^6/x^2)(x^2y)}{y^3} = \log y^4$

**15** $\ln y^3 + \dfrac{1}{3}\ln(x^9y^6) - 5\ln y = \ln y^3 + \ln(x^9y^6)^{1/3} - \ln y^5 = \ln y^3 + \ln(x^3y^2) - \ln y^5 = \ln\left[(x^3y^5)/y^5\right] = \ln x^3$

**16** $2\ln x - 4\ln(1/y) - 3\ln(xy) = \ln x^2 - \ln(1/y^4) - \ln(x^3y^3)$

$$= \ln x^2 - \left[\ln\dfrac{1}{y^4} + \ln(x^3y^3)\right] = \ln x^2 - \ln\dfrac{x^3}{y} = \ln\dfrac{x^2}{x^3/y} = \ln\dfrac{y}{x}$$

**17** $\log_6(2x-3) = \log_6 24 - \log_6 3 \Rightarrow \log_6(2x-3) = \log_6\frac{24}{3} \Rightarrow 2x-3 = 8 \Rightarrow 2x = 11 \Rightarrow x = \frac{11}{2}$

**18** $\log_4(3x+2) = \log_4 7 + \log_4 3 \Rightarrow \log_4(3x+2) = \log_4(7\cdot3) \Rightarrow 3x+2 = 21 \Rightarrow x = \frac{19}{3}$

**19** $2\log_3 x = 3\log_3 5 \Rightarrow \log_3 x^2 = \log_3 5^3 \Rightarrow x^2 = 125 \Rightarrow x = \pm\sqrt{125} = \pm5\sqrt{5};$

$-5\sqrt{5}$ is extraneous since it would make $\log_3 x$ undefined

**20** $3\log_2 x = 2\log_2 3 \Rightarrow \log_2 x^3 = \log_2 3^2 \Rightarrow x^3 = 9 \Rightarrow x = \sqrt[3]{9}$

**21** $\log x - \log(x+1) = 3\log 4 \Rightarrow \log\dfrac{x}{x+1} = \log 4^3 \Rightarrow \dfrac{x}{x+1} = 64 \Rightarrow x = 64(x+1) \Rightarrow$

$x = 64x + 64 \Rightarrow -63x = 64 \Rightarrow x = -\frac{64}{63}.$

But $-\frac{64}{63}$ is extraneous since it makes an argument negative, so there is **no solution** for the equation.

**22** $\log(x+2) - \log x = 2\log 4 \Rightarrow \log\dfrac{x+2}{x} = \log 16 \Rightarrow x+2 = 16x \Rightarrow x = \dfrac{2}{15}$

**23** $\ln(-4-x) + \ln 3 = \ln(2-x) \Rightarrow \ln[(-4-x)\cdot3] = \ln(2-x) \Rightarrow \ln(-12-3x) = \ln(2-x) \Rightarrow$

$-12 - 3x = 2 - x \Rightarrow 2x = -14 \Rightarrow x = -7.$

Remember, the solution of a logarithmic equation may be negative—you must examine what happens to the original logarithm expressions. In this case, we have $\ln 3 + \ln 3 = \ln 9$, which is true.

**24** $\ln x + \ln(x+6) = \frac{1}{2}\ln 9 \Rightarrow \ln(x^2+6x) = \ln 3 \Rightarrow x^2 + 6x - 3 = 0 \Rightarrow$

$$x = \dfrac{-6\pm\sqrt{48}}{2} = -3\pm2\sqrt{3};\ -3-2\sqrt{3}\text{ is extraneous}$$

**25** $\log_2(x+7) + \log_2 x = 3 \Rightarrow \log_2(x^2+7x) = 3 \Rightarrow x^2 + 7x = 2^3 \Rightarrow$

$x^2 + 7x - 8 = 0 \Rightarrow (x+8)(x-1) = 0 \Rightarrow x = -8, 1;\ -8$ is extraneous

**26** $\log_6(x+5) + \log_6 x = 2 \Rightarrow \log_6(x^2+5x) = 2 \Rightarrow x^2 + 5x = 36 \Rightarrow$

$(x+9)(x-4) = 0 \Rightarrow x = -9, 4;\ -9$ is extraneous

**27** $\log_2(-x) + \log_2(2-x) = 3 \Rightarrow \log_2(x^2-2x) = 3 \Rightarrow x^2 - 2x = 2^3 \Rightarrow$

$x^2 - 2x - 8 = 0 \Rightarrow (x+2)(x-4) = 0 \Rightarrow x = -2, 4;\ 4$ is extraneous

**28** $\log_3(-x) + \log_3(8-x) = 2 \;\Rightarrow\; \log_3(x^2 - 8x) = 2 \;\Rightarrow\; x^2 - 8x = 3^2 \;\Rightarrow$
$$x^2 - 8x - 9 = 0 \;\Rightarrow\; (x+1)(x-9) = 0 \;\Rightarrow\; x = -1, 9; 9 \text{ is extraneous}$$

**29** $\log_3(x+3) + \log_3(x+5) = 1 \;\Rightarrow\; \log_3[(x+3)(x+5)] = 1 \;\Rightarrow\; \log_3(x^2 + 8x + 15) = 1 \;\Rightarrow$
$$x^2 + 8x + 15 = 3 \;\Rightarrow\; x^2 + 8x + 12 = 0 \;\Rightarrow\; (x+2)(x+6) = 0 \;\Rightarrow\; x = -6, -2; -6 \text{ is extraneous}$$

**30** $\log_3(x-2) + \log_3(x-4) = 2 \;\Rightarrow\; \log_3(x^2 - 6x + 8) = 2 \;\Rightarrow\; x^2 - 6x + 8 = 9 \;\Rightarrow$
$$x^2 - 6x - 1 = 0 \;\Rightarrow\; x = \frac{6 \pm \sqrt{40}}{2} = 3 \pm \sqrt{10}; 3 - \sqrt{10} \text{ is extraneous}$$

**31** $\log(x+3) = 1 - \log(x-2) \;\Rightarrow\; \log(x+3) + \log(x-2) = 1 \;\Rightarrow\; \log[(x+3)(x-2)] = 1 \;\Rightarrow$
$$x^2 + x - 6 = 10^1 \;\Rightarrow\; x^2 + x - 16 = 0 \;\Rightarrow\; x = \frac{-1 + \sqrt{65}}{2} \approx 3.53; \frac{-1 - \sqrt{65}}{2} \approx -4.53 \text{ is extraneous}$$

**32** $\log(x+4) = 2 - \log(x-2) \;\Rightarrow\; \log(x+4) + \log(x-2) = 2 \;\Rightarrow\; \log[(x+4)(x-2)] = 2 \;\Rightarrow$
$$x^2 + 2x - 8 = 10^2 \;\Rightarrow\; x^2 + 2x - 108 = 0 \;\Rightarrow\; x = \frac{-2 + \sqrt{4 + 432}}{2} = \frac{-2 + 2\sqrt{109}}{2}.$$
$$x = -1 + \sqrt{109} \approx 9.44; -1 - \sqrt{109} \approx -11.44 \text{ is extraneous}$$

**33** $\log(20x) = 3 + \log(x-5) \;\Rightarrow\; \log(20x) - \log(x-5) = 3 \;\Rightarrow$
$$\log\frac{20x}{x-5} = 3 \;\Rightarrow\; \frac{20x}{x-5} = 10^3 \;\Rightarrow\; 20x = 1000x - 5000 \;\Rightarrow\; 5000 = 980x \;\Rightarrow\; x = \frac{250}{49}$$

**34** $\log(57x) = 2 + \log(x-2) \;\Rightarrow\; \log(57x) - \log(x-2) = 2 \;\Rightarrow$
$$\log\frac{57x}{x-2} = 2 \;\Rightarrow\; \frac{57x}{x-2} = 10^2 \;\Rightarrow\; 57x = 100x - 200 \;\Rightarrow\; 200 = 43x \;\Rightarrow\; x = \frac{200}{43}$$

**35** $\ln x = 1 - \ln(x+2) \;\Rightarrow\; \ln x + \ln(x+2) = 1 \;\Rightarrow\; \ln[x(x+2)] = 1 \;\Rightarrow\; x^2 + 2x = e^1 \;\Rightarrow$
$$x^2 + 2x - e = 0 \;\Rightarrow\; x = \frac{-2 \pm \sqrt{4 + 4e}}{2} = \frac{-2 \pm 2\sqrt{1+e}}{2} = -1 \pm \sqrt{1+e}.$$
$$x = -1 + \sqrt{1+e} \approx 0.93 \text{ is a valid solution, but } x = -1 - \sqrt{1+e} \approx -2.93 \text{ is extraneous.}$$

**36** $\ln x = 1 + \ln(x+1) \;\Rightarrow\; \ln x - \ln(x+1) = 1 \;\Rightarrow\; \ln\left(\frac{x}{x+1}\right) = 1 \;\Rightarrow\; \frac{x}{x+1} = e^1 \;\Rightarrow$
$$x = ex + e \;\Rightarrow\; (1-e)x = e \;\Rightarrow\; x = \frac{e}{1-e} \approx -1.58 \text{ and is extraneous, } \textbf{no solution}$$

**37**
$$\log_3(x-2) = \log_3 27 - \log_3(x-4) - 5^{\log_5 1} \qquad \{\text{given}\}$$
$$\log_3(x-2) + \log_3(x-4) = \log_3 3^3 - 1 \qquad \{5^{\log_5 1} = 1\}$$
$$\log_3[(x-2)(x-4)] = 3 - 1 \qquad \{\log_3 3^3 = 3\}$$
$$\log_3(x^2 - 6x + 8) = 2 \qquad \{\text{simplify}\}$$
$$x^2 - 6x + 8 = 3^2 \qquad \{\text{exponential form}\}$$
$$x^2 - 6x - 1 = 0 \qquad \{\text{subtract 9}\}$$

Now solve $x^2 - 6x - 1 = 0$ using the quadratic formula to get $x = \left(6 \pm \sqrt{40}\right)/2 = 3 \pm \sqrt{10}$.

Since $3 - \sqrt{10}$ makes the arguments of the logarithms negative, the only solution is $3 + \sqrt{10}$.

**38** $\log_2(x+3) = \log_2(x-3) + \log_3 9 + 4^{\log_4 3} \;\Rightarrow\; \log_2(x+3) - \log_2(x-3) = 2 + 3 \;\Rightarrow$
$$\log_2\frac{x+3}{x-3} = 5 \;\Rightarrow\; \frac{x+3}{x-3} = 2^5 \;\Rightarrow\; x + 3 = 32(x-3) \;\Rightarrow\; x + 3 = 32x - 96 \;\Rightarrow\; 99 = 31x \;\Rightarrow$$
$$x = \frac{99}{31}$$

**39** $f(x) = \log_3(3x) = \log_3 3 + \log_3 x = \log_3 x + 1$  •  shift $y = \log_3 x$ up 1 unit

*Figure 39*

*Figure 40*

**40** $f(x) = \log_4(16x) = \log_4 16 + \log_4 x = \log_4 x + 2$  •  shift $y = \log_4 x$ up 2 units

**41** $f(x) = 3\log_3 x$  •  vertically stretch $y = \log_3 x$ by a factor of 3

*Figure 41*

*Figure 42*

**42** $f(x) = \frac{1}{3}\log_3 x$  •  vertically compress $y = \log_3 x$ by a factor of 3

**43** $f(x) = \log_3(x^2) = 2\log_3 x$  •  Vertically stretch $y = \log_3 x$ by a factor of 2 and include its reflection through the $y$-axis since the domain of the original function, $f(x) = \log_3(x^2)$, is $\mathbb{R} - \{0\}$. Keep in mind that the laws of logarithms are established for positive real numbers, so that when we make the step $\log_3(x^2) = 2\log_3 x$, it is only for positive $x$.

*Figure 43*

*Figure 44*

**44** $f(x) = \log_2(x^2) = 2\log_2 x$  •  similar to Exercise 43

**45** $f(x) = \log_2(x^3) = 3\log_2 x$ • vertically stretch $y = \log_2 x$ by a factor of 3

*Figure 45*

*Figure 46*

**46** $f(x) = \log_3(x^3) = 3\log_3 x$ • vertically stretch $y = \log_3 x$ by a factor of 3

**47** $f(x) = \log_2 \sqrt{x} = \log_2 x^{1/2} = \frac{1}{2}\log_2 x$ • vertically compress $y = \log_2 x$ by a factor of $1/(1/2) = 2$

*Figure 47*

*Figure 48*

**48** $f(x) = \log_2 \sqrt[3]{x} = \frac{1}{3}\log_2 x$ • vertically compress $y = \log_2 x$ by a factor of 3

**49** $f(x) = \log_3\left(\dfrac{1}{x}\right) = \log_3 x^{-1} = -\log_3 x$ • reflect $y = \log_3 x$ through the $x$-axis.

*Figure 49*

*Figure 50*

**50** $f(x) = \log_2\left(\dfrac{1}{x}\right) = \log_2 x^{-1} = -\log_2 x$ • reflect $y = \log_2 x$ through the $x$-axis

**51** The values of $F(x) = \log_2 x$ are doubled and the reflection of $F$ through the $y$-axis is included.

The domain of $f$ is $\mathbb{R} - \{0\}$ and $f(x) = \log_2 x^2$.

**52** The domain of $f$ is $\mathbb{R} - \{0\}$ and $f$ has the same $y$-values as $F(x) = \log_2 x$.

Hence, $f(x) = \log_2 |x|$. {or $f(x) = \frac{1}{2} \log_2 x^2$}

**53** $F(x) = \log_2 x$ is shifted up 3 units since $(1, 0)$ on $F$ is $(1, 3)$ on the graph.

Hence, $f(x) = 3 + \log_2 x = \log_2 2^3 + \log_2 x = \log_2(8x)$.

**54** $F(x) = \log_2 x$ is reflected through the $x$-axis and shifted up 1 unit.

Hence, $f(x) = -\log_2 x + 1 = \log_2 2 - \log_2 x = \log_2 \dfrac{2}{x}$.

**55** $V_1 = 2$ and $V_2 = 4.5 \Rightarrow db = 20 \log \dfrac{V_2}{V_1} = 20 \log \dfrac{4.5}{2} \approx 7.04$, or $+7$.

**56** Let $\dfrac{V_2}{V_1} = k$. A $+20$ decibel gain $\Rightarrow +20 = 20 \log k \Rightarrow 1 = \log k \Rightarrow k = 10$.

A $+40$ decibel gain $\Rightarrow +40 = 20 \log k \Rightarrow 2 = \log k \Rightarrow k = 100$.

Note that a tenfold increase in the voltage ratio is needed to double the decibel gain.

**57** $\log y = \log b - k \log x \Rightarrow \log y = \log b - \log x^k \Rightarrow \log y = \log \dfrac{b}{x^k} \Rightarrow y = \dfrac{b}{x^k}$

**58** $p = p_0 e^{-ax} \Rightarrow \dfrac{p}{p_0} = e^{-ax} \Rightarrow \ln\left(\dfrac{p}{p_0}\right) = -ax \Rightarrow x(p) = -\dfrac{1}{a}\ln\left(\dfrac{p}{p_0}\right) = \dfrac{1}{a}\ln\left(\dfrac{p_0}{p}\right)$

**59** $c = 0.5$ and $z_0 = 0.1 \Rightarrow$

$v = c\ln(z/z_0)$

$= (0.5)\ln(z/0.1)$

$= \frac{1}{2}\ln(10z)$

$= \frac{1}{2}(\ln 10 + \ln z)$

$= \frac{1}{2}\ln 10 + \frac{1}{2}\ln z \approx \frac{1}{2}\ln z + 1.15.$

**60** $y = y_0 e^{-0.3821t}$ • $y = 50\%$ of $y_0 \Rightarrow \frac{1}{2}y_0 = y_0 e^{-0.3821t} \Rightarrow \frac{1}{2} = e^{-0.3821t} \Rightarrow \ln\frac{1}{2} = -0.3821t \Rightarrow$

$t = \dfrac{-\ln 2}{-0.3821} \approx 1.814$ yr.

**61** (a) $R(x) = a\log\left(\dfrac{x}{x_0}\right)$ • $R(x_0) = a\log\left(\dfrac{x_0}{x_0}\right) = a\log 1 = a \cdot 0 = 0$

(b) $R(2x) = a\log\left(\dfrac{2x}{x_0}\right) = a\log\left(2 \cdot \dfrac{x}{x_0}\right) = a\left[\log 2 + \log\left(\dfrac{x}{x_0}\right)\right] = a\log 2 + a\log\left(\dfrac{x}{x_0}\right) = R(x) + a\log 2$

**62** (a) $E(x) = E_0 e^{-x/x_0} \Rightarrow E(x_0) = E_0 e^{-x_0/x_0} = E_0 e^{-1} = \dfrac{1}{e}E_0$

(b) $E = E_0 - 99\% E_0 \Rightarrow (1 - 0.99)E_0 = E_0 e^{-x/x_0} \Rightarrow 0.01 = e^{-x/x_0} \Rightarrow$

$-\dfrac{x}{x_0} = \ln(0.01) \Rightarrow -\dfrac{x}{x_0} = -\ln 100 \Rightarrow x = (\ln 100)x_0 \approx 4.6\,x_0$

**63** $\ln I_0 - \ln I = kx \Rightarrow \ln \dfrac{I_0}{I} = kx \Rightarrow x = \dfrac{1}{k}\ln\dfrac{I_0}{I} = \dfrac{1}{0.39}\ln 1.12 \approx 0.29$ cm.

**64** $\ln I_0 - \ln I = kx \Rightarrow \ln \dfrac{I_0}{I} = kx \Rightarrow \dfrac{I_0}{I} = e^{kx} = e^{(0.39)(0.24)} \approx 1.10 \Rightarrow \dfrac{I}{I_0} \approx \dfrac{1}{1.10} \Rightarrow \dfrac{I}{I_0} \approx 0.91.$

The intensity decreases by approximately 9%.

**65** From the graph of $f(x) = x^3 - 3.5x^2 + 3x$ and $g(x) = \log 3x$, the coordinates of the points of intersection are approximately $(1.02, 0.48)$ and $(2.40, 0.86)$. $f(x) \geq g(x)$ on the intervals $(0, 1.02]$ and $[2.40, \infty)$.

$[0, 6]$ by $[-1, 3]$

*Figure 65*

$[0, 6]$ by $[-1, 3]$

*Figure 66*

**66** The domain of $g(x) = \log x$ is $x > 0$. The graphs of $f(x) = 3^{-0.5x}$ and $g$ intersect at $x \approx 2.08$.

The solution of the inequality $f(x) \geq g(x)$ is $(0, 2.08]$.

**67** Graph $y = e^{-x} - 2\log(1 + x^2) + 0.5x$ and estimate any $x$-intercepts.

From the graph, we see that the roots of the equation are approximately $x \approx 1.41, 6.59$.

$[0, 8]$ by $[-1.67, 3.67]$

*Figure 67*

$[-1, 5]$ by $[-1, 3]$

*Figure 68*

**68** Graph $y = 0.3\ln x + x^3 - 3.1x^2 + 1.3x + 0.8$ and estimate any $x$-intercepts. From the graph, we determine that the roots of the equation are approximately 0.056 and 2.359 as well as $x = 1$.

**69** (a) $f$ is increasing on $[0.2, 0.63]$ and $[6.87, 16]$. $f$ is decreasing on $[0.63, 6.87]$.

(b) The maximum value of $f$ is 4.61 when $x = 16$.

The minimum value of $f$ is approximately $-3.31$ when $x \approx 6.87$.

$[0.2, 16, 2]$ by $[-4.77, 5.77]$

*Figure 69*

$[0.2, 16, 2]$ by $[-6, 14]$

*Figure 70*

**70** (a) $f$ is increasing on $[0.44, 9.76]$. $f$ is decreasing on $[0.2, 0.44]$ and $[9.76, 16]$.

(b) The maximum value of $f$ is approximately 11.35 when $x \approx 9.76$.

The minimum value of $f$ is approximately $-4.9$ when $x = 16$.

**71** Graph $Y_1 = x \log x - \log x$ and $Y_2 = 5$. The graphs intersect at $x \approx 6.94$.

$[-5, 10]$ by $[-2, 8]$　　　　$[-5, 10]$ by $[-2, 8]$

*Figure 71*　　　　　*Figure 72*

**72** Graph $Y_1 = 0.3e^x - \ln x$ and $Y_2 = 4\ln(x+1)$. The graphs intersect at $x \approx 0.40$ and $3.12$.

**73** $I = I_0 - 20 \log d - kd$ • Let $d = x$. Graph $Y_1 = I_0 - 20 \log x - kx = 70 - 20 \log x - 0.076x$ and $Y_2 = 20$. At the point of intersection, $x \approx 115.3$. The distance is approximately 115 meters.

$[0, 150, 10]$ by $[0, 100, 10]$　　　$[0, 150, 10]$ by $[0, 100, 10]$

*Figure 73*　　　　　*Figure 74*

**74** $I = I_0 - 20 \log d - kd$ • Let $d = x$. Graph $Y_1 = I_0 - 20 \log x - kx = 60 - 20 \log x - 0.11x$ and $Y_2 = 15$. At the point of intersection, $x \approx 71.7$. The distance is approximately 72 meters.

## 4.6 Exercises

**1** (a) $5^x = 3 \;\Rightarrow\; \log 5^x = \log 3 \;\Rightarrow\; x \log 5 = \log 3 \;\Rightarrow\; x = \dfrac{\log 3}{\log 5} \approx 0.68$

　(b) $5^x = 3 \;\Rightarrow\; x = \log_5 3 = \dfrac{\log 3}{\log 5}$ {by the change of base formula} $\approx 0.68$

**2** (a) $4^x = 7 \;\Rightarrow\; \log 4^x = \log 7 \;\Rightarrow\; x \log 4 = \log 7 \;\Rightarrow\; x = \dfrac{\log 7}{\log 4} \approx 1.40$

　(b) $4^x = 7 \;\Rightarrow\; x = \log_4 7 = \dfrac{\log 7}{\log 4}$ {by the change of base formula} $\approx 1.40$

**3** (a) $3^{4-x} = 5 \;\Rightarrow\; \log(3^{4-x}) = \log 5 \;\Rightarrow\; (4-x)\log 3 = \log 5 \;\Rightarrow\; 4 - x = \dfrac{\log 5}{\log 3} \;\Rightarrow$
$$x = 4 - \frac{\log 5}{\log 3} \approx 2.54.$$

　***Note:*** The answer could also be written as $4 - \dfrac{\log 5}{\log 3} = \dfrac{4\log 3 - \log 5}{\log 3} = \dfrac{\log 81 - \log 5}{\log 3} = \dfrac{\log \frac{81}{5}}{\log 3}$.

　(b) $3^{4-x} = 5 \;\Rightarrow\; 4 - x = \log_3 5 \;\Rightarrow\; x = 4 - \dfrac{\log 5}{\log 3} \approx 2.54.$

**4** (a) $\left(\frac{1}{3}\right)^x = 100 \;\Rightarrow\; \log\left(\frac{1}{3}\right)^x = \log 100 \;\Rightarrow\; x \log \frac{1}{3} = 2 \;\Rightarrow\; x = \dfrac{2}{-\log 3} \approx -4.19$

　(b) $\left(\frac{1}{3}\right)^x = 100 \;\Rightarrow\; x = \log_{(1/3)} 100 = \dfrac{\log 100}{\log \frac{1}{3}} = \dfrac{2}{-\log 3} \approx -4.19$

**5** $\log_5 12 = \dfrac{\log 12}{\log 5} \left\{ \text{or, equivalently, } \dfrac{\ln 12}{\ln 5} \right\} \approx 1.5440$

Note that either log or ln can be used here. Try to get comfortable using either one.

**6** $\log_6 5 = \dfrac{\log 5}{\log 6} \left\{ \text{or, equivalently, } \dfrac{\ln 5}{\ln 6} \right\} \approx 0.8982$

**7** $\log_9 0.9 = \dfrac{\log 0.9}{\log 9} \left\{ \text{or, equivalently, } \dfrac{\ln 0.9}{\ln 9} \right\} \approx -0.0480$

**8** $\log_6 \frac{1}{3} = \dfrac{\log \frac{1}{3}}{\log 6} \left\{ \text{or, equivalently, } \dfrac{\ln \frac{1}{3}}{\ln 6} \right\} \approx -0.6131$

**9** $\dfrac{\log_5 16}{\log_5 4} = \log_4 16 = \log_4 4^2 = 2$

**10** $\dfrac{\log_7 243}{\log_7 3} = \log_3 243 = \log_3 3^5 = 5$

**11** $2^{-x} = 8 \;\Rightarrow\; 2^{-x} = 2^3 \;\Rightarrow\; -x = 3 \;\Rightarrow\; x = -3$

**12** $2^{-x^2} = 5 \;\Rightarrow\; -x^2 = \log_2 5 \;\Rightarrow\; x^2 = -\dfrac{\log 5}{\log 2}$, which is negative, but $x^2$ is nonnegative, so there is **no solution**

**13** $3^{-x^2} = 7 \;\Rightarrow\; -x^2 = \log_3 7 \;\Rightarrow\; x^2 = -\dfrac{\log 7}{\log 3}$, which is negative, but $x^2$ is nonnegative, so there is **no solution**

**14** $3^{-x} = 81 \;\Rightarrow\; 3^{-x} = 3^4 \;\Rightarrow\; -x = 4 \;\Rightarrow\; x = -4$

**15** The steps are similar to those in Example 4. $3^{x+4} = 2^{1-3x} \;\Rightarrow\; \log\big(3^{x+4}\big) = \log\big(2^{1-3x}\big) \;\Rightarrow$

$(x+4)\log 3 = (1-3x)\log 2 \;\Rightarrow\; x\log 3 + 4\log 3 = \log 2 - 3x\log 2 \;\Rightarrow$

$x\log 3 + 3x\log 2 = \log 2 - 4\log 3 \;\Rightarrow\; x(\log 3 + 3\log 2) = \log 2 - 4\log 3 \;\Rightarrow$

$$x = \dfrac{\log 2 - \log 81}{\log 3 + \log 8} \;\Rightarrow\; x = \dfrac{\log \frac{2}{81}}{\log 24} \approx -1.16$$

**16** $4^{2x+3} = 5^{x-2} \;\Rightarrow\; (2x+3)\log 4 = (x-2)\log 5 \;\Rightarrow\; 2x\log 4 + 3\log 4 = x\log 5 - 2\log 5 \;\Rightarrow$

$$2\log 5 + 3\log 4 = x(\log 5 - 2\log 4) \;\Rightarrow\; x = \dfrac{\log 25 + \log 64}{\log 5 - \log 16} \;\Rightarrow\; x = \dfrac{\log 1600}{\log \frac{5}{16}} \approx -6.34$$

**17** $2^{2x-3} = 5^{x-2} \;\Rightarrow\; \log(2^{2x-3}) = \log(5^{x-2}) \;\Rightarrow\; (2x-3)\log 2 = (x-2)\log 5 \;\Rightarrow$

$2x\log 2 - 3\log 2 = x\log 5 - 2\log 5 \;\Rightarrow\; 2x\log 2 - x\log 5 = 3\log 2 - 2\log 5 \;\Rightarrow$

$$x(2\log 2 - \log 5) = \log 2^3 - \log 5^2 \;\Rightarrow\; x = \dfrac{\log 8 - \log 25}{\log 4 - \log 5} \;\Rightarrow\; x = \dfrac{\log \frac{8}{25}}{\log \frac{4}{5}} \approx 5.11$$

**18** $3^{2-3x} = 4^{2x+1} \;\Rightarrow\; (2-3x)\log 3 = (2x+1)\log 4 \;\Rightarrow\; 2\log 3 - 3x\log 3 = 2x\log 4 + \log 4 \;\Rightarrow$

$$2\log 3 - \log 4 = x(2\log 4 + 3\log 3) \;\Rightarrow\; x = \dfrac{\log 9 - \log 4}{\log 16 + \log 27} \;\Rightarrow\; x = \dfrac{\log \frac{9}{4}}{\log 432} \approx 0.13$$

**19** $\log x = 1 - \log(x-3) \;\Rightarrow\; \log x + \log(x-3) = 1 \;\Rightarrow\; \log(x^2 - 3x) = 1 \;\Rightarrow\; x^2 - 3x = 10^1 \;\Rightarrow$

$x^2 - 3x - 10 = 0 \;\Rightarrow\; (x-5)(x+2) = 0 \;\Rightarrow\; x = 5, -2$. The solution $x = 5$ checks, but $-2$ is extraneous.

**20** $\log(5x+1) = 2 + \log(2x-3) \;\Rightarrow\; \log(5x+1) - \log(2x-3) = 2 \;\Rightarrow$

$$\log\left(\dfrac{5x+1}{2x-3}\right) = 2 \;\Rightarrow\; \dfrac{5x+1}{2x-3} = 10^2 \;\Rightarrow\; 5x+1 = 200x - 300 \;\Rightarrow\; x = \dfrac{301}{195} \approx 1.54$$

**21** $\log(x^2+4) - \log(x+2) = 2 + \log(x-2)$ $\Rightarrow$ $\log\left(\dfrac{x^2+4}{x+2}\right) - \log(x-2) = 2$ $\Rightarrow$

$\log\left(\dfrac{x^2+4}{x^2-4}\right) = 2$ $\Rightarrow$ $\dfrac{x^2+4}{x^2-4} = 10^2$ $\Rightarrow$ $x^2+4 = 100(x^2-4)$ $\Rightarrow$ $x^2+4 = 100x^2-400$ $\Rightarrow$

$\qquad 404 = 99x^2$ $\Rightarrow$ $x^2 = \frac{404}{99}$ $\Rightarrow$ $x = \pm\sqrt{\frac{4\cdot101}{9\cdot11}} = \pm\frac{2}{3}\sqrt{\frac{101}{11}} \approx \pm 2.02$; $-\frac{2}{3}\sqrt{\frac{101}{11}}$ is extraneous

**22** $\log(x+3) + \log(x-3) = \log(x^2+5) - 2$ $\Rightarrow$ $\log(x^2-9) = \log(x^2+5) - 2$ $\Rightarrow$

$\log(x^2-9) = \log(x^2+5) - \log 100$ $\Rightarrow$ $\log(x^2-9) = \log\left(\dfrac{x^2+5}{100}\right)$ $\Rightarrow$ $x^2-9 = \dfrac{x^2+5}{100}$ $\Rightarrow$

$\qquad 100x^2-900 = x^2+5$ $\Rightarrow$ $99x^2 = 905$ $\Rightarrow$ $x^2 = \frac{905}{99}$ $\Rightarrow$ $x = \pm\sqrt{\frac{905}{99}} \approx \pm 3.02$; $-\sqrt{\frac{905}{99}}$ is extraneous

**23** $\log(x-1) = \log(2/x) + \log(3x-5)$ $\Rightarrow$ $\log(x-1) = \log\left(\dfrac{2(3x-5)}{x}\right)$ $\Rightarrow$ $x-1 = \dfrac{6x-10}{x}$ $\Rightarrow$

$\qquad x(x-1) = 6x-10$ $\Rightarrow$ $x^2-x = 6x-10$ $\Rightarrow$ $x^2-7x+10 = 0$ $\Rightarrow$ $(x-2)(x-5) = 0$ $\Rightarrow$ $x = 2, 5$

**24** $\log(x-4) - \log(3x-10) = \log(1/x)$ $\Rightarrow$ $\log\left(\dfrac{x-4}{3x-10}\right) = \log\left(\dfrac{1}{x}\right)$ $\Rightarrow$ $\dfrac{x-4}{3x-10} = \dfrac{1}{x}$ $\Rightarrow$

$\qquad x^2-4x = 3x-10$ $\Rightarrow$ $(x-2)(x-5) = 0$ $\Rightarrow$ $x = 2, 5$; $2$ is extraneous

**25** See Example 5 for more detail concerning this type of exercise.

$\quad 5^x + 125(5^{-x}) = 30$ { multiply by $5^x$ } $\Rightarrow$ $(5^x)^2 + 125 = 30(5^x)$ $\Rightarrow$

$(5^x)^2 - 30(5^x) + 125 = 0$ {recognize as a quadratic in $5^x$ and factor} $\Rightarrow$

$\qquad (5^x - 5)(5^x - 25) = 0$ $\Rightarrow$ $5^x = 5, 25$ $\Rightarrow$ $5^x = 5^1, 5^2$ $\Rightarrow$ $x = 1, 2$

**26** $3(3^x) + 9(3^{-x}) = 28$ $\Rightarrow$ $3(3^x)^2 - 28(3^x) + 9 = 0$ $\Rightarrow$

$\qquad [3(3^x) - 1](3^x - 9) = 0$ $\Rightarrow$ $3^x = \frac{1}{3}, 9$ $\Rightarrow$ $3^x = 3^{-1}, 3^2$ $\Rightarrow$ $x = -1, 2$

**27** $4^x - 3(4^{-x}) = 8$ { multiply by $4^x$ } $\Rightarrow$ $(4^x)^2 - 3 = 8(4^x)$ $\Rightarrow$

$(4^x)^2 - 8(4^x) - 3 = 0$ {recognize as a quadratic in $4^x$ and use the quadratic formula} $\Rightarrow$

$4^x = \dfrac{-(-8) \pm \sqrt{(-8)^2 - 4(1)(-3)}}{2(1)} = \dfrac{8 \pm \sqrt{76}}{2} = \dfrac{8 \pm 2\sqrt{19}}{2} = 4 \pm \sqrt{19}.$

Since $4^x$ is positive and $4 - \sqrt{19}$ is negative, $4 - \sqrt{19}$ is discarded. Continuing, $4^x = 4 + \sqrt{19}$ $\Rightarrow$

$\qquad x = \log_4\left(4 + \sqrt{19}\right) = \dfrac{\log\left(4 + \sqrt{19}\right)}{\log 4}$ {use the change of base formula to approximate} $\approx 1.53$

**28** $2^x - 6(2^{-x}) = 6$ $\Rightarrow$ $(2^x)^2 - 6(2^x) - 6 = 0$ $\Rightarrow$ $2^x = \dfrac{6 + \sqrt{60}}{2}$ $\Rightarrow$

$\quad \left\{ \text{since } 2^x > 0 \text{ and } \dfrac{6 - \sqrt{60}}{2} < 0 \right\} = 3 + \sqrt{15}$ $\Rightarrow$ $x = \log_2\left(3 + \sqrt{15}\right) = \dfrac{\log\left(3 + \sqrt{15}\right)}{\log 2} \approx 2.78$

**29** $\log(x^2) = (\log x)^2$ $\Rightarrow$ $2\log x = (\log x)^2$ $\Rightarrow$ $(\log x)^2 - 2\log x = 0$ $\Rightarrow$

$\qquad (\log x)(\log x - 2) = 0$ $\Rightarrow$ $\log x = 0, 2$ $\Rightarrow$ $x = 10^0, 10^2$ $\Rightarrow$ $x = 1$ or $100$

**30** $\log\sqrt{x} = \sqrt{\log x}$ $\Rightarrow$ $\frac{1}{2}\log x = (\log x)^{1/2}$ $\Rightarrow$ $(\log x)^2 = 4\log x$ $\Rightarrow$

$\qquad (\log x)(\log x - 4) = 0$ $\Rightarrow$ $\log x = 0, 4$ $\Rightarrow$ $x = 10^0, 10^4$ $\Rightarrow$ $x = 1$ or $10{,}000$

**31** Don't confuse $\log(\log x)$ with $(\log x)(\log x)$.

The first expression is the log of the log of $x$, whereas the second expression is the log of $x$ times itself.

$\qquad \log(\log x) = 2$ $\Rightarrow$ $\log_{10}(\log x) = 2$ $\Rightarrow$ $\log x = 10^2 = 100$ $\Rightarrow$ $x = 10^{100}$

**32** $\log\sqrt{x^3-9}=2 \Rightarrow \sqrt{x^3-9}=10^2 \Rightarrow x^3-9=10^4 \Rightarrow x=\sqrt[3]{10{,}009}$

**33** $x^{\sqrt{\log x}}=10^8$ {take the log of both sides} $\Rightarrow \log\left(x^{\sqrt{\log x}}\right)=\log 10^8 \Rightarrow$

$\sqrt{\log x}(\log x)=8 \Rightarrow (\log x)^{1/2}(\log x)^1=8 \Rightarrow (\log x)^{3/2}=8 \Rightarrow$

$$\left[(\log x)^{3/2}\right]^{2/3}=(8)^{2/3} \Rightarrow \log x=\left(\sqrt[3]{8}\right)^2=4 \Rightarrow x=10{,}000$$

**34** $\log(x^3)=(\log x)^3 \Rightarrow 3\log x=(\log x)^3 \Rightarrow (\log x)\left[(\log x)^2-3\right]=0 \Rightarrow$

$$\log x=0,\pm\sqrt{3} \Rightarrow x=1,10^{\sqrt{3}},10^{-\sqrt{3}}$$

**35** Since $e^{2x}=(e^x)^2$, we recognize $e^{2x}+2e^x-15$ as a quadratic in $e^x$ and factor it.

$e^{2x}+2e^x-15=0 \Rightarrow (e^x+5)(e^x-3)=0 \Rightarrow e^x=-5,3$. But $e^x>0$, so $e^x=3 \Rightarrow x=\ln 3$.

**36** $e^x+4e^{-x}=5 \Rightarrow e^{2x}+4=5e^x$ {multiply by $e^x$} $\Rightarrow e^{2x}-5e^x+4=0 \Rightarrow (e^x-1)(e^x-4)=0 \Rightarrow$

$$e^x=1,4 \Rightarrow x=\ln 1,\ln 4 \Rightarrow x=0,\ln 4$$

**37** $\log_3 x-\log_9(x+42)=0 \Rightarrow \dfrac{\ln x}{\ln 3}-\dfrac{\ln(x+42)}{\ln 9}=0$ {change of base theorem} $\Rightarrow$

$\dfrac{2\ln x}{2\ln 3}-\dfrac{\ln(x+42)}{\ln 9}=0$ {get a common denominator, $2\ln 3=\ln 3^2=\ln 9$} $\Rightarrow$

$\ln x^2-\ln(x+42)=0$ {multiply by $\ln 9$ and change $2\ln x$ to $\ln x^2$} $\Rightarrow$

$\ln\left(\dfrac{x^2}{x+42}\right)=0 \Rightarrow \dfrac{x^2}{x+42}=e^0 \Rightarrow \dfrac{x^2}{x+42}=1 \Rightarrow x^2=x+42 \Rightarrow$

$$x^2-x-42=0 \Rightarrow (x-7)(x+6)=0 \Rightarrow x=7,\text{ and }-6\text{ is extraneous.}$$

**38** $\log_4 x+\log_8 x=1 \Rightarrow \dfrac{\ln x}{\ln 4}+\dfrac{\ln x}{\ln 8}=1 \Rightarrow \dfrac{\ln x}{\ln 2^2}+\dfrac{\ln x}{\ln 2^3}=1 \Rightarrow \dfrac{\ln x}{2\ln 2}+\dfrac{\ln x}{3\ln 2}=1 \Rightarrow$

$\dfrac{3\ln x}{6\ln 2}+\dfrac{2\ln x}{6\ln 2}=1 \Rightarrow 3\ln x+2\ln x=6\ln 2 \Rightarrow$

$$\ln x^3+\ln x^2=\ln 2^6 \Rightarrow \ln(x^3\cdot x^2)=\ln 2^6 \Rightarrow x^5=64 \Rightarrow x=\sqrt[5]{64}$$

**Note:** For Exercises 39–46 and Chapter Review Exercises 51–52, let $D$ denote the domain of the function determined by the original equation, and $R$ its range. These are then the range and domain, respectively, of the equation listed in the answer.

**39** $y=\dfrac{10^x+10^{-x}}{2}$ $\{D=\mathbb{R},R=[1,\infty)\} \Rightarrow$

$2y=10^x+10^{-x}$ $\left\{\text{since }10^{-x}=\dfrac{1}{10^x}\text{, multiply by }10^x\text{ to eliminate denominator}\right\} \Rightarrow$

$10^{2x}-2y\,10^x+1=0$ { treat as a quadratic in $10^x$ } $\Rightarrow 10^x=\dfrac{2y\pm\sqrt{4y^2-4}}{2}=y\pm\sqrt{y^2-1} \Rightarrow$

$$x=\log\left(y\pm\sqrt{y^2-1}\right)$$

**40** The solution is similar to that of Exercise 39. $y=\dfrac{10^x-10^{-x}}{2}$ $\{D=R=\mathbb{R}\} \Rightarrow 2y=10^x-10^{-x} \Rightarrow$

$10^{2x}-2y\,10^x-1=0 \Rightarrow 10^x=\dfrac{2y\pm\sqrt{4y^2+4}}{2}=y\pm\sqrt{y^2+1};$

$$\sqrt{y^2+1}>y,\text{ so }y-\sqrt{y^2+1}<0,\text{ but }10^x>0\text{ and thus, }x=\log\left(y+\sqrt{y^2+1}\right)$$

**41** $y=\dfrac{10^x-10^{-x}}{10^x+10^{-x}}$ $\{D=\mathbb{R},R=(-1,1)\} \Rightarrow y\,10^x+y\,10^{-x}=10^x-10^{-x} \Rightarrow y\,10^{2x}+y=10^{2x}-1 \Rightarrow$

$$(y-1)\,10^{2x}=-1-y \Rightarrow 10^{2x}=\dfrac{-1-y}{y-1} \Rightarrow 2x=\log\left(\dfrac{1+y}{1-y}\right) \Rightarrow x=\dfrac{1}{2}\log\left(\dfrac{1+y}{1-y}\right)$$

**42** $y = \dfrac{10^x + 10^{-x}}{10^x - 10^{-x}}$ $\{ D = \mathbb{R} - \{0\}, R = (-\infty, -1) \cup (1, \infty) \}$ $\Rightarrow$ $y\,10^x - y\,10^{-x} = 10^x + 10^{-x}$ $\Rightarrow$

$y\,10^{2x} - y = 10^{2x} + 1$ $\Rightarrow$ $(y-1)10^{2x} = y+1$ $\Rightarrow$ $10^{2x} = \dfrac{y+1}{y-1}$ $\Rightarrow$ $2x = \log\left(\dfrac{y+1}{y-1}\right)$ $\Rightarrow$

$$x = \tfrac{1}{2}\log\left(\dfrac{y+1}{y-1}\right)$$

**43** $y = \dfrac{e^x - e^{-x}}{2}$ $\{ D = R = \mathbb{R} \}$ $\Rightarrow$ $2y = e^x - e^{-x}$ $\Rightarrow$

$e^{2x} - 2y\,e^x - 1 = 0$ $\Rightarrow$ $e^x = \dfrac{2y \pm \sqrt{4y^2 + 4}}{2} = y \pm \sqrt{y^2 + 1};$

$\sqrt{y^2 + 1} > y$, so $y - \sqrt{y^2 + 1} < 0$, but $e^x > 0$ and thus, $x = \ln\left(y + \sqrt{y^2 + 1}\right)$

**44** Use ln instead of log in Exercise 39. $x = \ln\left(y \pm \sqrt{y^2 - 1}\right)$

**45** $y = \dfrac{e^x + e^{-x}}{e^x - e^{-x}}$

$\{ D = \mathbb{R} - \{0\}, R = (-\infty, -1) \cup (1, \infty) \}$ $\Rightarrow$ $ye^x - ye^{-x} = e^x + e^{-x}$ $\Rightarrow$ $ye^{2x} - y = e^{2x} + 1$ $\Rightarrow$

$(y-1)e^{2x} = y+1$ $\Rightarrow$ $e^{2x} = \dfrac{y+1}{y-1}$ $\Rightarrow$ $2x = \ln\left(\dfrac{y+1}{y-1}\right)$ $\Rightarrow$ $x = \dfrac{1}{2}\ln\left(\dfrac{y+1}{y-1}\right)$

**46** Use ln instead of log in Exercise 41. $x = \dfrac{1}{2}\ln\left(\dfrac{1+y}{1-y}\right)$

**47** $f(x) = \log_2(x+3)$ • $x = 0$ $\Rightarrow$ $y\text{-intercept} = \log_2 3 = \dfrac{\log 3}{\log 2} \approx 1.5850$

*Figure 47*

*Figure 48*

**48** $f(x) = \log_3(x+5)$ • $x = 0$ $\Rightarrow$ $y\text{-intercept} = \log_3 5 = \dfrac{\log 5}{\log 3} \approx 1.4650$

**49** $f(x) = 4^x - 3$ • $y = 0$ $\Rightarrow$ $4^x = 3$ $\Rightarrow$ $x\text{-intercept} = \log_4 3 = \dfrac{\log 3}{\log 4} \approx 0.7925$

*Figure 49*

*Figure 50*

**50** $f(x) = 3^x - 6$ • $y = 0$ $\Rightarrow$ $3^x = 6$ $\Rightarrow$ $x\text{-intercept} = \log_3 6 = \dfrac{\log 6}{\log 3} \approx 1.6309$

**51** (a) vinegar: pH $\approx -\log(6.3 \times 10^{-3}) = -(\log 6.3 + \log 10^{-3}) = -(\log 6.3 - 3) = 3 - \log 6.3 \approx 2.2$

(b) carrots: pH $\approx -\log(1.0 \times 10^{-5}) = -(\log 1.0 + \log 10^{-5}) = -(0 - 5\log 10) = 5(1) = 5$

(c) sea water: pH $\approx -\log(5.0 \times 10^{-9}) = -(\log 5.0 + \log 10^{-9}) = 9 - \log 5.0 \approx 8.3$

**52** pH $= -\log[H^+] \ \Rightarrow \ [H^+] = 10^{-\text{pH}}$  (a) apples: $[H^+] = 10^{-3} = 0.001$

(b) beer: $[H^+] = 10^{-4.2} \approx 0.0000631$  (c) milk: $[H^+] = 10^{-6.6} \approx 0.00000025$

**53** $[H^+] < 10^{-7} \ \Rightarrow \ \log[H^+] < \log 10^{-7}$ {since log is an increasing function} $\Rightarrow \ \log[H^+] < -7 \ \Rightarrow$
$-\log[H^+] > -(-7) \ \Rightarrow \ $ pH $> 7$ for basic solutions; similarly, pH $< 7$ for acidic solutions.

**54** $1 < \text{pH} < 14 \ \Rightarrow \ 1 < -\log[H^+] < 14 \ \Rightarrow \ -1 > \log[H^+] > -14 \ \Rightarrow$
$$10^{-1} > 10^{\log[H^+]} > 10^{-14} \ \Rightarrow \ 10^{-14} < [H^+] < 10^{-1}$$

**55** Solving $A = P\left(1 + \dfrac{r}{n}\right)^{nt}$ for $t$ with $A = 2P$, $r = 0.06$, and $n = 12$ yields

$2P = P\left(1 + \frac{0.06}{12}\right)^{12t}$ {divide by $P$} $\Rightarrow \ 2 = (1.005)^{12t}$ {take the ln of both sides} $\Rightarrow$

$\ln 2 = \ln(1.005)^{12t} \ \Rightarrow \ \ln 2 = 12t\ln(1.005) \ \Rightarrow \ t = \dfrac{\ln 2}{12\ln(1.005)} \approx 11.58$ yr, or about 11 years and 7 months.

**56** $A = P\left(1 + \dfrac{r}{n}\right)^{nt} \ \Rightarrow \ \dfrac{A}{P} = \left(1 + \dfrac{r}{n}\right)^{nt} \ \Rightarrow \ \ln\left(\dfrac{A}{P}\right) = nt\ln\left(1 + \dfrac{r}{n}\right) \ \Rightarrow \ t = \dfrac{\ln(A/P)}{n\ln\left(1 + \dfrac{r}{n}\right)}$

**57** 50% of the light reaching a depth of 13 meters corresponds to the equation $\frac{1}{2}I_0 = I_0 c^{13}$. Solving for $c$, we have

$c^{13} = \frac{1}{2} \ \Rightarrow \ c = \sqrt[13]{\frac{1}{2}} = 2^{-1/13}$. Now letting $I = 0.01\,I_0$, $c = 2^{-1/13}$, and using the formula from Example 8,

$$x = \frac{\log(I/I_0)}{\log c} = \frac{\log[(0.01\,I_0)/I_0]}{\log 2^{-1/13}} = \frac{\log 10^{-2}}{-\frac{1}{13}\log 2} = \frac{-2}{-\frac{1}{13}\log 2} = \frac{26}{\log 2} \approx 86.4 \text{ m.}$$

**58** Solving as in Exercise 57 with $x = 10$ cm $= 0.1$ m, $\frac{1}{2}I_0 = I_0 c^{0.1} \ \Rightarrow \ c^{1/10} = \frac{1}{2} \ \Rightarrow \ c = \left(\frac{1}{2}\right)^{10} = \frac{1}{1024}$.

$$x = \frac{\log(I/I_0)}{\log c} = \frac{\log[(0.01\,I_0)/I_0]}{\log\frac{1}{1024}} = \frac{\log 10^{-2}}{\log 1024^{-1}} = \frac{-2}{-\log 1024} \approx 0.664 \text{ m.}$$

**59** (a) The graph of $A = 100\left[1 - (0.9)^t\right]$ is an increasing exponential that
passes through $(0, 0)$, $(5, \approx 41)$, and $(10, \approx 65)$.

(b) $A = 50 \ \Rightarrow \ 50 = 100\left[1 - (0.9)^t\right] \ \Rightarrow$
$1 - (0.9)^t = \dfrac{50}{100} \ \Rightarrow \ (0.9)^t = 0.5 \ \Rightarrow$
$t = \log_{0.9}(0.5) = \dfrac{\log 0.5}{\log 0.9} \approx 6.58$ min.

**60** (a) $A(t) = 2 \ \Rightarrow \ 2 = 10(0.8)^t \ \Rightarrow \ 0.2 = (0.8)^t \ \Rightarrow \ t = \log_{0.8}(0.2) = \dfrac{\log 0.2}{\log 0.8} \approx 7.21$ hr

(b) $A(t) = \frac{1}{2}(10) \ \Rightarrow \ \frac{1}{2}(10) = 10(0.8)^t \ \Rightarrow \ t = \log_{0.8}(0.5) = \dfrac{\log 0.5}{\log 0.8} \approx 3.11$ hr

**61** (a) $F = F_0(1 - m)^t \ \Rightarrow \ (1 - m)^t = \dfrac{F}{F_0} \ \Rightarrow \ \log(1 - m)^t = \log\left(\dfrac{F}{F_0}\right) \ \Rightarrow$
$$t\log(1 - m) = \log\left(\dfrac{F}{F_0}\right) \ \Rightarrow \ t = \dfrac{\log(F/F_0)}{\log(1 - m)}$$

(b) Using part (a) with $F = \frac{1}{2}F_0$ and $m = 0.00005$,
$$t = \frac{\log(F/F_0)}{\log(1 - m)} = \frac{\log\left(\frac{1}{2}F_0/F_0\right)}{\log(1 - 0.00005)} = \frac{\log\frac{1}{2}}{\log 0.99995} \approx 13{,}863 \text{ generations.}$$

**62** (a) $f(n) = 3 + 20(1 - e^{-0.1n})$ •

$f(5) = 3 + 20\left[1 - e^{-0.1(5)}\right] \approx 10.87 \approx 11$;

$f(9) \approx 15$; $f(24) \approx 21$; $f(30) \approx 22$.

[0, 36, 2] by [0, 24, 2]

(b) The graph of $f(n) = 3 + 20(1 - e^{-0.1n})$ is shown in the figure.

(c) As $n \to \infty$, $e^{-0.1n} \to 0$, and $f(n) \to 23$.

Thus, there is a horizontal asymptote of $y = 23$.

**63** (a) $h = \dfrac{120}{1 + 200e^{-0.2t}}$ • $t = 10 \Rightarrow h = \dfrac{120}{1 + 200e^{-0.2(10)}} = \dfrac{120}{1 + 200e^{-2}} \approx 4.28$ ft

(b) $h = 50 \Rightarrow 50 = \dfrac{120}{1 + 200e^{-0.2t}} \Rightarrow 1 + 200e^{-0.2t} = \dfrac{120}{50} \Rightarrow 200e^{-0.2t} = \dfrac{12}{5} - 1 \Rightarrow$

$e^{-0.2t} = \dfrac{7}{5} \cdot \dfrac{1}{200} \Rightarrow e^{-0.2t} = 0.007 \Rightarrow -0.2t = \ln 0.007 \Rightarrow t = \dfrac{\ln 0.007}{-0.2} \approx 24.8$ yr

**64** (a) $T(2) = T_1 2^{-k} = (0.80)T_1 \Rightarrow 2^{-k} = 0.8 \Rightarrow -k = \log_2 0.8 \Rightarrow k = -\log_2 0.8 \approx 0.32$

(b) $T(4) = T_1(4)^{-k} = T_1(2^2)^{-k} = T_1(2^{-k})^2 = T_1(2^{\log_2 0.8})^2 = T_1(0.8)^2 = (0.64)T_1$

(c) $T(2n) = T_1(2n)^{-k} = 2^{-k}(T_1 n^{-k}) = 2^{\log_2 0.8} T(n) = (0.80)T(n)$

**65** $\dfrac{v_0}{v_1} = \left(\dfrac{h_0}{h_1}\right)^P \Rightarrow \ln \dfrac{v_0}{v_1} = \ln \left(\dfrac{h_0}{h_1}\right)^P \Rightarrow \ln \dfrac{v_0}{v_1} = P \ln \dfrac{h_0}{h_1} \Rightarrow P = \dfrac{\ln(v_0/v_1)}{\ln(h_0/h_1)} = \dfrac{\ln(25/6)}{\ln(200/35)} \approx 0.82$

**66** Without loss of generality, let $h_0 = 200$, $h_1 = 35$ and $v_0 > v_1$. Then $\dfrac{v_0}{v_1} > 1$ and $\ln \dfrac{v_0}{v_1}$ is positive.

Since $P = \dfrac{\ln(v_0/v_1)}{\ln(h_0/h_1)} \approx 0.57 \ln \dfrac{v_0}{v_1}$ and $y = \ln x$ is an increasing function, $P$ increases when the ratio $\dfrac{v_0}{v_1}$ increases.

Since $v_0 > v_1 > 1$, if $\dfrac{v_0}{v_1}$ increases, then $v_0 - v_1$ must also increase. Thus, $s = \dfrac{v_1 - v_0}{h_1 - h_0} = \dfrac{v_0 - v_1}{165}$ must increase.

Increasing values for $P$ correspond with larger values for $s$.

**67** If $y = c2^{kx}$ and $x = 0$, then $y = c2^0 = c = 4$. Thus, $y = 4(2)^{kx}$. Similarly, $x = 1 \Rightarrow$

$y = 4(2)^k = 3.249 \Rightarrow 2^k = \dfrac{3.249}{4} \Rightarrow k = \log_2 \left(\dfrac{3.249}{4}\right) \approx -0.300$. Thus, $y = 4(2)^{-0.3x}$.

Checking the remaining two points, we see that $x = 2 \Rightarrow y \approx 2.639$ and $x = 3 \Rightarrow y \approx 2.144$.

The four points *lie* on the graph of $y = 4(2)^{-0.3x}$ to within three-decimal-place accuracy.

**68** If $y = c2^{kx}$ and $x = 0$, then $y = c2^0 = c = -0.3$. Thus, $y = -0.3(2)^{kx}$.

Similarly, $x = 1 \Rightarrow y = -0.3(2)^k = -0.397 \Rightarrow 2^k = \dfrac{-0.397}{-0.3} \Rightarrow k = \log_2 \left(\dfrac{-0.397}{-0.3}\right) \approx 0.404$.

Thus, $y = -0.3(2)^{0.404x}$. Checking $x = 2$ gives us $y \approx -0.525$, not $-0.727$.

The points *do not lie* on the graph of $y = c2^{kx}$ to within three-decimal-place accuracy.

**69** If $y = c \log(kx + 10)$ and $x = 0$, then $y = c \log 10 = c = 1.5$. Thus, $y = 1.5 \log(kx + 10)$.

Similarly, $x = 1 \Rightarrow y = 1.5 \log(k + 10) = 1.619 \Rightarrow \dfrac{1.619}{1.5} = \log(k + 10) \Rightarrow k + 10 = 10^{1.619/1.5} \Rightarrow$

$k = 10^{1.619/1.5} - 10 \approx 2.004$. Thus, $y = 1.5 \log(2.004x + 10)$. Checking the remaining two points, we see that

$x = 2 \Rightarrow y \approx 1.720$, and $x = 3 \Rightarrow y \approx 1.807$, not $1.997$.

The points *do not lie* on the graph of $y = c \log(kx + 10)$ to within three-decimal-place accuracy.

**70** If $y = c \log(kx + 10)$ and $x = 0$, then $y = c \log 10 = c = 0.7$. Thus, $y = 0.7 \log(kx + 10)$. Similarly,

$x = 1 \Rightarrow y = 0.7 \log(k + 10) = 0.782 \Rightarrow k + 10 = 10^{0.782/0.7} \Rightarrow k = 10^{0.782/0.7} - 10 \approx 3.096$.

Thus, $y = 0.7 \log(3.096x + 10)$. Checking the remaining two points, we see that

$x = 2 \Rightarrow y \approx 0.847$ and $x = 4 \Rightarrow y \approx 0.945$.

The points *lie* on the graph of $y = 0.7 \log(3.096x + 10)$ to within three-decimal-place accuracy.

**71** $h(x) = \log_4 x - 2\log_8(1.2x)$  •  $h(5.3) = \log_4 5.3 - 2\log_8(1.2 \times 5.3) = \dfrac{\ln 5.3}{\ln 4} - \dfrac{2\ln 6.36}{\ln 8} \approx -0.5764$

**72** $h(52.6) = 3\log_3(2 \times 52.6 - 1) + 7\log_2(52.6 + 0.2) = \dfrac{3\ln 104.2}{\ln 3} + \dfrac{7\ln 52.8}{\ln 2} \approx 52.7450$

**73** The minimum point on the graph of $y = x - \ln(0.3x) - 3\log_3 x$ is about $(3.73, 0.023)$.

So there are no $x$-intercepts, and hence, no roots of the equation on $(0, 9)$.

$[0, 9]$ by $[-1, 5]$     $[0, 3]$ by $[-1, 1]$

*Figure 73*

*Figure 74*

**74** From the graph of $y = 2\log 2x - \log_3 x^2$, we see that the root of the equation on $(0, 3)$ is $x \approx 1.88$.

**75** The graphs of $f(x) = x$ and $g(x) = 3\log_2 x$ intersect at approximately $(1.37, 1.37)$ and $(9.94, 9.94)$.

Hence, the solutions of the equation $f(x) = g(x)$ are 1.37 and 9.94.

$[-1, 17]$ by $[-1, 11]$     $[-1, 2]$ by $[-1, 1]$

*Figure 75*

*Figure 76*

**76** The graphs of $f(x) = x$ and $g(x) = -x^2 - \log_5 x$ intersect at approximately $(0.40, 0.40)$.

Hence, the solution of the equation $f(x) = g(x)$ is 0.40.

**77** From the graphs, we see that the graphs of $f$ and $g$ intersect at three points. Their coordinates are approximately $(-0.32, 0.50)$, $(1.52, -1.33)$, and $(6.84, -6.65)$. The region near the origin in the first graph is enhanced in the second. Thus, $f(x) > g(x)$ on $(-\infty, -0.32)$ and $(1.52, 6.84)$.

$[-5, 10]$ by $[-8, 2]$     $[-1.53, 2.26]$ by $[-2.92, 1.05]$

**78** From the figure, we see that the graphs of $f(x) = 3\log_4 x - \log x$ and $g(x) = e^x - 0.25x^4$ intersect at two points. Their coordinates are approximately $(2.68, 1.70)$ and $(5.30, 2.88)$. Thus, $f(x) > g(x)$ on $(2.68, 5.30)$.

$[-8, 19, 2]$ by $[-13, 5, 2]$

**79** (1) The graph of $n(t) = 85e^{t/3}$ is increasing rapidly and soon becomes greater than 100. It is doubtful that the average score would improve dramatically without any review.

$[0, 5]$ by $[0, 200, 20]$     $[0, 5]$ by $[0, 100, 10]$

*Figure 79(1)*                      *Figure 79(2)*

(2) The graph of $n(t) = 70 + 10\ln(t + 1)$ is also increasing. It is incorrect because $n(0) = 70 \neq 85$. Also, one would not expect the average score to improve without any review.

(3) The graph of $n(t) = 86 - e^t$ decreases rapidly to zero. The average score probably would not be zero after 5 weeks.

$[0, 5]$ by $[0, 100, 10]$     $[0, 5]$ by $[0, 100, 10]$

*Figure 79(3)*                      *Figure 79(4)*

(4) The graph of $n(t) = 85 - 15\ln(t + 1)$ is decreasing. During the first weeks it decreases most rapidly and then starts to level off. Of the four functions, **this function seems to best model the situation.**

**80** (1) $T(t) = 212 - 50t$ decreases at a constant rate of 50°F each hour. Initially the temperature is 212°F, but after 3 hours the temperature of the water is 62°F, which is cooler than the room.

$[0, 5]$ by $[0, 250, 50]$     $[0, 5]$ by $[0, 250, 50]$

*Figure 80(1)*                      *Figure 80(2)*

(2) $T(t) = 140e^{-t} + 72$ is initially 212°F, cools rapidly at first and then gradually approaches a temperature of 72°F. This equation best models the situation.

(3) $T(t) = 212e^{-t}$ is initially 212°F, but decreases rapidly to temperatures cooler than 72°F.

$[0, 5]$ by $[0, 250, 50]$     $[0, 5]$ by $[0, 250, 50]$

*Figure 80(3)*                      *Figure 80(4)*

(4) $T(t) = 72 + 10\ln(140t + 1)$ is initially 72°F and is an increasing function.

## Chapter 4 Review Exercises

**1** Suppose $f(a) = f(b)$. $2a^3 - 5 = 2b^3 - 5 \Rightarrow 2a^3 = 2b^3 \Rightarrow a^3 = b^3 \Rightarrow a = b$.

Thus, $f$ is a one-to-one function.

**2** Reflect the graph of $y = f(x)$ through the line $y = x$ to obtain the graph of $y = f^{-1}(x)$. See *Figure 2* below.

**3** $f(x) = 10 - 15x \Rightarrow 15x = 10 - y \Rightarrow x = \dfrac{10 - y}{15} \Rightarrow f^{-1}(x) = \dfrac{10 - x}{15}$

Figure 2

Figure 3

Figure 4

**4** $f(x) = 9 - 2x^2,\ x \le 0 \Rightarrow y + 2x^2 = 9 \Rightarrow$

$$x^2 = \frac{9 - y}{2} \Rightarrow x = \pm\sqrt{\frac{9 - y}{2}} \ \{\text{choose minus since } x \le 0\} \Rightarrow f^{-1}(x) = -\sqrt{\frac{9 - x}{2}}$$

**5** (a) The point $(1, 2)$ is on the graph, so $f(1) = 2$.   (b) $(f \circ f)(1) = f(f(1)) = f(2) = 4$.

(c) $f(2) = 4$ and $f$ is one-to-one $\Rightarrow f^{-1}(4) = 2$.   (d) $y = 4$ when $x = 2$, so $f(x) = 4 \Rightarrow x = 2$.

(e) $y > 4$ when $x > 2$, so $f(x) > 4 \Rightarrow x > 2$.

**6** Since $f$ and $g$ are one-to-one functions, we know that $f(2) = 7$, $f(4) = 2$, and

$g(2) = 5$ imply that $f^{-1}(7) = 2$, $f^{-1}(2) = 4$, and $g^{-1}(5) = 2$, respectively.

(a) $(g \circ f^{-1})(7) = g(f^{-1}(7)) = g(2) = 5$   (b) $(f \circ g^{-1})(5) = f(g^{-1}(5)) = f(2) = 7$

(c) $(f^{-1} \circ g^{-1})(5) = f^{-1}(g^{-1}(5)) = f^{-1}(2) = 4$

(d) $(g^{-1} \circ f^{-1})(2) = g^{-1}(f^{-1}(2)) = g^{-1}(4)$, which is not known.

**7** $f(x) = 3^{x+2}$   • shift $y = 3^x$ left 2 units

Figure 7

Figure 8

**8** $f(x) = \left(\frac{3}{5}\right)^x$   • goes through $\left(-1, \frac{5}{3}\right)$, $(0, 1)$, and $\left(1, \frac{3}{5}\right)$

**9** $f(x) = \left(\frac{3}{2}\right)^{-x} = \left(\frac{2}{3}\right)^{x}$  •  goes through $\left(-1, \frac{3}{2}\right)$, $(0, 1)$, and $\left(1, \frac{2}{3}\right)$

*Figure 9*

*Figure 10*

**10** $f(x) = 3^{-2x} = (3^{-2})^{x} = \left(\frac{1}{9}\right)^{x}$  •  goes through $(-1, 9)$, $(0, 1)$, and $\left(1, \frac{1}{9}\right)$

Or: reflect $y = 3^{x}$ through the $y$-axis and horizontally compress it by a factor of 2

**11** Refer to Example 6 in Section 4.2 for the basic graph of $y = a^{-x^2} = (a^{-1})^{(x^2)} = \left(\frac{1}{a}\right)^{(x^2)}$, where $a > 1$.

$f(x) = 3^{-x^2} = (3^{-1})^{(x^2)} = \left(\frac{1}{3}\right)^{(x^2)}$  •

*Figure 11*

*Figure 12*

**12** $f(x) = 1 - 3^{-x} = -\left(\frac{1}{3}\right)^{x} + 1$  •  reflect $y = \left(\frac{1}{3}\right)^{x}$ through the $x$-axis and shift it up 1 unit

**13** $f(x) = e^{x/2} = (e^{1/2})^{x} \approx (1.65)^{x}$  •  goes through $\left(-1, 1/\sqrt{e}\right)$, $(0, 1)$, and $\left(1, \sqrt{e}\right)$;

or approximately $(-1, 0.61)$, $(0, 1)$, and $(1, 1.65)$

*Figure 13*

*Figure 14*

**14** $f(x) = \frac{1}{2}e^{x}$  •  vertically compress $y = e^{x}$ by a factor of 2

**15** $f(x) = e^{x-2}$ • shift $y = e^x$ right 2 units

*Figure 15*

*Figure 16*

**16** $f(x) = e^{2-x} = e^{-(x-2)} = \left(\frac{1}{e}\right)^{x-2}$ •

the graph of $y = \left(\frac{1}{e}\right)^x$ is the graph of $y = e^x$ reflected through the $y$-axis; shift it right 2 units

**17** $f(x) = \log_6 x$ • goes through $\left(\frac{1}{6}, -1\right), (1, 0),$ and $(6, 1)$

*Figure 17*

*Figure 18*

**18** $f(x) = \log_6(36x) = \log_6 36 + \log_6 x = \log_6 6^2 + \log_6 x = \log_6 x + 2$ • shift $y = \log_6 x$ up 2 units

**19** $f(x) = \log_4(x^2) = 2\log_4 x$ • stretch $y = \log_4 x$ by a factor of 2 and include its reflection through the $y$-axis

since the domain of the original function is $\mathbb{R} - \{0\}$

*Figure 19*

*Figure 20*

**20** $f(x) = \log_4 \sqrt[3]{x} = \log_4 x^{1/3} = \frac{1}{3}\log_4 x$ • vertically compress $y = \log_4 x$ by a factor of 3

**21** $f(x) = \log_2(x+4)$ • shift $y = \log_2 x$ left 4 units

*Figure 21*

*Figure 22*

**22** $f(x) = \log_2(4-x) = \log_2[-(x-4)]$ • shift $y = \log_2 x$ four units right and reflect through the line $x = 4$

**23** $f(x) = -3\log x$ • vertically stretch $y = \log x$ by a factor of 3 and reflect through the $x$-axis

*Figure 23*

*Figure 24*

**24** $f(x) = \ln x - 1$ • shift $y = \ln x$ one unit down

**25** (a) $\log_2 \frac{1}{16} = \log_2 2^{-4} = -4$    (b) $\log_\pi 1 = 0$

  (c) $\ln e = 1$    (d) $6^{\log_6 4} = 4$

  (e) $\log 1{,}000{,}000 = \log 10^6 = 6$    (f) $10^{3\log 2} = 10^{\log 2^3} = 2^3 = 8$

  (g) $\log_4 2 = \log_4 4^{1/2} = \dfrac{1}{2}$; *or,* $\log_4 2 = \dfrac{\log 2}{\log 4} = \dfrac{\log 2}{2\log 2} = \dfrac{1}{2}$

**26** (a) $\log_5 \sqrt[3]{5} = \log_5 5^{1/3} = \frac{1}{3}$    (b) $\log_5 1 = 0$

  (c) $\log 10 = 1$    (d) $e^{\ln 5} = 5$

  (e) $\log\log 10^{10} = \log(\log 10^{10}) = \log(10) = 1$    (f) $e^{2\ln 5} = e^{\ln 5^2} = 5^2 = 25$

  (g) $\log_{27} 3 = \log_{27} 27^{1/3} = \dfrac{1}{3}$; *or,* $\log_{27} 3 = \dfrac{\log 3}{\log 27} = \dfrac{\log 3}{3\log 3} = \dfrac{1}{3}$

**27** $2^{3x-1} = \frac{1}{2} \;\Rightarrow\; 2^{3x-1} = 2^{-1} \;\Rightarrow\; 3x - 1 = -1 \;\Rightarrow\; 3x = 0 \;\Rightarrow\; x = 0$

**28** $8^{2x} \cdot \left(\frac{1}{4}\right)^{x-2} = 4^{-x} \cdot \left(\frac{1}{2}\right)^{2-x} \;\Rightarrow\; (2^3)^{2x} \cdot (2^{-2})^{x-2} = (2^2)^{-x} \cdot (2^{-1})^{2-x} \;\Rightarrow$

  $2^{6x} \cdot 2^{-2x+4} = 2^{-2x} \cdot 2^{-2+x} \;\Rightarrow\; 2^{4x+4} = 2^{-2-x} \;\Rightarrow\; 4x + 4 = -2 - x \;\Rightarrow\; 5x = -6 \;\Rightarrow\; x = -\frac{6}{5}$

**29** $\log \sqrt{x} = \log(x-6) \;\Rightarrow\; \sqrt{x} = x - 6 \;\Rightarrow\; \left(\sqrt{x}\right)^2 = (x-6)^2 \;\Rightarrow$

  $x = x^2 - 12x + 36 \;\Rightarrow\; x^2 - 13x + 36 = 0 \;\Rightarrow\; (x-4)(x-9) = 0 \;\Rightarrow\; x = 4, 9;\ 4$ is extraneous

**30** $\log_8(x+6) = \frac{2}{3} \;\Rightarrow\; x + 6 = 8^{2/3} \;\Rightarrow\; x + 6 = 4 \;\Rightarrow\; x = -2$

**31** $\log_4(x+1) = 2 + \log_4(3x-2) \Rightarrow \log_4(x+1) - \log_4(3x-2) = 2 \Rightarrow$

$\log_4\left(\dfrac{x+1}{3x-2}\right) = 2 \Rightarrow \dfrac{x+1}{3x-2} = 4^2 \Rightarrow x+1 = 16(x-2) \Rightarrow$

$$x+1 = 48x - 32 \Rightarrow 33 = 47x \Rightarrow x = \tfrac{33}{47}$$

**32** $2\ln(x+3) - \ln(x+1) = 3\ln 2 \Rightarrow \ln\dfrac{(x+3)^2}{x+1} = \ln 2^3 \Rightarrow (x+3)^2 = 8(x+1) \Rightarrow$

$$x^2 + 6x + 9 = 8x + 8 \Rightarrow x^2 - 2x + 1 = 0 \Rightarrow (x-1)^2 = 0 \Rightarrow x = 1$$

**33** $\ln(x+2) = \ln e^{\ln 2} - \ln x \Rightarrow \ln(x+2) = \ln 2 - \ln x \Rightarrow$

$\ln(x+2) + \ln x = \ln 2 \Rightarrow \ln[x(x+2)] = \ln 2 \Rightarrow x^2 + 2x = 2 \Rightarrow$

$$x^2 + 2x - 2 = 0 \Rightarrow x = \dfrac{-2 \pm \sqrt{4+8}}{2} = \dfrac{-2 \pm \sqrt{12}}{2} = \dfrac{-2 \pm 2\sqrt{3}}{2} = -1 + \sqrt{3} \; \{x > 0\}$$

**34** $\log\sqrt[4]{x-3} = \tfrac{1}{2} \Rightarrow (x-3)^{1/4} = 10^{1/2} \Rightarrow \left[(x-3)^{1/4}\right]^4 = \left(10^{1/2}\right)^4 \Rightarrow x - 3 = 10^2 \Rightarrow x = 103$

**35** $2^{5-x} = 6 \Rightarrow 5 - x = \log_2 6 \Rightarrow 5 - \log_2 6 = x \Rightarrow$

$$x = 5 - \dfrac{\log 6}{\log 2}, \text{ or equivalently, } \dfrac{5\log 2 - \log 6}{\log 2} = \dfrac{\log 2^5 - \log 6}{\log 2} = \dfrac{\log\frac{32}{6}}{\log 2} = \dfrac{\log\frac{16}{3}}{\log 2} \approx 2.415$$

**36** $3^{(x^2)} = 7 \Rightarrow x^2 = \log_3 7 \Rightarrow x^2 = \dfrac{\log 7}{\log 3} \Rightarrow x = \pm\sqrt{\dfrac{\log 7}{\log 3}}$

**37** $2^{5x+3} = 3^{2x+1} \Rightarrow \log(2^{5x+3}) = \log(3^{2x+1}) \Rightarrow$

$(5x+3)\log 2 = (2x+1)\log 3 \Rightarrow 5x\log 2 + 3\log 2 = 2x\log 3 + \log 3 \Rightarrow$

$5x\log 2 - 2x\log 3 = \log 3 - 3\log 2 \Rightarrow x(5\log 2 - 2\log 3) = \log 3 - \log 2^3 \Rightarrow$

$$x = \dfrac{\log 3 - \log 8}{\log 32 - \log 9} = \dfrac{\log\frac{3}{8}}{\log\frac{32}{9}} \approx -0.773$$

**38** $\log_3(3x) = \log_3 x + \log_3(4-x) \Rightarrow \log_3(3x) = \log_3[x(4-x)] \Rightarrow$

$$3x = 4x - x^2 \Rightarrow x^2 - x = 0 \Rightarrow x(x-1) = 0 \Rightarrow x = 0, 1; \; 0 \text{ is extraneous}$$

**39** $\log_4 x = \sqrt[3]{\log_4 x} \Rightarrow \log_4 x = (\log_4 x)^{1/3} \Rightarrow (\log_4 x)^3 = \log_4 x \Rightarrow (\log_4 x)^3 - \log_4 x = 0 \Rightarrow$

$$\log_4 x\left[(\log_4 x)^2 - 1\right] = 0 \Rightarrow \log_4 x = 0 \text{ or } \log_4 x = \pm 1 \Rightarrow x = 1 \text{ or } x = 4, \tfrac{1}{4}$$

**40** $e^{x+\ln 4} = 3e^x \Rightarrow e^x e^{\ln 4} = 3e^x \Rightarrow 4e^x = 3e^x \Rightarrow e^x = 0$, which is never true. There is no real solution.

**41** $10^{2\log x} = 5 \Rightarrow 10^{\log x^2} = 5 \Rightarrow x^2 = 5 \Rightarrow x = \pm\sqrt{5}; -\sqrt{5}$ is extraneous

**42** $e^{\ln(x+1)} = 3 \Rightarrow x + 1 = 3 \Rightarrow x = 2$

**43** $x^2\left(-2xe^{-x^2}\right) + 2xe^{-x^2} = 0 \Rightarrow 2xe^{-x^2}(-x^2 + 1) = 0 \Rightarrow x = 0, \pm 1 \left\{e^{-x^2} \neq 0\right\}$

**44** $e^x + 2 = 8e^{-x} \Rightarrow e^x(e^x + 2) = e^x(8e^{-x}) \Rightarrow e^{2x} + 2e^x - 8 = 0 \Rightarrow (e^x + 4)(e^x - 2) = 0 \Rightarrow$

$$e^x = -4, 2 \Rightarrow x = \ln 2 \text{ since } e^x \neq -4$$

**45** (a) $\log x^2 = \log(6-x) \Rightarrow x^2 = 6 - x \Rightarrow x^2 + x - 6 = 0 \Rightarrow (x+3)(x-2) = 0 \Rightarrow x = -3, 2$

(b) $2\log x = \log(6-x) \Rightarrow \log x^2 = \log(6-x)$, which is the equation in part (a). This equation has the same

solutions provided they are in the domain. But $-3$ is extraneous, so $2$ is the only solution.

**46** (a) $\ln(e^x)^2 = 16 \Rightarrow 2\ln e^x = 16 \Rightarrow 2x = 16 \Rightarrow x = 8$

(b) $\ln e^{(x^2)} = 16 \Rightarrow x^2 = 16 \Rightarrow x = \pm 4$

**47** $\log x^4 \sqrt[3]{y^2/z} = \log(x^4 \, y^{2/3} \, z^{-1/3}) = \log x^4 + \log y^{2/3} + \log z^{-1/3} = 4 \log x + \frac{2}{3} \log y - \frac{1}{3} \log z$

**48** $\log(x^2/y^3) + 4 \log y - 6 \log \sqrt{xy} = \log\left(\dfrac{x^2}{y^3}\right) + \log y^4 - \log\left[(xy)^{1/2}\right]^6 = \log\left(\dfrac{x^2 \cdot y^4}{y^3}\right) - \log(x^3 y^3)$

$$= \log\left(\dfrac{x^2 y}{x^3 y^3}\right) = \log\left(\dfrac{1}{xy^2}\right) = \log 1 - \log(xy^2) = 0 - \log(xy^2)$$

$$= -\log(xy^2)$$

**49** We can assume that the graph has a horizontal asymptote of $y = 0$, and use the form $f(x) = ba^x$. The point $(0, 6)$ is on the graph, so $f(0) = 6 \;\Rightarrow\; 6 = ba^0 \;\Rightarrow\; 6 = b(1) \;\Rightarrow\; 6 = b$, and hence, $f(x) = 6a^x$. Since the point $P(1, 8)$ is on the graph, $f(1) = 8$. Thus, $8 = 6a^1 \;\Rightarrow\; a = \frac{4}{3}$, and the function is $f(x) = 6\left(\frac{4}{3}\right)^x$.

**50** $f(x) = \log_3(x + 2)$ •

$x = 0 \;\Rightarrow\; y\text{-intercept} = \log_3 2 = \dfrac{\log 2}{\log 3} \approx 0.6309$

**51** $y = \dfrac{1}{10^x + 10^{-x}} \;\left\{ D = \mathbb{R}, R = (0, \frac{1}{2}] \right\} \;\Rightarrow\; y\,10^x + y\,10^{-x} = 1 \;\Rightarrow$

$$y\,10^{2x} + y = 10^x \;\Rightarrow\; y\,10^{2x} - 10^x + y = 0 \;\Rightarrow\; 10^x = \dfrac{1 \pm \sqrt{1 - 4y^2}}{2y} \;\Rightarrow\; x = \log\left(\dfrac{1 \pm \sqrt{1 - 4y^2}}{2y}\right)$$

**52** $y = \dfrac{1}{10^x - 10^{-x}} \;\left\{ D = R = \mathbb{R} - \{0\} \right\} \;\Rightarrow\; y\,10^x - y\,10^{-x} = 1 \;\Rightarrow\; y\,10^{2x} - y = 10^x \;\Rightarrow$

$y\,10^{2x} - 10^x - y = 0 \;\Rightarrow\; 10^x = \dfrac{1 \pm \sqrt{1 + 4y^2}}{2y}$. There are 2 cases to consider.

(1)    If $y < 0$, then $\dfrac{1 - \sqrt{1 + 4y^2}}{2y} > 0$, so $x = \log\left(\dfrac{1 - \sqrt{1 + 4y^2}}{2y}\right)$.

(2)    If $y > 0$, then $\dfrac{1 + \sqrt{1 + 4y^2}}{2y} > 0$, so $x = \log\left(\dfrac{1 + \sqrt{1 + 4y^2}}{2y}\right)$.

**53** (a) $x = \ln 6.6 \approx 1.89$      (b) $\log x = 1.8938 \;\Rightarrow\; x = 10^{1.8938} \approx 78.3$

(c) $\ln x = -0.75 \;\Rightarrow\; x = e^{-0.75} \approx 0.472$      (d) $x = \log 52 \approx 1.72$

**54** (a) $x = \log 8.4 \approx 0.924$      (b) $\log x = -2.4260 \;\Rightarrow\; x = 10^{-2.4260} \approx 0.00375$

(c) $\ln x = 1.8 \;\Rightarrow\; x = e^{1.8} \approx 6.05$      (d) $x = \ln 0.8 \approx -0.223$

**55** (a) For $y = \log_2(x + 1)$, $D = (-1, \infty)$ and $R = \mathbb{R}$.

(b) $y = \log_2(x + 1) \;\Rightarrow\; x = \log_2(y + 1) \;\Rightarrow\; 2^x = y + 1 \;\Rightarrow\; y = 2^x - 1, D = \mathbb{R}, R = (-1, \infty)$

**56** (a) For $y = 2^{3-x} - 2$, $D = \mathbb{R}$ and $R = (-2, \infty)$.

(b) $y = 2^{3-x} - 2 \;\Rightarrow\; x = 2^{3-y} - 2 \;\Rightarrow\; x + 2 = 2^{3-y} \;\Rightarrow$

$$\log_2(x + 2) = 3 - y \;\Rightarrow\; y = 3 - \log_2(x + 2), D = (-2, \infty), R = \mathbb{R}$$

**57** (a) $Q(t) = 2(3^t)$ • $Q(0) = 2(3^0) = 2$ {in thousands}, or 2000

(b) $Q\left(\frac{10}{60}\right) = 2000\left(3^{1/6}\right) \approx 2401;\; Q\left(\frac{30}{60}\right) = 2000\left(3^{1/2}\right) \approx 3464;\; Q(1) = 2(3) = 6000$

**58** $A = P\left(1 + \dfrac{r}{n}\right)^{nt}$ • $A = 1000\left(1 + \dfrac{0.0325}{4}\right)^{4 \cdot 1} \approx \$1032.90$

**59** (a) $N = N_0(0.5)^{t/8}$ •

$\qquad N = 64(0.5)^{t/8} = 64\left[(0.5)^{1/8}\right]^t \approx 64(0.917)^t$

$N$ (amount remaining)

(b) $N = \frac{1}{2}N_0 \;\Rightarrow\; \frac{1}{2}N_0 = N_0(0.5)^{t/8} \;\Rightarrow$

$\qquad \left(\frac{1}{2}\right)^1 = \left(\frac{1}{2}\right)^{t/8} \;\Rightarrow\; 1 = t/8 \;\Rightarrow\; t = 8$ days

**60** $N = N_0 a^{ct}$ • $t = 0$ and $N = 1000 \;\Rightarrow\; N_0 = 1000.$ $t = 3$ and $N = 600 \;\Rightarrow\; 600 = 1000(a^c)^3 \;\Rightarrow$

$\qquad (a^c)^3 = \frac{600}{1000} \;\Rightarrow\; a^c = \left(\frac{3}{5}\right)^{1/3} \;\Rightarrow\; N = 1000\left(\frac{3}{5}\right)^{t/3},$ with $a = \frac{3}{5}$ and $c = \frac{1}{3}$.

**61** (a) Using $A = Pe^{rt}$ with $A = \$25{,}000$, $P = \$10{,}000$, and $r = 4.75\%$, we have

$\qquad 25{,}000 = 10{,}000e^{0.0475t} \;\Rightarrow\; e^{0.0475t} = 2.5 \;\Rightarrow\; 0.0475t = \ln 2.5 \;\Rightarrow\; t = \frac{1}{0.0475}\ln 2.5 \approx 19.3$ yr.

(b) $2 \cdot 10{,}000 = 10{,}000e^{0.0475t} \;\Rightarrow\; e^{0.0475t} = 2 \;\Rightarrow\; 0.0475t = \ln 2 \;\Rightarrow\; t \approx 14.6$ yr.

$\qquad\qquad$ Alternatively, using the doubling time formula, $t = (\ln 2)/r = (\ln 2)/0.0475 \approx 14.6$.

**62** The model is $y = 4000b^t$, with $t = 0$ corresponding to 1790. Use $t = 200$ and $y = 2{,}000{,}000$:

$\quad 2{,}000{,}000 = 4000b^{200} \;\Rightarrow\; 500 = b^{200} \;\Rightarrow\; b = \sqrt[200]{500} \approx 1.03156,$ so the annual interest rate is about 3.16%.

**63** $I(t) = I_0 e^{-Rt/L}$ • $I(t) = 1\%$ of $I_0 \;\Rightarrow\; \frac{1}{100}I_0 = I_0 e^{-Rt/L} \;\Rightarrow\; \frac{1}{100} = e^{-Rt/L} \;\Rightarrow\; \ln\frac{1}{100} = -\frac{Rt}{L} \;\Rightarrow$

$\qquad\qquad\qquad\qquad\qquad\qquad t = (-\ln 100)\left(-\dfrac{L}{R}\right) = (\ln 100)\dfrac{L}{R} \approx 4.6\dfrac{L}{R}$

**64** (a) $\alpha = 10\log\left(\dfrac{I}{I_0}\right) \;\Rightarrow\; \dfrac{\alpha}{10} = \log\left(\dfrac{I}{I_0}\right) \;\Rightarrow\; 10^{\alpha/10} = \dfrac{I}{I_0} \;\Rightarrow\; I = I_0 10^{\alpha/10}$

(b) Let $I(\alpha)$ be the intensity corresponding to $\alpha$ decibels.

$\qquad I(\alpha + 1) = I_0 10^{(\alpha+1)/10} = I_0 10^{\alpha/10} 10^{1/10} = I(\alpha)\,10^{1/10} \approx 1.26\,I(\alpha),$

$\qquad\qquad\qquad\qquad\qquad\qquad\qquad\qquad$ which represents a 26% increase in $I(\alpha)$.

**65** $L = a(1 - be^{-kt}) \;\Rightarrow\; \dfrac{L}{a} = 1 - be^{-kt} \;\Rightarrow\; be^{-kt} = 1 - \dfrac{L}{a} \;\Rightarrow\; be^{-kt} = \dfrac{a - L}{a} \;\Rightarrow$

$\qquad\qquad e^{-kt} = \dfrac{a - L}{ab} \;\Rightarrow\; -kt = \ln\left(\dfrac{a - L}{ab}\right) \;\Rightarrow\; t = -\dfrac{1}{k}\ln\left(\dfrac{a - L}{ab}\right)$

**66** $R = 2.3\log(A + 3000) - 5.1 \;\Rightarrow\; R + 5.1 = 2.3\log(A + 3000) \;\Rightarrow\; \dfrac{R + 5.1}{2.3} = \log(A + 3000) \;\Rightarrow$

$\qquad\qquad A + 3000 = 10^{(R+5.1)/2.3}$ {change to exponential form} $\;\Rightarrow\; A = 10^{(R+5.1)/2.3} - 3000$

**67** $R = 2.3\log(A + 34{,}000) - 7.5 \;\Rightarrow\; R + 7.5 = 2.3\log(A + 34{,}000) \;\Rightarrow\; \dfrac{R + 7.5}{2.3} = \log(A + 34{,}000) \;\Rightarrow$

$A + 34{,}000 = 10^{(R+7.5)/2.3}$ {change to exponential form} $\;\Rightarrow\; A = 10^{(R+7.5)/2.3} - 34{,}000.$

$\qquad\qquad$ From the previous exercise, $A = 10^{(R+5.1)/2.3} - 3000.$ Thus, $\dfrac{A_1}{A_2} = \dfrac{10^{(R+5.1)/2.3} - 3000}{10^{(R+7.5)/2.3} - 34{,}000}.$

**68** $R = 2.3\log(A + 14{,}000) - 6.6$ • $R = 4 \;\Rightarrow\; 2.3\log(A + 14{,}000) - 6.6 = 4 \;\Rightarrow$

$\qquad\qquad\qquad\qquad \log(A + 14{,}000) = \dfrac{10.6}{2.3} \;\Rightarrow\; A = 10^{106/23} - 14{,}000 \approx 26{,}615.9$ mi$^2$.

**69** $p = 29e^{-0.000\,034h}$ $\Rightarrow$ $\dfrac{p}{29} = e^{-0.000\,034h}$ $\Rightarrow$ $\ln\left(\dfrac{p}{29}\right) = -0.000\,034h$ $\Rightarrow$

$$h = \frac{\ln(p/29)}{-0.000\,034} \quad \Rightarrow \quad h = \frac{\ln(29/p)}{0.000\,034}$$

**70** $v = -a\ln m + b$  •  Substituting $v = 0$ and $m = m_1 + m_2$ yields $0 = -a\ln(m_1 + m_2) + b$.

Thus, $b = a\ln(m_1 + m_2)$. At burnout, $m = m_1$, and hence,

$$v = -a\ln m_1 + b = -a\ln m_1 + a\ln(m_1 + m_2) = a\left[\ln(m_1 + m_2) - \ln m_1\right] \quad \Rightarrow \quad v = a\ln\left(\frac{m_1 + m_2}{m_1}\right)$$

**71** (a) $\log n = 7.7 - (0.9)R$ $\Rightarrow$ $n = 10^{7.7 - 0.9R}$ {merely change the form}

(b) $R = 4, 5,$ and $6$ $\Rightarrow$ $n = 10^{7.7 - 0.9(4,\,5,\text{ and }6)} \approx 12{,}589;\ 1585;$ and 200 earthquakes

**72** (a) $\log E = 11.4 + (1.5)R$ $\Rightarrow$ $E = 10^{11.4 + 1.5R}$ {merely change the form}

(b) $R = 9.0$ $\Rightarrow$ $E = 10^{11.4 + 1.5(9.0)} = 10^{24.9} \approx 7.9 \times 10^{24}$ ergs

**73** $q(t) = q_0 e^{-0.0063t}$  •  Let $q(t) = \frac{1}{2}q_0$. $\frac{1}{2}q_0 = q_0 e^{-0.0063t}$ $\Rightarrow$ $\frac{1}{2} = e^{-0.0063t}$ $\Rightarrow$ $\ln\frac{1}{2} = -0.0063t$ $\Rightarrow$

$$-\ln 2 = -0.0063t \quad \Rightarrow \quad t = \frac{\ln 2}{0.0063} \approx 110 \text{ days}$$

**74** $h = 70.228 + 5.104t + 9.222\ln t$ and $R = 5.104 + (9.222/t)$. $t = 2$ $\Rightarrow$ $h \approx 86.8$ cm and $R = 9.715$ cm/yr.

**75** $I = \dfrac{V}{R}\left(1 - e^{-Rt/L}\right)$ $\Rightarrow$ $\dfrac{RI}{V} = 1 - e^{-Rt/L}$ $\Rightarrow$ $e^{-Rt/L} = 1 - \dfrac{RI}{V}$ $\Rightarrow$

$$e^{-Rt/L} = \left(\frac{V - RI}{V}\right) \quad \Rightarrow \quad -\frac{Rt}{L} = \ln\left(\frac{V - RI}{V}\right) \quad \Rightarrow \quad t = -\frac{L}{R}\ln\left(\frac{V - RI}{V}\right)$$

**76** (a) $T = -8310\ln x$  •  $x = 4\%$ $\Rightarrow$ $T = -8310\ln(0.04) \approx 26{,}749$ yr.

(b) $T = 10{,}000$ $\Rightarrow$ $10{,}000 = -8310\ln x$ $\Rightarrow$ $-\frac{10{,}000}{8310} = \ln x$ $\Rightarrow$ $x = e^{-1000/831} \approx 0.30,$ or 30%.

**77** $N = 30.7e^{0.022t}$  •  Using the doubling time formula, $t = (\ln 2)/r = (\ln 2)/0.022 \approx 31.5$ yr.

**78** $N(t) = N_0(0.805)^t$  •  $N(t) = \frac{1}{2}N_0$ $\Rightarrow$ $\frac{1}{2}N_0 = N_0(0.805)^t$ $\Rightarrow$ $2^{-1} = (0.805)^t$ $\Rightarrow$

$$\ln(2^{-1}) = \ln(0.805)^t \quad \Rightarrow \quad -\ln 2 = t\ln(0.805) \quad \Rightarrow \quad t = -\frac{\ln 2}{\ln(0.805)} \approx 3.196 \text{ millennia, or 3196 yr}$$

## Chapter 4 Discussion Exercises

**1** (a) $f(x) = -(x - 1)^3 + 1$ $\Rightarrow$ $y = -(x - 1)^3 + 1$ $\Rightarrow$

$(x - 1)^3 = 1 - y$ $\Rightarrow$ $x - 1 = \sqrt[3]{1 - y}$ $\Rightarrow$

$x = \sqrt[3]{1 - y} + 1$ $\Rightarrow$ $f^{-1}(x) = \sqrt[3]{1 - x} + 1$

(b) If $f$ is increasing, then $f^{-1}$ moves from left to right and increases.

If $f$ is decreasing, then $f^{-1}$ moves from right to left and decreases.

(c) If $P(a, b)$ is a point on $f$ and $P$ is an intersection point of $f$ and $f^{-1}$, then $Q(b, a)$ is a point on $f^{-1}$ (since $P$ is a point on $f$) and $Q$ is a point on $f$ (since $P$ is also a point on $f^{-1}$). If $a = b$, then $P$ lies on the line $y = x$. If $a \ne b$, then $m_{PQ} = -1$, and $P$ lies on a line perpendicular to $y = x$; that is, on a line of the form $y = -x + c$.

**2** The values for which $y = (-3)^x$ is defined correspond to points that are either on the graph of $y = 3^x$ or $y = -3^x$. There is no point on $y = (-3)^x$ for $x = 0.1$, but there is for $x = 0.2$ since $y = (-3)^{0.2} = (-3)^{1/5} = -\sqrt[5]{3}$. The base $a$ must be positive so that the function $f(x) = a^x$ is defined for all values of $x$.

[-4.7, 4.7] by [-3.1, 3.1]

**3** (a) The $y$-intercept is $a$, so it increases as $a$ does. The graph flattens out as $a$ increases.

(b) Graph $Y_1 = \frac{a}{2}\left(e^{x/a} + e^{-x/a}\right) + (30 - a)$ on $[-20, 20]$ by $[30, 32]$ and check for $Y_1 < 32$ at $x = 20$. In this case it turns out that $a = 101$ is the smallest integer value that satisfies the conditions, so an equation is

$$y = \tfrac{101}{2}\left(e^{x/101} + e^{-x/101}\right) - 71.$$

**4** $R = 65e^{0.02t}$ • Sum the values of $R$ for $t = 1$ to $t = x$ so that the sum is 50. Summing $R$ for $t = 1$ to $t = 7$ years gives 49.329 tons. The answer using the formula is about 7.16 years.

**5** (a) $x^y = y^x \;\Rightarrow\; \ln(x^y) = \ln(y^x) \;\Rightarrow\; y\ln x = x\ln y \;\Rightarrow\; \dfrac{\ln x}{x} = \dfrac{\ln y}{y}$

(b) Once you find two values of $(\ln x)/x$ that are the same (such as 0.36652), you know that the corresponding $x$-values, $x_1$ and $x_2$, satisfy the relationship $(x_1)^{x_2} \approx (x_2)^{x_1}$. In particular, when $(\ln x)/x \approx 0.36652$, we find that $x_1 \approx 2.50$ and $x_2 \approx 2.97$. Note that $2.50^{2.97} \approx 2.97^{2.50} \approx 15.20$.

(c) Note that $f(e) = \frac{1}{e}$. Any horizontal line $y = k$, with $0 < k < \frac{1}{e}$, will intersect the graph at the two points
$$\left(x_1, \frac{\ln x_1}{x_1}\right) \text{ and } \left(x_2, \frac{\ln x_2}{x_2}\right), \text{ where } 1 < x_1 < e \text{ and } x_2 > e.$$

**6** (a) $y_1 = (1.085)^x$ could be considered to be the value of an investment growing at 8.5% per year with no compounding. $y_2 = e^{0.085x}$ could be considered to be the value of an investment growing at 8.5% per year compounded continuously. In part (a) of the exercises, $x = 40 \;\Rightarrow\; y_1 \approx 26.13$ and $y_2 \approx 29.96$. In part (b) of the exercises, $y = 2 \;\Rightarrow\; x_1 \approx 8.50$ and $x_2 \approx 8.15$. The answers in part (b) could be considered to be the doubling time for the investments.

(b) $y_3 = (1 + 0.085/12)^{12x}$ would be greater than $y_1$, but less than $y_2$ (closer to $y_2$).

(c) An estimate of 29 and 8.2 would be reasonable. You would believe that these are correct because they are much closer to the continuously compounded interest values than the simple interest values. Actual values are 29.61 and 8.18.

**7** Logarithm law 3 states that it is valid only for positive real numbers, so $y = \log_3(x^2)$ is equivalent to $y = 2\log_3 x$ only for $x > 0$. The domain of $y = \log_3(x^2)$ is $\mathbb{R} - \{0\}$, whereas the domain of $y = 2\log_3 x$ is $x > 0$.

**8** (a) $U$ = compound interest amount − accumulated amount = $P\left(1 + \dfrac{r}{12}\right)^{12t} - \dfrac{12M\left[(1 + r/12)^{12t} - 1\right]}{r}$.

Note that $P$ is the loan amount $L$ and we use 12 for $n$ because there are monthly payments.

(b) $U = 90{,}000\left(1 + \dfrac{0.12}{12}\right)^{12x} - \dfrac{12(925.75)\left[(1 + 0.12/12)^{12x} - 1\right]}{0.12}$.

$[0, 35, 5]$ by $[0, 1\text{E}5, 1\text{E}4]$

(c) $x = 10$ years $\Rightarrow$ $U = \$84{,}076.50$. $U = \$45{,}000$ $\Rightarrow$ $x \approx 24.425$ years.

(d) The points $(0, 90{,}000)$ and $(30, 0)$ must be on the graph. The graph must be decreasing—more near $x = 30$ than in the beginning.

(e) It is an excellent approximation, but we must remember that payments are only made every month—not for every value of $x$.

**Note:** You may want to loosely discuss discrete vs. continuous models at this time.

**9** There are 4 points of intersection. Listed in order of difficulty to find we have: $(-0.9999011, 0.00999001)$, $(-0.0001, 0.01)$, $(100, 0.01105111)$, and $(36{,}102.844, 4.6928 \times 10^{13})$. Exponential function values (with base $> 1$) are greater than polynomial function values (with leading term positive) for very large values of $x$.

**10** There are 3 points of intersection. Listed in order of difficulty to find we have $(x, x)$ with $x \approx 0.44239443, 4.1770774$, and $5{,}503.6647$. The $y$-values for $y = x$ eventually will be larger than the $y$-values for $y = (\ln x)^n$.

**11** $60{,}000 = 40{,}000b^5$ $\Rightarrow$ $\dfrac{60{,}000}{40{,}000} = b^5$ $\Rightarrow$ $b = \sqrt[5]{1.5} \approx 1.0844717712$, or $8.44717712\%$. Mentally—it would take $70/8.5 \approx 8^+$ years to double and there would be about $40/8 = 5$ doubling periods, $2^5 = 32$ and $32 \cdot \$40{,}000 = \$1{,}280{,}000$. The actual value is $\$40{,}000(1 + 0.0844717712)^{40} = \$1{,}025{,}156.25$.

**12** (a) The formula in Exercise 72 of the review exercises, $\log E = 11.4 + 1.5\,R$, gives $E$ in terms of ergs and 1 joule = $10^7$ ergs. The earthquake released about $1.122 \times 10^{15}$ joules of energy, so about 3.5 earthquakes are equivalent to one 1-megaton bomb. About 425 1-megaton bombs are equivalent to the Mount St. Helens eruption.

(b) $E = 1.7 \times 10^{18}$ $\Rightarrow$ $R = (\log E - 11.4)/1.5 = 9.22$. Yes, the highest recorded reading is about 9.5 in the 1960 earthquake in Chile. The worst death toll by an earthquake was in 1201 in the Near East—it killed an estimated 1.1 million people.

**13** On the TI-83/4 Plus, enter the sum of the days, $\{0, 5168, 6728, 8136, 8407, 8735, 8857, 9010, 9274, 9631, 9666,$ $12{,}393, 12{,}580, 12{,}665\}$, and the averages, $\{1003.16, 2002.25, 3004.46, 4003.33, 5023.55, 6010.00, 7022.44,$ $8038.88, 9033.23, 10{,}006.78, 11{,}014.69, 12{,}011.73, 13{,}089.89, 14{,}000.41\}$, in $L_1$ and $L_2$, respectively. Use ExpReg under STAT CALC to obtain $y = ab^x$, where $a = 855.307\,849\,559\,44$ and $b = 1.000\,226\,119\,908\,8$. Plot the data along with the exponential function and the line $y = 20{,}000$. The functions intersect at approximately 13,941. This value corresponds to January 15, 2011 {it was less than 12,000 on that day}.

**Note:** The TI-83/4 has a convenient "day between dates" function for problems of this nature.

Using the first and last milestone figures and the continuously compounded interest formula gives us $A = Pe^{rt} \Leftrightarrow 14{,}000.41 = 1003.16e^{r(12{,}665)} \Rightarrow r \approx 0.000\,208\,127\,248\,1$ daily, or about 7.60% annually {obviously less if the most recent data is included}.

**Note:** The Dow was 100.25 on 1/12/1906. You may want to include this information and examine the differences it makes in any type of prediction. A discussion of practical considerations should lead to mention of crashes, corrections, and the validity of any model over too long of a period of time.

**14** On the TI-83/4 Plus, enter the sum of the days, $\{0, 3569, 7371, 8928, 10{,}023, 10{,}498, 10{,}554, 10{,}625\}$, and the averages, $\{100, 200.25, 501.62, 1005.89, 2000.56, 3028.51, 4041.46, 5046.86\}$, in $L_1$ and $L_2$, respectively. Use ExpReg under STAT CALC to obtain $y = ab^x$, where $a = 68.183\,323\,354\,785$ and $b = 1.000\,352\,623\,533\,9$.

A graph of the data and the model shows a poor fit. The phenomenal growth spurt makes it impossible to obtain a good fit over this long of a period of time.

**15** (a) $[-10, 110, 10]$ by $[0, 1E10, 1E9]$

(b) Based on the shape of the curve in part (a), a logistic model is definitely more appropriate.

(c) Using the logistic model feature, we obtain $y = c/\left(1 + ae^{-bx}\right)$ with $a = 3.637\,229\,245$, $b = 0.027\,809\,855\,7$, and $c = 1.154\,225\,9 \times 10^{10}$.

(d) As $x$ gets large, the term $ae^{-bx}$ gets closer to zero, so $y$ approaches $c/1 = c$.

**16** $\log_5 x + \log_7 x = 11$ • The left side is the sum of two simple increasing logarithms, so we would expect it to be an increasing function that would be equal to 11 exactly once, and there should be one solution.

$\log_5 x + \log_7 x = 11 \Rightarrow \dfrac{\ln x}{\ln 5} + \dfrac{\ln x}{\ln 7} = 11 \Rightarrow \dfrac{\ln x}{\ln 5} + \dfrac{\frac{\ln 5}{\ln 7} \cdot \ln x}{\ln 5} = 11 \Rightarrow \ln x \left(1 + \dfrac{\ln 5}{\ln 7}\right) =$
$11 \ln 5 \Rightarrow \ln x \left(\dfrac{\ln 7 + \ln 5}{\ln 7}\right) = 11 \ln 5 \Rightarrow \ln x = \dfrac{11 \ln 5 \cdot \ln 7}{\ln 35} \Rightarrow x = e^b$, where $b = \dfrac{11 \ln 5 \cdot \ln 7}{\ln 35}$.

**17** $y = \dfrac{9x}{\sqrt{x^2 + 1}} \Rightarrow y\sqrt{x^2 + 1} = 9x \Rightarrow y^2\left(x^2 + 1\right) = 81x^2 \Rightarrow y^2 x^2 + y^2 = 81x^2 \Rightarrow$

$y^2 x^2 - 81x^2 = -y^2 \Rightarrow x^2(y^2 - 81) = -y^2 \Rightarrow x^2 = \dfrac{y^2}{81 - y^2} \Rightarrow x = \pm\sqrt{\dfrac{y^2}{81 - y^2}} \Rightarrow$

$x = \pm\dfrac{|y|}{\sqrt{81 - y^2}} \Rightarrow x = \pm\dfrac{y}{\sqrt{81 - y^2}}$.

From the original equation, we see that $x$ and $y$ are always both positive or both negative, so the last equation can be simplified to $x = \dfrac{y}{\sqrt{81 - y^2}}$. Hence, $f^{-1}(y) = \dfrac{y}{\sqrt{81 - y^2}}$ or, equivalently, $f^{-1}(x) = \dfrac{x}{\sqrt{81 - x^2}}$. The denominator of $f^{-1}$ is zero for $x = \pm 9$, which are the vertical asymptotes. They are related to the horizontal asymptotes of $f$, which are $y = \pm 9$.

## Chapter 4 Test

**1** $y = f(x) = \dfrac{x-4}{x+2}$ $\Rightarrow$ $y(x+2) = x-4$ $\Rightarrow$ $yx + 2y = x-4$ $\Rightarrow$ $2y+4 = x - xy$ $\Rightarrow$

$2y+4 = x(1-y)$ $\Rightarrow$ $x = \dfrac{2y+4}{1-y}$ $\Rightarrow$ $f^{-1}(x) = \dfrac{2x+4}{1-x}$. The domain of $f^{-1}$ is $(-\infty, 1) \cup (1, \infty)$.

The range of $f^{-1}$ (the same as the domain of $f$) is $(-\infty, -2) \cup (-2, \infty)$.

**2** $y = 7 - x^2$ $\Rightarrow$ $x^2 = 7 - y$ $\Rightarrow$ $x = \pm\sqrt{7-y}$ $\Rightarrow$ $f^{-1}(x) = \pm\sqrt{7-x}$. Since $x \le 0$ for the domain of $f$, we must have $y \le 0$ range of $f^{-1}$, so choose the " $-$ " for the inverse. Since $7 - x$ must be nonnegative for $f^{-1}$ to be defined, we must have $x \le 7$ for the domain. So the inverse is $f^{-1}(x) = -\sqrt{7-x}$, the domain is $(-\infty, 7]$, and the range is $(-\infty, 0]$.

**3** First find $g^{-1}(x)$: $y = 2x - 3$ $\Rightarrow$ $2x = y + 3$ $\Rightarrow$ $x = \frac{1}{2}(y+3)$ $\Rightarrow$ $g^{-1}(x) = \frac{1}{2}(x+3)$.
Thus, $(f \circ g^{-1})(5) = f(g^{-1}(5)) = f(\frac{1}{2}(5+3)) = f(4) = 4^2 = 16$.

**4** $x$-intercept: let $y = 0$ to get $0 = -\left(\frac{3}{2}\right)^{-x} + \frac{4}{9}$ $\Rightarrow$ $\left(\frac{3}{2}\right)^{-x} = \frac{4}{9}$ $\Rightarrow$ $\left(\frac{2}{3}\right)^{x} = \frac{4}{9}$ $\Rightarrow$ $x = 2$.
$y$-intercept: $f(0) = -\left(\frac{3}{2}\right)^{0} + \frac{4}{9} = -1 + \frac{4}{9} = -\frac{5}{9}$.

**5** The horizontal asymptote is $y = 70$, so $f(x) = ba^{-x} + c$ has the form $f(x) = ba^{-x} + 70$. The $y$-intercept is 350, so $f(0) = 350$ $\Rightarrow$ $350 = ba^{-0} + 70$ $\Rightarrow$ $350 = b(1) + 70$ $\Rightarrow$ $280 = b$ $\Rightarrow$ $f(x) = 280a^{-x} + 70$. The function passes through the point $(3, 105)$, so $f(3) = 105$ $\Rightarrow$ $105 = 280a^{-3} + 70$ $\Rightarrow$ $35 = 280a^{-3}$ $\Rightarrow$ $35 = \frac{280}{a^3}$ $\Rightarrow$ $a^3 = \frac{280}{35}$ $\Rightarrow$ $a^3 = 8$ $\Rightarrow$ $a = 2$ $\Rightarrow$ $f(x) = 280(2)^{-x} + 70$.

**6** $q(t) = q_0 2^{kt}$ ● $q(t) = \frac{1}{2}q_0$ when $t = 300$ $\Rightarrow$ $\frac{1}{2}q_0 = q_0 2^{k(300)}$ $\Rightarrow$ $2^{-1} = 2^{300k}$ $\Rightarrow$ $300k = -1$ $\Rightarrow$
$$k = -\frac{1}{300}.$$

**7** (a) $M = \dfrac{Lrk}{12(k-1)}$ and $k = \left(1 + \dfrac{r}{12}\right)^{12t}$ ● $r = 0.07, t = 30, L = 270{,}000$ $\Rightarrow$
$$k = \left(1 + \frac{0.07}{12}\right)^{12 \cdot 30} \approx 8.116497 \text{ and } M = \frac{270{,}000(0.07)k}{12(k-1)} \approx \$1796.32.$$

(b) Total interest paid = total of payments − original loan amount
$$= (12 \cdot 30 \text{ payments}) \times \$1796.32 - \$270{,}000 = \$376{,}675.20$$

**8** The model is $y = 2b^t$, since $y = 2$ when $t = 0$. $y = 10$ when $t = 30$ $\Rightarrow$ $10 = 2b^{30}$ $\Rightarrow$ $5 = b^{30}$ $\Rightarrow$
$$b = \sqrt[30]{5} \approx 1.0551. \text{ The model is } y = 2(1.0551)^t.$$

**9** Apply the growth formula $q = q_0 e^{rt}$ with $q_0 = 100{,}000$, $r = 0.04$, and $t = 2020 - 1980 = 40$ years.
$$q = 100{,}000e^{0.04(40)} \approx 495{,}303.$$

**10** $100{,}000 = Pe^{(0.04)(10)}$ $\Rightarrow$ $P = \dfrac{100{,}000}{e^{0.4}} \approx \$67{,}032.00$ (Due to rounding, you actually need $\$67{,}032.01$.)

**11** Use the decay formula $q = q_0 e^{rt}$ with initial quantity $q_0$, rate of decay $r = -0.0375$, and time $t = 20$ hours.

The amount remaining after 20 hours is $q_0 e^{-0.0375(20)} = q_0 e^{-0.75} \approx 0.47q_0$, which is 47% of the initial amount.

**12** $\log_2 (5x+1) = 4$ $\Rightarrow$ $5x + 1 = 2^4$ $\Rightarrow$ $5x = 16 - 1$ $\Rightarrow$ $5x = 15$ $\Rightarrow$ $x = 3$.

Checking $x = 3$ gives $\log_2 16 = 4$, a true statement.

**13** $e^{\ln(2x-3)} = 2x - 3$ provided the argument is positive, that is,
$$2x - 3 > 0 \quad \Rightarrow \quad x > \tfrac{3}{2}, \text{ or, in interval notation, } \left(\tfrac{3}{2}, \infty\right).$$

**14** $C = Da^{t/E} - F \;\Rightarrow\; C + F = Da^{t/E} \;\Rightarrow\; \dfrac{C+F}{D} = a^{t/E} \;\Rightarrow\; \dfrac{t}{E} = \log_a \dfrac{C+F}{D} \;\Rightarrow\; t = E \log_a \dfrac{C+F}{D}$

**15** $A(t) = A_0 e^{-0.03t}$ • Since the field is *currently* 4 times the safe level $S$, we let $A_0 = 4S$ and $A(t) = S$.

$$S = 4Se^{-0.03t} \;\Rightarrow\; \tfrac{1}{4} = e^{-0.03t} \;\Rightarrow\; \ln 0.25 = -0.03t \;\Rightarrow\; t = \dfrac{\ln 0.25}{-0.03} \approx 46.2 \text{ yr.}$$

**16** $\log_4 (6 - x) + \log_4 (-x) = 2 \;\Rightarrow\; \log_4 (x^2 - 6x) = 2 \;\Rightarrow\; x^2 - 6x = 4^2 \;\Rightarrow\; x^2 - 6x - 16 = 0 \;\Rightarrow$

$(x - 8)(x + 2) = 0 \;\Rightarrow\; x = 8, -2.$ Checking gives $x = -2$ with $x = 8$ being extraneous.

**17** $\log(x + 3) = 1 - \log(x - 5) \;\Rightarrow\; \log(x + 3) + \log(x - 5) = 1 \;\Rightarrow\; \log[(x + 3)(x - 5)] = 1 \;\Rightarrow$

$(x + 3)(x - 5) = 10^1 \;\Rightarrow\; x^2 - 2x - 15 = 10 \;\Rightarrow\; x^2 - 2x - 25 = 0 \;\Rightarrow$

$x = \dfrac{2 \pm \sqrt{4 + 100}}{2} = \dfrac{2 \pm 2\sqrt{26}}{2} = 1 \pm \sqrt{26}.$

Checking gives $x = 1 + \sqrt{26} \approx 6.1$ with $x = 1 - \sqrt{26} \approx -4.1$ being extraneous.

**18** Losing 30% of the population is the same as retaining 70%. $y = 0.70y_0 \;\Rightarrow\; 0.70y_0 = y_0 e^{-0.015t} \;\Rightarrow$

$$0.70 = e^{-0.015t} \;\Rightarrow\; \ln(0.70) = -0.015t \;\Rightarrow\; t = \dfrac{\ln(0.70)}{-0.015} \approx 23.78 \text{ years.}$$

**19** $(e^x + 3)(e^x - 2)(4^x - 3) = 0$ • Set each factor equal to 0 and solve. $e^x + 3 > 3$, so there are no solutions from the first factor. $e^x - 2 = 0 \;\Rightarrow\; e^x = 2 \;\Rightarrow\; x = \ln 2.$ $4^x - 3 = 0 \;\Rightarrow\; 4^x = 3 \;\Rightarrow\; x = \log_4 3.$ The solutions are $\ln 2$ and $\log_4 3$.

**20** If $f(x) = \log x$, then $(f \circ f \circ f)(x) = 0 \;\Rightarrow$

$$\log \log \log x = 0 \;\Rightarrow\; \log \log x = 10^0 = 1 \;\Rightarrow\; \log x = 10^1 = 10 \;\Rightarrow\; x = 10^{10}.$$

**21** $f(x) = 0 \;\Rightarrow\; 2^x - 5 = 0 \;\Rightarrow\; 2^x = 5 \;\Rightarrow\; x = \log_2 5 = \dfrac{\log 5}{\log 2} \approx 2.3219.$

**22** $A = P\left(1 + \dfrac{r}{n}\right)^{nt}$ • $A = 3P, r = 0.05,$ and $n = 4 \;\Rightarrow\; 3P = P\left(1 + \dfrac{0.05}{4}\right)^{4t} \;\Rightarrow\; 3 = (1.0125)^{4t} \;\Rightarrow$

$$\log 3 = \log(1.0125)^{4t} \;\Rightarrow\; \log 3 = 4t \log(1.0125) \;\Rightarrow\; t = \dfrac{\log 3}{4 \log(1.0125)} \approx 22.11 \text{ years.}$$

## 5.1 Exercises

**Note:** In Exercises 1–4, the answers listed are the smallest (in magnitude) two positive coterminal angles and two negative coterminal angles.

**1** (a) $120° + 1(360°) = 480°$, $120° + 2(360°) = 840°$; $120° - 1(360°) = -240°$, $120° - 2(360°) = -600°$

(b) $135° + 1(360°) = 495°$, $135° + 2(360°) = 855°$; $135° - 1(360°) = -225°$, $135° - 2(360°) = -585°$

(c) $-30° + 1(360°) = 330°$, $-30° + 2(360°) = 690°$; $-30° - 1(360°) = -390°$, $-30° - 2(360°) = -750°$

**2** (a) $240° \rightarrow 600°, 960°, -120°, -480°$      (b) $315° \rightarrow 675°, 1035°, -45°, -405°$

(c) $-150° \rightarrow 210°, 570°, -510°, -870°$

**3** (a) $620° - 1(360°) = 260°$, $620° + 1(360°) = 980°$; $620° - 2(360°) = -100°$, $620° - 3(360°) = -460°$

(b) $\frac{5\pi}{6} + 1(2\pi) = \frac{5\pi}{6} + \frac{12\pi}{6} = \frac{17\pi}{6}$, $\frac{5\pi}{6} + 2(2\pi) = \frac{5\pi}{6} + \frac{24\pi}{6} = \frac{29\pi}{6}$;

$\frac{5\pi}{6} - 1(2\pi) = \frac{5\pi}{6} - \frac{12\pi}{6} = -\frac{7\pi}{6}$, $\frac{5\pi}{6} - 2(2\pi) = \frac{5\pi}{6} - \frac{24\pi}{6} = -\frac{19\pi}{6}$

(c) $-\frac{\pi}{4} + 1(2\pi) = -\frac{\pi}{4} + \frac{8\pi}{4} = \frac{7\pi}{4}$, $-\frac{\pi}{4} + 2(2\pi) = -\frac{\pi}{4} + \frac{16\pi}{4} = \frac{15\pi}{4}$;

$-\frac{\pi}{4} - 1(2\pi) = -\frac{\pi}{4} - \frac{8\pi}{4} = -\frac{9\pi}{4}$, $-\frac{\pi}{4} - 2(2\pi) = -\frac{\pi}{4} - \frac{16\pi}{4} = -\frac{17\pi}{4}$

**4** (a) $570° \rightarrow 210°, 930°, -150°, -510°$      (b) $\frac{2\pi}{3} \rightarrow \frac{8\pi}{3}, \frac{14\pi}{3}, -\frac{4\pi}{3}, -\frac{10\pi}{3}$

(c) $-\frac{5\pi}{4} \rightarrow \frac{3\pi}{4}, \frac{11\pi}{4}, -\frac{13\pi}{4}, -\frac{21\pi}{4}$

**5** (a) $90° - 12°37'24'' = 77°22'36''$      (b) $90° - 43.87° = 46.13°$

**6** (a) $90° - 76°4'53'' = 13°55'7''$      (b) $90° - 5.08° = 84.92°$

**7** (a) $180° - 125°16'27'' = 54°43'33''$      (b) $180° - 58.07° = 121.93°$

**8** (a) $180° - 87°13'52'' = 92°46'8''$      (b) $180° - 97.9° = 82.1°$

**Note:** Multiply each degree measure by $\frac{\pi}{180}$ to obtain the listed radian measure.

**9** (a) $150° \cdot \frac{\pi}{180} = \frac{5 \cdot 30\pi}{6 \cdot 30} = \frac{5\pi}{6}$      (b) $-60° \cdot \frac{\pi}{180} = -\frac{60\pi}{3 \cdot 60} = -\frac{\pi}{3}$

(c) $225° \cdot \frac{\pi}{180} = \frac{5 \cdot 45\pi}{4 \cdot 45} = \frac{5\pi}{4}$

**10** (a) $120° \cdot \frac{\pi}{180} = \frac{2 \cdot 60\pi}{3 \cdot 60} = \frac{2\pi}{3}$      (b) $-135° \cdot \frac{\pi}{180} = -\frac{3 \cdot 45\pi}{4 \cdot 45} = -\frac{3\pi}{4}$

(c) $210° \cdot \frac{\pi}{180} = \frac{7 \cdot 30\pi}{6 \cdot 30} = \frac{7\pi}{6}$

**11** (a) $450° \cdot \frac{\pi}{180} = \frac{5 \cdot 90\pi}{2 \cdot 90} = \frac{5\pi}{2}$      (b) $72° \cdot \frac{\pi}{180} = \frac{2 \cdot 36\pi}{5 \cdot 36} = \frac{2\pi}{5}$

(c) $100° \cdot \frac{\pi}{180} = \frac{5 \cdot 20\pi}{9 \cdot 20} = \frac{5\pi}{9}$

**12** (a) $630° \cdot \frac{\pi}{180} = \frac{7 \cdot 90\pi}{2 \cdot 90} = \frac{7\pi}{2}$      (b) $54° \cdot \frac{\pi}{180} = \frac{3 \cdot 18\pi}{10 \cdot 18} = \frac{3\pi}{10}$

(c) $95° \cdot \frac{\pi}{180} = \frac{19 \cdot 5\pi}{36 \cdot 5} = \frac{19\pi}{36}$

**Note:** Multiply each radian measure by $\frac{180}{\pi}$ to obtain the listed degree measure.

**13** (a) $\frac{2\pi}{3} \cdot \left(\frac{180}{\pi}\right)^\circ = \left(\frac{2 \cdot 3 \cdot 60\pi}{3\pi}\right)^\circ = 120^\circ$　　　　(b) $\frac{11\pi}{6} \cdot \left(\frac{180}{\pi}\right)^\circ = \left(\frac{11 \cdot 30 \cdot 6\pi}{6\pi}\right)^\circ = 330^\circ$

(c) $\frac{3\pi}{4} \cdot \left(\frac{180}{\pi}\right)^\circ = \left(\frac{3 \cdot 45 \cdot 4\pi}{4\pi}\right)^\circ = 135^\circ$

**14** (a) $\frac{5\pi}{6} \cdot \left(\frac{180}{\pi}\right)^\circ = \left(\frac{5 \cdot 30 \cdot 6\pi}{6\pi}\right)^\circ = 150^\circ$　　　　(b) $\frac{4\pi}{3} \cdot \left(\frac{180}{\pi}\right)^\circ = \left(\frac{4 \cdot 60 \cdot 3\pi}{3\pi}\right)^\circ = 240^\circ$

(c) $\frac{11\pi}{4} \cdot \left(\frac{180}{\pi}\right)^\circ = \left(\frac{11 \cdot 45 \cdot 4\pi}{4\pi}\right)^\circ = 495^\circ$

**15** (a) $-\frac{7\pi}{2} \cdot \left(\frac{180}{\pi}\right)^\circ = -\left(\frac{7 \cdot 90 \cdot 2\pi}{2\pi}\right)^\circ = -630^\circ$　　　　(b) $7\pi \cdot \left(\frac{180}{\pi}\right)^\circ = (7 \cdot 180)^\circ = 1260^\circ$

(c) $\frac{\pi}{9} \cdot \left(\frac{180}{\pi}\right)^\circ = \left(\frac{20 \cdot 9\pi}{9\pi}\right)^\circ = 20^\circ$

**16** (a) $-\frac{5\pi}{2} \cdot \left(\frac{180}{\pi}\right)^\circ = -\left(\frac{5 \cdot 90 \cdot 2\pi}{2\pi}\right)^\circ = -450^\circ$　　　　(b) $9\pi \cdot \left(\frac{180}{\pi}\right)^\circ = (9 \cdot 180)^\circ = 1620^\circ$

(c) $\frac{\pi}{16} \cdot \left(\frac{180}{\pi}\right)^\circ = \left(\frac{45 \cdot 4\pi}{4 \cdot 4\pi}\right)^\circ = \left(\frac{45}{4}\right)^\circ = 11.25^\circ$

**17** We first convert 1.57 radians to degrees. $1.57 \cdot \left(\frac{180}{\pi}\right)^\circ \approx 89.95437^\circ = 89^\circ + 0.95437^\circ$.

We now use the decimal portion, $0.95437^\circ$, and convert it to minutes.

Since $60' = 1^\circ$, we have $0.95437^\circ = 0.95437(60') = 57.2622'$.

Using the decimal portion, $0.2622'$, we convert it to seconds.

Since $60'' = 1'$, we have $0.2622' = 0.2622(60'') \approx 16''$.　　　　$\therefore$ 1.57 radians $\approx 89^\circ 57' 16''$

**18** $3.1 \cdot \left(\frac{180}{\pi}\right)^\circ \approx 177.616917^\circ$; $0.616917(60') = 37.01502'$; $0.01502(60'') \approx 1''$.　　　$\therefore$ 3.1 radians $\approx 177^\circ 37' 1''$

**19** $6.3 \cdot \left(\frac{180}{\pi}\right)^\circ \approx 360.96341^\circ$; $0.96341(60') = 57.8046'$; $0.8046(60'') \approx 48''$.　　　$\therefore$ 6.3 radians $\approx 360^\circ 57' 48''$

**20** $4.7 \cdot \left(\frac{180}{\pi}\right)^\circ \approx 269.29016^\circ$; $0.29016(60') = 17.4096'$; $0.4096(60'') \approx 25''$.　　　$\therefore$ 4.7 radians $\approx 269^\circ 17' 25''$

**21** Since $1' = \left(\frac{1}{60}\right)^\circ$, $16' = \left(\frac{16}{60}\right)^\circ$. Thus, $120^\circ 16' = \left(120 + \frac{16}{60}\right)^\circ \approx 120.2667^\circ$.

**22** Since $1' = \left(\frac{1}{60}\right)^\circ$, $47' = \left(\frac{47}{60}\right)^\circ$. Thus, $53^\circ 47' = \left(53 + \frac{47}{60}\right)^\circ \approx 53.7833^\circ$.

**23** Since $1'' = \left(\frac{1}{3600}\right)^\circ$, $31'' = \left(\frac{31}{3600}\right)^\circ$. Thus, $262^\circ 15' 31'' = \left(262 + \frac{15}{60} + \frac{31}{3600}\right)^\circ \approx 262.2586^\circ$.

**24** Since $1'' = \left(\frac{1}{3600}\right)^\circ$, $58'' = \left(\frac{58}{3600}\right)^\circ$. Thus, $320^\circ 7' 58'' = \left(320 + \frac{7}{60} + \frac{58}{3600}\right)^\circ \approx 320.1328^\circ$.

**25** We have $63^\circ$ and a portion of one more degree. Since $1^\circ = 60'$, $0.169^\circ = 0.169(60') = 10.14'$.

We now have $10'$ and a portion of one more minute.

Since $1' = 60''$, $0.14' = 0.14(60'') = 8.4''$. $\therefore$ $63.169^\circ \approx 63^\circ 10' 8''$

**26** $0.864(60') = 51.84'$; $0.84(60'') = 50.4''$;　　　　　　　　$\therefore$ $12.864^\circ \approx 12^\circ 51' 50''$

**27** $0.6215(60') = 37.29'$; $0.29(60'') = 17.4''$;　　　　　　　$\therefore$ $310.6215^\circ \approx 310^\circ 37' 17''$

**28** $0.7238(60') = 43.428'$; $0.428(60'') = 25.68''$;　　　　　　$\therefore$ $81.7238^\circ \approx 81^\circ 43' 26''$

**29** We will use the formula for the length of a circular arc. $s = r\theta \Rightarrow r = \frac{s}{\theta} = \frac{10}{4} = 2.5$ cm.

**30** $s = r\theta \Rightarrow r = \frac{s}{\theta} = \frac{3}{20 \cdot \frac{\pi}{180}} = \frac{27}{\pi} \approx 8.59$ km

**31** (a) $s = r\theta = 8 \cdot \left(45 \cdot \frac{\pi}{180}\right) = 8 \cdot \frac{\pi}{4} = 2\pi \approx 6.28$ cm

(b) $A = \frac{1}{2}r^2\theta = \frac{1}{2}(8)^2\left(\frac{\pi}{4}\right) = 8\pi \approx 25.13$ cm$^2$

**32** (a) $s = r\theta = 9 \cdot \left(120 \cdot \frac{\pi}{180}\right) = 9 \cdot \frac{2\pi}{3} = 6\pi \approx 18.85$ cm

(b) $A = \frac{1}{2}r^2\theta = \frac{1}{2}(9)^2\left(\frac{2\pi}{3}\right) = 27\pi \approx 84.82$ cm$^2$

**33** (a) Remember that $\theta$ is measured in radians. $s = r\theta \Rightarrow \theta = \frac{s}{r} = \frac{7}{4} = 1.75$ radians.
Converting to degrees, we have $\frac{7}{4} \cdot \left(\frac{180}{\pi}\right)^\circ = \left(\frac{315}{\pi}\right)^\circ \approx 100.27^\circ$.

(b) $A = \frac{1}{2}r^2\theta = \frac{1}{2}(4)^2\left(\frac{7}{4}\right) = 14$ cm$^2$

**34** (a) $\theta = \frac{s}{r} = \frac{3(12)}{20} = \frac{9}{5} = 1.8$ radians; $\frac{9}{5} \cdot \left(\frac{180}{\pi}\right)^\circ = \left(\frac{324}{\pi}\right)^\circ \approx 103.13^\circ$

(b) $A = \frac{1}{2}r^2\theta = \frac{1}{2}(20)^2\left(\frac{9}{5}\right) = 360$ in$^2$

**35** (a) A measure of $50^\circ$ is equivalent to $\left(50 \cdot \frac{\pi}{180}\right)$ radians. The radius is one-half of the diameter.
Thus, $s = r\theta = \left(\frac{1}{2} \cdot 16\right)\left(50 \cdot \frac{\pi}{180}\right) = 8 \cdot \frac{5\pi}{18} = \frac{20\pi}{9} \approx 6.98$ m.

(b) $A = \frac{1}{2}r^2\theta = \frac{1}{2}(8)^2\left(\frac{5\pi}{18}\right) = \frac{80\pi}{9} \approx 27.93$ m$^2$

**36** (a) $s = r\theta = \left(\frac{1}{2} \cdot 120\right)(2.2) = 60(2.2) = 132$ cm

(b) $A = \frac{1}{2}r^2\theta = \frac{1}{2}(60)^2(2.2) = 3960$ cm$^2$

**37** $s = r\theta$ and $s = 8 \Rightarrow 8 = r\theta \Rightarrow r = \frac{8}{\theta}$. $A = \frac{1}{2}r^2\theta = \frac{1}{2}\left(\frac{8}{\theta}\right)^2\theta = \frac{1}{2}\left(\frac{64}{\theta^2}\right)\theta = \frac{32}{\theta}$.

**38** $s = r\theta$ and $s = 14 \Rightarrow 14 = r\theta \Rightarrow r = \frac{14}{\theta}$. $A = \frac{1}{2}r^2\theta = \frac{1}{2}\left(\frac{14}{\theta}\right)^2\theta = \frac{1}{2}\left(\frac{196}{\theta^2}\right)\theta = \frac{98}{\theta}$.

**39** radius $= \frac{1}{2} \cdot 8000$ miles $= 4000$ miles

(a) $s = r\theta = 4000\left(60 \cdot \frac{\pi}{180}\right) = \frac{4000\pi}{3} \approx 4189$ miles    (b) $s = r\theta = 4000\left(45 \cdot \frac{\pi}{180}\right) = 1000\pi \approx 3142$ miles

(c) $s = r\theta = 4000\left(30 \cdot \frac{\pi}{180}\right) = \frac{2000\pi}{3} \approx 2094$ miles    (d) $s = r\theta = 4000\left(10 \cdot \frac{\pi}{180}\right) = \frac{2000\pi}{9} \approx 698$ miles

(e) $s = r\theta = 4000\left(1 \cdot \frac{\pi}{180}\right) = \frac{200\pi}{9} \approx 70$ miles

**40** $1' = \left(\frac{1}{60}\right)^\circ$; $s = r\theta = 4000\left(\frac{1}{60} \cdot \frac{\pi}{180}\right) = \frac{10\pi}{27} \approx 1.16$ mi

**41** $\theta = \frac{s}{r} = \frac{500}{4000} = \frac{1}{8}$ radian; $\left(\frac{1}{8}\right)\left(\frac{180}{\pi}\right)^\circ = \left(\frac{45}{2\pi}\right)^\circ \approx 7^\circ 10'$

**42** The area of equilateral $\triangle OAB$ is $\frac{1}{4}\sqrt{3}\,r^2$ (see the formula on the endpapers
of the text). The area of sector $OAB$ minus the area of $\triangle OAB$ is one-sixth
of the total difference; that is, $\frac{1}{6}(24) = 4$.
Sector $OAB_{\text{area}}$ − Triangle $OAB_{\text{area}} = 4 \Rightarrow$
$\frac{1}{2}r^2 \cdot \frac{\pi}{3} - \frac{1}{4}\sqrt{3}\,r^2 = 4 \Rightarrow 2\pi r^2 - 3\sqrt{3}\,r^2 = 48$ {multiply by 12} $\Rightarrow$
$r^2 = \dfrac{48}{2\pi - 3\sqrt{3}} \Rightarrow r = \sqrt{\dfrac{48}{2\pi - 3\sqrt{3}}} \approx 6.645$ m.

**43** The total rectangular area of the window is $T = 54 \times 24 = 1296$ in$^2$. The wiped area $W$ is the area of a sector with
radius $17 + 5 = 22$ inches minus the area of a sector with radius 5 inches; that is,

$$W = \frac{1}{2}(22)^2 \cdot \frac{2\pi}{3} - \frac{1}{2}(5)^2 \cdot \frac{2\pi}{3} = \frac{\pi}{3}(484 - 25) = \frac{459\pi}{3} \approx 480.66.$$

The percentage of the window's area that is wiped by the blade is $100 \times \frac{W}{T} \approx 37.1\%$.

**44** A point on the perimeter of the core is moving 264 ft in 1 sec. The radius of the core is 100 ft.

$$s = r\theta \quad \Rightarrow \quad \theta = \frac{s}{r} = \frac{264}{100} = 2.64 \text{ rad/sec} = 158.4 \text{ rad/min} = \frac{158.4}{2\pi} \text{ rev/min} \approx 25.2 \text{ rev/min.}$$

**45** 23 hours, 56 minutes, and 4 seconds $= 23(60)^2 + 56(60) + 4 = 86{,}164$ sec. Since Earth turns through

$2\pi$ radians in 86,164 seconds, it rotates through $\frac{2\pi}{86,164} \approx 7.29 \times 10^{-5}$ radians in one second.

**46** Using the result from Exercise 45, the distance $s$ traveled in 1 second will be

$$s = r\theta \approx (3963.3)\left(\frac{2\pi}{86,164}\right) \approx 0.29 \text{ mi/sec, or, } 1040 \text{ mi/hr.}$$

**47** (a) $\left(40 \dfrac{\text{revolutions}}{\text{minute}}\right)\left(2\pi \dfrac{\text{radians}}{\text{revolution}}\right) = 80\pi \dfrac{\text{radians}}{\text{minute}}$. **Note:** Remember to write out and "cancel" the units if

you are unsure about what units your answer is measured in.

(b) The distance that a point on the circumference travels is $s = r\theta = (5 \text{ in.}) \cdot 80\pi = 400\pi$ in.

Hence, its linear speed is $400\pi$ in./min $= \frac{100\pi}{3}$ ft/min $\{400\pi \cdot \frac{1}{12}\} \approx 104.72$ ft/min.

**48** (a) $\left(2400 \dfrac{\text{rev}}{\text{min}}\right)\left(2\pi \dfrac{\text{rad}}{\text{rev}}\right) = 4800\pi \dfrac{\text{rad}}{\text{min}}$

(b) $s = r\theta = (9 \text{ in}) \cdot 4800\pi = 43{,}200\pi$ in. Linear speed $= 43{,}200\pi$ in/min $= 3600\pi$ ft/min.

**49** (a) $200$ rpm $= 200 \dfrac{\text{rev}}{\text{min}} \cdot \dfrac{2\pi \text{ rad}}{1 \text{ rev}} = 400\pi \dfrac{\text{rad}}{\text{min}}$

(b) $s = r\theta = (5.7)(400\pi) = 2280\pi$ cm. Linear speed $= 2280\pi$ cm/min.

Divide by 60 to obtain cm/sec: $\frac{2280\pi}{60} = 38\pi \approx 119$ cm/sec

(c) Let $x$ be the desired angular speed. The linear speed at 5.7 cm must equal the linear speed at 3 cm, so

$2280\pi = 3x \quad \Rightarrow \quad x = 760\pi$ rad/min. Divide by $2\pi$ to obtain revolutions per minute: $\frac{760\pi}{2\pi} = 380$ rpm

(d) One approach is to simply return to part (c), replace 3 with $r$, and divide by $2\pi$ to create the function.

$2280\pi = rx \quad \Rightarrow \quad x = \dfrac{2280\pi}{r}$, so $S(r) = \dfrac{2280\pi}{r(2\pi)} = \dfrac{1140}{r}$. As the radius increases, the drive motor speed

decreases. Thus, $S$ and $r$ vary *inversely*.

**50** $\dfrac{60 \text{ miles}}{\text{hour}} = \dfrac{60 \text{ miles}}{\text{hour}} \cdot \dfrac{1 \text{ hour}}{60 \text{ minutes}} \cdot \dfrac{5280 \text{ feet}}{\text{mile}} \cdot \dfrac{12 \text{ inches}}{\text{foot}} = \dfrac{63{,}360 \text{ inches}}{\text{minute}}$.

A point of the circumference of the tire moves $2\pi r = 2\pi\left(\frac{1}{2} \cdot 22\right) = 22\pi$ inches each revolution.

Thus, the number of revolutions per minute is $\dfrac{63{,}360 \text{ inches}}{\text{minute}} \cdot \dfrac{1 \text{ revolution}}{22\pi \text{ inches}} = \dfrac{31{,}680 \text{ revolutions}}{11\pi \text{ minute}} \approx 916.73$ rpm.

**51** (a) The distance that the cargo is lifted is equal to the arc length that the cable is moved through.

$$s = r\theta = \left(\tfrac{1}{2} \cdot 3\right)\left(\tfrac{7\pi}{4}\right) = \dfrac{21\pi}{8} \approx 8.25 \text{ ft.}$$

(b) $s = r\theta \quad \Rightarrow \quad d = \left(\frac{1}{2} \cdot 3\right)\theta \quad \Rightarrow \quad \theta = \left(\frac{2}{3}d\right)$ radians.

For example, to lift the cargo 6 feet, the winch must rotate $\frac{2}{3} \cdot 6 = 4$ radians, or about $229°$.

**52** $\theta = \dfrac{s}{r} = \dfrac{6 \text{ in}}{4 \text{ ft}} = \dfrac{6 \text{ in}}{48 \text{ in}} = \dfrac{1}{8}$ radian $\approx 7.162°$ or $7°10'$

**53** Area$_{\text{small}} = \frac{1}{2}r^2\theta = \frac{1}{2}\left(\frac{1}{2} \cdot 18\right)^2 \cdot \left(\frac{2\pi}{6}\right) = \frac{27\pi}{2}$. Area$_{\text{large}} = \frac{1}{2}\left(\frac{1}{2} \cdot 26\right)^2 \cdot \left(\frac{2\pi}{8}\right) = \frac{169\pi}{8}$.

Cost$_{\text{small}}$ = Area$_{\text{small}} \div$ Cost $= \frac{27\pi}{2} \div 2 \approx 21.21$ in$^2$/dollar.

Cost$_{\text{large}}$ = Area$_{\text{large}} \div$ Cost $= \frac{169\pi}{8} \div 3 \approx 22.12$ in$^2$/dollar. The large slice provides slightly more pizza per dollar.

**54** Let $s_1$ and $s_2$ denote the lengths of the chain around the sprockets with radii $r_1$ and $r_2$, respectively. Thus,

$s_1 = r_1\theta_1$ and $s_2 = r_2\theta_2$. The lengths of chain $s_1$ and $s_2$ are equal. $s_2 = s_1 \Rightarrow r_2\theta_2 = r_1\theta_1 \Rightarrow \theta_2 = \dfrac{r_1\theta_1}{r_2}$.

**55** $\dfrac{40 \text{ miles}}{\text{hour}} = \dfrac{40 \text{ miles}}{\text{hour}} \cdot \dfrac{1 \text{ hour}}{3600 \text{ seconds}} \cdot \dfrac{5280 \text{ feet}}{\text{mile}} \cdot \dfrac{12 \text{ inches}}{\text{foot}} = \dfrac{704 \text{ inches}}{\text{second}}$.

The circumference of the wheel is $2\pi(14)$ inches. The back sprocket then rotates

$\dfrac{704 \text{ inches}}{\text{second}} \cdot \dfrac{1 \text{ revolution}}{28\pi \text{ inches}} = \dfrac{704 \text{ revolutions}}{28\pi \text{ second}}$ or $\dfrac{704}{28\pi} \cdot 2\pi = \dfrac{352}{7}$ radians per second.

From Exercise 54, the front sprocket's angular speed is given by $\theta_1 = \dfrac{r_2\theta_2}{r_1} = \dfrac{2 \cdot \frac{352}{7}}{5} = \dfrac{704}{35} \approx 20.114 \dfrac{\text{radians}}{\text{second}}$,

or 3.2 revolutions per second, or 192.08 revolutions per minute.

**56** $0.0017 \text{ rad/yr} = 0.0017\left(\dfrac{180}{\pi}\right)^{\circ}/\text{yr}$.

If $x$ is the number of years required, then $5 = \dfrac{0.0017(180)}{\pi}x \Rightarrow x = \dfrac{5\pi}{0.306} \approx 51.3$.

## 5.2 Exercises

**1** (a–b) From the figure, $\alpha$ is smaller than $\beta$. Since one radian is about $57°$, the only logical choices for the radian measures of $\alpha$ and $\beta$ are 0.28 and 1.29, respectively. The answers are (a) B and (b) D.

(c–e) The sides $x$, $y$, and $z$ must be 7, 24, and 25, respectively, since the legs $x$ and $y$ must be smaller than the hypotenuse $z$, and from the figure, $x$ is less than $y$. The answers are (c) A, (d) C, and (e) E.

**2** (c–e) The sides $x$, $y$, and $z$ must be 16, 17, and 23.35, respectively, since the legs $x$ and $y$ must be smaller than the hypotenuse $z$, and from the figure, $x < y$ (a measurement will show this). The answers are (c) B, (d) C, and (e) A.

(a–b) Since $x < y$, we have $\alpha < \beta$ since $\alpha$ is the angle opposite side $x$. The only logical choices for the radian measures of $\alpha$ and $\beta$ are 0.76 and 0.82, respectively. The answers are (a) E and (b) D.

**Note:** Answers are in the order *sin, cos, tan, cot, sec, csc* for any exercises that require the values of the six trigonometric functions.

**3** Using the definition of the trigonometric functions,

$$\sin\theta = \frac{\text{opp}}{\text{hyp}} = \frac{4}{5}, \quad \cos\theta = \frac{\text{adj}}{\text{hyp}} = \frac{3}{5}, \quad \text{and} \quad \tan\theta = \frac{\text{opp}}{\text{adj}} = \frac{4}{3}.$$

We now use the reciprocal identities to find the values of the other trigonometric functions:

$$\cot\theta = \frac{1}{\tan\theta} = \frac{3}{4}, \quad \sec\theta = \frac{1}{\cos\theta} = \frac{5}{3}, \quad \text{and} \quad \csc\theta = \frac{1}{\sin\theta} = \frac{5}{4}.$$

**4** $\sin\theta = \dfrac{\text{opp}}{\text{hyp}} = \dfrac{8}{17}$; $\cos\theta = \dfrac{\text{adj}}{\text{hyp}} = \dfrac{15}{17}$; $\tan\theta = \dfrac{\text{opp}}{\text{adj}} = \dfrac{8}{15}$    ★ $\dfrac{8}{17}, \dfrac{15}{17}, \dfrac{8}{15}, \dfrac{15}{8}, \dfrac{17}{15}, \dfrac{17}{8}$

**5** Using the Pythagorean theorem, $(\text{adj})^2 + (\text{opp})^2 = (\text{hyp})^2 \Rightarrow (\text{adj})^2 = (\text{hyp})^2 - (\text{opp})^2 \Rightarrow$

$\text{adj} = \sqrt{(\text{hyp})^2 - (\text{opp})^2} = \sqrt{5^2 - 2^2} = \sqrt{21}$.    ★ $\dfrac{2}{5}, \dfrac{\sqrt{21}}{5}, \dfrac{2}{\sqrt{21}}, \dfrac{\sqrt{21}}{2}, \dfrac{5}{\sqrt{21}}, \dfrac{5}{2}$

**6** Using the Pythagorean theorem, $\text{opp} = \sqrt{(\text{hyp})^2 - (\text{adj})^2} = \sqrt{3^2 - 1^2} = \sqrt{8}$.    ★ $\dfrac{\sqrt{8}}{3}, \dfrac{1}{3}, \sqrt{8}, \dfrac{1}{\sqrt{8}}, 3, \dfrac{3}{\sqrt{8}}$

**7** Using the Pythagorean theorem, $(\text{adj})^2 + (\text{opp})^2 = (\text{hyp})^2 \Rightarrow$
$\text{hyp} = \sqrt{(\text{adj})^2 + (\text{opp})^2} = \sqrt{b^2 + a^2} = \sqrt{a^2 + b^2}.$   ★ $\dfrac{a}{\sqrt{a^2+b^2}}, \dfrac{b}{\sqrt{a^2+b^2}}, \dfrac{a}{b}, \dfrac{b}{a}, \dfrac{\sqrt{a^2+b^2}}{b}, \dfrac{\sqrt{a^2+b^2}}{a}$

**8** $\text{opp} = \sqrt{c^2 - a^2}$   ★ $\dfrac{\sqrt{c^2-a^2}}{c}, \dfrac{a}{c}, \dfrac{\sqrt{c^2-a^2}}{a}, \dfrac{a}{\sqrt{c^2-a^2}}, \dfrac{c}{a}, \dfrac{c}{\sqrt{c^2-a^2}}$

**9** Using the Pythagorean theorem, $(\text{adj})^2 + (\text{opp})^2 = (\text{hyp})^2 \Rightarrow (\text{adj})^2 = (\text{hyp})^2 - (\text{opp})^2 \Rightarrow$
$\text{adj} = \sqrt{(\text{hyp})^2 - (\text{opp})^2} = \sqrt{c^2 - b^2}.$   ★ $\dfrac{b}{c}, \dfrac{\sqrt{c^2-b^2}}{c}, \dfrac{b}{\sqrt{c^2-b^2}}, \dfrac{\sqrt{c^2-b^2}}{b}, \dfrac{c}{\sqrt{c^2-b^2}}, \dfrac{c}{b}$

**10** $\text{hyp} = \sqrt{a^2 + a^2} = \sqrt{2a^2} = \sqrt{2}\,a \Rightarrow \sin\theta = \dfrac{a}{\sqrt{2}\,a} = \dfrac{1}{\sqrt{2}}, \text{ or, } \dfrac{\sqrt{2}}{2}.$
$\cos\theta = \dfrac{a}{\sqrt{2}\,a} = \dfrac{1}{\sqrt{2}}$ and $\tan\theta = \dfrac{a}{a} = 1.$   ★ $\dfrac{\sqrt{2}}{2}, \dfrac{\sqrt{2}}{2}, 1, 1, \sqrt{2}, \sqrt{2}$

**11** Since we want to find the value of the hypotenuse $x$, we need to use a trigonometric function which relates $x$ to two given parts of the triangle—in this case, the angle $30°$ and the opposite side of length 4. The sine function relates the opposite side and the hypotenuse. Hence, $\sin 30° = \dfrac{4}{x} \Rightarrow \dfrac{1}{2} = \dfrac{4}{x} \Rightarrow x = 8.$ The tangent function relates the opposite and the adjacent side. Hence, $\tan 30° = \dfrac{4}{y} \Rightarrow \dfrac{\sqrt{3}}{3} = \dfrac{4}{y} \Rightarrow y = 4\sqrt{3}.$

**12** $\sin 60° = \dfrac{3}{x} \Rightarrow \dfrac{\sqrt{3}}{2} = \dfrac{3}{x} \Rightarrow x = 2\sqrt{3}$ and $\tan 60° = \dfrac{3}{y} \Rightarrow \sqrt{3} = \dfrac{3}{y} \Rightarrow y = \sqrt{3}.$

**13** The easy way to find the values of $x$ and $y$ is to remember that the lengths of the legs in a $45°$–$45°$–$90°$ triangle must be the same; so $y = 7$. Also, the hypotenuse is $\sqrt{2}$ times the length of either leg; that is, $x = 7\sqrt{2}$. We can also use the trigonometric relationships as follows:
$\sin 45° = \dfrac{7}{x} \Rightarrow \dfrac{\sqrt{2}}{2} = \dfrac{7}{x} \Rightarrow x = 7\sqrt{2}$ and $\tan 45° = \dfrac{7}{y} \Rightarrow 1 = \dfrac{7}{y} \Rightarrow y = 7.$

**14** $\sin 30° = \dfrac{x}{10} \Rightarrow \dfrac{1}{2} = \dfrac{x}{10} \Rightarrow x = 5$ and $\cos 30° = \dfrac{y}{10} \Rightarrow \dfrac{\sqrt{3}}{2} = \dfrac{y}{10} \Rightarrow y = 5\sqrt{3}.$

**15** $\sin 60° = \dfrac{x}{8} \Rightarrow \dfrac{\sqrt{3}}{2} = \dfrac{x}{8} \Rightarrow x = 4\sqrt{3}$ and $\cos 60° = \dfrac{y}{8} \Rightarrow \dfrac{1}{2} = \dfrac{y}{8} \Rightarrow y = 4.$

**16** $\sin 45° = \dfrac{x}{4} \Rightarrow \dfrac{\sqrt{2}}{2} = \dfrac{x}{4} \Rightarrow x = 2\sqrt{2}$ and $\cos 45° = \dfrac{y}{4} \Rightarrow \dfrac{\sqrt{2}}{2} = \dfrac{y}{4} \Rightarrow y = 2\sqrt{2}.$

**Note:** It may help to sketch a triangle as shown for Exercises 17 and 21. Use the Pythagorean theorem to find the remaining side.

**17** $(\text{adj})^2 + (\text{opp})^2 = (\text{hyp})^2 \Rightarrow (\text{adj})^2 + 3^2 = 5^2 \Rightarrow \text{adj} = \sqrt{25 - 9} = 4.$   ★ $\dfrac{3}{5}, \dfrac{4}{5}, \dfrac{3}{4}, \dfrac{4}{3}, \dfrac{5}{4}, \dfrac{5}{3}$

*Figure 17*

*Figure 21*

**18** $(\text{adj})^2 + (\text{opp})^2 = (\text{hyp})^2 \;\Rightarrow\; 8^2 + (\text{opp})^2 = 17^2 \;\Rightarrow\; \text{opp} = \sqrt{289 - 64} = 15.$  ★ $\frac{15}{17}, \frac{8}{17}, \frac{15}{8}, \frac{8}{15}, \frac{17}{8}, \frac{17}{15}$

**19** $(\text{adj})^2 + (\text{opp})^2 = (\text{hyp})^2 \;\Rightarrow\; 12^2 + 5^2 = (\text{hyp})^2 \;\Rightarrow\; \text{hyp} = \sqrt{144 + 25} = 13.$  ★ $\frac{5}{13}, \frac{12}{13}, \frac{5}{12}, \frac{12}{5}, \frac{13}{12}, \frac{13}{5}$

**20** $(\text{adj})^2 + (\text{opp})^2 = (\text{hyp})^2 \;\Rightarrow\; 7^2 + 24^2 = (\text{hyp})^2 \;\Rightarrow\; \text{hyp} = \sqrt{49 + 576} = 25.$  ★ $\frac{24}{25}, \frac{7}{25}, \frac{24}{7}, \frac{7}{24}, \frac{25}{7}, \frac{25}{24}$

**21** $(\text{adj})^2 + (\text{opp})^2 = (\text{hyp})^2 \;\Rightarrow\; 5^2 + (\text{opp})^2 = 6^2 \;\Rightarrow\; \text{opp} = \sqrt{36 - 25} = \sqrt{11}.$  ★ $\frac{\sqrt{11}}{6}, \frac{5}{6}, \frac{\sqrt{11}}{5}, \frac{5}{\sqrt{11}}, \frac{6}{5}, \frac{6}{\sqrt{11}}$

**22** $(\text{adj})^2 + (\text{opp})^2 = (\text{hyp})^2 \;\Rightarrow\; (\text{adj})^2 + 3^2 = 4^2 \;\Rightarrow\; \text{adj} = \sqrt{16 - 9} = \sqrt{7}.$  ★ $\frac{3}{4}, \frac{\sqrt{7}}{4}, \frac{3}{\sqrt{7}}, \frac{\sqrt{7}}{3}, \frac{4}{\sqrt{7}}, \frac{4}{3}$

**23** Let $h$ denote the height of the tree.

$$\tan\theta = \frac{\text{opp}}{\text{adj}} \;\Rightarrow\; \tan 60° = \frac{h}{200} \;\Rightarrow\; h = 200\tan 60° = 200\sqrt{3} \approx 346.4 \text{ ft.}$$

**24** Let $d$ denote the distance to the base of the mountain.

$$\cot\theta = \frac{\text{adj}}{\text{opp}} \;\Rightarrow\; \cot 30° = \frac{d}{12{,}400} \;\Rightarrow\; d = 12{,}400\sqrt{3} \approx 21{,}477.4 \text{ ft.}$$

**25** Let $d$ be the distance that the stone was moved. The side opposite $9°$ is 30 feet and the hypotenuse is $d$.

$$\text{Thus, } \sin 9° = \frac{30}{d} \;\Rightarrow\; d = \frac{30}{\sin 9°} \approx 192 \text{ ft.}$$

**26** Let $h$ be the height of the top of the sign. $\tan 78.87° = \dfrac{h}{200} \;\Rightarrow\; h = 200\tan 78.87° \approx 1017$ ft

**27** $\sin\theta = \dfrac{1.22\lambda}{D} \;\Rightarrow\; D = \dfrac{1.22\lambda}{\sin\theta} = \dfrac{1.22 \times 550 \times 10^{-9}}{\sin 0.000\,037\,69°} \approx 1.02$ meters

**28** (a) $A = \frac{1}{2}\pi R^2(1 + \cos 0°) = \frac{1}{2}\pi R^2(2) = \pi R^2 = \pi(1080)^2 = 1{,}166{,}400\pi \approx 3{,}664{,}354 \text{ mi}^2$

(b) $A = \frac{1}{2}\pi R^2(1 + \cos 180°) = \frac{1}{2}\pi R^2(0) = 0 \text{ mi}^2$

(c) $A = \frac{1}{2}\pi R^2(1 + \cos 90°) = \frac{1}{2}\pi R^2(1) = \frac{1}{2}\pi R^2 = \frac{\pi}{2}(1080)^2 = 583{,}200\pi \approx 1{,}832{,}177 \text{ mi}^2$

(d) $A = \frac{1}{2}\pi R^2(1 + \cos 103°) \approx \frac{1}{2}\pi R^2(0.77505) \approx 0.38752\pi(1080)^2 \approx 1{,}420{,}027 \text{ mi}^2$

**29** *Note:* Be sure that your calculator is in degree mode.

(a) $\sin 73° \approx 0.9563$

(b) $\cos 61° \approx 0.4848$

(c) $\csc 105° = \dfrac{1}{\sin 105°} \approx 1.0353$

(d) $\sec(-215°) = \dfrac{1}{\cos(-215°)} \approx -1.2208$

**30** (a) $\tan 282° \approx -4.7046$

(b) $\cot(-81°) = \dfrac{1}{\tan(-81°)} \approx -0.1584$

(c) $\sec 202° = \dfrac{1}{\cos 202°} \approx -1.0785$

(d) $\sin 97° \approx 0.9925$

**31** *Note:* Be sure that your calculator is in radian mode.

(a) $\cot\dfrac{\pi}{13} = \dfrac{1}{\tan(\pi/13)} \approx 4.0572$

(b) $\csc 1.32 = \dfrac{1}{\sin 1.32} \approx 1.0323$

(c) $\cos(-8.54) \approx -0.6335$

(d) $\tan\dfrac{15}{8} \approx -3.1852$

**32** (a) $\sin(-0.11) \approx -0.1098$

(b) $\sec\dfrac{2\pi}{5} = \dfrac{1}{\cos(2\pi/5)} \approx 3.2361$

(c) $\tan\left(-\dfrac{3}{13}\right) \approx -0.2350$

(d) $\cos 2.4\pi \approx 0.3090$

**33** (a) $\sin 30° = 0.5$ (*not* $-0.9880$, that's the answer in radian mode)

(b) $\sin 30 \approx -0.9880$ (*not* $0.5$, that's the answer in degree mode)

(c) $\cos \pi° \approx 0.9985$ (*not* $-1$, that's the answer in radian mode)

(d) $\cos \pi = -1$ (*not* $-0.9985$, that's the answer in degree mode)

**Note:** In general, it's probably easiest to leave your calculator in radian mode and just attach the degree symbol (under the ANGLE menu on the TI-83/4 Plus) when needed.

**34** (a) $\sin 45° \approx 0.7071$                      (b) $\sin 45 \approx 0.8509$

(c) $\cos(3\pi/2)° \approx 0.9966$              (d) $\cos(3\pi/2) = 0$

**35** (a) Since $1 + \tan^2 4\beta = \sec^2 4\beta$, $\tan^2 4\beta - \sec^2 4\beta = -1$.

(b) $4 \tan^2 \beta - 4 \sec^2 \beta = 4(\tan^2 \beta - \sec^2 \beta) = 4(-1) = -4$

**36** (a) Since $1 + \cot^2 3\alpha = \csc^2 3\alpha$, $\csc^2 3\alpha - \cot^2 3\alpha = 1$.

(b) $3 \csc^2 \alpha - 3 \cot^2 \alpha = 3(\csc^2 \alpha - \cot^2 \alpha) = 3(1) = 3$

**37** (a) $5 \sin^2 \theta + 5 \cos^2 \theta = 5(\sin^2 \theta + \cos^2 \theta) = 5(1) = 5$

(b) $5 \sin^2 (\theta/4) + 5 \cos^2 (\theta/4) = 5 [\sin^2 (\theta/4) + \cos^2 (\theta/4)] = 5(1) = 5$

**38** (a) $7 \sec^2 \gamma - 7 \tan^2 \gamma = 7(\sec^2 \gamma - \tan^2 \gamma) = 7(1) = 7$

(b) $7 \sec^2 (\gamma/3) - 7 \tan^2 (\gamma/3) = 7 [\sec^2 (\gamma/3) - \tan^2 (\gamma/3)] = 7(1) = 7$

**39** $\dfrac{\sin^3 \theta + \cos^3 \theta}{\sin \theta + \cos \theta} = \dfrac{(\sin \theta + \cos \theta)(\sin^2 \theta - \sin \theta \cos \theta + \cos^2 \theta)}{\sin \theta + \cos \theta}$     {factor, sum of cubes}

$= \sin^2 \theta - \sin \theta \cos \theta + \cos^2 \theta$     {cancel $(\sin \theta + \cos \theta)$}

$= (\sin^2 \theta + \cos^2 \theta) - \sin \theta \cos \theta$     {group terms}

$= 1 - \sin \theta \cos \theta$     {Pythagorean identity}

**40** $\dfrac{\sin \theta - \cos \theta}{\sin^3 \theta - \cos^3 \theta} = \dfrac{\sin \theta - \cos \theta}{(\sin \theta - \cos \theta)(\sin^2 \theta + \sin \theta \cos \theta + \cos^2 \theta)}$     {factor, difference of cubes}

$= \dfrac{1}{\sin^2 \theta + \sin \theta \cos \theta + \cos^2 \theta}$     {cancel $(\sin \theta - \cos \theta)$}

$= \dfrac{1}{(\sin^2 \theta + \cos^2 \theta) + \sin \theta \cos \theta}$     {group terms}

$= \dfrac{1}{1 + \sin \theta \cos \theta}$     {Pythagorean identity}

**41** $\dfrac{9 - \tan^2 \theta}{\tan^2 \theta - 5 \tan \theta + 6} = \dfrac{(3 + \tan \theta)(3 - \tan \theta)}{(\tan \theta - 2)(\tan \theta - 3)} = \dfrac{3 + \tan \theta}{(\tan \theta - 2)(-1)} = \dfrac{3 + \tan \theta}{2 - \tan \theta}$

**42** $\dfrac{\cot^2 \alpha - 4}{\cot^2 \alpha - \cot \alpha - 6} = \dfrac{(\cot \alpha + 2)(\cot \alpha - 2)}{(\cot \alpha - 3)(\cot \alpha + 2)} = \dfrac{\cot \alpha - 2}{\cot \alpha - 3}$

**43** $\dfrac{2 - \tan\theta}{2\csc\theta - \sec\theta} = \dfrac{2 - \dfrac{\sin\theta}{\cos\theta}}{2 \cdot \dfrac{1}{\sin\theta} - \dfrac{1}{\cos\theta}}$  {tangent and reciprocal identities}

$\qquad = \dfrac{\dfrac{2\cos\theta - \sin\theta}{\cos\theta}}{\dfrac{2\cos\theta - \sin\theta}{\sin\theta\cos\theta}}$  {combine terms}

$\qquad = \dfrac{\dfrac{1}{1}}{\dfrac{1}{\sin\theta}}$  {cancel like terms}

$\qquad = \sin\theta$

**44** $\dfrac{\csc\theta + 1}{(1/\sin^2\theta) + \csc\theta} = \dfrac{\csc\theta + 1}{\csc^2\theta + \csc\theta} = \dfrac{\csc\theta + 1}{\csc\theta(\csc\theta + 1)} = \dfrac{1}{\csc\theta} = \sin\theta$

**45** $\cot\theta = \dfrac{\cos\theta}{\sin\theta}$ {cotangent identity} $= \dfrac{\sqrt{1 - \sin^2\theta}}{\sin\theta}$ {$\sin^2\theta + \cos^2\theta = 1$}

**46** $\tan\theta = \dfrac{\sin\theta}{\cos\theta}$ {tangent identity} $= \dfrac{\sqrt{1 - \cos^2\theta}}{\cos\theta}$ {$\sin^2\theta + \cos^2\theta = 1$}

**47** $\sec\theta = \dfrac{1}{\cos\theta}$ {reciprocal identity} $= \dfrac{1}{\sqrt{1 - \sin^2\theta}}$

**48** $\csc\theta = \dfrac{1}{\sin\theta}$ {reciprocal identity} $= \dfrac{1}{\sqrt{1 - \cos^2\theta}}$

**49** One solution is $\sin\theta = \sqrt{1 - \cos^2\theta} = \sqrt{1 - \dfrac{1}{\sec^2\theta}} = \dfrac{\sqrt{\sec^2\theta - 1}}{\sec\theta}$.

$\qquad$ Alternatively, $\sin\theta = \dfrac{\sin\theta/\cos\theta}{1/\cos\theta} = \dfrac{\tan\theta}{\sec\theta} = \dfrac{\sqrt{\sec^2\theta - 1}}{\sec\theta}$ {$1 + \tan^2\theta = \sec^2\theta$}.

**50** $\cos\theta = \dfrac{\cos\theta/\sin\theta}{1/\sin\theta} = \dfrac{\cot\theta}{\csc\theta} = \dfrac{\cot\theta}{\sqrt{1 + \cot^2\theta}}$ {$1 + \cot^2\theta = \csc^2\theta$}

**51** $\cos\theta\sec\theta = \cos\theta(1/\cos\theta)$ {reciprocal identity} $= 1$

**52** $\tan\theta\cot\theta = \tan\theta(1/\tan\theta) = 1$

**53** $\sin\theta\sec\theta = \sin\theta(1/\cos\theta) = \sin\theta/\cos\theta = \tan\theta$ {tangent identity}

**54** $\sin\theta\cot\theta = \sin\theta(\cos\theta/\sin\theta) = \cos\theta$

**55** $\dfrac{\csc\theta}{\sec\theta} = \dfrac{1/\sin\theta}{1/\cos\theta}$ {reciprocal identities} $= \dfrac{\cos\theta}{\sin\theta} = \cot\theta$ {cotangent identity}

**56** $\cot\theta\sec\theta = \dfrac{\cos\theta}{\sin\theta} \cdot \dfrac{1}{\cos\theta} = \dfrac{1}{\sin\theta} = \csc\theta$

**57** $(1 + \cos 2\theta)(1 - \cos 2\theta) = 1 - \cos^2 2\theta = \sin^2 2\theta$ {Pythagorean identity}

**58** $\cos^2 2\theta - \sin^2 2\theta = \cos^2 2\theta - (1 - \cos^2 2\theta) = 2\cos^2 2\theta - 1$

**59** $\cos^2\theta(\sec^2\theta - 1) = \cos^2\theta(\tan^2\theta)$ {Pythagorean identity} $= \cos^2\theta \cdot \dfrac{\sin^2\theta}{\cos^2\theta}$ {tangent identity} $= \sin^2\theta$

**60** $(\tan\theta + \cot\theta)\tan\theta = \tan^2\theta + \cot\theta\tan\theta = \tan^2\theta + 1 = \sec^2\theta$

**5.2 EXERCISES**

**61** $\dfrac{\sin(\theta/2)}{\csc(\theta/2)} + \dfrac{\cos(\theta/2)}{\sec(\theta/2)} = \dfrac{\sin(\theta/2)}{1/\sin(\theta/2)} + \dfrac{\cos(\theta/2)}{1/\cos(\theta/2)} = \sin^2(\theta/2) + \cos^2(\theta/2) = 1$

**62** $1 - 2\sin^2(\theta/2) = 1 - 2(1 - \cos^2(\theta/2)) = 1 - 2 + 2\cos^2(\theta/2) = 2\cos^2(\theta/2) - 1$

**63** $(1 + \sin\theta)(1 - \sin\theta) = 1 - \sin^2\theta \ \{\text{multiply as a difference of squares}\} = \cos^2\theta = \dfrac{1}{\sec^2\theta}$

**64** $(1 - \sin^2\theta)(1 + \tan^2\theta) = (\cos^2\theta)(\sec^2\theta) = \cos^2\theta(1/\cos^2\theta) = 1$

**65** $\sec\theta - \cos\theta = \dfrac{1}{\cos\theta} - \cos\theta = \dfrac{1 - \cos^2\theta}{\cos\theta} = \dfrac{\sin^2\theta}{\cos\theta} = \dfrac{\sin\theta}{\cos\theta} \cdot \sin\theta = \tan\theta\sin\theta$

**66** $\csc\theta - \sin\theta = \dfrac{1}{\sin\theta} - \sin\theta = \dfrac{1 - \sin^2\theta}{\sin\theta} = \dfrac{\cos^2\theta}{\sin\theta} = \dfrac{\cos\theta}{\sin\theta} \cdot \cos\theta = \cot\theta\cos\theta$

**67** $\dfrac{\sin\theta + \cos\theta}{\sin\theta} = \dfrac{\sin\theta}{\sin\theta} + \dfrac{\cos\theta}{\sin\theta} = 1 + \cot\theta$

**68** $\dfrac{\sin\theta + \cos\theta}{\cos\theta} = \dfrac{\sin\theta}{\cos\theta} + \dfrac{\cos\theta}{\cos\theta} = \tan\theta + 1 = 1 + \tan\theta$

**69** $(\cot\theta + \csc\theta)(\tan\theta - \sin\theta)$

$= \cot\theta\tan\theta - \cot\theta\sin\theta + \csc\theta\tan\theta - \csc\theta\sin\theta \qquad \{\text{multiply binomials}\}$

$= \dfrac{1}{\tan\theta}\tan\theta - \dfrac{\cos\theta}{\sin\theta}\sin\theta + \dfrac{1}{\sin\theta}\dfrac{\sin\theta}{\cos\theta} - \dfrac{1}{\sin\theta}\sin\theta \qquad \{\text{reciprocal, cotangent, and tangent identities}\}$

$= 1 - \cos\theta + \dfrac{1}{\cos\theta} - 1 \qquad \{\text{cancel terms}\}$

$= -\cos\theta + \sec\theta = \sec\theta - \cos\theta$

**70** $\cot\theta + \tan\theta = \dfrac{\cos\theta}{\sin\theta} + \dfrac{\sin\theta}{\cos\theta} = \dfrac{\cos^2\theta + \sin^2\theta}{\sin\theta\cos\theta} = \dfrac{1}{\sin\theta\cos\theta} = \dfrac{1}{\sin\theta} \cdot \dfrac{1}{\cos\theta} = \csc\theta\sec\theta$

**71** $\sec^2 3\theta \csc^2 3\theta = (1 + \tan^2 3\theta)(1 + \cot^2 3\theta) \qquad \{\text{Pythagorean identities}\}$

$\qquad = 1 + \tan^2 3\theta + \cot^2 3\theta + 1 \qquad \{\text{multiply binomials}\}$

$\qquad = (1 + \tan^2 3\theta) + (\cot^2 3\theta + 1) \qquad \{\text{group terms}\}$

$\qquad = \sec^2 3\theta + \csc^2 3\theta \qquad \{\text{Pythagorean identities}\}$

**72** $\dfrac{1 + \cos^2 3\theta}{\sin^2 3\theta} = \dfrac{1}{\sin^2 3\theta} + \dfrac{\cos^2 3\theta}{\sin^2 3\theta} = \csc^2 3\theta + \cot^2 3\theta = \csc^2 3\theta + (\csc^2 3\theta - 1) = 2\csc^2 3\theta - 1$

**73** $\log\csc\theta = \log\left(\dfrac{1}{\sin\theta}\right) \qquad \{\text{reciprocal identity}\}$

$\qquad = \log 1 - \log\sin\theta \qquad \{\text{property of logarithms}\}$

$\qquad = 0 - \log\sin\theta \qquad \{\log 1 = 0\}$

$\qquad = -\log\sin\theta$

**74** $\log\tan\theta = \log\left(\dfrac{\sin\theta}{\cos\theta}\right) = \log\sin\theta - \log\cos\theta$

**75** For the point $P(x, y)$, we let $r$ denote the distance from the origin to $P$. Applying the definition of trigonometric functions of any angle with $x = 12$, $y = -5$, and $r = \sqrt{x^2 + y^2} = \sqrt{12^2 + (-5)^2} = 13$, we obtain the following:

$$\sin\theta = \frac{y}{r} = \frac{-5}{13} = -\frac{5}{13} \qquad\qquad \cos\theta = \frac{x}{r} = \frac{12}{13}$$

$$\tan\theta = \frac{y}{x} = \frac{-5}{12} = -\frac{5}{12} \qquad\qquad \cot\theta = \frac{x}{y} = \frac{12}{-5} = -\frac{12}{5}$$

$$\sec\theta = \frac{r}{x} = \frac{13}{12} \qquad\qquad\qquad \csc\theta = \frac{r}{y} = \frac{13}{-5} = -\frac{13}{5}$$

**76** $x = -8$ and $y = -15 \ \Rightarrow \ r = \sqrt{(-8)^2 + (-15)^2} = 17.$ \qquad ★ $-\frac{15}{17}, -\frac{8}{17}, \frac{15}{8}, \frac{8}{15}, -\frac{17}{8}, -\frac{17}{15}$

$\boxed{77}$ $x = -2$ and $y = -5$ $\Rightarrow$ $r = \sqrt{x^2 + y^2} = \sqrt{(-2)^2 + (-5)^2} = \sqrt{29}$.

$$\sin \theta = \frac{y}{r} = \frac{-5}{\sqrt{29}}, \text{ or } -\frac{5}{29}\sqrt{29} \qquad \cos \theta = \frac{x}{r} = \frac{-2}{\sqrt{29}}, \text{ or } -\frac{2}{29}\sqrt{29}$$

$$\tan \theta = \frac{y}{x} = \frac{-5}{-2} = \frac{5}{2} \qquad \cot \theta = \frac{x}{y} = \frac{-2}{-5} = \frac{2}{5}$$

$$\sec \theta = \frac{r}{x} = \frac{\sqrt{29}}{-2}, \text{ or } -\frac{1}{2}\sqrt{29} \qquad \csc \theta = \frac{r}{y} = \frac{\sqrt{29}}{-5} = -\frac{1}{5}\sqrt{29}$$

$\boxed{78}$ $x = -2$ and $y = 3$ $\Rightarrow$ $r = \sqrt{(-2)^2 + 3^2} = \sqrt{13}$. $\qquad\qquad\qquad$ ★ $\frac{3}{\sqrt{13}}, -\frac{2}{\sqrt{13}}, -\frac{3}{2}, -\frac{2}{3}, -\frac{\sqrt{13}}{2}, \frac{\sqrt{13}}{3}$

**Note:** In the following exercises, we will only find the values of $x$, $y$, and $r$. The above definitions {in Exercises 75 and 77} can then be used to find the values of the trigonometric functions of $\theta$. These values are listed in the usual order in the answer.

$\boxed{79}$ On the line $y = -3x$ • Since the terminal side of $\theta$ is in QII, choose $x$ to be negative.

If $x = -1$, then $y = 3$ and $(-1, 3)$ is a point on the terminal side of $\theta$.

$x = -1$ and $y = 3$ $\Rightarrow$ $r = \sqrt{(-1)^2 + 3^2} = \sqrt{10}$. $\qquad$ ★ $\frac{3}{\sqrt{10}}, -\frac{1}{\sqrt{10}}, -3, -\frac{1}{3}, -\sqrt{10}, \frac{\sqrt{10}}{3}$

$\boxed{80}$ On the line $3y + 5x = 0$ • Since the terminal side of $\theta$ is in QIV, choose $x$ to be positive.

If $x = 3$, then $y = -5$ and $(3, -5)$ is a point on the terminal side of $\theta$.

$x = 3$ and $y = -5$ $\Rightarrow$ $r = \sqrt{3^2 + (-5)^2} = \sqrt{34}$. $\qquad$ ★ $-\frac{5}{\sqrt{34}}, \frac{3}{\sqrt{34}}, -\frac{5}{3}, -\frac{3}{5}, \frac{\sqrt{34}}{3}, -\frac{\sqrt{34}}{5}$

$\boxed{81}$ Remember that $y = mx$ is an equation of a line that passes through the origin and has slope $m$.

Thus, an equation of the line is $y = -\frac{3}{4}x$. If $x = 4$, then $y = -3$ and $(4, -3)$ is a point

in QIV on the terminal side of $\theta$. $x = 4$ and $y = -3$ $\Rightarrow$ $r = \sqrt{4^2 + (-3)^2} = 5$. $\qquad$ ★ $-\frac{3}{5}, \frac{4}{5}, -\frac{3}{4}, -\frac{4}{3}, \frac{5}{4}, -\frac{5}{3}$

$\boxed{82}$ An equation of the line bisecting the third quadrant is $y = x$.

If $x = -1$, then $y = -1$ and $(-1, -1)$ is a point on the terminal side of $\theta$.

$x = -1$ and $y = -1$ $\Rightarrow$ $r = \sqrt{(-1)^2 + (-1)^2} = \sqrt{2}$. $\qquad$ ★ $-\frac{\sqrt{2}}{2}, -\frac{\sqrt{2}}{2}, 1, 1, -\sqrt{2}, -\sqrt{2}$

$\boxed{83}$ $2y - 7x + 2 = 0$ $\Leftrightarrow$ $y = \frac{7}{2}x - 1$. Thus, the slope of the given line is $\frac{7}{2}$.

An equation of the line through the origin with that slope is $y = \frac{7}{2}x$.

If $x = -2$, then $y = -7$ and $(-2, -7)$ is a point on the terminal side of $\theta$.

$x = -2$ and $y = -7$ $\Rightarrow$ $r = \sqrt{(-2)^2 + (-7)^2} = \sqrt{53}$. $\qquad$ ★ $-\frac{7}{\sqrt{53}}, -\frac{2}{\sqrt{53}}, \frac{7}{2}, \frac{2}{7}, -\frac{\sqrt{53}}{2}, -\frac{\sqrt{53}}{7}$

$\boxed{84}$ $m_{AB} = \frac{-2-6}{3-1} = -4$. An equation of the line through the origin with a slope of $-4$ is $y = -4x$.

If $x = -1$, then $y = 4$ and $(-1, 4)$ is a point on the terminal side of $\theta$.

$x = -1$ and $y = 4$ $\Rightarrow$ $r = \sqrt{(-1)^2 + 4^2} = \sqrt{17}$. $\qquad$ ★ $\frac{4}{\sqrt{17}}, -\frac{1}{\sqrt{17}}, -4, -\frac{1}{4}, -\sqrt{17}, \frac{\sqrt{17}}{4}$

**Note:** U denotes *undefined*.

$\boxed{85}$ (a) For $\theta = 90°$, choose $x = 0$ and $y = 1$. $r = 1$. $\qquad\qquad\qquad\qquad\qquad\qquad$ ★ $1, 0, U, 0, U, 1$

$\quad$ (b) For $\theta = 0°$, choose $x = 1$ and $y = 0$. $r = 1$. $\qquad\qquad\qquad\qquad\qquad\qquad$ ★ $0, 1, 0, U, 1, U$

$\quad$ (c) For $\theta = \frac{7\pi}{2}$, choose $x = 0$ and $y = -1$. $r = 1$. $\qquad\qquad\qquad\qquad\qquad$ ★ $-1, 0, U, 0, U, -1$

$\quad$ (d) For $\theta = 3\pi$, choose $x = -1$ and $y = 0$. $r = 1$. $\qquad\qquad\qquad\qquad\qquad$ ★ $0, -1, 0, U, -1, U$

**86** (a) For $\theta = 180°$, choose $x = -1$ and $y = 0$. $r = 1$.                    ★ $0, -1, 0, U, -1, U$

(b) For $\theta = -90°$, choose $x = 0$ and $y = -1$. $r = 1$.                    ★ $-1, 0, U, 0, U, -1$

(c) For $\theta = 2\pi$, choose $x = 1$ and $y = 0$. $r = 1$.                    ★ $0, 1, 0, U, 1, U$

(d) For $\theta = \frac{5\pi}{2}$, choose $x = 0$ and $y = 1$. $r = 1$.                    ★ $1, 0, U, 0, U, 1$

**87** (a) $\cos\theta > 0$ $\{x > 0\}$ implies that the terminal side of $\theta$ is in QI or QIV.

$\sin\theta < 0$ $\{y < 0\}$ implies that the terminal side of $\theta$ is in QIII or QIV.

Thus, $\theta$ must be in quadrant IV to satisfy both conditions.

(b) $\sin\theta < 0$ $\Rightarrow$ $\theta$ is in QIII or QIV. $\cot\theta > 0$ $\Rightarrow$ $\theta$ is in QI or QIII.    $\therefore$ $\theta$ is in QIII.

(c) $\csc\theta > 0$ $\Rightarrow$ $\theta$ is in QI or QII. $\sec\theta < 0$ $\Rightarrow$ $\theta$ is in QII or QIII.    $\therefore$ $\theta$ is in QII.

(d) $\sec\theta < 0$ $\Rightarrow$ $\theta$ is in QII or QIII. $\tan\theta > 0$ $\Rightarrow$ $\theta$ is in QI or QIII.    $\therefore$ $\theta$ is in QIII.

**88** (a) $\tan\theta < 0$ $\Rightarrow$ $\theta$ is in QII or QIV. $\cos\theta > 0$ $\Rightarrow$ $\theta$ is in QI or QIV.    $\therefore$ $\theta$ is in QIV.

(b) $\sec\theta > 0$ $\Rightarrow$ $\theta$ is QI or QIV. $\tan\theta < 0$ $\Rightarrow$ $\theta$ is in QII or QIV.    $\therefore$ $\theta$ is in QIV.

(c) $\csc\theta > 0$ $\Rightarrow$ $\theta$ is in QI or QII. $\cot\theta < 0$ $\Rightarrow$ $\theta$ is in QII or QIV.    $\therefore$ $\theta$ is in QII.

(d) $\cos\theta < 0$ $\Rightarrow$ $\theta$ is in QII or QIII. $\csc\theta < 0$ $\Rightarrow$ $\theta$ is in QIII or QIV.    $\therefore$ $\theta$ is in QIII.

**Note:** For Exercises 89–96, steps to determine two function values using only the fundamental identities are shown. The other three function values are just the reciprocals of those given and are listed in the answer.

**89** $\tan\theta = -\frac{3}{4}$ and $\sin\theta > 0$ $\Rightarrow$ $\theta$ is in QII. $1 + \tan^2\theta = \sec^2\theta$ $\Rightarrow$ $\sec\theta = \pm\sqrt{1 + \tan^2\theta}$ {Use the "$-$" since the secant is negative in the second quadrant.} $= -\sqrt{1 + \tan^2\theta} = -\sqrt{1 + \frac{9}{16}} = -\frac{5}{4}$.

$\tan\theta = \dfrac{\sin\theta}{\cos\theta}$ $\Rightarrow$ $-\dfrac{3}{4} = \dfrac{\sin\theta}{-4/5}$ $\Rightarrow$ $\sin\theta = \left(-\frac{3}{4}\right)\left(-\frac{4}{5}\right) = \frac{3}{5}$.    ★ $\frac{3}{5}, -\frac{4}{5}, -\frac{3}{4}, -\frac{4}{3}, -\frac{5}{4}, \frac{5}{3}$

**90** $\cot\theta = \frac{3}{4}$ and $\cos\theta < 0$ $\Rightarrow$ $\theta$ is in QIII. $\csc\theta = -\sqrt{1 + \cot^2\theta} = -\sqrt{1 + \frac{9}{16}} = -\frac{5}{4}$;

$\cot\theta = \dfrac{\cos\theta}{\sin\theta}$ $\Rightarrow$ $\dfrac{3}{4} = \dfrac{\cos\theta}{-4/5}$ $\Rightarrow$ $\cos\theta = -\frac{3}{5}$    ★ $-\frac{4}{5}, -\frac{3}{5}, \frac{4}{3}, \frac{3}{4}, -\frac{5}{3}, -\frac{5}{4}$

**91** $\sin\theta = -\frac{5}{13}$ and $\sec\theta > 0$ $\Rightarrow$ $\theta$ is in QIV.

$\sin^2\theta + \cos^2\theta = 1$ $\Rightarrow$ $\cos^2\theta = 1 - \sin^2\theta$ $\Rightarrow$ $\cos\theta = \pm\sqrt{1 - \sin^2\theta} =$

{Use the "$+$" since the cosine is positive in the fourth quadrant.} $= \sqrt{1 - \frac{25}{169}} = \frac{12}{13}$.

$\tan\theta = \dfrac{\sin\theta}{\cos\theta} = \dfrac{-5/13}{12/13} = -\dfrac{5}{12}$.    ★ $-\frac{5}{13}, \frac{12}{13}, -\frac{5}{12}, -\frac{12}{5}, \frac{13}{12}, -\frac{13}{5}$

**92** $\cos\theta = \frac{1}{2}$ and $\sin\theta < 0$ $\Rightarrow$ $\theta$ is in QIV. $\sin\theta = -\sqrt{1 - \cos^2\theta} = -\sqrt{1 - \frac{1}{4}} = -\frac{\sqrt{3}}{2}$.

$\tan\theta = \dfrac{\sin\theta}{\cos\theta} = \dfrac{-\sqrt{3}/2}{1/2} = -\sqrt{3}$    ★ $-\frac{\sqrt{3}}{2}, \frac{1}{2}, -\sqrt{3}, -\frac{1}{\sqrt{3}}, 2, -\frac{2}{\sqrt{3}}$

**93** $\cos\theta = -\frac{1}{3}$ and $\sin\theta < 0$ $\Rightarrow$ $\theta$ is in QIII. $\sin\theta = -\sqrt{1 - \cos^2\theta} = -\sqrt{1 - \frac{1}{9}} = -\frac{\sqrt{8}}{3}$.

$\tan\theta = \dfrac{\sin\theta}{\cos\theta} = \dfrac{-\sqrt{8}/3}{-1/3} = \sqrt{8}$, or $2\sqrt{2}$.    ★ $-\frac{\sqrt{8}}{3}, -\frac{1}{3}, \sqrt{8}, \frac{1}{\sqrt{8}}, -3, -\frac{3}{\sqrt{8}}$

**94** $\csc\theta = 5$ and $\cot\theta < 0$ $\Rightarrow$ $\theta$ is in QII. $\cot\theta = -\sqrt{\csc^2\theta - 1} = -\sqrt{25 - 1} = -\sqrt{24}$.

$\cot\theta = \dfrac{\cos\theta}{\sin\theta}$ $\Rightarrow$ $-\sqrt{24} = \dfrac{\cos\theta}{1/5}$ $\Rightarrow$ $\cos\theta = -\frac{\sqrt{24}}{5}$    ★ $\frac{1}{5}, -\frac{\sqrt{24}}{5}, -\frac{1}{\sqrt{24}}, -\sqrt{24}, -\frac{5}{\sqrt{24}}, 5$

$\boxed{95}$ $\sec\theta = 4$ and $\csc\theta > 0$ $\Rightarrow$ $\theta$ is in QI. $\tan\theta = \sqrt{\sec^2\theta - 1} = \sqrt{16 - 1} = \sqrt{15}$.

$\tan\theta = \dfrac{\sin\theta}{\cos\theta}$ $\Rightarrow$ $\sqrt{15} = \dfrac{\sin\theta}{1/4}$ $\Rightarrow$ $\sin\theta = \dfrac{\sqrt{15}}{4}$. ★ $\dfrac{\sqrt{15}}{4}, \dfrac{1}{4}, \sqrt{15}, \dfrac{1}{\sqrt{15}}, 4, \dfrac{4}{\sqrt{15}}$

$\boxed{96}$ $\sin\theta = \frac{2}{5}$ and $\cos\theta > 0$ $\Rightarrow$ $\theta$ is in QI. $\cos\theta = \sqrt{1 - \sin^2\theta} = \sqrt{1 - \frac{4}{25}} = \dfrac{\sqrt{21}}{5}$.

$\tan\theta = \dfrac{\sin\theta}{\cos\theta} = \dfrac{2/5}{\sqrt{21}/5} = \dfrac{2}{\sqrt{21}}$ ★ $\dfrac{2}{5}, \dfrac{\sqrt{21}}{5}, \dfrac{2}{\sqrt{21}}, \dfrac{\sqrt{21}}{2}, \dfrac{5}{\sqrt{21}}, \dfrac{5}{2}$

$\boxed{97}$ $\sqrt{\sec^2\theta - 1} = \sqrt{\tan^2\theta}$ {Pythagorean identity}

$\qquad\qquad = |\tan\theta|$ $\left\{\sqrt{x^2} = |x|\right\}$

$\qquad\qquad = -\tan\theta$ {$\tan\theta < 0$ if $\pi/2 < \theta < \pi$}.

$\boxed{98}$ $\sqrt{1 + \cot^2\theta} = \sqrt{\csc^2\theta} = |\csc\theta| = \csc\theta$ since $\csc\theta > 0$ if $0 < \theta < \pi$.

$\boxed{99}$ $\sqrt{1 + \tan^2\theta} = \sqrt{\sec^2\theta}$ {Pythagorean identity}

$\qquad\qquad = |\sec\theta|$ $\left\{\sqrt{x^2} = |x|\right\}$

$\qquad\qquad = \sec\theta$ {$\sec\theta > 0$ if $3\pi/2 < \theta < 2\pi$}.

$\boxed{100}$ $\sqrt{\csc^2\theta - 1} = \sqrt{\cot^2\theta} = |\cot\theta| = -\cot\theta$ since $\cot\theta < 0$ if $3\pi/2 < \theta < 2\pi$.

$\boxed{101}$ $\sqrt{\sin^2(\theta/2)} = |\sin(\theta/2)|$ $\left\{\sqrt{x^2} = |x|\right\}$

$\qquad\qquad = -\sin(\theta/2)$ {$\sin(\theta/2) < 0$ if $2\pi < \theta < 4\pi$, that is, $\pi < \theta/2 < 2\pi$}.

$\boxed{102}$ $\sqrt{\cos^2(\theta/2)} = |\cos(\theta/2)| = \cos(\theta/2)$ since $\cos(\theta/2) > 0$ if $0 < \theta < \pi$ {$0 < \theta/2 < \pi/2$}.

## 5.3 Exercises

$\boxed{1}$ Using the definition of the trigonometric functions in terms of a unit circle with $P\left(-\frac{15}{17}, \frac{8}{17}\right)$, we have

$\quad \sin t = y = \frac{8}{17}$, $\qquad \cos t = x = -\frac{15}{17}$, $\qquad \tan t = \frac{y}{x} = \frac{8/17}{-15/17} = -\frac{8}{15}$,

$\quad \csc t = \frac{1}{y} = \frac{1}{8/17} = \frac{17}{8}$, $\qquad \sec t = \frac{1}{x} = \frac{1}{-15/17} = -\frac{17}{15}$, $\qquad \cot t = \frac{x}{y} = \frac{-15/17}{8/17} = -\frac{15}{8}$.

$\boxed{2}$ $P\left(\frac{4}{5}, \frac{3}{5}\right)$ gives us $\frac{3}{5}, \frac{4}{5}, \frac{3}{4}, \frac{4}{3}, \frac{5}{4}, \frac{5}{3}$.

$\boxed{3}$ Using the definition of the trigonometric functions in terms of a unit circle with $P\left(\frac{24}{25}, -\frac{7}{25}\right)$, we have

$\quad \sin t = y = -\frac{7}{25}$, $\qquad \cos t = x = \frac{24}{25}$, $\qquad \tan t = \frac{y}{x} = \frac{-7/25}{24/25} = -\frac{7}{24}$,

$\quad \csc t = \frac{1}{y} = \frac{1}{-7/25} = -\frac{25}{7}$, $\qquad \sec t = \frac{1}{x} = \frac{1}{24/25} = \frac{25}{24}$, $\qquad \cot t = \frac{x}{y} = \frac{24/25}{-7/25} = -\frac{24}{7}$.

$\boxed{4}$ $P\left(-\frac{5}{13}, -\frac{12}{13}\right)$ gives us $-\frac{12}{13}, -\frac{5}{13}, \frac{12}{5}, \frac{5}{12}, -\frac{13}{5}, -\frac{13}{12}$.

$\boxed{5}$ See *Figure 5*. $P(t) = \left(\frac{3}{5}, \frac{4}{5}\right)$.

(a) $(t + \pi)$ will be $\frac{1}{2}$ revolution from $(t)$ in the counterclockwise direction. Hence, $P(t + \pi) = \left(-\frac{3}{5}, -\frac{4}{5}\right)$.

(b) $(t - \pi)$ will be $\frac{1}{2}$ revolution from $(t)$ in the clockwise direction. Hence, $P(t - \pi) = \left(-\frac{3}{5}, -\frac{4}{5}\right)$.

$\qquad\qquad\qquad$ Observe that $P(t + \pi) = P(t - \pi)$ for any $t$.

(c) $(-t)$ is the angle measure in the opposite direction of $(t)$. Hence, $P(-t) = \left(\frac{3}{5}, -\frac{4}{5}\right)$.

(d) $(-t - \pi)$ will be $\frac{1}{2}$ revolution from $(-t)$ in the clockwise direction. Hence, $P(-t - \pi) = \left(-\frac{3}{5}, \frac{4}{5}\right)$.

**Figure 5**

**Figure 6**

**6** (a) $P(t) = \left(-\frac{8}{17}, \frac{15}{17}\right)$ $\Rightarrow$ $P(t+\pi) = \left(\frac{8}{17}, -\frac{15}{17}\right)$     (b) $P(t-\pi) = P(t+\pi) = \left(\frac{8}{17}, -\frac{15}{17}\right)$

(c) $P(-t) = \left(-\frac{8}{17}, -\frac{15}{17}\right)$                              (d) $P(-t-\pi) = \left(\frac{8}{17}, \frac{15}{17}\right)$

**7** (a) As in Exercise 5, $P(t) = \left(-\frac{12}{13}, -\frac{5}{13}\right)$ $\Rightarrow$ $P(t+\pi) = \left(\frac{12}{13}, \frac{5}{13}\right)$.

(b) $P(t-\pi) = P(t+\pi) = \left(\frac{12}{13}, \frac{5}{13}\right)$                   (c) $P(-t) = \left(-\frac{12}{13}, \frac{5}{13}\right)$

(d) $P(-t-\pi) = \left(\frac{12}{13}, -\frac{5}{13}\right)$

**Figure 7**

**Figure 8**

**8** (a) $P(t) = \left(\frac{7}{25}, -\frac{24}{25}\right)$ $\Rightarrow$ $P(t+\pi) = \left(-\frac{7}{25}, \frac{24}{25}\right)$     (b) $P(t-\pi) = P(t+\pi) = \left(-\frac{7}{25}, \frac{24}{25}\right)$

(c) $P(-t) = \left(\frac{7}{25}, \frac{24}{25}\right)$                               (d) $P(-t-\pi) = \left(-\frac{7}{25}, -\frac{24}{25}\right)$

**9** (a) The point $P$ on the unit circle $U$ that corresponds to $t = 2\pi$ has coordinates $(1, 0)$. Thus, we choose $x = 1$ and $y = 0$ and use the definition of the trigonometric functions in terms of a unit circle.

$\sin t = y$ $\Rightarrow$ $\sin 2\pi = 0$.                           $\cos t = x$ $\Rightarrow$ $\cos 2\pi = 1$.

$\tan t = \frac{y}{x}$ $\Rightarrow$ $\tan 2\pi = \frac{0}{1} = 0$.                      $\cot t = \frac{x}{y}$ $\Rightarrow$ $\cot 2\pi = \frac{1}{0}$ is undefined.

$\sec t = \frac{1}{x}$ $\Rightarrow$ $\sec 2\pi = \frac{1}{1} = 1$.                      $\csc t = \frac{1}{y}$ $\Rightarrow$ $\csc 2\pi = \frac{1}{0}$ is undefined.

(b) $t = -3\pi$ is coterminal with $t = \pi$. The point $P$ on the unit circle $U$ that corresponds to $t = -3\pi$ has coordinates $(-1, 0)$. Thus, we choose $x = -1$ and $y = 0$.

$\sin t = y$ $\Rightarrow$ $\sin(-3\pi) = 0$.                        $\cos t = x$ $\Rightarrow$ $\cos(-3\pi) = -1$.

$\tan t = \frac{y}{x}$ $\Rightarrow$ $\tan(-3\pi) = \frac{0}{-1} = 0$.                  $\cot t = \frac{x}{y}$ $\Rightarrow$ $\cot(-3\pi) = \frac{-1}{0}$ is undefined.

$\sec t = \frac{1}{x}$ $\Rightarrow$ $\sec(-3\pi) = \frac{1}{-1} = -1$.                 $\csc t = \frac{1}{y}$ $\Rightarrow$ $\csc(-3\pi) = \frac{1}{0}$ is undefined.

**Note:** U denotes *undefined*.

**10** (a) $t = -\pi$ $\Rightarrow$ $P(x, y) = (-1, 0)$.                                  ★ $0, -1, 0, U, -1, U$

(b) $t = 6\pi$ $\Rightarrow$ $P(x, y) = (1, 0)$.                                        ★ $0, 1, 0, U, 1, U$

**11** (a) The point $P$ on the unit circle $U$ that corresponds to $t = \frac{3\pi}{2}$ has coordinates $(0, -1)$.

Thus, we choose $x = 0$ and $y = -1$.

$\sin t = y \implies \sin \frac{3\pi}{2} = -1.$ $\qquad\qquad \cos t = x \implies \cos \frac{3\pi}{2} = 0.$

$\tan t = \frac{y}{x} \implies \tan \frac{3\pi}{2} = \frac{-1}{0}$ is und. $\qquad \cot t = \frac{x}{y} \implies \cot \frac{3\pi}{2} = \frac{0}{-1} = 0.$

$\sec t = \frac{1}{x} \implies \sec \frac{3\pi}{2} = \frac{1}{0}$ is und. $\qquad \csc t = \frac{1}{y} \implies \csc \frac{3\pi}{2} = \frac{1}{-1} = -1.$

(b) $t = -\frac{7\pi}{2}$ is coterminal with $t = \frac{\pi}{2}$. The point $P$ on the unit circle $U$ that corresponds to $t = -\frac{7\pi}{2}$ has coordinates $(0, 1)$. Thus, we choose $x = 0$ and $y = 1$.

$\sin t = y \implies \sin\left(-\frac{7\pi}{2}\right) = 1.$ $\qquad \cos t = x \implies \cos\left(-\frac{7\pi}{2}\right) = 0.$

$\tan t = \frac{y}{x} \implies \tan\left(-\frac{7\pi}{2}\right) = \frac{1}{0}$ is undefined. $\qquad \cot t = \frac{x}{y} \implies \cot\left(-\frac{7\pi}{2}\right) = \frac{0}{1} = 0.$

$\sec t = \frac{1}{x} \implies \sec\left(-\frac{7\pi}{2}\right) = \frac{1}{0}$ is undefined. $\qquad \csc t = \frac{1}{y} \implies \csc\left(-\frac{7\pi}{2}\right) = \frac{1}{1} = 1.$

**12** (a) $t = \frac{5\pi}{2} \implies P(x, y) = (0, 1).$ $\qquad\qquad\qquad\qquad\qquad\qquad\qquad$ ★ 1, 0, U, 0, U, 1

(b) $t = -\frac{\pi}{2} \implies P(x, y) = (0, -1).$ $\qquad\qquad\qquad\qquad\qquad\qquad\quad$ ★ −1, 0, U, 0, U, −1

**13** (a) $t = \frac{9\pi}{4}$ is coterminal with $t = \frac{\pi}{4}$. The point $P$ on the unit circle $U$ that corresponds to $t = \frac{9\pi}{4}$ has coordinates $\left(\frac{\sqrt{2}}{2}, \frac{\sqrt{2}}{2}\right)$. Thus, we choose $x = \frac{\sqrt{2}}{2}$ and $y = \frac{\sqrt{2}}{2}$.

$\sin t = y \implies \sin \frac{9\pi}{4} = \frac{\sqrt{2}}{2}.$ $\qquad \cos t = x \implies \cos \frac{9\pi}{4} = \frac{\sqrt{2}}{2}.$ $\qquad \tan t = \frac{y}{x} \implies \tan \frac{9\pi}{4} = \frac{\sqrt{2}/2}{\sqrt{2}/2} = 1.$

We now use the reciprocal relationships to find the values of the 3 remaining trigonometric functions.

$\cot t = \frac{1}{\tan t} = \frac{1}{1} = 1.$ $\qquad\qquad\qquad\qquad \sec t = \frac{1}{\cos t} = \frac{1}{\sqrt{2}/2} = \frac{2}{\sqrt{2}} = \frac{2^1}{2^{1/2}} = 2^{1/2} = \sqrt{2}.$

$\csc t = \frac{1}{\sin t} = \frac{1}{\sqrt{2}/2} = \sqrt{2}.$

(b) $t = -\frac{5\pi}{4}$ is coterminal with $t = \frac{3\pi}{4}$. The point $P$ on the unit circle $U$ that corresponds to $t = -\frac{5\pi}{4}$ has coordinates $\left(-\frac{\sqrt{2}}{2}, \frac{\sqrt{2}}{2}\right)$. Thus, we choose $x = -\frac{\sqrt{2}}{2}$ and $y = \frac{\sqrt{2}}{2}$.

$\sin t = y \implies \sin\left(-\frac{5\pi}{4}\right) = \frac{\sqrt{2}}{2}.$ $\qquad \cos t = x \implies \cos\left(-\frac{5\pi}{4}\right) = -\frac{\sqrt{2}}{2}.$

$\tan t = \frac{y}{x} \implies \tan\left(-\frac{5\pi}{4}\right) = \frac{\sqrt{2}/2}{-\sqrt{2}/2} = -1.$ $\qquad \cot t = \frac{1}{\tan t} = \frac{1}{-1} = -1.$

$\sec t = \frac{1}{\cos t} = \frac{1}{-\sqrt{2}/2} = -\sqrt{2}.$ $\qquad\qquad\qquad \csc t = \frac{1}{\sin t} = \frac{1}{\sqrt{2}/2} = \sqrt{2}.$

**14** (a) $t = \frac{3\pi}{4} \implies P(x, y) = \left(-\frac{\sqrt{2}}{2}, \frac{\sqrt{2}}{2}\right).$ $\frac{\sqrt{2}}{2}, -\frac{\sqrt{2}}{2}, -1, -1, -\sqrt{2}, \sqrt{2}$

(b) $t = -\frac{7\pi}{4} \implies P(x, y) = \left(\frac{\sqrt{2}}{2}, \frac{\sqrt{2}}{2}\right).$ $\frac{\sqrt{2}}{2}, \frac{\sqrt{2}}{2}, 1, 1, \sqrt{2}, \sqrt{2}$

**15** (a) The point $P$ on the unit circle $U$ that corresponds to $t = \frac{5\pi}{4}$ has coordinates $\left(-\frac{\sqrt{2}}{2}, -\frac{\sqrt{2}}{2}\right)$. Thus, we choose $x = -\frac{\sqrt{2}}{2}$ and $y = -\frac{\sqrt{2}}{2}$.

$\sin t = y \implies \sin \frac{5\pi}{4} = -\frac{\sqrt{2}}{2}.$ $\qquad\qquad \cos t = x \implies \cos \frac{5\pi}{4} = -\frac{\sqrt{2}}{2}.$

$\tan t = \frac{y}{x} \implies \tan \frac{5\pi}{4} = \frac{-\sqrt{2}/2}{-\sqrt{2}/2} = 1.$ $\qquad \cot t = \frac{1}{\tan t} = \frac{1}{1} = 1.$

$\sec t = \frac{1}{\cos t} = \frac{1}{-\sqrt{2}/2} = -\sqrt{2}.$ $\qquad\qquad \csc t = \frac{1}{\sin t} = \frac{1}{-\sqrt{2}/2} = -\sqrt{2}.$

(b) $t = -\frac{\pi}{4}$ is coterminal with $t = \frac{7\pi}{4}$. The point $P$ on the unit circle $U$ that corresponds to $t = -\frac{\pi}{4}$ has coordinates $\left(\frac{\sqrt{2}}{2}, -\frac{\sqrt{2}}{2}\right)$. Thus, we choose $x = \frac{\sqrt{2}}{2}$ and $y = -\frac{\sqrt{2}}{2}$.

$\sin t = y \implies \sin\left(-\frac{\pi}{4}\right) = -\frac{\sqrt{2}}{2}.$ $\qquad\qquad \cos t = x \implies \cos\left(-\frac{\pi}{4}\right) = \frac{\sqrt{2}}{2}.$

$\tan t = \frac{y}{x} \implies \tan\left(-\frac{\pi}{4}\right) = \frac{-\sqrt{2}/2}{\sqrt{2}/2} = -1.$ $\qquad \cot t = \frac{1}{\tan t} = \frac{1}{-1} = -1.$

$\sec t = \frac{1}{\cos t} = \frac{1}{\sqrt{2}/2} = \sqrt{2}.$ $\qquad\qquad\qquad \csc t = \frac{1}{\sin t} = \frac{1}{-\sqrt{2}/2} = -\sqrt{2}.$

**16** (a) $t = \frac{7\pi}{4}$ $\Rightarrow$ $P(x, y) = \left(\frac{\sqrt{2}}{2}, -\frac{\sqrt{2}}{2}\right)$. $-\frac{\sqrt{2}}{2}, \frac{\sqrt{2}}{2}, -1, -1, \sqrt{2}, -\sqrt{2}$

    (b) $t = -\frac{3\pi}{4}$ $\Rightarrow$ $P(x, y) = \left(-\frac{\sqrt{2}}{2}, -\frac{\sqrt{2}}{2}\right)$. $-\frac{\sqrt{2}}{2}, -\frac{\sqrt{2}}{2}, 1, 1, -\sqrt{2}, -\sqrt{2}$

**17** (a) $\sin(-90°) = -\sin 90°$ {since $\sin(-t) = -\sin t$} $= -1$

    (b) $\cos\left(-\frac{3\pi}{4}\right) = \cos\frac{3\pi}{4}$ {since $\cos(-t) = \cos t$} $= -\dfrac{\sqrt{2}}{2}$

    (c) $\tan(-135°) = -\tan 135°$ {since $\tan(-t) = -\tan t$} $= -(-1) = 1$

**18** (a) $\sin\left(-\frac{3\pi}{2}\right) = -\sin\frac{3\pi}{2} = -(-1) = 1$          (b) $\cos(-225°) = \cos 225° = -\dfrac{\sqrt{2}}{2}$

    (c) $\tan\left(-\frac{\pi}{4}\right) = -\tan\frac{\pi}{4} = -1$

**19** (a) $\cot\left(-\frac{3\pi}{4}\right) = -\cot\frac{3\pi}{4}$ {since $\cot(-t) = -\cot t$} $= -(-1) = 1$

    (b) $\sec(-45°) = \sec 45°$ {since $\sec(-t) = \sec t$} $= \sqrt{2}$

    (c) $\csc\left(-\frac{3\pi}{2}\right) = -\csc\frac{3\pi}{2}$ {since $\csc(-t) = -\csc t$} $= -(-1) = 1$

**20** (a) $\cot(-225°) = -\cot 225° = -1$          (b) $\sec(-\pi) = \sec\pi = -1$

    (c) $\csc(-45°) = -\csc 45° = -\sqrt{2}$

**21** $\sin(-x)\sec(-x) = (-\sin x)\sec x$        {formulas for negatives}

               $= (-\sin x)(1/\cos x)$       {reciprocal identity}

               $= -\tan x$               {tangent identity}

**22** $\csc(-x)\cos(-x) = (-\csc x)\cos x = (-1/\sin x)(\cos x) = -\cot x$

**23** $\dfrac{\cot(-x)}{\csc(-x)} = \dfrac{-\cot x}{-\csc x}$        {formulas for negatives}

           $= \dfrac{\cos x/\sin x}{1/\sin x}$       {cotangent identity and reciprocal identity}

           $= \cos x$           {simplify}

**24** $\dfrac{\sec(-x)}{\tan(-x)} = \dfrac{\sec x}{-\tan x} = -\dfrac{1/\cos x}{\sin x/\cos x} = -\dfrac{1}{\sin x} = -\csc x$

**25** $\dfrac{1}{\cos(-x)} - \tan(-x)\sin(-x) = \dfrac{1}{\cos x} - (-\tan x)(-\sin x)$       {formulas for negatives}

                               $= \dfrac{1}{\cos x} - \dfrac{\sin x}{\cos x}\sin x$       {tangent identity}

                               $= \dfrac{1 - \sin^2 x}{\cos x}$       {combine terms}

                               $= \dfrac{\cos^2 x}{\cos x}$       {Pythagorean identity}

                               $= \cos x$       {cancel $\cos x$}

**26** $\cot(-x)\cos(-x) + \sin(-x) = -\cot x \cos x - \sin x$

                       $= -\dfrac{\cos x}{\sin x}\cos x - \sin x = -\dfrac{\cos^2 x + \sin^2 x}{\sin x} = -\dfrac{1}{\sin x} = -\csc x$

**27** (a) Using Figure 9 in the text, we see that as $x$ gets close to 0 through numbers greater than 0 (from the *right* of 0), $\sin x$ approaches 0.

(b) As $x$ approaches $-\frac{\pi}{4}$ through numbers less than $-\frac{\pi}{4}$ (from the *left* of $-\frac{\pi}{4}$), $\sin x$ approaches $-\frac{\sqrt{2}}{2}$.

**28** (a) As $x \to -\frac{\pi}{2}$, $\sin x \to \underline{-1}$                        (b) As $x \to \frac{\pi}{6}^{-}$, $\sin x \to \underline{\frac{1}{2}}$

**29** (a) Using Figure 10 in the text, we see that as $x$ gets close to $\frac{\pi}{4}$ through numbers greater than $\frac{\pi}{4}$ (from the *right* of $\frac{\pi}{4}$), $\cos x$ approaches $\frac{\sqrt{2}}{2}$. Note that the value $\frac{\sqrt{2}}{2}$ is in the table containing specific values of the cosine function.

(b) As $x$ approaches $\frac{3\pi}{2}$, $\cos x$ approaches 0.

**30** (a) As $x \to \pi$, $\cos x \to \underline{-1}$                        (b) As $x \to -\frac{\pi}{3}^{-}$, $\cos x \to \underline{\frac{1}{2}}$

**31** (a) Using Figure 15 in the text, we see that as $x$ gets close to $\pi$, $\tan x$ approaches 0.

(b) As $x$ approaches $\frac{\pi}{2}$ through numbers greater than $\frac{\pi}{2}$ (from the *right* of $\frac{\pi}{2}$), $\tan x$ is approaching the vertical asymptote $x = \frac{\pi}{2}$. $\tan x$ is *decreasing* without bound, and we use the notation $\underline{\tan x \to -\infty}$ to denote this.

**32** (a) As $x \to \frac{\pi}{4}$, $\tan x \to \underline{1}$                        (b) As $x \to -\frac{\pi}{2}^{-}$, $\tan x \to \underline{\infty}$

**33** (a) Using Figure 19 in the text, we see that as $x$ gets close to $\frac{\pi}{6}$, $\cot x$ approaches $\sqrt{3}$.

(b) As $x$ approaches 0 through numbers greater than 0 (from the *right* of 0), $\cot x$ is approaching the vertical asymptote $x = 0$ {the $y$-axis}. $\cot x$ is *increasing* without bound, and we use the notation $\underline{\cot x \to \infty}$ to denote this.

**34** (a) As $x \to -\frac{\pi}{4}$, $\cot x \to \underline{-1}$                        (b) As $x \to \pi^{-}$, $\cot x \to \underline{-\infty}$

**35** (a) Using Figure 18 in the text, we see that as $x$ gets close to $\frac{\pi}{2}$ through numbers less than $\frac{\pi}{2}$ (from the *left* of $\frac{\pi}{2}$), $\sec x \to \infty$.

(b) As $x$ approaches 0, $\sec x$ approaches 1.

**36** (a) As $x \to \frac{\pi}{2}^{+}$, $\sec x \to \underline{-\infty}$                        (b) As $x \to \frac{\pi}{4}$, $\sec x \to \underline{\sqrt{2}}$

**37** (a) Using Figure 17 in the text, we see that as $x$ gets close to 0 through numbers less than 0 (from the *left* of 0), $\csc x \to -\infty$.

(b) As $x$ approaches $\frac{\pi}{4}$, $\csc x$ approaches $\sqrt{2}$.

**38** (a) As $x \to \pi^{+}$, $\csc x \to \underline{-\infty}$                        (b) As $x \to \frac{\pi}{2}$, $\csc x \to \underline{1}$

**39** Refer to Figure 9 in the text and the accompanying table. We see that $\sin \frac{3\pi}{2} = -1$.

Since the period of the sine is $2\pi$, the second value in $[0, 4\pi]$ is $\frac{3\pi}{2} + 2\pi = \frac{7\pi}{2}$.

**40** $\sin x = 1$ •                                                                                                   ★ $\frac{\pi}{2}, \frac{5\pi}{2}$

**41** Recall that $\sin \frac{\pi}{6} = \frac{1}{2}$ and $\sin \frac{5\pi}{6} = \frac{1}{2}$.

Since the period of the sine is $2\pi$, other values in $[0, 4\pi]$ are $\frac{\pi}{6} + 2\pi = \frac{13\pi}{6}$ and $\frac{5\pi}{6} + 2\pi = \frac{17\pi}{6}$.

**42** $\sin x = -\sqrt{2}/2$ •                                                                    ★ $\frac{5\pi}{4}, \frac{7\pi}{4}, \frac{13\pi}{4}, \frac{15\pi}{4}$

**43** Refer to Figure 1 in the text and the accompanying table. We see that $\cos 0 = \cos 2\pi = 1$.

Since the period of the cosine is $2\pi$, the other value in $[0, 4\pi]$ is $2\pi + 2\pi = 4\pi$.

**44** $\cos x = -1$ • ★ $\pi, 3\pi$

**45** Refer to Figure 11 in the text and the accompanying table. We see that $\cos \frac{\pi}{4} = \cos \frac{7\pi}{4} = \frac{\sqrt{2}}{2}$.

Since the period of the cosine is $2\pi$, other values in $[0, 4\pi]$ are $\frac{\pi}{4} + 2\pi = \frac{9\pi}{4}$ and $\frac{7\pi}{4} + 2\pi = \frac{15\pi}{4}$.

**46** $\cos x = -\frac{1}{2}$ • ★ $\frac{2\pi}{3}, \frac{4\pi}{3}, \frac{8\pi}{3}, \frac{10\pi}{3}$

**47** Refer to Figure 16 in the text. In the interval $\left(-\frac{\pi}{2}, \frac{\pi}{2}\right)$, $\tan x = 1$ only if $x = \frac{\pi}{4}$.

Since the period of the tangent is $\pi$, the desired value in the interval $\left(\frac{\pi}{2}, \frac{3\pi}{2}\right)$ is $\frac{\pi}{4} + \pi = \frac{5\pi}{4}$.

**48** $\tan x = \sqrt{3}$ • ★ $\frac{\pi}{3}, \frac{4\pi}{3}$

**49** Refer to Figure 16 in the text. In the interval $\left(-\frac{\pi}{2}, \frac{\pi}{2}\right)$, $\tan x = 0$ only if $x = 0$.

Since the period of the tangent is $\pi$, the desired value in the interval $\left(\frac{\pi}{2}, \frac{3\pi}{2}\right)$ is $0 + \pi = \pi$.

**50** $\tan x = -1/\sqrt{3}$ • ★ $-\frac{\pi}{6}, \frac{5\pi}{6}$

**51** $y = \sin x$; $[-2\pi, 2\pi]$; $a = \frac{1}{2}$ • Refer to Figure 9 in the text. $\sin x = \frac{1}{2}$ $\Rightarrow$ $x = \frac{\pi}{6}$ and $\frac{5\pi}{6}$.

Also, $\frac{\pi}{6} - 2\pi = -\frac{11\pi}{6}$ and $\frac{5\pi}{6} - 2\pi = -\frac{7\pi}{6}$.

$\sin x > \frac{1}{2}$ when the graph is *above* the horizontal line $y = \frac{1}{2}$.

$\sin x < \frac{1}{2}$ when the graph is *below* the horizontal line $y = \frac{1}{2}$.

(a) $-\frac{11\pi}{6}, -\frac{7\pi}{6}, \frac{\pi}{6}, \frac{5\pi}{6}$      (b) $-\frac{11\pi}{6} < x < -\frac{7\pi}{6}$ and $\frac{\pi}{6} < x < \frac{5\pi}{6}$

(c) $-2\pi \le x < -\frac{11\pi}{6}, -\frac{7\pi}{6} < x < \frac{\pi}{6}$, and $\frac{5\pi}{6} < x \le 2\pi$

**52** $y = \cos x$; $[0, 4\pi]$; $a = \frac{\sqrt{3}}{2}$ •

(a) $\frac{\pi}{6}, \frac{11\pi}{6}, \frac{13\pi}{6}, \frac{23\pi}{6}$      (b) $0 \le x < \frac{\pi}{6}, \frac{11\pi}{6} < x < \frac{13\pi}{6}$, and $\frac{23\pi}{6} < x \le 4\pi$

(c) $\frac{\pi}{6} < x < \frac{11\pi}{6}$ and $\frac{13\pi}{6} < x < \frac{23\pi}{6}$

**53** $y = \cos x$; $[-2\pi, 2\pi]$; $a = -\frac{1}{2}$ • Refer to Figure 11 in the text. $\cos x = -\frac{1}{2}$ $\Rightarrow$ $x = \frac{2\pi}{3}$ and $\frac{4\pi}{3}$.

Also, $\frac{2\pi}{3} - 2\pi = -\frac{4\pi}{3}$ and $\frac{4\pi}{3} - 2\pi = -\frac{2\pi}{3}$. $\cos x > -\frac{1}{2}$ when the graph is *above* the horizontal line $y = -\frac{1}{2}$.

$\cos x < -\frac{1}{2}$ when the graph is *below* the horizontal line $y = -\frac{1}{2}$.

(a) $-\frac{4\pi}{3}, -\frac{2\pi}{3}, \frac{2\pi}{3}, \frac{4\pi}{3}$

(b) $-2\pi \le x < -\frac{4\pi}{3}, -\frac{2\pi}{3} < x < \frac{2\pi}{3}$, and $\frac{4\pi}{3} < x \le 2\pi$

(c) $-\frac{4\pi}{3} < x < -\frac{2\pi}{3}$ and $\frac{2\pi}{3} < x < \frac{4\pi}{3}$

**54** $y = \sin x$; $[0, 4\pi]$; $a = -\frac{\sqrt{2}}{2}$ •

(a) $\frac{5\pi}{4}, \frac{7\pi}{4}, \frac{13\pi}{4}, \frac{15\pi}{4}$      (b) $0 \le x < \frac{5\pi}{4}, \frac{7\pi}{4} < x < \frac{13\pi}{4}$, and $\frac{15\pi}{4} < x \le 4\pi$

(c) $\frac{5\pi}{4} < x < \frac{7\pi}{4}$ and $\frac{13\pi}{4} < x < \frac{15\pi}{4}$

**55** $y = 2 + \sin x$ • Shift $y = \sin x$ up 2 units.

*Figure 55*

*Figure 56*

**56** $y = 3 + \cos x$ • Shift $y = \cos x$ up 3 units.

**57** $y = \cos x - 2$ • Shift $y = \cos x$ down 2 units.

*Figure 57*

*Figure 58*

**58** $y = \sin x - 1$ • Shift $y = \sin x$ down 1 unit. $x$-intercepts are at $x = \frac{\pi}{2} + 2\pi n$.

**59** $y = 1 + \tan x$ • Shift $y = \tan x$ up 1 unit.

Since $1 + \tan\left(-\frac{\pi}{4}\right) = 1 + (-1) = 0$, and the period of the tangent is $\pi$, there are $x$-intercepts at $x = -\frac{\pi}{4} + \pi n$.

*Figure 59*

*Figure 60*

**60** $y = \cot x - 1$ • Shift $y = \cot x$ down 1 unit. $x$-intercepts are at $x = \frac{\pi}{4} + \pi n$.

**61** $y = \sec x - 2$   • Shift $y = \sec x$ down 2 units. $x$-intercepts are at $x = \frac{\pi}{3} + 2\pi n, \frac{5\pi}{3} + 2\pi n$.

Figure 61

Figure 62

**62** $y = 1 + \csc x$   • Shift $y = \csc x$ up 1 unit. $x$-intercepts are at $x = \frac{3\pi}{2} + 2\pi n$.

**63** (a)  As we move from left to right, the secant function increases {goes up}

on the intervals $\left[-2\pi, -\frac{3\pi}{2}\right), \left(-\frac{3\pi}{2}, -\pi\right], \left[0, \frac{\pi}{2}\right), \left(\frac{\pi}{2}, \pi\right]$.

(b)  As we move from left to right, the secant function decreases {goes down}

on the intervals $\left[-\pi, -\frac{\pi}{2}\right), \left(-\frac{\pi}{2}, 0\right], \left[\pi, \frac{3\pi}{2}\right), \left(\frac{3\pi}{2}, 2\pi\right]$.

**64** (a)  $\left[-\frac{3\pi}{2}, -\pi\right), \left(-\pi, -\frac{\pi}{2}\right], \left[\frac{\pi}{2}, \pi\right), \left(\pi, \frac{3\pi}{2}\right]$           (b)  $\left(-2\pi, -\frac{3\pi}{2}\right], \left[-\frac{\pi}{2}, 0\right), \left(0, \frac{\pi}{2}\right], \left[\frac{3\pi}{2}, 2\pi\right)$

**65** (a)  The tangent function increases on *all* intervals on which it is defined.

Between $-2\pi$ and $2\pi$, these intervals are $\left[-2\pi, -\frac{3\pi}{2}\right), \left(-\frac{3\pi}{2}, -\frac{\pi}{2}\right), \left(-\frac{\pi}{2}, \frac{\pi}{2}\right), \left(\frac{\pi}{2}, \frac{3\pi}{2}\right)$, and $\left(\frac{3\pi}{2}, 2\pi\right]$.

(b)  The tangent function is *never* decreasing on any interval for which it is defined.

**66** (a)  The cotangent function is *never* increasing on any interval for which it is defined.

(b)  The cotangent function decreases on *all* intervals on which it is defined.

Between $-2\pi$ and $2\pi$, these intervals are $(-2\pi, -\pi), (-\pi, 0), (0, \pi)$, and $(\pi, 2\pi)$.

**67** This is good advice.

**69** (a)  From $(1, 0)$, move counterclockwise on the unit circle to the point at the tick marked 4. The projection of this point on the $y$-axis, approximately $-0.7$ or $-0.8$, is the value of $\sin 4$.

(b)  From $(1, 0)$, move clockwise 1.2 units to about 5.1. As in part (a), $\sin(-1.2)$ is about $-0.9$.

(c)  Draw the horizontal line $y = 0.5$. This line intersects the circle at about 0.5 and 2.6.

**70** (a)  As in part (a) of Exercise 69, $\sin 2$ is about 0.9.

(b)  As in part (b) of Exercise 69, $\sin(-2.3)$ is about $-0.8$.

(c)  As in part (c) of Exercise 69, the horizontal line $y = -0.2$ intersects the circle at about 3.3 and 6.1.

**71** (a)  From $(1, 0)$, move counterclockwise on the unit circle to the point at the tick marked 4.

The projection of this point on the $x$-axis, approximately $-0.6$ or $-0.7$, is the value of $\cos 4$.

(b)  Proceeding as in part (a), $\cos(-1.2)$ is about 0.4.

(c)  Draw the vertical line $x = -0.6$. This line intersects the circle at about 2.2 and 4.1.

**72** (a) As in part (a) of Exercise 71, cos 2 is about $-0.5$.

(b) As in part (b) of Exercise 71, cos$(-2.3)$ is about $-0.7$.

(c) As in part (c) of Exercise 71, the vertical line $x = 0.2$ intersects the circle at about 1.4 and 4.9.

**73** (a) Note that midnight occurs when $t = -6$.

| Time | Temperature | Humidity |
|---|---|---|
| 12 A.M. | 60 | 60 |
| 3 A.M. | 52 | 74 |
| 6 A.M. | 48 | 80 |
| 9 A.M. | 52 | 74 |

| Time | Temperature | Humidity |
|---|---|---|
| 12 P.M. | 60 | 60 |
| 3 P.M. | 68 | 46 |
| 6 P.M. | 72 | 40 |
| 9 P.M. | 68 | 46 |

(b) Since $T(t) = -12\cos\left(\frac{\pi}{12}t\right) + 60$, its maximum is $60 + 12 = 72°F$ at $t = 12$ or 6:00 P.M., and its minimum is $60 - 12 = 48°F$ at $t = 0$ or 6:00 A.M. Since $H(t) = 20\cos\left(\frac{\pi}{12}t\right) + 60$, its maximum is $60 + 20 = 80\%$ at $t = 0$ or 6:00 A.M., and its minimum is $60 - 20 = 40\%$ at $t = 12$ or 6:00 P.M.

(c) When the temperature increases, the relative humidity decreases and vice versa. As the temperature cools, the air can hold less moisture and the relative humidity increases. Because of this phenomenon, fog often occurs during the evening hours rather than in the middle of the day.

**74** (a) Since the elbow joint does not bend and the arm has a constant length, the robotic hand moves in a circular arc. Therefore, its height $h$ is equal to $h = 153\sin\theta + 50 = 153\sin\left(\frac{\pi}{12}t\right) + 50$. If $0 \le \theta \le \pi/2$, then $0 \le t \le 6$.

| $t$ (seconds) | 0 | 1 | 2 | 3 | 4 | 5 | 6 |
|---|---|---|---|---|---|---|---|
| $\theta$ (radians) | 0 | $\pi/12$ | $\pi/6$ | $\pi/4$ | $\pi/3$ | $5\pi/12$ | $\pi/2$ |
| $h$ (centimeters) | 50.00 | 89.60 | 126.50 | 158.19 | 182.50 | 197.79 | 203.00 |

(b) From the table, it is obvious that the height of the arm does not increase at a constant rate. Instead, it increases at a slower rate as $\theta$ increases at a constant rate. During the first second of time, the hand's height increases by $89.6 - 50 = 39.6$ cm, whereas during the sixth second its height increased by only $203 - 197.79 = 5.21$ cm.

(c) The total distance traveled by the hand is determined by the circular arc with a radius of 153 cm,

$$\text{subtending an angle of } \pi/2. \text{ Thus, } s = r\theta = 153(\pi/2) = 76.5\pi \approx 240.33 \text{ cm.}$$

**75** Graph $y = \sin(x^2)$ and $y = 0.5$ on the same coordinate plane. From the graph, we see that $\sin(x^2)$ assumes the value of 0.5 at $x \approx \pm 0.72, \pm 1.62$.

$[-2, 2]$ by $[-1.33, 1.33]$

*Figure 75*

$[0, 25, 2]$ by $[-8.33, 8.33]$

*Figure 76*

**76** Graph $y = \tan\left(\sqrt{x}\right)$ and $y = 5$ on the same coordinate plane. From the graph, we see that $\tan\left(\sqrt{x}\right)$ assumes the value of 5 at $x \approx 1.89, 20.39$. The figure was obtained by using Dot Mode. Note that the vertical asymptotes are at $\sqrt{x} = \dfrac{\pi}{2}, \dfrac{3\pi}{2}$ or $x = \dfrac{\pi^2}{4} \approx 2.47, \dfrac{9\pi^2}{4} \approx 22.21$.

**77** We see that the graph of $y = x \sin x$ assumes a maximum value of approximately 1.82 at $x \approx \pm 2.03$,

and a minimum value of $-4.81$ at $x \approx \pm 4.91$.

$[-2\pi, 2\pi, \pi/2]$ by $[-5.19, 3.19]$

*Figure 77*

$[-2.5, 2.5]$ by $[-1.67, 1.67]$

*Figure 78*

**78** We see that the graph of $y = \sin^2 x \cos x$ assumes a maximum value of approximately 0.38 at $x \approx \pm 0.96$,

and a minimum value of $-0.38$ at $x \approx \pm 2.19$.

**79** As $x \to 0^+$, $f(x) = \dfrac{1 - \cos x}{x} \to 0$.

$[-1, 1, 0.5]$ by $[-0.67, 0.67, 0.5]$

*Figure 79*

$[-2, 2, 0.5]$ by $[-1.33, 1.33, 0.5]$

*Figure 80*

**80** As $x \to 0^+$, $f(x) = \dfrac{6x - 6\sin x}{x^3} \to 1$.

**81** As $x \to 0^+$, $f(x) = x \cot x \to 1$.

$[-2, 2, 0.5]$ by $[-1.33, 1.33, 0.5]$

*Figure 81*

$[-1.5, 1.5]$ by $[0, 3]$

*Figure 82*

**82** As $x \to 0^+$, $f(x) = \dfrac{x + \tan x}{\sin x} \to 2$.

**83** As $x \to 0^+$, $f(x) = \dfrac{\tan x}{x} \to 1$.

$[-1.5, 1.5]$ by $[0, 3]$

*Figure 83*

$[-1, 1, 0.5]$ by $[-1.33, 0, 0.5]$

*Figure 84*

**84** As $x \to 0^+$, $f(x) = \dfrac{\cos\left(x + \frac{1}{2}\pi\right)}{x} \to -1$.

## 5.4 Exercises

**Note:** Let $\theta_C$ denote the coterminal angle of $\theta$ such that $0° \le \theta_C < 360°$ {or $0 \le \theta_C < 2\pi$}.

The following formulas from page 366 of the text are used in the following solutions.

(1) If $\theta_C$ is in QI, then $\theta_R = \theta_C$.

(2) If $\theta_C$ is in QII, then $\theta_R = 180° - \theta_C$ {or $\pi - \theta_C$}.

(3) If $\theta_C$ is in QIII, then $\theta_R = \theta_C - 180°$ {or $\theta_C - \pi$}.

(4) If $\theta_C$ is in QIV, then $\theta_R = 360° - \theta_C$ {or $2\pi - \theta_C$}.

**Note:** It is helpful to draw the angles when working these exercises.

$\boxed{1}$ (a) Since $310°$ is in QIV, $\theta_R = 360° - 310° = 50°$.　　(b) Since $260°$ is in QIII, $\theta_R = 260° - 180° = 80°$.

(c) $\theta_C = -235° + 1(360°) = 125° \in$ QII. $\theta_R = 180° - 125° = 55°$.

(d) $\theta_C = -660° + 2(360°) = 60° \in$ QI. $\theta_R = 60°$.

$\boxed{2}$ (a) Since $290°$ is in QIV, $\theta_R = 360° - 290° = 70°$.　　(b) Since $195°$ is in QIII, $\theta_R = 195° - 180° = 15°$.

(c) $\theta_C = -185° + 1(360°) = 175° \in$ QII. $\theta_R = 180° - 175° = 5°$.

(d) $\theta_C = 400° - 1(360°) = 40° \in$ QI. $\theta_R = 40°$.

$\boxed{3}$ (a) Since $\frac{3\pi}{4}$ is in QII, $\theta_R = \pi - \frac{3\pi}{4} = \frac{\pi}{4}$.　　(b) Since $\frac{4\pi}{3}$ is in QIII, $\theta_R = \frac{4\pi}{3} - \pi = \frac{\pi}{3}$.

(c) $\theta_C = -\frac{\pi}{6} + 1(2\pi) = \frac{11\pi}{6} \in$ QIV. $\theta_R = 2\pi - \frac{11\pi}{6} = \frac{\pi}{6}$.

(d) $\theta_C = \frac{9\pi}{4} - 1(2\pi) = \frac{\pi}{4} \in$ QI. $\theta_R = \frac{\pi}{4}$.

$\boxed{4}$ (a) Since $\frac{7\pi}{4}$ is in QIV, $\theta_R = 2\pi - \frac{7\pi}{4} = \frac{\pi}{4}$.　　(b) Since $\frac{2\pi}{3}$ is in QII, $\theta_R = \pi - \frac{2\pi}{3} = \frac{\pi}{3}$.

(c) $\theta_C = -\frac{3\pi}{4} + 1(2\pi) = \frac{5\pi}{4} \in$ QIII. $\theta_R = \frac{5\pi}{4} - \pi = \frac{\pi}{4}$. (d) $\theta_C = -\frac{23\pi}{6} + 2(2\pi) = \frac{\pi}{6} \in$ QI. $\theta_R = \frac{\pi}{6}$.

$\boxed{5}$ (a) Since $\frac{\pi}{2} < 3 < \pi$, $\theta$ is in QII and $\theta_R = \pi - 3 \approx 0.14$, or $8.1°$.

(b) $\theta_C = -2 + 1(2\pi) = 2\pi - 2 \approx 4.28$.

Since $\pi < 4.28 < \frac{3\pi}{2}$, $\theta_C$ is in QIII and $\theta_R = (2\pi - 2) - \pi = \pi - 2 \approx 1.14$, or $65.4°$.

(c) Since $\frac{3\pi}{2} < 5.5 < 2\pi$, $\theta$ is in QIV and $\theta_R = 2\pi - 5.5 \approx 0.78$, or $44.9°$.

(d) The number of revolutions made by $\theta$ is $\frac{100}{2\pi} \approx 15.92$, so $\theta_C = 100 - 15(2\pi) = 100 - 30\pi \approx 5.75$.

Since $\frac{3\pi}{2} < 5.75 < 2\pi$, $\theta_C$ is in QIV and $\theta_R = 2\pi - (100 - 30\pi) = 32\pi - 100 \approx 0.53$, or $30.4°$.

Alternatively, if your calculator is capable of computing trigonometric functions

of large values, then computing $\sin^{-1}(\sin 100) \approx -0.53 \quad \Rightarrow \quad \theta_R = 0.53$, or $30.4°$.

**6** (a) Since $\frac{3\pi}{2} < 6 < 2\pi$, $\theta$ is in QIV and $\theta_R = 2\pi - 6 \approx 0.28$, or $16.2°$.

  (b) $\theta_C = -4 + 1(2\pi) = 2\pi - 4 \approx 2.28$.

                   Since $\frac{\pi}{2} < 2.28 < \pi$, $\theta_C$ is in QII and $\theta_R = \pi - (2\pi - 4) = 4 - \pi \approx 0.86$, or $49.2°$.

  (c) Since $\pi < 4.5 < \frac{3\pi}{2}$, $\theta$ is in QIII and $\theta_R = 4.5 - \pi \approx 1.36$, or $77.8°$.

  (d) As in Exercise 5(d), $\frac{80}{2\pi} \approx 12.73$, so $\theta_C = 80 - 12(2\pi) = 80 - 24\pi \approx 4.60$.

       Since $\pi < 4.60 < \frac{3\pi}{2}$, $\theta_C$ is in QIII and $\theta_R = (80 - 24\pi) - \pi = 80 - 25\pi \approx 1.46$, or $83.7°$.

                      Alternatively, $\sin^{-1}(\sin 80) \approx -1.46 \implies \theta_R = 1.46$, or $83.7°$.

*Note:* For the following problems, we use the theorem on reference angles before evaluating.

**7** (a) $\sin \frac{2\pi}{3} = \sin \frac{\pi}{3}$ {since the sine is positive in QII and $\frac{\pi}{3}$ is the reference angle for $\frac{2\pi}{3}$} $= \frac{\sqrt{3}}{2}$

  (b) $\sin\left(-\frac{5\pi}{4}\right) = \sin \frac{3\pi}{4}$ {since $\frac{3\pi}{4}$ is coterminal with $-\frac{5\pi}{4}$} $=$

                 $\sin \frac{\pi}{4}$ {since the sine is positive in QII and $\frac{\pi}{4}$ is the reference angle for $\frac{3\pi}{4}$} $= \frac{\sqrt{2}}{2}$

**8** (a) $\sin 210° = -\sin 30° = -\frac{1}{2}$                (b) $\sin(-315°) = \sin 45° = \frac{\sqrt{2}}{2}$

**9** (a) $\cos 150° = -\cos 30°$ {since the cosine is negative in QII} $= -\frac{\sqrt{3}}{2}$

  (b) $\cos(-60°) = \cos 300° = \cos 60°$ {since the cosine is positive in QIV} $= \frac{1}{2}$

**10** (a) $\cos \frac{5\pi}{4} = -\cos \frac{\pi}{4} = -\frac{\sqrt{2}}{2}$        (b) $\cos\left(-\frac{11\pi}{6}\right) = \cos \frac{\pi}{6} = \frac{\sqrt{3}}{2}$

**11** (a) $\tan \frac{5\pi}{6} = -\tan \frac{\pi}{6}$ {since the tangent is negative in QII} $= -\frac{\sqrt{3}}{3}$

  (b) $\tan\left(-\frac{\pi}{3}\right) = \tan \frac{5\pi}{3} = -\tan \frac{\pi}{3}$ {since the tangent is negative in QIV} $= -\sqrt{3}$

**12** (a) $\tan 330° = -\tan 30° = -\frac{\sqrt{3}}{3}$       (b) $\tan(-225°) = \tan 135° = -\tan 45° = -1$

**13** (a) $\cot 120° = -\cot 60°$ {since the cotangent is negative in QII} $= -\frac{\sqrt{3}}{3}$

  (b) $\cot(-150°) = \cot 210° = \cot 30°$ {since the cotangent is positive in QIII} $= \sqrt{3}$

**14** (a) $\cot \frac{3\pi}{4} = -\cot \frac{\pi}{4} = -1$        (b) $\cot\left(-\frac{2\pi}{3}\right) = \cot \frac{4\pi}{3} = \cot \frac{\pi}{3} = \frac{\sqrt{3}}{3}$

**15** (a) $\sec \frac{2\pi}{3} = -\sec \frac{\pi}{3}$ {since the secant is negative in QII} $= -2$

  (b) $\sec\left(-\frac{\pi}{6}\right) = \sec \frac{11\pi}{6} = \sec \frac{\pi}{6}$ {since the secant is positive in QIV} $= \frac{2}{\sqrt{3}}$

**16** (a) $\sec 135° = -\sec 45° = -\sqrt{2}$       (b) $\sec(-210°) = \sec 150° = -\sec 30° = -\frac{2}{\sqrt{3}}$

**17** (a) $\csc 240° = -\csc 60°$ {since the cosecant is negative in QIII} $= -\frac{2}{\sqrt{3}}$

  (b) $\csc(-330°) = \csc 30° = 2$

**18** (a) $\csc \frac{3\pi}{4} = \csc \frac{\pi}{4} = \sqrt{2}$        (b) $\csc\left(-\frac{2\pi}{3}\right) = \csc \frac{4\pi}{3} = -\csc \frac{\pi}{3} = -\frac{2}{\sqrt{3}}$

**19** (a) Using the *degree* mode on a calculator, $\sin 24°20' \approx 0.412$.

  (b) Using the *radian* mode on a calculator, $\cos 0.68 \approx 0.778$.

**20** (a) $\cos 88°30' \approx 0.026$                      (b) $\sin 1.48 \approx 0.996$

**21** (a) Using the *degree* mode on a calculator, $\tan 73°10' \approx 3.305$.

(b) First compute $\tan 1.13$, obtaining $2.11975$. Now use the reciprocal key, usually labeled either $\boxed{1/x}$ or $\boxed{x^{-1}}$, to obtain $\cot 1.13 \approx 0.472$.

**22** (a) $\cot 9°10' \approx 6.197$  (b) $\tan 0.75 \approx 0.932$

**23** (a) First compute $\cos 67°50'$, obtaining $0.3773$. Now use the reciprocal key to obtain $\sec 67°50' \approx 2.650$.

(b) As in part (a), since $\sin 0.32 \approx 0.3146$, we have $\csc 0.32 \approx 3.179$.

**24** (a) $\csc 43°40' \approx 1.448$  (b) $\sec 0.26 \approx 1.035$

**25** (a) $\sin \theta = 0.42$ • Using the degree mode, calculate $\sin^{-1}(0.42)$ to obtain $24.83°$ to the nearest one-hundredth of a degree.

(b) Using the answer from part (a), subtract 24 and multiply that result by 60 to obtain $24°50'$ to the nearest minute.

**26** (a) $\sin \theta = 0.6612 \;\Rightarrow\; \theta = \sin^{-1}(0.6612) \approx 41.39°$  (b) $41.39° \approx 41°23'$

**27** (a) $\cos \theta = 0.8620$ • Using the degree mode, calculate $\cos^{-1}(0.8620)$ to obtain $30.46°$ to the nearest one-hundredth of a degree.

(b) Using the answer from part (a), subtract 30 and multiply that result by 60 to obtain $30°27'$ to the nearest minute.

**28** (a) $\cos \theta = 0.8 \;\Rightarrow\; \theta = \cos^{-1}(0.8) \approx 36.87°$  (b) $36.87° \approx 36°52'$

**29** (a) $\tan \theta = 3.7 \;\Rightarrow\; \theta = \tan^{-1}(3.7) \approx 74.88°$  (b) $74.88° \approx 74°53'$

**30** (a) $\tan \theta = 4.91 \;\Rightarrow\; \theta = \tan^{-1}(4.91) \approx 78.49°$  (b) $78.49° \approx 78°29'$

**31** (a) After entering 4, use $\boxed{1/x}$ and then $\boxed{\text{INV}}$ $\boxed{\text{TAN}}$, or, equivalently, $\boxed{\text{TAN}^{-1}}$. Similarly, for the cosecant function use $\boxed{1/x}$ and then $\boxed{\text{INV}}$ $\boxed{\text{SIN}}$ and for the secant function use $\boxed{1/x}$ and then $\boxed{\text{INV}}$ $\boxed{\text{COS}}$.
$\cot \theta = 4 \;\Rightarrow\; \tan \theta = \frac{1}{4} \;\Rightarrow\; \theta = \tan^{-1}\left(\frac{1}{4}\right) \approx 14.04°$.

(b) $\cot \theta = 4 \;\Rightarrow\; \tan \theta = \frac{1}{4} \;\Rightarrow\; \theta = \tan^{-1}\left(\frac{1}{4}\right) \approx 14°2'$

**32** (a) $\cot \theta = 0.361 \;\Rightarrow\; \tan \theta = \frac{1}{0.361} \;\Rightarrow\; \theta = \tan^{-1}\left(\frac{1}{0.361}\right) \approx 70.15°$  (b) $70.15° \approx 70°9'$

**33** (a) After entering 4.246, use $\boxed{1/x}$ and then $\boxed{\text{INV}}$ $\boxed{\text{COS}}$, or, equivalently, $\boxed{\text{COS}^{-1}}$. Similarly, for the cosecant function use $\boxed{1/x}$ and then $\boxed{\text{INV}}$ $\boxed{\text{SIN}}$ and for the cotangent function use $\boxed{1/x}$ and then $\boxed{\text{INV}}$ $\boxed{\text{TAN}}$. $\sec \theta = 4.246 \;\Rightarrow\; \cos \theta = \frac{1}{4.246} \;\Rightarrow\; \theta = \cos^{-1}\left(\frac{1}{4.246}\right) \approx 76.38°$.

(b) $\sec \theta = 4.246 \;\Rightarrow\; \cos \theta = \frac{1}{4.246} \;\Rightarrow\; \theta = \cos^{-1}\left(\frac{1}{4.246}\right) \approx 76°23'$

**34** (a) $\sec \theta = 1.15 \;\Rightarrow\; \cos \theta = \frac{1}{1.15} \;\Rightarrow\; \theta = \cos^{-1}\left(\frac{1}{1.15}\right) \approx 29.59°$.  (b) $29.59° \approx 29°36'$

**35** (a) $\csc \theta = 2.54 \;\Rightarrow\; \sin \theta = \frac{1}{2.54} \;\Rightarrow\; \theta = \sin^{-1}\left(\frac{1}{2.54}\right) \approx 23.18°$  (b) $23.18° \approx 23°11'$

**36** (a) $\csc \theta = 11 \;\Rightarrow\; \sin \theta = \frac{1}{11} \;\Rightarrow\; \theta = \sin^{-1}\left(\frac{1}{11}\right) \approx 5.22°$  (b) $5.22° \approx 5°13'$

**37** (a) $\sin 98°10' \approx 0.9899$  (b) $\cos 623.7° \approx -0.1097$

(c) $\tan 3 \approx -0.1425$  (d) $\cot 231°40' = \dfrac{1}{\tan 231°40'} \approx 0.7907$

(e) $\sec 1175.1° = \dfrac{1}{\cos 1175.1°} \approx -11.2493$  (f) $\csc 0.82 = \dfrac{1}{\sin 0.82} \approx 1.3677$

**38** (a)  $\sin 496.4° \approx 0.6896$     (b)  $\cos 0.65 \approx 0.7961$     (c)  $\tan 105°40' \approx -3.5656$

(d)  $\cot 1030.2° \approx -0.8451$     (e)  $\sec 1.46 \approx 9.0441$     (f)  $\csc 320°50' \approx -1.5833$

**39** (a)  Use degree mode.  $\sin\theta = -0.5640 \;\Rightarrow\; \theta = \sin^{-1}(-0.5640) \approx -34.3° \;\Rightarrow\; \theta_R \approx 34.3°$. Since the sine is negative in QIII and QIV, we use $\theta_R$ in those quadrants.  $180° + 34.3° = 214.3°$ and $360° - 34.3° = 325.7°$

(b)  $\cos\theta = 0.7490 \;\Rightarrow\; \theta = \cos^{-1}(0.7490) \approx 41.5°$.  $\theta_R \approx 41.5°$, QI: $41.5°$, QIV: $318.5°$

(c)  $\tan\theta = 2.798 \;\Rightarrow\; \theta = \tan^{-1}(2.798) \approx 70.3°$.  $\theta_R \approx 70.3°$, QI: $70.3°$, QIII: $250.3°$

(d)  $\cot\theta = -0.9601 \;\Rightarrow\; \tan\theta = -\dfrac{1}{0.9601} \;\Rightarrow\; \theta = \tan^{-1}\left(-\dfrac{1}{0.9601}\right) \approx -46.2°$.

$\theta_R \approx 46.2°$, QII: $133.8°$, QIV: $313.8°$

(e)  $\sec\theta = -1.116 \;\Rightarrow\; \cos\theta = -\dfrac{1}{1.116} \;\Rightarrow\; \theta = \cos^{-1}\left(-\dfrac{1}{1.116}\right) \approx 153.6°$.

$\theta_R \approx 180° - 153.6° = 26.4°$, QII: $153.6°$, QIII: $206.4°$

(f)  $\csc\theta = 1.485 \;\Rightarrow\; \sin\theta = \dfrac{1}{1.485} \;\Rightarrow\; \theta = \sin^{-1}\left(\dfrac{1}{1.485}\right) \approx 42.3°$.        $\theta_R \approx 42.3°$, QI: $42.3°$, QII: $137.7°$

**40** (a)  $\sin\theta = 0.8225 \;\Rightarrow\; \theta = \sin^{-1}(0.8225) \approx 55.3°$.  $\theta_R \approx 55.3°$, QI: $55.3°$, QII: $124.7°$

(b)  $\cos\theta = -0.6604 \;\Rightarrow\; \theta = \cos^{-1}(-0.6604) \approx 131.3°$.

$\theta_R \approx 180° - 131.3° = 48.7°$, QII: $131.3°$, QIII: $228.7°$

(c)  $\tan\theta = -1.5214 \;\Rightarrow\; \theta = \tan^{-1}(-1.5214) \approx -56.7°$.        $\theta_R \approx 56.7°$, QII: $123.3°$, QIV: $303.3°$

(d)  $\cot\theta = 1.3752 \;\Rightarrow\; \tan\theta = \dfrac{1}{1.3752} \;\Rightarrow\; \theta = \tan^{-1}\left(\dfrac{1}{1.3752}\right) \approx 36.0°$.  $\theta_R \approx 36.0°$, QI: $36.0°$, QIII: $216.0°$

(e)  $\sec\theta = 1.4291 \;\Rightarrow\; \cos\theta = \dfrac{1}{1.4291} \;\Rightarrow\; \theta = \cos^{-1}\left(\dfrac{1}{1.4291}\right) \approx 45.6°$.  $\theta_R \approx 45.6°$, QI: $45.6°$, QIV: $314.4°$

(f)  $\csc\theta = -2.3179 \;\Rightarrow\; \sin\theta = -\dfrac{1}{2.3179} \;\Rightarrow\; \theta = \sin^{-1}\left(-\dfrac{1}{2.3179}\right) \approx -25.6°$.

$\theta_R \approx 25.6°$, QIII: $205.6°$, QIV: $334.4°$

**41** (a)  Use radian mode.  $\sin\theta = 0.4195 \;\Rightarrow\; \theta = \sin^{-1}(0.4195) \approx 0.43$.  $\theta_R \approx 0.43$ is one answer.

Since sine is positive in QI and QII, we also use the reference angle for $\theta$ in quadrant II.  QII: $\pi - 0.43 \approx 2.71$

(b)  $\cos\theta = -0.1207 \;\Rightarrow\; \theta = \cos^{-1}(-0.1207) \approx 1.69$ is one answer.

Since 1.69 is in QII, $\theta_R \approx \pi - 1.69 \approx 1.45$.  The cosine is also negative in QIII.  QIII: $\pi + 1.45 \approx 4.59$

(c)  $\tan\theta = -3.2504 \;\Rightarrow\; \theta = \tan^{-1}(-3.2504) \approx -1.27 \;\Rightarrow\; \theta_R \approx 1.27$.

QII: $\pi - 1.27 \approx 1.87$, QIV: $2\pi - 1.27 \approx 5.01$

(d)  $\cot\theta = 2.6815 \;\Rightarrow\; \tan\theta = \dfrac{1}{2.6815} \;\Rightarrow\; \theta = \tan^{-1}\left(\dfrac{1}{2.6815}\right) \approx 0.36 \;\Rightarrow\;$

$\theta_R \approx 0.36$ is one answer.  QIII: $\pi + 0.36 \approx 3.50$

(e)  $\sec\theta = 1.7452 \;\Rightarrow\; \cos\theta = \dfrac{1}{1.7452} \;\Rightarrow\; \theta = \cos^{-1}\left(\dfrac{1}{1.7452}\right) \approx 0.96 \;\Rightarrow\;$

$\theta_R \approx 0.96$ is one answer.  QIV: $2\pi - 0.96 \approx 5.32$

(f)  $\csc\theta = -4.8521 \;\Rightarrow\; \sin\theta = -\dfrac{1}{4.8521} \;\Rightarrow\; \theta = \sin^{-1}\left(-\dfrac{1}{4.8521}\right) \approx -0.21 \;\Rightarrow\;$

$\theta_R \approx 0.21$.  QIII: $\pi + 0.21 \approx 3.35$, QIV: $2\pi - 0.21 \approx 6.07$

**42** (a)  $\sin\theta = -0.0135 \;\Rightarrow\; \theta = \sin^{-1}(-0.0135) \approx -0.01 \;\Rightarrow\; \theta_R \approx 0.01$.

QIII: $\pi + 0.01 \approx 3.15$; QIV: $2\pi - 0.01 \approx 6.27$

(b)  $\cos\theta = 0.9235 \;\Rightarrow\; \theta = \cos^{-1}(0.9235) \approx 0.39 \;\Rightarrow\; \theta_R \approx 0.39$ is one answer.        QIV: $2\pi - 0.39 \approx 5.89$

(c) $\tan\theta = 0.42 \;\Rightarrow\; \theta = \tan^{-1}(0.42) \approx 0.40 \;\Rightarrow\; \theta_R \approx 0.40$ is one answer.　　　QIII: $\pi + 0.40 \approx 3.54$

(d) $\cot\theta = -2.731 \;\Rightarrow\; \tan\theta = -\frac{1}{2.731} \;\Rightarrow\; \theta = \tan^{-1}\!\left(-\frac{1}{2.731}\right) \approx -0.35 \;\Rightarrow\; \theta_R \approx 0.35.$

QII: $\pi - 0.35 \approx 2.79$, QIV: $2\pi - 0.35 \approx 5.93$

(e) $\sec\theta = -3.51 \;\Rightarrow\; \cos\theta = -\frac{1}{3.51} \;\Rightarrow\; \theta = \cos^{-1}\!\left(-\frac{1}{3.51}\right) \approx 1.86$ is one answer.

Since 1.86 is in QII, $\theta_R \approx \pi - 1.86 \approx 1.28$. QIII: $\pi + 1.28 \approx 4.42$

(f) $\csc\theta = 1.258 \;\Rightarrow\; \sin\theta = \frac{1}{1.258} \;\Rightarrow\; \theta = \sin^{-1}\!\left(\frac{1}{1.258}\right) \approx 0.92 \;\Rightarrow\; \theta_R \approx 0.92$ is one answer.

QII: $\pi - 0.92 \approx 2.22$

**43** $\ln I_0 - \ln I = kx\sec\theta \;\Rightarrow\; \ln\dfrac{I_0}{I} = kx\sec\theta$ {property of logarithms} $\Rightarrow$

$x = \dfrac{1}{k\sec\theta}\ln\dfrac{I_0}{I}$ {solve for $x$} $= \dfrac{1}{1.88\sec 12°}\ln 1.72$ {substitute and approximate} $\approx 0.28$ cm.

**44** $\ln\dfrac{I_0}{I} = kx\sec\theta \;\Rightarrow\; \sec\theta = \dfrac{1}{kx}\ln\dfrac{I_0}{I} \;\Rightarrow\; \cos\theta = \dfrac{kx}{\ln(I_0/I)} = \dfrac{1.88(0.31)}{\ln 2.05} \approx 0.8119 \;\Rightarrow\; \theta \approx 35.7°.$

**45** (a) $R = R_0\cos\theta\sin\phi$ ● Since $\cos\theta$ and $\sin\phi$ are both less than or equal to 1, the solar radiation $R$ will equal its maximum $R_0$ when $\cos\theta = \sin\phi = 1$. This occurs when $\theta = 0°$ and $\phi = 90°$, and corresponds to when the sun is just rising in the east.

(b) The sun located in the southeast corresponds to $\phi = 45°$.

percentage of $R_0 = \dfrac{\text{amount of } R_0}{R_0} = \dfrac{R_0\cos 60°\sin 45°}{R_0} = \dfrac{1}{2}\cdot\dfrac{\sqrt{2}}{2} = \dfrac{\sqrt{2}}{4} \approx 35\%.$

**46** (a) $d = 2\pi\left(\dfrac{vR}{0.52\cos\phi}\right)^{1/3} = 2\pi\left(\dfrac{45\cdot 6369}{0.52\cos 48°}\right)^{1/3} \approx 589$ km.

(b) Since $\cos\phi$ decreases as $\phi$ increases from $0°$ to $90°$,

and $\cos\phi$ is in the denominator of the expression, $d$ increases as $\phi$ increases.

**47** $\sin\theta = \dfrac{b}{c} \;\Rightarrow\; \sin 60° = \dfrac{b}{18} \;\Rightarrow\; b = 18\sin 60° = 18\cdot\dfrac{\sqrt{3}}{2} = 9\sqrt{3} \approx 15.6.$

$\cos\theta = \dfrac{a}{c} \;\Rightarrow\; \cos 60° = \dfrac{a}{18} \;\Rightarrow\; a = 18\cos 60° = 18\cdot\dfrac{1}{2} = 9.$　　The hand is located at $\left(9, 9\sqrt{3}\right)$.

**48** The arm's initial length is $\sqrt{12^2 + 12^2} = \sqrt{288}$. $\tan\theta_1 = \dfrac{b}{a} = \dfrac{12}{12} = 1 \;\Rightarrow\; \theta_1 = 45°$ is the arm's initial angle.

The new arm length is $\sqrt{(-16)^2 + 10^2} = \sqrt{356}$. The new angle has $\tan\theta_2 = \dfrac{b}{a} = \dfrac{10}{-16} = -\dfrac{5}{8}$. Since $\theta_2$ is in

quadrant II, $\theta_2 \approx 148°$. Thus, the arm must increase its length by $\sqrt{356} - \sqrt{288} \approx 1.9$ inches and rotate

$\theta_2 - \theta_1 \approx 103°$ counterclockwise.

## 5.5 Exercises

**Note:** Exercises 1–4: We will refer to $y = \sin x$ as just $\sin x$, $y = \cos x$ as $\cos x$, etc. For the form $y = a\sin bx$, the amplitude is $|a|$ and the period is $\frac{2\pi}{|b|}$. These are merely listed in the answer along with the values of the $x$-intercepts. Let $n$ denote any integer.

[1] (a) $y = 4 \sin x$ • Vertically stretch $\sin x$ by a factor of 4. The $x$-intercepts are not affected by a vertical stretch or a vertical compression.

★ $4, 2\pi$, $x$-int. @ $\pi n$

(b) $y = \sin 4x$ • Horizontally compress $\sin x$ by a factor of 4. The $x$-intercepts are affected by a horizontal stretch or compression by the same factor—that is, a horizontal compression by a factor of $k$ will move the $x$-intercepts of $\sin x$ from $\pi n$ to $\frac{\pi}{k}n$, and a horizontal stretch by a factor of $k$ will move the $x$-intercepts of $\sin x$ from $\pi n$ to $k\pi n$.

★ $1, \frac{\pi}{2}$, $x$-int. @ $\frac{\pi}{4}n$

(c) $y = \frac{1}{4} \sin x$ • Vertically compress $\sin x$ by a factor of 4.

★ $\frac{1}{4}, 2\pi$, $x$-int. @ $\pi n$

Figure 1(a)

Figure 1(b)

Figure 1(c)

(d) $y = \sin \frac{1}{4}x$ • Horizontally stretch $\sin x$ by a factor of 4.

★ $1, 8\pi$, $x$-int. @ $4\pi n$

(e) $y = 2 \sin \frac{1}{4}x$ • Vertically stretch the graph in part (d) by a factor of 2.

★ $2, 8\pi$, $x$-int. @ $4\pi n$

(f) $y = \frac{1}{2} \sin 4x$ • Vertically compress the graph in part (b) by a factor of 2.

★ $\frac{1}{2}, \frac{\pi}{2}$, $x$-int. @ $\frac{\pi}{4}n$

Figure 1(d)

Figure 1(e)

Figure 1(f)

(g) $y = -4 \sin x$ • Reflect the graph in part (a) through the $x$-axis.

★ $4, 2\pi$, $x$-int. @ $\pi n$

(h) $y = \sin(-4x) = -\sin 4x$ using a formula for negatives. Reflect the graph in part (b) through the $x$-axis.

★ $1, \frac{\pi}{2}$, $x$-int. @ $\frac{\pi}{4}n$

Figure 1(g)

Figure 1(h)

☑ (a) $y = 4 \cos x$ • Vertically stretch $\cos x$ by a factor of 4.    ★ $4, 2\pi$, $x$-int. @ $\frac{\pi}{2} + \pi n$

(b) $y = \cos 4x$ • Horizontally compress $\cos x$ by a factor of 4.    ★ $1, \frac{\pi}{2}$, $x$-int. @ $\frac{\pi}{8} + \frac{\pi}{4} n$

(c) $y = \frac{1}{4} \cos x$ • Vertically compress $\cos x$ by a factor of 4.    ★ $\frac{1}{4}, 2\pi$, $x$-int. @ $\frac{\pi}{2} + \pi n$

*Figure 2(a)*

*Figure 2(b)*

*Figure 2(c)*

(d) $y = \cos \frac{1}{4} x$ • Horizontally stretch $\cos x$ by a factor of 4.    ★ $1, 8\pi$, $x$-int. @ $2\pi + 4\pi n$

(e) $y = 2 \cos \frac{1}{4} x$ • Vertically stretch the graph in part (d) by a factor of 2.    ★ $2, 8\pi$, $x$-int. @ $2\pi + 4\pi n$

(f) $y = \frac{1}{2} \cos 4x$ • Vertically compress the graph in part (b) by a factor of 2.    ★ $\frac{1}{2}, \frac{\pi}{2}$, $x$-int. @ $\frac{\pi}{8} + \frac{\pi}{4} n$

*Figure 2(d)*

*Figure 2(e)*

*Figure 2(f)*

(g) $y = -4 \cos x$ • Reflect the graph in part (a) through the $x$-axis.    ★ $4, 2\pi$, $x$-int. @ $\frac{\pi}{2} + \pi n$

(h) $y = \cos(-4x) = \cos 4x$ using a formula for negatives. This graph is the same as the graph in part (b).

★ $1, \frac{\pi}{2}$, $x$-int. @ $\frac{\pi}{8} + \frac{\pi}{4} n$

*Figure 2(g)*

*Figure 2(h)*

3  (a) $y = 3\cos x$  • Vertically stretch $\cos x$ by a factor of 3.                     ★ $3, 2\pi$, $x$-int. @ $\frac{\pi}{2} + \pi n$

(b) $y = \cos 3x$  • Horizontally compress $\cos x$ by a factor of 3. The $x$-intercepts are affected by a horizontal stretch or compression by the same factor—that is, horizontal compression by a factor of $k$ will move the $x$-intercepts of $\cos x$ from $\frac{\pi}{2} + \pi n$ to $\frac{\pi}{2k} + \frac{\pi}{k}n$, and a horizontal stretch by a factor of $k$ will move the $x$-intercepts of $\cos x$ from $\frac{\pi}{2} + \pi n$ to $\frac{k\pi}{2} + k\pi n$.                     ★ $1, \frac{2\pi}{3}$, $x$-int. @ $\frac{\pi}{6} + \frac{\pi}{3}n$

(c) $y = \frac{1}{3}\cos x$  • Vertically compress $\cos x$ by a factor of 3.                     ★ $\frac{1}{3}, 2\pi$, $x$-int. @ $\frac{\pi}{2} + \pi n$

Figure 3(a)

Figure 3(b)

Figure 3(c)

(d) $y = \cos \frac{1}{3}x$  • Horizontally stretch $\cos x$ by a factor of 3.                     ★ $1, 6\pi$, $x$-int. @ $\frac{3\pi}{2} + 3\pi n$

(e) $y = 2\cos \frac{1}{3}x$  • Vertically stretch the graph in part (d) by a factor of 2.                     ★ $2, 6\pi$, $x$-int. @ $\frac{3\pi}{2} + 3\pi n$

(f) $y = \frac{1}{2}\cos 3x$  • Vertically compress the graph in part (b) by a factor of 2.                     ★ $\frac{1}{2}, \frac{2\pi}{3}$, $x$-int. @ $\frac{\pi}{6} + \frac{\pi}{3}n$

Figure 3(d)

Figure 3(e)

Figure 3(f)

(g) $y = -3\cos x$  • Reflect the graph in part (a) through the $x$-axis.                     ★ $3, 2\pi$, $x$-int. @ $\frac{\pi}{2} + \pi n$

(h) $y = \cos(-3x) = \cos 3x$ using a formula for negatives. This graph is the same as the graph in part (b).                     ★ $1, \frac{2\pi}{3}$, $x$-int. @ $\frac{\pi}{6} + \frac{\pi}{3}n$

Figure 3(g)

Figure 3(h)

**4** (a) $y = 3 \sin x$ • Vertically stretch $\sin x$ by a factor of 3. ★ $3, 2\pi$, $x$-int. @ $\pi n$

(b) $y = \sin 3x$ • Horizontally compress $\sin x$ by a factor of 3. ★ $1, \frac{2\pi}{3}$, $x$-int. @ $\frac{\pi}{3}n$

(c) $y = \frac{1}{3} \sin x$ • Vertically compress $\sin x$ by a factor of 3. ★ $\frac{1}{3}, 2\pi$, $x$-int. @ $\pi n$

Figure 4(a)

Figure 4(b)

Figure 4(c)

(d) $y = \sin \frac{1}{3}x$ • Horizontally stretch $\sin x$ by a factor of 3. ★ $1, 6\pi$, $x$-int. @ $3\pi n$

(e) $y = 2 \sin \frac{1}{3}x$ • Vertically stretch the graph in part (d) by a factor of 2. ★ $2, 6\pi$, $x$-int. @ $3\pi n$

(f) $y = \frac{1}{2} \sin 3x$ • Vertically compress the graph in part (b) by a factor of 2. ★ $\frac{1}{2}, \frac{2\pi}{3}$, $x$-int. @ $\frac{\pi}{3}n$

Figure 4(d)

Figure 4(e)

Figure 4(f)

(g) $y = -3 \sin x$ • Reflect the graph in part (a) through the $x$-axis. ★ $3, 2\pi$, $x$-int. @ $\pi n$

(h) $y = \sin(-3x) = -\sin 3x$ • Reflect the graph in part (b) through the $x$-axis. ★ $1, \frac{2\pi}{3}$, $x$-int. @ $\frac{\pi}{3}n$

Figure 4(g)

Figure 4(h)

**Note:** We will write $y = a\sin(bx + c)$ in the form $y = a\sin\left[b\left(x + \frac{c}{b}\right)\right]$. From this form we have the amplitude, $|a|$, the period, $\frac{2\pi}{|b|}$, and the phase shift, $-\frac{c}{b}$. We will also list the interval that corresponds to $[0, 2\pi]$ for the sine functions and $\left[-\frac{\pi}{2}, \frac{3\pi}{2}\right]$ for the cosine functions—other intervals could certainly be used. See Exercises 17 and 29 for representative examples.

**5**   $y = \sin\left(x - \frac{\pi}{2}\right)$  •  $0 \le x - \frac{\pi}{2} \le 2\pi \Rightarrow \frac{\pi}{2} \le x \le \frac{5\pi}{2}$. Phase shift $= -\left(-\frac{\pi}{2}\right) = \frac{\pi}{2}$.    ★ $1, 2\pi, \frac{\pi}{2}, \left[\frac{\pi}{2}, \frac{5\pi}{2}\right]$

*Figure 5*                          *Figure 6*

**6**   $y = \sin\left(x + \frac{\pi}{4}\right)$  •  $0 \le x + \frac{\pi}{4} \le 2\pi \Rightarrow -\frac{\pi}{4} \le x \le \frac{7\pi}{4}$    ★ $1, 2\pi, -\frac{\pi}{4}, \left[-\frac{\pi}{4}, \frac{7\pi}{4}\right]$

**7**   $y = 3\sin\left(x + \frac{\pi}{6}\right)$  •  $0 \le x + \frac{\pi}{6} \le 2\pi \Rightarrow -\frac{\pi}{6} \le x \le \frac{11\pi}{6}$.
Phase shift $= -\left(\frac{\pi}{6}\right) = -\frac{\pi}{6}$.    ★ $3, 2\pi, -\frac{\pi}{6}, \left[-\frac{\pi}{6}, \frac{11\pi}{6}\right]$

*Figure 7*                          *Figure 8*

**8**   $y = 2\sin\left(x - \frac{\pi}{2}\right)$  •  $0 \le x - \frac{\pi}{2} \le 2\pi \Rightarrow \frac{\pi}{2} \le x \le \frac{5\pi}{2}$    ★ $2, 2\pi, \frac{\pi}{2}, \left[\frac{\pi}{2}, \frac{5\pi}{2}\right]$

**9**   $y = \cos\left(x + \frac{\pi}{3}\right)$  •  $-\frac{\pi}{2} \le x + \frac{\pi}{3} \le \frac{3\pi}{2} \Rightarrow -\frac{5\pi}{6} \le x \le \frac{7\pi}{6}$.
Phase shift $= -\left(\frac{\pi}{3}\right) = -\frac{\pi}{3}$.    ★ $1, 2\pi, -\frac{\pi}{3}, \left[-\frac{5\pi}{6}, \frac{7\pi}{6}\right]$

*Figure 9*                          *Figure 10*

**10**   $y = \cos\left(x - \frac{\pi}{3}\right)$  •  $-\frac{\pi}{2} \le x - \frac{\pi}{3} \le \frac{3\pi}{2} \Rightarrow -\frac{\pi}{6} \le x \le \frac{11\pi}{6}$    ★ $1, 2\pi, \frac{\pi}{3}, \left[-\frac{\pi}{6}, \frac{11\pi}{6}\right]$

**11**   $y = 4\cos\left(x - \frac{\pi}{4}\right)$  •  $-\frac{\pi}{2} \le x - \frac{\pi}{4} \le \frac{3\pi}{2} \Rightarrow -\frac{\pi}{4} \le x \le \frac{7\pi}{4}$.
Phase shift $= -\left(-\frac{\pi}{4}\right) = \frac{\pi}{4}$.    ★ $4, 2\pi, \frac{\pi}{4}, \left[-\frac{\pi}{4}, \frac{7\pi}{4}\right]$

*Figure 11*

*Figure 12*

**12** $y = 3\cos\left(x + \frac{\pi}{6}\right)$ • $-\frac{\pi}{2} \leq x + \frac{\pi}{6} \leq \frac{3\pi}{2}$ ⇒ $-\frac{2\pi}{3} \leq x \leq \frac{4\pi}{3}$ ★ $3, 2\pi, -\frac{\pi}{6}, \left[-\frac{2\pi}{3}, \frac{4\pi}{3}\right]$

**13** $y = \sin(2x - \pi) + 1 = \sin\left[2\left(x - \frac{\pi}{2}\right)\right] + 1$. • Period $= \frac{2\pi}{|2|} = \pi$. The normal range of the sine, $-1$ to $1$, is affected by the "+1" at the end of the equation. It shifts the graph up 1 unit and the resulting range is 0 to 2. It may be easiest to graph $y = \sin\left[2\left(x - \frac{\pi}{2}\right)\right]$ {1 period of a sine wave with endpoints at $\frac{\pi}{2}$ and $\frac{3\pi}{2}$} and then make a vertical shift of 1 unit up to complete the graph of $y = \sin\left[2\left(x - \frac{\pi}{2}\right)\right] + 1$.

$0 \leq 2x - \pi \leq 2\pi$ ⇒ $\pi \leq 2x \leq 3\pi$ ⇒ $\frac{\pi}{2} \leq x \leq \frac{3\pi}{2}$ ★ $1, \pi, \frac{\pi}{2}, \left[\frac{\pi}{2}, \frac{3\pi}{2}\right]$

*Figure 13*

*Figure 14*

**14** $y = -\sin(3x + \pi) - 1 = -\sin\left[3\left(x + \frac{\pi}{3}\right)\right] - 1$.

$0 \leq 3x + \pi \leq 2\pi$ ⇒ $-\pi \leq 3x \leq \pi$ ⇒ $-\frac{\pi}{3} \leq x \leq \frac{\pi}{3}$ ★ $1, \frac{2\pi}{3}, -\frac{\pi}{3}, \left[-\frac{\pi}{3}, \frac{\pi}{3}\right]$

**15** $y = -\cos(6x + \pi) - 2 = -\cos\left[6\left(x + \frac{\pi}{6}\right)\right] - 2$ • The "$-$" in front of cos has the effect of reflecting the graph of $y = \cos(6x + \pi)$ through the $x$-axis. The "$-2$" at the end of the equation lowers the range 2 units to $-3$ to $-1$. Period $= \frac{2\pi}{|6|} = \frac{\pi}{3}$, phase shift $= -\left(\frac{\pi}{6}\right) = -\frac{\pi}{6}$. $-\frac{\pi}{2} \leq 6x + \pi \leq \frac{3\pi}{2}$ ⇒ $-\frac{3\pi}{2} \leq 6x \leq \frac{\pi}{2}$ ⇒ $-\frac{\pi}{4} \leq x \leq \frac{\pi}{12}$

★ $1, \frac{\pi}{3}, -\frac{\pi}{6}, \left[-\frac{\pi}{4}, \frac{\pi}{12}\right]$

*Figure 15*

*Figure 16*

**16** $y = \cos(2x - \pi) + 2 = \cos\left[2\left(x - \frac{\pi}{2}\right)\right] + 2$.

$-\frac{\pi}{2} \leq 2x - \pi \leq \frac{3\pi}{2}$ ⇒ $\frac{\pi}{2} \leq 2x \leq \frac{5\pi}{2}$ ⇒ $\frac{\pi}{4} \leq x \leq \frac{5\pi}{4}$ ★ $1, \pi, \frac{\pi}{2}, \left[\frac{\pi}{4}, \frac{5\pi}{4}\right]$

**17** $y = -5\sin(3x + \pi) = -5\sin\left[3\left(x + \frac{\pi}{3}\right)\right]$.  • Amplitude $= |-5| = 5$.  The negative before the "5" has the effect of reflecting the graph of $y = 5\sin(3x + \pi)$ through the $x$-axis.  Period $= \frac{2\pi}{|3|} = \frac{2\pi}{3}$, phase shift $= -\left(\frac{\pi}{3}\right) = -\frac{\pi}{3}$,

$0 \le 3x + \pi \le 2\pi \ \Rightarrow\ -\pi \le 3x \le \pi \ \Rightarrow\ -\frac{\pi}{3} \le x \le \frac{\pi}{3}$.          ★$2, \frac{2\pi}{3}, -\frac{\pi}{3}, \left[-\frac{\pi}{3}, \frac{\pi}{3}\right]$

*Figure 17*

*Figure 18*

**18** $y = 3\cos(3x - \pi) = 3\cos\left[3\left(x - \frac{\pi}{3}\right)\right]$.

$-\frac{\pi}{2} \le 3x - \pi \le \frac{3\pi}{2} \ \Rightarrow\ \frac{\pi}{2} \le 3x \le \frac{5\pi}{2} \ \Rightarrow\ \frac{\pi}{6} \le x \le \frac{5\pi}{6}$          ★$3, \frac{2\pi}{3}, \frac{\pi}{3}, \left[\frac{\pi}{6}, \frac{5\pi}{6}\right]$

**19** $y = \sin\left(\frac{1}{2}x - \frac{\pi}{3}\right) = \sin\left[\frac{1}{2}\left(x - \frac{2\pi}{3}\right)\right]$.  • Period $= \frac{2\pi}{|1/2|} = 4\pi$.

$0 \le \frac{1}{2}x - \frac{\pi}{3} \le 2\pi \ \Rightarrow\ \frac{\pi}{3} \le \frac{1}{2}x \le \frac{7\pi}{3} \ \Rightarrow\ \frac{2\pi}{3} \le x \le \frac{14\pi}{3}$          ★$1, 4\pi, \frac{2\pi}{3}, \left[\frac{2\pi}{3}, \frac{14\pi}{3}\right]$

*Figure 19*

*Figure 20*

**20** $y = 7\sin\left(\frac{1}{2}x + \frac{\pi}{4}\right) = 7\sin\left[\frac{1}{2}\left(x + \frac{\pi}{2}\right)\right]$.

$0 \le \frac{1}{2}x + \frac{\pi}{4} \le 2\pi \ \Rightarrow\ -\frac{\pi}{4} \le \frac{1}{2}x \le \frac{7\pi}{4} \ \Rightarrow\ -\frac{\pi}{2} \le x \le \frac{7\pi}{2}$          ★$7, 4\pi, -\frac{\pi}{2}, \left[-\frac{\pi}{2}, \frac{7\pi}{2}\right]$

**21** $y = 6\sin\pi x$  • Period $= \frac{2\pi}{|\pi|} = 2$.  $0 \le \pi x \le 2\pi \ \Rightarrow\ 0 \le x \le 2$          ★$6, 2, 0, [0, 2]$

*Figure 21*

*Figure 22*

**22** $y = 3\cos\frac{\pi}{2}x$  • $-\frac{\pi}{2} \le \frac{\pi}{2}x \le \frac{3\pi}{2} \ \Rightarrow\ -1 \le x \le 3$          ★$3, 4, 0, [-1, 3]$

**23** $y = 2\cos\frac{\pi}{2}x$ • Period = $\frac{2\pi}{|\pi/2|} = 4$. $-\frac{\pi}{2} \le \frac{\pi}{2}x \le \frac{3\pi}{2}$ ⟹ $-1 \le x \le 3$ ★ $2, 4, 0, [-1, 3]$

Figure 23

Figure 24

**24** $y = 4\sin 2\pi x$ • $0 \le 2\pi x \le 2\pi$ ⟹ $0 \le x \le 1$ ★ $4, 1, 0, [0, 1]$

**25** $y = \frac{3}{4}\sin 2\pi x$ • $0 \le 2\pi x \le 2\pi$ ⟹ $0 \le x \le 1$ ★ $\frac{3}{4}, 1, 0, [0, 1]$

Figure 25

Figure 26

**26** $y = \frac{1}{2}\cos\frac{\pi}{3}x$ • $-\frac{\pi}{2} \le \frac{\pi}{3}x \le \frac{3\pi}{2}$ ⟹ $-\frac{3}{2} \le x \le \frac{9}{2}$ ★ $\frac{1}{2}, 6, 0, [-\frac{3}{2}, \frac{9}{2}]$

**27** $y = 5\sin\left(3x - \frac{\pi}{2}\right) = 5\sin\left[3\left(x - \frac{\pi}{6}\right)\right]$. • ★ $5, \frac{2\pi}{3}, \frac{\pi}{6}, [\frac{\pi}{6}, \frac{5\pi}{6}]$

$0 \le 3x - \frac{\pi}{2} \le 2\pi$ ⟹ $\frac{\pi}{2} \le 3x \le \frac{5\pi}{2}$ ⟹ $\frac{\pi}{6} \le x \le \frac{5\pi}{6}$. To graph this function, draw

one period of a sine wave with endpoints at $\frac{\pi}{6}$ and $\frac{5\pi}{6}$ and an amplitude of 5.

Figure 27

Figure 28

**28** $y = -4\cos\left(2x + \frac{\pi}{3}\right) = -4\cos\left[2\left(x + \frac{\pi}{6}\right)\right]$. •

$-\frac{\pi}{2} \le 2x + \frac{\pi}{3} \le \frac{3\pi}{2}$ ⟹ $-\frac{5\pi}{6} \le 2x \le \frac{7\pi}{6}$ ⟹ $-\frac{5\pi}{12} \le x \le \frac{7\pi}{12}$ ★ $4, \pi, -\frac{\pi}{6}, [-\frac{5\pi}{12}, \frac{7\pi}{12}]$

**29** $y = -3\cos\left(\frac{1}{2}x - \frac{\pi}{3}\right) = -3\cos\left[\frac{1}{2}\left(x - \frac{2\pi}{3}\right)\right]$. •

$-\frac{\pi}{2} \le \frac{1}{2}x - \frac{\pi}{3} \le \frac{3\pi}{2}$  ⇒  $-\frac{\pi}{6} \le \frac{1}{2}x \le \frac{11\pi}{6}$  ⇒  $-\frac{\pi}{3} \le x \le \frac{11\pi}{3}$  ★ $3, 4\pi, \frac{2\pi}{3}, \left[-\frac{\pi}{3}, \frac{11\pi}{3}\right]$

*Figure 29*

*Figure 30*

**30** $y = 2\sin\left(\frac{1}{2}x - \frac{\pi}{2}\right) = 2\sin\left[\frac{1}{2}(x - \pi)\right]$. •

$0 \le \frac{1}{2}x - \frac{\pi}{2} \le 2\pi$  ⇒  $\frac{\pi}{2} \le \frac{1}{2}x \le \frac{5\pi}{2}$  ⇒  $\pi \le x \le 5\pi$  ★ $2, 4\pi, \pi, [\pi, 5\pi]$

**31** $y = -5\cos\left(\frac{1}{3}x + \frac{\pi}{6}\right) = -5\cos\left[\frac{1}{3}\left(x + \frac{\pi}{2}\right)\right]$. •

$-\frac{\pi}{2} \le \frac{1}{3}x + \frac{\pi}{6} \le \frac{3\pi}{2}$  ⇒  $-\frac{2\pi}{3} \le \frac{1}{3}x \le \frac{4\pi}{3}$  ⇒  $-2\pi \le x \le 4\pi$  ★ $5, 6\pi, -\frac{\pi}{2}, [-2\pi, 4\pi]$

*Figure 31*

*Figure 32*

**32** $y = 4\sin\left(\frac{1}{3}x - \frac{\pi}{3}\right) = 4\sin\left[\frac{1}{3}(x - \pi)\right]$. •

$0 \le \frac{1}{3}x - \frac{\pi}{3} \le 2\pi$  ⇒  $\frac{\pi}{3} \le \frac{1}{3}x \le \frac{7\pi}{3}$  ⇒  $\pi \le x \le 7\pi$  ★ $4, 6\pi, \pi, [\pi, 7\pi]$

**33** $y = 3\cos(\pi x + 4\pi) = 3\cos[\pi(x + 4)]$. •

$-\frac{\pi}{2} \le \pi x + 4\pi \le \frac{3\pi}{2}$  ⇒  $-\frac{9\pi}{2} \le \pi x \le -\frac{5\pi}{2}$  ⇒  $-\frac{9}{2} \le x \le -\frac{5}{2}$  ★ $3, 2, -4, \left[-\frac{9}{2}, -\frac{5}{2}\right]$

*Figure 33*

*Figure 34*

**34** $y = -2\sin(2\pi x + \pi) = -2\sin\left[2\pi\left(x + \frac{1}{2}\right)\right]$. •

$0 \le 2\pi x + \pi \le 2\pi$  ⇒  $-\pi \le 2\pi x \le \pi$  ⇒  $-\frac{1}{2} \le x \le \frac{1}{2}$  ★ $2, 1, -\frac{1}{2}, \left[-\frac{1}{2}, \frac{1}{2}\right]$

**35** $y = -8\sin\left(\frac{\pi}{2}x - \frac{\pi}{4}\right) = -8\sin\left[\frac{\pi}{2}\left(x - \frac{1}{2}\right)\right]$. •

$0 \le \frac{\pi}{2}x - \frac{\pi}{4} \le 2\pi \;\Rightarrow\; \frac{\pi}{4} \le \frac{\pi}{2}x \le \frac{9\pi}{4} \;\Rightarrow\; \frac{1}{2} \le x \le \frac{9}{2}$

★ $8, 4, \frac{1}{2}, \left[\frac{1}{2}, \frac{9}{2}\right]$

*Figure 35*

*Figure 36*

**36** $y = 9\cos\left(\frac{\pi}{4}x - \frac{\pi}{2}\right) = 9\cos\left[\frac{\pi}{4}(x - 2)\right]$. •

$-\frac{\pi}{2} \le \frac{\pi}{4}x - \frac{\pi}{2} \le \frac{3\pi}{2} \;\Rightarrow\; 0 \le \frac{\pi}{4}x \le 2\pi \;\Rightarrow\; 0 \le x \le 8$

★ $9, 8, 2, [0, 8]$

**37** $y = -2\sin(2x - \pi) + 3 = -2\sin\left[2\left(x - \frac{\pi}{2}\right)\right] + 3$. • $0 \le 2x - \pi \le 2\pi \;\Rightarrow\; \pi \le 2x \le 3\pi \;\Rightarrow\; \frac{\pi}{2} \le x \le \frac{3\pi}{2}$.
The amplitude of 2 makes the normal sine range of $-1$ to $1$ change to $-2$ to $2$. The "$+3$" at the end of the equation raises the graph up 3 units and the range is 1 to 5.

★ $2, \pi, \frac{\pi}{2}, \left[\frac{\pi}{2}, \frac{3\pi}{2}\right]$

*Figure 37*

*Figure 38*

**38** $y = 3\cos(x + 3\pi) - 2$. • $-\frac{\pi}{2} \le x + 3\pi \le \frac{3\pi}{2} \;\Rightarrow\; -\frac{7\pi}{2} \le x \le -\frac{3\pi}{2}$

★ $3, 2\pi, -3\pi, \left[-\frac{7\pi}{2}, -\frac{3\pi}{2}\right]$

**39** $y = 5\cos(2x + 2\pi) + 2 = 5\cos\left[2(x + \pi)\right] + 2$. • $-\frac{\pi}{2} \le 2x + 2\pi \le \frac{3\pi}{2} \;\Rightarrow\; -\frac{5\pi}{2} \le 2x \le -\frac{\pi}{2} \;\Rightarrow$

$-\frac{5\pi}{4} \le x \le -\frac{\pi}{4}$

★ $5, \pi, -\pi, \left[-\frac{5\pi}{4}, -\frac{\pi}{4}\right]$

*Figure 39*

*Figure 40*

**40** $y = -4\sin(3x - \pi) - 3 = -4\sin\left[3\left(x - \frac{\pi}{3}\right)\right] - 3$. •

$0 \le 3x - \pi \le 2\pi \;\Rightarrow\; \pi \le 3x \le 3\pi \;\Rightarrow\; \frac{\pi}{3} \le x \le \pi$

★ $4, \frac{2\pi}{3}, \frac{\pi}{3}, \left[\frac{\pi}{3}, \pi\right]$

**41** (a)  The amplitude $a$ is 4 and the period {from $-\pi$ to $\pi$} is $2\pi$.

The phase shift is the first negative zero that occurs before a maximum, $-\pi$.

(b)  Period $= \frac{2\pi}{b} \Rightarrow 2\pi = \frac{2\pi}{b} \Rightarrow b = 1$. Phase shift $= -\frac{c}{b} \Rightarrow -\pi = -\frac{c}{1} \Rightarrow c = \pi$.

Hence, $y = a\sin(bx + c) = 4\sin(x + \pi)$.

**42** (a)  The amplitude $a$ is 3 and the period {from $-\frac{\pi}{4}$ to $\frac{3\pi}{4}$} is $\pi$.

The phase shift is the first negative zero that occurs before a maximum, $-\frac{\pi}{4}$.

(b)  Period $= \frac{2\pi}{b} \Rightarrow \pi = \frac{2\pi}{b} \Rightarrow b = 2$. Phase shift $= -\frac{c}{b} \Rightarrow -\frac{\pi}{4} = -\frac{c}{2} \Rightarrow c = \frac{\pi}{2}$.

Hence, $y = a\sin(bx + c) = 3\sin\left(2x + \frac{\pi}{2}\right)$.

**43** (a)  The amplitude $a$ is 2 and the period {from $-3$ to $1$} is 4.

The phase shift is the first negative zero that occurs before a maximum, $-3$.

(b)  Period $= \frac{2\pi}{b} \Rightarrow 4 = \frac{2\pi}{b} \Rightarrow b = \frac{\pi}{2}$. Phase shift $= -\frac{c}{b} \Rightarrow -3 = -\frac{c}{\pi/2} \Rightarrow$

$c = \frac{3\pi}{2}$. Hence, $y = a\sin(bx + c) = 2\sin\left(\frac{\pi}{2}x + \frac{3\pi}{2}\right)$.

**44** (a)  The amplitude $a$ is 3 and the period {from $-\frac{1}{4}$ to $\frac{3}{4}$ (or 0 to 1)} is 1.

The phase shift is the first negative zero that occurs before a maximum, $-\frac{1}{4}$.

(b)  Period $= \frac{2\pi}{b} \Rightarrow 1 = \frac{2\pi}{b} \Rightarrow b = 2\pi$. Phase shift $= -\frac{c}{b} \Rightarrow -\frac{1}{4} = -\frac{c}{2\pi} \Rightarrow$

$c = \frac{\pi}{2}$. Hence, $y = a\sin(bx + c) = 3\sin\left(2\pi x + \frac{\pi}{2}\right)$.

**45**  In the first second, there are 2 complete cycles. Hence 1 cycle is completed in $\frac{1}{2}$ second and thus, the period is $\frac{1}{2}$.

Also, the period is $\frac{2\pi}{b}$. Equating these expressions yields $\frac{2\pi}{b} = \frac{1}{2} \Rightarrow b = 4\pi$.

**46**  $\frac{2\pi}{b} = 24$ hours $\Rightarrow b = \frac{\pi}{12}$. The light intensity would be 0 at $t = 0$ and $t = 12$.

The light intensity is 510 at $t = 6$. $I = 510\sin\left(\frac{\pi}{12}t\right)$

**47**  We first note that $\frac{1}{2}$ period takes place in $\frac{1}{4}$ second and thus 1 period in $\frac{1}{2}$ second.

As in Exercise 45, $\frac{2\pi}{b} = \frac{1}{2} \Rightarrow b = 4\pi$. Since the maximum flow rate is 8 liters/minute, the amplitude is 8.

$a = 8$ and $b = 4\pi \Rightarrow y = 8\sin 4\pi t$.

**48** (a)  Period $= 23 \Rightarrow \frac{2\pi}{b} = 23 \Rightarrow b = \frac{2\pi}{23}$. Similarly, $b = \frac{2\pi}{28}$ and $b = \frac{2\pi}{33}$.

(b)  physical: $y = \sin\left(\frac{2\pi}{23}x\right) = \sin\left(\frac{2\pi}{23} \cdot 7670\right) \approx 0.136$, or 13.6%

emotional: $y = \sin\left(\frac{2\pi}{28}x\right) = \sin\left(\frac{2\pi}{28} \cdot 7670\right) \approx -0.434$, or $-43.4\%$

intellectual: $y = \sin\left(\frac{2\pi}{33}x\right) = \sin\left(\frac{2\pi}{33} \cdot 7670\right) \approx 0.458$, or 45.8%

**49** $f(t) = 0.5 \cos\left(\frac{\pi}{6}t - \frac{11\pi}{12}\right) = 0.5 \cos\left[\frac{\pi}{6}\left(t - \frac{11}{2}\right)\right]$, amplitude $= 0.5 = \frac{1}{2}$, period $= \frac{2\pi}{\pi/6} = 12$, phase shift $= \frac{11}{2}$

*Figure 49*　　　　　　　　　　　　*Figure 50*

**50** $f(t) = 0.2 \cos\left(\frac{\pi}{12}t - \frac{7\pi}{12}\right) = 0.2 \cos\left[\frac{\pi}{12}(t - 7)\right]$, amplitude $= 0.2 = \frac{1}{5}$, period $= \frac{2\pi}{\pi/12} = 24$, phase shift $= 7$

**51** From Example 12, $D(t) = \frac{K}{2} \sin\left[\frac{2\pi}{365}(t - 79)\right] + 12$. With $K \approx 12$, we have $D(t) = 6 \sin\left[\frac{2\pi}{365}(t - 79)\right] + 12$.

amplitude $= 6$, period $= \frac{2\pi}{2\pi/365} = 365$, phase shift $= 79$, range $= 12 - 6$ to $12 + 6$, or 6 to 18

*Figure 51*　　　　　　　　　　　　*Figure 52*

**52** (a) $T(t) = 36 \sin\left[\frac{2\pi}{365}(t - 101)\right] + 14$ •

amplitude $= 36$, period $= \frac{2\pi}{2\pi/365} = 365$, phase shift $= 101$, range $= 14 - 36$ to $14 + 36$ or $-22$ to 50

(b) The coldest day will occur when the argument of the sine is $-\frac{\pi}{2}$. $\{\frac{3\pi}{2}, \frac{7\pi}{2},$ etc. could also be used – they would result in another year's minimum.$\}$　$\frac{2\pi}{365}(t - 101) = -\frac{\pi}{2}$　$\Rightarrow$　$t - 101 = -\frac{365}{4}$　$\Rightarrow$　$t = 9.75$.

Since $t = 0$ corresponds to January 1, $t = 10$ would correspond to January 11.

**53** $y = 20 + 15 \sin\frac{\pi}{12}t$ • The temperature is 20°F at 9:00 A.M. ($t = 0$). It increases to a high of 35°F at 3:00 P.M. ($t = 6$) and then decreases to 20°F at 9:00 P.M. ($t = 12$). It continues to decrease to a low of 5°F at 3:00 A.M. ($t = 18$). It then rises to 20°F at 9:00 A.M. ($t = 24$).

$[0, 24, 4]$ by $[0, 40, 4]$　　　　　　　$[0, 24, 4]$ by $[40, 120, 20]$

*Figure 53*　　　　　　　　　　　　*Figure 54*

**54** $y = 80 + 22 \cos\left[\frac{\pi}{12}(t - 3)\right]$ • The temperature is approximately 95.6°F at 9:00 A.M. ($t = 0$). It increases to a high of 102°F at noon ($t = 3$) and then decreases to 58°F at midnight ($t = 15$). The temperature then rises to 95.6°F at 9:00 A.M. ($t = 24$).

**Note:** In Exercises 55–58, the period is 24 hours. Thus, $24 = \frac{2\pi}{b} \Rightarrow b = \frac{\pi}{12}$.

**55** A high of 10°C and a low of −10°C imply that $d = \dfrac{\text{high} + \text{low}}{2} = \dfrac{10 + (-10)}{2} = 0$ and

$a = \text{high} - \text{average} = 10 - 0 = 10$. The average temperature of 0°C will occur 6 hours {one-half of 12} after the low at 4 A.M., which corresponds to $t = 10$. Letting this correspond to the first zero of the sine function, we have

$$f(t) = 10\sin\left[\frac{\pi}{12}(t - 10)\right] + 0 = 10\sin\left(\frac{\pi}{12}t - \frac{5\pi}{6}\right) \text{ with } a = 10, b = \frac{\pi}{12}, c = -\frac{5\pi}{6}, d = 0.$$

*Figure 55*

*Figure 56*

**56** A high of 20°C and a low of 10°C imply that $d = 15$ and $a = 5$. Since $f(t)$ is decreasing at midnight, the average temperature of 15°C (before the high of 20°C) would occur at noon, which corresponds to $t = 12$. Letting this correspond to the first zero of the sine function, we have $f(t) = 5\sin\left[\frac{\pi}{12}(t - 12)\right] + 15 \Rightarrow$

$$f(t) = 5\sin\left(\frac{\pi}{12}t - \pi\right) + 15 \text{ with } a = 5, b = \frac{\pi}{12}, c = -\pi, d = 15.$$

**57** A high of 30°C and a low of 10°C imply that $d = \dfrac{30 + 10}{2} = 20$ and $a = 30 - 20 = 10$.

The average temperature of 20°C at 9 A.M. corresponds to $t = 9$.

Letting this correspond to the first zero of the sine function, we have

$$f(t) = 10\sin\left[\frac{\pi}{12}(t - 9)\right] + 20 = 10\sin\left(\frac{\pi}{12}t - \frac{3\pi}{4}\right) + 20 \text{ with } a = 10, b = \frac{\pi}{12}, c = -\frac{3\pi}{4}, d = 20.$$

*Figure 57*

*Figure 58*

**58** A high of 28°C with an average of 20°C imply that the low is 12°C, $d = 20$ and $a = 8$. It was 20°C at 8 A.M., which corresponds to $t = 8$. Letting this correspond to the first zero of the sine function, we have

$$f(t) = 8\sin\left[\frac{\pi}{12}(t - 8)\right] + 20 \Rightarrow f(t) = 8\sin\left(\frac{\pi}{12}t - \frac{2\pi}{3}\right) + 20 \text{ with } a = 8, b = \frac{\pi}{12}, c = -\frac{2\pi}{3}, d = 20.$$

**59** (a) See the figure.

(b) Since the period is 12 months, $12 = \frac{2\pi}{b} \Rightarrow b = \frac{\pi}{6}$. The maximum precipitation is 6.1 and the minimum is

0.2, so the sine wave is centered vertically at $d = \frac{6.1 + 0.2}{2} = 3.15$ and its amplitude is $a = \frac{6.1 - 0.2}{2} = 2.95$.

Since the maximum precipitation occurs at $t = 1$ (January), we must have $bt + c = \frac{\pi}{2} \Rightarrow$

$$\frac{\pi}{6}(1) + c = \frac{\pi}{2} \Rightarrow c = \frac{\pi}{3}. \text{ Thus, } P(t) = a\sin(bt + c) + d = 2.95\sin\left(\frac{\pi}{6}t + \frac{\pi}{3}\right) + 3.15.$$

[0.5, 24.5, 4] by [-1, 8]     [0, 23, 5] by [0, 50, 10]     [0, 30, 5] by [0, 50, 10]

*Figure 59*     *Figure 60(a–b)*     *Figure 60(c)*

**60** (a) See the figure.

(b) The maximum depth is 34.3 feet and the minimum depth is 18 feet. Thus, the amplitude of $D$ is $a = \frac{34.3 - 18}{2} = 8.15$ and it is centered vertically at $d = \frac{34.3 + 18}{2} = 26.15$. The time between maximum depths is approximately 13 hours. Thus, $b = \frac{2\pi}{13}$. The maximum of $D$ occurs at $t = 3$. It follows that $bt + c = \frac{\pi}{2}$ $\Rightarrow$ $\frac{2\pi}{13}(3) + c = \frac{\pi}{2}$ $\Rightarrow$ $c = \frac{\pi}{26}$. Thus, $D(t) = 8.15 \sin\left(\frac{2\pi}{13}t + \frac{\pi}{26}\right) + 26.15$.

(c) Graph $Y_1 = 8.15 \sin\left(\frac{2\pi}{13}x + \frac{\pi}{26}\right) + 26.15$ and $Y_2 = 24$ on $[0, 30]$. $Y_1 < Y_2$ {the depth is less than 24} $\Rightarrow$ $x \in (6.8, 12.2) \cup (19.8, 25.2)$. This corresponds to the time intervals from 6:48 A.M. to 12:12 P.M. and from 7:48 P.M. to 1:12 A.M.

**61** (a) See the figure.

(b) Since the period is 12 months, $b = \frac{2\pi}{12} = \frac{\pi}{6}$. From the table, the maximum number of daylight hours is 18.72 and the minimum is 5.88. Thus, the sine wave is centered vertically at $d = \frac{18.72 + 5.88}{2} = 12.3$ and its amplitude is $a = \frac{18.72 - 5.88}{2} = 6.42$. Since the maximum daylight occurs at $t = 7$ (July), we must have $bt + c = \frac{\pi}{2}$ $\Rightarrow$ $\frac{\pi}{6}(7) + c = \frac{\pi}{2}$ $\Rightarrow$ $c = -\frac{2\pi}{3}$. Thus, $D(t) = a \sin(bt + c) + d = 6.42 \sin\left(\frac{\pi}{6}t - \frac{2\pi}{3}\right) + 12.3$.

[0.5, 24.5, 4] by [0, 20, 4]     [0.5, 24.5, 4] by [0, 20, 4]

*Figure 61*     *Figure 62*

**62** (a) We have $a = \frac{15.02 - 9.32}{2} = 2.85$ and $d = \frac{15.02 + 9.32}{2} = 12.17$. Since the period is 12 months, $b = \frac{2\pi}{12} = \frac{\pi}{6}$. The maximum should occur on June 21 {when $t = 6.7$}. $\frac{\pi}{6}(6.7) + c = \frac{\pi}{2}$ $\Rightarrow$ $c = -\frac{3.7\pi}{6}$.

Thus, $D(t) = 2.85 \sin\left(\frac{\pi}{6}t - \frac{3.7\pi}{6}\right) + 12.17$.

(c) $D(2) \approx 9.96$ hr {true = 10.17} and $D(9) \approx 13.19$ hr {true = 13.08}.

**63** As $x \to 0^-$ or as $x \to 0^+$, $y$ oscillates between $-1$ and $1$ and does not approach a unique value.

[-2, 2, 0.5] by [-1.33, 1.33, 0.5]

**64** As $x \to 0^-$ or as $x \to 0^+$, $y$ appears to approach 0. You should zoom in at least once to obtain a better view of the region near the origin, as shown in the second figure.

$[-2, 2, 0.5]$ by $[-1.33, 1.33, 0.5]$     $[-0.2, 0.2, 0.05]$ by $[-0.13, 0.13, 0.05]$

**65** As $x \to 0^-$ or as $x \to 0^+$, $y$ appears to approach 2.

$[-2, 2, 0.5]$ by $[-0.33, 2.33, 0.5]$     $[-2, 2, 0.5]$ by $[-2.2, 2.2, 0.5]$

Figure 65     Figure 66

**66** As $x \to 0^-$ or as $x \to 0^+$, $y$ appears to approach 0.

**67** From Figure 67(1), we see that there is a horizontal asymptote of $y = 4$.

Figure 67(2) is a graph of the function near the origin.

$[-20, 20, 2]$ by $[-1, 5]$     $[-1, 1, 0.25]$ by $[-0.67, 0.67, 0.25]$     $[-20, 20, 2]$ by $[-2, 2]$

Figure 67(1)     Figure 67(2)     Figure 68

**68** From the graph, we see that there is a horizontal asymptote of $y = 0$.

**69** Graph $Y_1 = \cos 3x$ and $Y_2 = \frac{1}{3}x - \sin x$. From the graph, $Y_1$ intersects $Y_2$ at $x \approx 0.66, 1.39, 2.53$.

Thus, $\cos 3x \ge \frac{1}{3}x - \sin x$ on $[0, 0.66] \cup [1.39, 2.53]$.

$[0, \pi, 1]$ by $[-1.05, 1.05]$     $[0, \pi, 1]$ by $[-1.05, 1.05]$

Figure 69     Figure 70

**70** Graph $Y_1 = \frac{1}{4}\tan\left(\frac{1}{3}x^2\right)$ and $Y_2 = \frac{1}{2}\cos 2x + \frac{1}{20}x^2$. From the graph, $Y_1$ intersects $Y_2$ at $x \approx 0.77$.

$y = \frac{1}{4}\tan\left(\frac{1}{3}x^2\right)$ is undefined when $\frac{1}{3}x^2 = \frac{\pi}{2}$, or $x = \pm\sqrt{\frac{3\pi}{2}} \approx \pm 2.17$.

Thus, $\frac{1}{4}\tan\left(\frac{1}{3}x^2\right) < \frac{1}{2}\cos 2x + \frac{1}{20}x^2$ on $(0, 0.77) \cup \left(\sqrt{3\pi/2}, \pi\right]$.

The figure was run in Connected Mode—run it in Dot Mode to remove the vertical asymptote.

## 5.6 Exercises

**Note:** If $y = a\tan(bx + c)$ or $y = a\cot(bx + c)$, then the periods for the tangent and cotangent graphs are $\pi/|b|$.

If $y = a\sec(bx + c)$ or $y = a\csc(bx + c)$, then the periods for the secant and cosecant graphs are $2\pi/|b|$.

1. $y = 4\tan x$ • Vertically stretch $\tan x$ by a factor of 4. The *x-intercepts* of $\tan x$ and $\cot x$ are not affected by vertically stretching or compressing their graphs. The *vertical asymptotes* of $\tan x$, $\cot x$, $\sec x$, and $\csc x$ are not affected by vertically stretching or compressing their graphs.   ★ $\pi$

Figure 1

Figure 2

2. $y = \frac{1}{4}\tan x$ • Vertically compress $\tan x$ by a factor of 4.   ★ $\pi$

3. $y = \frac{1}{3}\cot x$ • Vertically compress $\cot x$ by a factor of 3.   ★ $\pi$

Figure 3

Figure 4

4. $y = 3\cot x$ • Vertically stretch $\cot x$ by a factor of 3.   ★ $\pi$

5. $y = 2\csc x$ • Vertically stretch $\csc x$ by a factor of 2. Note that there is now a minimum value of 2 at $x = \frac{\pi}{2}$.
The range of this function is $(-\infty, -2] \cup [2, \infty)$, or $|y| \geq 2$.   ★ $2\pi$

Figure 5

Figure 6

6. $y = \frac{1}{2}\csc x$ • Vertically compress $\csc x$ by a factor of 2, $f\left(\frac{\pi}{2}\right) = \frac{1}{2}$   ★ $2\pi$

**7**  $y = \frac{1}{4}\sec x$  •  Vertically compress $\sec x$ by a factor of 4, $f(0) = \frac{1}{4}$                                    ★ $2\pi$

*Figure 7*

*Figure 8*

**8**  $y = 4\sec x$  •  Vertically stretch $\sec x$ by a factor of 4. Note that there is now a minimum value of 4 at $x = 0$. The range of this function is $(-\infty, -4] \cup [4, \infty)$ or $|y| \geq 4$.                                    ★ $2\pi$

**Note:**  The vertical asymptotes of each function are denoted by $VA @ x =$. The work to determine two consecutive vertical asymptotes is shown for each exercise. The periods for the tangent and cotangent graphs are $\pi/|b|$. The periods for the secant and cosecant graphs are $2\pi/|b|$. For the tangent and secant functions, the region from $-\frac{\pi}{2}$ to $\frac{\pi}{2}$ is used. For the cotangent and cosecant functions, the region from 0 to $\pi$ is used.

**9**  $y = \tan\left(x - \frac{\pi}{4}\right)$  •  Shift $\tan x$ right $\frac{\pi}{4}$ units. $-\frac{\pi}{2} < x - \frac{\pi}{4} < \frac{\pi}{2}$ $\Rightarrow$ $-\frac{\pi}{4} < x < \frac{3\pi}{4}$, $VA @ x = -\frac{\pi}{4} + \pi n$. Note that the asymptotes remain $\pi$ units apart.                                    ★ $\pi$

*Figure 9*

*Figure 10*

**10**  $y = \tan\left(x + \frac{\pi}{2}\right)$  •  Shift $\tan x$ left $\frac{\pi}{2}$ units. $-\frac{\pi}{2} < x + \frac{\pi}{2} < \frac{\pi}{2}$ $\Rightarrow$ $-\pi < x < 0$, $VA @ x = \pi n$.                                    ★ $\pi$

**11**  $y = \tan 2x$  •  Horizontally compress $\tan x$ by a factor of 2. $-\frac{\pi}{2} < 2x < \frac{\pi}{2}$ $\Rightarrow$ $-\frac{\pi}{4} < x < \frac{\pi}{4}$, $VA @ x = -\frac{\pi}{4} + \frac{\pi}{2}n$. Note that the asymptotes are only $\frac{\pi}{2}$ units apart.                                    ★ $\frac{\pi}{2}$

*Figure 11*

*Figure 12*

**12**  $y = \tan \frac{1}{2}x$  •  Horizontally stretch $\tan x$ by a factor of 2. $-\frac{\pi}{2} < \frac{1}{2}x < \frac{\pi}{2}$ $\Rightarrow$ $-\pi < x < \pi$, $VA @ x = -\pi + 2\pi n$.                                    ★ $\frac{\pi}{1/2} = 2\pi$

**13** $y = \tan \frac{\pi}{6}x$ • Horizontally stretch $\tan x$ by a factor of $\frac{1}{\pi/6} = \frac{6}{\pi}$. $-\frac{\pi}{2} < \frac{\pi}{6}x < \frac{\pi}{2}$ ⟹ $-3 < x < 3$,

$VA$ @ $x = -3 + 6n$. Note that the asymptotes are 6 units apart. ★ $\frac{\pi}{\pi/6} = 6$

*Figure 13*

*Figure 14*

**14** $y = \tan \frac{\pi}{3}x$ • Horizontally compress $\tan x$ by a factor of $\frac{1}{\pi/3} = \frac{3}{\pi}$ $\{\frac{3}{\pi} < 1\}$. $-\frac{\pi}{2} < \frac{\pi}{3}x < \frac{\pi}{2}$ ⟹ $-\frac{3}{2} < x < \frac{3}{2}$,

$VA$ @ $x = -\frac{3}{2} + 3n$. Note that the asymptotes are 3 units apart. ★ $\frac{\pi}{\pi/3} = 3$

**15** $y = 2\tan\left(2x + \frac{\pi}{2}\right) = 2\tan\left[2\left(x + \frac{\pi}{4}\right)\right]$ • The phase shift is $-\frac{\pi}{4}$, the period is $\frac{\pi}{2}$, and we have a vertical stretching

factor of 2. $-\frac{\pi}{2} < 2x + \frac{\pi}{2} < \frac{\pi}{2}$ ⟹ $-\pi < 2x < 0$ ⟹ $-\frac{\pi}{2} < x < 0$, $VA$ @ $x = \frac{\pi}{2}n$. ★ $\frac{\pi}{2}$

*Figure 15*

*Figure 16*

**16** $y = \frac{1}{3}\tan\left(2x - \frac{\pi}{4}\right) = \frac{1}{3}\tan\left[2\left(x - \frac{\pi}{8}\right)\right]$ •

$-\frac{\pi}{2} < 2x - \frac{\pi}{4} < \frac{\pi}{2}$ ⟹ $-\frac{\pi}{4} < 2x < \frac{3\pi}{4}$ ⟹ $-\frac{\pi}{8} < x < \frac{3\pi}{8}$, $VA$ @ $x = -\frac{\pi}{8} + \frac{\pi}{2}n$. ★ $\frac{\pi}{2}$

**17** $y = -\frac{1}{4}\tan\left(\frac{1}{2}x + \frac{\pi}{3}\right) = -\frac{1}{4}\tan\left[\frac{1}{2}\left(x + \frac{2\pi}{3}\right)\right]$ • Note that the "$-$" in front of the $\frac{1}{4}$ reflects the graph through the

$x$-axis. This changes the appearance of a tangent graph to that of a cotangent graph {increasing to decreasing}.

$-\frac{\pi}{2} < \frac{1}{2}x + \frac{\pi}{3} < \frac{\pi}{2}$ ⟹ $-\frac{5\pi}{6} < \frac{1}{2}x < \frac{\pi}{6}$ ⟹ $-\frac{5\pi}{3} < x < \frac{\pi}{3}$, $VA$ @ $x = -\frac{5\pi}{3} + 2\pi n$. ★ $\frac{\pi}{1/2} = 2\pi$

*Figure 17*

*Figure 18*

**18** $y = -3\tan\left(\frac{1}{3}x - \frac{\pi}{3}\right) = -3\tan\left[\frac{1}{3}(x - \pi)\right]$ •

$-\frac{\pi}{2} < \frac{1}{3}x - \frac{\pi}{3} < \frac{\pi}{2}$ ⟹ $-\frac{\pi}{6} < \frac{1}{3}x < \frac{5\pi}{6}$ ⟹ $-\frac{\pi}{2} < x < \frac{5\pi}{2}$, $VA$ @ $x = -\frac{\pi}{2} + 3\pi n$. ★ $\frac{\pi}{1/3} = 3\pi$

**19** $y = \cot\left(x - \frac{\pi}{2}\right)$  •  $0 < x - \frac{\pi}{2} < \pi$  $\Rightarrow$  $\frac{\pi}{2} < x < \frac{3\pi}{2}$, $VA$ @ $x = \frac{\pi}{2} + \pi n$.          ★ $\pi$

*Figure 19*

*Figure 20*

**20** $y = \cot\left(x + \frac{\pi}{4}\right)$  •  $0 < x + \frac{\pi}{4} < \pi$  $\Rightarrow$  $-\frac{\pi}{4} < x < \frac{3\pi}{4}$, $VA$ @ $x = -\frac{\pi}{4} + \pi n$.          ★ $\pi$

**21** $y = \cot\frac{1}{2}x$  •  $0 < \frac{1}{2}x < \pi$  $\Rightarrow$  $0 < x < 2\pi$, $VA$ @ $x = 2\pi n$.          ★ $\frac{\pi}{1/2} = 2\pi$

*Figure 21*

*Figure 22*

**22** $y = \cot 2x$  •  $0 < 2x < \pi$  $\Rightarrow$  $0 < x < \frac{\pi}{2}$, $VA$ @ $x = \frac{\pi}{2}n$.          ★ $\frac{\pi}{2}$

**23** $y = \cot\frac{\pi}{2}x$  •  $0 < \frac{\pi}{2}x < \pi$  $\Rightarrow$  $0 < x < 2$, $VA$ @ $x = 2n$.          ★ $\frac{\pi}{\pi/2} = 2$

*Figure 23*

*Figure 24*

**24** $y = \cot\frac{\pi}{4}x$  •  $0 < \frac{\pi}{4}x < \pi$  $\Rightarrow$  $0 < x < 4$, $VA$ @ $x = 4n$.          ★ $\frac{\pi}{\pi/4} = 4$

25 $y = 2\cot\left(2x + \frac{\pi}{2}\right) = 2\cot\left[2\left(x + \frac{\pi}{4}\right)\right]$ •

$0 < 2x + \frac{\pi}{2} < \pi \;\Rightarrow\; -\frac{\pi}{2} < 2x < \frac{\pi}{2} \;\Rightarrow\; -\frac{\pi}{4} < x < \frac{\pi}{4},\, VA\ @\ x = -\frac{\pi}{4} + \frac{\pi}{2}n.$ ★ $\frac{\pi}{2}$

Figure 25

Figure 26

26 $y = -\frac{1}{3}\cot(3x - \pi) = -\frac{1}{3}\cot\left[3\left(x - \frac{\pi}{3}\right)\right]$ •

$0 < 3x - \pi < \pi \;\Rightarrow\; \pi < 3x < 2\pi \;\Rightarrow\; \frac{\pi}{3} < x < \frac{2\pi}{3},\, VA\ @\ x = \frac{\pi}{3} + \frac{\pi}{3}n.$ ★ $\frac{\pi}{3}$

27 $y = -\frac{1}{2}\cot\left(\frac{1}{2}x + \frac{\pi}{4}\right) = -\frac{1}{2}\cot\left[\frac{1}{2}\left(x + \frac{\pi}{2}\right)\right]$ •

$0 < \frac{1}{2}x + \frac{\pi}{4} < \pi \;\Rightarrow\; -\frac{\pi}{4} < \frac{1}{2}x < \frac{3\pi}{4} \;\Rightarrow\; -\frac{\pi}{2} < x < \frac{3\pi}{2},\, VA\ @\ x = -\frac{\pi}{2} + 2\pi n.$ ★ $\frac{\pi}{1/2} = 2\pi$

Figure 27

Figure 28

28 $y = 4\cot\left(\frac{1}{3}x - \frac{\pi}{6}\right) = 4\cot\left[\frac{1}{3}\left(x - \frac{\pi}{2}\right)\right]$ •

$0 < \frac{1}{3}x - \frac{\pi}{6} < \pi \;\Rightarrow\; \frac{\pi}{6} < \frac{1}{3}x < \frac{7\pi}{6} \;\Rightarrow\; \frac{\pi}{2} < x < \frac{7\pi}{2},\, VA\ @\ x = \frac{\pi}{2} + 3\pi n.$ ★ $\frac{\pi}{1/3} = 3\pi$

29 $y = \sec\left(x - \frac{\pi}{2}\right)$ • $-\frac{\pi}{2} < x - \frac{\pi}{2} < \frac{\pi}{2} \;\Rightarrow\; 0 < x < \pi,\, VA\ @\ x = \pi n.$

Note that this is the same graph as the graph of $y = \csc x$. ★ $2\pi$

Figure 29

Figure 30

30 $y = \sec\left(x - \frac{3\pi}{4}\right)$ • $-\frac{\pi}{2} < x - \frac{3\pi}{4} < \frac{\pi}{2} \;\Rightarrow\; \frac{\pi}{4} < x < \frac{5\pi}{4},\, VA\ @\ x = \frac{\pi}{4} + \pi n.$ ★ $2\pi$

**31** $y = \sec 2x$ • $-\frac{\pi}{2} < 2x < \frac{\pi}{2}$ $\Rightarrow$ $-\frac{\pi}{4} < x < \frac{\pi}{4}$, VA @ $x = -\frac{\pi}{4} + \frac{\pi}{2}n$.

Note that the asymptotes move closer together by a factor of 2.    ★ $\pi$

*Figure 31*

*Figure 32*

**32** $y = \sec \frac{1}{2}x$ • $-\frac{\pi}{2} < \frac{1}{2}x < \frac{\pi}{2}$ $\Rightarrow$ $-\pi < x < \pi$, VA @ $x = -\pi + 2\pi n$.    ★ $4\pi$

**33** $y = \sec \frac{\pi}{3}x$ • $-\frac{\pi}{2} < \frac{\pi}{3}x < \frac{\pi}{2}$ $\Rightarrow$ $-\frac{3}{2} < x < \frac{3}{2}$, VA @ $x = -\frac{3}{2} + 3n$.    ★ $\frac{2\pi}{\pi/3} = 6$

*Figure 33*

*Figure 34*

**34** $y = \sec \frac{2\pi}{3}x$ • $-\frac{\pi}{2} < \frac{2\pi}{3}x < \frac{\pi}{2}$ $\Rightarrow$ $-\frac{3}{4} < x < \frac{3}{4}$, VA @ $x = -\frac{3}{4} + \frac{3}{2}n$.    ★ $\frac{2\pi}{2\pi/3} = 3$

**35** $y = 2\sec\left(2x - \frac{\pi}{2}\right) = 2\sec\left[2\left(x - \frac{\pi}{4}\right)\right]$ •

$-\frac{\pi}{2} < 2x - \frac{\pi}{2} < \frac{\pi}{2}$ $\Rightarrow$ $0 < 2x < \pi$ $\Rightarrow$ $0 < x < \frac{\pi}{2}$, VA @ $x = \frac{\pi}{2}n$.    ★ $\frac{2\pi}{2} = \pi$

*Figure 35*

*Figure 36*

**36** $y = \frac{1}{2}\sec\left(2x - \frac{\pi}{2}\right) = \frac{1}{2}\sec\left[2\left(x - \frac{\pi}{4}\right)\right]$ •

$-\frac{\pi}{2} < 2x - \frac{\pi}{2} < \frac{\pi}{2}$ $\Rightarrow$ $0 < 2x < \pi$ $\Rightarrow$ $0 < x < \frac{\pi}{2}$, VA @ $x = \frac{\pi}{2}n$.    ★ $\frac{2\pi}{2} = \pi$

**37** $y = -\frac{1}{3}\sec\left(\frac{1}{2}x + \frac{\pi}{4}\right) = -\frac{1}{3}\sec\left[\frac{1}{2}\left(x + \frac{\pi}{2}\right)\right]$ •

$-\frac{\pi}{2} < \frac{1}{2}x + \frac{\pi}{4} < \frac{\pi}{2} \Rightarrow -\frac{3\pi}{4} < \frac{1}{2}x < \frac{\pi}{4} \Rightarrow -\frac{3\pi}{2} < x < \frac{\pi}{2}, \text{VA @ } x = -\frac{3\pi}{2} + 2\pi n.$  ★ $\frac{2\pi}{1/2} = 4\pi$

*Figure 37*

*Figure 38*

**38** $y = -3\sec\left(\frac{1}{3}x + \frac{\pi}{3}\right) = -3\sec\left[\frac{1}{3}\left(x + \pi\right)\right]$ •

$-\frac{\pi}{2} < \frac{1}{3}x + \frac{\pi}{3} < \frac{\pi}{2} \Rightarrow -\frac{5\pi}{6} < \frac{1}{3}x < \frac{\pi}{6} \Rightarrow -\frac{5\pi}{2} < x < \frac{\pi}{2}, \text{VA @ } x = -\frac{5\pi}{2} + 3\pi n.$  ★ $\frac{2\pi}{1/3} = 6\pi$

**39** $y = \csc\left(x - \frac{\pi}{2}\right)$ • $0 < x - \frac{\pi}{2} < \pi \Rightarrow \frac{\pi}{2} < x < \frac{3\pi}{2}, \text{VA @ } x = \frac{\pi}{2} + \pi n.$  ★ $2\pi$

*Figure 39*

*Figure 40*

**40** $y = \csc\left(x + \frac{3\pi}{4}\right)$ • $0 < x + \frac{3\pi}{4} < \pi \Rightarrow -\frac{3\pi}{4} < x < \frac{\pi}{4}, \text{VA @ } x = -\frac{3\pi}{4} + \pi n.$  ★ $2\pi$

**41** $y = \csc\frac{1}{2}x$ • $0 < \frac{1}{2}x < \pi \Rightarrow 0 < x < 2\pi, \text{VA @ } x = 2\pi n.$  ★ $\frac{2\pi}{1/2} = 4\pi$

*Figure 41*

*Figure 42*

**42** $y = \csc 2x$ • $0 < 2x < \pi \Rightarrow 0 < x < \frac{\pi}{2}, \text{VA @ } x = \frac{\pi}{2}n.$  ★ $\frac{2\pi}{2} = \pi$

**43** $y = \csc \pi x$ • $0 < \pi x < \pi$ ⇒ $0 < x < 1$, VA @ $x = 1n = n$.　　★ $\frac{2\pi}{\pi} = 2$

*Figure 43*

*Figure 44*

**44** $y = \csc \frac{\pi}{4}x$ • $0 < \frac{\pi}{4}x < \pi$ ⇒ $0 < x < 4\pi$, VA @ $x = 4\pi n$.　　★ $\frac{2\pi}{\pi/4} = 8$

**45** $y = 2\csc\left(2x + \frac{\pi}{2}\right) = 2\csc\left[2\left(x + \frac{\pi}{4}\right)\right]$ •

$0 < 2x + \frac{\pi}{2} < \pi$ ⇒ $-\frac{\pi}{2} < 2x < \frac{\pi}{2}$ ⇒ $-\frac{\pi}{4} < x < \frac{\pi}{4}$, VA @ $x = -\frac{\pi}{4} + \frac{\pi}{2}n$.　　★ $\frac{2\pi}{2} = \pi$

*Figure 45*

*Figure 46*

**46** $y = -\frac{1}{2}\csc(2x - \pi) = -\frac{1}{2}\csc\left[2\left(x - \frac{\pi}{2}\right)\right]$ •

$0 < 2x - \pi < \pi$ ⇒ $\pi < 2x < 2\pi$ ⇒ $\frac{\pi}{2} < x < \pi$, VA @ $x = \frac{\pi}{2}n$.　　★ $\frac{2\pi}{2} = \pi$

**47** $y = -\frac{1}{4}\csc\left(\frac{1}{2}x + \frac{\pi}{2}\right) = -\frac{1}{4}\csc\left[\frac{1}{2}(x + \pi)\right]$ •

$0 < \frac{1}{2}x + \frac{\pi}{2} < \pi$ ⇒ $-\frac{\pi}{2} < \frac{1}{2}x < \frac{\pi}{2}$ ⇒ $-\pi < x < \pi$, VA @ $x = -\pi + 2\pi n$.　　★ $\frac{2\pi}{1/2} = 4\pi$

*Figure 47*

*Figure 48*

**48** $y = 4\csc\left(\frac{1}{2}x - \frac{\pi}{4}\right) = 4\csc\left[\frac{1}{2}\left(x - \frac{\pi}{2}\right)\right]$ •

$0 < \frac{1}{2}x - \frac{\pi}{4} < \pi$ ⇒ $\frac{\pi}{4} < \frac{1}{2}x < \frac{5\pi}{4}$ ⇒ $\frac{\pi}{2} < x < \frac{5\pi}{2}$, VA @ $x = \frac{\pi}{2} + 2\pi n$.　　★ $\frac{2\pi}{1/2} = 4\pi$

**49** One cycle of $y = f(x) = \cot(2x - \pi)$ can be found by solving $0 < 2x - \pi < \pi \Rightarrow \pi < 2x < 2\pi \Rightarrow$ $\frac{\pi}{2} < x < \pi$. The equations of two successive vertical asymptotes of the graph of $y = \cot(2x - \pi)$ are $x = \frac{\pi}{2}$ and $x = \pi$. Other answers are possible.

**50** One cycle of $y = f(x) = \tan(3x + 1)$ can be found by solving $-\frac{\pi}{2} < 3x + 1 < \frac{\pi}{2} \Rightarrow$ $-1 - \frac{\pi}{2} < 3x < -1 + \frac{\pi}{2} \Rightarrow \frac{1}{3}(-1 - \frac{\pi}{2}) < x < \frac{1}{3}(-1 + \frac{\pi}{2})$. The equations of two successive vertical asymptotes of the graph of $y = \tan(3x + 1)$ are $x = \frac{1}{3}(-1 - \frac{\pi}{2})$ and $x = \frac{1}{3}(-1 + \frac{\pi}{2})$. Other answers are possible.

**51** One $x$-intercept of $y = \tan x$ is 0  Solving $4x - 3 = 0$ gives us $4x = 3 \Rightarrow x = \frac{3}{4}$. So $\frac{3}{4}$ is an $x$-intercept of the graph of $y = \tan(4x - 3)$ and there are infinitely many others. Your answer will be of the form $\frac{3}{4} + \frac{\pi}{4}n$, where $n$ is an integer, depending on your choice for the $x$-intercept of $y = \tan x$. If you're looking at a graph of $f$, note that 0 is *not* an $x$-intercept, but $\frac{3}{4} - \frac{\pi}{4}$ is.

**52** One $x$-intercept of $y = \cot x$ is $\frac{\pi}{2}$. Solving $3x + \frac{\pi}{4} = \frac{\pi}{2}$ gives us $3x = \frac{\pi}{4} \Rightarrow x = \frac{\pi}{12}$. So $\frac{\pi}{12}$ is an $x$-intercept of the graph of $y = \cot(3x + \frac{\pi}{4})$ and there are infinitely many others. Your answer will be of the form $\frac{\pi}{12} + \frac{\pi}{3}n$, where $n$ is an integer, depending on your choice for the $x$-intercept of $y = \cot x$.

**53** For $y = \csc x$, the upper branch on the interval $(0, \pi)$ has its lowest point of $(\frac{\pi}{2}, 1)$. Solving $\frac{1}{2}x - \frac{\pi}{2} = \frac{\pi}{2}$ gives us $x = 2\pi$. Since $y = 3\csc(\frac{1}{2}x - \frac{\pi}{2})$ has a 3 multiplier, the lowest point on an upper branch is $(2\pi, 3)$. Your answer will be of the form $(2\pi + 4\pi n, 3) \left\{ \frac{2\pi}{1/2} = 4\pi \right\}$, where $n$ is an integer, depending on your choice for the lowest point on an upper branch of $y = \csc x$.

**54** For $y = \sec x$, the upper branch on the interval $(-\frac{\pi}{2}, \frac{\pi}{2})$ has its lowest point of $(0, 1)$. Solving $4x + \frac{\pi}{6} = 0$ gives us $x = -\frac{\pi}{24}$. Since $y = 4\sec(4x + \frac{\pi}{6})$ has a 4 multiplier, the lowest point on an upper branch is $(-\frac{\pi}{24}, 4)$. Your answer will be of the form $(-\frac{\pi}{24} + \frac{\pi}{2}n, 4) \left\{ \frac{2\pi}{4} = \frac{\pi}{2} \right\}$, where $n$ is an integer, depending on your choice for the lowest point on an upper branch of $y = \sec x$.

**55** $f(x) = 3\sec(2x + 5) + 1$  •  The range of $y = \sec x$ is $(-\infty, -1] \cup [1, \infty)$. Multiplying by 3 changes the range to $(-\infty, -3] \cup [3, \infty)$, and adding 1 results in a final range of $(-\infty, -2] \cup [4, \infty)$.

**56** $f(x) = 4\csc(2x - \pi) - 3$  •  The range of $y = \csc x$ is $(-\infty, -1] \cup [1, \infty)$. Multiplying by 4 changes the range to $(-\infty, -4] \cup [4, \infty)$, and subtracting 3 results in a final range of $(-\infty, -7] \cup [1, \infty)$.

**57** Reflecting the graph of $y = \cot x$ about the $x$-axis, which is $y = -\cot x$, gives us the graph of $y = \tan(x + \frac{\pi}{2})$. If we shift this graph to the left (or right), we will obtain the graph of $y = \tan x$.

Thus, one equation is $y = -\cot(x + \frac{\pi}{2})$.

**58** Shifting the graph of $y = \csc x$ to the left $\frac{\pi}{2}$ units gives us the graph of $y = \sec x$.

Thus, one equation is $y = \csc(x + \frac{\pi}{2})$.

**59** $y = |\sin x|$  •  Reflect the negative values of $y = \sin x$ through the $x$-axis. In general, when sketching the graph of $y = |f(x)|$, reflect the negative values of $f(x)$ through the $x$-axis. The absolute value does not affect the nonnegative values.

*Figure 59*

*Figure 60*

**60** $y = |\cos x|$  •  Reflect the negative values of $y = \cos x$ through the $x$-axis.

**61** $y = |\sin x| + 2$  •  Shift $y = |\sin x|$ up 2 units.

*Figure 61*

*Figure 62*

**62** $y = |\cos x| - 3$  •  Shift $y = |\cos x|$ down 3 units.

**63** $y = -|\cos x| + 1$  •  Similar to Exercise 59, we first reflect the negative values of $y = \cos x$ through the $x$-axis. The "$-$" in front of $|\cos x|$ has the effect of reflecting $y = |\cos x|$ through the $x$-axis. Finally, we shift that graph 1 unit up to obtain the graph of $y = -|\cos x| + 1$.

*Figure 63*

*Figure 64*

**64** $y = -|\sin x| - 2$  •  Reflect the negative values of $y = \sin x$ through the $x$-axis. Reflect that graph through the $x$-axis and then shift that graph down 2 units.

**65** $y = x + \cos x$ • The value of $\cos x$ is between $-1$ and $1$—adding this relatively small amount to the value of $x$ has the effect of oscillating the graph about the line $y = x$.

*Figure 65*

*Figure 66*

**66** $y = x - \sin x$ • The value of $\sin x$ is between $-1$ and $1$—subtracting this relatively small amount to the value of $x$ has the effect of oscillating the graph about the line $y = x$.

**67** $y = 2^{-x}\cos x$ • This graph is similar to the graph in Example 8. It oscillates between the graphs of $y = 2^{-x}$ and $y = -2^{-x}$.

*Figure 67*

*Figure 68*

**68** $y = e^x \sin x$ • This graph oscillates between the graphs of $y = e^x$ and $y = -e^x$.

**69** $y = |x| \sin x$ • The graph will coincide with the graph of $y = |x|$ if $\sin x = 1$—that is, if $x = \frac{\pi}{2} + 2\pi n$.
The graph will coincide with the graph of $y = -|x|$ if $\sin x = -1$—that is, if $x = \frac{3\pi}{2} + 2\pi n$.

*Figure 69*

*Figure 70*

**70** $y = |x| \cos x$ • The graph will coincide with the graph of $y = |x|$ if $\cos x = 1$—that is, if $x = 2\pi n$.
The graph will coincide with the graph of $y = -|x|$ if $\cos x = -1$—that is, if $x = \pi + 2\pi n$.

**71** $f(x) = \tan(0.5x)$; $g(x) = \tan[0.5(x + \pi/2)]$ •

Since $g(x) = f(x + \pi/2)$, the graph of $g$ can be obtained by shifting the graph of $f$ left a distance of $\frac{\pi}{2}$.

$[-2\pi, 2\pi, \pi/2]$ by $[-4, 4]$

*Figure 71*

$[-2\pi, 2\pi, \pi/2]$ by $[-4, 4]$

*Figure 72*

**72** $f(x) = 0.5 \csc(0.5x)$; $g(x) = 0.5 \csc(0.5x) - 2$ •

Since $g(x) = f(x) - 2$, the graph of $g$ can be obtained by shifting the graph of $f$ downward a distance of 2.

**73** $f(x) = 0.5 \sec 0.5x$; $g(x) = 0.5 \sec[0.5(x - \pi/2)] - 1$ • Since $g(x) = f(x - \pi/2) - 1$, the graph of $g$ can be obtained by shifting the graph of $f$ horizontally to the right a distance of $\frac{\pi}{2}$ and vertically downward a distance of 1.

$[-2\pi, 2\pi, \pi/2]$ by $[-4, 4]$

*Figure 73*

$[-2\pi, 2\pi, \pi/2]$ by $[-4, 4]$

*Figure 74*

**74** $f(x) = \tan x - 1$; $g(x) = -\tan x + 1$ •

Since $g(x) = -f(x)$, the graph of $g$ can be obtained by reflecting the graph of $f$ through the $x$–axis.

**75** $f(x) = 3 \cos 2x$; $g(x) = |3 \cos 2x| - 1$ • Since $g(x) = |f(x)| - 1$, the graph of $g$ can be obtained from the graph of $f$ by reflecting it through the $x$–axis when $f(x) < 0$ and then shifting that graph downward a distance of 1.

$[-2\pi, 2\pi, \pi/2]$ by $[-4, 4]$

*Figure 75*

$[-2\pi, 2\pi, \pi/2]$ by $[-4, 4]$

*Figure 76*

**76** $f(x) = 1.2^{-x} \cos x$; $g(x) = 1.2^x \cos x$ • Since $g(x) = 1.2^x \cos x = 1.2^{-(-x)} \cos(-x) = f(-x)$, the graph of $g$ can be obtained from the graph of $f$ by reflecting the graph of $f$ through the $y$–axis.

**77** The damping factor of $y = e^{-x/4} \sin 4x$ is $e^{-x/4}$.

$[-2\pi, 2\pi, \pi/2]$ by $[-4.19, 4.19]$

$[-2\pi, 2\pi, \pi/2]$ by $[-4.19, 4.19]$

*Figure 77*                                    *Figure 78*

**78** The damping factor of $y = 3^{-x/5} \cos 2x$ is $3^{-x/5}$.

**79** From the graph, we see that the maximum occurs at the approximate coordinates $(-2.76, 3.09)$,

and the minimum occurs at the approximate coordinates $(1.23, -3.68)$.

$[-\pi, \pi, \pi/4]$ by $[-4, 4]$

*Figure 79*

$[-\pi, \pi, \pi/4]$ by $[-4, 4]$

*Figure 80*

**80** From the graph, we see that the maximum occurs at the approximate coordinates $(2.40, 2.68)$,

and the minimum occurs at the approximate coordinates $(-2.40, -2.68)$.

**81** From the graph, we see that $f$ is increasing and one-to-one between $a \approx -0.70$ and $b \approx 0.12$.

Thus, the interval is approximately $[-0.70, 0.12]$.

$[-2, 2]$ by $[-1.33, 1.33]$

*Figure 81*

$[-3, 3]$ by $[-1, 3]$

*Figure 82*

**82** From the graph, we see that $f$ is increasing and one-to-one between $a \approx -1.70$ and $b \approx 0.70$.

Thus, the interval is approximately $[-1.70, 0.70]$.

**83** Graph $Y_1 = \cos(2x - 1) + \sin 3x$ and $Y_2 = \sin \frac{1}{3}x + \cos x$.

From the graph, $Y_1$ intersects $Y_2$ at $x \approx -1.31, 0.11, 0.95, 2.39$.

Thus, $\cos(2x - 1) + \sin 3x \geq \sin \frac{1}{3}x + \cos x$ on $[-\pi, -1.31] \cup [0.11, 0.95] \cup [2.39, \pi]$.

$[-\pi, \pi, \pi/4]$ by $[-2.09, 2.09]$

*Figure 83*

$[-\pi, \pi, \pi/4]$ by $[-2.09, 2.09]$

*Figure 84*

**84** Graph $Y_1 = \frac{1}{2} \cos 2x + 2 \cos(x - 2)$ and $Y_2 = 2 \cos(1.5x + 1) + \sin(x - 1)$.

From the graph, $Y_1$ intersects $Y_2$ at $x \approx -2.16, 0.15, 2.76$.

Thus, $\frac{1}{2} \cos 2x + 2 \cos(x - 2) < 2 \cos(1.5x + 1) + \sin(x - 1)$ on $(-2.16, 0.15) \cup (2.76, \pi]$.

**85** (a) $\theta = 0 \Rightarrow I = \frac{1}{2}I_0[1 + \cos(\pi \sin 0)] = \frac{1}{2}I_0[1 + \cos(0)] = \frac{1}{2}I_0(2) = I_0$.

(b) $\theta = \pi/3 \Rightarrow I = \frac{1}{2}I_0[1 + \cos(\pi \sin(\pi/3))] \approx 0.044I_0$.

(c) $\theta = \pi/7 \Rightarrow I = \frac{1}{2}I_0[1 + \cos(\pi \sin(\pi/7))] \approx 0.603I_0$.

**86** (a) The intensity $I = \frac{1}{2}I_0[1 + \cos(\pi \sin\theta)]$ will be maximum when $\cos(\pi\sin\theta) = 1 \Rightarrow \pi\sin\theta = 0 \Rightarrow$ $\sin\theta = 0 \Rightarrow \theta = 0, \pi$. Thus, the intensity is maximum in the east and west directions. The intensity $I$ will be minimum when $\cos(\pi\sin\theta) = -1 \Rightarrow \pi\sin\theta = \pm\pi \Rightarrow \sin\theta = \pm 1 \Rightarrow \theta = \frac{\pi}{2}, \frac{3\pi}{2}$. There is no signal in the north and south directions so that it wouldn't interfere with a radio station at the same wavelength to the north or south.

$[0, 2\pi, \pi/2]$ by $[0, 1.5, 0.5]$

(b) Graph $Y_1 = \frac{1}{2}[1 + \cos(\pi\sin\theta)]$ and $Y_2 = \frac{1}{3}$.

There are four points of intersection on $[0, 2\pi)$.

They occur at $\theta \approx 0.654, 2.488, 3.795, 5.629$.

**87** (a) The damping factor of $S = A_0 e^{-\alpha z}\sin(kt - \alpha z)$ is $A_0 e^{-\alpha z}$.

(b) The phase shift at depth $z_0$ can be found by solving the equation $kt - \alpha z_0 = 0$ for $t$.

Doing so gives us $kt = \alpha z_0$, and hence, $t = \dfrac{\alpha}{k} z_0$.

(c) At the surface, $z = 0$. Hence, $S = A_0 \sin kt$ and the amplitude at the surface is $A_0$.

$\text{Amplitude}_{\text{wave}} = \frac{1}{2}\text{Amplitude}_{\text{surface}} \Rightarrow A_0 e^{-\alpha z} = \frac{1}{2}A_0 \Rightarrow e^{-\alpha z} = \frac{1}{2} \Rightarrow -\alpha z = \ln\frac{1}{2} \Rightarrow$

$$z = \frac{-\ln 2}{-\alpha} = \frac{\ln 2}{\alpha}.$$

## 5.7 Exercises

**Note:** The missing values are found in terms of the given values. We could also use proportions to find the remaining parts.

**1** Since $\alpha$ is given and $\gamma = 90°$, we can easily find $\beta$. $\beta = 90° - \alpha = 90° - 30° = 60°$.

To find $a$, we will relate it to the given parts, $\alpha$ and $b$, using the tangent function.

$\tan\alpha = \dfrac{a}{b} \Rightarrow a = b\tan\alpha = 20\tan 30° = 20\left(\dfrac{1}{3}\sqrt{3}\right) = \dfrac{20}{3}\sqrt{3}$.

$\sec\alpha = \dfrac{c}{b} \Rightarrow c = b\sec\alpha = 20\sec 30° = 20\left(\dfrac{2}{3}\sqrt{3}\right) = \dfrac{40}{3}\sqrt{3}$.

**2** $\alpha = 90° - \beta = 45°$. $\cot\beta = \dfrac{a}{b} \Rightarrow a = b\cot\beta = 35(1) = 35$.

$\csc\beta = \dfrac{c}{b} \Rightarrow c = b\csc\beta = 35\left(\sqrt{2}\right) = 35\sqrt{2}$.

**3** $\alpha = 90° - \beta = 90° - 45° = 45°$.

$\cos\beta = \dfrac{a}{c} \Rightarrow a = c\cos\beta = 30\cos 45° = 30\left(\dfrac{1}{2}\sqrt{2}\right) = 15\sqrt{2}$. $b = a$ in a 45°-45°-90° triangle.

**4** $\beta = 90° - \alpha = 30°$.

$\sin\alpha = \dfrac{a}{c} \Rightarrow a = c\sin\alpha = 6\left(\dfrac{1}{2}\sqrt{3}\right) = 3\sqrt{3}$. $\cos\alpha = \dfrac{b}{c} \Rightarrow b = c\cos\alpha = 6\left(\dfrac{1}{2}\right) = 3$.

**5** $\tan\alpha = \dfrac{a}{b} = \dfrac{5}{5} = 1 \Rightarrow \alpha = 45°$. $\beta = 90° - \alpha = 90° - 45° = 45°$.

Using the Pythagorean theorem, $a^2 + b^2 = c^2 \Rightarrow c = \sqrt{a^2 + b^2} = \sqrt{25 + 25} = \sqrt{50} = 5\sqrt{2}$.

**6** $\sin\alpha = \dfrac{a}{c} = \dfrac{4\sqrt{3}}{8} = \dfrac{\sqrt{3}}{2} \Rightarrow \alpha = 60°$. $\beta = 90° - \alpha = 30°$. $b = \sqrt{c^2 - a^2} = \sqrt{64 - 48} = \sqrt{16} = 4$.

**7** $\cos\alpha = \dfrac{b}{c} = \dfrac{5\sqrt{3}}{10\sqrt{3}} = \dfrac{1}{2} \;\Rightarrow\; \alpha = 60°.\;\; \beta = 90° - \alpha = 90° - 60° = 30°.$

$$a = \sqrt{c^2 - b^2} = \sqrt{300 - 75} = \sqrt{225} = 15.$$

**8** $\cos\alpha = \dfrac{b}{c} = \dfrac{7\sqrt{2}}{14} = \dfrac{\sqrt{2}}{2} \;\Rightarrow\; \alpha = 45°.\;\; \beta = 90° - \alpha = 45°.\;\; a = \sqrt{c^2 - b^2} = \sqrt{196 - 98} = \sqrt{98} = 7\sqrt{2}.$

**9** $\beta = 90° - \alpha = 90° - 37° = 53°.\;\; \tan\alpha = \dfrac{a}{b} \;\Rightarrow\; a = b\tan\alpha = 24\tan 37° \approx 18.$

$$\sec\alpha = \dfrac{c}{b} \;\Rightarrow\; c = b\sec\alpha = 24\sec 37° \approx 30.$$

**10** $\alpha = 90° - \beta = 25°40'.\;\; \tan\beta = \dfrac{b}{a} \;\Rightarrow\; b = a\tan\beta = 20.1\tan 64°20' \approx 41.8.$

$$\sec\beta = \dfrac{c}{a} \;\Rightarrow\; c = a\sec\beta = 20.1\sec 64°20' \approx 46.4.$$

**11** $\alpha = 90° - \beta = 90° - 71°51' = 18°9'.\;\; \cot\beta = \dfrac{a}{b} \;\Rightarrow\; a = b\cot\beta = 240.0\cot 71°51' \approx 78.7.$

$$\csc\beta = \dfrac{c}{b} \;\Rightarrow\; c = b\csc\beta = 240.0\csc 71°51' \approx 252.6.$$

**12** $\beta = 90° - \alpha = 58°50'.\;\; \cot\alpha = \dfrac{b}{a} \;\Rightarrow\; b = a\cot\alpha = 510\cot 31°10' \approx 843.$

$$\csc\alpha = \dfrac{c}{a} \;\Rightarrow\; c = a\csc\alpha = 510\csc 31°10' \approx 985.$$

**13** $\tan\alpha = \dfrac{a}{b} = \dfrac{25}{45} \;\Rightarrow\; \alpha = \tan^{-1}\dfrac{25}{45} \approx 29°.\;\; \beta = 90° - \alpha \approx 90° - 29° = 61°.$

$$c = \sqrt{a^2 + b^2} = \sqrt{25^2 + 45^2} = \sqrt{625 + 2025} = \sqrt{2650} \approx 51.$$

**14** $\tan\alpha = \dfrac{a}{b} = \dfrac{31}{9.0} \;\Rightarrow\; \alpha \approx 74°.\;\; \beta = 90° - \alpha \approx 16°.\;\; c = \sqrt{a^2 + b^2} = \sqrt{961 + 81} = \sqrt{1042} \approx 32.$

**15** $\cos\alpha = \dfrac{b}{c} = \dfrac{2.1}{5.8} \;\Rightarrow\; \alpha = \cos^{-1}\dfrac{21}{58} \approx 69°.\;\; \beta = 90° - \alpha \approx 90° - 69° = 21°.$

$$a = \sqrt{c^2 - b^2} = \sqrt{(5.8)^2 - (2.1)^2} = \sqrt{33.64 - 4.41} = \sqrt{29.23} \approx 5.4.$$

**16** $\sin\alpha = \dfrac{a}{c} = \dfrac{0.42}{0.68} \;\Rightarrow\; \alpha \approx 38°.\;\; \beta = 90° - \alpha \approx 52°.\;\; b = \sqrt{c^2 - a^2} = \sqrt{0.4624 - 0.1764} = \sqrt{0.286} \approx 0.53.$

**Note:** Refer to Figures 1 and 2 in the text for the labeling of the sides and angles.

**17** We need to find a relationship involving $b$, $c$, and $\alpha$. We want angle $\alpha$ with its adjacent side $b$ and hypotenuse $c$. The cosine or secant are the functions of $\alpha$ that involve $b$ and $c$. We choose the cosine since it is easier to solve for $b$ {$b$ is in the numerator}. $\cos\alpha = \dfrac{b}{c} \;\Rightarrow\; b = c\cos\alpha.$

**18** $\sin\beta = \dfrac{b}{c} \;\Rightarrow\; b = c\sin\beta$

**19** We want angle $\beta$ with its adjacent side $a$ and opposite side $b$. The tangent or cotangent are the functions of $\beta$ that involve $a$ and $b$. $\cot\beta = \dfrac{a}{b} \;\Rightarrow\; a = b\cot\beta.$

**20** $\tan\alpha = \dfrac{a}{b} \;\Rightarrow\; a = b\tan\alpha$

**21** We want angle $\alpha$ with its opposite side $a$ and hypotenuse $c$. The sine or cosecant are the functions of $\alpha$ that involve $a$ and $c$. $\csc\alpha = \dfrac{c}{a} \;\Rightarrow\; c = a\csc\alpha.$

**22** $\sec\beta = \dfrac{c}{a} \;\Rightarrow\; c = a\sec\beta$

**23** $a^2 + b^2 = c^2 \;\Rightarrow\; b^2 = c^2 - a^2 \;\Rightarrow\; b = \sqrt{c^2 - a^2}$

**24** $a^2 + b^2 = c^2 \Rightarrow c = \sqrt{a^2 + b^2}$

**25** Let $h$ denote the height of the kite and $x = h - 4$.

$$\sin 60° = \frac{x}{500} \Rightarrow x = 500 \sin 60° = 500\left(\tfrac{1}{2}\sqrt{3}\right) = 250\sqrt{3}. \quad h = x + 4 = 250\sqrt{3} + 4 \approx 437 \text{ ft.}$$

**26** $\cot 68° = \dfrac{x}{15} \Rightarrow x = 15 \cot 68° \approx 6.1 \text{ m.}$

*Figure 26*

*Figure 27*

**27** $\sin 10° = \dfrac{5000}{x} \Rightarrow x = \dfrac{5000}{\sin 10°} \Rightarrow x = 5000 \csc 10° \approx 28{,}793.85, \text{ or } 28{,}800 \text{ ft.}$

**28** Let $L$ denote the length of the wire. $\cos 58°20' = \dfrac{40}{L} \Rightarrow L = 40 \sec 58°20' \approx 76.2 \text{ m}$

**29** $\tan \angle PRQ = \dfrac{d}{50.0} \Rightarrow \tan 72°40' = \dfrac{d}{50} \Rightarrow d = 50 \tan 72°40' \approx 160 \text{ m.}$

**30** (a) $\tan \theta = \dfrac{h}{d} \Rightarrow h = d \tan \theta$    (b) $h = 1000 \tan 59° \approx 1664 \text{ m}$

**31** The 10,000 feet would represent the hypotenuse in a triangle depicting this information. Let $h$ denote the altitude.

$$\sin 75° = \frac{h}{10{,}000} \Rightarrow h = 10{,}000 \sin 75° \Rightarrow h \approx 9659 \text{ ft.}$$

**32** Let $d$ denote the distance the plane travels. $\sin 10° = 15{,}000/d \Rightarrow d = 15{,}000 \csc 10°.$

$$\text{At 250 ft/sec, it will take } \frac{d}{250} = \frac{15{,}000 \csc 10°}{250} \approx 345.5 \text{ seconds or } 5.76 \text{ minutes.}$$

**33** (a)  The bridge section is 75 feet long. Using the right triangle with the 75 foot section as its hypotenuse and $(d - 15)$ as the side opposite the 35° angle, we have

$$\sin 35° = \frac{d - 15}{75} \Rightarrow d - 15 = 75 \sin 35° \Rightarrow d = 75 \sin 35° + 15 \approx 58 \text{ ft.}$$

(b)  Let $x$ be the horizontal distance from the end of a bridge section to a point directly underneath the end of the section. $\cos 35° = \dfrac{x}{75} \Rightarrow x = 75 \cos 35°.$ The distance between the ends of the two sections is

(total distance) − (the 2 horizontal distances under the bridge sections) $= 150 - 2x \approx 27 \text{ ft.}$

**34** The *lower section* has a horizontal length of $x_1 = 15 \cot 25°$ and a slide length of $s_1 = 15 \csc 25° \approx 35.5$.

The *upper section* has a horizontal length of $x_2 = 15 \cot 35°$ and a slide length of $s_2 = 15 \csc 35° \approx 26.2$.

The *middle section* has a slide length of $s_3 = 100 - x_1 - x_2 \approx 46.4$.

                    The **total slide length** is $s_1 + s_2 + s_3 \approx 35.5 + 26.2 + 46.4 = 108.1 \text{ ft.}$

**35** Let $\alpha$ denote the angle of elevation. $\tan \alpha = \frac{5}{4} \Rightarrow \alpha \approx 51°20'.$

**36** $\sin \alpha = \frac{5}{24} \Rightarrow \alpha \approx 12°$

**37** Let $D$ denote the position of the duck and $t$ the number of seconds required for a direct hit.

The duck will move $(7t)$ cm. and the bullet will travel $(25t)$ cm.

$$\sin\varphi = \frac{\overline{AD}}{\overline{OD}} = \frac{7t}{25t} \quad \Rightarrow \quad \sin\varphi = \frac{7}{25} \quad \Rightarrow \quad \varphi \approx 16.3°.$$

**38** (a) $\sin\alpha = \dfrac{4}{9} \quad \Rightarrow \quad \alpha \approx 26.4°$ (b) $\sin 40° = \dfrac{h}{9} \quad \Rightarrow \quad h = 9\sin 40° \approx 5.8$ m

**39** Let $h$ denote the height of the tower. $\tan 21°20'24'' = \tan 21.34° = \dfrac{h}{5280} \quad \Rightarrow \quad h = 5280\tan 21.34° \approx 2063$ ft.

**40** Maximum elongation $\theta_{max}$ will occur when the line of sight from Earth to Venus is tangent to the orbit of Venus. Since a tangent line to a circle is perpendicular to a radius, maximum elongation will occur when the angle determined by the sun, Venus, and Earth is 90°. $\sin(\theta_{max}) = \dfrac{D_v}{D_e} = \dfrac{68{,}000{,}000}{91{,}500{,}000} = \dfrac{68}{91.5} \quad \Rightarrow \quad \theta_{max} \approx 48°.$

**41** The central angle of a section of the Pentagon has measure $\dfrac{360°}{5} = 72°.$

Bisecting that angle, we have an angle of 36° whose opposite side is $\dfrac{921}{2}$.

The height $h$ is given by $\tan 36° = \dfrac{\frac{921}{2}}{h} \quad \Rightarrow \quad h = \dfrac{921}{2\tan 36°}.$

$$\text{Area} = 5\left(\tfrac{1}{2}bh\right) = 5\left(\tfrac{1}{2}\right)(921)\left(\frac{921}{2\tan 36°}\right) \approx 1{,}459{,}379 \text{ ft}^2.$$

**42** The central angle of a section of the octagon has an angle measure of $\dfrac{360°}{8} = 45°.$ Bisecting that angle forms a right triangle with a hypotenuse of 12 cm. $\sin 22.5° = \dfrac{x}{12} \quad \Rightarrow \quad x = 12\sin 22.5°.$ There are 8 sides of length $2x$. Hence, the perimeter is $16x = 192\sin 22.5° \approx 73.5$ cm.

**43** The diagonal of the base is $\sqrt{8^2 + 6^2} = 10.$ $\tan\theta = \dfrac{4}{10} \quad \Rightarrow \quad \theta \approx 21.8°$

**44** $V = \tfrac{1}{3}\pi r^2 h \quad \Leftrightarrow \quad 20 = \tfrac{1}{3}\pi(2)^2 h \quad \Rightarrow \quad h = \dfrac{15}{\pi}.$ $\tan\dfrac{\beta}{2} = \dfrac{r}{h} = \dfrac{2}{15/\pi} \quad \Rightarrow \quad \dfrac{\beta}{2} \approx 22.728°,$ and $\beta \approx 45.5°.$

**45** $\cot 53°30' = \dfrac{x}{h} \quad \Rightarrow \quad x = h\cot 53°30'.$ $\cot 26°50' = \dfrac{x+25}{h} \quad \Rightarrow \quad x + 25 = h\cot 26°50' \quad \Rightarrow$

$x = h\cot 26°50' - 25.$ We now have two expressions for $x$. We will set these equal to each other and solve for $h$.

Thus, $h\cot 53°30' = h\cot 26°50' - 25 \quad \Rightarrow \quad 25 = h\cot 26°50' - h\cot 53°30' \quad \Rightarrow$

$h = \dfrac{25}{\cot 26°50' - \cot 53°30'} \approx 20.2$ m.

*Figure 45*

*Figure 46*

**46** (a) $\sin 22° = \dfrac{x}{20} \Rightarrow x = 20 \sin 22° \approx 7.49$ ft.

(b) $\cos 22° = \dfrac{h}{20} \Rightarrow h \approx 18.54$ ft, the original height of the ladder. Let $x = 20 \sin 22° + 3$ and then

$h = \sqrt{20^2 - x^2} \approx 17.03$ ft. Hence, the top of the ladder moved from 18.54 to 17.03 or approximately 1.51 ft.

**47** When the angle of elevation is $19°20'$, $\tan 19°20' = \dfrac{h_1}{110} \Rightarrow h_1 = 110 \tan 19°20'$.

When the angle of elevation is $31°50'$, $\tan 31°50' = \dfrac{h_2}{110} \Rightarrow h_2 = 110 \tan 31°50'$.

The change in elevation is $h_2 - h_1 \approx 68.29 - 38.59 = 29.7$ km.

**48** $\tan 12°50' = \dfrac{8.2}{y} \Rightarrow y \approx 36.0$. $\tan 31°20' = \dfrac{x}{y} \Rightarrow x \approx 21.9$. The height is $x + 8.2$, or 30.1 m.

*Figure 48*

*Figure 52*

**49** The distance from the spacelab to the center of Earth is $(380 + r)$ miles.

$\sin 65.8° = \dfrac{r}{r + 380} \Rightarrow r \sin 65.8° + 380 \sin 65.8° = r \Rightarrow r - r \sin 65.8° = 380 \sin 65.8° \Rightarrow$

$$r(1 - \sin 65.8°) = 380 \sin 65.8° \Rightarrow r = \dfrac{380 \sin 65.8°}{1 - \sin 65.8°} \approx 3944 \text{ mi.}$$

**50** Let $h$ denote the length of the antenna and $\theta$ the angle opposite the garage.

$\tan \theta = \frac{16}{100} \Rightarrow \theta \approx 9.09°$. $\alpha = 12° + 9.09° = 21.09°$. $\tan 21.09° = \dfrac{h + 16}{100} \Rightarrow$

$$h + 16 = 100 \tan 21.09° \Rightarrow h = 100 \tan 21.09° - 16 \approx 22.6 \text{ ft.}$$

**51** Let $d$ be the distance traveled. $\tan 42° = \dfrac{10{,}000}{d} \Rightarrow d = 10{,}000 \cot 42°$.

Converting to mi/hr, we have $\dfrac{10{,}000 \cot 42° \text{ ft}}{1 \text{ minute}} \cdot \dfrac{60 \text{ minutes}}{1 \text{ hour}} \cdot \dfrac{1 \text{ mile}}{5280 \text{ ft}} \approx 126$ mi/hr.

**52** The motorist travels a distance of 10 km. Now $\tan 10° = \dfrac{h}{x + 10} \Rightarrow x = h \cot 10° - 10$ and $\tan 70° = \dfrac{h}{x} \Rightarrow$

$$x = h \cot 70°. \quad h \cot 10° - 10 = h \cot 70° \Rightarrow h = \dfrac{10}{\cot 10° - \cot 70°} \approx 1.88 \text{ km.}$$

**53** (a) As in Exercise 49, there is a right angle formed on Earth's surface. Bisecting angle $\theta$ and forming a right

triangle, we have $\cos \dfrac{\theta}{2} = \dfrac{R}{R + a} = \dfrac{4000}{26{,}300}$. Thus, $\dfrac{\theta}{2} \approx 81.25° \Rightarrow \theta \approx 162.5°$.

The percentage of the equator that is within signal range is $\dfrac{162.5°}{360°} \times 100 \approx 45\%$.

(b) Each satellite has a signal range of more than 120°, and thus all 3 will cover all points on the equator.

**54** (a) Bisect $\theta$ and form a right triangle with angle $\dfrac{\theta}{2}$, adjacent side $R - d$, and hypotenuse $R$.

$$\cos \dfrac{\theta}{2} = \dfrac{R - d}{R} \Rightarrow R \cos \dfrac{\theta}{2} = R - d \Rightarrow d = R - R \cos \dfrac{\theta}{2} \Rightarrow d = R \left(1 - \cos \dfrac{\theta}{2}\right).$$

(b) From Exercise 53, $\cos \dfrac{\theta}{2} = \dfrac{40}{263}$. The portion of the planet's surface that is within signal range is

$$\dfrac{\text{surface area of spherical cap}}{\text{surface area of Earth}} = \dfrac{2\pi R d}{4\pi R^2} = \dfrac{d}{2R} = \dfrac{R\left(1 - \cos \dfrac{\theta}{2}\right)}{2R} = \dfrac{1 - \cos \dfrac{\theta}{2}}{2} = \dfrac{1 - \dfrac{40}{263}}{2} = \dfrac{223}{526} \approx 0.424,$$

or 42.4%.

**55** Let $x = h - c$. $\sin \alpha = \dfrac{x}{d}$ $\Rightarrow$ $x = d \sin \alpha$. $h = x + c = d \sin \alpha + c$.

**56** $\cot \alpha = \dfrac{x}{d}$ $\Rightarrow$ $x = d \cot \alpha$

**57** Let $x$ denote the distance from the base of the tower to the closer point.

$\cot \beta = \dfrac{x}{h}$ $\Rightarrow$ $x = h \cot \beta$. $\cot \alpha = \dfrac{x + d}{h}$ $\Rightarrow$ $x + d = h \cot \alpha$ $\Rightarrow$ $x = h \cot \alpha - d$.

Thus, $h \cot \beta = h \cot \alpha - d$ $\Rightarrow$ $d = h \cot \alpha - h \cot \beta$ $\Rightarrow$ $d = h(\cot \alpha - \cot \beta)$ $\Rightarrow$ $h = \dfrac{d}{\cot \alpha - \cot \beta}$.

**58** The central angle of a section of an $n$-sided polygon has an angle measure of $\dfrac{360°}{n}$.

Bisecting that angle forms a right triangle with a hypotenuse $r$ and opposite side $x$.

$\sin \left( \dfrac{1}{2} \cdot \dfrac{360°}{n} \right) = \sin \left( \dfrac{180}{n} \right)^{\circ} = \dfrac{x}{r}$ $\Rightarrow$ $x = r \sin \left( \dfrac{180}{n} \right)^{\circ}$. There are $n$ sides of length $2x$.

Hence, the perimeter $P$ is $2nx = 2nr \sin \left( \dfrac{180}{n} \right)^{\circ}$.

**59** When the angle of elevation is $\alpha$, $\tan \alpha = \dfrac{h_1}{d}$ $\Rightarrow$ $h_1 = d \tan \alpha$. When the angle of elevation is $\beta$,

$\tan \beta = \dfrac{h_2}{d}$ $\Rightarrow$ $h_2 = d \tan \beta$. $h = h_2 - h_1 = d \tan \beta - d \tan \alpha = d(\tan \beta - \tan \alpha)$.

**60** Let $x$ and $y$ denote the sides as labeled in Figure 48. We see that $\cot \beta = \dfrac{y}{d}$ $\Rightarrow$ $y = d \cot \beta$.

Also, $\tan \alpha = \dfrac{x}{y}$ $\Rightarrow$ $x = y \tan \alpha = d \cot \beta \tan \alpha$. Hence, $h = d + x = d + d \cot \beta \tan \alpha = d(1 + \cot \beta \tan \alpha)$.

**61** The bearing from $P$ to $A$ is $90° - 20° = 70°$ east of north and is denoted by N70°E.

The bearing from $P$ to $B$ is $40°$ west of north and is denoted by N40°W.

The bearing from $P$ to $C$ is $90° - 75° = 15°$ west of south and is denoted by S15°W.

The bearing from $P$ to $D$ is $25°$ east of south and is denoted by S25°E.

**62** The bearings for $A$, $B$, $C$, and $D$ are N15°E, N30°W, S80°W, and S55°E, respectively.

**63** (a) The first ship travels 2 hours @ 24 mi/hr for a distance of 48 miles.

The second ship travels $1\frac{1}{2}$ hours @ 18 mi/hr for a distance of 27 miles.

The paths form a right triangle with legs of 48 miles and 27 miles.

The distance between the two ships is $\sqrt{27^2 + 48^2} \approx 55$ miles.

(b) The angle between the side of length 48 and the hypotenuse is found by solving $\tan \alpha = \frac{27}{48}$ for $\alpha$. Now $\alpha \approx 29°$, so the second ship is approximately $29° + 34° = $ S63°E of the first ship.

**64** Let $F$ denote the point of the fire. $\angle BAF = 90° - 35°50' = 54°10'$ and $\angle ABF = 90° - 54°10' = 35°50'$.

Thus, $\angle BFA = 90°$. If $d$ denotes the distance $AF$, then $\cos 54°10' = \dfrac{d}{5}$ $\Rightarrow$ $d \approx 2.9$ mi.

**65** 30 minutes @ 360 mi/hr = 180 miles. 45 minutes @ 360 mi/hr = 270 miles. $227° - 137° = 90°$, and hence, the plane's flight forms a right triangle with legs 180 miles and 270 miles. The distance from $A$ to the airplane is equal to the hypotenuse of the triangle—that is, $\sqrt{180^2 + 270^2} \approx 324.5$ mi.

**66** (a) The plane's flight forms two legs (400 mi each) of a right triangle. The hypotenuse of this 45°–45°–90° triangle is $400\sqrt{2}$. The plane is in the direction $153° - 45° = 108°$ from point $A$ (18° below the horizontal). It must take the direction $270° + 18° = 288°$ to get back to $A$.

(b) At 400 mi/hr, it will take the plane $\sqrt{2}$ hr to travel $400\sqrt{2}$ mi.

**67** $d = 10 \sin 6\pi t$ • Amplitude, 10 cm; period $= \frac{2\pi}{6\pi} = \frac{1}{3}$ sec; frequency $= \frac{6\pi}{2\pi} = 3$ oscillations/sec. The point is at the origin at $t = 0$. It moves upward with decreasing speed, reaching the point with coordinate 10 when $6\pi t = \frac{\pi}{2}$ or $t = \frac{1}{12}$. It then reverses direction and moves downward, gaining speed until it reaches the origin when $6\pi t = \pi$ or $t = \frac{1}{6}$. It continues downward with decreasing speed, reaching the point with coordinate $-10$ when $6\pi t = \frac{3\pi}{2}$ or $t = \frac{1}{4}$. It then reverses direction and moves upward with increasing speed, returning to the origin when $6\pi t = 2\pi$ or $t = \frac{1}{3}$ to complete one oscillation.

Another approach is to simply model this movement in terms of proportions of the sine curve. For one period, the sine increases for $\frac{1}{4}$ period, decreases for $\frac{1}{2}$ period, and increases for its last $\frac{1}{4}$ period.

**68** $d = \frac{1}{3} \cos \frac{\pi}{4} t$ • Amplitude, $\frac{1}{3}$ cm; period $= \frac{2\pi}{\pi/4} = 8$ sec; frequency $= \frac{\pi/4}{2\pi} = \frac{1}{8}$ oscillation/sec. The point is at $d = \frac{1}{3}$ cm when $t = 0$. It then decreases in height until $\frac{\pi}{4} t = \pi$ or $t = 4$ where it obtains a minimum of $d = -\frac{1}{3}$. It then reverses direction and increases to a height of $d = \frac{1}{3}$ when $\frac{\pi}{4} t = 2\pi$ or $t = 8$ to complete one oscillation.

**69** $d = 4 \cos \frac{3\pi}{2} t$ • Amplitude, 4 cm; period $= \frac{2\pi}{3\pi/2} = \frac{4}{3}$ sec; frequency $= \frac{3\pi/2}{2\pi} = \frac{3}{4}$ oscillation/sec. The point is at $d = 4$ when $t = 0$. It then decreases in height until $\frac{3\pi}{2} t = \pi$ or $t = \frac{2}{3}$ where it obtains a minimum of $d = -4$.
It then reverses direction and increases to a height of $d = 4$ when $\frac{3\pi}{2} t = 2\pi$ or $t = \frac{4}{3}$ to complete one oscillation.

**70** $d = 6 \sin \frac{2\pi}{3} t$ • Amplitude, 6 cm; period $= \frac{2\pi}{2\pi/3} = 3$ sec; frequency $= \frac{2\pi/3}{2\pi} = \frac{1}{3}$ oscillation/sec. The point is at the origin at $t = 0$. It will obtain a maximum height of 6 when $\frac{2\pi}{3} t = \frac{\pi}{2}$ or $t = \frac{3}{4}$. It then decreases in height until it obtains a minimum of $-6$ when $\frac{2\pi}{3} t = \frac{3\pi}{2}$ or $t = \frac{9}{4}$. It then reverses direction and returns to the origin when $\frac{2\pi}{3} t = 2\pi$ or $t = 3$ to complete one oscillation.

**71** Period $= 3 \Rightarrow \frac{2\pi}{\omega} = 3 \Rightarrow \omega = \frac{2\pi}{3}$. Amplitude $= 5 \Rightarrow a = 5$. $d = 5 \cos \frac{2\pi}{3} t$

**72** $\frac{1}{2}$ oscillation per minute $\Rightarrow \frac{\omega}{2\pi} = \frac{1}{2} \Rightarrow \omega = \pi$. Amplitude $= 4 \Rightarrow a = 4$. $d = 4 \sin \pi t$

**73** (a) Period $= 30 \Rightarrow \frac{2\pi}{\omega} = 30 \Rightarrow \omega = \frac{\pi}{15}$. When $t = 0$, the wave is at its highest point, thus, we use the cosine function. $y = 25 \cos \frac{\pi}{15} t$, where $t$ is in minutes.

(b) 180 ft/sec $= 10{,}800$ ft/min. $10{,}800$ ft/min for 30 minutes is a distance of 324,000 ft, or $61\frac{4}{11}$ miles.

**74** (a) $y = a \sin bt = 8 \sin \frac{\pi}{6} t \Rightarrow a = 8$ and $b = \frac{\pi}{6}$.

Thus, the wave has an amplitude of 8 ft and its period is $\frac{2\pi}{b} = \frac{2\pi}{\pi/6} = 12$ min.

(b) The wave moves 21 km every 12 min. The wave's velocity is $\frac{21}{12} = 1.75$ km/min, or, 105 km/hr.

## Chapter 5 Review Exercises

**1** $330° \cdot \frac{\pi}{180} = \frac{11 \cdot 30\pi}{6 \cdot 30} = \frac{11\pi}{6}$; $\qquad 405° \cdot \frac{\pi}{180} = \frac{9 \cdot 45\pi}{4 \cdot 45} = \frac{9\pi}{4}$; $\qquad -150° \cdot \frac{\pi}{180} = -\frac{5 \cdot 30\pi}{6 \cdot 30} = -\frac{5\pi}{6}$; $240° \cdot \frac{\pi}{180} = \frac{4 \cdot 60\pi}{3 \cdot 60} = \frac{4\pi}{3}$; $\qquad 36° \cdot \frac{\pi}{180} = \frac{36\pi}{5 \cdot 36} = \frac{\pi}{5}$

**2** $\frac{9\pi}{2} \cdot \left(\frac{180}{\pi}\right)° = \left(\frac{9 \cdot 90 \cdot 2\pi}{2\pi}\right)° = 810°$; $\qquad -\frac{2\pi}{3} \cdot \left(\frac{180}{\pi}\right)° = -\left(\frac{2 \cdot 60 \cdot 3\pi}{3\pi}\right)° = -120°$ $\frac{7\pi}{4} \cdot \left(\frac{180}{\pi}\right)° = \left(\frac{7 \cdot 45 \cdot 4\pi}{4\pi}\right)° = 315°$; $\qquad 5\pi \cdot \left(\frac{180}{\pi}\right)° = \left(\frac{5 \cdot 180 \cdot \pi}{\pi}\right)° = 900°$ $\qquad \frac{\pi}{5} \cdot \left(\frac{180}{\pi}\right)° = \left(\frac{36 \cdot 5\pi}{5\pi}\right)° = 36°$

**3** (a) $\theta = \frac{s}{r} = \frac{20 \text{ cm}}{2 \text{ m}} = \frac{20 \text{ cm}}{2(100)\text{cm}} = 0.1$ radian $\qquad$ (b) $A = \frac{1}{2} r^2 \theta = \frac{1}{2}(2)^2(0.1) = 0.2$ m$^2$

**4** (a) $s = r\theta = \left(15 \cdot \frac{1}{2}\right)\left(70 \cdot \frac{\pi}{180}\right) = \frac{35\pi}{12} \approx 9.16$ cm

(b) $A = \frac{1}{2} r^2 \theta = \frac{1}{2}\left(15 \cdot \frac{1}{2}\right)^2\left(70 \cdot \frac{\pi}{180}\right) = \frac{175\pi}{16} \approx 34.4$ cm$^2$

**5**  We take the number of revolutions per minute times the number of radians per revolution and obtain

$$\left(33\tfrac{1}{3}\right)(2\pi) = \tfrac{200\pi}{3} \text{ radians/minute and } 45(2\pi) = 90\pi \text{ radians/minute.}$$

**6**  $s = r\theta = \left(\tfrac{1}{2}\cdot 12\right)\left(\tfrac{200\pi}{3}\right) = 400\pi$ in.  Linear speed $= 400\pi$ in/min $= \tfrac{400\pi}{12} = \tfrac{100\pi}{3}$ ft/min.

$s = r\theta = \left(\tfrac{1}{2}\cdot 7\right)(90\pi) = 315\pi$ in.  Linear speed $= 315\pi$ in/min $= \tfrac{315\pi}{12} = \tfrac{105\pi}{4}$ ft/min.

**7**  $\sin 60^\circ = \dfrac{9}{x} \;\Rightarrow\; \dfrac{\sqrt{3}}{2} = \dfrac{9}{x} \;\Rightarrow\; x = 6\sqrt{3}; \tan 60^\circ = \dfrac{9}{y} \;\Rightarrow\; \sqrt{3} = \dfrac{9}{y} \;\Rightarrow\; y = 3\sqrt{3}$

**8**  $\sin 45^\circ = \dfrac{x}{7} \;\Rightarrow\; \dfrac{\sqrt{2}}{2} = \dfrac{x}{7} \;\Rightarrow\; x = \dfrac{7}{2}\sqrt{2}; \cos 45^\circ = \dfrac{y}{7} \;\Rightarrow\; \dfrac{\sqrt{2}}{2} = \dfrac{y}{7} \;\Rightarrow\; y = \dfrac{7}{2}\sqrt{2}$

**9**  $1 + \tan^2\theta = \sec^2\theta \;\Rightarrow\; \tan^2\theta = \sec^2\theta - 1 \;\Rightarrow\; \tan\theta = \sqrt{\sec^2\theta - 1}$

**10**  $1 + \cot^2\theta = \csc^2\theta \;\Rightarrow\; \cot^2\theta = \csc^2\theta - 1 \;\Rightarrow\; \cot\theta = \sqrt{\csc^2\theta - 1}$

**11**  $\begin{aligned} \sin\theta(\csc\theta - \sin\theta) &= \sin\theta\csc\theta - \sin^2\theta && \{\text{multiply terms}\} \\ &= \sin\theta\cdot\dfrac{1}{\sin\theta} - \sin^2\theta && \{\text{reciprocal identity}\} \\ &= 1 - \sin^2\theta && \{\text{simplify}\} \\ &= \cos^2\theta && \{\text{Pythagorean identity}\} \end{aligned}$

**12**  $\cos\theta(\tan\theta + \cot\theta) = \cos\theta\cdot\dfrac{\sin\theta}{\cos\theta} + \cos\theta\cdot\dfrac{\cos\theta}{\sin\theta} = \sin\theta + \dfrac{\cos^2\theta}{\sin\theta} = \dfrac{\sin^2\theta + \cos^2\theta}{\sin\theta} = \dfrac{1}{\sin\theta} = \csc\theta$

**13**  $\begin{aligned} \left(\cos^2\theta - 1\right)\left(\tan^2\theta + 1\right) &= \left(\cos^2\theta - 1\right)\left(\sec^2\theta\right) && \{\text{Pythagorean identity}\} \\ &= \cos^2\theta\sec^2\theta - \sec^2\theta && \{\text{multiply terms}\} \\ &= 1 - \sec^2\theta && \{\text{reciprocal identity}\} \end{aligned}$

**14**  $\dfrac{\sec\theta - \cos\theta}{\tan\theta} = \dfrac{\dfrac{1}{\cos\theta} - \cos\theta}{\dfrac{\sin\theta}{\cos\theta}} = \dfrac{\dfrac{1 - \cos^2\theta}{\cos\theta}}{\dfrac{\sin\theta}{\cos\theta}} = \dfrac{\dfrac{\sin^2\theta}{\cos\theta}}{\dfrac{\sin\theta}{\cos\theta}} = \dfrac{\dfrac{\sin\theta}{\cos\theta}}{\dfrac{1}{\cos\theta}} = \dfrac{\tan\theta}{\sec\theta}$

**15**  $\begin{aligned} \dfrac{1 + \tan^2\theta}{\tan^2\theta} &= \dfrac{1}{\tan^2\theta} + \dfrac{\tan^2\theta}{\tan^2\theta} && \{\text{split up the fraction}\} \\ &= \cot^2\theta + 1 && \{\text{reciprocal identity, simplify}\} \\ &= \csc^2\theta && \{\text{Pythagorean identity}\} \end{aligned}$

**16**  $\dfrac{\sec\theta + \csc\theta}{\sec\theta - \csc\theta} = \dfrac{\dfrac{1}{\cos\theta} + \dfrac{1}{\sin\theta}}{\dfrac{1}{\cos\theta} - \dfrac{1}{\sin\theta}} = \dfrac{\dfrac{\sin\theta + \cos\theta}{\cos\theta\sin\theta}}{\dfrac{\sin\theta - \cos\theta}{\cos\theta\sin\theta}} = \dfrac{\sin\theta + \cos\theta}{\sin\theta - \cos\theta}$

**17**  $\begin{aligned} \dfrac{\cot\theta - 1}{1 - \tan\theta} &= \dfrac{\dfrac{\cos\theta}{\sin\theta} - 1}{1 - \dfrac{\sin\theta}{\cos\theta}} && \{\text{put in terms of sines and cosines}\} \\[2mm] &= \dfrac{\dfrac{\cos\theta - \sin\theta}{\sin\theta}}{\dfrac{\cos\theta - \sin\theta}{\cos\theta}} && \{\text{make the numerator and the denominator each a single fraction}\} \\[2mm] &= \dfrac{(\cos\theta - \sin\theta)\cos\theta}{(\cos\theta - \sin\theta)\sin\theta} && \{\text{simplify a complex fraction}\} \\[2mm] &= \dfrac{\cos\theta}{\sin\theta} && \{\text{cancel like term}\} \\[2mm] &= \cot\theta && \{\text{cotangent identity}\} \end{aligned}$

**18** $\dfrac{1 + \sec\theta}{\tan\theta + \sin\theta} = \dfrac{1 + \dfrac{1}{\cos\theta}}{\dfrac{\sin\theta}{\cos\theta} + \dfrac{\sin\theta\cos\theta}{\cos\theta}} = \dfrac{\dfrac{\cos\theta + 1}{\cos\theta}}{\dfrac{\sin\theta(1 + \cos\theta)}{\cos\theta}} = \dfrac{1}{\sin\theta} = \csc\theta$

**19** $\dfrac{\tan(-\theta) + \cot(-\theta)}{\tan\theta} = \dfrac{-\tan\theta - \cot\theta}{\tan\theta}$ 　　{formulas for negatives}

$= -\dfrac{\tan\theta}{\tan\theta} - \dfrac{\cot\theta}{\tan\theta}$ 　　{split up fraction}

$= -1 - \cot^2\theta$ 　　{simplify, reciprocal identity}

$= -(1 + \cot^2\theta)$ 　　{factor out $-1$}

$= -\csc^2\theta$ 　　{Pythagorean identity}

**20** $-\dfrac{1}{\csc(-\theta)} - \dfrac{\cot(-\theta)}{\sec(-\theta)} = -\dfrac{1}{-\csc\theta} - \dfrac{-\cot\theta}{\sec\theta} = \sin\theta + \dfrac{\frac{\cos\theta}{\sin\theta}}{\frac{1}{\cos\theta}} = \sin\theta + \dfrac{\cos^2\theta}{\sin\theta} = \dfrac{\sin^2\theta + \cos^2\theta}{\sin\theta} = \dfrac{1}{\sin\theta} = \csc\theta$

**21** $\text{opp} = \sqrt{\text{hyp}^2 - \text{adj}^2} = \sqrt{7^2 - 4^2} = \sqrt{33}.$ 　　★ $\dfrac{\sqrt{33}}{7}, \dfrac{4}{7}, \dfrac{\sqrt{33}}{4}, \dfrac{4}{\sqrt{33}}, \dfrac{7}{4}, \dfrac{7}{\sqrt{33}}$

**22** (a) $x = 30$ and $y = -40 \;\Rightarrow\; r = \sqrt{30^2 + (-40)^2} = 50.$ 　　★ (a) $-\dfrac{4}{5}, \dfrac{3}{5}, -\dfrac{4}{3}, -\dfrac{3}{4}, \dfrac{5}{3}, -\dfrac{5}{4}$

(b) $2x + 3y + 6 = 0 \;\Leftrightarrow\; y = -\frac{2}{3}x - 2$, so the slope of the given line is $-\frac{2}{3}$. The line through the origin with that

slope is $y = -\frac{2}{3}x$. If $x = -3$, then $y = 2$ and $(-3, 2)$ is a point on the terminal side of $\theta$.

$x = -3$ and $y = 2 \;\Rightarrow\; r = \sqrt{(-3)^2 + 2^2} = \sqrt{13}.$ 　　★ $\dfrac{2}{\sqrt{13}}, -\dfrac{3}{\sqrt{13}}, -\dfrac{2}{3}, -\dfrac{3}{2}, -\dfrac{\sqrt{13}}{3}, \dfrac{\sqrt{13}}{2}$

(c) For $\theta = -90°$, choose $x = 0$ and $y = -1$. $r$ is 1. 　　★ (c) $-1, 0, \text{U}, 0, \text{U}, -1$

**23** (a) $\sec\theta < 0 \;\Rightarrow\;$ terminal side of $\theta$ is in QII or QIII.

$\sin\theta > 0 \;\Rightarrow\;$ terminal side of $\theta$ is in QI or QII. Hence, $\theta$ is in QII.

(b) $\cot\theta > 0 \;\Rightarrow\;$ terminal side of $\theta$ is in QI or QIII.

$\csc\theta < 0 \;\Rightarrow\;$ terminal side of $\theta$ is in QIII or QIV. Hence, $\theta$ is in QIII.

(c) $\cos\theta > 0 \;\Rightarrow\;$ terminal side of $\theta$ is in QI or QIV.

$\tan\theta < 0 \;\Rightarrow\;$ terminal side of $\theta$ is in QII or QIV. Hence, $\theta$ is in QIV.

**24** (a) $\tan\theta = \dfrac{\sin\theta}{\cos\theta} = \dfrac{-4/5}{3/5} = -\dfrac{4}{3}$, and the other values are just the reciprocals. 　　★ $-\dfrac{4}{5}, \dfrac{3}{5}, -\dfrac{4}{3}, -\dfrac{3}{4}, \dfrac{5}{3}, -\dfrac{5}{4}$

(b) $\cot\theta = \dfrac{\cos\theta}{\sin\theta} = \dfrac{\csc\theta}{\sec\theta} \;\Rightarrow\; -\dfrac{3}{2} = \dfrac{\sqrt{13}/2}{\sec\theta} \;\Rightarrow\; \sec\theta = -\dfrac{\sqrt{13}}{3}$; the other values are just the reciprocals.

★ $\dfrac{2}{\sqrt{13}}, -\dfrac{3}{\sqrt{13}}, -\dfrac{2}{3}, -\dfrac{3}{2}, -\dfrac{\sqrt{13}}{3}, \dfrac{\sqrt{13}}{2}$

**25** $7\pi$ is coterminal with $\pi$. $P(7\pi) = P(\pi) = (-1, 0)$. $-\frac{5\pi}{2}$ is coterminal with $-\frac{\pi}{2}$. $P\!\left(-\frac{5\pi}{2}\right) = P\!\left(-\frac{\pi}{2}\right) = (0, -1)$.

$P\!\left(\frac{9\pi}{2}\right) = P\!\left(\frac{\pi}{2}\right) = (0, 1)$. $P\!\left(-\frac{3\pi}{4}\right) = \left(-\frac{\sqrt{2}}{2}, -\frac{\sqrt{2}}{2}\right)$. $P(18\pi) = P(0) = (1, 0)$. $P\!\left(\frac{\pi}{6}\right) = \left(\frac{\sqrt{3}}{2}, \frac{1}{2}\right)$.

**26** $P(t) = \left(-\frac{3}{5}, -\frac{4}{5}\right)$ is in QIII. $P(t + \pi)$ is in QI and will have the same coordinates as $P(t)$,

but with opposite (positive) signs, so $P(t + 3\pi) = P(t + \pi) = P(t - \pi) = \left(\frac{3}{5}, \frac{4}{5}\right)$.

$P(-t) = \left(-\frac{3}{5}, \frac{4}{5}\right)$ is in QII. $P(2\pi - t) = P(-t + 2\pi) = \left(-\frac{3}{5}, \frac{4}{5}\right)$.

**27** (a) $\theta = \frac{5\pi}{4} \;\Rightarrow\; \theta_R = \frac{5\pi}{4} - \pi = \frac{\pi}{4}.$ 　　$\theta = -\frac{5\pi}{6} \;\Rightarrow\; \theta_C = \frac{7\pi}{6}$ and $\theta_R = \frac{7\pi}{6} - \pi = \frac{\pi}{6}.$

$\theta = -\frac{9\pi}{8} \;\Rightarrow\; \theta_C = \frac{7\pi}{8}$ and $\theta_R = \pi - \frac{7\pi}{8} = \frac{\pi}{8}.$

(b) $\theta = 245° \;\Rightarrow\; \theta_R = 245° - 180° = 65°.$ 　　$\theta = 137° \;\Rightarrow\; \theta_R = 180° - 137° = 43°.$

$\theta = 892° \;\Rightarrow\; \theta_C = 172°$ and $\theta_R = 180° - 172° = 8°.$

**28** (a) For $\theta = \frac{9\pi}{2}$, choose $x = 0$ and $y = 1$. $r = 1$.     ★ (a) 1, 0, U, 0, U, 1

    (b) For $\theta = -\frac{5\pi}{4}$, choose $x = -1$ and $y = 1$. $r = \sqrt{2}$.     ★ $\frac{\sqrt{2}}{2}$, $-\frac{\sqrt{2}}{2}$, $-1$, $-1$, $-\sqrt{2}$, $\sqrt{2}$

    (c) For $\theta = 0$, choose $x = 1$ and $y = 0$. $r = 1$.     ★ (c) 0, 1, 0, U, 1, U

    (d) For $\theta = \frac{11\pi}{6}$, choose $x = \sqrt{3}$ and $y = -1$. $r = 2$.     ★ $-\frac{1}{2}$, $\frac{\sqrt{3}}{2}$, $-\frac{\sqrt{3}}{3}$, $-\sqrt{3}$, $\frac{2}{\sqrt{3}}$, $-2$

**29** (a) $\cos 225° = -\cos 45° = -\frac{\sqrt{2}}{2}$       (b) $\tan 150° = -\tan 30° = -\frac{\sqrt{3}}{3}$

    (c) $\sin\left(-\frac{\pi}{6}\right) = -\sin\frac{\pi}{6} = -\frac{1}{2}$       (d) $\sec\frac{4\pi}{3} = -\sec\frac{\pi}{3} = -2$

    (e) $\cot\frac{7\pi}{4} = -\cot\frac{\pi}{4} = -1$       (f) $\csc 300° = -\csc 60° = -\frac{2}{\sqrt{3}}$

**30** $\sin\theta = -0.7604 \Rightarrow \theta = \sin^{-1}(-0.7604) \approx -49.5° \Rightarrow \theta_R \approx 49.5°$.

Since the sine is negative in QIII and QIV, and the secant is positive in QIV,

          we want the fourth-quadrant angle having $\theta_R = 49.5°$. $360° - 49.5° = 310.5°$

**31** $\tan\theta = 2.7381 \Rightarrow \theta = \tan^{-1}(2.7381) \approx 1.2206 \Rightarrow \theta_R \approx 1.2206$. Since the tangent is positive in QI and QIII, we need to add $\pi$ to $\theta_R$ to find the value in QIII. $\pi + \theta_R \approx 4.3622$

**32** $\sec\theta = 1.6403 \Rightarrow \cos\theta = \frac{1}{1.6403} \Rightarrow \theta = \cos^{-1}\left(\frac{1}{1.6403}\right) \approx 52.44° \Rightarrow \theta_R \approx 52.44°$. Since the secant is positive in QI and QIV, we need to subtract $\theta_R$ from $360°$ to find the value in QIV. $360° - \theta_R \approx 307.56°$

**33** $y = 5\cos x$ • Vertically stretch $\cos x$ by a factor of 5.     ★ $5, 2\pi$, $x$-int. @ $\frac{\pi}{2} + \pi n$

Figure 33

Figure 34

**34** $y = \frac{2}{3}\sin x$ • Vertically compress $\sin x$ by a factor of $\frac{3}{2}$ {or multiply by $\frac{2}{3}$}.     ★ $\frac{2}{3}, 2\pi$, $x$-int. @ $\pi n$

**35** $y = \frac{1}{3}\sin 3x$ • Horizontally compress $\sin x$ by a factor of 3 and vertically compress that graph by a factor of 3.     ★ $\frac{1}{3}, \frac{2\pi}{3}$, $x$-int. @ $\frac{\pi}{3} n$

Figure 35

Figure 36

**36** $y = -\frac{1}{2}\cos\frac{1}{3}x$ • Horizontally stretch $\cos x$ by a factor of 3, vertically compress by a factor of 2, and reflect that graph through the $x$-axis.     ★ $\frac{1}{2}, 6\pi$, $x$-int. @ $\frac{3\pi}{2} + 3\pi n$

**37** $y = -3\cos\frac{1}{2}x$ • Horizontally stretch $\cos x$ by a factor of 2, vertically stretch that graph by a factor of 3, and reflect that graph through the $x$-axis. ★ 3, $4\pi$, $x$-int. @ $\pi + 2\pi n$

*Figure 37*

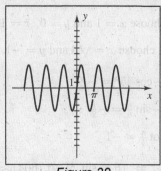

*Figure 38*

**38** $y = 4\sin 2x$ • Horizontally compress $\sin x$ by a factor of 2 and vertically stretch that graph by a factor of 4. ★ 4, $\pi$, $x$-int. @ $\frac{\pi}{2}n$

**39** $y = 2\sin\pi x$ • Horizontally compress $\sin x$ by a factor of $\pi$, and then vertically stretch that graph by a factor of 2. ★ 2, 2, $x$-int. @ $n$

*Figure 39*

*Figure 40*

**40** $y = 4\cos\frac{\pi}{2}x - 2$ • Horizontally compress $\cos x$ by a factor of $\pi/2$, vertically stretch that graph by a factor of 4, and shift the last graph 2 units down. ★ 4, 4, $x$-int. @ $\frac{2}{3} + 4n$, $\frac{10}{3} + 4n$

**Note:** Let $a$ denote the amplitude and $p$ the period.

**41** (a) $a = |-1.43| = 1.43$. We have $\frac{3}{4}$ of a period from $(0,0)$ to $(1.5, -1.43)$. $\frac{3}{4}p = 1.5 \Rightarrow p = 2$.

(b) Since the period $p$ is given by $\frac{2\pi}{b}$, we can solve for $b$, obtaining $b = \frac{2\pi}{p}$.

Hence, $b = \frac{2\pi}{p} = \frac{2\pi}{2} = \pi$ and consequently, $y = 1.43\sin\pi x$.

**42** (a) $a = |-3.27| = 3.27$, $\frac{1}{4}p = \frac{3\pi}{4} \Rightarrow p = 3\pi$.

(b) $b = \frac{2\pi}{p} = \frac{2\pi}{3\pi} = \frac{2}{3}$, $y = -3.27\sin\frac{2}{3}x$.

**43** (a) Since the $y$-intercept is $-3$, $a = |-3| = 3$. The second positive $x$-intercept is $\pi$,

so $\frac{3}{4}$ of a period occurs from $(0, -3)$ to $(\pi, 0)$. Thus, $\frac{3}{4}p = \pi \Rightarrow p = \frac{4\pi}{3}$.

(b) $b = \frac{2\pi}{p} = \frac{2\pi}{4\pi/3} = \frac{3}{2}$, $y = -3\cos\frac{3}{2}x$.

**44** (a) Since the $y$-intercept is 2, $a = |2| = 2$. The first positive $x$-intercept is 1, so $\frac{1}{4}p = 1 \Rightarrow p = 4$.

(b) $b = \frac{2\pi}{p} = \frac{2\pi}{4} = \frac{\pi}{2}$, $y = 2\cos\frac{\pi}{2}x$.

**45** $y = 2\sin\left(x - \frac{2\pi}{3}\right)$ • $0 \le x - \frac{2\pi}{3} \le 2\pi$ $\Rightarrow$ $\frac{2\pi}{3} \le x \le \frac{8\pi}{3}$. There are $x$-intercepts at $x = \frac{2\pi}{3} + \pi n$.

*Figure 45*

*Figure 46*

**46** $y = -3\sin\left(\frac{1}{2}x - \frac{\pi}{4}\right) = -3\sin\left[\frac{1}{2}\left(x - \frac{\pi}{2}\right)\right]$ • $0 \le \frac{1}{2}x - \frac{\pi}{4} \le 2\pi$ $\Rightarrow$ $\frac{\pi}{4} \le \frac{1}{2}x \le \frac{9\pi}{4}$ $\Rightarrow$ $\frac{\pi}{2} \le x \le \frac{9\pi}{2}$

**47** $y = -4\cos\left(x + \frac{\pi}{6}\right)$ • $-\frac{\pi}{2} \le x + \frac{\pi}{6} \le \frac{3\pi}{2}$ $\Rightarrow$ $-\frac{2\pi}{3} \le x \le \frac{4\pi}{3}$. There are $x$-intercepts at $x = -\frac{2\pi}{3} + \pi n$.

*Figure 47*

*Figure 48*

**48** $y = 5\cos\left(2x + \frac{\pi}{2}\right) = 5\cos\left[2\left(x + \frac{\pi}{4}\right)\right]$ • $-\frac{\pi}{2} \le 2x + \frac{\pi}{2} \le \frac{3\pi}{2}$ $\Rightarrow$ $-\pi \le 2x \le \pi$ $\Rightarrow$ $-\frac{\pi}{2} \le x \le \frac{\pi}{2}$

**49** $y = 2\tan\left(\frac{1}{2}x - \pi\right) = 2\tan\left[\frac{1}{2}(x - 2\pi)\right]$ •

$$-\frac{\pi}{2} < \frac{1}{2}x - \pi < \frac{\pi}{2} \Rightarrow \frac{\pi}{2} < \frac{1}{2}x < \frac{3\pi}{2} \Rightarrow \pi < x < 3\pi, \, VA \; @ \; x = \pi + 2\pi n.$$

*Figure 49*

*Figure 50*

**50** $y = -3\tan\left(2x + \frac{\pi}{3}\right) = -3\tan\left[2\left(x + \frac{\pi}{6}\right)\right]$ •

$$-\frac{\pi}{2} < 2x + \frac{\pi}{3} < \frac{\pi}{2} \Rightarrow -\frac{5\pi}{6} < 2x < \frac{\pi}{6} \Rightarrow -\frac{5\pi}{12} < x < \frac{\pi}{12}, \, VA \; @ \; x = -\frac{5\pi}{12} + \frac{\pi}{2}n.$$

**51** $y = -4\cot\left(2x - \frac{\pi}{2}\right) = -4\cot\left[2\left(x - \frac{\pi}{4}\right)\right]$ •

$0 < 2x - \frac{\pi}{2} < \pi \;\Rightarrow\; \frac{\pi}{2} < 2x < \frac{3\pi}{2} \;\Rightarrow\; \frac{\pi}{4} < x < \frac{3\pi}{4},\; VA @ x = \frac{\pi}{4} + \frac{\pi}{2}n.$

Figure 51

Figure 52

**52** $y = 2\cot\left(\frac{1}{2}x + \frac{\pi}{4}\right) = 2\cot\left[\frac{1}{2}\left(x + \frac{\pi}{2}\right)\right]$ •

$0 < \frac{1}{2}x + \frac{\pi}{4} < \pi \;\Rightarrow\; -\frac{\pi}{4} < \frac{1}{2}x < \frac{3\pi}{4} \;\Rightarrow\; -\frac{\pi}{2} < x < \frac{3\pi}{2},\; VA @ x = -\frac{\pi}{2} + 2\pi n.$

**53** $y = \sec\left(\frac{1}{2}x + \pi\right) = \sec\left[\frac{1}{2}(x + 2\pi)\right]$ •

$-\frac{\pi}{2} < \frac{1}{2}x + \pi < \frac{\pi}{2} \;\Rightarrow\; -\frac{3\pi}{2} < \frac{1}{2}x < -\frac{\pi}{2} \;\Rightarrow\; -3\pi < x < -\pi,\; VA @ x = -3\pi + 2\pi n.$

Figure 53

Figure 54

**54** $y = \sec\left(2x - \frac{\pi}{2}\right) = \sec\left[2\left(x - \frac{\pi}{4}\right)\right]$ • $-\frac{\pi}{2} < 2x - \frac{\pi}{2} < \frac{\pi}{2} \;\Rightarrow\; 0 < 2x < \pi \;\Rightarrow\; 0 < x < \frac{\pi}{2},\; VA @ x = \frac{\pi}{2}n.$

**55** $y = \csc\left(2x - \frac{\pi}{4}\right) = \csc\left[2\left(x - \frac{\pi}{8}\right)\right]$ •

$0 < 2x - \frac{\pi}{4} < \pi \;\Rightarrow\; \frac{\pi}{4} < 2x < \frac{5\pi}{4} \;\Rightarrow\; \frac{\pi}{8} < x < \frac{5\pi}{8},\; VA @ x = \frac{\pi}{8} + \frac{\pi}{2}n.$

Figure 55

Figure 56

**56** $y = \csc\left(\frac{1}{2}x + \frac{\pi}{4}\right) = \csc\left[\frac{1}{2}\left(x + \frac{\pi}{2}\right)\right]$ •

$0 < \frac{1}{2}x + \frac{\pi}{4} < \pi \;\Rightarrow\; -\frac{\pi}{4} < \frac{1}{2}x < \frac{3\pi}{4} \;\Rightarrow\; -\frac{\pi}{2} < x < \frac{3\pi}{2},\; VA @ x = -\frac{\pi}{2} + 2\pi n.$

**57** $\alpha$ and $\beta$ are complementary, so $\alpha = 90° - \beta = 90° - 60° = 30°$.

$$\cot \beta = \frac{a}{b} \quad \Rightarrow \quad a = b \cot \beta = 40 \cot 60° = 40 \left( \frac{1}{3} \sqrt{3} \right) \approx 23.$$

$$\csc \beta = \frac{c}{b} \quad \Rightarrow \quad c = b \csc \beta = 40 \csc 60° = 40 \left( \frac{2}{3} \sqrt{3} \right) \approx 46.$$

**58** $\beta = 90° - \alpha = 35°20'$. $\tan \alpha = \frac{a}{b} \quad \Rightarrow \quad a = b \tan \alpha = 220 \tan 54°40' \approx 310$.

$$\sec \alpha = \frac{c}{b} \quad \Rightarrow \quad c = b \sec \alpha = 220 \sec 54°40' \approx 380.$$

**59** $\tan \alpha = \frac{a}{b} = \frac{62}{25} \quad \Rightarrow \quad \alpha \approx 68°$. $\beta = 90° - \alpha \approx 90° - 68° = 22°$.

$$c = \sqrt{a^2 + b^2} = \sqrt{62^2 + 25^2} = \sqrt{3844 + 625} = \sqrt{4469} \approx 67.$$

**60** $\sin \alpha = \frac{a}{c} = \frac{9.0}{41} \quad \Rightarrow \quad \alpha \approx 13°$. $\beta = 90° - \alpha \approx 77°$. $b = \sqrt{c^2 - a^2} = \sqrt{1681 - 81} = \sqrt{1600} = 40$.

**61** (a) $\left( \dfrac{545 \text{ rev}}{1 \text{ min}} \right) \left( \dfrac{2\pi \text{ rad}}{1 \text{ rev}} \right) \left( \dfrac{1 \text{ min}}{60 \text{ sec}} \right) = \dfrac{109\pi}{6}$ rad/sec $\approx 57$ rad/sec

(b) $d = 22.625 \text{ ft} \quad \Rightarrow \quad C = \pi d = 22.625\pi \text{ ft}$. $\left( \dfrac{22.625\pi \text{ ft}}{1 \text{ rev}} \right) \left( \dfrac{545 \text{ rev}}{1 \text{ min}} \right) \left( \dfrac{1 \text{ mile}}{5280 \text{ ft}} \right) \left( \dfrac{60 \text{ min}}{1 \text{ hour}} \right) \approx 440.2 \text{ mi/hr}$

**62** Let $h$ denote the height of the tower. $\tan 79.2° = \dfrac{h}{200} \quad \Rightarrow \quad h \approx 1048 \text{ ft}$.

**63** $\Delta f = \dfrac{2fv}{c} \quad \Rightarrow \quad v = \dfrac{c(\Delta f)}{2f} = \dfrac{186{,}000 \times 10^8}{2 \times 10^{14}} = 93{,}000 \times 10^{-6} = 0.093 \text{ mi/sec}$

**64** The angle $\varphi$ has an adjacent side of $\frac{1}{2}(230 \text{ m})$, or 115 m. $\tan \varphi = \frac{147}{115} \quad \Rightarrow \quad \varphi \approx 52°$.

**65** Let $d$ denote the distance from Venus to the sun in the third figure.

$$\sin 47° = \frac{d}{92{,}900{,}000} \quad \Rightarrow \quad d \approx 67{,}942{,}759 \text{ mi., or approximately } 67{,}900{,}000 \text{ mi.}$$

**66** $\cot 17° = \dfrac{x}{233} \quad \Rightarrow \quad x = 233 \cot 17° \approx 762.1 \text{ ft}$.

**67** (a) $\sin 25° = \frac{x}{16} \quad \Rightarrow \quad x = 16 \sin 25° \approx 6.76 \text{ ft}$.

(b) $\cos 25° = \frac{h}{16} \quad \Rightarrow \quad h \approx 14.50 \text{ ft}$, the original height of the ladder.

Let $x = 16 \sin 25° - 1.5 \approx 5.26$ and then $h = \sqrt{16^2 - x^2} \approx 15.11 \text{ ft}$.

Hence, the top of the ladder moved from 14.50 to 15.11 or

approximately 0.61 ft.

**68** The depth of the cone is 4 inches and its slant height is 5 inches. Thus, $4^2 + r^2 = 5^2 \quad \Rightarrow \quad r = 3$ inches.

The circumference of the rim of the cone is $2\pi r = 6\pi$. On the circle, $\theta = \dfrac{s}{r} = \dfrac{6\pi}{5}$ radians $= 216°$.

**69** Let $A$ denote the point at the 36° angle. Let $Q$ denote the highest point of the mountain and $P$ denote $Q$'s projection such that $\angle APQ = 90°$. Let $x$ denote the distance from the left end of the mountain to $P$ and let $y$ denote the distance from the right end of the mountain to $P$.

$$\cot 36° = \frac{x + 200}{260} \quad \Rightarrow \quad 260 \cot 36° = x + 200 \quad \Rightarrow \quad x = 260 \cot 36° - 200.$$

$$\cot 47° = \frac{y + 150}{260} \quad \Rightarrow \quad 260 \cot 47° = y + 150 \quad \Rightarrow \quad y = 260 \cot 47° - 150. \quad x + y \approx 250 \text{ ft}.$$

**70** (a) Let $h$ denote the height of the building and $x$ the distance between the two buildings.

$\tan 59° = \dfrac{h - 50}{x}$ and $\tan 62° = \dfrac{h}{x}$ $\Rightarrow$ $h = x \tan 59° + 50$ and

$h = x \tan 62°$ $\Rightarrow$ $x \tan 62° - x \tan 59° = 50$ $\Rightarrow$ $x = \dfrac{50}{\tan 62° - \tan 59°} \approx 231.0$ ft.

(b) From part (a), $h = x \tan 62° \approx 434.5$ ft.

**71** (a) Let $x = \overline{QR}$. $\cot \beta = \dfrac{x}{h}$ $\Rightarrow$ $x = h \cot \beta$. $\cot \alpha = \dfrac{d + x}{h}$ $\Rightarrow$ $x = h \cot \alpha - d$.

Thus, $h \cot \beta = h \cot \alpha - d$ $\Rightarrow$ $d = h(\cot \alpha - \cot \beta)$ $\Rightarrow$ $h = \dfrac{d}{\cot \alpha - \cot \beta}$.

(b) $d = 2$ miles, $\alpha = 15°$, and $\beta = 20°$ $\Rightarrow$ $h = \dfrac{2}{\cot 15° - \cot 20°} \approx 2.03$, or 2 miles.

**72** (a) Extend the two boundary lines for $h$ {call these $l_{\text{top}}$ and $l_{\text{bottom}}$} to the right until they intersect a line $l$ extended down from the front edge of the building. Let $x$ denote the distance from the intersection of the incline and $l_{\text{bottom}}$ to $l$ and $y$ the distance on $l$ from $l_{\text{top}}$ to the lower left corner of the building.

$\cos \alpha = \dfrac{x}{d}$ $\Rightarrow$ $x = d \cos \alpha$. $\sin \alpha = \dfrac{h + y}{d}$ $\Rightarrow$ $y = d \sin \alpha - h$.

$\tan \theta = \dfrac{y + T}{x}$ $\Rightarrow$ $T = x \tan \theta - y = d \cos \alpha \tan \theta - d \sin \alpha + h$ $\Rightarrow$ $T = h + d(\cos \alpha \tan \theta - \sin \alpha)$.

(b) $T = 6 + 50(\cos 15° \tan 31.4° - \sin 15°) \approx 6 + 50(0.3308) \approx 22.54$ ft.

**73** (a) $\cos \theta = \dfrac{15}{s}$ $\Rightarrow$ $s = \dfrac{15}{\cos \theta}$. $E = \dfrac{5000 \cos \theta}{s^2} = \dfrac{5000 \cos \theta}{225/\cos^2 \theta} = \dfrac{200}{9} \cos^3 \theta$.

$\theta = 30°$ $\Rightarrow$ $E = \dfrac{200}{9} \left(\dfrac{1}{2}\sqrt{3}\right)^3 = \dfrac{200}{9} \left(\dfrac{3}{8}\sqrt{3}\right) = \dfrac{25}{3}\sqrt{3} \approx 14.43$ ft-candles

(b) $E = \dfrac{1}{2} E_{\max}$ $\Rightarrow$ $\dfrac{200}{9} \cos^3 \theta = \dfrac{1}{2}\left(\dfrac{200}{9} \cos^3 0°\right)$ $\Rightarrow$ $\cos^3 \theta = \dfrac{1}{2}$ $\Rightarrow$ $\cos \theta = \sqrt[3]{\dfrac{1}{2}}$ $\Rightarrow$

$\theta = \cos^{-1} \sqrt[3]{\dfrac{1}{2}}$ $\Rightarrow$ $\theta \approx 37.47°$

**74** (a) Let $x = \overline{PT}$ and $y = \overline{QT}$. Now $x^2 + d^2 = y^2$, $h = x \sin \alpha$, and $h = y \sin \beta$.

$d^2 = y^2 - x^2 = \dfrac{h^2}{\sin^2 \beta} - \dfrac{h^2}{\sin^2 \alpha} = \dfrac{h^2(\sin^2 \alpha - \sin^2 \beta)}{\sin^2 \alpha \sin^2 \beta}$ $\Rightarrow$ $h^2 = \dfrac{d^2 \sin^2 \alpha \sin^2 \beta}{\sin^2 \alpha - \sin^2 \beta}$ $\Rightarrow$

$h = \dfrac{d \sin \alpha \sin \beta}{\sqrt{\sin^2 \alpha - \sin^2 \beta}}$.

(b) $\alpha = 30°$, $\beta = 20°$, and $d = 10$ $\Rightarrow$ $h = \dfrac{10 \sin 30° \sin 20°}{\sqrt{\sin^2 30° - \sin^2 20°}} \approx 4.69$ miles.

**75** (a) Let $d$ denote the distance from the end of the bracket to the wall.

$\cos 30° = \dfrac{d}{85.5}$ $\Rightarrow$ $d = (85.5)\left(\dfrac{1}{2}\sqrt{3}\right) \approx 74.05$ in.

(b) Let $y$ denote the side opposite 30°. $\sin 30° = \dfrac{y}{85.5}$ $\Rightarrow$ $y = 42.75$ in.

Thus, the distance from the ceiling to the top of the screen is

(length of the bracket + $y$ − one-half the height of the screen) $= (18'' + 42.75'' - 36'') = 24.75''$.

**76** (a) $\sin \theta = \dfrac{\frac{1}{2}x}{a}$ $\Rightarrow$ $x = 2a \sin \theta$. The area of one face is $\frac{1}{2}$(base)(height) $= \frac{1}{2}xa$.

$S = 4\left(\frac{1}{2}ax\right) = 2ax = 2a(2a \sin \theta) = 4a^2 \sin \theta$.

(b) $\cos \theta = \dfrac{y}{a}$ $\Rightarrow$ $y = a \cos \theta$. $V = \frac{1}{3}$(base area)(height) $= \frac{1}{3}x^2 y = \frac{1}{3}(2a \sin \theta)^2(a \cos \theta) = \frac{4}{3}a^3 \sin^2 \theta \cos \theta$.

**77** (a) Let $\theta = \angle PCQ$. Since $\angle BPC = 90°$, $\cos \theta = \dfrac{R}{R+h}$ $\Rightarrow$

$R + h = R \sec \theta$ $\Rightarrow$ $h = R \sec \theta - R$. Since $\theta = \dfrac{s}{R}$, $h = R \sec \dfrac{s}{R} - R$.

(b) $h = R\left(\sec \dfrac{s}{R} - 1\right) = 4000\left(\sec \dfrac{50}{4000} - 1\right) \approx 0.31252 \,\text{mi} \approx 1650 \,\text{ft}$.

**78** $y = a - a \cos \dfrac{\pi}{2L} x$ • $a = 1$ and $L = 10$ $\Rightarrow$

$y = 1 - 1\cos\left(\frac{1}{2}\pi x / 10\right) = -\cos\left(\frac{\pi}{20}x\right) + 1$.

For $0 \le x \le 10$, $0 \le \frac{\pi}{20}x \le \frac{\pi}{2}$ $\Rightarrow$ $1 \ge \cos\left(\frac{\pi}{20}x\right) \ge 0$ $\Rightarrow$

$-1 \le -\cos\left(\frac{\pi}{20}x\right) \le 0$ $\Rightarrow$ $0 \le -\cos\left(\frac{\pi}{20}x\right) + 1 \le 1$ $\Rightarrow$ $0 \le y \le 1$.

**79** The range of temperatures is 0.6°F, so $a = 0.3$. $\frac{2\pi}{b} = 24$ $\Rightarrow$ $b = \frac{\pi}{12}$. The average temperature occurs at 11 A.M., 6 hours before the high at 5 P.M., which corresponds to $t = 11$. The argument of the sine is then $\frac{\pi}{12}(t - 11)$, or $\frac{\pi}{12}t - \frac{11\pi}{12}$.

Thus, $y = 98.6 + (0.3)\sin\left(\frac{\pi}{12}t - \frac{11\pi}{12}\right)$ {or equivalently, $y = 98.6 + (0.3)\sin\left(\frac{\pi}{12}t + \frac{13\pi}{12}\right)$}.

**80** (a) For $T(t) = 15.8 \sin\left[\frac{\pi}{6}(t - 3)\right] + 5$, the period $p = \frac{2\pi}{\pi/6} = 12$ months.

(b) The highest temperature will occur when the argument of the sine is $\frac{\pi}{2}$. $\frac{\pi}{6}(t - 3) = \frac{\pi}{2}$ $\Rightarrow$ $t - 3 = 3$ $\Rightarrow$ $t = 6$ months. This is July 1st and the temperature is 20.8°C, or 69.44°F.

*Figure 80*

*Figure 81*

**81** (a) For $D(t) = 2000 \sin \frac{\pi}{90}t + 4000$, the period $p = \frac{2\pi}{\pi/90} = 180$ days.

(b) The greatest demand will occur when the argument of the sine is $\frac{\pi}{2}$. $\frac{\pi}{90}t = \frac{\pi}{2}$ $\Rightarrow$ $t = 45$ days into summer.

**82** (a) $s(t) = 12 + \cos \pi t$ • The cork is in simple harmonic motion. At $t = 0$, its height is 13 ft.

It decreases until $t = 1$, reaching a minimum of 11 ft. It then increases, reaching a maximum of 13 ft at $t = 2$.

(b) From part (a), the cork is rising for $1 \le t \le 2$.

## Chapter 5 Discussion Exercises

**1** On the TI-83/4 Plus with $a = 15$, there is an indication that there are 15 sine waves on each side of the $y$-axis, but the minimums and maximums do not get to $-1$ and 1, respectively. With $a = 30$, the number of sine waves is undetectable—there simply aren't enough pixels for any degree of clarity. With $a = 45$, there are 2 sine waves on each side of the $y$-axis—there should be 45!

2  Divide $10^{k+1}$ by $2\pi$, subtract the greatest integer of that result from itself, leaving only a fractional part of $2\pi$ radians. Multiply that result by $2\pi$ to give you a number between $0$ and $2\pi$, and then take the sine of that value. On the TI-83/4 Plus, $k = 11$. To find $\sin(10^{12})$, enter $10^{12}$, divide by $2\pi$, take fPart Ans to obtain $0.89$ {fPart is under the NUM submenu from the MATH key}, multiply by $2\pi$, and take the sine of that result. Thus, $\sin 10^{12} \approx \sin 5.59203 \approx -0.6374$.

3  The sum on the left, $\cos x + \cos 2x + \cos 3x$, can never be greater than $1 + 1 + 1 = 3 < \pi$,

so there are no solutions.

4  A discussion should bring out the following comments:

(1) the trigonometric functions are all periodic functions,

(2) periodic functions can't be one-to-one functions,

(3) for a function to have an inverse it must be one-to-one;

and come up with the conclusion that any one of the trigonometric functions cannot have an inverse unless its domain is restricted.

5  The graph of $y_1 = x$, $y_2 = \sin x$, and $y_3 = \tan x$ in the suggested viewing rectangle, $[-0.1, 0.1]$ by $[-0.1, 0.1]$, indicates that their values are very close to each other near $x = 0$—in fact, the graphs of the functions are indistinguishable. Creating a table of values on the order of $10^{-10}$ also shows that all three functions are nearly equal.

6  (a)  Consider the track as a unit circle. The 2 km can then be thought of as an angle measurement of 2 radians. Thus, $x = \cos 2 \approx -0.4161$ and $y = \sin 2 \approx 0.9093$.

(b)  Since the diameter is 2 km, the radius is 1 km and the circumference is $2\pi$ km. $\frac{500}{2\pi} \approx 79.577472$ revolutions. Subtracting the 79 whole laps and multiplying the remainder by $2\pi$ we obtain $(2\pi)(0.577472) \approx 3.6283607$ radians. Thus, $x \approx \cos(3.6283607) \approx -0.8838$ and $y \approx \sin(3.6283607) \approx -0.4678$. Alternatively, $x = \cos 500 \approx -0.8838$ and $y = \sin 500 \approx -0.4678$.

7  (a)  $S$ is at $(0, -1)$ on the rectangular coordinate system. Starting at $S$, subtract 1 from the 2 km to get to the circular portion of the track. Now consider $t = \left(1 + \frac{3\pi}{2}\right)$ as the radian measurement (starting from $S$) of the circular track in Discussion Exercise 6. $\left\{ \frac{3\pi}{2} \text{ to get to the bottom of the circle and 1 to make the second km.} \right\}$ $x = \cos t + 1 \approx 1.8415$ and $y = \sin t \approx -0.5403$.

(b)  The perimeter of the track is $(4 + 2\pi)$ km. $\frac{500}{4 + 2\pi} \approx 48.623066$ laps. Subtracting the 48 whole laps, we have a portion of a lap left, $0.623066$ lap. Multiply by $4 + 2\pi$ to see how many km we are from $S$. $(4 + 2\pi)(0.623066) \approx 6.4071052$. To determine where this places us on the track, start at $S$ and subtract 1 {to get to $(1, -1)$}, subtract $\pi$ {to get to $(1, 1)$}, and subtract 2 {to get to $(-1, 1)$}. $6.4071052 - (3 + \pi) \approx 0.2655126$. Now consider $t = 0.2655126 + \frac{\pi}{2}$ as the radian measurement of the circular track in Discussion Exercise 6 (but with $S$ at the bottom).

$x \approx \cos t - 1 \approx -1.2624$ and $y \approx \sin t \approx 0.9650$.

8  (a)  $\omega = \dfrac{5000 \text{ rev}}{1 \text{ minute}} \times \dfrac{1 \text{ minute}}{60 \text{ seconds}} \times \dfrac{2\pi \text{ radians}}{1 \text{ revolution}} = \dfrac{500\pi}{3} \approx 523.6 \text{ radian/sec}$.

(b) Since the depth is 18, we have $d = 18$. The radius is 5 inches, so $a = 5$. Thus, $D(t) = a\cos(\omega t + c) + d = 5\cos\left(\frac{500\pi}{3}t + c\right) + 18$. Since the point is initially at a depth of 23 inches, $D = 23$ when $t = 0$. Substituting, we have $23 = 5\cos(c) + 18 \Rightarrow \cos c = 1 \Rightarrow c = 0$.

Hence, $D(t) = 5\cos\left(\frac{500\pi}{3}t\right) + 18$.

(c) Graph $Y_1 = 5\cos\left(\frac{500\pi}{3}x\right) + 18$ on the interval $[0, 0.12]$. From the graph, we see that the propeller completes approximately 10 revolutions in 0.12 seconds.

$[0, 0.12, 0.01]$ by $[0, 25, 5]$

## Chapter 5 Test

1. $s = r\theta \Rightarrow r = \dfrac{s}{\theta} = \dfrac{14}{35 \cdot \frac{\pi}{180}} \approx 22.92$ cm

2. The angle $32°17'$ in radians is $\left(32 + \frac{17}{60}\right)\left(\frac{\pi}{180}\right)$.

The area of the sector is $A = \frac{1}{2}r^2\theta = \frac{1}{2}(8)^2\left(32 + \frac{17}{60}\right)\left(\frac{\pi}{180}\right) \approx 18.03$ square inches.

3. The radius is $\frac{1}{2}(4) = 2$ feet. Find the central angle in radians. $s = r\theta \Rightarrow \theta = \dfrac{s}{r} = \dfrac{6}{2} = 3$ radians.

The area is $A = \frac{1}{2}r^2\theta = \frac{1}{2}(2)^2(3) = 6$ square feet.

4. Find the central angle in radians. $s = r\theta \Rightarrow \theta = \dfrac{s}{r} = \dfrac{9}{4} = 2.25$ rad.

The degree measure is $2.25\left(\frac{180}{\pi}\right) \approx 128.92 \approx 128°55'$.

5. (a) The angular speed is $\left(1200\,\dfrac{\text{rev}}{\text{min}}\right)\left(2\pi\,\dfrac{\text{rad}}{\text{rev}}\right) = 2400\pi\,\dfrac{\text{rad}}{\text{min}}$.

(b) $s = r\theta = (7\text{ in})(2400\pi) = 16{,}800\pi$ in. Linear speed $= 16{,}800\pi$ in/min $= 1400\pi$ ft/min $\approx 4398$ ft/min.

6. Use the Pythagorean theorem to find the remaining side.

$(\text{adj})^2 + (\text{opp})^2 = (\text{hyp})^2 \Rightarrow (\text{adj})^2 + 5^2 = 8^2 \Rightarrow \text{adj} = \sqrt{64 - 25} = \sqrt{39}$. Thus, $\sin\theta = \dfrac{5}{8}$,

$\cos\theta = \dfrac{\text{adj}}{\text{hyp}} = \dfrac{\sqrt{39}}{8}$, $\tan\theta = \dfrac{\text{opp}}{\text{adj}} = \dfrac{5}{\sqrt{39}}$, $\cot\theta = \dfrac{\text{adj}}{\text{opp}} = \dfrac{\sqrt{39}}{5}$, $\sec\theta = \dfrac{\text{hyp}}{\text{adj}} = \dfrac{8}{\sqrt{39}}$, $\csc\theta = \dfrac{\text{hyp}}{\text{opp}} = \dfrac{8}{5}$.

7. $\sin^2\theta + \cos^2\theta = 1 \Rightarrow \sin^2\theta = 1 - \cos^2\theta \Rightarrow \sin\theta = +\sqrt{1 - \cos^2\theta}$ {use the positive sign since $\theta$ is acute}.

Thus, $\cot\theta = \dfrac{\cos\theta}{\sin\theta}$ { cotangent identity } $= \dfrac{\cos\theta}{\sqrt{1 - \cos^2\theta}}$.

8. $\text{LS} = \left(\dfrac{\csc\theta - 1}{\csc\theta}\right)\left(\dfrac{\csc\theta + 1}{\csc\theta}\right) = \dfrac{\csc^2\theta - 1}{\csc^2\theta} = 1 - \dfrac{1}{\csc^2\theta} = 1 - \sin^2\theta = \cos^2\theta = \dfrac{1}{\sec^2\theta} = \text{RS}$

9. $x = 12$ and $y = -5 \Rightarrow r = \sqrt{12^2 + (-5)^2} = 13$. $\sin\theta = y/r = -\frac{5}{13}$, $\cos\theta = x/r = \frac{12}{13}$, $\tan\theta = y/x = -\frac{5}{12}$, $\cot\theta = x/y = -\frac{12}{5}$, $\sec\theta = r/x = \frac{13}{12}$, and $\csc\theta = r/y = -\frac{13}{5}$.

10. $\tan\theta = \frac{3}{4}$ and $\sin\theta < 0 \Rightarrow \theta$ is in QIII. $\sec\theta = -\sqrt{1 + \tan^2\theta} = -\sqrt{1 + \frac{9}{16}} = -\frac{5}{4}$.

$\tan\theta = \dfrac{\sin\theta}{\cos\theta} \Rightarrow \dfrac{3}{4} = \dfrac{\sin\theta}{-4/5} \Rightarrow \sin\theta = -\dfrac{3}{5}$. The values are $-\dfrac{3}{5}, -\dfrac{4}{5}, \dfrac{3}{4}, \dfrac{4}{3}, -\dfrac{5}{4}, -\dfrac{5}{3}$.

**11** $\sqrt{1-\sin^2\theta} = \sqrt{\cos^2\theta} = |\cos\theta| = -\cos\theta$ since $\cos\theta < 0$ if $\pi/2 < \theta < \pi$.

**12** $P(t) = \left(-\frac{15}{17}, \frac{8}{17}\right) \Rightarrow P(-t) = \left(-\frac{15}{17}, -\frac{8}{17}\right) \Rightarrow P(-t-\pi) = \left(\frac{15}{17}, \frac{8}{17}\right)$

**13** LS $= \sin(-x)\sec^2(-x) = -\sin x \sec^2 x = -\sin x \dfrac{1}{\cos^2 x} = -\dfrac{\sin x}{\cos x}\dfrac{1}{\cos x} = -\tan x \sec x = $ RS

**14** $\sin x = -\frac{1}{2} \Rightarrow x = \frac{7\pi}{6}$ and $x = \frac{11\pi}{6}$ in $[\pi, 2\pi]$.

Thus, $\sin x > -\frac{1}{2}$ {the graph of $y = \sin x$ is above the horizontal line $y = -\frac{1}{2}$} for $\pi \le x < \frac{7\pi}{6}$ and $\frac{11\pi}{6} < x \le 2\pi$.

**15** The number of revolutions formed by $\theta$ is $\frac{60}{2\pi} \approx 9.55$, so $\theta_C = 60 - 9(2\pi) = 60 - 18\pi \approx 3.45$.

Since $\pi < 3.45 < \frac{3\pi}{2}$, $\theta_C$ is in QIII and $\theta_R = (60 - 18\pi) - \pi = 60 - 19\pi \approx 0.31$ radians, or $17.7°$.

**16** $\csc\dfrac{4\pi}{3} = -\csc\dfrac{\pi}{3} = -\dfrac{1}{\sin(\pi/3)} = -\dfrac{1}{\sqrt{3}/2} = -\dfrac{2}{\sqrt{3}}$

**17** Use the degree mode. $\cos\theta = 0.6357 \Rightarrow \theta = \cos^{-1}(0.6357) \approx 50.5°$. $\theta_R \approx 50.5°$.

Since the cosine is positive in QI and QIV, we get $360° - 50.5° = 309.5°$.

**18** Use the radian mode. $\tan\theta = -1.8224 \Rightarrow \theta = \tan^{-1}(-1.8224) \approx -1.07 \Rightarrow \theta_R \approx 1.07$.

Since the tangent is negative in QII and QIV, we get $\pi - 1.07 \approx 2.07$ and $2\pi - 1.07 \approx 5.21$.

**19** The period of $y = f(x) = 4\sin 3\pi x + 2$ is $\frac{2\pi}{3\pi} = \frac{2}{3}$, so there are $\frac{50-0}{2/3} = 75$ cycles of $f$ on the interval $[0, 50]$.

**20** One cycle of $y = f(x) = 3\cos\left(\frac{1}{3}x - \frac{\pi}{6}\right) - 1$ can be found by solving $0 \le \frac{1}{3}x - \frac{\pi}{6} \le 2\pi \Rightarrow$
$\frac{\pi}{6} \le \frac{1}{3}x \le 2\pi + \frac{\pi}{6} \Rightarrow \frac{\pi}{2} \le x \le 6\pi + \frac{\pi}{2}$. Since 0 and $2\pi$ correspond to high points on the graph of $y = \cos x$, $\frac{\pi}{2}$ and $6\pi + \frac{\pi}{2}$ correspond to high points on the graph of $f$. Now $f\left(\frac{\pi}{2}\right) = 3\cos 0 - 1 = 3 - 1 = 2$, so $\left(\frac{\pi}{2}, 2\right)$ is one of the highest points on the graph. The other high points are multiples of $6\pi$ away from $\frac{\pi}{2}$, so we could summarize all of the high points as $(a, 2)$, where $a = \frac{\pi}{2} + 6\pi n$ and $n$ is an integer.

**21** One cycle of $y = f(x) = -2\sin\left(\frac{1}{2}x - \frac{\pi}{4}\right)$ can be found by solving
$0 \le \frac{1}{2}x - \frac{\pi}{4} \le 2\pi \Rightarrow \frac{\pi}{4} \le \frac{1}{2}x \le 2\pi + \frac{\pi}{4} \Rightarrow \frac{\pi}{2} \le x \le 4\pi + \frac{\pi}{2}$.
Multiplying by "$-2$" reflects the graph of the sine about the $x$-axis, so it will decrease to its low point and then increase to its high point. The middle of the cycle is the average of $\frac{\pi}{2}$ and $\frac{9\pi}{2}$, which is $\frac{5\pi}{2}$. Halfway between $\frac{\pi}{2}$ and $\frac{5\pi}{2}$, $f$ will attain its low point, which is $\left(\frac{3\pi}{2}, f\left(\frac{3\pi}{2}\right)\right) = \left(\frac{3\pi}{2}, -2\right)$. Halfway between $\frac{5\pi}{2}$ and $\frac{9\pi}{2}$, $f$ will attain its high point, which is $\left(\frac{7\pi}{2}, f\left(\frac{7\pi}{2}\right)\right) = \left(\frac{7\pi}{2}, 2\right)$. The endpoints are $\left(\frac{\pi}{2}, 0\right)$ and $\left(\frac{9\pi}{2}, 0\right)$.

**22** The distance from the low point to the high point is $5 - (-1) = 6$, so the value of $a$ is one-half of 6, or 3.

To get to the high value of 5, $d$ must be 2. The sine function attains a maximum at $x = \frac{\pi}{2}$, so for $x = \pi$, we can have $bx = \frac{\pi}{2} \Rightarrow b\pi = \frac{\pi}{2} \Rightarrow b = \frac{1}{2}$. Thus, an equation is $y = 3\sin\frac{1}{2}x + 2$. There are other equations that satisfy the conditions, such as $y = -3\sin\frac{3}{2}x + 2$.

**23** One cycle of $y = \tan(3x - 7)$ can be found by solving $-\frac{\pi}{2} < 3x - 7 < \frac{\pi}{2} \Rightarrow 7 - \frac{\pi}{2} < 3x < 7 + \frac{\pi}{2} \Rightarrow$
$\frac{1}{3}\left(7 - \frac{\pi}{2}\right) < x < \frac{1}{3}\left(7 + \frac{\pi}{2}\right)$. The equations of two successive vertical asymptotes of the graph of $y = \tan(3x - 7)$ are $x = \frac{1}{3}\left(7 - \frac{\pi}{2}\right)$ and $x = \frac{1}{3}\left(7 + \frac{\pi}{2}\right)$. Other answers are possible.

**24** One $x$-intercept of $y = \cot x$ is $\frac{\pi}{2}$. Solving $\frac{1}{8}x + \frac{\pi}{4} = \frac{\pi}{2}$ gives us $\frac{1}{8}x = \frac{\pi}{4}$ $\Rightarrow$ $x = 2\pi$. So $2\pi$ is an $x$-intercept of the graph of $y = \cot\left(\frac{1}{8}x + \frac{\pi}{4}\right)$ and there are infinitely many others. Your answer will be of the form $2\pi + 8\pi n$, where $n$ is an integer, depending on your choice for the $x$-intercept of $y = \cot x$.

**25** For $y = \sec x$, the upper branch on the interval $\left(-\frac{\pi}{2}, \frac{\pi}{2}\right)$ has its lowest point of $(0, 1)$. Solving $2x + \pi = 0$ gives us $x = -\frac{\pi}{2}$. Since $y = 2\sec(2x + \pi)$ has a 2 multiplier, the lowest point on an upper branch is $\left(-\frac{\pi}{2}, 2\right)$. Your answer will be of the form $\left(-\frac{\pi}{2} + \pi n, 2\right)$, where $n$ is an integer, depending on your choice for the lowest point on an upper branch of $y = \sec x$.

**26** $y = 3\csc(x - \pi) - 2$ • The range of $y = \csc x$ is $(-\infty, -1] \cup [1, \infty)$. Multiplying by 3 changes the range to $(-\infty, -3] \cup [3, \infty)$, and subtracting 2 results in a final range of $(-\infty, -5] \cup [1, \infty)$.

**27** The graph of $y = |\sec x|$ has only upper branches. The same graph results for $y = \left|\csc\left(x - \frac{\pi}{2}\right)\right|$, or $y = \left|\csc\left(x + \frac{\pi}{2}\right)\right|$, or in general, $y = \left|\csc\left(x + (2n+1)\frac{\pi}{2}\right)\right|$.

**28** $\alpha = 90° - \beta = 45°$. $\cos\beta = \frac{a}{c}$ $\Rightarrow$ $a = c\cos\beta = 20\left(\frac{1}{2}\sqrt{2}\right) = 10\sqrt{2}$. $b = a$ in a $45° - 45° - 90°$ $\triangle$.

**29** $\alpha = 90° - \beta = 90° - 73°14' = 16°46'$. $\cot\beta = \frac{a}{b}$ $\Rightarrow$ $a = b\cot\beta = 821.0\cot 73°14' \approx 247.4$.

$\qquad\qquad\qquad\qquad\qquad\qquad$ $\csc\beta = \frac{c}{b}$ $\Rightarrow$ $c = b\csc\beta = 821.0\csc 73°14' \approx 857.5$.

**30** $\tan\alpha = \frac{a}{b}$ $\Rightarrow$ $a = b\tan\alpha$

**31** The central angle of a section of the pentagon has an angle measure of $\frac{360°}{5} = 72°$. Bisecting that angle forms a right triangle with a hypotenuse of 18 inches. $\sin 36° = \frac{x}{18}$ $\Rightarrow$ $x = 18\sin 36°$. There are 5 sides of length $2x$. Hence, the perimeter is $10x = 180\sin 36° \approx 105.8$ inches.

**32** Let $x$ denote the height of the building from eye level at point $A$ so that the total height of the building is $x + 10$. Let $y$ denote the distance along eye level from point $A$ to the building. Then $\tan 8° = \frac{10}{y}$ $\Rightarrow$ $y = 10\cot 8°$ and $\tan 42° = \frac{x}{y}$ $\Rightarrow$ $x = y\tan 42° = 10\cot 8°\tan 42° \approx 64.1$. The height of the building is $x + 10$, or 74.1 meters.

## 6.1 Exercises

**1** $\csc\theta - \sin\theta = \dfrac{1}{\sin\theta} - \sin\theta = \dfrac{1-\sin^2\theta}{\sin\theta} = \dfrac{\cos^2\theta}{\sin\theta} = \dfrac{\cos\theta}{\sin\theta}\cdot\cos\theta = \cot\theta\cos\theta$

**2** $\sin x + \cos x\cot x = \sin x + \cos x\cdot\dfrac{\cos x}{\sin x} = \dfrac{\sin^2 x + \cos^2 x}{\sin x} = \dfrac{1}{\sin x} = \csc x$

**3** $\dfrac{\sec^2 2u - 1}{\sec^2 2u} = 1 - \dfrac{1}{\sec^2 2u}$ {split up fraction} $= 1 - \cos^2 2u = \sin^2 2u$

**4** $\tan t + 2\cos t\csc t = \dfrac{\sin t}{\cos t} + \dfrac{2\cos t}{\sin t} = \dfrac{\sin^2 t + 2\cos^2 t}{\cos t\sin t} = \dfrac{1-\cos^2 t + 2\cos^2 t}{\cos t\sin t}$

$\qquad\qquad = \dfrac{1+\cos^2 t}{\cos t\sin t} = \dfrac{1}{\cos t\sin t} + \dfrac{\cos t}{\sin t} = \sec t\csc t + \cot t$

**5** $\dfrac{\csc^2\theta}{1+\tan^2\theta} = \dfrac{\csc^2\theta}{\sec^2\theta} = \dfrac{1/\sin^2\theta}{1/\cos^2\theta} = \dfrac{\cos^2\theta}{\sin^2\theta} = \left(\dfrac{\cos\theta}{\sin\theta}\right)^2 = \cot^2\theta$

**6** $(\tan u + \cot u)(\cos u + \sin u) = \left(\dfrac{\sin u}{\cos u} + \dfrac{\cos u}{\sin u}\right)(\cos u + \sin u)$

$\qquad\qquad = \left(\dfrac{\sin^2 u + \cos^2 u}{\cos u\sin u}\right)(\cos u + \sin u)$

$\qquad\qquad = \left(\dfrac{1}{\cos u\sin u}\right)(\cos u + \sin u)$

$\qquad\qquad = \dfrac{\cos u}{\cos u\sin u} + \dfrac{\sin u}{\cos u\sin u}$

$\qquad\qquad = \dfrac{1}{\sin u} + \dfrac{1}{\cos u} = \csc u + \sec u$

**7** $\dfrac{1+\cos 3t}{\sin 3t} + \dfrac{\sin 3t}{1+\cos 3t} = \dfrac{(1+\cos 3t)^2 + \sin^2 3t}{\sin 3t(1+\cos 3t)}$  {combine fractions}

$\qquad\qquad = \dfrac{1 + 2\cos 3t + \cos^2 3t + \sin^2 3t}{\sin 3t(1+\cos 3t)}$  {expand}

$\qquad\qquad = \dfrac{2 + 2\cos 3t}{\sin 3t(1+\cos 3t)}$  {$\cos^2 3t + \sin^2 3t = 1$}

$\qquad\qquad = \dfrac{2(1+\cos 3t)}{\sin 3t(1+\cos 3t)}$  {factor out 2}

$\qquad\qquad = \dfrac{2}{\sin 3t}$  {cancel like term}

$\qquad\qquad = 2\csc 3t$  {reciprocal identity}

**8** $\tan^2\alpha - \sin^2\alpha = \dfrac{\sin^2\alpha}{\cos^2\alpha} - \sin^2\alpha = \sin^2\alpha\left(\dfrac{1}{\cos^2\alpha} - 1\right) = (\sec^2\alpha - 1)\sin^2\alpha = \tan^2\alpha\sin^2\alpha$

**9** $\dfrac{1}{1-\cos\gamma} + \dfrac{1}{1+\cos\gamma} = \dfrac{1+\cos\gamma + 1 - \cos\gamma}{1-\cos^2\gamma} = \dfrac{2}{\sin^2\gamma} = 2\csc^2\gamma$

**10** $\dfrac{1+\csc 3\beta}{\sec 3\beta} - \cot 3\beta = \dfrac{1}{\sec 3\beta} + \dfrac{\csc 3\beta}{\sec 3\beta} - \cot 3\beta = \cos 3\beta + \dfrac{\cos 3\beta}{\sin 3\beta} - \cot 3\beta = \cos 3\beta$

**339**

**11** $(\sec u - \tan u)(\csc u + 1) = \left(\dfrac{1}{\cos u} - \dfrac{\sin u}{\cos u}\right)\left(\dfrac{1}{\sin u} + 1\right)$     {change to sines and cosines}

$$= \left(\dfrac{1 - \sin u}{\cos u}\right)\left(\dfrac{1 + \sin u}{\sin u}\right) \quad \text{\{combine fractions\}}$$

$$= \dfrac{1 - \sin^2 u}{\cos u \sin u} \quad \text{\{multiply terms\}}$$

$$= \dfrac{\cos^2 u}{\cos u \sin u} = \dfrac{\cos u}{\sin u} = \cot u$$

**12** $\dfrac{\cot\theta - \tan\theta}{\sin\theta + \cos\theta} = \dfrac{\dfrac{\cos\theta}{\sin\theta} - \dfrac{\sin\theta}{\cos\theta}}{\sin\theta + \cos\theta} = \dfrac{\dfrac{\cos^2\theta - \sin^2\theta}{\sin\theta\cos\theta}}{\sin\theta + \cos\theta}$

$$= \dfrac{(\cos\theta + \sin\theta)(\cos\theta - \sin\theta)}{\sin\theta\cos\theta(\sin\theta + \cos\theta)}$$

$$= \dfrac{\cos\theta - \sin\theta}{\sin\theta\cos\theta} = \dfrac{\cos\theta}{\sin\theta\cos\theta} - \dfrac{\sin\theta}{\sin\theta\cos\theta} = \dfrac{1}{\sin\theta} - \dfrac{1}{\cos\theta} = \csc\theta - \sec\theta$$

**13** $\csc^4 t - \cot^4 t = \left(\csc^2 t\right)^2 - \left(\cot^2 t\right)^2$     {recognize as a difference of squares}

$$= \left(\csc^2 t + \cot^2 t\right)\left(\csc^2 t - \cot^2 t\right) \quad \text{\{factor\}}$$

$$= \left(\csc^2 t + \cot^2 t\right)(1) \quad \text{\{Pythagorean identity, } 1 + \cot^2 t = \csc^2 t\text{\}}$$

$$= \csc^2 t + \cot^2 t$$

**14** $\cos^4 2\theta + \sin^2 2\theta = \left(\cos^2 2\theta\right)^2 + \sin^2 2\theta = \left(1 - \sin^2 2\theta\right)^2 + \sin^2 2\theta$

$$= 1 - 2\sin^2 2\theta + \sin^4 2\theta + \sin^2 2\theta = 1 - \sin^2 2\theta + \sin^4 2\theta = \cos^2 2\theta + \sin^4 2\theta$$

**15** The first step in the following verification is to multiply the denominator, $1 - \sin\beta$, by its conjugate, $1 + \sin\beta$. This procedure will give us the difference of two squares, $1 - \sin^2\beta$, which is equal to $\cos^2\beta$. This step is often helpful when simplifying trigonometric expressions because manipulation of the Pythagorean identities often allows us to reduce the resulting expression to a single term.

$$\dfrac{\cos\beta}{1 - \sin\beta} = \dfrac{\cos\beta}{1 - \sin\beta} \cdot \dfrac{1 + \sin\beta}{1 + \sin\beta}$$

$$= \dfrac{\cos\beta(1 + \sin\beta)}{1 - \sin^2\beta} = \dfrac{\cos\beta(1 + \sin\beta)}{\cos^2\beta} = \dfrac{1 + \sin\beta}{\cos\beta} = \dfrac{1}{\cos\beta} + \dfrac{\sin\beta}{\cos\beta} = \sec\beta + \tan\beta$$

**16** $\dfrac{1}{\csc y - \cot y} = \dfrac{1}{\csc y - \cot y} \cdot \dfrac{\csc y + \cot y}{\csc y + \cot y} = \dfrac{\csc y + \cot y}{\csc^2 y - \cot^2 y} = \dfrac{\csc y + \cot y}{1} = \csc y + \cot y$

**17** $\dfrac{\tan^2 x}{\sec x + 1} = \dfrac{\sec^2 x - 1}{\sec x + 1} = \dfrac{(\sec x + 1)(\sec x - 1)}{\sec x + 1} = \sec x - 1 = \dfrac{1}{\cos x} - 1 = \dfrac{1 - \cos x}{\cos x}$

**18** $\dfrac{\cot x}{\csc x + 1} = \dfrac{\cot x}{\csc x + 1} \cdot \dfrac{\csc x - 1}{\csc x - 1} = \dfrac{\cot x(\csc x - 1)}{\csc^2 x - 1} = \dfrac{\cot x(\csc x - 1)}{\cot^2 x} = \dfrac{\csc x - 1}{\cot x}$

**19** $\dfrac{\cot 4u - 1}{\cot 4u + 1} = \dfrac{\dfrac{1}{\tan 4u} - 1}{\dfrac{1}{\tan 4u} + 1} = \dfrac{\dfrac{1}{\tan 4u} - \dfrac{\tan 4u}{\tan 4u}}{\dfrac{1}{\tan 4u} + \dfrac{\tan 4u}{\tan 4u}} = \dfrac{\dfrac{1 - \tan 4u}{\tan 4u}}{\dfrac{1 + \tan 4u}{\tan 4u}} = \dfrac{1 - \tan 4u}{1 + \tan 4u}$

**20** $\dfrac{1 + \sec 4x}{\sin 4x + \tan 4x} = \dfrac{1 + \dfrac{1}{\cos 4x}}{\sin 4x + \dfrac{\sin 4x}{\cos 4x}} = \dfrac{\dfrac{\cos 4x + 1}{\cos 4x}}{\dfrac{\sin 4x \cos 4x + \sin 4x}{\cos 4x}} = \dfrac{\cos 4x + 1}{\sin 4x(\cos 4x + 1)} = \dfrac{1}{\sin 4x} = \csc 4x$

**21** $\sin^4 r - \cos^4 r = (\sin^2 r - \cos^2 r)(\sin^2 r + \cos^2 r) = (\sin^2 r - \cos^2 r)(1) = \sin^2 r - \cos^2 r$

**22** $\sin^4\theta + 2\sin^2\theta\cos^2\theta + \cos^4\theta = \left(\sin^2\theta + \cos^2\theta\right)^2 = (1)^2 = 1$

**23** $\tan^4 k - \sec^4 k = (\tan^2 k - \sec^2 k)(\tan^2 k + \sec^2 k)$ {factor as a difference of squares}

$\qquad = (-1)(\sec^2 k - 1 + \sec^2 k)$ {Pythagorean identity}

$\qquad = (-1)(2\sec^2 k - 1) = 1 - 2\sec^2 k$

**24** $\sec^4 u - \sec^2 u = \sec^2 u(\sec^2 u - 1) = (1 + \tan^2 u)(\tan^2 u) = \tan^2 u + \tan^4 u$

**25** $(\sec t + \tan t)^2 = \left(\dfrac{1}{\cos t} + \dfrac{\sin t}{\cos t}\right)^2$

$\qquad = \left(\dfrac{1 + \sin t}{\cos t}\right)^2 = \dfrac{(1 + \sin t)^2}{\cos^2 t} = \dfrac{(1 + \sin t)^2}{1 - \sin^2 t} = \dfrac{(1 + \sin t)^2}{(1 + \sin t)(1 - \sin t)} = \dfrac{1 + \sin t}{1 - \sin t}$

**26** $\mathrm{RS} = (1 - \sin^4 \gamma)\sec^4 \gamma = \sec^4 \gamma - \dfrac{\sin^4 \gamma}{\cos^4 \gamma}$

$\qquad = \sec^4 \gamma - \tan^4 \gamma = (\sec^2 \gamma - \tan^2 \gamma)(\sec^2 \gamma + \tan^2 \gamma) = (1)(\sec^2 \gamma + \tan^2 \gamma) = \sec^2 \gamma + \tan^2 \gamma = \mathrm{LS}$

**27** $(\sin^2 \theta + \cos^2 \theta)^3 = (1)^3 = 1$

**28** $\dfrac{\sin t}{1 - \cos t} = \dfrac{\sin t}{1 - \cos t} \cdot \dfrac{1 + \cos t}{1 + \cos t} = \dfrac{\sin t(1 + \cos t)}{1 - \cos^2 t} = \dfrac{\sin t(1 + \cos t)}{\sin^2 t} = \dfrac{1 + \cos t}{\sin t} = \dfrac{1}{\sin t} + \dfrac{\cos t}{\sin t} = \csc t + \cot t$

**29** $\dfrac{1 + \csc \beta}{\cot \beta + \cos \beta} = \dfrac{1 + \dfrac{1}{\sin \beta}}{\dfrac{\cos \beta}{\sin \beta} + \cos \beta} = \dfrac{\dfrac{\sin \beta + 1}{\sin \beta}}{\dfrac{\cos \beta + \cos \beta \sin \beta}{\sin \beta}} = \dfrac{\sin \beta + 1}{\cos \beta(1 + \sin \beta)} = \dfrac{1}{\cos \beta} = \sec \beta$

**30** $\dfrac{\cos^3 x - \sin^3 x}{\cos x - \sin x} = \dfrac{(\cos x - \sin x)(\cos^2 x + \cos x \sin x + \sin^2 x)}{\cos x - \sin x} = 1 + \sin x \cos x$

**31** As demonstrated in the following verification, it may be beneficial to try to combine expressions rather than expand them. $(\csc t - \cot t)^4 (\csc t + \cot t)^4 = [(\csc t - \cot t)(\csc t + \cot t)]^4 = (\csc^2 t - \cot^2 t)^4 = (1)^4 = 1$

**32** $(a\cos t - b\sin t)^2 + (a\sin t + b\cos t)^2$

$\qquad = (a^2 \cos^2 t - 2ab \cos t \sin t + b^2 \sin^2 t) + (a^2 \sin^2 t + 2ab \sin t \cos t + b^2 \cos^2 t)$

$\qquad = a^2(\cos^2 t + \sin^2 t) + b^2(\sin^2 t + \cos^2 t) = a^2 + b^2$

**33** $\mathrm{RS} = \dfrac{\tan \alpha + \tan \beta}{1 - \tan \alpha \tan \beta} = \dfrac{\dfrac{\sin \alpha}{\cos \alpha} + \dfrac{\sin \beta}{\cos \beta}}{1 - \dfrac{\sin \alpha}{\cos \alpha} \cdot \dfrac{\sin \beta}{\cos \beta}} = \dfrac{\dfrac{\sin \alpha \cos \beta + \cos \alpha \sin \beta}{\cos \alpha \cos \beta}}{\dfrac{\cos \alpha \cos \beta - \sin \alpha \sin \beta}{\cos \alpha \cos \beta}} = \dfrac{\sin \alpha \cos \beta + \cos \alpha \sin \beta}{\cos \alpha \cos \beta - \sin \alpha \sin \beta} = \mathrm{LS}$

**Note:** We could obtain the RS by dividing the numerator and denominator of the LS by $\cos \alpha \cos \beta$.

**34** $\dfrac{\tan u - \tan v}{1 + \tan u \tan v} = \dfrac{\dfrac{1}{\cot u} - \dfrac{1}{\cot v}}{1 + \dfrac{1}{\cot u} \cdot \dfrac{1}{\cot v}} = \dfrac{\dfrac{\cot v - \cot u}{\cot u \cot v}}{\dfrac{\cot u \cot v + 1}{\cot u \cot v}} = \dfrac{\cot v - \cot u}{\cot u \cot v + 1}$

**35** $\dfrac{\tan \alpha}{1 + \sec \alpha} + \dfrac{1 + \sec \alpha}{\tan \alpha} = \dfrac{\tan^2 \alpha + (1 + \sec \alpha)^2}{(1 + \sec \alpha)\tan \alpha}$

$\qquad = \dfrac{(\sec^2 \alpha - 1) + (1 + 2\sec \alpha + \sec^2 \alpha)}{(1 + \sec \alpha)\tan \alpha}$

$\qquad = \dfrac{2\sec^2 \alpha + 2\sec \alpha}{(1 + \sec \alpha)\tan \alpha} = \dfrac{2\sec \alpha(\sec \alpha + 1)\cot \alpha}{1 + \sec \alpha} = \dfrac{2}{\cos \alpha} \cdot \dfrac{\cos \alpha}{\sin \alpha} = \dfrac{2}{\sin \alpha} = 2\csc \alpha$

**36** $\dfrac{\csc x}{1 + \csc x} - \dfrac{\csc x}{1 - \csc x} = \dfrac{\csc x(1 - \csc x) - \csc x(1 + \csc x)}{1 - \csc^2 x}$

$\qquad = \dfrac{\csc x - \csc^2 x - \csc x - \csc^2 x}{1 - \csc^2 x} = \dfrac{-2\csc^2 x}{-\cot^2 x} = \dfrac{2/\sin^2 x}{\cos^2 x/\sin^2 x} = \dfrac{2}{\cos^2 x} = 2\sec^2 x$

**37** $\dfrac{1}{\tan\beta+\cot\beta}=\dfrac{1}{\dfrac{\sin\beta}{\cos\beta}+\dfrac{\cos\beta}{\sin\beta}}=\dfrac{1}{\dfrac{\sin^2\beta+\cos^2\beta}{\cos\beta\sin\beta}}=\dfrac{1}{\dfrac{1}{\cos\beta\sin\beta}}=\sin\beta\cos\beta$

**38** $\dfrac{\cot y-\tan y}{\sin y\cos y}=\dfrac{\dfrac{\cos y}{\sin y}-\dfrac{\sin y}{\cos y}}{\sin y\cos y}=\dfrac{\cos^2 y-\sin^2 y}{\sin^2 y\cos^2 y}=\dfrac{\cos^2 y}{\sin^2 y\cos^2 y}-\dfrac{\sin^2 y}{\sin^2 y\cos^2 y}=\dfrac{1}{\sin^2 y}-\dfrac{1}{\cos^2 y}=\csc^2 y-\sec^2 y$

**39** $\sec\theta+\csc\theta-\cos\theta-\sin\theta=\dfrac{1}{\cos\theta}+\dfrac{1}{\sin\theta}-\cos\theta-\sin\theta$

$=\left(\dfrac{1}{\cos\theta}-\cos\theta\right)+\left(\dfrac{1}{\sin\theta}-\sin\theta\right)$

$=\dfrac{1-\cos^2\theta}{\cos\theta}+\dfrac{1-\sin^2\theta}{\sin\theta}$

$=\dfrac{\sin^2\theta}{\cos\theta}+\dfrac{\cos^2\theta}{\sin\theta}$

$=\left(\sin\theta\cdot\dfrac{\sin\theta}{\cos\theta}\right)+\left(\cos\theta\cdot\dfrac{\cos\theta}{\sin\theta}\right)=\sin\theta\tan\theta+\cos\theta\cot\theta$

**40** $\sin^3 t+\cos^3 t=(\sin t+\cos t)(\sin^2 t-\sin t\cos t+\cos^2 t)=(1-\sin t\cos t)(\sin t+\cos t)$

**41** $RS=\sec^4\phi-4\tan^2\phi$

$=\left(\sec^2\phi\right)^2-4\tan^2\phi$

$=\left(1+\tan^2\phi\right)^2-4\tan^2\phi$

$=\left(1+2\tan^2\phi+\tan^4\phi\right)-4\tan^2\phi=1-2\tan^2\phi+\tan^4\phi=\left(1-\tan^2\phi\right)^2=LS$

**42** $\cos^4 w+1-\sin^4 w=\cos^4 w+1-\left(1-\cos^2 w\right)^2=\cos^4 w+1-\left(1-2\cos^2 w+\cos^4 w\right)=2\cos^2 w$

**43** $\dfrac{\cot(-t)+\tan(-t)}{\cot t}=\dfrac{-\cot t-\tan t}{\cot t}=-\dfrac{\cot t}{\cot t}-\dfrac{\tan t}{\cot t}=-\left(1+\tan^2 t\right)=-\sec^2 t$

**44** $\dfrac{\csc(-t)-\sin(-t)}{\sin(-t)}=\dfrac{-\csc t+\sin t}{-\sin t}=\dfrac{\csc t}{\sin t}-\dfrac{\sin t}{\sin t}=\csc^2 t-1=\cot^2 t$

**45** $\log 10^{\tan t}=\log_{10}10^{\tan t}=\tan t$, since $\log_a a^x=x$

**46** $10^{\log|\sin t|}=10^{\log_{10}|\sin t|}=|\sin t|$, since $a^{\log_a x}=x$

**47** $\ln\cot x=\ln(\cot x)=\ln(\tan x)^{-1}=-\ln(\tan x)$ {since $\ln a^x=x\ln a$} $=-\ln\tan x$

**48** $\ln\sec\theta=\ln(\sec\theta)=\ln(\cos\theta)^{-1}=-\ln(\cos\theta)=-\ln\cos\theta$

**49** $\ln|\sec\theta+\tan\theta|=\ln\left|\dfrac{(\sec\theta+\tan\theta)(\sec\theta-\tan\theta)}{\sec\theta-\tan\theta}\right|$　　multiply by the conjugate

$=\ln\left|\dfrac{\sec^2\theta-\tan^2\theta}{\sec\theta-\tan\theta}\right|$　　simplify

$=\ln\left|\dfrac{1}{\sec\theta-\tan\theta}\right|$　　Pythagorean identity

$=\ln\dfrac{|1|}{|\sec\theta-\tan\theta|}$　　$\left|\dfrac{a}{b}\right|=\dfrac{|a|}{|b|}$

$=\ln|1|-\ln|\sec\theta-\tan\theta|$　　$\ln\dfrac{a}{b}=\ln a-\ln b$

$=-\ln|\sec\theta-\tan\theta|$　　$\ln 1=0$

**50** $\ln|\csc x - \cot x| = \ln\left|\dfrac{(\csc x - \cot x)(\csc x + \cot x)}{\csc x + \cot x}\right|$

$= \ln\left|\dfrac{\csc^2 x - \cot^2 x}{\csc x + \cot x}\right| = \ln\left|\dfrac{1}{\csc x + \cot x}\right| = \ln|1| - \ln|\csc x + \cot x| = -\ln|\csc x + \cot x|$

**51** $\cos^2 t = 1 - \sin^2 t \ \Rightarrow \ \cos t = \pm\sqrt{1 - \sin^2 t}$. Since the given equation is $\cos t = +\sqrt{1 - \sin^2 t}$, we may choose any $t$ such that $\cos t < 0$. Using $t = \pi$, LS $= \cos\pi = -1$. RS $= \sqrt{1 - \sin^2\pi} = 1$. Since $-1 \neq 1$, LS $\neq$ RS.

**52** $(\sin t + \cos t)^2 = \sin^2 t + 2\cos t\sin t + \cos^2 t$. Hence, choose any $t$ except $0$ or $\frac{\pi}{2}$ and their coterminal angles. Using $t = \pi$, LS $= \sqrt{\sin^2\pi + \cos^2\pi} = 1$. RS $= \sin\pi + \cos\pi = 0 + (-1) = -1$. Since $1 \neq -1$, LS $\neq$ RS.

**53** $\sqrt{\sin^2 t} = |\sin t| = \pm\sin t$. Hence, choose any $t$ such that $\sin t < 0$.

Using $t = \frac{3\pi}{2}$, LS $= \sqrt{(-1)^2} = 1$. RS $= \sin\frac{3\pi}{2} = -1$. Since $1 \neq -1$, LS $\neq$ RS.

**54** $\sec^2 t = \tan^2 t + 1 \ \Rightarrow \ \sec t = \pm\sqrt{\tan^2 t + 1}$. Hence, choose any $t$ such that $\sec t < 0$.

Using $t = \frac{3\pi}{4}$, LS $= \sec\frac{3\pi}{4} = -\sqrt{2}$. RS $= \sqrt{(-1)^2 + 1} = \sqrt{2}$. Since $-\sqrt{2} \neq \sqrt{2}$, LS $\neq$ RS.

**55** $(\sin\theta + \cos\theta)^2 = \sin^2\theta + 2\sin\theta\cos\theta + \cos^2\theta$. Since the right side of the given equation is only $\sin^2\theta + \cos^2\theta$, we may choose any $\theta$ such that $2\sin\theta\cos\theta \neq 0$. Using $\theta = \frac{\pi}{4}$, LS $= \left(\frac{1}{2}\sqrt{2} + \frac{1}{2}\sqrt{2}\right)^2 = \left(\sqrt{2}\right)^2 = 2$.

RS $= \left(\frac{1}{2}\sqrt{2}\right)^2 + \left(\frac{1}{2}\sqrt{2}\right)^2 = \frac{1}{2} + \frac{1}{2} = 1$. Since $2 \neq 1$, LS $\neq$ RS.

**56** $\log(1/\sin t) = -\log\sin t \neq (\log\sin t)^{-1}$. $\log\sin t$ is defined if $\sin t > 0$. If $\sin t > 0$, $\log\sin t \leq 0$ since $\sin t \leq 1$ and $-\log\sin t \geq 0$. $(\log\sin t)^{-1} < 0$ when defined so LS is never equal to RS. Using $t = \frac{\pi}{6}$, LS $= \log 2$.

RS $= 1/\log\frac{1}{2} = -1/\log 2$. Since $\log 2 \neq -1/\log 2$, LS $\neq$ RS.

**57** $\cos(-t) = -\cos t$ $\bullet$ Since $\cos(-t) = \cos t$, we may choose any $t$ such that $\cos t \neq -\cos t$—that is, any $t$ such that $\cos t \neq 0$. Using $t = \pi$, LS $= \cos(-\pi) = -1$. RS $= -\cos\pi = -(-1) = 1$. Since $-1 \neq 1$, LS $\neq$ RS.

**58** From the unit circle, $\sin(t + \pi) = -\sin t$. Choose any $t$ such that $-\sin t \neq \sin t$, i.e., any $t$ such that $\sin t \neq 0$.

Using $t = \frac{\pi}{2}$, LS $= \sin\frac{3\pi}{2} = -1$. RS $= \sin\frac{\pi}{2} = 1$. Since $-1 \neq 1$, LS $\neq$ RS.

**59** Don't confuse $\cos(\sec t) = 1$ with $\cos t \cdot \sec t = 1$. The former is true if $\sec t = 2\pi$ or an integer multiple of $2\pi$. The latter is true for any value of $t$ as long as $\sec t$ is defined. Choose any $t$ such that $\sec t \neq 2\pi n$.

Using $t = \frac{\pi}{4}$, LS $= \cos\left(\sec\frac{\pi}{4}\right) = \cos\sqrt{2} \neq 1 =$ RS.

**60** Don't confuse $\cot(\tan\theta) = 1$ with $\cot\theta \cdot \tan\theta = 1$. Choose any $\theta$ such that

$\tan\theta \neq \frac{\pi}{4} + \pi n$. Using $\theta = \frac{\pi}{4}$, LS $= \cot\left(\tan\frac{\pi}{4}\right) = \cot 1 \neq 1 =$ RS.

**61** LS $= (\sec x + \tan x)^2$

$= \sec^2 x + 2\sec x\tan x + \tan^2 x = (\tan^2 x + 1) + 2\sec x\tan x + \tan^2 x = 2\tan^2 x + 2\sec x\tan x + 1$

RS $= 2\tan x(\tan x + \sec x) = 2\tan^2 x + 2\tan x\sec x$

Thus, LS $=$ RS $+ 1$, and the equation *is not* an identity.

**62** LS $= \dfrac{\tan^2 x}{\sec x - 1} = \dfrac{\tan^2 x}{\sec x - 1} \cdot \dfrac{\sec x + 1}{\sec x + 1}$

$= \dfrac{(\tan^2 x)(\sec x + 1)}{(\sec x - 1)(\sec x + 1)} = \dfrac{(\tan^2 x)(\sec x + 1)}{\sec^2 x - 1} = \dfrac{(\tan^2 x)(\sec x + 1)}{\tan^2 x} = \sec x + 1 \neq \sec x =$ RS

Thus, LS $=$ RS $+ 1$, and the equation *is not* an identity.

**63** $LS = \cos x(\tan x + \cot x) = \cos x\left(\dfrac{\sin x}{\cos x} + \dfrac{\cos x}{\sin x}\right) = \sin x + \dfrac{\cos^2 x}{\sin x} = \dfrac{\sin^2 x + \cos^2 x}{\sin x} = \dfrac{1}{\sin x} = \csc x = RS$,

so the equation *is* an identity.

**64** $LS = \csc^2 x + \sec^2 x = \dfrac{1}{\sin^2 x} + \dfrac{1}{\cos^2 x} = \dfrac{\cos^2 x + \sin^2 x}{\sin^2 x \cos^2 x} = \dfrac{1}{\sin^2 x \cos^2 x} = \dfrac{1}{\sin^2 x} \cdot \dfrac{1}{\cos^2 x} = \csc^2 x \sec^2 x = RS$,

so the equation *is* an identity.

**Note:** In Exercises 65–68, use $\sqrt{a^2 - x^2} = a\cos\theta$ because

$\sqrt{a^2 - x^2} = \sqrt{a^2 - a^2\sin^2\theta} = \sqrt{a^2(1 - \sin^2\theta)} = \sqrt{a^2\cos^2\theta} = |a||\cos\theta| = a\cos\theta$

since $\cos\theta > 0$ if $-\frac{\pi}{2} < \theta < \frac{\pi}{2}$ and $a > 0$.

**65** $\dfrac{x^2}{a^2 - x^2} = \dfrac{(a\sin\theta)^2}{\left(\sqrt{a^2 - x^2}\right)^2} = \dfrac{a^2\sin^2\theta}{(a\cos\theta)^2}$ {see note above} $= \dfrac{a^2\sin^2\theta}{a^2\cos^2\theta} = \dfrac{\sin^2\theta}{\cos^2\theta} = \left(\dfrac{\sin\theta}{\cos\theta}\right)^2 = \tan^2\theta$

**66** $\dfrac{(a^2 - x^2)^2}{x^3} = \dfrac{\left[\left(\sqrt{a^2 - x^2}\right)^2\right]^2}{(a\sin\theta)^3} = \dfrac{(a\cos\theta)^4}{a^3\sin^3\theta} = \dfrac{a^4\cos^4\theta}{a^3\sin^3\theta} = a\cdot\left(\dfrac{\cos\theta}{\sin\theta}\right)^3\cdot\cos\theta = a\cot^3\theta\cos\theta$

**67** $\dfrac{\sqrt{a^2 - x^2}}{x^2} = \dfrac{a\cos\theta}{(a\sin\theta)^2} = \dfrac{a\cos\theta}{a^2\sin^2\theta} = \dfrac{1}{a}\cdot\dfrac{\cos\theta}{\sin\theta}\cdot\dfrac{1}{\sin\theta} = \dfrac{1}{a}\cot\theta\csc\theta$

**68** $\dfrac{x}{\sqrt{a^2 - x^2}} = \dfrac{a\sin\theta}{a\cos\theta} = \dfrac{\sin\theta}{\cos\theta} = \tan\theta$

**Note:** In Exercises 69–72, use $\sqrt{a^2 + x^2} = a\sec\theta$ because

$\sqrt{a^2 + x^2} = \sqrt{a^2 + a^2\tan^2\theta} = \sqrt{a^2(1 + \tan^2\theta)} = \sqrt{a^2\sec^2\theta} = |a||\sec\theta| = a\sec\theta$

since $\sec\theta > 0$ if $-\frac{\pi}{2} < \theta < \frac{\pi}{2}$ and $a > 0$.

**69** $\dfrac{x^4}{(a^2 + x^2)^2} = \dfrac{(a\tan\theta)^4}{\left[\left(\sqrt{a^2 + x^2}\right)^2\right]^2} = \dfrac{a^4\tan^4\theta}{(a\sec\theta)^4}$ {see note above} $= \dfrac{a^4\tan^4\theta}{a^4\sec^4\theta} = \left(\dfrac{\sin\theta/\cos\theta}{1/\cos\theta}\right)^4 = (\sin\theta)^4 = \sin^4\theta$

**70** $\dfrac{a^2 + x^2}{x^2} = \dfrac{\left(\sqrt{a^2 + x^2}\right)^2}{(a\tan\theta)^2} = \dfrac{(a\sec\theta)^2}{a^2\tan^2\theta} = \dfrac{a^2\sec^2\theta}{a^2\tan^2\theta} = \left(\dfrac{1/\cos\theta}{\sin\theta/\cos\theta}\right)^2 = \left(\dfrac{1}{\sin\theta}\right)^2 = \csc^2\theta$

**71** $\dfrac{x^2}{\sqrt{a^2 + x^2}} = \dfrac{(a\tan\theta)^2}{a\sec\theta} = \dfrac{a^2\tan^2\theta}{a\sec\theta} = \dfrac{a\tan^2\theta}{\sec\theta} = \dfrac{a(\sin\theta/\cos\theta)^2}{1/\cos\theta} = a\cdot\dfrac{\sin\theta}{\cos\theta}\cdot\dfrac{\sin\theta}{1} = a\tan\theta\sin\theta$

**72** $\dfrac{\sqrt{a^2 + x^2}}{x} = \dfrac{a\sec\theta}{a\tan\theta} = \dfrac{\sec\theta}{\tan\theta} = \dfrac{1/\cos\theta}{\sin\theta/\cos\theta} = \dfrac{1}{\sin\theta} = \csc\theta$

**Note:** In Exercises 73–76, use $\sqrt{x^2 - a^2} = a\tan\theta$ because

$\sqrt{x^2 - a^2} = \sqrt{a^2\sec^2\theta - a^2} = \sqrt{a^2(\sec^2\theta - 1)} = \sqrt{a^2\tan^2\theta} = |a||\tan\theta| = a\tan\theta$

since $\tan\theta > 0$ if $0 < \theta < \frac{\pi}{2}$ and $a > 0$.

**73** $\dfrac{(x^2 - a^2)^2}{x^2} = \dfrac{\left[\left(\sqrt{x^2 - a^2}\right)^2\right]^2}{(a\sec\theta)^2} = \dfrac{(a\tan\theta)^4}{a^2\sec^2\theta}$ {see note above}

$= \dfrac{a^4\tan^4\theta}{a^2\sec^2\theta} = \dfrac{a^2(\sin\theta/\cos\theta)^4}{(1/\cos\theta)^2} = a^2\left(\dfrac{\sin\theta}{\cos\theta}\right)^2\dfrac{\sin^2\theta}{1} = a^2\tan^2\theta\sin^2\theta$

**74** $\dfrac{x}{x^2-a^2} = \dfrac{a\sec\theta}{\left(\sqrt{x^2-a^2}\right)^2} = \dfrac{a\sec\theta}{(a\tan\theta)^2} = \dfrac{a\sec\theta}{a^2\tan^2\theta} = \dfrac{1/\cos\theta}{a(\sin\theta/\cos\theta)^2}$

$$= \dfrac{1}{a}\cdot\dfrac{\cos\theta}{\sin\theta}\cdot\dfrac{1}{\sin\theta} = \dfrac{1}{a}\cdot\dfrac{\cos\theta}{\sin\theta}\cdot\dfrac{1}{\sin\theta} = \dfrac{1}{a}\cot\theta\csc\theta$$

**75** $\dfrac{\sqrt{x^2-a^2}}{x} = \dfrac{a\tan\theta}{a\sec\theta} = \dfrac{\tan\theta}{\sec\theta} = \dfrac{\sin\theta/\cos\theta}{1/\cos\theta} = \dfrac{\sin\theta}{1} = \sin\theta$

**76** $\dfrac{x^2}{\sqrt{x^2-a^2}} = \dfrac{(a\sec\theta)^2}{a\tan\theta} = \dfrac{a^2\sec^2\theta}{a\tan\theta} = \dfrac{a(1/\cos\theta)^2}{\sin\theta/\cos\theta} = \dfrac{a}{\sin\theta\cos\theta} = a\cdot\dfrac{1}{\cos\theta}\cdot\dfrac{1}{\sin\theta} = a\sec\theta\csc\theta$

**77** The graph of $f(x) = \dfrac{\sin^2 x - \sin^4 x}{(1-\sec^2 x)\cos^4 x}$ appears to be that of the horizontal line $y = g(x) = -1$.

Verifying this identity, we have

$$\dfrac{\sin^2 x - \sin^4 x}{(1-\sec^2 x)\cos^4 x} = \dfrac{\sin^2 x(1-\sin^2 x)}{-\tan^2 x\cos^4 x} = \dfrac{\sin^2 x\cos^2 x}{-(\sin^2 x/\cos^2 x)\cos^4 x} = \dfrac{\sin^2 x\cos^2 x}{-\sin^2 x\cos^2 x} = -1.$$

**78** The graph of $f$ appears to be that of $y = g(x) = \sin x$.

$$\dfrac{\sin x - \sin^3 x}{\cos^4 x + \cos^2 x\sin^2 x} = \dfrac{\sin x(1-\sin^2 x)}{\cos^2 x(\cos^2 x + \sin^2 x)} = \dfrac{\sin x\cos^2 x}{\cos^2 x(1)} = \sin x$$

**79** The graph of $f(x) = \sec x(\sin x\cos x + \cos^2 x) - \sin x$ appears to be that of $y = g(x) = \cos x$.

Verifying this identity, we have

$$\sec x(\sin x\cos x + \cos^2 x) - \sin x = \sec x\cos x(\sin x + \cos x) - \sin x = (\sin x + \cos x) - \sin x = \cos x.$$

**80** The graph of $f$ appears to be that of $y = g(x) = 1$.

$$\dfrac{\sin^3 x + \sin x\cos^2 x}{\csc x} + \dfrac{\cos^3 x + \cos x\sin^2 x}{\sec x} = \dfrac{\sin x(\sin^2 x + \cos^2 x)}{\csc x} + \dfrac{\cos x(\cos^2 x + \sin^2 x)}{\sec x}$$

$$= \dfrac{\sin x}{\csc x} + \dfrac{\cos x}{\sec x} = \sin^2 x + \cos^2 x = 1$$

## *6.2 Exercises*

**1** In $[0, 2\pi)$, $\sin x = -\dfrac{\sqrt{2}}{2}$ only if $x = \dfrac{5\pi}{4}, \dfrac{7\pi}{4}$.

*All solutions* would include these angles plus all angles coterminal with them. Hence, $x = \dfrac{5\pi}{4} + 2\pi n, \dfrac{7\pi}{4} + 2\pi n$.

**2** $\cos t = -1 \;\Rightarrow\; t = \pi + 2\pi n$, or, equivalently, $(2n+1)\pi$.

**3** $\tan\theta = \sqrt{3} \;\Rightarrow\; \theta = \dfrac{\pi}{3} + \pi n$

**Note:** This solution could be written as $\dfrac{\pi}{3} + 2\pi n$ and $\dfrac{4\pi}{3} + 2\pi n$. Since the period of the tangent (and the cotangent) is $\pi$, we use the abbreviated form $\dfrac{\pi}{3} + \pi n$ to describe all solutions. We will use "$\pi n$" for solutions of exercises involving the tangent and cotangent functions.

**4** $\cot\alpha = -\dfrac{1}{\sqrt{3}} \;\Rightarrow\; \tan\alpha = -\sqrt{3} \;\Rightarrow\; \alpha = \dfrac{2\pi}{3} + \pi n$

**5** $\sec\beta = 2 \;\Rightarrow\; \cos\beta = \dfrac{1}{2} \;\Rightarrow\; \beta = \dfrac{\pi}{3} + 2\pi n, \dfrac{5\pi}{3} + 2\pi n$

**6** $\csc\gamma = \sqrt{2} \;\Rightarrow\; \sin\gamma = \dfrac{1}{\sqrt{2}} \;\Rightarrow\; \gamma = \dfrac{\pi}{4} + 2\pi n, \dfrac{3\pi}{4} + 2\pi n$

$\boxed{7}$ $\sin x = \frac{\pi}{2}$ has **no solution** since $\frac{\pi}{2} > 1$, which is not in the range $[-1, 1]$. Your calculator will give some kind of error message if you attempt to find a solution to this or any similar problem.

$\boxed{8}$ $\cos x = -\frac{\pi}{3}$ has **no solution** since $-\frac{\pi}{3} < -1$, which is not in the range $[-1, 1]$.

$\boxed{9}$ $\cos \theta = \dfrac{1}{\sec \theta}$ is true for all values *for which the equation is defined.*     ★ All $\theta$ *except* $\theta = \frac{\pi}{2} + \pi n$

$\boxed{10}$ $\csc \theta \sin \theta = 1$ is true for all values for which the equation is defined.     ★ All $\theta$ except $\theta = \pi n$

$\boxed{11}$ $2\cos 2\theta - \sqrt{3} = 0 \;\Rightarrow\; \cos 2\theta = \frac{\sqrt{3}}{2}$ {$2\theta$ is just an angle — so we solve this equation for $2\theta$ and then divide those solutions by 2} $\;\Rightarrow\; 2\theta = \frac{\pi}{6} + 2\pi n, \frac{11\pi}{6} + 2\pi n \;\Rightarrow\; \theta = \frac{\pi}{12} + \pi n, \frac{11\pi}{12} + \pi n$

$\boxed{12}$ $2\sin 3\theta + \sqrt{2} = 0 \;\Rightarrow\; \sin 3\theta = -\frac{\sqrt{2}}{2} \;\Rightarrow\; 3\theta = \frac{5\pi}{4} + 2\pi n, \frac{7\pi}{4} + 2\pi n \;\Rightarrow\; \theta = \frac{5\pi}{12} + \frac{2\pi}{3}n, \frac{7\pi}{12} + \frac{2\pi}{3}n$

$\boxed{13}$ $\sqrt{3}\tan \frac{1}{3}t = 1 \;\Rightarrow\; \tan \frac{1}{3}t = \frac{1}{\sqrt{3}} \;\Rightarrow\; \frac{1}{3}t = \frac{\pi}{6} + \pi n \;\Rightarrow\; t = \frac{\pi}{2} + 3\pi n$

$\boxed{14}$ $\cos \frac{1}{4}x = -\frac{\sqrt{2}}{2} \;\Rightarrow\; \frac{1}{4}x = \frac{3\pi}{4} + 2\pi n, \frac{5\pi}{4} + 2\pi n \;\Rightarrow\; x = 3\pi + 8\pi n, 5\pi + 8\pi n$

$\boxed{15}$ $\sin\left(\theta + \frac{\pi}{4}\right) = \frac{1}{2} \;\Rightarrow\; \theta + \frac{\pi}{4} = \frac{\pi}{6} + 2\pi n, \frac{5\pi}{6} + 2\pi n \;\Rightarrow\; \theta = -\frac{\pi}{12} + 2\pi n, \frac{7\pi}{12} + 2\pi n$

$\boxed{16}$ $\cos\left(x - \frac{\pi}{3}\right) = -1 \;\Rightarrow\; x - \frac{\pi}{3} = \pi + 2\pi n \;\Rightarrow\; x = \frac{4\pi}{3} + 2\pi n$

$\boxed{17}$ $\sin\left(2x - \frac{\pi}{3}\right) = \frac{1}{2} \;\Rightarrow\; 2x - \frac{\pi}{3} = \frac{\pi}{6} + 2\pi n, \frac{5\pi}{6} + 2\pi n \;\Rightarrow\; 2x = \frac{\pi}{2} + 2\pi n, \frac{7\pi}{6} + 2\pi n \;\Rightarrow$
$$x = \frac{\pi}{4} + \pi n, \frac{7\pi}{12} + \pi n$$

$\boxed{18}$ $\cos\left(4x - \frac{\pi}{4}\right) = \frac{\sqrt{2}}{2} \;\Rightarrow\; 4x - \frac{\pi}{4} = \frac{\pi}{4} + 2\pi n, \frac{7\pi}{4} + 2\pi n \;\Rightarrow\; 4x = \frac{\pi}{2} + 2\pi n, 2\pi + 2\pi n$ {or just $2\pi n$} $\;\Rightarrow$
$$x = \frac{\pi}{8} + \frac{\pi}{2}n, \frac{\pi}{2}n$$

$\boxed{19}$ $2\cos t + 1 = 0 \;\Rightarrow\; 2\cos t = -1 \;\Rightarrow\; \cos t = -\frac{1}{2} \;\Rightarrow\; t = \frac{2\pi}{3} + 2\pi n, \frac{4\pi}{3} + 2\pi n$

$\boxed{20}$ $4\cos \theta - 2 = 0 \;\Rightarrow\; \cos \theta = \frac{1}{2} \;\Rightarrow\; \theta = \frac{\pi}{3} + 2\pi n, \frac{5\pi}{3} + 2\pi n$

$\boxed{21}$ $\sqrt{3} + 2\sin \beta = 0 \;\Rightarrow\; 2\sin \beta = -\sqrt{3} \;\Rightarrow\; \sin \beta = -\frac{\sqrt{3}}{2} \;\Rightarrow\; \beta = \frac{4\pi}{3} + 2\pi n, \frac{5\pi}{3} + 2\pi n$

$\boxed{22}$ $2\cos x = \sqrt{3} \;\Rightarrow\; \cos x = \frac{\sqrt{3}}{2} \;\Rightarrow\; x = \frac{\pi}{6} + 2\pi n, \frac{11\pi}{6} + 2\pi n$

$\boxed{23}$ $(\cos \theta - 1)\sin \theta = 0 \;\Rightarrow\; \cos \theta = 1$ or $\sin \theta = 0 \;\Rightarrow\; \theta = 2\pi n$ or $\theta = \pi n$, or simply $\pi n$

$\boxed{24}$ $(\sin t - 1)\cos t = 0 \;\Rightarrow\; \sin t = 1$ or $\cos t = 0 \;\Rightarrow\; t = \frac{\pi}{2} + 2\pi n$ or $t = \frac{\pi}{2} + \pi n$, or simply $\frac{\pi}{2} + \pi n$

$\boxed{25}$ $\tan^2 x = 1 \;\Rightarrow\; \tan x = \pm 1 \;\Rightarrow\; x = \frac{\pi}{4} + \pi n, \frac{3\pi}{4} + \pi n$, or simply $\frac{\pi}{4} + \frac{\pi}{2}n$

$\boxed{26}$ $\cot^2 \theta - 1 = 0 \;\Rightarrow\; \cot^2 \theta = 1 \;\Rightarrow\; \cot \theta = \pm 1 \;\Rightarrow\; \theta = \frac{\pi}{4} + \pi n, \frac{3\pi}{4} + \pi n$, or simply $\frac{\pi}{4} + \frac{\pi}{2}n$

$\boxed{27}$ $\sec^2 \alpha - 4 = 0 \;\Rightarrow\; \sec^2 \alpha = 4 \;\Rightarrow\; \sec \alpha = \pm 2 \;\Rightarrow\; \alpha = \frac{\pi}{3} + 2\pi n, \frac{5\pi}{3} + 2\pi n, \frac{2\pi}{3} + 2\pi n, \frac{4\pi}{3} + 2\pi n,$
$$\text{or simply } \tfrac{\pi}{3} + \pi n, \tfrac{2\pi}{3} + \pi n$$

$\boxed{28}$ $3 - \tan^2 \beta = 0 \;\Rightarrow\; \tan^2 \beta = 3 \;\Rightarrow\; \tan \beta = \pm\sqrt{3} \;\Rightarrow\; \beta = \frac{\pi}{3} + \pi n, \frac{2\pi}{3} + \pi n$

$\boxed{29}$ $\cot^2 x - 3 = 0 \;\Rightarrow\; \cot^2 x = 3 \;\Rightarrow\; \cot x = \pm\sqrt{3} \;\Rightarrow\; x = \frac{\pi}{6} + \pi n, \frac{5\pi}{6} + \pi n$

$\boxed{30}$ $4\sin^2 x - 3 = 0 \;\Rightarrow\; \sin^2 x = \frac{3}{4} \;\Rightarrow\; \sin x = \pm\frac{\sqrt{3}}{2} \;\Rightarrow\; x = \frac{\pi}{3} + \pi n, \frac{2\pi}{3} + \pi n$

$\boxed{31}$ $(2\sin \theta + 1)(2\cos \theta + 3) = 0 \;\Rightarrow\; \sin \theta = -\frac{1}{2}$ or $\cos \theta = -\frac{3}{2} \;\Rightarrow$
$$\theta = \tfrac{7\pi}{6} + 2\pi n, \tfrac{11\pi}{6} + 2\pi n \; \{\cos \theta = -\tfrac{3}{2} \text{ has no solutions}\}$$

**32** $(2\sin u - 1)\left(\cos u - \sqrt{2}\right) = 0 \;\Rightarrow\; \sin u = \frac{1}{2}$ or $\cos u = \sqrt{2} \;\Rightarrow$

$$u = \frac{\pi}{6} + 2\pi n, \frac{5\pi}{6} + 2\pi n \;\{\cos u = \sqrt{2} \text{ has no solutions}\}$$

**33** $\cos x + 1 = 2\sin^2 x \;\Rightarrow\; \cos x + 1 = 2(1 - \cos^2 x) \;\Rightarrow\; \cos x + 1 = 2 - 2\cos^2 x \;\Rightarrow$

$2\cos^2 x + \cos x - 1 = 0 \;\Rightarrow\; (2\cos x - 1)(\cos x + 1) = 0 \;\Rightarrow\; \cos x = \frac{1}{2}, -1 \;\Rightarrow$

$$x = \frac{\pi}{3} + 2\pi n, \frac{5\pi}{3} + 2\pi n, \pi + 2\pi n$$

**34** $2\cos^2 x + \sin x = 1 \;\Rightarrow\; 2(1 - \sin^2 x) + \sin x - 1 = 0 \;\Rightarrow\; 2 - 2\sin^2 x + \sin x - 1 = 0 \;\Rightarrow$

$2\sin^2 x - \sin x - 1 = 0 \;\Rightarrow\; (2\sin x + 1)(\sin x - 1) = 0 \;\Rightarrow\; \sin x = -\frac{1}{2}, 1 \;\Rightarrow$

$$x = \frac{7\pi}{6} + 2\pi n, \frac{11\pi}{6} + 2\pi n, \frac{\pi}{2} + 2\pi n$$

**35** $\sin 2x(\csc 2x - 2) = 0 \;\Rightarrow\; 1 - 2\sin 2x \;\{\text{multiply}\} = 0 \;\Rightarrow\; \sin 2x = \frac{1}{2} \;\Rightarrow$

$$2x = \frac{\pi}{6} + 2\pi n, \frac{5\pi}{6} + 2\pi n \;\Rightarrow\; x = \frac{\pi}{12} + \pi n, \frac{5\pi}{12} + \pi n$$

**36** $\cos 2x(\sec 2x + 2) = 0 \;\Rightarrow\; 1 + 2\cos 2x \;\{\text{multiply}\} = 0 \;\Rightarrow\; \cos 2x = -\frac{1}{2} \;\Rightarrow$

$$2x = \frac{2\pi}{3} + 2\pi n, \frac{4\pi}{3} + 2\pi n \;\Rightarrow\; x = \frac{\pi}{3} + \pi n, \frac{2\pi}{3} + \pi n$$

**37** $\cot x + \cot^2 x = 0 \;\Rightarrow\; \cot x(1 + \cot x) = 0 \;\Rightarrow\; \cot x = 0, -1 \;\Rightarrow\; x = \frac{\pi}{2} + \pi n, \frac{3\pi}{4} + \pi n$

**38** $\tan \alpha + \tan^2 \alpha = 0 \;\Rightarrow\; \tan \alpha(1 + \tan \alpha) = 0 \;\Rightarrow\; \tan \alpha = 0, -1 \;\Rightarrow\; \alpha = \pi n, \frac{3\pi}{4} + \pi n$

**39** $\cos(\ln x) = 0 \;\Rightarrow\; \ln x = \frac{\pi}{2} + \pi n \;\Rightarrow\; x = e^{(\pi/2) + \pi n} \;\{\text{since } \ln x = y \;\Leftrightarrow\; x = e^y\}$

**40** $\sin(\log x) = 0 \;\Rightarrow\; \log x = \pi n \;\Rightarrow\; x = 10^{\pi n} \;\{\text{since } \log x = y \;\Leftrightarrow\; x = 10^y\}$

**41** $\log(\cos x) = 0 \;\Rightarrow\; \cos x = 10^0 = 1 \;\Rightarrow\; x = 2\pi n$

**42** $\ln(\sin x) = 0 \;\Rightarrow\; \sin x = e^0 = 1 \;\Rightarrow\; x = \frac{\pi}{2} + 2\pi n$

**43** $\cos\left(2x - \frac{\pi}{4}\right) = 0 \;\Rightarrow\; 2x - \frac{\pi}{4} = \frac{\pi}{2} + \pi n \;\Rightarrow\; 2x = \frac{3\pi}{4} + \pi n \;\Rightarrow\; x = \frac{3\pi}{8} + \frac{\pi}{2}n.$

$x$ will be in the interval $[0, 2\pi)$ if $n = 0, 1, 2,$ or $3$. Thus, $x = \frac{3\pi}{8}, \frac{7\pi}{8}, \frac{11\pi}{8}, \frac{15\pi}{8}.$

**44** $\sin\left(3x - \frac{\pi}{4}\right) = 1 \;\Rightarrow\; 3x - \frac{\pi}{4} = \frac{\pi}{2} + 2\pi n \;\Rightarrow\; 3x = \frac{3\pi}{4} + 2\pi n \;\Rightarrow\; x = \frac{\pi}{4} + \frac{2\pi}{3}n.$

$x$ will be in the interval $[0, 2\pi)$ if $n = 0, 1,$ or $2$. Thus, $x = \frac{\pi}{4}, \frac{11\pi}{12}, \frac{19\pi}{12}.$

**45** $2 - 8\cos^2 t = 0 \;\Rightarrow\; \cos^2 t = \frac{1}{4} \;\Rightarrow\; \cos t = \pm\frac{1}{2} \;\Rightarrow\; t = \frac{\pi}{3}, \frac{2\pi}{3}, \frac{4\pi}{3}, \frac{5\pi}{3}$

**46** $1 + 8\sin^3 x = 0 \;\Rightarrow\; \sin^3 x = -\frac{1}{8} \;\Rightarrow\; \sin x = -\frac{1}{2} \;\Rightarrow\; x = \frac{7\pi}{6}, \frac{11\pi}{6}$

**47** $\tan^2 x = \tan x \;\Rightarrow\; \tan^2 x - \tan x = 0 \;\Rightarrow\; \tan x(\tan x - 1) = 0 \;\Rightarrow\; \tan x = 0, 1 \;\Rightarrow\; \theta = \frac{\pi}{2}, \frac{3\pi}{2}, \frac{\pi}{4}, \frac{5\pi}{4}$

**48** $\cot^2 \theta - \cot \theta = 0 \;\Rightarrow\; \cot \theta(\cot \theta - 1) = 0 \;\Rightarrow\; \cot \theta = 0, 1 \;\Rightarrow\; \theta = \frac{\pi}{2}, \frac{3\pi}{2}, \frac{\pi}{4}, \frac{5\pi}{4}$

**49** $2\sin^2 u = 1 - \sin u \;\Rightarrow\; 2\sin^2 u + \sin u - 1 = 0 \;\Rightarrow\; (2\sin u - 1)(\sin u + 1) = 0 \;\Rightarrow$

$$\sin u = \frac{1}{2}, -1 \;\Rightarrow\; u = \frac{\pi}{6}, \frac{5\pi}{6}, \frac{3\pi}{2}$$

**50** $2\cos^2 t + 3\cos t = -1 \;\Rightarrow\; 2\cos^2 t + 3\cos t + 1 = 0 \;\Rightarrow\; (2\cos t + 1)(\cos t + 1) = 0 \;\Rightarrow$

$$\cos t = -\frac{1}{2}, -1 \;\Rightarrow\; t = \frac{2\pi}{3}, \frac{4\pi}{3}, \pi$$

**51** $\tan^2 x \sin x = \sin x \;\Rightarrow\; \tan^2 x \sin x - \sin x = 0 \;\Rightarrow\; \sin x(\tan^2 x - 1) = 0 \;\Rightarrow$

$\sin x = 0$ or $\tan x = \pm 1 \;\Rightarrow\; x = 0, \pi, \frac{\pi}{4}, \frac{3\pi}{4}, \frac{5\pi}{4}, \frac{7\pi}{4}.$ ***Note:*** A common mistake is to divide both sides of the given equation by $\sin x$—doing so results in losing the solutions for $\sin x = 0$.

**52** $\sec^2 x \cos x = \cos x \Rightarrow \sec^2 x \cos x - \cos x = 0 \Rightarrow \cos x(\sec^2 x - 1) = 0 \Rightarrow$
$\cos x = 0$ or $\sec x = \pm 1 \Rightarrow x = \frac{\pi}{2}, \frac{3\pi}{2}, 0, \pi$, but the original equation is not defined when $x = \frac{\pi}{2}$ or $\frac{3\pi}{2}$,
so the solutions are $0$ and $\pi$.

**53** $\sec x \csc x = \sqrt{2} \sec x \Rightarrow \sec x \csc x - \sqrt{2} \sec x = 0 \Rightarrow \sec x\left(\csc x - \sqrt{2}\right) = 0 \Rightarrow$
$\sec x = 0$ or $\csc x = \sqrt{2} \Rightarrow x = \frac{\pi}{4}, \frac{3\pi}{4}$ {$\sec x = 0$ has no solutions}

**54** $\sec \beta \csc \beta = 2 \csc \beta \Rightarrow \sec \beta \csc \beta - 2 \csc \beta = 0 \Rightarrow \csc \beta(\sec \beta - 2) = 0 \Rightarrow$
$\csc \beta = 0$ or $\sec \beta = 2 \Rightarrow \beta = \frac{\pi}{3}, \frac{5\pi}{3}$ {$\csc \beta = 0$ has no solutions}

**55** $2 \cos^2 \gamma + \cos \gamma = 0 \Rightarrow \cos \gamma(2 \cos \gamma + 1) = 0 \Rightarrow \cos \gamma = 0, -\frac{1}{2} \Rightarrow \gamma = \frac{\pi}{2}, \frac{3\pi}{2}, \frac{2\pi}{3}, \frac{4\pi}{3}$

**56** $\sin x - \cos x = 0 \Rightarrow \sin x = \cos x \Rightarrow \tan x = 1 \Rightarrow x = \frac{\pi}{4}, \frac{5\pi}{4}$

**57** $\sin^2 \theta + \sin \theta - 6 = 0 \Rightarrow (\sin \theta + 3)(\sin \theta - 2) = 0 \Rightarrow \sin \theta = -3, 2.$
There are **no solutions** for either equation.

**58** $2 \sin^2 u + \sin u - 6 = 0 \Rightarrow (2 \sin u - 3)(\sin u + 2) = 0 \Rightarrow \sin u = \frac{3}{2}, -2.$
There are **no solutions** for either equation.

**59** $1 - \sin t = \sqrt{3} \cos t$ • Square both sides to obtain an equation in either sin or cos.
$(1 - \sin t)^2 = \left(\sqrt{3} \cos t\right)^2 \Rightarrow 1 - 2 \sin t + \sin^2 t = 3 \cos^2 t \Rightarrow \sin^2 t - 2 \sin t + 1 = 3(1 - \sin^2 t) \Rightarrow$
$4 \sin^2 t - 2 \sin t - 2 = 0 \Rightarrow 2 \sin^2 t - \sin t - 1 = 0 \Rightarrow (2 \sin t + 1)(\sin t - 1) = 0 \Rightarrow \sin t = -\frac{1}{2}, 1 \Rightarrow$
$t = \frac{7\pi}{6}, \frac{11\pi}{6}, \frac{\pi}{2}$. Since each side of the equation was squared, the solutions must be checked in the original equation.
**Check $\frac{7\pi}{6}$:** LS $= 1 - \sin \frac{7\pi}{6} = 1 - \left(-\frac{1}{2}\right) = \frac{3}{2}$ and RS $= \sqrt{3} \cos \frac{7\pi}{6} = \sqrt{3}\left(-\frac{\sqrt{3}}{2}\right) = -\frac{3}{2}$.
Since LS $\ne$ RS, $\frac{7\pi}{6}$ is an *extraneous solution*.
**Check $\frac{11\pi}{6}$:** LS $= 1 - \sin \frac{11\pi}{6} = 1 - \left(-\frac{1}{2}\right) = \frac{3}{2}$ and RS $= \sqrt{3} \cos \frac{11\pi}{6} = \sqrt{3}\left(\frac{\sqrt{3}}{2}\right) = \frac{3}{2}$.
Since LS $=$ RS, $\frac{11\pi}{6}$ is a *valid solution*.
**Check $\frac{\pi}{2}$:** LS $= 1 - 1 = 0$ and RS $= \sqrt{3} \cdot 0 = 0$.     Since LS $=$ RS, $\frac{\pi}{2}$ is a *valid solution*.
Thus, $t = \frac{\pi}{2}$ and $t = \frac{11\pi}{6}$ are the only solutions of the equation.

**60** $\cos \theta - \sin \theta = 1 \Rightarrow \cos \theta = 1 + \sin \theta \Rightarrow \cos^2 \theta = 1 + 2 \sin \theta + \sin^2 \theta \Rightarrow$
$1 - \sin^2 \theta = 1 + 2 \sin \theta + \sin^2 \theta \Rightarrow 2 \sin^2 \theta + 2 \sin \theta = 0 \Rightarrow 2 \sin \theta(\sin \theta + 1) = 0 \Rightarrow$
$\sin \theta = 0, -1 \Rightarrow \theta = 0, \pi, \frac{3\pi}{2}$. $\pi$ is an extraneous solution.

**61** $\cos \alpha + \sin \alpha = 1 \Rightarrow \cos \alpha = 1 - \sin \alpha$ {square both sides} $\Rightarrow$
$\cos^2 \alpha = 1 - 2 \sin \alpha + \sin^2 \alpha$ {change $\cos^2 \alpha$ to $1 - \sin^2 \alpha$ to obtain an equation involving only $\sin \alpha$} $\Rightarrow$
$1 - \sin^2 \alpha = 1 - 2 \sin \alpha + \sin^2 \alpha \Rightarrow 2 \sin^2 \alpha - 2 \sin \alpha = 0 \Rightarrow 2 \sin \alpha(\sin \alpha - 1) = 0 \Rightarrow$
$\sin \alpha = 0, 1 \Rightarrow \alpha = 0, \pi, \frac{\pi}{2}$. $\pi$ is an extraneous solution.

**62** $\sqrt{3} \sin t + \cos t = 1 \Rightarrow \sqrt{3} \sin t = 1 - \cos t \Rightarrow 3 \sin^2 t = 1 - 2 \cos t + \cos^2 t \Rightarrow$
$3(1 - \cos^2 t) = 1 - 2 \cos t + \cos^2 t \Rightarrow 4 \cos^2 t - 2 \cos t - 2 = 0 \Rightarrow 2 \cos^2 t - \cos t - 1 = 0 \Rightarrow$
$(2 \cos t + 1)(\cos t - 1) = 0 \Rightarrow \cos t = -\frac{1}{2}, 1 \Rightarrow t = \frac{2\pi}{3}, \frac{4\pi}{3}, 0$. $\frac{4\pi}{3}$ is an extraneous solution.

**63** $2 \tan t - \sec^2 t = 0 \Rightarrow 2 \tan t - (1 + \tan^2 t) = 0 \Rightarrow \tan^2 t - 2 \tan t + 1 = 0 \Rightarrow (\tan t - 1)^2 = 0 \Rightarrow$
$\tan t = 1 \Rightarrow t = \frac{\pi}{4}, \frac{5\pi}{4}$

**64** $\tan\theta + \sec\theta = 1 \Rightarrow \sec^2\theta = (1-\tan\theta)^2 \Rightarrow 1 + \tan^2\theta = 1 - 2\tan\theta + \tan^2\theta \Rightarrow$

$\qquad\qquad\qquad\qquad\qquad\qquad 2\tan\theta = 0 \Rightarrow \theta = 0, \pi. \; \pi$ is an extraneous solution.

**65** $\cot\alpha + \tan\alpha = \csc\alpha\sec\alpha \Rightarrow \dfrac{\cos\alpha}{\sin\alpha} + \dfrac{\sin\alpha}{\cos\alpha} = \dfrac{1}{\sin\alpha\cos\alpha} \Rightarrow \dfrac{\cos^2\alpha + \sin^2\alpha}{\sin\alpha\cos\alpha} = \dfrac{1}{\sin\alpha\cos\alpha}$. This is an

identity and is true for *all numbers in* $[0, 2\pi)$ *except* $0$, $\frac{\pi}{2}$, $\pi$, and $\frac{3\pi}{2}$ since these values make the original equation

undefined.

**66** $\sin x + \cos x \cot x = \csc x \Rightarrow \sin x + \cos x \cdot \dfrac{\cos x}{\sin x} = \dfrac{1}{\sin x} \Rightarrow \dfrac{\sin^2 x + \cos^2 x}{\sin x} = \dfrac{1}{\sin x}$. This is an identity

and is true for *all numbers in* $[0, 2\pi)$ *except* $0$ and $\pi$ since these values make the original equation undefined.

**67** $2\sin^3 x + \sin^2 x - 2\sin x - 1 = 0$ {factor by grouping since there are four terms} $\Rightarrow$

$\sin^2 x(2\sin x + 1) - 1(2\sin x + 1) = 0 \Rightarrow (\sin^2 x - 1)(2\sin x + 1) = 0 \Rightarrow \sin x = \pm 1, -\frac{1}{2} \Rightarrow$

$\qquad\qquad\qquad\qquad\qquad\qquad\qquad\qquad\qquad\qquad\qquad x = \frac{\pi}{2}, \frac{3\pi}{2}, \frac{7\pi}{6}, \frac{11\pi}{6}$

**68** $\sec^5\theta = 4\sec\theta \Rightarrow \sec\theta(\sec^4\theta - 4) = 0 \Rightarrow \sec\theta = 0$ or $\sec^2\theta = \pm 2 \Rightarrow$

$\qquad\qquad\qquad \sec\theta = \pm\sqrt{2}$ {since $\sec\theta \neq 0$ and $\sec^2\theta \neq -2$} $\Rightarrow \theta = \frac{\pi}{4}, \frac{3\pi}{4}, \frac{5\pi}{4}, \frac{7\pi}{4}$

**69** $2\tan t \csc t + 2\csc t + \tan t + 1 = 0 \Rightarrow 2\csc t(\tan t + 1) + 1(\tan t + 1) \Rightarrow$

$\qquad (2\csc t + 1)(\tan t + 1) = 0 \Rightarrow \csc t = -\frac{1}{2}$ or $\tan t = -1 \Rightarrow t = \frac{3\pi}{4}, \frac{7\pi}{4}$ {since $\csc t \neq -\frac{1}{2}$}

**70** $2\sin v \csc v - \csc v = 4\sin v - 2 \Rightarrow 2\sin v \csc v - \csc v - 4\sin v + 2 = 0 \Rightarrow$

$\csc v(2\sin v - 1) - 2(2\sin v - 1) = 0 \Rightarrow (\csc v - 2)(2\sin v - 1) = 0 \Rightarrow \csc v = 2$ or $\sin v = \frac{1}{2} \Rightarrow$

$\qquad\qquad\qquad\qquad\qquad \sin v = \frac{1}{2}$ {since $\csc v = 2$ has the same solutions} $\Rightarrow v = \frac{\pi}{6}, \frac{5\pi}{6}$.

**71** $\sin^2 t - 4\sin t + 1 = 0 \Rightarrow \sin t = \dfrac{4 \pm \sqrt{12}}{2} = 2 \pm \sqrt{3}. \; 2 + \sqrt{3} > 1$ is not in the range of the sine,

$\qquad\qquad\qquad\qquad \text{so } \sin t = 2 - \sqrt{3} \Rightarrow t = 15°30'$ or $164°30'$ {to the nearest ten minutes}

**72** $\cos^2 t - 4\cos t + 2 = 0 \Rightarrow \cos t = \frac{4 \pm \sqrt{8}}{2} = 2 \pm \sqrt{2}. \; 2 + \sqrt{2} > 1$ is not in the range of the cosine,

$\qquad\qquad\qquad\qquad \text{so } \cos t = 2 - \sqrt{2} \Rightarrow t = 54°10'$ or $305°50'$ {to the nearest ten minutes}

**73** $\tan^2\theta + 3\tan\theta + 2 = 0 \Rightarrow (\tan\theta + 1)(\tan\theta + 2) = 0 \Rightarrow \tan\theta = -1, -2 \Rightarrow$

$\qquad\qquad\qquad\qquad\qquad\qquad\qquad\qquad\qquad\qquad \theta = 135°, 315°, 116°30', 296°30'$

**74** $2\tan^2 x - 3\tan x - 1 = 0 \Rightarrow \tan x = \frac{3 \pm \sqrt{17}}{4} \Rightarrow x = 60°40', 240°40', 164°20', 344°20'$

**75** $12\sin^2 u - 5\sin u - 2 = 0 \Rightarrow (3\sin u - 2)(4\sin u + 1) = 0 \Rightarrow \sin u = \frac{2}{3}, -\frac{1}{4} \Rightarrow$

$\qquad\qquad\qquad\qquad\qquad\qquad\qquad\qquad\qquad u = 41°50', 138°10', 194°30', 345°30'$

**76** $5\cos^2\alpha + 3\cos\alpha - 2 = 0 \Rightarrow (5\cos\alpha - 2)(\cos\alpha + 1) = 0 \Rightarrow \cos\alpha = \frac{2}{5}, -1 \Rightarrow$

$\qquad\qquad\qquad\qquad\qquad\qquad\qquad\qquad\qquad\qquad\qquad \alpha = 66°30', 293°30', 180°$

**77** $y = 25\cos\frac{\pi}{15}t \; \bullet$ The top of the wave will be above the sea wall when its height is greater than 12.5.

$y > 12.5 \Rightarrow 25\cos\frac{\pi}{15}t > 12.5 \Rightarrow \cos\frac{\pi}{15}t > \frac{1}{2} \Rightarrow$

{To visualize this step, it may help to look at a unit circle and draw a vertical line through 0.5 on the $x$-axis—

$\qquad\qquad\qquad\qquad\qquad\qquad\qquad\qquad\qquad x > 0.5$ is the same as $\cos\frac{\pi}{15}t > 0.5$.}

$-\frac{\pi}{3} < \frac{\pi}{15}t < \frac{\pi}{3} \Rightarrow -5 < t < 5$ {multiply by $\frac{15}{\pi}$} $\Rightarrow$

$\qquad\qquad\qquad\qquad\qquad y > 12.5$ for about $5 - (-5) = 10$ minutes of each 30-minute period.

**78** $T = 36 \sin\left[\frac{2\pi}{365}(t - 101)\right] + 14$ • The low temperature will be below $-4°$F when $T < -4$. $T < -4 \Rightarrow$

$36 \sin\left[\frac{2\pi}{365}(t - 101)\right] + 14 < -4 \Rightarrow \sin\left[\frac{2\pi}{365}(t - 101)\right] < -\frac{1}{2} \Rightarrow \frac{7\pi}{6} < \frac{2\pi}{365}(t - 101) < \frac{11\pi}{6} \Rightarrow$

$\frac{2555}{12} < t - 101 < \frac{4015}{12} \Rightarrow \frac{3767}{12} < t < \frac{5227}{12} \Rightarrow 313\frac{11}{12} < t < 435\frac{7}{12} \Rightarrow$

$T < -4$ for $435\frac{7}{12} - 313\frac{11}{12} = 121\frac{2}{3}$ days.

**79** (a) $T(t) = 26.5 \sin\left(\frac{\pi}{6}t - \frac{2\pi}{3}\right) + 56.5$ • See the figure.

(b) July: $T(7) = 83°$F; October: $T(10) = 56.5°$F.

(c) Graph $Y_1 = 26.5 \sin\left(\frac{\pi}{6}x - \frac{2\pi}{3}\right) + 56.5$ and $Y_2 = 69$. Their graphs intersect at $t \approx 4.94, 9.06$ on $[1, 13]$. The average high temperature is above $69°$F approximately May through September.

(d) A sine function is periodic and varies between a maximum and minimum value. Average monthly high temperatures are also seasonal with a 12-month period. Therefore, a sine function is a reasonable function to model these temperatures.

$[1, 25, 5]$ by $[0, 100, 10]$　　　　　　$[1, 25, 5]$ by $[0, 100, 10]$

*Figure 79*　　　　　　　　　*Figure 80*

**80** (a) $T(t) = 17 \cos\left(\frac{\pi}{6}t - \frac{7\pi}{6}\right) + 75$ • See the figure.

(b) April: $T(4) = 75°$F; December: $T(12) \approx 60.3°$F.

(c) Graph $Y_1 = 17 \cos\left(\frac{\pi}{6}x - \frac{7\pi}{6}\right) + 75$ and $Y_2 = 67$. Their graphs intersect at $t \approx 3.06, 10.94$ on the interval $[1, 13]$. The average high temperature is below $67°$F approximately November through March.

**81** $I = I_M \sin^3 \frac{\pi t}{D}$ • $I = \frac{1}{2}I_M$ and $D = 12 \Rightarrow \frac{1}{2}I_M = I_M \sin^3 \frac{\pi}{12}t \Rightarrow \sin^3 \frac{\pi}{12}t = \frac{1}{2} \Rightarrow \sin \frac{\pi}{12}t = \sqrt[3]{\frac{1}{2}} \Rightarrow$

$\frac{\pi}{12}t \approx 0.9169$ and $2.2247$ {$\pi - 0.9169 \approx 2.2247$ is the reference angle for $0.9169$ in QII.} $\Rightarrow$

$t \approx 3.50$ and $t \approx 8.50$

**82** $I = I_M \sin^2 \frac{\pi t}{D}$ • $I = \frac{1}{2}I_M$ and $D = 12 \Rightarrow \frac{1}{2}I_M = I_M \sin^2 \frac{\pi}{12}t \Rightarrow \sin^2 \frac{\pi}{12}t = \frac{1}{2} \Rightarrow \sin \frac{\pi}{12}t = \pm\sqrt{\frac{1}{2}}$.

The sine is positive since if $0 \le t \le D$, then $0 \le \frac{\pi t}{D} \le \pi$. Thus, $\frac{\pi}{12}t = \frac{\pi}{4}$ and $\frac{\pi}{12}t = \frac{3\pi}{4} \Rightarrow t = 3$ and $t = 9$.

**83** (a) 75% of the maximum intensity $= 0.75 I_M$. $I > 0.75 I_M \Rightarrow I_M \sin^3 \frac{\pi}{12}t > 0.75 I_M \Rightarrow \sin^3 \frac{\pi}{12}t > \frac{3}{4} \Rightarrow$

$\sin \frac{\pi}{12}t > \sqrt[3]{\frac{3}{4}} \Rightarrow 1.1398 < \frac{\pi}{12}t < 2.0018 \Rightarrow 4.3538 < t < 7.6462$, or approximately 3.29 hours.

(b) $I > 0.75 I_M \Rightarrow I_M \sin^2 \frac{\pi}{12}t > 0.75 I_M \Rightarrow \sin^2 \frac{\pi}{12}t > \frac{3}{4} \Rightarrow \sin \frac{\pi}{12}t > \frac{1}{2}\sqrt{3} \Rightarrow$

$\frac{\pi}{3} < \frac{\pi}{12}t < \frac{2\pi}{3} \Rightarrow 4 < t < 8$, or 4 hours.

**84** (a) $T = T_0 e^{-\lambda x} \sin(\omega t - \lambda x)$ • On the surface, $x = 0$. Thus, $T = T_0 e^{-\lambda(0)} \sin(\omega t - \lambda(0)) = T_0 \sin\omega t$.

Since the period is 24 hours, $24 = \frac{2\pi}{\omega}$, or $\omega = \frac{\pi}{12}$.

The formula for the temperature at the surface is then $T = T_0 \sin \frac{\pi}{12}t$.

(b) $T$ will be a minimum when $\sin \frac{\pi}{12}t$ equals $-1$.

$\sin \frac{\pi}{12}t = -1 \Rightarrow \frac{\pi}{12}t = \frac{3\pi}{2} + 2\pi n \Rightarrow t = 18 + 24n$ for $n = 0, 1, 2, \ldots$.

(c) If $\lambda = 2.5$ and $x = 1$, then $T = T_0 e^{-2.5} \sin\left(\frac{\pi}{12}t - 2.5\right)$. As in part (b), $\sin\left(\frac{\pi}{12}t - 2.5\right) = -1 \Rightarrow$

$\frac{\pi}{12}t - \frac{5}{2} = -\frac{\pi}{2} + 2\pi n \Rightarrow \frac{\pi}{12}t = \frac{5-\pi}{2} + 2\pi n \Rightarrow t = \frac{6(5-\pi)}{\pi} + 24n$ for

$n = 0, 1, 2, \ldots \approx 3.55 + 24n$ for $n = 0, 1, 2, \ldots$ . $\{$If $\frac{3\pi}{2}$ is used instead of $-\frac{\pi}{2}$, then $n = -1, 0, 1, 2, \ldots \}$

**85** (a) $N(t) = 1000\cos\frac{\pi}{5}t + 4000$ •

amplitude $= 1000$, period $= \frac{2\pi}{\pi/5} = 10$ years

(b) $N > 4500 \Rightarrow 1000\cos\frac{\pi}{5}t + 4000 > 4500 \Rightarrow$

$\cos\frac{\pi}{5}t > \frac{1}{2} \Rightarrow$ {The cosine function is greater

than $\frac{1}{2}$ on $[0, \frac{\pi}{3})$ and $(\frac{5\pi}{3}, 2\pi]$.} $0 \le \frac{\pi}{5}t < \frac{\pi}{3}$ and

$\frac{5\pi}{3} < \frac{\pi}{5}t \le 2\pi \Rightarrow 0 \le t < \frac{5}{3}$ and $\frac{25}{3} < t \le 10$

**86** $F(t) = 26{,}000\sin\left[\frac{\pi}{6}(t-5.5)\right] + 34{,}000$ • $F > 55{,}000 \Rightarrow 26{,}000\sin\left[\frac{\pi}{6}(t-5.5)\right] + 34{,}000 > 55{,}000 \Rightarrow$

$\sin\left[\frac{\pi}{6}(t-5.5)\right] > \frac{21}{26} \Rightarrow$ {approximate values} $0.94 < \frac{\pi}{6}(t-5.5) < 2.20 \Rightarrow 1.8 < t - 5.5 < 4.2 \Rightarrow$

$7.3 < t < 9.7 \Rightarrow F > 55{,}000$ for about 2.4 months.

**87** $\frac{1}{2} + \cos x = 0 \Rightarrow \cos x = -\frac{1}{2} \Rightarrow x = -\frac{4\pi}{3}, -\frac{2\pi}{3}, \frac{2\pi}{3},$ and $\frac{4\pi}{3}$ {for $x$ in $[-2\pi, 2\pi]$} for $A, B, C,$ and $D$,

respectively. The corresponding $y$ values are found by using $y = \frac{1}{2}x + \sin x$ with each of the above values.

The points are: $A\left(-\frac{4\pi}{3}, -\frac{2\pi}{3} + \frac{1}{2}\sqrt{3}\right)$, $B\left(-\frac{2\pi}{3}, -\frac{\pi}{3} - \frac{1}{2}\sqrt{3}\right)$, $C\left(\frac{2\pi}{3}, \frac{\pi}{3} + \frac{1}{2}\sqrt{3}\right)$, and $D\left(\frac{4\pi}{3}, \frac{2\pi}{3} - \frac{1}{2}\sqrt{3}\right)$.

**88** $4\cos 2x - \sin 2x = 0 \Rightarrow 4\cos 2x = \sin 2x \Rightarrow 4 = \tan 2x \Rightarrow 2x \approx 1.3258 + \pi n \Rightarrow$

$x \approx 0.6629 + \frac{\pi}{2}n$ for $n = 0, 1, 2, \ldots$, or $0.66, 2.23, 3.80, 5.38, \ldots$ .

**89** $I(t) = k \Rightarrow 20\sin(60\pi t - 6\pi) = -10 \Rightarrow \sin(60\pi t - 6\pi) = -\frac{1}{2} \Rightarrow 60\pi t_1 - 6\pi = \frac{7\pi}{6} + 2\pi n$ or

$60\pi t_2 - 6\pi = \frac{11\pi}{6} + 2\pi n$ {We use $t_1$ and $t_2$ to distinguish between angles coterminal with $\frac{7\pi}{6}$ and those coterminal

with $\frac{11\pi}{6}$.} $\Rightarrow 60t_1 = \frac{43}{6} + 2n$ or $60t_2 = \frac{47}{6} + 2n \Rightarrow t_1 = \frac{43}{360} + \frac{1}{30}n$ or $t_2 = \frac{47}{360} + \frac{1}{30}n$. We must now find

the smallest positive value of $t_1$ or $t_2$. $t_1 > 0 \Rightarrow \frac{1}{30}n > -\frac{43}{360} \Rightarrow n > -\frac{43}{12} \approx -3.58$. The last result

indicates that $n$ must be an integer in the set $\{ -3, -2, -1, \ldots \}$. If $n = -3$, then $t_1 = \frac{7}{360}$. Greater values of $n$

yield greater values of $t_1$. Similarly, for $t_2$, $t_2 > 0 \Rightarrow \frac{1}{30}n > -\frac{47}{360} \Rightarrow n > -\frac{47}{12}$. If $n = -3$, then $t_1 = \frac{11}{360}$.

Thus, the smallest exact value of $t$ for which $I(t) = -10$ is $t = \frac{7}{360}$ sec.

**90** $I(t) = k \Rightarrow 40\sin(100\pi t - 4\pi) = 20 \Rightarrow \sin(100\pi t - 4\pi) = \frac{1}{2} \Rightarrow 100\pi t_1 - 4\pi = \frac{\pi}{6} + 2\pi n$ or

$100\pi t_2 - 4\pi = \frac{5\pi}{6} + 2\pi n \Rightarrow 100t_1 = \frac{25}{6} + 2n$ or $100t_2 = \frac{29}{6} + 2n \Rightarrow t_1 = \frac{25}{600} + \frac{1}{50}n$ or $t_2 = \frac{29}{600} + \frac{1}{50}n$.

$t_1 > 0 \Rightarrow \frac{1}{50}n > -\frac{25}{600} \Rightarrow n > -\frac{25}{12}$. If $n = -2$, then $t_1 = \frac{1}{600}$. $t_2 > 0 \Rightarrow \frac{1}{50}n > -\frac{29}{600} \Rightarrow n > -\frac{29}{12}$.

If $n = -2$, then $t_2 = \frac{5}{600}$. Thus, $t = \frac{1}{600}$ sec.

**91** Graph $y = \cos x$ and $y = 0.3$ on the same coordinate plane. The points of intersection are located at $x \approx 1.27, 5.02$,

and $\cos x$ is less than 0.3 between these values. Therefore, $\cos x \ge 0.3$ on $[0, 1.27] \cup [5.02, 2\pi]$.

$[0, 2\pi, \pi/4]$ by $[-2.09, 2.09]$     $[0, 2\pi, \pi/4]$ by $[-2.09, 2.09]$

*Figure 91*     *Figure 92*

**92** Graph $y = \sin x$ and $y = -0.6$ on the same coordinate plane.

The points of intersection are located at $x \approx 3.79, 5.64$. From the figure, we see that $\sin x < -0.6$ on $(3.79, 5.64)$.

**93** Graph $y = \cos 3x$ and $y = 2\sin x$ on the same coordinate plane. The points of intersection are located at $x \approx 0.31$ and $x \approx 3.45$. From the graph, we see that $\cos 3x < 2\sin x$ on $(0.31, 3.45)$.

$[0, 2\pi, \pi/4]$ by $[-2.09, 2.09]$

*Figure 93*

$[0, 2\pi, \pi/4]$ by $[-2.09, 2.09]$

*Figure 94*

**94** Graph $y = \tan \frac{1}{2}x$ and $y = \sin 2x$ on the same coordinate plane. The points of intersection are located at $x \approx 1.20, 5.09$, and $x = 0, 2\pi$. $\tan \frac{1}{2}x$ is undefined at $\pi$. From the graph, we see that $\tan \frac{1}{2}x \le \sin 2x$ on $[0, 1.20] \cup (\pi, 5.09] \cup \{2\pi\}$.

**95** (a) The largest zero occurs when $x \approx 0.6366$.

   (b) As $x$ becomes large, the graph of $f(x) = \cos(1/x)$ approaches the horizontal asymptote $y = 1$.

   (c) There appear to be an infinite number of zeros on $[0, c]$ for any $c > 0$.

$[0, 3]$ by $[-1.5, 1.5]$

*Figure 95*

$[0, 3]$ by $[-1.5, 1.5]$

*Figure 96*

**96** (a) The largest zero occurs when $x \approx 0.5642$.

   (b) As $x$ becomes large, the graph of $f(x) = \sin(1/x^2)$ approaches the horizontal asymptote $y = 0$.

   (c) There appear to be an infinite number of zeros on $[0, c]$ for any $c > 0$.

**Note:** In Exercises 97–100, graph $Y_1 = M$ and $Y_2 = \theta + e\sin\theta$ and approximate the value of $\theta$ such that $Y_1 = Y_2$.

**97** Mercury: $Y_1 = 5.241$ and $Y_2 = \theta + 0.206\sin\theta$ intersect when $\theta \approx 5.400$ (radians).

$[0, 12]$ by $[0, 8]$

*Figure 97*

$[0, 12]$ by $[0, 8]$

*Figure 98*

**98** Mars: $Y_1 = 4.028$ and $Y_2 = \theta + 0.093\sin\theta$ intersect when $\theta \approx 4.104$.

**99** Earth: $Y_1 = 3.611$ and $Y_2 = \theta + 0.0167 \sin\theta$ intersect when $\theta \approx 3.619$.

$[0, 12]$ by $[0, 8]$              $[0, 0.3, 0.1]$ by $[0, 0.2, 0.1]$

*Figure 99*                    *Figure 100*

**100** Pluto: $Y_1 = 0.09424$ and $Y_2 = \theta + 0.255 \sin\theta$ intersect when $\theta \approx 0.075$

**101** Graph $y = \sin 2x$ and $y = 2 - x^2$. From the graph, we see that there are two points of intersection.

The $x$-coordinates of these points are $x \approx -1.48, 1.08$.

$[-\pi, \pi, \pi/4]$ by $[-2.09, 2.09]$         $[-\pi, \pi, \pi/4]$ by $[-2.09, 2.09]$

*Figure 101*                  *Figure 102*

**102** Graph $y = \cos^3 x + \cos 3x - 2\sin^3 x$. The graph has $x$-intercepts at $x \approx -2.55, 0.60$.

**103** Graph $y = \ln(1 + \sin^2 x)$ and $y = \cos x$. From the graph, we see that there are two points of intersection.

The $x$-coordinates of these points are $x \approx \pm 1.00$.

$[-\pi, \pi, \pi/4]$ by $[-2.09, 2.09]$         $[-\pi, \pi, \pi/4]$ by $[-2.09, 2.09]$

*Figure 103*                  *Figure 104*

**104** Graph $y = e^{\sin x}$ and $y = \sec\left(\frac{1}{3}x - \frac{1}{2}\right)$. From the graph, we see that there are two points of intersection.

The $x$-coordinates of these points are $x \approx 0.11, 3.01$.

**105** Graph $y = 3\cos^4 x - 2\cos^3 x + \cos x - 1$. The graph has $x$-intercepts at $x \approx \pm 0.64, \pm 2.42$.

$[-\pi, \pi, \pi/4]$ by $[-2.09, 2.09]$         $[-\pi, \pi, \pi/4]$ by $[-2.09, 2.09]$

*Figure 105*                  *Figure 106*

**106** Graph $y = \cos 2x + \sin 3x + \tan \frac{1}{3}x$. The graph has $x$-intercepts at $x \approx -0.28, 1.02, 2.03$.

**107** (a) $g = 9.8$ $\Rightarrow$ $9.8 = 9.8066(1 - 0.00264\cos 2\theta)$ $\Rightarrow$ $\frac{9.8}{9.8066} = 1 - 0.00264\cos 2\theta$ $\Rightarrow$

$0.00264\cos 2\theta = 1 - \frac{9.8}{9.8066}$ $\Rightarrow$ $0.00264\cos 2\theta = \frac{0.0066}{9.8066}$ $\Rightarrow$ $\cos 2\theta = \frac{0.0066}{(9.8066)(0.00264)}$ $\Rightarrow$

$2\theta = \cos^{-1}\left(\frac{0.0066}{0.025889424}\right) \approx 75.2°$ $\Rightarrow$ $\theta \approx 37.6°$

(b) At the equator, $g_0 = 9.8066(1 - 0.00264\cos 0°) = 9.8066(0.99736)$. Since the weight $W$ of a person on Earth's surface is directly proportional to the force of gravity, we have $W = kg$.

At $\theta = 0°$, $W = kg$ $\Rightarrow$ $150 = kg_0$ $\Rightarrow$ $k = \frac{150}{g_0}$ $\Rightarrow$ $W = \frac{150}{g_0}g$.

$W = 150.5$ $\Rightarrow$ $150.5 = \frac{150}{g_0}g$ $\Rightarrow$ $150.5 = \frac{150 \cdot 9.8066(1 - 0.00264\cos 2\theta)}{9.8066(0.99736)}$ $\Rightarrow$

$150.5 = \frac{150}{0.99736}(1 - 0.00264\cos 2\theta)$ $\Rightarrow$ $0.00264\cos 2\theta = 1 - \frac{150.5(0.99736)}{150}$ $\Rightarrow$

$\cos 2\theta \approx -0.2593$ $\Rightarrow$ $2\theta \approx 105.0°$ $\Rightarrow$ $\theta \approx 52.5°$.

## 6.3 Exercises

**1** **Note:** Use the cofunction formulas with $\left(\frac{\pi}{2} - u\right)$ for the argument if you're working with radian measure, $(90° - u)$ if you're working with degree measure.

(a) $\sin 15°20' = \cos(90° - 15°20') = \cos 74°40'$

(b) $\cos 73°12' = \sin(90° - 73°12') = \sin 16°48'$

(c) $\tan\frac{\pi}{6} = \cot\left(\frac{\pi}{2} - \frac{\pi}{6}\right) = \cot\left(\frac{3\pi}{6} - \frac{\pi}{6}\right) = \cot\frac{2\pi}{6} = \cot\frac{\pi}{3}$

(d) $\sec 17.28° = \csc(90° - 17.28°) = \csc 72.72°$

**2** (a) $\tan 37°50' = \cot(90° - 37°50') = \cot 52°10'$

(b) $\sin 89°41' = \cos(90° - 89°41') = \cos 0°19'$

(c) $\cos\frac{\pi}{3} = \sin\left(\frac{\pi}{2} - \frac{\pi}{3}\right) = \sin\left(\frac{3\pi}{6} - \frac{2\pi}{6}\right) = \sin\frac{\pi}{6}$

(d) $\cot 61.87° = \tan(90° - 61.87°) = \tan 28.13°$

**3** (a) $\cos\frac{\pi}{8} = \sin\left(\frac{\pi}{2} - \frac{\pi}{8}\right) = \sin\frac{3\pi}{8}$

(b) $\sin\frac{1}{4} = \cos\left(\frac{\pi}{2} - \frac{1}{4}\right) = \cos\left(\frac{2\pi - 1}{4}\right)$

(c) $\tan 1 = \cot\left(\frac{\pi}{2} - 1\right) = \cot\left(\frac{\pi - 2}{2}\right)$

(d) $\csc 0.53 = \sec\left(\frac{\pi}{2} - 0.53\right)$

**4** (a) $\sin\frac{\pi}{12} = \cos\left(\frac{\pi}{2} - \frac{\pi}{12}\right) = \cos\frac{5\pi}{12}$

(b) $\cos\frac{1}{5} = \sin\left(\frac{\pi}{2} - \frac{1}{5}\right) = \sin\left(\frac{5\pi - 2}{10}\right)$

(c) $\tan\sqrt{2} = \cot\left(\frac{\pi}{2} - \sqrt{2}\right)$

(d) $\sec 1.2 = \csc\left(\frac{\pi}{2} - 1.2\right)$

**5** (a) $\cos\frac{\pi}{4} + \cos\frac{\pi}{6} = \frac{\sqrt{2}}{2} + \frac{\sqrt{3}}{2} = \frac{\sqrt{2} + \sqrt{3}}{2}$

(b) $\cos\frac{5\pi}{12} = \cos\left(\frac{\pi}{4} + \frac{\pi}{6}\right) = \cos\frac{\pi}{4}\cos\frac{\pi}{6} - \sin\frac{\pi}{4}\sin\frac{\pi}{6} = \frac{\sqrt{2}}{2}\cdot\frac{\sqrt{3}}{2} - \frac{\sqrt{2}}{2}\cdot\frac{1}{2} = \frac{\sqrt{6} - \sqrt{2}}{4}$

**6** (a) $\sin\frac{2\pi}{3} + \sin\frac{\pi}{4} = \frac{\sqrt{3}}{2} + \frac{\sqrt{2}}{2} = \frac{\sqrt{3} + \sqrt{2}}{2}$

(b) $\sin\frac{11\pi}{12} = \sin\left(\frac{2\pi}{3} + \frac{\pi}{4}\right) = \sin\frac{2\pi}{3}\cos\frac{\pi}{4} + \cos\frac{2\pi}{3}\sin\frac{\pi}{4} = \frac{\sqrt{3}}{2}\cdot\frac{\sqrt{2}}{2} + \left(-\frac{1}{2}\right)\cdot\frac{\sqrt{2}}{2} = \frac{\sqrt{6} - \sqrt{2}}{4}$

**7** (a) $\tan 60° + \tan 225° = \sqrt{3} + 1$

(b) $\tan 285° = \tan(60° + 225°) = \frac{\tan 60° + \tan 225°}{1 - \tan 60°\tan 225°} = \frac{\sqrt{3} + 1}{1 - \left(\sqrt{3}\right)(1)}\cdot\frac{1 + \sqrt{3}}{1 + \sqrt{3}} = \frac{4 + 2\sqrt{3}}{-2} = -2 - \sqrt{3}$

**8** (a) $\cos 225° - \cos 30° = -\frac{\sqrt{2}}{2} - \frac{\sqrt{3}}{2} = \frac{-\sqrt{2} - \sqrt{3}}{2}$

(b) $\cos 195° = \cos(225° - 30°) = \cos 225°\cos 30° + \sin 225°\sin 30° = -\frac{\sqrt{2}}{2}\cdot\frac{\sqrt{3}}{2} + \left(-\frac{\sqrt{2}}{2}\right)\cdot\frac{1}{2} = \frac{-\sqrt{6} - \sqrt{2}}{4}$

**9** (a) $\sin\frac{\pi}{4} - \sin\frac{\pi}{6} = \frac{\sqrt{2}}{2} - \frac{1}{2} = \frac{\sqrt{2}-1}{2}$

(b) $\sin\frac{\pi}{12} = \sin\left(\frac{\pi}{4} - \frac{\pi}{6}\right) = \sin\frac{\pi}{4}\cos\frac{\pi}{6} - \cos\frac{\pi}{4}\sin\frac{\pi}{6} = \frac{\sqrt{2}}{2}\cdot\frac{\sqrt{3}}{2} - \frac{\sqrt{2}}{2}\cdot\frac{1}{2} = \frac{\sqrt{6}-\sqrt{2}}{4}$

**10** (a) $\tan\frac{3\pi}{4} - \tan\frac{\pi}{6} = -1 - \frac{\sqrt{3}}{3} = \frac{-3-\sqrt{3}}{3}$

(b) $\tan\frac{7\pi}{12} = \tan\left(\frac{3\pi}{4} - \frac{\pi}{6}\right)$

$$= \frac{\tan\frac{3\pi}{4} - \tan\frac{\pi}{6}}{1 + \tan\frac{3\pi}{4}\tan\frac{\pi}{6}} = \frac{-1 - \sqrt{3}/3}{1 + (-1)\cdot\left(\sqrt{3}/3\right)}\cdot\frac{3}{3} = \frac{-3-\sqrt{3}}{3-\sqrt{3}}\cdot\frac{3+\sqrt{3}}{3+\sqrt{3}} = \frac{-12-6\sqrt{3}}{6} = -2 - \sqrt{3}$$

**11** Since the expression is of the form "cos cos plus sin sin", we recognize it as the subtraction formula for the cosine.

$$\cos 70° \cos 53° + \sin 70° \sin 53° = \cos(70° - 53°) = \cos 17°$$

**12** $\cos 6° \cos 25° - \sin 6° \sin 25° = \cos(6° + 25°) = \cos 31°$

**13** $\cos 61° \sin 82° - \sin 61° \cos 82° = \sin 82° \cos 61° - \cos 82° \sin 61° = \sin(82° - 61°) = \sin 21°$

**14** $\sin 57° \cos 4° + \cos 57° \sin 4° = \sin(57° + 4°) = \sin 61°$

**15** Since we have angle arguments of 2, 3, and $-2$, we want to change one of them so that we can apply one of the formulas. We recognize that $\cos 2 = \cos(-2)$ and this is probably the simplest change.

$$\cos 3 \sin(-2) - \cos 2 \sin 3 = \sin(-2)\cos 3 - \cos(-2)\sin 3 = \sin(-2 - 3) = \sin(-5)$$

**16** $\sin(-5)\cos 2 + \cos 5 \sin(-2) = \sin(-5)\cos(-2) + \cos(-5)\sin(-2) = \sin[-2 + (-5)] = \sin(-7)$

**17** Since $\sin\alpha = -\frac{5}{13} < 0$ and $\tan\alpha > 0$, $\alpha$ is in QIII, and $\cos\alpha = -\sqrt{1 - \left(-\frac{5}{13}\right)^2} = -\frac{12}{13}$.

$$\sin\left(\alpha - \frac{\pi}{3}\right) = \sin\alpha\cos\frac{\pi}{3} - \cos\alpha\sin\frac{\pi}{3} = -\frac{5}{13}\cdot\frac{1}{2} - \left(-\frac{12}{13}\right)\cdot\frac{\sqrt{3}}{2} = -\frac{5}{26} + \frac{12\sqrt{3}}{26} = \frac{12\sqrt{3}-5}{26}$$

**18** Since $\cos\alpha = \frac{24}{25} > 0$ and $\sin\alpha < 0$, $\alpha$ is in QIV, and $\sin\alpha = -\sqrt{1 - \left(\frac{24}{25}\right)^2} = -\frac{7}{25}$.

$$\cos\left(\alpha + \frac{\pi}{6}\right) = \cos\alpha\cos\frac{\pi}{6} - \sin\alpha\sin\frac{\pi}{6} = \frac{24}{25}\cdot\frac{\sqrt{3}}{2} - \left(-\frac{7}{25}\right)\cdot\frac{1}{2} = \frac{24\sqrt{3}}{50} + \frac{7}{50} = \frac{24\sqrt{3}+7}{50}$$

**19** Since $\sec x = 3 > 0$ and $\csc x < 0$, $x$ is in QIV, and $\sin x = -\sqrt{1 - \left(-\frac{1}{3}\right)^2} = -\sqrt{\frac{8}{9}} = -\frac{\sqrt{8}}{3}$.

$$\cos\left(x - \frac{\pi}{4}\right) = \cos x\cos\frac{\pi}{4} + \sin x\sin\frac{\pi}{4} = \frac{1}{3}\cdot\frac{\sqrt{2}}{2} + \left(-\frac{\sqrt{8}}{3}\right)\cdot\frac{\sqrt{2}}{2} = \frac{\sqrt{2}}{6} - \frac{\sqrt{16}}{6} = \frac{\sqrt{2}-4}{6}$$

**20** Since $\tan x = \frac{1}{4} > 0$ and $\sec x > 0$, $x$ is in QI. As in Example 2 with $\tan x = \frac{1}{4}$, $r^2 = 1^2 + 4^2 \Rightarrow r = \sqrt{17}$.

$$\sin\left(x + \frac{\pi}{3}\right) = \sin x\cos\frac{\pi}{3} + \cos x\sin\frac{\pi}{3} = \frac{1}{\sqrt{17}}\cdot\frac{1}{2} + \frac{4}{\sqrt{17}}\cdot\frac{\sqrt{3}}{2} = \frac{4\sqrt{3}+1}{2\sqrt{17}}$$

**21** Since $\cot x = \sqrt{3} > 0$ and $\cos x < 0$, $x$ is in QIII.

$$\tan\left(x + \frac{\pi}{6}\right) = \frac{\tan x + \tan\frac{\pi}{6}}{1 - \tan x\tan\frac{\pi}{6}} = \frac{\frac{1}{\sqrt{3}} + \frac{1}{\sqrt{3}}}{1 - \frac{1}{\sqrt{3}}\cdot\frac{1}{\sqrt{3}}} = \frac{\frac{2}{\sqrt{3}}}{1 - \frac{1}{3}} = \frac{\frac{2}{\sqrt{3}}}{\frac{2}{3}} = \sqrt{3}$$

You may have recognized that $x = \frac{7\pi}{6}$ and that $\tan\left(x + \frac{\pi}{6}\right) = \tan\left(\frac{7\pi}{6} + \frac{\pi}{6}\right) = \tan\frac{4\pi}{3} = \sqrt{3}$

**22** Since $\csc x = -\frac{5}{3} < 0$ and $\cot x > 0$, $x$ is in QIII.

As in Example 2 with $\csc x = -\frac{5}{3}$, $5^2 = x_1^2 + (-3)^2 \Rightarrow x_1^2 = 25 - 9 \Rightarrow x_1 = -4$, so $\tan x = \frac{y}{x_1} = \frac{-3}{-4}$.

$$\tan\left(x - \frac{\pi}{4}\right) = \frac{\tan x - \tan\frac{\pi}{4}}{1 + \tan x\tan\frac{\pi}{4}} = \frac{\frac{3}{4} - 1}{1 + \frac{3}{4}\cdot 1} = \frac{-\frac{1}{4}}{\frac{7}{4}} = -\frac{1}{7}$$

**23** See the figure for a drawing of angles $\alpha$ and $\beta$.

(a) $\sin(\alpha + \beta) = \sin\alpha\cos\beta + \cos\alpha\sin\beta = \frac{3}{5}\cdot\frac{15}{17} + \frac{4}{5}\cdot\frac{8}{17} = \frac{77}{85}$

(b) $\cos(\alpha + \beta) = \cos\alpha\cos\beta - \sin\alpha\sin\beta = \frac{4}{5}\cdot\frac{15}{17} - \frac{3}{5}\cdot\frac{8}{17} = \frac{36}{85}$

(c) Since the sine and cosine of $(\alpha + \beta)$ are positive, $(\alpha + \beta)$ is in QI.

*Figure 23*

**24** (a) $\sin(\alpha + \beta) = \sin\alpha\cos\beta + \cos\alpha\sin\beta = \frac{12}{13}\cdot\frac{4}{5} + \frac{5}{13}\cdot\frac{3}{5} = \frac{63}{65}$

(b) $\tan(\alpha + \beta) = \dfrac{\tan\alpha + \tan\beta}{1 - \tan\alpha\tan\beta} = \dfrac{\frac{12}{5} + \frac{3}{4}}{1 - \frac{12}{5}\cdot\frac{3}{4}}\cdot\dfrac{20}{20} = \dfrac{48 + 15}{20 - 36} = -\dfrac{63}{16}$

(c) Since the sine is positive and the tangent is negative, $(\alpha + \beta)$ is in QII.

**25** See the figure for a drawing of angles $\alpha$ and $\beta$.

(a) $\sin(\alpha + \beta) = \sin\alpha\cos\beta + \cos\alpha\sin\beta = \left(-\frac{4}{5}\right)\cdot\frac{3}{5} + \left(-\frac{3}{5}\right)\cdot\frac{4}{5} = -\frac{24}{25}$

(b) $\tan(\alpha + \beta) = \dfrac{\tan\alpha + \tan\beta}{1 - \tan\alpha\tan\beta} = \dfrac{\frac{4}{3} + \frac{4}{3}}{1 - \frac{4}{3}\cdot\frac{4}{3}}\cdot\dfrac{9}{9} = \dfrac{12 + 12}{9 - 16} = -\dfrac{24}{7}$

(c) Since the sine and tangent of $(\alpha + \beta)$ are negative, $(\alpha + \beta)$ is in QIV.

*Figure 25*

**26** (a) $\sin(\alpha + \beta) = \sin\alpha\cos\beta + \cos\alpha\sin\beta = \frac{7}{25}\cdot\left(-\frac{3}{5}\right) + \left(-\frac{24}{25}\right)\cdot\left(-\frac{4}{5}\right) = \frac{75}{125} = \frac{3}{5}$

(b) $\cos(\alpha + \beta) = \cos\alpha\cos\beta - \sin\alpha\sin\beta = \left(-\frac{24}{25}\right)\cdot\left(-\frac{3}{5}\right) - \frac{7}{25}\cdot\left(-\frac{4}{5}\right) = \frac{100}{125} = \frac{4}{5}$

(c) $\tan(\alpha + \beta) = \dfrac{\sin(\alpha + \beta)}{\cos(\alpha + \beta)} = \dfrac{3/5}{4/5} = \dfrac{3}{4}$

(d) $\sin(\alpha - \beta) = \sin\alpha\cos\beta - \cos\alpha\sin\beta = \frac{7}{25}\cdot\left(-\frac{3}{5}\right) - \left(-\frac{24}{25}\right)\cdot\left(-\frac{4}{5}\right) = -\frac{117}{125}$

(e) $\cos(\alpha - \beta) = \cos\alpha\cos\beta + \sin\alpha\sin\beta = \left(-\frac{24}{25}\right)\cdot\left(-\frac{3}{5}\right) + \frac{7}{25}\cdot\left(-\frac{4}{5}\right) = \frac{44}{125}$

(f) $\tan(\alpha - \beta) = \dfrac{\sin(\alpha - \beta)}{\cos(\alpha - \beta)} = \dfrac{-117/125}{44/125} = -\dfrac{117}{44}$

**27** (a) $\sin(\alpha - \beta) = \sin \alpha \cos \beta - \cos \alpha \sin \beta = \left(-\frac{\sqrt{21}}{5}\right) \cdot \left(-\frac{3}{5}\right) - \left(-\frac{2}{5}\right) \cdot \left(-\frac{4}{5}\right) = \frac{3\sqrt{21}-8}{25} \approx 0.23$

(b) $\cos(\alpha - \beta) = \cos \alpha \cos \beta + \sin \alpha \sin \beta = \left(-\frac{2}{5}\right) \cdot \left(-\frac{3}{5}\right) + \left(-\frac{\sqrt{21}}{5}\right) \cdot \left(-\frac{4}{5}\right) = \frac{4\sqrt{21}+6}{25} \approx 0.97$

(c) Since the sine and cosine of $(\alpha - \beta)$ are positive, $(\alpha - \beta)$ is in QI.

**28** (a) $\sin(\alpha + \beta) = \sin \alpha \cos \beta + \cos \alpha \sin \beta = \frac{2}{3} \cdot \left(-\frac{1}{3}\right) + \left(-\frac{\sqrt{5}}{3}\right) \cdot \left(\frac{2\sqrt{2}}{3}\right) = \frac{-2-2\sqrt{10}}{9} \approx -0.92$

(b) $\tan(\alpha + \beta) = \dfrac{\tan \alpha + \tan \beta}{1 - \tan \alpha \tan \beta} = \dfrac{-\frac{2}{\sqrt{5}} + \left(-2\sqrt{2}\right)}{1 - \left(-\frac{2}{\sqrt{5}}\right) \cdot \left(-2\sqrt{2}\right)} \cdot \dfrac{\sqrt{5}}{\sqrt{5}} = \dfrac{-2 - 2\sqrt{10}}{\sqrt{5} - 4\sqrt{2}} \approx 2.43$

(c) Since the sine is negative and the tangent is positive, $(\alpha + \beta)$ is in QIII.

**29** $\sin(\theta + \pi) = \sin \theta \cos \pi + \cos \theta \sin \pi = \sin \theta(-1) + \cos \theta(0) = -\sin \theta$

**30** $\sin\left(x + \frac{\pi}{2}\right) = \sin x \cos \frac{\pi}{2} + \cos x \sin \frac{\pi}{2} = \sin x(0) + \cos x(1) = \cos x$

  Alternatively, we could use the cofunction identity: $\sin\left(x + \frac{\pi}{2}\right) = \cos\left[\frac{\pi}{2} - \left(x + \frac{\pi}{2}\right)\right] = \cos(-x) = \cos x$.

**31** $\sin\left(x - \frac{5\pi}{2}\right) = \sin x \cos \frac{5\pi}{2} - \cos x \sin \frac{5\pi}{2} = \sin x(0) - \cos x(1) = -\cos x$

**32** $\sin\left(\theta - \frac{3\pi}{2}\right) = \sin \theta \cos \frac{3\pi}{2} - \cos \theta \sin \frac{3\pi}{2} = \sin \theta(0) - \cos \theta(-1) = \cos \theta$

**33** $\cos(\theta - \pi) = \cos \theta \cos \pi + \sin \theta \sin \pi = \cos \theta(-1) + \sin \theta(0) = -\cos \theta$

**34** $\cos\left(x + \frac{\pi}{2}\right) = \sin\left[\frac{\pi}{2} - \left(x + \frac{\pi}{2}\right)\right] = \sin(-x) = -\sin x$

**35** $\cos\left(x + \frac{3\pi}{2}\right) = \cos x \cos \frac{3\pi}{2} - \sin x \sin \frac{3\pi}{2} = \cos x(0) - \sin x(-1) = \sin x$

**36** $\cos\left(\theta - \frac{5\pi}{2}\right) = \cos \theta \cos \frac{5\pi}{2} + \sin \theta \sin \frac{5\pi}{2} = \cos \theta(0) + \sin \theta(1) = \sin \theta$

**37** $\tan\left(x - \frac{\pi}{2}\right) = \dfrac{\sin\left(x - \frac{\pi}{2}\right)}{\cos\left(x - \frac{\pi}{2}\right)} = \dfrac{\sin x \cos \frac{\pi}{2} - \cos x \sin \frac{\pi}{2}}{\cos x \cos \frac{\pi}{2} + \sin x \sin \frac{\pi}{2}} = \dfrac{-\cos x}{\sin x} = -\cot x$

**38** $\tan(\pi - \theta) = \dfrac{\tan \pi - \tan \theta}{1 + \tan \pi \tan \theta} = \dfrac{0 - \tan \theta}{1 + (0)\tan \theta} = -\tan \theta$

**39** The tangent of a sum formula won't work here since $\tan \frac{\pi}{2}$ is undefined.
We will use a cofunction identity to verify the identity.

$$\tan\left(\theta + \frac{\pi}{2}\right) = \cot\left[\frac{\pi}{2} - \left(\theta + \frac{\pi}{2}\right)\right] = \cot(-\theta) = -\cot \theta$$

Alternatively, we could also write $\tan\left(\theta + \frac{\pi}{2}\right)$ as $\dfrac{\sin\left(\theta + \frac{\pi}{2}\right)}{\cos\left(\theta + \frac{\pi}{2}\right)}$ and then simplify.

**40** $\tan(x + \pi) = \dfrac{\tan x + \tan \pi}{1 - \tan x \tan \pi} = \dfrac{\tan x + 0}{1 - (\tan x)(0)} = \tan x$

**41** $\sin\left(\theta + \frac{\pi}{4}\right) = \sin \theta \cos \frac{\pi}{4} + \cos \theta \sin \frac{\pi}{4} = \frac{\sqrt{2}}{2} \sin \theta + \frac{\sqrt{2}}{2} \cos \theta = \frac{\sqrt{2}}{2}(\sin \theta + \cos \theta)$

**42** $\cos\left(\theta + \frac{\pi}{4}\right) = \cos \theta \cos \frac{\pi}{4} - \sin \theta \sin \frac{\pi}{4} = \frac{\sqrt{2}}{2} \cos \theta - \frac{\sqrt{2}}{2} \sin \theta = \frac{\sqrt{2}}{2}(\cos \theta - \sin \theta)$

**43** $\tan\left(u + \frac{\pi}{4}\right) = \dfrac{\tan u + \tan \frac{\pi}{4}}{1 - \tan u \tan \frac{\pi}{4}} = \dfrac{\tan u + 1}{1 - \tan u(1)} = \dfrac{1 + \tan u}{1 - \tan u}$

**44** $\tan\left(x - \frac{\pi}{4}\right) = \dfrac{\tan x - \tan \frac{\pi}{4}}{1 + \tan x \tan \frac{\pi}{4}} = \dfrac{\tan x - 1}{1 + \tan x(1)} = \dfrac{\tan x - 1}{\tan x + 1}$

**45** $\cos(u + v) + \cos(u - v) = (\cos u \cos v - \sin u \sin v) + (\cos u \cos v + \sin u \sin v) = 2 \cos u \cos v$

**46** $\sin(u+v) + \sin(u-v) = (\sin u \cos v + \cos u \sin v) + (\sin u \cos v - \cos u \sin v) = 2 \sin u \cos v$

**47** $\sin(u+v) \cdot \sin(u-v)$

$\quad = (\sin u \cos v + \cos u \sin v) \cdot (\sin u \cos v - \cos u \sin v)$ {addition and subtraction formulas for sine}

$\quad = \sin^2 u \cos^2 v - \cos^2 u \sin^2 v$ {recognize as the difference of two squares}

$\quad = \sin^2 u (1 - \sin^2 v) - (1 - \sin^2 u) \sin^2 v$ {change to terms involving only sine}

$\quad = \sin^2 u - \sin^2 u \sin^2 v - \sin^2 v + \sin^2 u \sin^2 v$

$\quad = \sin^2 u - \sin^2 v$

**48** $\cos(u+v) \cdot \cos(u-v)$

$\quad = (\cos u \cos v - \sin u \sin v) \cdot (\cos u \cos v + \sin u \sin v)$ {addition and subtraction formulas for cosine}

$\quad = \cos^2 u \cos^2 v - \sin^2 u \sin^2 v$ {recognize as the difference of two squares}

$\quad = \cos^2 u (1 - \sin^2 v) - (1 - \cos^2 u) \sin^2 v$

$\quad = \cos^2 u - \cos^2 u \sin^2 v - \sin^2 v + \cos^2 u \sin^2 v$

$\quad = \cos^2 u - \sin^2 v$

**49** $\dfrac{1}{\cot\alpha - \cot\beta} = \dfrac{1}{\dfrac{\cos\alpha}{\sin\alpha} - \dfrac{\cos\beta}{\sin\beta}} = \dfrac{1}{\dfrac{\cos\alpha\sin\beta - \cos\beta\sin\alpha}{\sin\alpha\sin\beta}} = \dfrac{\sin\alpha\sin\beta}{\sin(\beta-\alpha)}$

**50** $\dfrac{1}{\tan\alpha + \tan\beta} = \dfrac{1}{\dfrac{\sin\alpha}{\cos\alpha} + \dfrac{\sin\beta}{\cos\beta}} = \dfrac{1}{\dfrac{\sin\alpha\cos\beta + \sin\beta\cos\alpha}{\cos\alpha\cos\beta}} = \dfrac{\cos\alpha\cos\beta}{\sin(\alpha+\beta)}$

**51** $\sin(u+v+w) = \sin[(u+v)+w]$

$\quad = \sin(u+v)\cos w + \cos(u+v)\sin w$

$\quad = (\sin u \cos v + \cos u \sin v)\cos w + (\cos u \cos v - \sin u \sin v)\sin w$

$\quad = \sin u \cos v \cos w + \cos u \sin v \cos w + \cos u \cos v \sin w - \sin u \sin v \sin w$

**52** $\tan(u+v+w) = \tan[(u+v)+w]$

$\quad = \dfrac{\tan(u+v) + \tan w}{1 - \tan(u+v)\tan w}$

$\quad = \dfrac{\dfrac{\tan u + \tan v}{1 - \tan u \tan v} + \tan w}{1 - \left(\dfrac{\tan u + \tan v}{1 - \tan u \tan v}\right)\tan w}$

$\quad = \dfrac{\dfrac{\tan u + \tan v + \tan w - \tan u \tan v \tan w}{1 - \tan u \tan v}}{\dfrac{(1 - \tan u \tan v) - \tan u \tan w - \tan v \tan w}{1 - \tan u \tan v}} = \dfrac{\tan u + \tan v + \tan w - \tan u \tan v \tan w}{1 - (\tan u \tan v + \tan u \tan w + \tan v \tan w)}$

**53** The question usually asked here is "Why divide by $\sin u \sin v$?" Since we know the form we want to end up with, we need to "force" the term "$-\sin u \sin v$" to equal "$-1$", hence divide all terms by "$\sin u \sin v$."

$$\cot(u+v) = \frac{\cos(u+v)}{\sin(u+v)} = \frac{(\cos u \cos v - \sin u \sin v)(1/\sin u \sin v)}{(\sin u \cos v + \cos u \sin v)(1/\sin u \sin v)} = \frac{\cot u \cot v - 1}{\cot v + \cot u}$$

**54** $\alpha + \beta = 90° \Rightarrow \alpha = 90° - \beta$.

$\quad \sin^2\alpha + \cos^2\alpha = 1 \Rightarrow \sin^2\alpha + \cos^2(90° - \beta) = 1 \Rightarrow \sin^2\alpha + \sin^2\beta = 1$, since $\cos(90° - \beta) = \sin\beta$.

**55** $\sin(u-v) = \sin[u + (-v)] = \sin u \cos(-v) + \cos u \sin(-v) = \sin u \cos v - \cos u \sin v$

**56** $\tan(u - v) = \tan[u + (-v)] = \dfrac{\tan u + \tan(-v)}{1 - \tan u \tan(-v)} = \dfrac{\tan u - \tan v}{1 + \tan u \tan v}$

**57** $\dfrac{f(x+h) - f(x)}{h} = \dfrac{\cos(x+h) - \cos x}{h} = \dfrac{\cos x \cos h - \sin x \sin h - \cos x}{h}$

$= \dfrac{\cos x \cos h - \cos x}{h} - \dfrac{\sin x \sin h}{h} = \cos x \left(\dfrac{\cos h - 1}{h}\right) - \sin x \left(\dfrac{\sin h}{h}\right)$

**58** $\dfrac{f(x+h) - f(x)}{h} = \dfrac{\tan(x+h) - \tan x}{h} = \dfrac{\dfrac{\tan x + \tan h}{1 - \tan x \tan h} - \tan x}{h}$

$= \dfrac{\tan x + \tan h - \tan x + \tan^2 x \tan h}{h(1 - \tan x \tan h)} = \dfrac{\tan h(\tan^2 x + 1)}{h(1 - \tan x \tan h)}$

$= \sec^2 x \left(\dfrac{\sin h}{h}\right)\left(\dfrac{1}{\cos h}\right)\left(\dfrac{1}{1 - \tan x \tan h}\right) = \sec^2 x \left(\dfrac{\sin h}{h}\right)\dfrac{1}{\cos h - \sin h \tan x}$

**59** (a) Both sides, $\sin 63° - \sin 57°$ and $\sin 3°$, are approximately equal to 0.0523.

(b) LS $= \sin(\alpha + \beta) - \sin(\alpha - \beta) = (\sin \alpha \cos \beta + \cos \alpha \sin \beta) - (\sin \alpha \cos \beta - \cos \alpha \sin \beta) = 2 \cos \alpha \sin \beta$
RS $= \sin \beta$. For $2 \cos \alpha \sin \beta$ to equal $\sin \beta$, $2 \cos \alpha$ must equal 1, so $\cos \alpha = \frac{1}{2}$ and $\alpha = 60°$.

(c) $\alpha = 60°$ and $\beta = 3°$.

**60** (a) Both sides, $\sin 35° + \sin 25°$ and $\cos 5°$, are approximately equal to 0.9962.

(b) LS $= \sin(\alpha + \beta) + \sin(\alpha - \beta) = (\sin \alpha \cos \beta + \cos \alpha \sin \beta) + (\sin \alpha \cos \beta - \cos \alpha \sin \beta) = 2 \sin \alpha \cos \beta$
RS $= \cos \beta$. For $2 \sin \alpha \cos \beta$ to equal $\cos \beta$, $2 \sin \alpha$ must equal 1, so $\sin \alpha = \frac{1}{2}$ and $\alpha = 30°$.

(c) $\alpha = 30°$ and $\beta = 5°$.

**61** $\sin 4t \cos t = \sin t \cos 4t \Rightarrow \sin 4t \cos t - \sin t \cos 4t = 0 \Rightarrow \sin(4t - t) = 0 \Rightarrow \sin 3t = 0 \Rightarrow$
$\quad 3t = \pi n \Rightarrow t = \frac{\pi}{3}n$. In $[0, \pi)$, $t = 0, \frac{\pi}{3}, \frac{2\pi}{3}$.

**62** $\cos 5t \cos 3t = \frac{1}{2} + \sin(-5t)\sin 3t \Rightarrow \cos 5t \cos 3t + \sin 5t \sin 3t = \frac{1}{2} \Rightarrow \cos(5t - 3t) = \frac{1}{2} \Rightarrow$
$\quad \cos 2t = \frac{1}{2} \Rightarrow 2t = \frac{\pi}{3} + 2\pi n, \frac{5\pi}{3} + 2\pi n \Rightarrow t = \frac{\pi}{6} + \pi n, \frac{5\pi}{6} + \pi n$. In $[0, \pi)$, $t = \frac{\pi}{6}, \frac{5\pi}{6}$.

**63** $\cos 5t \cos 2t = -\sin 5t \sin 2t \Rightarrow \cos 5t \cos 2t + \sin 5t \sin 2t = 0 \Rightarrow \cos(5t - 2t) = 0 \Rightarrow$
$\quad \cos 3t = 0 \Rightarrow 3t = \frac{\pi}{2} + \pi n \Rightarrow t = \frac{\pi}{6} + \frac{\pi}{3}n$. In $[0, \pi)$, $t = \frac{\pi}{6}, \frac{\pi}{2}, \frac{5\pi}{6}$.

**64** $\sin 3t \cos t + \cos 3t \sin t = -\frac{1}{2} \Rightarrow \sin(3t + t) = -\frac{1}{2} \Rightarrow \sin 4t = -\frac{1}{2} \Rightarrow$
$\quad 4t = \frac{7\pi}{6} + 2\pi n, \frac{11\pi}{6} + 2\pi n \Rightarrow t = \frac{7\pi}{24} + \frac{\pi}{2}n, \frac{11\pi}{24} + \frac{\pi}{2}n$. In $[0, \pi)$, $t = \frac{7\pi}{24}, \frac{19\pi}{24}, \frac{11\pi}{24}, \frac{23\pi}{24}$.

**65** $\tan 2t + \tan t = 1 - \tan 2t \tan t \Rightarrow \dfrac{\tan 2t + \tan t}{1 - \tan 2t \tan t} = 1 \Rightarrow \tan(2t + t) = 1 \Rightarrow \tan 3t = 1 \Rightarrow$
$\quad 3t = \frac{\pi}{4} + \pi n \Rightarrow t = \frac{\pi}{12} + \frac{\pi}{3}n$. In $[0, \pi)$, $t = \frac{\pi}{12}, \frac{5\pi}{12}, \frac{3\pi}{4}$.

$\quad$ However, $\tan 2t$ is undefined if $t = \frac{3\pi}{4}$, so exclude this value of $t$.

**66** $\tan t - \tan 4t = 1 + \tan 4t \tan t \Rightarrow \dfrac{\tan t - \tan 4t}{1 + \tan t \tan 4t} = 1 \Rightarrow \tan(t - 4t) = 1 \Rightarrow \tan(-3t) = 1 \Rightarrow$
$\quad -\tan 3t = 1 \Rightarrow \tan 3t = -1 \Rightarrow 3t = \frac{3\pi}{4} + \pi n \Rightarrow t = \frac{\pi}{4} + \frac{\pi}{3}n$. In $[0, \pi)$, $t = \frac{\pi}{4}, \frac{7\pi}{12}, \frac{11\pi}{12}$.

**67** (a) $f(x) = \sqrt{3}\cos 2x + \sin 2x$ • $A = \sqrt{\left(\sqrt{3}\right)^2 + 1^2} = 2$. $\tan C = \frac{1}{\sqrt{3}}$ $\Rightarrow$ $C = \frac{\pi}{6}$.

$$f(x) = 2\cos\left(2x - \frac{\pi}{6}\right) = 2\cos\left[2\left(x - \frac{\pi}{12}\right)\right]$$

(b) amplitude $= 2$, period $= \frac{2\pi}{2} = \pi$, phase shift $= \frac{\pi}{12}$

Figure 67

Figure 68

**68** (a) $f(x) = \cos 4x + \sqrt{3}\sin 4x$ • $A = \sqrt{1^2 + \left(\sqrt{3}\right)^2} = 2$. $\tan C = \frac{\sqrt{3}}{1}$ $\Rightarrow$ $C = \frac{\pi}{3}$.

$$f(x) = 2\cos\left(4x - \frac{\pi}{3}\right) = 2\cos\left[4\left(x - \frac{\pi}{12}\right)\right]$$

(b) amplitude $= 2$, period $= \frac{2\pi}{4} = \frac{\pi}{2}$, phase shift $= \frac{\pi}{12}$

**69** (a) $f(x) = 2\cos 3x - 2\sin 3x$ • $A = \sqrt{2^2 + 2^2} = 2\sqrt{2}$. $\tan C = \frac{-2}{2} = -1$ $\Rightarrow$ $C = -\frac{\pi}{4}$.

$$f(x) = 2\sqrt{2}\cos\left(3x + \frac{\pi}{4}\right) = 2\sqrt{2}\cos\left[3\left(x + \frac{\pi}{12}\right)\right]$$

(b) amplitude $= 2\sqrt{2}$, period $= \frac{2\pi}{3}$, phase shift $= -\frac{\pi}{12}$

Figure 69

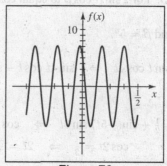

Figure 70

**70** (a) $f(x) = 5\cos 10x - 5\sin 10x$ • $A = \sqrt{5^2 + (-5)^2} = 5\sqrt{2}$. $\tan C = \frac{-5}{5} = -1$ $\Rightarrow$ $C = -\frac{\pi}{4}$.

$$f(x) = 5\sqrt{2}\cos\left(10x + \frac{\pi}{4}\right) = 5\sqrt{2}\cos\left[10\left(x + \frac{\pi}{40}\right)\right]$$

(b) amplitude $= 5\sqrt{2}$, period $= \frac{2\pi}{10} = \frac{\pi}{5}$, phase shift $= -\frac{\pi}{40}$

**71** $y = 50\sin 60\pi t + 40\cos 60\pi t$ • $A = \sqrt{50^2 + 40^2} = 10\sqrt{41}$. $\tan C = \frac{50}{40}$ $\Rightarrow$ $C = \tan^{-1}\frac{5}{4} \approx 0.8961$.

$$y = 10\sqrt{41}\cos\left(60\pi t - \tan^{-1}\frac{5}{4}\right) \approx 10\sqrt{41}\cos(60\pi t - 0.8961).$$

**72** $y = 10\sin\left(120\pi t - \frac{\pi}{2}\right) + 5\sin 120\pi t$ • $\sin\left(120\pi t - \frac{\pi}{2}\right) = \sin 120\pi t \cos\frac{\pi}{2} - \cos 120\pi t \sin\frac{\pi}{2} = -\cos 120\pi t$.

Now, $y = -10\cos 120\pi t + 5\sin 120\pi t = -(10\cos 120\pi t - 5\sin 120\pi t)$.

{$a$, the coefficient of the cosine term, must be positive to apply the formula in Example 7.}.

$A = \sqrt{10^2 + (-5)^2} = 5\sqrt{5}$. $\tan C = \frac{-5}{10}$ $\Rightarrow$ $C = \tan^{-1}\left(-\frac{1}{2}\right) \approx -0.4636$.

$$y = -5\sqrt{5}\cos\left[120\pi t - \tan^{-1}\left(-\frac{1}{2}\right)\right] \approx -5\sqrt{5}\cos(120\pi t + 0.4636).$$

**73** (a) $y = y_0 \cos \omega t + \dfrac{v_0}{\omega} \sin \omega t$ • $\omega = 1$, $y_0 = 2$, and $v_0 = 3$ $\Rightarrow$ $y = 2\cos t + 3\sin t$. $A = \sqrt{2^2 + 3^2} = \sqrt{13}$;

$\tan C = \frac{3}{2}$ $\Rightarrow$ $C \approx 0.98$; $y = \sqrt{13}\cos(t - C)$; amplitude $= \sqrt{13}$, period $= \frac{2\pi}{1} = 2\pi$

(b) $y = 0$ $\Rightarrow$ $\sqrt{13}\cos(t - C) = 0$ $\Rightarrow$ $t - C = \frac{\pi}{2} + \pi n$ $\Rightarrow$

$t = C + \frac{\pi}{2} + \pi n \approx 2.5536 + \pi n$ for every nonnegative integer $n$.

**74** $4 =$ amplitude $\Rightarrow$ $4 = \sqrt{(y_0)^2 + \left(\dfrac{v_0}{\omega}\right)^2}$ $\Rightarrow$ $4 = \sqrt{1^2 + \left(\dfrac{v_0}{2}\right)^2}$ $\{y_0 = 1$ and $\omega = 2\}$ $\Rightarrow$

$16 = 1 + \frac{1}{4}v_0^2$ $\Rightarrow$ $v_0^2 = 60$ $\Rightarrow$ $v_0 = \pm 2\sqrt{15}$ ft/sec

**75** (a) $p(t) = A \sin \omega t + B \sin(\omega t + \tau)$

$= A \sin \omega t + B(\sin \omega t \cos \tau + \cos \omega t \sin \tau)$

$= A \sin \omega t + B \cos \tau \sin \omega t + B \sin \tau \cos \omega t$

$= (B \sin \tau)\cos \omega t + (A + B \cos \tau)\sin \omega t$

$= a \cos \omega t + b \sin \omega t$, with $a = B \sin \tau$ and $b = A + B \cos \tau$

(b) $C^2 = (B \sin \tau)^2 + (A + B \cos \tau)^2$

$= B^2 \sin^2 \tau + A^2 + 2AB \cos \tau + B^2 \cos^2 \tau$

$= A^2 + B^2(\sin^2 \tau + \cos^2 \tau) + 2AB \cos \tau$

$= A^2 + B^2 + 2AB \cos \tau$

**76** (a) Using $C^2 = A^2 + B^2 + 2AB \cos \tau$ from Exercise 75(b) and letting $A = B$ yields $C^2 = 2A^2 + 2A^2 \cos \tau$,

or $C^2 = 2A^2(1 + \cos \tau)$. If the amplitude $C$ of $p$ is zero, then $1 + \cos \tau = 0$, i.e., $\cos \tau = -1$. Hence, $\tau = \pi$.

(b) Destructive interference occurs if $C < A$. If $A$, $C > 0$, then $C < A$ $\Rightarrow$ $C^2 < A^2$ $\Rightarrow$

$2A^2(1 + \cos \tau) < A^2$ $\Rightarrow$ $1 + \cos \tau < \frac{1}{2}$ $\Rightarrow$ $\cos \tau < -\frac{1}{2}$ $\Rightarrow$ $\frac{2\pi}{3} < \tau < \frac{4\pi}{3}$.

**77** (a) $C^2 = A^2 + B^2 + 2AB \cos \tau \le A^2 + B^2 + 2AB$, since $\cos \tau \le 1$ and

$A > 0$, $B > 0$. Thus, $C^2 \le (A + B)^2$, and hence $C \le A + B$.

(b) $C = A + B$ if $\cos \tau = 1$, or $\tau = 0, 2\pi$.

(c) Constructive interference will occur if $C > A$. $C > A$ $\Rightarrow$ $C^2 > A^2$ $\Rightarrow$

$A^2 + B^2 + 2AB \cos \tau > A^2$ $\Rightarrow$ $B^2 + 2AB \cos \tau > 0$ $\Rightarrow$ $B(B + 2A \cos \tau) > 0$.

Since $B > 0$, the product will be positive if $B + 2A \cos \tau > 0$, i.e., $\cos \tau > -\dfrac{B}{2A}$.

**78** (a) $A = B = 2$, $\omega_1 = 1$, $\omega_2 = 20$, and $\tau = 3$ $\Rightarrow$ $p(t) = 2\sin t + 2\sin(20t + 3)$.

(b) The tone of the tuning fork with the shortest period will fade in and out at intervals equal to the period of the tuning fork with the longest period.

$[-2\pi, 2\pi, \pi/2]$ by $[-4.19, 4.19]$  $[-\pi, \pi, \pi/4]$ by $[-5, 5]$  $[-\pi, \pi, \pi/4]$ by $[-5, 5]$

*Figure 78*

*Figure 79*

*Figure 80*

**79** Graph $y = 3\sin 2t + 2\sin(4t + 1)$. Constructive interference will occur when $y > 3$ or $y < -3$. From the graph, we see that this occurs on the intervals $(-2.97, -2.69)$, $(-1.00, -0.37)$, $(0.17, 0.46)$, and $(2.14, 2.77)$.

**80** Graph $y = 2\sin t + 2\sin(3t + 3)$. Constructive interference will occur when $y > 2$ or $y < -2$.

From the graph (see Figure 80), we see that this occurs on the intervals $(-2.01, -1.05)$ and $(1.13, 2.10)$.

## 6.4 Exercises

**1** From the figure, $\sin\theta = \frac{4}{5}$ and $\cos\theta = \frac{3}{5}$. Thus, $\sin 2\theta = 2\sin\theta\cos\theta = 2\left(\frac{4}{5}\right)\left(\frac{3}{5}\right) = \frac{24}{25}$,

$$\cos 2\theta = \cos^2\theta - \sin^2\theta = \left(\tfrac{3}{5}\right)^2 - \left(\tfrac{4}{5}\right)^2 = -\tfrac{7}{25}, \text{ and } \tan 2\theta = \frac{\sin 2\theta}{\cos 2\theta} = \frac{24/25}{-7/25} = -\frac{24}{7}.$$

**Figure 1**

**Figure 2**

**2** From the figure, $\sin\theta = -\frac{3}{5}$ and $\cos\theta = -\frac{4}{5}$. Thus, $\sin 2\theta = 2\sin\theta\cos\theta = 2\left(-\frac{3}{5}\right)\left(-\frac{4}{5}\right) = \frac{24}{25}$,

$$\cos 2\theta = \cos^2\theta - \sin^2\theta = \left(-\tfrac{4}{5}\right)^2 - \left(-\tfrac{3}{5}\right)^2 = \tfrac{7}{25}, \text{ and } \tan 2\theta = \frac{\sin 2\theta}{\cos 2\theta} = \frac{24/25}{7/25} = \frac{24}{7}.$$

**3** $\sec\theta = -\frac{13}{12} \;\Rightarrow\; \cos\theta = -\frac{12}{13}$. $\sin\theta = \pm\sqrt{1 - \left(-\frac{12}{13}\right)^2} = \pm\sqrt{\frac{25}{169}} = \frac{5}{13}$, since $\theta$ is in QII.

Thus, $\sin 2\theta = 2\sin\theta\cos\theta = 2\left(\frac{5}{13}\right)\left(-\frac{12}{13}\right) = -\frac{120}{169}$,

$$\cos 2\theta = \cos^2\theta - \sin^2\theta = \left(-\tfrac{12}{13}\right)^2 - \left(\tfrac{5}{13}\right)^2 = \tfrac{144}{169} - \tfrac{25}{169} = \tfrac{119}{169}, \text{ and } \tan 2\theta = \frac{\sin 2\theta}{\cos 2\theta} = \frac{-120/169}{119/169} = -\frac{120}{119}.$$

**4** $\sin\theta = -\frac{12}{13} \;\Rightarrow\; \cos\theta = \pm\sqrt{1 - \left(-\frac{12}{13}\right)^2} = \pm\sqrt{\frac{25}{169}} = \frac{5}{13}$, since $\theta$ is in QIV.

Thus, $\sin 2\theta = 2\sin\theta\cos\theta = 2\left(-\frac{12}{13}\right)\left(\frac{5}{13}\right) = -\frac{120}{169}$,

$$\cos 2\theta = \cos^2\theta - \sin^2\theta = \left(\tfrac{5}{13}\right)^2 - \left(-\tfrac{12}{13}\right)^2 = \tfrac{25}{169} - \tfrac{144}{169} = -\tfrac{119}{169}, \text{ and } \tan 2\theta = \frac{\sin 2\theta}{\cos 2\theta} = \frac{-120/169}{-119/169} = \frac{120}{119}.$$

**5** $\tan\alpha = 3 \;\Rightarrow\; \dfrac{y}{x} = \dfrac{3}{1}$. $r^2 = x^2 + y^2 = 1^2 + 3^2 = 10 \;\Rightarrow\; r = \sqrt{10}$,

so $\sin 2\alpha = 2\sin\alpha\cos\alpha = 2\left(\dfrac{3}{\sqrt{10}}\right)\left(\dfrac{1}{\sqrt{10}}\right)$ {$\alpha$ acute} $= \dfrac{6}{10} = \dfrac{3}{5}$.

**6** $\cot\alpha = 2 \;\Rightarrow\; \dfrac{x}{y} = \dfrac{2}{1}$. $r^2 = x^2 + y^2 = 2^2 + 1^2 = 5 \;\Rightarrow\; r = \sqrt{5}$,

so $\cos 2\alpha = \cos^2\alpha - \sin^2\alpha = \left(\dfrac{2}{\sqrt{5}}\right)^2 - \left(\dfrac{1}{\sqrt{5}}\right)^2$ {$\alpha$ acute} $= \dfrac{4}{5} - \dfrac{1}{5} = \dfrac{3}{5}$.

**7** $\sec\theta = \frac{5}{4} \;\Rightarrow\; \cos\theta = \frac{4}{5}$. $\theta$ acute implies that $\frac{\theta}{2}$ is acute, so all six trigonometric functions of $\frac{\theta}{2}$ are positive and we use the "$+$" sign for the sine and cosine.

$$\sin\frac{\theta}{2} = \sqrt{\frac{1 - \cos\theta}{2}} = \sqrt{\frac{1 - \frac{4}{5}}{2}} = \sqrt{\frac{\frac{1}{5}}{2}} = \sqrt{\frac{1}{10}} = \sqrt{\frac{1}{10}\cdot\frac{10}{10}} = \frac{\sqrt{10}}{10}.$$

$$\cos\frac{\theta}{2} = \sqrt{\frac{1 + \cos\theta}{2}} = \sqrt{\frac{1 + \frac{4}{5}}{2}} = \sqrt{\frac{\frac{9}{5}}{2}} = \sqrt{\frac{9}{10}} = \sqrt{\frac{9}{10}\cdot\frac{10}{10}} = \frac{3\sqrt{10}}{10}. \quad \tan\frac{\theta}{2} = \frac{\sin\frac{\theta}{2}}{\cos\frac{\theta}{2}} = \frac{\sqrt{10}/10}{3\sqrt{10}/10} = \frac{1}{3}.$$

**8** From the figure $\left(\text{with } \csc\theta = -\dfrac{5}{3}\right)$, $\cos\theta = \dfrac{4}{5}$ and $\dfrac{\theta}{2}$ is in QIV. Hence, $\sin\dfrac{\theta}{2} < 0$ and $\cos\dfrac{\theta}{2} > 0$.

$$\sin\frac{\theta}{2} = -\sqrt{\frac{1-\cos\theta}{2}} = -\sqrt{\frac{1-\frac{4}{5}}{2}} = -\sqrt{\frac{\frac{1}{5}}{2}} = -\sqrt{\frac{1}{10}\cdot\frac{10}{10}} = -\frac{\sqrt{10}}{10}.$$

$$\cos\frac{\theta}{2} = \sqrt{\frac{1+\cos\theta}{2}} = \sqrt{\frac{1+\frac{4}{5}}{2}} = \sqrt{\frac{\frac{9}{5}}{2}} = \sqrt{\frac{9}{10}\cdot\frac{10}{10}} = \frac{3\sqrt{10}}{10}. \quad \tan\frac{\theta}{2} = \frac{\sin\frac{\theta}{2}}{\cos\frac{\theta}{2}} = \frac{-\sqrt{10}/10}{3\sqrt{10}/10} = -\frac{1}{3}.$$

*Figure 8*

*Figure 11*

**9** $\sin\theta = \dfrac{12}{13}$ and $\theta$ in QII $\Rightarrow$ $\cos\theta = -\sqrt{1-\left(\dfrac{12}{13}\right)^2} = -\sqrt{\dfrac{25}{169}} = -\dfrac{5}{13}.$

$90° < \theta < 180° \Rightarrow 45° < \dfrac{\theta}{2} < 90° \Rightarrow \dfrac{\theta}{2}$ is in QI.

$$\sin\frac{\theta}{2} = \sqrt{\frac{1-\cos\theta}{2}} = \sqrt{\frac{1+\frac{5}{13}}{2}} = \sqrt{\frac{\frac{18}{13}}{2}} = \sqrt{\frac{9}{13}} = \frac{3}{\sqrt{13}}.$$

$$\cos\frac{\theta}{2} = \sqrt{\frac{1+\cos\theta}{2}} = \sqrt{\frac{1-\frac{5}{13}}{2}} = \sqrt{\frac{\frac{8}{13}}{2}} = \sqrt{\frac{4}{13}} = \frac{2}{\sqrt{13}}. \quad \tan\frac{\theta}{2} = \frac{\sin\frac{\theta}{2}}{\cos\frac{\theta}{2}} = \frac{3/\sqrt{13}}{2/\sqrt{13}} = \frac{3}{2}.$$

**10** $\tan\theta = -\dfrac{5}{12} \Rightarrow r^2 = (-5)^2 + 12^2 \Rightarrow r = 13.$ $\theta$ in QIV $\Rightarrow \cos\theta = \dfrac{12}{13}.$

$270° < \theta < 360° \Rightarrow 135° < \dfrac{\theta}{2} < 180° \Rightarrow \dfrac{\theta}{2}$ is in QII.

$$\sin\frac{\theta}{2} = \sqrt{\frac{1-\cos\theta}{2}} = \sqrt{\frac{1-\frac{12}{13}}{2}} = \sqrt{\frac{\frac{1}{13}}{2}} = \sqrt{\frac{1}{26}} = \frac{1}{\sqrt{26}}.$$

$$\cos\frac{\theta}{2} = -\sqrt{\frac{1+\cos\theta}{2}} = -\sqrt{\frac{1+\frac{12}{13}}{2}} = -\sqrt{\frac{\frac{25}{13}}{2}} = -\sqrt{\frac{25}{26}} = -\frac{5}{\sqrt{26}}.$$

$$\tan\frac{\theta}{2} = \frac{\sin\frac{\theta}{2}}{\cos\frac{\theta}{2}} = \frac{1/\sqrt{26}}{-5/\sqrt{26}} = -\frac{1}{5}.$$

**11** From the figure (with $a > 0$ and $\tan\theta = 1$), $\cos\theta = -\dfrac{a}{\sqrt{2}\,a} = -\dfrac{\sqrt{2}}{2}$ and $\dfrac{\theta}{2}$ is in QIV.

$$\sin\frac{\theta}{2} = -\sqrt{\frac{1-\cos\theta}{2}} = -\sqrt{\frac{1+\sqrt{2}/2}{2}} = -\sqrt{\frac{2+\sqrt{2}}{4}} = -\frac{1}{2}\sqrt{2+\sqrt{2}}.$$

$$\cos\frac{\theta}{2} = \sqrt{\frac{1+\cos\theta}{2}} = \sqrt{\frac{1-\sqrt{2}/2}{2}} = \sqrt{\frac{2-\sqrt{2}}{4}} = \frac{1}{2}\sqrt{2-\sqrt{2}}.$$

$$\tan\frac{\theta}{2} = \frac{1-\cos\theta}{\sin\theta} = \frac{1+\sqrt{2}/2}{-\sqrt{2}/2}\cdot\frac{2}{2} = \frac{2+\sqrt{2}}{-\sqrt{2}} = -\sqrt{2}-1.$$

**12** $\sec\theta = -4 \;\Rightarrow\; \cos\theta = -\frac{1}{4}.\; 180° < \theta < 270° \;\Rightarrow\; 90° < \frac{\theta}{2} < 135° \;\Rightarrow\; \frac{\theta}{2}$ is in QII.

$$\sin\frac{\theta}{2} = \sqrt{\frac{1-\cos\theta}{2}} = \sqrt{\frac{1+\frac{1}{4}}{2}} = \sqrt{\frac{\frac{5}{4}}{2}} = \sqrt{\frac{5}{8}\cdot\frac{2}{2}} = \frac{\sqrt{10}}{4}.$$

$$\cos\frac{\theta}{2} = -\sqrt{\frac{1+\cos\theta}{2}} = -\sqrt{\frac{1-\frac{1}{4}}{2}} = -\sqrt{\frac{\frac{3}{4}}{2}} = -\sqrt{\frac{3}{8}\cdot\frac{2}{2}} = -\frac{\sqrt{6}}{4}.$$

$$\tan\frac{\theta}{2} = \frac{\sin\frac{\theta}{2}}{\cos\frac{\theta}{2}} = \frac{\sqrt{10}/4}{-\sqrt{6}/4} = -\sqrt{\frac{5}{3}\cdot\frac{3}{3}} = -\frac{\sqrt{15}}{3}.$$

**13** $\cos\beta = \frac{9}{41} \;\Rightarrow\; \sin\beta = \pm\sqrt{1-\left(\frac{9}{41}\right)^2} = \pm\sqrt{\frac{1600}{1681}} = -\frac{40}{41}$, since $\beta$ is in QIV.

$$\tan\frac{\beta}{2} = \frac{1-\cos\beta}{\sin\beta} = \frac{1-\frac{9}{41}}{-\frac{40}{41}}\cdot\frac{41}{41} = \frac{41-9}{-40} = -\frac{32}{40} = -\frac{4}{5}.$$

**14** $\sec\theta = -\frac{25}{7} \;\Rightarrow\; \cos\theta = -\frac{7}{25}.\; \sin\theta = \pm\sqrt{1-\left(-\frac{7}{25}\right)^2} = \pm\sqrt{\frac{576}{625}} = \pm\frac{24}{25}.$

$$\tan\frac{\theta}{2} = \frac{1-\cos\theta}{\sin\theta} = \frac{1-\left(-\frac{7}{25}\right)}{\pm\frac{24}{25}}\cdot\frac{25}{25} = \frac{25+7}{\pm 24} = \pm\frac{32}{24} = \pm\frac{4}{3}.$$

**15** (a) $\cos 67°30' = \sqrt{\dfrac{1+\cos 135°}{2}} = \sqrt{\dfrac{1-\sqrt{2}/2}{2}} = \sqrt{\dfrac{2-\sqrt{2}}{4}} = \dfrac{1}{2}\sqrt{2-\sqrt{2}}.$

(b) $\sin 15° = \sqrt{\dfrac{1-\cos 30°}{2}} = \sqrt{\dfrac{1-\sqrt{3}/2}{2}} = \sqrt{\dfrac{2-\sqrt{3}}{4}} = \dfrac{1}{2}\sqrt{2-\sqrt{3}}.$

(c) $\tan\dfrac{3\pi}{8} = \dfrac{1-\cos\frac{3\pi}{4}}{\sin\frac{3\pi}{4}} = \dfrac{1+\sqrt{2}/2}{\sqrt{2}/2}\cdot\dfrac{2}{2} = \dfrac{2+\sqrt{2}}{\sqrt{2}} = \sqrt{2}+1.$

**16** (a) $\cos 165° = -\sqrt{\dfrac{1+\cos 330°}{2}} = -\sqrt{\dfrac{1+\sqrt{3}/2}{2}} = -\sqrt{\dfrac{2+\sqrt{3}}{4}} = -\dfrac{1}{2}\sqrt{2+\sqrt{3}}.$

(b) $\sin 157°30' = \sqrt{\dfrac{1-\cos 315°}{2}} = \sqrt{\dfrac{1-\sqrt{2}/2}{2}} = \sqrt{\dfrac{2-\sqrt{2}}{4}} = \dfrac{1}{2}\sqrt{2-\sqrt{2}}.$

(c) $\tan\dfrac{\pi}{8} = \dfrac{1-\cos\frac{\pi}{4}}{\sin\frac{\pi}{4}} = \dfrac{1-\sqrt{2}/2}{\sqrt{2}/2}\cdot\dfrac{2}{2} = \dfrac{2-\sqrt{2}}{\sqrt{2}} = \sqrt{2}-1.$

**17** Recognize that $10\theta = 2\cdot 5\theta$ and use the double-angle formula for the sine. $\sin 10\theta = \sin(2\cdot 5\theta) = 2\sin 5\theta\cos 5\theta$

**18** $\cos^2 3x - \sin^2 3x = \cos(2\cdot 3x) = \cos 6x$

**19** We recognize the product of the sine and the cosine as being of the form of the right side of the double-angle formula for the sine, and apply that formula "in reverse."

$$4\sin\frac{x}{2}\cos\frac{x}{2} = 2\cdot 2\sin\frac{x}{2}\cos\frac{x}{2} = 2\sin\left(2\cdot\frac{x}{2}\right) = 2\sin x$$

**20** $\dfrac{\sin^2 2\alpha}{\sin^2\alpha} = \dfrac{(2\sin\alpha\cos\alpha)^2}{\sin^2\alpha} = \dfrac{4\sin^2\alpha\cos^2\alpha}{\sin^2\alpha} = 4\cos^2\alpha = 4\left(1-\sin^2\alpha\right) = 4 - 4\sin^2\alpha$

**21** $\sin^2\dfrac{x}{2} = \dfrac{1-\cos x}{2} = \dfrac{1-\cos x}{2}\cdot\dfrac{1+\cos x}{1+\cos x} = \dfrac{1-\cos^2 x}{2(1+\cos x)} = \dfrac{\sin^2 x}{2(1+\cos x)}$

**22** $\cos^2\dfrac{x}{2} = \dfrac{1+\cos x}{2} = \dfrac{1+\cos x}{2}\cdot\dfrac{1-\cos x}{1-\cos x} = \dfrac{1-\cos^2 x}{2(1-\cos x)} = \dfrac{\sin^2 x}{2(1-\cos x)}$

**23** $(\sin t + \cos t)^2 = \sin^2 t + 2\sin t \cos t + \cos^2 t = (\sin^2 t + \cos^2 t) + (2\sin t \cos t) = 1 + \sin 2t$

**24** $\csc 2u = \dfrac{1}{\sin 2u} = \dfrac{1}{2\sin u \cos u} = \dfrac{1}{2}\csc u \sec u$

**25** $\sin 3u = \sin(2u + u)$        {addition formula for sine}

$\qquad = \sin 2u \cos u + \cos 2u \sin u$

$\qquad = (2\sin u \cos u)\cos u + (1 - 2\sin^2 u)\sin u$     {double-angle formulas for sine and cosine}

$\qquad = 2\sin u \cos^2 u + \sin u - 2\sin^3 u$

$\qquad = 2\sin u(1 - \sin^2 u) + \sin u - 2\sin^3 u$     {$\sin^2 u + \cos^2 u = 1$}

$\qquad = 2\sin u - 2\sin^3 u + \sin u - 2\sin^3 u$

$\qquad = 3\sin u - 4\sin^3 u$

$\qquad = \sin u(3 - 4\sin^2 u)$

**26** $\sin 4t = \sin(2 \cdot 2t) = 2\sin 2t \cos 2t = 2(2\sin t \cos t)(1 - 2\sin^2 t) = 4\sin t \cos t(1 - 2\sin^2 t)$

**27** $\cos 4\theta = \cos(2 \cdot 2\theta) = 2\cos^2 2\theta - 1$     {double-angle formula for cosine}

$\qquad = 2(2\cos^2\theta - 1)^2 - 1$     {double-angle formula for cosine}

$\qquad = 2(4\cos^4\theta - 4\cos^2\theta + 1) - 1$     {square binomial}

$\qquad = (8\cos^4\theta - 8\cos^2\theta + 2) - 1$

$\qquad = 8\cos^4\theta - 8\cos^2\theta + 1$

**28** $\cos 6t = \cos(2 \cdot 3t) = 2\cos^2 3t - 1$

$\qquad = 2(4\cos^3 t - 3\cos t)^2 - 1$     {using Example 2}

$\qquad = 2(16\cos^6 t - 24\cos^4 t + 9\cos^2 t) - 1$

$\qquad = 32\cos^6 t - 48\cos^4 t + 18\cos^2 t - 1$

**29** $\sin^4 t = (\sin^2 t)^2 = \left(\dfrac{1 - \cos 2t}{2}\right)^2$

$\qquad = \tfrac{1}{4}(1 - 2\cos 2t + \cos^2 2t)$

$\qquad = \tfrac{1}{4} - \tfrac{1}{2}\cos 2t + \tfrac{1}{4}\left(\dfrac{1 + \cos 4t}{2}\right)$     {half-angle identity (2)}

$\qquad = \tfrac{1}{4} - \tfrac{1}{2}\cos 2t + \tfrac{1}{8} + \tfrac{1}{8}\cos 4t$

$\qquad = \tfrac{3}{8} - \tfrac{1}{2}\cos 2t + \tfrac{1}{8}\cos 4t$

**30** $\cos^4 x - \sin^4 x = (\cos^2 x + \sin^2 x)(\cos^2 x - \sin^2 x) = \cos^2 x - \sin^2 x = \cos 2x$

**31** We do not have a formula for $\sec 2\theta$, so we will write $\sec 2\theta$ in terms of $\cos 2\theta$ in order to apply the double-angle formula for the cosine.

$$\sec 2\theta = \frac{1}{\cos 2\theta} = \frac{1}{2\cos^2\theta - 1} = \frac{1}{2\left(\dfrac{1}{\sec^2\theta}\right) - 1} = \frac{1}{\dfrac{2 - \sec^2\theta}{\sec^2\theta}} = \frac{\sec^2\theta}{2 - \sec^2\theta}$$

**32** $\cot 2u = \dfrac{1}{\tan 2u} = \dfrac{1 - \tan^2 u}{2\tan u} = \dfrac{1 - \dfrac{1}{\cot^2 u}}{\dfrac{2}{\cot u}} \cdot \dfrac{\cot^2 u}{\cot^2 u} = \dfrac{\cot^2 u - 1}{2\cot u}$

**33** We need to match the arguments of the trigonometric functions involved—that is, either write both of them in terms of $2t$ or in terms of $4t$. Converting $\cos 4t$ to an expression with $2t$ as the angle argument gives us

$$2\sin^2 2t + \cos 4t = 2\sin^2 2t + \cos(2 \cdot 2t) = 2\sin^2 2t + \left(1 - 2\sin^2 2t\right) = 1.$$

Alternatively, if we write both arguments in terms of $4t$, we have

$$2\sin^2 2t + \cos 4t = 2 \cdot \frac{1 - \cos 4t}{2} + \cos 4t = 1 - \cos 4t + \cos 4t = 1.$$

**34** $\tan\theta + \cot\theta = \dfrac{\sin\theta}{\cos\theta} + \dfrac{\cos\theta}{\sin\theta} = \dfrac{\sin^2\theta + \cos^2\theta}{\cos\theta\sin\theta} = \dfrac{2}{2\sin\theta\cos\theta} = \dfrac{2}{\sin 2\theta} = 2\csc 2\theta$

**35** $\tan 3u = \tan(2u + u) = \dfrac{\tan 2u + \tan u}{1 - \tan 2u \tan u}$

$$= \frac{\dfrac{2\tan u}{1 - \tan^2 u} + \tan u}{1 - \dfrac{2\tan u}{1 - \tan^2 u} \cdot \tan u} = \frac{\dfrac{2\tan u + \tan u - \tan^3 u}{1 - \tan^2 u}}{\dfrac{1 - \tan^2 u - 2\tan^2 u}{1 - \tan^2 u}} = \frac{3\tan u - \tan^3 u}{1 - 3\tan^2 u} = \frac{\tan u(3 - \tan^2 u)}{1 - 3\tan^2 u}$$

**36** $\dfrac{1 + \sin 2v + \cos 2v}{1 + \sin 2v - \cos 2v} = \dfrac{1 + 2\sin v\cos v + 2\cos^2 v - 1}{1 + 2\sin v\cos v - 1 + 2\sin^2 v} = \dfrac{2\cos^2 v + 2\sin v\cos v}{2\sin^2 v + 2\sin v\cos v} = \dfrac{2\cos v(\cos v + \sin v)}{2\sin v(\sin v + \cos v)} = \cot v$

**37** $\tan\dfrac{\theta}{2} = \dfrac{1 - \cos\theta}{\sin\theta} = \dfrac{1}{\sin\theta} - \dfrac{\cos\theta}{\sin\theta} = \csc\theta - \cot\theta$

**38** $\tan^2\dfrac{\theta}{2} = \dfrac{1 - \cos\theta}{1 + \cos\theta} \cdot \dfrac{1 - \cos\theta}{1 - \cos\theta} = \dfrac{(1 - \cos\theta)^2}{1 - \cos^2\theta} = \dfrac{1 - 2\cos\theta + \cos^2\theta}{\sin^2\theta} = \dfrac{1}{\sin^2\theta} - \dfrac{2\cos\theta}{\sin^2\theta} + \dfrac{\cos^2\theta}{\sin^2\theta}$

$\quad = \csc^2\theta - 2\cot\theta\csc\theta + \cot^2\theta = (1 + \cot^2\theta) - 2\cot\theta\csc\theta + \cot^2\theta = 1 - 2\cot\theta\csc\theta + 2\cot^2\theta$

**39** $\cos^4\dfrac{\theta}{2} = \left(\cos^2\dfrac{\theta}{2}\right)^2 = \left(\dfrac{1 + \cos\theta}{2}\right)^2 = \dfrac{1 + 2\cos\theta + \cos^2\theta}{4}$

$\quad = \dfrac{1}{4} + \dfrac{1}{2}\cos\theta + \dfrac{1}{4}\left(\dfrac{1 + \cos 2\theta}{2}\right) = \dfrac{1}{4} + \dfrac{1}{2}\cos\theta + \dfrac{1}{8} + \dfrac{1}{8}\cos 2\theta = \dfrac{3}{8} + \dfrac{1}{2}\cos\theta + \dfrac{1}{8}\cos 2\theta$

**40** $\cos^4 2x = \left(\cos^2 2x\right)^2 = \left(\dfrac{1 + \cos 4x}{2}\right)^2 = \dfrac{1 + 2\cos 4x + \cos^2 4x}{4}$

$\quad = \dfrac{1}{4} + \dfrac{1}{2}\cos 4x + \dfrac{1}{4}\left(\dfrac{1 + \cos 8x}{2}\right) = \dfrac{1}{4} + \dfrac{1}{2}\cos 4x + \dfrac{1}{8} + \dfrac{1}{8}\cos 8x = \dfrac{3}{8} + \dfrac{1}{2}\cos 4x + \dfrac{1}{8}\cos 8x$

**41** $\sin^4 2x = \left(\sin^2 2x\right)^2 = \left(\dfrac{1 - \cos 4x}{2}\right)^2 = \dfrac{1 - 2\cos 4x + \cos^2 4x}{4} = \dfrac{1}{4} - \dfrac{2}{4}\cos 4x + \dfrac{1}{4}\cos^2 4x$

$\quad = \dfrac{1}{4} - \dfrac{1}{2}\cos 4x + \dfrac{1}{4}\left(\dfrac{1 + \cos 8x}{2}\right) = \dfrac{1}{4} - \dfrac{1}{2}\cos 4x + \dfrac{1}{8} + \dfrac{1}{8}\cos 8x = \dfrac{3}{8} - \dfrac{1}{2}\cos 4x + \dfrac{1}{8}\cos 8x$

**42** $\sin^4\dfrac{\theta}{2} = \left(\sin^2\dfrac{\theta}{2}\right)^2 = \left(\dfrac{1 - \cos\theta}{2}\right)^2 = \dfrac{1 - 2\cos\theta + \cos^2\theta}{4}$

$\quad = \dfrac{1}{4} - \dfrac{1}{2}\cos\theta + \dfrac{1}{4}\left(\dfrac{1 + \cos 2\theta}{2}\right) = \dfrac{1}{4} - \dfrac{1}{2}\cos\theta + \dfrac{1}{8} + \dfrac{1}{8}\cos 2\theta = \dfrac{3}{8} - \dfrac{1}{2}\cos\theta + \dfrac{1}{8}\cos 2\theta$

**43** $\sin 2t + \sin t = 0 \;\Rightarrow\; 2\sin t\cos t + \sin t = 0 \;\Rightarrow\; \sin t(2\cos t + 1) = 0 \;\Rightarrow$

$\qquad\qquad\qquad \sin t = 0 \text{ or } \cos t = -\tfrac{1}{2} \;\Rightarrow\; t = 0, \pi \text{ or } \tfrac{2\pi}{3}, \tfrac{4\pi}{3}$

**44** $\cos t - \sin 2t = 0 \;\Rightarrow\; \cos t - 2\sin t\cos t = 0 \;\Rightarrow\; \cos t(1 - 2\sin t) = 0 \;\Rightarrow$

$\qquad\qquad\qquad \cos t = 0 \text{ or } \sin t = \tfrac{1}{2} \;\Rightarrow\; t = \tfrac{\pi}{2}, \tfrac{3\pi}{2} \text{ or } \tfrac{\pi}{6}, \tfrac{5\pi}{6}$

**45** $\cos u + \cos 2u = 0 \;\Rightarrow\; \cos u + 2\cos^2 u - 1 = 0 \;\Rightarrow\; 2\cos^2 u + \cos u - 1 = 0 \;\Rightarrow$

$$(2\cos u - 1)(\cos u + 1) = 0 \;\Rightarrow\; \cos u = \tfrac{1}{2}, -1 \;\Rightarrow\; u = \tfrac{\pi}{3}, \tfrac{5\pi}{3}, \pi$$

**46** $\cos 2\theta - \tan\theta = 1 \;\Rightarrow\; 1 - 2\sin^2\theta - \dfrac{\sin\theta}{\cos\theta} = 1 \;\Rightarrow\; 2\sin^2\theta\cos\theta + \sin\theta = 0 \;\Rightarrow$

$\sin\theta\,(2\sin\theta\cos\theta + 1) = 0 \;\Rightarrow\; \sin\theta = 0$ or $\sin 2\theta = -1 \;\Rightarrow$

$$\theta = 0, \pi \text{ or } 2\theta = \tfrac{3\pi}{2}, \tfrac{7\pi}{2} \text{ \{If } \theta \in [0, 2\pi), \text{ then } 2\theta \in [0, 4\pi).\} \;\Rightarrow\; \theta = 0, \pi, \tfrac{3\pi}{4}, \tfrac{7\pi}{4}$$

**47** A first approach uses the concept that if $\tan\alpha = \tan\beta$, then $\alpha = \beta + \pi n$.

$$\tan 2x = \tan x \;\Rightarrow\; 2x = x + \pi n \;\Rightarrow\; x = \pi n \;\Rightarrow\; x = 0, \pi.$$

Another approach is: $\tan 2x = \tan x \;\Rightarrow\; \dfrac{\sin 2x}{\cos 2x} = \dfrac{\sin x}{\cos x} \;\Rightarrow\; \sin 2x\cos x = \sin x \cos 2x \;\Rightarrow$

$$\sin 2x \cos x - \sin x \cos 2x = 0 \;\Rightarrow\; \sin(2x - x) = 0 \;\Rightarrow\; \sin x = 0 \;\Rightarrow\; x = 0, \pi.$$

**48** $\tan 2t - 2\cos t = 0 \;\Rightarrow\; \dfrac{\sin 2t}{\cos 2t} - 2\cos t = 0 \;\Rightarrow\; \dfrac{2\sin t \cos t}{\cos 2t} - \dfrac{(1 - 2\sin^2 t)(2\cos t)}{\cos 2t} = 0 \;\Rightarrow$

$2\sin t\cos t - 2\cos t + 4\cos t\sin^2 t = 0 \;\Rightarrow\; 2\cos t(2\sin^2 t + \sin t - 1) = 0 \;\Rightarrow$

$$(2\cos t)(2\sin t - 1)(\sin t + 1) \;\Rightarrow\; \cos t = 0 \text{ or } \sin t = \tfrac{1}{2}, -1 \;\Rightarrow\; t = \tfrac{\pi}{2}, \tfrac{3\pi}{2} \text{ or } t = \tfrac{\pi}{6}, \tfrac{5\pi}{6}, \tfrac{3\pi}{2}$$

**49** $\sin\tfrac{1}{2}u + \cos u = 1 \;\Rightarrow\; \sin\tfrac{1}{2}u + \cos\left[2 \cdot \left(\tfrac{1}{2}u\right)\right] = 1 \;\Rightarrow\; \sin\tfrac{1}{2}u + \left(1 - 2\sin^2\tfrac{1}{2}u\right) = 1 \;\Rightarrow$

$\sin\tfrac{1}{2}u - 2\sin^2\tfrac{1}{2}u = 0 \;\Rightarrow\; \sin\tfrac{1}{2}u\left(1 - 2\sin\tfrac{1}{2}u\right) = 0 \;\Rightarrow\; \sin\tfrac{1}{2}u = 0, \tfrac{1}{2} \;\Rightarrow\; \tfrac{1}{2}u = 0, \tfrac{\pi}{6}, \tfrac{5\pi}{6} \;\Rightarrow$

$$u = 0, \tfrac{\pi}{3}, \tfrac{5\pi}{3}$$

**50** $2 - \cos^2 x = 4\sin^2\tfrac{1}{2}x \;\Rightarrow\; 2 - \cos^2 x = 4\left(\dfrac{1 - \cos x}{2}\right) \;\Rightarrow\; 2 - \cos^2 x = 2 - 2\cos x \;\Rightarrow$

$$\cos^2 x - 2\cos x = 0 \;\Rightarrow\; \cos x(\cos x - 2) = 0 \;\Rightarrow\; \cos x = 0 \text{ \{} \cos x \neq 2 \text{\}} \;\Rightarrow\; x = \tfrac{\pi}{2}, \tfrac{3\pi}{2}$$

**51** $\tan\dfrac{x}{2} = \sin x \;\Rightarrow\; \dfrac{1 - \cos x}{\sin x} = \sin x \;\Rightarrow\; 1 - \cos x = \sin^2 x \;\Rightarrow\; 1 - \cos x = 1 - \cos^2 x \;\Rightarrow$

$$\cos^2 x - \cos x = 0 \;\Rightarrow\; \cos x(1 - \cos x) = 0 \;\Rightarrow\; \cos x = 0 \text{ or } \cos x = 1 \;\Rightarrow\; x = 0, \tfrac{\pi}{2}, \tfrac{3\pi}{2}$$

**52** $\tan\dfrac{x}{2} = \cot x \;\Rightarrow\; \dfrac{1 - \cos x}{\sin x} = \dfrac{\cos x}{\sin x} \;\Rightarrow\; 1 - \cos x = \cos x \;\Rightarrow\; 1 = 2\cos x \;\Rightarrow$

$$\cos x = \tfrac{1}{2} \;\Rightarrow\; x = \tfrac{\pi}{3}, \tfrac{5\pi}{3}$$

**53** $RS = \sqrt{a^2 + b^2}\,\sin(u + v) = \sqrt{a^2 + b^2}\,(\sin u\cos v + \cos u\sin v)$

$= \sqrt{a^2 + b^2}\,\sin u\cos v + \sqrt{a^2 + b^2}\,\cos u\sin v = \left(\sqrt{a^2 + b^2}\,\cos v\right)\sin u + \left(\sqrt{a^2 + b^2}\,\sin v\right)\cos u$

$LS = a\sin u + b\cos u$. Equating coefficients of $\sin u$ and $\cos u$ gives us $a = \sqrt{a^2 + b^2}\,\cos v$ and

$b = \sqrt{a^2 + b^2}\,\sin v \;\Rightarrow\; \cos v = \dfrac{a}{\sqrt{a^2 + b^2}}$ and $\sin v = \dfrac{b}{\sqrt{a^2 + b^2}}$. Since $0 < u < \tfrac{\pi}{2}$, $\sin u > 0$ and $\cos v > 0$.

Now $a > 0$ and $b > 0$ combine with the above to imply that $\cos v > 0$ and $\sin v > 0$. Thus, $0 < v < \tfrac{\pi}{2}$.

**54** $\sqrt{8^2 + 15^2} = 17$. $\sin v = \tfrac{15}{17}$ and $\cos v = \tfrac{8}{17} \;\Rightarrow\; v = \approx 1.08$ radians, or $v \approx 62°$.

$$8\sin u + 15\cos u \approx 17\sin(u + 1.08).$$

**55** (a) $\cos 2x + 2\cos x = 0 \;\Rightarrow\; 2\cos^2 x + 2\cos x - 1 = 0 \;\Rightarrow$

$$\cos x = \dfrac{-2 \pm \sqrt{12}}{4} = \dfrac{-1 \pm \sqrt{3}}{2} \approx 0.366 \left\{\cos x \neq \dfrac{-1 - \sqrt{3}}{2} < -1\right\}. \text{ Thus, } x \approx 1.20 \text{ and } 5.09.$$

(b) $\sin 2x + \sin x = 0 \;\Rightarrow\; 2\sin x\cos x + \sin x = 0 \;\Rightarrow\; \sin x(2\cos x + 1) = 0 \;\Rightarrow$

$$\sin x = 0 \text{ or } \cos x = -\tfrac{1}{2} \;\Rightarrow\; x = 0, \pi, 2\pi \text{ or } \tfrac{2\pi}{3}, \tfrac{4\pi}{3}. \; P\left(\tfrac{2\pi}{3}, -1.5\right), Q(\pi, -1), R\left(\tfrac{4\pi}{3}, -1.5\right)$$

**56** (a) $\cos x - \sin 2x = 0 \;\Rightarrow\; \cos x - 2\sin x \cos x = 0 \;\Rightarrow\; \cos x(1 - 2\sin x) = 0 \;\Rightarrow$

$$\cos x = 0 \text{ or } \sin x = \tfrac{1}{2} \;\Rightarrow\; x = \tfrac{\pi}{2}, \tfrac{3\pi}{2} \text{ or } \tfrac{\pi}{6}, \tfrac{5\pi}{6} \text{ for } x \text{ in } [0, 2\pi].$$

(b) $\sin x + 2\cos 2x = 0 \;\Rightarrow\; \sin x + 2(1 - 2\sin^2 x) = 0 \;\Rightarrow\; 4\sin^2 x - \sin x - 2 = 0 \;\Rightarrow$

$$\sin x = \tfrac{1 \pm \sqrt{33}}{8} \approx 0.843, -0.593 \;\Rightarrow\; x \approx 1.00, 2.14, 5.65, 3.78$$

**57** (a) $\cos 3x - 3\cos x = 0 \;\Rightarrow\; 4\cos^3 x - 3\cos x - 3\cos x = 0 \;\Rightarrow\; 4\cos^3 x - 6\cos x = 0 \;\Rightarrow$

$$2\cos x(2\cos^2 x - 3) = 0 \;\Rightarrow\; \cos x = 0, \pm\sqrt{3/2} \left\{\cos x \neq \pm\sqrt{3/2} \text{ since } \sqrt{3/2} > 1\right\} \;\Rightarrow$$

$$x = \tfrac{\pi}{2}, \tfrac{3\pi}{2} \text{ for } x \text{ in } [0, 2\pi].$$

(b) $\sin 3x - \sin x = 0 \;\Rightarrow\; 3\sin x - 4\sin^3 x - \sin x = 0 \;\Rightarrow\; 4\sin^3 x - 2\sin x = 0 \;\Rightarrow$

$$2\sin x(2\sin^2 x - 1) = 0 \;\Rightarrow\; \sin x = 0, \pm 1/\sqrt{2} \;\Rightarrow\; x = 0, \pi, 2\pi, \tfrac{\pi}{4}, \tfrac{3\pi}{4}, \tfrac{5\pi}{4}, \tfrac{7\pi}{4}$$

**58** $\sin 4x - 4\sin x = 0 \;\Rightarrow\; 4\sin x \cos x(1 - 2\sin^2 x) - 4\sin x = 0 \;\Rightarrow\; 4\sin x\left[\cos x(1 - 2\sin^2 x) - 1\right] = 0 \;\Rightarrow$

$4\sin x\left[\cos x(2\cos^2 x - 1) - 1\right] = 0 \;\Rightarrow\; 4\sin x(2\cos^3 x - \cos x - 1) = 0 \;\Rightarrow$

$4\sin x(\cos x - 1)(2\cos^2 x + 2\cos x + 1) = 0 \;\Rightarrow\; \sin x = 0 \text{ or } \cos x = 1 \; \{2\cos^2 x + 2\cos x + 1 \neq 0\} \;\Rightarrow$

$$x = 0, \pi, 2\pi \text{ for } x \text{ in } [0, 2\pi].$$

**59** (a) Let $y = \overline{BC}$. Form a right triangle with hypotenuse $y$, side opposite $\theta$, 20, and side adjacent $\theta$, $x$.

$\sin\theta = \dfrac{20}{y} \;\Rightarrow\; y = \dfrac{20}{\sin\theta}. \; \cos\theta = \dfrac{x}{y} \;\Rightarrow\; x = y\cos\theta = \dfrac{20}{\sin\theta} \cdot \cos\theta = \dfrac{20\cos\theta}{\sin\theta}.$

Now $d = (40 - x) + y = 40 - \dfrac{20\cos\theta}{\sin\theta} + \dfrac{20}{\sin\theta} = 20\left(\dfrac{1 - \cos\theta}{\sin\theta}\right) + 40 = 20\tan\dfrac{\theta}{2} + 40.$

(b) $50 = 20\tan\dfrac{\theta}{2} + 40 \;\Rightarrow\; \tan\dfrac{\theta}{2} = \dfrac{1}{2} \;\Rightarrow\; \dfrac{1 - \cos\theta}{\sin\theta} = \dfrac{1}{2} \;\Rightarrow\; 2 - 2\cos\theta = \sin\theta \;\Rightarrow$

$4 - 8\cos\theta + 4\cos^2\theta = \sin^2\theta = 1 - \cos^2\theta \;\Rightarrow\; 5\cos^2\theta - 8\cos\theta + 3 = 0 \;\Rightarrow$

$(5\cos\theta - 3)(\cos\theta - 1) = 0 \;\Rightarrow\; \cos\theta = \tfrac{3}{5}, 1. \; \{\cos\theta = 1 \;\Rightarrow\; \theta = 0 \text{ and } 0 \text{ is extraneous}\}.$

$\cos\theta = \dfrac{3}{5} \;\Rightarrow\; \sin\theta = \dfrac{4}{5} \text{ and } y = \dfrac{20}{4/5} = 25. \; \cos\theta = \dfrac{x}{y} \text{ and } \cos\theta = \dfrac{3}{5} \;\Rightarrow\; \dfrac{x}{25} = \dfrac{3}{5} \;\Rightarrow$

$$x = 15, \text{ which means that } B \text{ would be 25 miles from } A.$$

**60** $R = \dfrac{v^2}{16}\sin\theta\cos\theta \;\bullet\; R = 150 \text{ and } v = 80 \;\Rightarrow\; 150 = \dfrac{80^2}{16}\sin\theta\cos\theta \;\Rightarrow\; \dfrac{3}{8} = \dfrac{1}{2}(2\sin\theta\cos\theta) \;\Rightarrow$

$$\sin 2\theta = \tfrac{3}{4} \;\Rightarrow\; 2\theta \approx 48.59° \text{ or } 131.41° \;\Rightarrow\; \theta \approx 24.30° \text{ or } 65.70°.$$

**61** (a) From Example 8, the area $A$ of a cross section is $A = \tfrac{1}{2}(\text{side})^2(\text{sine of included angle}) = \tfrac{1}{2}\left(\tfrac{1}{2}\right)^2 \sin\theta = \tfrac{1}{8}\sin\theta.$

The volume $V = (\text{length of gutter})(\text{area of cross section}) = 20\left(\tfrac{1}{8}\sin\theta\right) = \tfrac{5}{2}\sin\theta.$

(b) $V = 2 \;\Rightarrow\; \tfrac{5}{2}\sin\theta = 2 \;\Rightarrow\; \sin\theta = \tfrac{4}{5} \;\Rightarrow\; \theta \approx 53.13°.$

**62** (a) Let $D$ denote the center of the circle. $\angle ACB = 180 - \phi.$ $\triangle DAC$ is a right triangle since the circle is

tangent to the highway. $\angle DCA = \tfrac{1}{2}\angle ACB = 90° - \dfrac{\phi}{2},$ so $\angle CDA = \dfrac{\phi}{2}. \; \tan\dfrac{\phi}{2} = \dfrac{d}{R} \;\Rightarrow\; d = R\tan\dfrac{\phi}{2}.$

(b) $20 = R\tan\dfrac{45°}{2} \;\Rightarrow\; 20 = R\left(\dfrac{1 - \cos 45°}{\sin 45°}\right) \;\Rightarrow$

$$R = \dfrac{20\sin 45°}{1 - \cos 45°} = \dfrac{20 \cdot \sqrt{2}/2}{1 - \sqrt{2}/2} \cdot \dfrac{2}{2} = \dfrac{20\sqrt{2}}{2 - \sqrt{2}} \cdot \dfrac{2 + \sqrt{2}}{2 + \sqrt{2}} = \dfrac{20\left(2\sqrt{2} + 2\right)}{2} = 20\sqrt{2} + 20 \approx 48.28 \text{ ft.}$$

The length of the curbing can be treated as an arc length.

The radius is $R$ and the central angle is $45°$. $s = r\theta = \left(20 + 20\sqrt{2}\right)\left(\dfrac{\pi}{4}\right) \approx 37.92 \text{ ft.}$

**63** (a) Let $y = \overline{DB}$ and $x$ denote the distance from $D$ to the midpoint of $\overline{BC}$.

$$\sin\frac{\theta}{2} = \frac{b/2}{y} \implies y = \frac{b}{2}\cdot\frac{1}{\sin(\theta/2)} \text{ and } \tan\frac{\theta}{2} = \frac{b/2}{x} \implies x = \frac{b}{2}\cdot\frac{\cos(\theta/2)}{\sin(\theta/2)}.$$

$$l = (a-x)+y = a - \frac{b}{2}\cdot\frac{\cos(\theta/2)}{\sin(\theta/2)} + \frac{b}{2}\cdot\frac{1}{\sin(\theta/2)} = a + \frac{b}{2}\cdot\frac{1-\cos(\theta/2)}{\sin(\theta/2)} = a + \frac{b}{2}\tan\left(\frac{\theta/2}{2}\right)$$

$$= a + \frac{b}{2}\tan\frac{\theta}{4}.$$

(b) $a = 10$ mm, $b = 6$ mm, and $\theta = 156° \implies l = 10 + 3\tan 39° \approx 12.43$ mm.

**64** (a) $f(t) = \sin^2\omega t = \dfrac{1-\cos 2\omega t}{2} = \dfrac{1}{2} - \dfrac{1}{2}\cos 2\omega t$. Now $\cos 2\omega t$ has period $\dfrac{2\pi}{2\omega} = \dfrac{\pi}{\omega}$. Since $0 \le t \le 2\left(\dfrac{\pi}{\omega}\right)$,

we see that $f$ will complete 2 cycles on the given interval. Thus, the average value is $c = \frac{1}{2}$.

(b) $r = RI^2 = RI_0^2 \sin^2\omega t = RI_0^2\left(\frac{1}{2} - \frac{1}{2}\cos 2\omega t\right) = \frac{1}{2}RI_0^2 - \frac{1}{2}RI_0^2\cos 2\omega t$.

Thus, the average rate at which heat is produced is $\frac{1}{2}RI_0^2$.

**65** The graph of $f$ appears to be that of $y = g(x) = \tan x$.

$$\frac{\sin 2x + \sin x}{\cos 2x + \cos x + 1} = \frac{2\sin x\cos x + \sin x}{(2\cos^2 x - 1) + \cos x + 1} = \frac{\sin x(2\cos x + 1)}{\cos x(2\cos x + 1)} = \frac{\sin x}{\cos x} = \tan x$$

**66** The graph of $f$ appears to be that of $y = g(x) = \cos x$.

$$\frac{\sin x(1 + \cos 2x)}{\sin 2x} = \frac{\sin x[1 + (2\cos^2 x - 1)]}{2\sin x\cos x} = \frac{2\cos^2 x}{2\cos x} = \cos x$$

**67** Graph $Y_1 = \tan(0.5x + 1)$ and $Y_2 = \sin 0.5x$ on $[-2\pi, 2\pi]$ in Dot mode. There are two points of intersection. They occur at $x \approx -3.55, 5.22$.

$[-2\pi, 2\pi, \pi/2]$ by $[-4, 4]$          $[-\pi/2, \pi/2, \pi/4]$ by $[-4, 4]$

*Figure 67*          *Figure 68*

**68** Graph $Y_1 = 1/\cos(2x + 1)$ and $Y_2 = \cos(0.5x) + 1$ on $[-\pi/2, \pi/2]$ in Dot mode. There are two points of intersection. They occur at $x \approx -1.00, 0.02$.

**69** Graph $Y_1 = 1/\sin(0.25x + 1)$ and $Y_2 = 1.5 - \cos 2x$ on $[-\pi, \pi]$. There are four points of intersection. They occur at $x \approx -2.03, -0.72, 0.58, 2.62$.

$[-\pi, \pi, \pi/4]$ by $[-4, 4]$          $[-\pi, \pi, \pi/4]$ by $[-4, 4]$

*Figure 69*          *Figure 70*

**70** Graph $Y_1 = 3\sin(2x) + 0.5$ and $Y_2 = 2\sin\left(\frac{1}{2}x + 1\right)$ on $[-\pi, \pi]$. There are three points of intersection. They occur at $x \approx -1.56, 0.22, 1.31$.

**71** Graph $Y_1 = 2/\tan(.25x)$ and $Y_2 = 1 - 1/\cos(.5x)$ on $[-2\pi, 2\pi]$ in Dot mode. There is one point of intersection. It occurs at $x \approx -2.59$.

$[-2\pi, 2\pi, \pi/2]$ by $[-4, 4]$

*Figure 71*

$[-\pi, \pi, \pi/4]$ by $[-4, 4]$

*Figure 72*

**72** Graph $Y_1 = \tan(1.5x + .5)$ and $Y_2 = 1.5\sin(2x)$ on $[-\pi, \pi]$ in Dot mode. There are three points of intersection. They occur at $x \approx -1.92, -0.97, 1.63$.

## 6.5 Exercises

*Note:* We will reference the product-to-sum formulas as [P1]–[P4] and the sum-to-product formulas as [S1]–[S4] in the order they appear in the text. The formulas $\cos(-kx) = \cos kx$ and $\sin(-kx) = -\sin kx$ will be used without mention.

**1** $\sin 7t \sin t = $ [P4] $\frac{1}{2}[\cos(7t - t) - \cos(7t + t)] = \frac{1}{2}\cos 6t - \frac{1}{2}\cos 8t$

**2** $\sin(-4x)\cos 8x = $ [P1] $\frac{1}{2}[\sin(-4x + 8x) + \sin(-4x - 8x)] = \frac{1}{2}\sin 4x + \frac{1}{2}\sin(-12x) = \frac{1}{2}\sin 4x - \frac{1}{2}\sin 12x$

**3** $\cos 6u \cos(-4u) = $ [P3] $\frac{1}{2}\{\cos[6u + (-4u)] + \cos[6u - (-4u)]\} = \frac{1}{2}\cos 2u + \frac{1}{2}\cos 10u$

**4** $\cos 2t \sin 6t = $ [P2] $\frac{1}{2}[\sin(2t + 6t) - \sin(2t - 6t)] = \frac{1}{2}\sin 8t - \frac{1}{2}\sin(-4t) = \frac{1}{2}\sin 8t + \frac{1}{2}\sin 4t$

**5** $2\sin 5\theta \cos 3\theta = $ [P1] $2 \cdot \frac{1}{2}[\sin(5\theta + 3\theta) + \sin(5\theta - 3\theta)] = \sin 8\theta + \sin 2\theta$

**6** $2\sin 7\theta \sin 5\theta = $ [P4] $2 \cdot \frac{1}{2}[\cos(7\theta - 5\theta) - \cos(7\theta + 5\theta)] = \cos 2\theta - \cos 12\theta$

**7** $3\cos x \sin 2x = $ [P2] $3 \cdot \frac{1}{2}[\sin(x + 2x) - \sin(x - 2x)] = \frac{3}{2}\sin 3x - \frac{3}{2}\sin(-x) = \frac{3}{2}\sin 3x + \frac{3}{2}\sin x$

**8** $5\cos 4u \cos 5u = $ [P3] $5 \cdot \frac{1}{2}[\cos(4u + 5u) + \cos(4u - 5u)] = \frac{5}{2}\cos 9u + \frac{5}{2}\cos(-u) = \frac{5}{2}\cos 9u + \frac{5}{2}\cos u$

**9** $\sin 2\theta + \sin 4\theta = $ [S1] $2\sin\dfrac{2\theta + 4\theta}{2}\cos\dfrac{2\theta - 4\theta}{2} = 2\sin 3\theta \cos(-\theta) = 2\sin 3\theta \cos\theta$

**10** $\sin 2\theta - \sin 8\theta = $ [S2] $2\cos\dfrac{2\theta + 8\theta}{2}\sin\dfrac{2\theta - 8\theta}{2} = 2\cos 5\theta \sin(-3\theta) = -2\cos 5\theta \sin 3\theta$

**11** $\cos 5x - \cos 3x = $ [S4] $-2\sin\dfrac{5x + 3x}{2}\sin\dfrac{5x - 3x}{2} = -2\sin 4x \sin x$

**12** $\cos 5t + \cos 6t = $ [S3] $2\cos\dfrac{5t + 6t}{2}\cos\dfrac{5t - 6t}{2} = 2\cos\frac{11}{2}t \cos(-\frac{1}{2}t) = 2\cos\frac{11}{2}t \cos\frac{1}{2}t$

**13** $\sin 3t - \sin 9t = $ [S2] $2\cos\dfrac{3t + 9t}{2}\sin\dfrac{3t - 9t}{2} = 2\cos 6t \sin(-3t) = -2\cos 6t \sin 3t$

**14** $\cos 3\theta - \cos 5\theta = $ [S4] $-2\sin\dfrac{3\theta + 5\theta}{2}\sin\dfrac{3\theta - 5\theta}{2} = -2\sin 4\theta \sin(-\theta) = 2\sin 4\theta \sin\theta$

**15** $\cos x + \cos 2x = $ [S3] $2\cos\dfrac{x + 2x}{2}\cos\dfrac{x - 2x}{2} = 2\cos\frac{3}{2}x \cos(-\frac{1}{2}x) = 2\cos\frac{3}{2}x \cos\frac{1}{2}x$

$\boxed{16}$ $\sin 8t + \sin 2t = $ [S1] $2 \sin \dfrac{8t + 2t}{2} \cos \dfrac{8t - 2t}{2} = 2 \sin 5t \cos 3t$

$\boxed{17}$ $\dfrac{\sin 4t + \sin 6t}{\cos 4t - \cos 6t} = \dfrac{\text{[S1]} \ 2 \sin 5t \cos(-t)}{\text{[S4]} \ -2 \sin 5t \sin(-t)} = \dfrac{\cos t}{-(-\sin t)} = \dfrac{\cos t}{\sin t} = \cot t$

$\boxed{18}$ $\dfrac{\sin \theta + \sin 3\theta}{\cos \theta + \cos 3\theta} = \dfrac{\text{[S1]} \ 2 \sin 2\theta \cos(-\theta)}{\text{[S3]} \ 2 \cos 2\theta \cos(-\theta)} = \dfrac{\sin 2\theta}{\cos 2\theta} = \tan 2\theta$

$\boxed{19}$ $\dfrac{\sin u + \sin v}{\cos u + \cos v} = \dfrac{\text{[S1]} \ 2 \sin \frac{1}{2}(u+v) \cos \frac{1}{2}(u-v)}{\text{[S3]} \ 2 \cos \frac{1}{2}(u+v) \cos \frac{1}{2}(u-v)} = \dfrac{\sin \frac{1}{2}(u+v)}{\cos \frac{1}{2}(u+v)} = \tan \tfrac{1}{2}(u+v)$

$\boxed{20}$ $\dfrac{\sin u - \sin v}{\cos u - \cos v} = \dfrac{\text{[S2]} \ 2 \cos \frac{1}{2}(u+v) \sin \frac{1}{2}(u-v)}{\text{[S4]} \ -2 \sin \frac{1}{2}(u+v) \sin \frac{1}{2}(u-v)} = \dfrac{\cos \frac{1}{2}(u+v)}{-\sin \frac{1}{2}(u+v)} = -\cot \tfrac{1}{2}(u+v)$

$\boxed{21}$ $\dfrac{\sin u - \sin v}{\sin u + \sin v} = \dfrac{\text{[S2]} \ 2 \cos \frac{1}{2}(u+v) \sin \frac{1}{2}(u-v)}{\text{[S1]} \ 2 \sin \frac{1}{2}(u+v) \cos \frac{1}{2}(u-v)} = \cot \tfrac{1}{2}(u+v) \tan \tfrac{1}{2}(u-v) = \dfrac{\tan \frac{1}{2}(u-v)}{\tan \frac{1}{2}(u+v)}$

$\boxed{22}$ $\dfrac{\cos u - \cos v}{\cos u + \cos v} = \dfrac{\text{[S4]} \ -2 \sin \frac{1}{2}(u+v) \sin \frac{1}{2}(u-v)}{\text{[S3]} \ 2 \cos \frac{1}{2}(u+v) \cos \frac{1}{2}(u-v)} = -\tan \tfrac{1}{2}(u+v) \tan \tfrac{1}{2}(u-v)$

$\boxed{23}$ Since the arguments on the right side are all even multiples of $x$ ($2x$, $4x$, and $6x$), we begin by grouping the terms with the odd multiples of $x$ together, and operate on them with a product-to-sum formula, which will convert these expressions to expressions with even multiples of $x$.

$$\begin{aligned} 4 \cos x \cos 2x \sin 3x &= 2 \cos 2x \,(2 \sin 3x \cos x) \\ &= 2 \cos 2x \,(\,[\text{P1}] \sin 4x + \sin 2x) \\ &= (2 \cos 2x \sin 4x) + (2 \cos 2x \sin 2x) \\ &= [\,[\text{P2}] \sin 6x - \sin(-2x)] + (\,[\text{P2}] \sin 4x - \sin 0) \\ &= \sin 2x + \sin 4x + \sin 6x \end{aligned}$$

$\boxed{24}$ $\dfrac{\cos t + \cos 4t + \cos 7t}{\sin t + \sin 4t + \sin 7t} = \dfrac{\cos 4t + \text{[S3]} \ 2 \cos 4t \cos(-3t)}{\sin 4t + \text{[S1]} \ 2 \sin 4t \cos(-3t)} = \dfrac{\cos 4t \,(1 + 2 \cos 3t)}{\sin 4t \,(1 + 2 \cos 3t)} = \cot 4t$

$\boxed{25}$ $(\sin ax)(\cos bx) = [\text{P1}] \ \frac{1}{2}[\sin(ax + bx) + \sin(ax - bx)] = \frac{1}{2} \sin[(a+b)x] + \frac{1}{2} \sin[(a-b)x]$

$\boxed{26}$ $(\cos au)(\cos bu) = [\text{P3}] \ \frac{1}{2}[\cos(au + bu) + \cos(au - bu)] = \frac{1}{2} \cos[(a+b)u] + \frac{1}{2} \cos[(a-b)u]$

$\boxed{27}$ $\sin 5t + \sin 3t = 0 \ \Rightarrow \ [\text{S1}] \ 2 \sin 4t \cos t = 0 \ \Rightarrow \ \sin 4t = 0 \text{ or } \cos t = 0 \ \Rightarrow$

$\quad 4t = \pi n \text{ or } t = \frac{\pi}{2} + \pi n \ \Rightarrow \ t = \frac{\pi}{4} n \text{ \{which includes } t = \frac{\pi}{2} + \pi n\}$

$\boxed{28}$ $\sin t + \sin 3t = \sin 2t \ \Rightarrow \ [\text{S1}] \ 2 \sin 2t \cos(-t) = \sin 2t \ \Rightarrow \ \sin 2t \,(2 \cos t - 1) = 0 \ \Rightarrow$

$\quad \sin 2t = 0 \text{ or } \cos t = \frac{1}{2} \ \Rightarrow \ 2t = \pi n \text{ \{i.e., } t = \frac{\pi}{2} n\} \text{ or } t = \frac{\pi}{3} + 2\pi n, \frac{5\pi}{3} + 2\pi n$

$\boxed{29}$ $\cos x = \cos 3x \ \Rightarrow \ \cos x - \cos 3x = 0 \ \Rightarrow \ [\text{S4}] \ -2 \sin 2x \sin(-x) = 0 \ \Rightarrow$

$\quad \sin 2x = 0 \text{ or } \sin x = 0 \ \Rightarrow \ 2x = \pi n \text{ or } x = \pi n \ \Rightarrow \ x = \frac{\pi}{2} n \text{ \{which includes } x = \pi n\}$

$\boxed{30}$ $\cos 4x - \cos 3x = 0 \ \Rightarrow \ [\text{S4}] \ -2 \sin \frac{7}{2}x \sin \frac{1}{2}x = 0 \ \Rightarrow \ \sin \frac{7}{2}x = 0 \text{ or } \sin \frac{1}{2}x = 0 \ \Rightarrow$

$\quad \frac{7}{2}x = \pi n \text{ or } \frac{1}{2}x = \pi n \ \Rightarrow \ x = \frac{2\pi}{7} n \text{ or } x = 2\pi n \ \Rightarrow \ x = \frac{2\pi}{7} n \text{ \{which includes } x = 2\pi n\}$

$\boxed{31}$ $\cos 3x + \cos 5x = \cos x \ \Rightarrow \ [\text{S3}] \ 2 \cos 4x \cos(-x) - \cos x = 0 \ \Rightarrow \ \cos x \,(2 \cos 4x - 1) = 0 \ \Rightarrow$

$\quad \cos x = 0 \text{ or } \cos 4x = \frac{1}{2} \ \Rightarrow \ x = \frac{\pi}{2} + \pi n \text{ or } 4x = \frac{\pi}{3} + 2\pi n, \frac{5\pi}{3} + 2\pi n \ \Rightarrow \ x = \frac{\pi}{2} + \pi n, \frac{\pi}{12} + \frac{\pi}{2} n, \frac{5\pi}{12} + \frac{\pi}{2} n$

$\boxed{32}$ $\cos 3x = -\cos 6x \ \Rightarrow \ \cos 3x + \cos 6x = 0 \ \Rightarrow \ [\text{S3}] \ 2 \cos \frac{9}{2}x \cos(-\frac{3}{2}x) = 0 \ \Rightarrow$

$\quad \frac{9}{2}x = \frac{\pi}{2} + \pi n \text{ or } \frac{3}{2}x = \frac{\pi}{2} + \pi n \ \Rightarrow \ x = \frac{\pi}{9} + \frac{2\pi}{9} n \text{ or } x = \frac{\pi}{3} + \frac{2\pi}{3} n \ \Rightarrow$

$\qquad\qquad\qquad\qquad x = \frac{\pi}{9} + \frac{2\pi}{9} n \text{ \{which includes } x = \frac{\pi}{3} + \frac{2\pi}{3} n\}$

**33** $\sin 2x - \sin 5x = 0 \;\Rightarrow\;$ [S2] $2\cos\frac{7}{2}x \sin\left(-\frac{3}{2}x\right) = 0 \;\Rightarrow\; \frac{7}{2}x = \frac{\pi}{2} + \pi n$ or $\frac{3}{2}x = \pi n \;\Rightarrow\;$

$$x = \frac{\pi}{7} + \frac{2\pi}{7}n \text{ or } x = \frac{2\pi}{3}n$$

**34** $\sin 5x - \sin x = 2\cos 3x \;\Rightarrow\;$ [S2] $2\cos 3x \sin 2x - 2\cos 3x = 0 \;\Rightarrow\; 2\cos 3x (\sin 2x - 1) = 0 \;\Rightarrow$

$\cos 3x = 0$ or $\sin 2x = 1 \;\Rightarrow\; 3x = \frac{\pi}{2} + \pi n$ or $2x = \frac{\pi}{2} + 2\pi n \;\Rightarrow\; x = \frac{\pi}{6} + \frac{\pi}{3}n$ or $x = \frac{\pi}{4} + \pi n$

**35** $\cos x + \cos 3x = 0 \;\Rightarrow\;$ [S3] $2\cos 2x \cos(-x) = 0 \;\Rightarrow\; \cos 2x = 0$ or $\cos x = 0 \;\Rightarrow$

$2x = \frac{\pi}{2} + \pi n$ or $x = \frac{\pi}{2} + \pi n \;\Rightarrow\; x = \frac{\pi}{4} + \frac{\pi}{2}n$ or $x = \frac{\pi}{2} + \pi n \;\Rightarrow\; x = \frac{\pi}{4}, \frac{3\pi}{4}, \frac{5\pi}{4}, \frac{7\pi}{4}, \frac{\pi}{2}, \frac{3\pi}{2}$ for $0 \le x \le 2\pi$

**36** $\sin 4x - \sin x = 0 \;\Rightarrow\;$ [S2] $2\cos\frac{5}{2}x \sin\frac{3}{2}x \;\Rightarrow\; \cos\frac{5}{2}x = 0$ or $\sin\frac{3}{2}x = 0 \;\Rightarrow$

$\frac{5}{2}x = \frac{\pi}{2} + \pi n$ or $\frac{3}{2}x = \pi n \;\Rightarrow\; x = \frac{\pi}{5} + \frac{2\pi}{5}n$ or $x = \frac{2\pi}{3}n \;\Rightarrow\; x = \frac{\pi}{5}, \frac{3\pi}{5}, \pi, \frac{7\pi}{5}, \frac{9\pi}{5}, 0, \frac{2\pi}{3}, \frac{4\pi}{3}, 2\pi$ for

$0 \le x \le 2\pi$. **Note:** $\frac{3\pi}{5} \approx 1.88$, $\frac{2\pi}{3} \approx 2.09$, $\frac{4\pi}{3} \approx 4.19$, and $\frac{7\pi}{5} \approx 4.40$ are the intercepts that are close together.

**37** $\sin 3x - \sin x = 0 \;\Rightarrow\;$ [S2] $2\cos 2x \sin x = 0 \;\Rightarrow\; \cos 2x = 0$ or $\sin x = 0 \;\Rightarrow$

$2x = \frac{\pi}{2} + \pi n$ or $x = \pi n \;\Rightarrow\; x = \frac{\pi}{4} + \frac{\pi}{2}n$ or $x = \pi n \;\Rightarrow\; x = 0, \pi, 2\pi, \frac{\pi}{4}, \frac{3\pi}{4}, \frac{5\pi}{4}, \frac{7\pi}{4}$ for $0 \le x \le 2\pi$.

**38** $\cos 4x - \cos x = 0 \;\Rightarrow\;$ [S4] $-2\sin\frac{5}{2}x \sin\frac{3}{2}x = 0 \;\Rightarrow\; \sin\frac{5}{2}x = 0$ or $\sin\frac{3}{2}x = 0 \;\Rightarrow$

$\frac{5}{2}x = \pi n$ or $\frac{3}{2}x = \pi n \;\Rightarrow\; x = \frac{2\pi}{5}n$ or $x = \frac{2\pi}{3}n \;\Rightarrow\; x = 0, \frac{2\pi}{5}, \frac{4\pi}{5}, \frac{6\pi}{5}, \frac{8\pi}{5}, 2\pi, \frac{2\pi}{3}, \frac{4\pi}{3}$ for $0 \le x \le 2\pi$.

**39** $f(x) = \sin\left(\frac{\pi n}{l}x\right)\cos\left(\frac{k\pi n}{l}t\right) =$ [P1] $\frac{1}{2}\left[\sin\left(\frac{\pi n}{l}x + \frac{k\pi n}{l}t\right) + \sin\left(\frac{\pi n}{l}x - \frac{k\pi n}{l}t\right)\right]$

$= \frac{1}{2}\left[\sin\frac{\pi n}{l}(x + kt) + \sin\frac{\pi n}{l}(x - kt)\right] = \frac{1}{2}\sin\frac{\pi n}{l}(x + kt) + \frac{1}{2}\sin\frac{\pi n}{l}(x - kt)$

**40** (a) $p(t) = a\cos\omega_1 t + a\cos\omega_2 t = a(\cos\omega_1 t + \cos\omega_2 t)$

$=$ [S3] $a \cdot 2\cos\left[\frac{1}{2}(\omega_1 + \omega_2)t\right]\cos\left[\frac{1}{2}(\omega_1 - \omega_2)t\right] = 2a\cos\frac{1}{2}(\omega_1 + \omega_2)t \cos\frac{1}{2}(\omega_1 - \omega_2)t$

(b) From part (a), $p(t) = \left[2a\cos\frac{1}{2}(\omega_1 - \omega_2)t\right]\cos\frac{1}{2}(\omega_1 + \omega_2)t = f(t)\cos\frac{1}{2}(\omega_1 + \omega_2)t$.

Since $\omega_1 \approx \omega_2$, $\frac{1}{2}(\omega_1 + \omega_2) \approx \omega_1$, and the period is approximately $2\pi/\omega_1$.

The maximum amplitude occurs when $\cos\frac{1}{2}(\omega_1 - \omega_2)t = 1$, i.e., $f(t) = 2a$.

(c) $p(t) = 0 \;\Rightarrow\; \cos 4.5t + \cos 3.5t = 0 \;\Rightarrow\;$ [S3] $2\cos 4t \cos\frac{1}{2}t = 0 \;\Rightarrow\; \left[2\cos\frac{1}{2}t\right]\cos 4t = 0$.

From part (b), we want to know when the amplitude is zero. $2\cos\frac{1}{2}t = 0 \;\Rightarrow\; \frac{1}{2}t = \frac{\pi}{2} + \pi n \;\Rightarrow$

$t = \pi + 2\pi n$. $A = (-\pi, 0)$ and $B = (\pi, 0)$. Near-silence occurs every $2\pi$ units of time.

(d) From the graph, we see that one-half period occurs on the interval from $A$ to $B$.

$$\tfrac{1}{2}(period) = \pi - (-\pi) \;\Rightarrow\; \tfrac{1}{2}(period) = 2\pi \;\Rightarrow\; period = 4\pi.$$

**41** (a) $f(x) = \sin 4x + \sin 2x$ • Estimating the $x$-intercepts, we have $x \approx 0, \pm 1.05, \pm 1.57, \pm 2.09, \pm 3.14$.

(b) $\sin 4x + \sin 2x =$ [S1] $2\sin 3x \cos x = 0 \;\Rightarrow\; \sin 3x = 0$ or $\cos x = 0$.

$\sin 3x = 0 \;\Rightarrow\; 3x = \pi n \;\Rightarrow\; x = \frac{\pi}{3}n \;\Rightarrow\; x = 0, \pm\frac{\pi}{3}, \pm\frac{2\pi}{3}, \pm\pi$.

$\cos x = 0 \;\Rightarrow\; x = \pm\frac{\pi}{2}$.        The $x$-intercepts are $0, \pm\frac{\pi}{3}, \pm\frac{\pi}{2}, \pm\frac{2\pi}{3}, \pm\pi$.

$[-\pi, \pi, \pi/4]$ by $[-2.09, 2.09]$            $[-\pi, \pi, \pi/4]$ by $[-2.09, 2.09]$

*Figure 41*                 *Figure 42*

**42** (a) $f(x) = \cos 3x - \cos 2x$ • Estimating the $x$-intercepts, we have $x \approx 0, \pm 1.26, \pm 2.51$.

(b) $\cos 3x - \cos 2x = \text{[S4]} -2 \sin \frac{5}{2}x \sin \frac{1}{2}x = 0 \Rightarrow \sin \frac{5}{2}x = 0$ or $\sin \frac{1}{2}x = 0$.

$\sin \frac{5}{2}x = 0 \Rightarrow \frac{5}{2}x = \pi n \Rightarrow x = \frac{2\pi}{5}n \Rightarrow x = 0, \pm\frac{2\pi}{5}, \pm\frac{4\pi}{5}$.

$\sin \frac{1}{2}x = 0 \Rightarrow x = 0$.  The $x$-intercepts are $0, \pm\frac{2\pi}{5}, \pm\frac{4\pi}{5}$.

**43** Graphing on an interval of $[-\pi, \pi]$ gives us a figure that resembles a tangent function. It appears that there is a vertical asymptote at about 0.78. Recognizing that this value is about $\frac{\pi}{4}$, we might make the conjecture that we have "halved" the period of the tangent and that the graph of $f(x) = \dfrac{\sin x + \sin 2x + \sin 3x}{\cos x + \cos 2x + \cos 3x}$ appears to be that of $y = g(x) = \tan 2x$. Verifying this identity, we have the following:

$$\frac{\sin x + \sin 2x + \sin 3x}{\cos x + \cos 2x + \cos 3x} = \frac{\sin 2x + (\sin 3x + \sin x)}{\cos 2x + (\cos 3x + \cos x)}$$

$$= \frac{\sin 2x + 2\sin 2x \cos x}{\cos 2x + 2\cos 2x \cos x} = \frac{\sin 2x \, (1 + 2\cos x)}{\cos 2x \, (1 + 2\cos x)} = \frac{\sin 2x}{\cos 2x} = \tan 2x$$

**44** The graph of $f$ appears to be that of $y = g(x) = \cot 2x$.

$$\frac{\cos x - \cos 2x + \cos 3x}{\sin x - \sin 2x + \sin 3x} = \frac{-\cos 2x + (\cos 3x + \cos x)}{-\sin 2x + (\sin 3x + \sin x)}$$

$$= \frac{-\cos 2x + 2\cos 2x \cos x}{-\sin 2x + 2\sin 2x \cos x} = \frac{\cos 2x \, (-1 + 2\cos x)}{\sin 2x \, (-1 + 2\cos x)} = \frac{\cos 2x}{\sin 2x} = \cot 2x$$

## *6.6 Exercises*

**1** (a) $\sin^{-1}\left(-\frac{\sqrt{2}}{2}\right) = -\frac{\pi}{4}$ since $\sin\left(-\frac{\pi}{4}\right) = -\frac{\sqrt{2}}{2}$ and $-\frac{\pi}{2} \leq -\frac{\pi}{4} \leq \frac{\pi}{2}$

(b) $\cos^{-1}\left(-\frac{1}{2}\right) = \frac{2\pi}{3}$ since $\cos \frac{2\pi}{3} = -\frac{1}{2}$ and $0 \leq \frac{2\pi}{3} \leq \pi$

(c) $\tan^{-1}\left(-\sqrt{3}\right) = -\frac{\pi}{3}$ since $\tan\left(-\frac{\pi}{3}\right) = -\sqrt{3}$ and $-\frac{\pi}{2} < -\frac{\pi}{3} < \frac{\pi}{2}$

**2** (a) $\sin^{-1}\left(-\frac{1}{2}\right) = -\frac{\pi}{6}$      (b) $\cos^{-1}\left(-\frac{\sqrt{2}}{2}\right) = \frac{3\pi}{4}$      (c) $\tan^{-1}(-1) = -\frac{\pi}{4}$

**3** (a) $\arcsin \frac{\sqrt{3}}{2} = \frac{\pi}{3}$ since $\sin \frac{\pi}{3} = \frac{\sqrt{3}}{2}$ and $-\frac{\pi}{2} \leq \frac{\pi}{3} \leq \frac{\pi}{2}$

(b) $\arccos \frac{\sqrt{2}}{2} = \frac{\pi}{4}$ since $\cos \frac{\pi}{4} = \frac{\sqrt{2}}{2}$ and $0 \leq \frac{\pi}{4} \leq \pi$

(c) $\arctan \frac{1}{\sqrt{3}} = \frac{\pi}{6}$ since $\tan \frac{\pi}{6} = \frac{1}{\sqrt{3}}$ and $-\frac{\pi}{2} < \frac{\pi}{6} < \frac{\pi}{2}$

**4** (a) $\arcsin 0 = 0$      (b) $\arccos(-1) = \pi$      (c) $\arctan 0 = 0$

**5** (a) $\sin^{-1} \frac{\pi}{3}$ is *not defined* since $\frac{\pi}{3} > 1$, that is, $\frac{\pi}{3} \notin [-1, 1]$

(b) $\cos^{-1} \frac{\pi}{2}$ is *not defined* since $\frac{\pi}{2} > 1$, that is, $\frac{\pi}{2} \notin [-1, 1]$

(c) $\tan^{-1} 1 = \frac{\pi}{4}$ since $\tan \frac{\pi}{4} = 1$ and $-\frac{\pi}{2} < \frac{\pi}{4} < \frac{\pi}{2}$

**6** (a) $\arcsin \frac{\pi}{2}$ is *not defined* since $\frac{\pi}{2} > 1$, i.e., $\frac{\pi}{2} \notin [-1, 1]$

(b) $\arccos \frac{\pi}{3}$ is *not defined* since $\frac{\pi}{3} > 1$, that is, $\frac{\pi}{3} \notin [-1, 1]$      (c) $\arctan\left(-\frac{\sqrt{3}}{3}\right) = -\frac{\pi}{6}$

**Note:** Exercises 7–10 refer to the boxed properties of $\sin^{-1}$, $\cos^{-1}$, and $\tan^{-1}$.

7  (a) $\sin\left[\arcsin\left(-\frac{3}{10}\right)\right] = -\frac{3}{10}$ since $-1 \le -\frac{3}{10} \le 1$      (b) $\cos\left(\arccos\frac{1}{2}\right) = \frac{1}{2}$ since $-1 \le \frac{1}{2} \le 1$

   (c) $\tan(\arctan 14) = 14$ since $\tan(\arctan x) = x$ for every $x$

8  (a) $\sin\left(\sin^{-1}\frac{2}{3}\right) = \frac{2}{3}$ since $-1 \le \frac{2}{3} \le 1$      (b) $\cos\left[\cos^{-1}\left(-\frac{1}{5}\right)\right] = -\frac{1}{5}$ since $-1 \le -\frac{1}{5} \le 1$

   (c) $\tan\left[\tan^{-1}(-9)\right] = -9$ since $\tan(\arctan x) = x$ for every $x$

9  (a) $\sin^{-1}\left(\sin\frac{\pi}{3}\right) = \frac{\pi}{3}$ since $-\frac{\pi}{2} \le \frac{\pi}{3} \le \frac{\pi}{2}$      (b) $\cos^{-1}\left[\cos\left(\frac{5\pi}{6}\right)\right] = \frac{5\pi}{6}$ since $0 \le \frac{5\pi}{6} \le \pi$

   (c) $\tan^{-1}\left[\tan\left(-\frac{\pi}{6}\right)\right] = -\frac{\pi}{6}$ since $-\frac{\pi}{2} < -\frac{\pi}{6} < \frac{\pi}{2}$

10  (a) $\arcsin\left[\sin\left(-\frac{\pi}{2}\right)\right] = -\frac{\pi}{2}$ since $-\frac{\pi}{2} \le -\frac{\pi}{2} \le \frac{\pi}{2}$      (b) $\arccos(\cos 0) = 0$ since $0 \le 0 \le \pi$

    (c) $\arctan\left(\tan\frac{\pi}{4}\right) = \frac{\pi}{4}$ since $-\frac{\pi}{2} < \frac{\pi}{4} < \frac{\pi}{2}$

11  (a) $\arcsin\left(\sin\frac{5\pi}{4}\right) = \arcsin\left(-\frac{\sqrt{2}}{2}\right) = -\frac{\pi}{4}$      (b) $\arccos\left(\cos\frac{5\pi}{4}\right) = \arccos\left(-\frac{\sqrt{2}}{2}\right) = \frac{3\pi}{4}$

    (c) $\arctan\left(\tan\frac{7\pi}{4}\right) = \arctan(-1) = -\frac{\pi}{4}$

12  (a) $\sin^{-1}\left(\sin\frac{2\pi}{3}\right) = \sin^{-1}\frac{\sqrt{3}}{2} = \frac{\pi}{3}$      (b) $\cos^{-1}\left(\cos\frac{4\pi}{3}\right) = \cos^{-1}\left(-\frac{1}{2}\right) = \frac{2\pi}{3}$

    (c) $\tan^{-1}\left(\tan\frac{7\pi}{6}\right) = \tan^{-1}\frac{\sqrt{3}}{3} = \frac{\pi}{6}$

13  (a) $\sin\left[\cos^{-1}\left(-\frac{1}{2}\right)\right] = \sin\frac{2\pi}{3} = \frac{\sqrt{3}}{2}$      (b) $\cos(\tan^{-1} 1) = \cos\frac{\pi}{4} = \frac{\sqrt{2}}{2}$

    (c) $\tan\left[\sin^{-1}(-1)\right] = \tan\left(-\frac{\pi}{2}\right)$, which is *not defined*.

14  (a) $\sin\left(\tan^{-1}\sqrt{3}\right) = \sin\frac{\pi}{3} = \frac{\sqrt{3}}{2}$      (b) $\cos(\sin^{-1} 1) = \cos\frac{\pi}{2} = 0$

    (c) $\tan(\cos^{-1} 0) = \tan\frac{\pi}{2}$, which is *not defined*.

**Note:** Triangles could be used for the figures, and may be easier to work with.

15  (a) Let $\theta = \sin^{-1}\frac{2}{3}$. From the figure, $\cot\left(\sin^{-1}\frac{2}{3}\right) = \cot\theta = \dfrac{x}{y} = \dfrac{\sqrt{5}}{2}$.

    (b) Let $\theta = \tan^{-1}\left(-\frac{3}{5}\right)$. From the figure, $\sec\left[\tan^{-1}\left(-\frac{3}{5}\right)\right] = \sec\theta = \dfrac{r}{x} = \dfrac{\sqrt{34}}{5}$.

    (c) Let $\theta = \cos^{-1}\left(-\frac{1}{4}\right)$. From the figure, $\csc\left[\cos^{-1}\left(-\frac{1}{4}\right)\right] = \csc\theta = \dfrac{r}{y} = \dfrac{4}{\sqrt{15}}$.

*Figure 15(a)*

*Figure 15(b)*

*Figure 15(c)*

**16** (a) Let $\theta = \sin^{-1}\left(-\frac{2}{5}\right)$. From the figure, $\cot\left[\sin^{-1}\left(-\frac{2}{5}\right)\right] = \cot\theta = \frac{x}{y} = \frac{\sqrt{21}}{-2} = -\frac{\sqrt{21}}{2}$.

(b) Let $\theta = \tan^{-1}\frac{7}{4}$. From the figure, $\sec\left(\tan^{-1}\frac{7}{4}\right) = \sec\theta = \frac{r}{x} = \frac{\sqrt{65}}{4}$.

(c) Let $\theta = \cos^{-1}\frac{1}{5}$. From the figure, $\csc\left(\cos^{-1}\frac{1}{5}\right) = \csc\theta = \frac{r}{y} = \frac{5}{\sqrt{24}}$.

*Figure 16(a)*

*Figure 16(b)*

*Figure 16(c)*

**17** (a) $\sin\left(\arcsin\frac{1}{2} + \arccos 0\right) = \sin\left(\frac{\pi}{6} + \frac{\pi}{2}\right) = \sin\frac{2\pi}{3} = \frac{\sqrt{3}}{2}$.

(b) Remember, $\arctan\left(-\frac{3}{4}\right)$ and $\arcsin\frac{4}{5}$ are *angles*. To abbreviate this solution, we let $\alpha = \arctan\left(-\frac{3}{4}\right)$ and $\beta = \arcsin\frac{4}{5}$. Using the difference identity for the cosine and figures as in Exercises 15 and 16, we have

$$\cos\left[\arctan\left(-\tfrac{3}{4}\right) - \arcsin\tfrac{4}{5}\right] = \cos(\alpha - \beta) = \cos\alpha\cos\beta + \sin\alpha\sin\beta = \tfrac{4}{5}\cdot\tfrac{3}{5} + \left(-\tfrac{3}{5}\right)\cdot\tfrac{4}{5} = 0.$$

(c) Let $\alpha = \arctan\frac{4}{3}$ and $\beta = \arccos\frac{8}{17}$. Use the sum identity for the tangent.

$$\tan\left(\arctan\tfrac{4}{3} + \arccos\tfrac{8}{17}\right) = \tan(\alpha + \beta) = \frac{\tan\alpha + \tan\beta}{1 - \tan\alpha\tan\beta} = \frac{\tfrac{4}{3} + \tfrac{15}{8}}{1 - \tfrac{4}{3}\cdot\tfrac{15}{8}}\cdot\frac{24}{24} = \frac{32 + 45}{24 - 60} = -\frac{77}{36}.$$

**18** (a) Let $\alpha = \sin^{-1}\frac{5}{13}$ and $\beta = \cos^{-1}\left(-\frac{3}{5}\right)$.
$$\sin\left[\sin^{-1}\tfrac{5}{13} - \cos^{-1}\left(-\tfrac{3}{5}\right)\right] = \sin(\alpha - \beta) = \sin\alpha\cos\beta - \cos\alpha\sin\beta = \tfrac{5}{13}\cdot\left(-\tfrac{3}{5}\right) - \tfrac{12}{13}\cdot\tfrac{4}{5} = -\tfrac{63}{65}.$$

(b) Let $\alpha = \sin^{-1}\frac{4}{5}$ and $\beta = \tan^{-1}\frac{3}{4}$.
$$\cos\left(\sin^{-1}\tfrac{4}{5} + \tan^{-1}\tfrac{3}{4}\right) = \cos(\alpha + \beta) = \cos\alpha\cos\beta - \sin\alpha\sin\beta = \tfrac{3}{5}\cdot\tfrac{4}{5} - \tfrac{4}{5}\cdot\tfrac{3}{5} = 0.$$

(c) $\tan\left(\cos^{-1}\frac{1}{2} - \sin^{-1}\frac{1}{2}\right) = \tan\left(\frac{\pi}{3} - \frac{\pi}{6}\right) = \tan\frac{\pi}{6} = \frac{1}{\sqrt{3}}$.

**19** (a) We first recognize this expression as being of the form $\sin(\textit{twice an angle})$; where $\arccos\left(-\frac{24}{25}\right)$ is the angle. Let $\alpha = \arccos\left(-\frac{24}{25}\right)$. It may help to draw a figure as in Exercise 15 to determine that $\alpha$ is a second quadrant angle and that $\sin\alpha = \frac{7}{25}$. Applying the double-angle formula for the sine gives us

$$\sin\left[2\arccos\left(-\tfrac{24}{25}\right)\right] = \sin 2\alpha = 2\sin\alpha\cos\alpha = 2\left(\tfrac{7}{25}\right)\left(-\tfrac{24}{25}\right) = -\tfrac{336}{625}.$$

(b) Let $\alpha = \sin^{-1}\frac{15}{17}$. Thus, $\cos\alpha = \frac{8}{17}$ and we apply the double-angle formula for the cosine.
$$\cos\left(2\sin^{-1}\tfrac{15}{17}\right) = \cos 2\alpha = \cos^2\alpha - \sin^2\alpha = \left(\tfrac{8}{17}\right)^2 - \left(\tfrac{15}{17}\right)^2 = -\tfrac{161}{289}.$$

(c) Let $\alpha = \tan^{-1}\frac{3}{4}$. Thus, $\tan\alpha = \frac{3}{4}$ and we apply the double-angle formula for the tangent.
$$\tan\left(2\tan^{-1}\tfrac{3}{4}\right) = \tan 2\alpha = \frac{2\tan\alpha}{1 - \tan^2\alpha} = \frac{2\cdot\tfrac{3}{4}}{1 - \left(\tfrac{3}{4}\right)^2}\cdot\frac{16}{16} = \frac{24}{16 - 9} = \frac{24}{7}.$$

**20** (a) Let $\alpha = \tan^{-1}\frac{5}{12}$. $\sin\left(2\tan^{-1}\frac{5}{12}\right) = \sin 2\alpha = 2\sin\alpha\cos\alpha = 2\left(\frac{5}{13}\right)\left(\frac{12}{13}\right) = \frac{120}{169}$.

(b) Let $\alpha = \arccos\frac{9}{41}$. $\cos\left(2\arccos\frac{9}{41}\right) = \cos 2\alpha = \cos^2\alpha - \sin^2\alpha = \left(\frac{9}{41}\right)^2 - \left(\frac{40}{41}\right)^2 = -\frac{1519}{1681}$.

(c) Let $\alpha = \arcsin\left(-\frac{15}{17}\right)$. $\tan\left[2\arcsin\left(-\frac{15}{17}\right)\right] = \tan 2\alpha = \frac{2\tan\alpha}{1 - \tan^2\alpha} = \frac{2\cdot\left(-\frac{15}{8}\right)}{1 - \left(-\frac{15}{8}\right)^2}\cdot\frac{64}{64} = -\frac{240}{64 - 225} = \frac{240}{161}$.

**21** (a) We first recognize this expression as being of the form $\sin(\textit{one-half an angle})$, where $\sin^{-1}\left(-\frac{7}{25}\right)$ is the angle. Let $\alpha = \sin^{-1}\left(-\frac{7}{25}\right)$. Hence, $\alpha$ is a fourth quadrant angle and $\cos\alpha = \frac{24}{25}$. $-\frac{\pi}{2} < \alpha < 0 \;\Rightarrow\; -\frac{\pi}{4} < \frac{1}{2}\alpha < 0$.

We need to know the sign of $\sin\frac{1}{2}\alpha$ in order to correctly apply the half-angle formula for sine.

Since $-\frac{\pi}{4} < \frac{1}{2}\alpha < 0$ {QIV}, $\sin\frac{1}{2}\alpha < 0$.

$$\sin\left[\tfrac{1}{2}\sin^{-1}\left(-\tfrac{7}{25}\right)\right] = \sin\tfrac{1}{2}\alpha = -\sqrt{\frac{1-\cos\alpha}{2}} = -\sqrt{\frac{1-\frac{24}{25}}{2}} = -\sqrt{\frac{1}{50}\cdot\frac{2}{2}} = -\frac{\sqrt{2}}{10}.$$

(b) Let $\alpha = \tan^{-1}\frac{8}{15}$. $0 < \alpha < \frac{\pi}{2} \;\Rightarrow\; 0 < \frac{1}{2}\alpha < \frac{\pi}{4}$ and $\cos\frac{1}{2}\alpha > 0$. Apply the half-angle formula for cosine.

$$\cos\left(\tfrac{1}{2}\tan^{-1}\tfrac{8}{15}\right) = \cos\tfrac{1}{2}\alpha = \sqrt{\frac{1+\cos\alpha}{2}} = \sqrt{\frac{1+\frac{15}{17}}{2}} = \sqrt{\frac{16}{17}\cdot\frac{17}{17}} = \frac{4\sqrt{17}}{17}.$$

(c) Let $\alpha = \cos^{-1}\frac{3}{5}$. Apply the half-angle formula for the tangent.

$$\tan\left(\tfrac{1}{2}\cos^{-1}\tfrac{3}{5}\right) = \tan\tfrac{1}{2}\alpha = \frac{1-\cos\alpha}{\sin\alpha} = \frac{1-\frac{3}{5}}{\frac{4}{5}} = \frac{1}{2}.$$

**22** (a) Let $\alpha = \cos^{-1}\left(-\frac{3}{5}\right)$. $\frac{\pi}{2} < \alpha < \pi \;\Rightarrow\; \frac{\pi}{4} < \frac{1}{2}\alpha < \frac{\pi}{2}$ and $\sin\frac{1}{2}\alpha > 0$.

$$\sin\left[\tfrac{1}{2}\cos^{-1}\left(-\tfrac{3}{5}\right)\right] = \sin\tfrac{1}{2}\alpha = \sqrt{\frac{1-\cos\alpha}{2}} = \sqrt{\frac{1-\left(-\frac{3}{5}\right)}{2}} = \sqrt{\frac{4}{5}\cdot\frac{5}{5}} = \frac{2\sqrt{5}}{5}.$$

(b) Let $\alpha = \sin^{-1}\frac{12}{13}$. $0 < \alpha < \frac{\pi}{2} \;\Rightarrow\; 0 < \frac{1}{2}\alpha < \frac{\pi}{4}$ and $\cos\frac{1}{2}\alpha > 0$.

$$\cos\left(\tfrac{1}{2}\sin^{-1}\tfrac{12}{13}\right) = \cos\tfrac{1}{2}\alpha = \sqrt{\frac{1+\cos\alpha}{2}} = \sqrt{\frac{1+\frac{5}{13}}{2}} = \sqrt{\frac{9}{13}\cdot\frac{13}{13}} = \frac{3\sqrt{13}}{13}.$$

(c) Let $\alpha = \tan^{-1}\frac{40}{9}$. $\tan\left(\tfrac{1}{2}\tan^{-1}\tfrac{40}{9}\right) = \tan\tfrac{1}{2}\alpha = \frac{1-\cos\alpha}{\sin\alpha} = \frac{1-\frac{9}{41}}{\frac{40}{41}} = \frac{4}{5}.$

**23** We recognize this expression as being of the form $\sin(\textit{some angle})$. The angle is *the angle whose tangent is* $\alpha$. The easiest way to picture this angle is to consider it as being the angle whose ratio of opposite side to adjacent side is $x$ to 1. Let $\alpha = \tan^{-1}x$. From the figure, $\sin(\tan^{-1}x) = \sin\alpha = \dfrac{x}{\sqrt{x^2+1}}$.

*Figure 23*

*Figure 24*

**24** Let $\alpha = \arccos x$. From the figure, $\tan(\arccos x) = \tan\alpha = \dfrac{\sqrt{1-x^2}}{x}$.

**25** Let $\alpha = \tan^{-1}\dfrac{\sqrt{x^2-9}}{3}$. From the figure, $\sec\left(\tan^{-1}\dfrac{\sqrt{x^2-9}}{3}\right) = \sec\alpha = \dfrac{x}{3}$.

*Figure 25*

*Figure 26*

**26** Let $\alpha = \tan^{-1}\dfrac{x}{2}$. From the figure, $\csc\left(\tan^{-1}\dfrac{x}{2}\right) = \csc\alpha = \dfrac{\sqrt{x^2+4}}{x}$.

**27** Let $\alpha = \sin^{-1} \dfrac{x}{\sqrt{x^2+4}}$. From the figure, $\sec\left(\sin^{-1}\dfrac{x}{\sqrt{x^2+4}}\right) = \sec\alpha = \dfrac{\sqrt{x^2+4}}{2}$.

*Figure 27*

*Figure 28*

**28** Let $\alpha = \sin^{-1} \dfrac{\sqrt{x^2-9}}{x}$. From the figure, $\cot\left(\sin^{-1}\dfrac{\sqrt{x^2-9}}{x}\right) = \cot\alpha = \dfrac{3}{\sqrt{x^2-9}}$.

**29** Let $\alpha = \sin^{-1} x$. From the figure, $\sin(2\sin^{-1}x) = \sin 2\alpha = 2\sin\alpha\cos\alpha = 2\cdot\dfrac{x}{1}\cdot\dfrac{\sqrt{1-x^2}}{1} = 2x\sqrt{1-x^2}$.

*Figure 29*

*Figure 30*

**30** Let $\alpha = \tan^{-1} x$. From the figure,

$$\cos(2\tan^{-1}x) = \cos 2\alpha = \cos^2\alpha - \sin^2\alpha = \left(\frac{1}{\sqrt{x^2+1}}\right)^2 - \left(\frac{x}{\sqrt{x^2+1}}\right)^2 = \frac{1}{x^2+1} - \frac{x^2}{x^2+1} = \frac{1-x^2}{x^2+1}.$$

**31** Let $\alpha = \cos^{-1} \dfrac{1}{x}$.

From the figure, $\tan\left(2\cos^{-1}\dfrac{1}{x}\right) = \tan 2x = \dfrac{2\tan x}{1-\tan^2 x} = \dfrac{2\cdot\sqrt{x^2-1}}{1-\left(\sqrt{x^2-1}\right)^2} = \dfrac{2\sqrt{x^2-1}}{1-(x^2-1)} = \dfrac{2\sqrt{x^2-1}}{2-x^2}.$

*Figure 31*

*Figure 32*

**32** Let $\alpha = \sin^{-1} x$.

From the figure, $\cos(2\sin^{-1}x) = \cos 2\alpha = \cos^2\alpha - \sin^2\alpha = \left(\dfrac{\sqrt{1-x^2}}{1}\right)^2 - \left(\dfrac{x}{1}\right)^2 = 1-x^2-x^2 = 1-2x^2.$

**33** Let $\alpha = \arccos x$. $0 \le \alpha \le \pi \;\Rightarrow\; 0 \le \frac{1}{2}\alpha \le \frac{\pi}{2}$. Thus $\cos\frac{1}{2}\alpha > 0$ and we use the "+" in the half-angle formula

for the cosine. $\cos\left(\frac{1}{2}\arccos x\right) = \cos\frac{1}{2}\alpha = \sqrt{\dfrac{1 + \cos\alpha}{2}} = \sqrt{\dfrac{1 + x}{2}}$.

Figure 33

Figure 34

**34** Let $\alpha = \cos^{-1}\frac{1}{x}$. From the figure, $\tan\left(\frac{1}{2}\cos^{-1}\frac{1}{x}\right) = \tan\frac{1}{2}\alpha = \dfrac{1 - \cos\alpha}{\sin\alpha} = \dfrac{1 - \frac{1}{x}}{\frac{\sqrt{x^2-1}}{x}} \cdot \dfrac{x}{x} = \dfrac{x - 1}{\sqrt{x^2 - 1}}$.

**35** (a) See Figure 2 in the text. As $x \to -1^+$, $\sin^{-1} x \to -\frac{\pi}{2}$.

   (b) See Figure 5 in the text. As $x \to 1^-$, $\cos^{-1} x \to 0$.

   (c) See Figure 8 in the text. As $x \to \infty$, $\tan^{-1} x \to \frac{\pi}{2}$.

**36** (a) As $x \to 1^-$, $\sin^{-1} x \to \underline{\frac{\pi}{2}}$.    (b) As $x \to -1^+$, $\cos^{-1} x \to \underline{\pi}$.     (c) As $x \to -\infty$, $\tan^{-1} x \to \underline{-\frac{\pi}{2}}$.

**37** $y = \sin^{-1} 2x$  •  Horizontally compress $y = \sin^{-1} x$ by a factor of 2.

Note that the domain changes from $[-1, 1]$ to $\left[-\frac{1}{2}, \frac{1}{2}\right]$.

Figure 37

Figure 38

**38** $y = \frac{1}{2}\sin^{-1} x$  •  Vertically compress $y = \sin^{-1} x$ by a factor of 2. The range changes from $\left[-\frac{\pi}{2}, \frac{\pi}{2}\right]$ to $\left[-\frac{\pi}{4}, \frac{\pi}{4}\right]$.

**39** $y = \sin^{-1}(x + 1)$  •  Shift $y = \sin^{-1} x$ left 1 unit. The domain changes from $[-1, 1]$ to $[-2, 0]$.

Figure 39

Figure 40

**40** $y = \sin^{-1}(x - 2) + \frac{\pi}{2}$  •  Shift $y = \sin^{-1} x$ right 2 units and up $\frac{\pi}{2}$ units.

The range changes from $\left[-\frac{\pi}{2}, \frac{\pi}{2}\right]$ to $[0, \pi]$.

**41** $y = \cos^{-1} \frac{1}{2}x$ • Horizontally stretch $y = \cos^{-1} x$ by a factor of 2. The domain changes from $[-1, 1]$ to $[-2, 2]$.

*Figure 41*

*Figure 42*

**42** $y = 2\cos^{-1} x$ • Vertically stretch $y = \cos^{-1} x$ by a factor of 2. The range changes from $[0, \pi]$ to $[0, 2\pi]$.

**43** $y = \frac{\pi}{2} - \cos^{-1} x = -\cos^{-1} x + \frac{\pi}{2}$ • Reflect $y = \cos^{-1} x$ through the $x$-axis and then shift it up $\frac{\pi}{2}$ units.

Note that this is the same graph as that of $y = \sin^{-1} x$.

*Figure 43*

*Figure 44*

**44** $y = \cos^{-1}(x + 1)$ • Horizontally shift $y = \cos^{-1} x$ one unit to the left.

The domain changes from $[-1, 1]$ to $[-2, 0]$.

**45** $y = 2 + \tan^{-1} x$ • Shift $y = \tan^{-1} x$ up 2 units. The range changes from $\left(-\frac{\pi}{2}, \frac{\pi}{2}\right)$ to $\left(2 - \frac{\pi}{2}, 2 + \frac{\pi}{2}\right)$,

which is approximately $(0.43, 3.57)$.

*Figure 45*

*Figure 46*

**46** $y = \tan^{-1} 2x$ • Horizontally compress $y = \tan^{-1} x$ by a factor of 2.

**47** $y = \frac{6}{\pi} \tan^{-1} x$ • Vertically stretch $y = \tan^{-1} x$ by a factor of $\frac{6}{\pi}$. The range changes from $\left(-\frac{\pi}{2}, \frac{\pi}{2}\right)$ to $(-3, 3)$.

Figure 47

Figure 48

**48** $y = \tan^{-1}(x - \pi)$ • Horizontally shift $y = \tan^{-1} x$ to the right $\pi$ units.

**49** If $\alpha = \arccos x$, then $\cos \alpha = x$, where $0 \le \alpha \le \pi$. Hence, $y = \sin(\arccos x) = \sin \alpha = \sqrt{1 - \cos^2 \alpha} = \sqrt{1 - x^2}$.
Thus, we have the graph of the semicircle $y = \sqrt{1 - x^2}$ on the interval $[-1, 1]$.

Figure 49

Figure 50

**50** By a property of $\sin^{-1}$, $\sin(\sin^{-1} x) = x$ for $-1 \le x \le 1$.

Thus, we have the graph of the line $y = x$ on the interval $[-1, 1]$.

**51** (a) $y = \frac{1}{2} \sin^{-1}(x - 3)$ • Since the domain of the arcsine function is $[-1, 1]$,

we know that $x - 3$ must be in that interval. Thus, $-1 \le x - 3 \le 1 \;\Rightarrow\; 2 \le x \le 4$.

(b) The range of the arcsine function is $\left[-\frac{\pi}{2}, \frac{\pi}{2}\right]$.

Thus, $-\frac{\pi}{2} \le \sin^{-1}(x - 3) \le \frac{\pi}{2} \;\Rightarrow\; -\frac{\pi}{4} \le \frac{1}{2} \sin^{-1}(x - 3) \le \frac{\pi}{4} \;\Rightarrow\; -\frac{\pi}{4} \le y \le \frac{\pi}{4}$.

(c) $y = \frac{1}{2} \sin^{-1}(x - 3) \;\Rightarrow\; 2y = \sin^{-1}(x - 3) \;\Rightarrow\; \sin 2y = x - 3 \;\Rightarrow\; x = \sin 2y + 3$

**52** (a) $y = 3 \tan^{-1}(2x + 1)$ • Since the domain of $\tan^{-1}$ is $\mathbb{R}$, $x$ can be any real number.

(b) $-\frac{\pi}{2} < \tan^{-1}(2x + 1) < \frac{\pi}{2} \;\Rightarrow\; -\frac{3\pi}{2} < 3 \tan^{-1}(2x + 1) < \frac{3\pi}{2} \;\Rightarrow\; -\frac{3\pi}{2} < y < \frac{3\pi}{2}$

(c) $y = 3 \tan^{-1}(2x + 1) \;\Rightarrow\; \frac{1}{3} y = \tan^{-1}(2x + 1) \;\Rightarrow\; \tan \frac{1}{3} y = 2x + 1 \;\Rightarrow\; 2x = \tan \frac{1}{3} y - 1 \;\Rightarrow$

$$x = \frac{1}{2}\left(\tan \tfrac{1}{3} y - 1\right)$$

**53** (a) $y = 4 \cos^{-1} \frac{2}{3} x$ • $-1 \le \frac{2}{3} x \le 1 \;\Rightarrow\; -\frac{3}{2} \le x \le \frac{3}{2}$

(b) $0 \le \cos^{-1} \frac{2}{3} x \le \pi \;\Rightarrow\; 0 \le 4 \cos^{-1} \frac{2}{3} x \le 4\pi \;\Rightarrow\; 0 \le y \le 4\pi$

(c) $y = 4 \cos^{-1} \frac{2}{3} x \;\Rightarrow\; \frac{1}{4} y = \cos^{-1} \frac{2}{3} x \;\Rightarrow\; \cos \frac{1}{4} y = \frac{2}{3} x \;\Rightarrow\; x = \frac{3}{2} \cos \frac{1}{4} y$

**54** (a) $y = 2\sin^{-1}(3x-4)$ • $-1 \le 3x-4 \le 1 \Rightarrow 3 \le 3x \le 5 \Rightarrow 1 \le x \le \frac{5}{3}$

(b) $-\frac{\pi}{2} \le \sin^{-1}(3x-4) \le \frac{\pi}{2} \Rightarrow -\pi \le 2\sin^{-1}(3x-4) \le \pi \Rightarrow -\pi \le y \le \pi$

(c) $y = 2\sin^{-1}(3x-4) \Rightarrow \frac{1}{2}y = \sin^{-1}(3x-4) \Rightarrow \sin\frac{1}{2}y = 3x-4 \Rightarrow$

$$3x = \sin\frac{1}{2}y + 4 \Rightarrow x = \frac{1}{3}\sin\frac{1}{2}y + \frac{4}{3}$$

**55** $y = -3 - \sin x \Rightarrow y + 3 = -\sin x \Rightarrow -(y+3) = \sin x \Rightarrow x = \sin^{-1}(-y-3)$

**56** $y = 2 + 3\sin x \Rightarrow y - 2 = 3\sin x \Rightarrow \frac{1}{3}(y-2) = \sin x \Rightarrow x = \sin^{-1}\left[\frac{1}{3}(y-2)\right]$

**57** $y = 15 - 2\cos x \Rightarrow 2\cos x = 15 - y \Rightarrow \cos x = \frac{1}{2}(15-y) \Rightarrow x = \cos^{-1}\left[\frac{1}{2}(15-y)\right]$

**58** $y = 6 - 3\cos x \Rightarrow 3\cos x = 6 - y \Rightarrow \cos x = \frac{1}{3}(6-y) \Rightarrow x = \cos^{-1}\left[\frac{1}{3}(6-y)\right]$

**59** $\dfrac{\sin x}{3} = \dfrac{\sin y}{4} \Rightarrow \sin x = \frac{3}{4}\sin y$. Since $0 < y < \pi$, we know that $\sin y > 0$. Thus, solving $\sin x = \frac{3}{4}\sin y$ is similar to solving $\sin x = a$, where $0 < a < 1$. Remember that when solving equations of this form, there are two solutions, a first quadrant angle and a second quadrant angle. The reference angle for $x$ is $x_R = \sin^{-1}\left(\frac{3}{4}\sin y\right)$, where $0 < \frac{3}{4}\sin y \le \frac{3}{4} < 1$. If $0 < x < \frac{\pi}{2}$, then $x = x_R$. If $\frac{\pi}{2} < x < \pi$, then $x = \pi - x_R$.

**60** $\dfrac{4}{\sin x} = \dfrac{7}{\sin y} \Rightarrow \dfrac{\sin x}{4} = \dfrac{\sin y}{7} \Rightarrow \sin x = \frac{4}{7}\sin y$. The reference angle for $x$ is $x_R = \sin^{-1}\left(\frac{4}{7}\sin y\right)$, where $0 < \frac{4}{7}\sin y \le \frac{4}{7} < 1$. If $0 < x < \frac{\pi}{2}$, then $x = x_R$. If $\frac{\pi}{2} < x < \pi$, then $x = \pi - x_R$.

**61** $\cos^2 x + 2\cos x - 1 = 0 \Rightarrow \cos x = -1 \pm \sqrt{2} \approx 0.4142, -2.4142$.

Since $-2.4142 < -1$, $x = \cos^{-1}\left(-1 + \sqrt{2}\right) \approx 1.1437$ is one answer.

$$x = 2\pi - \cos^{-1}\left(-1 + \sqrt{2}\right) \approx 2\pi - 1.1437 \approx 5.1395 \text{ is the other answer.}$$

**62** $\sin^2 x - \sin x - 1 = 0 \Rightarrow \sin x = \dfrac{1 \pm \sqrt{5}}{2} \approx 1.6180, -0.6180$. Since $1.6180 > 1$,

$x_0 = \sin^{-1}\left(\dfrac{1-\sqrt{5}}{2}\right) \approx -0.6662$, but this is not in $[0, 2\pi)$. The reference angle is $x_R = -x_0 \approx 0.6662$.

Since the sine is negative in quadrants III and IV, the values are $\pi + x_R \approx 3.8078$ and $2\pi - x_R \approx 5.6170$.

**63** $2\tan^2 t + 9\tan t + 3 = 0 \Rightarrow \tan t = \dfrac{-9 \pm \sqrt{81 - 24}}{4} \Rightarrow t = \tan^{-1}\frac{1}{4}\left(-9 \pm \sqrt{57}\right)$

$\tan^{-1}\frac{1}{4}\left(-9 + \sqrt{57}\right) \approx -0.3478$, $\tan^{-1}\frac{1}{4}\left(-9 - \sqrt{57}\right) \approx -1.3337$

**64** $3\sin^2 t + 7\sin t + 3 = 0 \Rightarrow \sin t = \dfrac{-7 \pm \sqrt{49 - 36}}{6} \Rightarrow$

$t = \sin^{-1}\frac{1}{6}\left(-7 + \sqrt{13}\right)$ $\{\sin t \ne \frac{1}{6}\left(-7 - \sqrt{13}\right) < -1\}$; $\sin^{-1}\frac{1}{6}\left(-7 + \sqrt{13}\right) \approx -0.6013$

**65** $15\cos^4 x - 14\cos^2 x + 3 = 0 \Rightarrow (5\cos^2 x - 3)(3\cos^2 x - 1) = 0 \Rightarrow \cos^2 x = \frac{3}{5}, \frac{1}{3} \Rightarrow$

$\cos x = \pm\frac{1}{5}\sqrt{15}, \pm\frac{1}{3}\sqrt{3} \Rightarrow x = \cos^{-1}\left(\pm\frac{1}{5}\sqrt{15}\right), \cos^{-1}\left(\pm\frac{1}{3}\sqrt{3}\right)$.

$\cos^{-1}\frac{1}{5}\sqrt{15} \approx 0.6847$, $\cos^{-1}\left(-\frac{1}{5}\sqrt{15}\right) \approx 2.4569$, $\cos^{-1}\frac{1}{3}\sqrt{3} \approx 0.9553$, $\cos^{-1}\left(-\frac{1}{3}\sqrt{3}\right) \approx 2.1863$

**66** $3\tan^4\theta - 19\tan^2\theta + 2 = 0 \Rightarrow \tan^2\theta = \dfrac{19 \pm \sqrt{361 - 24}}{6} \Rightarrow \theta = \tan^{-1}\left(\pm\sqrt{\frac{1}{6}\left(19 \pm \sqrt{337}\right)}\right)$.

$\tan^{-1}\left(\pm\sqrt{\frac{1}{6}\left(19 + \sqrt{337}\right)}\right) \approx \pm 1.1896$, $\tan^{-1}\left(\pm\sqrt{\frac{1}{6}\left(19 - \sqrt{337}\right)}\right) \approx \pm 0.3162$

**67** $6\sin^3\theta + 18\sin^2\theta - 5\sin\theta - 15 = 0 \Rightarrow 6\sin^2\theta(\sin\theta + 3) - 5(\sin\theta + 3) = 0 \Rightarrow$

$(6\sin^2\theta - 5)(\sin\theta + 3) = 0 \Rightarrow \sin\theta = \pm\frac{1}{6}\sqrt{30} \Rightarrow \theta = \sin^{-1}\left(\pm\frac{1}{6}\sqrt{30}\right) \approx \pm 1.1503$

**68** $6\sin 2x - 8\cos x + 9\sin x - 6 = 0 \;\Rightarrow\; 12\sin x\cos x - 8\cos x + 9\sin x - 6 = 0 \;\Rightarrow$

$4\cos x(3\sin x - 2) + 3(3\sin x - 2) = 0 \;\Rightarrow\; (4\cos x + 3)(3\sin x - 2) = 0 \;\Rightarrow$

$x = \cos^{-1}\left(-\frac{3}{4}\right), \sin^{-1}\frac{2}{3} \approx 0.7297.$ However, $\cos^{-1}\left(-\frac{3}{4}\right)$ is in $\left(\frac{\pi}{2}, \pi\right)$, and *not* in $\left(-\frac{\pi}{2}, \frac{\pi}{2}\right)$.

**69** $(\cos x)(15\cos x + 4) = 3 \;\Rightarrow\; 15\cos^2 x + 4\cos x - 3 = 0 \;\Rightarrow\; (5\cos x + 3)(3\cos x - 1) = 0 \;\Rightarrow$

$\cos x = -\frac{3}{5}, \frac{1}{3} \;\Rightarrow\; x = \cos^{-1}\left(-\frac{3}{5}\right) \approx 2.2143, \cos^{-1}\frac{1}{3} \approx 1.2310.$ These angles are in the second quadrant and the first quadrant. In $[0, 2\pi)$, we must also have a third quadrant angle and a fourth quadrant angle that satisfy the original equation. These angles are $2\pi - \cos^{-1}\left(-\frac{3}{5}\right) \approx 4.0689$ and $2\pi - \cos^{-1}\frac{1}{3} \approx 5.0522.$

**70** $6\sin^2 x = \sin x + 2 \;\Rightarrow\; 6\sin^2 x - \sin x - 2 = 0 \;\Rightarrow\; (3\sin x - 2)(2\sin x + 1) = 0 \;\Rightarrow\; \sin x = \frac{2}{3}, -\frac{1}{2} \;\Rightarrow$

$x = \sin^{-1}\frac{2}{3} \approx 0.7297, \pi - \sin^{-1}\frac{2}{3} \approx 2.4119, \frac{7\pi}{6} \approx 3.6652, \frac{11\pi}{6} \approx 5.7596.$

**71** $3\cos 2x - 7\cos x + 5 = 0 \;\Rightarrow\; 3(2\cos^2 x - 1) - 7\cos x + 5 = 0 \;\Rightarrow\; 6\cos^2 x - 7\cos x + 2 = 0 \;\Rightarrow$

$(3\cos x - 2)(2\cos x - 1) = 0 \;\Rightarrow\; \cos x = \frac{2}{3}, \frac{1}{2} \;\Rightarrow$

$x = \cos^{-1}\frac{2}{3} \approx 0.8411, 2\pi - \cos^{-1}\frac{2}{3} \approx 5.4421, \frac{\pi}{3} \approx 1.0472, \frac{5\pi}{3} \approx 5.2360.$

**72** $\sin 2x = -1.5\cos x \;\Rightarrow\; \sin 2x + 1.5\cos x = 0 \;\Rightarrow\; 2\sin x\cos x + 1.5\cos x = 0 \;\Rightarrow$

$(\cos x)(2\sin x + 1.5) = 0 \;\Rightarrow\; \cos x = 0 \text{ or } \sin x = -\frac{3}{4} \;\Rightarrow$

$x = \frac{\pi}{2} \approx 1.5708, \frac{3\pi}{2} \approx 4.7124, \sin^{-1}\left(-\frac{3}{4}\right) \{\text{not in } [0, 2\pi)\}, 2\pi + \sin^{-1}\left(-\frac{3}{4}\right) \approx 5.4351, \pi - \sin^{-1}\left(-\frac{3}{4}\right) \approx 3.9897.$

**73** (a) $M = \frac{S}{2}\left(1 - \frac{2}{\pi}\tan^{-1}\frac{d}{D}\right)$ • $S = 4, D = 3.5, d = 1 \;\Rightarrow\; M = \frac{4}{2}\left(1 - \frac{2}{\pi}\tan^{-1}\frac{1}{3.5}\right) \approx 1.65$ m

(b) $S = 4, D = 3.5, d = 4 \;\Rightarrow\; M = \frac{4}{2}\left(1 - \frac{2}{\pi}\tan^{-1}\frac{4}{3.5}\right) \approx 0.92$ m

(c) $S = 4, D = 3.5, d = 10 \;\Rightarrow\; M = \frac{4}{2}\left(1 - \frac{2}{\pi}\tan^{-1}\frac{10}{3.5}\right) \approx 0.43$ m

**74** First solve for $D$: $M = \frac{S}{2}\left(1 - \frac{2}{\pi}\tan^{-1}\frac{d}{D}\right) \;\Rightarrow\; \frac{2M}{S} = 1 - \frac{2}{\pi}\tan^{-1}\frac{d}{D} \;\Rightarrow\; \frac{2}{\pi}\tan^{-1}\frac{d}{D} = 1 - \frac{2M}{S} \;\Rightarrow$

$\tan^{-1}\frac{d}{D} = \frac{\pi}{2}\left(1 - \frac{2M}{S}\right) \;\Rightarrow\; \frac{d}{D} = \tan\left[\frac{\pi}{2}\left(1 - \frac{2M}{S}\right)\right] \;\Rightarrow\; D = d\cot\left[\frac{\pi}{2}\left(1 - \frac{2M}{S}\right)\right].$

Now $S = 3, M = 0.6, d = 5 \;\Rightarrow\; D = 5\cot\left[\frac{\pi}{2}\left(1 - \frac{2(0.6)}{3}\right)\right] \approx 3.63$ km.

**75** Form a right triangle with the center line of the fairway and half the width of the fairway as the legs of the triangle.

$$\text{opp} = \tfrac{1}{2}(30) = 15 \text{ and hyp} = 280 \;\Rightarrow\; \sin\theta = \frac{15}{280} \;\Rightarrow\; \theta = \sin^{-1}\frac{15}{280} \approx 3.07°$$

**76** $\tan\alpha = \dfrac{4'}{11'10''} \;\Rightarrow\; \alpha = \tan^{-1}\frac{48}{142} \approx 18.7°. \;\; \alpha + \beta = 90° \;\Rightarrow\; \beta \approx 71.3°.$

**77** (a) Let $\beta$ denote the angle by the sailboat with opposite side $d$ and hypotenuse $k$.

Now $\sin\beta = \frac{d}{k} \;\Rightarrow\; \beta = \sin^{-1}\frac{d}{k}.$ Using alternate interior angles, we see that $\alpha + \beta = \theta.$

Thus, $\alpha = \theta - \beta = \theta - \sin^{-1}\frac{d}{k}.$

(b) $d = 50, k = 210,$ and $\theta = 53.4° \;\Rightarrow\; \alpha = 53.4° - \sin^{-1}\frac{50}{210} \approx 39.63°$, or $40°$.

**78** (a) Draw a line from the art critic's eyes to the painting. This forms two right triangles with opposite sides 8 {upper $\triangle$ } and 2 {lower $\triangle$ } and adjacent side $x$. Let $\alpha$ be the angle of elevation to the top of the painting and $\beta$ be the angle of depression to the bottom of the painting.

Since $\tan\alpha = \dfrac{8}{x}$ and $\tan\beta = \dfrac{2}{x}, \theta = \alpha + \beta = \tan^{-1}\dfrac{8}{x} + \tan^{-1}\dfrac{2}{x}.$

(b) $\tan\theta = \tan(\alpha+\beta) = \dfrac{\tan\alpha + \tan\beta}{1 - \tan\alpha\tan\beta} = \dfrac{8/x + 2/x}{1 - (8/x)(2/x)} \cdot \dfrac{x^2}{x^2} = \dfrac{8x + 2x}{x^2 - 16} = \dfrac{10x}{x^2 - 16} \cdot \Rightarrow$

$\theta = \tan^{-1}\left(\dfrac{10x}{x^2 - 16}\right)$. Note that if $0 < x < 4$, $\dfrac{10x}{x^2 - 16} < 0$ and $90° < \theta < 180°$, *not* $-90° < \theta < 0°$ since $0° < \theta < 180°$ in any triangle.

If $x = 4$, $\dfrac{10x}{x^2 - 16}$ is undefined and $\theta = 90°$. If $x > 4$, $\dfrac{10x}{x^2 - 16} > 0$ and $0 < \theta < 90°$.

(c) $45° = \tan^{-1}\left(\dfrac{10x}{x^2 - 16}\right) \Rightarrow \tan 45° = \dfrac{10x}{x^2 - 16} \Rightarrow (1)(x^2 - 16) = 10x \Rightarrow$

$$x^2 - 10x - 16 = 0 \Rightarrow x = \dfrac{10 \pm \sqrt{164}}{2} = \{x > 0\}\ x = 5 + \sqrt{41} \approx 11.4 \text{ ft.}$$

**Note:** The following is a general outline that can be used for verifying trigonometric identities involving inverse trigonometric functions.

(1) Define angles and their ranges—make sure the range of values for one side of the equation is equal to the range of values for the other side.

(2) Choose a trigonometric function $T$ that is one-to-one on the range of values listed in part (1).

(3) Show that $T(\text{LS}) = T(\text{RS})$. Note that $T(\text{LS}) = T(\text{RS}) \;\not\Rightarrow\; \text{LS} = \text{RS}$.

(4) Conclude that since $T$ is one-to-one on the range of values, LS = RS.

**79** Let $\alpha = \sin^{-1}x$ and $\beta = \tan^{-1}\dfrac{x}{\sqrt{1 - x^2}}$ with $-\frac{\pi}{2} < \alpha < \frac{\pi}{2}$ and $-\frac{\pi}{2} < \beta < \frac{\pi}{2}$. Thus, $\sin\alpha = x$ and $\sin\beta = x$.

Since the sine function is one-to-one on $\left(-\frac{\pi}{2}, \frac{\pi}{2}\right)$, we have $\alpha = \beta$—that is, $\sin^{-1}x = \tan^{-1}\dfrac{x}{\sqrt{1 - x^2}}$.

**80** Let $\alpha = \arccos x$ and $\beta = \arccos\sqrt{1 - x^2}$. Since $0 \le x \le 1$, we have $0 \le \alpha \le \frac{\pi}{2}$ and $0 \le \beta \le \frac{\pi}{2}$,

and hence $0 \le \alpha + \beta \le \pi$. Thus, $\cos(\alpha + \beta) = \cos\alpha\cos\beta - \sin\alpha\sin\beta = x \cdot \sqrt{1 - x^2} - \sqrt{1 - x^2} \cdot x = 0$.

Since the cosine function is one-to-one on $[0, \pi]$, we have $\alpha + \beta = \frac{\pi}{2}$.

**81** Let $\alpha = \arcsin(-x)$ and $\beta = \arcsin x$ with $-\frac{\pi}{2} \le \alpha \le \frac{\pi}{2}$ and $-\frac{\pi}{2} \le \beta \le \frac{\pi}{2}$. Thus, $\sin\alpha = -x$ and $\sin\beta = x$.

Consequently, $\sin\alpha = -\sin\beta = \sin(-\beta)$.

Since the sine function is one-to-one on $\left[-\frac{\pi}{2}, \frac{\pi}{2}\right]$, we have $\alpha = -\beta$—that is, $\arcsin(-x) = -\arcsin x$.

**82** Let $\alpha = \arccos(-x)$ and $\beta = \pi - \arccos x$ with $0 \le \alpha \le \pi$ and $0 \le \beta \le \pi$ since $0 \le \arccos x \le \pi \;\Rightarrow\;$

$0 \ge -\arccos x \ge -\pi \;\Rightarrow\; \pi \ge \pi - \arccos x \ge 0$.

Thus, $\cos\alpha = -x$ and $\cos\beta = \cos(\pi - \arccos x) = \cos\pi \cdot x + \sin\pi \cdot \sin(\arccos x) = -x$.

Since the cosine function is one-to-one on $[0, \pi]$, we have $\alpha = \beta$.

**83** Let $\alpha = \arctan x$ and $\beta = \arctan(1/x)$. Since $x > 0$, we have $0 < \alpha < \frac{\pi}{2}$ and $0 < \beta < \frac{\pi}{2}$,

and hence $0 < \alpha + \beta < \pi$. Thus, $\tan(\alpha + \beta) = \dfrac{\tan\alpha + \tan\beta}{1 - \tan\alpha\tan\beta} = \dfrac{x + (1/x)}{1 - x \cdot (1/x)} = \dfrac{x + (1/x)}{0}$.

Since the denominator is 0, $\tan(\alpha + \beta)$ is undefined and hence,

$\alpha + \beta = \frac{\pi}{2}$ since $\frac{\pi}{2}$ is the only value between 0 and $\pi$ for which the tangent is undefined.

**84** Let $\alpha = \cos^{-1}x$ and $\beta = \cos^{-1}(2x^2 - 1)$. Since $0 \le x \le 1$, $0 \le \alpha \le \frac{\pi}{2}$ and $0 \le 2\alpha \le \pi$.

Also, $0 \le x \le 1 \;\Rightarrow\; 0 \le 2x^2 \le 2 \;\Rightarrow\; -1 \le 2x^2 - 1 \le 1$ and $0 \le \beta \le \pi$.

Thus, $\cos 2\alpha = \cos^2\alpha - \sin^2\alpha = (x)^2 - \left(\sqrt{1 - x^2}\right)^2 = x^2 - (1 - x^2) = 2x^2 - 1$ and $\cos\beta = 2x^2 - 1$.

Since the cosine function is one-to-one on $[0, \pi]$, we have $2\alpha = \beta$.

**85** $f(x) = 2\sin^{-1}(x-1) + \cos^{-1}\frac{1}{2}x$ ● The domain of $\sin^{-1}(x-1)$ is $[0, 2]$ and the domain of $\cos^{-1}\frac{1}{2}x$ is $[-2, 2]$. The domain of $f$ is the intersection of $[0, 2]$ and $[-2, 2]$, i.e., $[0, 2]$. From the graph, we see that the function is increasing and its range is $\left[-\frac{\pi}{2}, \pi\right]$.

$[-3, 6]$ by $[-2, 4]$

*Figure 85*

$[-3, 12]$ by $[-4, 6]$

*Figure 86*

**86** $f(x) = \frac{1}{2}\tan^{-1}(1-2x) + 3\tan^{-1}\sqrt{x+2}$ ● The domain of $\frac{1}{2}\tan^{-1}(1-2x)$ is $(-\infty, \infty)$ and the domain of $3\tan^{-1}\sqrt{x+2}$ is $[-2, \infty)$. The domain of $f$ is $[-2, \infty)$. The minimum value of approximately $\frac{1}{2}\tan^{-1}5 \approx 0.69$ occurs at $x = -2$. The maximum value of the function does not occur at $x \approx -0.13$. Rather for large $x$, $\frac{1}{2}\tan^{-1}(1-2x)$ approaches $-\frac{\pi}{4}$ and $3\tan^{-1}\sqrt{x+2}$ approaches $\frac{3\pi}{2}$. Thus, the function increases asymptotically to $\frac{5\pi}{4} \approx 3.93$. The range of the function is $\left[\frac{1}{2}\tan^{-1}5, \frac{5\pi}{4}\right)$.

**87** Graph $y = \sin^{-1}2x$ and $y = \tan^{-1}(1-x)$. From the graph, we see that there is one solution at $x \approx 0.29$.

$[-3, 3]$ by $[-2, 2]$

*Figure 87*

$[-6, 6]$ by $[-4.5, 4.5]$

*Figure 88*

**88** Graph $y = \cos^{-1}\left(x - \frac{1}{5}\right)$ and $y = 2\sin^{-1}\left(\frac{1}{2} - x\right)$. From the graph, we see that there is one solution at $x \approx -0.39$.

**89** $f(\theta) = \frac{1}{2}\left(\frac{\sin^2\alpha}{\sin^2\beta} + \frac{\tan^2\alpha}{\tan^2\beta}\right)$, where $\alpha = \theta - \gamma$, $\beta = \theta + \gamma$, and $\gamma = \sin^{-1}\left(\frac{\sin\theta}{1.52}\right)$ ● We'll let $X = \theta$, $Y_1 = \gamma$, $Y_2 = \alpha$, and $Y_3 = \beta$. Make the assignments $Y_1 = \sin^{-1}(\sin X/1.52)$, $Y_2 = X - Y_1$, $Y_3 = X + Y_1$, and $Y_4 = 0.5\left((\sin Y_2)^2/(\sin Y_3)^2 + (\tan Y_2)^2/(\tan Y_3)^2\right)$. Now turn *off* $Y_1$, $Y_2$, and $Y_3$—leaving only $Y_4$ *on* to graph. From the graph, we see that when $f(\theta) = 0.2$, $\theta \approx 1.25$, or approximately $72°$.

$[0, \pi/2, 0.2]$ by $[0, 1.05, 0.2]$

*Figure 89*

$[-\pi/2, \pi/2, 0.5]$ by $[-1.05, 1.05, 0.5]$

*Figure 90*

**90** (a) $\sin\phi = \sin 23.5° \sin 51.7° + \cos 23.5° \cos 51.7° \cos H$ $\Rightarrow$
$$\phi = \sin^{-1}(\sin 23.5° \sin 51.7° + \cos 23.5° \cos 51.7° \cos H)$$

(b) From Figure, we find that $\phi = 45° = \frac{\pi}{4} \approx 0.785398$ at $H \approx \pm 0.8044$.

Since 6 hours corresponds to $\frac{\pi}{2}$, 1 hour corresponds to $\frac{\pi}{12}$. $\pm 0.8044 \div \frac{\pi}{12} \approx \pm 3.07$ hr $\approx \pm 3$ hr and 4 min.

         The times are approximately 8:56 A.M. and 3:04 P.M.

**91** Actual distance between $x$-ticks is equal to $x_A = \dfrac{3 \text{ units}}{3 \text{ ticks}} = 1$ unit between ticks.

Actual distance between $y$-ticks is equal to $y_A = \dfrac{2 \text{ units}}{2 \text{ ticks}} = 1$ unit between ticks.

The ratio is $m_A = \dfrac{y_A}{x_A} = \dfrac{1}{1} = 1$. The graph will make an angle of $\theta = \tan^{-1} 1 = 45°$.

[0, 3] by [0, 2]      [0, 6] by [0, 2]

*Figure 91*      *Figure 92*

**92** $x_A = \dfrac{3 \text{ units}}{6 \text{ ticks}} = \dfrac{1}{2},\ y_A = \dfrac{2 \text{ units}}{2 \text{ ticks}} = 1 \ \Rightarrow\ m_A = \dfrac{1}{1/2} = 2 \ \Rightarrow\ \theta = \tan^{-1} 2 \approx 63.4°.$

**93** $x_A = \dfrac{3 \text{ units}}{3 \text{ ticks}} = 1,\ y_A = \dfrac{2 \text{ units}}{4 \text{ ticks}} = \dfrac{1}{2} \ \Rightarrow\ m_A = \dfrac{1/2}{1} = \dfrac{1}{2} \ \Rightarrow\ \theta = \tan^{-1} \dfrac{1}{2} \approx 26.6°.$

[0, 3] by [0, 4]      [0, 2] by [0, 2]

*Figure 93*      *Figure 94*

**94** $x_A = \dfrac{3 \text{ units}}{2 \text{ ticks}} = \dfrac{3}{2},\ y_A = \dfrac{2 \text{ units}}{2 \text{ ticks}} = 1 \ \Rightarrow\ m_A = \dfrac{1}{3/2} = \dfrac{2}{3} \ \Rightarrow\ \theta = \tan^{-1} \dfrac{2}{3} \approx 33.7°.$

## Chapter 6 Review Exercises

**1** $(\cot^2 x + 1)(1 - \cos^2 x) = (\csc^2 x)(\sin^2 x) = (1/\sin^2 x)(\sin^2 x) = 1$

**2** $\cos\theta + \sin\theta \tan\theta = \cos\theta + \sin\theta \cdot \dfrac{\sin\theta}{\cos\theta} = \dfrac{\cos^2\theta + \sin^2\theta}{\cos\theta} = \dfrac{1}{\cos\theta} = \sec\theta$

**3** $\dfrac{(\sec^2\theta - 1)\cot\theta}{\tan\theta \sin\theta + \cos\theta} = \dfrac{(\tan^2\theta)\cot\theta}{\dfrac{\sin\theta}{\cos\theta}\cdot \sin\theta + \cos\theta}$      {Pythagorean and tangent identities}

$= \dfrac{\tan\theta\,(\tan\theta \cot\theta)}{\dfrac{\sin^2\theta}{\cos\theta} + \cos\theta}$      {combine terms}

$= \dfrac{\tan\theta}{\dfrac{\sin^2\theta + \cos^2\theta}{\cos\theta}}$      {reciprocal identity, common denominator}

$= \dfrac{\sin\theta / \cos\theta}{1/\cos\theta}$      {Pythagorean and tangent identities}

$= \sin\theta$      {simplify}

**4** $(\tan x + \cot x)^2 = \left(\dfrac{\sin x}{\cos x} + \dfrac{\cos x}{\sin x}\right)^2 = \left(\dfrac{\sin^2 x + \cos^2 x}{\cos x \sin x}\right)^2 = \dfrac{1}{\cos^2 x \sin^2 x} = \sec^2 x \csc^2 x$

**5**    $\dfrac{1}{1+\sin t} = \dfrac{1}{1+\sin t} \cdot \dfrac{1-\sin t}{1-\sin t}$    $\left\{ \begin{array}{c} \text{multiply the numerator and the denominator} \\ \text{by conjugate of the denominator} \end{array} \right\}$

$= \dfrac{1-\sin t}{1-\sin^2 t}$    {the difference of two squares}

$= \dfrac{1-\sin t}{\cos^2 t}$    {Pythagorean identity}

$= \dfrac{1-\sin t}{\cos t} \cdot \dfrac{1}{\cos t}$    {break up since we want sec $t$ on the right side}

$= \left( \dfrac{1}{\cos t} - \dfrac{\sin t}{\cos t} \right) \cdot \sec t$    {split up fraction}

$= (\sec t - \tan t)\sec t$    {reciprocal and tangent identities}

**6**    $\dfrac{\sin(\alpha - \beta)}{\cos(\alpha + \beta)} = \dfrac{\sin\alpha\cos\beta - \cos\alpha\sin\beta}{\cos\alpha\cos\beta - \sin\alpha\sin\beta}$    $\left\{ \begin{array}{c} \text{subtraction formula for the sine} \\ \text{addition formula for the cosine} \end{array} \right\}$

The first term in the denominator is $\cos\alpha\cos\beta$, but looking ahead, we see that the first term in the denominator of the expression we want to obtain is 1. Hence, we will divide both the numerator and the denominator by $\cos\alpha\cos\beta$. Continuing, we have:

$$\frac{\sin(\alpha - \beta)}{\cos(\alpha + \beta)} = \frac{(\sin\alpha\cos\beta - \cos\alpha\sin\beta)\,/\,\cos\alpha\cos\beta}{(\cos\alpha\cos\beta - \sin\alpha\sin\beta)\,/\,\cos\alpha\cos\beta}$$

$$= \frac{\dfrac{\sin\alpha\cos\beta}{\cos\alpha\cos\beta} - \dfrac{\cos\alpha\sin\beta}{\cos\alpha\cos\beta}}{\dfrac{\cos\alpha\cos\beta}{\cos\alpha\cos\beta} - \dfrac{\sin\alpha\sin\beta}{\cos\alpha\cos\beta}} = \frac{\dfrac{\sin\alpha}{\cos\alpha} - \dfrac{\sin\beta}{\cos\beta}}{1 - \dfrac{\sin\alpha}{\cos\alpha} \cdot \dfrac{\sin\beta}{\cos\beta}} = \frac{\tan\alpha - \tan\beta}{1 - \tan\alpha\tan\beta}$$

**7**    $\tan 2u = \dfrac{2\tan u}{1 - \tan^2 u}$    {apply the double-angle formula for the tangent}

$= \dfrac{2 \cdot \dfrac{1}{\cot u}}{1 - \dfrac{1}{\cot^2 u}}$    {put in terms of cot since it appears on the right side}

$= \dfrac{\dfrac{2}{\cot u}}{\dfrac{\cot^2 u - 1}{\cot^2 u}}$    {combine into one fraction}

$= \dfrac{2\cot u}{\cot^2 u - 1}$    {simplify complex fraction}

$= \dfrac{2\cot u}{(\csc^2 u - 1) - 1}$    {Pythagorean identity}

$= \dfrac{2\cot u}{\csc^2 u - 2}$    {simplify}

**8**    $\cos^2 \dfrac{v}{2} = \dfrac{1 + \cos v}{2} = \dfrac{1 + \dfrac{1}{\sec v}}{2} = \dfrac{\dfrac{\sec v + 1}{\sec v}}{2} = \dfrac{1 + \sec v}{2\sec v}$

**9**    Factor the numerator using the difference of two cubes formula.

$\dfrac{\tan^3\phi - \cot^3\phi}{\tan^2\phi + \csc^2\phi} = \dfrac{(\tan\phi - \cot\phi)(\tan^2\phi + \tan\phi\cot\phi + \cot^2\phi)}{\tan^2\phi + (1 + \cot^2\phi)} = \dfrac{(\tan\phi - \cot\phi)(\tan^2\phi + 1 + \cot^2\phi)}{\tan^2\phi + 1 + \cot^2\phi}$

$= \tan\phi - \cot\phi$

**10**    LS $= \dfrac{\sin u + \sin v}{\csc u + \csc v} = \dfrac{\sin u + \sin v}{\dfrac{1}{\sin u} + \dfrac{1}{\sin v}} = \dfrac{\sin u + \sin v}{\dfrac{\sin v + \sin u}{\sin u \sin v}} = \sin u \sin v$.   At this point, there is no apparent "next step."

Thus, we will stop working with the left side and try to simplify the right side to the same expression, $\sin u \sin v$.

$$RS = \frac{1 - \sin u \sin v}{-1 + \csc u \csc v} = \frac{1 - \sin u \sin v}{-1 + \dfrac{1}{\sin u \sin v}} = \frac{1 - \sin u \sin v}{\dfrac{1 - \sin u \sin v}{\sin u \sin v}} = \sin u \sin v.$$

Since the LS and RS equal the same expression and the steps are reversible, the identity is verified.

$\boxed{11}$ $\left(\dfrac{\sin^2 x}{\tan^4 x}\right)^3 \left(\dfrac{\csc^3 x}{\cot^6 x}\right)^2 = \left(\dfrac{\sin^6 x}{\tan^{12} x}\right)\left(\dfrac{\csc^6 x}{\cot^{12} x}\right) = \dfrac{(\sin x \csc x)^6}{(\tan x \cot x)^{12}} = \dfrac{(1)^6}{(1)^{12}} = \dfrac{1}{1} = 1$

$\boxed{12}$ $\dfrac{\cos\gamma}{1 - \tan\gamma} + \dfrac{\sin\gamma}{1 - \cot\gamma} = \dfrac{\cos\gamma}{1 - \dfrac{\sin\gamma}{\cos\gamma}} + \dfrac{\sin\gamma}{1 - \dfrac{\cos\gamma}{\sin\gamma}} = \dfrac{\cos\gamma}{\dfrac{\cos\gamma - \sin\gamma}{\cos\gamma}} + \dfrac{\sin\gamma}{\dfrac{\sin\gamma - \cos\gamma}{\sin\gamma}}$

$$= \frac{\cos^2\gamma}{\cos\gamma - \sin\gamma} + \frac{\sin^2\gamma}{\sin\gamma - \cos\gamma} = \frac{\cos^2\gamma}{\cos\gamma - \sin\gamma} - \frac{\sin^2\gamma}{-(\sin\gamma - \cos\gamma)}$$

$$= \frac{\cos^2\gamma}{\cos\gamma - \sin\gamma} - \frac{\sin^2\gamma}{\cos\gamma - \sin\gamma} = \frac{\cos^2\gamma - \sin^2\gamma}{\cos\gamma - \sin\gamma}$$

$$= \frac{(\cos\gamma + \sin\gamma)(\cos\gamma - \sin\gamma)}{\cos\gamma - \sin\gamma} = \cos\gamma + \sin\gamma$$

$\boxed{13}$ $\dfrac{\cos(-t)}{\sec(-t) + \tan(-t)} = \dfrac{\cos t}{\sec t + (-\tan t)} = \dfrac{\cos t}{\sec t - \tan t}$

$$= \frac{\cos t}{\dfrac{1}{\cos t} - \dfrac{\sin t}{\cos t}} = \frac{\cos t}{\dfrac{1 - \sin t}{\cos t}} = \frac{\cos^2 t}{1 - \sin t} = \frac{1 - \sin^2 t}{1 - \sin t} = \frac{(1 - \sin t)(1 + \sin t)}{1 - \sin t} = 1 + \sin t$$

$\boxed{14}$ $\dfrac{\cot(-t) + \csc(-t)}{\sin(-t)} = \dfrac{-\cot t - \csc t}{-\sin t}$

$$= \frac{\dfrac{\cos t}{\sin t} + \dfrac{1}{\sin t}}{\sin t} = \frac{\cos t + 1}{\sin^2 t} = \frac{\cos t + 1}{1 - \cos^2 t} = \frac{\cos t + 1}{(1 - \cos t)(1 + \cos t)} = \frac{1}{1 - \cos t}$$

$\boxed{15}$ In the following solution, we could multiply both the numerator and the denominator by *either* the conjugate of the numerator *or* the conjugate of the denominator. Since the numerator on the right side looks like the numerator on the left side, we'll change the denominator.

$$\sqrt{\frac{1 - \cos t}{1 + \cos t}} = \sqrt{\frac{(1 - \cos t)}{(1 + \cos t)} \cdot \frac{(1 - \cos t)}{(1 - \cos t)}} = \sqrt{\frac{(1 - \cos t)^2}{1 - \cos^2 t}}$$

$$= \sqrt{\frac{(1 - \cos t)^2}{\sin^2 t}} = \frac{\sqrt{(1 - \cos t)^2}}{\sqrt{\sin^2 t}} = \frac{|1 - \cos t|}{|\sin t|} = \frac{1 - \cos t}{|\sin t|}, \text{ since } (1 - \cos t) \ge 0.$$

$\boxed{16}$ $\sqrt{\dfrac{1 - \sin\theta}{1 + \sin\theta}} = \sqrt{\dfrac{(1 - \sin\theta)}{(1 + \sin\theta)} \cdot \dfrac{(1 + \sin\theta)}{(1 + \sin\theta)}} = \sqrt{\dfrac{1 - \sin^2\theta}{(1 + \sin\theta)^2}} = \sqrt{\dfrac{\cos^2\theta}{(1 + \sin\theta)^2}} = \dfrac{|\cos\theta|}{|1 + \sin\theta|} = \dfrac{|\cos\theta|}{1 + \sin\theta},$

since $(1 + \sin\theta) \ge 0$.

$\boxed{17}$ $\cos\left(x - \dfrac{5\pi}{2}\right) = \cos x \cos\dfrac{5\pi}{2} + \sin x \sin\dfrac{5\pi}{2} = (\cos x)(0) + (\sin x)(1) = \sin x$

$\boxed{18}$ $\tan\left(x + \dfrac{3\pi}{4}\right) = \dfrac{\tan x + \tan\dfrac{3\pi}{4}}{1 - \tan x \tan\dfrac{3\pi}{4}} = \dfrac{\tan x - 1}{1 + \tan x}$

$\boxed{19}$ We need to break down the angle argument of $4\beta$ into terms with only $\beta$ as their argument. We can do this by using either the double-angle formula for the sine or the addition formula for the sine.

$$\tfrac{1}{4}\sin 4\beta = \tfrac{1}{4}\sin(2 \cdot 2\beta) = \tfrac{1}{4}(2\sin 2\beta \cos 2\beta) = \tfrac{1}{2}(2\sin\beta\cos\beta)(\cos^2\beta - \sin^2\beta) = \sin\beta\cos^3\beta - \cos\beta\sin^3\beta$$

**20** $\tan \frac{1}{2}\theta = \dfrac{1 - \cos\theta}{\sin\theta}$　　　　{apply the half-angle formula for the tangent}

$\qquad = \dfrac{1}{\sin\theta} - \dfrac{\cos\theta}{\sin\theta}$　　{split up the fraction}

$\qquad = \csc\theta - \cot\theta$　　{reciprocal and cotangent identities}

**21** $\sin 8\theta = \sin(2 \cdot 4\theta)$

$\qquad = 2(\sin 4\theta)(\cos 4\theta)$　　　　　　　　　　　　　{double angle formula for sine}

$\qquad = 2\left(2\underline{\sin 2\theta}\cos 2\theta\right)\left(1 - 2\sin^2 2\theta\right)$　　　　　{double angle formulas for sine and cosine}

$\qquad = 2\left[2 \cdot \underline{2\sin\theta\cos\theta}\left(1 - 2\sin^2\theta\right)\right]\left[1 - 2(\sin 2\theta)^2\right]$　　{double angle formulas for sine and cosine}

$\qquad = 8\sin\theta\cos\theta\left(1 - 2\sin^2\theta\right)\left[1 - 2(2\sin\theta\cos\theta)^2\right]$　　{double angle formula for sine}

$\qquad = 8\sin\theta\cos\theta\left(1 - 2\sin^2\theta\right)\left[1 - 2(4\sin^2\theta\cos^2\theta)\right]$

$\qquad = 8\sin\theta\cos\theta\left(1 - 2\sin^2\theta\right)\left(1 - 8\sin^2\theta\cos^2\theta\right)$

**22** Let $\alpha = \arctan x$ and $\beta = \arctan \dfrac{2x}{1 - x^2}$. Because $-1 < x < 1$, $\arctan(-1) < \arctan(x) < \arctan(1)$, and hence $-\frac{\pi}{4} < \alpha < \frac{\pi}{4}$. Thus, $\tan\alpha = x$ and $\tan\beta = \dfrac{2x}{1 - x^2} = \dfrac{2\tan\alpha}{1 - \tan^2\alpha} = \tan 2\alpha$.

Since the tangent function is one-to-one on $\left(-\frac{\pi}{2}, \frac{\pi}{2}\right)$, we have $\beta = 2\alpha$ or, equivalently, $\alpha = \frac{1}{2}\beta$.

$\qquad\qquad\qquad\qquad\qquad\qquad$ In terms of $x$, we have $\arctan x = \dfrac{1}{2}\arctan\dfrac{2x}{1 - x^2}$.

**23** $2\cos^3\theta - \cos\theta = 0 \;\Rightarrow\; \cos\theta\left(2\cos^2\theta - 1\right) = 0 \;\Rightarrow\; \cos\theta = 0, \pm\frac{\sqrt{2}}{2} \;\Rightarrow\; \theta = \frac{\pi}{2}, \frac{3\pi}{2}, \frac{\pi}{4}, \frac{7\pi}{4}, \frac{3\pi}{4}, \frac{5\pi}{4}$

**24** $2\cos\alpha + \tan\alpha = \sec\alpha \;\Rightarrow\; 2\cos\alpha + \dfrac{\sin\alpha}{\cos\alpha} = \dfrac{1}{\cos\alpha} \;\Rightarrow\;$ {multiply by the lcd, $\cos\alpha$}

$2\cos^2\alpha + \sin\alpha = 1 \;\Rightarrow\; 2(1 - \sin^2\alpha) + \sin\alpha = 1 \;\Rightarrow\; 2 - 2\sin^2\alpha + \sin\alpha = 1 \;\Rightarrow\;$

$2\sin^2\alpha - \sin\alpha - 1 = 0 \;\Rightarrow\; (2\sin\alpha + 1)(\sin\alpha - 1) = 0 \;\Rightarrow\; \sin\alpha = -\frac{1}{2}, 1 \;\Rightarrow\; \alpha = \frac{7\pi}{6}, \frac{11\pi}{6}, \frac{\pi}{2}$.

Checking these values in the original equation,

$\qquad\qquad\qquad\qquad$ we see that $\tan\frac{\pi}{2}$ is undefined so exclude $\frac{\pi}{2}$ and our solution is $\alpha = \frac{7\pi}{6}, \frac{11\pi}{6}$.

**25** $\sin\theta = \tan\theta \;\Rightarrow\; \sin\theta - \dfrac{\sin\theta}{\cos\theta} = 0 \;\Rightarrow\; \sin\theta\left(1 - \dfrac{1}{\cos\theta}\right) = 0 \;\Rightarrow\; \sin\theta = 0 \text{ or } 1 = \dfrac{1}{\cos\theta} \;\Rightarrow\;$

$\qquad\qquad\qquad\qquad\qquad \sin\theta = 0 \text{ or } \cos\theta = 1 \;\Rightarrow\; \theta = 0, \pi \text{ or } \theta = 0 \;\Rightarrow\; \theta = 0, \pi$

**26** $\csc^5\theta - 4\csc\theta = 0 \;\Rightarrow\; \csc\theta\left(\csc^4\theta - 4\right) = 0 \;\Rightarrow\; \csc^2\theta = 2 \,\{\csc\theta \neq 0, \csc^2\theta \neq -2\} \;\Rightarrow\;$

$\qquad\qquad\qquad\qquad\qquad\qquad\qquad\qquad \csc\theta = \pm\sqrt{2} \;\Rightarrow\; \theta = \frac{\pi}{4}, \frac{3\pi}{4}, \frac{5\pi}{4}, \frac{7\pi}{4}$

**27** $2\cos^3 t + \cos^2 t - 2\cos t - 1 = 0 \;\Rightarrow\; \cos^2 t\left(2\cos t + 1\right) - 1\left(2\cos t + 1\right) = 0 \;\Rightarrow\;$

$\qquad\qquad\qquad (\cos^2 t - 1)(2\cos t + 1) = 0 \;\Rightarrow\; \cos t = \pm 1, -\frac{1}{2} \;\Rightarrow\; t = 0, \pi, \frac{2\pi}{3}, \frac{4\pi}{3}$

**28** $\cos x \cot^2 x = \cos x \;\Rightarrow\; \cos x \cot^2 x - \cos x = 0 \;\Rightarrow\; \cos x\left(\cot^2 x - 1\right) = 0 \;\Rightarrow\;$

$\qquad\qquad\qquad\qquad \cos x = 0 \text{ or } \cot x = \pm 1 \;\Rightarrow\; x = \frac{\pi}{2}, \frac{3\pi}{2}, \frac{\pi}{4}, \frac{5\pi}{4}, \frac{3\pi}{4}, \frac{7\pi}{4}$

**29** $\sin\beta + 2\cos^2\beta = 1 \;\Rightarrow\; \sin\beta + 2(1 - \sin^2\beta) = 1 \;\Rightarrow\; 2\sin^2\beta - \sin\beta - 1 = 0 \;\Rightarrow\;$

$\qquad\qquad\qquad (2\sin\beta + 1)(\sin\beta - 1) = 0 \;\Rightarrow\; \sin\beta = -\frac{1}{2}, 1 \;\Rightarrow\; \beta = \frac{7\pi}{6}, \frac{11\pi}{6}, \frac{\pi}{2}$

**30** $\cos 2x + 3\cos x + 2 = 0 \;\Rightarrow\; 2\cos^2 x + 3\cos x + 1 = 0 \;\Rightarrow\; (2\cos x + 1)(\cos x + 1) = 0 \;\Rightarrow\;$

$\qquad\qquad\qquad\qquad\qquad\qquad \cos x = -\frac{1}{2}, -1 \;\Rightarrow\; x = \frac{2\pi}{3}, \frac{4\pi}{3}, \pi$

**31** $2 \sec u \sin u + 2 = 4 \sin u + \sec u \Rightarrow 2 \sec u \sin u - 4 \sin u - \sec u + 2 = 0 \Rightarrow$

$2 \sin u (\sec u - 2) - 1(\sec u - 2) = 0 \Rightarrow (2 \sin u - 1)(\sec u - 2) = 0 \Rightarrow$

$\sin u = \frac{1}{2}$ or $\sec u = 2 \left\{ \text{which is the same as } \cos u = \frac{1}{2} \right\} \Rightarrow u = \frac{\pi}{6}, \frac{5\pi}{6}, \frac{\pi}{3}, \frac{5\pi}{3}$

**32** $\tan 2x \cos 2x = \sin 2x \Rightarrow \sin 2x = \sin 2x$. This is an identity and is true for all values of $x$ in $[0, 2\pi)$ except those that make $\tan 2x$ undefined, or, equivalently, those that make $\cos 2x$ equal to 0.

$\cos 2x = 0 \Rightarrow 2x = \frac{\pi}{2} + \pi n \Rightarrow x = \frac{\pi}{4} + \frac{\pi}{2}n$. Hence, the solutions are all $x$ in $[0, 2\pi)$ except $\frac{\pi}{4}, \frac{3\pi}{4}, \frac{5\pi}{4}, \frac{7\pi}{4}$.

**33** $2 \cos 3x \cos 2x = 1 - 2 \sin 3x \sin 2x \Rightarrow 2 \cos 3x \cos 2x + 2 \sin 3x \sin 2x = 1 \Rightarrow$

$2(\cos 3x \cos 2x + \sin 3x \sin 2x) = 1 \Rightarrow \cos(3x - 2x) = \frac{1}{2} \Rightarrow \cos x = \frac{1}{2} \Rightarrow x = \frac{\pi}{3}, \frac{5\pi}{3}$

**34** $\sin x \cos 2x + \cos x \sin 2x = 0 \Rightarrow \sin(x + 2x) = 0 \Rightarrow \sin 3x = 0 \Rightarrow$

$3x = \pi n \Rightarrow x = \frac{\pi}{3}n \Rightarrow x = 0, \frac{\pi}{3}, \frac{2\pi}{3}, \pi, \frac{4\pi}{3}, \frac{5\pi}{3}$

**35** $\cos \pi x + \sin \pi x = 0 \Rightarrow \sin \pi x = -\cos \pi x \Rightarrow \dfrac{\sin \pi x}{\cos \pi x} = \dfrac{-\cos \pi x}{\cos \pi x}$ {divide by $\cos \pi x$} $\Rightarrow$

$\tan \pi x = -1 \Rightarrow \pi x = \frac{3\pi}{4} + \pi n \Rightarrow x = \frac{3}{4} + n \Rightarrow x = \frac{3}{4}, \frac{7}{4}, \frac{11}{4}, \frac{15}{4}, \frac{19}{4}, \frac{23}{4}$

**36** $\sin 2u = \sin u \Rightarrow 2 \sin u \cos u = \sin u \Rightarrow 2 \sin u \cos u - \sin u = 0 \Rightarrow$

$\sin u (2 \cos u - 1) = 0 \Rightarrow \sin u = 0$ or $\cos u = \frac{1}{2} \Rightarrow u = 0, \pi, \frac{\pi}{3}, \frac{5\pi}{3}$

**37** $2 \cos^2 \frac{1}{2}\theta - 3 \cos \theta = 0 \Rightarrow 2 \left( \dfrac{1 + \cos \theta}{2} \right) - 3 \cos \theta = 0 \Rightarrow (1 + \cos \theta) - 3 \cos \theta = 0 \Rightarrow$

$1 - 2 \cos \theta = 0 \Rightarrow \cos \theta = \frac{1}{2} \Rightarrow \theta = \frac{\pi}{3}, \frac{5\pi}{3}$

**38** $\sec 2x \csc 2x = 2 \csc 2x \Rightarrow \sec 2x \csc 2x - 2 \csc 2x = 0 \Rightarrow \csc 2x (\sec 2x - 2) = 0 \Rightarrow$

$\cos 2x = \frac{1}{2}$ {$\csc 2x \neq 0$} $\Rightarrow 2x = \frac{\pi}{3}, \frac{5\pi}{3}, \frac{7\pi}{3}, \frac{11\pi}{3} \Rightarrow x = \frac{\pi}{6}, \frac{5\pi}{6}, \frac{7\pi}{6}, \frac{11\pi}{6}$

**39** $\sin 5x = \sin 3x \Rightarrow \sin 5x - \sin 3x = 0 \Rightarrow$ [S2] $2 \cos \dfrac{5x + 3x}{2} \sin \dfrac{5x - 3x}{2} = 0 \Rightarrow$

$\cos 4x \sin x = 0 \Rightarrow 4x = \frac{\pi}{2} + \pi n$ or $x = \pi n \Rightarrow x = \frac{\pi}{8} + \frac{\pi}{4}n$ or $x = 0, \pi \Rightarrow$

$x = 0, \frac{\pi}{8}, \frac{3\pi}{8}, \frac{5\pi}{8}, \frac{7\pi}{8}, \pi, \frac{9\pi}{8}, \frac{11\pi}{8}, \frac{13\pi}{8}, \frac{15\pi}{8}$

**40** $\cos 3x = -\cos 2x \Rightarrow \cos 3x + \cos 2x = 0 \Rightarrow 2 \cos \dfrac{3x + 2x}{2} \cos \dfrac{3x - 2x}{2} = 0 \Rightarrow$

$\cos \frac{5}{2}x \cos \frac{1}{2}x = 0 \Rightarrow \frac{5}{2}x = \frac{\pi}{2} + \pi n$ or $\frac{1}{2}x = \frac{\pi}{2} + \pi n \Rightarrow x = \frac{\pi}{5} + \frac{2\pi}{5}n$ or $x = \pi + 2\pi n \Rightarrow$

$x = \frac{\pi}{5}, \frac{3\pi}{5}, \pi, \frac{7\pi}{5}, \frac{9\pi}{5}$

**41** $\cos 75° = \cos(45° + 30°) = \cos 45° \cos 30° - \sin 45° \sin 30° = \frac{\sqrt{2}}{2} \cdot \frac{\sqrt{3}}{2} - \frac{\sqrt{2}}{2} \cdot \frac{1}{2} = \frac{\sqrt{6} - \sqrt{2}}{4}$

**42** $\tan 285° = \tan(225° + 60°) = \dfrac{\tan 225° + \tan 60°}{1 - \tan 225° \tan 60°} = \dfrac{1 + \sqrt{3}}{1 - \sqrt{3}} \cdot \dfrac{1 + \sqrt{3}}{1 + \sqrt{3}} = \dfrac{4 + 2\sqrt{3}}{-2} = -2 - \sqrt{3}$

**43** $\sin 195° = \sin(135° + 60°) = \sin 135° \cos 60° + \cos 135° \sin 60° = \frac{\sqrt{2}}{2} \cdot \frac{1}{2} + \left( -\frac{\sqrt{2}}{2} \right) \cdot \frac{\sqrt{3}}{2} = \frac{\sqrt{2} - \sqrt{6}}{4}$

**44** $\csc \frac{\pi}{8} = \dfrac{1}{\sin \frac{\pi}{8}} = \dfrac{1}{\sin \left( \frac{1}{2} \cdot \frac{\pi}{4} \right)} = \dfrac{1}{\sqrt{\dfrac{1 - \cos \frac{\pi}{4}}{2}}} = \dfrac{1}{\sqrt{\dfrac{1 - \sqrt{2}/2}{2}}} = \dfrac{1}{\sqrt{\dfrac{2 - \sqrt{2}}{4}}} = \dfrac{2}{\sqrt{2 - \sqrt{2}}}$

**45** $\csc \theta = \frac{5}{3}$ and $\cos \phi = \frac{8}{17} \Rightarrow \sin \theta = \frac{3}{5}, \cos \theta = \frac{4}{5}, \tan \theta = \frac{3}{4}$ and $\sin \phi = \frac{15}{17}, \tan \phi = \frac{15}{8}$.

$\sin(\theta + \phi) = \sin \theta \cos \phi + \cos \theta \sin \phi = \frac{3}{5} \cdot \frac{8}{17} + \frac{4}{5} \cdot \frac{15}{17} = \frac{84}{85}$

**46** $\cos(\theta + \phi) = \cos \theta \cos \phi - \sin \theta \sin \phi = \frac{4}{5} \cdot \frac{8}{17} - \frac{3}{5} \cdot \frac{15}{17} = -\frac{13}{85}$

**47** $\tan(\phi + \theta) = \tan(\theta + \phi) = \dfrac{\sin(\theta + \phi)}{\cos(\theta + \phi)} = \dfrac{84/85 \;\{\text{from Exercise 45}\}}{-13/85 \;\{\text{from Exercise 46}\}} = -\dfrac{84}{13}$

**48** $\tan(\theta - \phi) = \dfrac{\tan\theta - \tan\phi}{1 + \tan\theta\,\tan\phi} = \dfrac{\frac{3}{4} - \frac{15}{8}}{1 + \frac{3}{4} \cdot \frac{15}{8}} \cdot \dfrac{32}{32} = \dfrac{24 - 60}{32 + 45} = -\dfrac{36}{77}$

**49** $\sin(\phi - \theta) = \sin\phi\cos\theta - \cos\phi\sin\theta = \frac{15}{17} \cdot \frac{4}{5} - \frac{8}{17} \cdot \frac{3}{5} = \frac{36}{85}$

**50** First recognize the relationship to Exercise 49. $\sin(\theta - \phi) = \sin[-(\phi - \theta)] = -\sin(\phi - \theta) = -\frac{36}{85}$

**51** $\cos(\phi - \theta) = \cos\phi\cos\theta - \sin\phi\sin\theta = \frac{8}{17} \cdot \frac{4}{5} + \frac{15}{17} \cdot \frac{3}{5} = \frac{77}{85}$

**52** $\cos(\theta - \phi) = \cos\theta\cos\phi + \sin\theta\sin\phi = \frac{4}{5} \cdot \frac{8}{17} + \frac{3}{5} \cdot \frac{15}{17} = \frac{77}{85}$

{or notice that $\cos(\theta - \phi)$ is equivalent to $\cos(\phi - \theta)$ in the previous exercise}

**53** $\sin 2\phi = 2\sin\phi\cos\phi = 2 \cdot \frac{15}{17} \cdot \frac{8}{17} \;\{\text{from Exercise 45}\} = \frac{240}{289}$

**54** $\cos 2\phi = \cos^2\phi - \sin^2\phi = \left(\frac{8}{17}\right)^2 - \left(\frac{15}{17}\right)^2 = -\frac{161}{289}$

**55** $\tan 2\theta = \dfrac{2\tan\theta}{1 - \tan^2\theta} = \dfrac{2 \cdot \frac{3}{4}}{1 - \left(\frac{3}{4}\right)^2} = \dfrac{\frac{3}{2}}{1 - \frac{9}{16}} \cdot \dfrac{16}{16} = \dfrac{24}{16 - 9} = \dfrac{24}{7}$

**56** $\sin\frac{1}{2}\theta = \sqrt{\dfrac{1 - \cos\theta}{2}} = \sqrt{\dfrac{1 - \frac{4}{5}}{2}} = \sqrt{\dfrac{\frac{1}{5}}{2}} = \sqrt{\dfrac{1}{10} \cdot \dfrac{10}{10}} = \dfrac{\sqrt{10}}{10}$

**57** $\tan\frac{1}{2}\theta = \dfrac{1 - \cos\theta}{\sin\theta} = \dfrac{1 - \frac{4}{5}}{\frac{3}{5}} = \dfrac{\frac{1}{5}}{\frac{3}{5}} = \dfrac{1}{3}$

**58** $\cos\frac{1}{2}\phi = \sqrt{\dfrac{1 + \cos\phi}{2}} = \sqrt{\dfrac{1 + \frac{8}{17}}{2}} = \sqrt{\dfrac{\frac{25}{17}}{2}} = \sqrt{\dfrac{25}{34} \cdot \dfrac{34}{34}} = \dfrac{5\sqrt{34}}{34}$

**59** (a) $\sin 7t \sin 4t = $ [P4] $\frac{1}{2}[\cos(7t - 4t) - \cos(7t + 4t)] = \frac{1}{2}\cos 3t - \frac{1}{2}\cos 11t$

   (b) $\cos\frac{1}{4}u \cos\left(-\frac{1}{6}u\right) = $ [P3] $\frac{1}{2}\left\{\cos\left[\frac{1}{4}u + \left(-\frac{1}{6}u\right)\right] + \cos\left[\frac{1}{4}u - \left(-\frac{1}{6}u\right)\right]\right\} = \frac{1}{2}\left(\cos\frac{2}{24}u + \cos\frac{10}{24}u\right)$
   $= \frac{1}{2}\cos\frac{1}{12}u + \frac{1}{2}\cos\frac{5}{12}u$

   (c) $6\cos 5x \sin 3x = $ [P2] $6 \cdot \frac{1}{2}[\sin(5x + 3x) - \sin(5x - 3x)] = 3\sin 8x - 3\sin 2x$

   (d) $4\sin 3\theta \cos 7\theta = $ [P1] $4 \cdot \frac{1}{2}[\sin(3\theta + 7\theta) + \sin(3\theta - 7\theta)] = 2\sin 10\theta - 2\sin 4\theta$

**60** (a) $\sin 8u + \sin 2u = $ [S1] $2\sin\dfrac{8u + 2u}{2}\cos\dfrac{8u - 2u}{2} = 2\sin 5u \cos 3u$

   (b) $\cos 3\theta - \cos 8\theta = $ [S4] $-2\sin\dfrac{3\theta + 8\theta}{2}\sin\dfrac{3\theta - 8\theta}{2} = -2\sin\frac{11}{2}\theta\sin\left(-\frac{5}{2}\theta\right) = 2\sin\frac{11}{2}\theta\sin\frac{5}{2}\theta$

   (c) $\sin\frac{1}{4}t - \sin\frac{1}{5}t = $ [S2] $2\cos\dfrac{\frac{1}{4}t + \frac{1}{5}t}{2}\sin\dfrac{\frac{1}{4}t - \frac{1}{5}t}{2} = 2\cos\dfrac{\frac{5}{20}t + \frac{4}{20}t}{2}\sin\dfrac{\frac{5}{20}t - \frac{4}{20}t}{2} = 2\cos\frac{9}{40}t\sin\frac{1}{40}t$

   (d) $3\cos 2x + 3\cos 6x = $ [S3] $3 \cdot 2\cos\dfrac{2x + 6x}{2}\cos\dfrac{2x - 6x}{2} = 6\cos 4x \cos(-2x) = 6\cos 4x \cos 2x$

**61** $\cos^{-1}\left(\frac{\sqrt{3}}{2}\right) = \frac{\pi}{6}$ since $\cos\frac{\pi}{6} = \frac{\sqrt{3}}{2}$ and $0 \le \frac{\pi}{6} \le \pi$

**62** $\arcsin\left(\frac{\sqrt{2}}{2}\right) = \frac{\pi}{4}$ since $\sin\frac{\pi}{4} = \frac{\sqrt{2}}{2}$ and $-\frac{\pi}{2} \le \frac{\pi}{4} \le \frac{\pi}{2}$

**63** $\arctan\sqrt{3} = \frac{\pi}{3}$ since $\tan\frac{\pi}{3} = \sqrt{3}$ and $-\frac{\pi}{2} < \frac{\pi}{3} < \frac{\pi}{2}$

**64** $\arccos\left(\tan\frac{3\pi}{4}\right) = \arccos(-1) = \pi$          **65** $\arcsin\left(\sin\frac{5\pi}{4}\right) = \arcsin\left(-\frac{\sqrt{2}}{2}\right) = -\frac{\pi}{4}$

**66** $\cos^{-1}\left(\cos\frac{5\pi}{4}\right) = \cos^{-1}\left(-\frac{\sqrt{2}}{2}\right) = \frac{3\pi}{4}$      **67** $\sin\left[\arccos\left(-\frac{\sqrt{3}}{2}\right)\right] = \sin\frac{5\pi}{6} = \frac{1}{2}$

**68** $\tan(\tan^{-1} 2) = 2$ since $\tan(\arctan x) = x$ for every $x$

**69** $\cos^{-1}\left(\tan\frac{\pi}{3}\right) = \cos^{-1}\sqrt{3}$, which is *not defined* since $\sqrt{3} > 1$ and the domain of $\cos^{-1}$ is $[-1, 1]$.

**70** $\sec(2\tan^{-1} 1) = \sec\left(2 \cdot \frac{\pi}{4}\right) = \sec\frac{\pi}{2}$, which is *not defined*.

**71** $\sec\left(\sin^{-1}\frac{3}{2}\right)$ is *not defined* since $\frac{3}{2} > 1$ and the domain of $\sin^{-1}$ is $[-1, 1]$.

**72** $\cos^{-1}(\sin 0) = \cos^{-1} 0 = \frac{\pi}{2}$.

**73** Let $\alpha = \sin^{-1}\frac{15}{17}$ and $\beta = \sin^{-1}\frac{8}{17}$.
$$\cos\left(\sin^{-1}\frac{15}{17} - \sin^{-1}\frac{8}{17}\right) = \cos(\alpha - \beta) = \cos\alpha\cos\beta + \sin\alpha\sin\beta = \frac{8}{17}\cdot\frac{15}{17} + \frac{15}{17}\cdot\frac{8}{17} = \frac{240}{289}.$$

**74** Let $\alpha = \sin^{-1}\frac{4}{5}$. $\cos\left(2\sin^{-1}\frac{4}{5}\right) = \cos 2\alpha = \cos^2\alpha - \sin^2\alpha = \left(\frac{3}{5}\right)^2 - \left(\frac{4}{5}\right)^2 = -\frac{7}{25}$.

**75** Let $\alpha = \tan^{-1} 7$. $\sin(2\tan^{-1} 7) = \sin 2\alpha = 2\sin\alpha\cos\alpha = 2\left(\frac{7}{\sqrt{50}}\right)\left(\frac{1}{\sqrt{50}}\right) = \frac{14}{50} = \frac{7}{25}$.

**76** Let $\alpha = \sin^{-1}\frac{4}{5}$. $\tan\left(\frac{1}{2}\sin^{-1}\frac{4}{5}\right) = \tan\frac{1}{2}\alpha = \frac{1 - \cos\alpha}{\sin\alpha} = \frac{1 - \frac{3}{5}}{\frac{4}{5}} = \frac{\frac{2}{5}}{\frac{4}{5}} = \frac{2}{4} = \frac{1}{2}$.

**77** $y = \cos^{-1} 3x$  •  Horizontally compress $y = \cos^{-1} x$ by a factor of 3.

The domain changes from $[-1, 1]$ to $\left[-\frac{1}{3}, \frac{1}{3}\right]$.

*Figure 77*

*Figure 78*

**78** $y = 4\sin^{-1} x$  •  Vertically stretch $y = \sin^{-1} x$ by a factor of 4. The range changes from $\left[-\frac{\pi}{2}, \frac{\pi}{2}\right]$ to $[-2\pi, 2\pi]$.

**79** $y = 1 - \sin^{-1} x = -\sin^{-1} x + 1$  •  Reflect $y = \sin^{-1} x$ through the $x$-axis and shift it up 1 unit.

*Figure 79*

*Figure 80*

**80** If $\alpha = \cos^{-1} x$, then $\cos\alpha = x$, where $0 \le \alpha \le \pi$.

Hence, $y = \sin\left(\frac{1}{2}\cos^{-1} x\right) = \sin\frac{1}{2}\alpha = \sqrt{\frac{1 - \cos\alpha}{2}} = \sqrt{\frac{1 - x}{2}}$.

Thus, we have the graph of the half-parabola $y = \sqrt{\frac{1}{2}(1 - x)}$ on the interval $[-1, 1]$.

**81** $\cos(\alpha + \beta + \gamma) = \cos[(\alpha + \beta) + \gamma]$

$\qquad = \cos(\alpha + \beta)\cos\gamma - \sin(\alpha + \beta)\sin\gamma$

$\qquad = (\cos\alpha\cos\beta - \sin\alpha\sin\beta)\cos\gamma - (\sin\alpha\cos\beta + \cos\alpha\sin\beta)\sin\gamma$

$\qquad = \cos\alpha\cos\beta\cos\gamma - \sin\alpha\sin\beta\cos\gamma - \sin\alpha\cos\beta\sin\gamma - \cos\alpha\sin\beta\sin\gamma$

**82** (a) $t = -\frac{\pi}{2b} \Rightarrow F = A\left[\cos\left(-\frac{\pi}{2}\right) - a\cos\left(-\frac{3\pi}{2}\right)\right] = A(0 - a\cdot 0) = 0$

$\qquad\qquad\qquad\qquad\qquad t = \frac{\pi}{2b} \Rightarrow F = A\left(\cos\frac{\pi}{2} - a\cos\frac{3\pi}{2}\right) = A(0 - a\cdot 0) = 0$

(b) $a = \frac{1}{3} \Rightarrow \sin 3bt = \sin bt \Rightarrow \sin 3bt - \sin bt = 0 \Rightarrow$ [S2] $2\cos\dfrac{3bt + bt}{2}\sin\dfrac{3bt - bt}{2} = 0 \Rightarrow$

$\cos 2bt \sin bt = 0 \Rightarrow \cos 2bt = 0$ or $\sin bt = 0 \Rightarrow 2bt = \frac{\pi}{2} + \pi n$ or $bt = \pi n \Rightarrow$

$\qquad\qquad t = \frac{\pi}{4b} + \frac{\pi}{2b}n$ or $t = \frac{\pi}{b}n$. Since $-\frac{\pi}{2b} < t < \frac{\pi}{2b}$, $t = \pm\frac{\pi}{4b}, 0$.

(c) Using the values from part (b), $t = 0 \Rightarrow F = A\left(\cos 0 - \frac{1}{3}\cos 0\right) = A\left(1 - \frac{1}{3}\right) = \frac{2}{3}A$.

$t = \pm\frac{\pi}{4b} \Rightarrow F = A\left[\cos\left(\pm\frac{\pi}{4}\right) - \frac{1}{3}\cos\left(\pm\frac{3\pi}{4}\right)\right] = A\left(\frac{\sqrt{2}}{2} + \frac{\sqrt{2}}{6}\right) = \frac{4\sqrt{2}}{6}A = \frac{2}{3}\sqrt{2}A$.

$\qquad\qquad$ The second value is $\sqrt{2}$ times the first, hence $\frac{2}{3}\sqrt{2}A$ is the maximum force.

**83** $\cos x - \cos 2x + \cos 3x = 0 \Rightarrow (\cos x + \cos 3x) - \cos 2x \Rightarrow$

[S3] $2\cos\dfrac{x + 3x}{2}\cos\dfrac{x - 3x}{2} - \cos 2x = 0 \Rightarrow 2\cos 2x\cos x - \cos 2x = 0 \Rightarrow$

$\cos 2x(2\cos x - 1) = 0 \Rightarrow \cos 2x = 0$ or $\cos x = \frac{1}{2} \Rightarrow 2x = \frac{\pi}{2} + \pi n$ (or $x = \frac{\pi}{4} + \frac{\pi}{2}n$) or

$\qquad\qquad x = \frac{\pi}{3} + 2\pi n,\ \frac{5\pi}{3} + 2\pi n$. In the figure, for $[0, 2\pi]$, $x = \frac{\pi}{4}, \frac{3\pi}{4}, \frac{5\pi}{4}, \frac{7\pi}{4}, \frac{\pi}{3}, \frac{5\pi}{3}$.

**84** (a) Bisect $\theta$ to form two right triangles. $\tan\frac{1}{2}\theta = \dfrac{\frac{1}{2}x}{d} \Rightarrow x = 2d\tan\frac{1}{2}\theta$.

(b) Using part (a) with $x = 0.5$ ft and $\theta = 0.0005$ radian, we have $d = \dfrac{x}{2\tan\frac{1}{2}\theta} \approx 1000$ ft, so $d \le 1000$ ft.

**85** (a) Bisect $\theta$ to form two right triangles.

$\qquad\qquad \cos\frac{1}{2}\theta = \dfrac{r}{d + r} \Rightarrow d + r = \dfrac{r}{\cos\frac{1}{2}\theta} \Rightarrow d = r\sec\frac{1}{2}\theta - r = r\left(\sec\frac{1}{2}\theta - 1\right).$

(b) $d = 300$ and $r = 4000 \Rightarrow \cos\frac{1}{2}\theta = \dfrac{r}{d + r} = \dfrac{4000}{4300} \Rightarrow \frac{1}{2}\theta \approx 21.5° \Rightarrow \theta \approx 43°$.

**86** (a) $N = \dfrac{h}{w}$ and $\tan\theta = N \Rightarrow \tan\theta = \dfrac{h}{w} \bullet \tan\theta = \dfrac{h}{w} = \dfrac{400}{80} = 5 \Rightarrow \theta = \tan^{-1}5 \approx 78.7°$

(b) $\tan\theta = \dfrac{h}{w} = \dfrac{55}{30} = \dfrac{11}{6} \Rightarrow \theta = \tan^{-1}\dfrac{11}{6} \approx 61.4°$

## Chapter 6 Discussion Exercises

**1** $\dfrac{\tan x}{1 - \cot x} + \dfrac{\cot x}{1 - \tan x} = \dfrac{\frac{\sin x}{\cos x}}{1 - \frac{\cos x}{\sin x}} + \dfrac{\frac{\cos x}{\sin x}}{1 - \frac{\sin x}{\cos x}} = \dfrac{\sin^2 x}{\cos x(\sin x - \cos x)} + \dfrac{\cos^2 x}{\sin x(\cos x - \sin x)}$

$\qquad\qquad = \dfrac{\sin^2 x}{\cos x(\sin x - \cos x)} - \dfrac{\cos^2 x}{\sin x(\sin x - \cos x)} = \dfrac{\sin^3 x - \cos^3 x}{\cos x\sin x(\sin x - \cos x)}$

$\qquad\qquad = \dfrac{(\sin x - \cos x)(\sin^2 x + \sin x\cos x + \cos^2 x)}{\cos x\sin x(\sin x - \cos x)} = \dfrac{1 + \sin x\cos x}{\cos x\sin x}$

$\qquad\qquad = \dfrac{1}{\cos x\sin x} + 1 = 1 + \sec x\csc x$

**2** $\sqrt{a^2 - x^2} = \begin{cases} a\cos\theta & \text{if } 0 \le \theta \le \pi/2 \text{ or } 3\pi/2 \le \theta < 2\pi \\ -a\cos\theta & \text{if } \pi/2 < \theta < 3\pi/2 \end{cases}$

**3** *Note:* Graphing on a TI-83/4 doesn't really help to solve this problem.

$3\cos 45x + 4\sin 45x = 5 \Rightarrow$ {by Example 7 in Section 6.3} $5\cos\left(45x - \tan^{-1}\frac{4}{3}\right) = 5 \Rightarrow$

$\cos\left(45x - \tan^{-1}\frac{4}{3}\right) = 1 \Rightarrow 45x - \tan^{-1}\frac{4}{3} = 2\pi n \Rightarrow 45x = 2\pi n + \tan^{-1}\frac{4}{3} \Rightarrow x = \dfrac{2\pi n + \tan^{-1}\frac{4}{3}}{45}.$

$n = 0, 1, \ldots, 44$ will yield $x$ values in $[0, 2\pi)$.

*Note:* After using Example 7, you might notice that this is a function with period $2\pi/45$, and it will obtain 45 maximums on an interval of length $2\pi$. The largest value of $x$ is approximately 6.164 {when $n = 44$}.

**4** The difference quotient for the sine function appears to be the cosine function.

$\dfrac{f(x+h) - f(x)}{h} = \dfrac{\sin(x+h) - \sin x}{h} = \dfrac{\sin x \cos h + \cos x \sin h - \sin x}{h} = \sin x\left(\dfrac{\cos h - 1}{h}\right) + \cos x\left(\dfrac{\sin h}{h}\right)$

The figure shows the graph of $y = \dfrac{\sin(x+h) - \sin x}{h}$ for $h = 0.5, 0.1$, and $0.001$ on the viewing rectangle $[0, 2\pi, \pi/2]$ by $[-1, 1]$.

**5** Let $\alpha = \tan^{-1}\left(\frac{1}{239}\right)$ and $\theta = \tan^{-1}\left(\frac{1}{5}\right)$. $\frac{\pi}{4} = 4\theta - \alpha \Rightarrow \frac{\pi}{4} + \alpha = 4\theta$. Both sides are acute angles, and we will show that the tangent of each side is equal to the same value, hence proving the identity.

$LS = \tan\left(\frac{\pi}{4} + \alpha\right) = \dfrac{\tan\frac{\pi}{4} + \tan\alpha}{1 - \tan\frac{\pi}{4}\tan\alpha} = \dfrac{1 + \frac{1}{239}}{1 - 1 \cdot \frac{1}{239}} = \dfrac{\frac{240}{239}}{\frac{238}{239}} = \dfrac{240}{238} = \dfrac{120}{119}.$

$RS = \tan 4\theta = \dfrac{2\tan 2\theta}{1 - \tan^2(2\theta)} = \dfrac{2 \cdot \dfrac{2\tan\theta}{1 - \tan^2\theta}}{1 - \left(\dfrac{2\tan\theta}{1 - \tan^2\theta}\right)^2} = \dfrac{2 \cdot \dfrac{\frac{2}{5}}{1 - \frac{1}{25}}}{1 - \left(\dfrac{\frac{2}{5}}{1 - \frac{1}{25}}\right)^2} = \dfrac{\frac{4}{5} \cdot \frac{24}{25}}{1 - \frac{4}{25} \cdot \frac{24 \cdot 24}{25 \cdot 25}} = \dfrac{\frac{5}{6}}{\frac{119}{144}} = \dfrac{120}{119}.$

Similarly, for the second relationship, we could write $\frac{\pi}{4} = \alpha + \beta + \gamma$ and show that $\tan\left(\frac{\pi}{4} - \alpha\right) = \tan(\beta + \gamma) = \frac{1}{3}$.

For the third relationship, write $\pi - \tan^{-1}1 = \tan^{-1}2 + \tan^{-1}3 \Rightarrow \tan\left(\pi - \frac{\pi}{4}\right) = \tan(\alpha + \beta) \Rightarrow$

$\tan\frac{3\pi}{4} = \dfrac{\tan\alpha + \tan\beta}{1 - \tan\alpha\tan\beta} \Rightarrow -1 = \dfrac{2 + 3}{1 - 2 \cdot 3}$ {true}.

**6** (a) The **inverse sawtooth function**, denoted by $\text{saw}^{-1}$ or arcsaw, is defined by $y = \text{saw}^{-1}x$ iff $x = \text{saw}\,y$ for $-2 \le x \le 2$ and $-1 \le y \le 1$.

(b) $\text{arcsaw}(1.7) = 0.85$ since $\text{saw}(0.85) = 1.7$. $\text{arcsaw}(-0.8) = -0.4$ since $\text{saw}(-0.4) = -0.8$

(c) $\text{saw}(\text{saw}^{-1}x) = \text{saw}(\text{arcsaw}\,x) = x$ if $-2 \le x \le 2$.

$\text{saw}^{-1}(\text{saw}\,y) = \text{arcsaw}(\text{saw}\,y) = y$ if $-1 \le y \le 1$

(d)

**7** $\dfrac{\sin^4(x/2) - \cos^4(x/2)}{\sin^4(x/2)\cos^4(x/2)} = \dfrac{\left[\sin^2(x/2)\right]^2 - \left[\cos^2(x/2)\right]^2}{\left[\sin^2(x/2)\right]^2 \left[\cos^2(x/2)\right]^2} = \dfrac{\dfrac{(1-\cos x)^2}{4} - \dfrac{(1+\cos x)^2}{4}}{\dfrac{(1-\cos x)^2}{4} \cdot \dfrac{(1+\cos x)^2}{4}}$

$$= \dfrac{\dfrac{1 - 2\cos x + \cos^2 x - 1 - 2\cos x - \cos^2 x}{4}}{\dfrac{(1-\cos^2 x)^2}{16}} = \dfrac{-4\cos x \cdot 4}{(\sin^2 x)^2} = \dfrac{-16\cos x}{\sin^4 x}$$

## Chapter 6 Test

**1** $\text{LS} = \left(\dfrac{1}{\sin x} - \dfrac{1}{\tan x}\right)^{-1} = (\csc x - \cot x)^{-1} = \dfrac{1}{\csc x - \cot x} = \dfrac{1}{\csc x - \cot x} \cdot \dfrac{\csc x + \cot x}{\csc x + \cot x}$

$\qquad = \dfrac{\csc x + \cot x}{\csc^2 x - \cot^2 x} = \dfrac{\csc x + \cot x}{1} = \csc x + \cot x = \text{RS}$

**2** $\text{LS} = \dfrac{\tan x}{1 + \sec x} + \dfrac{1 + \cos x}{\sin x} = \dfrac{\dfrac{\sin x}{\cos x}}{1 + \dfrac{1}{\cos x}} + \dfrac{1 + \cos x}{\sin x} = \dfrac{\dfrac{\sin x}{\cos x}}{\dfrac{\cos x + 1}{\cos x}} + \dfrac{1 + \cos x}{\sin x}$

$\qquad = \dfrac{\sin x}{1 + \cos x} + \dfrac{1 + \cos x}{\sin x} = \dfrac{\sin^2 x + (1 + \cos x)^2}{(1 + \cos x)\sin x} = \dfrac{\sin^2 x + 1 + 2\cos x + \cos^2 x}{(1 + \cos x)\sin x}$

$\qquad = \dfrac{2 + 2\cos x}{(1 + \cos x)\sin x} = \dfrac{2(1 + \cos x)}{(1 + \cos x)\sin x} = \dfrac{2}{\sin x} = 2\csc x = \text{RS}$

**3** $\sec^2 x = \tan^2 x + 1 \ \Rightarrow \ \sec^2 x - 1 = \tan^2 x \ \Rightarrow \ \tan x = \pm\sqrt{\sec^2 x - 1}$. Hence, choose any $x$ such that

$\tan x < 0$. Using $x = \frac{3\pi}{4}$, $\text{LS} = \tan\frac{3\pi}{4} = -1$. $\text{RS} = \sqrt{(-\sqrt{2})^2 - 1} = 1$. Since $-1 \neq 1$, $\text{LS} \neq \text{RS}$.

**4** $\dfrac{\sqrt{a^2 - x^2}}{a^2 x^2} = \dfrac{\sqrt{a^2 - a^2\sin^2\theta}}{a^2 \cdot a^2\sin^2\theta} = \dfrac{\sqrt{a^2(1 - \sin^2\theta)}}{a^4\sin^2\theta} = \dfrac{\sqrt{a^2\cos^2\theta}}{a^4\sin^2\theta} = \dfrac{|a|\,|\cos\theta|}{a^4\sin^2\theta} = \dfrac{a\cos\theta}{a^4\sin^2\theta}$,

$\qquad$ since $\cos\theta > 0$ if $-\frac{\pi}{2} < \theta < \frac{\pi}{2}$ and $a > 0$. This simplifies to $\dfrac{\cos\theta}{a^3\sin\theta\sin\theta} = \dfrac{1}{a^3}\cot\theta\csc\theta$.

**5** Since the secant function equals $-\sqrt{2}$ when $x = \frac{3\pi}{4}$ and $x = \frac{5\pi}{4}$ for $0 \leq x < 2\pi$, we have $\sec\frac{\pi}{4}x = -\sqrt{2} \ \Rightarrow$

$\qquad \frac{\pi}{4}x = \frac{3\pi}{4} + 2\pi n$ or $\frac{5\pi}{4} + 2\pi n \ \Rightarrow \ x = 3 + 8n$ or $5 + 8n$, where $n$ is an integer.

**6** The highest points on the cosine have $y = 1$. $\cos(4x + 3) = 1 \ \Rightarrow \ 4x + 3 = 2\pi n \ \Rightarrow \ 4x = 2\pi n - 3 \ \Rightarrow$

$\qquad x = \frac{1}{4}(2\pi n - 3)$, where $n$ is an integer.

**7** $f(x) = 0 \ \Rightarrow \ \sec\left(2x + \frac{\pi}{3}\right) = 2 \ \Rightarrow \ 2x + \frac{\pi}{3} = -\frac{\pi}{3} + 2\pi n$ or $\frac{\pi}{3} + 2\pi n \ \Rightarrow \ 2x = -\frac{2\pi}{3} + 2\pi n$ or $2\pi n \ \Rightarrow$

$\qquad x = -\frac{\pi}{3} + \pi n$ or $\pi n$, where $n$ is an integer.

**8** $-\cos x + 1 = 2\sin^2 x \ \Rightarrow \ -\cos x + 1 = 2(1 - \cos^2 x) \ \Rightarrow \ -\cos x + 1 = 2 - 2\cos^2 x \ \Rightarrow$

$\qquad 2\cos^2 x - \cos x - 1 = 0 \ \Rightarrow \ (2\cos x + 1)(\cos x - 1) = 0 \ \Rightarrow \ \cos x = -\frac{1}{2}, 1 \ \Rightarrow$

$\qquad x = \frac{2\pi}{3} + 2\pi n, \frac{4\pi}{3} + 2\pi n, 2\pi n$

**9** $\cos\frac{\pi}{12} = \cos\left(\frac{\pi}{3} - \frac{\pi}{4}\right) = \cos\frac{\pi}{3}\cos\frac{\pi}{4} + \sin\frac{\pi}{3}\sin\frac{\pi}{4} = \frac{1}{2}\frac{\sqrt{2}}{2} + \frac{\sqrt{3}}{2}\frac{\sqrt{2}}{2} = \frac{1}{4}\left(\sqrt{2} + \sqrt{6}\right)$

**10** Since $\sin\alpha = -\frac{12}{13} < 0$ and $\tan\alpha < 0$, $\alpha$ is in QIV, and $\cos\alpha = \sqrt{1 - (-\frac{12}{13})^2} = \frac{5}{13}$.

$\qquad \sin\left(\alpha + \frac{\pi}{6}\right) = \sin\alpha\cos\frac{\pi}{6} + \cos\alpha\sin\frac{\pi}{6} = -\frac{12}{13}\frac{\sqrt{3}}{2} + \frac{5}{13}\frac{1}{2} = \frac{1}{26}\left(5 - 12\sqrt{3}\right)$.

**11** $\sin\alpha = \frac{3}{5}$ and $\alpha$ in QII $\Rightarrow$ $\cos\alpha = -\sqrt{1-\left(\frac{3}{5}\right)^2} = -\frac{4}{5}$.

$\cos\beta = -\frac{8}{17}$ and $\beta$ in QII $\Rightarrow$ $\sin\beta = \sqrt{1-\left(-\frac{8}{17}\right)^2} = \frac{15}{17}$.

$\tan(\alpha+\beta) = \dfrac{\tan\alpha+\tan\beta}{1-\tan\alpha\tan\beta} = \dfrac{-\frac{3}{4}+\left(-\frac{15}{8}\right)}{1-\left(-\frac{3}{4}\right)\left(-\frac{15}{8}\right)} \cdot \dfrac{32}{32} = \dfrac{-24-60}{32-45} = \dfrac{84}{13}$.

**12** $\cos\left(x+\frac{5\pi}{2}\right) = \cos x\cos\frac{5\pi}{2} - \sin x\sin\frac{5\pi}{2} = (\cos x)(0) - (\sin x)(1) = -\sin x$

**13** $\sin\pi x\cos\frac{\pi}{2}x = \sin\frac{\pi}{2}x\cos\pi x + 1$ $\Rightarrow$ $\sin\pi x\cos\frac{\pi}{2}x - \sin\frac{\pi}{2}x\cos\pi x = 1$ $\Rightarrow$ $\sin\left(\pi x - \frac{\pi}{2}x\right) = 1$ $\Rightarrow$

$\sin\frac{\pi}{2}x = 1$ $\Rightarrow$ $\frac{\pi}{2}x = \frac{\pi}{2} + 2\pi n$ $\Rightarrow$ $x = 1 + 4n$. In $[0,10)$, $x = 1, 5, 9$.

**14** $\sin 2\theta = 2\sin\theta\cos\theta = 2\left(-\frac{5}{13}\right)\left(\frac{12}{13}\right) = -\frac{120}{169}$.

$\cos 2\theta = \cos^2\theta - \sin^2\theta = \left(\frac{12}{13}\right)^2 - \left(-\frac{5}{13}\right)^2 = \frac{144}{169} - \frac{25}{169} = \frac{119}{169}$. $\tan 2\theta = \dfrac{\sin 2\theta}{\cos 2\theta} = \dfrac{-120/169}{119/169} = -\dfrac{120}{119}$.

**15** $\cos\theta = \frac{3}{5}$ and $\frac{\theta}{2}$ is in QIV. Hence, $\sin\frac{\theta}{2} < 0$ and $\cos\frac{\theta}{2} > 0$.

$\sin\dfrac{\theta}{2} = -\sqrt{\dfrac{1-\cos\theta}{2}} = -\sqrt{\dfrac{1-\frac{3}{5}}{2}} = -\sqrt{\dfrac{\frac{2}{5}}{2}} = -\sqrt{\dfrac{1}{5}} = -\dfrac{1}{\sqrt{5}}$.

$\cos\dfrac{\theta}{2} = \sqrt{\dfrac{1+\cos\theta}{2}} = \sqrt{\dfrac{1+\frac{3}{5}}{2}} = \sqrt{\dfrac{\frac{8}{5}}{2}} = \sqrt{\dfrac{4}{5}} = \dfrac{2}{\sqrt{5}}$. $\tan\dfrac{\theta}{2} = \dfrac{\sin\frac{\theta}{2}}{\cos\frac{\theta}{2}} = \dfrac{-1/\sqrt{5}}{2/\sqrt{5}} = -\dfrac{1}{2}$.

**16** LS $= \sin 3x = \sin(2x + x)$

$= \sin 2x\cos x + \cos 2x\sin x$

$= (2\sin x\cos x)\cos x + (2\cos^2 x - 1)\sin x$

$= \sin x[2\cos^2 x + (2\cos^2 x - 1)] = \sin x(4\cos^2 x - 1) =$ RS

**17** $\cos 2x + 3\cos x = -2$ $\Rightarrow$ $(2\cos^2 x - 1) + 3\cos x + 2 = 0$ $\Rightarrow$ $2\cos^2 x + 3\cos x + 1 = 0$ $\Rightarrow$

$(2\cos x + 1)(\cos x + 1) = 0$ $\Rightarrow$ $\cos x = -\frac{1}{2}$ or $\cos x = -1$ $\Rightarrow$ $x = \frac{2\pi}{3}, \frac{4\pi}{3}, \pi$

**18** Use product-to-sum formula 3 [P3]. $4\cos x\cos 7x = 4\cdot\frac{1}{2}[\cos(x+7x) + \cos(x-7x)]$

$= 2[\cos(8x) + \cos(-6x)]$

$= 2[\cos(8x) + \cos(6x)] = 2\cos 8x + 2\cos 6x$

**19** Use sum-to-product formula 4 [S4]. $\cos x - \cos 7x = -2\sin\dfrac{x+7x}{2}\sin\dfrac{x-7x}{2}$

$= -2\sin\dfrac{8x}{2}\sin\dfrac{-6x}{2}$

$= -2\sin 4x\sin(-3x) = 2\sin 4x\sin 3x$

**20** LS $= \dfrac{\cos 8x + \cos 4x}{\sin 8x - \sin 4x} = \dfrac{2\cos\dfrac{8x+4x}{2}\cos\dfrac{8x-4x}{2}\ \text{[S3]}}{2\cos\dfrac{8x+4x}{2}\sin\dfrac{8x-4x}{2}\ \text{[S2]}} = \dfrac{\cos\dfrac{4x}{2}}{\sin\dfrac{4x}{2}} = \dfrac{\cos 2x}{\sin 2x} = \cot 2x =$ RS

**21** $\sin 7x + \sin x = 0$ $\Rightarrow$ [S1] $2\sin\dfrac{7x+x}{2}\cos\dfrac{7x-x}{2} = 0$ $\Rightarrow$ $2\sin 4x\cos 3x = 0$ $\Rightarrow$

$\sin 4x = 0$ or $\cos 3x = 0$ $\Rightarrow$ $4x = \pi n$ or $3x = \frac{\pi}{2} + \pi n$ $\Rightarrow$ $x = \frac{\pi}{4}n$ or $x = \frac{\pi}{6} + \frac{\pi}{3}n$

**22** $\arcsin\left(\sin\frac{11\pi}{6}\right) = \arcsin\left(-\frac{1}{2}\right) = -\frac{\pi}{6}$

**23** The domain of the arctan function is $\mathbb{R}$ and the range of the arctan function is $-\frac{\pi}{2} < \theta < \frac{\pi}{2}$,

so the property $\arctan(\tan\theta) = \theta$ is valid for $-\frac{\pi}{2} < \theta < \frac{\pi}{2}$.

**24** Let $\alpha = \arccos\frac{7}{25}$. $\cos\left(2\arccos\frac{7}{25}\right) = \cos 2\alpha = 2\cos^2\alpha - 1 = 2\left(\frac{7}{25}\right)^2 - 1 = -\frac{527}{625}$.

**25** Let $\alpha = \arccos\dfrac{a}{c}$. $\cos\left(2\arccos\dfrac{a}{c}\right) = \cos 2\alpha = 2\cos^2\alpha - 1 = 2\left(\dfrac{a}{c}\right)^2 - 1$, or $\dfrac{2a^2 - c^2}{c^2}$.

**26** As $x \to 2$, $\dfrac{x^3 - 7}{2} \to \dfrac{1}{2}$, so $\sin^{-1}\left(\dfrac{x^3 - 7}{2}\right) \to \dfrac{\pi}{6}$.

**27** $y = 3\cos^{-1}\frac{2}{5}x \;\Rightarrow\; \frac{1}{3}y = \cos^{-1}\frac{2}{5}x \;\Rightarrow\; \cos\frac{1}{3}y = \frac{2}{5}x \;\Rightarrow\; x = \frac{5}{2}\cos\frac{1}{3}y$. *Note:* No domain restrictions are asked for in this question, but the function $y = 3\cos^{-1}\frac{2}{5}x$ has domain $-2.5 \le x \le 2.5$.

**28** $\cos^2 x + 4\cos x + 1 = 0 \;\Rightarrow\; \cos x = \dfrac{-4 \pm \sqrt{16 - 4}}{2} = \dfrac{-4 \pm 2\sqrt{3}}{2} = -2 \pm \sqrt{3} \;\Rightarrow\; x = \cos^{-1}(-2 \pm \sqrt{3})$. Reject $-2 - \sqrt{3}$ since it is not in $[-1, 1]$. $x = \cos^{-1}(-2 + \sqrt{3}) \approx 1.84$ and $2\pi - \cos^{-1}(-2 + \sqrt{3}) \approx 4.44$ are the exact and approximate solutions in $[0, 2\pi)$.

## 7.1 Exercises

**1**   $\beta = 180° - \alpha - \gamma = 180° - 52° - 65° = 63°.$

$\dfrac{b}{\sin\beta} = \dfrac{a}{\sin\alpha} \;\Rightarrow\; b = \dfrac{a\sin\beta}{\sin\alpha} = \dfrac{23.7\sin 63°}{\sin 52°} \approx 26.8. \quad \dfrac{c}{\sin\gamma} = \dfrac{a}{\sin\alpha} \;\Rightarrow\; c = \dfrac{a\sin\gamma}{\sin\alpha} = \dfrac{23.7\sin 65°}{\sin 52°} \approx 27.3.$

**2**   $\alpha = 180° - \beta - \gamma = 180° - 25° - 41° = 114°.$

$\dfrac{a}{\sin\alpha} = \dfrac{b}{\sin\beta} \;\Rightarrow\; a = \dfrac{b\sin\alpha}{\sin\beta} = \dfrac{170\sin 114°}{\sin 25°} \approx 367,\ \text{or } 370 \text{ to 2 significant figures.}$

$\dfrac{c}{\sin\gamma} = \dfrac{b}{\sin\beta} \;\Rightarrow\; c = \dfrac{b\sin\gamma}{\sin\beta} = \dfrac{170\sin 41°}{\sin 25°} \approx 264,\ \text{or } 260.$

**3**   $\gamma = 180° - \alpha - \beta = 180° - 27°40' - 52°10' = 100°10'.$

$\dfrac{b}{\sin\beta} = \dfrac{a}{\sin\alpha} \;\Rightarrow\; b = \dfrac{a\sin\beta}{\sin\alpha} = \dfrac{32.4\sin 52°10'}{\sin 27°40'} \approx 55.1.$

$\dfrac{c}{\sin\gamma} = \dfrac{a}{\sin\alpha} \;\Rightarrow\; c = \dfrac{a\sin\gamma}{\sin\alpha} = \dfrac{32.4\sin 100°10'}{\sin 27°40'} \approx 68.7.$

**4**   $\alpha = 180° - \beta - \gamma = 180° - 50°50' - 70°30' = 58°40'.$

$\dfrac{a}{\sin\alpha} = \dfrac{c}{\sin\gamma} \;\Rightarrow\; a = \dfrac{c\sin\alpha}{\sin\gamma} = \dfrac{537\sin 58°40'}{\sin 70°30'} \approx 487.$

$\dfrac{b}{\sin\beta} = \dfrac{c}{\sin\gamma} \;\Rightarrow\; b = \dfrac{c\sin\beta}{\sin\gamma} = \dfrac{537\sin 50°50'}{\sin 70°30'} \approx 442.$

**5**   $\beta = 180° - \alpha - \gamma = 180° - 42°10' - 61°20' = 76°30'.$

$\dfrac{a}{\sin\alpha} = \dfrac{b}{\sin\beta} \;\Rightarrow\; a = \dfrac{b\sin\alpha}{\sin\beta} = \dfrac{19.7\sin 42°10'}{\sin 76°30'} \approx 13.6.$

$\dfrac{c}{\sin\gamma} = \dfrac{b}{\sin\beta} \;\Rightarrow\; c = \dfrac{b\sin\gamma}{\sin\beta} = \dfrac{19.7\sin 61°20'}{\sin 76°30'} \approx 17.8.$

**6**   $\beta = 180° - \alpha - \gamma = 180° - 103.45° - 27.19° = 49.36°.$

$\dfrac{a}{\sin\alpha} = \dfrac{b}{\sin\beta} \;\Rightarrow\; a = \dfrac{b\sin\alpha}{\sin\beta} = \dfrac{38.84\sin 103.45°}{\sin 49.36°} \approx 49.78.$

$\dfrac{c}{\sin\gamma} = \dfrac{b}{\sin\beta} \;\Rightarrow\; c = \dfrac{b\sin\gamma}{\sin\beta} = \dfrac{38.84\sin 27.19°}{\sin 49.36°} \approx 23.39.$

**7**   $\dfrac{\sin\beta}{b} = \dfrac{\sin\gamma}{c} \;\Rightarrow\; \beta = \sin^{-1}\left(\dfrac{b\sin\gamma}{c}\right) = \sin^{-1}\left(\dfrac{12\sin 81°}{11}\right) \approx \sin^{-1}(1.0775).$

Since 1.0775 is not in the domain of the inverse sine function, which is $[-1, 1]$, *no triangle exists.*

**8**   $\dfrac{\sin\gamma}{c} = \dfrac{\sin\alpha}{a} \;\Rightarrow\; \gamma = \sin^{-1}\left(\dfrac{c\sin\alpha}{a}\right) = \sin^{-1}\left(\dfrac{75\sin 27°}{34}\right) \approx \sin^{-1}(1.0014).$

Since 1.0014 is not in the domain of the inverse sine function, which is $[-1, 1]$, *no triangle exists.*

**9**   $\dfrac{\sin\alpha}{a} = \dfrac{\sin\gamma}{c} \;\Rightarrow\; \alpha = \sin^{-1}\left(\dfrac{a\sin\gamma}{c}\right) = \sin^{-1}\left(\dfrac{140\sin 53°20'}{115}\right) \approx \sin^{-1}(0.9765) \approx 77°30' \text{ or } 102°30'$

{rounded to the nearest 10 minutes}. When using the inverse sine function to solve for an angle, remember that there are always *two* values if $\theta \neq 90°$. The first angle is the one you obtain using your calculator, and the second is the reference angle for the first angle in the second quadrant. After obtaining these values, we need to check the sum of the angles. If this sum is less than $180°$, a triangle is formed. If this sum is greater than or equal to $180°$, no

**397**

triangle is formed. For this exercise, there are two triangles possible since in either case $\alpha + \gamma < 180°$.

$\beta = (180° - \gamma) - \alpha \approx (180° - 53°20') - (77°30' \text{ or } 102°30') = 49°10' \text{ or } 24°10'.$

$$\frac{b}{\sin \beta} = \frac{c}{\sin \gamma} \Rightarrow b = \frac{c \sin \beta}{\sin \gamma} \approx \frac{115 \sin(49°10' \text{ or } 24°10')}{\sin 53°20'} \approx 108 \text{ or } 58.7.$$

**10**   $\dfrac{\sin \gamma}{c} = \dfrac{\sin \alpha}{a} \Rightarrow \gamma = \sin^{-1}\left(\dfrac{c \sin \alpha}{a}\right) = \sin^{-1}\left(\dfrac{52.8 \sin 27°30'}{28.1}\right) \Rightarrow \gamma \approx \sin^{-1}(0.8676) \approx 60°10'$ or

119°50′ {rounded to the nearest 10 minutes}. There are two triangles possible since in either case $\alpha + \gamma < 180°$.

$\beta = (180° - \alpha) - \gamma \approx (180° - 27°30') - (60°10' \text{ or } 119°50') = 92°20' \text{ or } 32°40'.$

$$\frac{b}{\sin \beta} = \frac{a}{\sin \alpha} \Rightarrow b = \frac{a \sin \beta}{\sin \alpha} \approx \frac{28.1 \sin(92°20' \text{ or } 32°40')}{\sin 27°30'} \approx 60.8 \text{ or } 32.8.$$

**11**   $\dfrac{\sin \alpha}{a} = \dfrac{\sin \gamma}{c} \Rightarrow \alpha = \sin^{-1}\left(\dfrac{a \sin \gamma}{c}\right) = \sin^{-1}\left(\dfrac{131.08 \sin 47.74°}{97.84}\right) \approx \sin^{-1}(0.9915) \approx 82.54° \text{ or } 97.46°.$

There are two triangles possible since in either case $\alpha + \gamma < 180°$.

$\beta = (180° - \gamma) - \alpha \approx (180° - 47.74°) - (82.54° \text{ or } 97.46°) = 49.72° \text{ or } 34.80°.$

$$\frac{b}{\sin \beta} = \frac{c}{\sin \gamma} \Rightarrow b = \frac{c \sin \beta}{\sin \gamma} \approx \frac{97.84 \sin(49.72° \text{ or } 34.80°)}{\sin 47.74°} \approx 100.85 \text{ or } 75.45.$$

**12**   $\dfrac{\sin \beta}{b} = \dfrac{\sin \alpha}{a} \Rightarrow \beta = \sin^{-1}\left(\dfrac{b \sin \alpha}{a}\right) = \sin^{-1}\left(\dfrac{6.12 \sin 42.17°}{5.01}\right) \approx \sin^{-1}(0.8201) \approx 55.09° \text{ or } 124.91°.$

There are two triangles possible since in either case $\alpha + \beta < 180°$.

$\gamma = (180° - \alpha) - \beta \approx (180° - 42.17°) - (55.09° \text{ or } 124.91°) = 82.74° \text{ or } 12.92°.$

$$\frac{c}{\sin \gamma} = \frac{a}{\sin \alpha} \Rightarrow c = \frac{a \sin \gamma}{\sin \alpha} \approx \frac{5.01 \sin(82.74° \text{ or } 12.92°)}{\sin 42.17°} \approx 7.40 \text{ or } 1.67.$$

**13**   $\dfrac{\sin \beta}{b} = \dfrac{\sin \alpha}{a} \Rightarrow \beta = \sin^{-1}\left(\dfrac{b \sin \alpha}{a}\right) = \sin^{-1}\left(\dfrac{77.7 \sin 47°20'}{86.3}\right) \approx \sin^{-1}(0.6620) \approx 41°30' \text{ or } 138°30'$

{rounded to the nearest 10 minutes}. Reject 138°30′ because then $\alpha + \beta \geq 180°$.

$\gamma = 180° - \alpha - \beta \approx 180° - 47°20' - 41°30' = 91°10'.$

$$\frac{c}{\sin \gamma} = \frac{a}{\sin \alpha} \Rightarrow c = \frac{a \sin \gamma}{\sin \alpha} \approx \frac{86.3 \sin 91°10'}{\sin 47°20'} \approx 117.3.$$

**14**   $\dfrac{\sin \gamma}{c} = \dfrac{\sin \beta}{b} \Rightarrow \gamma = \sin^{-1}\left(\dfrac{c \sin \beta}{b}\right) = \sin^{-1}\left(\dfrac{195 \sin 113°10'}{248}\right) \approx \sin^{-1}(0.7229) \approx 46°20' \text{ or } 133°40'$

{rounded to the nearest 10 minutes}. Reject 133°40′ because then $\beta + \gamma \geq 180°$.

$\alpha = 180° - \beta - \gamma \approx 180° - 113°10' - 46°20' = 20°30'.$

$$\frac{a}{\sin \alpha} = \frac{b}{\sin \beta} \Rightarrow a = \frac{b \sin \alpha}{\sin \beta} \approx \frac{248 \sin 20°30'}{\sin 113°10'} \approx 94.5.$$

**15**   $\dfrac{\sin \gamma}{c} = \dfrac{\sin \beta}{b} \Rightarrow \gamma = \sin^{-1}\left(\dfrac{c \sin \beta}{b}\right) = \sin^{-1}\left(\dfrac{0.178 \sin 121.624°}{0.283}\right) \approx \sin^{-1}(0.5356) \approx 32.383° \text{ or } 147.617°.$

Reject 147.617° because then $\beta + \gamma \geq 180°$. $\alpha = 180° - \beta - \gamma \approx 180° - 121.624° - 32.383° = 25.993°.$

$$\frac{a}{\sin \alpha} = \frac{b}{\sin \beta} \Rightarrow a = \frac{b \sin \alpha}{\sin \beta} \approx \frac{0.283 \sin 25.993°}{\sin 121.624°} \approx 0.146.$$

**16**   $\dfrac{\sin \alpha}{a} = \dfrac{\sin \gamma}{c} \Rightarrow \alpha = \sin^{-1}\left(\dfrac{a \sin \gamma}{c}\right) = \sin^{-1}\left(\dfrac{17.31 \sin 73.01°}{20.24}\right) \Rightarrow \alpha \approx \sin^{-1}(0.8179) \approx 54.88°$ or

125.12°. Reject 125.12° because then $\alpha + \gamma \geq 180°$. $\beta = 180° - \gamma - \alpha \approx 180° - 73.01° - 54.88° = 52.11°.$

$$\frac{b}{\sin \beta} = \frac{c}{\sin \gamma} \Rightarrow b = \frac{c \sin \beta}{\sin \gamma} \approx \frac{20.24 \sin 52.11°}{\sin 73.01°} \approx 16.70.$$

**17**   $\angle ABC = 180° - 54°10' - 63°20' = 62°30'.$   $\dfrac{\overline{AB}}{\sin 54°10'} = \dfrac{240}{\sin 62°30'} \Rightarrow \overline{AB} \approx 219.36 \text{ yd}$

**18** $\dfrac{\sin \angle ABC}{375} = \dfrac{\sin 49°30'}{530} \;\Rightarrow\; \angle ABC \approx 32°30'.$

$\angle ACB \approx 180° - 49°30' - 32°30' = 98°.$

$\dfrac{\overline{AB}}{\sin 98°} = \dfrac{530}{\sin 49°30'} \;\Rightarrow\; \overline{AB} \approx 690 \text{ yards.}$

**19** (a) $\angle ABP = 180° - 65° = 115°.$ $\angle APB = 180° - 21° - 115° = 44°.$

$\dfrac{\overline{AP}}{\sin 115°} = \dfrac{1.2}{\sin 44°} \;\Rightarrow\; \overline{AP} \approx 1.57, \text{ or } 1.6 \text{ mi.}$

(b) $\sin 21° = \dfrac{\text{height of } P}{\overline{AP}} \;\Rightarrow\; \text{height of } P = \dfrac{1.2 \sin 115° \sin 21°}{\sin 44°} \; \text{\{from part (a)\}} \; \approx 0.56, \text{ or } 0.6 \text{ mi.}$

**20** The angle between the road and the dashed line to the sun is $57° - 15° = 42°.$

The angle between the road and the pole is $90° + 15° = 105°.$

Hence, the angle between the pole and the dashed line is $180° - 42° - 105° = 33°.$

Let $l$ denote the length of the pole. $\dfrac{l}{\sin 42°} = \dfrac{75}{\sin 33°} \;\Rightarrow\; l = \dfrac{75 \sin 42°}{\sin 33°} \approx 92.14 \text{ ft.}$

**21** Let $C$ denote the base of the balloon and $P$ its projection on the ground.

$\angle ACB = 180° - 24°10' - 47°40' = 108°10'.$ $\dfrac{\overline{AC}}{\sin 47°40'} = \dfrac{8.4}{\sin 108°10'} \;\Rightarrow\; \overline{AC} \approx 6.5 \text{ mi.}$

$\sin 24°10' = \dfrac{\overline{PC}}{\overline{AC}} \;\Rightarrow\; \overline{PC} = \dfrac{8.4 \sin 47°40' \sin 24°10'}{\sin 108°10'} \approx 2.7 \text{ mi.}$

**22** The angle between the panel and the roof is $45° - 25° = 20°.$

The angle between the brace and the roof is $90° + 25° = 115°.$ $\dfrac{d}{\sin 20°} = \dfrac{10}{\sin 115°} \;\Rightarrow\; d = \dfrac{10 \sin 20°}{\sin 115°} \approx 3.77 \text{ ft.}$

**23** $\angle APQ = 57° - 22° = 35°.$ $\angle AQP = 180° - (63° - 22°) = 139°.$

$\angle PAQ = 180° - 139° - 35° = 6°.$ $\dfrac{\overline{AP}}{\sin 139°} = \dfrac{100}{\sin 6°} \;\Rightarrow\; \overline{AP} = \dfrac{100 \sin 139°}{\sin 6°} \approx 628 \text{ m.}$

**24** Let $\gamma = \angle BCA.$ $\angle BAC = 63° - 38° = 25°.$ $\dfrac{\sin \gamma}{239} = \dfrac{\sin 25°}{374} \;\Rightarrow\; \gamma \approx 15°40'.$

$\angle ABC \approx 180° - 15°40' - 25° = 139°20'.$ $\dfrac{\overline{AC}}{\sin 139°20'} = \dfrac{374}{\sin 25°} \;\Rightarrow\; \overline{AC} \approx 577 \text{ yards.}$

*Figure 24*

*Figure 25*

**25** $\angle FAB = 90° - 27°10' = 62°50',$ $\angle FBA = 90° - 52°40' = 37°20',$ and

$\angle AFB = 180° - 62°50' - 37°20' = 79°50'.$

$\dfrac{\overline{AF}}{\sin 37°20'} = \dfrac{6}{\sin 79°50'} \;\Rightarrow\; \overline{AF} \approx 3.70 \text{ mi. and } \dfrac{\overline{BF}}{\sin 62°50'} = \dfrac{6}{\sin 79°50'} \;\Rightarrow\; \overline{BF} \approx 5.42 \text{ mi.}$

**26** (a) Label the base of the tower $A$, the top of the tower $B$, and the observation point $C$. Let $\alpha = \angle BAC$ and

$\beta = \angle ABC$. $\dfrac{\sin \beta}{150} = \dfrac{\sin 53°}{179}$ $\Rightarrow$ $\beta \approx 42°$. $\alpha \approx 180° - 42° - 53° = 85°$. $\theta = 90° - \alpha \approx 5°$.

(b) $\theta = 5°$ and $\sin \theta = \dfrac{d}{179}$ $\Rightarrow$ $d \approx 15.6$ ft.

**27** Let $A$ denote the base of the hill, $B$ the base of the cathedral, and $C$ the top of the spire.

The angle at the base of the hill is $180° - 48° = 132°$. The angle at the top of the spire is $180° - 132° - 41° = 7°$.

$\dfrac{\overline{AC}}{\sin 41°} = \dfrac{200}{\sin 7°}$ $\Rightarrow$ $\overline{AC} = \dfrac{200 \sin 41°}{\sin 7°} \approx 1077$ ft. $\angle BAC = 48° - 32° = 16°$. $\angle ACB = 90° - 48° = 42°$.

$\angle ABC = 180° - 42° - 16° = 122°$. $\dfrac{\overline{BC}}{\sin 16°} = \dfrac{\overline{AC}}{\sin 122°}$ $\Rightarrow$ $\overline{BC} = \dfrac{200 \sin 41° \sin 16°}{\sin 7° \sin 122°} \approx 350$ ft.

**28** (a) Let $A$ denote the shorter mountain peak, $B$ the higher mountain peak, and $C$ the helicopter.

$\angle BAC = 90° - 18° = 72°$. $\angle ACB = 90° - 43° = 47°$. $\angle ABC = 180° - 72° - 47° = 61°$.

$\dfrac{\overline{AB}}{\sin 47°} = \dfrac{1000}{\sin 61°}$ $\Rightarrow$ $\overline{AB} = \dfrac{1000 \sin 47°}{\sin 61°} \approx 836$ ft.

(b) Let $h$ denote the height that $B$ is above the 5210 foot level.

$\sin 18° = \dfrac{h}{\overline{AB}}$ $\Rightarrow$ $h \approx 258$ ft, so the height of $B$ is $5210 + 258 = 5468$ ft.

**29** (a) In the triangle that forms the base, the third angle is $180° - 103° - 52° = 25°$. Let $l$ denote the length of the

dashed line. $\dfrac{l}{\sin 103°} = \dfrac{12.0}{\sin 25°}$ $\Rightarrow$ $l \approx 27.7$ units. Now $\tan 34° = \dfrac{h}{l}$ $\Rightarrow$ $h \approx 18.7$ units.

(b) Draw a line from the $103°$ angle that is perpendicular to $l$ and call it $d$. $\sin 52° = \dfrac{d}{12}$ $\Rightarrow$ $d \approx 9.5$ units.

The area of the triangular base is $B = \frac{1}{2}ld$.

The volume $V$ is $\frac{1}{3}\left(\frac{1}{2}ld\right)h = 288 \sin 52° \sin^2 103° \tan 34° \csc^2 25° \approx 814$ cubic units.

**30** (a) $\angle CBA = 180° - 153° = 27°$. $\dfrac{\sin \angle BAC}{35.9} = \dfrac{\sin 27°}{16.7}$ $\Rightarrow$ $\angle BAC \approx 77.4°$. $\phi = 180° - \angle BAC \approx 102.6°$.

(b) Let $h$ denote the perpendicular distance from $\overline{BA}$ to $C$.

$\sin \angle BAC = \dfrac{h}{16.7}$ $\Rightarrow$ $h \approx 16.30$ ft. The wing span $CC'$ is $2h + 4.80 \approx 37.4$ ft.

(c) $\angle BCA \approx 180° - 27° - 77.4° = 75.6°$. $\dfrac{\overline{BA}}{\sin 75.6°} = \dfrac{16.7}{\sin 27°}$ $\Rightarrow$ $\overline{BA} \approx 35.6$ ft.

The area of $\triangle ABC$ is then $\frac{1}{2}\left(\overline{BA}\right)h \approx 290.3$ ft$^2$.

**31** Draw a line through $P$ perpendicular to the $x$-axis. Locate points $A$ and $B$ on this line so that

$\angle PAQ = \angle PBR = 90°$. $\overline{AP} = 5127.5 - 3452.8 = 1674.7$, $\overline{AQ} = 3145.8 - 1487.7 = 1658.1$; and

$\tan \angle APQ = \dfrac{1658.1}{1674.7}$ $\Rightarrow$ $\angle APQ \approx 44°43'$. Thus, $\angle BPR \approx 180° - 55°50' - 44°43' = 79°27'$.

By the distance formula, $\overline{PQ} \approx \sqrt{(1674.7)^2 + (1658.1)^2} \approx 2356.7$.

Now $\dfrac{\overline{PR}}{\sin 65°22'} = \dfrac{\overline{PQ}}{\sin(180° - 55°50' - 65°22')}$ $\Rightarrow$ $\overline{PR} = \dfrac{2356.7 \sin 65°22'}{\sin 58°48'} \approx 2504.5$.

$\sin \angle BPR = \dfrac{\overline{BR}}{\overline{PR}}$ $\Rightarrow$ $\overline{BR} \approx (2504.5)(\sin 79°27') \approx 2462.2$. $\cos \angle BPR = \dfrac{\overline{BP}}{\overline{PR}}$ $\Rightarrow$

$\overline{BP} \approx (2504.5)(\cos 79°27') \approx 458.6$. Using the coordinates of $P$, we see that

$$R(x, y) \approx (1487.7 + 2462.2, 3452.8 - 458.6) = (3949.9, 2994.2).$$

## 7.2 Exercises

1. (d–f) The sides correspond to the three largest values and the angles correspond to the three smallest values. The sides $x$, $y$, and $z$ must be $13.45, 12.60$, and $10$, respectively, since it appears that $x > y > z$. Answers: (d) **E** (e) **A** (f) **C**.

   (a–c) The angles $\beta$ (opposite $x$), $\alpha$ (opposite $y$), and $\gamma$ (opposite $z$) must be $1.26, 1.10$, and $0.79$, respectively, since the largest angle is opposite the largest side, etc. Answers: (a) **B** (b) **F** (c) **D**

2. (d–f) The sides correspond to the three largest values and the angles correspond to the three smallest values. The sides $x$, $y$, and $z$ must be $8.24, 6.72$, and $3$, respectively, since it appears that $x > y > z$. Answers: (d) **C** (e) **E** (f) **A**

   (a–c) The angles $\beta$ (opposite $x$), $\alpha$ (opposite $y$), and $\gamma$ (opposite $z$) must be $1.92, 0.87$, and $0.35$, respectively, since the largest angle is opposite the largest side, etc. Answers: (a) **B** (b) **D** (c) **F**

3. (a) Given: side $c$, side $a$, angle $\gamma$ (opposite side $c$). We are given two sides and an angle opposite one of them (SSA), so use the law of sines to find $\alpha$. $\left( \dfrac{\sin \alpha}{a} = \dfrac{\sin \gamma}{c} \right)$

   (b) Given: side $c$, side $b$, angle $\alpha$ (between sides $c$ and $b$). We are given two sides and the angle between them (SAS), so use the law of cosines to find $a$. $(a^2 = b^2 + c^2 - 2bc \cos \alpha)$

   (c) Given: the three sides $a$, $b$, and $c$ (SSS), use the law of cosines to find any angle. (To find $\alpha$, use $a^2 = b^2 + c^2 - 2bc \cos \alpha$.)

   (d) Given: the three angles $\alpha$, $\beta$, and $\gamma$. There is *not enough information given* to find any side.

   (e) Given: angle $\alpha$, angle $\beta$, and side $c$. We are given the two angles $\alpha$ and $\beta$, so we can easily find the third angle $\gamma$ using $\alpha + \beta + \gamma = 180°$.

   (f) Given: angle $\beta$, angle $\gamma$, and side $b$. We are given two angles and a side (AAS or ASA), so we could use the law of sines to find $c$. $\left( \dfrac{c}{\sin \gamma} = \dfrac{b}{\sin \beta} \right)$ Also, since we are given the two angles $\beta$ and $\gamma$, we could easily find the third angle $\alpha$ using $\alpha + \beta + \gamma = 180°$.

4. (a) Given: side $a$, side $b$, angle $\gamma$ (between sides $a$ and $b$). We are given two sides and the angle between them (SAS), so use the law of cosines to find $c$. $(c^2 = a^2 + b^2 - 2ab \cos \gamma)$

   (b) Given: side $c$, side $b$, angle $\beta$ (opposite side $b$). We are given two sides and an angle opposite one of them (SSA), so use the law of sines to find $\gamma$. $\left( \dfrac{\sin \gamma}{c} = \dfrac{\sin \beta}{b} \right)$

   (c) Given: angle $\alpha$, angle $\gamma$, and side $b$. We are given the two angles $\alpha$ and $\gamma$, so we can easily find the third angle $\beta$ using $\alpha + \beta + \gamma = 180°$.

   (d) Given: angle $\alpha$, angle $\gamma$, and side $c$. We are given two angles and a side (AAS or ASA), so we could use the law of sines to find $a$. $\left( \dfrac{a}{\sin \alpha} = \dfrac{c}{\sin \gamma} \right)$ Also, since we are given the two angles $\alpha$ and $\gamma$, we could easily find the third angle $\beta$ using $\alpha + \beta + \gamma = 180°$.

   (e) Given: the three angles $\alpha$, $\beta$, and $\gamma$. There is *not enough information given* to find any side.

   (f) Given: the three sides $a$, $b$, and $c$ (SSS), use the law of cosines to find any angle. (To find $\alpha$, use $a^2 = b^2 + c^2 - 2bc \cos \alpha$.)

# 7.2 EXERCISES

**Note:** These formulas will be used to solve problems that involve the law of cosines.

(1) $\quad a^2 = b^2 + c^2 - 2bc \cos \alpha \quad \Rightarrow \quad a = \sqrt{b^2 + c^2 - 2bc \cos \alpha}$ (Similar formulas are used for $b$ and $c$.)

(2) $\quad a^2 = b^2 + c^2 - 2bc \cos \alpha \quad \Rightarrow \quad 2bc \cos \alpha = b^2 + c^2 - a^2 \quad \Rightarrow$

$\cos \alpha = \dfrac{b^2 + c^2 - a^2}{2bc}, \quad \Rightarrow \quad \alpha = \cos^{-1}\left(\dfrac{b^2 + c^2 - a^2}{2bc}\right)$ (Similar formulas are used for $\beta$ and $\gamma$.)

**5** $\quad a = \sqrt{b^2 + c^2 - 2bc \cos \alpha} = \sqrt{20^2 + 30^2 - 2(20)(30)\cos 60^\circ} = \sqrt{700} \approx 26.$

$\beta = \cos^{-1}\left(\dfrac{a^2 + c^2 - b^2}{2ac}\right) = \cos^{-1}\left(\dfrac{700 + 30^2 - 20^2}{2 \cdot \sqrt{700} \cdot 30}\right) \approx \cos^{-1}(0.7559) \approx 41^\circ.$

$\gamma = 180^\circ - \alpha - \beta \approx 180^\circ - 60^\circ - 41^\circ = 79^\circ.$

**6** $\quad c = \sqrt{a^2 + b^2 - 2ab \cos \gamma} = \sqrt{325 - 150\sqrt{2}} \approx 10.6. \quad \alpha = \cos^{-1}\left(\dfrac{b^2 + c^2 - a^2}{2bc}\right) \approx \cos^{-1}(-0.0571) \approx 93^\circ 20'.$

$\beta = 180^\circ - \alpha - \gamma \approx 180^\circ - 93^\circ 20' - 45^\circ = 41^\circ 40'.$

**7** $\quad b = \sqrt{a^2 + c^2 - 2ac \cos \beta} = \sqrt{23{,}400 + 4500\sqrt{3}} \approx 177,$ or $180.$

$\alpha = \cos^{-1}\left(\dfrac{b^2 + c^2 - a^2}{2bc}\right) \approx \cos^{-1}(0.9054) \approx 25^\circ 10',$ or $25^\circ.$

**Note:** We do not have to worry about an "ambiguous" case of the law of cosines as we did with the law of sines. This is true because the inverse cosine function gives us a unique angle from $0^\circ$ to $180^\circ$ for all values in its domain.

$\gamma = 180^\circ - \alpha - \beta \approx 180^\circ - 25^\circ 10' - 150^\circ = 4^\circ 50',$ or $5^\circ.$

**8** $\quad b = \sqrt{a^2 + c^2 - 2ac \cos \beta} \approx \sqrt{7086.74} \approx 84.2. \quad \alpha = \cos^{-1}\left(\dfrac{b^2 + c^2 - a^2}{2bc}\right) \approx \cos^{-1}(-0.1214) \approx 97^\circ 00'.$

$\gamma = 180^\circ - \alpha - \beta \approx 180^\circ - 97^\circ - 73^\circ 50' = 9^\circ 10'.$

**9** $\quad c = \sqrt{a^2 + b^2 - 2ab \cos \gamma} \approx \sqrt{7.58} \approx 2.75. \quad \alpha = \cos^{-1}\left(\dfrac{b^2 + c^2 - a^2}{2bc}\right) \approx \cos^{-1}(0.9324) \approx 21^\circ 10'.$

$\beta = 180^\circ - \alpha - \gamma \approx 180^\circ - 21^\circ 10' - 115^\circ 10' = 43^\circ 40'.$

**10** $\quad a = \sqrt{b^2 + c^2 - 2bc \cos \alpha} \approx \sqrt{4367} \approx 66.1. \quad \beta = \cos^{-1}\left(\dfrac{a^2 + c^2 - b^2}{2ac}\right) \approx \cos^{-1}(-0.9051) \approx 154^\circ 50'.$

$\gamma = 180^\circ - \alpha - \beta \approx 180^\circ - 23^\circ 40' - 154^\circ 50' = 1^\circ 30'.$

**11** $\quad \alpha = \cos^{-1}\left(\dfrac{b^2 + c^2 - a^2}{2bc}\right) = \cos^{-1}\left(\dfrac{11^2 + 22^2 - 10^2}{2 \cdot 11 \cdot 22}\right) \approx \cos^{-1}(1.0434).$

Since 1.0434 is not in the domain of the inverse cosine function, which is $[-1, 1]$, *no triangle exists.*

**12** $\quad \alpha = \cos^{-1}\left(\dfrac{b^2 + c^2 - a^2}{2bc}\right) = \cos^{-1}\left(\dfrac{5.6^2 + 9.8^2 - 3.7^2}{2 \cdot 5.6 \cdot 9.8}\right) \approx \cos^{-1}(1.0360).$

Since 1.0360 is not in the domain of the inverse cosine function, which is $[-1, 1]$, *no triangle exists.*

**13** $\quad \alpha = \cos^{-1}\left(\dfrac{b^2 + c^2 - a^2}{2bc}\right) = \cos^{-1}(0.875) \approx 29^\circ. \quad \beta = \cos^{-1}\left(\dfrac{a^2 + c^2 - b^2}{2ac}\right) = \cos^{-1}(0.6875) \approx 47^\circ.$

$\gamma = 180^\circ - \alpha - \beta \approx 180^\circ - 29^\circ - 47^\circ = 104^\circ.$

**14** $\quad \alpha = \cos^{-1}\left(\dfrac{b^2 + c^2 - a^2}{2bc}\right) \approx \cos^{-1}(0.7472) \approx 41^\circ 40',$ or $42^\circ.$

$\beta = \cos^{-1}\left(\dfrac{a^2 + c^2 - b^2}{2ac}\right) \approx \cos^{-1}(0.0792) \approx 85^\circ 30',$ or $85^\circ.$

$\gamma = 180^\circ - \alpha - \beta \approx 180^\circ - 41^\circ 40' - 85^\circ 30' = 52^\circ 50',$ or $53^\circ.$

**15** $\alpha = \cos^{-1}\left(\dfrac{b^2 + c^2 - a^2}{2bc}\right) \approx \cos^{-1}(0.9766) \approx 12°30'.$   $\beta = \cos^{-1}\left(\dfrac{a^2 + c^2 - b^2}{2ac}\right) = \cos^{-1}(-0.725) \approx 136°30'.$

$$\gamma = 180° - \alpha - \beta \approx 180° - 12°30' - 136°30' = 31°00'.$$

**16** $\alpha = \cos^{-1}\left(\dfrac{b^2 + c^2 - a^2}{2bc}\right) = \cos^{-1}\left(\dfrac{11.7^2 + 13.1^2 - 8.5^2}{2 \cdot 11.7 \cdot 13.1}\right) \approx \cos^{-1}(0.7707) \approx 39°30'.$

$\beta = \cos^{-1}\left(\dfrac{a^2 + c^2 - b^2}{2ac}\right) = \cos^{-1}\left(\dfrac{8.5^2 + 13.1^2 - 11.7^2}{2 \cdot 8.5 \cdot 13.1}\right) \approx \cos^{-1}(0.4803) \approx 61°20'.$

$$\gamma = 180° - \alpha - \beta \approx 180° - 39°30' - 61°20' = 79°10'.$$

**17** $\alpha = \cos^{-1}\left(\dfrac{b^2 + c^2 - a^2}{2bc}\right) = \cos^{-1}\left(\dfrac{286.5^2 + 10.0^2 - 286.5^2}{2 \cdot 286.5 \cdot 10.0}\right) \approx \cos^{-1}(0.0175) \approx 89°00'.$

By symmetry, $\beta = \alpha$.   $\gamma = 180° - \alpha - \beta \approx 180° - 89°00' - 89°00' = 2°00'.$

**18** $\alpha = \cos^{-1}\left(\dfrac{b^2 + c^2 - a^2}{2bc}\right) = \cos^{-1}(0.25) \approx 75°30'.$   $\beta = \alpha$ since $b = a$.

$$\gamma = 180° - \alpha - \beta \approx 180° - 75°30' - 75°30' = 29°00'.$$

**Note:** When deciding whether to use the law of cosines or the law of sines, it may be helpful to remember that the law of cosines must be used when you have:

   (1)  three sides, or

   (2)  two sides and the angle between them.

**19** We have two sides and the angle between them. Hence, we apply the law of cosines.

$$\text{Third side} = \sqrt{175^2 + 150^2 - 2(175)(150)\cos 73°40'} \approx 196 \text{ feet.}$$

**20** $\overline{AB} = \sqrt{420^2 + 540^2 - 2(420)(540)\cos 63°10'} \approx 513$ yards.

**21** 20 minutes $= \frac{1}{3}$ hour $\Rightarrow$ the cars have traveled $60\left(\frac{1}{3}\right) = 20$ miles and $45\left(\frac{1}{3}\right) = 15$ miles, respectively.

$$\text{The distance } d \text{ apart is } d = \sqrt{20^2 + 15^2 - 2(20)(15)\cos 84°} \approx 24 \text{ miles.}$$

**22** The smallest angle $\alpha$ between the sides is the angle opposite the shortest side (180 ft).

$$\alpha = \cos^{-1}\left(\dfrac{420^2 + 350^2 - 180^2}{2(420)(350)}\right) \approx \cos^{-1}(0.9065) \approx 25°.$$

**23** The first ship travels $(24)(2) = 48$ miles in two hours. The second ship travels $(18)\left(1\frac{1}{2}\right) = 27$ miles in $1\frac{1}{2}$ hours. The angle between the paths is $20° + 35° = 55°$. $\overline{AB} = \sqrt{27^2 + 48^2 - 2(27)(48)\cos 55°} \approx 39$ miles.

*Figure 23*

*Figure 24*

**24** The angle between the two paths is $40° + 25° = 65°$. $\overline{AB} = \sqrt{165^2 + 80^2 - 2(165)(80)\cos 65°} \approx 150$ miles.

**25** $\angle ABC = 40° + 20° = 60°$.

$\overline{AB} = \left(\dfrac{1 \text{ mile}}{8 \text{ min}} \cdot 20 \text{ min}\right) = 2.5 \text{ miles}$ and $\overline{BC} = \left(\dfrac{1 \text{ mile}}{8 \text{ min}} \cdot 16 \text{ min}\right) = 2 \text{ miles}$.

$$\overline{AC} = \sqrt{2.5^2 + 2^2 - 2(2)(2.5)\cos 60°} = \sqrt{5.25} \approx 2.3 \text{ miles}.$$

Figure 25

Figure 27

**26** $PQ = \sqrt{300^2 + 438^2 - 2(300)(438)\cos 37°40'} \approx 271.7$, or 272 feet

**27** See Figure 27. $\gamma = \cos^{-1}\left(\dfrac{2^2 + 3^2 - 4^2}{2 \cdot 2 \cdot 3}\right) = \cos^{-1}(-0.25) \approx 104°29'$. $\phi \approx 104°29' - 70° = 34°29'$.

The direction that the third side was traversed is approximately $N(90° - 34°29')E = N55°31'E$.

**28** The length of the diagonal in the base is $\sqrt{6^2 + 8^2} = \sqrt{100} = 10$ inches.

The length of the diagonal of the $6'' \times 4''$ side is $\sqrt{6^2 + 4^2} = \sqrt{52}$ inches.

The length of the diagonal of the $8'' \times 4''$ side is $\sqrt{8^2 + 4^2} = \sqrt{80}$ inches, and it is the

side opposite angle $\theta$. $\theta = \cos^{-1}\left(\dfrac{100 + 52 - 80}{2(10)\sqrt{52}}\right) \approx \cos^{-1}(0.4992) \approx 60.05°$, or 60°.

**29** Let $H$ denote home plate, $M$ the mound, $F$ first base, $S$ second base, and $T$ third base.

$\overline{HS} = \sqrt{90^2 + 90^2} = 90\sqrt{2} \approx 127.3$ ft. $\overline{MS} = 90\sqrt{2} - 60.5 \approx 66.8$ ft. $\angle MHF = 45°$ so

$\overline{MF} = \sqrt{60.5^2 + 90^2 - 2(60.5)(90)\cos 45°} \approx 63.7$ ft. $\overline{MT} = \overline{MF}$ by the symmetry of the field.

Figure 29

Figure 30

**30** $\overline{AC} = \sqrt{100^2 + 100^2 - 2(100)(100)\cos 70°} \approx 114.7$ cm.

$$\overline{BD} = \sqrt{100^2 + 100^2 - 2(100)(100)\cos 110°} \approx 163.8 \text{ cm}.$$

**31** $\angle RTP = 21°$ and $\angle RSP = 37°$. $\sin \angle RSP = \dfrac{10,000}{\overline{SP}} \Rightarrow \overline{SP} = 10,000 \csc 37° \approx 16,616$ ft.

$\sin \angle RTP = \dfrac{10,000}{\overline{TP}} \Rightarrow \overline{TP} = 10,000 \csc 21° \approx 27,904$ ft.

$$\overline{ST} = \sqrt{\overline{SP}^2 + \overline{TP}^2 - 2(\overline{SP})(\overline{TP})\cos 110°} \approx 37,039 \text{ ft} \approx 7 \text{ miles}.$$

**32** (a) The angle between the ship's path and its intended path is $14°$.

Let $d$ denote the distance from $P$ to the port.

$d = \sqrt{80^2 + 150^2 - 2(80)(150)\cos 14°} \approx 74.9$ mi.

(b) $\angle P = \cos^{-1}\left(\dfrac{80^2 + d^2 - 150^2}{2(80)d}\right) \approx \cos^{-1}(-0.8749) \approx 151°$.

From the figure, $\angle P = 33° + 90° + 28° \{ = 151°\}$.

The angle that should then be taken is N$(90° - 28°)$E, or N62°E.

**33** Let $d = \overline{ES}$. $d^2 = R^2 + R^2 - 2RR\cos\theta \Rightarrow d^2 = 2R^2(1 - \cos\theta) \Rightarrow d^2 = 4R^2\left(\dfrac{1 - \cos\theta}{2}\right) \Rightarrow$

$d = 2R\sqrt{\dfrac{1 - \cos\theta}{2}} \Rightarrow d = 2R\sin\dfrac{\theta}{2}$. Since $d = vt$, $t = \dfrac{d}{v} = \dfrac{2R}{v}\sin\dfrac{\theta}{2}$.

**34** (a) In $\triangle CBD$, $\angle CBD = \cos^{-1}\left(\dfrac{\overline{BC}^2 + \overline{BD}^2 - \overline{CD}^2}{2(\overline{BC})(\overline{BD})}\right) = \cos^{-1}\left(\dfrac{184^2 + 102^2 - 236^2}{2(184)(102)}\right) \approx 107.74°$.

In $\triangle BCE$, $\angle BCE = \cos^{-1}\left(\dfrac{\overline{BC}^2 + \overline{CE}^2 - \overline{BE}^2}{2(\overline{BC})(\overline{CE})}\right) = \cos^{-1}\left(\dfrac{184^2 + 80^2 - 218^2}{2(184)(80)}\right) \approx 104.29°$.

In $\triangle ABC$, $\angle BCA = 180° - \angle BCE \approx 75.71°$, $\angle CBA = 180° - \angle CBD \approx 72.26°$,

and $\angle BAC = 180° - \angle BCA - \angle CBA \approx 32.03°$. We now use the law of sines to find $\overline{AB}$ and $\overline{AC}$.

$\dfrac{\overline{AB}}{\sin\angle BCA} = \dfrac{\overline{BC}}{\sin\angle BAC} \Rightarrow \overline{AB} = \dfrac{184\sin 75.71°}{\sin 32.03°} \approx 336.2$ ft.

$\dfrac{\overline{AC}}{\sin\angle CBA} = \dfrac{\overline{BC}}{\sin\angle BAC} \Rightarrow \overline{AC} = \dfrac{184\sin 72.26°}{\sin 32.03°} \approx 330.4$ ft.

(b) Let $h$ denote the perpendicular distance from $A$ to $\overline{BC}$.

$\sin\angle BCA = \dfrac{h}{\overline{AC}} \Rightarrow h \approx (330.4)(\sin 75.71°) \approx 320.2$ ft.

**35** (a) $\angle BCP = \frac{1}{2}(\angle BCD) = \frac{1}{2}(72°) = 36°$. $\triangle BPC$ is isosceles so $\angle BPC = \angle PBC$ and

$2\angle BPC = 180° - 36° \Rightarrow \angle BPC = \underline{72°}$. $\angle APB = 180° - \angle BPC = 180° - 72° = \underline{108°}$.

$\angle ABP = 180° - \angle APB - \angle BAP = 180° - 108° - 36° = \underline{36°}$.

(b) $\overline{BP} = \sqrt{\overline{BC}^2 + \overline{PC}^2 - 2(\overline{BC})(\overline{PC})\cos 36°} = \sqrt{1^2 + 1^2 - 2(1)(1)\cos 36°} \approx 0.62$.

(c) Area$_{\text{kite}}$ = 2(Area of $\triangle BPC$) = $2 \cdot \frac{1}{2}(\overline{CB})(\overline{CP})\sin\angle BCP = \sin 36° \approx 0.59$.

Area$_{\text{dart}}$ = 2(Area of $\triangle ABP$) = $2 \cdot \frac{1}{2}(\overline{AB})(\overline{BP})\sin\angle ABP = \overline{BP}\sin 36° \approx 0.36$.

$\{\overline{BP}$ was found in part (b).$\}$

**36** Note that $\triangle TPQ$ is similar to $\triangle THB$. $\dfrac{\overline{TQ}}{\overline{TB}} = \dfrac{\overline{PQ}}{\overline{HB}} \Rightarrow \dfrac{\overline{TQ}}{42} = \dfrac{24}{32} \Rightarrow \overline{TQ} = 31.5$ in.

$\overline{TP} = \sqrt{\overline{TQ}^2 + \overline{PQ}^2 - 2(\overline{TQ})(\overline{PQ})\cos\angle TQP} = \sqrt{31.5^2 + 24^2 - 2(31.5)(24)\cos(90° - 26°)} \approx 30.1$ in.

**Note:** In Exercises 37–44, $\mathcal{A}$ (the area) is measured in square units.

**37** Since $\alpha$ is the angle between sides $b$ and $c$, we may apply the area of a triangle formula listed in this section.

$\mathcal{A} = \frac{1}{2}bc\sin\alpha = \frac{1}{2}(20)(30)\sin 60° = 300\left(\sqrt{3}/2\right) \approx 260$.

**38** $\mathcal{A} = \frac{1}{2}ab\sin\gamma = \frac{1}{2}(15.0)(10.0)\sin 45° = 75\left(\sqrt{2}/2\right) \approx 53.0$.

**39** $\gamma = 180° - \alpha - \beta = 180° - 40.3° - 62.9° = 76.8°.$

$$\frac{a}{\sin \alpha} = \frac{b}{\sin \beta} \quad\Rightarrow\quad a = \frac{b \sin \alpha}{\sin \beta} = \frac{5.63 \sin 40.3°}{\sin 62.9°}. \quad \mathcal{A} = \frac{1}{2}ab \sin \gamma \approx 11.21.$$

**40** $\beta = 180° - \alpha - \gamma = 180° - 35.7° - 105.2° = 39.1°.$

$$\frac{a}{\sin \alpha} = \frac{b}{\sin \beta} \quad\Rightarrow\quad a = \frac{b \sin \alpha}{\sin \beta} = \frac{17.2 \sin 35.7°}{\sin 39.1°}. \quad \mathcal{A} = \frac{1}{2}ab \sin \gamma \approx 132.1.$$

**41** $\dfrac{\sin \beta}{b} = \dfrac{\sin \alpha}{a} \;\Rightarrow\; \sin \beta = \dfrac{b \sin \alpha}{a} = \dfrac{3.4 \sin 80.1°}{8.0} \approx 0.4187 \;\Rightarrow\; \beta \approx 24.8°$ or $155.2°.$ Reject $155.2°$ because

then $\alpha + \beta = 235.3° \geq 180°.$ $\gamma \approx 180° - 80.1° - 24.8° = 75.1°.$ $\mathcal{A} = \frac{1}{2}ab \sin \gamma = \frac{1}{2}(8.0)(3.4)\sin 75.1° \approx 13.1.$

**42** $\dfrac{\sin \alpha}{a} = \dfrac{\sin \gamma}{c} \;\Rightarrow\; \sin \alpha = \dfrac{a \sin \gamma}{c} = \dfrac{14.6 \sin 32.1°}{15.8} \approx 0.4910 \;\Rightarrow\; \alpha \approx 29.4°$ or $150.6°.$

Reject $150.6°$ because then $\alpha + \gamma = 182.7° \geq 180°.$ $\beta \approx 180° - 29.4° - 32.1° = 118.5°.$

$$\mathcal{A} = \tfrac{1}{2}ac \sin \beta = \tfrac{1}{2}(14.6)(15.8)\sin 118.5° \approx 101.4.$$

**43** Given the lengths of the 3 sides of a triangle, we compute the semiperimeter and then use Heron's formula to find

the area of the triangle. $s = \frac{1}{2}(a + b + c) = \frac{1}{2}(25.0 + 80.0 + 60.0) = 82.5.$

$$\mathcal{A} = \sqrt{s(s-a)(s-b)(s-c)} = \sqrt{(82.5)(57.5)(2.5)(22.5)} \approx 516.56, \text{ or } 517.0.$$

**44** $s = \frac{1}{2}(a + b + c) = \frac{1}{2}(50.0 + 50.0 + 25.0) = 62.5.$

$$\mathcal{A} = \sqrt{s(s-a)(s-b)(s-c)} = \sqrt{(62.5)(12.5)(12.5)(37.5)} \approx 605.2.$$

**45** $s = \frac{1}{2}(a + b + c) = \frac{1}{2}(600 + 700 + 724) = 1012.$

$$\mathcal{A} = \sqrt{s(s-a)(s-b)(s-c)} = \sqrt{(1012)(412)(312)(288)} \approx 193,559 \text{ yd}^2, \text{ or } \mathcal{A}/4840 \approx 40.0 \text{ acres.}$$

**46** $s = \frac{1}{2}(a + b + c) = \frac{1}{2}(320 + 350 + 500) = 585.$

$$\mathcal{A} = \sqrt{s(s-a)(s-b)(s-c)} = \sqrt{(585)(265)(235)(85)} \approx 55,647.3 \text{ yd}^2, \text{ or } \mathcal{A}/4840 \approx 11.5 \text{ acres.}$$

**47** The area of the parallelogram is twice the area of the triangle formed by the two sides and the included angle.

$$\mathcal{A} = 2\left(\tfrac{1}{2}\right)(12.0)(16.0)\sin 40° \approx 123.4 \text{ ft}^2.$$

**48** As in Exercise 47, $\mathcal{A} = 2\left(\frac{1}{2}\right)(40.3)(52.6)\sin 100° \approx 2087.6 \text{ ft}^2.$

## 7.3 Exercises

**1** $\mathbf{a} + \mathbf{b} = \langle 2, -3 \rangle + \langle -5, -1 \rangle = \langle 2 + (-5), -3 + (-1) \rangle = \langle -3, -4 \rangle.$

$\mathbf{a} - \mathbf{b} = \langle 2, -3 \rangle - \langle -5, -1 \rangle = \langle 2 - (-5), -3 - (-1) \rangle = \langle 7, -2 \rangle.$

$4\mathbf{a} + 5\mathbf{b} = 4\langle 2, -3 \rangle + 5\langle -5, -1 \rangle = \langle 4(2), 4(-3) \rangle + \langle 5(-5), 5(-1) \rangle$

$\qquad = \langle 8, -12 \rangle + \langle -25, -5 \rangle = \langle 8 + (-25), -12 + (-5) \rangle = \langle -17, -17 \rangle.$

From above, $4\mathbf{a} - 5\mathbf{b} = \langle 8, -12 \rangle - \langle -25, -5 \rangle = \langle 8 - (-25), -12 - (-5) \rangle = \langle 33, -7 \rangle.$

$\|\mathbf{a}\| = \|\langle 2, -3 \rangle\| = \sqrt{2^2 + (-3)^2} = \sqrt{4 + 9} = \sqrt{13}.$

**2** With $\mathbf{a} = \langle -2, -3 \rangle$ and $\mathbf{b} = \langle 2, 3 \rangle,$

$$\mathbf{a} + \mathbf{b} = \langle 0, 0 \rangle, \mathbf{a} - \mathbf{b} = \langle -4, -6 \rangle, 4\mathbf{a} + 5\mathbf{b} = \langle 2, 3 \rangle, 4\mathbf{a} - 5\mathbf{b} = \langle -18, -27 \rangle, \text{ and } \|\mathbf{a}\| = \sqrt{13}.$$

**3**  Simplifying **a** and **b** first, we have $\mathbf{a} = -\langle 7, -2 \rangle = \langle -(7), -(-2) \rangle = \langle -7, 2 \rangle$ and
$$\mathbf{b} = 3\langle 0, -2 \rangle = \langle 3(0), 3(-2) \rangle = \langle 0, -6 \rangle.$$

$\mathbf{a} + \mathbf{b} = \langle -7, 2 \rangle + \langle 0, -6 \rangle = \langle -7 + 0, 2 + (-6) \rangle = \langle -7, -4 \rangle.$

$\mathbf{a} - \mathbf{b} = \langle -7, 2 \rangle - \langle 0, -6 \rangle = \langle -7 - 0, 2 - (-6) \rangle = \langle -7, 8 \rangle.$

$4\mathbf{a} + 5\mathbf{b} = 4\langle -7, 2 \rangle + 5\langle 0, -6 \rangle = \langle -28, 8 \rangle + \langle 0, -30 \rangle = \langle -28, -22 \rangle.$

From above, $4\mathbf{a} - 5\mathbf{b} = \langle -28, 8 \rangle - \langle 0, -30 \rangle = \langle -28, 38 \rangle.$

$\|\mathbf{a}\| = \|\langle -7, 2 \rangle\| = \sqrt{(-7)^2 + 2^2} = \sqrt{49 + 4} = \sqrt{53}.$

**4**  With $\mathbf{a} = 2\langle 5, -4 \rangle = \langle 10, -8 \rangle$ and $\mathbf{b} = -\langle 6, 0 \rangle = \langle -6, 0 \rangle,$
$$\mathbf{a} + \mathbf{b} = \langle 4, -8 \rangle, \mathbf{a} - \mathbf{b} = \langle 16, -8 \rangle, 4\mathbf{a} + 5\mathbf{b} = \langle 10, -32 \rangle, 4\mathbf{a} - 5\mathbf{b} = \langle 70, -32 \rangle, \text{ and } \|\mathbf{a}\| = \sqrt{164}.$$

**5**  $\mathbf{a} + \mathbf{b} = (\mathbf{i} + 2\mathbf{j}) + (3\mathbf{i} - 5\mathbf{j}) = (1 + 3)\mathbf{i} + (2 - 5)\mathbf{j} = 4\mathbf{i} - 3\mathbf{j}.$

$\mathbf{a} - \mathbf{b} = (\mathbf{i} + 2\mathbf{j}) - (3\mathbf{i} - 5\mathbf{j}) = (1 - 3)\mathbf{i} + (2 - (-5))\mathbf{j} = -2\mathbf{i} + 7\mathbf{j}.$

$4\mathbf{a} + 5\mathbf{b} = 4(\mathbf{i} + 2\mathbf{j}) + 5(3\mathbf{i} - 5\mathbf{j}) = (4\mathbf{i} + 8\mathbf{j}) + (15\mathbf{i} - 25\mathbf{j}) = 19\mathbf{i} - 17\mathbf{j}.$

From above, $4\mathbf{a} - 5\mathbf{b} = (4\mathbf{i} + 8\mathbf{j}) - (15\mathbf{i} - 25\mathbf{j}) = -11\mathbf{i} + 33\mathbf{j}.$

$\|\mathbf{a}\| = \|\mathbf{i} + 2\mathbf{j}\| = \|1\mathbf{i} + 2\mathbf{j}\| = \sqrt{1^2 + 2^2} = \sqrt{1 + 4} = \sqrt{5}.$

**6**  With $\mathbf{a} = -3\mathbf{i} + \mathbf{j}$ and $\mathbf{b} = -3\mathbf{i} + \mathbf{j},$
$$\mathbf{a} + \mathbf{b} = -6\mathbf{i} + 2\mathbf{j}, \mathbf{a} - \mathbf{b} = 0\mathbf{i} + 0\mathbf{j}, 4\mathbf{a} + 5\mathbf{b} = -27\mathbf{i} + 9\mathbf{j}, 4\mathbf{a} - 5\mathbf{b} = 3\mathbf{i} - \mathbf{j}, \text{ and } \|\mathbf{a}\| = \sqrt{10}.$$

**7**  $\mathbf{a} = 3\mathbf{i} + 2\mathbf{j}$ and $\mathbf{b} = -\mathbf{i} + 5\mathbf{j} \Rightarrow \mathbf{a} + \mathbf{b} = 2\mathbf{i} + 7\mathbf{j}, 2\mathbf{a} = 6\mathbf{i} + 4\mathbf{j}, \text{ and } -3\mathbf{b} = 3\mathbf{i} - 15\mathbf{j}.$

Terminal points of the vectors are $(3, 2), (-1, 5), (2, 7), (6, 4),$ and $(3, -15).$

*Figure 7*

*Figure 8*

**8**  $\mathbf{a} = -5\mathbf{i} + 2\mathbf{j}$ and $\mathbf{b} = \mathbf{i} - 3\mathbf{j} \Rightarrow \mathbf{a} + \mathbf{b} = -4\mathbf{i} - \mathbf{j}, 2\mathbf{a} = -10\mathbf{i} + 4\mathbf{j}, \text{ and } -3\mathbf{b} = -3\mathbf{i} + 9\mathbf{j}.$

Terminal points of the vectors are $(-5, 2), (1, -3), (-4, -1), (-10, 4),$ and $(-3, 9).$

**9**  $\mathbf{a} = \langle -4, 6 \rangle$ and $\mathbf{b} = \langle -2, 3 \rangle \Rightarrow \mathbf{a} + \mathbf{b} = \langle -6, 9 \rangle, 2\mathbf{a} = \langle -8, 12 \rangle, \text{ and } -3\mathbf{b} = \langle 6, -9 \rangle.$

Terminal points of the vectors are $(-4, 6), (-2, 3), (-6, 9), (-8, 12),$ and $(6, -9).$

*Figure 9*

*Figure 10*

**10**  $\mathbf{a} = \langle 2, 0 \rangle$ and $\mathbf{b} = \langle -2, 0 \rangle \Rightarrow \mathbf{a} + \mathbf{b} = \langle 0, 0 \rangle, 2\mathbf{a} = \langle 4, 0 \rangle, \text{ and } -3\mathbf{b} = \langle 6, 0 \rangle.$

Terminal points of the vectors are $(2, 0), (-2, 0), (0, 0), (4, 0),$ and $(6, 0).$

$\boxed{11}$ $\mathbf{a} + \mathbf{b} = \langle 2, 0 \rangle + \langle -1, 0 \rangle = \langle 1, 0 \rangle = -\langle -1, 0 \rangle = -\mathbf{b}$

$\boxed{12}$ $\mathbf{c} - \mathbf{d} = \langle 0, 2 \rangle - \langle 0, -1 \rangle = \langle 0, 3 \rangle = -3\langle 0, -1 \rangle = -3\mathbf{d}$

$\boxed{13}$ $\mathbf{b} + \mathbf{e} = \langle -1, 0 \rangle + \langle 2, 2 \rangle = \langle 1, 2 \rangle = \mathbf{f}$

$\boxed{14}$ $\mathbf{f} - \mathbf{b} = \langle 1, 2 \rangle - \langle -1, 0 \rangle = \langle 2, 2 \rangle = \mathbf{e}$

$\boxed{15}$ $\mathbf{b} + \mathbf{d} = \langle -1, 0 \rangle + \langle 0, -1 \rangle = \langle -1, -1 \rangle = -\frac{1}{2}\langle 2, 2 \rangle = -\frac{1}{2}\mathbf{e}$

$\boxed{16}$ $\mathbf{e} + \mathbf{c} = \langle 2, 2 \rangle + \langle 0, 2 \rangle = \langle 2, 4 \rangle = 2\langle 1, 2 \rangle = 2\mathbf{f}$

$\boxed{17}$ $\begin{aligned} \mathbf{a} + (\mathbf{b} + \mathbf{c}) &= \langle a_1, a_2 \rangle + (\langle b_1, b_2 \rangle + \langle c_1, c_2 \rangle) \\ &= \langle a_1, a_2 \rangle + \langle b_1 + c_1, b_2 + c_2 \rangle \\ &= \langle a_1 + b_1 + c_1, a_2 + b_2 + c_2 \rangle \\ &= \langle a_1 + b_1, a_2 + b_2 \rangle + \langle c_1, c_2 \rangle \\ &= (\langle a_1, a_2 \rangle + \langle b_1, b_2 \rangle) + \langle c_1, c_2 \rangle \\ &= (\mathbf{a} + \mathbf{b}) + \mathbf{c} \end{aligned}$

$\boxed{18}$ $\mathbf{a} + \mathbf{0} = \langle a_1, a_2 \rangle + \langle 0, 0 \rangle = \langle a_1 + 0, a_2 + 0 \rangle = \langle a_1, a_2 \rangle = \mathbf{a}$

$\boxed{19}$ $\begin{aligned} \mathbf{a} + (-\mathbf{a}) &= \langle a_1, a_2 \rangle + (-\langle a_1, a_2 \rangle) \\ &= \langle a_1, a_2 \rangle + \langle -a_1, -a_2 \rangle \\ &= \langle a_1 - a_1, a_2 - a_2 \rangle \\ &= \langle 0, 0 \rangle = \mathbf{0} \end{aligned}$

$\boxed{20}$ $\begin{aligned} (m + n)\mathbf{a} &= (m + n)\langle a_1, a_2 \rangle \\ &= \langle (m + n)a_1, (m + n)a_2 \rangle \\ &= \langle ma_1 + na_1, ma_2 + na_2 \rangle \\ &= \langle ma_1, ma_2 \rangle + \langle na_1, na_2 \rangle \\ &= m\langle a_1, a_2 \rangle + n\langle a_1, a_2 \rangle = m\mathbf{a} + n\mathbf{a} \end{aligned}$

$\boxed{21}$ $\begin{aligned} (mn)\mathbf{a} &= (mn)\langle a_1, a_2 \rangle \\ &= \langle (mn)a_1, (mn)a_2 \rangle \\ &= \langle mna_1, mna_2 \rangle \\ &= m\langle na_1, na_2 \rangle && \text{or } n\langle ma_1, ma_2 \rangle \\ &= m(n\langle a_1, a_2 \rangle) && \text{or } n(m\langle a_1, a_2 \rangle) \\ &= m(n\mathbf{a}) && \text{or } n(m\mathbf{a}) \end{aligned}$

$\boxed{22}$ $1\mathbf{a} = 1\langle a_1, a_2 \rangle = \langle 1a_1, 1a_2 \rangle = \langle a_1, a_2 \rangle = \mathbf{a}$

$\boxed{23}$ $0\mathbf{a} = 0\langle a_1, a_2 \rangle = \langle 0a_1, 0a_2 \rangle = \langle 0, 0 \rangle = \mathbf{0}$. Also, $m\mathbf{0} = m\langle 0, 0 \rangle = \langle m0, m0 \rangle = \langle 0, 0 \rangle = \mathbf{0}$.

$\boxed{24}$ $\begin{aligned} (-m)\mathbf{a} &= (-m)\langle a_1, a_2 \rangle \\ &= \langle (-m)a_1, (-m)a_2 \rangle \\ &= \langle -(ma_1), -(ma_2) \rangle \\ &= -(\langle ma_1, ma_2 \rangle) \\ &= -(m\langle a_1, a_2 \rangle) \\ &= -m\langle a_1, a_2 \rangle = -m\mathbf{a} \end{aligned}$

**25** $-(\mathbf{a}+\mathbf{b}) = -(\langle a_1, a_2\rangle + \langle b_1, b_2\rangle)$
$= -(\langle a_1 + b_1, a_2 + b_2\rangle)$
$= \langle -(a_1 + b_1), -(a_2 + b_2)\rangle$
$= \langle -a_1 - b_1, -a_2 - b_2\rangle$
$= \langle -a_1, -a_2\rangle + \langle -b_1, -b_2\rangle$
$= -\mathbf{a} + (-\mathbf{b}) = -\mathbf{a} - \mathbf{b}$

**26** $m(\mathbf{a}-\mathbf{b}) = m(\langle a_1, a_2\rangle - \langle b_1, b_2\rangle)$
$= m\langle a_1 - b_1, a_2 - b_2\rangle$
$= \langle m(a_1 - b_1), m(a_2 - b_2)\rangle$
$= \langle ma_1 - mb_1, ma_2 - mb_2\rangle$
$= \langle ma_1, ma_2\rangle + \langle -mb_1, -mb_2\rangle$
$= m\langle a_1, a_2\rangle + (-m)\langle b_1, b_2\rangle = m\mathbf{a} - m\mathbf{b}$

**27** $\|2\mathbf{v}\| = \|2\langle a, b\rangle\|$
$= \|\langle 2a, 2b\rangle\| = \sqrt{(2a)^2 + (2b)^2} = \sqrt{4a^2 + 4b^2} = \sqrt{4(a^2 + b^2)} = 2\sqrt{a^2 + b^2} = 2\|\langle a, b\rangle\| = 2\|\mathbf{v}\|$

**28** $\|k\mathbf{v}\| = \|k\langle a, b\rangle\| = \|\langle ka, kb\rangle\| = \sqrt{(ka)^2 + (kb)^2} = \sqrt{k^2a^2 + k^2b^2} = \sqrt{k^2}\sqrt{a^2 + b^2} = |k|\|\langle a, b\rangle\| = |k|\|\mathbf{v}\|$

**29** $\|\mathbf{a}\| = \|\langle 0, -5\rangle\| = \sqrt{0^2 + (-5)^2} = \sqrt{25} = 5$. The terminal side of $\theta$ is on the negative $y$-axis $\Rightarrow$ $\theta = \frac{3\pi}{2}$.

**30** $\|\mathbf{a}\| = \|\langle 0, 10\rangle\| = \sqrt{0^2 + 10^2} = \sqrt{100} = 10$. The terminal side of $\theta$ is on the positive $y$-axis $\Rightarrow$ $\theta = \frac{\pi}{2}$.

**31** $\|\mathbf{a}\| = \|\langle 3, -3\rangle\| = \sqrt{3^2 + (-3)^2} = \sqrt{18} = 3\sqrt{2}$. $\tan\theta = \frac{-3}{3} = -1$ and $\theta$ in QIV $\Rightarrow$ $\theta = \frac{7\pi}{4}$.

**32** $\|\mathbf{a}\| = \left\|\langle -2, -2\sqrt{3}\rangle\right\| = \sqrt{(-2)^2 + \left(-2\sqrt{3}\right)^2} = \sqrt{16} = 4$. $\tan\theta = \frac{-2\sqrt{3}}{-2} = \sqrt{3}$ and $\theta$ in QIII $\Rightarrow$ $\theta = \frac{4\pi}{3}$.

**33** $\|\mathbf{a}\| = \|-4\mathbf{i} + 5\mathbf{j}\| = \sqrt{(-4)^2 + 5^2} = \sqrt{41}$. $\tan\theta = \frac{5}{-4}$ and $\theta$ in QII $\Rightarrow$ $\theta = \tan^{-1}\left(-\frac{5}{4}\right) + \pi$.

**34** $\|\mathbf{a}\| = \|-3\mathbf{i} + 7\mathbf{j}\| = \sqrt{(-3)^2 + 7^2} = \sqrt{58}$. $\tan\theta = \frac{7}{-3}$ and $\theta$ in QII $\Rightarrow$ $\theta = \tan^{-1}\left(-\frac{7}{3}\right) + \pi$.

**35** $\|\mathbf{a}\| = \|6\mathbf{i} - 5\mathbf{j}\| = \sqrt{6^2 + (-5)^2} = \sqrt{61}$. $\tan\theta = \frac{-5}{6}$ and $\theta$ in QIV $\Rightarrow$ $\theta = \tan^{-1}\left(-\frac{5}{6}\right) + 2\pi$.

**36** $\|\mathbf{a}\| = \|2\mathbf{i} - 3\mathbf{j}\| = \sqrt{2^2 + (-3)^2} = \sqrt{13}$. $\tan\theta = \frac{-3}{2}$ and $\theta$ in QIV $\Rightarrow$ $\theta = \tan^{-1}\left(-\frac{3}{2}\right) + 2\pi$.

**Note:** In Exercises 37–42, each resultant force is found by completing the parallelogram and then applying the law of cosines.

**37** $\|\mathbf{r}\| = \sqrt{40^2 + 70^2 - 2(40)(70)\cos 135°} = \sqrt{6500 + 2800\sqrt{2}} \approx 102.3$, or 102 lb.

*Figure 37*

*Figure 38*

**38** $\|\mathbf{r}\| = \sqrt{5.5^2 + 6.2^2 - 2(5.5)(6.2)\cos 120°} = \sqrt{102.79} \approx 10.1$ lb.

**39** $\|\mathbf{r}\| = \sqrt{2^2 + 8^2 - 2(2)(8)\cos 60°} = \sqrt{68 - 16} = \sqrt{52} \approx 7.2$ lb.

*Figure 39*

*Figure 40*

**40** $\|\mathbf{r}\| = \sqrt{30^2 + 50^2 - 2(30)(50)\cos 30°} = \sqrt{3400 - 1500\sqrt{3}} \approx 28.3,$ or 28 lb.

**41** $\|\mathbf{r}\| = \sqrt{90^2 + 60^2 - 2(90)(60)\cos 70°} \approx 89.48,$ or 89 lb.  Using the law of cosines,

$\alpha = \cos^{-1}\left(\dfrac{90^2 + \|\mathbf{r}\|^2 - 60^2}{2(90)(\|\mathbf{r}\|)}\right) \approx \cos^{-1}(0.7765) \approx 39°,$ which is 24° under the negative $x$-axis.

This angle is 204°, or S 66° W.

*Figure 41*

*Figure 42*

**42** $\|\mathbf{r}\| = \sqrt{50^2 + 20^2 - 2(50)(20)\cos 99°} \approx 56.68,$ or 57 lb.  Using the law of cosines,

$\alpha = \cos^{-1}\left(\dfrac{50^2 + \|\mathbf{r}\|^2 - 20^2}{2(50)(\|\mathbf{r}\|)}\right) \approx \cos^{-1}(0.9373) \approx 20°,$ which is 12° under the negative $x$-axis.

This angle is 192°, or S78° W.

**43** We use a component approach for this exercise.

$\mathbf{a} = \langle 6.0\cos 110°, 6.0\sin 110°\rangle \approx \langle -2.05, 5.64\rangle.$  $\mathbf{b} = \langle 2.0\cos 215°, 2.0\sin 215°\rangle \approx \langle -1.64, -1.15\rangle.$

$\mathbf{a} + \mathbf{b} \approx \langle -3.69, 4.49\rangle$ and $\|\mathbf{a} + \mathbf{b}\| \approx 5.8$ lb.  $\tan\theta \approx \frac{4.49}{-3.69} \Rightarrow \theta \approx 129°$ since $\theta$ is in QII.

**44** We use a component approach for this exercise.

$\mathbf{a} = \langle 30\cos 280°, 30\sin 280°\rangle \approx \langle 5.21, -29.54\rangle.$  $\mathbf{b} = \langle 80\cos 10°, 80\sin 10°\rangle \approx \langle 78.78, 13.89\rangle.$

$\mathbf{a} + \mathbf{b} \approx \langle 83.99, -15.65\rangle$ and $\|\mathbf{a} + \mathbf{b}\| \approx 85.44,$ or 85 lb.  $\tan\theta \approx \frac{-15.65}{83.99} \Rightarrow \theta \approx 349°$ since $\theta$ is in QIV.

**45** Horizontal $= 50\cos 35° \approx 40.96.$  Vertical $= 50\sin 35° \approx 28.68.$

**46** Horizontal $= 20\cos 40° \approx 15.32.$  Vertical $= 20\sin 40° \approx 12.86.$

**47** Horizontal $= 20\cos 108° \approx -6.18.$  Vertical $= 20\sin 108° \approx 19.02.$

**48** Horizontal $= 160\cos 7.5° \approx 158.63.$  Vertical $= 160\sin 7.5° \approx 20.88.$

***Note:*** In Exercises 49–52, let **u** denote the unit vector in the direction of **a**.

**49** (a)  The unit vector **u** in the direction of **a** is $\mathbf{u} = \dfrac{1}{\|\mathbf{a}\|}\,\mathbf{a}$.

$$\mathbf{a} = -8\mathbf{i} + 15\mathbf{j} \ \Rightarrow\ \|\mathbf{a}\| = \sqrt{(-8)^2 + 15^2} = \sqrt{64 + 225} = \sqrt{289} = 17.$$

$$\mathbf{u} = \frac{1}{\|\mathbf{a}\|}\,\mathbf{a} = \tfrac{1}{17}(-8\mathbf{i} + 15\mathbf{j}) = -\tfrac{8}{17}\mathbf{i} + \tfrac{15}{17}\mathbf{j}.$$

(b)  The unit vector $-\mathbf{u}$ has the opposite direction of **u** and hence, the opposite direction of **a**.

$$-\mathbf{u} = -\left(-\tfrac{8}{17}\mathbf{i} + \tfrac{15}{17}\mathbf{j}\right) = \tfrac{8}{17}\mathbf{i} - \tfrac{15}{17}\mathbf{j}.$$

**50** (a)  $\mathbf{a} = 5\mathbf{i} - 3\mathbf{j} \ \Rightarrow\ \|\mathbf{a}\| = \sqrt{5^2 + (-3)^2} = \sqrt{34};\ \mathbf{u} = \dfrac{\mathbf{a}}{\|\mathbf{a}\|} = \tfrac{5}{\sqrt{34}}\mathbf{i} - \tfrac{3}{\sqrt{34}}\mathbf{j}$

(b)  $-\mathbf{u} = -\left(\tfrac{5}{\sqrt{34}}\mathbf{i} - \tfrac{3}{\sqrt{34}}\mathbf{j}\right) = -\tfrac{5}{\sqrt{34}}\mathbf{i} + \tfrac{3}{\sqrt{34}}\mathbf{j}$

**51** (a)  As in Exercise 49, $\mathbf{a} = \langle 2, -5\rangle \ \Rightarrow\ \|\mathbf{a}\| = \sqrt{2^2 + (-5)^2} = \sqrt{29}$ and $\mathbf{u} = \dfrac{\mathbf{a}}{\|\mathbf{a}\|} = \left\langle \tfrac{2}{\sqrt{29}}, -\tfrac{5}{\sqrt{29}}\right\rangle$.

(b)  $-\mathbf{u} = -\left\langle \tfrac{2}{\sqrt{29}}, -\tfrac{5}{\sqrt{29}}\right\rangle = \left\langle -\tfrac{2}{\sqrt{29}}, \tfrac{5}{\sqrt{29}}\right\rangle$

**52** (a)  $\mathbf{a} = \langle -12, 5\rangle \ \Rightarrow\ \|\mathbf{a}\| = \sqrt{(-12)^2 + 5^2} = 13;\ \mathbf{u} = \dfrac{\mathbf{a}}{\|\mathbf{a}\|} = \dfrac{\langle -12, 5\rangle}{13} = \left\langle -\tfrac{12}{13}, \tfrac{5}{13}\right\rangle$

(b)  $-\mathbf{u} = -\left\langle -\tfrac{12}{13}, \tfrac{5}{13}\right\rangle = \left\langle \tfrac{12}{13}, -\tfrac{5}{13}\right\rangle$

**53** (a)  $2\mathbf{a}$ has twice the magnitude of **a** and the same direction as **a**.  Hence, $2\langle -8, 2\rangle = \langle -16, 4\rangle$.

(b)  $\tfrac{1}{2}\mathbf{a}$ has one-half the magnitude of **a** and the same direction as **a**.  Hence, $\tfrac{1}{2}\langle -8, 2\rangle = \langle -4, 1\rangle$.

**54** (a)  $-3\mathbf{a}$ has three times the magnitude of **a** and the opposite direction of **a**.  Hence, $-3(8\mathbf{i} - 5\mathbf{j}) = -24\mathbf{i} + 15\mathbf{j}$.

(b)  $-\tfrac{1}{3}\mathbf{a}$ has one-third the magnitude of **a** and the opposite direction of **a**.  Hence, $-\tfrac{1}{3}(8\mathbf{i} - 5\mathbf{j}) = -\tfrac{8}{3}\mathbf{i} + \tfrac{5}{3}\mathbf{j}$.

**55**  Let **v** denote the desired vector.  The unit vector $\dfrac{\mathbf{a}}{\|\mathbf{a}\|}$ has the same direction as **a**.

The vector $-6\left(\dfrac{\mathbf{a}}{\|\mathbf{a}\|}\right)$ will have a magnitude of 6 and the opposite direction of **a**.

$$\mathbf{a} = 4\mathbf{i} - 7\mathbf{j} \ \Rightarrow\ \|\mathbf{a}\| = \sqrt{16 + 49} = \sqrt{65}.\ \text{Thus, } -6\left(\frac{\mathbf{a}}{\|\mathbf{a}\|}\right) = -6\left(\tfrac{4}{\sqrt{65}}\mathbf{i} - \tfrac{7}{\sqrt{65}}\mathbf{j}\right) = -\tfrac{24}{\sqrt{65}}\mathbf{i} + \tfrac{42}{\sqrt{65}}\mathbf{j}.$$

**56**  Let **v** denote the desired vector.  $\mathbf{a} = \langle -3, -1\rangle \ \Rightarrow\ \|\mathbf{a}\| = \sqrt{10}.\ \mathbf{v} = -5\left(\dfrac{\mathbf{a}}{\|\mathbf{a}\|}\right) = \left\langle \tfrac{15}{\sqrt{10}}, \tfrac{5}{\sqrt{10}}\right\rangle.$

**57** (a)  $\mathbf{F} = \mathbf{F}_1 + \mathbf{F}_2 + \mathbf{F}_3 = \langle 4, 3\rangle + \langle -2, -3\rangle + \langle 5, 2\rangle = \langle 7, 2\rangle$.

(b)  $\mathbf{F} + \mathbf{G} = 0 \ \Rightarrow\ \mathbf{G} = -\mathbf{F} = \langle -7, -2\rangle$.

**58** (a)  $\mathbf{F} = \mathbf{F}_1 + \mathbf{F}_2 + \mathbf{F}_3 = \langle -3, -1\rangle + \langle 0, -3\rangle + \langle 3, 4\rangle = \langle 0, 0\rangle$.

(b)  No additional force is needed since the system is in equilibrium.

**59** (a)  $\mathbf{F} = \mathbf{F}_1 + \mathbf{F}_2 = \langle 6\cos 130°, 6\sin 130°\rangle + \langle 4\cos(-120°), 4\sin(-120°)\rangle \approx \langle -5.86, 1.13\rangle$.

(b)  $\mathbf{F} + \mathbf{G} = 0 \ \Rightarrow\ \mathbf{G} = -\mathbf{F} \approx \langle 5.86, -1.13\rangle$.

**60** (a)  $\mathbf{F} = \mathbf{F}_1 + \mathbf{F}_2 + \mathbf{F}_3 = \langle 8\cos 50°, 8\sin 50°\rangle + \langle 7\cos 130°, 7\sin 130°\rangle + \langle 5\cos 200°, 5\sin 200°\rangle$
$$\approx \langle -4.06, 9.78\rangle$$

(b)  $\mathbf{F} + \mathbf{G} = 0 \ \Rightarrow\ \mathbf{G} = -\mathbf{F} \approx \langle 4.06, -9.78\rangle$.

**61** The vertical components of the forces must add up to zero for the large ship to move along the line segment $AB$.

The vertical component of the smaller tug is $3200 \sin(-30°) = -1600$.

The vertical component of the larger tug is $4000 \sin \theta$.

$4000 \sin \theta = 1600 \quad \Rightarrow \quad \theta = \sin^{-1}\left(\frac{1600}{4000}\right) = \sin^{-1}(0.4) \approx 23.6°.$

**62** (a) Consider the force of 160 pounds to be the resultant vector of two vectors whose initial point is at the astronaut's feet, one along the positive $x$-axis and the other along the negative $y$-axis.

The angle formed by the resultant vector and the positive $x$-axis is the complement of $\theta$, $90° - \theta$.

$$\text{Now } \cos(90° - \theta) = \frac{x\text{-component}}{160} \quad \Rightarrow \quad x\text{-component} = 160 \sin \theta$$
$$\text{and } \sin(90° - \theta) = \frac{y\text{-component}}{160} \quad \Rightarrow \quad y\text{-component} = 160 \cos \theta.$$

(b) $27 = 160 \cos \theta \quad \Rightarrow \quad \theta = \cos^{-1}\left(\frac{27}{160}\right) \approx 80.28°$ on the moon. $60 = 160 \cos \theta \quad \Rightarrow$
$$\theta = \cos^{-1}\left(\frac{60}{160}\right) = \cos^{-1}\left(\frac{3}{8}\right) \approx 67.98° \text{ on Mars.}$$

**Note:** In Exercises 63–68, measure angles from the positive $x$-axis.

**63** $\mathbf{p} = \langle 200 \cos 40°, 200 \sin 40° \rangle \approx \langle 153.21, 128.56 \rangle.$ $\mathbf{w} = \langle 40 \cos 0°, 40 \sin 0° \rangle = \langle 40, 0 \rangle.$

$\mathbf{p} + \mathbf{w} \approx \langle 193.21, 128.56 \rangle$ and $\|\mathbf{p} + \mathbf{w}\| \approx 232.07$, or 232 mi/hr. $\tan \theta \approx \frac{128.56}{193.21} \quad \Rightarrow \quad \theta \approx 34°.$

The true course is then N$(90° - 34°)$E, or N$56°$E.

**64** $\mathbf{p} = \langle 500 \cos 310°, 500 \sin 310° \rangle \approx \langle 321.39, -383.02 \rangle.$

$\mathbf{w} = \langle 30 \cos 25°, 30 \sin 25° \rangle \approx \langle 27.19, 12.68 \rangle.$

$\mathbf{p} + \mathbf{w} \approx \langle 348.58, -370.34 \rangle$ and $\|\mathbf{p} + \mathbf{w}\| \approx 508.59$, or 509 mi/hr.

$\tan \theta \approx \dfrac{-370.34}{348.58} \quad \Rightarrow \quad \theta \approx -46.7°$, or $-47°$, or, equivalently, $137°.$

**65** $\mathbf{w} = \langle 50 \cos 90°, 50 \sin 90° \rangle = \langle 0, 50 \rangle.$

$\mathbf{r} = \langle 400 \cos 200°, 400 \sin 200° \rangle \approx \langle -375.88, -136.81 \rangle$, where $\mathbf{r}$ is the desired resultant of $\mathbf{p} + \mathbf{w}$.

Since $\mathbf{r} = \mathbf{p} + \mathbf{w}$, $\mathbf{p} = \mathbf{r} - \mathbf{w} \approx \langle -375.88, -186.81 \rangle.$ $\|\mathbf{p}\| \approx 419.74$, or 420 mi/hr.

$\tan \theta \approx \frac{-186.81}{-375.88}$ and $\theta$ is in QIII $\quad \Rightarrow \quad \theta \approx 206°$ from the positive $x$-axis, or $244°$ using the directional form.

*Figure 65*

*Figure 66*

**66** $\mathbf{p} = \langle 300 \cos 70°, 300 \sin 70° \rangle \approx \langle 102.61, 281.91 \rangle.$ $\mathbf{r} = \langle 350 \cos 60°, 350 \sin 60° \rangle \approx \langle 175, 303.11 \rangle.$

$\mathbf{w} = \mathbf{r} - \mathbf{p} \approx \langle 72.39, 21.20 \rangle$ and $\|\mathbf{w}\| \approx 75.43$, or 75 mi/hr.

$\tan \theta \approx \frac{21.20}{72.39} \quad \Rightarrow \quad \theta \approx 16°$, or in the direction of $74°.$

**67** Let the vectors **c**, **b**, and **r** denote the current, the boat, and the resultant,
respectively. $\mathbf{c} = \langle 1.5\cos 0°, 1.5\sin 0° \rangle = \langle 1.5, 0 \rangle$. $\mathbf{r} = \langle s\cos 90°, s\sin 90° \rangle = \langle 0, s \rangle$,
where $s$ is the resulting speed. $\mathbf{b} = \langle 4\cos\theta, 4\sin\theta \rangle$. Also, $\mathbf{b} = \mathbf{r} - \mathbf{c} = \langle -1.5, s \rangle$.

$$4\cos\theta = -1.5 \quad \Rightarrow \quad \theta \approx 112°, \text{ or N22°W.}$$

*Figure 67*

*Figure 68*

**68** Let the vectors **c**, **b**, and **r** denote the current, the boat, and the resultant, respectively. Let $s$ denote the rate of the
current and $t$ the resulting speed. $\mathbf{b} = \langle 30\cos 75°, 30\sin 75° \rangle \approx \langle 7.76, 28.98 \rangle$.

$$\mathbf{c} = \langle s\cos 180°, s\sin 180° \rangle = \langle -s, 0 \rangle. \quad \mathbf{r} = \langle t\cos 90°, t\sin 90° \rangle = \langle 0, t \rangle.$$

$$\text{Since } \mathbf{c} = \mathbf{r} - \mathbf{b}, \text{ we have } -s = 0 - 7.76 \quad \Rightarrow \quad s = 7.76, \text{ or } 8 \text{ mi/hr.}$$

**69** In the figure in the text, suppose $\mathbf{v}_1$ was pointing upwards instead of downwards. If we then write $\mathbf{v}_1$ in terms of its
vertical and horizontal components, we have $\mathbf{v}_1 = \|\mathbf{v}_1\|\cos\theta_1\,\mathbf{j} - \|\mathbf{v}_1\|\sin\theta_1\,\mathbf{i}$. We want the negative of this vector
since $\mathbf{v}_1$ is actually pointing downward, so using $\|\mathbf{v}_1\| = 8.2$ and $\theta_1 = 30°$, we obtain

$$\mathbf{v}_1 = \|\mathbf{v}_1\|\sin\theta_1\,\mathbf{i} - \|\mathbf{v}_1\|\cos\theta_1\,\mathbf{j} = 8.2\left(\tfrac{1}{2}\right)\mathbf{i} - 8.2\left(\sqrt{3}/2\right)\mathbf{j} = 4.1\,\mathbf{i} - 4.1\sqrt{3}\,\mathbf{j} \approx 4.1\,\mathbf{i} - 7.10\,\mathbf{j}.$$

The angle $\theta_2$ can now be computed using the given relationship in the text.

$$\frac{\|\mathbf{v}_1\|}{\|\mathbf{v}_2\|} = \frac{\tan\theta_1}{\tan\theta_2} \quad \Rightarrow \quad \tan\theta_2 = \frac{\|\mathbf{v}_2\|}{\|\mathbf{v}_1\|}\tan\theta_1 = \frac{3.8}{8.2} \times \frac{1}{\sqrt{3}} \quad \Rightarrow \quad \tan\theta_2 \approx 0.2676 \quad \Rightarrow \quad \theta_2 \approx 14.98°.$$

We now write $\mathbf{v}_2$ in terms of its horizontal and vertical components, and using $\|\mathbf{v}_2\| = 3.8$, it follows that

$$\mathbf{v}_2 = \|\mathbf{v}_2\|\sin\theta_2\,\mathbf{i} - \|\mathbf{v}_2\|\cos\theta_2\,\mathbf{j} \approx 0.98\,\mathbf{i} - 3.67\,\mathbf{j}.$$

**70** Since $\theta_1$ is an acute angle, $\mathbf{v}_1 = 20\,\mathbf{i} - 82\,\mathbf{j} \quad \Rightarrow \quad \tan\theta_1 = \tfrac{20}{82} \quad \Rightarrow \quad \theta_1 \approx 13.71°.$

$$\|\mathbf{v}_1\| = \sqrt{20^2 + (-82)^2} = \sqrt{7124} \approx 84.40 \text{ cm/day.}$$

$$\frac{\|\mathbf{v}_1\|}{\|\mathbf{v}_2\|} = \frac{\tan\theta_1}{\tan\theta_2} \quad \Rightarrow \quad \tan\theta_2 = \frac{\|\mathbf{v}_2\|}{\|\mathbf{v}_1\|}\tan\theta_1 \approx \frac{725}{\sqrt{7124}}\left(\frac{20}{82}\right) \approx 2.095 \quad \Rightarrow \quad \theta_2 \approx 64.48°.$$

**71** (a) $\mathbf{a} = 15\cos 40°\,\mathbf{i} + 15\sin 40°\,\mathbf{j} \approx 11.49\,\mathbf{i} + 9.64\,\mathbf{j}$. $\mathbf{b} = 17\cos 40°\,\mathbf{i} + 17\sin 40°\,\mathbf{j} \approx 13.02\,\mathbf{i} + 10.93\,\mathbf{j}$.

$$\overrightarrow{PR} = \mathbf{a} + \mathbf{b} \approx 24.51\,\mathbf{i} + 20.57\,\mathbf{j} \quad \Rightarrow \quad R \approx (24.51, 20.57).$$

  (b) $\mathbf{c} = 15\cos(40° + 85°)\,\mathbf{i} + 15\sin 125°\,\mathbf{j} \approx -8.60\,\mathbf{i} + 12.29\,\mathbf{j}$.

  $\mathbf{d} = 17\cos(40° + 85° + 35°)\,\mathbf{i} + 17\sin 160°\,\mathbf{j} \approx -15.97\,\mathbf{i} + 5.81\,\mathbf{j}$.

$$\overrightarrow{PR} = \mathbf{c} + \mathbf{d} \approx -24.57\,\mathbf{i} + 18.10\,\mathbf{j} \quad \Rightarrow \quad R \approx (-24.57, 18.10).$$

**72** (a) $\mathbf{a} = 15\cos(-50°)\,\mathbf{i} + 15\sin(-50°)\,\mathbf{j} \approx 9.64\,\mathbf{i} - 11.49\,\mathbf{j}$. $\mathbf{b} = 10\cos(-50°)\,\mathbf{i} + 10\sin(-50°)\,\mathbf{j} \approx 6.43\,\mathbf{i} - 7.66\,\mathbf{j}$.

  $\mathbf{c} = 7\cos(-50°)\,\mathbf{i} + 7\sin(-50°)\,\mathbf{j} \approx 4.50\,\mathbf{i} - 5.36\,\mathbf{j}$.

$$\overrightarrow{PR} = \mathbf{a} + \mathbf{b} + \mathbf{c} \approx 20.57\,\mathbf{i} - 24.51\,\mathbf{j} \quad \Rightarrow \quad R \approx (20.57, -24.51).$$

(b) $\mathbf{d} = 15\cos(-50° + 75°)\mathbf{i} + 15\sin 25°\,\mathbf{j} \approx 13.59\,\mathbf{i} + 6.34\,\mathbf{j}$.

$\mathbf{e} = 10\cos(-50° + 75° - 80°)\mathbf{i} + 10\sin(-55°)\mathbf{j} \approx 5.74\,\mathbf{i} - 8.19\,\mathbf{j}$.

$\mathbf{f} = 7\cos(-50° + 75° - 80° + 40°)\mathbf{i} + 7\sin(-15°)\mathbf{j} \approx 6.76\,\mathbf{i} - 1.81\,\mathbf{j}$.

$$\overrightarrow{PR} = \mathbf{d} + \mathbf{e} + \mathbf{f} \approx 26.09\,\mathbf{i} - 3.66\,\mathbf{j} \quad \Rightarrow \quad R \approx (26.09, -3.66).$$

[73] Break the force into a horizontal and a vertical component. The group of 550 people had to contribute a force equal to the vertical component up the ramp. The vertical component is $99,000\sin 9° \approx 15,487$ lb.

$$\frac{15,487}{550} \approx 28.2 \text{ lb/person.} \quad \text{(Since friction was ignored, the actual force would have been greater.)}$$

## 7.4 Exercises

[1] (a) The dot product of the two vectors is $\langle -2, 5\rangle \cdot \langle 3, 6\rangle = (-2)(3) + (5)(6) = -6 + 30 = 24$.

(b) The angle between the two vectors is $\theta = \cos^{-1}\left(\dfrac{\langle -2, 5\rangle \cdot \langle 3, 6\rangle}{\|\langle -2, 5\rangle\|\,\|\langle 3, 6\rangle\|}\right) = \cos^{-1}\left(\dfrac{24}{\sqrt{29}\,\sqrt{45}}\right) \approx 48°22'$.

[2] (a) $\langle 4, -7\rangle \cdot \langle -6, 1\rangle = (4)(-6) + (-7)(1) = -24 - 7 = -31$

(b) $\theta = \cos^{-1}\left(\dfrac{\langle 4, -7\rangle \cdot \langle -6, 1\rangle}{\|\langle 4, -7\rangle\|\,\|\langle -6, 1\rangle\|}\right) = \cos^{-1}\left(\dfrac{-31}{\sqrt{65}\,\sqrt{37}}\right) \approx 129°12'$

[3] (a) $(4\mathbf{i} - \mathbf{j}) \cdot (-3\mathbf{i} + 2\mathbf{j}) = (4)(-3) + (-1)(2) = -12 - 2 = -14$

(b) $\theta = \cos^{-1}\left(\dfrac{(4\mathbf{i} - \mathbf{j}) \cdot (-3\mathbf{i} + 2\mathbf{j})}{\|4\mathbf{i} - \mathbf{j}\|\,\|-3\mathbf{i} + 2\mathbf{j}\|}\right) = \cos^{-1}\left(\dfrac{-14}{\sqrt{17}\,\sqrt{13}}\right) \approx 160°21'$

[4] (a) $(8\mathbf{i} - 3\mathbf{j}) \cdot (2\mathbf{i} - 7\mathbf{j}) = (8)(2) + (-3)(-7) = 16 + 21 = 37$

(b) $\theta = \cos^{-1}\left(\dfrac{(8\mathbf{i} - 3\mathbf{j}) \cdot (2\mathbf{i} - 7\mathbf{j})}{\|8\mathbf{i} - 3\mathbf{j}\|\,\|2\mathbf{i} - 7\mathbf{j}\|}\right) = \cos^{-1}\left(\dfrac{37}{\sqrt{73}\,\sqrt{53}}\right) \approx 53°30'$

[5] (a) $(9\mathbf{i}) \cdot (5\mathbf{i} + 4\mathbf{j}) = (9)(5) + (0)(4) = 45 + 0 = 45$

(b) $\theta = \cos^{-1}\left(\dfrac{(9\mathbf{i}) \cdot (5\mathbf{i} + 4\mathbf{j})}{\|9\mathbf{i}\|\,\|5\mathbf{i} + 4\mathbf{j}\|}\right) = \cos^{-1}\left(\dfrac{45}{\sqrt{81}\,\sqrt{41}}\right) \approx 38°40'$

[6] (a) $(6\mathbf{j}) \cdot (-4\mathbf{i}) = (0)(-4) + (6)(0) = 0 + 0 = 0$

(b) $\theta = \cos^{-1}\left(\dfrac{(6\mathbf{j}) \cdot (-4\mathbf{i})}{\|6\mathbf{j}\|\,\|-4\mathbf{i}\|}\right) = \cos^{-1}\left(\dfrac{0}{\sqrt{36}\,\sqrt{16}}\right) = \cos^{-1}(0) = 90°$

[7] (a) $\langle -9, -3\rangle \cdot \langle 3, 1\rangle = (-9)(3) + (-3)(1) = -27 - 3 = -30$

(b) $\theta = \cos^{-1}\left(\dfrac{\langle -9, -3\rangle \cdot \langle 3, 1\rangle}{\|\langle -9, -3\rangle\|\,\|\langle 3, 1\rangle\|}\right) = \cos^{-1}\left(\dfrac{-30}{\sqrt{90}\,\sqrt{10}}\right) = \cos^{-1}(-1) = 180°$

This result $\{\theta = 180°\}$ indicates that the vectors have the opposite direction.

[8] (a) $\langle -3, 6\rangle \cdot \langle -1, 2\rangle = (-3)(-1) + (6)(2) = 15$

(b) $\theta = \cos^{-1}\left(\dfrac{\langle -3, 6\rangle \cdot \langle -1, 2\rangle}{\|\langle -3, 6\rangle\|\,\|\langle -1, 2\rangle\|}\right) = \cos^{-1}\left(\dfrac{15}{\sqrt{45}\,\sqrt{5}}\right) = \cos^{-1}(1) = 0°$

This result $\{\theta = 0°\}$ indicates that the vectors have the same direction.

**9** $\langle 4, -1 \rangle \cdot \langle 2, 8 \rangle = 8 - 8 = 0 \implies$ vectors are orthogonal since their dot product is zero.

**10** $\langle -2, 5 \rangle \cdot \langle 10, 4 \rangle = -20 + 20 = 0 \implies$ vectors are orthogonal since their dot product is zero.

**11** $(-4\mathbf{j}) \cdot (-7\mathbf{i}) = 0 + 0 = 0 \implies$ vectors are orthogonal since their dot product is zero.

**12** $(7\mathbf{i} - 14\mathbf{j}) \cdot (2\mathbf{i} + \mathbf{j}) = 14 - 14 = 0 \implies$ vectors are orthogonal since their dot product is zero.

**13** We first find the angle between the two vectors. If this angle is 0 or $\pi$, then the vectors are parallel.

$$\cos\theta = \frac{\mathbf{a} \cdot \mathbf{b}}{\|\mathbf{a}\|\|\mathbf{b}\|} = \frac{(3)\left(-\frac{12}{7}\right) + (-5)\left(\frac{20}{7}\right)}{\sqrt{9 + 25}\sqrt{\frac{144}{49} + \frac{400}{49}}} = \frac{-\frac{136}{7}}{\sqrt{\frac{18,496}{49}}} = \frac{-\frac{136}{7}}{\frac{136}{7}} = -1 \implies \theta = \cos^{-1}(-1) = \pi.$$

$\mathbf{b} = m\mathbf{a} \implies -\frac{12}{7}\mathbf{i} + \frac{20}{7}\mathbf{j} = 3m\mathbf{i} - 5m\mathbf{j} \implies 3m = -\frac{12}{7}$ and $-5m = \frac{20}{7} \implies m = -\frac{4}{7} < 0 \implies$

$\mathbf{a}$ and $\mathbf{b}$ have opposite directions. Showing either $\theta = \pi$ or $m < 0$ is sufficient.

**14** $\cos\theta = \dfrac{\mathbf{a} \cdot \mathbf{b}}{\|\mathbf{a}\|\|\mathbf{b}\|} = \dfrac{\left(-\frac{5}{2}\right)(-10) + (6)(24)}{\sqrt{\frac{25}{4} + 36}\sqrt{100 + 576}} = \dfrac{169}{\sqrt{\frac{169}{4}} \cdot 26} = 1 \implies \theta = \cos^{-1} 1 = 0.$

$\mathbf{b} = m\mathbf{a} \implies -10\mathbf{i} + 24\mathbf{j} = -\frac{5}{2}m\mathbf{i} + 6m\mathbf{j} \implies -\frac{5}{2}m = -10$ and $6m = 24 \implies m = 4 > 0 \implies$

$\mathbf{a}$ and $\mathbf{b}$ have the same direction. Showing either $\theta = 0$ or $m > 0$ is sufficient.

**15** $\cos\theta = \dfrac{\mathbf{a} \cdot \mathbf{b}}{\|\mathbf{a}\|\|\mathbf{b}\|} = \dfrac{\left(\frac{2}{3}\right)(8) + \left(\frac{3}{4}\right)(9)}{\sqrt{\frac{4}{9} + \frac{9}{16}}\sqrt{64 + 81}} = \dfrac{\frac{145}{12}}{\sqrt{\frac{145}{144}} \cdot \sqrt{145}} = 1 \implies \theta = \cos^{-1} 1 = 0.$

$\mathbf{b} = m\mathbf{a} \implies 8\mathbf{i} + 9\mathbf{j} = \frac{2}{3}m\mathbf{i} + \frac{3}{4}m\mathbf{j} \implies 8 = \frac{2}{3}m$ and $9 = \frac{3}{4}m \implies m = 12 > 0 \implies$

$\mathbf{a}$ and $\mathbf{b}$ have the same direction. Showing either $\theta = 0$ or $m > 0$ is sufficient.

**16** $\cos\theta = \dfrac{\mathbf{a} \cdot \mathbf{b}}{\|\mathbf{a}\|\|\mathbf{b}\|} = \dfrac{(6)(-4) + (18)(-12)}{\sqrt{36 + 324}\sqrt{16 + 144}} = \dfrac{-240}{\sqrt{57,600}} = -1 \implies \theta = \cos^{-1}(-1) = \pi.$

$\mathbf{b} = m\mathbf{a} \implies -4\mathbf{i} - 12\mathbf{j} = 6m\mathbf{i} + 18m\mathbf{j} \implies 6m = -4$ and $18m = -12 \implies m = -\frac{2}{3} < 0 \implies$

$\mathbf{a}$ and $\mathbf{b}$ have opposite directions. Showing either $\theta = \pi$ or $m < 0$ is sufficient.

**17** We need to have the dot product of the two vectors equal 0.

$$(3\mathbf{i} - 2\mathbf{j}) \cdot (4\mathbf{i} + 5m\mathbf{j}) = 0 \implies 12 - 10m = 0 \implies m = \frac{6}{5}.$$

**18** $(4m\mathbf{i} + \mathbf{j}) \cdot (9m\mathbf{i} - 25\mathbf{j}) = 0 \implies 36m^2 - 25 = 0 \implies m^2 = \frac{25}{36} \implies m = \pm\frac{5}{6}.$

**19** $(9\mathbf{i} - 16m\mathbf{j}) \cdot (\mathbf{i} + 4m\mathbf{j}) = 0 \implies 9 - 64m^2 = 0 \implies m^2 = \frac{9}{64} \implies m = \pm\frac{3}{8}.$

**20** $(5m\mathbf{i} + 3\mathbf{j}) \cdot (2\mathbf{i} + 7\mathbf{j}) = 0 \implies 10m + 21 = 0 \implies m = -\frac{21}{10}.$

**21** (a) $\mathbf{a} \cdot (\mathbf{b} + \mathbf{c}) = \langle 2, -3 \rangle \cdot (\langle 3, 4 \rangle + \langle -1, 5 \rangle) = \langle 2, -3 \rangle \cdot \langle 2, 9 \rangle = 4 - 27 = -23$

    (b) $\mathbf{a} \cdot \mathbf{b} + \mathbf{a} \cdot \mathbf{c} = \langle 2, -3 \rangle \cdot \langle 3, 4 \rangle + \langle 2, -3 \rangle \cdot \langle -1, 5 \rangle = (6 - 12) + (-2 - 15) = -23$

**22** (a) $\mathbf{b} \cdot (\mathbf{a} - \mathbf{c}) = \langle 3, 4 \rangle \cdot (\langle 2, -3 \rangle - \langle -1, 5 \rangle) = \langle 3, 4 \rangle \cdot \langle 3, -8 \rangle = 9 - 32 = -23$

    (b) $\mathbf{b} \cdot \mathbf{a} - \mathbf{b} \cdot \mathbf{c} = \langle 3, 4 \rangle \cdot \langle 2, -3 \rangle - \langle 3, 4 \rangle \cdot \langle -1, 5 \rangle = (6 - 12) - (-3 + 20) = -23$

**23** $(\mathbf{a} + \mathbf{c}) \cdot (\mathbf{a} - \mathbf{c}) = (\langle 2, -3 \rangle + \langle -1, 5 \rangle) \cdot (\langle 2, -3 \rangle - \langle -1, 5 \rangle)$

       $= \langle 1, 2 \rangle \cdot \langle 3, -8 \rangle = 3 - 16 = -13$

**24** $(\mathbf{a} - \mathbf{b}) \cdot (\mathbf{b} + \mathbf{c}) = (\langle 2, -3 \rangle - \langle 3, 4 \rangle) \cdot (\langle 3, 4 \rangle + \langle -1, 5 \rangle) = \langle -1, -7 \rangle \cdot \langle 2, 9 \rangle = -2 - 63 = -65$

**25** $\text{comp}_\mathbf{c} \mathbf{b} = \dfrac{\mathbf{b} \cdot \mathbf{c}}{\|\mathbf{c}\|} = \dfrac{\langle 3, 4 \rangle \cdot \langle -1, 5 \rangle}{\|\langle -1, 5 \rangle\|} = \dfrac{17}{\sqrt{26}} \approx 3.33$

**26** $\text{comp}_b\,\mathbf{c} = \dfrac{\mathbf{c}\cdot\mathbf{b}}{\|\mathbf{b}\|} = \dfrac{\langle -1,5\rangle\cdot\langle 3,4\rangle}{\|\langle 3,4\rangle\|} = \dfrac{17}{5} = 3.4$

**27** $\text{comp}_b(\mathbf{a}+\mathbf{c}) = \dfrac{(\mathbf{a}+\mathbf{c})\cdot\mathbf{b}}{\|\mathbf{b}\|} = \dfrac{(\langle 2,-3\rangle + \langle -1,5\rangle)\cdot\langle 3,4\rangle}{\|\langle 3,4\rangle\|} = \dfrac{\langle 1,2\rangle\cdot\langle 3,4\rangle}{5} = \dfrac{11}{5} = 2.2$

**28** $\text{comp}_c\,\mathbf{c} = \dfrac{\mathbf{c}\cdot\mathbf{c}}{\|\mathbf{c}\|} = \dfrac{\langle -1,5\rangle\cdot\langle -1,5\rangle}{\|\langle -1,5\rangle\|} = \dfrac{26}{\sqrt{26}} = \sqrt{26} \approx 5.10.$

Note that, in general, the component of a vector along itself is just the magnitude of the vector.

**29** $\mathbf{c}\cdot\overrightarrow{PQ} = (3\mathbf{i}+4\mathbf{j})\cdot\langle 5-0,-2-0\rangle = \langle 3,4\rangle\cdot\langle 5,-2\rangle = 15-8 = 7.$

**30** $\mathbf{c}\cdot\overrightarrow{PQ} = (-4\mathbf{i}+2\mathbf{j})\cdot\langle 3-0,9-0\rangle = \langle -4,2\rangle\cdot\langle 3,9\rangle = -12+18 = 6.$

**31** We want a vector with initial point at the origin and terminal point located so that this vector has the same magnitude and direction as $\overrightarrow{PQ}$.

Following the hint in the text, $\mathbf{b} = \overrightarrow{PQ} \;\Rightarrow\; \langle b_1,b_2\rangle = \langle 4-2, 3-(-1)\rangle \;\Rightarrow\; \langle b_1,b_2\rangle = \langle 2,4\rangle.$

$$\mathbf{c}\cdot\mathbf{b} = \langle 6,4\rangle\cdot\langle 2,4\rangle = 12+16 = 28.$$

**32** As in Exercise 31, $\mathbf{c}\cdot\overrightarrow{PQ} = \langle -1,7\rangle\cdot\langle 6-(-2),1-5\rangle = -36.$

**33** The force is described by the vector $\langle 0,4\rangle$. The work done is $\langle 0,4\rangle\cdot\langle 8,3\rangle = 0+12 = 12.$

**34** The force is described by the vector $\langle -10,0\rangle$. The work done is $\langle -10,0\rangle\cdot\langle 1-0,0-1\rangle = -10+0 = -10.$

**35** $\mathbf{a}\cdot\mathbf{a} = \langle a_1,a_2\rangle\cdot\langle a_1,a_2\rangle = a_1^2 + a_2^2 = \left(\sqrt{a_1^2+a_2^2}\right)^2 = \|\mathbf{a}\|^2$

**36** $\mathbf{a}\cdot\mathbf{b} = \langle a_1,a_2\rangle\cdot\langle b_1,b_2\rangle = a_1b_1+a_2b_2 = b_1a_1+b_2a_2 = \langle b_1,b_2\rangle\cdot\langle a_1,a_2\rangle = \mathbf{b}\cdot\mathbf{a}$

**37** $(m\mathbf{a})\cdot\mathbf{b} = (m\langle a_1,a_2\rangle)\cdot\langle b_1,b_2\rangle$

$\qquad\qquad = \langle ma_1,ma_2\rangle\cdot\langle b_1,b_2\rangle$

$\qquad\qquad = ma_1b_1 + ma_2b_2$

$\qquad\qquad = m(a_1b_1+a_2b_2) = m(\mathbf{a}\cdot\mathbf{b})$

**38** $m(\mathbf{a}\cdot\mathbf{b}) = m(\langle a_1,a_2\rangle\cdot\langle b_1,b_2\rangle)$

$\qquad\qquad = m(a_1b_1+a_2b_2)$

$\qquad\qquad = ma_1b_1 + ma_2b_2$

$\qquad\qquad = a_1(mb_1) + a_2(mb_2)$

$\qquad\qquad = \langle a_1,a_2\rangle\cdot\langle mb_1,mb_2\rangle$

$\qquad\qquad = \mathbf{a}\cdot(m\langle b_1,b_2\rangle) = \mathbf{a}\cdot(m\mathbf{b})$

**39** $\mathbf{0}\cdot\mathbf{a} = \langle 0,0\rangle\cdot\langle a_1,a_2\rangle = 0(a_1)+0(a_2) = 0+0 = 0$

**40** $(\mathbf{a}+\mathbf{b})\cdot(\mathbf{a}-\mathbf{b}) = (\langle a_1,a_2\rangle + \langle b_1,b_2\rangle)\cdot(\langle a_1,a_2\rangle - \langle b_1,b_2\rangle)$

$\qquad\qquad = \langle a_1+b_1, a_2+b_2\rangle\cdot\langle a_1-b_1, a_2-b_2\rangle$

$\qquad\qquad = (a_1+b_1)(a_1-b_1) + (a_2+b_2)(a_2-b_2)$

$\qquad\qquad = a_1^2 - b_1^2 + a_2^2 - b_2^2$

$\qquad\qquad = (a_1^2+a_2^2) - (b_1^2+b_2^2)$

$\qquad\qquad = (\langle a_1,a_2\rangle\cdot\langle a_1,a_2\rangle) - (\langle b_1,b_2\rangle\cdot\langle b_1,b_2\rangle) = \mathbf{a}\cdot\mathbf{a} - \mathbf{b}\cdot\mathbf{b}$

**41** Using the horizontal and vertical components of a vector from Section 7.3, we have the force vector as $\langle 20\cos 30°, 20\sin 30°\rangle = \langle 10\sqrt{3}, 10\rangle$. The distance (direction vector) can be described by the vector $\langle 100,0\rangle$.

The work done is $\langle 10\sqrt{3},10\rangle\cdot\langle 100,0\rangle = 1000\sqrt{3} \approx 1732$ ft-lb.

**42** The force vector is now $\langle 20\cos 60°, 20\sin 60° \rangle = \langle 10, 10\sqrt{3} \rangle$.

The direction vector is $\langle 100\cos 30°, 100\sin 30° \rangle = \langle 50\sqrt{3}, 50 \rangle$.

The work done is $\langle 10, 10\sqrt{3} \rangle \cdot \langle 50\sqrt{3}, 50 \rangle = 500\sqrt{3} + 500\sqrt{3} = 1000\sqrt{3} \approx 1732$ ft-lb.

Note that the force in relation to the direction of movement is exactly the same as in Exercise 41.

**43** (a) The horizontal component has magnitude $93 \times 10^6$ and the vertical component has magnitude $0.432 \times 10^6$.

Thus, $\mathbf{v} = (93 \times 10^6)\mathbf{i} + (0.432 \times 10^6)\mathbf{j}$ and $\mathbf{w} = (93 \times 10^6)\mathbf{i} - (0.432 \times 10^6)\mathbf{j}$.

(b) $\cos\theta = \dfrac{\mathbf{v} \cdot \mathbf{w}}{\|\mathbf{v}\|\|\mathbf{w}\|} = \dfrac{(93 \times 10^6)^2 - (0.432 \times 10^6)^2}{\sqrt{(93 \times 10^6)^2 + (0.432 \times 10^6)^2}\,\sqrt{(93 \times 10^6)^2 + (0.432 \times 10^6)^2}} \approx 0.99995685 \Rightarrow$

$$\theta \approx 0.53°.$$

**44** Let the vector $\mathbf{I}$ represent the magnitude and direction of the sun's rays and $\mathbf{h}$ a horizontal vector.

Then, $\text{comp}_{\mathbf{h}}\,\mathbf{I} = \|\mathbf{I}\|\cos\phi = I\cos\phi$, so $\text{comp}_{\mathbf{h}}\,\mathbf{I} = 978\,e^{-0.136/\sin 30°}\cos 30° \approx 645$ watts/m$^2$.

The total amount of radiation striking the wall is approximately $160 \times 645 = 103{,}200$ watts.

**45** $\mathbf{R} = 2(\mathbf{N} \cdot \mathbf{L})\mathbf{N} - \mathbf{L} = 2\big(\langle 0, 1 \rangle \cdot \langle -\tfrac{4}{5}, \tfrac{3}{5} \rangle\big)\langle 0, 1 \rangle - \langle -\tfrac{4}{5}, \tfrac{3}{5} \rangle$

$\qquad = 2\big(\tfrac{3}{5}\big)\langle 0, 1 \rangle - \langle -\tfrac{4}{5}, \tfrac{3}{5} \rangle$

$\qquad = \langle 0, \tfrac{6}{5} \rangle - \langle -\tfrac{4}{5}, \tfrac{3}{5} \rangle = \langle \tfrac{4}{5}, \tfrac{3}{5} \rangle$

**46** $\mathbf{R} = 2(\mathbf{N} \cdot \mathbf{L})\mathbf{N} - \mathbf{L} = 2\big(\langle \tfrac{1}{2}\sqrt{2}, \tfrac{1}{2}\sqrt{2} \rangle \cdot \langle \tfrac{12}{13}, -\tfrac{5}{13} \rangle\big)\langle \tfrac{1}{2}\sqrt{2}, \tfrac{1}{2}\sqrt{2} \rangle - \langle \tfrac{12}{13}, -\tfrac{5}{13} \rangle$

$\qquad = 2\big(\tfrac{7}{26}\sqrt{2}\big)\langle \tfrac{1}{2}\sqrt{2}, \tfrac{1}{2}\sqrt{2} \rangle - \langle \tfrac{12}{13}, -\tfrac{5}{13} \rangle$

$\qquad = \langle \tfrac{7}{13}, \tfrac{7}{13} \rangle - \langle \tfrac{12}{13}, -\tfrac{5}{13} \rangle = \langle -\tfrac{5}{13}, \tfrac{12}{13} \rangle$

**47** Let horizontal ground be represented by $\mathbf{b} = \langle 1, 0 \rangle$ (it could be any vector of the form $\langle a, 0 \rangle$).

$$\text{comp}_{\mathbf{b}}\,\mathbf{a} = \frac{\mathbf{a} \cdot \mathbf{b}}{\|\mathbf{b}\|} = \frac{\langle 2.6, 4.5 \rangle \cdot \langle 1, 0 \rangle}{\|\langle 1, 0 \rangle\|} = \frac{2.6}{1} = 2.6 \Rightarrow |\text{comp}_{\mathbf{b}}\,\mathbf{a}| = 2.6$$

**48** Let horizontal ground be represented by $\mathbf{b} = \langle 1, 0 \rangle$.

$$\text{comp}_{\mathbf{b}}\,\mathbf{a} = \frac{\mathbf{a} \cdot \mathbf{b}}{\|\mathbf{b}\|} = \frac{\langle -3.1, 7.9 \rangle \cdot \langle 1, 0 \rangle}{\|\langle 1, 0 \rangle\|} = \frac{-3.1}{1} = -3.1 \Rightarrow |\text{comp}_{\mathbf{b}}\,\mathbf{a}| = 3.1$$

**49** Let the direction of the ground be represented by $\mathbf{b} = \langle \cos\theta, \sin\theta \rangle = \langle \cos 12°, \sin 12° \rangle$.

$$\text{comp}_{\mathbf{b}}\,\mathbf{a} = \frac{\mathbf{a} \cdot \mathbf{b}}{\|\mathbf{b}\|} = \frac{\langle 25.7, -3.9 \rangle \cdot \langle \cos 12°, \sin 12° \rangle}{\|\langle \cos 12°, \sin 12° \rangle\|} \approx \frac{24.33}{1} = 24.33 \Rightarrow |\text{comp}_{\mathbf{b}}\,\mathbf{a}| = 24.33$$

**50** Let the direction of the ground be represented by $\mathbf{b} = \langle \cos\theta, \sin\theta \rangle = \langle \cos(-17°), \sin(-17°) \rangle$.

$$\text{comp}_{\mathbf{b}}\,\mathbf{a} = \frac{\mathbf{a} \cdot \mathbf{b}}{\|\mathbf{b}\|} = \frac{\langle -13.8, 19.4 \rangle \cdot \langle \cos(-17°), \sin(-17°) \rangle}{\|\langle \cos(-17°), \sin(-17°) \rangle\|} \approx \frac{-18.87}{1} = -18.87 \Rightarrow |\text{comp}_{\mathbf{b}}\,\mathbf{a}| = 18.87$$

**51** From the "Theorem on the Dot Product," we know that $\mathbf{F} \cdot \mathbf{v} = \|\mathbf{F}\|\|\mathbf{v}\|\cos\theta$,

so $P = \tfrac{1}{550}(\mathbf{F} \cdot \mathbf{v}) = \tfrac{1}{550}\|\mathbf{F}\|\|\mathbf{v}\|\cos\theta = \tfrac{1}{550}(2200)(8)\cos 30° = 16\sqrt{3} \approx 27.7$ horsepower.

## 7.5 Exercises

**1** $|3 - 4i| = \sqrt{3^2 + (-4)^2} = \sqrt{9 + 16} = \sqrt{25} = 5$

**2** $|5 + 8i| = \sqrt{5^2 + 8^2} = \sqrt{25 + 64} = \sqrt{89}$

**3**   $|-6 - 7i| = \sqrt{(-6)^2 + (-7)^2} = \sqrt{36 + 49} = \sqrt{85}$

**4**   $|1 - i| = \sqrt{1^2 + (-1)^2} = \sqrt{1 + 1} = \sqrt{2}$

**5**   $|0| = |0 + 0i| = \sqrt{0^2 + 0^2} = \sqrt{0} = 0$

**6**   $|-8| = |-8 + 0i| = \sqrt{(-8)^2 + 0^2} = \sqrt{64} = 8$

**7**   $|8i| = |0 + 8i| = \sqrt{0^2 + 8^2} = \sqrt{64} = 8$

**8**   $|-8i| = |0 - 8i| = \sqrt{0^2 + (-8)^2} = \sqrt{64} = 8$

**9**   From Section 1.5, $i^m = i, -1, -i,$ or $1$. Since all of these are 1 unit from the origin, $|i^m| = 1$ for any integer $m$.

         As an alternate solution, $\left|i^{500}\right| = \left|\left(i^4\right)^{125}\right| = \left|(1)^{125}\right| = |1| = |1 + 0i| = \sqrt{1^2 + 0^2} = \sqrt{1} = 1.$

**10**   $\left|i^7\right| = \left|i^4 \cdot i^2 \cdot i\right| = |(1)(-1)(i)| = |-i| = |0 - i| = \sqrt{0^2 + (-1)^2} = \sqrt{1} = 1$

*Figure for Odd Exercises 11–20*

*Figure for Even Exercises 11–20*

**11**   $4 + 2i$        **12**   $-5 + 3i$        **13**   $3 - 5i$        **14**   $-2 - 6i$        **15**   $-(3 - 6i) = -3 + 6i$

**16**   $(1 + 2i)^2 = 1 + 2(1)(2i) + (2i)^2 = 1 + 4i - 4 = -3 + 4i$

**17**   $-2i(3 - 2i) = -6i + 4i^2 = -6i - 4 = -4 - 6i$

**18**   $-3i(2 - i) = -6i + 3i^2 = -6i - 3 = -3 - 6i$

**19**   $(1 + i)^2 = 1 + 2(1)(i) + i^2 = 1 + 2i - 1 = 2i$

**20**   $4(-1 + 2i) = -4 + 8i$

***Note:*** For each of the following exercises, we need to find $r$ and $\theta$. If $z = a + bi$, then $r = \sqrt{a^2 + b^2}$. To find $\theta$, we

       will use the fact that $\tan \theta = b/a$ and our knowledge of what quadrant the terminal side of $\theta$ is in.

**21**   $z = 1 - i \;\Rightarrow\; r = \sqrt{1 + (-1)^2} = \sqrt{2}.\;\; \tan \theta = \frac{-1}{1} = -1$ and $\theta$ in QIV $\;\Rightarrow\;\; \theta = \frac{7\pi}{4}.$

                   Thus, $z = 1 - i = \sqrt{2}\left(\cos \frac{7\pi}{4} + i \sin \frac{7\pi}{4}\right)$, or simply $\sqrt{2} \operatorname{cis} \frac{7\pi}{4}.$

**22**   $z = \sqrt{3} + i \;\Rightarrow\; r = \sqrt{\left(\sqrt{3}\right)^2 + 1^2} = \sqrt{4} = 2.\;\; \tan \theta = \frac{1}{\sqrt{3}}$ and $\theta$ in QI $\;\Rightarrow\;\; \theta = \frac{\pi}{6}.\;\; z = 2 \operatorname{cis} \frac{\pi}{6}.$

**23**   $z = -4\sqrt{3} + 4i \;\Rightarrow\; r = \sqrt{\left(-4\sqrt{3}\right)^2 + 4^2} = \sqrt{64} = 8.$

                   $\tan \theta = \frac{4}{-4\sqrt{3}} = -\frac{1}{\sqrt{3}}$ and $\theta$ in QII $\;\Rightarrow\;\; \theta = \frac{5\pi}{6}.\;\; z = 8 \operatorname{cis} \frac{5\pi}{6}.$

**24**   $z = -2 - 2i \;\Rightarrow\; r = \sqrt{(-2)^2 + (-2)^2} = \sqrt{8} = 2\sqrt{2}.$

                   $\tan \theta = \frac{-2}{-2} = 1$ and $\theta$ in QIII $\;\Rightarrow\;\; \theta = \frac{5\pi}{4}.\;\; z = 2\sqrt{2} \operatorname{cis} \frac{5\pi}{4}.$

**25** $z = 2\sqrt{3} + 2i \Rightarrow r = \sqrt{\left(2\sqrt{3}\right)^2 + 2^2} = \sqrt{16} = 4.$

$\tan\theta = \frac{2}{2\sqrt{3}} = \frac{1}{\sqrt{3}}$ and $\theta$ in QI $\Rightarrow \theta = \frac{\pi}{6}.$ $z = 4\operatorname{cis}\frac{\pi}{6}.$

**26** $z = 3 - 3\sqrt{3}\,i \Rightarrow r = \sqrt{3^2 + \left(-3\sqrt{3}\right)^2} = \sqrt{36} = 6.$

$\tan\theta = \frac{-3\sqrt{3}}{3} = -\sqrt{3}$ and $\theta$ in QIV $\Rightarrow \theta = \frac{5\pi}{3}.$ $z = 6\operatorname{cis}\frac{5\pi}{3}.$

**27** $z = -4 - 4i \Rightarrow r = \sqrt{(-4)^2 + (-4)^2} = \sqrt{32} = 4\sqrt{2}.$

$\tan\theta = \frac{-4}{-4} = 1$ and $\theta$ in QIII $\Rightarrow \theta = \frac{5\pi}{4}.$ $z = 4\sqrt{2}\operatorname{cis}\frac{5\pi}{4}.$

**28** $z = -8 + 8i \Rightarrow r = \sqrt{(-8)^2 + 8^2} = \sqrt{128} = 8\sqrt{2}.$

$\tan\theta = \frac{8}{-8} = -1$ and $\theta$ in QII $\Rightarrow \theta = \frac{3\pi}{4}.$ $z = 8\sqrt{2}\operatorname{cis}\frac{3\pi}{4}.$

**29** $z = -20i \Rightarrow r = 20.$ $\theta$ on the negative $y$-axis $\Rightarrow \theta = \frac{3\pi}{2}.$ $z = 20\operatorname{cis}\frac{3\pi}{2}.$

**30** $z = -6i \Rightarrow r = 6.$ $\theta$ on the negative $y$-axis $\Rightarrow \theta = \frac{3\pi}{2}.$ $z = 6\operatorname{cis}\frac{3\pi}{2}.$

**31** $z = 12 \Rightarrow r = 12.$ $\theta$ on the positive $x$-axis $\Rightarrow \theta = 0.$ $z = 12\operatorname{cis}0.$

**32** $z = 15 \Rightarrow r = 15.$ $\theta$ on the positive $x$-axis $\Rightarrow \theta = 0.$ $z = 15\operatorname{cis}0.$

**33** $z = -7 \Rightarrow r = 7.$ $\theta$ on the negative $x$-axis $\Rightarrow \theta = \pi.$ $z = 7\operatorname{cis}\pi.$

**34** $z = -5 \Rightarrow r = 5.$ $\theta$ on the negative $x$-axis $\Rightarrow \theta = \pi.$ $z = 5\operatorname{cis}\pi.$

**35** $z = 6i \Rightarrow r = 6.$ $\theta$ on the positive $y$-axis $\Rightarrow \theta = \frac{\pi}{2}.$ $z = 6\operatorname{cis}\frac{\pi}{2}.$

**36** $z = 4i \Rightarrow r = 4.$ $\theta$ on the positive $y$-axis $\Rightarrow \theta = \frac{\pi}{2}.$ $z = 4\operatorname{cis}\frac{\pi}{2}.$

**37** $z = -5 - 5\sqrt{3}\,i \Rightarrow r = \sqrt{(-5)^2 + \left(-5\sqrt{3}\right)^2} = \sqrt{100} = 10.$

$\tan\theta = \frac{-5\sqrt{3}}{-5} = \sqrt{3}$ and $\theta$ in QIII $\Rightarrow \theta = \frac{4\pi}{3}.$ $z = 10\operatorname{cis}\frac{4\pi}{3}.$

**38** $z = \sqrt{3} - i \Rightarrow r = \sqrt{\left(\sqrt{3}\right)^2 + (-1)^2} = \sqrt{4} = 2.$ $\tan\theta = \frac{-1}{\sqrt{3}}$ and $\theta$ in QIV $\Rightarrow \theta = \frac{11\pi}{6}.$ $z = 2\operatorname{cis}\frac{11\pi}{6}.$

**39** $z = 5 + 2i \Rightarrow r = \sqrt{5^2 + 2^2} = \sqrt{29}.$ $\tan\theta = \frac{2}{5}$ and $\theta$ in QI $\Rightarrow \theta = \tan^{-1}\frac{2}{5}.$ $z = \sqrt{29}\operatorname{cis}\left(\tan^{-1}\frac{2}{5}\right).$

**40** $z = 3 + 2i \Rightarrow r = \sqrt{3^2 + 2^2} = \sqrt{13}.$ $\tan\theta = \frac{2}{3}$ and $\theta$ in QI $\Rightarrow \theta = \tan^{-1}\frac{2}{3}.$ $z = \sqrt{13}\operatorname{cis}\left(\tan^{-1}\frac{2}{3}\right).$

**41** $z = -3 + i \Rightarrow r = \sqrt{(-3)^2 + 1^2} = \sqrt{10}.$ $\tan\theta = \frac{1}{-3}$ and $\theta$ in QII $\Rightarrow \theta = \tan^{-1}\left(-\frac{1}{3}\right) + \pi.$

We must add $\pi$ to $\tan^{-1}\left(-\frac{1}{3}\right)$ because $-\frac{\pi}{2} < \tan^{-1}\left(-\frac{1}{3}\right) < 0$ and we want $\theta$ to be in the interval $\left(\frac{\pi}{2}, \pi\right)$.

$z = \sqrt{10}\operatorname{cis}\left[\tan^{-1}\left(-\frac{1}{3}\right) + \pi\right].$

**42** $z = -4 + 2i \Rightarrow r = \sqrt{(-4)^2 + 2^2} = \sqrt{20} = 2\sqrt{5}.$ $\tan\theta = \frac{2}{-4} = -\frac{1}{2}$ and $\theta$ in QII $\Rightarrow \theta = \tan^{-1}\left(-\frac{1}{2}\right) + \pi.$

$z = 2\sqrt{5}\operatorname{cis}\left[\tan^{-1}\left(-\frac{1}{2}\right) + \pi\right].$

**43** $z = -5 - 3i \Rightarrow r = \sqrt{(-5)^2 + (-3)^2} = \sqrt{34}.$ $\tan\theta = \frac{-3}{-5} = \frac{3}{5}$ and $\theta$ in QIII $\Rightarrow \theta = \tan^{-1}\frac{3}{5} + \pi.$

We must add $\pi$ to $\tan^{-1}\frac{3}{5}$ because $0 < \tan^{-1}\frac{3}{5} < \frac{\pi}{2}$ and we want $\theta$ to be in the interval $\left(\pi, \frac{3\pi}{2}\right)$.

$z = \sqrt{34}\operatorname{cis}\left(\tan^{-1}\frac{3}{5} + \pi\right).$

**44** $z = -2 - 7i \Rightarrow r = \sqrt{(-2)^2 + (-7)^2} = \sqrt{53}.$ $\tan\theta = \frac{-7}{-2} = \frac{7}{2}$ and $\theta$ in QIII $\Rightarrow \theta = \tan^{-1}\frac{7}{2} + \pi.$

$z = \sqrt{53}\operatorname{cis}\left(\tan^{-1}\frac{7}{2} + \pi\right).$

**45** $z = 4 - 3i \Rightarrow r = \sqrt{4^2 + (-3)^2} = \sqrt{25} = 5.$ $\tan\theta = \frac{-3}{4}$ and $\theta$ in QIV $\Rightarrow$ $\theta = \tan^{-1}\left(-\frac{3}{4}\right) + 2\pi.$

We must add $2\pi$ to $\tan^{-1}\left(-\frac{3}{4}\right)$ because $-\frac{\pi}{2} < \tan^{-1}\left(-\frac{3}{4}\right) < 0$ and we want $\theta$ to be in the interval $\left(\frac{3\pi}{2}, 2\pi\right).$

$$z = 5\operatorname{cis}\left[\tan^{-1}\left(-\frac{3}{4}\right) + 2\pi\right].$$

**46** $z = 12 - 5i \Rightarrow r = \sqrt{12^2 + (-5)^2} = \sqrt{169} = 13.$ $\tan\theta = \frac{-5}{12}$ and $\theta$ in QIV $\Rightarrow$ $\theta = \tan^{-1}\left(-\frac{5}{12}\right) + 2\pi.$

$$z = 13\operatorname{cis}\left[\tan^{-1}\left(-\frac{5}{12}\right) + 2\pi\right].$$

**47** $4\left(\cos\frac{\pi}{4} + i\sin\frac{\pi}{4}\right) = 4\left(\frac{\sqrt{2}}{2} + \frac{\sqrt{2}}{2}i\right) = 2\sqrt{2} + 2\sqrt{2}\,i$

**48** $8\left(\cos\frac{7\pi}{4} + i\sin\frac{7\pi}{4}\right) = 8\left(\frac{\sqrt{2}}{2} - \frac{\sqrt{2}}{2}i\right) = 4\sqrt{2} - 4\sqrt{2}\,i$

**49** $6\left(\cos\frac{2\pi}{3} + i\sin\frac{2\pi}{3}\right) = 6\left(-\frac{1}{2} + \frac{\sqrt{3}}{2}i\right) = -3 + 3\sqrt{3}\,i$

**50** $12\left(\cos\frac{4\pi}{3} + i\sin\frac{4\pi}{3}\right) = 12\left(-\frac{1}{2} - \frac{\sqrt{3}}{2}i\right) = -6 - 6\sqrt{3}\,i$

**51** $5(\cos\pi + i\sin\pi) = 5(-1 + 0i) = -5$

**52** $3\left(\cos\frac{3\pi}{2} + i\sin\frac{3\pi}{2}\right) = 3(0 - 1i) = -3i$

**53** For any given angle $\theta$, where $\theta = \tan^{-1}\frac{y}{x}$, we have $r = \sqrt{x^2 + y^2}.$

In this case, $\theta = \tan^{-1}\frac{3}{5}$, so $r = \sqrt{3^2 + 5^2} = \sqrt{34}.$ You may want to draw a figure to represent $x$, $y$, and $r$, as we did in previous chapters. Also, note that $\cos\theta = \frac{x}{r}$ and $\sin\theta = \frac{y}{r}.$

$$\sqrt{34}\operatorname{cis}\left(\tan^{-1}\tfrac{3}{5}\right) = \sqrt{34}\left[\cos\left(\tan^{-1}\tfrac{3}{5}\right) + i\sin\left(\tan^{-1}\tfrac{3}{5}\right)\right] = \sqrt{34}\left(\frac{5}{\sqrt{34}} + \frac{3}{\sqrt{34}}i\right) = 5 + 3i$$

**54** $\sqrt{53}\operatorname{cis}\left[\tan^{-1}\left(-\frac{2}{7}\right)\right] = \sqrt{53}\left\{\cos\left[\tan^{-1}\left(-\frac{2}{7}\right)\right] + i\sin\left[\tan^{-1}\left(-\frac{2}{7}\right)\right]\right\} = \sqrt{53}\left(\frac{7}{\sqrt{53}} - \frac{2}{\sqrt{53}}i\right) = 7 - 2i$

**55** Since $\tan^{-1}\left(-\frac{1}{2}\right)$ is a QIV angle, it may help to think of it as $\tan^{-1}\left(\frac{-1}{2}\right)$, so that $x = 2$, $y = -1$, and $r = \sqrt{5}.$

$$\sqrt{5}\operatorname{cis}\left[\tan^{-1}\left(-\tfrac{1}{2}\right)\right] = \sqrt{5}\left\{\cos\left[\tan^{-1}\left(-\tfrac{1}{2}\right)\right] + i\sin\left[\tan^{-1}\left(-\tfrac{1}{2}\right)\right]\right\} = \sqrt{5}\left(\frac{2}{\sqrt{5}} - \frac{1}{\sqrt{5}}i\right) = 2 - i$$

**56** $\sqrt{10}\operatorname{cis}\left(\tan^{-1}3\right) = \sqrt{10}\left[\cos\left(\tan^{-1}3\right) + i\sin\left(\tan^{-1}3\right)\right] = \sqrt{10}\left(\frac{1}{\sqrt{10}} + \frac{3}{\sqrt{10}}i\right) = 1 + 3i$

**57** Since $\tan^{-1}\left(-\frac{7}{4}\right) + \pi$ is a QII angle, we have $x = -4$, $y = 7$, and $r = \sqrt{65}.$

$$\sqrt{65}\operatorname{cis}\left[\tan^{-1}\left(-\tfrac{7}{4}\right) + \pi\right] = \sqrt{65}\left\{\cos\left[\tan^{-1}\left(-\tfrac{7}{4}\right) + \pi\right] + i\sin\left[\tan^{-1}\left(-\tfrac{7}{4}\right) + \pi\right]\right\}$$
$$= \sqrt{65}\left(-\frac{4}{\sqrt{65}} + \frac{7}{\sqrt{65}}i\right) = -4 + 7i$$

**58** $\sqrt{61}\operatorname{cis}\left[\tan^{-1}\left(-\frac{6}{5}\right) + \pi\right] = \sqrt{61}\left\{\cos\left[\tan^{-1}\left(-\frac{6}{5}\right) + \pi\right] + i\sin\left[\tan^{-1}\left(-\frac{6}{5}\right) + \pi\right]\right\}$
$$= \sqrt{61}\left(-\frac{5}{\sqrt{61}} + \frac{6}{\sqrt{61}}i\right) = -5 + 6i$$

**59** Since $\tan^{-1}\frac{3}{7} + \pi$ is a QIII angle, we have $x = -7$, $y = -3$, and $r = \sqrt{58}.$

$$\sqrt{58}\operatorname{cis}\left(\tan^{-1}\tfrac{3}{7} + \pi\right) = \sqrt{58}\left[\cos\left(\tan^{-1}\tfrac{3}{7} + \pi\right) + i\sin\left(\tan^{-1}\tfrac{3}{7} + \pi\right)\right]$$
$$= \sqrt{58}\left(-\frac{7}{\sqrt{58}} - \frac{3}{\sqrt{58}}i\right) = -7 - 3i$$

**60** $\sqrt{85}\operatorname{cis}\left(\tan^{-1}\frac{9}{2} + \pi\right) = \sqrt{85}\left[\cos\left(\tan^{-1}\frac{9}{2} + \pi\right) + i\sin\left(\tan^{-1}\frac{9}{2} + \pi\right)\right]$
$$= \sqrt{85}\left(-\frac{2}{\sqrt{85}} - \frac{9}{\sqrt{85}}i\right) = -2 - 9i$$

**Note:** For Exercises 61–70, the trigonometric forms for $z_1$ and $z_2$ are listed and then used in the theorem in this section. The trigonometric forms can be found as in Exercises 21–46.

**61** $z_1 = -1 + i = \sqrt{2} \operatorname{cis} \frac{3\pi}{4}$ and $z_2 = 1 + i = \sqrt{2} \operatorname{cis} \frac{\pi}{4}$. $z_1 z_2 = \sqrt{2} \cdot \sqrt{2} \operatorname{cis}\left(\frac{3\pi}{4} + \frac{\pi}{4}\right) = 2 \operatorname{cis} \pi = -2 + 0i$.

$$\frac{z_1}{z_2} = \frac{\sqrt{2}}{\sqrt{2}} \operatorname{cis}\left(\frac{3\pi}{4} - \frac{\pi}{4}\right) = 1 \operatorname{cis} \frac{\pi}{2} = 0 + i$$

**62** $z_1 = \sqrt{3} - i = 2 \operatorname{cis} \frac{11\pi}{6}$ and $z_2 = -\sqrt{3} - i = 2 \operatorname{cis} \frac{7\pi}{6}$. $z_1 z_2 = 2 \cdot 2 \operatorname{cis}\left(\frac{11\pi}{6} + \frac{7\pi}{6}\right) = 4 \operatorname{cis} 3\pi = -4 + 0i$.

$$\frac{z_1}{z_2} = \frac{2}{2} \operatorname{cis}\left(\frac{11\pi}{6} - \frac{7\pi}{6}\right) = 1 \operatorname{cis} \frac{2\pi}{3} = -\frac{1}{2} + \frac{\sqrt{3}}{2} i$$

**63** $z_1 = -2 - 2\sqrt{3}i = 4 \operatorname{cis} \frac{4\pi}{3}$ and $z_2 = 5i = 5 \operatorname{cis} \frac{\pi}{2}$. $z_1 z_2 = 4 \cdot 5 \operatorname{cis}\left(\frac{4\pi}{3} + \frac{\pi}{2}\right) = 20 \operatorname{cis} \frac{11\pi}{6} = 10\sqrt{3} - 10i$.

$$\frac{z_1}{z_2} = \frac{4}{5} \operatorname{cis}\left(\frac{4\pi}{3} - \frac{\pi}{2}\right) = \frac{4}{5} \operatorname{cis} \frac{5\pi}{6} = -\frac{2}{5}\sqrt{3} + \frac{2}{5} i$$

**64** $z_1 = -5 + 5i = 5\sqrt{2} \operatorname{cis} \frac{3\pi}{4}$ and $z_2 = -3i = 3 \operatorname{cis} \frac{3\pi}{2}$. $z_1 z_2 = 5\sqrt{2} \cdot 3 \operatorname{cis}\left(\frac{3\pi}{4} + \frac{3\pi}{2}\right) = 15\sqrt{2} \operatorname{cis} \frac{9\pi}{4} = 15 + 15i$.

$$\frac{z_1}{z_2} = \frac{5\sqrt{2}}{3} \operatorname{cis}\left(\frac{3\pi}{4} - \frac{3\pi}{2}\right) = \frac{5\sqrt{2}}{3} \operatorname{cis}\left(-\frac{3\pi}{4}\right) = -\frac{5}{3} - \frac{5}{3} i$$

**65** $z_1 = -10 = 10 \operatorname{cis} \pi$ and $z_2 = -4 = 4 \operatorname{cis} \pi$. $z_1 z_2 = 10 \cdot 4 \operatorname{cis}(\pi + \pi) = 40 \operatorname{cis} 2\pi = 40 + 0i$.

$$\frac{z_1}{z_2} = \frac{10}{4} \operatorname{cis}(\pi - \pi) = \frac{5}{2} \operatorname{cis} 0 = \frac{5}{2} + 0i$$

**66** $z_1 = 2i = 2 \operatorname{cis} \frac{\pi}{2}$ and $z_2 = -3i = 3 \operatorname{cis} \frac{3\pi}{2}$. $z_1 z_2 = 2 \cdot 3 \operatorname{cis}\left(\frac{\pi}{2} + \frac{3\pi}{2}\right) = 6 \operatorname{cis} 2\pi = 6 + 0i$.

$$\frac{z_1}{z_2} = \frac{2}{3} \operatorname{cis}\left(\frac{\pi}{2} - \frac{3\pi}{2}\right) = \frac{2}{3} \operatorname{cis}(-\pi) = -\frac{2}{3} + 0i$$

**67** $z_1 = 4 = 4 \operatorname{cis} 0$ and $z_2 = 2 - i = \sqrt{5} \operatorname{cis}\left[\tan^{-1}\left(-\frac{1}{2}\right)\right]$. Let $\theta = \tan^{-1}\left(-\frac{1}{2}\right)$. Thus $\cos\theta = \frac{2}{\sqrt{5}}$ and $\sin\theta = -\frac{1}{\sqrt{5}}$.

$z_1 z_2 = 4 \cdot \sqrt{5} \operatorname{cis}(0 + \theta) = 4\sqrt{5}(\cos\theta + i\sin\theta) = 4\sqrt{5}\left(\frac{2}{\sqrt{5}} + \frac{-1}{\sqrt{5}} i\right) = 8 - 4i$.

$\frac{z_1}{z_2} = \frac{4}{\sqrt{5}} \operatorname{cis}(0 - \theta) = \frac{4}{\sqrt{5}}[\cos(-\theta) + i\sin(-\theta)] = \frac{4}{\sqrt{5}}(\cos\theta - i\sin\theta) = \frac{4}{\sqrt{5}}\left(\frac{2}{\sqrt{5}} + \frac{1}{\sqrt{5}} i\right) = \frac{8}{5} + \frac{4}{5} i$.

**68** $z_1 = 7 = 7 \operatorname{cis} 0$ and $z_2 = 3 + 5i = \sqrt{34} \operatorname{cis}\left(\tan^{-1} \frac{5}{3}\right)$. Let $\theta = \tan^{-1} \frac{5}{3}$.

$z_1 z_2 = 7 \cdot \sqrt{34} \operatorname{cis}(0 + \theta) = 7\sqrt{34}(\cos\theta + i\sin\theta) = 7\sqrt{34}\left(\frac{3}{\sqrt{34}} + \frac{5}{\sqrt{34}} i\right) = 21 + 35i$.

$\frac{z_1}{z_2} = \frac{7}{\sqrt{34}} \operatorname{cis}(0 - \theta) = \frac{7}{\sqrt{34}}[\cos(-\theta) + i\sin(-\theta)] = \frac{7}{\sqrt{34}}\left(\frac{3}{\sqrt{34}} - \frac{5}{\sqrt{34}} i\right) = \frac{21}{34} - \frac{35}{34} i$.

**69** $z_1 = -5 = 5 \operatorname{cis} \pi$ and $z_2 = 3 - 2i = \sqrt{13} \operatorname{cis}\left[\tan^{-1}\left(-\frac{2}{3}\right)\right]$. Let $\theta = \tan^{-1}\left(-\frac{2}{3}\right)$.

$z_1 z_2 = 5 \cdot \sqrt{13} \operatorname{cis}(\pi + \theta) = 5\sqrt{13}[\cos(\pi + \theta) + i\sin(\pi + \theta)] = 5\sqrt{13}\left(\frac{-3}{\sqrt{13}} + \frac{2}{\sqrt{13}} i\right) = -15 + 10i$.

We simplify the above using the addition formulas for the sine and cosine as follows:

$$\cos(\pi + \theta) = \cos\pi\cos\theta - \sin\pi\sin\theta = -\cos\theta = \frac{-3}{\sqrt{13}} \text{ and}$$

$$\sin(\pi + \theta) = \sin\pi\cos\theta + \cos\pi\sin\theta = -\sin\theta = \frac{2}{\sqrt{13}}.$$

$\frac{z_1}{z_2} = \frac{5}{\sqrt{13}} \operatorname{cis}(\pi - \theta) = \frac{5}{\sqrt{13}}\left(\frac{-3}{\sqrt{13}} - \frac{2}{\sqrt{13}} i\right)$ {since $\cos(\pi - \theta) = -\cos\theta$ and $\sin(\pi - \theta) = \sin\theta$} $= -\frac{15}{13} - \frac{10}{13} i$.

**70** $z_1 = -3 = 3 \operatorname{cis} \pi$ and $z_2 = 5 + 2i = \sqrt{29} \operatorname{cis}\left(\tan^{-1} \frac{2}{5}\right)$. Let $\theta = \tan^{-1} \frac{2}{5}$.

$z_1 z_2 = 3 \cdot \sqrt{29} \operatorname{cis}(\pi + \theta) = 3\sqrt{29}[\cos(\pi + \theta) + i\sin(\pi + \theta)] = 3\sqrt{29}\left(\frac{-5}{\sqrt{29}} + \frac{-2}{\sqrt{29}} i\right) = -15 - 6i$.

We simplify the above using the addition formulas for the sine and cosine as follows:

$$\cos(\pi + \theta) = \cos\pi\cos\theta - \sin\pi\sin\theta = -\cos\theta = \frac{-5}{\sqrt{29}} \text{ and}$$

$$\sin(\pi + \theta) = \sin\pi\cos\theta + \cos\pi\sin\theta = -\sin\theta = \frac{-2}{\sqrt{29}}.$$

$\frac{z_1}{z_2} = \frac{3}{\sqrt{29}} \operatorname{cis}(\pi - \theta) = \frac{3}{\sqrt{29}}\left(\frac{-5}{\sqrt{29}} + \frac{2}{\sqrt{29}} i\right)$ {since $\cos(\pi - \theta) = -\cos\theta$ and $\sin(\pi - \theta) = \sin\theta$} $= -\frac{15}{29} + \frac{6}{29} i$.

**71** Let $z_1 = r_1 \operatorname{cis} \theta_1$ and $z_2 = r_2 \operatorname{cis} \theta_2$.

$$\frac{z_1}{z_2} = \frac{r_1 \operatorname{cis} \theta_1}{r_2 \operatorname{cis} \theta_2} = \frac{r_1(\cos \theta_1 + i \sin \theta_1)(\cos \theta_2 - i \sin \theta_2)}{r_2(\cos \theta_2 + i \sin \theta_2)(\cos \theta_2 - i \sin \theta_2)} \qquad \{\text{multiplying by the conjugate of the denominator}\}$$

$$= \frac{r_1[(\cos \theta_1 \cos \theta_2 + \sin \theta_1 \sin \theta_2) + i(\sin \theta_1 \cos \theta_2 - \sin \theta_2 \cos \theta_1)]}{r_2[(\cos^2 \theta_2 + \sin^2 \theta_2) + i(\sin \theta_2 \cos \theta_2 - \cos \theta_2 \sin \theta_2)]}$$

$$= \frac{r_1[\cos(\theta_1 - \theta_2) + i \sin(\theta_1 - \theta_2)]}{r_2(1 + 0i)} = \frac{r_1}{r_2} \operatorname{cis}(\theta_1 - \theta_2).$$

**72** (a) Let $z_1 = r_1 \operatorname{cis} \theta_1$, $z_2 = r_2 \operatorname{cis} \theta_2$, and $z_3 = r_3 \operatorname{cis} \theta_3$. Then

$$z_1 z_2 z_3 = (z_1 z_2) z_3 = [r_1 r_2 \operatorname{cis}(\theta_1 + \theta_2)](r_3 \operatorname{cis} \theta_3) = [(r_1 r_2) r_3] \operatorname{cis}[(\theta_1 + \theta_2) + \theta_3] = (r_1 r_2 r_3) \operatorname{cis}(\theta_1 + \theta_2 + \theta_3).$$

(b) The generalization is $z_1 z_2 \cdots z_n = (r_1 r_2 \cdots r_n) \operatorname{cis}(\theta_1 + \theta_2 + \cdots + \theta_n)$.

**73** The unknown quantity is $V$: $I = V/Z \Rightarrow$

$$V = IZ = (10 \operatorname{cis} 35°)(3 \operatorname{cis} 20°) = (10 \times 3) \operatorname{cis}(35° + 20°) = 30 \operatorname{cis} 55° \approx 17.21 + 24.57i.$$

**74** The unknown quantity is $V$: $I = V/Z \Rightarrow$

$$V = IZ = (12 \operatorname{cis} 5°)(100 \operatorname{cis} 90°) = (12 \times 100) \operatorname{cis}(5° + 90°) = 1200 \operatorname{cis} 95° \approx -104.59 + 1195.43i.$$

**75** The unknown quantity is $Z$: $I = V/Z \Rightarrow$

$$Z = \frac{V}{I} = \frac{115 \operatorname{cis} 45°}{8 \operatorname{cis} 5°} = (115 \div 8) \operatorname{cis}(45° - 5°) = 14.375 \operatorname{cis} 40° \approx 11.01 + 9.24i.$$

**76** The unknown quantity is $I$: $I = \dfrac{V}{Z} = \dfrac{163 \operatorname{cis} 17°}{78 \operatorname{cis} 61°} = (163 \div 78) \operatorname{cis}(17° - 61°) = \frac{163}{78} \operatorname{cis}(-44°) \approx 1.50 - 1.45i.$

**77** $Z = 14 - 13i \Rightarrow |Z| = \sqrt{14^2 + (-13)^2} = \sqrt{365} \approx 19.1$ ohms

**78** $I = \dfrac{V}{Z} \Rightarrow Z = \dfrac{V}{I} = \dfrac{220 \operatorname{cis} 34°}{5 \operatorname{cis} 90°} = 44 \operatorname{cis}(-56°) \approx 24.60 - 36.48i.$

The resistance is 24.60 ohms and the reactance is 36.48 ohms.

**79** $I = \dfrac{V}{Z} \Rightarrow V = IZ = (4 \operatorname{cis} 90°)[18 \operatorname{cis}(-78°)] = 72 \operatorname{cis} 12° \approx 70.43 + 14.97i$

**80** $I = \dfrac{V}{Z} = \dfrac{163 \operatorname{cis} 43°}{100 \operatorname{cis} 17°} = 1.63 \operatorname{cis} 26° \approx 1.47 + 0.71i.$ The actual current is 1.47 amps.

## 7.6 Exercises

**Note:** In this section, it is assumed that the reader can transform complex numbers to their trigonometric from. If this is not the case, see Exercises 7.5.

**1** $(3 + 3i)^5 = \left(3\sqrt{2} \operatorname{cis} \frac{\pi}{4}\right)^5 = \left(3\sqrt{2}\right)^5 \operatorname{cis}\left(5 \cdot \frac{\pi}{4}\right) = \left(3\sqrt{2}\right)^5 \operatorname{cis} \frac{5\pi}{4} = 972\sqrt{2}\left(-\frac{\sqrt{2}}{2} - \frac{\sqrt{2}}{2} i\right) = -972 - 972i$

**2** $(1 + i)^{11} = \left(\sqrt{2} \operatorname{cis} \frac{\pi}{4}\right)^{11} = \left(\sqrt{2}\right)^{11} \operatorname{cis} \frac{11\pi}{4} = \left(\sqrt{2}\right)^{11} \operatorname{cis} \frac{11\pi}{4} = 32\sqrt{2}\left(-\frac{\sqrt{2}}{2} + \frac{\sqrt{2}}{2} i\right) = -32 + 32i$

**3** $(1 - i)^{10} = \left(\sqrt{2} \operatorname{cis} \frac{7\pi}{4}\right)^{10} = \left(\sqrt{2}\right)^{10} \operatorname{cis}\left(10 \cdot \frac{7\pi}{4}\right) = \left(\sqrt{2}\right)^{10} \operatorname{cis} \frac{35\pi}{2} = 2^5 \operatorname{cis}\left(16\pi + \frac{3\pi}{2}\right)$

$$= 32 \operatorname{cis} \frac{3\pi}{2} = 32(0 - i) = -32i$$

**4** $(-1 + i)^8 = \left(\sqrt{2} \operatorname{cis} \frac{3\pi}{4}\right)^8 = \left(\sqrt{2}\right)^8 \operatorname{cis} 6\pi = 16 \operatorname{cis} 0 = 16(1 + 0i) = 16$

**5** $\left(1 - \sqrt{3}\,i\right)^3 = \left(2\operatorname{cis}\frac{5\pi}{3}\right)^3 = 2^3\operatorname{cis}5\pi = 8\operatorname{cis}\pi = 8(-1+0i) = -8$

**6** $\left(1 - \sqrt{3}\,i\right)^5 = \left(2\operatorname{cis}\frac{5\pi}{3}\right)^5 = 2^5\operatorname{cis}\frac{25\pi}{3} = 32\operatorname{cis}\frac{\pi}{3} = 32\left(\frac{1}{2}+\frac{\sqrt{3}}{2}\,i\right) = 16 + 16\sqrt{3}\,i$

**7** $\left(-\frac{\sqrt{2}}{2}+\frac{\sqrt{2}}{2}\,i\right)^{15} = \left(1\operatorname{cis}\frac{3\pi}{4}\right)^{15} = 1^{15}\operatorname{cis}\frac{45\pi}{4} = \operatorname{cis}\frac{5\pi}{4} = -\frac{\sqrt{2}}{2} - \frac{\sqrt{2}}{2}\,i$

**8** $\left(\frac{\sqrt{2}}{2}+\frac{\sqrt{2}}{2}\,i\right)^{25} = \left(1\operatorname{cis}\frac{\pi}{4}\right)^{25} = 1^{25}\operatorname{cis}\frac{25\pi}{4} = \operatorname{cis}\frac{\pi}{4} = \frac{\sqrt{2}}{2}+\frac{\sqrt{2}}{2}\,i$

**9** $\left(-\frac{\sqrt{3}}{2}-\frac{1}{2}\,i\right)^{20} = \left(1\operatorname{cis}\frac{7\pi}{6}\right)^{20} = 1^{20}\operatorname{cis}\frac{70\pi}{3} = \operatorname{cis}\frac{4\pi}{3} = -\frac{1}{2} - \frac{\sqrt{3}}{2}\,i$

**10** $\left(-\frac{\sqrt{3}}{2}-\frac{1}{2}\,i\right)^{50} = \left(1\operatorname{cis}\frac{7\pi}{6}\right)^{50} = 1^{50}\operatorname{cis}\frac{175\pi}{3} = \operatorname{cis}\frac{\pi}{3} = \frac{1}{2} + \frac{\sqrt{3}}{2}\,i$

**11** $\left(\sqrt{3}+i\right)^7 = \left(2\operatorname{cis}\frac{\pi}{6}\right)^7 = 2^7\operatorname{cis}\frac{7\pi}{6} = 128\left(-\frac{\sqrt{3}}{2}-\frac{1}{2}i\right) = -64\sqrt{3} - 64i$

**12** $(-2-2i)^{10} = \left(2\sqrt{2}\operatorname{cis}\frac{5\pi}{4}\right)^{10} = \left(2\sqrt{2}\right)^{10}\operatorname{cis}\frac{25\pi}{2} = 32{,}768\operatorname{cis}\frac{\pi}{2} = 32{,}768(0+i) = 32{,}768i$

**13** $1 + \sqrt{3}\,i = 2\operatorname{cis}60°.$   $w_k = \sqrt{2}\operatorname{cis}\left(\frac{60°+360°\,k}{2}\right)$ for $k = 0, 1.$

$w_0 = \sqrt{2}\operatorname{cis}30° = \sqrt{2}\left(\frac{\sqrt{3}}{2}+\frac{1}{2}i\right) = \frac{\sqrt{6}}{2}+\frac{\sqrt{2}}{2}\,i.$     $w_1 = \sqrt{2}\operatorname{cis}210° = \sqrt{2}\left(-\frac{\sqrt{3}}{2}-\frac{1}{2}i\right) = -\frac{\sqrt{6}}{2}-\frac{\sqrt{2}}{2}\,i.$

**14** $-9i = 9\operatorname{cis}270°.$   $w_k = \sqrt{9}\operatorname{cis}\left(\frac{270°+360°\,k}{2}\right)$ for $k = 0, 1.$

$w_0 = 3\operatorname{cis}135° = 3\left(-\frac{\sqrt{2}}{2}+\frac{\sqrt{2}}{2}i\right) = -\frac{3\sqrt{2}}{2}+\frac{3\sqrt{2}}{2}\,i.$     $w_1 = 3\operatorname{cis}315° = 3\left(\frac{\sqrt{2}}{2}-\frac{\sqrt{2}}{2}i\right) = \frac{3\sqrt{2}}{2}-\frac{3\sqrt{2}}{2}\,i.$

**15** $-1 - \sqrt{3}\,i = 2\operatorname{cis}240°.$   $w_k = \sqrt[4]{2}\operatorname{cis}\left(\frac{240°+360°\,k}{4}\right)$ for $k = 0, 1, 2, 3.$

$w_0 = \sqrt[4]{2}\operatorname{cis}60° = \sqrt[4]{2}\left(\frac{1}{2}+\frac{\sqrt{3}}{2}i\right) = \frac{\sqrt[4]{2}}{2}+\frac{\sqrt[4]{18}}{2}\,i$ {since $\sqrt[4]{2}\cdot\sqrt{3} = \sqrt[4]{2}\cdot\sqrt[4]{9} = \sqrt[4]{18}$}.

$w_1 = \sqrt[4]{2}\operatorname{cis}150° = \sqrt[4]{2}\left(-\frac{\sqrt{3}}{2}+\frac{1}{2}i\right) = -\frac{\sqrt[4]{18}}{2}+\frac{\sqrt[4]{2}}{2}\,i.$

$w_2 = \sqrt[4]{2}\operatorname{cis}240° = \sqrt[4]{2}\left(-\frac{1}{2}-\frac{\sqrt{3}}{2}i\right) = -\frac{\sqrt[4]{2}}{2}-\frac{\sqrt[4]{18}}{2}\,i.$

$w_3 = \sqrt[4]{2}\operatorname{cis}330° = \sqrt[4]{2}\left(\frac{\sqrt{3}}{2}-\frac{1}{2}i\right) = \frac{\sqrt[4]{18}}{2}-\frac{\sqrt[4]{2}}{2}\,i.$

**16** $-8 + 8\sqrt{3}i = 16\operatorname{cis}120°.$   $w_k = \sqrt[4]{16}\operatorname{cis}\left(\frac{120°+360°\,k}{4}\right)$ for $k = 0, 1, 2, 3.$

$w_0 = 2\operatorname{cis}30° = 2\left(\frac{\sqrt{3}}{2}+\frac{1}{2}i\right) = \sqrt{3}+i.$     $w_1 = 2\operatorname{cis}120° = 2\left(-\frac{1}{2}+\frac{\sqrt{3}}{2}i\right) = -1+\sqrt{3}\,i.$

$w_2 = 2\operatorname{cis}210° = 2\left(-\frac{\sqrt{3}}{2}-\frac{1}{2}i\right) = -\sqrt{3}-i.$     $w_3 = 2\operatorname{cis}300° = 2\left(\frac{1}{2}-\frac{\sqrt{3}}{2}i\right) = 1-\sqrt{3}\,i.$

**17** $-27i = 27\operatorname{cis}270°.$   $w_k = \sqrt[3]{27}\operatorname{cis}\left(\frac{270°+360°\,k}{3}\right)$ for $k = 0, 1, 2.$ $w_0 = 3\operatorname{cis}90° = 3(0+i) = 3i.$

$w_1 = 3\operatorname{cis}210° = 3\left(-\frac{\sqrt{3}}{2}-\frac{1}{2}i\right) = -\frac{3\sqrt{3}}{2}-\frac{3}{2}i.$     $w_2 = 3\operatorname{cis}330° = 3\left(\frac{\sqrt{3}}{2}-\frac{1}{2}i\right) = \frac{3\sqrt{3}}{2}-\frac{3}{2}i.$

**18** $64i = 64\operatorname{cis}90°.$   $w_k = \sqrt[3]{64}\operatorname{cis}\left(\frac{90°+360°\,k}{3}\right)$ for $k = 0, 1, 2.$   $w_0 = 4\operatorname{cis}30° = 4\left(\frac{\sqrt{3}}{2}+\frac{1}{2}i\right) = 2\sqrt{3}+2i.$

$w_1 = 4\operatorname{cis}150° = 4\left(-\frac{\sqrt{3}}{2}+\frac{1}{2}i\right) = -2\sqrt{3}+2i.$     $w_2 = 4\operatorname{cis}270° = 4(0-i) = -4i.$

**19** $1 = 1 \operatorname{cis} 0°$. $w_k = \sqrt[6]{1} \operatorname{cis}\left(\dfrac{0° + 360° k}{6}\right)$ for $k = 0, 1, 2, 3, 4, 5$. $w_0 = 1 \operatorname{cis} 0° = 1 + 0i$.

$w_1 = 1 \operatorname{cis} 60° = \frac{1}{2} + \frac{\sqrt{3}}{2} i$.      $w_2 = 1 \operatorname{cis} 120° = -\frac{1}{2} + \frac{\sqrt{3}}{2} i$.      $w_3 = 1 \operatorname{cis} 180° = -1 + 0i$.

$w_4 = 1 \operatorname{cis} 240° = -\frac{1}{2} - \frac{\sqrt{3}}{2} i$.      $w_5 = 1 \operatorname{cis} 300° = \frac{1}{2} - \frac{\sqrt{3}}{2} i$.

*Figure 19*

*Figure 20*

**20** $1 = 1 \operatorname{cis} 0°$. $w_k = \sqrt[8]{1} \operatorname{cis}\left(\dfrac{0° + 360° k}{8}\right)$ for $k = 0, 1, 2, 3, 4, 5, 6, 7$.

$w_0 = 1 \operatorname{cis} 0° = 1 + 0i$.      $w_1 = 1 \operatorname{cis} 45° = \frac{\sqrt{2}}{2} + \frac{\sqrt{2}}{2} i$.      $w_2 = 1 \operatorname{cis} 90° = 0 + i$.

$w_3 = 1 \operatorname{cis} 135° = -\frac{\sqrt{2}}{2} + \frac{\sqrt{2}}{2} i$.      $w_4 = 1 \operatorname{cis} 180° = -1 + 0i$.      $w_5 = 1 \operatorname{cis} 225° = -\frac{\sqrt{2}}{2} - \frac{\sqrt{2}}{2} i$.

$w_6 = 1 \operatorname{cis} 270° = 0 - i$.      $w_7 = 1 \operatorname{cis} 315° = \frac{\sqrt{2}}{2} - \frac{\sqrt{2}}{2} i$.

**21** $1 + i = \sqrt{2} \operatorname{cis} 45°$. $w_k = \sqrt{\sqrt[5]{2}} \operatorname{cis}\left(\dfrac{45° + 360° k}{5}\right)$ for $k = 0, 1, 2, 3, 4$.

$$w_k = \sqrt[10]{2} \operatorname{cis} \theta \text{ with } \theta = 9°, 81°, 153°, 225°, 297°.$$

*Figure 21*

*Figure 22*

**22** $-\sqrt{3} - i = 2 \operatorname{cis} 210°$. $w_k = \sqrt[5]{2} \operatorname{cis}\left(\dfrac{210° + 360° k}{5}\right)$ for $k = 0, 1, 2, 3, 4$.

$$w_k = \sqrt[5]{2} \operatorname{cis} \theta \text{ with } \theta = 42°, 114°, 186°, 258°, 330°.$$

**23** $x^4 - 16 = 0 \Rightarrow x^4 = 16$. The problem is now to find the 4 fourth roots of 16.

$16 = 16 + 0i = 16 \operatorname{cis} 0°$. $w_k = \sqrt[4]{16} \operatorname{cis}\left(\dfrac{0° + 360° k}{4}\right)$ for $k = 0, 1, 2, 3$.

$w_0 = 2 \operatorname{cis} 0° = 2(1 + 0i) = 2$.      $w_1 = 2 \operatorname{cis} 90° = 2(0 + i) = 2i$.

$w_2 = 2 \operatorname{cis} 180° = 2(-1 + 0i) = -2$.      $w_3 = 2 \operatorname{cis} 270° = 2(0 - i) = -2i$.

**24** $x^6 - 64 = 0 \Rightarrow x^6 = 64$. The problem is now to find the 6 sixth roots of 64.

$64 = 64 + 0i = 64 \operatorname{cis} 0°$. $w_k = \sqrt[6]{64} \operatorname{cis}\left(\dfrac{0° + 360° k}{6}\right)$ for $k = 0, 1, 2, 3, 4, 5$.

$w_0 = 2 \operatorname{cis} 0° = 2(1 + 0i) = 2$.      $w_1 = 2 \operatorname{cis} 60° = 2\left(\frac{1}{2} + \frac{\sqrt{3}}{2} i\right) = 1 + \sqrt{3}\, i$.

$w_2 = 2 \operatorname{cis} 120° = 2\left(-\frac{1}{2} + \frac{\sqrt{3}}{2} i\right) = -1 + \sqrt{3}\, i.$ $\qquad$ $w_3 = 2 \operatorname{cis} 180° = 2(-1 + 0i) = -2.$

$w_4 = 2 \operatorname{cis} 240° = 2\left(-\frac{1}{2} - \frac{\sqrt{3}}{2} i\right) = -1 - \sqrt{3}\, i.$ $\qquad$ $w_5 = 2 \operatorname{cis} 300° = 2\left(\frac{1}{2} - \frac{\sqrt{3}}{2} i\right) = 1 - \sqrt{3}\, i.$

**25** $x^6 + 64 = 0 \;\Rightarrow\; x^6 = -64.$ The problem is now to find the 6 sixth roots of $-64$.

$-64 = -64 + 0i = 64 \operatorname{cis} 180°.$ $w_k = \sqrt[6]{64} \operatorname{cis}\left(\dfrac{180° + 360°\, k}{6}\right)$ for $k = 0, 1, \ldots, 5$.

$w_0 = 2 \operatorname{cis} 30° = 2\left(\frac{\sqrt{3}}{2} + \frac{1}{2} i\right) = \sqrt{3} + i.$ $\qquad$ $w_1 = 2 \operatorname{cis} 90° = 2(0 + i) = 2i.$

$w_2 = 2 \operatorname{cis} 150° = 2\left(-\frac{\sqrt{3}}{2} + \frac{1}{2} i\right) = -\sqrt{3} + i.$ $\qquad$ $w_3 = 2 \operatorname{cis} 210° = 2\left(-\frac{\sqrt{3}}{2} - \frac{1}{2} i\right) = -\sqrt{3} - i.$

$w_4 = 2 \operatorname{cis} 270° = 2(0 - i) = -2i.$ $\qquad$ $w_5 = 2 \operatorname{cis} 330° = 2\left(\frac{\sqrt{3}}{2} - \frac{1}{2} i\right) = \sqrt{3} - i.$

**26** $x^5 + 1 = 0 \;\Rightarrow\; x^5 = -1.$ The problem is now to find the 5 fifth roots of $-1$.

$-1 = -1 + 0i = 1 \operatorname{cis} 180°.$ $w_k = \sqrt[5]{1} \operatorname{cis}\left(\dfrac{180° + 360°\, k}{5}\right)$ for $k = 0, 1, 2, 3, 4$.

$w_k = 1 \operatorname{cis} \theta$ with $\theta = 36°, 108°, 180°, 252°, 324°$.

**27** $x^3 + 8i = 0 \;\Rightarrow\; x^3 = -8i.$ The problem is now to find the 3 cube roots of $-8i$.

$-8i = 0 - 8i = 8 \operatorname{cis} 270°.$ $w_k = \sqrt[3]{8} \operatorname{cis}\left(\dfrac{270° + 360°\, k}{3}\right)$ for $k = 0, 1, 2$.

$w_0 = 2 \operatorname{cis} 90° = 2(0 + i) = 2i.$ $\qquad$ $w_1 = 2 \operatorname{cis} 210° = 2\left(-\frac{\sqrt{3}}{2} - \frac{1}{2} i\right) = -\sqrt{3} - i.$

$w_2 = 2 \operatorname{cis} 330° = 2\left(\frac{\sqrt{3}}{2} - \frac{1}{2} i\right) = \sqrt{3} - i.$

**28** $x^3 - 216i = 0 \;\Rightarrow\; x^3 = 216i.$ The problem is now to find the 3 cube roots of $216i$.

$216i = 0 + 216i = 216 \operatorname{cis} 90°.$

$w_k = \sqrt[3]{216} \operatorname{cis}\left(\dfrac{90° + 360°\, k}{3}\right)$ for $k = 0, 1, 2$. $\qquad$ $w_0 = 6 \operatorname{cis} 30° = 6\left(\frac{\sqrt{3}}{2} + \frac{1}{2} i\right) = 3\sqrt{3} + 3i.$

$w_1 = 6 \operatorname{cis} 150° = 6\left(-\frac{\sqrt{3}}{2} + \frac{1}{2} i\right) = -3\sqrt{3} + 3i.$ $\qquad$ $w_2 = 6 \operatorname{cis} 270° = 6(0 - i) = -6i.$

**29** $x^5 - 243 = 0 \;\Rightarrow\; x^5 = 243.$ The problem is now to find the 5 fifth roots of $243$. $243 = 243 + 0i = 243 \operatorname{cis} 0°.$

$w_k = \sqrt[5]{243} \operatorname{cis}\left(\dfrac{0° + 360°\, k}{5}\right)$ for $k = 0, 1, 2, 3, 4$. $w_k = 3 \operatorname{cis} \theta$ with $\theta = 0°, 72°, 144°, 216°, 288°$.

**30** $x^4 + 81 = 0 \;\Rightarrow\; x^4 = -81.$ The problem is now to find the 4 fourth roots of $-81$.

$-81 = -81 + 0i = 81 \operatorname{cis} 180°.$ $w_k = \sqrt[4]{81} \operatorname{cis}\left(\dfrac{180° + 360°\, k}{4}\right)$ for $k = 0, 1, 2, 3$.

$w_0 = 3 \operatorname{cis} 45° = 3\left(\frac{\sqrt{2}}{2} + \frac{\sqrt{2}}{2} i\right) = \frac{3\sqrt{2}}{2} + \frac{3\sqrt{2}}{2} i.$

$w_1 = 3 \operatorname{cis} 135° = 3\left(-\frac{\sqrt{2}}{2} + \frac{\sqrt{2}}{2} i\right) = -\frac{3\sqrt{2}}{2} + \frac{3\sqrt{2}}{2} i.$

$w_2 = 3 \operatorname{cis} 225° = 3\left(-\frac{\sqrt{2}}{2} - \frac{\sqrt{2}}{2} i\right) = -\frac{3\sqrt{2}}{2} - \frac{3\sqrt{2}}{2} i.$

$w_3 = 3 \operatorname{cis} 315° = 3\left(\frac{\sqrt{2}}{2} - \frac{\sqrt{2}}{2} i\right) = \frac{3\sqrt{2}}{2} - \frac{3\sqrt{2}}{2} i.$

**31** $x^4 = 8 + 8\sqrt{3}i$ • The problem is to find the 4 fourth roots of $8 + 8\sqrt{3}i = 16 \operatorname{cis} 60°$.

$w_k = \sqrt[4]{16} \operatorname{cis}\left(\dfrac{60° + 360°\, k}{4}\right)$ for $k = 0, 1, 2, 3$. $w_k = 2 \operatorname{cis} \theta$ with $\theta = 15°, 105°, 195°, 285°$.

**32** $x^6 = -1 + \sqrt{3}i$ • The problem is to find the 6 sixth roots of $-1 + \sqrt{3}i = 2 \operatorname{cis} 120°$.

$w_k = \sqrt[6]{2} \operatorname{cis}\left(\dfrac{120° + 360°\, k}{6}\right)$ for $k = 0, 1, 2, 3, 4, 5$. $w_k = \sqrt[6]{2} \operatorname{cis} \theta$ with $\theta = 20°, 80°, 140°, 200°, 260°, 320°$.

**33** $[r(\cos\theta + i\sin\theta)]^n = \left[r\left(e^{i\theta}\right)\right]^n = r^n\left(e^{i\theta}\right)^n = r^n e^{i(n\theta)} = r^n(\cos n\theta + i\sin n\theta)$

## Chapter 7 Review Exercises

1. We are given two sides of a triangle and the angle between them—so we use the law of cosines to find the third side.

$$a = \sqrt{b^2 + c^2 - 2bc \cos \alpha} = \sqrt{6^2 + 7^2 - 2(6)(7) \cos 60°} = \sqrt{43}.$$

$$\beta = \cos^{-1}\left(\frac{a^2 + c^2 - b^2}{2ac}\right) = \cos^{-1}\left(\frac{43 + 49 - 36}{2\sqrt{43}(7)}\right) = \cos^{-1}\left(\frac{4}{\sqrt{43}}\right).$$

$$\gamma = \cos^{-1}\left(\frac{a^2 + b^2 - c^2}{2ab}\right) = \cos^{-1}\left(\frac{43 + 36 - 49}{2\sqrt{43}(6)}\right) = \cos^{-1}\left(\frac{5}{2\sqrt{43}}\right).$$

2. $\dfrac{\sin \alpha}{a} = \dfrac{\sin \gamma}{c} \Rightarrow \alpha = \sin^{-1}\left(\dfrac{a \sin \gamma}{c}\right) = \sin^{-1}\left(\dfrac{2\sqrt{3} \cdot \frac{1}{2}}{2}\right) = \sin^{-1}\left(\dfrac{\sqrt{3}}{2}\right) = 60°$ or $120°$.

There are two triangles possible since in either case $\alpha + \gamma < 180°$.

$\beta = (180° - \gamma) - \alpha = (180° - 30°) - (60°$ or $120°) = 90°$ or $30°$.

$$\frac{b}{\sin \beta} = \frac{c}{\sin \gamma} \Rightarrow b = \frac{c \sin \beta}{\sin \gamma} = \frac{2 \sin(90° \text{ or } 30°)}{\sin 30°} = 4 \text{ or } 2.$$

3. $\gamma = 180° - \alpha - \beta = 180° - 60° - 45° = 75°$.

$$\frac{a}{\sin \alpha} = \frac{b}{\sin \beta} \Rightarrow a = \frac{b \sin \alpha}{\sin \beta} = \frac{100 \sin 60°}{\sin 45°} = \frac{100 \cdot \left(\sqrt{3}/2\right)}{\sqrt{2}/2} \cdot \frac{\sqrt{2}}{\sqrt{2}} = 50\sqrt{6}.$$

$$\frac{c}{\sin \gamma} = \frac{b}{\sin \beta} \Rightarrow c = \frac{b \sin \gamma}{\sin \beta} = \frac{100 \sin(45° + 30°)}{\sqrt{2}/2} = 100\sqrt{2}(\sin 45° \cos 30° + \cos 45° \sin 30°), \text{ so}$$

$$c = 100\sqrt{2}\left(\frac{\sqrt{2}}{2} \cdot \frac{\sqrt{3}}{2} + \frac{\sqrt{2}}{2} \cdot \frac{1}{2}\right) = \frac{100}{4}\sqrt{2}\left(\sqrt{6} + \sqrt{2}\right) = 25\left(2\sqrt{3} + 2\right) = 50\left(1 + \sqrt{3}\right).$$

4. $\alpha = \cos^{-1}\left(\dfrac{b^2 + c^2 - a^2}{2bc}\right) = \cos^{-1}\left(\dfrac{9 + 16 - 4}{2(3)(4)}\right) = \cos^{-1}\left(\frac{7}{8}\right)$.

$\beta = \cos^{-1}\left(\dfrac{a^2 + c^2 - b^2}{2ac}\right) = \cos^{-1}\left(\dfrac{4 + 16 - 9}{2(2)(4)}\right) = \cos^{-1}\left(\frac{11}{16}\right)$.

$\gamma = \cos^{-1}\left(\dfrac{a^2 + b^2 - c^2}{2ab}\right) = \cos^{-1}\left(\dfrac{4 + 9 - 16}{2(2)(3)}\right) = \cos^{-1}\left(-\frac{1}{4}\right)$.

5. $\alpha = 180° - \beta - \gamma = 180° - 67° - 75° = 38°$. $\dfrac{a}{\sin \alpha} = \dfrac{b}{\sin \beta} \Rightarrow a = \dfrac{b \sin \alpha}{\sin \beta} = \dfrac{12 \sin 38°}{\sin 67°} \approx 8.0$.

$\dfrac{c}{\sin \gamma} = \dfrac{b}{\sin \beta} \Rightarrow c = \dfrac{b \sin \gamma}{\sin \beta} = \dfrac{12 \sin 75°}{\sin 67°} \approx 12.6$, or 13.

6. $\dfrac{\sin \gamma}{c} = \dfrac{\sin \alpha}{a} \Rightarrow \gamma = \sin^{-1}\left(\dfrac{c \sin \alpha}{a}\right) = \sin^{-1}\left(\dfrac{125 \sin 23°30'}{152}\right) \approx \sin^{-1}(0.3279) \approx 19°10'$ or $160°50'$

{rounded to the nearest 10 minutes}. Reject $160°50'$ because then $\alpha + \gamma \geq 180°$.

$\beta = 180° - \alpha - \gamma \approx 180° - 23°30' - 19°10' = 137°20'$.

$$\frac{b}{\sin \beta} = \frac{a}{\sin \alpha} \Rightarrow b = \frac{a \sin \beta}{\sin \alpha} = \frac{152 \sin 137°20'}{\sin 23°30'} \approx 258.3, \text{ or } 258.$$

7. $b = \sqrt{a^2 + c^2 - 2ac \cos \beta} = \sqrt{(4.6)^2 + (7.3)^2 - 2(4.6)(7.3) \cos 115°} \approx \sqrt{102.8} \approx 10.1$.

$\alpha = \cos^{-1}\left(\dfrac{b^2 + c^2 - a^2}{2bc}\right) \approx \cos^{-1}(0.9116) \approx 24°$. $\gamma = 180° - \alpha - \beta \approx 180° - 24° - 115° = 41°$.

8. $\alpha = \cos^{-1}\left(\dfrac{b^2 + c^2 - a^2}{2bc}\right) \approx \cos^{-1}(0.7410) \approx 42°$. $\beta = \cos^{-1}\left(\dfrac{a^2 + c^2 - b^2}{2ac}\right) \approx \cos^{-1}(0.0607) \approx 87°$.

$\gamma = 180° - \alpha - \beta \approx 180° - 42° - 87° = 51°$.

**9**   Since we are given two sides and the included angle of a triangle, we use the formula for the area of a triangle from Section 7.2. $\mathcal{A} = \frac{1}{2}bc\sin\alpha = \frac{1}{2}(20)(30)\sin 75° \approx 289.8$, or 290 square units.

**10**   Given the three sides of a triangle, we apply Heron's formula to find the area.

$s = \frac{1}{2}(a+b+c) = \frac{1}{2}(5+8+12) = 12.5.$

$$\mathcal{A} = \sqrt{s(s-a)(s-b)(s-c)} = \sqrt{(12.5)(7.5)(4.5)(0.5)} \approx 14.5 \text{ square units.}$$

**11**   (a)   $\mathbf{a} = \langle -4, 5\rangle$ and $\mathbf{b} = \langle 2, -8\rangle \Rightarrow$

$\mathbf{a} + \mathbf{b} = \langle -4+2, 5+(-8)\rangle = \langle -2, -3\rangle.$

(b)   $\mathbf{a} - \mathbf{b} = \langle -4-2, 5-(-8)\rangle = \langle -6, 13\rangle.$

(c)   $2\mathbf{a} = 2\langle -4, 5\rangle = \langle -8, 10\rangle.$

(d)   $-\frac{1}{2}\mathbf{b} = -\frac{1}{2}\langle 2, -8\rangle = \langle -1, 4\rangle.$

Terminal points are $(-2, -3)$, $(-6, 13)$, $(-8, 10)$, $(-1, 4)$.

**12**   (a)   $4\mathbf{a} + \mathbf{b} = 4(2\mathbf{i} + 5\mathbf{j}) + (4\mathbf{i} - \mathbf{j}) = 8\mathbf{i} + 20\mathbf{j} + 4\mathbf{i} - \mathbf{j} = 12\mathbf{i} + 19\mathbf{j}.$

(b)   $2\mathbf{a} - 3\mathbf{b} = 2(2\mathbf{i} + 5\mathbf{j}) - 3(4\mathbf{i} - \mathbf{j}) = 4\mathbf{i} + 10\mathbf{j} - 12\mathbf{i} + 3\mathbf{j} = -8\mathbf{i} + 13\mathbf{j}.$

(c)   $\|\mathbf{a} - \mathbf{b}\| = \|(2\mathbf{i} + 5\mathbf{j}) - (4\mathbf{i} - \mathbf{j})\| = \|-2\mathbf{i} + 6\mathbf{j}\| = \sqrt{40} = 2\sqrt{10} \approx 6.32.$

(d)   $\|\mathbf{a}\| - \|\mathbf{b}\| = \|2\mathbf{i} + 5\mathbf{j}\| - \|4\mathbf{i} - \mathbf{j}\| = \sqrt{29} - \sqrt{17} \approx 1.26.$

**13**   S 50° E is the same as 320°, or $-40°$, on the $xy$-plane.

$$\langle 14\cos(-40°), 14\sin(-40°)\rangle = \langle 14\cos 40°, -14\sin 40°\rangle \approx \langle 10.72, -9.00\rangle.$$

**14**   S 60° E is equivalent to 330° and N 74° E is equivalent to 16°.

$$\langle 72\cos 330°, 72\sin 330°\rangle + \langle 46\cos 16°, 46\sin 16°\rangle = \mathbf{r} \approx \langle 106.57, -23.32\rangle.$$

$\|\mathbf{r}\| \approx 109$ kg. $\tan\theta \approx \dfrac{-23.32}{106.57} \Rightarrow \theta \approx -12°$, or equivalently, S78°E.

**15**   To find a vector that has the opposite direction of $\mathbf{a}$ and twice the magnitude, multiply $\mathbf{a}$ by $-2$.

$$-2\mathbf{a} = -2(5\mathbf{i} + 7\mathbf{j}) = -10\mathbf{i} - 14\mathbf{j}$$

**16**   $\mathbf{a} = \langle -3, 7\rangle \Rightarrow \|\mathbf{a}\| = \sqrt{58}.$ $\mathbf{v} = 4\left(\dfrac{\mathbf{a}}{\|\mathbf{a}\|}\right) = \left\langle -\dfrac{12}{\sqrt{58}}, \dfrac{28}{\sqrt{58}}\right\rangle.$

**17**   $\|\mathbf{r} - \mathbf{a}\| = c \Rightarrow \|\langle x, y\rangle - \langle a_1, a_2\rangle\| = c \Rightarrow \|\langle x - a_1, y - a_2\rangle\| = c \Rightarrow$

$\sqrt{(x-a_1)^2 + (y-a_2)^2} = c \Rightarrow (x-a_1)^2 + (y-a_2)^2 = c^2.$ This is a circle with center $(a_1, a_2)$ and radius $c$.

**18**   The vectors $\mathbf{a}$, $\mathbf{b}$, and $\mathbf{a} - \mathbf{b}$ form a triangle with the vector $\mathbf{a} - \mathbf{b}$ opposite angle $\theta$. The conclusion is a direct application of the law of cosines with sides $\|\mathbf{a}\|$, $\|\mathbf{b}\|$, and $\|\mathbf{a} - \mathbf{b}\|$.

**19**   $\mathbf{p} = \langle 400\cos 10°, 400\sin 10°\rangle \approx \langle 393.92, 69.46\rangle.$

$\mathbf{r} = \langle 390\cos 0°, 390\sin 0°\rangle = \langle 390, 0\rangle.$

$\mathbf{w} = \mathbf{r} - \mathbf{p} \approx \langle -3.92, -69.46\rangle$ and $\|\mathbf{w}\| \approx 69.57$, or 70 mi/hr.

$\tan\theta \approx \dfrac{-69.46}{-3.92} \Rightarrow \theta \approx 267°$, or in the direction of 183°.

**20** (a) $\mathbf{a} \cdot \mathbf{b} = \langle 2, -3 \rangle \cdot \langle -1, -4 \rangle = (2)(-1) + (-3)(-4) = -2 + 12 = 10$

(b) The angle between $\mathbf{a}$ and $\mathbf{b}$ is $\theta = \cos^{-1}\left(\dfrac{\mathbf{a} \cdot \mathbf{b}}{\|\mathbf{a}\|\|\mathbf{b}\|}\right) = \cos^{-1}\left(\dfrac{10}{\sqrt{13}\sqrt{17}}\right) \approx 47°44'$.

(c) $\operatorname{comp}_{\mathbf{a}}\mathbf{b} = \dfrac{\mathbf{b} \cdot \mathbf{a}}{\|\mathbf{a}\|} = \dfrac{10}{\sqrt{13}} \approx 2.77$

**21** (a) $(2\mathbf{a} - 3\mathbf{b}) \cdot \mathbf{a} = [2(6\mathbf{i} - 2\mathbf{j}) - 3(-2\mathbf{i} + 3\mathbf{j})] \cdot (6\mathbf{i} - 2\mathbf{j}) = (18\mathbf{i} - 13\mathbf{j}) \cdot (6\mathbf{i} - 2\mathbf{j}) = 108 + 26 = 134$.

(b) $\mathbf{c} = \mathbf{a} + \mathbf{b} = (6\mathbf{i} - 2\mathbf{j}) + (-2\mathbf{i} + 3\mathbf{j}) = 4\mathbf{i} + \mathbf{j}$. The angle between $\mathbf{a}$ and $\mathbf{c}$ is
$$\theta = \cos^{-1}\left(\frac{\mathbf{a} \cdot \mathbf{c}}{\|\mathbf{a}\|\|\mathbf{c}\|}\right) = \cos^{-1}\left[\frac{(6\mathbf{i} - 2\mathbf{j}) \cdot (4\mathbf{i} + \mathbf{j})}{\|6\mathbf{i} - 2\mathbf{j}\|\|4\mathbf{i} + \mathbf{j}\|}\right] = \cos^{-1}\left(\frac{22}{\sqrt{40}\sqrt{17}}\right) \approx 32°28'.$$

(c) $\operatorname{comp}_{\mathbf{a}}(\mathbf{a} + \mathbf{b}) = \operatorname{comp}_{\mathbf{a}}\mathbf{c} = \dfrac{\mathbf{c} \cdot \mathbf{a}}{\|\mathbf{a}\|} = \dfrac{22}{\sqrt{40}} = \dfrac{22}{2\sqrt{10}} = \dfrac{11}{\sqrt{10}} \approx 3.48$.

**22** $\mathbf{a} \cdot \overrightarrow{PQ} = \langle 7, 4 \rangle \cdot \langle 3 - (-5), 0 - 0 \rangle = 56 + 0 = 56$.

**23** $z = -10 + 10i \;\Rightarrow\; r = \sqrt{(-10)^2 + 10^2} = \sqrt{200} = 10\sqrt{2}$. $\tan\theta = \dfrac{10}{-10} = -1$ and $\theta$ in QII $\;\Rightarrow\; \theta = \dfrac{3\pi}{4}$.
$$z = 10\sqrt{2}\operatorname{cis}\frac{3\pi}{4}.$$

**24** $z = 2 - 2\sqrt{3}\,i \;\Rightarrow\; r = \sqrt{2^2 + \left(-2\sqrt{3}\right)^2} = \sqrt{16} = 4$. $\tan\theta = \dfrac{-2\sqrt{3}}{2} = -\sqrt{3}$ and $\theta$ in QIV $\;\Rightarrow\; \theta = \dfrac{5\pi}{3}$.
$$z = 4\operatorname{cis}\frac{5\pi}{3}.$$

**25** $z = -17 \;\Rightarrow\; r = 17$. $\theta$ on the negative $x$-axis $\;\Rightarrow\; \theta = \pi$. $z = 17\operatorname{cis}\pi$.

**26** $z = -12i \;\Rightarrow\; r = 12$. $\theta$ on the negative $y$-axis $\;\Rightarrow\; \theta = \dfrac{3\pi}{2}$. $z = 12\operatorname{cis}\dfrac{3\pi}{2}$.

**27** $z = -5\sqrt{3} - 5i \;\Rightarrow\; r = \sqrt{\left(-5\sqrt{3}\right)^2 + (-5)^2} = \sqrt{100} = 10$.
$$\tan\theta = \frac{-5}{-5\sqrt{3}} = \frac{1}{\sqrt{3}} \text{ and } \theta \text{ in QIII} \;\Rightarrow\; \theta = \frac{7\pi}{6}. \; z = 10\operatorname{cis}\frac{7\pi}{6}.$$

**28** $z = 4 + 5i \;\Rightarrow\; r = \sqrt{4^2 + 5^2} = \sqrt{41}$. $\tan\theta = \dfrac{5}{4}$ and $\theta$ in QI $\;\Rightarrow\; \theta = \tan^{-1}\dfrac{5}{4}$. $z = \sqrt{41}\operatorname{cis}\left(\tan^{-1}\dfrac{5}{4}\right)$.

**29** $z = -2 + 5i \;\Rightarrow\; r = \sqrt{(-2)^2 + 5^2} = \sqrt{29}$. $\tan\theta = \dfrac{5}{-2} = -\dfrac{5}{2}$ and $\theta$ in QII $\;\Rightarrow\; \theta = \tan^{-1}\left(-\dfrac{5}{2}\right) + \pi$.
$$z = \sqrt{29}\operatorname{cis}\left[\tan^{-1}\left(-\frac{5}{2}\right) + \pi\right].$$

**30** $z = 8 - 15i \;\Rightarrow\; r = \sqrt{8^2 + (-15)^2} = \sqrt{289} = 17$. $\tan\theta = \dfrac{-15}{8}$ and $\theta$ in QIV $\;\Rightarrow\; \theta = \tan^{-1}\left(-\dfrac{15}{8}\right) + 2\pi$.
$$z = 17\operatorname{cis}\left[\tan^{-1}\left(-\frac{15}{8}\right) + 2\pi\right].$$

**31** $20\left(\cos\dfrac{11\pi}{6} + i\sin\dfrac{11\pi}{6}\right) = 20\left(\dfrac{\sqrt{3}}{2} - \dfrac{1}{2}i\right) = 10\sqrt{3} - 10i$

**32** $13\operatorname{cis}\left(\tan^{-1}\dfrac{5}{12}\right) = 13\left[\cos\left(\tan^{-1}\dfrac{5}{12}\right) + i\sin\left(\tan^{-1}\dfrac{5}{12}\right)\right] = 13\left(\dfrac{12}{13} + \dfrac{5}{13}i\right) = 12 + 5i$

**33** $z_1 = -3\sqrt{3} - 3i = 6\operatorname{cis}\dfrac{7\pi}{6}$ and $z_2 = 2\sqrt{3} + 2i = 4\operatorname{cis}\dfrac{\pi}{6}$.
$$z_1 z_2 = 6 \cdot 4\operatorname{cis}\left(\frac{7\pi}{6} + \frac{\pi}{6}\right) = 24\operatorname{cis}\frac{4\pi}{3} = 24\left(-\frac{1}{2} - \frac{\sqrt{3}}{2}i\right) = -12 - 12\sqrt{3}\,i.$$
$$\frac{z_1}{z_2} = \frac{6}{4}\operatorname{cis}\left(\frac{7\pi}{6} - \frac{\pi}{6}\right) = \frac{3}{2}\operatorname{cis}\pi = \frac{3}{2}(-1 + 0i) = -\frac{3}{2}.$$

**34** $z_1 = 2\sqrt{2} + 2\sqrt{2}i = 4\operatorname{cis}\dfrac{\pi}{4}$ and $z_2 = -1 - i = \sqrt{2}\operatorname{cis}\dfrac{5\pi}{4}$.
$$z_1 z_2 = 4 \cdot \sqrt{2}\operatorname{cis}\left(\frac{\pi}{4} + \frac{5\pi}{4}\right) = 4\sqrt{2}\operatorname{cis}\frac{3\pi}{2} = 4\sqrt{2}(0 - i) = -4\sqrt{2}\,i.$$
$$\frac{z_1}{z_2} = \frac{4}{\sqrt{2}}\operatorname{cis}\left(\frac{\pi}{4} - \frac{5\pi}{4}\right) = 2\sqrt{2}\operatorname{cis}(-\pi) = 2\sqrt{2}(-1 + 0i) = -2\sqrt{2}.$$

$\boxed{35}$ $\left(-\sqrt{3}+i\right)^9 = \left(2\operatorname{cis}\frac{5\pi}{6}\right)^9 = 2^9\operatorname{cis}\left(9\cdot\frac{5\pi}{6}\right) = 2^9\operatorname{cis}\frac{15\pi}{2} = 512\operatorname{cis}\frac{3\pi}{2} = 512(0-i) = -512i$

$\boxed{36}$ $\left(\frac{\sqrt{2}}{2}-\frac{\sqrt{2}}{2}i\right)^{30} = \left(1\operatorname{cis}\frac{7\pi}{4}\right)^{30} = 1^{30}\operatorname{cis}\frac{105\pi}{2} = \operatorname{cis}\frac{\pi}{2} = 0+i$

$\boxed{37}$ $(3-3i)^5 = \left(3\sqrt{2}\operatorname{cis}\frac{7\pi}{4}\right)^5 = \left(3\sqrt{2}\right)^5\operatorname{cis}\frac{35\pi}{4} = 972\sqrt{2}\operatorname{cis}\frac{3\pi}{4} = 972\sqrt{2}\left(-\frac{\sqrt{2}}{2}+\frac{\sqrt{2}}{2}i\right) = -972+972i$

$\boxed{38}$ $\left(2+2\sqrt{3}i\right)^{10} = \left(4\operatorname{cis}\frac{\pi}{3}\right)^{10} = 4^{10}\operatorname{cis}\frac{10\pi}{3} = 2^{20}\operatorname{cis}\frac{4\pi}{3} = 2^{20}\left(-\frac{1}{2}-\frac{\sqrt{3}}{2}i\right) = -2^{19}-2^{19}\sqrt{3}i$

$\boxed{39}$ $-27 = -27+0i = 27\operatorname{cis}180°$. $w_k = \sqrt[3]{27}\operatorname{cis}\left(\dfrac{180°+360°k}{3}\right)$ for $k = 0,1,2$.

$w_0 = 3\operatorname{cis}60° = 3\left(\frac{1}{2}+\frac{\sqrt{3}}{2}i\right) = \frac{3}{2}+\frac{3\sqrt{3}}{2}i$. $\qquad$ $w_1 = 3\operatorname{cis}180° = 3(-1+0i) = -3$.

$w_2 = 3\operatorname{cis}300° = 3\left(\frac{1}{2}-\frac{\sqrt{3}}{2}i\right) = \frac{3}{2}-\frac{3\sqrt{3}}{2}i$.

$\boxed{40}$ (a) $z^{24} = \left(1-\sqrt{3}i\right)^{24} = \left(2\operatorname{cis}\frac{5\pi}{3}\right)^{24} = 2^{24}\operatorname{cis}40\pi = 2^{24}(1+0i) = 2^{24}$

(b) $1-\sqrt{3}i = 2\operatorname{cis}300°$. $w_k = \sqrt[3]{2}\operatorname{cis}\left(\dfrac{300°+360°k}{3}\right)$ for $k = 0,1,2$.

$\qquad\qquad\qquad\qquad\qquad\qquad\qquad\qquad$ $w_k = \sqrt[3]{2}\operatorname{cis}\theta$ with $\theta = 100°, 220°, 340°$.

$\boxed{41}$ $x^5+32i = 0 \Rightarrow x^5 = -32i$. The problem is now to find the 5 fifth roots of $-32i$.

$-32i = 0-32i = 32\operatorname{cis}270°$. $w_k = \sqrt[5]{32}\operatorname{cis}\left(\dfrac{270°+360°k}{5}\right)$ for $k = 0,1,2,3,4$.

$\qquad\qquad\qquad\qquad\qquad\qquad\qquad$ $w_k = 2\operatorname{cis}\theta$ with $\theta = 54°, 126°, 198°, 270°, 342°$.

$\boxed{42}$ $\dfrac{\sin\gamma}{150} = \dfrac{\sin 27.4°}{200} \Rightarrow$

$\gamma = \sin^{-1}\left(\dfrac{150\sin 27.4°}{200}\right) \approx \sin^{-1}(0.3451) \approx 20.2°$.

$\beta = 180° - \alpha - \beta \approx 180° - 27.4° - 20.2° = 132.4°$.

The angle between the hill and the horizontal is then $180° - 132.4° = 47.6°$.

$\boxed{43}$ $\angle ABT = 180° - 59° = 121°$. $\angle BTA = 180° - 121° - 40° = 19°$.

$\dfrac{\overline{BT}}{\sin 40°} = \dfrac{100}{\sin 19°} \Rightarrow \overline{BT} = \dfrac{100\sin 40°}{\sin 19°} \approx 197.4$ yards.

Figure 43

Figure 44

$\boxed{44}$ The angle between the two paths is $30° + 90° + 10° = 130°$.

$\qquad\qquad\qquad\qquad\qquad$ $\overline{AB} = \sqrt{120^2+140^2-2(120)(140)\cos 130°} \approx 235.8$ miles.

**45** Let $a$ be the Earth-Venus distance, $b$ the Earth-sun distance, and $c$ the Venus-sun distance.

Then, by the law of cosines (with $a$, $b$, and $c$ in millions),

$$a^2 = b^2 + c^2 - 2bc \cos \alpha = 93^2 + 67^2 - 2(93)(67) \cos 34° \approx 2807 \quad \Rightarrow \quad a \approx 53 \text{—that is, } 53,000,000 \text{ miles.}$$

**46** Let $P$ denote the point at the base of the shorter building, $S$ the point at the top of the shorter building, $T$ the point at the top of the skyscraper, $Q$ the point 50 feet up the side of the skyscraper, and $h$ the height of the skyscraper.

(a) $\angle SPT = 90° - 62° = 28°$. $\angle PST = 90° + 59° = 149°$. Thus, $\angle STP = 180° - 28° - 149° = 3°$.

$$\frac{\overline{ST}}{\sin 28°} = \frac{50}{\sin 3°} \quad \Rightarrow \quad \overline{ST} \approx 448.52, \text{ or } 449 \text{ ft.}$$

(b) $h = \overline{QT} + 50 = \overline{ST} \sin 59° + 50 \approx 434.45$, or 434 ft.

**47** (a) $\angle LAS = 180° - 47.2° - 66.4° = 66.4°$. $\dfrac{\overline{AL}}{\sin 47.2°} = \dfrac{41}{\sin 66.4°} \quad \Rightarrow$

$$\overline{AL} = \frac{41 \sin 47.2°}{\sin 66.4°} \approx 32.83, \text{ or } 33 \text{ miles.} \quad \overline{AS} = \overline{LS} = 41 \text{ since } \triangle LAS \text{ is isosceles.}$$

(b) Let $\overline{AP}$ be perpendicular to $\overline{LS}$. $\sin 47.2° = \dfrac{\overline{AP}}{\overline{AS}} \quad \Rightarrow \quad \overline{AP} \approx 30.08$, or 30 miles.

**48** Let $E$ denote the middle point. $\angle CDA = \angle BDC - \angle BDA = 125° - 100° = 25°$.

In $\triangle CAD$, $\angle CAD = 180° - \angle ACD - \angle CDA = 180° - 115° - 25° = 40°$.

$\dfrac{\overline{AD}}{\sin 115°} = \dfrac{120}{\sin 40°} \quad \Rightarrow \quad \overline{AD} \approx 169.20$. $\angle DCB = \angle ACD - \angle ACB = 115° - 92° = 23°$.

In $\triangle DBC$, $\angle DBC = 180° - \angle BDC - \angle DCB = 180° - 125° - 23° = 32°$.

$\dfrac{\overline{BD}}{\sin 23°} = \dfrac{120}{\sin 32°} \quad \Rightarrow \quad \overline{BD} \approx 88.48$. In $\triangle ADB$, $\overline{AB}^2 = \overline{AD}^2 + \overline{BD}^2 - 2(\overline{AD})(\overline{BD}) \cos \angle BDA \quad \Rightarrow$

$$\overline{AB} \approx \sqrt{(169.20)^2 + (88.48)^2 - 2(169.20)(88.48) \cos 100°} \approx 204.1, \text{ or } 204 \text{ ft.}$$

**49** If $d$ denotes the distance each girl walks before losing contact with each other, then $d = 5t$, where $t$ is in hours.

Using the law of cosines, $10^2 = d^2 + d^2 - 2(d)(d) \cos 105° \quad \Rightarrow \quad 100 = 2d^2(1 - \cos 105°) \quad \Rightarrow$

$$d^2 = \frac{50}{1 - \cos 105°} \quad \Rightarrow \quad d \approx 6.30. \text{ Now } t = d/5 \approx 1.26 \text{ hours, or 1 hour and 16 minutes.}$$

**50** (a) Draw a vertical line $l$ through $C$ and label its $x$-intercept $D$.

Since we have alternate interior angles, $\angle ACD = \theta_1$. $\angle DCP = 180° - \theta_2$.

$$\text{Thus, } \angle ACP = \angle ACD + \angle DCP = \theta_1 + (180° - \theta_2) = 180° - (\theta_2 - \theta_1).$$

(b) Let $k = d(A, P)$. $k^2 = 17^2 + 17^2 - 2(17)(17) \cos [180° - (\theta_2 - \theta_1)]$.

Since $\cos(180° - \alpha) = \cos 180° \cos \alpha + \sin 180° \sin \alpha = -\cos \alpha$, we have

$k^2 = 578 + 578 \cos(\theta_2 - \theta_1) = 578 [1 + \cos(\theta_2 - \theta_1)]$.

Using the distance formula with the points $A(0, 26)$ and $P(x, y)$, we also have $k^2 = x^2 + (y - 26)^2$.

$$\text{Hence, } 578 [1 + \cos(\theta_2 - \theta_1)] = x^2 + (y - 26)^2 \quad \Rightarrow \quad 1 + \cos(\theta_2 - \theta_1) = \frac{x^2 + (y - 26)^2}{578}.$$

(c) If $x = 25$, $y = 4$, and $\theta_1 = 135°$, then $1 + \cos(\theta_2 - 135°) = \dfrac{25^2 + (-22)^2}{578} = \dfrac{1109}{578} \quad \Rightarrow$

$$\cos(\theta_2 - 135°) = \tfrac{531}{578} \quad \Rightarrow \quad \theta_2 - 135° \approx 23.3° \quad \Rightarrow \quad \theta_2 \approx 158.3°, \text{ or } 158°.$$

**51** (a) Let $d$ denote the length of the rescue tunnel.

Using the law of cosines, $d^2 = 45^2 + 50^2 - 2(45)(50) \cos 78° \quad \Rightarrow \quad d \approx 59.91$ ft.

$$\text{Now using the law of sines, } \frac{\sin \theta}{45} = \frac{\sin 78°}{d} \quad \Rightarrow \quad \theta = \sin^{-1}\left(\frac{45 \sin 78°}{d}\right) \approx 47.28°, \text{ or } 47°.$$

(b) If $x$ denotes the number of hours needed, then $d$ ft $= (3 \text{ ft/hr})(x \text{ hr}) \Rightarrow x = \frac{1}{3}d = \frac{1}{3}(59.91) \approx 20$ hr.

$\boxed{52}$ (a) $\angle CBA = 180° - 136° = 44°$ and $d = \overline{AC} = \sqrt{22.9^2 + 17.2^2 - 2(22.9)(17.2)\cos 44°} \approx 15.9$.

Let $\alpha = \angle BAC$. Using the law of sines, $\dfrac{\sin \alpha}{22.9} = \dfrac{\sin 44°}{d} \Rightarrow \alpha = \sin^{-1}\left(\dfrac{22.9 \sin 44°}{d}\right) \approx 87.4°$.

Let $\beta = \angle CAD$. Using the law of cosines, $5.7^2 = d^2 + 16^2 - 2(d)(16)\cos \beta \Rightarrow$

$$\beta = \cos^{-1}\left(\frac{d^2 + 16^2 - 5.7^2}{2(d)(16)}\right) \approx 20.6°. \quad \phi \approx 180° - 87.4° - 20.6° = 72°.$$

(b) The area of $ABCD$ is the sum of the areas of $\triangle CBA$ and $\triangle ADC$.

$$\text{Area} = \tfrac{1}{2}\left(\text{base } \overline{BC}\right)(\text{height to } A) + \tfrac{1}{2}\left(\text{base } \overline{AC}\right)(\text{height to } D)$$
$$= \tfrac{1}{2}\left(\overline{BC}\right)\left(\overline{BA}\right)\sin \angle CBA + \tfrac{1}{2}\left(\overline{AC}\right)\left(\overline{AD}\right)\sin \angle CAD$$
$$= \tfrac{1}{2}(22.9)(17.2)\sin 44° + \tfrac{1}{2}(15.9)(16)\sin 20.6° \approx 136.8 + 44.8 = 181.6 \text{ ft}^2.$$

(c) Let $h$ denote the perpendicular distance from $\overline{BA}$ to $C$.

$$\sin 44° = \frac{h}{22.9} \Rightarrow h \approx 15.9. \text{ The wing span } \overline{CC'} \text{ is } 2h + 5.8 \approx 37.6 \text{ ft.}$$

## Chapter 7 Discussion Exercises

$\boxed{1}$ (a) $\dfrac{a}{\sin \alpha} = \dfrac{c}{\sin \gamma} \Rightarrow \dfrac{a}{c} = \dfrac{\sin \alpha}{\sin \gamma}$ and $\dfrac{b}{\sin \beta} = \dfrac{c}{\sin \gamma} \Rightarrow \dfrac{b}{c} = \dfrac{\sin \beta}{\sin \gamma}$.

Adding the equations yields $\dfrac{a}{c} + \dfrac{b}{c} = \dfrac{\sin \alpha}{\sin \gamma} + \dfrac{\sin \beta}{\sin \gamma} \Rightarrow \dfrac{a+b}{c} = \dfrac{\sin \alpha + \sin \beta}{\sin \gamma}$.

(b) $\dfrac{a+b}{c} = \dfrac{\sin \alpha + \sin \beta}{\sin \gamma} \Rightarrow \dfrac{a+b}{c} = \dfrac{\text{[S1] } 2\sin \frac{1}{2}(\alpha + \beta)\cos \frac{1}{2}(\alpha - \beta)}{2\sin \frac{1}{2}\gamma \cos \frac{1}{2}\gamma}$. Now $\gamma = 180° - (\alpha + \beta) \Rightarrow$

$\frac{1}{2}\gamma = \left[90° - \frac{1}{2}(\alpha + \beta)\right]$ and $\sin \frac{1}{2}(\alpha + \beta) = \cos\left[90° - \frac{1}{2}(\alpha + \beta)\right] = \cos \frac{1}{2}\gamma$. Thus, $\dfrac{a+b}{c} = \dfrac{\cos \frac{1}{2}(\alpha - \beta)}{\sin \frac{1}{2}\gamma}$.

**Note:** This is an interesting result and gives an answer to the question, "How can I check these triangle problems?" Some of my students have written programs for their graphing calculators to utilize this check.

$\boxed{2}$ $z^{-n} = r^{-n}[\cos(-n\theta) + i\sin(-n\theta)] = \dfrac{\cos n\theta - i\sin n\theta}{r^n}$        {cos is even, sin is odd}

$= \dfrac{(\cos n\theta - i\sin n\theta)(\cos n\theta + i\sin n\theta)}{r^n(\cos n\theta + i\sin n\theta)} = \dfrac{\cos^2 n\theta - i^2\sin^2 n\theta}{r^n(\cos n\theta + i\sin n\theta)}$

$= \dfrac{\cos^2 n\theta + \sin^2 n\theta}{r^n(\cos n\theta + i\sin n\theta)} = \dfrac{1}{r^n(\cos n\theta + i\sin n\theta)} = \dfrac{1}{z^n}$

$\boxed{3}$ Example 3 in Section 7.6 illustrates the case $a = 1$.

Algebraic: $\sqrt[3]{a}, \; \sqrt[3]{a}\operatorname{cis}\frac{2\pi}{3}, \; \sqrt[3]{a}\operatorname{cis}\frac{4\pi}{3}$

Geometric: All roots lie on a circle of radius $\sqrt[3]{a}$, they are all 120° apart,

one is on the real axis, one is on $\theta = \frac{2\pi}{3}$, and one is on $\theta = \frac{4\pi}{3}$.

$\boxed{4}$ (a) The vector $\mathbf{v} - \mathbf{w}$ is the vector that would need to be added to $\mathbf{w}$ to equal $\mathbf{v}$. That is, if the initial point of $\mathbf{v} - \mathbf{w}$ (assuming $\mathbf{v}$ and $\mathbf{w}$ have the same initial point) is placed on the terminal point of $\mathbf{w}$, the terminal point of $\mathbf{v} - \mathbf{w}$ would coincide with the terminal point of $\mathbf{v}$ and "complete the triangle."

(b) Use the law of cosines to obtain $\|\mathbf{v} - \mathbf{w}\| = \sqrt{\|\mathbf{v}\|^2 + \|\mathbf{w}\|^2 - 2\|\mathbf{v}\|\|\mathbf{w}\|\cos \theta}$.

[5] (a) $\mathbf{c} = \mathbf{b} + \mathbf{a} = (\|\mathbf{b}\| \cos\alpha\, \mathbf{i} + \|\mathbf{b}\| \sin\alpha\, \mathbf{j}) + (\|\mathbf{a}\| \cos(-\beta)\mathbf{i} + \|\mathbf{a}\| \sin(-\beta)\mathbf{j})$

$\qquad = \|\mathbf{b}\| \cos\alpha\, \mathbf{i} + \|\mathbf{b}\| \sin\alpha\, \mathbf{j} + \|\mathbf{a}\| \cos\beta\, \mathbf{i} - \|\mathbf{a}\| \sin\beta\, \mathbf{j}$

$\qquad = (\|\mathbf{b}\| \cos\alpha + \|\mathbf{a}\| \cos\beta)\mathbf{i} + (\|\mathbf{b}\| \sin\alpha - \|\mathbf{a}\| \sin\beta)\mathbf{j}$

(b) $\|\mathbf{c}\|^2 = (\|\mathbf{b}\| \cos\alpha + \|\mathbf{a}\| \cos\beta)^2 + (\|\mathbf{b}\| \sin\alpha - \|\mathbf{a}\| \sin\beta)^2$

$\qquad = \|\mathbf{b}\|^2 \cos^2\alpha + 2\|\mathbf{a}\|\|\mathbf{b}\| \cos\alpha \cos\beta + \|\mathbf{a}\|^2 \cos^2\beta + \|\mathbf{b}\|^2 \sin^2\alpha - 2\|\mathbf{a}\|\|\mathbf{b}\| \sin\alpha \sin\beta + \|\mathbf{a}\|^2 \sin^2\beta$

$\qquad = (\|\mathbf{b}\|^2 \cos^2\alpha + \|\mathbf{b}\|^2 \sin^2\alpha) + (\|\mathbf{a}\|^2 \cos^2\beta + \|\mathbf{a}\|^2 \sin^2\beta) + 2\|\mathbf{a}\|\|\mathbf{b}\| \cos\alpha \cos\beta$

$\qquad\qquad\qquad\qquad\qquad\qquad\qquad\qquad\qquad\qquad\qquad\qquad\qquad\qquad - 2\|\mathbf{a}\|\|\mathbf{b}\| \sin\alpha \sin\beta$

$\qquad = \|\mathbf{b}\|^2 + \|\mathbf{a}\|^2 + 2\|\mathbf{a}\|\|\mathbf{b}\|(\cos\alpha \cos\beta - \sin\alpha \sin\beta)$

$\qquad = \|\mathbf{a}\|^2 + \|\mathbf{b}\|^2 + 2\|\mathbf{a}\|\|\mathbf{b}\| \cos(\alpha + \beta)$

$\qquad = \|\mathbf{a}\|^2 + \|\mathbf{b}\|^2 + 2\|\mathbf{a}\|\|\mathbf{b}\| \cos(\pi - \gamma) \quad \{\alpha + \beta + \gamma = \pi\}$

$\qquad = \|\mathbf{a}\|^2 + \|\mathbf{b}\|^2 - 2\|\mathbf{a}\|\|\mathbf{b}\| \cos\gamma \quad \{\cos(\pi - \gamma) = -\cos\gamma\}$

(c) From part (a), we let $\|\mathbf{b}\| \sin\alpha - \|\mathbf{a}\| \sin\beta = 0$. Thus, $\|\mathbf{b}\| \sin\alpha = \|\mathbf{a}\| \sin\beta$, and $\dfrac{\sin\alpha}{\|\mathbf{a}\|} = \dfrac{\sin\beta}{\|\mathbf{b}\|}$.

[6] (a) $e^{2\pi i} = \cos 2\pi + i \sin 2\pi = 1 + i \cdot 0 = 1$

(b) $\mathrm{LN}(-1) = \mathrm{LN}(-1 + 0i) = \ln|-1 + 0i| + i(\pi + 2\pi \cdot 0) = \ln\sqrt{(-1)^2 + 0^2} + i(\pi) = \ln 1 + \pi i = 0 + \pi i = \pi i$

$\mathrm{LN}\, i = \mathrm{LN}(0 + i) = \ln|0 + i| + i\left(\frac{\pi}{2} + 2\pi \cdot 0\right) = \ln\sqrt{0^2 + 1^2} + i\left(\frac{\pi}{2}\right) = \ln 1 + \frac{\pi}{2}i = 0 + \frac{\pi}{2}i = \frac{\pi}{2}i$

(c) $\sqrt{i} = i^{1/2} = e^{(1/2)\mathrm{LN}\, i} = e^{(1/2)(\ln 1 + i(\pi/2))} = e^{(1/2)(i(\pi/2))} = e^{(\pi/4)i} = \cos\frac{\pi}{4} + i\sin\frac{\pi}{4} = \frac{\sqrt{2}}{2} + \frac{\sqrt{2}}{2}i$

$i^i = e^{i\mathrm{LN}\, i} = e^{i(\ln 1 + i(\pi/2))} = e^{i(i(\pi/2))} = e^{-\pi/2} \approx 0.2079 \ \{\text{a real number!}\}$

[7] If we check the statement

$$\tan\alpha + \tan\beta + \tan\gamma = \tan\alpha \tan\beta \tan\gamma \qquad (*)$$

for a couple sets of values of $\alpha$, $\beta$, and $\gamma$ such that $\alpha + \beta + \gamma = \pi$, we find that the statement is true, so we'll try to prove that (*) is an identity.

$\mathrm{LS} = \tan\alpha + \tan\beta + \tan\gamma$

$\qquad = \dfrac{\sin\alpha}{\cos\alpha} + \dfrac{\sin\beta}{\cos\beta} + \dfrac{\sin\gamma}{\cos\gamma}$

$\qquad = \dfrac{\sin\alpha \cos\beta \cos\gamma + \sin\beta \cos\alpha \cos\gamma + \sin\gamma \cos\alpha \cos\beta}{\cos\alpha \cos\beta \cos\gamma}$

$\qquad = \dfrac{\cos\gamma(\sin\alpha \cos\beta + \sin\beta \cos\alpha) + \sin\gamma \cos\alpha \cos\beta}{\cos\alpha \cos\beta \cos\gamma}$

$\qquad = \dfrac{\cos\gamma \sin(\alpha + \beta) + \sin\gamma \cos\alpha \cos\beta}{\cos\alpha \cos\beta \cos\gamma}$

Note that $\sin(\alpha + \beta) = \sin(\pi - \gamma) = \sin\pi \cos\gamma - \cos\pi \sin\gamma = 0 - (-1)\sin\gamma = \sin\gamma$. Continuing,

$\mathrm{LS} = \dfrac{\cos\gamma \sin\gamma + \sin\gamma \cos\alpha \cos\beta}{\cos\alpha \cos\beta \cos\gamma}$

$\qquad = \dfrac{\sin\gamma(\cos\gamma + \cos\alpha \cos\beta)}{\cos\alpha \cos\beta \cos\gamma}$

Note that

$\cos\gamma = \cos[\pi - (\alpha + \beta)] = \cos\pi \cos(\alpha + \beta) + \sin\pi \sin(\alpha + \beta) = -\cos(\alpha + \beta) = -\cos\alpha \cos\beta + \sin\alpha \sin\beta$.

Continuing,

$\mathrm{LS} = \dfrac{\sin\gamma(-\cos\alpha \cos\beta + \sin\alpha \sin\beta + \cos\alpha \cos\beta)}{\cos\alpha \cos\beta \cos\gamma}$

$\qquad = \dfrac{\sin\gamma(\sin\alpha \sin\beta)}{\cos\alpha \cos\beta \cos\gamma} = \dfrac{\sin\alpha}{\cos\alpha} \cdot \dfrac{\sin\beta}{\cos\beta} \cdot \dfrac{\sin\gamma}{\cos\gamma} = \tan\alpha \tan\beta \tan\gamma = \mathrm{RS}$

**8** If **W** represents the force of the ornament, then because

$\cos(180° - \alpha) = \cos 180° \cos\alpha + \sin 180° \sin\alpha = -1 \cdot \cos\alpha + 0 \cdot \sin\alpha = -\cos\alpha$, we have

$\mathbf{T_1} = \|\mathbf{T_1}\| \langle -\cos\alpha, \sin\alpha \rangle$, $\mathbf{T_2} = \|\mathbf{T_2}\| \langle \cos\beta, \sin\beta \rangle$, and $\mathbf{W} = \langle 0, -5 \rangle$.

The sum of the forces is $\mathbf{0} = \langle 0, 0 \rangle$, so

$$-\|\mathbf{T_1}\| \cos\alpha + \|\mathbf{T_2}\| \cos\beta = 0 \quad (E_1) \qquad \text{and} \qquad \|\mathbf{T_1}\| \sin\alpha + \|\mathbf{T_2}\| \sin\beta - 5 = 0 \quad (E_2).$$

Solve $E_1$ for $\|\mathbf{T_2}\|$ and substitute into $E_2$. $\|\mathbf{T_2}\| \cos\beta = \|\mathbf{T_1}\| \cos\alpha \Rightarrow \|\mathbf{T_2}\| = \dfrac{\|\mathbf{T_1}\| \cos\alpha}{\cos\beta}$, so $E_2$ becomes

$\|\mathbf{T_1}\| \sin\alpha + \dfrac{\|\mathbf{T_1}\| \cos\alpha}{\cos\beta} \cdot \sin\beta = 5 \Rightarrow \|\mathbf{T_1}\| \sin\alpha \cos\beta + \|\mathbf{T_1}\| \cos\alpha \sin\beta = 5 \cos\beta \Rightarrow$

$\|\mathbf{T_1}\|(\sin\alpha \cos\beta + \cos\alpha \sin\beta) = 5 \cos\beta \Rightarrow \|\mathbf{T_1}\| \sin(\alpha + \beta) = 5 \cos\beta \Rightarrow \|\mathbf{T_1}\| = \dfrac{5 \cos\beta}{\sin(\alpha + \beta)}$.

Thus, $\|\mathbf{T_2}\| = \dfrac{\|\mathbf{T_1}\| \cos\alpha}{\cos\beta} = \dfrac{5 \cos\beta \cos\alpha}{\sin(\alpha + \beta) \cos\beta} = \dfrac{5 \cos\alpha}{\sin(\alpha + \beta)}$.

## Chapter 7 Test

**1** $\dfrac{\sin\alpha}{a} = \dfrac{\sin\gamma}{c} \Rightarrow \alpha = \sin^{-1}\left(\dfrac{a \sin\gamma}{c}\right) = \sin^{-1}\left(\dfrac{5 \sin\gamma}{3}\right)$

(a) $\gamma = 35° \Rightarrow \alpha \approx 73°$ or $107°$, so **2 triangles** are possible.

(b) $\gamma = 39° \Rightarrow \alpha \approx \sin^{-1}(1.05)$, but $1.05$ is not in the domain of the arcsin function,

so **0 triangles** are possible.

(c) $\gamma = 158° \Rightarrow \alpha \approx 39°$ or $141°$, but we reject $141°$ because then $\gamma + \alpha \geq 180°$, so **1 triangle** is possible.

**2** Let $C$ denote the base of the object and $P$ its projection on the ground. $\angle ACB = 180° - 25° - 57° = 98°$.

$\dfrac{\overline{AC}}{\sin 57°} = \dfrac{6}{\sin 98°} \Rightarrow \overline{AC} = \dfrac{6 \sin 57°}{\sin 98°}$. $\sin 25° = \dfrac{\overline{PC}}{\overline{AC}} \Rightarrow \overline{PC} = \dfrac{6 \sin 57° \sin 25°}{\sin 98°} \approx 2.15$ mi.

**3** $\angle FAB = 90° - 15°50' = 74°10'$. $\angle FBA = 90° - 48°20' = 41°40'$.

$\angle AFB = 180° - 74°10' - 41°40' = 64°10'$. $\dfrac{\overline{AF}}{\sin 41°40'} = \dfrac{7.3}{\sin 64°10'} \Rightarrow \overline{AF} = \dfrac{7.3 \sin 41°40'}{\sin 64°10'} \approx 5.39$ mi.

**4** Given the three sides $a$, $b$, and $c$ (SSS), use *the law of cosines* to find *any angle*.

For example, to find $\alpha$, use $a^2 = b^2 + c^2 - 2bc \cos\alpha$.

**5** Third side $= \sqrt{300^2 + 250^2 - 2(300)(250) \cos 75°} \approx 337$ feet.

**6** The largest angle $\alpha$ between the sides is the angle opposite the longest side (80 ft).

$80^2 = 70^2 + 60^2 - 2(70)(60) \cos\alpha \Rightarrow \alpha = \cos^{-1}\left(\dfrac{70^2 + 60^2 - 80^2}{2(70)(60)}\right) = \cos^{-1}(0.25) \approx 75.5°$.

**7** $s = \frac{1}{2}(a + b + c) = \frac{1}{2}(26.0 + 30.0 + 40.0) = 48$. $\mathcal{A} = \sqrt{s(s-a)(s-b)(s-c)} = \sqrt{(48)(22)(18)(8)} \approx 390$ ft$^2$.

**8** $2\mathbf{a} - 3\mathbf{b} = 2\langle 3, -2 \rangle - 3\langle 4, 1 \rangle = \langle 6, -4 \rangle - \langle 12, 3 \rangle = \langle -6, -7 \rangle$,

so $\| 2\mathbf{a} - 3\mathbf{b} \| = \| \langle -6, -7 \rangle \| = \sqrt{(-6)^2 + (-7)^2} = \sqrt{36 + 49} = \sqrt{85}$.

**9** The resultant force is found by completing the parallelogram and then applying the law of cosines.

$\|\mathbf{r}\| = \sqrt{10.2^2 + 15.7^2 - 2(10.2)(15.7) \cos(180° - 33°)}$
$= \sqrt{350.53 - 320.28 \cos 147°} \approx 24.9$, or 25 lb.

**10** The unit vector $\dfrac{\mathbf{a}}{\|\mathbf{a}\|}$ has the same direction as $\mathbf{a}$. The vector $-7\left(\dfrac{\mathbf{a}}{\|\mathbf{a}\|}\right)$ will have a magnitude of 7 and the opposite direction of $\mathbf{a}$. $\mathbf{a} = -3\mathbf{i} + 8\mathbf{j} \;\Rightarrow\; \|\mathbf{a}\| = \sqrt{9+64} = \sqrt{73}$.

$$\text{Thus, } -7\left(\frac{\mathbf{a}}{\|\mathbf{a}\|}\right) = -7\left(-\frac{3}{\sqrt{73}}\mathbf{i} + \frac{8}{\sqrt{73}}\mathbf{j}\right) = \frac{21}{\sqrt{73}}\mathbf{i} - \frac{56}{\sqrt{73}}\mathbf{j}.$$

**11** For wind: $\mathbf{w} = \langle 30\cos 90°, 30\sin 90°\rangle = \langle 0, 30\rangle$. Measuring from the positive $x$-axis, the angle for the plane is $180° + 25° = 205°$. $\mathbf{r} = \langle 450\cos 205°, 450\sin 205°\rangle \approx \langle -407.84, -190.18\rangle$, where $\mathbf{r}$ is the desired resultant of $\mathbf{p} + \mathbf{w}$. Since $\mathbf{r} = \mathbf{p} + \mathbf{w}$, $\mathbf{p} = \mathbf{r} - \mathbf{w} \approx \langle -407.84, -220.18\rangle$. $\|\mathbf{p}\| \approx 463.48$, or 463 mi/hr.

$\tan\theta \approx \dfrac{-220.18}{-407.84}$ and $\theta$ is in QIII $\;\Rightarrow\;$ $\theta \approx 208°$ from the positive $x$-axis, or 242° using the directional form.

**12** $\cos\theta = \dfrac{\mathbf{a}\cdot\mathbf{b}}{\|\mathbf{a}\|\,\|\mathbf{b}\|} \;\Rightarrow\; \theta = \cos^{-1}\left(\dfrac{(5\mathbf{i}-3\mathbf{j})\cdot(4\mathbf{i}+2\mathbf{j})}{\|5\mathbf{i}-3\mathbf{j}\|\,\|4\mathbf{i}+2\mathbf{j}\|}\right) = \cos^{-1}\left(\dfrac{20-6}{\sqrt{25+9}\,\sqrt{16+4}}\right) \approx 57.53°$

**13** We need to have the dot product of the two vectors equal 0.

$$(4m\mathbf{i}+\mathbf{j})\cdot(9m\mathbf{i}-25\mathbf{j}) = 0 \;\Rightarrow\; 36m^2 - 25 = 0 \;\Rightarrow\; m^2 = \tfrac{25}{36} \;\Rightarrow\; m = \pm\tfrac{5}{6}$$

**14** $(3\mathbf{a}-\mathbf{b})\cdot(2\mathbf{c}) = (3\langle 6,-5\rangle - \langle 7,1\rangle)\cdot(2\langle -2,4\rangle)$
$= (\langle 18,-15\rangle - \langle 7,1\rangle)\cdot\langle -4,8\rangle = \langle 11,-16\rangle\cdot\langle -4,8\rangle = -44-128 = -172$

**15** $\text{comp}_{\mathbf{a}}\,\mathbf{b} = \dfrac{\mathbf{b}\cdot\mathbf{a}}{\|\mathbf{a}\|} = \dfrac{\langle -4,5\rangle\cdot\langle -8,3\rangle}{\|\langle -8,3\rangle\|} = \dfrac{47}{\sqrt{73}} \approx 5.5$

**16** Using the horizontal and vertical components of a vector from Section 7.3,

we have the *force vector* as $\langle 20\cos(25°+27°), 20\sin 52°\rangle$.

The *distance (direction vector)* can be described by the vector $\langle 200\cos 25°, 200\sin 25°\rangle$.

The *work* done is $\langle 20\cos 52°, 20\sin 52°\rangle \cdot \langle 200\cos 25°, 200\sin 25°\rangle \approx 3564$ ft-lb.

**17** $(2-3i)^2 = 4 - 12i + 9i^2 = -5 - 12i$,

$$\text{so } |(2-3i)^2| = |-5-12i| = \sqrt{(-5)^2 + (-12)^2} = \sqrt{25+144} = \sqrt{169} = 13.$$

**18** $z = -3+2i \;\Rightarrow\; r = \sqrt{(-3)^2 + 2^2} = \sqrt{13}$. $\tan\theta = \dfrac{2}{-3}$ and $\theta$ in QII $\;\Rightarrow\;$ $\theta = \tan^{-1}\left(-\tfrac{2}{3}\right) + \pi$.

We must add $\pi$ to $\tan^{-1}\left(-\tfrac{1}{3}\right)$ because $-\tfrac{\pi}{2} < \tan^{-1}\left(-\tfrac{1}{3}\right) < 0$ and we want $\theta$ to be in the interval $\left(\tfrac{\pi}{2}, \pi\right)$.

$$z = \sqrt{13}\operatorname{cis}\left[\tan^{-1}\left(-\tfrac{2}{3}\right) + \pi\right].$$

**19** $\sqrt{106}\operatorname{cis}\left(\tan^{-1}\tfrac{2}{7}\right) = \sqrt{106}\left[\cos\left(\tan^{-1}\tfrac{2}{7}\right) + i\sin\left(\tan^{-1}\tfrac{2}{7}\right)\right] = \sqrt{106}\left(\dfrac{7}{\sqrt{53}} + \dfrac{2}{\sqrt{53}}i\right) = 7\sqrt{2} + 2\sqrt{2}i$

**20** $z_1 = -4 - 4\sqrt{3}i = 8\operatorname{cis}\tfrac{4\pi}{3}$ and $z_2 = 7i = 7\operatorname{cis}\tfrac{\pi}{2}$.   $z_1 z_2 = 8\cdot 7\operatorname{cis}\left(\tfrac{4\pi}{3} + \tfrac{\pi}{2}\right) = 56\operatorname{cis}\tfrac{11\pi}{6} = 28\sqrt{3} - 28i$.

$$\frac{z_1}{z_2} = \frac{8}{7}\operatorname{cis}\left(\frac{4\pi}{3} - \frac{\pi}{2}\right) = \frac{8}{7}\operatorname{cis}\frac{5\pi}{6} = -\frac{4}{7}\sqrt{3} + \frac{4}{7}i.$$

**21** $\left(-\tfrac{1}{2} - \tfrac{\sqrt{3}}{2}i\right)^{32} = (1\operatorname{cis}\tfrac{4\pi}{3})^{32} = 1^{32}\operatorname{cis}\tfrac{128\pi}{3} = \operatorname{cis}\tfrac{2\pi}{3} = -\tfrac{1}{2} + \tfrac{\sqrt{3}}{2}i$

**22** $-64i = 64 \operatorname{cis} 270°$. $w_k = \sqrt[3]{64} \operatorname{cis}\left(\dfrac{270° + 360° \, k}{3}\right)$ for $k = 0, 1, 2$.

$$w_0 = 4 \operatorname{cis} 90° = 4(0 + i) = 4i.$$

$$w_1 = 4 \operatorname{cis} 210° = 4\left(-\frac{\sqrt{3}}{2} - \frac{1}{2}i\right) = -2\sqrt{3} - 2i.$$

$$w_2 = 4 \operatorname{cis} 330° = 4\left(\frac{\sqrt{3}}{2} - \frac{1}{2}i\right) = 2\sqrt{3} - 2i.$$

**23** $x^5 - 7i = 0 \;\Rightarrow\; x^5 = 7i$. The problem is now to find the 5 fifth roots of $7i$.

$7i = 0 + 7i = 7 \operatorname{cis} 90°$. $w_k = \sqrt[5]{7} \operatorname{cis}\left(\dfrac{90° + 360° \, k}{5}\right)$ for $k = 0, 1, 2, 3, 4$.

$$w_k = \sqrt[5]{7} \operatorname{cis} \theta \text{ with } \theta = 18°, 90°, 162°, 234°, 306°.$$

# Chapter 8: Systems of Equations and Inequalities

## 8.1 Exercises

*Note:* The expressions $E_1$ and $E_2$ refer to the first and second equation, respectively.

$\boxed{1}$ Substituting $y$ in $E_2$ into $E_1$ yields $2x - 1 = x^2 - 4$ $\Rightarrow$ $x^2 - 2x - 3 = 0$ $\Rightarrow$ $(x - 3)(x + 1) = 0$ $\Rightarrow$ $x = 3, -1$. Substituting $x = 3$ into $E_2$ gives us $y = 5$, so $(3, 5)$ is a solution of the system.

Similarly, $(-1, -3)$ is a solution.

$\boxed{2}$ Substituting $y$ in $E_1$ into $E_2$ yields $x + x^2 + 1 = 3$ $\Rightarrow$ $x^2 + x - 2 = 0$ $\Rightarrow$ $(x + 2)(x - 1) = 0$ $\Rightarrow$ $x = -2, 1; y = 5, 2$. $\qquad \bigstar \ (-2, 5), (1, 2)$

$\boxed{3}$ Solving $E_2$ for $x$, $x = 1 - 2y$, and substituting into $E_1$ yields $y^2 = 1 - (1 - 2y)$ $\Rightarrow$ $y^2 - 2y = 0$ $\Rightarrow$ $y(y - 2) = 0$ $\Rightarrow$ $y = 0, 2; x = 1, -3$. $\qquad \bigstar \ (1, 0), (-3, 2)$

$\boxed{4}$ Solving $E_2$ for $x$, $x = -2y - 3$, and substituting into $E_1$ yields $y^2 = -2y - 3$ $\Rightarrow$ $y^2 + 2y + 3 = 0$ $\Rightarrow$ $y = -1 \pm \sqrt{2}\, i$. There are **no real solutions**.

$\boxed{5}$ Substituting $y$ in $E_2$ into $E_1$ yields $2(4x^3) = x^2$ $\Rightarrow$ $8x^3 = x^2$ $\Rightarrow$ $8x^3 - x^2 = 0$ $\Rightarrow$ $x^2(8x - 1) = 0$ $\Rightarrow$ $x = 0, \frac{1}{8}; y = 0, \frac{1}{128}$. $\qquad \bigstar \ (0, 0), \left(\frac{1}{8}, \frac{1}{128}\right)$

$\boxed{6}$ Solving $E_1$ for $x$ and substituting into $E_2$ yields $2(y^3 + 1) = 9y^2 + 2$ $\Rightarrow$ $2y^3 - 9y^2 = 0$ $\Rightarrow$ $y^2(2y - 9) = 0$ $\Rightarrow$ $y = 0, \frac{9}{2}; x = 1, \frac{737}{8}$. $\qquad \bigstar \ (1, 0), \left(\frac{737}{8}, \frac{9}{2}\right)$

$\boxed{7}$ Solving $E_1$ for $x$, $x = -2y - 1$, and substituting into $E_2$ yields $2(-2y - 1) - 3y = 12$ $\Rightarrow$ $-7y = 14$ $\Rightarrow$ $y = -2; x = 3$. $\qquad \bigstar \ (3, -2)$

$\boxed{8}$ Solving $E_2$ for $y$ and substituting into $E_1$ yields $3x - 4\left(-4 - \frac{3}{2}x\right) + 20 = 0$ $\Rightarrow$ $9x = -36$ $\Rightarrow$ $x = -4; y = 2$. $\qquad \bigstar \ (-4, 2)$

$\boxed{9}$ Solving $E_1$ for $x$, $2x = 3y + 1$ $\Rightarrow$ $x = \frac{3}{2}y + \frac{1}{2}$, and substituting into $E_2$ yields $-6\left(\frac{3}{2}y + \frac{1}{2}\right) + 9y = 4$ $\Rightarrow$ $-9y - 3 + 9y = 4$ $\Rightarrow$ $-3 = 4$, a contradiction. There are **no solutions**.

$\boxed{10}$ Solving $E_1$ for $x$ and substituting into $E_2$ yields $8\left(\frac{1}{2} + \frac{5}{4}y\right) - 10y = -5$ $\Rightarrow$ $4 = -5$. There are **no solutions**.

$\boxed{11}$ Solving $E_1$ for $y$, $y = x + 2$, and substituting into $E_2$ yields $x^2 + (x + 2)^2 = 20$ $\Rightarrow$ $x^2 + x^2 + 4x + 4 = 20$ $\Rightarrow$ $2x^2 + 4x - 16 = 0$ $\Rightarrow$ $x^2 + 2x - 8 = 0$ $\Rightarrow$ $(x + 4)(x - 2) = 0$ $\Rightarrow$ $x = -4, 2; y = -2, 4$. $\qquad \bigstar \ (-4, -2), (2, 4)$

$\boxed{12}$ Solving $E_1$ for $y$, $y = 1 - x$, and substituting into $E_2$ yields $x^2 + (1 - x)^2 = 85$ $\Rightarrow$ $x^2 + 1 - 2x + x^2 = 85$ $\Rightarrow$ $2x^2 - 2x - 84 = 0$ $\Rightarrow$ $x^2 - x - 42 = 0$ $\Rightarrow$ $(x + 6)(x - 7) = 0$ $\Rightarrow$ $x = -6, 7; y = 7, -6$. $\qquad \bigstar \ (-6, 7), (7, -6)$

$\boxed{13}$ Solving $E_1$ for $x$, $x = 5 - 3y$, and substituting into $E_2$ yields $(5 - 3y)^2 + y^2 = 25$ $\Rightarrow$ $25 - 30y + 9y^2 + y^2 = 25$ $\Rightarrow$ $10y^2 - 30y = 0$ $\Rightarrow$ $10y(y - 3) = 0$ $\Rightarrow$ $y = 0, 3; x = 5, -4$. $\qquad \bigstar \ (-4, 3), (5, 0)$

**14** Solving $E_2$ for $x$, $x = 2y - 4$, and substituting into $E_1$ yields $(2y - 4)^2 + y^2 = 16$ $\Rightarrow$

$4y^2 - 16y + 16 + y^2 = 16$ $\Rightarrow$ $5y^2 - 16y = 0$ $\Rightarrow$ $y(5y - 16) = 0$ $\Rightarrow$

$y = 0, \frac{16}{5}$; $x = -4, \frac{12}{5}$. $\qquad\qquad\qquad\qquad\qquad\qquad$ $\bigstar\ (-4, 0), \left(\frac{12}{5}, \frac{16}{5}\right)$

**15** Solving $E_2$ for $y$, $y = x + 4$, and substituting into $E_1$ yields $x^2 + (x + 4)^2 = 8$ $\Rightarrow$ $x^2 + x^2 + 8x + 16 = 8$ $\Rightarrow$

$2x^2 + 8x + 8 = 0$ $\Rightarrow$ $x^2 + 4x + 4 = 0$ $\Rightarrow$ $(x + 2)^2 = 0$ $\Rightarrow$ $x = -2$; $y = 2$. $\qquad\qquad$ $\bigstar\ (-2, 2)$

**16** Solving $E_2$ for $x$ and substituting into $E_1$ yields $\left(-\frac{4}{3}y - \frac{25}{3}\right)^2 + y^2 = 25$ $\Rightarrow$ $\frac{25}{9}y^2 + \frac{200}{9}y + \frac{400}{9} = 0$ $\Rightarrow$

$y^2 + 8y + 16 = 0$ $\Rightarrow$ $(y + 4)^2 = 0$ $\Rightarrow$ $y = -4$; $x = -3$. $\qquad\qquad\qquad$ $\bigstar\ (-3, -4)$

**17** Solving $E_2$ for $y$, $y = 3x + 2$, and substituting into $E_1$ yields $x^2 + (3x + 2)^2 = 9$ $\Rightarrow$

$x^2 + 9x^2 + 12x + 4 = 9$ $\Rightarrow$ $10x^2 + 12x - 5 = 0$ $\Rightarrow$

$$x = \frac{-12 \pm \sqrt{344}}{20} = \frac{-12 \pm \sqrt{4 \cdot 86}}{20} = \frac{-12 \pm 2\sqrt{86}}{20} = \frac{-6 \pm \sqrt{86}}{10} = -\frac{3}{5} \pm \frac{1}{10}\sqrt{86}.$$

Now we'll substitute the values of $x$ into $y = 3x + 2$ to get the corresponding values of $y$.

$$y = 3\left(\frac{-6 \pm \sqrt{86}}{10}\right) + 2 = \frac{-18 \pm 3\sqrt{86}}{10} + \frac{20}{10} = \frac{2 \pm 3\sqrt{86}}{10} = \frac{1}{5} \pm \frac{3}{10}\sqrt{86}.$$

$\bigstar\ \left(-\frac{3}{5} + \frac{1}{10}\sqrt{86}, \frac{1}{5} + \frac{3}{10}\sqrt{86}\right), \left(-\frac{3}{5} - \frac{1}{10}\sqrt{86}, \frac{1}{5} - \frac{3}{10}\sqrt{86}\right)$

**18** Solving $E_2$ for $y$, $y = -2x - 1$, and substituting into $E_1$ yields $x^2 + (-2x - 1)^2 = 16$ $\Rightarrow$

$5x^2 + 4x - 15 = 0$ $\Rightarrow$ $x = -\frac{2}{5} \pm \frac{1}{5}\sqrt{79}$; $y = -2\left(-\frac{2}{5} \pm \frac{1}{5}\sqrt{79}\right) - 1 = \frac{4}{5} \mp \frac{2}{5}\sqrt{79} - \frac{5}{5} = -\frac{1}{5} \mp \frac{2}{5}\sqrt{79}$.

$\bigstar\ \left(-\frac{2}{5} \pm \frac{1}{5}\sqrt{79}, -\frac{1}{5} \mp \frac{2}{5}\sqrt{79}\right)$

**19** Solving $E_2$ for $y$, $y = -x + 9$, and substituting into $E_1$ yields $x^2 + (-x + 9)^2 = 36$ $\Rightarrow$

$x^2 + x^2 - 18x + 81 = 36$ $\Rightarrow$ $2x^2 - 18x - 45 = 0$ $\Rightarrow$

$$x = \frac{18 \pm \sqrt{684}}{4} = \frac{18 \pm \sqrt{36 \cdot 19}}{4} = \frac{18 \pm 6\sqrt{19}}{4} = \frac{9 \pm 3\sqrt{19}}{2} = \frac{9}{2} \pm \frac{3}{2}\sqrt{19} \approx 11.04, -2.04.$$

Substituting those values into $E_2$ gives us $y \approx -2.04, 11.04$.

Neither ordered pair checks in $E_2$, so there are **no real solutions**.

**20** Solving $E_2$ for $y$, $y = -2x - 3$, and substituting into $E_1$ yields $x^2 + (-2x - 3)^2 = 1$ $\Rightarrow$

$5x^2 + 12x + 8 = 0$ $\Rightarrow$ $x = -\frac{6}{5} \pm \frac{2}{5}i$. There are **no real solutions**.

**21** Solving $E_2$ for $x$, $x = 1 - y$, and substituting into $E_1$ yields $(1 - y - 1)^2 + (y + 2)^2 = 10$ $\Rightarrow$

$y^2 + (y^2 + 4y + 4) = 10$ $\Rightarrow$ $2y^2 + 4y - 6 = 0$ $\Rightarrow$ $2(y^2 + 2y - 3) = 0$ $\Rightarrow$

$2(y + 3)(y - 1) = 0$ $\Rightarrow$ $y = -3, 1$; $x = 4, 0$. $\qquad\qquad\qquad\qquad$ $\bigstar\ (0, 1), (4, -3)$

**22** Solving $E_1$ for $y$ and substituting into $E_2$ yields $3x - \frac{2}{x} + 5 = 0$ $\Rightarrow$ $3x^2 + 5x - 2 = 0$ $\Rightarrow$

$(3x - 1)(x + 2) = 0$ $\Rightarrow$ $x = \frac{1}{3}, -2$; $y = 6, -1$. $\qquad\qquad\qquad$ $\bigstar\ \left(\frac{1}{3}, 6\right), (-2, -1)$

**23** Substituting $y$ in $E_1$ into $E_2$ yields $\frac{4}{x + 2} = x + 5$ $\Rightarrow$ $4 = (x + 2)(x + 5)$ $\Rightarrow$ $4 = x^2 + 7x + 10$ $\Rightarrow$

$0 = x^2 + 7x + 6$ $\Rightarrow$ $0 = (x + 6)(x + 1)$ $\Rightarrow$ $x = -6, -1$; $y = -1, 4$. $\qquad\qquad$ $\bigstar\ (-6, -1), (-1, 4)$

**24** Substituting $y$ in $E_1$ into $E_2$ yields $\dfrac{10}{x+3} = -x + 8 \Rightarrow 10 = (x+3)(-x+8) \Rightarrow$

$10 = -x^2 + 5x + 24 \Rightarrow x^2 - 5x - 14 = 0 \Rightarrow (x-7)(x+2) = 0 \Rightarrow$

$x = 7, -2; y = 1, 10.$ ★ $(7, 1), (-2, 10)$

**25** Substituting $y$ in $E_1$ into $E_2$ yields $20/x^2 = 9 - x^2$ {multiply by $x^2$} $\Rightarrow 20 = 9x^2 - x^4 \Rightarrow$

$x^4 - 9x^2 + 20 = 0 \Rightarrow (x^2 - 4)(x^2 - 5) = 0 \Rightarrow x^2 = 4, 5 \Rightarrow x = \pm 2, \pm\sqrt{5}.$

If $x^2 = 4$, then $y = \frac{20}{4} = 5$. If $x^2 = 5$, then $y = \frac{20}{5} = 4$. Thus, we get the *four* solutions $(\pm 2, 5)$ and $\left(\pm\sqrt{5}, 4\right)$.

**26** Solving $E_2$ for $x$ and substituting into $E_1$ yields $y + 1 = y^2 - 4y + 5 \Rightarrow y^2 - 5y + 4 = 0 \Rightarrow$

$(y-1)(y-4) = 0 \Rightarrow y = 1, 4; x = 2, 5.$ ★ $(2, 1), (5, 4)$

**27** Solving $E_1$ for $y^2$, $y^2 = 4x^2 + 4$, and substituting into $E_2$ yields $9(4x^2 + 4) + 16x^2 = 140 \Rightarrow 52x^2 = 104 \Rightarrow$

$x^2 = 2 \Rightarrow x = \pm\sqrt{2}; y = \pm 2\sqrt{3}.$ There are *four* solutions. ★ $\left(\sqrt{2}, \pm 2\sqrt{3}\right), \left(-\sqrt{2}, \pm 2\sqrt{3}\right)$

**28** Solving $E_1$ for $y^2$, $y^2 = 4 - x^2$, and substituting into $E_2$ yields $6x^2 + 7(4 - x^2) = 28 \Rightarrow$

$-x^2 = 0 \Rightarrow x = 0$, so $y^2 = 4 \Rightarrow y = \pm 2.$ ★ $(0, \pm 2)$

**29** Solving $E_1$ for $x^2$, $\dfrac{36 - 9y^2}{4}$, and substituting into $E_2$ yields $8\left(\dfrac{36 - 9y^2}{4}\right) + 16y^2 = 128 \Rightarrow$

$72 - 18y^2 + 16y^2 = 128 \Rightarrow -2y^2 = 56 \Rightarrow y^2 = -28.$ There are **no real solutions**.

**30** Solving $E_2$ for $x^2$ and substituting into $E_1$ yields $25y^2 - 16\left(\frac{9}{4}y^2 - 9\right) = 400 \Rightarrow$

$25y^2 - 36y^2 + 144 = 400 \Rightarrow -11y^2 = 256 \Rightarrow y^2 = -\frac{256}{11}.$ There are **no real solutions**.

**31** Solving $E_1$ for $x^2$ and substituting into $E_2$ yields $(y^2 + 4) + y^2 = 12 \Rightarrow 2y^2 = 8 \Rightarrow y^2 = 4 \Rightarrow$

$y = \pm 2; x = \pm\sqrt{8} = \pm 2\sqrt{2}.$ There are *four* solutions. ★ $\left(2\sqrt{2}, \pm 2\right), \left(-2\sqrt{2}, \pm 2\right)$

**32** Solving $E_1$ for $y^3$ and substituting into $E_2$ yields $3x^3 + 4(6x^3 - 1) = 5 \Rightarrow 27x^3 = 9 \Rightarrow x^3 = \frac{1}{3} \Rightarrow$

$x = \sqrt[3]{\frac{1}{3}}$ or $\frac{1}{3}\sqrt[3]{9}; y = 1.$ ★ $\left(\frac{1}{3}\sqrt[3]{9}, 1\right)$

**33** Solving $E_2$ for $y$, $y = 2x + z - 9$, and substituting into $E_1$ and $E_3$ yields

$$\begin{cases} x + 2(2x + z - 9) - z = -1 \\ x + 3(2x + z - 9) + 3z = 6 \end{cases} \Rightarrow \begin{cases} 5x + z = 17 \quad (E_4) \\ 7x + 6z = 33 \quad (E_5) \end{cases}$$

Solving $E_4$ for $z$, $z = 17 - 5x$, and substituting into $E_5$ yields $7x + 6(17 - 5x) = 33 \Rightarrow$

$7x + 102 - 30x = 33 \Rightarrow -23x = -69 \Rightarrow x = 3$. Now $z = 17 - 5x = 17 - 5(3) = 2$ and

$y = 2x + z - 9 = 2(3) + 2 - 9 = -1.$ ★ $(3, -1, 2)$

**34** Solving $E_2$ for $z^2$ and substituting into $E_1$ yields $\begin{cases} x - 2y = 1 \quad (E_4) \\ x^2 - xy = 0 \quad (E_3) \end{cases}$

Now solve $E_4$ for $x$ and substitute into $E_3$ yielding $(2y + 1)^2 - (2y + 1)y = 0 \Rightarrow$

$2y^2 + 3y + 1 = 0 \Rightarrow (2y + 1)(y + 1) = 0 \Rightarrow y = -\frac{1}{2}, -1.$

$x = 2y + 1 = 0, -1; z^2 = x - y + 1 = \frac{3}{2}, 1 \Rightarrow z = \pm\sqrt{\frac{3}{2}}, \pm 1.$ ★ $\left(0, -\frac{1}{2}, \pm\sqrt{\frac{3}{2}}\right), (-1, -1, \pm 1)$

**35** Solving $E_3$ for $y$, $y = 1 - z$, and substituting into $E_2$ yields $\begin{cases} x^2 + z^2 = 5 \quad (E_1) \\ 2x - z = 0 \quad (E_4) \end{cases}$

Now solve $E_4$ for $z$, $z = 2x$, and substitute into $E_1$ yielding $x^2 + (2x)^2 = 5 \Rightarrow x^2 + 4x^2 = 5 \Rightarrow$

$5x^2 = 5 \Rightarrow x^2 = 1 \Rightarrow x = \pm 1; z = 2x = \pm 2; y = 1 - z = -1, 3.$ ★ $(1, -1, 2), (-1, 3, -2)$

**36** From $E_3$, $xyz = 0$, we see that $x = 0$, $y = 0$, or $z = 0$. Substituting 0 for $x$ in $E_1$ gives us $2z = 1$ $\Rightarrow$ $z = \frac{1}{2}$;

substituting $\frac{1}{2}$ for $z$ in $E_2$ gives us $2y = \frac{9}{2}$ $\Rightarrow$ $y = \frac{9}{4}$. $\quad\quad\quad\quad\quad$ ★ $(0, \frac{9}{4}, \frac{1}{2})$

Substituting 0 for $y$ in $E_2$ gives us $-z = 4$ $\Rightarrow$ $z = -4$;

substituting $-4$ for $z$ in $E_1$ gives us $x - 8 = 1$ $\Rightarrow$ $x = 9$. $\quad\quad\quad\quad\quad$ ★ $(9, 0, -4)$

Substituting 0 for $z$ in $E_1$ gives us $x = 1$; substituting 0 for $z$ in $E_2$ gives us $2y = 4$ $\Rightarrow$ $y = 2$. $\quad\quad$ ★ $(1, 2, 0)$

**37** Substituting $y = 4x - b$ into $y = x^2$ yields $4x - b = x^2$ $\Rightarrow$ $x^2 - 4x + b = 0$ $\Rightarrow$

$x = \dfrac{4 \pm \sqrt{16 - 4b}}{2} = 2 \pm \sqrt{4 - b}$. For $x$ to have 1, 2, or no values, the discriminant $4 - b$ must be equal to zero,

greater than zero, or less than zero, respectively. Graphically, the line would be tangent to the parabola, intersect

the parabola in two points, and not intersect the parabola, respectively.

(a) $4 - b = 0$ $\Rightarrow$ $b = 4$. $\quad\quad\quad\quad\quad$ (b) $4 - b > 0$ $\Rightarrow$ $4 > b$ $\Rightarrow$ $b < 4$.

(c) $4 - b < 0$ $\Rightarrow$ $4 < b$ $\Rightarrow$ $b > 4$.

**38** Substituting $y = x + b$ into $x^2 + y^2 = 4$ yields $x^2 + (x + b)^2 = 4$ $\Rightarrow$ $2x^2 + 2bx + (b^2 - 4) = 0$ $\Rightarrow$

$x = \dfrac{-2b \pm \sqrt{4b^2 - 8(b^2 - 4)}}{4} = \dfrac{-b \pm \sqrt{8 - b^2}}{2}$. For $x$ to have 1, 2, or no values, the discriminant $8 - b^2$ must be

equal to zero, greater than zero, or less than zero, respectively. Graphically, the line would be tangent to the circle,

intersect the circle in two points, and not intersect the circle, respectively.

(a) $8 - b^2 = 0$ $\Rightarrow$ $b = \pm\sqrt{8} = \pm 2\sqrt{2}$.

(b) $8 - b^2 > 0$ $\Rightarrow$ $b^2 < 8$ $\Rightarrow$ $|b| < 2\sqrt{2}$ $\Rightarrow$ $-2\sqrt{2} < b < 2\sqrt{2}$.

(c) $8 - b^2 < 0$ $\Rightarrow$ $b > 2\sqrt{2}$ or $b < -2\sqrt{2}$ from parts (a) and (b).

**39** From the graph of $y = x$ and $y = 2^{-x}$, it is clear that there is a point of intersection and therefore a single solution

between 0 and 1.

*Figure 39*

*Figure 40*

**40** From the graph, it is clear that there are no intersection points of the two graphs, and therefore there are no

solutions.

**41** The equation of the line is $y - 2 = m(x - 4)$. Substituting $y^2$ for $x$ gives us $y - 2 = m(y^2 - 4)$ $\Rightarrow$

$0 = my^2 - y + (2 - 4m)$ $\Rightarrow$ $y = \dfrac{1 \pm \sqrt{1 - 4m(2 - 4m)}}{2m}$. For there to be only one value of $y$, the

discriminant $1 - 4m(2 - 4m)$ must be equal to zero, i.e., $1 - 4m(2 - 4m) = 0$ $\Rightarrow$ $1 - 8m + 16m^2 = 0$ $\Rightarrow$

$(4m - 1)^2 = 0$ $\Rightarrow$ $m = \frac{1}{4}$. This line, $y - 2 = \frac{1}{4}(x - 4)$, or $y = \frac{1}{4}x + 1$, is tangent to the parabola.

[42] The equation of the line is $y - 1 = m(x - 1)$, or $y = mx + (1 - m)$. Setting this expression equal to $x^2$ yields $x^2 - mx + m - 1 = 0 \Rightarrow x = \dfrac{m \pm \sqrt{m^2 - 4m + 4}}{2}$. For there to be only one value of $x$, the discriminant $m^2 - 4m + 4 = (m - 2)^2$ must be zero, i.e., $m = 2$. This line, $y = 2x - 1$, is tangent to the parabola.

[43] Use the fact that $(0, 3)$, $\left(-1, \frac{5}{3}\right)$, and $(1, 7)$ are on the graph of $f(x) = ba^x + c$.
$$\begin{cases} f(0) = 3 \\ f(-1) = \frac{5}{3} \\ f(1) = 7 \end{cases} \Rightarrow \begin{cases} 3 = ba^0 + c & (E_1) \\ \frac{5}{3} = ba^{-1} + c & (E_2) \\ 7 = ba^1 + c & (E_3) \end{cases}$$
From $E_1$, $3 = b + c \Rightarrow c = 3 - b$. Substitute $3 - b$ for $c$ in $E_2$ and $E_3$.

$E_2$: $\frac{5}{3} = ba^{-1} + 3 - b \Rightarrow b - ba^{-1} = \frac{4}{3} \Rightarrow b\left(1 - \frac{1}{a}\right) = \frac{4}{3} \Rightarrow b\left(\frac{a-1}{a}\right) = \frac{4}{3}$

$E_3$: $7 = ba^1 + 3 - b \Rightarrow b - ba = -4 \Rightarrow b(1 - a) = -4 \Rightarrow b(a - 1) = 4$

Solving both equations for $b$ and equating the expressions gives us $\dfrac{4a}{3(a-1)} = \dfrac{4}{a-1} \Rightarrow \dfrac{a}{3} = \dfrac{1}{1} \Rightarrow a = 3$.

Substituting 3 for $a$ in $b(a - 1) = 4$ gives us $2b = 4 \Rightarrow b = 2$.

Substituting 2 for $b$ in $c = 3 - b$ gives us $c = 1$, so the function is $f(x) = 2(3)^x + 1$.

[44] Use the fact that $(0, 3)$, $(-1, 9)$, and $\left(1, \frac{3}{2}\right)$ are on the graph of $f(x) = ba^x + c$.
$$\begin{cases} f(0) = 3 \\ f(-1) = 9 \\ f(1) = \frac{3}{2} \end{cases} \Rightarrow \begin{cases} 3 = ba^0 + c & (E_1) \\ 9 = ba^{-1} + c & (E_2) \\ \frac{3}{2} = ba^1 + c & (E_3) \end{cases}$$
From $E_1$, $3 = b + c \Rightarrow c = 3 - b$. Substitute $3 - b$ for $c$ in $E_2$ and $E_3$.

$E_2$: $9 = ba^{-1} + 3 - b \Rightarrow b - ba^{-1} = -6 \Rightarrow b\left(1 - \frac{1}{a}\right) = -6 \Rightarrow b\left(\frac{a-1}{a}\right) = -6$

$E_3$: $\frac{3}{2} = ba^1 + 3 - b \Rightarrow b - ba = \frac{3}{2} \Rightarrow b(1 - a) = \frac{3}{2} \Rightarrow b(1 - a) = \frac{3}{2}$

Solving both equations for $b$ and equating the expressions gives us

$\dfrac{-6a}{a-1} = \dfrac{3}{2(1-a)} \Rightarrow \dfrac{6a}{1-a} = \dfrac{3}{2(1-a)} \Rightarrow \dfrac{6a}{1} = \dfrac{3}{2} \Rightarrow 12a = 3 \Rightarrow a = \dfrac{1}{4}$.

Substituting $\frac{1}{4}$ for $a$ in $b(1 - a) = \frac{3}{2}$ gives us $\frac{3}{4}b = \frac{3}{2} \Rightarrow b = 2$.

Substituting 2 for $b$ in $c = 3 - b$ gives us $c = 1$, so the function is $f(x) = 2\left(\frac{1}{4}\right)^x + 1$.

[45] Let $x$ and $y$ denote two numbers whose difference is 8 and quotient is 3. A system is $\begin{cases} x - y = 8 & (E_1) \\ x/y = 3 & (E_2) \end{cases}$

Solving $E_1$ for $x$, $x = y + 8$, and substituting into $E_2$ yields $(y + 8)/y = 3 \Rightarrow$

$y + 8 = 3y \Rightarrow 8 = 2y \Rightarrow 4 = y$; $x = 12$. The numbers are 12 and 4.

[46] Let $x$ and $y$ denote two numbers whose sum is 10 and product is 22. A system is $\begin{cases} x + y = 10 & (E_1) \\ xy = 22 & (E_2) \end{cases}$

Solving $E_1$ for $x$, $x = 10 - y$, and substituting into $E_2$ yields $(10 - y)y = 22 \Rightarrow$

$10y - y^2 = 22 \Rightarrow y^2 - 10y + 22 = 0 \Rightarrow y = \dfrac{10 \pm \sqrt{12}}{2} = 5 \pm \sqrt{3}$. Substituting into $E_1$ gives us

$x = 10 - \left(5 \pm \sqrt{3}\right) = 5 \mp \sqrt{3}$. In either case, the numbers are $5 + \sqrt{3}$ and $5 - \sqrt{3}$.

[47] Using $P = 40 = 2l + 2w$ and $A = 96 = lw$, we have $\begin{cases} 2l + 2w = 40 & (E_1) \\ lw = 96 & (E_2) \end{cases}$

Solving $E_1$ for $l$, $l = 20 - w$, and substituting into $E_2$ yields $(20 - w)w = 96 \Rightarrow 20w - w^2 = 96 \Rightarrow$

$w^2 - 20w + 96 = 0 \Rightarrow (w - 8)(w - 12) = 0 \Rightarrow w = 8, 12$; $l = 12, 8$.

In either case, the rectangle is 12 inches $\times$ 8 inches.

**48** $A = 200 = (2\pi r)h \Rightarrow \pi rh = 100.$ $V = 200 = \pi r^2 h \Rightarrow h = 200/(\pi r^2)$.

Substituting $h$ into $\pi rh = 100$ yields $200/r = 100 \Rightarrow r = 2$ in.; $h = 50/\pi \approx 15.9$ in.

**49** (a) We have $R = aS/(S + b)$ and for 2009, let $S = 40{,}000$ and $R = 60{,}000$.

Then for 2010, let $S = 60{,}000$ and $R = 72{,}000$.

$$\begin{cases} 60{,}000 = (40{,}000a)/(40{,}000 + b) \\ 72{,}000 = (60{,}000a)/(60{,}000 + b) \end{cases} \Rightarrow \begin{cases} 120{,}000 + 3b = 2a & (E_1) \\ 360{,}000 + 6b = 5a & (E_2) \end{cases}$$

Solving $E_1$ for $a$ and substituting into $E_2$ yields

$$360{,}000 + 6b = 5\left(60{,}000 + \tfrac{3}{2}b\right) \Rightarrow 60{,}000 = \tfrac{3}{2}b \Rightarrow b = 40{,}000;\ a = 120{,}000.$$

(b) Now let $S = 72{,}000$ and thus $R = \dfrac{(120{,}000)(72{,}000)}{72{,}000 + 40{,}000} = \dfrac{540{,}000}{7} \approx 77{,}143$.

**50** Follow the outline of the solution in Exercise 49 with $R = aSe^{-bS}$.

(a) $\begin{cases} 60{,}000 = a(40{,}000)e^{(-b)(40{,}000)} \\ 72{,}000 = a(60{,}000)e^{(-b)(60{,}000)} \end{cases} \Rightarrow \begin{cases} 3 = 2ae^{-40{,}000b} \\ 6 = 5ae^{-60{,}000b} \end{cases} \Rightarrow 6 = 5\left(\dfrac{3}{2e^{-40{,}000b}}\right)e^{-60{,}000b} \Rightarrow$

$0.8 = e^{-20{,}000b} \Rightarrow -20{,}000b = \ln 0.8 \Rightarrow b = \dfrac{\ln 0.8}{-20{,}000} \approx 0.00001116$;

$$a = \frac{3}{2e^{-40{,}000\,[\ln 0.8/(-20{,}000)]}} = \frac{3}{2\left(e^{\ln 0.8}\right)^2} = \frac{75}{32}$$

(b) $R = \tfrac{75}{32}(72{,}000)e^{-[\ln 0.8/(-20{,}000)](72{,}000)} = 168{,}750\left(e^{\ln 0.8}\right)^{3.6} = 168{,}750(0.8)^{3.6} \approx 75{,}573$

**51** Let $R_1$ and $R_2$ equal 0. The system is then $\begin{cases} 0 = 0.01x(50 - x - y) \\ 0 = 0.02y(100 - y - 0.5x) \end{cases}$

The first equation is zero if $x = 0$ or if $50 - x - y = 0$. The second equation is zero if $y = 0$ or if $100 - y - 0.5x = 0$. Hence, there are 4 possible solutions.

(1) One solution is $x = 0$ and $y = 0$, or $(0, 0)$.

(2) A second solution is $x = 0$ and $100 - y - 0.5x = 0$ {$y = 100$}, or $(0, 100)$.

(3) A third solution is $y = 0$ and $50 - x - y = 0$ {$x = 50$}, or $(50, 0)$.

(4) A fourth solution occurs if $50 - x - y = 0$ and $100 - y - 0.5x = 0$.

Solve the first equation for $y$ {$y = 50 - x$} and substitute into the second equation:

$100 - (50 - x) - 0.5x = 0 \Rightarrow 50 = -\tfrac{1}{2}x \Rightarrow x = -100;\ y = 150$.

This solution is meaningless for this problem since $x$ and $y$ are nonnegative.

**52** Let $l$ be the length of the side opposite the river and $w$ the length of the other two sides. {10 acres $= 435{,}600$ ft$^2$}

$\begin{cases} l + 2w = 2420 & (E_1) \\ \quad lw = 435{,}600 & (E_2) \end{cases}$ Solve $E_1$ for $l$ and substitute into $E_2$. $(2420 - 2w)w = 435{,}600 \Rightarrow$

$2w^2 - 2420w + 435{,}600 = 0 \Rightarrow w^2 - 1210w + 217{,}800 = 0 \Rightarrow (w - 990)(w - 220) = 0 \Rightarrow$

$w = 990$ or $220$; $l = 2420 - 2w = 440$ or $1980$.

**53** Since we have an *open* top instead of a closed top, we use $3xy$ instead of $4xy$ {as in Example 5} for the surface area

formula. $\begin{cases} \quad x^2y = 2 & volume \\ 2x^2 + 3xy = 8 & surface\ area \end{cases}$ Solving $E_1$ for $y$ and substituting into $E_2$ yields

$2x^2 + 3x(2/x^2) = 8 \Rightarrow 2x^2 + (6/x) = 8$ {multiply by $x$} $\Rightarrow 2x^3 - 8x + 6 = 0 \Rightarrow$

$2(x^3 - 4x + 3) = 0$. We know that $x = 1$ is a solution of $x^3 - 4x + 3 = 0$ since the sum of the coefficients is

zero. Continuing, $2(x - 1)(x^2 + x - 3) = 0 \Rightarrow$ {$x > 0$} $x = 1, \dfrac{-1 + \sqrt{13}}{2}$. There are two solutions:

$$1\ \text{ft} \times 1\ \text{ft} \times 2\ \text{ft, or } \frac{\sqrt{13}-1}{2}\ \text{ft} \times \frac{\sqrt{13}-1}{2}\ \text{ft} \times \frac{8}{\left(\sqrt{13}-1\right)^2}\ \text{ft} \approx 1.30\ \text{ft} \times 1.30\ \text{ft} \times 1.18\ \text{ft}.$$

**54** Let $r$ denote the radius of a circle, and $l$ and $w$ the length and width of a rectangle.

If the rectangle and circle have equal perimeters and areas, then $\begin{cases} 2l + 2w = 2\pi r & perimeter \\ lw = \pi r^2 & area \end{cases}$

Solve $E_1$ for $l$ and substitute into $E_2$. $(\pi r - w)w = \pi r^2 \Rightarrow \pi r w - w^2 = \pi r^2 \Rightarrow w^2 - \pi r w + \pi r^2 = 0 \Rightarrow$

$w = \dfrac{\pi r \pm \sqrt{\pi^2 r^2 - 4\pi r^2}}{2} = \dfrac{\pi r \pm r\sqrt{\pi(\pi - 4)}}{2}$. Since the discriminant is negative, there are no real roots.

**55** We eliminate $n$ from the equations to determine all intersection points.

(a) $x^2 + y^2 = n^2$ and $y = n - 1$ {so $n = y + 1$} $\Rightarrow x^2 + y^2 = (y+1)^2 \Rightarrow x^2 + y^2 = y^2 + 2y + 1 \Rightarrow$

$x^2 = 2y + 1 \Rightarrow 2y = x^2 - 1 \Rightarrow y = \frac{1}{2}x^2 - \frac{1}{2}$. The points are on the parabola $y = \frac{1}{2}x^2 - \frac{1}{2}$.

(b) As in part (a), $x^2 + y^2 = (y + 2)^2 \Rightarrow x^2 = 4y + 4 \Rightarrow y = \frac{1}{4}x^2 - 1$.

**56** (a) $\begin{cases} \frac{4}{3}\pi\left(\frac{1}{2}\right)^3 = \pi r^2 h & volume \\ 2\left[4\pi\left(\frac{1}{2}\right)^2\right] = 2\pi rh + 2\pi r^2 & surface\ area \end{cases} \Rightarrow \begin{cases} 1 = 6r^2 h & (E_1) \\ 1 = r^2 + rh & (E_2) \end{cases}$

Solve $E_1$ for $h$, $h = \dfrac{1}{6r^2}$, and substitute into $E_2$. $r^2 + r\left(\dfrac{1}{6r^2}\right) = 1 \Rightarrow 6r^3 - 6r + 1 = 0$.

(b) $r = 0.172 \Rightarrow h \approx 5.63$ (unreasonable) and $r = 0.903 \Rightarrow h \approx 0.204$ (reasonable).

**57** (a) The slope of the line from $(-4, -3)$ to the origin is $\frac{3}{4}$ so the slope of the tangent line (which is perpendicular to the line to the origin) is $-\frac{4}{3}$. An equation of the line through $(-4, -3)$ with slope $-\frac{4}{3}$ is $y + 3 = -\frac{4}{3}(x + 4)$, or, equivalently, $4x + 3y = -25$. Letting $y = -50$, we find that $x = 31.25$.

(b) The slope of the line from an arbitrary point $(x, y)$ on the circle to the origin is $\dfrac{y}{x}$, so the slope of the tangent line is $-\dfrac{x}{y}$. The line through $(0, -50)$ is $y + 50 = \left(-\dfrac{x}{y}\right)(x - 0)$, or, equivalently, $y^2 + 50y = -x^2$.

The equation of the circle is $x^2 + y^2 = 25$. Substituting $x^2 = 25 - y^2$ into $y^2 + 50y = -x^2$ gives us $50y = -25$, or $y = -\frac{1}{2}$. Substituting $y = -\frac{1}{2}$ into $x^2 = 25 - y^2$ gives us $x^2 = \frac{99}{4}$ and hence $x = \pm\frac{3}{2}\sqrt{11}$. The positive solution corresponds to releasing the hammer from a clockwise spin, whereas the negative solution corresponds to releasing the hammer from a counterclockwise spin as depicted in the figures.

Hence, the hammer should be released at $\left(-\frac{3}{2}\sqrt{11}, -\frac{1}{2}\right) \approx (-4.975, -0.5)$.

**58** (a) Since $y = -\frac{3}{4}x$ is a line that describes the slope, and $x^2 + y^2 = 50^2$, the point where the ball hits the ground can be found by solving $(x)^2 + \left(-\frac{3}{4}x\right)^2 = 50^2$ for $x$. $x^2 + \frac{9}{16}x^2 = 2500 \Rightarrow \frac{25}{16}x^2 = 2500 \Rightarrow$

$x^2 = 1600 \Rightarrow x = 40 \ \{x > 0\}$ and $y = -\frac{3}{4}(40) = -30$, so the point is $(40, -30)$. $c$ is 0, so substitute $(40, -30)$ for $(x, y)$ in $y = ax^2 + x$ to get $-30 = 1600a + 40 \Rightarrow -70 = 1600a \Rightarrow a = -\frac{7}{160}$. Thus, the equation is $y = -\frac{7}{160}x^2 + x$.

(b) The maximum height off the ground is found when the difference $d$ between the parabola and the line is greatest. $d = \left(-\frac{7}{160}x^2 + x\right) - \left(-\frac{3}{4}x\right) = -\frac{7}{160}x^2 + \frac{7}{4}x$.

$d$ will be a maximum when $x = \dfrac{-b}{2a} = \dfrac{-7/4}{2(-7/160)} = 20$. $x = 20 \Rightarrow d = 17.5$ ft.

Note that the vertex of the parabola is $\left(\frac{80}{7}, \frac{40}{7}\right) \approx (11.4, 5.7)$.

**59** **Graphically:** $x^2 + y^2 = 4 \Rightarrow y = \pm\sqrt{4 - x^2}$ and $x + y = 1 \Rightarrow y = 1 - x$.

Graph $Y_1 = \sqrt{4 - x^2}$, $Y_2 = -Y_1$, and $Y_3 = 1 - x$.

There are two points of intersection at approximately $(-0.82, 1.82)$ and $(1.82, -0.82)$.

**Algebraically:** $y = 1 - x$ and $x^2 + y^2 = 4 \Rightarrow x^2 + (1 - x)^2 = 4 \Rightarrow x^2 + 1 - 2x + x^2 = 4 \Rightarrow$

$2x^2 - 2x - 3 = 0$. Using the quadratic formula, $x = \dfrac{2 \pm \sqrt{4 - 4(2)(-3)}}{4} = \dfrac{1 \pm \sqrt{7}}{2}$.

To find the value of $y$ we use $y = 1 - x \Rightarrow y = 1 - \dfrac{1 \pm \sqrt{7}}{2} = \dfrac{1 \mp \sqrt{7}}{2}$.

The points of intersection are $\left(\dfrac{1}{2} \pm \dfrac{\sqrt{7}}{2}, \dfrac{1}{2} \mp \dfrac{\sqrt{7}}{2}\right)$. The graphical solution approximates the algebraic solution.

$[-6, 6]$ by $[-4, 4]$

*Figure 59*

$[-9, 9]$ by $[-6, 6]$

*Figure 60*

**60** **Graphically:** $x^2 y^2 = 9 \Rightarrow y = \pm\dfrac{3}{x}$ and $2x + y = 0 \Rightarrow y = -2x$. Graph $Y_1 = \dfrac{3}{x}$, $Y_2 = -Y_1$, and

$Y_3 = -2x$. There are two points of intersection at approximately $(-1.22, 2.45)$ and $(1.22, -2.45)$.

**Algebraically:** $y = -2x$, $x^2 y^2 = 9 \Rightarrow x^2(-2x)^2 = 9 \Rightarrow 4x^4 = 9 \Rightarrow x = \pm\sqrt{\dfrac{3}{2}} = \pm\dfrac{1}{2}\sqrt{6}$.

$y = -2x = \mp\sqrt{6}$. The points of intersection are $\left(\pm\dfrac{1}{2}\sqrt{6}, \mp\sqrt{6}\right)$.

The graphical solution approximates the algebraic solution.

**61** After zooming in near the region of interest in the second quadrant, we see that the cubic intersects the circle twice.

Due to the symmetry, we know there are two more points of intersection in the fourth quadrant.

Thus, the six points of intersection are approximately $(\mp 0.56, \pm 1.92)$, $(\mp 0.63, \pm 1.90)$, and $(\pm 1.14, \pm 1.65)$.

$[-6, 6]$ by $[-4, 4]$

*Figure 61*

$[-4.5, 4.5]$ by $[-3, 3]$

*Figure 62*

**62** From the graphs of $Y_1 = \sqrt{9 - 9x^2}$, $Y_2 = -Y_1$, and $Y_3 = e^x$, there are two points of intersection for $Y_1$ and $Y_3$.

They are approximately $(-0.992, 0.371)$ and $(0.725, 2.065)$.

**63** $|x + \ln|x|| - y^2 = 0 \Rightarrow y^2 = |x + \ln|x|| \Rightarrow y = \pm\sqrt{|x + \ln|x||}$ and $\dfrac{x^2}{4} + \dfrac{y^2}{2.25} = 1 \Rightarrow$

$\dfrac{y^2}{2.25} = 1 - \dfrac{x^2}{4} \Rightarrow y^2 = 2.25\left(1 - x^2/4\right) \Rightarrow y = \pm 1.5\sqrt{1 - x^2/4}$.

The graph is symmetric with respect to $x$-axis. There are 8 points of intersection.

Their coordinates are approximately $(-1.44, \pm 1.04)$, $(-0.12, \pm 1.50)$, $(0.10, \pm 1.50)$, and $(1.22, \pm 1.19)$.

Figure 63  Figure 64

**64** $y^3 - e^{x/2} = x \Rightarrow y = (x + e^{x/2})^{1/3}$ and $y + 0.85x^2 = 2.1 \Rightarrow y = 2.1 - 0.85x^2$.

There are 2 points of intersection. Their coordinates are approximately $(-1.96, -1.17)$ and $(0.93, 1.36)$.

**65** If $f(x) = ae^{-bx}$ and $x = 1$, then $f(1) = ae^{-b} = 0.80487 \Rightarrow a = 0.80487e^b$.

When $x = 2$, $f(2) = ae^{-2b} = 0.53930 \Rightarrow a = 0.53930e^{2b}$. Let $a = y$ and $b = x$ and then graph

$Y_1 = 0.80487e^x$ and $Y_2 = 0.53930e^{2x}$. The graphs intersect at approximately $(0.4004, 1.2012) = (b, a)$.

Thus, $a \approx 1.2012$, $b \approx 0.4004$, and $f(x) = 1.2012e^{-0.4004x}$. The function $f$ is also accurate at $x = 3, 4$.

[0, 3] by [0, 2]

[1, 13] by [-7, 1]

Figure 65  Figure 66

**66** If $f(x) = a \ln bx$ and $x = 1$, then $f(1) = a \ln b = -8.208 \Rightarrow a = \dfrac{-8.208}{\ln b}$.

When $x = 2$, $f(2) = a \ln 2b = -11.74 \Rightarrow a = \dfrac{-11.74}{\ln 2b}$. Graph $Y_1 = \dfrac{-8.208}{\ln x}$ and $Y_2 = \dfrac{-11.74}{\ln 2x}$.

The graphs intersect at approximately $(5.0068, -5.0956)$.

Thus, $a \approx -5.0956$, $b \approx 5.0068$, and $f(x) = -5.0956 \ln(5.0068x)$. The function $f$ is also accurate at $x = 3, 4$.

**67** If $f(x) = ax^2 + e^{bx}$ and $x = 2$, then $f(2) = 4a + e^{2b} = 17.2597 \Rightarrow a = (17.2597 - e^{2b})/4$.

When $x = 3$, $f(3) = 9a + e^{3b} = 40.1058 \Rightarrow a = (40.1058 - e^{3b})/9$.

Graph $Y_1 = (17.2597 - e^{2x})/4$ and $Y_2 = (40.1058 - e^{3x})/9$.

The graphs intersect at approximately $(0.9002, 2.8019)$.

Thus, $a \approx 2.8019$, $b \approx 0.9002$, and $f(x) = 2.8019x^2 + e^{0.9002x}$. The function $f$ is also accurate at $x = 4$.

[0, 4] by [0, 4]

[0, 12] by [0, 8]

Figure 67  Figure 68

**68** If $f(x) = \sqrt{ax + b}$ and $x = 2$, then $f(2) = \sqrt{2a + b} = 3.8859 \Rightarrow 2a + b = (3.8859)^2 \Rightarrow$

$b = (3.8859)^2 - 2a$. When $x = 4$, $f(4) = \sqrt{4a + b} = 5.1284 \Rightarrow 4a + b = (5.1284)^2 \Rightarrow$

$b = (5.1284)^2 - 4a$.

*(continued)*

Graph $Y_1 = (3.8859)^2 - 2x$ and $Y_2 = (5.1284)^2 - 4x$. The graphs intersect at approximately $(5.6001, 3.9000)$. Thus, $a \approx 5.6001$, $b \approx 3.9000$, and $f(x) = \sqrt{5.6001x + 3.9000}$. The function $f$ is also accurate at $x = 6$.

## 8.2 Exercises

**Note:** The expressions $E_1$ and $E_2$ refer to the first and second equation, respectively. The expression $3E_2$ symbolizes "3 times equation 2". After the value of one variable is found, the value(s) of the other variable(s) will be stated and can be found by substituting the known value(s) back into the original equation(s).

1. The easiest choice for multipliers is to take $-2$ times the second equation and eliminate $x$.

$-2E_2 + E_1 \Rightarrow 4y + 3y = -16 + 2 \Rightarrow 7y = -14 \Rightarrow y = -2; x = 4$.

Another way to write this is as follows: $\begin{cases} 2x + 3y = 2 & (E_1) \\ x - 2y = 8 & (E_2) \end{cases} \Rightarrow \begin{cases} 2x + 3y = 2 & (E_1) \\ -2x + 4y = -16 & (-2E_2) \end{cases}$

Alternatively, if we wanted to eliminate $y$ instead of $x$, we could add 2 times the first equation to 3 times the second equation, giving us $2E_1 + 3E_2 \Rightarrow 4x + 3x = 4 + 24 \Rightarrow 7x = 28 \Rightarrow x = 4; y = -2$   ★ $(4, -2)$

2. $-5E_2 + E_1 \Rightarrow -5(3x + y = -4) + (4x + 5y = 13) \Rightarrow -11x = 33 \Rightarrow x = -3$.

From the second equation, we see that $3(-3) + y = -4 \Rightarrow y = 5$.   ★ $(-3, 5)$

3. $3E_1 + 2E_2 \Rightarrow 3(3x + 2y = -45) + 2(-4x - 3y = 30) \Rightarrow 9x - 8x = -135 + 60 \Rightarrow x = -75$.

From the first equation, we see that $3(-75) + 2y = -45 \Rightarrow 2y = 180 \Rightarrow y = 90$.   ★ $(-75, 90)$

4. $2E_1 + E_2 \Rightarrow 2(-2x + y = -28) + (3x - 2y = 11) \Rightarrow -4x + 3x = -56 + 11 \Rightarrow -x = -45 \Rightarrow$

$x = 45$. From the second equation, we see that $3(45) - 2y = 11 \Rightarrow 124 = 2y \Rightarrow 62 = y$.   ★ $(45, 62)$

5. $2E_2 + E_1 \Rightarrow 2(r - 2s = -4) + (3r + 4s = 3) \Rightarrow 2r + 3r = -8 + 3 \Rightarrow 5r = -5 \Rightarrow r = -1$.

From the second equation, we see that $-1 - 2s = -4 \Rightarrow -2s = -3 \Rightarrow s = \frac{3}{2}$.   ★ $\left(-1, \frac{3}{2}\right)$

6. $-3E_2 + E_1 \Rightarrow -3(3u - 5v = 17) + (9u + 2v = 0) \Rightarrow 17v = -51 \Rightarrow v = -3; u = \frac{2}{3}$   ★ $\left(\frac{2}{3}, -3\right)$

7. $3E_1 - 5E_2 \Rightarrow 3(5x - 6y = 4) - 5(3x + 7y = 8) \Rightarrow -18y - 35y = 12 - 40 \Rightarrow -53y = -28 \Rightarrow$

$y = \frac{28}{53}$. Instead of substituting into one of the equations to find the value of the other variable, it is usually easier to pick different multipliers and re-solve the system for the other variable, as in Example 4. $7E_1 + 6E_2 \Rightarrow$

$7(5x - 6y = 4) + 6(3x + 7y = 8) \Rightarrow 35x + 18x = 28 + 48 \Rightarrow 53x = 76 \Rightarrow x = \frac{76}{53}$.   ★ $\left(\frac{76}{53}, \frac{28}{53}\right)$

8. $3E_1 - 2E_2 \Rightarrow 3(2x + 8y = 7) - 2(3x - 5y = 4) \Rightarrow 34y = 13 \Rightarrow y = \frac{13}{34}$.

$5E_1 + 8E_2 \Rightarrow 5(2x + 8y = 7) + 8(3x - 5y = 4) \Rightarrow 34x = 67 \Rightarrow x = \frac{67}{34}$.   ★ $\left(\frac{67}{34}, \frac{13}{34}\right)$

9. We will first eliminate all fractions by multiplying both sides of each equation by its lcd.

$\begin{cases} 6E_1 \\ 3E_2 \end{cases} \Rightarrow \begin{cases} 6\left(\frac{1}{3}c + \frac{1}{2}d = 5\right) \\ 3\left(c - \frac{2}{3}d = -1\right) \end{cases} \Rightarrow \begin{cases} 2c + 3d = 30 & (E_3) \\ 3c - 2d = -3 & (E_4) \end{cases}$

Eliminate $c$: $3E_3 - 2E_4 \Rightarrow 3(2c + 3d = 30) - 2(3c - 2d = -3) \Rightarrow 13d = 96 \Rightarrow d = \frac{96}{13}$.

Eliminate $d$: $2E_3 + 3E_4 \Rightarrow 2(2c + 3d = 30) + 3(3c - 2d = -3) \Rightarrow 13c = 51 \Rightarrow c = \frac{51}{13}$.   ★ $\left(\frac{51}{13}, \frac{96}{13}\right)$

10. $\begin{cases} 10E_1 \\ 12E_2 \end{cases} \Rightarrow \begin{cases} 10\left(\frac{1}{2}t - \frac{1}{5}v = \frac{3}{2}\right) \\ 12\left(\frac{2}{3}t + \frac{1}{4}v = \frac{5}{12}\right) \end{cases} \Rightarrow \begin{cases} 5t - 2v = 15 & (E_3) \\ 8t + 3v = 5 & (E_4) \end{cases}$

$8E_3 - 5E_4 \Rightarrow -31v = 95 \Rightarrow v = -\frac{95}{31}; 3E_3 + 2E_4 \Rightarrow 31t = 55 \Rightarrow t = \frac{55}{31}$   ★ $\left(\frac{55}{31}, -\frac{95}{31}\right)$

**11** To eliminate $y$: the least common multiple of 2 and 3 is 6, so we will multiply the first equation by $\sqrt{3}$ and the second equation by $\sqrt{2}$ so that the coefficients of $y$ are $\sqrt{6}$ and $-\sqrt{6}$. $\sqrt{3}\,E_1 + \sqrt{2}\,E_2 \Rightarrow$

$$\sqrt{3}\left(\sqrt{3}x - \sqrt{2}y = 2\sqrt{3}\right) + \sqrt{2}\left(2\sqrt{2}x + \sqrt{3}y = \sqrt{2}\right) \Rightarrow 3x + 4x = 6 + 2 \Rightarrow 7x = 8 \Rightarrow x = \tfrac{8}{7}.$$

We will now re-solve the system by eliminating $x$ to obtain a value for $y$.

$$2\sqrt{2}\,E_1 - \sqrt{3}\,E_2 \Rightarrow 2\sqrt{2}\left(\sqrt{3}x - \sqrt{2}y = 2\sqrt{3}\right) - \sqrt{3}\left(2\sqrt{2}x + \sqrt{3}y = \sqrt{2}\right) \Rightarrow$$

$$-4y - 3y = 4\sqrt{6} - \sqrt{6} \Rightarrow -7y = 3\sqrt{6} \Rightarrow y = -\tfrac{3}{7}\sqrt{6}. \qquad \bigstar \left(\tfrac{8}{7}, -\tfrac{3}{7}\sqrt{6}\right)$$

**12** Eliminate $x$: $\sqrt{3}\,E_1 - \sqrt{5}\,E_2 \Rightarrow \sqrt{3}\left(\sqrt{5}x + \sqrt{3}y = 14\sqrt{3}\right) - \sqrt{5}\left(\sqrt{3}x - 2\sqrt{5}y = -2\sqrt{5}\right) \Rightarrow$

$$3y + 10y = 42 + 10 \Rightarrow 13y = 52 \Rightarrow y = 4;$$

Eliminate $y$: $2\sqrt{5}\,E_1 + \sqrt{3}\,E_2 \Rightarrow 2\sqrt{5}\left(\sqrt{5}x + \sqrt{3}y = 14\sqrt{3}\right) + \sqrt{3}\left(\sqrt{3}x - 2\sqrt{5}y = -2\sqrt{5}\right) \Rightarrow$

$$10x + 3x = 28\sqrt{15} - 2\sqrt{15} \Rightarrow 13x = 26\sqrt{15} \Rightarrow x = 2\sqrt{15} \qquad \bigstar \left(2\sqrt{15}, 4\right)$$

**13** Eliminate decimals: $\begin{cases} 100E_1 \\ 100E_2 \end{cases} \Rightarrow \begin{cases} 100(-0.03x + 0.07y = 0.23) \\ 100(0.04x - 0.05y = 0.15) \end{cases} \Rightarrow \begin{cases} -3x + 7y = 23 & (E_3) \\ 4x - 5y = 15 & (E_4) \end{cases}$

Eliminate $x$: $4\,E_3 + 3\,E_4 \Rightarrow 4(-3x + 7y = 23) + 3(4x - 5y = 15) \Rightarrow 28y - 15y = 92 + 45 \Rightarrow$

$13y = 137 \Rightarrow y = \tfrac{137}{13}$;

Eliminate $y$: $5\,E_3 + 7\,E_4 \Rightarrow 5(-3x + 7y = 23) + 7(4x - 5y = 15) \Rightarrow -15x + 28x = 115 + 105 \Rightarrow$

$13x = 220 \Rightarrow x = \tfrac{220}{13}$ $\qquad \bigstar \left(\tfrac{220}{13}, \tfrac{137}{13}\right)$

**14** Eliminate decimals: $\begin{cases} 100E_1 \\ 100E_2 \end{cases} \Rightarrow \begin{cases} 100(0.11x - 0.03y = 0.25) \\ 100(0.12x + 0.05y = 0.70) \end{cases} \Rightarrow \begin{cases} 11x - 3y = 25 & (E_3) \\ 12x + 5y = 70 & (E_4) \end{cases}$

Eliminate $x$: $12\,E_3 - 11\,E_4 \Rightarrow 12(11x - 3y = 25) - 11(12x + 5y = 70) \Rightarrow$

$-36y - 55y = 300 - 770 \Rightarrow -91y = -470 \Rightarrow y = \tfrac{470}{91}$;

Eliminate $y$: $5\,E_3 + 3\,E_4 \Rightarrow 5(11x - 3y = 25) + 3(12x + 5y = 70) \Rightarrow 55x + 36x = 125 + 210 \Rightarrow$

$91x = 335 \Rightarrow x = \tfrac{335}{91}$ $\qquad \bigstar \left(\tfrac{335}{91}, \tfrac{470}{91}\right)$

**15** $3E_1 + E_2 \Rightarrow 3(2x - 3y = 5) + (-6x + 9y = 12) \Rightarrow 6x - 6x - 9y + 9y = 15 + 12 \Rightarrow 0 = 27$;

this statement is never true so there are **no solutions**.

**16** $4E_1 + E_2 \Rightarrow 4(3p - q = 7) + (-12p + 4q = 3) \Rightarrow 12p - 4q - 12p + 4q = 28 + 3 \Rightarrow 0 = 31$;

this statement is never true so there are **no solutions**.

**17** $2E_1 + E_2 \Rightarrow 2(3m - 4n = 2) + (-6m + 8n = -4) \Rightarrow 6m - 6m - 8n + 8n = 4 - 4 \Rightarrow 0 = 0$;

this statement is always true so the solution is all ordered pairs $(m, n)$ such that $3m - 4n = 2$. We could also say that the solution is all ordered pairs $(m, n)$ such that $-6m + 8n = -4$. Either statement is correct.

**18** $-3E_1 + E_2 \Rightarrow -3(x - 5y = 2) + (3x - 15y = 6) \Rightarrow -3x + 3x + 15y - 15y = -6 + 6 \Rightarrow 0 = 0$;

the solution is all ordered pairs $(x, y)$ such that $x - 5y = 2$.

**19** $3E_1 - 2E_2 \Rightarrow 3(2y - 5x = 0) - 2(3y + 4x = 0) \Rightarrow 6y - 6y - 15x - 8x = 0 - 0 \Rightarrow$

$-23x = 0 \Rightarrow x = 0; \ y = 0$ $\qquad \bigstar (0, 0)$

**20** $-7E_2 + E_1 \Rightarrow -7(y = 5) + (3x + 7y = 9) \Rightarrow -7y + 7y + 3x = -35 + 9 \Rightarrow$

$3x = -26 \Rightarrow x = -\tfrac{26}{3}; \ y = 5$ $\qquad \bigstar \left(-\tfrac{26}{3}, 5\right)$

**21** Let $u = 1/x$ and $v = 1/y$. $\begin{cases} 2/x + 3/y = -2 & (E_1) \\ 4/x - 5/y = 1 & (E_2) \end{cases} \Rightarrow \begin{cases} 2u + 3v = -2 & (E_3) \\ 4u - 5v = 1 & (E_4) \end{cases}$

$-2\,E_3 + E_4 \Rightarrow -2(2u + 3v = -2) + (4u - 5v = 1) \Rightarrow -11v = 5 \Rightarrow v = -\frac{5}{11}.$

$5\,E_3 + 3\,E_4 \Rightarrow 5(2u + 3v = -2) + 3(4u - 5v = 1) \Rightarrow 22u = -7 \Rightarrow u = -\frac{7}{22}.$

Resubstituting, we have $x = 1/u = -\frac{22}{7}$ and $y = 1/v = -\frac{11}{5}$.  $\bigstar \left(-\frac{22}{7}, -\frac{11}{5}\right)$

**22** Let $u = 1/x$ and $v = 1/y$. $\begin{cases} 6/x + 10/y = -1 & (E_1) \\ 4/x - 5/y = -3 & (E_2) \end{cases} \Rightarrow \begin{cases} 6u + 10v = -1 & (E_3) \\ 4u - 5v = -3 & (E_4) \end{cases}$

$2\,E_3 - 3\,E_4 \Rightarrow 2(6u + 10v = -1) - 3(4u - 5v = -3) \Rightarrow 35v = 7 \Rightarrow v = \frac{1}{5}.$

$E_3 + 2\,E_4 \Rightarrow (6u + 10v = -1) + 2(4u - 5v = -3) \Rightarrow 14u = -7 \Rightarrow u = -\frac{1}{2}.$

Resubstituting, we have $x = 1/u = -2$ and $y = 1/v = 5$.  $\bigstar (-2, 5)$

**23** Let $u = \dfrac{1}{x+2}$ and $v = \dfrac{1}{y-5}$. $\begin{cases} \dfrac{8}{x+2} - \dfrac{6}{y-5} = 3 & (E_1) \\ \dfrac{4}{x+2} + \dfrac{12}{y-5} = -1 & (E_2) \end{cases} \Rightarrow \begin{cases} 8u - 6v = 3 & (E_3) \\ 4u + 12v = -1 & (E_4) \end{cases}$

$E_3 - 2\,E_4 \Rightarrow (8u - 6v = 3) - 2(4u + 12v = -1) \Rightarrow -30v = 5 \Rightarrow v = -\frac{1}{6}.$

$2\,E_3 + E_4 \Rightarrow 2(8u - 6v = 3) + (4u + 12v = -1) \Rightarrow 20u = 5 \Rightarrow u = \frac{1}{4}.$

Solve for $x$ and $y$: $u(x + 2) = 1 \Rightarrow ux + 2u = 1 \Rightarrow ux = 1 - 2u \Rightarrow x = \frac{1}{u} - 2$

$v(y - 5) = 1 \Rightarrow vy - 5v = 1 \Rightarrow vy = 1 + 5v \Rightarrow y = \frac{1}{v} + 5$

Resubstituting, we have $x = \frac{1}{u} - 2 = 4 - 2 = 2$ and $y = \frac{1}{v} + 5 = -6 + 5 = -1.$  $\bigstar (2, -1)$

**24** Let $u = \dfrac{1}{x-1}$ and $v = \dfrac{1}{y+2}$. $\begin{cases} \dfrac{3}{x-1} + \dfrac{4}{y+2} = 2 & (E_1) \\ \dfrac{6}{x-1} - \dfrac{7}{y+2} = -3 & (E_2) \end{cases} \Rightarrow \begin{cases} 3u + 4v = 2 & (E_3) \\ 6u - 7v = -3 & (E_4) \end{cases}$

$-2\,E_3 + E_4 \Rightarrow -2(3u + 4v = 2) + (6u - 7v = -3) \Rightarrow -15v = -7 \Rightarrow v = \frac{7}{15}.$

$7\,E_3 + 4\,E_4 \Rightarrow 7(3u + 4v = 2) + 4(6u - 7v = -3) \Rightarrow 45u = 2 \Rightarrow u = \frac{2}{45}.$

Solve for $x$ and $y$: $u(x - 1) = 1 \Rightarrow ux - u = 1 \Rightarrow ux = 1 + u \Rightarrow x = \frac{1}{u} + 1$

$v(y + 2) = 1 \Rightarrow vy + 2v = 1 \Rightarrow vy = 1 - 2v \Rightarrow y = \frac{1}{v} - 2$

Resubstituting, we have $x = \frac{1}{u} + 1 = \frac{45}{2} + 1 = \frac{47}{2}$ and $y = \frac{1}{v} - 2 = \frac{15}{7} - 2 = \frac{1}{7}.$  $\bigstar \left(\frac{47}{2}, \frac{1}{7}\right)$

**25** $\begin{cases} 2^{x+1} + 3^y = 11 & (E_1) \\ 2^x - 3^{y+1} = -26 & (E_2) \end{cases} \Rightarrow \begin{cases} 2^x 2^1 + 3^y = 11 \\ 2^x - 3^y 3^1 = -26 \end{cases} \Rightarrow \begin{cases} 2 \cdot 2^x + 3^y = 11 \\ 2^x - 3 \cdot 3^y = -26 \end{cases}$

Let $u = 2^x$ and $v = 3^y$. $\begin{cases} 2u + v = 11 & (E_3) \\ u - 3v = -26 & (E_4) \end{cases}$

$E_3 - 2\,E_4 \Rightarrow (2u + v = 11) - 2(u - 3v = -26) \Rightarrow 7v = 63 \Rightarrow v = 9.$

$3\,E_3 + E_4 \Rightarrow 3(2u + v = 11) + (u - 3v = -26) \Rightarrow 7u = 7 \Rightarrow u = 1.$

Resubstituting, we have $x = \log_2 u = \log_2 1 = 0$ and $y = \log_3 v = \log_3 9 = 2.$  $\bigstar (0, 2)$

**26** $\begin{cases} 4 \cdot 2^x + 3^{y-1} = 5 & (E_1) \\ 8 \cdot 2^{x-2} - 3^y = -8 & (E_2) \end{cases} \Rightarrow \begin{cases} 4 \cdot 2^x + 3^y 3^{-1} = 5 \\ 8 \cdot 2^x 2^{-2} - 3^y = -8 \end{cases} \Rightarrow \begin{cases} 4 \cdot 2^x + \frac{1}{3} \cdot 3^y = 5 \\ 2 \cdot 2^x - 3^y = -8 \end{cases}$

Let $u = 2^x$ and $v = 3^y$. $\begin{cases} 4u + \frac{1}{3}v = 5 & (E_3) \\ 2u - v = -8 & (E_4) \end{cases}$

$E_3 - 2\,E_4 \Rightarrow \left(4u + \frac{1}{3}v = 5\right) - 2(2u - v = -8) \Rightarrow \frac{7}{3}v = 21 \Rightarrow v = 9.$

$3\,E_3 + E_4 \Rightarrow 3\left(4u + \frac{1}{3}v = 5\right) + (2u - v = -8) \Rightarrow 14u = 7 \Rightarrow u = \frac{1}{2}.$

Resubstituting, we have $x = \log_2 u = \log_2 \frac{1}{2} = -1$ and $y = \log_3 v = \log_3 9 = 2.$  $\bigstar (-1, 2)$

**27** Let $x$ denote the number of \$3.00 tickets and $y$ the number of \$4.50 tickets.

$$\begin{cases} x + y = 450 & quantity \\ 3.00x + 4.50y = 1555.50 & value \end{cases}$$

$E_2 - 3E_1 \Rightarrow 4.50y - 3y = 1555.50 - 1350 \Rightarrow 1.5y = 205.50 \Rightarrow y = \frac{205.50}{1.5} = 137.$

Since $x + y = 450$, $x = 450 - 137 = 313$.

**28** Let $x$ denote the number of passengers that purchased a ticket to Phoenix and $y$ the number of passengers that purchased a ticket to Albuquerque.

$$\begin{cases} x + y = 185 & quantity \\ 90x + 120y = 21,000 & value \end{cases}$$

$E_2 - 90E_1 \Rightarrow 30y = 4350 \Rightarrow y = 145; x = 40$

**29** The volume for a cylinder is $\pi r^2 h$ and the volume for a cone is $\frac{1}{3}\pi r^2 h$. The radius of the cylinder is $\frac{1}{2}$ cm.

$$\begin{cases} x + y = 8 & length \\ \pi\left(\frac{1}{2}\right)^2 x + \frac{1}{3}\pi\left(\frac{1}{2}\right)^2 y = 5 & volume \end{cases}$$

Solving $E_1$ for $y$, $y = 8 - x$, and substituting into $E_2$ yields

$\frac{\pi}{4}x + \frac{\pi}{12}(8 - x) = 5 \Rightarrow \frac{\pi}{4}x + \frac{8\pi}{12} - \frac{\pi}{12}x = \frac{15}{3} \Rightarrow \frac{3\pi}{12}x - \frac{\pi}{12}x = \frac{15}{3} - \frac{2\pi}{3} \Rightarrow \frac{\pi}{6}x = \frac{15 - 2\pi}{3} \Rightarrow$

$x = \frac{6}{\pi} \cdot \frac{15 - 2\pi}{3} = \frac{30 - 4\pi}{\pi} = \frac{30}{\pi} - 4 \approx 5.55$ cm.

$y = 8 - x = 8 - \left(\frac{30 - 4\pi}{\pi}\right) = \frac{8\pi}{\pi} - \frac{30}{\pi} + \frac{4\pi}{\pi} = \frac{12\pi - 30}{\pi} = 12 - \frac{30}{\pi} \approx 2.45$ cm.

**30** Let $x$ denote the rate at which he can row in still water and $y$ the speed of the current. $d = rt$ yields

$$\begin{cases} 500 = (x - y)10 & upstream \\ 300 = (x + y)5 & downstream \end{cases} \Rightarrow \begin{cases} 50 = x - y \\ 60 = x + y \end{cases}$$

$E_1 + E_2 \Rightarrow 2x = 110 \Rightarrow x = 55$ ft/min; $y = 5$ ft/min

**31** The perimeter is composed of 2 sides of the rectangular portion of the table, $2l$, and 2 edges of the semicircular regions, $2 \cdot \frac{1}{2}(2\pi r) = 2\pi r$. Since the radius is $\frac{1}{2}w$, the system can be represented by

$$\begin{cases} 2l + 2\pi\left(\frac{1}{2}w\right) = 40 & perimeter \\ lw = 2\left[\pi\left(\frac{1}{2}w\right)^2\right] & area \end{cases}$$

Solving $E_1$ for $l$, $l = \frac{40 - \pi w}{2}$, and substituting into $E_2$ yields $\left(\frac{40 - \pi w}{2}\right)w = \frac{\pi w^2}{2} \Rightarrow$

$(40 - \pi w)w = \pi w^2 \Rightarrow 40w - \pi w^2 = \pi w^2 \Rightarrow 40w - 2\pi w^2 = 0 \Rightarrow 2w(20 - \pi w) = 0 \Rightarrow$

$w = 0, \frac{20}{\pi}$. We discard $w = 0$ and use $w = \frac{20}{\pi} \approx 6.37$ ft. Thus, $l = \frac{40 - \pi(20/\pi)}{2} = \frac{20}{2} = 10$ ft.

**32** Let $x$ denote the amount invested in the 4% fund and $y$ the amount in the 6% fund.

$$\begin{cases} x + y = 19,000 & amount \\ 0.04x + 0.06y = 1000 & interest \end{cases}$$

$100E_2 - 4E_1 \Rightarrow 2y = 24,000 \Rightarrow y = \$12,000; x = \$7000$

**33** Let $x$ denote the number of adults and $y$ the number of kittens. Thus, $\frac{1}{2}x$ is the number of adult females.

$$\begin{cases} x + y = 6000 & total \\ y = 3\left(\frac{1}{2}x\right)3 & kittens\ per\ adult\ female \end{cases}$$

Substituting $y$ from $E_2$ into $E_1$ yields $x + \frac{3}{2}x = 6000 \Rightarrow \frac{5}{2}x = 6000 \Rightarrow x = \frac{2}{5} \cdot 6000 = 2400; y = 3600.$

**34** Let $x$ denote the flow rate of the inlet pipe and $y$ the flow rate of one of the outlet pipes.

$\{(\text{inlet rate} - \text{outlet rate})(\text{hours}) = \text{gallons}\}$

$$\begin{cases} (x - 2y)5 = 300 & \textit{both open} \\ (x - y)3 = 300 & \textit{one closed} \end{cases} \Rightarrow \begin{cases} x - 2y = 60 \\ x - y = 100 \end{cases} \quad E_2 - E_1 \Rightarrow y = 40 \text{ gal/hr}; x = 140 \text{ gal/hr}$$

**35** Let $x$ denote the number of grams of the 35% alloy and $y$ the number of grams of the 60% alloy.

$$\begin{cases} x + y = 100 & \textit{quantity} \\ 0.35x + 0.60y = 0.50 \cdot 100 & \textit{quality} \end{cases}$$

Multiply the second equation by 100 to obtain $35x + 60y = 5000$ ($E_3$).

$$E_3 - 35E_1 \Rightarrow 25y = 1500 \Rightarrow y = 60; x = 40$$

**36** Let $x$ denote the number of pounds of peanuts used and $y$ the number of pounds of cashews used.

$$\begin{cases} x + y = 60 & \textit{quantity} \\ 3x + 8y = 5 \cdot 60 & \textit{quality} \end{cases} \quad E_2 - 3E_1 \Rightarrow 5y = 120 \Rightarrow y = 24; x = 36$$

**37** Let $x$ denote the speed of the plane and $y$ the speed of the wind. Use $d = rt$.

$$\begin{cases} 1200 = (x + y)(2) & \textit{with the wind} \\ 1200 = (x - y)(2\frac{1}{2}) & \textit{against the wind} \end{cases} \Rightarrow \begin{cases} 600 = x + y \\ 480 = x - y \end{cases}$$

$$E_1 + E_2 \Rightarrow 2x = 1080 \Rightarrow x = 540 \text{ mi/hr}; y = 60 \text{ mi/hr}$$

**38** Let $x$ denote the number of $0.50 notebooks and $y$ the number of $0.70 notebooks.

$$\begin{cases} x + y = 500 & \textit{quantity} \\ 0.50x + 0.70y = 286 & \textit{value} \end{cases} \quad 10E_2 - 5E_1 \Rightarrow 2y = 360 \Rightarrow y = 180; x = 320$$

**39** $v(t) = v_0 + at \bullet \begin{cases} v(2) = 16 \\ v(5) = 25 \end{cases} \Rightarrow \begin{cases} 16 = v_0 + 2a & (E_1) \\ 25 = v_0 + 5a & (E_2) \end{cases} \quad E_2 - E_1 \Rightarrow 9 = 3a \Rightarrow a = 3; v_0 = 10$

**40** $s(t) = -16t^2 + v_0t + s_0 \bullet \begin{cases} s(1) = 84 \\ s(2) = 116 \end{cases} \Rightarrow \begin{cases} 84 = -16 + v_0 + s_0 & (E_1) \\ 116 = -64 + 2v_0 + s_0 & (E_2) \end{cases}$

$$E_2 - E_1 \Rightarrow v_0 = 80; s_0 = 20$$

**41** Let $x$ denote the number of sofas produced and $y$ the number of recliners produced.

$$\begin{cases} 8x + 6y = 340 & \textit{labor hours} \\ 180x + 105y = 6750 & \textit{cost of materials} \end{cases}$$

$$6E_2 - 105E_1 \Rightarrow 1080x - 840x = 40{,}500 - 35{,}700 \Rightarrow 240x = 4800 \Rightarrow x = 20; y = 30$$

**42** Let $x$ denote the number of ounces of oats used and $y$ the number of ounces of cornmeal used.

$$\begin{cases} 4x + 3y = 200 & \textit{protein} \\ 18x + 24y = 1320 & \textit{carbohydrates} \end{cases} \quad E_2 - 8E_1 \Rightarrow -14x = -280 \Rightarrow x = 20; y = 40$$

**43** (a) The expression $6x + 5y$ represents the total bill for the plumber's business. This should equal the plumber's income, which is the plumber's number of hours times the hourly wage—that is, $(6 + 4)(x) = 10x$.

The expression $4x + 6y$ represents the total bill for the electrician's business. This should equal the electrician's income, that is, $(5 + 6)(y) = 11y$.

$$\begin{cases} 6x + 5y = 10x \\ 4x + 6y = 11y \end{cases} \Rightarrow \begin{cases} 5y = 4x \\ 4x = 5y \end{cases} \Rightarrow y = \frac{4}{5}x, \text{ or equivalently, } y = 0.80x$$

(b) The electrician should charge 80% of what the plumber charges—80% of $35 per hour is $28 per hour.

**44** We want the equations of the 3 lines that are perpendicular to a side and pass through the opposite vertex. $m_{AB} = \frac{1}{4}$; the equation of the line through $C$ with a slope of $-4$ is $y + 8 = -4(x - 3)$ $\Leftrightarrow$ $4x + y = 4$ (E$_1$). Similarly, the other two altitudes are:

$$m_{BC} = 6; \quad y - 2 = -\tfrac{1}{6}(x + 3) \quad \Leftrightarrow \quad x + 6y = 9 \quad (E_2)$$
$$m_{AC} = -\tfrac{5}{3}; \quad y - 4 = \tfrac{3}{5}(x - 5) \quad \Leftrightarrow \quad 3x - 5y = -5 \quad (E_3)$$

Finding the intersection of E$_1$ and E$_2$, we have E$_1$ $-$ 4 E$_2$ $\Rightarrow$ $-23y = -32$ $\Rightarrow$ $y = \frac{32}{23}; x = \frac{15}{23}$.

$\left(\frac{15}{23}, \frac{32}{23}\right)$ also lies on E$_3$.

**45** Let $t = 0$ correspond to the year 1891. The average daily maximum can then be approximated by the linear equation $y_1 = 0.011t + 15.1$ and the average daily minimum by the linear equation $y_2 = 0.019t + 5.8$. We must determine $t$ when $y_1$ and $y_2$ differ by 9. $y_1 - y_2 = 9$ $\Rightarrow$ $(0.011t + 15.1) - (0.019t + 5.8) = 9$ $\Rightarrow$ $-0.008t + 9.3 = 9$ $\Rightarrow$ $-0.008t = -0.3$ $\Rightarrow$ $t = 37.5$. $1891 + 37.5 = 1928.5$, or during the year 1928. Now we find the corresponding average maximum temperature:

$$t = 37.5 \quad \Rightarrow \quad y_1 = 0.011(37.5) + 15.1 = 15.5125 \approx 15.5°C.$$

**46** (a) Let $x$ denote the cost of the first minute and $y$ the cost of each additional minute.
$$\begin{cases} x + 35y = 2.93 & 36 \text{ minute call} \\ x + 12y = 1.09 & 13 \text{ minute call} \end{cases} \qquad E_1 - E_2 \Rightarrow 23y = 1.84 \Rightarrow y = \$0.08; x = \$0.13$$

(b) If $C$ denotes the cost of an $n$ minute phone call, then $C = 0.13 + 0.08(n - 1)$.

The total cost $T$ of the call is $T = (\text{cost}) + (\text{federal tax}) + (\text{state tax}) = C + 0.032C + 0.072C = 1.104C$.

$$T = 5.00 \quad \Rightarrow \quad 1.104C = 5.00 \quad \Rightarrow \quad C = \tfrac{5.00}{1.104} \quad \Rightarrow \quad 0.13 + 0.08(n - 1) = \tfrac{5.00}{1.104} \quad \Rightarrow$$
$$0.08(n - 1) = \tfrac{5.00}{1.104} - 0.13 \quad \Rightarrow \quad n = \frac{\frac{5.00}{1.104} - 0.13}{0.08} + 1 \approx 55.99 \text{ min, or } 55 \text{ min.}$$

**47** Let $x$ and $y$ denote the amount of time in hours at the LP and SLP speeds, respectively. 5 hours and 20 minutes $= 5\frac{1}{3}$ hours, so $\dfrac{x}{5\frac{1}{3}}$ is the portion of the tape used at the LP speed. $\dfrac{y}{8}$ is the portion of the tape used at the SLP speed, and together, these fractions add up to 1 whole tape.

$$\begin{cases} x + y = 6 & \text{total time} \\ \dfrac{x}{5\frac{1}{3}} + \dfrac{y}{8} = 1 & \text{portions of tape} \end{cases} \Rightarrow \begin{cases} x + y = 6 & (E_1) \\ \tfrac{3}{16}x + \tfrac{1}{8}y = 1 & (E_2) \end{cases}$$
$$16\,E_2 - 2E_1 \quad \Rightarrow \quad 3x - 2x = 16 - 12 \quad \Rightarrow \quad x = 4; y = 2$$

**Note:** If you convert hours to minutes, the equations can be written as $x + y = 360$ and $x/320 + y/480 = 1$ with the solution $x = 240$ and $y = 120$.

**48** (a) Model this as a line through the two points $(15, 1{,}000{,}000)$ and $(16, 900{,}000)$.
$$Q - 1{,}000{,}000 = \frac{900{,}000 - 1{,}000{,}000}{16 - 15}(p - 15) \quad \Rightarrow \quad Q = -100{,}000p + 2{,}500{,}000$$

(b) $K - 2{,}000{,}000 = \frac{150{,}000}{1}(p - 20) \quad \Rightarrow \quad K = 150{,}000p - 1{,}000{,}000$

(c) $Q = K \quad \Rightarrow \quad -100{,}000p + 2{,}500{,}000 = 150{,}000p - 1{,}000{,}000 \quad \Rightarrow \quad 250{,}000p = 3{,}500{,}000 \quad \Rightarrow$

$$p = \$14.00$$

**49** $\begin{cases} ae^{3x} + be^{-3x} = 0 & (E_1) \\ a(3e^{3x}) + b(-3e^{-3x}) = e^{3x} & (E_2) \end{cases}$

Following the hint in the text, think of this system as a system of two equations in the variables $a$ and $b$.

In $E_1$, we have "$e^{3x}$" times $a$, and in $E_2$, we have "$3e^{3x}$" times $a$. Hence, we will multiply $E_1$ by $-3$ and add this equation to $E_2$ to eliminate $a$ and then solve the system for $b$.

$-3E_1 + E_2 \Rightarrow -3b\,e^{-3x} - 3b\,e^{-3x} = e^{3x} \Rightarrow -6be^{-3x} = e^{3x} \Rightarrow b = -\frac{1}{6}e^{6x}$.

Substituting back into $E_1$ yields $ae^{3x} + \left(-\frac{1}{6}e^{6x}\right)e^{-3x} = 0 \Rightarrow ae^{3x} = \frac{1}{6}e^{3x} \Rightarrow a = \frac{1}{6}$.

**50** $\begin{cases} ae^{-x} + be^{4x} = 0 & (E_1) \\ -ae^{-x} + b(4e^{4x}) = 2 & (E_2) \end{cases}$   $E_1 + E_2 \Rightarrow be^{4x} + 4be^{4x} = 2 \Rightarrow 5be^{4x} = 2 \Rightarrow b = \frac{2}{5}e^{-4x}$.

Substituting back into $E_1$ yields $ae^{-x} + \left(\frac{2}{5}e^{-4x}\right)e^{4x} = 0 \Rightarrow ae^{-x} + \frac{2}{5} = 0 \Rightarrow ae^{-x} = -\frac{2}{5} \Rightarrow a = -\frac{2}{5}e^{x}$.

**51** $\begin{cases} a\cos x + b\sin x = 0 & (E_1) \\ -a\sin x + b\cos x = \tan x & (E_2) \end{cases}$ $(\sin x)(E_1)$ and $(\cos x)(E_2)$ yield $\begin{cases} a\sin x\cos x + b\sin^2 x = 0 & (E_3) \\ -a\sin x\cos x + b\cos^2 x = \sin x & (E_4) \end{cases}$

$E_3 + E_4 \Rightarrow b\sin^2 x + b\cos^2 x = \sin x \Rightarrow b(\sin^2 x + \cos^2 x) = \sin x \Rightarrow b(1) = \sin x \Rightarrow b = \sin x$.

Substituting back into $E_1$ yields

$a\cos x + \sin^2 x = 0 \Rightarrow a = -\frac{\sin^2 x}{\cos x} = -\frac{1 - \cos^2 x}{\cos x} = -\frac{1}{\cos x} + \frac{\cos^2 x}{\cos x} = -\sec x + \cos x = \cos x - \sec x$.

**52** $\begin{cases} a\cos x + b\sin x = 0 & (E_1) \\ -a\sin x + b\cos x = \sin x & (E_2) \end{cases}$

$(\sin x)(E_1)$ and $(\cos x)(E_2)$ yield $\begin{cases} a\sin x\cos x + b\sin^2 x = 0 & (E_3) \\ -a\sin x\cos x + b\cos^2 x = \sin x\cos x & (E_4) \end{cases}$

$E_3 + E_4 \Rightarrow b\sin^2 x + b\cos^2 x = \sin x\cos x \Rightarrow b = \sin x\cos x$.

Substituting back into $E_1$ yields $a\cos x = -\sin^2 x\cos x \Rightarrow a = -\sin^2 x$.

## 8.3 Exercises

**1** $3x - 2y < 6 \Leftrightarrow y > \frac{3}{2}x - 3$. Sketch the graph of $y = \frac{3}{2}x - 3$ with dashes. The point $(0, 0)$ is clearly on one side of the line, so we will substitute $x = 0$ and $y = 0$ into the inequality $y > \frac{3}{2}x - 3$. Checking, we have $0 > -3$, a *true* statement. Hence, we shade *all* points that are on the *same* side of the line as $(0, 0)$.

Figure 1                Figure 2

**2** $4x + 3y < 12 \Leftrightarrow y < -\frac{4}{3}x + 4$; test point $(0, 0) \rightarrow$ True

$\boxed{3}$ $2x + 3y \geq 2y + 1$ $\Leftrightarrow$ $y \geq -2x + 1$. Sketch the graph of $y = -2x + 1$ as a solid line. Checking the test point $(0, 0)$ in $y \geq -2x + 1$ gives us $0 \geq 1$, a *false* statement. Hence, we shade *all* points that are on the *opposite* side of the line as $(0, 0)$.

*Figure 3*

*Figure 4*

$\boxed{4}$ $2x + 2y > 3y + 3$ $\Leftrightarrow$ $2x > y + 3$ $\Leftrightarrow$ $y < 2x - 3$; test point $(0, 0) \rightarrow$ False

$\boxed{5}$ $y + 2 < x^2$ $\Leftrightarrow$ $y < x^2 - 2$. Sketch the graph of the parabola $y = x^2 - 2$ with dashes. Checking the test point $(0, 0)$ in $y < x^2 - 2$ gives us $0 < -2$, a *false* statement. Hence, we shade *all* points that are on the *opposite* side of the parabola as $(0, 0)$.

*Figure 5*

*Figure 6*

$\boxed{6}$ $y^2 - x \leq 0$ $\Leftrightarrow$ $x \geq y^2$; test point $(1, 0) \rightarrow$ True

$\boxed{7}$ $x^2 + 1 \leq y$ $\Leftrightarrow$ $y \geq x^2 + 1$. Sketch the graph of the parabola $y = x^2 + 1$ with a solid curve. Checking the test point $(0, 0)$ in $y \geq x^2 + 1$ gives us $0 \geq 1$, a *false* statement. Hence, we shade *all* points that are on the *opposite* side of the parabola as $(0, 0)$.

*Figure 7*

*Figure 8*

$\boxed{8}$ $y - x^3 < 1$ $\Leftrightarrow$ $y < x^3 + 1$; test point $(0, 0) \rightarrow$ True

**9** $yx^2 \geq 1 \Leftrightarrow y \geq 1/x^2 \{x \neq 0\}$. Sketch the graph of $y = 1/x^2$ with a solid curve. The point $(1, 0)$ is clearly not on the graph. Substituting $x = 1$ and $y = 0$ into $y \geq 1/x^2$ yields $0 \geq 1$, a false statement. Hence, we do not shade the region containing $(1, 0)$, but we do shade the regions in the first and second quadrants that are above the graph.

*Figure 9*

*Figure 10*

**10** $x^2 + 4 \geq y \Leftrightarrow y \leq x^2 + 4$; test point $(0, 0) \to$ True

**Note:** The will use the notation $V @ (a, b), (c, d), \dots$ to denote the intersection point(s) of the solution region of the graph. These can be found by solving the system of *equalities* that correspond to the given system of inequalities.

**11** $\begin{cases} x - y > -2 \\ x + y > -2 \end{cases} \Leftrightarrow \begin{cases} y < x + 2 \\ y > -x - 2 \end{cases} \quad V @ (-2, 0)$

Solving the system $y = x + 2$ and $y = -x - 2$ gives us the solution $(-2, 0)$. Testing the point $(0, 0)$ in both inequalities, we see that we need to shade below $y = x + 2$ and above $y = -x - 2$, as shown in the figure.

*Figure 11*

*Figure 12*

**12** $\begin{cases} x - y > -1 \\ x + y < 3 \end{cases} \Leftrightarrow \begin{cases} y < x + 1 \\ y < -x + 3 \end{cases} \quad V @ (1, 2)$

**13** $\begin{cases} 3x - y \geq -19 \\ 2x + 5y < 10 \end{cases} \Leftrightarrow \begin{cases} y \leq 3x + 19 \\ y < -\frac{2}{5}x + 2 \end{cases} \quad V @ (-5, 4)$

Solving the system $y = 3x + 19$ and $y = -\frac{2}{5}x + 2$ gives us the solution $(-5, 4)$.

We need to shade below $y = 3x + 19$ and below $y = -\frac{2}{5}x + 2$.

*Figure 13*

*Figure 14*

**14** $\begin{cases} 2y - x \le 4 \\ 3y + 2x < 6 \end{cases}$ ⟺ $\begin{cases} y \le \frac{1}{2}x + 2 \\ y < -\frac{2}{3}x + 2 \end{cases}$   $V @ \ (0, 2)$

**15** $\begin{cases} 3x + y \le 6 \\ y - 2x \ge 1 \\ x \ge -2 \\ y \le 4 \end{cases}$ ⟺ $\begin{cases} y \le -3x + 6 \\ y \ge 2x + 1 \\ x \ge -2 \\ y \le 4 \end{cases}$   $V @ \ (-2, -3), \ (-2, 4), \ (\frac{2}{3}, 4), \ (1, 3)$

We need to shade below $y = -3x + 6$, above $y = 2x + 1$, to the right of $x = -2$, and

below $y = 4$. Include all the boundaries in the solution region.

*Figure 15*

*Figure 16*

**16** $\begin{cases} 2x + y \ge 2 \\ y \ge x \\ y \le 6 \\ x \le 4 \end{cases}$ ⟺ $\begin{cases} y \ge -2x + 2 \\ y \ge x \\ y \le 6 \\ x \le 4 \end{cases}$   $V @ \ (\frac{2}{3}, \frac{2}{3}), \ (4, 4), \ (4, 6), \ (-2, 6)$

**17** $\begin{cases} x + 2y \le 8 \\ 0 \le x \le 4 \\ 0 \le y \le 3 \end{cases}$ • $V @ \ (0, 0), \ (4, 0), \ (4, 2), \ (2, 3), \ (0, 3)$

We can write $x + 2y \le 8$ as $y \le -\frac{1}{2}x + 4$. Shade below $y = -\frac{1}{2}x + 4$, between $x = 0$ and $x = 4$, and between

$y = 0$ and $y = 3$. Include all the boundaries in the solution region.

*Figure 17*

*Figure 18*

**18** $\begin{cases} 2x + 3y \ge 6 \\ 0 \le x \le 5 \\ 0 \le y \le 4 \end{cases}$ • $V @ \ (3, 0), \ (5, 0), \ (5, 4), \ (0, 4), \ (0, 2)$

**19** $|x| \geq 2 \iff x \geq 2$ or $x \leq -2$.

This region is bounded on the left by the vertical line $x = 2$ and on the right by $x = -2$, including the lines.

$|y| < 3 \iff -3 < y < 3$.

This region is bounded below by the horizontal line $y = -3$ and above by $y = 3$, excluding the lines.

*Figure 19*

*Figure 20*

**20** $|x| \geq 4 \iff x \geq 4$ or $x \leq -4$; $|y| \geq 3 \iff y \geq 3$ or $y \leq -3$

**21** $|x + 1| < 3 \iff -3 \leq x + 1 \leq 3 \iff -4 \leq x \leq 2$.

This region is bounded by the vertical lines $x = -4$ and $x = 2$, excluding the lines.

$|y - 2| \leq 4 \iff -4 < y - 2 < 4 \iff -2 < y < 6$.

This region is bounded by the horizontal lines $y = -2$ and $y = 6$, including the lines.

*Figure 21*

*Figure 22*

**22** $|x - 2| \leq 5 \iff -5 \leq x - 2 \leq 5 \iff -3 \leq x \leq 7$;

$|y - 4| > 2 \iff y - 4 > 2$ or $y - 4 < -2 \iff y > 6$ or $y < 2$

**23** $\begin{cases} x^2 + y^2 \leq 45 \\ x + y \leq -3 \end{cases} \iff \begin{cases} x^2 + y^2 \leq \left(\sqrt{45}\right)^2 \\ y \leq -x - 3 \end{cases}$    $V @ (-6, 3), (3, -6)$

Shade inside the circle $x^2 + y^2 = 45$ and below the line $y = -x - 3$.

*Figure 23*

*Figure 24*

$\boxed{24}$ $\begin{cases} x^2 + y^2 > 1 \\ x^2 + y^2 < 4 \end{cases}$

$\boxed{25}$ $\begin{cases} x^2 \leq 1 - y \\ x \geq 1 + y \end{cases} \Leftrightarrow \begin{cases} y \leq -x^2 + 1 \\ y \leq x - 1 \end{cases}$  $V @ (-2, -3), (1, 0)$

Shade below {or inside} the parabola $y = -x^2 + 1$ and below the line $y = x - 1$.

*Figure 25*

*Figure 26*

$\boxed{26}$ $\begin{cases} x - y^2 < 0 \\ x + y^2 > 0 \end{cases} \Leftrightarrow \begin{cases} x < y^2 \\ x > -y^2 \end{cases}$

$\boxed{27}$ The shaded region lies between $x = 0$ and $x = 3$, including $x = 0$ and excluding $x = 3$. This region is described by $0 \leq x < 3$.

The dashed line goes through $(0, 4)$ and $(4, 0)$. Hence, its slope is $-1$, its $y$-intercept is 4, and an equation for it is $y = -x + 4$. Substituting $x = 0$ and $y = 0$ into $y = -x + 4$ gives us $0 = 4$. We replace $=$ by $<$ {the line is dashed} to make this statement a true statement. Hence, we have the inequality $y < -x + 4$.

The solid line goes through $(0, -4)$ and $(4, 0)$. Hence, its slope is 1, its $y$-intercept is $-4$, and an equation for it is $y = x - 4$. Substituting $x = 0$ and $y = 0$ into $y = x - 4$ gives us $0 = -4$. We replace $=$ by $\geq$ {the line is solid} to make this statement a true statement. Hence, we have the inequality $y \geq x - 4$. Thus, the graph may be described by the system $\begin{cases} 0 \leq x < 3 \\ y < -x + 4 \\ y \geq x - 4 \end{cases}$

$\boxed{28}$ $\begin{cases} x^2 + y^2 \leq 9 & \text{center is } (0, 0), \text{ radius is } 3 \\ (x - 1)^2 + y^2 < 9 & \text{center is } (1, 0), \text{ radius is } 3 \end{cases}$

$\boxed{29}$ The shaded region lies *inside* the circle $x^2 + y^2 = 3^2$, so we can describe it with the inequality $x^2 + y^2 \leq 9$.

The dashed line goes through $(0, 4)$ and $(2, 0)$. Hence, its slope is $-2$, its $y$-intercept is 4, and an equation for it is $y = -2x + 4$. We want the region shaded *above* the line, so replace $=$ by $>$ {the line is dashed} to make this statement a true statement. Hence, we have the inequality $y > -2x + 4$. Thus, the graph may be described by the system $\begin{cases} x^2 + y^2 \leq 9 \\ y > -2x + 4 \end{cases}$

$\boxed{30}$ $\begin{cases} 0 \leq y \leq 3 \\ x \geq 0 \\ y < -x + 4 & \text{slope between } (0, 4) \text{ and } (4, 0) \text{ is } -1, y\text{-intercept is } 4 \\ y \geq \frac{3}{2}x - 3 & \text{slope between } (0, -3) \text{ and } (2, 0) \text{ is } \frac{3}{2}, y\text{-intercept is } -3 \end{cases}$

**31** The center of the circle is $(2, 2)$ and it passes through $(0, 0)$. The radius is the distance from $(0, 0)$ to $(2, 2)$, which is $\sqrt{8}$. An equation of the circle is $(x - 2)^2 + (y - 2)^2 = 8$. The center is clearly inside the circle, and if we substitute $x = 2$ and $y = 2$ in the equation of the circle, we get $0 = 8$. Since we want to make this a true statement and include the boundary, we use $(x - 2)^2 + (y - 2)^2 \le 8$ to describe the shaded circular region and its boundary. For the dashed line $y = x$, test the point $(1, 0)$. This test gives us $0 = 1$, which we can make true by replacing $=$ by $<$. Hence $y < x$ describes the shaded region below the line $y = x$. The other inequality may be found as in Exercise 27. Thus, the graph may be described by the system $\begin{cases} y < x \\ y \le -x + 4 \\ (x - 2)^2 + (y - 2)^2 \le 8 \end{cases}$

**32** $\begin{cases} y < x^2 \\ x^2 + y^2 \le 9 \end{cases}$  center is $(0, 0)$, radius is 3

**33** For the dashed line through $(-4, 0)$ and $(4, 1)$, we can use the point-slope form to find an equation of the line. $y - 0 = \dfrac{1 - 0}{4 - (-4)}(x - (-4)) \iff y = \dfrac{1}{8}x + \dfrac{1}{2}$. Checking the point $(0, 1)$ {which is in the shaded region} gives us $1 = \frac{1}{2}$, so we change $=$ to $>$ to obtain $y > \frac{1}{8}x + \frac{1}{2}$.

Similarly, for the solid line with $x$-intercept $-4$ and $y$-intercept 4, the shaded region can be described by $y \le x + 4$. Lastly, the solid line passing through $(4, 1)$ has slope $-\frac{3}{4}$, $y$-intercept 4, and its shaded region can be described by $y \le -\frac{3}{4}x + 4$. Thus, the system is $\begin{cases} y > \frac{1}{8}x + \frac{1}{2} \\ y \le x + 4 \\ y \le -\frac{3}{4}x + 4 \end{cases}$

**34** $\begin{cases} y < \frac{4}{3}x + 4 \\ y \le -x + 2 \end{cases}$  slope between $(-3, 0)$ and $(0, 4)$ is $\frac{4}{3}$, $y$-intercept is 4
slope between $(2, 0)$ and $(0, 2)$ is $-1$, $y$-intercept is 2

**35** Let $x$ and $y$ denote the number of sets of brand A and brand B, respectively.

"Necessary to stock at least twice as many sets of brand A as of brand B" may be symbolized as $x \ge 2y$.

"Necessary to have on hand at least 10 sets of brand B" may be symbolized as $y \ge 10$.

Consequently, $x \ge 20$ from the first inequality.

"Room for not more than 100 sets in the store" may be symbolized as $x + y \le 100$.

We now sketch the system of inequalities and shade the region that they have in common. The graph is the region bounded by the triangle with vertices $(20, 10)$, $(90, 10)$, and $\left(\frac{200}{3}, \frac{100}{3}\right)$.

*Figure 35*

*Figure 36*

**36** If $x$ and $y$ denote the number of $8.00 and $5.00 seats, respectively, then a system is $x + y \le 600$, $y \ge 225$, $8x + 5y \ge 3000$. The graph is the region bounded by the triangle with vertices $(0, 600)$, $(375, 225)$, $\left(\frac{1875}{8} \{= 234.375\}, 225\right)$.

**37** If $x$ and $y$ denote the amount placed in the high-risk and low-risk investment, respectively, then a system is $x \geq 2000$, $y \geq 3x$, $x + y \leq 15{,}000$. The graph is the region bounded by the triangle with vertices $(2000, 6000)$, $(2000, 13{,}000)$, and $(3750, 11{,}250)$.

*Figure 37*

*Figure 38*

**38** If $x$ and $y$ denote the number of 55¢ and 85¢ notebooks, respectively, then a system is $0.55x + 0.85y \leq 600$, $y \geq 300$, $x \geq 400$. The graph is the region bounded by the triangle with vertices $(400, 300)$, $\left(400, \frac{7600}{17} \{ \approx 447.1\}\right)$, $\left(\frac{6900}{11} \{ \approx 627.3\}, 300\right)$.

**39** A system is $x + y \leq 9$, $y \geq x$, $x \geq 1$. To justify the condition $y \geq x$, start with $\dfrac{\text{cylinder volume}}{\text{total volume}} \geq 0.75 \Rightarrow$

$$\frac{\pi r^2 y}{\pi r^2 y + \frac{1}{3}\pi r^2 x} \geq \frac{3}{4} \Rightarrow 4\pi r^2 y \geq 3\pi r^2 y + \pi r^2 x \Rightarrow \pi r^2 y \geq \pi r^2 x \Rightarrow y \geq x.$$

The graph is the region bounded by the triangle with vertices $(1, 1)$, $(1, 8)$, and $\left(\frac{9}{2}, \frac{9}{2}\right)$.

*Figure 39*

*Figure 40*

**40** If $\ell$ denotes the length of the rectangle (the height of the rectangular portion of the window), then a system is $\frac{1}{2}d + \ell \leq 6$, $\ell \geq \frac{\pi}{4}d$, $d \geq 2$. The figure has $\ell = y$ and $d = x$. To justify the condition $\ell \geq \frac{\pi}{4}d$, start with (area of rectangle) $\geq 2$(area of semicircle) $\Rightarrow d\ell \geq 2\left[\frac{1}{2}\pi\left(\frac{1}{2}d\right)^2\right] \Rightarrow d\ell \geq \frac{\pi}{4}d^2 \Rightarrow \ell \geq \frac{\pi}{4}d$. The graph is the region bounded by the triangle with vertices $(2, 5)$, $\left(2, \frac{\pi}{2}\right)$, and $\left(\dfrac{24}{\pi + 2}, \dfrac{6\pi}{\pi + 2}\right) \approx (4.67, 3.67)$.

**41** If the plant is located at $(x, y)$, then a system is $(60)^2 \leq x^2 + y^2 \leq (100)^2$, $(60)^2 \leq (x - 100)^2 + y^2 \leq (100)^2$, $y \geq 0$. The graph is the region in the first quadrant that lies between the two concentric circles with center $(0, 0)$ and radii 60 and 100, and also between the two concentric circles with center $(100, 0)$ and radii 60 and 100. Equating the different circle equations, we obtain the vertices of the solution region $\left(50, 50\sqrt{3}\right)$, $\left(50, 10\sqrt{11}\right)$, $\left(18, 6\sqrt{91}\right)$, and $\left(82, 6\sqrt{91}\right)$. For example, to determine where the circle $x^2 + y^2 = 100^2$ intersects the circle $(x - 100)^2 + y^2 = 60^2$, we subtract the first equation from the second to obtain $\left[(x - 100)^2 + y^2\right] - (x^2 + y^2) = 60^2 - 100^2 \Rightarrow -200x + 10{,}000 = -6400 \Rightarrow$

$200x = 16,400 \ \Rightarrow \ x = 82.$ Substituting $x = 82$ into $x^2 + y^2 = 100^2$ gives us $y^2 = 100^2 - 82^2 = 3276 \ \Rightarrow$
$y = \pm\sqrt{3276} = \pm 6\sqrt{91} \approx \pm 57.2.$

| Figure 41 | Figure 42 |

**42** If $x$ and $y$ denote the depths of the patio and pool areas, respectively, then a system is $y \geq 10$, $x + y \leq 60$ {sum of depths cannot exceed 60}, $x \geq y$ {patio area $\geq$ pool area}, $2x + 25y \leq 675$ {$4(50x) + 50(50y) \leq 67{,}500$}. The graph is the region bounded by the quadrilateral with vertices $(10, 10)$, $(25, 25)$, $\left(35\frac{20}{23}, 24\frac{3}{23}\right)$, $(50, 10)$.

**43** $64y^3 - x^3 \leq e^{1-2x} \ \Rightarrow \ 64y^3 \leq e^{1-2x} + x^3 \ \Rightarrow \ y^3 \leq \frac{1}{64}(e^{1-2x} + x^3) \ \Rightarrow \ y \leq \frac{1}{4}(e^{1-2x} + x^3)^{1/3}.$
Graph the curve $y = \frac{1}{4}(e^{1-2x} + x^3)^{1/3}$. The solution includes the curve and the region below it.

$[-3.5, 4]$ by $[-1, 4]$          $[-3.5, 4]$ by $[-1, 4]$

| Figure 43 | Figure 44 |

**44** $e^{5y} - e^{-x} \geq x^4 \ \Rightarrow \ e^{5y} \geq x^4 + e^{-x} \ \Rightarrow \ 5y \geq \ln(x^4 + e^{-x}) \ \Rightarrow \ y \geq \frac{1}{5}\ln(x^4 + e^{-x}).$
Graph the curve $y = \frac{1}{5}\ln(x^4 + e^{-x})$. The solution includes the curve and the region above it.

**45** $5^{1-y} \geq x^4 + x^2 + 1 \ \Rightarrow \ 1 - y \geq \log_5(x^4 + x^2 + 1) \ \Rightarrow \ y \leq 1 - \log_5(x^4 + x^2 + 1).$
$x + 3y \geq x^{5/3} \ \Rightarrow \ y \geq \frac{1}{3}(x^{5/3} - x).$ Graph $Y_1 = 1 - \log_5(x^4 + x^2 + 1)$ and $Y_2 = \frac{1}{3}(x^{5/3} - x)$. The curves intersect at approximately $(-1.32, -0.09)$ and $(1.21, 0.05)$. The solution is located between the points of intersection. It includes the curves and the region below the first curve and above the second curve.

$[-1.5, 1.5, 0.5]$ by $[-1, 1, 0.5]$          $[-3, 3]$ by $[-2, 2]$

| Figure 45 | Figure 46 |

**46** $x^4 + y^5 < 2^x \ \Rightarrow \ y < (2^x - x^4)^{1/5}.$ $y^3 > \ln(x^2 + 1) \ \Rightarrow \ y > [\ln(x^2 + 1)]^{1/3}.$ Graph $Y_1 = (2^x - x^4)^{1/5}$ and $Y_2 = [\ln(x^2 + 1)]^{1/3}$. The curves intersect at approximately $(-0.76, 0.77)$ and $(1.10, 0.93)$. The solution does not include the curves. It includes the region located between the points of intersection that is below the first curve and above the second curve.

**47** $x^4 - 2x < 3y \Rightarrow y > \frac{1}{3}(x^4 - 2x)$. $x + 2y < x^3 - 5 \Rightarrow y < \frac{1}{2}(x^3 - x - 5)$. Graph $Y_1 = \frac{1}{3}(x^4 - 2x)$ and $Y_2 = \frac{1}{2}(x^3 - x - 5)$. The curves do not intersect. The solution must be above the first curve and below the second curve. Since the regions do not intersect, there is no solution.

$[-4.5, 4.5]$ by $[-3, 3]$

*Figure 47*

$[0, 9]$ by $[-3, 3]$

*Figure 48*

**48** $e^x + x^2 \leq 2^{x+2y} \Rightarrow \log_2(e^x + x^2) \leq x + 2y \Rightarrow y \geq \frac{1}{2}\left[\log_2(e^x + x^2) - x\right]$. $2^{x+2y} \leq x^3 2^y \Rightarrow x + 2y \leq \log_2(x^3 2^y) \Rightarrow 2y \leq \log_2 x^3 + \log_2 2^y - x \Rightarrow y \leq 3\log_2 x - x$.

Graph $Y_1 = \frac{1}{2}\left[\log_2(e^x + x^2) - x\right]$ and $Y_2 = 3\log_2 x - x$. The curves intersect at approximately $(1.77, 0.70)$ and $(6.72, 1.53)$. The solution is located between the points of intersection. It includes the curves and the region above the first curve and below the second curve.

**49** (a) $29T - 39P < 450 \Rightarrow 29(37) - 39(21.2) < 450 \Rightarrow 246.2 < 450$ (true). Yes, forests can grow.

(b) $29T - 39P < 450 \Rightarrow -39P < -29T + 450 \Rightarrow P > \frac{29}{39}T - \frac{150}{13}$.

Graph $Y_1 = \frac{29}{39}x - \frac{150}{13}$, $Y_3 = 13$, $Y_4 = 45$, and use $\text{Shade}(Y_1, 45, 33, 76)$.

(c) Forests can grow whenever the point $(T, P)$ lies in the shaded region with vertices $(33, 13)$, $(\approx 76, 45)$, and $(33, 45)$.

$[33, 80, 5]$ by $[0, 50, 5]$

*Figure 49*

$[33, 80, 5]$ by $[0, 50, 5]$

*Figure 50*

**50** (a) $22P - 3T > 33 \Rightarrow 22(7.8) - 3(70) > 33 \Rightarrow -38.4 > 33$ (false). No, grasslands will not grow.

(b) $22P - 3T > 33 \Rightarrow 22P > 3T + 33 \Rightarrow P > \frac{3}{22}T + \frac{3}{2}$. Graph $Y_2 = \frac{3}{22}x + \frac{3}{2}$ together with $Y_1$, $Y_3$, and $Y_4$ from the previous exercise, and use $\text{Shade}(13, Y_1, 33, 76)$ and $\text{Shade}(13, 45, 76, 80)$.

(c) Grasslands can grow, but not forests, whenever the point $(T, P)$ lies in the shaded region with vertices $(33, 13)$, $(\approx 76, 45)$, $(80, 45)$, and $(80, 13)$.

## 8.4 Exercises

**1** We substitute the $x$ and $y$ values of each vertex into $C = 3x + 2y + 5$ and summarize the results in the following table. We see that there is a maximum of 27 at $(6, 2)$, and a minimum of 9 at $(0, 2)$. The maximum or minimum value is denoted by a ■.

| $(x,y)$ | $(0,2)$ | $(0,4)$ | $(3,5)$ | $(6,2)$ | $(5,0)$ | $(2,0)$ |
|---|---|---|---|---|---|---|
| $C$ | 9 ■ | 13 | 24 | 27 ■ | 20 | 11 |

**2** $C = 2x + 7y + 3$ •

| $(x,y)$ | $(1,3)$ | $(0,5)$ | $(2,5)$ | $(6,2)$ | $(6,0)$ | $(3,1)$ |
|---|---|---|---|---|---|---|
| $C$ | 26 | 38 | 42 ■ | 29 | 15 ■ | 16 |

There is a maximum of 42 at $(2,5)$, and a minimum of 15 at $(6,0)$.

**3** The vertices of $R$ are found by obtaining the intersection points of the system of equations corresponding to the given inequalities. $C = 3x + y$ •

| $(x,y)$ | $(0,0)$ | $(0,3)$ | $(4,6)$ | $(6,3)$ | $(5,0)$ |
|---|---|---|---|---|---|
| $C$ | 0 | 3 | 18 | 21 ■ | 15 |

There is a maximum of 21 at $(6,3)$.

*Figure 3*

*Figure 4*

**4** $C = 4x - 2y$ •

| $(x,y)$ | $(0,4)$ | $(6,7)$ | $(4,0)$ |
|---|---|---|---|
| $C$ | −8 | 10 | 16 ■ |

There is a maximum of 16 at $(4,0)$.

**5** $C = 3x + 6y$ •

| $(x,y)$ | $(8,0)$ | $(3,2)$ | $(0,4)$ |
|---|---|---|---|
| $C$ | 24 | 21 ■ | 24 |

There is a minimum of 21 at $(3,2)$.

*Figure 5*

*Figure 6*

**6** $C = 2x + 6y$ •

| $(x,y)$ | $(0,9)$ | $(4,5)$ | $(12,0)$ |
|---|---|---|---|
| $C$ | 54 | 38 | 24 ■ |

There is a minimum of 3 at $(0,3)$.

**7** $C = 2x + 4y$ •

| $(x,y)$ | $(0,0)$ | $(0,4)$ | $(2,5)$ | $(6,3)$ | $(8,0)$ |
|---|---|---|---|---|---|
| $C$ | 0 | 16 | 24 ■ | 24 ■ | 16 |

As in Example 2, $C = 2x + 4y$ has the maximum value 24 for *any* point on the line segment from $(2,5)$ to $(6,3)$. To show that the last statement is true, we will substitute $6 - \frac{1}{2}x$ for $y$ in $C$.

$C = 2x + 4y = 2x + 4\left(6 - \frac{1}{2}x\right) = 2x + 24 - 2x = 24.$

Figure 7

Figure 8

**8** $C = 6x + 3y$ •

| $(x, y)$ | $(2, 1)$ | $(2, 5)$ | $(5, 3)$ | $(6, 1)$ |
|---|---|---|---|---|
| $C$ | 15 | 27 | 39 ■ | 39 ■ |

$C = 6x + 3y$ has the maximum value 39 for any point on the line segment from $(6, 1)$ to $(5, 3)$.
On this line segment, $C = 6x + 3y = 6(6.5 - 0.5y) + 3y = 39 - 3y + 3y = 39$.

**9** The slopes for $x + 2y = 16$, $x + y = 9$, and $3x + 2y = 24$ are $-\frac{1}{2}$, $-1$, and $-\frac{3}{2}$, respectively. Note the order of the slopes: $-2 < -\frac{3}{2} < -1 < -\frac{1}{2}$. A slope of $-2$ would give the largest $y$-intercept, $P/350$, when the objective function passes through the vertex $(8, 0)$.

**10** See the solution for Exercise 9. Since $-1 < -\frac{3}{4} < -\frac{1}{2}$, a slope of $-\frac{3}{4}$ would give the largest $y$-intercept, $P/350$, when the objective function passes through the vertex $(2, 7)$.

**11** An objective function with a slope of $-1$ will coincide with the line $x + y = 9$, and all points on the line segment between $(2, 7)$ and $(6, 3)$, inclusive, will give the same maximum profit.

**12** An objective function with a slope of $-\frac{3}{2}$ will coincide with the line $3x + 2y = 24$, and all points on the line segment between $(6, 3)$ and $(8, 0)$, inclusive, will give the same maximum profit.

**13** $P = 500x + by \iff y = (-500/b)x + P/b$. The maximum profit occurs at $(2, 7)$ if the slope of the objective function satisfies the inequality $-1 < -\frac{500}{b} < -\frac{1}{2} \Rightarrow 2b > 1000 > b$ {multiply by $-2b$, $b > 0$} $\Rightarrow 2b > 1000$ and $1000 > b \Rightarrow b > 500$ and $b < 1000$. So any value of $b$ such that $500 < b < 1000$ yields a maximum profit at $(2, 7)$. One example is $P = 500x + 600y$.

**14** See the solution for Exercise 13. Here, $-\frac{500}{b} < -\frac{3}{2} \Rightarrow 1000 > 3b \Rightarrow 0 < b < 333\frac{1}{3}$. So any value of $b$ such that $0 < b < 333\frac{1}{3}$ yields a maximum profit at $(8, 0)$. One example is $P = 500x + 300y$.

**Note:** For the linear programming application exercises, the solution outline is as follows:

(1) Define the variables used in the problem.

(2) Define the function to be maximized or minimized.

(3) List the system of inequalities that determine the solution region $R$.

(4) A table of intersection points and values of the function in step 2 at those points is given. The maximum or minimum value is denoted by a ■.

(5) A summarizing statement is given.

(6) A figure is shown for the system of inequalities.

**15** Let $x$ and $y$ denote the number of oversized and standard rackets, respectively. Profit function: $P = 15x + 8y$

$$\begin{cases} 30 \leq y \leq 80 \\ 10 \leq x \leq 30 \\ x + y \leq 80 \end{cases}$$

| $(x, y)$ | $(10, 30)$ | $(30, 30)$ | $(30, 50)$ | $(10, 70)$ |
|----------|-----------|-----------|-----------|-----------|
| $P$ | 390 | 690 | 850 ∎ | 710 |

The maximum profit of $850 per day occurs when 30 oversized rackets and 50 standard rackets are manufactured.

*Figure 15*

*Figure 16*

**16** Let $x$ and $y$ denote the number of deluxe and standard model cell phones, respectively.

Profit function: $P = 25x + 30y$

$$\begin{cases} x + y \leq 200 \\ x \geq 80 \\ y \geq 100 \end{cases}$$

| $(x, y)$ | $(80, 100)$ | $(100, 100)$ | $(80, 120)$ |
|----------|------------|-------------|------------|
| $P$ | 5000 | 5500 | 5600 ∎ |

The maximum profit of $5,600 per day occurs when 80 deluxe models and 120 standard models are produced.

**17** Let $x$ and $y$ denote the number of pounds of S and T, respectively. Cost function: $C = 3x + 4y$

$$\begin{cases} 2x + 2y \geq 9 & \textit{amount of } I \\ 4x + 6y \geq 20 & \textit{amount of } G \\ x \geq 0, y \geq 0 \end{cases}$$

| $(x, y)$ | $(0, 4.5)$ | $(3.5, 1)$ | $(5, 0)$ |
|----------|-----------|-----------|----------|
| $C$ | 18 | 14.5 ∎ | 15 |

The minimum cost of $14.50 occurs when 3.5 pounds of S and 1 pound of T are used.

*Figure 17*

*Figure 18*

**18** Let $x$ and $y$ denote the number of deluxe and regular notebooks, respectively.

Difference function: $D = 0.80x + 0.40y$

$$\begin{cases} 2000 \leq x \leq 3000 \\ 3000 \leq y \leq 6000 \\ x + y \leq 7000 \end{cases}$$

| $(x, y)$ | $(2000, 3000)$ | $(3000, 3000)$ | $(3000, 4000)$ | $(2000, 5000)$ |
|----------|---------------|---------------|---------------|---------------|
| $D$ | 2800 | 3600 | 4000 ∎ | 3600 |

The maximum difference of $4000 occurs when 3000 deluxe notebooks and 4000 regular notebooks are produced.

**19** Let $x$ and $y$ denote the number of units sent to A and B, respectively, from $W_1$.

Cost function: $C = 12x + 10(35 - x) + 16y + 12(60 - y) = 2x + 4y + 1070$

The points are the same as those in Example 4.

$$\begin{cases} 0 \le x \le 35 \\ 0 \le y \le 60 \\ x + y \le 80 \\ x + y \ge 25 \end{cases}$$

| $(x, y)$ | $(0, 25)$ | $(0, 60)$ | $(20, 60)$ | $(25, 0)$ | $(35, 45)$ | $(35, 0)$ |
|---|---|---|---|---|---|---|
| $C$ | 1170 | 1310 | 1350 | 1320 | 1140 | 1120 ■ |

To minimize the shipping costs, send 25 units from $W_1$ to A and 0 from $W_1$ to B.

Send 10 {35 − 25} units from $W_2$ to A and 60 {60 − 0} units from $W_2$ to B.

Figure 19

Figure 20

**20** Let $x$ and $y$ denote the number of tons purchased from supplier A and B, respectively.

Cost function: $C = 900x + 1200y$

$$\begin{cases} 0.20x + 0.40y \ge 280 & \textit{premium grade} \\ 0.50x + 0.20y \ge 200 & \textit{regular grade} \\ x \ge 0, y \ge 0 \end{cases} \Rightarrow \begin{cases} x + 2y \ge 1400 \\ 5x + 2y \ge 2000 \\ x \ge 0, y \ge 0 \end{cases}$$

| $(x, y)$ | $(0, 1000)$ | $(150, 625)$ | $(1400, 0)$ |
|---|---|---|---|
| $C$ | 1,200,000 | 885,000 ■ | 1,260,000 |

The minimum cost of $885,000 occurs when 150 tons are purchased from supplier A and 625 tons are purchased from supplier B.

**21** Let $x$ and $y$ denote the number of acres planted with alfalfa and corn, respectively.

Profit function: $P = 500x - 32x - 60x + 700y - 48y - 30y = 408x + 622y$

$$\begin{cases} 32x + 48y \le 3840 & \textit{seed cost} \\ 60x + 30y \le 4200 & \textit{labor cost} \\ x + y \le 90 & \textit{area} \\ x, y \ge 0 \end{cases} \Rightarrow \begin{cases} 2x + 3y \le 240 & \textit{seed cost} \\ 2x + y \le 140 & \textit{labor cost} \\ x + y \le 90 & \textit{area} \\ x, y \ge 0 \end{cases}$$

| $(x, y)$ | $(70, 0)$ | $(50, 40)$ | $(30, 60)$ | $(0, 80)$ | $(0, 0)$ |
|---|---|---|---|---|---|
| $P$ | 28,560 | 45,280 | 49,560 | 49,760 ■ | 0 |

The maximum profit of $49,760 occurs when 0 acres of alfalfa are planted and 80 acres of corn are planted.

Figure 21

Figure 22

**22** Let $x$ and $y$ denote the number of bookshelves and desks manufactured, respectively.

Profit function: $P = 20x + 50y$

$$\begin{cases} 1x + 2y \leq 12 & \text{router use} \\ \frac{1}{2}x + 2y \leq 8 & \text{saw use} \\ x, y \geq 0 \end{cases}$$

| $(x, y)$ | $(12, 0)$ | $(8, 2)$ | $(0, 4)$ | $(0, 0)$ |
|---|---|---|---|---|
| $P$ | 240 | 260 ■ | 200 | 0 |

The maximum profit of \$260 occurs when 8 bookshelves and 2 desks are manufactured daily. See Figure.

**23** Let $x$, $y$, and $z$ denote the number of ounces of X, Y, and Z, respectively.

Cost function: $C = 0.25x + 0.35y + 0.50z = 0.25x + 0.35y + 0.50(20 - x - y) = 10 - 0.25x - 0.15y$

$$\begin{cases} 0.20x + 0.20y + 0.10z \geq 0.14(20) & \text{amount of A} \\ 0.10x + 0.40y + 0.20z \geq 0.16(20) & \text{amount of B} \\ 0.25x + 0.15y + 0.25z \geq 0.20(20) & \text{amount of C} \end{cases} \Rightarrow \begin{cases} x + y \geq 8 \\ x - 2y \leq 8 \\ y \leq 10 \\ x + y \leq 20 \\ 0 \leq x, y \leq 20 \end{cases}$$

The new restrictions are found by substituting $z = 20 - x - y$ into the 3 inequalities, simplifying, and adding the last 2 inequalities.

| $(x, y)$ | $(8, 0)$ | $(16, 4)$ | $(10, 10)$ | $(0, 10)$ | $(0, 8)$ |
|---|---|---|---|---|---|
| $C$ | 8.00 | 5.40 ■ | 6.00 | 8.50 | 8.80 ■ |

The minimum cost of \$5.40 requires 16 oz of X, 4 oz of Y, and 0 oz of Z.

The maximum cost of \$8.80 requires 0 oz of X, 8 oz of Y, and 12 oz of Z.

*Figure 23*

*Figure 24*

**24** Let $x$ and $y$ denote the number of bags of peanuts and candy, respectively.

Profit function: $P = (3.00 - 2.00)x + (5.50 - 4.00)y = x + 1.5y$

$$\begin{cases} 2x + 4y \leq 2000 & \text{purchase} \\ x + y \leq 700 & \text{sell} \\ 0 \leq x \leq 500 \\ 0 \leq y \leq 400 \end{cases} \Rightarrow \begin{cases} x + 2y \leq 1000 \\ x + y \leq 700 \\ 0 \leq x \leq 500 \\ 0 \leq y \leq 400 \end{cases}$$

| $(x, y)$ | $(500, 0)$ | $(500, 200)$ | $(400, 300)$ | $(200, 400)$ | $(0, 400)$ | $(0, 0)$ |
|---|---|---|---|---|---|---|
| $P$ | 500 | 800 | 850 ■ | 800 | 600 | 0 |

The maximum profit of \$850 occurs when he sells 400 bags of peanuts and 300 bags of candy.

**25** Let $x$ and $y$ denote the number of vans and buses purchased, respectively.

Passenger capacity function: $P = 15x + 25y$

$$\begin{cases} 10,000x + 20,000y \leq 100,000 & \text{purchase} \\ 100x + 75y \leq 500 & \text{maintenance} \\ x \geq 0, \ y \geq 0 \end{cases} \Rightarrow \begin{cases} x + 2y \leq 10 \\ 4x + 3y \leq 20 \\ x \geq 0, y \geq 0 \end{cases}$$

| $(x,y)$ | $(5,0)$ | $(2,4)$ | $(0,5)$ | $(0,0)$ |
|---|---|---|---|---|
| $P$ | 75 | 103 ■ | 125 | 0 |

The maximum passenger capacity of 130 would occur if the community purchases 2 vans and 4 buses.

Figure 25

Figure 26

**26** Let $x$ and $y$ denote the number of vans and buses purchased, respectively.

Cost function: $C = 550x + 850y$

$$\begin{cases} 10{,}000x + 20{,}000y \le 100{,}000 \quad purchase \\ 100x + 75y \le 500 \qquad\qquad maintenance \\ 15x + 25y \ge 75 \qquad\qquad passengers \\ x, y \ge 0 \end{cases} \Rightarrow \begin{cases} x + 2y \le 10 \\ 4x + 3y \le 20 \\ 3x + 5y \ge 15 \\ x, y \ge 0 \end{cases}$$

| $(x,y)$ | $(5,0)$ | $(2,4)$ | $(0,5)$ | $(0,3)$ |
|---|---|---|---|---|
| $P$ | 2750 | 4500 | 4250 | 2550 ■ |

The minimum cost of \$2550 per month would occur if the community purchases 3 buses and no vans.

**27** Let $x$ and $y$ denote the number of trout and bass, respectively. Pound function: $P = 3x + 4y$

$$\begin{cases} x + y \le 5000 \quad number\ of\ fish \\ 0.50x + 0.75y \le 3000 \quad cost \\ x \ge 0, y \ge 0 \end{cases} \Rightarrow \begin{cases} x + y \le 5000 \\ 2x + 3y \le 12{,}000 \\ x \ge 0, y \ge 0 \end{cases}$$

| $(x,y)$ | $(5000,0)$ | $(3000,2000)$ | $(0,4000)$ | $(0,0)$ |
|---|---|---|---|---|
| $P$ | 15,000 | 17,000 ■ | 16,000 | 0 |

The total number of pounds of fish will be a maximum of 17,000 if 3000 trout and 2000 bass are purchased.

Figure 27

Figure 28

**28** Let $x$ and $y$ denote the number of ounces of corn and squash, respectively.

$$\begin{cases} \frac{1}{2}x + \frac{1}{4}y \ge 3 \quad protein \\ 4x + 3y \le 36 \quad cost \\ x \ge 2 \qquad\quad corn \\ y \ge x \qquad\quad ratio \end{cases} \Rightarrow \begin{cases} 2x + y \ge 12 \\ 4x + 3y \le 36 \\ x \ge 2 \\ y \ge x \end{cases}$$

| $(x,y)$ | $(4,4)$ | $\left(\frac{36}{7}, \frac{36}{7}\right)$ | $\left(2, \frac{28}{3}\right)$ | $(2,8)$ |
|---|---|---|---|---|
| $W$ | 8 ■ | $10\frac{2}{7}$ | $11\frac{1}{3}$ | 10 |

The weight is a minimum of 8 ounces when 4 ounces of each are used.

**29** Let $x$ and $y$ denote the number of basic and deluxe units constructed, respectively.

Revenue function: $R = 75x + 120y$

$$\begin{cases} 800x + 1600y \le 80,000 & cost \\ x \ge 2y & ratio \\ 80x + 120y \le 7200 & area \\ x, y \ge 0 \end{cases} \Rightarrow \begin{cases} x + 2y \le 100 \\ y \le \frac{1}{2}x \\ 2x + 3y \le 180 \\ x, y \ge 0 \end{cases}$$

| $(x, y)$ | $(90, 0)$ | $(60, 20)$ | $(50, 25)$ | $(0, 0)$ |
|---|---|---|---|---|
| $W$ | 6750 | 6900 ■ | 6750 | 0 |

The maximum monthly revenue of \$6900 occurs if 60 basic units and 20 deluxe units are constructed.

**Figure 29**

**Figure 30**

**30** Let $x$ and $y$ denote the number of kg of tree leaves and aquatic plants, respectively. Energy function: $E = 4x + y$

$$\begin{cases} x + y \le 33 \\ y \ge 17 \\ x \ge 0 \end{cases}$$

| $(x, y)$ | $(0, 17)$ | $(0, 33)$ | $(16, 17)$ |
|---|---|---|---|
| $E$ | 17 | 33 | 81 ■ |

The maximum daily energy intake of 81 units occurs if the moose eats 16 kg of tree leaves and 17 kg of aquatic plants.

## 8.5 Exercises

**Note:** Some equations are interchanged to obtain the matrix in the first step. Most systems are solved using the back substitution method. The solution for Exercise 7 uses the reduced echelon method. To avoid fractions, some solutions include linear combinations of rows—that is, $mR_i + nR_j$.

**1**
$$\begin{bmatrix} 1 & -2 & -3 & | & -1 \\ 2 & 1 & 1 & | & 6 \\ 1 & 3 & -2 & | & 13 \end{bmatrix} \begin{matrix} \\ R_2 - 2R_1 \to R_2 \\ R_3 - R_1 \to R_3 \end{matrix} \begin{bmatrix} 1 & -2 & -3 & | & -1 \\ 0 & 5 & 7 & | & 8 \\ 0 & 5 & 1 & | & 14 \end{bmatrix} \begin{matrix} \\ \\ R_3 - R_2 \to R_3 \end{matrix} \begin{bmatrix} 1 & -2 & -3 & | & -1 \\ 0 & 5 & 7 & | & 8 \\ 0 & 0 & -6 & | & 6 \end{bmatrix}$$

$R_3: -6z = 6 \Rightarrow z = -1$

$R_2: 5y + 7z = 8 \Rightarrow 5y + 7(-1) = 8 \Rightarrow 5y = 15 \Rightarrow y = 3$      ★ $(2, 3, -1)$

$R_1: x - 2y - 3z = -1 \Rightarrow x - 2(3) - 3(-1) = -1 \Rightarrow x = 2$

**2**
$$\begin{bmatrix} 1 & 3 & -1 & | & -3 \\ 3 & -1 & 2 & | & 1 \\ 2 & -1 & 1 & | & -1 \end{bmatrix} \begin{matrix} \\ R_2 - 3R_1 \to R_2 \\ R_3 - 2R_1 \to R_3 \end{matrix} \begin{bmatrix} 1 & 3 & -1 & | & -3 \\ 0 & -10 & 5 & | & 10 \\ 0 & -7 & 3 & | & 5 \end{bmatrix} \begin{matrix} \\ 2R_2 - 3R_3 \to R_2 \\ \\ \end{matrix}$$

$$\begin{bmatrix} 1 & 3 & -1 & | & -3 \\ 0 & 1 & 1 & | & 5 \\ 0 & -7 & 3 & | & 5 \end{bmatrix} \begin{matrix} \\ \\ R_3 + 7R_2 \to R_3 \end{matrix} \begin{bmatrix} 1 & 3 & -1 & | & -3 \\ 0 & 1 & 1 & | & 5 \\ 0 & 0 & 10 & | & 40 \end{bmatrix} \begin{matrix} \\ \\ \frac{1}{10}R_3 \to R_3 \end{matrix} \begin{bmatrix} 1 & 3 & -1 & | & -3 \\ 0 & 1 & 1 & | & 5 \\ 0 & 0 & 1 & | & 4 \end{bmatrix}$$

$R_3: z = 4$

$R_2: y + z = 5 \Rightarrow y = 1$      ★ $(-2, 1, 4)$

$R_1: x + 3y - z = -3 \Rightarrow x = -2$

**3**
$$\begin{bmatrix} 1 & -2 & 2 & | & 0 \\ 5 & 2 & -1 & | & -7 \\ 0 & 3 & 1 & | & 17 \end{bmatrix} \quad R_2 - 5R_1 \to R_2 \quad \begin{bmatrix} 1 & -2 & 2 & | & 0 \\ 0 & 12 & -11 & | & -7 \\ 0 & 3 & 1 & | & 17 \end{bmatrix} \quad 4R_3 - R_2 \to R_3 \quad \begin{bmatrix} 1 & -2 & 2 & | & 0 \\ 0 & 12 & -11 & | & -7 \\ 0 & 0 & 15 & | & 75 \end{bmatrix}$$

$R_3: 15z = 75 \Rightarrow z = 5$

$R_2: 12y - 11z = -7 \Rightarrow 12y - 11(5) = -7 \Rightarrow 12y = 48 \Rightarrow y = 4$ ★ $(-2, 4, 5)$

$R_1: x - 2y + 2z = 0 \Rightarrow x - 2(4) + 2(5) = 0 \Rightarrow x = -2$

**4**
$$\begin{bmatrix} 4 & -1 & 3 & | & 6 \\ -8 & 3 & -5 & | & -6 \\ 5 & -4 & 0 & | & -9 \end{bmatrix} \quad R_3 - R_1 \to R_3 \quad \begin{bmatrix} 4 & -1 & 3 & | & 6 \\ -8 & 3 & -5 & | & -6 \\ 1 & -3 & -3 & | & -15 \end{bmatrix} \quad \begin{matrix} R_1 - 4R_3 \to R_1 \\ R_2 + 8R_3 \to R_2 \end{matrix}$$

$$\begin{bmatrix} 0 & 11 & 15 & | & 66 \\ 0 & -21 & -29 & | & -126 \\ 1 & -3 & -3 & | & -15 \end{bmatrix} \quad R_2 + 2R_1 \to R_2 \quad \begin{bmatrix} 0 & 11 & 15 & | & 66 \\ 0 & 1 & 1 & | & 6 \\ 1 & -3 & -3 & | & -15 \end{bmatrix} \quad R_1 - 11R_2 \to R_1$$

$$\begin{bmatrix} 0 & 0 & 4 & | & 0 \\ 0 & 1 & 1 & | & 6 \\ 1 & -3 & -3 & | & -15 \end{bmatrix} \quad \tfrac{1}{4}R_1 \to R_1 \quad \begin{bmatrix} 0 & 0 & 1 & | & 0 \\ 0 & 1 & 1 & | & 6 \\ 1 & -3 & -3 & | & -15 \end{bmatrix}$$

$R_1: z = 0$

$R_2: y + z = 6 \Rightarrow y = 6$ ★ $(3, 6, 0)$

$R_3: x - 3y - 3z = -15 \Rightarrow x = 3$

**5**
$$\begin{bmatrix} 2 & 6 & -4 & | & 1 \\ 1 & 3 & -2 & | & 4 \\ 2 & 1 & -3 & | & -7 \end{bmatrix} \quad R_1 \leftrightarrow R_2 \quad \begin{bmatrix} 1 & 3 & -2 & | & 4 \\ 2 & 6 & -4 & | & 1 \\ 2 & 1 & -3 & | & -7 \end{bmatrix} \quad \begin{matrix} R_2 - 2R_1 \to R_2 \\ R_3 - 2R_1 \to R_3 \end{matrix} \quad \begin{bmatrix} 1 & 3 & -2 & | & 4 \\ 0 & 0 & 0 & | & -7 \\ 0 & -5 & 1 & | & -15 \end{bmatrix}$$

The second row, $0x + 0y + 0z = -7$, has *no solution*.

**6**
$$\begin{bmatrix} 1 & 3 & -3 & | & -5 \\ 2 & -1 & 1 & | & -3 \\ -6 & 3 & -3 & | & 4 \end{bmatrix} \quad \begin{matrix} R_2 - 2R_1 \to R_2 \\ R_3 + 6R_1 \to R_3 \end{matrix} \quad \begin{bmatrix} 1 & 3 & -3 & | & -5 \\ 0 & -7 & 7 & | & 7 \\ 0 & 21 & -21 & | & -26 \end{bmatrix} \quad -\tfrac{1}{7}R_2 \to R_2$$

$$\begin{bmatrix} 1 & 3 & -3 & | & -5 \\ 0 & 1 & -1 & | & -1 \\ 0 & 21 & -21 & | & -26 \end{bmatrix} \quad R_3 - 21R_2 \to R_3 \quad \begin{bmatrix} 1 & 3 & -3 & | & -5 \\ 0 & 1 & -1 & | & -1 \\ 0 & 0 & 0 & | & -5 \end{bmatrix}$$

The third row, $0x + 0y + 0z = -5$, has *no solution*.

**7**
$$\begin{bmatrix} 2 & -3 & 2 & | & -3 \\ -3 & 2 & 1 & | & 1 \\ 4 & 1 & -3 & | & 4 \end{bmatrix} \quad R_1 \leftrightarrow R_2 \text{ and then } R_2 \leftrightarrow R_3 \quad \begin{bmatrix} -3 & 2 & 1 & | & 1 \\ 4 & 1 & -3 & | & 4 \\ 2 & -3 & 2 & | & -3 \end{bmatrix} \quad R_1 + R_2 \to R_1$$

$$\begin{bmatrix} 1 & 3 & -2 & | & 5 \\ 4 & 1 & -3 & | & 4 \\ 2 & -3 & 2 & | & -3 \end{bmatrix} \quad \begin{matrix} R_2 - 4R_1 \to R_2 \\ R_3 - 2R_1 \to R_3 \end{matrix} \quad \begin{bmatrix} 1 & 3 & -2 & | & 5 \\ 0 & -11 & 5 & | & -16 \\ 0 & -9 & 6 & | & -13 \end{bmatrix} \quad 4R_2 - 5R_3 \to R_2 \,(*)$$

$$\begin{bmatrix} 1 & 3 & -2 & | & 5 \\ 0 & 1 & -10 & | & 1 \\ 0 & -9 & 6 & | & -13 \end{bmatrix} \quad R_3 + 9R_2 \to R_3 \quad \begin{bmatrix} 1 & 3 & -2 & | & 5 \\ 0 & 1 & -10 & | & 1 \\ 0 & 0 & -84 & | & -4 \end{bmatrix}$$

$R_3: -84z = -4 \Rightarrow z = \tfrac{1}{21}$

$R_2: y - 10z = 1 \Rightarrow y = \tfrac{31}{21}$

$R_1: x + 3y - 2z = 5 \Rightarrow x = \tfrac{14}{21} = \tfrac{2}{3}$

★ $\left(\tfrac{2}{3}, \tfrac{31}{21}, \tfrac{1}{21}\right)$

(*) We could have just used $-\tfrac{1}{11}R_2 \to R_2$, but we would then have to work with many fractions and increase our chance of making a mistake. We will solve this system again, but this time we will obtain the reduced echelon form. The first 4 matrices are exactly the same. Starting with the fourth matrix we have:

$$\begin{bmatrix} 1 & 3 & -2 & | & 5 \\ 0 & 1 & -10 & | & 1 \\ 0 & -9 & 6 & | & -13 \end{bmatrix} \quad \begin{matrix} R_1 - 3R_2 \to R_1 \\ R_3 + 9R_2 \to R_3 \end{matrix} \quad \begin{bmatrix} 1 & 0 & 28 & | & 2 \\ 0 & 1 & -10 & | & 1 \\ 0 & 0 & -84 & | & -4 \end{bmatrix} \quad -\tfrac{1}{84}R_3 \to R_3$$

$$\begin{bmatrix} 1 & 0 & 28 & | & 2 \\ 0 & 1 & -10 & | & 1 \\ 0 & 0 & 1 & | & \tfrac{1}{21} \end{bmatrix} \quad \begin{matrix} R_1 - 28R_3 \to R_1 \\ R_2 + 10R_3 \to R_2 \end{matrix} \quad \begin{bmatrix} 1 & 0 & 0 & | & \tfrac{14}{21} \\ 0 & 1 & 0 & | & \tfrac{31}{21} \\ 0 & 0 & 1 & | & \tfrac{1}{21} \end{bmatrix} \qquad R_1: x = \tfrac{14}{21} = \tfrac{2}{3}; \; R_2: y = \tfrac{31}{21}; \; R_3: z = \tfrac{1}{21}$$

**8**
$$\begin{bmatrix} 2 & -3 & 1 & | & 2 \\ 3 & 2 & -1 & | & -5 \\ 5 & -2 & 1 & | & 0 \end{bmatrix} \quad -R_1 + R_2 \to R_1 \quad \begin{bmatrix} 1 & 5 & -2 & | & -7 \\ 3 & 2 & -1 & | & -5 \\ 5 & -2 & 1 & | & 0 \end{bmatrix} \begin{array}{l} R_2 - 3R_1 \to R_2 \\ R_3 - 5R_1 \to R_3 \end{array}$$

$$\begin{bmatrix} 1 & 5 & -2 & | & -7 \\ 0 & -13 & 5 & | & 16 \\ 0 & -27 & 11 & | & 35 \end{bmatrix} \quad 2R_2 - R_3 \to R_2 \quad \begin{bmatrix} 1 & 5 & -2 & | & -7 \\ 0 & 1 & -1 & | & -3 \\ 0 & -27 & 11 & | & 35 \end{bmatrix} \quad R_3 + 27R_2 \to R_3$$

$$\begin{bmatrix} 1 & 5 & -2 & | & -7 \\ 0 & 1 & -1 & | & -3 \\ 0 & 0 & -16 & | & -46 \end{bmatrix} \quad \begin{array}{l} R_3: z = \frac{23}{8} \\ R_2: y - z = -3 \;\Rightarrow\; y = -\frac{1}{8} \\ R_1: x + 5y - 2z = -7 \;\Rightarrow\; x = -\frac{5}{8} \end{array} \quad -\tfrac{1}{16}R_3 \to R_3 \qquad \bigstar \left(-\tfrac{5}{8}, -\tfrac{1}{8}, \tfrac{23}{8}\right)$$

**9**
$$\begin{bmatrix} 1 & 3 & -1 & | & 0 \\ -1 & -2 & 1 & | & 0 \\ -2 & 1 & 3 & | & 0 \end{bmatrix} \begin{array}{l} R_2 + R_1 \to R_2 \\ R_3 + 2R_1 \to R_3 \end{array} \begin{bmatrix} 1 & 3 & -1 & | & 0 \\ 0 & 1 & 0 & | & 0 \\ 0 & 7 & 1 & | & 0 \end{bmatrix} \quad R_3 - 7R_2 \to R_3 \quad \begin{bmatrix} 1 & 3 & -1 & | & 0 \\ 0 & 1 & 0 & | & 0 \\ 0 & 0 & 1 & | & 0 \end{bmatrix}$$

$R_3: z = 0$
$R_2: y = 0$
$R_1: x + 3y - z = 0 \;\Rightarrow\; x = 0$ ★ $(0, 0, 0)$

**10**
$$\begin{bmatrix} 1 & -1 & -2 & | & 0 \\ 2 & -1 & 1 & | & 0 \\ 2 & -3 & -1 & | & 0 \end{bmatrix} \begin{array}{l} R_2 - 2R_1 \to R_2 \\ R_3 - 2R_1 \to R_3 \end{array} \begin{bmatrix} 1 & -1 & -2 & | & 0 \\ 0 & 1 & 5 & | & 0 \\ 0 & -1 & 3 & | & 0 \end{bmatrix} \quad R_3 + R_2 \to R_3 \quad \begin{bmatrix} 1 & -1 & -2 & | & 0 \\ 0 & 1 & 5 & | & 0 \\ 0 & 0 & 8 & | & 0 \end{bmatrix}$$

$$\tfrac{1}{8}R_3 \to R_3 \quad \begin{bmatrix} 1 & -1 & -2 & | & 0 \\ 0 & 1 & 5 & | & 0 \\ 0 & 0 & 1 & | & 0 \end{bmatrix} \begin{array}{l} R_3: z = 0 \\ R_2: y + 5z = 0 \;\Rightarrow\; y = 0 \\ R_1: x - y - 2z = 0 \;\Rightarrow\; x = 0 \end{array} \qquad \bigstar (0, 0, 0)$$

**Note:** In Exercises 11–18, there are other forms for the answers; $c$ is any real number.

**11**
$$\begin{bmatrix} 1 & 3 & 1 & | & 0 \\ 1 & 1 & -1 & | & 0 \\ 1 & -2 & -4 & | & 0 \end{bmatrix} \begin{array}{l} R_2 - R_1 \to R_2 \\ R_3 - R_1 \to R_3 \end{array} \begin{bmatrix} 1 & 3 & 1 & | & 0 \\ 0 & -2 & -2 & | & 0 \\ 0 & -5 & -5 & | & 0 \end{bmatrix} \begin{array}{l} -\tfrac{1}{2}R_2 \to R_2 \\ \\ -\tfrac{1}{5}R_3 \to R_3 \end{array} \begin{bmatrix} 1 & 3 & 1 & | & 0 \\ 0 & 1 & 1 & | & 0 \\ 0 & 1 & 1 & | & 0 \end{bmatrix} \begin{array}{l} R_1 - 3R_2 \to R_1 \\ \\ R_3 - R_2 \to R_3 \end{array}$$

$$\begin{bmatrix} 1 & 0 & -2 & | & 0 \\ 0 & 1 & 1 & | & 0 \\ 0 & 0 & 0 & | & 0 \end{bmatrix} \begin{array}{l} R_1: x - 2z = 0 \;\Rightarrow\; x = 2z \\ R_2: y + z = 0 \;\Rightarrow\; y = -z \end{array} \qquad \bigstar (2c, -c, c)$$

**12**
$$\begin{bmatrix} 1 & 1 & -2 & | & 0 \\ 1 & -1 & -4 & | & 0 \\ 0 & 1 & 1 & | & 0 \end{bmatrix} \quad R_2 - R_1 \to R_2 \quad \begin{bmatrix} 1 & 1 & -2 & | & 0 \\ 0 & -2 & -2 & | & 0 \\ 0 & 1 & 1 & | & 0 \end{bmatrix} \quad -\tfrac{1}{2}R_2 \to R_2 \quad \begin{bmatrix} 1 & 1 & -2 & | & 0 \\ 0 & 1 & 1 & | & 0 \\ 0 & 1 & 1 & | & 0 \end{bmatrix} \begin{array}{l} R_1 - R_2 \to R_1 \\ \\ R_3 - R_2 \to R_3 \end{array}$$

$$\begin{bmatrix} 1 & 0 & -3 & | & 0 \\ 0 & 1 & 1 & | & 0 \\ 0 & 0 & 0 & | & 0 \end{bmatrix} \begin{array}{l} R_1: x - 3z = 0 \;\Rightarrow\; x = 3z \\ R_2: y + z = 0 \;\Rightarrow\; y = -z \end{array} \qquad \bigstar (3c, -c, c)$$

**13**
$$\begin{bmatrix} 2 & 1 & 1 & | & 0 \\ 1 & -2 & -2 & | & 0 \\ 1 & 1 & 1 & | & 0 \end{bmatrix} \quad R_1 \leftrightarrow R_2 \quad \begin{bmatrix} 1 & -2 & -2 & | & 0 \\ 2 & 1 & 1 & | & 0 \\ 1 & 1 & 1 & | & 0 \end{bmatrix} \begin{array}{l} R_2 - 2R_1 \to R_2 \\ R_3 - R_1 \to R_3 \end{array} \begin{bmatrix} 1 & -2 & -2 & | & 0 \\ 0 & 5 & 5 & | & 0 \\ 0 & 3 & 3 & | & 0 \end{bmatrix} \begin{array}{l} \tfrac{1}{5}R_2 \to R_2 \\ \\ \tfrac{1}{3}R_3 \to R_3 \end{array}$$

$$\begin{bmatrix} 1 & -2 & -2 & | & 0 \\ 0 & 1 & 1 & | & 0 \\ 0 & 1 & 1 & | & 0 \end{bmatrix} \begin{array}{l} R_1 + 2R_2 \to R_1 \\ \\ R_3 - R_2 \to R_3 \end{array} \begin{bmatrix} 1 & 0 & 0 & | & 0 \\ 0 & 1 & 1 & | & 0 \\ 0 & 0 & 0 & | & 0 \end{bmatrix} \begin{array}{l} R_1: x = 0 \\ R_2: y + z = 0 \;\Rightarrow\; y = -z \end{array} \qquad \bigstar (0, -c, c)$$

**14**
$$\begin{bmatrix} 1 & 2 & -2 & | & 4 \\ -1 & -3 & 2 & | & -6 \\ 2 & 1 & -4 & | & 2 \end{bmatrix} \begin{array}{l} R_2 + R_1 \to R_2 \\ R_3 - 2R_1 \to R_3 \end{array} \begin{bmatrix} 1 & 2 & -2 & | & 4 \\ 0 & -1 & 0 & | & -2 \\ 0 & -3 & 0 & | & -6 \end{bmatrix} \begin{array}{l} -R_2 \to R_2 \\ \\ -\tfrac{1}{3}R_3 \to R_3 \end{array} \begin{bmatrix} 1 & 2 & -2 & | & 4 \\ 0 & 1 & 0 & | & 2 \\ 0 & 1 & 0 & | & 2 \end{bmatrix}$$

$R_2: y = 2$
$R_1: x + 2y - 2z = 4 \;\Rightarrow\; x + 2(2) - 2z = 4 \;\Rightarrow\; x = 2z$ ★ $(2c, 2, c)$

**15** $\begin{bmatrix} 1 & 4 & -1 & | & -2 \\ 3 & 13 & 5 & | & 7 \end{bmatrix}$   $R_2 - 3R_1 \rightarrow R_2$   $\begin{bmatrix} 1 & 4 & -1 & | & -2 \\ 0 & 1 & 8 & | & 13 \end{bmatrix}$

$R_2 : y + 8z = 13 \Rightarrow y = -8z + 13$
$R_1 : x + 4y - z = -2 \Rightarrow x = -4(-8z + 13) + z - 2 = 33z - 54$   $\bigstar (33c - 54, -8c + 13, c)$

**16** $\begin{bmatrix} 2 & -1 & 4 & | & 8 \\ -3 & 1 & -2 & | & 5 \end{bmatrix}$   $-R_1 - R_2 \rightarrow R_1$   $\begin{bmatrix} 1 & 0 & -2 & | & -13 \\ -3 & 1 & -2 & | & 5 \end{bmatrix}$   $R_2 + 3R_1 \rightarrow R_2$   $\begin{bmatrix} 1 & 0 & -2 & | & -13 \\ 0 & 1 & -8 & | & -34 \end{bmatrix}$

$R_2 : y - 8z = -34 \Rightarrow y = 8z - 34$
$R_1 : x - 2z = -13 \Rightarrow x = 2z - 13$   $\bigstar (2c - 13, 8c - 34, c)$

**17** $\begin{bmatrix} 4 & -2 & 1 & | & 5 \\ 3 & 1 & -4 & | & 0 \end{bmatrix}$   $R_1 - R_2 \rightarrow R_1$   $\begin{bmatrix} 1 & -3 & 5 & | & 5 \\ 3 & 1 & -4 & | & 0 \end{bmatrix}$   $R_2 - 3R_1 \rightarrow R_2$   $\begin{bmatrix} 1 & -3 & 5 & | & 5 \\ 0 & 10 & -19 & | & -15 \end{bmatrix}$

$R_2 : 10y - 19z = -15 \Rightarrow y = \frac{19}{10}z - \frac{3}{2}$
$R_1 : x - 3y + 5z = 5 \Rightarrow x = 3\left(\frac{19}{10}z - \frac{3}{2}\right) - 5z + 5 = \frac{7}{10}z + \frac{1}{2}$   $\bigstar \left(\frac{7}{10}c + \frac{1}{2}, \frac{19}{10}c - \frac{3}{2}, c\right)$

**18** $\begin{bmatrix} 5 & 2 & -1 & | & 10 \\ 0 & 1 & 1 & | & -3 \end{bmatrix}$   $R_2 : y + z = -3 \Rightarrow y = -z - 3$
$R_1 : 5x + 2y - z = 10 \Rightarrow x = -\frac{2}{5}(-z - 3) + \frac{1}{5}z + 2 = \frac{3}{5}z + \frac{16}{5}$

$\bigstar \left(\frac{3}{5}c + \frac{16}{5}, -c - 3, c\right)$

**19** $\begin{bmatrix} 5 & 0 & 2 & | & 1 \\ 0 & 1 & -3 & | & 2 \\ 2 & 1 & 0 & | & 3 \end{bmatrix}$   $R_1 - 2R_3 \rightarrow R_1$   $\begin{bmatrix} 1 & -2 & 2 & | & -5 \\ 0 & 1 & -3 & | & 2 \\ 2 & 1 & 0 & | & 3 \end{bmatrix}$   $R_3 - 2R_1 \rightarrow R_3$

$\begin{bmatrix} 1 & -2 & 2 & | & -5 \\ 0 & 1 & -3 & | & 2 \\ 0 & 5 & -4 & | & 13 \end{bmatrix}$   $R_3 - 5R_2 \rightarrow R_3$   $\begin{bmatrix} 1 & -2 & 2 & | & -5 \\ 0 & 1 & -3 & | & 2 \\ 0 & 0 & 11 & | & 3 \end{bmatrix}$   $R_3 : 11z = 3 \Rightarrow z = \frac{3}{11}$
$R_2 : y - 3z = 2 \Rightarrow y = \frac{31}{11}$
$R_1 : x - 2y + 2z = -5 \Rightarrow x = \frac{1}{11}$

$\bigstar \left(\frac{1}{11}, \frac{31}{11}, \frac{3}{11}\right)$

**20** $\begin{bmatrix} 2 & -3 & 0 & | & 12 \\ 0 & 3 & 1 & | & -2 \\ 5 & 0 & -3 & | & 3 \end{bmatrix}$   $3R_1 - R_3 \rightarrow R_1$   $\begin{bmatrix} 1 & -9 & 3 & | & 33 \\ 0 & 3 & 1 & | & -2 \\ 5 & 0 & -3 & | & 3 \end{bmatrix}$   $R_3 - 5R_1 \rightarrow R_3$   $\begin{bmatrix} 1 & -9 & 3 & | & 33 \\ 0 & 3 & 1 & | & -2 \\ 0 & 45 & -18 & | & -162 \end{bmatrix}$

$\frac{1}{9}R_3 \rightarrow R_3$   $\begin{bmatrix} 1 & -9 & 3 & | & 33 \\ 0 & 3 & 1 & | & -2 \\ 0 & 5 & -2 & | & -18 \end{bmatrix}$   $2R_2 - R_3 \rightarrow R_2$   $\begin{bmatrix} 1 & -9 & 3 & | & 33 \\ 0 & 1 & 4 & | & 14 \\ 0 & 5 & -2 & | & -18 \end{bmatrix}$   $R_1 + 9R_2 \rightarrow R_1$   $R_3 - 5R_2 \rightarrow R_3$

$\begin{bmatrix} 1 & 0 & 39 & | & 159 \\ 0 & 1 & 4 & | & 14 \\ 0 & 0 & -22 & | & -88 \end{bmatrix}$   $-\frac{1}{22}R_3 \rightarrow R_3$   $\begin{bmatrix} 1 & 0 & 39 & | & 159 \\ 0 & 1 & 4 & | & 14 \\ 0 & 0 & 1 & | & 4 \end{bmatrix}$   $R_1 - 39R_3 \rightarrow R_1$   $R_2 - 4R_3 \rightarrow R_2$   $\begin{bmatrix} 1 & 0 & 0 & | & 3 \\ 0 & 1 & 0 & | & -2 \\ 0 & 0 & 1 & | & 4 \end{bmatrix}$   $\bigstar (3, -2, 4)$

**21** $\begin{bmatrix} 4 & -3 & | & 1 \\ 2 & 1 & | & -7 \\ -1 & 1 & | & -1 \end{bmatrix}$   $R_1 + 3R_3 \rightarrow R_1$   $\begin{bmatrix} 1 & 0 & | & -2 \\ 2 & 1 & | & -7 \\ -1 & 1 & | & -1 \end{bmatrix}$   $R_2 - 2R_1 \rightarrow R_2$   $R_3 + R_1 \rightarrow R_3$   $\begin{bmatrix} 1 & 0 & | & -2 \\ 0 & 1 & | & -3 \\ 0 & 1 & | & -3 \end{bmatrix}$   $R_3 - R_2 \rightarrow R_3$

$\begin{bmatrix} 1 & 0 & | & -2 \\ 0 & 1 & | & -3 \\ 0 & 0 & | & 0 \end{bmatrix}$   $R_1 : x = -2$
$R_2 : y = -3$   $\bigstar (-2, -3)$

**22** $\begin{bmatrix} 1 & 1 & | & 1 \\ 2 & 3 & | & -2 \\ 1 & -2 & | & 13 \end{bmatrix}$   $R_2 - 2R_1 \rightarrow R_2$   $R_3 - R_1 \rightarrow R_3$   $\begin{bmatrix} 1 & 1 & | & 1 \\ 0 & 1 & | & -4 \\ 0 & -3 & | & 12 \end{bmatrix}$   $R_1 - R_2 \rightarrow R_1$   $R_3 + 3R_2 \rightarrow R_3$   $\begin{bmatrix} 1 & 0 & | & 5 \\ 0 & 1 & | & -4 \\ 0 & 0 & | & 0 \end{bmatrix}$

$R_2 : y = -4 ; R_1 : x = 5$   $\bigstar (5, -4)$

**23**
$$\begin{bmatrix} 2 & 3 & | & 5 \\ 1 & -3 & | & 4 \\ 1 & 1 & | & -2 \end{bmatrix} \quad R_1 \leftrightarrow R_2 \quad \begin{bmatrix} 1 & -3 & | & 4 \\ 2 & 3 & | & 5 \\ 1 & 1 & | & -2 \end{bmatrix} \quad \begin{array}{c} R_2 - 2R_1 \to R_2 \\ R_3 - R_1 \to R_3 \end{array} \quad \begin{bmatrix} 1 & -3 & | & 4 \\ 0 & 9 & | & -3 \\ 0 & 4 & | & -6 \end{bmatrix} \quad R_2 - 2R_3 \to R_2$$

$$\begin{bmatrix} 1 & -3 & | & 4 \\ 0 & 1 & | & 9 \\ 0 & 4 & | & -6 \end{bmatrix} \quad \begin{array}{c} R_1 + 3R_2 \to R_1 \\ R_3 - 4R_2 \to R_3 \end{array} \quad \begin{bmatrix} 1 & 0 & | & 31 \\ 0 & 1 & | & 9 \\ 0 & 0 & | & -42 \end{bmatrix}$$ There is a contradiction in row 3, therefore there is *no solution*.

**24**
$$\begin{bmatrix} 4 & -1 & | & 2 \\ 2 & 2 & | & 1 \\ 4 & -5 & | & 3 \end{bmatrix} \quad \begin{array}{c} 2R_2 - R_1 \to R_2 \\ R_3 - R_1 \to R_3 \end{array} \quad \begin{bmatrix} 4 & -1 & | & 2 \\ 0 & 5 & | & 0 \\ 0 & -4 & | & 1 \end{bmatrix}$$

$$R_2 \Rightarrow \quad y = 0 \text{ and } R_3 \Rightarrow \quad y = -\tfrac{1}{4}, \text{ a contradiction, there is } no \ solution.$$

**25** Let $x$, $y$, and $z$ denote the number of liters of the 10% acid, 30% acid, and 50% acid.

$$\begin{cases} x + \quad y + \quad z = 50 & \text{quantity} \quad (E_1) \\ 0.10x + 0.30y + 0.50z = (0.32)(50) & \text{quality} \quad (E_2) \\ \qquad\qquad\qquad z = 2y & \text{constraint} \quad (E_3) \end{cases}$$

Substitute $z = 2y$ into $E_1$ and $100E_2$ to obtain $\begin{cases} x + \quad 3y = \quad 50 \quad (E_4) \\ 10x + 130y = 1600 \quad (E_5) \end{cases}$

$$E_5 - 10E_4 \quad \Rightarrow \quad 100y = 1100 \quad \Rightarrow \quad y = 11; \ x = 17; \ z = 22$$

**26** Let $z$ denote the number of hours it takes for pipe C to fill the pool alone. By adding the hourly rates, that is, how much of the pool each pipe fills in one hour, we have $\dfrac{1}{8} + \dfrac{1}{z} = \dfrac{1}{6} \quad \Rightarrow \quad \dfrac{1}{z} = \dfrac{4}{24} - \dfrac{3}{24} \quad \Rightarrow \quad z = 24$. Let $y$ denote the number of hours it takes for pipe B to fill the pool alone. Then $\dfrac{1}{y} + \dfrac{1}{24} = \dfrac{1}{10} \quad \Rightarrow \quad \dfrac{1}{y} = \dfrac{12}{120} - \dfrac{5}{120} \quad \Rightarrow \quad y = \dfrac{120}{7}$. Let $x$ denote the number of hours it takes for all three pipes to fill the pool. Then

$$\frac{1}{8} + \frac{7}{120} + \frac{1}{24} = \frac{1}{x} \quad \Rightarrow \quad \frac{1}{x} = \frac{15}{120} + \frac{7}{120} + \frac{5}{120} \quad \Rightarrow \quad x = \frac{120}{27} = \frac{40}{9}.$$

**27** Let $x$, $y$, and $z$ denote the number of hours needed for A, B, and C, respectively, to produce 1000 items. In one hour, A, B, and C produce $\dfrac{1000}{x}$, $\dfrac{1000}{y}$, and $\dfrac{1000}{z}$ items, respectively. In 6 hours, A and B produce $\dfrac{6000}{x}$ and $\dfrac{6000}{y}$ items. From the table, this sum must equal 4500. The system of equations is then:

$$\begin{cases} \dfrac{6000}{x}x + \dfrac{6000}{y} \qquad\qquad = 4500 \\[2mm] \dfrac{8000}{x} \qquad\qquad + \dfrac{8000}{z} = 3600 \\[2mm] \qquad\qquad \dfrac{7000}{y} + \dfrac{7000}{z} = 4900 \end{cases}$$

To simplify, let $a = \dfrac{1}{x}$, $b = \dfrac{1}{y}$, $c = \dfrac{1}{z}$ and divide each equation by its greatest common factor $\{1500, 400, \text{ and } 700\}$.

$$\begin{cases} 4a + 4b \qquad = 3 \quad (E_1) \\ 20a + \qquad 20c = 9 \quad (E_2) \\ \qquad 10b + 10c = 7 \quad (E_3) \end{cases} \quad E_2 - 5E_1 \quad \Rightarrow \quad 20c - 20b = -6 \quad (E_4)$$

$$E_4 + 2E_3 \quad \Rightarrow \quad 40c = 8 \quad \Rightarrow \quad c = \tfrac{1}{5}; \ b = \tfrac{1}{2}; \ a = \tfrac{1}{4}. \text{ Resubstituting, } x = 4, \ y = 2, \text{ and } z = 5.$$

**28**
$$\begin{cases} \dfrac{1}{A} + \dfrac{1}{B} = \dfrac{1}{48} \\ \dfrac{1}{B} + \dfrac{1}{C} = \dfrac{1}{80} \\ \dfrac{1}{A} + \dfrac{1}{C} = \dfrac{1}{60} \end{cases} \Rightarrow \begin{cases} 48x + 48y = 1 \quad (E_1) \\ 80y + 80z = 1 \quad (E_2) \\ 60x + 60z = 1 \quad (E_3) \end{cases} \text{ where } x = \dfrac{1}{A}, y = \dfrac{1}{B}, \text{ and } z = \dfrac{1}{C}.$$

$5E_1 - 4E_3 \Rightarrow 240y - 240z = 1$ (E$_4$) and $E_4 + 3E_2 \Rightarrow 480y = 4 \Rightarrow y = \dfrac{1}{120}; z = \dfrac{1}{240}; x = \dfrac{1}{80}.$

Resubstituting, A = 80, B = 120, and C = 240.

**29** Let $x$, $y$, and $z$ denote the amounts of G$_1$, G$_2$, and G$_3$, respectively.
$$\begin{cases} x + y + z = 600 & \textit{quantity} & (E_1) \\ 0.30x + 0.20y + 0.15z = (0.25)(600) & \textit{quality} & (E_2) \\ z = 100 + y & \textit{constraint} & (E_3) \end{cases}$$

Substitute $z = 100 + y$ into E$_1$ and 100E$_2$ to obtain $\begin{cases} x + 2y = 500 & (E_4) \\ 30x + 35y = 13,500 & (E_5) \end{cases}$

$E_5 - 30E_4 \Rightarrow -25y = -1500 \Rightarrow y = 60; z = 160; x = 380.$

**30** $s\left(\dfrac{1}{2}\right) = 7 \Rightarrow 7 = \dfrac{1}{8}a + \dfrac{1}{2}v_0 + s_0$ (E$_1$)

$\quad s(1) = 11 \Rightarrow 11 = \dfrac{1}{2}a + v_0 + s_0$ (E$_2$)

$\quad s\left(\dfrac{3}{2}\right) = 17 \Rightarrow 17 = \dfrac{9}{8}a + \dfrac{3}{2}v_0 + s_0$ (E$_3$)

Solving E$_2$ for $s_0$ and substituting into E$_1$ and E$_3$ yields $\begin{cases} -4 = -\dfrac{3}{8}a - \dfrac{1}{2}v_0 & (E_4) \\ 6 = \dfrac{5}{8}a + \dfrac{1}{2}v_0 & (E_5) \end{cases}$

$E_4 + E_5 \Rightarrow 2 = \dfrac{1}{4}a \Rightarrow a = 8; v_0 = 2; s_0 = 5.$

**31** (a) Let $R_1 = R_2 = R_3 = 3$ in the given system of equations.
$$\begin{cases} I_1 - I_2 + I_3 = 0 \\ 3I_1 + 3I_2 = 6 \\ 3I_2 + 3I_3 = 12 \end{cases} \Rightarrow \begin{cases} I_1 - I_2 + I_3 = 0 & (E_1) \\ I_1 + I_2 = 2 & (E_2) \\ I_2 + I_3 = 4 & (E_3) \end{cases}$$

Substitute $I_1 = I_2 - I_3$ from E$_1$ into E$_2$ to obtain $2I_2 - I_3 = 2$ (E$_4$).

Now $E_4 + E_3 \Rightarrow 3I_2 = 6 \Rightarrow I_2 = 2; I_3 = 2; I_1 = 0.$

(b) Let $R_1 = 4$, $R_2 = 1$, and $R_3 = 4$ in the given system of equations.
$$\begin{cases} I_1 - I_2 + I_3 = 0 & (E_1) \\ 4I_1 + 1I_2 = 6 & (E_2) \\ 1I_2 + 4I_3 = 12 & (E_3) \end{cases}$$

Substitute $I_1 = I_2 - I_3$ from E$_1$ into E$_2$ to obtain $4(I_2 - I_3) + I_2 = 6 \Rightarrow$

$5I_2 - 4I_3 = 6$ (E$_4$). Now $E_4 + E_3 \Rightarrow 6I_2 = 18 \Rightarrow I_2 = 3; I_3 = \dfrac{9}{4}; I_1 = \dfrac{3}{4}.$

**32** Let $x$, $y$, and $z$ denote the number of birds on island A, B, and C, respectively.
$$\begin{cases} x + y + z = 35,000 & \textit{quantity} & (E_1) \\ x - 0.10x + 0.05z = x & \textit{island A} & (E_2) \\ y - 0.20y + 0.10x = y & \textit{island B} & (E_3) \\ z - 0.05z + 0.20y = z & \textit{island C} & (E_4) \end{cases}$$

Solve E$_2$ for $z$ $\{z = 2x\}$, E$_3$ for $y$ $\{y = \dfrac{1}{2}x\}$, and substitute both expressions into E$_1$ to obtain

$x + \dfrac{1}{2}x + 2x = 35,000 \Rightarrow \dfrac{7}{2}x = 35,000 \Rightarrow x = 10,000; y = 5000; z = 20,000.$

**33** Let $x$, $y$, and $z$ denote the amount of Colombian, Costa Rican, and Kenyan coffee used, respectively.

$$\begin{cases} x + y + z = 1 & \text{quantity} \quad (\text{E}_1) \\ 14x + 10y + 12z = (12.50)(1) & \text{quality} \quad (\text{E}_2) \\ x = 3y & \text{constraint} \quad (\text{E}_3) \end{cases}$$

Substitute $x = 3y$ into $\text{E}_1$ and $\text{E}_2$ to obtain $\begin{cases} 4y + z = 1 & (\text{E}_4) \\ 52y + 12z = 12.50 & (\text{E}_5) \end{cases}$

$$\text{E}_5 - 12\text{E}_4 \Rightarrow 4y = \tfrac{1}{2} \Rightarrow y = \tfrac{1}{8}; z = \tfrac{1}{2}; x = \tfrac{3}{8}.$$

**34** Let $x$, $y$, and $z$ denote the weight of the small, medium, and large links, respectively.

$$\begin{cases} 10x + 20y + 30z = 450 & 450\text{-}ounce\ chain \quad (\text{E}_1) \\ 10x + 30y + 40z = 610 & 610\text{-}ounce\ chain \quad (\text{E}_2) \\ 10x + 40y + 70z = 950 & 950\text{-}ounce\ chain \quad (\text{E}_3) \end{cases}$$

Divide each equation by 10 and write the system in matrix form.

$$\begin{bmatrix} 1 & 2 & 3 & | & 45 \\ 1 & 3 & 4 & | & 61 \\ 1 & 4 & 7 & | & 95 \end{bmatrix} \begin{matrix} \\ R_2 - R_1 \to R_2 \\ R_3 - R_1 \to R_3 \end{matrix} \begin{bmatrix} 1 & 2 & 3 & | & 45 \\ 0 & 1 & 1 & | & 16 \\ 0 & 2 & 4 & | & 50 \end{bmatrix} \begin{matrix} R_1 - 2R_2 \to R_1 \\ \\ R_3 - 2R_2 \to R_3 \end{matrix} \begin{bmatrix} 1 & 0 & 1 & | & 13 \\ 0 & 1 & 1 & | & 16 \\ 0 & 0 & 2 & | & 18 \end{bmatrix} \tfrac{1}{2}R_3 \to R_3$$

$$\begin{bmatrix} 1 & 0 & 1 & | & 13 \\ 0 & 1 & 1 & | & 16 \\ 0 & 0 & 1 & | & 9 \end{bmatrix} \begin{matrix} R_1 - R_3 \to R_1 \\ R_2 - R_3 \to R_2 \end{matrix} \begin{bmatrix} 1 & 0 & 0 & | & 4 \\ 0 & 1 & 0 & | & 7 \\ 0 & 0 & 1 & | & 9 \end{bmatrix}$$

The weights of the small, medium, and large links, are 4, 7, & 9 ounces, respectively.

**35** (a) A: $x_1 + x_4 = 50 + 25 = 75$, B: $x_1 + x_2 = 100 + 50 = 150$, C: $x_2 + x_3 = 150 + 75 = 225$,

D: $x_3 + x_4 = 100 + 50 = 150$

(b) From C, $x_3 = 100 \Rightarrow x_2 = 225 - 100 = 125$. From D, $x_3 = 100 \Rightarrow x_4 = 150 - 100 = 50$.

From A, $x_4 = 50 \Rightarrow x_1 = 75 - 50 = 25$.

(c) From D in part (a), $x_3 = 150 - x_4 \Rightarrow x_3 \le 150$ **(1)** since $x_4 \ge 0$.

From C, $x_3 = 225 - x_2 = 225 - (150 - x_1)$ {from B} $= 75 + x_1 \Rightarrow x_3 \ge 75$ **(2)** since $x_1 \ge 0$.

From **(1)** and **(2)**, we get $75 \le x_3 \le 150$.

**36** $f(x) = ax^3 + bx + c$ • $\begin{cases} f(-3) = -12 \\ f(-1) = 22 \\ f(2) = 13 \end{cases} \Rightarrow \begin{cases} -27a - 3b + c = -12 & (\text{E}_1) \\ -a - b + c = 22 & (\text{E}_2) \\ 8a + 2b + c = 13 & (\text{E}_3) \end{cases}$

Solving $\text{E}_2$ for $c$ and substituting into $\text{E}_1$ and $\text{E}_3$ yields $\begin{cases} -13a - b = -17 & (\text{E}_4) \\ 3a + b = -3 & (\text{E}_5) \end{cases}$

$$\text{E}_4 + \text{E}_5 \Rightarrow -10a = -20 \Rightarrow a = 2; b = -9; c = 15.$$

**37** $t = 2070 - 1990 = 80$. $rt = (0.025)(80) = 2$ and $A = 800$ for $\text{E}_1$, $(0.015)(80) = 1.2$ and $A = 560$ for $\text{E}_2$, and $(0.01)(0) = 0$ and $A = 340$ for $\text{E}_3$. Substituting into $A = a + ct + ke^{rt}$ and summarizing as a system, we have:

$$\begin{cases} a + 80c + ke^2 = 800 & (\text{E}_1) \\ a + 80c + ke^{1.2} = 560 & (\text{E}_2) \\ a + k = 340 & (\text{E}_3) \end{cases}$$

We want to find $t$ when $A$ has doubled—that is, $A = 2(340)$. First we find $c$ and $k$.

$\text{E}_1 - \text{E}_2 \Rightarrow e^2 k - e^{1.2} k = 240 \Rightarrow k = \dfrac{240}{e^2 - e^{1.2}} \approx 58.98$. Substituting into $\text{E}_3$ gives

$a = 340 - k \approx 281.02$. Substituting into $\text{E}_1$ gives $c = \dfrac{800 - a - e^2 k}{80} \approx \dfrac{800 - 281.02 - (58.98)e^2}{80} \approx 1.04$.

Thus, $A = 281.02 + 1.04t + 58.98e^{rt}$. If $A = 680$ and $r = 0.01$, then $680 = 281.02 + 1.04t + 58.98e^{0.01t} \Rightarrow$

$1.04t + 58.98e^{0.01t} - 398.98 = 0$. Graphing $y = 1.04t + 58.98e^{0.01t} - 398.98$,

we see there is an $x$-intercept at $x \approx 144.08$. $1990 + 144.08 = 2134.08$, or during the year 2134.

$[0, 1050, 100]$ by $[-350, 350, 100]$        $[0, 1050, 100]$ by $[-350, 350, 100]$

**Figure 37**        **Figure 38**

**38** $A = a + ct + ke^{rt}$ • $\begin{cases} t = 40, r = 0.020, A = 455 \\ t = 40, r = 0.015, A = 430 \\ t = 0, A = 340 \end{cases} \Rightarrow \begin{cases} a + 40c + ke^{0.8} = 455 & (E_1) \\ a + 40c + ke^{0.6} = 430 & (E_2) \\ a \phantom{ + 40c} + k \phantom{e^{0.6}} = 340 & (E_3) \end{cases}$

$E_1 - E_2 \Rightarrow e^{0.8}k - e^{0.6}k = 25 \Rightarrow k = \dfrac{25}{e^{0.8} - e^{0.6}} \approx 61.97$. Substituting into $E_3$ gives

$a = 340 - k \approx 278.03$. Substituting into $E_1$ gives $c = \dfrac{455 - a - ke^{0.8}}{40} \approx \dfrac{455 - 278.03 - (61.97)e^{0.8}}{40} \approx 0.98$.

Thus, $A = 278.03 + 0.98t + 61.97e^{rt}$. If $A = 680$ and $r = 0.025$, then $680 = 278.03 + 0.98t + 61.97e^{rt} \Rightarrow$

$0.98t + 61.97e^{0.025t} - 401.97 = 0$. Graphing $y = 0.98t + 61.97e^{0.025t} - 401.97$,

we see there is an $x$-intercept at $x \approx 67.59$. $1990 + 67.59 = 2057.59$, or during the year 2057.

**39** The parabola has an equation of the form $y = ax^2 + bx + c$. Substituting the $x$- and $y$-values of $P(-1, 9)$, $Q(1, 7)$,

and $R(2, 15)$ into this equation yields $\begin{cases} a - b + c = 9 & P & (E_1) \\ a + b + c = 7 & Q & (E_2) \\ 4a + 2b + c = 15 & R & (E_3) \end{cases}$

Solving $E_1$ for $c$ $\{c = 9 - a + b\}$ and substituting into $E_2$ and $E_3$ yields

$\begin{cases} 2b = -2 & (E_4) \\ 3a + 3b = 6 & (E_5) \end{cases} \Rightarrow \begin{cases} b = -1 & (E_6) \\ a + b = 2 & (E_7) \end{cases}$   $E_7 - E_6 \Rightarrow a = 3; b = -1; c = 5$.

The equation is $y = 3x^2 - x + 5$.

**40** The parabola has an equation of the form $y = ax^2 + bx + c$. Substituting the $x$- and $y$-values of $P(-1, -12)$,

$Q(1, -6)$, and $R(2, -9)$ into this equation yields $\begin{cases} a - b + c = -12 & P & (E_1) \\ a + b + c = -6 & Q & (E_2) \\ 4a + 2b + c = -9 & R & (E_3) \end{cases}$

Solving $E_1$ for $c$ $\{c = -12 - a + b\}$ and substituting into $E_2$ and $E_3$ yields

$\begin{cases} 2b = 6 & (E_4) \\ 3a + 3b = 3 & (E_5) \end{cases} \Rightarrow \begin{cases} b = 3 & (E_6) \\ a + b = 1 & (E_7) \end{cases}$   $E_7 - E_6 \Rightarrow a = -2; b = 3; c = -7$.

The equation is $y = -2x^2 + 3x - 7$.

**41** The circle has an equation of the form $x^2 + y^2 + ax + by + c = 0$. Substituting the $x$- and $y$-values of $P(2, 1)$,

$Q(-1, -4)$, and $R(3, 0)$ into this equation yields $\begin{cases} 2a + b + c = -5 & P & (E_1) \\ -a - 4b + c = -17 & Q & (E_2) \\ 3a \phantom{ + b} + c = -9 & R & (E_3) \end{cases}$

Solving $E_3$ for $c$ $\{c = -9 - 3a\}$ and substituting into $E_1$ and $E_2$ yields

$\begin{cases} -a + b = 4 & (E_4) \\ -4a - 4b = -8 & (E_5) \end{cases} \Rightarrow \begin{cases} -a + b = 4 & (E_6) \\ a + b = 2 & (E_7) \end{cases}$   $E_6 + E_7 \Rightarrow 2b = 6 \Rightarrow b = 3; a = -1; c = -6$.

The equation is $x^2 + y^2 - x + 3y - 6 = 0$.

**42** The circle has an equation of the form $x^2 + y^2 + ax + by + c = 0$. Substituting the $x$- and $y$-values of $P(-5, 5)$, $Q(-2, -4)$, and $R(2, 4)$ into this equation yields 
$$\begin{cases} -5a + 5b + c = -50 & P \quad (E_1) \\ -2a - 4b + c = -20 & Q \quad (E_2) \\ 2a + 4b + c = -20 & R \quad (E_3) \end{cases}$$

Solving $E_2$ for $c$ $\{c = 2a + 4b - 20\}$ and substituting into $E_1$ and $E_3$ yields
$$\begin{cases} -3a + 9b = -30 & (E_4) \\ 4a + 8b = \phantom{-}0 & (E_5) \end{cases} \Rightarrow \begin{cases} -a + 3b = -10 & (E_6) \\ a + 2b = \phantom{-}0 & (E_7) \end{cases}$$

$E_6 + E_7 \Rightarrow 5b = -10 \Rightarrow b = -2; a = 4; c = -20$. The equation is $x^2 + y^2 + 4x - 2y - 20 = 0$.

**43** Using $y = f(x) = ax^3 + bx^2 + cx + d$ and the point $P(0, -6)$, we should recognize that $d = -6$ since substituting 0 for $x$ leaves only the constant term. Now use the points $Q(1, -11)$, $R(-1, -5)$, and $S(2, -14)$ to obtain the system
$$\begin{cases} a + b + c - 6 = -11 & Q \quad (E_1) \\ -a + b - c - 6 = \phantom{-}-5 & R \quad (E_2) \\ 8a + 4b - 2c - 6 = -14 & S \quad (E_3) \end{cases}$$

Add 6 to each equation and divide the resulting third equation by 2 to obtain

$\begin{bmatrix} 1 & 1 & 1 & -5 \\ -1 & 1 & -1 & 1 \\ 4 & 2 & 1 & -4 \end{bmatrix}$ $\begin{matrix} \\ R_2 + R_1 \to R_2 \\ R_3 - 4R_1 \to R_3 \end{matrix}$ $\begin{bmatrix} 1 & 1 & 1 & -5 \\ 0 & 2 & 0 & -4 \\ 0 & -2 & -3 & 16 \end{bmatrix}$ $\frac{1}{2}R_2 \to R_2$ $\begin{bmatrix} 1 & 1 & 1 & -5 \\ 0 & 1 & 0 & -2 \\ 0 & -2 & -3 & 16 \end{bmatrix}$

$\begin{matrix} R_1 - R_2 \to R_1 \\ \\ R_3 + 2R_2 \to R_3 \end{matrix}$ $\begin{bmatrix} 1 & 0 & 1 & -3 \\ 0 & 1 & 0 & -2 \\ 0 & 0 & -3 & 12 \end{bmatrix}$ $-\frac{1}{3}R_3 \to R_3$ $\begin{bmatrix} 1 & 0 & 1 & -3 \\ 0 & 1 & 0 & -2 \\ 0 & 0 & 1 & -4 \end{bmatrix}$ $R_1 - R_3 \to R_1$ $\begin{bmatrix} 1 & 0 & 0 & 1 \\ 0 & 1 & 0 & -2 \\ 0 & 0 & 1 & -4 \end{bmatrix}$

Thus, $a = 1$, $b = -2$, and $c = -4$, so $f(x) = x^3 - 2x^2 - 4x - 6$.

**44** Using $y = f(x) = ax^3 + bx^2 + cx + d$ and the point $P(0, 4)$, we should recognize that $d = 4$ since substituting 0 for $x$ leaves only the constant term. Now use the points $Q(1, 2)$, $R(-1, 10)$, and $S(2, -2)$ to obtain the system
$$\begin{cases} a + b + c + 4 = \phantom{-}2 & Q \quad (E_1) \\ -a + b - c + 4 = 10 & R \quad (E_2) \\ 8a + 4b + 2c + 4 = -2 & S \quad (E_3) \end{cases}$$

Solving the system yields $a = -1$, $b = 2$, and $c = -3$, so $f(x) = -x^3 + 2x^2 - 3x + 4$.

**45** For $y = f(x) = ax^3 + bx^2 + cx + d$ and the points $(-1, 2)$, $(0.5, 2)$, $(1, 3)$, and $(2, 4.5)$, we obtain the system
$$\begin{cases} -a + b - c + d = 2 & (-1, 2) \\ 0.125a + 0.25b + 0.5c + d = 2 & (0.5, 2) \\ a + b + c + d = 3 & (1, 3) \\ 8a + 4b + 2c + d = 4.5 & (2, 4.5) \end{cases}$$

Solving the system yields $a = -\frac{4}{9}$, $b = \frac{11}{9}$, $c = \frac{17}{18}$, and $d = \frac{23}{18}$.

**46** For $y = f(x) = ax^4 + bx^3 + cx^2 + dx + e$ and the points $(-2, 1.5)$, $(-1, -2)$, $(1, -3)$, $(2, -3.5)$, and $(3, -4.8)$, we obtain the system 
$$\begin{cases} 16a - 8b + 4c - 2d + e = \phantom{-}1.5 & (-2, 1.5) \\ a - b + c - d + e = \phantom{-}-2 & (-1, -2) \\ a + b + c + d + e = \phantom{-}-3 & (1, -3) \\ 16a + 8b + 4c + 2d + e = -3.5 & (2, -3.5) \\ 81a + 27b + 9c + 3d + e = -4.8 & (3, -4.8) \end{cases}$$

Solving the system yields $a = 0.03$, $b = -0.25$, $c = 0.35$, $d = -0.25$, and $e = -2.88$.

## 8.6 Exercises

**Note:** For Exercises 1–8, $A + B$ and $A - B$ are possible only if $A$ and $B$ have the same number of rows and columns. {The calculations in Exercises 7 and 8 are not possible.} However, $2A$ and $-3B$ are always possible by simply multiplying the elements of $A$ and $B$ by 2 and $-3$, respectively.

**1** $A + B = \begin{bmatrix} 5 & -2 \\ 1 & 3 \end{bmatrix} + \begin{bmatrix} 4 & 1 \\ -3 & 2 \end{bmatrix} = \begin{bmatrix} 5+4 & -2+1 \\ 1+(-3) & 3+2 \end{bmatrix} = \begin{bmatrix} 9 & -1 \\ -2 & 5 \end{bmatrix}$

$A - B = \begin{bmatrix} 5 & -2 \\ 1 & 3 \end{bmatrix} - \begin{bmatrix} 4 & 1 \\ -3 & 2 \end{bmatrix} = \begin{bmatrix} 5-4 & -2-1 \\ 1-(-3) & 3-2 \end{bmatrix} = \begin{bmatrix} 1 & -3 \\ 4 & 1 \end{bmatrix}$

$2A = 2 \begin{bmatrix} 5 & -2 \\ 1 & 3 \end{bmatrix} = \begin{bmatrix} 2(5) & 2(-2) \\ 2(1) & 2(3) \end{bmatrix} = \begin{bmatrix} 10 & -4 \\ 2 & 6 \end{bmatrix}$

$-3B = -3 \begin{bmatrix} 4 & 1 \\ -3 & 2 \end{bmatrix} = \begin{bmatrix} -3(4) & -3(1) \\ -3(-3) & -3(2) \end{bmatrix} = \begin{bmatrix} -12 & -3 \\ 9 & -6 \end{bmatrix}$

**2** $A + B = \begin{bmatrix} 3 & 0 \\ -1 & 2 \end{bmatrix} + \begin{bmatrix} 3 & -4 \\ 1 & 1 \end{bmatrix} = \begin{bmatrix} 6 & -4 \\ 0 & 3 \end{bmatrix}$, $A - B = \begin{bmatrix} 0 & 4 \\ -2 & 1 \end{bmatrix}$, $2A = \begin{bmatrix} 6 & 0 \\ -2 & 4 \end{bmatrix}$, $-3B = \begin{bmatrix} -9 & 12 \\ -3 & -3 \end{bmatrix}$

**3** $A + B = \begin{bmatrix} 6 & -1 \\ 2 & 0 \\ -3 & 4 \end{bmatrix} + \begin{bmatrix} 3 & 1 \\ -1 & 5 \\ 6 & 0 \end{bmatrix} = \begin{bmatrix} 6+3 & -1+1 \\ 2+(-1) & 0+5 \\ -3+6 & 4+0 \end{bmatrix} = \begin{bmatrix} 9 & 0 \\ 1 & 5 \\ 3 & 4 \end{bmatrix}$

$A - B = \begin{bmatrix} 6 & -1 \\ 2 & 0 \\ -3 & 4 \end{bmatrix} - \begin{bmatrix} 3 & 1 \\ -1 & 5 \\ 6 & 0 \end{bmatrix} = \begin{bmatrix} 6-3 & -1-1 \\ 2-(-1) & 0-5 \\ -3-6 & 4-0 \end{bmatrix} = \begin{bmatrix} 3 & -2 \\ 3 & -5 \\ -9 & 4 \end{bmatrix}$

$2A = 2 \begin{bmatrix} 6 & -1 \\ 2 & 0 \\ -3 & 4 \end{bmatrix} = \begin{bmatrix} 2(6) & 2(-1) \\ 2(2) & 2(0) \\ 2(-3) & 2(4) \end{bmatrix} = \begin{bmatrix} 12 & -2 \\ 4 & 0 \\ -6 & 8 \end{bmatrix}$

$-3B = -3 \begin{bmatrix} 3 & 1 \\ -1 & 5 \\ 6 & 0 \end{bmatrix} = \begin{bmatrix} -3(3) & -3(1) \\ -3(-1) & -3(5) \\ -3(6) & -3(0) \end{bmatrix} = \begin{bmatrix} -9 & -3 \\ 3 & -15 \\ -18 & 0 \end{bmatrix}$

**4** $A + B = \begin{bmatrix} 0 & -2 & 7 \\ 5 & 4 & -3 \end{bmatrix} + \begin{bmatrix} 8 & 4 & 0 \\ 0 & 1 & 4 \end{bmatrix} = \begin{bmatrix} 8 & 2 & 7 \\ 5 & 5 & 1 \end{bmatrix}$, $A - B = \begin{bmatrix} -8 & -6 & 7 \\ 5 & 3 & -7 \end{bmatrix}$,

$2A = \begin{bmatrix} 0 & -4 & 14 \\ 10 & 8 & -6 \end{bmatrix}$, $-3B = \begin{bmatrix} -24 & -12 & 0 \\ 0 & -3 & -12 \end{bmatrix}$

**5** $A + B = \begin{bmatrix} 4 & -3 & 2 \end{bmatrix} + \begin{bmatrix} 7 & 0 & -5 \end{bmatrix} = \begin{bmatrix} 11 & -3 & -3 \end{bmatrix}$,

$A - B = \begin{bmatrix} -3 & -3 & 7 \end{bmatrix}$, $2A = \begin{bmatrix} 8 & -6 & 4 \end{bmatrix}$, $-3B = \begin{bmatrix} -21 & 0 & 15 \end{bmatrix}$

**6** $A + B = \begin{bmatrix} 7 \\ -16 \end{bmatrix} + \begin{bmatrix} -11 \\ 9 \end{bmatrix} = \begin{bmatrix} -4 \\ -7 \end{bmatrix}$, $A - B = \begin{bmatrix} 18 \\ -25 \end{bmatrix}$, $2A = \begin{bmatrix} 14 \\ -32 \end{bmatrix}$, $-3B = \begin{bmatrix} 33 \\ -27 \end{bmatrix}$

**7** $A + B$ and $A - B$ are not possible since $A$ and $B$ are different sizes.

$2A = 2 \begin{bmatrix} 3 & -2 & 2 \\ 0 & 1 & -4 \\ -3 & 2 & -1 \end{bmatrix} = \begin{bmatrix} 6 & -4 & 4 \\ 0 & 2 & -8 \\ -6 & 4 & -2 \end{bmatrix}$, $-3B = -3 \begin{bmatrix} 4 & 0 \\ 2 & -1 \\ -1 & 3 \end{bmatrix} = \begin{bmatrix} -12 & 0 \\ -6 & 3 \\ 3 & -9 \end{bmatrix}$

**8** $A + B$ and $A - B$ are not possible since $A$ and $B$ are different sizes.

$2A = 2 \begin{bmatrix} 2 & 1 \end{bmatrix} = \begin{bmatrix} 4 & 2 \end{bmatrix}$, $-3B = -3 \begin{bmatrix} 3 & -1 & 5 \end{bmatrix} = \begin{bmatrix} -9 & 3 & -15 \end{bmatrix}$

**9** $2C = A \Leftrightarrow C = \frac{1}{2}A \Leftrightarrow \begin{bmatrix} x & y \\ z & w \end{bmatrix} = \frac{1}{2} \begin{bmatrix} 4 & 0 \\ -8 & 16 \end{bmatrix} \Leftrightarrow \begin{bmatrix} x & y \\ z & w \end{bmatrix} = \begin{bmatrix} 2 & 0 \\ -4 & 8 \end{bmatrix}$

**10** $-3C = B \Leftrightarrow C = -\frac{1}{3}B \Leftrightarrow \begin{bmatrix} x & y \\ z & w \end{bmatrix} = -\frac{1}{3} \begin{bmatrix} 9 & -3 \\ 12 & 0 \end{bmatrix} \Leftrightarrow \begin{bmatrix} x & y \\ z & w \end{bmatrix} = \begin{bmatrix} -3 & 1 \\ -4 & 0 \end{bmatrix}$

**11** $A + C = B \Leftrightarrow C = B - A \Leftrightarrow \begin{bmatrix} x & y \\ z & w \end{bmatrix} = \begin{bmatrix} 9 & -3 \\ 12 & 0 \end{bmatrix} - \begin{bmatrix} 4 & 0 \\ -8 & 16 \end{bmatrix} \Leftrightarrow \begin{bmatrix} x & y \\ z & w \end{bmatrix} = \begin{bmatrix} 5 & -3 \\ 20 & -16 \end{bmatrix}$.

**12** $A - C = B \Leftrightarrow C = A - B \Leftrightarrow \begin{bmatrix} x & y \\ z & w \end{bmatrix} = \begin{bmatrix} 4 & 0 \\ -8 & 16 \end{bmatrix} - \begin{bmatrix} 9 & -3 \\ 12 & 0 \end{bmatrix} \Leftrightarrow \begin{bmatrix} x & y \\ z & w \end{bmatrix} = \begin{bmatrix} -5 & 3 \\ -20 & 16 \end{bmatrix}$

**13** To find $c_{21}$ in Exercise 19, use the second row of $A$ and the first column of $B$.

$$c_{21} = (-5)(2) + (2)(0) + (2)(-4) = -10 + 0 - 8 = -18.$$

**14** To find $c_{23}$ in Exercise 22, use the second row of $A$ and the third column of $B$.

$$c_{23} = (3)(1) + (-2)(0) + (0)(4) + (5)(3) = 3 + 0 + 0 + 15 = 18.$$

**Note:** For Exercises 15–28, $AB$ is possible only if the number of columns of $A$ equal the number of rows of $B$. {$BA$ is not possible in Exercise 27, $AB$ is not possible in Exercise 28.} Multiplying an $\boxed{m} \times n$ matrix with an $n \times \boxed{k}$ matrix will result in an $m \times k$ matrix.

**15** $AB = \begin{bmatrix} 2 & 6 \\ 3 & -4 \end{bmatrix} \begin{bmatrix} 5 & -2 \\ 1 & 7 \end{bmatrix} = \begin{bmatrix} 2(5) + 6(1) & 2(-2) + 6(7) \\ 3(5) + (-4)(1) & 3(-2) + (-4)(7) \end{bmatrix} = \begin{bmatrix} 10+6 & -4+42 \\ 15-4 & -6-28 \end{bmatrix} = \begin{bmatrix} 16 & 38 \\ 11 & -34 \end{bmatrix}$

$BA = \begin{bmatrix} 5 & -2 \\ 1 & 7 \end{bmatrix} \begin{bmatrix} 2 & 6 \\ 3 & -4 \end{bmatrix} = \begin{bmatrix} 5(2) + (-2)(3) & 5(6) + (-2)(-4) \\ 1(2) + 7(3) & 1(6) + 7(-4) \end{bmatrix} = \begin{bmatrix} 4 & 38 \\ 23 & -22 \end{bmatrix}$

**16** $AB = \begin{bmatrix} 4 & -2 \\ -2 & 1 \end{bmatrix} \begin{bmatrix} 2 & 1 \\ 4 & 2 \end{bmatrix} = \begin{bmatrix} 0 & 0 \\ 0 & 0 \end{bmatrix}, BA = \begin{bmatrix} 6 & -3 \\ 12 & -6 \end{bmatrix}$

**17** $AB = \begin{bmatrix} 3 & 0 & -1 \\ 0 & 4 & 2 \\ 5 & -3 & 1 \end{bmatrix} \begin{bmatrix} 1 & -5 & 0 \\ 4 & 1 & -2 \\ 0 & -1 & 3 \end{bmatrix}$

$= \begin{bmatrix} 3(1) + 0(4) + (-1)(0) & 3(-5) + 0(1) + (-1)(-1) & 3(0) + 0(-2) + (-1)(3) \\ 0(1) + 4(4) + 2(0) & 0(-5) + 4(1) + 2(-1) & 0(0) + 4(-2) + 2(3) \\ 5(1) + (-3)(4) + 1(0) & 5(-5) + (-3)(1) + 1(-1) & 5(0) + (-3)(-2) + 1(3) \end{bmatrix} = \begin{bmatrix} 3 & -14 & -3 \\ 16 & 2 & -2 \\ -7 & -29 & 9 \end{bmatrix}$

$BA = \begin{bmatrix} 1 & -5 & 0 \\ 4 & 1 & -2 \\ 0 & -1 & 3 \end{bmatrix} \begin{bmatrix} 3 & 0 & -1 \\ 0 & 4 & 2 \\ 5 & -3 & 1 \end{bmatrix}$

$= \begin{bmatrix} 1(3) + (-5)(0) + 0(5) & 1(0) + (-5)(4) + 0(-3) & 1(-1) + (-5)(2) + 0(1) \\ 4(3) + 1(0) + (-2)(5) & 4(0) + 1(4) + (-2)(-3) & 4(-1) + 1(2) + (-2)(1) \\ 0(3) + (-1)(0) + 3(5) & 0(0) + (-1)(4) + 3(-3) & 0(-1) + (-1)(2) + 3(1) \end{bmatrix} = \begin{bmatrix} 3 & -20 & -11 \\ 2 & 10 & -4 \\ 15 & -13 & 1 \end{bmatrix}$.

**18** $AB = \begin{bmatrix} 5 & 0 & 0 \\ 0 & -3 & 0 \\ 0 & 0 & 2 \end{bmatrix} \begin{bmatrix} 3 & 0 & 0 \\ 0 & 4 & 0 \\ 0 & 0 & -2 \end{bmatrix} = \begin{bmatrix} 15 & 0 & 0 \\ 0 & -12 & 0 \\ 0 & 0 & -4 \end{bmatrix}, BA = \begin{bmatrix} 15 & 0 & 0 \\ 0 & -12 & 0 \\ 0 & 0 & -4 \end{bmatrix}$

**19** $AB = \begin{bmatrix} 4 & -3 & 1 \\ -5 & 2 & 2 \end{bmatrix} \begin{bmatrix} 2 & 1 \\ 0 & 1 \\ -4 & 7 \end{bmatrix} = \begin{bmatrix} 4(2) + (-3)(0) + 1(-4) & 4(1) + (-3)(1) + 1(7) \\ -5(2) + 2(0) + 2(-4) & -5(1) + 2(1) + 2(7) \end{bmatrix} = \begin{bmatrix} 4 & 8 \\ -18 & 11 \end{bmatrix}$

$BA = \begin{bmatrix} 2 & 1 \\ 0 & 1 \\ -4 & 7 \end{bmatrix} \begin{bmatrix} 4 & -3 & 1 \\ -5 & 2 & 2 \end{bmatrix} = \begin{bmatrix} 2(4) + 1(-5) & 2(-3) + 1(2) & 2(1) + 1(2) \\ 0(4) + 1(-5) & 0(-3) + 1(2) & 0(1) + 1(2) \\ -4(4) + 7(-5) & -4(-3) + 7(2) & -4(1) + 7(2) \end{bmatrix} = \begin{bmatrix} 3 & -4 & 4 \\ -5 & 2 & 2 \\ -51 & 26 & 10 \end{bmatrix}$

**20** $AB = \begin{bmatrix} 3 & 1 & -5 \\ 0 & 6 & 7 \end{bmatrix} \begin{bmatrix} 4 & 2 \\ -3 & 1 \\ 5 & 0 \end{bmatrix} = \begin{bmatrix} 3(4) + 1(-3) + (-5)(5) & 3(2) + 1(1) + (-5)(0) \\ 0(4) + 6(-3) + 7(5) & 0(2) + 6(1) + 7(0) \end{bmatrix} = \begin{bmatrix} -16 & 7 \\ 17 & 6 \end{bmatrix}$

$BA = \begin{bmatrix} 4 & 2 \\ -3 & 1 \\ 5 & 0 \end{bmatrix} \begin{bmatrix} 3 & 1 & -5 \\ 0 & 6 & 7 \end{bmatrix} = \begin{bmatrix} 4(3) + 2(0) & 4(1) + 2(6) & 4(-5) + 2(7) \\ -3(3) + 1(0) & -3(1) + 1(6) & -3(-5) + 1(7) \\ 5(3) + 0(0) & 5(1) + 0(6) & 5(-5) + 0(7) \end{bmatrix} = \begin{bmatrix} 12 & 16 & -6 \\ -9 & 3 & 22 \\ 15 & 5 & -25 \end{bmatrix}$

**21** $AB = \begin{bmatrix} 2 & 0 & -1 & 0 \\ 0 & 5 & 1 & -2 \\ 1 & 3 & 0 & 4 \end{bmatrix} \begin{bmatrix} -2 & 7 & 1 \\ 0 & 3 & 3 \\ -1 & 4 & 0 \\ 5 & 0 & 2 \end{bmatrix} = \begin{bmatrix} -3 & 10 & 2 \\ -11 & 19 & 11 \\ 18 & 16 & 18 \end{bmatrix}, BA = \begin{bmatrix} -3 & 38 & 9 & -10 \\ 3 & 24 & 3 & 6 \\ -2 & 20 & 5 & -8 \\ 12 & 6 & -5 & 8 \end{bmatrix}$

**22** $AB = \begin{bmatrix} 2 & 1 & -1 & 0 \\ 3 & -2 & 0 & 5 \\ -2 & 1 & 4 & 2 \end{bmatrix} \begin{bmatrix} 5 & -3 & 1 \\ 1 & 2 & 0 \\ -1 & 0 & 4 \\ 0 & -2 & 3 \end{bmatrix} = \begin{bmatrix} 12 & -4 & -2 \\ 13 & -23 & 18 \\ -13 & 4 & 20 \end{bmatrix}, BA = \begin{bmatrix} -1 & 12 & -1 & -13 \\ 8 & -3 & -1 & 10 \\ -10 & 3 & 17 & 8 \\ -12 & 7 & 12 & -4 \end{bmatrix}$

**23** $AB = \begin{bmatrix} 1 & 2 & 3 \\ 4 & 5 & 6 \\ 7 & 8 & 9 \end{bmatrix} \begin{bmatrix} 1 & 0 & 0 \\ 0 & 1 & 0 \\ 0 & 0 & 1 \end{bmatrix} = \begin{bmatrix} 1 & 2 & 3 \\ 4 & 5 & 6 \\ 7 & 8 & 9 \end{bmatrix}, BA = \begin{bmatrix} 1 & 2 & 3 \\ 4 & 5 & 6 \\ 7 & 8 & 9 \end{bmatrix}$

**24** $AB = \begin{bmatrix} 1 & 2 & 3 \\ 2 & 3 & 1 \\ 3 & 1 & 2 \end{bmatrix} \begin{bmatrix} 2 & 0 & 0 \\ 0 & 2 & 0 \\ 0 & 0 & 2 \end{bmatrix} = \begin{bmatrix} 2 & 4 & 6 \\ 4 & 6 & 2 \\ 6 & 2 & 4 \end{bmatrix}, BA = \begin{bmatrix} 2 & 4 & 6 \\ 4 & 6 & 2 \\ 6 & 2 & 4 \end{bmatrix}$

**25** $AB = \begin{bmatrix} -3 & 7 & 2 \end{bmatrix} \begin{bmatrix} 1 \\ 4 \\ -5 \end{bmatrix} = \begin{bmatrix} -3(1) + 7(4) + 2(-5) \end{bmatrix} = \begin{bmatrix} 15 \end{bmatrix},$

$BA = \begin{bmatrix} 1 \\ 4 \\ -5 \end{bmatrix} \begin{bmatrix} -3 & 7 & 2 \end{bmatrix} = \begin{bmatrix} 1(-3) & 1(7) & 1(2) \\ 4(-3) & 4(7) & 4(2) \\ -5(-3) & -5(7) & -5(2) \end{bmatrix} = \begin{bmatrix} -3 & 7 & 2 \\ -12 & 28 & 8 \\ 15 & -35 & -10 \end{bmatrix}$

**26** $AB = \begin{bmatrix} 4 & 8 \end{bmatrix} \begin{bmatrix} -3 \\ 2 \end{bmatrix} = \begin{bmatrix} 4 \end{bmatrix}, BA = \begin{bmatrix} -12 & -24 \\ 8 & 16 \end{bmatrix}$

**27** $AB = \begin{bmatrix} 2 & 0 & 1 \\ -1 & 2 & 0 \end{bmatrix} \begin{bmatrix} 1 & -1 & 2 \\ 3 & 1 & 0 \\ 0 & 2 & 1 \end{bmatrix}$

$= \begin{bmatrix} 2(1) + 0(3) + 1(0) & 2(-1) + 0(1) + 1(2) & 2(2) + 0(0) + 1(1) \\ -1(1) + 2(3) + 0(0) & -1(-1) + 2(1) + 0(2) & -1(2) + 2(0) + 0(1) \end{bmatrix} = \begin{bmatrix} 2 & 0 & 5 \\ 5 & 3 & -2 \end{bmatrix}$

$BA$ is a $3 \times 3$ matrix times a $2 \times 3$ matrix.

Since the number of columns of $B$, 3, is not equal to the number of rows of $A$, 2, $BA$ is *not possible*.

**28** $AB$ is *not possible*, $BA = \begin{bmatrix} -2 \\ 5 \end{bmatrix} \begin{bmatrix} 3 & -1 & 4 \end{bmatrix} = \begin{bmatrix} -6 & 2 & -8 \\ 15 & -5 & 20 \end{bmatrix}.$

**29** $AB = \begin{bmatrix} 4 & -2 \\ 0 & 3 \\ -7 & 5 \end{bmatrix} \begin{bmatrix} 3 \\ 4 \end{bmatrix} = \begin{bmatrix} 4(3) + (-2)(4) \\ 0(3) + 3(4) \\ (-7)(3) + 5(4) \end{bmatrix} = \begin{bmatrix} 4 \\ 12 \\ -1 \end{bmatrix}$

**30** $AB = \begin{bmatrix} 4 \\ -3 \\ 2 \end{bmatrix} \begin{bmatrix} 5 & 1 \end{bmatrix} = \begin{bmatrix} 20 & 4 \\ -15 & -3 \\ 10 & 2 \end{bmatrix}$

**31** $AB = \begin{bmatrix} 2 & 1 & 0 & -3 \\ -7 & 0 & -2 & 4 \end{bmatrix} \begin{bmatrix} 4 & -2 & 0 \\ 1 & 1 & -2 \\ 0 & 0 & 5 \\ -3 & -1 & 0 \end{bmatrix} = \begin{bmatrix} c_{11} & c_{12} & c_{13} \\ c_{21} & c_{22} & c_{23} \end{bmatrix},$ where

$c_{11} = 2(4) + 1(1) + 0(0) + (-3)(-3),$      $c_{12} = 2(-2) + 1(1) + 0(0) + (-3)(-1),$

$c_{13} = 2(0) + 1(-2) + 0(5) + (-3)(0),$      $c_{21} = -7(4) + 0(1) + (-2)(0) + 4(-3),$

$c_{22} = -7(-2) + 0(1) + (-2)(0) + 4(-1),$ and      $c_{23} = -7(0) + 0(-2) + (-2)(5) + 4(0).$

Hence, $AB = \begin{bmatrix} 18 & 0 & -2 \\ -40 & 10 & -10 \end{bmatrix}.$

**32** $AB = \begin{bmatrix} 1 & 2 & -3 \\ 4 & -5 & 6 \end{bmatrix} \begin{bmatrix} 1 & -1 & 0 & 2 \\ -2 & 3 & 1 & 0 \\ 0 & 4 & 0 & -3 \end{bmatrix} = \begin{bmatrix} -3 & -7 & 2 & 11 \\ 14 & 5 & -5 & -10 \end{bmatrix}$

**33** $A + B = \begin{bmatrix} 1 & 2 \\ 0 & -3 \end{bmatrix} + \begin{bmatrix} 2 & -1 \\ 3 & 1 \end{bmatrix} = \begin{bmatrix} 3 & 1 \\ 3 & -2 \end{bmatrix}$ and $A - B = \begin{bmatrix} 1 & 2 \\ 0 & -3 \end{bmatrix} - \begin{bmatrix} 2 & -1 \\ 3 & 1 \end{bmatrix} = \begin{bmatrix} -1 & 3 \\ -3 & -4 \end{bmatrix}$, so

$(A + B)(A - B) = \begin{bmatrix} 3 & 1 \\ 3 & -2 \end{bmatrix} \begin{bmatrix} -1 & 3 \\ -3 & -4 \end{bmatrix} = \begin{bmatrix} -6 & 5 \\ 3 & 17 \end{bmatrix}$.

$A^2 = AA = \begin{bmatrix} 1 & 2 \\ 0 & -3 \end{bmatrix} \begin{bmatrix} 1 & 2 \\ 0 & -3 \end{bmatrix} = \begin{bmatrix} 1 & -4 \\ 0 & 9 \end{bmatrix}$ and $B^2 = BB = \begin{bmatrix} 2 & -1 \\ 3 & 1 \end{bmatrix} \begin{bmatrix} 2 & -1 \\ 3 & 1 \end{bmatrix} = \begin{bmatrix} 1 & -3 \\ 9 & -2 \end{bmatrix}$, so

$A^2 - B^2 = \begin{bmatrix} 1 & -4 \\ 0 & 9 \end{bmatrix} - \begin{bmatrix} 1 & -3 \\ 9 & -2 \end{bmatrix} = \begin{bmatrix} 0 & -1 \\ -9 & 11 \end{bmatrix}$.

Thus, $(A + B)(A - B) \neq A^2 - B^2$ since $\begin{bmatrix} -6 & 5 \\ 3 & 17 \end{bmatrix} \neq \begin{bmatrix} 0 & -1 \\ -9 & 11 \end{bmatrix}$.

**34** $(A + B)(A + B) = \begin{bmatrix} 3 & 1 \\ 3 & -2 \end{bmatrix} \begin{bmatrix} 3 & 1 \\ 3 & -2 \end{bmatrix} = \begin{bmatrix} 12 & 1 \\ 3 & 7 \end{bmatrix}$;

$A^2 + 2AB + B^2 = \begin{bmatrix} 1 & -4 \\ 0 & 9 \end{bmatrix} + \begin{bmatrix} 16 & 2 \\ -18 & -6 \end{bmatrix} + \begin{bmatrix} 1 & -3 \\ 9 & -2 \end{bmatrix} = \begin{bmatrix} 18 & -5 \\ -9 & 1 \end{bmatrix}$

**35** $A(B + C) = \begin{bmatrix} 1 & 2 \\ 0 & -3 \end{bmatrix} \begin{bmatrix} 5 & 0 \\ 1 & 1 \end{bmatrix} = \begin{bmatrix} 7 & 2 \\ -3 & -3 \end{bmatrix}$; $AB + AC = \begin{bmatrix} 8 & 1 \\ -9 & -3 \end{bmatrix} + \begin{bmatrix} -1 & 1 \\ 6 & 0 \end{bmatrix} = \begin{bmatrix} 7 & 2 \\ -3 & -3 \end{bmatrix}$

**36** $A(BC) = \begin{bmatrix} 1 & 2 \\ 0 & -3 \end{bmatrix} \begin{bmatrix} 8 & 2 \\ 7 & 3 \end{bmatrix} = \begin{bmatrix} 22 & 8 \\ -21 & -9 \end{bmatrix}$; $(AB)C = \begin{bmatrix} 8 & 1 \\ -9 & -3 \end{bmatrix} \begin{bmatrix} 3 & 1 \\ -2 & 0 \end{bmatrix} = \begin{bmatrix} 22 & 8 \\ -21 & -9 \end{bmatrix}$

**37** $m(A + B) = m \begin{bmatrix} a+p & b+q \\ c+r & d+s \end{bmatrix} = \begin{bmatrix} m(a+p) & m(b+q) \\ m(c+r) & m(d+s) \end{bmatrix} = \begin{bmatrix} ma+mp & mb+mq \\ mc+mr & md+ms \end{bmatrix}$

$= \begin{bmatrix} ma & mb \\ mc & md \end{bmatrix} + \begin{bmatrix} mp & mq \\ mr & ms \end{bmatrix} = m \begin{bmatrix} a & b \\ c & d \end{bmatrix} + m \begin{bmatrix} p & q \\ r & s \end{bmatrix} = mA + mB$

**38** $(m + n)A = (m + n) \begin{bmatrix} a & b \\ c & d \end{bmatrix} = \begin{bmatrix} (m+n)a & (m+n)b \\ (m+n)c & (m+n)d \end{bmatrix} = \begin{bmatrix} ma+na & mb+nb \\ mc+nc & md+nd \end{bmatrix}$

$= \begin{bmatrix} ma & mb \\ mc & md \end{bmatrix} + \begin{bmatrix} na & nb \\ nc & nd \end{bmatrix} = m \begin{bmatrix} a & b \\ c & d \end{bmatrix} + n \begin{bmatrix} a & b \\ c & d \end{bmatrix} = mA + nA$

**39** $A(B + C) = \begin{bmatrix} a & b \\ c & d \end{bmatrix} \begin{bmatrix} p+w & q+x \\ r+y & s+z \end{bmatrix} = \begin{bmatrix} a(p+w)+b(r+y) & a(q+x)+b(s+z) \\ c(p+w)+d(r+y) & c(q+x)+d(s+z) \end{bmatrix}$

$= \begin{bmatrix} ap+aw+br+by & aq+ax+bs+bz \\ cp+cw+dr+dy & cq+cx+ds+dz \end{bmatrix} = \begin{bmatrix} ap+br & aq+bs \\ cp+dr & cq+ds \end{bmatrix} + \begin{bmatrix} aw+by & ax+bz \\ cw+dy & cx+dz \end{bmatrix}$

$= \begin{bmatrix} a & b \\ c & d \end{bmatrix} \begin{bmatrix} p & q \\ r & s \end{bmatrix} + \begin{bmatrix} a & b \\ c & d \end{bmatrix} \begin{bmatrix} w & x \\ y & z \end{bmatrix} = AB + AC$

**40** $A(BC) = \begin{bmatrix} a & b \\ c & d \end{bmatrix} \left( \begin{bmatrix} p & q \\ r & s \end{bmatrix} \begin{bmatrix} w & x \\ y & z \end{bmatrix} \right) = \begin{bmatrix} a & b \\ c & d \end{bmatrix} \begin{bmatrix} pw+qy & px+qz \\ rw+sy & rx+sz \end{bmatrix}$

$= \begin{bmatrix} a(pw+qy)+b(rw+sy) & a(px+qz)+b(rx+sz) \\ c(pw+qy)+d(rw+sy) & c(px+qz)+d(rx+sz) \end{bmatrix}$

$= \begin{bmatrix} apw+aqy+brw+bsy & apx+aqz+brx+bsz \\ cpw+cqy+drw+dsy & cpx+cqz+drx+dsz \end{bmatrix}$

$= \begin{bmatrix} (ap+br)w+(aq+bs)y & (ap+br)x+(aq+bs)z \\ (cp+dr)w+(cq+ds)y & (cp+dr)x+(cq+ds)z \end{bmatrix}$

$= \begin{bmatrix} ap+br & aq+bs \\ cp+dr & cq+ds \end{bmatrix} \begin{bmatrix} w & x \\ y & z \end{bmatrix} = \left( \begin{bmatrix} a & b \\ c & d \end{bmatrix} \begin{bmatrix} p & q \\ r & s \end{bmatrix} \right) \begin{bmatrix} w & x \\ y & z \end{bmatrix} = (AB)C$

**Note:** For Exercises 41–44, $A = \begin{bmatrix} 3 & -3 & 7 \\ 2 & 6 & -2 \\ 4 & 2 & 5 \end{bmatrix}$ and $B = \begin{bmatrix} -9 & 5 & -8 \\ 3 & -7 & 1 \\ -1 & 2 & 6 \end{bmatrix}$.

**41** $A^2 = AA = \begin{bmatrix} 3 & -3 & 7 \\ 2 & 6 & -2 \\ 4 & 2 & 5 \end{bmatrix} \begin{bmatrix} 3 & -3 & 7 \\ 2 & 6 & -2 \\ 4 & 2 & 5 \end{bmatrix} = \begin{bmatrix} 31 & -13 & 62 \\ 10 & 26 & -8 \\ 36 & 10 & 49 \end{bmatrix}$

$B^2 = BB = \begin{bmatrix} -9 & 5 & -8 \\ 3 & -7 & 1 \\ -1 & 2 & 6 \end{bmatrix} \begin{bmatrix} -9 & 5 & -8 \\ 3 & -7 & 1 \\ -1 & 2 & 6 \end{bmatrix} = \begin{bmatrix} 104 & -96 & 29 \\ -49 & 66 & -25 \\ 9 & -7 & 46 \end{bmatrix}$

$A^2 + B^2 = \begin{bmatrix} 31 & -13 & 62 \\ 10 & 26 & -8 \\ 36 & 10 & 49 \end{bmatrix} + \begin{bmatrix} 104 & -96 & 29 \\ -49 & 66 & -25 \\ 9 & -7 & 46 \end{bmatrix} = \begin{bmatrix} 135 & -109 & 91 \\ -39 & 92 & -33 \\ 45 & 3 & 95 \end{bmatrix}$

**42** $3A - BA = \begin{bmatrix} 9 & -9 & 21 \\ 6 & 18 & -6 \\ 12 & 6 & 15 \end{bmatrix} - \begin{bmatrix} -49 & 41 & -113 \\ -1 & -49 & 40 \\ 25 & 27 & 19 \end{bmatrix} = \begin{bmatrix} 58 & -50 & 134 \\ 7 & 67 & -46 \\ -13 & -21 & -4 \end{bmatrix}$

**43** $A^2 - 5B = \begin{bmatrix} 31 & -13 & 62 \\ 10 & 26 & -8 \\ 36 & 10 & 49 \end{bmatrix} - \begin{bmatrix} -45 & 25 & -40 \\ 15 & -35 & 5 \\ -5 & 10 & 30 \end{bmatrix} = \begin{bmatrix} 76 & -38 & 102 \\ -5 & 61 & -13 \\ 41 & 0 & 19 \end{bmatrix}$

**44** $A + A^2 + B + B^2 = \begin{bmatrix} 3 & -3 & 7 \\ 2 & 6 & -2 \\ 4 & 2 & 5 \end{bmatrix} + \begin{bmatrix} 31 & -13 & 62 \\ 10 & 26 & -8 \\ 36 & 10 & 49 \end{bmatrix} + \begin{bmatrix} -9 & 5 & -8 \\ 3 & -7 & 1 \\ -1 & 2 & 6 \end{bmatrix} + \begin{bmatrix} 104 & -96 & 29 \\ -49 & 66 & -25 \\ 9 & -7 & 46 \end{bmatrix}$

$= \begin{bmatrix} 129 & -107 & 90 \\ -34 & 91 & -34 \\ 48 & 7 & 106 \end{bmatrix}$

**45** (a) For the inventory matrix, we have 5 colors and 3 sizes of towels, and for each size of towel, we have 1 price. We choose a $5 \times 3$ matrix $A$ and a $3 \times 1$ matrix $B$.

inventory matrix $A = \begin{bmatrix} 400 & 550 & 500 \\ 400 & 450 & 500 \\ 300 & 500 & 600 \\ 250 & 200 & 300 \\ 100 & 100 & 200 \end{bmatrix}$ price matrix $B = \begin{bmatrix} \$8.99 \\ \$10.99 \\ \$12.99 \end{bmatrix}$

(b) $C = AB = \begin{bmatrix} 400 & 550 & 500 \\ 400 & 450 & 500 \\ 300 & 500 & 600 \\ 250 & 200 & 300 \\ 100 & 100 & 200 \end{bmatrix} \begin{bmatrix} \$8.99 \\ \$10.99 \\ \$12.99 \end{bmatrix} = \begin{bmatrix} \$16,135.50 \\ \$15,036.50 \\ \$15,986.00 \\ \$8342.50 \\ \$4596.00 \end{bmatrix}$

(c) The \$4596.00 represents the amount the store would receive if all the yellow towels were sold.

**46** (a) For the cost matrix, we have 3 sizes and 2 types of cost, and for the order matrix, we have 3 quantities. We choose a $1 \times 3$ matrix $A$ and a $3 \times 2$ matrix $B$.

order matrix $A = \begin{bmatrix} 4 & 10 & 6 \end{bmatrix}$ cost matrix $B = \begin{bmatrix} 70 & 90 \\ 95 & 105 \\ 117 & 223 \end{bmatrix}$

(b) $C = AB = \begin{bmatrix} 4 & 10 & 6 \end{bmatrix} \begin{bmatrix} 70 & 90 \\ 95 & 105 \\ 117 & 223 \end{bmatrix} = \begin{bmatrix} 1932 & 2748 \end{bmatrix}$

(c) The \$1,932,000 represents the amount needed for labor and the \$2,748,000 represents the amount needed for materials.

## 8.7 Exercises

**1**   $AB = \begin{bmatrix} 5 & 7 \\ 2 & 3 \end{bmatrix} \begin{bmatrix} 3 & -7 \\ -2 & 5 \end{bmatrix} = \begin{bmatrix} 1 & 0 \\ 0 & 1 \end{bmatrix} = I_2$ and $BA = \begin{bmatrix} 3 & -7 \\ -2 & 5 \end{bmatrix} \begin{bmatrix} 5 & 7 \\ 2 & 3 \end{bmatrix} = \begin{bmatrix} 1 & 0 \\ 0 & 1 \end{bmatrix} = I_2$.

Since $AB = I_2$ and $BA = I_2$, $B$ is the inverse of $A$.

**2**   $AB = \begin{bmatrix} 8 & -5 \\ -3 & 2 \end{bmatrix} \begin{bmatrix} 2 & 5 \\ 3 & 8 \end{bmatrix} = \begin{bmatrix} 1 & 0 \\ 0 & 1 \end{bmatrix} = I_2$ and $BA = \begin{bmatrix} 2 & 5 \\ 3 & 8 \end{bmatrix} \begin{bmatrix} 8 & -5 \\ -3 & 2 \end{bmatrix} = \begin{bmatrix} 1 & 0 \\ 0 & 1 \end{bmatrix} = I_2$.

Since $AB = I_2$ and $BA = I_2$, $B$ is the inverse of $A$.

**Note:** In Exercises 3–16, let $A$ denote the given matrix.

**3**   $\begin{bmatrix} 2 & -4 & | & 1 & 0 \\ 1 & 3 & | & 0 & 1 \end{bmatrix}$   $R_1 - R_2 \rightarrow R_1$   $\begin{bmatrix} 1 & -7 & | & 1 & -1 \\ 1 & 3 & | & 0 & 1 \end{bmatrix}$   $R_2 - R_1 \rightarrow R_2$   $\begin{bmatrix} 1 & -7 & | & 1 & -1 \\ 0 & 10 & | & -1 & 2 \end{bmatrix}$   $\frac{1}{10}R_2 \rightarrow R_2$

$\begin{bmatrix} 1 & -7 & | & 1 & -1 \\ 0 & 1 & | & -\frac{1}{10} & \frac{2}{10} \end{bmatrix}$   $R_1 + 7R_2 \rightarrow R_1$   $\begin{bmatrix} 1 & 0 & | & \frac{3}{10} & \frac{4}{10} \\ 0 & 1 & | & -\frac{1}{10} & \frac{2}{10} \end{bmatrix}$   $\Rightarrow$   $A^{-1} = \frac{1}{10}\begin{bmatrix} 3 & 4 \\ -1 & 2 \end{bmatrix}$

**4**   $\begin{bmatrix} 3 & 2 & | & 1 & 0 \\ 4 & 5 & | & 0 & 1 \end{bmatrix}$   $-R_1 + R_2 \rightarrow R_1$   $\begin{bmatrix} 1 & 3 & | & -1 & 1 \\ 4 & 5 & | & 0 & 1 \end{bmatrix}$   $R_2 - 4R_1 \rightarrow R_2$   $\begin{bmatrix} 1 & 3 & | & -1 & 1 \\ 0 & -7 & | & 4 & -3 \end{bmatrix}$   $-\frac{1}{7}R_2 \rightarrow R_2$

$\begin{bmatrix} 1 & 3 & | & -1 & 1 \\ 0 & 1 & | & -\frac{4}{7} & \frac{3}{7} \end{bmatrix}$   $R_1 - 3R_2 \rightarrow R_1$   $\begin{bmatrix} 1 & 0 & | & \frac{5}{7} & -\frac{2}{7} \\ 0 & 1 & | & -\frac{4}{7} & \frac{3}{7} \end{bmatrix}$   $\Rightarrow$   $A^{-1} = \frac{1}{7}\begin{bmatrix} 5 & -2 \\ -4 & 3 \end{bmatrix}$

**5**   $\begin{bmatrix} 2 & 4 & | & 1 & 0 \\ 4 & 8 & | & 0 & 1 \end{bmatrix}$   $\frac{1}{2}R_1 \rightarrow R_1$   $\begin{bmatrix} 1 & 2 & | & \frac{1}{2} & 0 \\ 4 & 8 & | & 0 & 1 \end{bmatrix}$   $R_2 - 4R_1 \rightarrow R_2$   $\begin{bmatrix} 1 & 2 & | & \frac{1}{2} & 0 \\ 0 & 0 & | & -2 & 1 \end{bmatrix}$

Since the identity matrix cannot be obtained on the left, *no inverse exists*.

**6**   $\begin{bmatrix} 3 & -1 & | & 1 & 0 \\ 6 & -2 & | & 0 & 1 \end{bmatrix}$   $R_2 - 2R_1 \rightarrow R_2$   $\begin{bmatrix} 3 & -1 & | & 1 & 0 \\ 0 & 0 & | & -2 & 1 \end{bmatrix}$

Since the identity matrix cannot be obtained on the left, *no inverse exists*.

**7**   $\begin{bmatrix} 3 & -1 & 0 & | & 1 & 0 & 0 \\ 2 & 2 & 0 & | & 0 & 1 & 0 \\ 0 & 0 & 4 & | & 0 & 0 & 1 \end{bmatrix}$   $R_1 - R_2 \rightarrow R_1$   $\begin{bmatrix} 1 & -3 & 0 & | & 1 & -1 & 0 \\ 2 & 2 & 0 & | & 0 & 1 & 0 \\ 0 & 0 & 4 & | & 0 & 0 & 1 \end{bmatrix}$   $R_2 - 2R_1 \rightarrow R_2$

$\begin{bmatrix} 1 & -3 & 0 & | & 1 & -1 & 0 \\ 0 & 8 & 0 & | & -2 & 3 & 0 \\ 0 & 0 & 4 & | & 0 & 0 & 1 \end{bmatrix}$   $\frac{1}{8}R_2 \rightarrow R_2$   $\frac{1}{4}R_3 \rightarrow R_3$   $\begin{bmatrix} 1 & -3 & 0 & | & 1 & -1 & 0 \\ 0 & 1 & 0 & | & -\frac{2}{8} & \frac{3}{8} & 0 \\ 0 & 0 & 1 & | & 0 & 0 & \frac{1}{4} \end{bmatrix}$   $R_1 + 3R_2 \rightarrow R_1$

$\begin{bmatrix} 1 & 0 & 0 & | & \frac{2}{8} & \frac{1}{8} & 0 \\ 0 & 1 & 0 & | & -\frac{2}{8} & \frac{3}{8} & 0 \\ 0 & 0 & 1 & | & 0 & 0 & \frac{2}{8} \end{bmatrix}$   $\Rightarrow$   $A^{-1} = \frac{1}{8}\begin{bmatrix} 2 & 1 & 0 \\ -2 & 3 & 0 \\ 0 & 0 & 2 \end{bmatrix}$

**8**   $\begin{bmatrix} 3 & 0 & 2 & | & 1 & 0 & 0 \\ 0 & 1 & 0 & | & 0 & 1 & 0 \\ -4 & 0 & 2 & | & 0 & 0 & 1 \end{bmatrix}$   $-R_1 - R_3 \rightarrow R_1$   $\begin{bmatrix} 1 & 0 & -4 & | & -1 & 0 & -1 \\ 0 & 1 & 0 & | & 0 & 1 & 0 \\ -4 & 0 & 2 & | & 0 & 0 & 1 \end{bmatrix}$   $R_3 + 4R_1 \rightarrow R_3$

$\begin{bmatrix} 1 & 0 & -4 & | & -1 & 0 & -1 \\ 0 & 1 & 0 & | & 0 & 1 & 0 \\ 0 & 0 & -14 & | & -4 & 0 & -3 \end{bmatrix}$   $-\frac{1}{14}R_3 \rightarrow R_3$   $\begin{bmatrix} 1 & 0 & -4 & | & -1 & 0 & -1 \\ 0 & 1 & 0 & | & 0 & 1 & 0 \\ 0 & 0 & 1 & | & \frac{4}{14} & 0 & \frac{3}{14} \end{bmatrix}$   $R_1 + 4R_3 \rightarrow R_1$

$\begin{bmatrix} 1 & 0 & 0 & | & \frac{2}{14} & 0 & -\frac{2}{14} \\ 0 & 1 & 0 & | & 0 & 1 & 0 \\ 0 & 0 & 1 & | & \frac{4}{14} & 0 & \frac{3}{14} \end{bmatrix}$   $\Rightarrow$   $A^{-1} = \frac{1}{14}\begin{bmatrix} 2 & 0 & -2 \\ 0 & 14 & 0 \\ 4 & 0 & 3 \end{bmatrix}$

**9** $\begin{bmatrix} -2 & 2 & 3 & | & 1 & 0 & 0 \\ 1 & -1 & 0 & | & 0 & 1 & 0 \\ 0 & 1 & 4 & | & 0 & 0 & 1 \end{bmatrix}$ $R_1 + 2R_2 \leftrightarrow R_2$ $\begin{bmatrix} 1 & -1 & 0 & | & 0 & 1 & 0 \\ 0 & 0 & 3 & | & 1 & 2 & 0 \\ 0 & 1 & 4 & | & 0 & 0 & 1 \end{bmatrix}$ $R_1 + R_3 \rightarrow R_1$

$\begin{bmatrix} 1 & 0 & 4 & | & 0 & 1 & 1 \\ 0 & 0 & 3 & | & 1 & 2 & 0 \\ 0 & 1 & 4 & | & 0 & 0 & 1 \end{bmatrix}$ $\frac{1}{3}R_2 \leftrightarrow R_3$ $\begin{bmatrix} 1 & 0 & 4 & | & 0 & 1 & 1 \\ 0 & 1 & 4 & | & 0 & 0 & 1 \\ 0 & 0 & 1 & | & \frac{1}{3} & \frac{2}{3} & 0 \end{bmatrix}$ $R_1 - 4R_3 \rightarrow R_1$ $R_2 - 4R_3 \rightarrow R_2$

$\begin{bmatrix} 1 & 0 & 0 & | & -\frac{4}{3} & -\frac{5}{3} & 1 \\ 0 & 1 & 0 & | & -\frac{4}{3} & -\frac{8}{3} & 1 \\ 0 & 0 & 1 & | & \frac{1}{3} & \frac{2}{3} & 0 \end{bmatrix}$ $\Rightarrow$ $\qquad A^{-1} = \frac{1}{3}\begin{bmatrix} -4 & -5 & 3 \\ -4 & -8 & 3 \\ 1 & 2 & 0 \end{bmatrix}$

**10** $\begin{bmatrix} 1 & 2 & 3 & | & 1 & 0 & 0 \\ -2 & 1 & 0 & | & 0 & 1 & 0 \\ 3 & -1 & 1 & | & 0 & 0 & 1 \end{bmatrix}$ $\begin{matrix} R_2 + 2R_1 \rightarrow R_2 \\ R_3 - 3R_1 \rightarrow R_3 \end{matrix}$ $\begin{bmatrix} 1 & 2 & 3 & | & 1 & 0 & 0 \\ 0 & 5 & 6 & | & 2 & 1 & 0 \\ 0 & -7 & -8 & | & -3 & 0 & 1 \end{bmatrix}$ $3R_2 + 2R_3 \rightarrow R_2$

$\begin{bmatrix} 1 & 2 & 3 & | & 1 & 0 & 0 \\ 0 & 1 & 2 & | & 0 & 3 & 2 \\ 0 & -7 & -8 & | & -3 & 0 & 1 \end{bmatrix}$ $\begin{matrix} R_1 - 2R_2 \rightarrow R_1 \\ R_3 + 7R_2 \rightarrow R_3 \end{matrix}$ $\begin{bmatrix} 1 & 0 & -1 & | & 1 & -6 & -4 \\ 0 & 1 & 2 & | & 0 & 3 & 2 \\ 0 & 0 & 6 & | & -3 & 21 & 15 \end{bmatrix}$ $\frac{1}{6}R_3 \rightarrow R_3$

$\begin{bmatrix} 1 & 0 & -1 & | & 1 & -6 & -4 \\ 0 & 1 & 2 & | & 0 & 3 & 2 \\ 0 & 0 & 1 & | & -\frac{1}{2} & \frac{7}{2} & \frac{5}{2} \end{bmatrix}$ $\begin{matrix} R_1 + R_3 \rightarrow R_1 \\ R_2 - 2R_3 \rightarrow R_2 \end{matrix}$ $\begin{bmatrix} 1 & 0 & 0 & | & \frac{1}{2} & -\frac{5}{2} & -\frac{3}{2} \\ 0 & 1 & 0 & | & 1 & -4 & -3 \\ 0 & 0 & 1 & | & -\frac{1}{2} & \frac{7}{2} & \frac{5}{2} \end{bmatrix}$ $\Rightarrow$

$$A^{-1} = \frac{1}{2}\begin{bmatrix} 1 & -5 & -3 \\ 2 & -8 & -6 \\ -1 & 7 & 5 \end{bmatrix}$$

**11** $\begin{bmatrix} 2 & 0 & 0 & | & 1 & 0 & 0 \\ 0 & 4 & 0 & | & 0 & 1 & 0 \\ 0 & 0 & 6 & | & 0 & 0 & 1 \end{bmatrix}$ $\begin{matrix} \frac{1}{2}R_1 \rightarrow R_1 \\ \frac{1}{4}R_2 \rightarrow R_2 \\ \frac{1}{6}R_3 \rightarrow R_3 \end{matrix}$ $\begin{bmatrix} 1 & 0 & 0 & | & \frac{1}{2} & 0 & 0 \\ 0 & 1 & 0 & | & 0 & \frac{1}{4} & 0 \\ 0 & 0 & 1 & | & 0 & 0 & \frac{1}{6} \end{bmatrix}$ $\Rightarrow$ $\quad A^{-1} = \frac{1}{12}\begin{bmatrix} 6 & 0 & 0 \\ 0 & 3 & 0 \\ 0 & 0 & 2 \end{bmatrix}$

**12** $\begin{bmatrix} 0 & 0 & -3 & | & 1 & 0 & 0 \\ 0 & -2 & 0 & | & 0 & 1 & 0 \\ -1 & 0 & 0 & | & 0 & 0 & 1 \end{bmatrix}$ $\begin{matrix} -\frac{1}{3}R_1 \rightarrow R_1 \\ -\frac{1}{2}R_2 \rightarrow R_2 \\ -R_3 \rightarrow R_3 \end{matrix}$ $\begin{bmatrix} 0 & 0 & 1 & | & -\frac{1}{3} & 0 & 0 \\ 0 & 1 & 0 & | & 0 & -\frac{1}{2} & 0 \\ 1 & 0 & 0 & | & 0 & 0 & -1 \end{bmatrix}$ $R_1 \leftrightarrow R_3$

$\begin{bmatrix} 1 & 0 & 0 & | & 0 & 0 & -1 \\ 0 & 1 & 0 & | & 0 & -\frac{1}{2} & 0 \\ 0 & 0 & 1 & | & -\frac{1}{3} & 0 & 0 \end{bmatrix}$ $\Rightarrow$ $\qquad A^{-1} = -\frac{1}{6}\begin{bmatrix} 0 & 0 & 6 \\ 0 & 3 & 0 \\ 2 & 0 & 0 \end{bmatrix}$

**13** $\begin{bmatrix} -2 & 1 & 2 & | & 1 & 0 & 0 \\ 0 & 1 & 3 & | & 0 & 1 & 0 \\ -2 & 2 & 5 & | & 0 & 0 & 1 \end{bmatrix}$ $R_1 - R_3 \rightarrow R_1$ $\begin{bmatrix} 0 & -1 & -3 & | & 1 & 0 & -1 \\ 0 & 1 & 3 & | & 0 & 1 & 0 \\ -2 & 2 & 5 & | & 0 & 0 & 1 \end{bmatrix}$ $R_1 + R_2 \rightarrow R_1$

$\begin{bmatrix} 0 & 0 & 0 & | & 1 & 1 & -1 \\ 0 & 1 & 3 & | & 0 & 1 & 0 \\ -2 & 2 & 5 & | & 0 & 0 & 1 \end{bmatrix}$  Since the identity matrix cannot be obtained on the left, *no inverse exists.*

**14** $\begin{bmatrix} 1 & 1 & 1 & | & 1 & 0 & 0 \\ 2 & 2 & 2 & | & 0 & 1 & 0 \\ 3 & 3 & 3 & | & 0 & 0 & 1 \end{bmatrix}$ $\begin{matrix} R_2 - 2R_1 \rightarrow R_2 \\ R_3 - 3R_1 \rightarrow R_3 \end{matrix}$ $\begin{bmatrix} 1 & 1 & 1 & | & 1 & 0 & 0 \\ 0 & 0 & 0 & | & -2 & 1 & 0 \\ 0 & 0 & 0 & | & -3 & 0 & 1 \end{bmatrix}$  *No inverse exists.*

**15** $\begin{bmatrix} 1 & 0 & 2 & | & 1 & 0 & 0 \\ 0 & 1 & 3 & | & 0 & 1 & 0 \\ 0 & 0 & 0 & | & 0 & 0 & 1 \end{bmatrix}$  Since the identity matrix cannot be obtained on the left, *no inverse exists.*

**16** $\begin{bmatrix} 0 & 1 & -2 & | & 1 & 0 & 0 \\ 1 & 0 & 1 & | & 0 & 1 & 0 \\ 0 & 0 & 0 & | & 0 & 0 & 1 \end{bmatrix}$  Since the identity matrix cannot be obtained on the left, *no inverse exists.*

$\boxed{17}$ $\begin{bmatrix} a & 0 & | & 1 & 0 \\ 0 & b & | & 0 & 1 \end{bmatrix}$ $\begin{array}{l} \frac{1}{a}R_1 \to R_1 \\ \frac{1}{b}R_2 \to R_2 \end{array}$ $\Rightarrow$ $\begin{bmatrix} 1 & 0 & | & 1/a & 0 \\ 0 & 1 & | & 0 & 1/b \end{bmatrix}$

The inverse is the matrix with main diagonal elements $1/a$ and $1/b$.

The required conditions are that $a$ and $b$ are nonzero to avoid division by zero.

$\boxed{18}$ Refer to Exercise 17. Generalizing, we have the inverse $\begin{bmatrix} 1/a & 0 & 0 \\ 0 & 1/b & 0 \\ 0 & 0 & 1/c \end{bmatrix}$.

$\boxed{19}$ $AI_3 = \begin{bmatrix} a_{11} & a_{12} & a_{13} \\ a_{21} & a_{22} & a_{23} \\ a_{31} & a_{32} & a_{33} \end{bmatrix} \begin{bmatrix} 1 & 0 & 0 \\ 0 & 1 & 0 \\ 0 & 0 & 1 \end{bmatrix} = \begin{bmatrix} a_{11} & a_{12} & a_{13} \\ a_{21} & a_{22} & a_{23} \\ a_{31} & a_{32} & a_{33} \end{bmatrix} = A$

$I_3A = \begin{bmatrix} 1 & 0 & 0 \\ 0 & 1 & 0 \\ 0 & 0 & 1 \end{bmatrix} \begin{bmatrix} a_{11} & a_{12} & a_{13} \\ a_{21} & a_{22} & a_{23} \\ a_{31} & a_{32} & a_{33} \end{bmatrix} = \begin{bmatrix} a_{11} & a_{12} & a_{13} \\ a_{21} & a_{22} & a_{23} \\ a_{31} & a_{32} & a_{33} \end{bmatrix} = A$

$\boxed{20}$ Show that the same conditions in Exercise 19 hold using a square matrix of order 4.

$\boxed{21}$ (a) $X = A^{-1}B = \frac{1}{10}\begin{bmatrix} 3 & 4 \\ -1 & 2 \end{bmatrix}\begin{bmatrix} 3 \\ 1 \end{bmatrix}\{A^{-1} \text{ from Exercise 3}\} = \frac{1}{10}\begin{bmatrix} 13 \\ -1 \end{bmatrix}$; solution is $\left(\frac{13}{10}, -\frac{1}{10}\right)$

(b) $X = A^{-1}B = \frac{1}{10}\begin{bmatrix} 3 & 4 \\ -1 & 2 \end{bmatrix}\begin{bmatrix} -2 \\ 5 \end{bmatrix} = \frac{1}{10}\begin{bmatrix} 14 \\ 12 \end{bmatrix}$; solution is $\left(\frac{7}{5}, \frac{6}{5}\right)$

$\boxed{22}$ (a) $X = A^{-1}B = \frac{1}{7}\begin{bmatrix} 5 & -2 \\ -4 & 3 \end{bmatrix}\begin{bmatrix} -1 \\ 1 \end{bmatrix}\{A^{-1} \text{ from Exercise 4}\} = \frac{1}{7}\begin{bmatrix} -7 \\ 7 \end{bmatrix}$; solution is $(-1, 1)$

(b) $X = A^{-1}B = \frac{1}{7}\begin{bmatrix} 5 & -2 \\ -4 & 3 \end{bmatrix}\begin{bmatrix} 4 \\ 3 \end{bmatrix} = \frac{1}{7}\begin{bmatrix} 14 \\ -7 \end{bmatrix}$; solution is $(2, -1)$

$\boxed{23}$ (a) $X = A^{-1}B = \frac{1}{3}\begin{bmatrix} -4 & -5 & 3 \\ -4 & -8 & 3 \\ 1 & 2 & 0 \end{bmatrix}\begin{bmatrix} 1 \\ 3 \\ -2 \end{bmatrix}\{A^{-1} \text{ from Exercise 9}\} = \frac{1}{3}\begin{bmatrix} -25 \\ -34 \\ 7 \end{bmatrix}$; solution is $\left(-\frac{25}{3}, -\frac{34}{3}, \frac{7}{3}\right)$

(b) $X = A^{-1}B = \frac{1}{3}\begin{bmatrix} -4 & -5 & 3 \\ -4 & -8 & 3 \\ 1 & 2 & 0 \end{bmatrix}\begin{bmatrix} -1 \\ 0 \\ 4 \end{bmatrix} = \frac{1}{3}\begin{bmatrix} 16 \\ 16 \\ -1 \end{bmatrix}$; solution is $\left(\frac{16}{3}, \frac{16}{3}, -\frac{1}{3}\right)$

$\boxed{24}$ (a) $X = A^{-1}B = \frac{1}{2}\begin{bmatrix} 1 & -5 & -3 \\ 2 & -8 & -6 \\ -1 & 7 & 5 \end{bmatrix}\begin{bmatrix} -1 \\ 4 \\ 2 \end{bmatrix}\{A^{-1} \text{ from Exercise 10}\} = \frac{1}{2}\begin{bmatrix} -27 \\ -46 \\ 39 \end{bmatrix}$;

solution is $\left(-\frac{27}{2}, -23, \frac{39}{2}\right)$

(b) $X = A^{-1}B = \frac{1}{2}\begin{bmatrix} 1 & -5 & -3 \\ 2 & -8 & -6 \\ -1 & 7 & 5 \end{bmatrix}\begin{bmatrix} -3 \\ -2 \\ 1 \end{bmatrix} = \frac{1}{2}\begin{bmatrix} 4 \\ 4 \\ -6 \end{bmatrix}$; solution is $(2, 2, -3)$

$\boxed{25}$ The inverse should be found using some type of computational device. If you are using a TI-83/4, enter the nine values into the matrix [A]. Change Float to 3 via MODE. Now find $[A]^{-1}$ {be sure to use the $\boxed{x^{-1}}$ key}. Use the right arrow key to see the rightmost elements in [A].

$A = \begin{bmatrix} 2 & -5 & 8 \\ 3 & 7 & -1 \\ 0 & 2 & 1 \end{bmatrix}$ $\Rightarrow$ $A^{-1} \approx \begin{bmatrix} 0.111 & 0.259 & -0.630 \\ -0.037 & 0.025 & 0.321 \\ 0.074 & -0.049 & 0.358 \end{bmatrix}$

$\boxed{26}$ $A = \begin{bmatrix} 0 & 1.2 & 4.1 \\ -1 & 0 & -1 \\ 5.9 & 2 & 0 \end{bmatrix}$ $\Rightarrow$ $A^{-1} \approx \begin{bmatrix} -0.131 & -0.537 & 0.079 \\ 0.386 & 1.583 & 0.268 \\ 0.131 & -0.463 & -0.079 \end{bmatrix}$

27 $A = \begin{bmatrix} 2 & -1 & 1 & 4 \\ 7 & 1.2 & -8 & 0 \\ 2.5 & 0 & 1.9 & 7.9 \\ 1 & -1 & 3 & 1 \end{bmatrix} \Rightarrow A^{-1} \approx \begin{bmatrix} -0.223 & 0.129 & 0.065 & 0.378 \\ -1.178 & 0.095 & 0.559 & 0.292 \\ -0.372 & 0.002 & 0.141 & 0.374 \\ 0.160 & -0.042 & 0.072 & -0.210 \end{bmatrix}$

28 $A = \begin{bmatrix} -3 & -7 & 4 & 0 \\ -7 & 0 & 5.5 & 9 \\ 3 & 1 & 0 & 0 \\ 9 & -11 & 4 & 1 \end{bmatrix} \Rightarrow A^{-1} \approx \begin{bmatrix} -0.031 & -0.004 & 0.184 & 0.036 \\ 0.092 & 0.012 & 0.448 & -0.109 \\ 0.389 & 0.018 & 0.921 & -0.163 \\ -0.261 & 0.097 & -0.420 & 0.128 \end{bmatrix}$

29 (a) $AX = B \Leftrightarrow \begin{bmatrix} 4.0 & 7.1 \\ 2.2 & -4.9 \end{bmatrix} \begin{bmatrix} x \\ y \end{bmatrix} = \begin{bmatrix} 6.2 \\ 2.9 \end{bmatrix}$

(b) On your calculator, find $[A]^{-1}$ and STOre this matrix as [B] for use in part (c). $A^{-1} \approx \begin{bmatrix} 0.1391 & 0.2016 \\ 0.0625 & -0.1136 \end{bmatrix}$

(c) Following the instructions in part (b), enter the three values into [C] {a $3 \times 1$ matrix}, and then evaluate

$[B]*[C].$ $X = A^{-1}B \approx \begin{bmatrix} 0.1391 & 0.2016 \\ 0.0625 & -0.1136 \end{bmatrix} \begin{bmatrix} 6.2 \\ 2.9 \end{bmatrix} \approx \begin{bmatrix} 1.4472 \\ 0.0579 \end{bmatrix}.$

30 (a) $AX = B \Leftrightarrow \begin{bmatrix} 1.9 & -3.2 \\ 2.6 & 0.4 \end{bmatrix} \begin{bmatrix} x \\ y \end{bmatrix} = \begin{bmatrix} 5.7 \\ 3.8 \end{bmatrix}$

(b) $A^{-1} \approx \begin{bmatrix} 0.0441 & 0.3524 \\ -0.2863 & 0.2093 \end{bmatrix}$

(c) $X = A^{-1}B \approx \begin{bmatrix} 0.0441 & 0.3524 \\ -0.2863 & 0.2093 \end{bmatrix} \begin{bmatrix} 5.7 \\ 3.8 \end{bmatrix} \approx \begin{bmatrix} 1.5903 \\ -0.8370 \end{bmatrix}$

31 (a) $AX = B \Leftrightarrow \begin{bmatrix} 3.1 & 6.7 & -8.7 \\ 4.1 & -5.1 & 0.2 \\ 0.6 & 1.1 & -7.4 \end{bmatrix} \begin{bmatrix} x \\ y \\ z \end{bmatrix} = \begin{bmatrix} 1.5 \\ 2.1 \\ 3.9 \end{bmatrix}$

(b) $A^{-1} \approx \begin{bmatrix} 0.1474 & 0.1572 & -0.1691 \\ 0.1197 & -0.0696 & -0.1426 \\ 0.0297 & 0.0024 & -0.1700 \end{bmatrix}$

(c) $X = A^{-1}B \approx \begin{bmatrix} 0.1474 & 0.1572 & -0.1691 \\ 0.1197 & -0.0696 & -0.1426 \\ 0.0297 & 0.0024 & -0.1700 \end{bmatrix} \begin{bmatrix} 1.5 \\ 2.1 \\ 3.9 \end{bmatrix} \approx \begin{bmatrix} -0.1081 \\ -0.5227 \\ -0.6135 \end{bmatrix}$

32 (a) $AX = B \Leftrightarrow \begin{bmatrix} 5.1 & 8.7 & 2.5 \\ 9.9 & 15 & 12 \\ -4.3 & -2.2 & -1 \end{bmatrix} \begin{bmatrix} x \\ y \\ z \end{bmatrix} = \begin{bmatrix} 1.1 \\ 3.8 \\ -7.1 \end{bmatrix}$

(b) $A^{-1} \approx \begin{bmatrix} -0.0576 & -0.0162 & -0.3381 \\ 0.2108 & -0.0286 & 0.1842 \\ -0.2159 & 0.1324 & 0.0487 \end{bmatrix}$

(c) $X = A^{-1}B \approx \begin{bmatrix} -0.0576 & -0.0162 & -0.3381 \\ 0.2108 & -0.0286 & 0.1842 \\ -0.2159 & 0.1324 & 0.0487 \end{bmatrix} \begin{bmatrix} 1.1 \\ 3.8 \\ -7.1 \end{bmatrix} = \begin{bmatrix} 2.2759 \\ -1.1847 \\ -0.0801 \end{bmatrix}$

33 (a) $f(x) = ax^2 + bx + c$ • $f(2) = 4a + 2b + c = 19;$

$f(8) = 64a + 8b + c = 59;$ $f(11) = 121a + 11b + c = 26$

Solve the $3 \times 3$ linear system using the inverse method.

$\begin{bmatrix} 4 & 2 & 1 \\ 64 & 8 & 1 \\ 121 & 11 & 1 \end{bmatrix} \begin{bmatrix} a \\ b \\ c \end{bmatrix} = \begin{bmatrix} 19 \\ 59 \\ 26 \end{bmatrix} \Rightarrow \begin{bmatrix} a \\ b \\ c \end{bmatrix} \approx \begin{bmatrix} -1.9630 \\ 26.2963 \\ -25.7407 \end{bmatrix}$

(b) [1, 12] by [−15, 70, 5]

Thus, let $f(x) = -1.9630x^2 + 26.2963x - 25.7407.$

(c) For June, $f(6) \approx 61°F$ and for October, $f(10) \approx 41°F.$

**34** (a) $f(x) = ax^2 + bx + c$  •  $f(2) = 4a + 2b + c = 9$;

   $f(7) = 49a + 7b + c = 60$; $f(11) = 121a + 11b + c = 21$

   Solve the $3 \times 3$ linear system using the inverse method.

$$\begin{bmatrix} 4 & 2 & 1 \\ 49 & 7 & 1 \\ 121 & 11 & 1 \end{bmatrix} \begin{bmatrix} a \\ b \\ c \end{bmatrix} = \begin{bmatrix} 9 \\ 60 \\ 21 \end{bmatrix} \Rightarrow \begin{bmatrix} a \\ b \\ c \end{bmatrix} \approx \begin{bmatrix} -2.2167 \\ 30.1500 \\ -42.4333 \end{bmatrix}$$

   Thus, let $f(x) = -2.2167x^2 + 30.15x - 42.4333$.

(b)

$[1, 12]$ by $[-15, 70, 5]$

(c) For June, $f(6) \approx 59°F$ and for October, $f(10) \approx 37°F$.

## 8.8 Exercises

**Note:** The minor $M_{ij}$ and the cofactor $A_{ij}$ are equal if $i + j$ is even and opposites if $i + j$ is odd.

**1** The minor $M_{11}$ is obtained by deleting the first row and first column from $A = \begin{bmatrix} 7 & -1 \\ 5 & 0 \end{bmatrix}$. Thus, $M_{11} = 0 = A_{11}$.

Similarly, $M_{12} = 5$ and $A_{12} = -5$; $M_{21} = -1$ and $A_{21} = 1$; and $M_{22} = 7 = A_{22}$.

**2** $A = \begin{bmatrix} -6 & 4 \\ 3 & 2 \end{bmatrix}$; $M_{11} = 2 = A_{11}$; $M_{12} = 3$ and $A_{12} = -3$; $M_{21} = 4$ and $A_{21} = -4$; $M_{22} = -6 = A_{22}$

**3** Let $A = \begin{bmatrix} 2 & 4 & -1 \\ 0 & 3 & 2 \\ -5 & 7 & 0 \end{bmatrix}$. Be sure you understand the note preceding the solution to Exercise 1.

$M_{11} = \begin{vmatrix} 3 & 2 \\ 7 & 0 \end{vmatrix} = (3)(0) - (7)(2) = 0 - 14 = -14 = A_{11}$;

$M_{12} = \begin{vmatrix} 0 & 2 \\ -5 & 0 \end{vmatrix} = (0)(0) - (-5)(2) = 0 - (-10) = 10$; $A_{12} = -10$;

$M_{13} = \begin{vmatrix} 0 & 3 \\ -5 & 7 \end{vmatrix} = (0)(7) - (-5)(3) = 0 - (-15) = 15 = A_{13}$;

$M_{21} = \begin{vmatrix} 4 & -1 \\ 7 & 0 \end{vmatrix} = 7$; $A_{21} = -7$;   $M_{22} = \begin{vmatrix} 2 & -1 \\ -5 & 0 \end{vmatrix} = -5 = A_{22}$;   $M_{23} = \begin{vmatrix} 2 & 4 \\ -5 & 7 \end{vmatrix} = 34$; $A_{23} = -34$;

$M_{31} = \begin{vmatrix} 4 & -1 \\ 3 & 2 \end{vmatrix} = 11 = A_{31}$;   $M_{32} = \begin{vmatrix} 2 & -1 \\ 0 & 2 \end{vmatrix} = 4$; $A_{32} = -4$;   $M_{33} = \begin{vmatrix} 2 & 4 \\ 0 & 3 \end{vmatrix} = 6 = A_{33}$.

**4** Let $A = \begin{bmatrix} 5 & -2 & 1 \\ 4 & 7 & 0 \\ -3 & 4 & -1 \end{bmatrix}$.

$M_{11} = \begin{vmatrix} 7 & 0 \\ 4 & -1 \end{vmatrix} = -7 = A_{11}$;   $M_{12} = \begin{vmatrix} 4 & 0 \\ -3 & -1 \end{vmatrix} = -4$; $A_{12} = 4$; $M_{13} = \begin{vmatrix} 4 & 7 \\ -3 & 4 \end{vmatrix} = 37 = A_{13}$;

$M_{21} = \begin{vmatrix} -2 & 1 \\ 4 & -1 \end{vmatrix} = -2$; $A_{21} = 2$;   $M_{22} = \begin{vmatrix} 5 & 1 \\ -3 & -1 \end{vmatrix} = -2 = A_{22}$;   $M_{23} = \begin{vmatrix} 5 & -2 \\ -3 & 4 \end{vmatrix} = 14$; $A_{23} = -14$;

$M_{31} = \begin{vmatrix} -2 & 1 \\ 7 & 0 \end{vmatrix} = -7 = A_{31}$;   $M_{32} = \begin{vmatrix} 5 & 1 \\ 4 & 0 \end{vmatrix} = -4$; $A_{32} = 4$;   $M_{33} = \begin{vmatrix} 5 & -2 \\ 4 & 7 \end{vmatrix} = 43 = A_{33}$

**Note:** In Exercises 5–24, let $A$ denote the given matrix.

**5** $|A| = \begin{vmatrix} 7 & -1 \\ 5 & 0 \end{vmatrix} = (7)(0) - (-1)(5) = 0 + 5 = 5$

**6** $|A| = \begin{vmatrix} -6 & 4 \\ 3 & 2 \end{vmatrix} = (-6)(2) - (4)(3) = -12 - 12 = -24$

**7** Expanding $|A|$ by the first column and using the cofactor values from Exercise 3, we obtain

$$|A| = a_{11}A_{11} + a_{21}A_{21} + a_{31}A_{31} = 2(-14) + 0(A_{21}) - 5(11) = -83.$$

**8** Expand by the third column. $|A| = a_{13}A_{13} + a_{23}A_{23} + a_{33}A_{33} = 1(37) + 0(A_{23}) - 1(43) = -6$

**9** By the definition of the determinant of a $2 \times 2$ matrix $A$ on page 607 of the text,

$$|A| = \begin{vmatrix} -5 & 4 \\ -3 & 2 \end{vmatrix} = (-5)(2) - (4)(-3) = -10 + 12 = 2.$$

**10** $|A| = \begin{vmatrix} 6 & 4 \\ -3 & 2 \end{vmatrix} = (6)(2) - (4)(-3) = 12 + 12 = 24$

**11** $|A| = \begin{vmatrix} a & -a \\ b & -b \end{vmatrix} = (a)(-b) - (-a)(b) = -ab + ab = 0$

**12** $|A| = \begin{vmatrix} c & d \\ -d & c \end{vmatrix} = (c)(c) - (d)(-d) = c^2 + d^2$

**13** Expand by the first row.

$$|A| = \begin{vmatrix} 3 & 1 & -2 \\ 4 & 2 & 5 \\ -6 & 3 & -1 \end{vmatrix} = a_{11}A_{11} + a_{12}A_{12} + a_{13}A_{13}$$

$$= (3)(-1)^{1+1}\begin{vmatrix} 2 & 5 \\ 3 & -1 \end{vmatrix} + (1)(-1)^{1+2}\begin{vmatrix} 4 & 5 \\ -6 & -1 \end{vmatrix} + (-2)(-1)^{1+3}\begin{vmatrix} 4 & 2 \\ -6 & 3 \end{vmatrix}$$

$$= (3)(1)(-17) + (1)(-1)(26) + (-2)(1)(24) = -51 - 26 - 48 = -125$$

**14** Expand by the first row.

$$|A| = \begin{vmatrix} 2 & -5 & 1 \\ -3 & 1 & 6 \\ 4 & -2 & 3 \end{vmatrix} = a_{11}A_{11} + a_{12}A_{12} + a_{13}A_{13} = 2(15) - 5(33) + 1(2) = -133$$

**15** Expand by the third row.

$$|A| = \begin{vmatrix} -5 & 4 & 1 \\ 3 & -2 & 7 \\ 2 & 0 & 6 \end{vmatrix} = a_{31}A_{31} + a_{32}A_{32} + a_{33}A_{33} = 2(30) + 0(A_{32}) + 6(-2) = 48$$

**16** Expand by the second row.

$$|A| = \begin{vmatrix} 2 & 7 & -3 \\ 1 & 0 & 4 \\ 4 & -1 & -2 \end{vmatrix} = a_{21}A_{21} + a_{22}A_{22} + a_{23}A_{23} = 1(17) + 0(A_{22}) + 4(30) = 137$$

**17** Expand $|A|$ by the third row. $|A| = 6\,A_{32} = -6\,M_{32} = -6\begin{vmatrix} 3 & 2 & 0 \\ 4 & -3 & 5 \\ 1 & -4 & 2 \end{vmatrix}$.

Expand $M_{32}$ by the first row. $M_{32} = 3(14) + 2(-3) + 0(-13) = 36 \implies |A| = -6(36) = -216.$

**18** Expand $|A|$ by the fourth column. $|A| = 6\,A_{34} = -6\,M_{34} = -6\begin{vmatrix} 2 & 5 & 1 \\ -4 & 0 & -3 \\ -1 & 4 & 2 \end{vmatrix}$.

Expand $M_{34}$ by the second column. $5(11) + 0(5) + 4(2) = 63$, $\therefore |A| = -6(63) = -378$

**19** Expand by the first row. $|A| = -b\begin{vmatrix} 0 & c & 0 \\ a & 0 & 0 \\ 0 & 0 & d \end{vmatrix}$.

Expand again by the first row. $|A| = (-b)(-c)\begin{vmatrix} a & 0 \\ 0 & d \end{vmatrix} = bc(ad - 0) = abcd.$

**20** Expand by the first column. $|A| = a \begin{vmatrix} b & x & y \\ 0 & c & z \\ 0 & 0 & d \end{vmatrix}$.

Expand again by the first column. $|A| = (ab) \begin{vmatrix} c & z \\ 0 & d \end{vmatrix} = abcd$.

**21** $|A| = \begin{vmatrix} e^{2x} & e^{3x} \\ 2e^{2x} & 3e^{3x} \end{vmatrix} = (e^{2x})(3e^{3x}) - (e^{3x})(2e^{2x}) = 3e^{5x} - 2e^{5x} = e^{5x}$

**22** $|A| = \begin{vmatrix} x^2 & x^3 \\ 2x & 3x^2 \end{vmatrix} = (x^2)(3x^2) - (x^3)(2x) = 3x^4 - 2x^4 = x^4$

**23** $|A| = \begin{vmatrix} \sin x & \cos x \\ \cos x & -\sin x \end{vmatrix} = (\sin x)(-\sin x) - (\cos x)(\cos x) = -\sin^2 x - \cos^2 x = -(\sin^2 x + \cos^2 x) = -1$

**24** $|A| = \begin{vmatrix} \tan x & \sec x \\ \sec^2 x & \sec x \tan x \end{vmatrix} = (\tan x)(\sec x \tan x) - (\sec x)(\sec^2 x)$

$= \sec x \tan^2 x - \sec^3 x = \sec x(\tan^2 x - \sec^2 x) = \sec x(-1) = -\sec x$

**25** $LS = \begin{vmatrix} a & b \\ c & d \end{vmatrix} = ad - bc;$    $RS = -\begin{vmatrix} c & d \\ a & b \end{vmatrix} = -(bc - ad) = ad - bc$

**26** $LS = \begin{vmatrix} a & b \\ c & d \end{vmatrix} = ad - bc;$    $RS = -\begin{vmatrix} b & a \\ d & c \end{vmatrix} = -(bc - ad) = ad - bc$

**27** $LS = \begin{vmatrix} a & kb \\ c & kd \end{vmatrix} = adk - bck;$    $RS = k\begin{vmatrix} a & b \\ c & d \end{vmatrix} = k(ad - bc) = adk - bck$

**28** $LS = \begin{vmatrix} a & b \\ kc & kd \end{vmatrix} = adk - bck;$    $RS = k\begin{vmatrix} a & b \\ c & d \end{vmatrix} = k(ad - bc) = adk - bck$

**29** $LS = \begin{vmatrix} a & b \\ c & d \end{vmatrix} = ad - bc;$    $RS = \begin{vmatrix} a & b \\ ka+c & kb+d \end{vmatrix} = abk + ad - abk - bc = ad - bc$

**30** $LS = \begin{vmatrix} a & b \\ c & d \end{vmatrix} = ad - bc;$    $RS = \begin{vmatrix} a & ka+b \\ c & kc+d \end{vmatrix} = ack + ad - ack - bc = ad - bc$

**31** $LS = \begin{vmatrix} a & b \\ c & d \end{vmatrix} + \begin{vmatrix} a & e \\ c & f \end{vmatrix} = ad - bc + af - ce;$ $RS = \begin{vmatrix} a & b+e \\ c & d+f \end{vmatrix} = ad + af - bc - ce$

**32** $LS = \begin{vmatrix} a & b \\ c & d \end{vmatrix} + \begin{vmatrix} a & b \\ e & f \end{vmatrix} = ad - bc + af - be;$ $RS = \begin{vmatrix} a & b \\ c+e & d+f \end{vmatrix} = ad + af - bc - be$

**33** Consider the matrix in Exercise 20. If we expanded along the first column, we would obtain $a$ times its cofactor. Expanding along the first column again, we obtain $ab$ times another cofactor. This exercise is similar since all elements in $A$ *above* {rather than below} the main diagonal are zero. We can evaluate the determinant using $n$ expansions by the first row, and obtain $|A| = a_{11} a_{22} \cdots a_{nn}$.

**34** $\begin{bmatrix} a_{11} & a_{12} & | & 1 & 0 \\ a_{21} & a_{22} & | & 0 & 1 \end{bmatrix}$    $(1/a_{11})R_1 \to R_1$    {$a_{11}$ or $a_{21}$ must be nonzero since $|A| \neq 0$.}
                                                                                   {The rows could be swapped.}

$\begin{bmatrix} 1 & a_{12}/a_{11} & | & 1/a_{11} & 0 \\ a_{21} & a_{22} & | & 0 & 1 \end{bmatrix}$    $R_2 - a_{21}R_1 \to R_2$

$\begin{bmatrix} 1 & a_{12}/a_{11} & | & 1/a_{11} & 0 \\ 0 & (a_{11}a_{22} - a_{12}a_{21})/a_{11} & | & -a_{21}/a_{11} & 1 \end{bmatrix}$    $(a_{11}/|A|)R_2 \to R_2$, where $|A| = a_{11}a_{22} - a_{12}a_{21}$

$\begin{bmatrix} 1 & a_{12}/a_{11} & | & 1/a_{11} & 0 \\ 0 & 1 & | & -a_{21}/|A| & a_{11}/|A| \end{bmatrix}$    $R_1 - (a_{12}/a_{11})R_2 \to R_1$

$$\begin{bmatrix} 1 & 0 & 1/a_{11} + (a_{12}a_{21})/(a_{11}|A|) & -a_{12}/|A| \\ 0 & 1 & -a_{21}/|A| & a_{11}/|A| \end{bmatrix}$$

$$\begin{bmatrix} 1 & 0 & (|A| + a_{12}a_{21})/(a_{11}|A|) & -a_{12}/|A| \\ 0 & 1 & -a_{21}/|A| & a_{11}/|A| \end{bmatrix} \{\text{Use the definition of } |A| \text{ above}\}$$

$$\begin{bmatrix} 1 & 0 & a_{22}/|A| & -a_{12}/|A| \\ 0 & 1 & -a_{21}/|A| & a_{11}/|A| \end{bmatrix} \Rightarrow \qquad A^{-1} = \frac{1}{|A|} \begin{bmatrix} a_{22} & -a_{12} \\ -a_{21} & a_{11} \end{bmatrix}$$

**35** (a) $A - xI = \begin{bmatrix} 1 & 2 \\ 3 & 2 \end{bmatrix} - x\begin{bmatrix} 1 & 0 \\ 0 & 1 \end{bmatrix} = \begin{bmatrix} 1-x & 2 \\ 3 & 2-x \end{bmatrix}.$

$f(x) = |A - xI| = \begin{vmatrix} 1-x & 2 \\ 3 & 2-x \end{vmatrix} = (1-x)(2-x) - (3)(2) = (2 - 3x + x^2) - 6 = x^2 - 3x - 4.$

(b) $x^2 - 3x - 4 = 0 \Rightarrow (x-4)(x+1) = 0 \Rightarrow x = -1, 4$

**36** (a) $f(x) = |A - xI| = \begin{vmatrix} 3-x & 1 \\ 2 & 2-x \end{vmatrix} = (3-x)(2-x) - (1)(2) = (6 - 5x + x^2) - 2 = x^2 - 5x + 4.$

(b) $(x-1)(x-4) = 0 \Rightarrow x = 1, 4$

**37** (a) $f(x) = |A - xI| = \begin{vmatrix} 1-x & 6 \\ 2 & 7-x \end{vmatrix} = (1-x)(7-x) - (6)(2) = (7 - 8x + x^2) - 12 = x^2 - 8x - 5.$

(b) $x^2 - 8x - 5 = 0 \Rightarrow x = \dfrac{8 \pm \sqrt{64 + 20}}{2} = \dfrac{8 \pm 2\sqrt{21}}{2} = 4 \pm \sqrt{21} \approx 8.58, -0.58$

**38** (a) $f(x) = |A - xI| = \begin{vmatrix} 2-x & -4 \\ -3 & 5-x \end{vmatrix} = (2-x)(5-x) - (-4)(-3) = (10 - 7x + x^2) - 12 = x^2 - 7x - 2.$

(b) $x^2 - 7x - 2 = 0 \Rightarrow x = \dfrac{7 \pm \sqrt{49 + 8}}{2} = \dfrac{7 \pm \sqrt{57}}{2} \approx 7.27, -0.27$

**39** (a) Expand by the first row.

$f(x) = \begin{vmatrix} 1-x & 0 & 0 \\ 1 & 0-x & -2 \\ -1 & 1 & -3-x \end{vmatrix} = (1-x)[(-x)(-3-x) - (-2)] = (1-x)(x^2 + 3x + 2)$

$= (1-x)(x+1)(x+2)$ or $(-x^3 - 2x^2 + x + 2)$

(b) $(1-x)(x+1)(x+2) = 0 \Rightarrow x = -2, -1, 1$

**40** (a) Expand by the third column.

$f(x) = \begin{vmatrix} 2-x & 1 & 0 \\ -1 & 0-x & 0 \\ 1 & 3 & 2-x \end{vmatrix} = (2-x)[(2-x)(-x) - (-1)]$

$= (2-x)(x^2 - 2x + 1) = (2-x)(x-1)^2$ or $(-x^3 + 4x^2 - 5x + 2).$

(b) $(2-x)(x-1)^2 = 0 \Rightarrow x = 1, 2$

**41** (a) Expand by the first row.

$f(x) = \begin{vmatrix} 0-x & 2 & -2 \\ -1 & 3-x & 1 \\ -3 & 3 & 1-x \end{vmatrix} = (-x)[(3-x)(1-x) - 3] - 2[(x-1) + 3] - 2[-3 + 3(3-x)]$

$= (-x)[(3 - 4x + x^2) - 3] - 2(x+2) - 2(-3x + 6)$

$= (-x^3 + 4x^2) - 2x - 4 + 6x - 12 = -x^3 + 4x^2 + 4x - 16$

(b) By trying possible rational roots, we determine that 2 is a zero of $f$. Thus, $-x^3 + 4x^2 + 4x - 16 = 0 \Rightarrow$

$(x-2)(-x^2 + 2x + 8) = 0 \Rightarrow (x+2)(x-2)(-x+4) = 0 \Rightarrow x = -2, 2, 4.$

**42** (a) Expand by the first row.

$$f(x) = \begin{vmatrix} 3-x & 2 & 2 \\ 1 & 0-x & 2 \\ -1 & -1 & 0-x \end{vmatrix} = (3-x)(x^2+2) - 2(-x+2) + 2(-1-x)$$

$$= -x^3 + 3x^2 - 2x = (-x)(x^2 - 3x + 2) = (-x)(x-1)(x-2)$$

(b) $(-x)(x-1)(x-2) = 0 \implies x = 0, 1, 2$

**Note:** In Exercises 43–46, expand by the first row.

**43** $\begin{vmatrix} i & j & k \\ 2 & -1 & 6 \\ -3 & 5 & 1 \end{vmatrix} = i\begin{vmatrix} -1 & 6 \\ 5 & 1 \end{vmatrix} - j\begin{vmatrix} 2 & 6 \\ -3 & 1 \end{vmatrix} + k\begin{vmatrix} 2 & -1 \\ -3 & 5 \end{vmatrix} = -31i - 20j + 7k$

**44** $\begin{vmatrix} i & j & k \\ 1 & -2 & 3 \\ 2 & 1 & -4 \end{vmatrix} = i\begin{vmatrix} -2 & 3 \\ 1 & -4 \end{vmatrix} - j\begin{vmatrix} 1 & 3 \\ 2 & -4 \end{vmatrix} + k\begin{vmatrix} 1 & -2 \\ 2 & 1 \end{vmatrix} = 5i + 10j + 5k$

**45** $\begin{vmatrix} i & j & k \\ 5 & -6 & -1 \\ 3 & 0 & 1 \end{vmatrix} = i\begin{vmatrix} -6 & -1 \\ 0 & 1 \end{vmatrix} - j\begin{vmatrix} 5 & -1 \\ 3 & 1 \end{vmatrix} + k\begin{vmatrix} 5 & -6 \\ 3 & 0 \end{vmatrix} = -6i - 8j + 18k$

**46** $\begin{vmatrix} i & j & k \\ 4 & -6 & 2 \\ -2 & 3 & -1 \end{vmatrix} = i\begin{vmatrix} -6 & 2 \\ 3 & -1 \end{vmatrix} - j\begin{vmatrix} 4 & 2 \\ -2 & -1 \end{vmatrix} + k\begin{vmatrix} 4 & -6 \\ -2 & 3 \end{vmatrix} = 0i + 0j + 0k$

**47** $A = \begin{bmatrix} 1 & -2.1 & 5 \\ -4 & 3.2 & 2 \\ 8 & 5.9 & -7 \end{bmatrix} \implies |A| = -225$

**48** $A = \begin{bmatrix} -2 & 5.5 & 8 \\ -0.3 & 8.5 & 7 \\ 4.9 & 6.7 & 11 \end{bmatrix} \implies |A| = -235.68$

**49** $A = \begin{bmatrix} 29 & -17 & 90 \\ -34 & 91 & -34 \\ 48 & 7 & 10 \end{bmatrix} \implies |A| = -359,284$

**50** $A = \begin{bmatrix} 15 & -21 & 32 \\ -40 & 17 & 9 \\ 30 & 25 & -11 \end{bmatrix} \implies |A| = -50,930$

**51** (a) $f(x) = |A - xI| = \begin{vmatrix} 1-x & 0 & 1 \\ 0 & 2-x & 1 \\ 1 & 1 & -2-x \end{vmatrix} = (1-x)[(2-x)(-2-x) - 1] + 1[0 - (2-x)]$

$$= (1-x)[-5 + x^2] + (x-2) = -x^3 + x^2 + 6x - 7$$

(b) The characteristic values of $A$ are equal to the zeros of $f$.

From the graph, we see that the zeros are approximately $-2.51, 1.22,$ and $2.29$.

$[-10, 11]$ by $[-12, 2]$

$[-15, 15, 2]$ by $[-10, 10, 2]$

*Figure 51*

*Figure 52*

[52] (a)  $f(x) = |A - xI| = \begin{vmatrix} 3-x & -1 & -1 \\ -1 & 1-x & 0 \\ -1 & 0 & -2-x \end{vmatrix}$

$$= (3-x)[(1-x)(-2-x) - 0] + 1[-1(-2-x) - 0] - 1[0 + 1(1-x)]$$

$$= (3-x)[-2 + x + x^2] + 1[x+2] - 1[1-x]$$

$$= -x^3 + 2x^2 + 5x - 6 + (x+2) + (x-1) = -x^3 + 2x^2 + 7x - 5$$

(b) The characteristic values of $A$ are equal to the zeros of $f$.

From the graph, we see that the zeros are approximately $-2.20, 0.64,$ and $3.57$.

## 8.9 Exercises

[1] $R_2$ and $R_3$ are interchanged. The determinant value is multiplied by $-1$.

[2] $R_1$ and $R_3$ are interchanged. The determinant value is multiplied by $-1$.

[3] $C_2$ and $C_3$ are interchanged. The determinant value is multiplied by $-1$.

[4] $C_1$ and $C_3$ are interchanged. The determinant value is multiplied by $-1$.

[5] $R_3$ is replaced by $-R_1 + R_3$. There is no change in the determinant value.

[6] $R_1$ is replaced by $-R_2 + R_1$. There is no change in the determinant value.

[7] The number 2 can be factored out of $R_1$, yielding $2 \begin{vmatrix} 1 & 2 & 1 \\ 1 & 2 & 4 \\ 2 & 6 & 4 \end{vmatrix}$.

Next, the number 2 can be factored out of $R_3$, yielding $4 \begin{vmatrix} 1 & 2 & 1 \\ 1 & 2 & 4 \\ 1 & 3 & 2 \end{vmatrix}$.

[8] 2 is a common factor of $C_1$ and 3 is a common factor of $C_3$

[9] $R_1$ and $R_3$ are identical. The determinant is 0.

[10] $C_1$ and $C_3$ are identical. The determinant is 0.

[11] $-1$ is a common factor of $R_2$.

[12] $-1$ is a common factor of $R_1$.

[13] Every number in $C_2$ is 0. The determinant is zero.

[14] Every number in $R_2$ is 0. The determinant is zero.

[15] $C_3$ is replaced by $(2C_1 + C_3)$. There is no change in the determinant value.

[16] $C_3$ is replaced by $(2C_2 + C_3)$. There is no change in the determinant value.

*Note:* $\{R_i\}$ and $\{C_i\}$ indicate that the determinant is expanded by the $i$th row or column, respectively.

[17] Since there are two zeros in the third column, we expand by the third column.

$\begin{vmatrix} 1 & 2 & 0 \\ -4 & 3 & 0 \\ \pi & a & 5 \end{vmatrix}$ $\{C_3\} = (5) \begin{vmatrix} 1 & 2 \\ -4 & 3 \end{vmatrix} = (5)(3+8) = 5(11) = 55$

**18** Since there are two zeros in the second column, we expand by the second column.

$$\begin{vmatrix} 4 & 0 & 2 \\ e & 7 & x \\ 1 & 0 & -3 \end{vmatrix} \{C_2\} = (7)\begin{vmatrix} 4 & 2 \\ 1 & -3 \end{vmatrix} = (7)(-12-2) = 7(-14) = -98$$

**19** There are many possibilities for introducing zeros. In this case, obtaining a zero in the third row, second column would lead to an easy evaluation using the second column.

$$\begin{vmatrix} 3 & 1 & 0 \\ -2 & 0 & 1 \\ 1 & 3 & -1 \end{vmatrix} \begin{matrix} \\ \\ R_3 - 3R_1 \to R_3 \end{matrix} = \begin{vmatrix} 3 & 1 & 0 \\ -2 & 0 & 1 \\ -8 & 0 & -1 \end{vmatrix} \{C_2\} = (-1)\begin{vmatrix} -2 & 1 \\ -8 & -1 \end{vmatrix} = (-1)(2+8) = -10$$

**20** $$\begin{vmatrix} -3 & 0 & 4 \\ 1 & 2 & 0 \\ 4 & 1 & -1 \end{vmatrix} \begin{matrix} \\ R_2 - 2R_3 \to R_2 \\ \end{matrix} = \begin{vmatrix} -3 & 0 & 4 \\ -7 & 0 & 2 \\ 4 & 1 & -1 \end{vmatrix} \{C_2\} = (-1)\begin{vmatrix} -3 & 4 \\ -7 & 2 \end{vmatrix} = (-1)(-6+28) = -22$$

**21** $$\begin{vmatrix} 5 & 4 & 3 \\ -3 & 2 & 1 \\ 0 & 7 & -2 \end{vmatrix} \begin{matrix} R_1 - 3R_2 \to R_1 \\ \\ R_3 + 2R_2 \to R_3 \end{matrix} = \begin{vmatrix} 14 & -2 & 0 \\ -3 & 2 & 1 \\ -6 & 11 & 0 \end{vmatrix} \{C_3\} = (-1)\begin{vmatrix} 14 & -2 \\ -6 & 11 \end{vmatrix} = (-1)(154-12) = -142$$

**22** $$\begin{vmatrix} 0 & 2 & -6 \\ 5 & 1 & -3 \\ 6 & -2 & 5 \end{vmatrix} \begin{matrix} R_1 - 2R_2 \to R_1 \\ \\ R_3 + 2R_2 \to R_3 \end{matrix} = \begin{vmatrix} -10 & 0 & 0 \\ 5 & 1 & -3 \\ 16 & 0 & -1 \end{vmatrix} \{C_2\} = (1)\begin{vmatrix} -10 & 0 \\ 16 & -1 \end{vmatrix} = (1)(10-0) = 10$$

**23** $$\begin{vmatrix} 2 & 2 & -3 \\ 3 & 6 & 9 \\ -2 & 5 & 4 \end{vmatrix} \{3 \text{ is a common factor of } R_2\} = (3)\begin{vmatrix} 2 & 2 & -3 \\ 1 & 2 & 3 \\ -2 & 5 & 4 \end{vmatrix}$$

Since there is a "1" in the second row, first column, we will obtain zeros in the other two locations of the first column.

$$(3)\begin{vmatrix} 2 & 2 & -3 \\ 1 & 2 & 3 \\ -2 & 5 & 4 \end{vmatrix} \begin{matrix} R_1 - 2R_2 \to R_1 \\ \\ R_3 + 2R_2 \to R_3 \end{matrix} = (3)\begin{vmatrix} 0 & -2 & -9 \\ 1 & 2 & 3 \\ 0 & 9 & 10 \end{vmatrix} \{C_1\} = (3)(-1)\begin{vmatrix} -2 & -9 \\ 9 & 10 \end{vmatrix} = (-3)(-20+81) = -183$$

**24** $$\begin{vmatrix} 3 & 8 & 5 \\ 5 & 3 & -6 \\ 2 & 4 & -2 \end{vmatrix} \{2 \text{ is a common factor of } R_3\} = (2)\begin{vmatrix} 3 & 8 & 5 \\ 5 & 3 & -6 \\ 1 & 2 & -1 \end{vmatrix} \begin{matrix} R_1 - 3R_3 \to R_1 \\ R_2 - 5R_3 \to R_2 \\ \end{matrix} = (2)\begin{vmatrix} 0 & 2 & 8 \\ 0 & -7 & -1 \\ 1 & 2 & -1 \end{vmatrix} \{C_1\}$$

$$= (2)(1)\begin{vmatrix} 2 & 8 \\ -7 & -1 \end{vmatrix} = (2)(-2+56) = 108$$

**25** $$\begin{vmatrix} 3 & 1 & -2 & 2 \\ 2 & 0 & 1 & 4 \\ 0 & 1 & 3 & 5 \\ -1 & 2 & 0 & -3 \end{vmatrix} \begin{matrix} \\ \\ R_3 - R_1 \to R_3 \\ R_4 - 2R_1 \to R_4 \end{matrix} = \begin{vmatrix} 3 & 1 & -2 & 2 \\ 2 & 0 & 1 & 4 \\ -3 & 0 & 5 & 3 \\ -7 & 0 & 4 & -7 \end{vmatrix} \{C_2\} = (-1)\begin{vmatrix} 2 & 1 & 4 \\ -3 & 5 & 3 \\ -7 & 4 & -7 \end{vmatrix} \begin{matrix} \\ R_2 - 5R_1 \to R_2 \\ R_3 - 4R_1 \to R_3 \end{matrix}$$

$$= (-1)\begin{vmatrix} 2 & 1 & 4 \\ -13 & 0 & -17 \\ -15 & 0 & -23 \end{vmatrix} \{C_2\} = (-1)(-1)\begin{vmatrix} -13 & -17 \\ -15 & -23 \end{vmatrix}$$

$$= (1)(299-255) = 44$$

**26** $$\begin{vmatrix} 3 & 2 & 0 & 4 \\ -2 & 0 & 5 & 0 \\ 4 & -3 & 1 & 6 \\ 2 & -1 & 2 & 0 \end{vmatrix} \begin{matrix} \\ R_2 - 5R_3 \to R_2 \\ \\ R_4 - 2R_3 \to R_4 \end{matrix} = \begin{vmatrix} 3 & 2 & 0 & 4 \\ -22 & 15 & 0 & -30 \\ 4 & -3 & 1 & 6 \\ -6 & 5 & 0 & -12 \end{vmatrix} \{C_3\} = (1)\begin{vmatrix} 3 & 2 & 4 \\ -22 & 15 & -30 \\ -6 & 5 & -12 \end{vmatrix} \begin{matrix} C_1 - C_2 \to C_1 \\ \\ \end{matrix}$$

$$= \begin{vmatrix} 1 & 2 & 4 \\ -37 & 15 & -30 \\ -11 & 5 & -12 \end{vmatrix} \begin{matrix} \\ R_2 + 37R_1 \to R_2 \\ R_3 + 11R_1 \to R_3 \end{matrix} = \begin{vmatrix} 1 & 2 & 4 \\ 0 & 89 & 118 \\ 0 & 27 & 32 \end{vmatrix} \{C_1\} = (1)\begin{vmatrix} 89 & 118 \\ 27 & 32 \end{vmatrix} = (1)(2848-3186) = -338$$

**27** $\begin{vmatrix} 2 & -2 & 0 & 0 & -3 \\ 3 & 0 & 3 & 2 & -1 \\ 0 & 1 & -2 & 0 & 2 \\ -1 & 2 & 0 & 3 & 0 \\ 0 & 4 & 1 & 0 & 0 \end{vmatrix}$ $\begin{matrix} C_2 - 4C_3 \to C_2 \\ \\ = \end{matrix}$ $\begin{vmatrix} 2 & -2 & 0 & 0 & -3 \\ 3 & -12 & 3 & 2 & -1 \\ 0 & 9 & -2 & 0 & 2 \\ -1 & 2 & 0 & 3 & 0 \\ 0 & 0 & 1 & 0 & 0 \end{vmatrix}$ $\{R_5\}$

$= (1)\begin{vmatrix} 2 & -2 & 0 & -3 \\ 3 & -12 & 2 & -1 \\ 0 & 9 & 0 & 2 \\ -1 & 2 & 3 & 0 \end{vmatrix}$ $\begin{matrix} R_1 + 2R_4 \to R_1 \\ R_2 + 3R_4 \to R_2 \\ = \end{matrix}$ $\begin{vmatrix} 0 & 2 & 6 & -3 \\ 0 & -6 & 11 & -1 \\ 0 & 9 & 0 & 2 \\ -1 & 2 & 3 & 0 \end{vmatrix}$ $\{C_1\}$

$= (1)\begin{vmatrix} 2 & 6 & -3 \\ -6 & 11 & -1 \\ 9 & 0 & 2 \end{vmatrix}$ $\begin{matrix} R_1 - 3R_2 \to R_1 \\ \\ R_3 + 2R_2 \to R_3 \end{matrix}$ $= \begin{vmatrix} 20 & -27 & 0 \\ -6 & 11 & -1 \\ -3 & 22 & 0 \end{vmatrix}$ $\{C_3\} = (1)\begin{vmatrix} 20 & -27 \\ -3 & 22 \end{vmatrix} = (1)(440 - 81) = 359$

**28** $\begin{vmatrix} 2 & 0 & -1 & 0 & 2 \\ 1 & 3 & 0 & 0 & 1 \\ 0 & 4 & 3 & 0 & -1 \\ -1 & 2 & 0 & -2 & 0 \\ 0 & 1 & 5 & 0 & -4 \end{vmatrix}$ $\{C_4\} = (-2)\begin{vmatrix} 2 & 0 & -1 & 2 \\ 1 & 3 & 0 & 1 \\ 0 & 4 & 3 & -1 \\ 0 & 1 & 5 & -4 \end{vmatrix}$ $\begin{matrix} R_1 - 2R_2 \to R_1 \\ \\ \\ \end{matrix}$

$= (-2)\begin{vmatrix} 0 & -6 & -1 & 0 \\ 1 & 3 & 0 & 1 \\ 0 & 4 & 3 & -1 \\ 0 & 1 & 5 & -4 \end{vmatrix}$ $\{C_1\} = (-2)(-1)\begin{vmatrix} -6 & -1 & 0 \\ 4 & 3 & -1 \\ 1 & 5 & -4 \end{vmatrix}$ $\begin{matrix} R_1 + 6R_3 \to R_1 \\ R_2 - 4R_3 \to R_2 \\ = \end{matrix}$ $(2)\begin{vmatrix} 0 & 29 & -24 \\ 0 & -17 & 15 \\ 1 & 5 & -4 \end{vmatrix}$ $\{C_1\}$

$= (2)(1)\begin{vmatrix} 29 & -24 \\ -17 & 15 \end{vmatrix} = (2)(435 - 408) = 54$

**29** $\begin{vmatrix} 1 & 1 & 1 \\ a & b & c \\ a^2 & b^2 & c^2 \end{vmatrix}$ $\begin{matrix} C_1 - C_2 \to C_1 \\ \\ C_3 - C_2 \to C_3 \end{matrix}$ $= \begin{vmatrix} 0 & 1 & 0 \\ a-b & b & c-b \\ a^2-b^2 & b^2 & c^2-b^2 \end{vmatrix}$ $\begin{matrix} a-b \text{ is a common factor of } C_1 \\ c-b \text{ is a common factor of } C_3 \end{matrix}$

$= (a-b)(c-b)\begin{vmatrix} 0 & 1 & 0 \\ 1 & b & 1 \\ a+b & b^2 & c+b \end{vmatrix}$ $\{R_1\} = (a-b)(c-b)(-1)\begin{vmatrix} 1 & 1 \\ a+b & c+b \end{vmatrix}$

$= (a-b)(b-c)(c+b-a-b) = (a-b)(b-c)(c-a)$

**30** $\begin{vmatrix} 1 & 1 & 1 \\ a & b & c \\ a^3 & b^3 & c^3 \end{vmatrix}$ $\begin{matrix} R_2 - aR_1 \to R_2 \\ \\ R_3 - a^3R_1 \to R_3 \end{matrix}$ $= \begin{vmatrix} 1 & 1 & 1 \\ 0 & b-a & c-a \\ 0 & b^3-a^3 & c^3-a^3 \end{vmatrix}$ $\{C_1\} = (1)\begin{vmatrix} b-a & c-a \\ b^3-a^3 & c^3-a^3 \end{vmatrix}$

$= (b-a)(c^3-a^3) - (c-a)(b^3-a^3) = (b-a)(c-a)(c^2+ac+a^2) - (c-a)(b-a)(b^2+ab+a^2)$

$= (b-a)(c-a)(c^2+ac+a^2-b^2-ab-a^2) = (b-a)(c-a)(c^2+ac-b^2-ab)$

$= (b-a)(c-a)[(c-b)(c+b) + a(c-b)] = (b-a)(c-a)[(c-b)(c+b+a)]$

$= (a-b)(b-c)(c-a)(a+b+c)$

**31** $\begin{vmatrix} a_{11} & a_{12} & a_{13} & a_{14} \\ 0 & a_{22} & a_{23} & a_{24} \\ 0 & 0 & a_{33} & a_{34} \\ 0 & 0 & 0 & a_{44} \end{vmatrix}$ $\{C_1\} = (a_{11})\begin{vmatrix} a_{22} & a_{23} & a_{24} \\ 0 & a_{33} & a_{34} \\ 0 & 0 & a_{44} \end{vmatrix}$ $\{C_1\} = (a_{11})(a_{22})\begin{vmatrix} a_{33} & a_{34} \\ 0 & a_{44} \end{vmatrix}$

$= (a_{11}a_{22})(a_{33}a_{44} - 0) = a_{11}a_{22}a_{33}a_{44}$

**32** $|A| = \begin{vmatrix} a & b & 0 & 0 \\ c & d & 0 & 0 \\ 0 & 0 & e & f \\ 0 & 0 & g & h \end{vmatrix}$ $\{C_1\} = a\begin{vmatrix} d & 0 & 0 \\ 0 & e & f \\ 0 & g & h \end{vmatrix} - c\begin{vmatrix} b & 0 & 0 \\ 0 & e & f \\ 0 & g & h \end{vmatrix}$ $\{R_1 \text{ for both determinants}\}$

$= ad\begin{vmatrix} e & f \\ g & h \end{vmatrix} - cb\begin{vmatrix} e & f \\ g & h \end{vmatrix} = (ad - bc)\begin{vmatrix} e & f \\ g & h \end{vmatrix} = \begin{vmatrix} a & b \\ c & d \end{vmatrix}\begin{vmatrix} e & f \\ g & h \end{vmatrix}$

**33** $|AB| = \begin{vmatrix} a_{11}b_{11} + a_{12}b_{21} & a_{11}b_{12} + a_{12}b_{22} \\ a_{21}b_{11} + a_{22}b_{21} & a_{21}b_{12} + a_{22}b_{22} \end{vmatrix}$

$= (a_{11}b_{11} + a_{12}b_{21})(a_{21}b_{12} + a_{22}b_{22}) - (a_{11}b_{12} + a_{12}b_{22})(a_{21}b_{11} + a_{22}b_{21})$

$= a_{11}b_{11}a_{21}b_{12} + a_{11}b_{11}a_{22}b_{22} + a_{12}b_{21}a_{21}b_{12} + a_{12}b_{21}a_{22}b_{22}$

$\qquad\qquad\qquad - a_{11}b_{12}a_{21}b_{11} - a_{11}b_{12}a_{22}b_{21} - a_{12}b_{22}a_{21}b_{11} - a_{12}b_{22}a_{22}b_{21}$

$= a_{11}a_{22}b_{11}b_{22} - a_{11}a_{22}b_{21}b_{12} - a_{21}a_{12}b_{11}b_{22} + a_{21}a_{12}b_{21}b_{12} = (a_{11}a_{22} - a_{21}a_{12})(b_{11}b_{22} - b_{21}b_{12}) = |A||B|$

**34** Let $B = kA$. Since $k$ is a factor of each of the $n$ rows of $A$, $n$ repeated applications of property (2) of the theorem on row and column transformations of a determinant yields $|B| = k^n|A|$.

**35** Expanding by the first row yields $Ax + By + C = 0$ {an equation of a line} where $A$, $B$, and $C$ are constants. To show that the line contains $(x_1, y_1)$ and $(x_2, y_2)$, we must show that these points are solutions of the equation. Substituting $x_1$ for $x$ and $y_1$ for $y$, we obtain two identical rows and the determinant is zero. Hence, $(x_1, y_1)$ is a solution of the equation and a similar argument can be made for $(x_2, y_2)$.

**36** Expanding by the first row yields $A(x^2 + y^2) + Bx + Cy + D = 0$ {an equation of a circle} where $A$, $B$, $C$, and $D$ are constants. To show that the circle contains $(x_1, y_1)$, $(x_2, y_2)$, and $(x_3, y_3)$ we must show that these points are solutions of the equation. Substituting $x_1$ for $x$ and $y_1$ for $y$, we obtain two identical rows and the determinant is zero. Hence, $(x_1, y_1)$ is a solution of the equation and similar arguments can be made for $(x_2, y_2)$ and $(x_3, y_3)$.

**37** For the system $\begin{cases} 2x + 3y = 2 \\ x - 2y = 8 \end{cases}$ we have $|D| = \begin{vmatrix} 2 & 3 \\ 1 & -2 \end{vmatrix} = -4 - 3 = -7$.

Since $|D| = -7 \neq 0$, we may solve the system using Cramer's rule.

$|D_x| = \begin{vmatrix} 2 & 3 \\ 8 & -2 \end{vmatrix} = -4 - 24 = -28$. $|D_y| = \begin{vmatrix} 2 & 2 \\ 1 & 8 \end{vmatrix} = 16 - 2 = 14$.

$x = \dfrac{|D_x|}{|D|} = \dfrac{-28}{-7} = 4$ and $y = \dfrac{|D_y|}{|D|} = \dfrac{14}{-7} = -2$. ★ $(4, -2)$

**38** $\begin{cases} 4x + 5y = 13 \\ 3x + y = -4 \end{cases}$ • $|D_x| = 33$, $|D_y| = -55$, $|D| = -11$; $x = -3$, $y = 5$

**39** For the system $\begin{cases} 2x + 5y = 16 \\ 3x - 7y = 24 \end{cases}$ we have $|D| = \begin{vmatrix} 2 & 5 \\ 3 & -7 \end{vmatrix} = -14 - 15 = -29$.

Since $|D| = -29 \neq 0$, we may solve the system using Cramer's rule.

$|D_x| = \begin{vmatrix} 16 & 5 \\ 24 & -7 \end{vmatrix} = -112 - 120 = -232$. $|D_y| = \begin{vmatrix} 2 & 16 \\ 3 & 24 \end{vmatrix} = 48 - 48 = 0$.

$x = \dfrac{|D_x|}{|D|} = \dfrac{-232}{-29} = 8$ and $y = \dfrac{|D_y|}{|D|} = \dfrac{0}{-29} = 0$. ★ $(8, 0)$

**40** $\begin{cases} 7x - 8y = 9 \\ 4x + 3y = -10 \end{cases}$ • $|D_x| = -53$, $|D_y| = -106$, $|D| = 53$; $x = -1$, $y = -2$

**41** $\begin{cases} 2x - 3y = 5 \\ -6x + 9y = 12 \end{cases}$ • $|D| = \begin{vmatrix} 2 & -3 \\ -6 & 9 \end{vmatrix} = 18 - 18 = 0$, so Cramer's rule cannot be used.

**42** $\begin{cases} 3p - q = 7 \\ -12p + 4q = 3 \end{cases}$ • $|D| = \begin{vmatrix} 3 & -1 \\ -12 & 4 \end{vmatrix} = 12 - 12 = 0$, so Cramer's rule cannot be used.

**43** $\begin{cases} x - 2y - 3z = -1 \\ 2x + y + z = 6 \\ x + 3y - 2z = 13 \end{cases}$ • $|D| = \begin{vmatrix} 1 & -2 & -3 \\ 2 & 1 & 1 \\ 1 & 3 & -2 \end{vmatrix}$ $\{R_1\} = 1(-5) - (-2)(-5) + (-3)(5) = -30,$

$|D_x| = \begin{vmatrix} -1 & -2 & -3 \\ 6 & 1 & 1 \\ 13 & 3 & -2 \end{vmatrix}$ $\{R_1\} = (-1)(-5) - (-2)(-25) + (-3)(5) = -60$

$|D_y| = \begin{vmatrix} 1 & -1 & -3 \\ 2 & 6 & 1 \\ 1 & 13 & -2 \end{vmatrix}$ $\{R_1\} = 1(-25) - (-1)(-5) + (-3)(20) = -90,$

$|D_z| = \begin{vmatrix} 1 & -2 & -1 \\ 2 & 1 & 6 \\ 1 & 3 & 13 \end{vmatrix}$ $\{R_1\} = 1(-5) - (-2)(20) + (-1)(5) = 30$

$x = \dfrac{|D_x|}{|D|} = \dfrac{-60}{-30} = 2; \ y = \dfrac{|D_y|}{|D|} = \dfrac{-90}{-30} = 3; \ z = \dfrac{|D_z|}{|D|} = \dfrac{30}{-30} = -1.$ ★ $(2, 3, -1)$

**44** $\begin{cases} x + 3y - z = -3 \\ 3x - y + 2z = 1 \\ 2x - y + z = -1 \end{cases}$ • $|D_x| = -10, |D_y| = 5, |D_z| = 20, |D| = 5; \ x = -2, y = 1, z = 4$

**45** $\begin{cases} 5x + 2y - z = -7 \\ x - 2y + 2z = 0 \\ 3y + z = 17 \end{cases}$ • $|D| = \begin{vmatrix} 5 & 2 & -1 \\ 1 & -2 & 2 \\ 0 & 3 & 1 \end{vmatrix}$ $\{R_3\} = -3(11) + 1(-12) = -45,$

$|D_x| = \begin{vmatrix} -7 & 2 & -1 \\ 0 & -2 & 2 \\ 17 & 3 & 1 \end{vmatrix}$ $\{C_1\} = -7(-8) + 17(2) = 90,$

$|D_y| = \begin{vmatrix} 5 & -7 & -1 \\ 1 & 0 & 2 \\ 0 & 17 & 1 \end{vmatrix}$ $\{R_2\} = -1(10) - 2(85) = -180,$

$|D_z| = \begin{vmatrix} 5 & 2 & -7 \\ 1 & -2 & 0 \\ 0 & 3 & 17 \end{vmatrix}$ $\{C_1\} = 5(-34) - 1(55) = -225$

$x = \dfrac{|D_x|}{|D|} = \dfrac{90}{-45} = -2; \ y = \dfrac{|D_y|}{|D|} = \dfrac{-180}{-45} = 4; \ z = \dfrac{|D_z|}{|D|} = \dfrac{-225}{-45} = 5.$ ★ $(-2, 4, 5)$

**46** $\begin{cases} 4x - y + 3z = 6 \\ -8x + 3y - 5z = -6 \\ 5x - 4y = -9 \end{cases}$ • $|D_x| = -12, |D_y| = -24, |D_z| = 0, |D| = -4; \ x = 3, y = 6, z = 0$

**47** To solve for $x$, find $|D|$ and $|D_x|$, and then use Cramer's Rule.

$|D| = \begin{vmatrix} a & b & c \\ e & 0 & f \\ h & i & 0 \end{vmatrix}$ $\begin{array}{c}(1/c)R_1 \to R_1\end{array}$ $= \begin{vmatrix} a/c & b/c & 1 \\ e & 0 & f \\ h & i & 0 \end{vmatrix}$ $R_2 - fR_1 \to R_2 = \begin{vmatrix} a/c & b/c & 1 \\ e - af/c & -bf/c & 0 \\ h & i & 0 \end{vmatrix} \{C_3\}$

$= (1) \begin{vmatrix} e - af/c & -bf/c \\ h & i \end{vmatrix} = \dfrac{ce - af}{c} \cdot i - \left( -\dfrac{bf}{c} \cdot h \right) = \dfrac{cei - afi + bfh}{c}$

$|D_x| = \begin{vmatrix} d & b & c \\ g & 0 & f \\ j & i & 0 \end{vmatrix}$ $\begin{array}{c}(1/c)R_1 \to R_1\end{array}$ $= \begin{vmatrix} d/c & b/c & 1 \\ g & 0 & f \\ j & i & 0 \end{vmatrix}$ $R_2 - fR_1 \to R_2 = \begin{vmatrix} d/c & b/c & 1 \\ g - df/c & -bf/c & 0 \\ j & i & 0 \end{vmatrix} \{C_3\}$

$= (1) \begin{vmatrix} g - df/c & -bf/c \\ j & i \end{vmatrix} = \dfrac{cg - df}{c} \cdot i - \left( -\dfrac{bf}{c} \cdot j \right) = \dfrac{cgi - dfi + bfj}{c}$

Thus, $x = \dfrac{|D_x|}{|D|} = \dfrac{cgi - dfi + bfj}{cei - afi + bfh}.$

## 8.10 Exercises

**Note:** The general outline for the solutions in this section is as follows:

(1)   The expression is shown on the left side of the equation and its decomposition is on the right side.

(2)   The equation in the first line is multiplied by its least common denominator and left in factored form.

(3)   On third and subsequent lines, values are substituted into the equation in the second line and the coefficients are found by solving the resulting equations.  The method of equating coefficients is noted if used.

$\boxed{1}$  $\dfrac{8x - 1}{(x - 2)(x + 3)} = \dfrac{A}{x - 2} + \dfrac{B}{x + 3}$

$8x - 1 = A(x + 3) + B(x - 2)$

$x = -3: -25 = -5B \Rightarrow B = 5$

$x = 2: 15 = 5A \Rightarrow A = 3$                                    $\bigstar \dfrac{3}{x - 2} + \dfrac{5}{x + 3}$

$\boxed{2}$  $\dfrac{x - 29}{(x - 4)(x + 1)} = \dfrac{A}{x - 4} + \dfrac{B}{x + 1}$

$x - 29 = A(x + 1) + B(x - 4)$

$x = -1: -30 = -5B \Rightarrow B = 6$

$x = 4: -25 = 5A \Rightarrow A = -5$                                    $\bigstar -\dfrac{5}{x - 4} + \dfrac{6}{x + 1}$

$\boxed{3}$  $\dfrac{x + 34}{(x - 6)(x + 2)} = \dfrac{A}{x - 6} + \dfrac{B}{x + 2}$

$x + 34 = A(x + 2) + B(x - 6)$

$x = -2: 32 = -8B \Rightarrow B = -4$

$x = 6: 40 = 8A \Rightarrow A = 5$                                    $\bigstar \dfrac{5}{x - 6} - \dfrac{4}{x + 2}$

$\boxed{4}$  $\dfrac{5x - 12}{x(x - 4)} = \dfrac{A}{x} + \dfrac{B}{x - 4}$

$5x - 12 = A(x - 4) + Bx$

$x = 4: 8 = 4B \Rightarrow B = 2$

$x = 0: -12 = -4A \Rightarrow A = 3$                                    $\bigstar \dfrac{3}{x} + \dfrac{2}{x - 4}$

$\boxed{5}$  $\dfrac{4x^2 - 15x - 1}{(x - 1)(x + 2)(x - 3)} = \dfrac{A}{x - 1} + \dfrac{B}{x + 2} + \dfrac{C}{x - 3}$

$4x^2 - 15x - 1 = A(x + 2)(x - 3) + B(x - 1)(x - 3) + C(x - 1)(x + 2)$

$x = -2: 45 = 15B \Rightarrow B = 3$

$x = 1: -12 = -6A \Rightarrow A = 2$

$x = 3: -10 = 10C \Rightarrow C = -1$                                    $\bigstar \dfrac{2}{x - 1} + \dfrac{3}{x + 2} - \dfrac{1}{x - 3}$

$\boxed{6}$  $\dfrac{x^2 + 19x + 20}{x(x + 2)(x - 5)} = \dfrac{A}{x} + \dfrac{B}{x + 2} + \dfrac{C}{x - 5}$

$x^2 + 19x + 20 = A(x + 2)(x - 5) + Bx(x - 5) + Cx(x + 2)$

$x = -2: -14 = 14B \Rightarrow B = -1$

$x = 5: 140 = 35C \Rightarrow C = 4$

$x = 0: 20 = -10A \Rightarrow A = -2$                                    $\bigstar -\dfrac{2}{x} - \dfrac{1}{x + 2} + \dfrac{4}{x - 5}$

**7** $\dfrac{4x^2 - 5x - 15}{x(x-5)(x+1)} = \dfrac{A}{x} + \dfrac{B}{x-5} + \dfrac{C}{x+1}$

$4x^2 - 5x - 15 = A(x-5)(x+1) + Bx(x+1) + Cx(x-5)$

$x = -1: -6 = 6C \;\Rightarrow\; C = -1$

$x = 0: -15 = -5A \;\Rightarrow\; A = 3$

$x = 5: 60 = 30B \;\Rightarrow\; B = 2$

$\bigstar\; \dfrac{3}{x} + \dfrac{2}{x-5} - \dfrac{1}{x+1}$

**8** $\dfrac{37 - 11x}{(x+1)(x-2)(x-3)} = \dfrac{A}{x+1} + \dfrac{B}{x-2} + \dfrac{C}{x-3}$

$37 - 11x = A(x-2)(x-3) + B(x+1)(x-3) + C(x+1)(x-2)$

$x = -1: 48 = 12A \;\Rightarrow\; A = 4$

$x = 2: 15 = -3B \;\Rightarrow\; B = -5$

$x = 3: 4 = 4C \;\Rightarrow\; C = 1$

$\bigstar\; \dfrac{4}{x+1} - \dfrac{5}{x-2} + \dfrac{1}{x-3}$

**9** $\dfrac{2x+3}{(x-1)^2} = \dfrac{A}{x-1} + \dfrac{B}{(x-1)^2}$

$2x + 3 = A(x-1) + B$

$x = 1: 5 = B$

$x = 0: 3 = -A + B \;\Rightarrow\; A = 2$

$\bigstar\; \dfrac{2}{x-1} + \dfrac{5}{(x-1)^2}$

**10** $\dfrac{5x^2 - 4}{x^2(x+2)} = \dfrac{A}{x} + \dfrac{B}{x^2} + \dfrac{C}{x+2}$

$5x^2 - 4 = Ax(x+2) + B(x+2) + Cx^2$

$x = -2: 16 = 4C \;\Rightarrow\; C = 4$

$x = 0: -4 = 2B \;\Rightarrow\; B = -2$

$x = 1: 1 = 3A + 3B + C \;\Rightarrow\; A = 1$

$\bigstar\; \dfrac{1}{x} - \dfrac{2}{x^2} + \dfrac{4}{x+2}$

**11** $\dfrac{19x^2 + 50x - 25}{x^2(3x-5)} = \dfrac{A}{x} + \dfrac{B}{x^2} + \dfrac{C}{3x-5}$

$19x^2 + 50x - 25 = Ax(3x-5) + B(3x-5) + Cx^2$

$x = \tfrac{5}{3}: \dfrac{1000}{9} = \dfrac{25}{9}C \;\Rightarrow\; C = 40$

$x = 0: -25 = -5B \;\Rightarrow\; B = 5$

$x = 1: 44 = -2A - 2B + C \;\Rightarrow\; A = -7$

$\bigstar\; -\dfrac{7}{x} + \dfrac{5}{x^2} + \dfrac{40}{3x-5}$

**12** $\dfrac{10 - x}{(x+5)^2} = \dfrac{A}{x+5} + \dfrac{B}{(x+5)^2}$

$10 - x = A(x+5) + B$

$x = -5: 15 = B$

$x = 0: 10 = 5A + B \;\Rightarrow\; A = -1$

$\bigstar\; -\dfrac{1}{x+5} + \dfrac{15}{(x+5)^2}$

**13** $\dfrac{x^2 - 6}{(x+2)^2(2x-1)} = \dfrac{A}{x+2} + \dfrac{B}{(x+2)^2} + \dfrac{C}{2x-1}$

$x^2 - 6 = A(x+2)(2x-1) + B(2x-1) + C(x+2)^2$

$x = -2: -2 = -5B \;\Rightarrow\; B = \tfrac{2}{5}$

$x = \tfrac{1}{2}: -\dfrac{23}{4} = \dfrac{25}{4}C \;\Rightarrow\; C = -\dfrac{23}{25}$

$x = 1: -5 = 3A + B + 9C \;\Rightarrow\; A = \dfrac{24}{25}$

$\bigstar\; \dfrac{\frac{24}{25}}{x+2} + \dfrac{\frac{2}{5}}{(x+2)^2} - \dfrac{\frac{23}{25}}{2x-1}$

**14** $\dfrac{2x^2 + x}{(x-1)^2(x+1)^2} = \dfrac{A}{x-1} + \dfrac{B}{(x-1)^2} + \dfrac{C}{x+1} + \dfrac{D}{(x+1)^2}$

$2x^2 + x = A(x-1)(x+1)^2 + B(x+1)^2 + C(x+1)(x-1)^2 + D(x-1)^2$

$x = -1 : 1 = 4D \Rightarrow D = \frac{1}{4}$

$x = 1 : 3 = 4B \Rightarrow B = \frac{3}{4}$

$x = 0 : 0 = -A + B + C + D$ (E$_1$)

$x = 2 : 10 = 9A + 9B + 3C + D$ (E$_2$)

Substituting the values for $B$ and $D$ into E$_1$ and E$_2$ yields $\begin{cases} -A + \phantom{9}C = -1 \\ 9A + 3C = \phantom{-}3 \end{cases} \Rightarrow \begin{cases} A - C = 1 & \text{(E}_3) \\ 3A + C = 1 & \text{(E}_4) \end{cases}$

E$_3$ + E$_4$ $\Rightarrow$ $4A = 2 \Rightarrow A = \frac{1}{2}; C = -\frac{1}{2}$ $\quad\bigstar\ \dfrac{\frac{1}{2}}{x-1} + \dfrac{\frac{3}{4}}{(x-1)^2} - \dfrac{\frac{1}{2}}{x+1} + \dfrac{\frac{1}{4}}{(x+1)^2}$

**15** $\dfrac{3x^3 + 11x^2 + 16x + 5}{x(x+1)^3} = \dfrac{A}{x} + \dfrac{B}{x+1} + \dfrac{C}{(x+1)^2} + \dfrac{D}{(x+1)^3}$

$3x^3 + 11x^2 + 16x + 5 = A(x+1)^3 + Bx(x+1)^2 + Cx(x+1) + Dx$

$x = -1 : -3 = -D \Rightarrow D = 3$

$x = 0 : 5 = A$

$x = 1 : 35 = 8A + 4B + 2C + D$ (E$_1$)

$x = -2 : -7 = -A - 2B + 2C - 2D$ (E$_2$)

Substituting the values for $A$ and $D$ into E$_1$ and E$_2$ yields $\begin{cases} \phantom{-}4B + 2C = -8 \\ -2B + 2C = \phantom{-}4 \end{cases} \Rightarrow \begin{cases} 2B + C = -4 & \text{(E}_3) \\ -B + C = \phantom{-}2 & \text{(E}_4) \end{cases}$

E$_3$ + 2E$_4$ $\Rightarrow$ $3C = 0 \Rightarrow C = 0; B = -2$ $\quad\bigstar\ \dfrac{5}{x} - \dfrac{2}{x+1} + \dfrac{3}{(x+1)^3}$

**16** $\dfrac{4x^3 + 3x^2 + 5x - 2}{x^3(x+2)} = \dfrac{A}{x} + \dfrac{B}{x^2} + \dfrac{C}{x^3} + \dfrac{D}{x+2}$

$4x^3 + 3x^2 + 5x - 2 = Ax^2(x+2) + Bx(x+2) + C(x+2) + Dx^3$

$x = -2 : -32 = -8D \Rightarrow D = 4$

$x = 0 : -2 = 2C \Rightarrow C = -1$

$x = -1 : -8 = A - B + C - D$ (E$_1$)

$x = 1 : 10 = 3A + 3B + 3C + D$ (E$_2$)

Substituting the values for $C$ and $D$ into E$_1$ and E$_2$ yields $\begin{cases} A - \phantom{3}B = -3 \\ 3A + 3B = \phantom{-}9 \end{cases} \Rightarrow \begin{cases} A - B = -3 & \text{(E}_3) \\ A + B = \phantom{-}3 & \text{(E}_4) \end{cases}$

E$_3$ + E$_4$ $\Rightarrow$ $2A = 0 \Rightarrow A = 0; B = 3$ $\quad\bigstar\ \dfrac{3}{x^2} - \dfrac{1}{x^3} + \dfrac{4}{x+2}$

**17** $\dfrac{x^2 + x - 6}{(x^2+1)(x-1)} = \dfrac{Ax + B}{x^2+1} + \dfrac{C}{x-1}$

$x^2 + x - 6 = (Ax + B)(x-1) + C(x^2+1)$

$x = 1 : -4 = 2C \Rightarrow C = -2$

$x = 0 : -6 = -B + C \Rightarrow B = 4$

$x = 2 : 0 = 2A + B + 5C \Rightarrow A = 3$ $\quad\bigstar\ -\dfrac{2}{x-1} + \dfrac{3x+4}{x^2+1}$

**18** $\dfrac{x^2 - x - 21}{(x^2 + 4)(2x - 1)} = \dfrac{Ax + B}{x^2 + 4} + \dfrac{C}{2x - 1}$

$x^2 - x - 21 = (Ax + B)(2x - 1) + C(x^2 + 4)$

$x = \frac{1}{2}: -\frac{85}{4} = \frac{17}{4}C \;\Rightarrow\; C = -5$

$x = 0: -21 = -B + 4C \;\Rightarrow\; B = 1$

$x = 1: -21 = A + B + 5C \;\Rightarrow\; A = 3$

$\bigstar \; -\dfrac{5}{2x - 1} + \dfrac{3x + 1}{x^2 + 4}$

**19** $\dfrac{9x^2 - 3x + 8}{x(x^2 + 2)} = \dfrac{A}{x} + \dfrac{Bx + C}{x^2 + 2}$

$9x^2 - 3x + 8 = A(x^2 + 2) + (Bx + C)x$

$x = 0: 8 = 2A \;\Rightarrow\; A = 4$

$x = 1: 14 = 3A + B + C \quad (\text{E}_1)$

$x = -1: 20 = 3A + B - C \quad (\text{E}_2)$

$\text{E}_1 - \text{E}_2 \;\Rightarrow\; -6 = 2C \;\Rightarrow\; C = -3; B = 5$

$\bigstar \; \dfrac{4}{x} + \dfrac{5x - 3}{x^2 + 2}$

**20** $\dfrac{5x^2 - x + 12}{x^3 + 4x} = \dfrac{5x^2 - x + 12}{x(x^2 + 4)} = \dfrac{A}{x} + \dfrac{Bx + C}{x^2 + 4}$

$5x^2 - x + 12 = A(x^2 + 4) + (Bx + C)x$

$x = 0: 12 = 4A \;\Rightarrow\; A = 3$

$x = 1: 16 = 5A + B + C \quad (\text{E}_1)$

$x = -1: 18 = 5A + B - C \quad (\text{E}_2)$

$\text{E}_1 - \text{E}_2 \;\Rightarrow\; -2 = 2C \;\Rightarrow\; C = -1; B = 2$

$\bigstar \; \dfrac{3}{x} + \dfrac{2x - 1}{x^2 + 4}$

**21** $\dfrac{3x^3 - 4x^2 + 3x - 3}{x^4 + 3x^2} = \dfrac{3x^3 - 4x^2 + 3x - 3}{x^2(x^2 + 3)} = \dfrac{A}{x} + \dfrac{B}{x^2} + \dfrac{Cx + D}{x^2 + 3}$

$3x^3 - 4x^2 + 3x - 3 = Ax(x^2 + 3) + B(x^2 + 3) + (Cx + D)x^2 = (A + C)x^3 + (B + D)x^2 + 3Ax + 3B$

Equating coefficients (like terms must have equal coefficients on each side), we have the following:

constant terms: $3B = -3 \;\Rightarrow\; B = -1$;

$x$-terms: $3A = 3 \;\Rightarrow\; A = 1$

$x^2$-terms: $B + D = -4 \;\Rightarrow\; D = -3$

$x^3$-terms: $A + C = 3 \;\Rightarrow\; C = 2$

$\bigstar \; \dfrac{1}{x} - \dfrac{1}{x^2} + \dfrac{2x - 3}{x^2 + 3}$

**22** $\dfrac{2x^3 + 2x^2 + 4x - 3}{x^2(x^2 + 1)} = \dfrac{A}{x} + \dfrac{B}{x^2} + \dfrac{Cx + D}{x^2 + 1}$

$2x^3 + 2x^2 + 4x - 3 = Ax(x^2 + 1) + B(x^2 + 1) + (Cx + D)x^2 = (A + C)x^3 + (B + D)x^2 + Ax + B$

Equating coefficients (like terms must have equal coefficients on each side), we have the following:

constant terms: $B = -3$;

$x$-terms: $A = 4$

$x^2$-terms: $B + D = 2 \;\Rightarrow\; D = 5$

$x^3$-terms: $A + C = 2 \;\Rightarrow\; C = -2$

$\bigstar \; \dfrac{4}{x} - \dfrac{3}{x^2} + \dfrac{-2x + 5}{x^2 + 1}$

**23** $\dfrac{4x^3 - x^2 + 4x + 2}{(x^2+1)^2} = \dfrac{Ax+B}{x^2+1} + \dfrac{Cx+D}{(x^2+1)^2}$

$4x^3 - x^2 + 4x + 2 = (Ax+B)(x^2+1) + Cx + D = Ax^3 + Bx^2 + (A+C)x + (B+D)$

Equating coefficients (like terms must have equal coefficients on each side), we have the following:

$x^3$-terms: $A = 4$

$x^2$-terms: $B = -1$

$x$-terms: $A + C = 4 \Rightarrow C = 0$

constant terms: $B + D = 2 \Rightarrow D = 3$       $\bigstar \dfrac{4x-1}{x^2+1} + \dfrac{3}{(x^2+1)^2}$

**24** $\dfrac{3x^3 + 13x - 1}{(x^2+4)^2} = \dfrac{Ax+B}{x^2+4} + \dfrac{Cx+D}{(x^2+4)^2}$

$3x^3 + 13x - 1 = (Ax+B)(x^2+4) + Cx + D = Ax^3 + Bx^2 + (4A+C)x + (4B+D)$

Equating coefficients (like terms must have equal coefficients on each side), we have the following:

$x^3$-terms: $A = 3$

$x^2$-terms: $B = 0$

$x$-terms: $4A + C = 13 \Rightarrow C = 1$

constant terms: $4B + D = -1 \Rightarrow D = -1$       $\bigstar \dfrac{3x}{x^2+4} + \dfrac{x-1}{(x^2+4)^2}$

**25** The degree of the numerator is not lower than the degree of the denominator.

Thus, we must first use long division and then decompose the remaining expression.

Hence, by first dividing and then factoring, we get $2x + \dfrac{4x^2 - 3x + 1}{(x^2+1)(x-1)} = 2x + \dfrac{Ax+B}{x^2+1} + \dfrac{C}{x-1}$.

$4x^2 - 3x + 1 = (Ax+B)(x-1) + C(x^2+1)$

$x = 1: 2 = 2C \Rightarrow C = 1$

$x = 0: 1 = -B + C \Rightarrow B = 0$

$x = -1: 8 = 2A - 2B + 2C \Rightarrow A = 3$       $\bigstar 2x + \dfrac{1}{x-1} + \dfrac{3x}{x^2+1}$

**26** By first dividing and then factoring, we get $1 + \dfrac{3x^2 - 9x + 27}{(x^2+9)(x-3)} = 1 + \dfrac{Ax+B}{x^2+9} + \dfrac{C}{x-3}$.

$3x^2 - 9x + 27 = (Ax+B)(x-3) + C(x^2+9)$

$x = 3: 27 = 18C \Rightarrow C = \frac{3}{2}$

$x = 0: 27 = -3B + 9C \Rightarrow B = -\frac{9}{2}$

$x = 2: 21 = -2A - B + 13C \Rightarrow A = \frac{3}{2}$       $\bigstar 1 + \dfrac{\frac{3}{2}}{x-3} + \dfrac{\frac{3}{2}x - \frac{9}{2}}{x^2+9}$

**27** By first dividing and then factoring, we get $3 + \dfrac{12x - 16}{x(x-4)} = 3 + \dfrac{A}{x} + \dfrac{B}{x-4}$.

$12x - 16 = A(x-4) + Bx$

$x = 0: -16 = -4A \Rightarrow A = 4$

$x = 4: 32 = 4B \Rightarrow B = 8$       $\bigstar 3 + \dfrac{4}{x} + \dfrac{8}{x-4}$

**28** By first dividing and then factoring, we get $2 + \dfrac{-5x - 18}{(x+3)^2} = 2 + \dfrac{A}{x+3} + \dfrac{B}{(x+3)^2}$.

$-5x - 18 = A(x+3) + B$

$x = -3: -3 = B \Rightarrow B = -3$

Equating coefficients of $x$, we see that $A = -5$.       $\bigstar 2 - \dfrac{5}{x+3} - \dfrac{3}{(x+3)^2}$

**29** By first dividing and then factoring, we get $2x + 3 + \dfrac{x+5}{(2x+1)(x-1)} = 2x + 3 + \dfrac{A}{2x+1} + \dfrac{B}{x-1}$.

$x + 5 = A(x-1) + B(2x+1)$

$x = 1: 6 = 3B \Rightarrow B = 2$

$x = -\frac{1}{2}: \frac{9}{2} = -\frac{3}{2}A \Rightarrow A = -3$ 
$\qquad \qquad \qquad \qquad \qquad \qquad \bigstar\; 2x + 3 + \dfrac{2}{x-1} - \dfrac{3}{2x+1}$

**30** By first dividing and then factoring, we get $x^2 - 2x + 1 + \dfrac{2x^2 - 4x + 12}{x^2(x-3)} = x^2 - 2x + 1 + \dfrac{A}{x} + \dfrac{B}{x^2} + \dfrac{C}{x-3}$.

$2x^2 - 4x + 12 = Ax(x-3) + B(x-3) + Cx^2$

$x = 3: 18 = 9C \Rightarrow C = 2$

$x = 0: 12 = -3B \Rightarrow B = -4$

$x = 1: 10 = -2A - 2B + C \Rightarrow A = 0$ 
$\qquad \qquad \qquad \bigstar\; x^2 - 2x + 1 - \dfrac{4}{x^2} + \dfrac{2}{x-3}$

## Chapter 8 Review Exercises

**1** $4E_1 + 3E_2 \Rightarrow 4(2x - 3y = 4) + 3(5x + 4y = 1) \Rightarrow 8x + 15x = 16 + 3 \Rightarrow 23x = 19 \Rightarrow x = \frac{19}{23}$;

$-5E_1 + 2E_2 \Rightarrow -5(2x - 3y = 4) + 2(5x + 4y = 1) \Rightarrow 15y + 8y = -20 + 2 \Rightarrow$

$23y = -18 \Rightarrow y = -\frac{18}{23}$ 
$\qquad \qquad \qquad \qquad \qquad \qquad \bigstar \left(\frac{19}{23}, -\frac{18}{23}\right)$

**2** $2E_1 + E_2 \Rightarrow 2(x - 3y = 4) + (-2x + 6y = 2) \Rightarrow 0 = 10$; **no solution**.

**3** Solve $E_2$ for $y$, $y = -2x - 1$, and substitute into $E_1$ to yield $-2x - 1 + 4 = x^2 \Rightarrow x^2 + 2x - 3 = 0 \Rightarrow$

$(x+3)(x-1) = 0 \Rightarrow x = -3, 1$ and $y = 5, -3$. 
$\qquad \qquad \bigstar\; (-3, 5), (1, -3)$

**4** Solve $E_2$ for $x$, $x = y + 7$, and substitute into $E_1$ to yield $(y+7)^2 + y^2 = 25 \Rightarrow 2y^2 + 14y + 49 = 25 \Rightarrow$

$y^2 + 7y + 12 = 0 \Rightarrow (y+3)(y+4) = 0 \Rightarrow y = -3, -4$ and $x = 4, 3$. 
$\qquad \bigstar\; (4, -3), (3, -4)$

**5** $4E_2 + E_1 \Rightarrow 4(x^2 - 4y^2 = 4) + (9x^2 + 16y^2 = 140) \Rightarrow 4x^2 + 9x^2 = 16 + 140 \Rightarrow$

$13x^2 = 156 \Rightarrow x^2 = 12 \Rightarrow x = \pm\sqrt{12} = \pm 2\sqrt{3}$.

Substituting 12 for $x^2$ in $E_2$ gives us $12 - 4y^2 = 4 \Rightarrow 8 = 4y^2 \Rightarrow 2 = y^2 \Rightarrow y = \pm\sqrt{2}$.

There are *four* solutions: $\left(2\sqrt{3}, \pm\sqrt{2}\right), \left(-2\sqrt{3}, \pm\sqrt{2}\right)$.

**6** From $E_3$, $x^2 = xz$, $x^2 - xz = 0 \Rightarrow x(x-z) = 0 \Rightarrow x = 0$ **(1)** or $x = z$ **(2)**.

**(1)** If $x = 0$, $E_1$, $2x = y^2 + 3z$, is $0 = y^2 + 3z$ and $E_2$, $x = y^2 + z - 1$, is $z = 1 - y^2$.

Substituting $1 - y^2$ for $z$ into $0 = y^2 + 3z$ yields $2y^2 = 3$ or $y = \pm\frac{1}{2}\sqrt{6}$ and $z$ is $-\frac{1}{2}$ for both values of $y$.

**(2)** If $x = z$, $E_1$, $2x = y^2 + 3z$, is $0 = y^2 + z$ and $E_2$, $x = y^2 + z - 1$, is $y^2 = 1$.

Thus, $y = \pm 1$ and in either case, $x = z = -1$. 
$\qquad$ There are *four* solutions: $(-1, \pm 1, -1), \left(0, \pm\frac{1}{2}\sqrt{6}, -\frac{1}{2}\right)$.

**7** $-4E_1 + E_2 \Rightarrow -4(1/x + 3/y = 7) + (4/x - 2/y = 1) \Rightarrow -12/y - 2/y = -28 + 1 \Rightarrow$

$-14/y = -27 \Rightarrow y = \frac{14}{27}$;

$2E_1 + 3E_2 \Rightarrow 2(1/x + 3/y = 7) + 3(4/x - 2/y = 1) \Rightarrow 2/x + 12/x = 14 + 3 \Rightarrow$

$14/x = 17 \Rightarrow x = \frac{14}{17}$ 
$\qquad \qquad \qquad \qquad \qquad \qquad \bigstar \left(\frac{14}{17}, \frac{14}{27}\right)$

**8** Treat $3^{y+1}$ as $3 \cdot 3^y$ and $2^{x+1}$ as $2 \cdot 2^x$. Thus, $E_1$ is $1(2^x) + 3(3^y) = 10$ and $E_2$ is $2(2^x) - 1(3^y) = 5$.

Now $E_1 + 3E_2 \Rightarrow [1(2^x) + 3(3^y) = 10] + 3[2(2^x) - 1(3^y) = 5] \Rightarrow 7 \cdot 2^x = 25 \Rightarrow 2^x = \frac{25}{7} \Rightarrow$

$x = \log_2 \frac{25}{7} = \dfrac{\log \frac{25}{7}}{\log 2} \approx 1.84$. Resolving the original system for $y$, we have $-2E_1 + E_2 \Rightarrow$

$-2[1(2^x) + 3(3^y) = 10] + [2(2^x) - 1(3^y) = 5] \Rightarrow -7 \cdot 3^y = -15 \Rightarrow 3^y = \frac{15}{7} \Rightarrow$

$y = \log_3 \frac{15}{7} = \dfrac{\log \frac{15}{7}}{\log 3} \approx 0.69$.     $\star \left( \log_2 \frac{25}{7}, \log_3 \frac{15}{7} \right)$

**9** Solve $E_3$ for $z$, $z = 4x + 5y + 2$, and substitute into $E_1$ and $E_2$ to obtain

$$\begin{cases} 3x + y - 2(4x + 5y + 2) = -1 \\ 2x - 3y + (4x + 5y + 2) = 4 \end{cases} \Rightarrow \begin{cases} -5x - 9y = 3 & (E_4) \\ 6x + 2y = 2 & (E_5) \end{cases}$$

$6E_4 + 5E_5 \Rightarrow 6(-5x - 9y = 3) + 5(6x + 2y = 2) \Rightarrow -44y = 28 \Rightarrow y = -\frac{7}{11}$;

$2E_4 + 9E_5 \Rightarrow 2(-5x - 9y = 3) + 9(6x + 2y = 2) \Rightarrow 44x = 24 \Rightarrow x = \frac{6}{11}$; $z = 1$     $\star \left( \frac{6}{11}, -\frac{7}{11}, 1 \right)$

**10** Solve $E_1$ for $x$, $x = -3y$, and substitute into $E_3$ to obtain $\begin{cases} y - 5z = 3 & (E_2) \\ -6y + z = -1 & (E_4) \end{cases}$

$6E_2 + E_4 \Rightarrow 6(y - 5z = 3) + (-6y + z = -1) \Rightarrow -29z = 17 \Rightarrow z = -\frac{17}{29}$;

$E_2 + 5E_4 \Rightarrow (y - 5z = 3) + 5(-6y + z = -1) \Rightarrow -29y = -2 \Rightarrow y = \frac{2}{29}$; $x = -\frac{6}{29}$ $\star \left( -\frac{6}{29}, \frac{2}{29}, -\frac{17}{29} \right)$

**11** Solve $E_2$ for $x$, $x = y + z$, and substitute into $E_1$ and $E_3$ to obtain

$$\begin{cases} 4(y + z) - 3y - z = 0 \\ 3(y + z) - y + 3z = 0 \end{cases} \Rightarrow \begin{cases} y + 3z = 0 & (E_4) \\ 2y + 6z = 0 & (E_5) \end{cases}$$

Now $E_5$ is $2E_4$, hence $y = -3z$ and $x = y + z = -3z + z = -2z$.

The general solution is $(-2c, -3c, c)$ for any real number $c$.

**12** Solve $E_2$ for $x$, $x = 2y - z$, and substitute into $E_1$ and $E_3$ to obtain

$$\begin{cases} 2(2y - z) + y - z = 0 \\ 3(2y - z) + 3y + 2z = 0 \end{cases} \Rightarrow \begin{cases} 5y - 3z = 0 & (E_4) \\ 9y - z = 0 & (E_5) \end{cases}$$

$E_4 - 3E_5 \Rightarrow (5y - 3z = 0) - 3(9y - z = 0) \Rightarrow -22y = 0 \Rightarrow y = 0, z = 0, x = 0$;     $\star (0, 0, 0)$

**13** $E_1 - E_2 \Rightarrow (4x + 2y - z = 1) - (3x + 2y + 4z = 2) \Rightarrow x - 5z = -1 \Rightarrow x = 5z - 1$.

Substitute $5z - 1$ for $x$ into $E_1$ to obtain $4(5z - 1) + 2y - z = 1 \Rightarrow 19z + 2y = 5 \Rightarrow y = \dfrac{-19z + 5}{2}$.

$\left( 5c - 1, \dfrac{-19c + 5}{2}, c \right)$ is the general solution, where $c$ is any real number.

**14** $3E_1 + E_2 \Rightarrow 3(2x + y = 6) + (x - 3y = 17) \Rightarrow 7x = 35 \Rightarrow x = 5$, and from $E_2$, $y = -4$.

This solution, $(5, -4)$, also satisfies $E_3$, $3x + 2y = 7$.     $\star (5, -4)$

**15** Let $a = \dfrac{1}{x}$, $b = \dfrac{1}{y}$, and $c = \dfrac{1}{z}$ to obtain the system $\begin{cases} 4a + b + 2c = 4 & (E_1) \\ 2a + 3b - c = 1 & (E_2) \\ a + b + c = 4 & (E_3) \end{cases}$

Solving $E_2$ for $c$, $c = 2a + 3b - 1$, and substituting into $E_1$ and $E_3$ yields

$$\begin{cases} 4a + b + 2(2a + 3b - 1) = 4 \\ a + b + (2a + 3b - 1) = 4 \end{cases} \Rightarrow \begin{cases} 8a + 7b = 6 & (E_4) \\ 3a + 4b = 5 & (E_5) \end{cases}$$

$3E_4 - 8E_5 \Rightarrow 3(8a + 7b = 6) - 8(3a + 4b = 5) \Rightarrow -11b = -22 \Rightarrow b = 2$.

$4E_4 - 7E_5 \Rightarrow 4(8a + 7b = 6) - 7(3a + 4b = 5) \Rightarrow 11a = -11 \Rightarrow a = -1$.

Now $c = 2(-1) + 3(2) - 1 = 3$ and $x$, $y$, and $z$ are the reciprocals of $a$, $b$, and $c$.     $\star \left( -1, \frac{1}{2}, \frac{1}{3} \right)$

**16** Solve $E_1$ for $w$, $w = 2x - y + 3z + 3$, and substitute into $E_2$, $E_3$, and $E_4$ to obtain

$$\begin{cases} 3x + 2y - z + 1(2x - y + 3z + 3) = 13 \\ x - 3y + z - 2(2x - y + 3z + 3) = -4 \\ -x + y + 4z + 3(2x - y + 3z + 3) = 0 \end{cases} \Rightarrow \begin{cases} 5x + y + 2z = 10 \quad (E_5) \\ -3x - y - 5z = 2 \quad (E_6) \\ 5x - 2y + 13z = -9 \quad (E_7) \end{cases}$$

Solve $E_6$ for $y$, $y = -3x - 5z - 2$, and substitute into $E_5$ and $E_7$ to obtain

$$\begin{cases} 5x + (-3x - 5z - 2) + 2z = 10 \\ 5x - 2(-3x - 5z - 2) + 13z = -9 \end{cases} \Rightarrow \begin{cases} 2x - 3z = 12 \quad (E_8) \\ 11x + 23z = -13 \quad (E_9) \end{cases}$$

$11\,E_8 - 2E_9 \Rightarrow 11(2x - 3z = 12) - 2(11x + 23z = -13) \Rightarrow -79z = 158 \Rightarrow z = -2.$

$23E_8 + 3E_9 \Rightarrow 23(2x - 3z = 12) + 3(11x + 23z = -13) \Rightarrow 79x = 237 \Rightarrow x = 3.$

Now $y = -3(3) - 5(-2) - 2 = -1$ and $w = 2(3) - (-1) + 3(-2) + 3 = 4.$   ★ $(3, -1, -2, 4)$

**17** $\begin{cases} x^2 + y^2 < 16 \\ y - x^2 > 0 \end{cases} \Leftrightarrow \begin{cases} x^2 + y^2 < 4^2 \\ y > x^2 \end{cases}$     $V @ \left( \pm\sqrt{-\tfrac{1}{2} + \tfrac{1}{2}\sqrt{65}}, -\tfrac{1}{2} + \tfrac{1}{2}\sqrt{65} \right) \approx (\pm 1.88, 3.53)$

Shade inside the dashed circle $x^2 + y^2 = 4^2$ and inside the dashed parabola $y = x^2$.

*Figure 17*

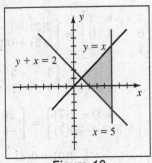

*Figure 18*

**18** $\begin{cases} y - x \le 0 \\ y + x \ge 2 \\ x \le 5 \end{cases} \Leftrightarrow \begin{cases} y \le x \\ y \ge -x + 2 \\ x \le 5 \end{cases}$     $V @ (1, 1),\ (5, 5),\ (5, -3)$

Shade below the solid line $y = x$, above the solid line $y = -x + 2$, and to the left of the solid line $x = 5$.

**19** $\begin{cases} x - 2y \le 2 \\ y - 3x \le 4 \\ 2x + y \le 4 \end{cases} \Leftrightarrow \begin{cases} y \ge \tfrac{1}{2}x - 1 \\ y \le 3x + 4 \\ y \le -2x + 4 \end{cases}$     $V @ (-2, -2),\ (0, 4),\ (2, 0)$

Shade above the solid line $y = \tfrac{1}{2}x - 1$, below the solid line $y = 3x + 4$, and below the solid line $y = -2x + 4$.

*Figure 19*

*Figure 20*

**20** $\begin{cases} x^2 - y < 0 \\ y - 2x < 5 \\ xy < 0 \end{cases} \Leftrightarrow \begin{cases} y > x^2 \\ y < 2x + 5 \\ xy < 0 \end{cases}$     $V @ \left( 1 - \sqrt{6}, 7 - 2\sqrt{6} \right) \approx (-1.45, 2.10),\ (0, 5),\ (0, 0)$

Shade below the dashed line $y = 2x + 5$ and inside the dashed parabola $y = x^2$. For $xy < 0$, either $x$ or $y$ must be negative. We want to shade on the left of the $y$-axis, where $y < 0$. The solution does not include any boundaries.

**21** The shaded region lies *outside* the circle $x^2 + y^2 = 5^2$, so we can describe it with the inequality $x^2 + y^2 \geq 25$. The shaded region lies to the right of $x = 3$ and to the left of $x = -3$, and since those lines are dashed, we can describe it with the inequality $|x| > 3$. The shaded region lies below $y = 6$ and above $y = -6$, and since those lines are solid, we can describe it with the inequality $|y| \leq 6$. Thus, the graph may be described by the system
$$\begin{cases} x^2 + y^2 \geq 25 \\ |x| > 3 \\ |y| \leq 6 \end{cases}$$

**22** The dashed curve is $x = y^2$. Substituting $x = 0$ and $y = -2$ into $x = y^2$ gives us $0 = 4$. We replace $=$ by $<$ to make this statement a true statement. Hence, we have the inequality $x < y^2$. The solid line goes through $(0, -1)$ and $(1, 0)$. Hence, its slope is 1, its $y$-intercept is $-1$, and an equation for it is $y = x - 1$. Substituting $x = 0$ and $y = -2$ into $y = x - 1$ gives us $-2 = -1$. We replace $=$ by $\leq$ {the line is solid} to make this statement a true statement. Hence, we have the inequality $y \leq x - 1$. Thus, the graph may be described by the system $\begin{cases} x < y^2 \\ y \leq x - 1 \end{cases}$

**23** $\begin{bmatrix} 2 & -1 & 0 \\ 3 & 0 & -2 \end{bmatrix}\begin{bmatrix} 2 & -1 & 3 \\ 0 & 3 & 0 \\ 1 & 4 & 2 \end{bmatrix} = \begin{bmatrix} 2(2) + (-1)(0) + 0(1) & 2(-1) + (-1)(3) + 0(4) & 2(3) + (-1)(0) + 0(2) \\ 3(2) + 0(0) + (-2)(1) & 3(-1) + 0(3) + (-2)(4) & 3(3) + 0(0) + (-2)(2) \end{bmatrix}$

$$= \begin{bmatrix} 4 & -5 & 6 \\ 4 & -11 & 5 \end{bmatrix}$$

**24** $\begin{bmatrix} 4 & 2 \\ 5 & -3 \end{bmatrix}\begin{bmatrix} 3 \\ 7 \end{bmatrix} = \begin{bmatrix} 4(3) + 2(7) \\ 5(3) + (-3)(7) \end{bmatrix} = \begin{bmatrix} 26 \\ -6 \end{bmatrix}$

**25** $\begin{bmatrix} 2 & 0 \\ 1 & 4 \\ -2 & 3 \end{bmatrix}\begin{bmatrix} 0 & 2 & -3 \\ 4 & 5 & 1 \end{bmatrix} = \begin{bmatrix} 2(0) + 0(4) & 2(2) + 0(5) & 2(-3) + 0(1) \\ 1(0) + 4(4) & 1(2) + 4(5) & 1(-3) + 4(1) \\ -2(0) + 3(4) & -2(2) + 3(5) & -2(-3) + 3(1) \end{bmatrix} = \begin{bmatrix} 0 & 4 & -6 \\ 16 & 22 & 1 \\ 12 & 11 & 9 \end{bmatrix}$

**26** $\begin{bmatrix} 0 & -2 & 3 \\ 4 & 1 & 2 \end{bmatrix}\begin{bmatrix} 2 & 0 \\ 3 & 8 \\ 2 & -7 \end{bmatrix} = \begin{bmatrix} 0(2) + (-2)(3) + 3(2) & 0(0) + (-2)(8) + 3(-7) \\ 4(2) + 1(3) + 2(2) & 4(0) + 1(8) + 2(-7) \end{bmatrix} = \begin{bmatrix} 0 & -37 \\ 15 & -6 \end{bmatrix}$

**27** $2\begin{bmatrix} 0 & -1 & -4 \\ 3 & 2 & 1 \end{bmatrix} - 3\begin{bmatrix} 4 & -2 & 1 \\ 0 & 5 & -1 \end{bmatrix} = \begin{bmatrix} 0 & -2 & -8 \\ 6 & 4 & 2 \end{bmatrix} + \begin{bmatrix} -12 & 6 & -3 \\ 0 & -15 & 3 \end{bmatrix} = \begin{bmatrix} -12 & 4 & -11 \\ 6 & -11 & 5 \end{bmatrix}$

**28** $\begin{bmatrix} 1 & 3 \\ 2 & 4 \end{bmatrix}\begin{bmatrix} a & 0 \\ 0 & a \end{bmatrix} = \begin{bmatrix} 1(a) + 3(0) & 1(0) + 3(a) \\ 2(a) + 4(0) & 2(0) + 4(a) \end{bmatrix} = \begin{bmatrix} a & 3a \\ 2a & 4a \end{bmatrix}$

**29** $\begin{bmatrix} a & 0 \\ 0 & b \end{bmatrix}\begin{bmatrix} 1 & 3 \\ 2 & 4 \end{bmatrix} = \begin{bmatrix} a(1) + 0(2) & a(3) + 0(4) \\ 0(1) + b(2) & 0(3) + b(4) \end{bmatrix} = \begin{bmatrix} a & 3a \\ 2b & 4b \end{bmatrix}$

**30** $\begin{bmatrix} 3 & 2 \\ 0 & 0 \end{bmatrix}\begin{bmatrix} -2 & 0 \\ 3 & 0 \end{bmatrix} = \begin{bmatrix} 3(-2) + 2(3) & 3(0) + 2(0) \\ 0(-2) + 0(3) & 0(0) + 0(0) \end{bmatrix} = \begin{bmatrix} 0 & 0 \\ 0 & 0 \end{bmatrix}$

**31** $\begin{bmatrix} 1 & 2 \\ 3 & 4 \end{bmatrix}\left(\begin{bmatrix} 2 & -4 \\ 3 & 7 \end{bmatrix} + \begin{bmatrix} 1 & 5 \\ -2 & -3 \end{bmatrix}\right) = \begin{bmatrix} 1 & 2 \\ 3 & 4 \end{bmatrix}\begin{bmatrix} 3 & 1 \\ 1 & 4 \end{bmatrix} = \begin{bmatrix} 1(3) + 2(1) & 1(1) + 2(4) \\ 3(3) + 4(1) & 3(1) + 4(4) \end{bmatrix} = \begin{bmatrix} 5 & 9 \\ 13 & 19 \end{bmatrix}$

**32** Don't multiply, just remember that $AA^{-1} = I_3$.

***Note:*** Let $A$ denote each of the matrices in Exercises 33–48.

**33** $\begin{bmatrix} 5 & -4 & | & 1 & 0 \\ -3 & 2 & | & 0 & 1 \end{bmatrix}$ $\begin{array}{c} 2R_1 + 3R_2 \to R_1 \end{array}$ $\begin{bmatrix} 1 & -2 & | & 2 & 3 \\ -3 & 2 & | & 0 & 1 \end{bmatrix}$ $\begin{array}{c} R_2 + 3R_1 \to R_2 \end{array}$ $\begin{bmatrix} 1 & -2 & | & 2 & 3 \\ 0 & -4 & | & 6 & 10 \end{bmatrix}$

$\begin{array}{c} -\frac{1}{4}R_2 \to R_2 \end{array}$ $\begin{bmatrix} 1 & -2 & | & 2 & 3 \\ 0 & 1 & | & -\frac{3}{2} & -\frac{5}{2} \end{bmatrix}$ $\begin{array}{c} R_1 + 2R_2 \to R_1 \end{array}$ $\begin{bmatrix} 1 & 0 & | & -1 & -2 \\ 0 & 1 & | & -\frac{3}{2} & -\frac{5}{2} \end{bmatrix}$ $\Rightarrow$ $A^{-1} = -\frac{1}{2}\begin{bmatrix} 2 & 4 \\ 3 & 5 \end{bmatrix}$

**34** $\begin{bmatrix} 2 & -1 & 0 & | & 1 & 0 & 0 \\ 1 & 4 & 2 & | & 0 & 1 & 0 \\ 3 & -2 & 1 & | & 0 & 0 & 1 \end{bmatrix}$ $\begin{array}{l} R_1 - 2R_2 \leftrightarrow R_2 \\ \\ R_3 - 3R_2 \rightarrow R_3 \end{array}$ $\begin{bmatrix} 1 & 4 & 2 & | & 0 & 1 & 0 \\ 0 & -9 & -4 & | & 1 & -2 & 0 \\ 0 & -14 & -5 & | & 0 & -3 & 1 \end{bmatrix}$ $3R_2 - 2R_3 \rightarrow R_2$

$\begin{bmatrix} 1 & 4 & 2 & | & 0 & 1 & 0 \\ 0 & 1 & -2 & | & 3 & 0 & -2 \\ 0 & -14 & -5 & | & 0 & -3 & 1 \end{bmatrix}$ $\begin{array}{l} R_1 - 4R_2 \rightarrow R_1 \\ \\ R_3 + 14R_2 \rightarrow R_3 \end{array}$ $\begin{bmatrix} 1 & 0 & 10 & | & -12 & 1 & 8 \\ 0 & 1 & -2 & | & 3 & 0 & -2 \\ 0 & 0 & -33 & | & 42 & -3 & -27 \end{bmatrix}$ $-\tfrac{1}{33}R_3 \rightarrow R_3$

$\begin{bmatrix} 1 & 0 & 10 & | & -12 & 1 & 8 \\ 0 & 1 & -2 & | & 3 & 0 & -2 \\ 0 & 0 & 1 & | & -\tfrac{14}{11} & \tfrac{1}{11} & \tfrac{9}{11} \end{bmatrix}$ $\begin{array}{l} R_1 - 10R_3 \rightarrow R_1 \\ R_2 + 2R_3 \rightarrow R_2 \end{array}$ $\begin{bmatrix} 1 & 0 & 0 & | & \tfrac{8}{11} & \tfrac{1}{11} & -\tfrac{2}{11} \\ 0 & 1 & 0 & | & \tfrac{5}{11} & \tfrac{2}{11} & -\tfrac{4}{11} \\ 0 & 0 & 1 & | & -\tfrac{14}{11} & \tfrac{1}{11} & \tfrac{9}{11} \end{bmatrix}$ $\Rightarrow$

$$A^{-1} = \frac{1}{11}\begin{bmatrix} 8 & 1 & -2 \\ 5 & 2 & -4 \\ -14 & 1 & 9 \end{bmatrix}$$

**35** $\begin{bmatrix} 1 & 0 & 0 & | & 1 & 0 & 0 \\ 0 & 4 & 7 & | & 0 & 1 & 0 \\ 0 & 1 & 2 & | & 0 & 0 & 1 \end{bmatrix}$ $R_3 \leftrightarrow R_2$ $\begin{bmatrix} 1 & 0 & 0 & | & 1 & 0 & 0 \\ 0 & 1 & 2 & | & 0 & 0 & 1 \\ 0 & 4 & 7 & | & 0 & 1 & 0 \end{bmatrix}$ $R_3 - 4R_2 \rightarrow R_3$ $\begin{bmatrix} 1 & 0 & 0 & | & 1 & 0 & 0 \\ 0 & 1 & 2 & | & 0 & 0 & 1 \\ 0 & 0 & -1 & | & 0 & 1 & -4 \end{bmatrix}$

$-R_3 \rightarrow R_3$ $\begin{bmatrix} 1 & 0 & 0 & | & 1 & 0 & 0 \\ 0 & 1 & 2 & | & 0 & 0 & 1 \\ 0 & 0 & 1 & | & 0 & -1 & 4 \end{bmatrix}$ $R_2 - 2R_3 \rightarrow R_2$ $\begin{bmatrix} 1 & 0 & 0 & | & 1 & 0 & 0 \\ 0 & 1 & 0 & | & 0 & 2 & -7 \\ 0 & 0 & 1 & | & 0 & -1 & 4 \end{bmatrix}$ $\Rightarrow$

$$A^{-1} = \begin{bmatrix} 1 & 0 & 0 \\ 0 & 2 & -7 \\ 0 & -1 & 4 \end{bmatrix}$$

**36** $\begin{bmatrix} 2 & 0 & 5 & | & 1 & 0 & 0 \\ 0 & 3 & -1 & | & 0 & 1 & 0 \\ 3 & 4 & 0 & | & 0 & 0 & 1 \end{bmatrix}$ $R_3 - R_1 \leftrightarrow R_1$ $\begin{bmatrix} 1 & 4 & -5 & | & -1 & 0 & 1 \\ 0 & 3 & -1 & | & 0 & 1 & 0 \\ 2 & 0 & 5 & | & 1 & 0 & 0 \end{bmatrix}$ $R_3 - 2R_1 \rightarrow R_3$

$\begin{bmatrix} 1 & 4 & -5 & | & -1 & 0 & 1 \\ 0 & 3 & -1 & | & 0 & 1 & 0 \\ 0 & -8 & 15 & | & 3 & 0 & -2 \end{bmatrix}$ $3R_2 + R_3 \rightarrow R_2$ $\begin{bmatrix} 1 & 4 & -5 & | & -1 & 0 & 1 \\ 0 & 1 & 12 & | & 3 & 3 & -2 \\ 0 & -8 & 15 & | & 3 & 0 & -2 \end{bmatrix}$ $\begin{array}{l} R_1 - 4R_2 \rightarrow R_1 \\ \\ R_3 + 8R_2 \rightarrow R_3 \end{array}$

$\begin{bmatrix} 1 & 0 & -53 & | & -13 & -12 & 9 \\ 0 & 1 & 12 & | & 3 & 3 & -2 \\ 0 & 0 & 111 & | & 27 & 24 & -18 \end{bmatrix}$ $\tfrac{1}{111}R_3 \rightarrow R_3$ $\begin{bmatrix} 1 & 0 & -53 & | & -13 & -12 & 9 \\ 0 & 1 & 12 & | & 3 & 3 & -2 \\ 0 & 0 & 1 & | & \tfrac{9}{37} & \tfrac{8}{37} & -\tfrac{6}{37} \end{bmatrix}$ $\begin{array}{l} R_1 + 53R_3 \rightarrow R_1 \\ R_2 - 12R_3 \rightarrow R_2 \end{array}$

$\begin{bmatrix} 1 & 0 & 0 & | & -\tfrac{4}{37} & -\tfrac{20}{37} & \tfrac{15}{37} \\ 0 & 1 & 0 & | & \tfrac{3}{37} & \tfrac{15}{37} & -\tfrac{2}{37} \\ 0 & 0 & 1 & | & \tfrac{9}{37} & \tfrac{8}{37} & -\tfrac{6}{37} \end{bmatrix}$ $\Rightarrow$ $\qquad A^{-1} = \frac{1}{37}\begin{bmatrix} -4 & -20 & 15 \\ 3 & 15 & -2 \\ 9 & 8 & -6 \end{bmatrix}$

**37** $X = A^{-1}B = -\dfrac{1}{2}\begin{bmatrix} 2 & 4 \\ 3 & 5 \end{bmatrix}\begin{bmatrix} 30 \\ -16 \end{bmatrix}\{A^{-1} \text{ from Exercise 33}\} = -\dfrac{1}{2}\begin{bmatrix} -4 \\ 10 \end{bmatrix} = \begin{bmatrix} 2 \\ -5 \end{bmatrix};\ (x, y) = (2, -5)$

**38** $X = A^{-1}B = \dfrac{1}{11}\begin{bmatrix} 8 & 1 & -2 \\ 5 & 2 & -4 \\ -14 & 1 & 9 \end{bmatrix}\begin{bmatrix} -5 \\ 15 \\ -7 \end{bmatrix}\{A^{-1} \text{ from Exercise 34}\} = \dfrac{1}{11}\begin{bmatrix} -11 \\ 33 \\ 22 \end{bmatrix} = \begin{bmatrix} -1 \\ 3 \\ 2 \end{bmatrix};\ (x, y, z) = (-1, 3, 2)$

**39** An equation for the left half of the circle $x^2 + y^2 = 25$ is $x = -\sqrt{25 - y^2}$. An equation of the "v-shaped" graph is $y = |x| - 1$. Since we only want the left side, we use $y = -x - 1$. Substituting $-\sqrt{25 - y^2}$ for $x$ in $y = -x - 1$

gives us $y = \sqrt{25 - y^2} - 1 \;\Rightarrow\; y + 1 = \sqrt{25 - y^2} \;\Rightarrow\; (y + 1)^2 = 25 - y^2 \;\Rightarrow$

$y^2 + 2y + 1 = 25 - y^2 \;\Rightarrow\; 2y^2 + 2y - 24 = 0 \;\Rightarrow\; y^2 + y - 12 = 0 \;\Rightarrow\; (y + 4)(y - 3) = 0 \;\Rightarrow$

$y = -4, 3$. From the figure, we see that $y = 3$ and hence, $3 = -x - 1 \;\Rightarrow\; x = -4$.

So the only point of intersection is $(-4, 3)$.

**40** The line through $(-2, -2)$ and $(0, 4)$ has slope $\frac{4-(-2)}{0-(-2)} = \frac{6}{2} = 3$, so its slope-intercept form is $y = 3x + 4$. The parabola has an equation of the form $y = ax^2 + bx + c$. Substituting the $x$ and $y$ values of $(-1, 6)$, $(0, 0)$, and $(3, 6)$ into this equation yields $\begin{cases} a - b + c = 6 \ (E_1) \\ \quad\quad\quad c = 0 \ (E_2) \\ 9a + 3b + c = 6 \ (E_3) \end{cases}$ Using 0 for $c$ and adding $3E_1$ to $E_3$ yields

$12a = 24 \ \Rightarrow \ a = 2$, and hence, $b = -4$. An equation of the parabola is $y = 2x^2 - 4x$. Solving for the points of intersection, we get $2x^2 - 4x = 3x + 4 \ \Rightarrow \ 2x^2 - 7x - 4 = 0 \ \Rightarrow \ (2x + 1)(x - 4) = 0 \ \Rightarrow \ x = -\frac{1}{2}, 4$.

So the points of intersection are $\left(-\frac{1}{2}, \frac{5}{2}\right)$ and $(4, 16)$.

**41** $A = \begin{bmatrix} 3 & 4 \\ -6 & -5 \end{bmatrix} \ \Rightarrow \ |A| = \begin{vmatrix} 3 & 4 \\ -6 & -5 \end{vmatrix} = 3(-5) - 4(-6) = -15 + 24 = 9$

**42** $A = \begin{bmatrix} 3 & -4 \\ 6 & 8 \end{bmatrix} \ \Rightarrow \ |A| = \begin{vmatrix} 3 & -4 \\ 6 & 8 \end{vmatrix} = 3(8) - 6(-4) = 24 + 24 = 48$

**43** $|A| = \begin{vmatrix} 0 & 4 & -3 \\ 2 & 0 & 4 \\ -5 & 1 & 0 \end{vmatrix} \ \{R_1\} = 0(A_{11}) - 4(20) - 3(2) = -80 - 6 = -86$

**44** $|A| = \begin{vmatrix} 2 & -3 & 5 \\ -4 & 1 & 3 \\ 3 & 2 & -1 \end{vmatrix} \ \{R_1\} = 2(-7) + 3(-5) + 5(-11) = -14 - 15 - 55 = -84$

**45** $|A| = \begin{vmatrix} 3 & 1 & -2 \\ -5 & 2 & -4 \\ 7 & 3 & -6 \end{vmatrix} \ \{R_1\} = 3(0) - 1(58) - 2(-29) = 0 - 58 + 58 = 0$

**46** From Exercise 33 in Section 8.8, the determinant of $A$ is the product of the main diagonal elements of $A$—that is,

$$|A| = (5)(-3)(-4)(2) = 120.$$

**47** $\begin{vmatrix} 1 & 2 & 0 & 3 & 1 \\ -2 & -1 & 4 & 1 & 2 \\ 3 & 0 & -1 & 0 & -1 \\ 2 & -3 & 2 & -4 & 2 \\ -1 & 1 & 0 & 1 & 3 \end{vmatrix} \quad \begin{matrix} R_2 + 4R_3 \to R_2 \\ \\ = \\ \\ R_4 + 2R_3 \to R_4 \end{matrix} \quad \begin{vmatrix} 1 & 2 & 0 & 3 & 1 \\ 10 & -1 & 0 & 1 & -2 \\ 3 & 0 & -1 & 0 & -1 \\ 8 & -3 & 0 & -4 & 0 \\ -1 & 1 & 0 & 1 & 3 \end{vmatrix} \{C_3\}$

$= (-1) \begin{vmatrix} 1 & 2 & 3 & 1 \\ 10 & -1 & 1 & -2 \\ 8 & -3 & -4 & 0 \\ -1 & 1 & 1 & 3 \end{vmatrix} \quad \begin{matrix} R_2 + 2R_1 \to R_2 \\ \\ R_4 - 3R_1 \to R_4 \end{matrix} \quad = (-1) \begin{vmatrix} 1 & 2 & 3 & 1 \\ 12 & 3 & 7 & 0 \\ 8 & -3 & -4 & 0 \\ -4 & -5 & -8 & 0 \end{vmatrix} \{C_4\}$

$= (-1)(-1) \begin{vmatrix} 12 & 3 & 7 \\ 8 & -3 & -4 \\ -4 & -5 & -8 \end{vmatrix} \quad \{4 \text{ is a common factor of } C_1 \text{ and } -1 \text{ of } R_3\}$

$= (-4) \begin{vmatrix} 3 & 3 & 7 \\ 2 & -3 & -4 \\ 1 & 5 & 8 \end{vmatrix} \quad \begin{matrix} R_1 - 3R_3 \to R_1 \\ R_2 - 2R_3 \to R_2 \end{matrix} \quad = (-4) \begin{vmatrix} 0 & -12 & -17 \\ 0 & -13 & -20 \\ 1 & 5 & 8 \end{vmatrix} \{C_1\}$

$= (-4) \begin{vmatrix} -12 & -17 \\ -13 & -20 \end{vmatrix} = (-4)(240 - 221) = -76$

**48** As in Exercise 32 in Section 8.9, $|A| = \begin{vmatrix} 1 & 2 \\ 3 & 4 \end{vmatrix} \begin{vmatrix} 1 & 2 & 3 \\ 2 & -1 & 1 \\ 1 & 3 & -1 \end{vmatrix}$. Expand the $3 \times 3$ determinant by $R_1$.

$$|A| = (-2)[1(-2) - 2(-3) + 3(7)] = -50$$

**49** $|A - xI| = \begin{vmatrix} 2-x & 3 \\ 1 & -4-x \end{vmatrix} = 0 \Rightarrow (2-x)(-4-x) - 3 = 0 \Rightarrow$

$$x^2 + 2x - 11 = 0 \Rightarrow x = \frac{-2 \pm \sqrt{4+44}}{2} = \frac{-2 \pm 4\sqrt{3}}{2} = -1 \pm 2\sqrt{3}$$

**50** $|A - xI| = \begin{vmatrix} 2-x & -1 & 3 \\ 0 & 4-x & 0 \\ 1 & 0 & -2-x \end{vmatrix} = 0 \Rightarrow \{C_1\} (2-x)(4-x)(-2-x) - 3(4-x) = 0 \Rightarrow$

$$(4-x)[(2-x)(-2-x) - 3] = 0 \Rightarrow (4-x)(x^2 - 7) = 0 \Rightarrow x = 4, \pm\sqrt{7}$$

**51** 2 is a common factor of $R_1$, 2 is a common factor of $C_2$, and 3 is a common factor of $C_3$.

**52** Interchange $R_1$ with $R_2$ and then $R_2$ with $R_3$ to obtain the determinant on the right.

The effect is to multiply by $-1$ twice.

**53** This is an extension of Exercise 33 of §8.8. Expanding by $C_1$, only $a_{11}$ is not 0. Expanding by the new $C_1$ again, only $a_{22}$ is not 0. Repeating this process yields $|A| = a_{11}a_{22}a_{33}\cdots a_{nn}$, the product of the main diagonal elements.

**54** $\begin{vmatrix} 1 & a & b+c \\ 1 & b & a+c \\ 1 & c & a+b \end{vmatrix}$ $C_3 + C_2 \to C_2$ $= \begin{vmatrix} 1 & a & a+b+c \\ 1 & b & a+b+c \\ 1 & c & a+b+c \end{vmatrix}$ $C_3 - (a+b+c)C_1 \to C_3$ $= \begin{vmatrix} 1 & a & 0 \\ 1 & b & 0 \\ 1 & c & 0 \end{vmatrix} = 0,$

since $C_3$ consists of all zeros.

**55** For the system $\begin{cases} 5x - 6y = 4 \\ 3x + 7y = 8 \end{cases}$ we have $|D| = \begin{vmatrix} 5 & -6 \\ 3 & 7 \end{vmatrix} = 35 + 18 = 53.$

Since $|D| = 53 \neq 0$, we may solve the system using Cramer's rule.

$|D_x| = \begin{vmatrix} 4 & -6 \\ 8 & 7 \end{vmatrix} = 28 + 48 = 76$ and $|D_y| = \begin{vmatrix} 5 & 4 \\ 3 & 8 \end{vmatrix} = 40 - 12 = 28,$ so

$x = \dfrac{|D_x|}{|D|} = \dfrac{76}{53}$ and $y = \dfrac{|D_y|}{|D|} = \dfrac{28}{53}.$ $\bigstar \left(\dfrac{76}{53}, \dfrac{28}{53}\right)$

**56** $\begin{cases} 2x - 3y + 2z = -3 \\ -3x + 2y + z = 1 \\ 4x + y - 3z = 4 \end{cases}$ • $|D| = \begin{vmatrix} 2 & -3 & 2 \\ -3 & 2 & 1 \\ 4 & 1 & -3 \end{vmatrix}$ $\{R_1\} = 2(-7) + 3(5) + 2(-11) = -21,$

$|D_x| = \begin{vmatrix} -3 & -3 & 2 \\ 1 & 2 & 1 \\ 4 & 1 & -3 \end{vmatrix}$ $\{R_1\} = -3(-7) + 3(-7) + 2(-7) = -14,$

$|D_y| = \begin{vmatrix} 2 & -3 & 2 \\ -3 & 1 & 1 \\ 4 & 4 & -3 \end{vmatrix}$ $\{R_1\} = 2(-7) + 3(5) + 2(-16) = -31,$

$|D_z| = \begin{vmatrix} 2 & -3 & -3 \\ -3 & 2 & 1 \\ 4 & 1 & 4 \end{vmatrix}$ $\{R_1\} = 2(7) + 3(-16) - 3(-11) = -1.$

$x = \dfrac{|D_x|}{|D|} = \dfrac{-14}{-21} = \dfrac{2}{3}, y = \dfrac{|D_y|}{|D|} = \dfrac{31}{21}, z = \dfrac{|D_z|}{|D|} = \dfrac{1}{21}.$ $\bigstar \left(\dfrac{2}{3}, \dfrac{31}{21}, \dfrac{1}{21}\right)$

**57** $\dfrac{4x^2 + 54x + 134}{(x+3)(x^2 + 4x - 5)} = \dfrac{A}{x+3} + \dfrac{B}{x+5} + \dfrac{C}{x-1}$

$4x^2 + 54x + 134 = A(x+5)(x-1) + B(x+3)(x-1) + C(x+3)(x+5)$

$x = 1: 192 = 24C \Rightarrow C = 8$

$x = -3: 8 = -8A \Rightarrow A = -1$

$x = -5: -36 = 12B \Rightarrow B = -3$ $\bigstar \dfrac{8}{x-1} - \dfrac{3}{x+5} - \dfrac{1}{x+3}$

**58** By first dividing and then factoring, we get $\dfrac{2x^2 + 7x + 9}{x^2 + 2x + 1} = 2 + \dfrac{3x + 7}{(x + 1)^2} = 2 + \dfrac{A}{x + 1} + \dfrac{B}{(x + 1)^2}$.

$3x + 7 = A(x + 1) + B$

$x = -1 : 4 = B \Rightarrow B = 4$

$x = 0 : 7 = A + B \Rightarrow A = 3$

$\bigstar\ 2 + \dfrac{3}{x + 1} + \dfrac{4}{(x + 1)^2}$

**59** $\dfrac{x^2 + 14x - 13}{x^3 + 5x^2 + 4x + 20} = \dfrac{A}{x + 5} + \dfrac{Bx + C}{x^2 + 4}$

$x^2 + 14x - 13 = A(x^2 + 4) + (Bx + C)(x + 5)$

$x = -5 : -58 = 29A \Rightarrow A = -2$

$x = 0 : -13 = 4A + 5C \Rightarrow C = -1$

$x = 1 : 2 = 5A + 6B + 6C \Rightarrow B = 3$

$\bigstar\ -\dfrac{2}{x + 5} + \dfrac{3x - 1}{x^2 + 4}$

**60** $\dfrac{x^3 + 2x^2 + 2x + 16}{x^4 + 7x^2 + 10} = \dfrac{Ax + B}{x^2 + 2} + \dfrac{Cx + D}{x^2 + 5}$

$x^3 + 2x^2 + 2x + 16 = (Ax + B)(x^2 + 5) + (Cx + D)(x^2 + 2)$

$\qquad\qquad\qquad\qquad\ = (A + C)x^3 + (B + D)x^2 + (5A + 2C)x + (5B + 2D)$

Equating coefficients (like terms must have equal coefficients on each side), we have the following:

$x^3$-terms: $A + C = 1$

$x^2$-terms: $B + D = 2$

$x$-terms: $5A + 2C = 2\ \{A + C = 1\} \Rightarrow A = 0$ and $C = 1$

constant terms: $5B + 2D = 16\ \{B + D = 2\} \Rightarrow 3B = 12 \Rightarrow B = 4$ and $D = -2 \quad \bigstar\ \dfrac{4}{x^2 + 2} + \dfrac{x - 2}{x^2 + 5}$

**61** Let $x$ and $y$ denote the length and width, respectively, of the rectangle. A diagonal of the field is 100 ft.

We can use the Pythagorean theorem to formulate an equation that relates the sides and a diagonal.

$$\begin{cases} \quad xy = 4000 \quad & area \quad & (\text{E}_1) \\ x^2 + y^2 = 100^2 \quad & diagonal \quad & (\text{E}_2) \end{cases}$$

Solve $\text{E}_1$ for $y$, $y = 4000/x$, and substitute into $\text{E}_2$. $x^2 + \dfrac{4000^2}{x^2} = 100^2 \Rightarrow$

$x^4 - 10{,}000x^2 + 16{,}000{,}000 = 0 \Rightarrow (x^2 - 2000)(x^2 - 8000) = 0 \Rightarrow$

$x = 20\sqrt{5},\ 40\sqrt{5}$ and $y = 40\sqrt{5},\ 20\sqrt{5}$. The dimensions are $20\sqrt{5}$ ft $\times\ 40\sqrt{5}$ ft.

**62** Substitute $mx + 3$ for $y$ in $x^2 + y^2 = 1$ to get $x^2 + (mx + 3)^2 = 1 \Rightarrow x^2 + m^2x^2 + 6xm + 9 = 1 \Rightarrow$

$(m^2 + 1)x^2 + (6m)x + (8) = 0 \Rightarrow x = \dfrac{-6m \pm \sqrt{36m^2 - 32m^2 - 32}}{2(m^2 + 1)}$. If there is to be only one solution to

the system, i.e., one point of intersection between the circle and the line, then the discriminant must equal 0.

$\qquad\quad 4m^2 - 32 = 0 \Rightarrow m^2 = 8 \Rightarrow m = \pm 2\sqrt{2}$, and the equations of the lines are $y = \pm 2\sqrt{2}\,x + 3$.

**63** Let $r_1$ and $r_2$ denote the inside radius and the outside radius, respectively.

Inside distance $= 90\%$(outside distance) $\Rightarrow 2\pi r_1 = 0.90(2\pi r_2) \Rightarrow r_1 = 0.90(r_2) \Rightarrow$

$r_1 = 0.90(r_1 + 10)\ \{\text{since } r_2 = r_1 + 10\} \Rightarrow r_1 = 0.9r_1 + 9 \Rightarrow 0.1r_1 = 9 \Rightarrow$

$$r_1 = \dfrac{9}{0.1} = 90 \text{ ft and } r_2 = 90 + 10 = 100 \text{ ft}$$

**64** Let $x$ and $y$ denote the total amount of taxes paid and bonus money, respectively.

$$\begin{cases} x = 0.40(2{,}000{,}000 - y) & \textit{taxes} \\ y = 0.10(2{,}000{,}000 - x) & \textit{bonuses} \end{cases} \Rightarrow \begin{cases} 10x + 4y = 8{,}000{,}000 & (E_1) \\ x + 10y = 2{,}000{,}000 & (E_2) \end{cases}$$

$E_1 - 10E_2 \Rightarrow (10x + 4y = 8{,}000{,}000) - 10(x + 10y = 2{,}000{,}000) \Rightarrow -96y = -12{,}000{,}000 \Rightarrow$

$y = \$125{,}000$. From $E_2$, $x = 2{,}000{,}000 - 10(125{,}000) = \$750{,}000$.

**65** Let $x$ denote the rate at which she can row in still water and $y$ the speed of the current.

$$D = RT \begin{cases} 1.75 = (x - y)\frac{35}{60} & \textit{upstream} \\ 1.75 = (x + y)\frac{15}{60} & \textit{downstream} \end{cases} \Rightarrow \begin{cases} 3 = x - y & (E_1) \\ 7 = x + y & (E_2) \end{cases}$$

$E_1 + E_2 \Rightarrow (x - y = 3) + (x + y = 7) \Rightarrow 2x = 10 \Rightarrow x = 5 \text{ mi/hr}; y = 2 \text{ mi/hr}$

**66** Let $x$ denote the number of pounds of peanuts used and $y$ the number of pounds of raisins used.

$$\begin{cases} x + y = 55 & \textit{quantity} \\ 1.85x + 1.30y = 1.55(55) & \textit{quality} \end{cases} \Rightarrow \begin{cases} x + y = 55 & (E_1) \\ 185x + 130y = 8525 & (E_2) \end{cases}$$

$E_2 - 130E_1 \Rightarrow (185x + 130y = 8525) - 130(x + y = 55) \Rightarrow 55x = 1375 \Rightarrow x = 25; y = 30$

**67** Let $x$ denote the speed of the plane and $y$ the speed of the wind.

$$D = RT \begin{cases} 3470 = (x + y)(2.5) & \textit{with the wind} \\ 3470 = (x - y)(2.75) & \textit{against the wind} \end{cases} \Rightarrow \begin{cases} x + y = 1388 & (E_1) \\ x - y \approx 1261.8 & (E_2) \end{cases}$$

$E_1 + E_2 \Rightarrow (x + y = 1388) + (x - y \approx 1261.8) \Rightarrow 2x \approx 2649.8 \Rightarrow$

$x \approx 1324.9 \approx 1325 \text{ mi/hr}; y \approx 63 \text{ mi/hr}$

**68** Let $x$, $y$, and $z$ denote the number of ft$^3$/hr flowing through pipes A, B, and C, respectively.

$$\begin{cases} 10x + 10y + 10z = 1000 & \textit{all three working} \\ 20x + 20y = 1000 & \textit{only A and B working} \\ 12.5x + 12.5z = 1000 & \textit{only A and C working} \end{cases} \Rightarrow \begin{cases} x + y + z = 100 & (E_1) \\ x + y = 50 & (E_2) \\ x + z = 80 & (E_3) \end{cases}$$

$E_1 - E_2 \Rightarrow (x + y + z = 100) - (x + y = 50) \Rightarrow z = 50$.

$E_1 - E_3 \Rightarrow (x + y + z = 100) - (x + z = 80) \Rightarrow y = 20$, and then from $E_2$, $x = 30$.

**69** Let $x$ and $y$ denote the number of desks shipped from the western warehouse and the eastern warehouse, respectively. $\begin{cases} x + y = 150 & \textit{quantity} \quad (E_1) \\ 48x + 70y = 8410 & \textit{price} \quad (E_2) \end{cases}$

$E_2 - 48E_1 \Rightarrow (48x + 70y = 8410) - 48(x + y = 150) \Rightarrow 22y = 1210 \Rightarrow y = 55; x = 95$

**70** If $x$ and $y$ denote the length and the width, respectively, then a system is $x \le 12$, $y \le 8$, $y \ge \frac{1}{2}x$.

The graph is the region bounded by the quadrilateral with vertices $(0, 0)$, $(0, 8)$, $(12, 8)$, and $(12, 6)$.

*Figure 70*

*Figure 71*

**71** The number of hours spent resting is $24 - x - y$.

A system is $24 - x - y \ge 6$ {hours resting}, $x \ge 2y$, $x \ge 0$, $y \ge 0$. The first inequality is $x + y \le 18$.

The graph is the region bounded by the triangle with vertices $(0, 0)$, $(18, 0)$, and $(12, 6)$.

**72** Let $x$ and $y$ denote the number of lawn mowers and edgers produced, respectively.

Profit function: $P = 100x + 80y$

$$\begin{cases} 6x + 4y \le 600 & \textit{machining} \\ 2x + 3y \le 300 & \textit{welding} \\ 5x + 5y \le 550 & \textit{assembly} \\ x, y \ge 0 \end{cases}$$

| $(x, y)$ | $(100, 0)$ | $(80, 30)$ | $(30, 80)$ | $(0, 100)$ | $(0, 0)$ |
|---|---|---|---|---|---|
| $P$ | 10,000 | 10,400 ■ | 9400 | 8000 | 0 |

The maximum weekly profit of \$10,400 occurs when 80 lawn mowers and 30 edgers are produced.

*Figure 72*

*Figure 73*

**73** Let $x$ and $y$ denote the amount in the high- and low-risk investments, respectively.

The amount in bonds is $750,000 - x - y$.

Profit function: $P = 0.12x + 0.08y + 0.04(750,000 - x - y) = 30,000 + 0.08x + 0.04y$

$$\begin{cases} x + y \le 750,000 \\ y \ge 2x \\ x, y \ge 0 \end{cases}$$

| $(x, y)$ | $(0, 0)$ | $(0, 750,000)$ | $(250,000, 500,000)$ |
|---|---|---|---|
| $P$ | 30,000 | 60,000 | 70,000 ■ |

The maximum return of \$70,000 occurs when \$250,000 is invested in the high-risk investment, \$500,000 is invested in the low-risk investment, and \$0 is invested in bonds.

## Chapter 8 Discussion Exercises

**1**  (a)  For $b = 1.99$, we get $x = 204$ and $y = -100$. For $b = 1.999$, we get $x = 2004$ and $y = -1000$.

(b)  Solving $\begin{cases} x + 2y = 4 \\ x + by = 5 \end{cases}$ for $y$ gives us $y = \dfrac{1}{b - 2}$ and then solving for $x$ we obtain $x = \dfrac{4b - 10}{b - 2}$.

Both $x$ and $y$ are rational functions of $b$ and as $b \to 2^-$, $x \to \infty$ and $y \to -\infty$.

(c)  If $b$ gets very large, $(x, y)$ gets close to $(4, 0)$.

**2**  (a)  $D = \begin{bmatrix} 12,000 & 9000 & 14,000 \end{bmatrix}$; $E = \begin{bmatrix} 0.90 & 0.10 & 0.00 \\ 0.00 & 0.80 & 0.20 \\ 0.05 & 0.00 & 0.95 \end{bmatrix}$

(b)  $F = DE = \begin{bmatrix} 12,000 & 9000 & 14,000 \end{bmatrix} \begin{bmatrix} 0.90 & 0.10 & 0.00 \\ 0.00 & 0.80 & 0.20 \\ 0.05 & 0.00 & 0.95 \end{bmatrix} = \begin{bmatrix} 11,500 & 8400 & 15,100 \end{bmatrix}$.

The elements of $F$ represent the populations on islands A, B, and C, respectively, after one year.

(c) After repeated multiplications of the population matrix by the proportion matrix, we obtain the matrix $G = [\,10{,}000 \quad 5000 \quad 20{,}000\,]$. Our conclusion is that the population stabilizes with 10,000 birds on A, 5000 birds on B, and 20,000 birds on C.

(d) If we begin with $D = [\,34{,}000 \quad 500 \quad 500\,]$, multiply by $E$, and continue to multiply the result by $E$, we eventually get the values in $G$. Our conclusion is that regardless of the initial population distribution of the 35,000 birds, the populations tend toward the distribution described in part (c).

$\boxed{3}$  If we let $A$ be an $m \times n$ matrix ($m \ne n$), then $B$ would have to be an $n \times m$ matrix so that $AB$ and $BA$ are both defined. But then $AB = I_m$ and $BA = I_n$, different orders of the identity matrix, which we can't have (they must be the same).

$\boxed{4}$  $AX = B \;\Leftrightarrow\; \begin{bmatrix} 0.5 & 0.4 & 0.1 \\ 0.3 & 0.2 & 0.5 \\ 0.2 & 0.4 & 0.4 \end{bmatrix} \begin{bmatrix} x \\ y \\ z \end{bmatrix} = \begin{bmatrix} 0.34 \\ 0.33 \\ 0.33 \end{bmatrix} \;\Rightarrow\; X = A^{-1}B = \begin{bmatrix} 0.35 \\ 0.3\overline{3} \\ 0.31\overline{6} \end{bmatrix}.$

Give 35% to the AD, $33\frac{1}{3}\%$ to the DS, and $31\frac{2}{3}\%$ to the SP.

$\boxed{5}$  Synthetically dividing $x^4 + ax^2 + bx + c$ by $x + 1$, $x - 2$, and $x - 3$ yields the remainders $a - b + c + 1$, $4a + 2b + c + 16$, and $9a + 3b + c + 81$, respectively. Setting each of the remainders equal to 0 gives us the following system of equations in matrix form.

$$AX = B \;\Leftrightarrow\; \begin{bmatrix} 1 & -1 & 1 \\ 4 & 2 & 1 \\ 9 & 3 & 1 \end{bmatrix} \begin{bmatrix} a \\ b \\ c \end{bmatrix} = \begin{bmatrix} -1 \\ -16 \\ -81 \end{bmatrix} \;\Rightarrow\; X = A^{-1}B = \begin{bmatrix} -15 \\ 10 \\ 24 \end{bmatrix}.$$

Hence, $a = -15$, $b = 10$, $c = 24$, and we graph $Y_1 = x^4 - 15x^2 + 10x + 24$. The roots of $Y_1$ are $-1, 2, 3$, and $-4$.

$\boxed{6}$  With $y = ax^3 + bx^2 + cx + d$ and the points $(-6, -6)$, $(-4, 3)$, $(2, 2)$, and $(6, 6)$, we have

$$AX = B \;\Leftrightarrow\; \begin{bmatrix} -216 & 36 & -6 & 1 \\ 8 & 4 & 2 & 1 \\ 216 & 36 & 6 & 1 \\ -64 & 16 & -4 & 1 \end{bmatrix} \begin{bmatrix} a \\ b \\ c \\ d \end{bmatrix} = \begin{bmatrix} -6 \\ 2 \\ 6 \\ 3 \end{bmatrix} \;\Rightarrow\; X = A^{-1}B = \begin{bmatrix} 0.058\overline{3} \\ -0.11\overline{6} \\ -1.1 \\ 4.2 \end{bmatrix}$$

So the equation is $y = 0.058\overline{3}x^3 - 0.11\overline{6}x^2 - 1.1x + 4.2$. As $y$ gets large positive, the values of $a$ and $d$ get larger positively and the values of $b$ and $c$ get larger negatively. As $y$ gets large negative, the values of $a$ and $d$ get larger negatively and the values of $b$ and $c$ get larger positively. In either case, changing the $y$-value for $(-4, y)$ makes the graph appear nearly vertical through the other three points.

$\boxed{7}$  Using $a_{11}x + a_{12}y = k_1$ and the value of $y$ that was found, we substitute for $y$ and solve for $x$.

Let $|A| = \begin{vmatrix} a_{11} & a_{12} \\ a_{21} & a_{22} \end{vmatrix}$ and $|K| = \begin{vmatrix} a_{11} & k_1 \\ a_{21} & k_2 \end{vmatrix}$. $a_{11}x + a_{12}y = k_1 \;\Rightarrow\; a_{11}x + a_{12} \cdot \dfrac{|K|}{|A|} = k_1 \;\Rightarrow$

$$x = \frac{k_1 - a_{12} \cdot \dfrac{|K|}{|A|}}{a_{11}} = \frac{|A| \cdot k_1 - a_{12} \cdot |K|}{a_{11} \cdot |A|} = \frac{(a_{11}a_{22} - a_{12}a_{21})k_1 - a_{12}(a_{11}k_2 - k_1 a_{21})}{a_{11} \cdot |A|}$$

$$= \frac{a_{11}a_{22}k_1 - a_{12}a_{21}k_1 - a_{12}a_{11}k_2 - a_{12}a_{21}k_1}{a_{11} \cdot |A|} = \frac{a_{11}a_{22}k_1 - a_{12}a_{11}k_2}{a_{11} \cdot |A|} = \frac{a_{11}(a_{22}k_1 - a_{12}k_2)}{a_{11} \cdot |A|}$$

$$= \frac{\begin{vmatrix} k_1 & a_{12} \\ k_2 & a_{22} \end{vmatrix}}{|A|}, \text{ which is what we wanted to show.}$$

**8** The points are $P(-1, 3)$, $Q(0, 4)$, and $R(3, 2)$.

(a) $m_{PQ} = 1$ and $m_{QR} = -\frac{2}{3}$, so we cannot have a line through $P$, $Q$, and $R$.

(b) The circle has an equation of the form $x^2 + y^2 + ax + by + c = 0$. Substituting the $x$ and $y$ values of $P(-1, 3)$, $Q(0, 4)$, and $R(3, 2)$ into this equation yields:

$$\begin{cases} -a + 3b + c = -10 & P & (E_1) \\ 4b + c = -16 & Q & (E_2) \\ 3a + 2b + c = -13 & R & (E_3) \end{cases}$$

Solving the system gives us $a = -1.8$, $b = -4.2$, and $c = 0.8$, so an equation of the circle is $x^2 + y^2 - 1.8x - 4.2y + 0.8 = 0$.

(c) The parabola with vertical axis has an equation of the form $f(x) = ax^2 + bx + c$.

Substituting the $x$ and $y$ values of $P(-1, 3)$, $Q(0, 4)$, and $R(3, 2)$ into this equation yields:

$$\begin{cases} a - b + c = 3 & P & (E_1) \\ c = 4 & Q & (E_2) \\ 9a + 3b + c = 2 & R & (E_3) \end{cases}$$

Solving the system gives us $a = -\frac{5}{12}$, $b = \frac{7}{12}$, and $c = 4$, so an equation of the parabola is $f(x) = -\frac{5}{12}x^2 + \frac{7}{12}x + 4$.

(d) For a cubic, $f(x) = ax^3 + bx^2 + cx + d$, we see that $d = 4$ from $Q(0, 4)$.

Substituting the $x$ and $y$ values of $P(-1, 3)$ and $R(3, 2)$ gives us

$$\begin{cases} -a + b - c = -1 & P & (E_1) \\ 27a + 9b + 3c = -2 & Q & (E_2) \end{cases}$$

$3E_1 + E_2 \Rightarrow 24a + 12b = -5 \Rightarrow b = -2a - \frac{5}{12}$.

Using $E_1$, $-a + \left(-2a - \frac{5}{12}\right) - c = -1 \Rightarrow c = -3a + \frac{7}{12}$. Thus, we can use any cubic of the form

$$f(x) = ax^3 + \left(-2a - \tfrac{5}{12}\right)x^2 + \left(-3a + \tfrac{7}{12}\right)x + 4, \ a \neq 0.$$

(e) Use $f(x) = ba^x + c$ with the points $P(-1, 3)$, $Q(0, 4)$, and $R(3, 2)$.

$$\begin{aligned} f(0) &= 4 \\ f(-1) &= 3 \\ f(3) &= 2 \end{aligned} \Rightarrow \begin{cases} 4 = ba^0 + c & Q & (E_1) \\ 3 = ba^{-1} + c & P & (E_2) \\ 2 = ba^3 + c & R & (E_3) \end{cases}$$

From $E_1$, $4 = b + c \Rightarrow c = 4 - b$. Substitute $4 - b$ for $c$ in $E_2$ and $E_3$.

$E_2$: $3 = ba^{-1} + 4 - b \Rightarrow b - ba^{-1} = 1 \Rightarrow b\left(1 - \dfrac{1}{a}\right) = 1 \Rightarrow b\left(\dfrac{a - 1}{a}\right) = 1$

$E_3$: $2 = ba^3 + 4 - b \Rightarrow b - ba^3 = 2 \Rightarrow b(1 - a^3) = 2 \Rightarrow b(a^3 - 1) = -2$

Solving both equations for $b$ and equating the expressions gives us

$\dfrac{a}{a - 1} = \dfrac{-2}{a^3 - 1} \Rightarrow \dfrac{a}{a - 1} = \dfrac{-2}{(a - 1)(a^2 + a + 1)} \Rightarrow a(a^2 + a + 1) = -2 \Rightarrow$

$a^3 + a^2 + a + 2 = 0$. The last equation is true only for a value of $a$ that is negative, but $a$ is the base and it must be positive, so we cannot have an exponential of the form $f(x) = ba^x + c$ through the three points.

## Chapter 8 Test

**1** $\begin{cases} x^2 + y^2 = 13 & (E_1) \\ y - x = 1 & (E_2) \end{cases}$ • Solve $E_2$ for $y$: $y = x + 1$. Substituting $x + 1$ for $y$ in $E_1$ we get

$x^2 + (x+1)^2 = 13 \Rightarrow x^2 + x^2 + 2x + 1 = 13 \Rightarrow 2x^2 + 2x - 12 = 0 \Rightarrow x^2 + x - 6 = 0 \Rightarrow$

$(x+3)(x-2) = 0 \Rightarrow x = -3, 2$ and so $y = -2, 3$. The solutions are $(-3, -2)$ and $(2, 3)$.

**2** $\begin{cases} x^2 - y^2 = 40 & (E_1) \\ 2x^2 + y^2 = 107 & (E_2) \end{cases}$ • Adding the two equations gives us $3x^2 = 147 \Rightarrow x^2 = 49 \Rightarrow x = \pm 7$.

Substituting $x^2 = 49$ in $E_1$ gives us $49 - y^2 = 40 \Rightarrow y^2 = 9 \Rightarrow y = \pm 3$.

There are *four* solutions: $(-7, -3), (-7, 3), (7, -3),$ and $(7, 3)$.

**3** If $x$ and $y$ denote the numbers, then we can describe the problem statement with the system $\begin{cases} x - y = 8 \\ x/y = 3 \end{cases}$

The second equation is equivalent to $x = 3y$ for $y \neq 0$. Substituting $3y$ for $x$ into the first equation gives

$3y - y = 8 \Rightarrow 2y = 8 \Rightarrow y = 4$, so $x = 3(4) = 12$. The numbers are 12 and 4.

**4** The slope of the line from $(x, y)$ (the point of tangency) to the origin is $\frac{y}{x}$ so the slope of the tangent line is $-\frac{x}{y}$.

The line through $(0, 5)$ has equation $y = \left(-\frac{x}{y}\right)x + 5 \Rightarrow y^2 = -x^2 + 5y \Rightarrow x^2 = 5y - y^2$.

Substituting $5y - y^2$ for $x^2$ in $x^2 + y^2 = 10$ gives us $5y - y^2 + y^2 = 10 \Rightarrow 5y = 10 \Rightarrow y = 2$.

Now $x^2 = 10 - y^2 \Rightarrow x = \pm\sqrt{10 - 2^2} = \pm\sqrt{6}$. The possible points of tangency are $(\pm\sqrt{6}, 2)$.

**5** $\begin{cases} 4x - 7y = 9 \\ 5x + 3y = 11 \end{cases}$ • 3 times the first equation and 7 times the second equation

gives us the system $\begin{cases} 12x - 21y = 27 \\ 35x + 21y = 77 \end{cases}$ Adding these equations gives us $47x = 104 \Rightarrow x = \frac{104}{47}$.

$-5$ times the first equation and 4 times the second equation gives us the system $\begin{cases} -20x + 35y = -45 \\ 20x + 12y = 44 \end{cases}$

Adding these equations gives us $47y = -1 \Rightarrow y = -\frac{1}{47}$. The solution is $\left(\frac{104}{47}, -\frac{1}{47}\right)$.

**6** $\begin{cases} -0.3x + 0.4y = -0.9 \\ 9x - 12y = 28 \end{cases}$ • 30 times the first equation (you might multiply by 10 and then by 3)

gives us the system $\begin{cases} -9x + 12y = -27 \\ 9x - 12y = 28 \end{cases}$ Adding these equations gives us $0 = 1$, which indicates that the system

has no solution.

**7** $\begin{cases} \frac{3}{5}x - \frac{1}{5}y = -1 \\ -12x + 4y = 20 \end{cases}$ • 20 times the first equation (you might multiply by 5 to get $3x - y = -5$ and then multiply

by 4) gives us the system $\begin{cases} 12x - 4y = -20 \\ -12x + 4y = 20 \end{cases}$ Adding these equations gives us $0 = 0$, which indicates that the

system has an infinite number of solutions, namely, all ordered pairs $(x, y)$ such that $3x - y = -5$ (or some

equivalent equation).

**8** Let $s$ denote the number of sofas produced and $r$ the number of recliners produced.

$\begin{cases} 6s + 7r = 495 & \text{\textit{labor hours}} & (E_1) \\ 150s + 135r = 10{,}575 & \text{\textit{cost of materials}} & (E_2) \end{cases}$

$E_2 - 25 E_1 \Rightarrow (150s + 135r = 10{,}575) - 25(6s + 7r = 495) \Rightarrow 135r - 175r = 10{,}575 - 12{,}375 \Rightarrow$

$-40r = -1800 \Rightarrow r = 45; s = 30.$ 30 sofas and 45 recliners can be produced.

**9**   $|y| < 2 \implies -2 < y < 2$. Shade between the dashed lines $y = -2$ and $y = 2$. Shade the exterior of the solid circle $x^2 + y^2 = 25$.

*Figure 9*

*Figure 11*

**10**   The solid circle has intercepts 4 units from the origin, and since it is shaded on the inside, an inequality for it is $x^2 + y^2 \le 4^2$. The dashed line has $y$-intercept 2, a slope of 1, and since it is shaded above the line, an inequality for it is $y > 1x + 2$. A system is $\begin{cases} y > x + 2 \\ x^2 + y^2 \le 16 \end{cases}$

**11**   If $x$ and $y$ denote the amount placed in the high-risk and low-risk investment, respectively, then a system is $x \ge 3000$, $y \ge 4x$, $x + y \le 25,000$. The graph is the region bounded by the triangle with vertices $(3000, 12,000)$, $(3000, 22,000)$, and $(5000, 20,000)$. See *Figure 11* above.

**12**   $x + y \le 6 \implies y \le -x + 6$ and $x + 2y \le 8 \implies y \le -\frac{1}{2}x + 4$. The corresponding lines intersect at $(4, 2)$.

The other vertices are $(0, 4)$, $(6, 0)$, and $(0, 0)$:

| $(x, y)$ | $(0,0)$ | $(0,4)$ | $(4,2)$ | $(6,0)$ |
|---|---|---|---|---|
| $C = 2x + y$ | 0 | 4 | 10 | 12 ■ |

The maximum of $C = 2x + y$ is 12 and it occurs at $(6, 0)$.

*Figure 12*

*Figure 13*

**13**   Let $x$ and $y$ denote the number of vans and buses purchased, respectively.

$$\begin{cases} 20,000x + 60,000y \le 360,000 & purchase \\ 200x + 160y \le 1400 & maintenance \\ \qquad\qquad\quad x \ge 0 \\ \qquad\qquad\quad y \ge 0 \end{cases} \implies \begin{cases} x + 3y \le 18 \\ 5x + 4y \le 35 \\ \quad x \ge 0 \\ \quad y \ge 0 \end{cases}$$

Passenger capacity function: $P = 20x + 50y$

| $(x, y)$ | $(7, 0)$ | $(3, 5)$ | $(0, 6)$ | $(0, 0)$ |
|---|---|---|---|---|
| $P$ | 140 | 310 ■ | 300 | 0 |

The maximum passenger capacity of 310 would occur if the community purchases 3 vans and 5 buses.

**14** $\begin{cases} 3x + 2y - z = -1 \\ x - 4y + 2z = 30 \\ 5y + z = -8 \end{cases}$ • $\begin{bmatrix} 3 & 2 & -1 & | & -1 \\ 1 & -4 & 2 & | & 30 \\ 0 & 5 & 1 & | & -8 \end{bmatrix}$ $\begin{matrix} R_1 \leftrightarrow R_2 \\ \\ \end{matrix}$ $\begin{bmatrix} 1 & -4 & 2 & | & 30 \\ 3 & 2 & -1 & | & -1 \\ 0 & 5 & 1 & | & -8 \end{bmatrix}$ $R_2 - 3R_1 \rightarrow R_2$

$\begin{bmatrix} 1 & -4 & 2 & | & 30 \\ 0 & 14 & -7 & | & -91 \\ 0 & 5 & 1 & | & -8 \end{bmatrix}$ $3R_3 - R_2 \rightarrow R_2$ $\begin{bmatrix} 1 & -4 & 2 & | & 30 \\ 0 & 1 & 10 & | & 67 \\ 0 & 5 & 1 & | & -8 \end{bmatrix}$ $R_3 - 5R_2 \rightarrow R_3$ $\begin{bmatrix} 1 & -4 & 2 & | & 30 \\ 0 & 1 & 10 & | & 67 \\ 0 & 0 & -49 & | & -343 \end{bmatrix}$

$-\frac{1}{49}R_3 \rightarrow R_3$ $\begin{bmatrix} 1 & -4 & 2 & | & 30 \\ 0 & 1 & 10 & | & 67 \\ 0 & 0 & 1 & | & 7 \end{bmatrix}$ $\begin{matrix} R_3: z = 7 \\ R_2: y + 10z = 67 \Rightarrow y = -3 \\ R_1: x - 4y + 2z = 30 \Rightarrow x = 4 \end{matrix}$ ★ $(4, -3, 7)$

**15** $\begin{cases} x + 2y + z = 0 \\ x - 2y - 7z = 0 \\ x + 3y + 3z = 0 \end{cases}$ • $\begin{bmatrix} 1 & 2 & 1 & | & 0 \\ 1 & -2 & -7 & | & 0 \\ 1 & 3 & 3 & | & 0 \end{bmatrix}$ $\begin{matrix} R_2 - R_1 \rightarrow R_2 \\ R_3 - R_1 \rightarrow R_3 \end{matrix}$ $\begin{bmatrix} 1 & 2 & 1 & | & 0 \\ 0 & -4 & -8 & | & 0 \\ 0 & 1 & 2 & | & 0 \end{bmatrix}$ $-\frac{1}{4}R_2 \rightarrow R_2$

$\begin{bmatrix} 1 & 2 & 1 & | & 0 \\ 0 & 1 & 2 & | & 0 \\ 0 & 1 & 2 & | & 0 \end{bmatrix}$ $\begin{matrix} R_1 - R_2 \rightarrow R_1 \\ R_3 - R_2 \rightarrow R_3 \end{matrix}$ $\begin{bmatrix} 1 & 1 & -1 & | & 0 \\ 0 & 1 & 2 & | & 0 \\ 0 & 0 & 0 & | & 0 \end{bmatrix}$ $\begin{matrix} R_2: y + 2z = 0 \Rightarrow y = -2z \\ R_1: x + y - z = 0 \Rightarrow x = 3z \end{matrix}$ ★ $(3c, -2c, c)$

**16** Let $x$, $y$, and $z$ denote the weight of the rope per linear foot, the chain per linear foot, and an anchor, respectively.

$\begin{cases} 100x + 4y + z = 51 & \text{100-ft rope } (E_1) \\ 60x + 8y + z = 49 & \text{60-ft rope } (E_2) \\ 40x + z = 28 & \text{40-ft rope } (E_3) \end{cases}$  Solving $E_3$ for $z$ and substituting into $E_1$ and $E_2$ yields

$\begin{cases} 60x + 4y = 23 & (E_4) \\ 20x + 8y = 21 & (E_5) \end{cases}$ $E_4 - 3E_5 \Rightarrow -20y = -40 \Rightarrow y = 2; x = \frac{1}{4}; z = 18.$ The weights of the rope per

linear foot, the chain per linear foot, and an anchor, are $\frac{1}{4}$, 2, and 18 pounds, respectively.

**17** Using $y = f(x) = ax^3 + bx^2 + cx + d$ and the point $P(0, -7)$, we should recognize that $d = -7$ since substituting

0 for $x$ leaves only the constant term. Now use the points $Q(1, -8)$, $R(2, -1)$, and $S(3, 32)$ to obtain the system:

$\begin{cases} a + b + c - 7 = -8 & Q & (E_1) \\ 8a + 4b + 2c - 7 = -1 & R & (E_2) \\ 27a + 9b + 3c - 7 = 32 & S & (E_3) \end{cases}$ $\Rightarrow$ $\begin{cases} a + b + c = -1 & Q & (E_1) \\ 8a + 4b + 2c = 6 & R & (E_2) \\ 27a + 9b + 3c = 39 & S & (E_3) \end{cases}$

Solving the system yields $a = 3$, $b = -5$, and $c = 1$, so $f(x) = 3x^3 - 5x^2 + x - 7$.

**18** $A - 2B = \begin{bmatrix} 4 & 0 & -3 \\ -2 & 1 & 5 \end{bmatrix} - 2\begin{bmatrix} 5 & 7 & -1 \\ 4 & -2 & 0 \end{bmatrix}$

$= \begin{bmatrix} 4 & 0 & -3 \\ -2 & 1 & 5 \end{bmatrix} - \begin{bmatrix} 10 & 14 & -2 \\ 8 & -4 & 0 \end{bmatrix} = \begin{bmatrix} 4-10 & 0-14 & -3+2 \\ -2-8 & 1+4 & 5-0 \end{bmatrix} = \begin{bmatrix} -6 & -14 & -1 \\ -10 & 5 & 5 \end{bmatrix}$

**19** $AB = \begin{bmatrix} 0 & 4 & -1 \\ -7 & 8 & 2 \end{bmatrix}\begin{bmatrix} 2 & 7 \\ -4 & 6 \\ 1 & -3 \end{bmatrix}$

$= \begin{bmatrix} 0(2) + 4(-4) + (-1)(1) & 0(7) + 4(6) + (-1)(-3) \\ -7(2) + 8(-4) + 2(1) & -7(7) + 8(6) + 2(-3) \end{bmatrix} = \begin{bmatrix} -17 & 27 \\ -44 & -7 \end{bmatrix}$

**20** To find $c_{23}$, use the second row of $A$ and the third column of $B$.

$c_{23} = -1(-2) + (-7)(3) + 6(0) = 2 - 21 = -19.$

**21** Let $A = \begin{bmatrix} 23 & 7 \\ 35 & 12 \\ 40 & 19 \end{bmatrix}$. Since $A$ is $3 \times 2$, we'll define $B$ as the $2 \times 3$ matrix $\begin{bmatrix} 100 & 80 & 30 \\ 90 & 75 & 20 \end{bmatrix}$.

$C = AB = \begin{bmatrix} 23 & 7 \\ 35 & 12 \\ 40 & 19 \end{bmatrix} \begin{bmatrix} 100 & 80 & 30 \\ 90 & 75 & 20 \end{bmatrix} = \begin{bmatrix} 2930 & 2365 & 830 \\ 4580 & 3700 & 1290 \\ 5710 & 4625 & 1580 \end{bmatrix}$. The numbers on the main diagonal represent

the total value of the iron sets, wood sets, and hybrids—$2930, $3700, and $1580, respectively. A less likely

answer is to define $A$ as $\begin{bmatrix} 23 & 35 & 40 \\ 7 & 12 & 19 \end{bmatrix}$, $B$ as $\begin{bmatrix} 100 & 90 \\ 80 & 75 \\ 30 & 20 \end{bmatrix}$, and then $C$ is $\begin{bmatrix} 6300 & 5495 \\ 2230 & 1910 \end{bmatrix}$. In this case, the

numbers on the main diagonal represent the total value of the men's and women's equipment—$6300 and $1910,

respectively. In either case, the sum of the main diagonal elements is $8210—the total value of all the equipment,

and the other values are meaningless.

**22** $A = \begin{bmatrix} 1 & 2 \\ -4 & -7 \end{bmatrix}$ • $\begin{bmatrix} 1 & 2 & | & 1 & 0 \\ -4 & -7 & | & 0 & 1 \end{bmatrix}$ $\begin{matrix} \\ R_2 + 4R_1 \to R_2 \end{matrix}$ $\begin{bmatrix} 1 & 2 & | & 1 & 0 \\ 0 & 1 & | & 4 & 1 \end{bmatrix}$ $\begin{matrix} R_1 - 2R_2 \to R_1 \\ \end{matrix}$

$\begin{bmatrix} 1 & 0 & | & -7 & -2 \\ 0 & 1 & | & 4 & 1 \end{bmatrix}$ $\Rightarrow$ $A^{-1} = \begin{bmatrix} -7 & -2 \\ 4 & 1 \end{bmatrix}$.

**23** $A = \begin{bmatrix} 5 & 3 \\ 2 & -1 \end{bmatrix}$ $\Rightarrow$ $A^{-1} = -\frac{1}{11} \begin{bmatrix} -1 & -3 \\ -2 & 5 \end{bmatrix}$.

$X = A^{-1}B$ $\Rightarrow$ $\begin{bmatrix} x \\ y \end{bmatrix} = -\frac{1}{11} \begin{bmatrix} -1 & -3 \\ -2 & 5 \end{bmatrix} \begin{bmatrix} -8 \\ 10 \end{bmatrix} = -\frac{1}{11} \begin{bmatrix} -22 \\ 66 \end{bmatrix} = \begin{bmatrix} 2 \\ -6 \end{bmatrix}$

**24** The fourth row of $A$ contains only zeros, so the determinant of $A$ is zero, and hence, $A$ is not invertible.

**25** $\begin{bmatrix} 2 & -3 & 8 \\ -4 & 3 & 1 \\ 5 & 4 & -1 \end{bmatrix}$ • $M_{23} = \begin{vmatrix} 2 & -3 \\ 5 & 4 \end{vmatrix} = 2(4) - 5(-3) = 8 + 15 = 23$

**26** $\begin{bmatrix} -9 & -4 & 5 \\ 7 & 1 & -3 \\ -6 & -2 & 4 \end{bmatrix}$ • $M_{23} = \begin{vmatrix} -9 & -4 \\ -6 & -2 \end{vmatrix} = -9(-2) - (-6)(-4) = 18 - 24 = -6$.

$A_{23} = (-1)^{2+3} M_{23} = (-1)^5 (-6) = -1(-6) = 6$.

**27** $\begin{bmatrix} 2 & -5 & -1 \\ 4 & 6 & 5 \\ -2 & 0 & 3 \end{bmatrix}$ • Expand by the third row. 

$\begin{aligned} |A| &= a_{31}A_{31} + a_{32}A_{32} + a_{33}A_{33} \\ &= -2(-25 + 6) + 0(A_{32}) + 3(12 + 20) \\ &= -2(-19) + 0 + 3(32) \\ &= 38 + 96 = 134 \end{aligned}$

**28** $A - xI = \begin{bmatrix} 1 & 8 \\ 2 & 1 \end{bmatrix} - x \begin{bmatrix} 1 & 0 \\ 0 & 1 \end{bmatrix} = \begin{bmatrix} 1-x & 8 \\ 2 & 1-x \end{bmatrix}$.

$f(x) = |A - xI| = \begin{vmatrix} 1-x & 8 \\ 2 & 1-x \end{vmatrix} = (1-x)^2 - 16 = x^2 - 2x - 15$.

$f(x) = 0$ $\Rightarrow$ $(x+3)(x-5) = 0$ $\Rightarrow$ $x = -3, 5$

**29** $R_1$ and $R_3$ are identical.

**30** $|A| = \begin{vmatrix} 3 & 5 & -4 \\ 3 & 6 & 9 \\ -2 & 1 & 0 \end{vmatrix}$ { 3 is a common factor of $R_2$ }

$= (3) \begin{vmatrix} 3 & 5 & -4 \\ 1 & 2 & 3 \\ -2 & 1 & 0 \end{vmatrix}$ $\begin{array}{l} R_1 - 3R_2 \to R_1 \\ \\ R_3 + 2R_2 \to R_3 \end{array}$

$= (3) \begin{vmatrix} 0 & -1 & -13 \\ 1 & 2 & 3 \\ 0 & 5 & 6 \end{vmatrix}$ { Expand along $C_1$ }

$= (3)(-1) \begin{vmatrix} -1 & -13 \\ 5 & 6 \end{vmatrix} = (-3)(-6 + 65) = -177$

**31** For the system $\begin{cases} 6x - 5y = 38 \\ -2x + 3y = -18 \end{cases}$, $|D| = \begin{vmatrix} 6 & -5 \\ -2 & 3 \end{vmatrix} = 18 - 10 = 8$.

Since $|D| = 8 \neq 0$, we may solve the system using Cramer's rule. $|D_x| = \begin{vmatrix} 38 & -5 \\ -18 & 3 \end{vmatrix} = 114 - 90 = 24$.

$|D_y| = \begin{vmatrix} 6 & 38 \\ -2 & -18 \end{vmatrix} = -108 + 76 = -32$. $x = \dfrac{|D_x|}{|D|} = \dfrac{24}{8} = 3$. $y = \dfrac{|D_y|}{|D|} = \dfrac{-32}{8} = -4$.

The solution is $(3, -4)$.

**32** $\dfrac{-x + 11}{(x - 2)(x + 1)} = \dfrac{A}{x - 2} + \dfrac{B}{x + 1}$

$-x + 11 = A(x + 1) + B(x - 2)$

$x = -1: 12 = -3B \Rightarrow B = -4$

$x = 2: 9 = 3A \Rightarrow A = 3$

$\bigstar \ \dfrac{3}{x - 2} - \dfrac{4}{x + 1}$

**33** $\dfrac{-x^2 + 11x + 15}{x^2(x + 3)} = \dfrac{A}{x} + \dfrac{B}{x^2} + \dfrac{C}{x + 3}$

$-x^2 + 11x + 15 = Ax(x + 3) + B(x + 3) + Cx^2$

$x = -3: -27 = 9C \Rightarrow C = -3$

$x = 0: 15 = 3B \Rightarrow B = 5$

$\bigstar \ \dfrac{2}{x} + \dfrac{5}{x^2} - \dfrac{3}{x + 3}$

$x = 1: 25 = 4A + 4B + C \Rightarrow 25 = 4A + 20 - 3 \Rightarrow A = 2$

**34** $\dfrac{2x^3 - 5x^2 + 2x - 2}{(x^2 + 1)^2} = \dfrac{Ax + B}{x^2 + 1} + \dfrac{Cx + D}{(x^2 + 1)^2}$

$\begin{aligned} 2x^3 - 5x^2 + 2x - 2 &= (Ax + B)(x^2 + 1) + Cx + D \\ &= Ax^3 + Bx^2 + (A + C)x + (B + D) \end{aligned}$

Equating coefficients (like terms must have equal coefficients on each side), we have the following:

$x^3$-terms: $A = 2$

$x^2$-terms: $B = -5$

$x$-terms: $A + C = 2 \Rightarrow C = 0$

$\bigstar \ \dfrac{2x - 5}{x^2 + 1} + \dfrac{3}{(x^2 + 1)^2}$

constant terms: $B + D = -2 \Rightarrow D = 3$

## 9.1 Exercises

**Note:** For Exercises 1–16, the answers are listed in the order $a_1$, $a_2$, $a_3$, $a_4$; and $a_8$. Simply substitute 1, 2, 3, 4, and 8 for $n$ in the formula for $a_n$ to obtain the results.

**1** $a_n = 12 - 3n$ • $a_1 = 12 - 3(1) = 9,$ $a_2 = 12 - 3(2) = 6,$
$a_3 = 12 - 3(3) = 3,$ $a_4 = 12 - 3(4) = 0;$ and $a_8 = 12 - 3(8) = -12$ ★ $9, 6, 3, 0; -12$

**2** $a_n = \dfrac{3}{5n - 2}$ • ★ $1, \dfrac{3}{8}, \dfrac{3}{13}, \dfrac{1}{6}; \dfrac{3}{38}$

**3** $a_n = \dfrac{3n - 2}{n^2 + 1}$ • $a_1 = \dfrac{3(1) - 2}{(1)^2 + 1} = \dfrac{1}{2},$ $a_2 = \dfrac{3(2) - 2}{(2)^2 + 1} = \dfrac{4}{5},$
$a_3 = \dfrac{3(3) - 2}{(3)^2 + 1} = \dfrac{7}{10},$ $a_4 = \dfrac{3(4) - 2}{(4)^2 + 1} = \dfrac{10}{17};$ and $a_8 = \dfrac{3(8) - 2}{(8)^2 + 1} = \dfrac{22}{65}$ ★ $\dfrac{1}{2}, \dfrac{4}{5}, \dfrac{7}{10}, \dfrac{10}{17}; \dfrac{22}{65}$

**4** $a_n = 10 + \dfrac{1}{n}$ • ★ $11, \dfrac{21}{2}, \dfrac{31}{3}, \dfrac{41}{4}; \dfrac{81}{8}$

**5** $a_n = 9$ • $a_{\text{(any allowable value)}} = 9$ ★ $9, 9, 9, 9; 9$

**6** $a_n = \sqrt{2}$ • $a_{\text{(any allowable value)}} = \sqrt{2}$ ★ $\sqrt{2}, \sqrt{2}, \sqrt{2}, \sqrt{2}; \sqrt{2}$

**7** $a_n = 2 + (-0.1)^n$ • $a_1 = 2 + (-0.1)^1 = 2 - 0.1 = 1.9,$ $a_2 = 2 + (-0.1)^2 = 2 + 0.01 = 2.01,$
$a_3 = 2 + (-0.1)^3 = 2 - 0.001 = 1.999,$ $a_4 = 2 + (-0.1)^4 = 2 + 0.0001 = 2.0001;$ and
$a_8 = 2 + (-0.1)^8 = 2 + 0.00000001 = 2.00000001$ ★ $1.9, 2.01, 1.999, 2.0001; 2.00000001$

**8** $a_n = 4 + (0.1)^n$ • ★ $4.1, 4.01, 4.001, 4.0001; 4.00000001$

**9** $a_n = (-1)^{n-1}\left(\dfrac{n + 7}{2n}\right)$ • $a_1 = (-1)^{1-1}\left(\dfrac{1 + 7}{2(1)}\right) = (-1)^0\left(\dfrac{8}{2}\right) = (1)(4) = 4,$
$a_2 = (-1)^{2-1}\left(\dfrac{2 + 7}{2(2)}\right) = (-1)^1\left(\dfrac{9}{4}\right) = -\dfrac{9}{4},$ $a_3 = (-1)^{3-1}\left(\dfrac{3 + 7}{2(3)}\right) = (-1)^2\left(\dfrac{10}{6}\right) = \dfrac{5}{3},$
$a_4 = (-1)^{4-1}\left(\dfrac{4 + 7}{2(4)}\right) = (-1)^3\left(\dfrac{11}{8}\right) = -\dfrac{11}{8};$ and $a_8 = (-1)^{8-1}\left(\dfrac{8 + 7}{2(8)}\right) = (-1)^7\left(\dfrac{15}{16}\right) = -\dfrac{15}{16}$
★ $4, -\dfrac{9}{4}, \dfrac{5}{3}, -\dfrac{11}{8}; -\dfrac{15}{16}$

**10** $a_n = (-1)^n\dfrac{6 - 2n}{\sqrt{n + 1}}$ • ★ $-2\sqrt{2}, \dfrac{2}{3}\sqrt{3}, 0, -\dfrac{2}{5}\sqrt{5}; -\dfrac{10}{3}$

**11** $a_n = 1 + (-1)^{n+1}$ • $a_1 = 1 + (-1)^{1+1} = 1 + (-1)^2 = 1 + 1 = 2,$
$a_2 = 1 + (-1)^{2+1} = 1 + (-1)^3 = 1 - 1 = 0,$ $a_3 = 1 + (-1)^{3+1} = 1 + (-1)^4 = 1 + 1 = 2,$
$a_4 = 1 + (-1)^{4+1} = 1 + (-1)^5 = 1 - 1 = 0;$ and $a_8 = 1 + (-1)^{8+1} = 1 + (-1)^9 = 1 - 1 = 0$ ★ $2, 0, 2, 0; 0$

**12** $a_n = (-1)^{n+1} + (0.1)^{n-1}$ • ★ $2, -0.9, 1.01, -0.999; -0.9999999$

**13** $a_n = \dfrac{2^n}{n^2 + 2}$ • $a_1 = \dfrac{2^1}{1^2 + 2} = \dfrac{2}{3},$ $a_2 = \dfrac{2^2}{2^2 + 2} = \dfrac{4}{6} = \dfrac{2}{3},$ $a_3 = \dfrac{2^3}{3^2 + 2} = \dfrac{8}{11},$ $a_4 = \dfrac{2^4}{4^2 + 2} = \dfrac{16}{18} = \dfrac{8}{9};$ and
$a_8 = \dfrac{2^8}{8^2 + 2} = \dfrac{256}{66} = \dfrac{128}{33}$ ★ $\dfrac{2}{3}, \dfrac{2}{3}, \dfrac{8}{11}, \dfrac{8}{9}; \dfrac{128}{33}$

**519**

**14** $a_n = (n-1)(n-2)(n-3)$ • ★ $0, 0, 0, 6; 210$

**15** $a_n$ is the number of decimal places in $(0.1)^n$. • $(0.1)^1 = 0.1$ {1 decimal place} $\Rightarrow$ $a_1 = 1,$
$(0.1)^2 = 0.01$ {2 decimal places} $\Rightarrow$ $a_2 = 2,$ $(0.1)^3 = 0.001$ {3 decimal places} $\Rightarrow$ $a_3 = 3,$
$(0.1)^4 = 0.0001$ {4 decimal places} $\Rightarrow$ $a_4 = 4;$ $(0.1)^8 = 0.00000001$ {8 decimal places} $\Rightarrow$ $a_8 = 8$
★ $1, 2, 3, 4; 8$

**16** $a_n$ is the number of positive integers less than $n^3$. • The values of $n^3$ are 1, 8, 27, 64, 125, 216, 343, and 512.
★ $0, 7, 26, 63; 511$

**17** $\left\{ \dfrac{1}{\sqrt{n}} \right\} = \dfrac{1}{\sqrt{1}}, \dfrac{1}{\sqrt{2}}, \dfrac{1}{\sqrt{3}}, \dfrac{1}{\sqrt{4}}, \dfrac{1}{\sqrt{5}}, \ldots \approx 1, 0.71, 0.58, 0.5, 0.45, \ldots$

*Figure 17*

*Figure 18*

**18** $\left\{ \dfrac{1}{n} \right\} = \dfrac{1}{1}, \dfrac{1}{2}, \dfrac{1}{3}, \dfrac{1}{4}, \dfrac{1}{5}, \ldots = 1, 0.5, 0.\overline{3}, 0.25, 0.2, \ldots$

**19** $\{ (-1)^{n+1} n^2 \} = 1 \cdot 1^2, -1 \cdot 2^2, 1 \cdot 3^2, -1 \cdot 4^2, \ldots = 1, -4, 9, -16, \ldots$

*Figure 19*

*Figure 20*

**20** $\{ (-1)^n (2n+1) \} = -1 \cdot 3, 1 \cdot 5, -1 \cdot 7, 1 \cdot 9, \ldots = -3, 5, -7, 9, \ldots$

**Note:** For Exercises 21–28, the answers are listed in the order $a_1, a_2, a_3, a_4, a_5$.

**21** $a_1 = 2, a_{k+1} = 3a_k - 5$ • $a_2 = a_{1+1}$ {$k = 1$} $= 3a_1 - 5 = 3(2) - 5 = 1, a_3 = 3a_2 - 5 = 3(1) - 5 = -2,$
$a_4 = 3a_3 - 5 = 3(-2) - 5 = -11, a_5 = 3a_4 - 5 = 3(-11) - 5 = -38$ ★ $2, 1, -2, -11, -38$

**22** $a_1 = 5, a_{k+1} = 7 - 2a_k$ • $a_2 = a_{1+1}$ {$k = 1$} $= 7 - 2a_1 = 7 - 2(5) = -3, a_3 = 7 - 2a_2 = 7 - 2(-3) = 13,$
$a_4 = 7 - 2a_3 = 7 - 2(13) = -19, a_5 = 7 - 2a_4 = 7 - 2(-19) = 45$ ★ $5, -3, 13, -19, 45$

**23** $a_1 = -3$, $a_{k+1} = a_k^2$ • $a_2 = a_{1+1}$ $\{k = 1\} = a_1^2 = (-3)^2 = 3^2 = 9$, $a_3 = a_2^2 = (3^2)^2 = 3^4$,
$a_4 = a_3^2 = (3^4)^2 = 3^8$, $a_5 = a_4^2 = (3^8)^2 = 3^{16}$ ★ $-3, 3^2, 3^4, 3^8, 3^{16}$

**24** $a_1 = 128$, $a_{k+1} = \frac{1}{4} a_k$ • $a_2 = a_{1+1}$ $\{k = 1\} = \frac{1}{4} a_1 = \frac{1}{4}(128) = 32$, $a_3 = \frac{1}{4} a_2 = \frac{1}{4}(32) = 8$,
$a_4 = \frac{1}{4} a_3 = \frac{1}{4}(8) = 2$, $a_5 = \frac{1}{4} a_4 = \frac{1}{4}(2) = \frac{1}{2}$ ★ $128, 32, 8, 2, \frac{1}{2}$

**25** $a_1 = 5$, $a_{k+1} = k a_k$ • $a_2 = a_{1+1}$ $\{k = 1\} = 1 a_1 = 1(5) = 5$, $a_3 = 2 a_2 = 2(5) = 10$,
$a_4 = 3 a_3 = 3(10) = 30$, $a_5 = 4 a_4 = 4(30) = 120$ ★ $5, 5, 10, 30, 120$

**26** $a_1 = 3$, $a_{k+1} = \frac{1}{a_k}$ • $a_2 = \frac{1}{a_1} = \frac{1}{3}$, $a_3 = \frac{1}{a_2} = \frac{1}{1/3} = 3$, $a_4 = \frac{1}{a_3} = \frac{1}{3}$, $a_5 = \frac{1}{a_4} = \frac{1}{1/3} = 3$ ★ $3, \frac{1}{3}, 3, \frac{1}{3}, 3$

**27** $a_1 = 2$, $a_{k+1} = (a_k)^k$ • $a_2 = a_{1+1}$ $\{k = 1\} = (a_1)^1 = (2)^1 = 2$, $a_3 = (a_2)^2 = (2)^2 = 4$,
$a_4 = (a_3)^3 = (4)^3 = 4^3$ or $64$, $a_5 = (a_4)^4 = (4^3)^4 = 4^{12}$ or $16{,}777{,}216$ ★ $2, 2, 4, 64, 4^{12}$

**28** $a_1 = 2$, $a_{k+1} = (a_k)^{1/k}$ • $a_2 = a_{1+1}$ $\{k = 1\} = (a_1)^{1/1} = (2)^1 = 2$, $a_3 = (a_2)^{1/2} = 2^{1/2}$,
$a_4 = (a_3)^{1/3} = (2^{1/2})^{1/3} = 2^{1/6}$, $a_5 = (a_4)^{1/4} = (2^{1/6})^{1/4} = 2^{1/24}$ ★ $2, 2, 2^{1/2}, 2^{1/6}, 2^{1/24}$

**29** $a_1 = 1$, $a_2 = 2$, $a_{k+1} = 2a_k + 3a_{k-1}$ for $k \geq 2$ {given formula} ★ $7, 20, 61$
$\qquad a_3 = 2a_2 + 3a_1 = 2(2) + 3(1) = 7$ $\{k = 2\}$
$\qquad a_4 = 2a_3 + 3a_2 = 2(7) + 3(2) = 20$ $\{k = 3\}$
$\qquad a_5 = 2a_4 + 3a_3 = 2(20) + 3(7) = 61$ $\{k = 4\}$

**30** $a_1 = 3$, $a_2 = 1$, $a_{k+1} = 3a_k - 2a_{k-1}$ for $k \geq 2$ {given formula} ★ $-3, -11, -27$
$\qquad a_3 = 3a_2 - 2a_1 = 3(1) - 2(3) = -3$ $\{k = 2\}$
$\qquad a_4 = 3a_3 - 2a_2 = 3(-3) - 2(1) = -11$ $\{k = 3\}$
$\qquad a_5 = 3a_4 - 2a_3 = 3(-11) - 2(-3) = -27$ $\{k = 4\}$

**31** $a_1 = 4$, $a_2 = -2$, $a_{k+2} = a_{k+1} a_k$ for $k \geq 1$ {given formula} ★ $-8, 16, -128$
$\qquad a_3 = a_2 \cdot a_1 = -2(4) = -8$ $\{k = 1\}$
$\qquad a_4 = a_3 \cdot a_2 = -8(-2) = 16$ $\{k = 2\}$
$\qquad a_5 = a_4 \cdot a_3 = 16(-8) = -128$ $\{k = 3\}$

**32** $a_1 = 2$, $a_2 = -3$, $a_{k+2} = a_{k+1} a_k^2$ for $k \geq 1$ {given formula} ★ $-12, -108, -15{,}552$
$\qquad a_3 = a_2 \cdot a_1^2 = -3(2^2) = -12$ $\{k = 1\}$
$\qquad a_4 = a_3 \cdot a_2^2 = -12(-3)^2 = -108$ $\{k = 2\}$
$\qquad a_5 = a_4 \cdot a_3^2 = -108(-12)^2 = -15{,}552$ $\{k = 3\}$

**33** $a_n = 3 + \frac{1}{2}n$ • $S_1 = a_1 = 3 + \frac{1}{2} = \frac{7}{2}$. $S_2 = S_1 + a_2 = \frac{7}{2} + 4 = \frac{15}{2}$. Alternatively, to find $S_2$ we could use $a_1 + a_2$. However, in most cases, it is easier to compute $S_{n+1}$ by using $S_n + a_{n+1}$. $S_3 = S_2 + a_3 = \frac{15}{2} + \frac{9}{2} = 12$. $S_4 = S_3 + a_4 = 12 + 5 = 17$.

**34** $\{1/n^2\}$ • $S_1 = a_1 = 1$. $S_2 = S_1 + a_2 = 1 + \frac{1}{4} = \frac{5}{4}$. $S_3 = S_2 + a_3 = \frac{5}{4} + \frac{1}{9} = \frac{49}{36}$.
$\qquad\qquad\qquad S_4 = S_3 + a_4 = \frac{49}{36} + \frac{1}{16} = \frac{205}{144}$.

**35** $\{(-1)^n n^{-1/2}\} = \left\{ (-1)^n \frac{1}{\sqrt{n}} \right\}$ • $S_1 = a_1 = -1$. $S_2 = S_1 + a_2 = -1 + \frac{1}{\sqrt{2}}$.
$S_3 = S_2 + a_3 = -1 + \frac{1}{\sqrt{2}} - \frac{1}{\sqrt{3}}$. $S_4 = S_3 + a_4 = -1 + \frac{1}{\sqrt{2}} - \frac{1}{\sqrt{3}} + \frac{1}{2} = -\frac{1}{2} + \frac{1}{\sqrt{2}} - \frac{1}{\sqrt{3}}$.

**36** $\{(-1)^n (1/2)^n\}$ • $S_1 = a_1 = -\frac{1}{2}$. $S_2 = S_1 + a_2 = -\frac{1}{2} + \frac{1}{4} = -\frac{1}{4}$. $S_3 = S_2 + a_3 = -\frac{1}{4} - \frac{1}{8} = -\frac{3}{8}$.
$\qquad\qquad\qquad S_4 = S_3 + a_4 = -\frac{3}{8} + \frac{1}{16} = -\frac{5}{16}$.

**37** Substitute $k = 1, 2, 3, 4,$ and 5 into $2k - 7$ and then add the results.

$$\sum_{k=1}^{5}(2k - 7) = (-5) + (-3) + (-1) + 1 + 3 = -5$$

**38** $\displaystyle\sum_{k=1}^{6}(10 - 3k) = 7 + 4 + 1 + (-2) + (-5) + (-8) = -3$

**39** $\displaystyle\sum_{k=1}^{4}(k^2 - 5) = (1^2 - 5) + (2^2 - 5) + (3^2 - 5) + (4^2 - 5) = (-4) + (-1) + 4 + 11 = 10$

**40** $\displaystyle\sum_{k=1}^{10}\left[1 + (-1)^k\right] = 0 + 2 + 0 + 2 + 0 + 2 + 0 + 2 + 0 + 2 = 10$

**41** $\displaystyle\sum_{k=0}^{5}k(k - 2) = 0(-2) + 1(-1) + 2(0) + 3(1) + 4(2) + 5(3) = 0 + (-1) + 0 + 3 + 8 + 15 = 25$

**42** $\displaystyle\sum_{k=0}^{4}(k - 1)(k - 3) = 3 + 0 + (-1) + 0 + 3 = 5$

**43** $\displaystyle\sum_{k=3}^{6}\frac{k - 5}{k - 1} = \frac{-2}{2} + \frac{-1}{3} + \frac{0}{4} + \frac{1}{5} = -\frac{15}{15} - \frac{5}{15} + \frac{3}{15} = -\frac{17}{15}$

**44** $\displaystyle\sum_{k=1}^{6}\frac{3}{k + 1} = \frac{3}{2} + 1 + \frac{3}{4} + \frac{3}{5} + \frac{1}{2} + \frac{3}{7} = \frac{669}{140}$

**45** $\displaystyle\sum_{k=1}^{5}(-3)^{k-1} = (-3)^0 + (-3)^1 + (-3)^2 + (-3)^3 + (-3)^4 = 1 + (-3) + 9 + (-27) + 81 = 61$

**46** $\displaystyle\sum_{k=0}^{4}3\left(2^k\right) = 3 + 6 + 12 + 24 + 48 = 93$

**47** By part (1) of the theorem on the sum of a constant, we have $\displaystyle\sum_{k=1}^{100}100 = 100(100) = 10{,}000.$

**48** By part (1) of the theorem on the sum of a constant, we have $\displaystyle\sum_{k=1}^{1000}5 = 1000(5) = 5000.$

**49** By part (2) of the theorem on the sum of a constant, we have $\displaystyle\sum_{k=253}^{571}\frac{1}{3} = (571 - 253 + 1)\left(\frac{1}{3}\right) = 319\left(\frac{1}{3}\right) = \frac{319}{3}.$

**50** By part (2) of the theorem on the sum of a constant, we have

$$\sum_{k=137}^{428}2.1 = (428 - 137 + 1)(2.1) = 292(2.1) = 613.2.$$

**51** Note that $j$, not $k$, is the summation variable. Hence, we again use part (1) of the theorem on the sum of a constant,

obtaining $\displaystyle\sum_{j=1}^{7}\frac{1}{2}k^2 = 7\left(\frac{1}{2}k^2\right) = \frac{7}{2}k^2.$

**52** $\displaystyle\sum_{k=0}^{5}(3j + 2) = 6(3j + 2) = 18j + 12$ {note that $k$, not $j$, is the summation variable}

**53** $\displaystyle\sum_{k=1}^{n}(a_k - b_k) = (a_1 - b_1) + (a_2 - b_2) + \cdots + (a_n - b_n) = (a_1 + a_2 + \cdots + a_n) + (-b_1 - b_2 - \cdots - b_n)$

$$= (a_1 + a_2 + \cdots + a_n) - (b_1 + b_2 + \cdots + b_n) = \sum_{k=1}^{n}a_k - \sum_{k=1}^{n}b_k$$

**54** $\displaystyle\sum_{k=1}^{n}(a_k + b_k + c_k) = \sum_{k=1}^{n}\left[(a_k + b_k) + c_k\right] = \sum_{k=1}^{n}(a_k + b_k) + \sum_{k=1}^{n}c_k = \sum_{k=1}^{n}a_k + \sum_{k=1}^{n}b_k + \sum_{k=1}^{n}c_k$

**55** $a_1 = 5$, $a_{k+1} = \sqrt{a_k}$ for $k \geq 1$ • $a_1 = 5$, $a_2 = 5^{1/2}$, $a_3 = \left(5^{1/2}\right)^{1/2} = 5^{1/4}$, $a_4 = \left(5^{1/4}\right)^{1/2} = 5^{1/8}$, ....

As $k$ increases, the exponent gets closer to zero and the terms approach 1.

**56** (a) $x_1 = 3$, $x_{k+1} = x_k - \tan x_k$ • $3, 3.142546543, 3.141592653, 3.141592654, 3.141592654$ {approach $\pi$}

(b) When $x_1 = 6$, the terms of the sequence approach $2\pi$.

**57** $a_1 = 0.4$, $a_k = 0.1\left(3 \cdot 2^{k-2} + 4\right)$ for $k \geq 2$ •

$a_2 = 0.1\left(3 \cdot 2^{2-2} + 4\right) = 0.1\left(3 \cdot 2^0 + 4\right) = 0.1(3 \cdot 1 + 4) = 0.1(7) = 0.7$

$a_3 = 0.1\left(3 \cdot 2^{3-2} + 4\right) = 0.1\left(3 \cdot 2^1 + 4\right) = 0.1(3 \cdot 2 + 4) = 0.1(10) = 1$

$a_4 = 0.1\left(3 \cdot 2^{4-2} + 4\right) = 0.1\left(3 \cdot 2^2 + 4\right) = 0.1(3 \cdot 4 + 4) = 0.1(16) = 1.6$

$a_5 = 0.1\left(3 \cdot 2^{5-2} + 4\right) = 0.1\left(3 \cdot 2^3 + 4\right) = 0.1(3 \cdot 8 + 4) = 0.1(28) = 2.8$

**58** (a) The initial number of bacteria is 500. After one day, 1000; two days, 2000; three days, 4000.

(b) After $n$ days, $a_n = 500(2)^n$.

**59** (a) $a_1 = 1$, $a_2 = 1$, $a_{k+1} = a_k + a_{k-1}$ for $k \geq 2$. Thus, $a_3 = a_2 + a_1 = 1 + 1 = 2$, $a_4 = a_3 + a_2 = 2 + 1 = 3$,

$a_5 = a_4 + a_3 = 3 + 2 = 5$, $\qquad a_6 = a_5 + a_4 = 5 + 3 = 8$, $\qquad a_7 = a_6 + a_5 = 8 + 5 = 13$,

$a_8 = a_7 + a_6 = 13 + 8 = 21$, $\qquad a_9 = a_8 + a_7 = 21 + 13 = 34$, $\qquad a_{10} = a_9 + a_8 = 34 + 21 = 55$.

The following screens show the assignment needed to generate the Fibonacci sequence on the TI-83/4 Plus and a listing of the first 14 Fibonacci numbers.

```
Plot1 Plot2 Plot3
nMin=1
·u(n)◘u(n-1)+u(n
-2)
u(nMin)◘{1,1}
·v(n)=
v(nMin)=
·w(n)=
```

```
u(1,7)
  {1 1 2 3 5 8 13}
u(8,11)
      {21 34 55 89}
u(12,14)
       {144 233 377}
```

(b) $r_1 = \frac{1}{1} = 1$, $\quad r_2 = \frac{2}{1} = 2$, $\quad r_3 = \frac{3}{2} = 1.5$, $\quad r_4 = \frac{5}{3} = 1.\overline{6}$, $\quad r_5 = \frac{8}{5} = 1.6$, $\quad r_6 = \frac{13}{8} = 1.625$,

$r_7 = \frac{21}{13} \approx 1.6153846$, $\quad r_8 = \frac{34}{21} \approx 1.6190476$, $\quad r_9 = \frac{55}{34} \approx 1.6176471$, $\quad r_{10} = \frac{89}{55} \approx 1.6181818$.

**60** $a_n = \frac{1}{\sqrt{5}}\left(\frac{1+\sqrt{5}}{2}\right)^n - \frac{1}{\sqrt{5}}\left(\frac{1-\sqrt{5}}{2}\right)^n$ •

$a_1 = \frac{1}{\sqrt{5}}\left(\frac{1+\sqrt{5}}{2}\right)^1 - \frac{1}{\sqrt{5}}\left(\frac{1-\sqrt{5}}{2}\right)^1 = \frac{1}{2\sqrt{5}} + \frac{1}{2} - \frac{1}{2\sqrt{5}} + \frac{1}{2} = 1$.

$a_2 = \frac{1}{\sqrt{5}}\left(\frac{1+\sqrt{5}}{2}\right)^2 - \frac{1}{\sqrt{5}}\left(\frac{1-\sqrt{5}}{2}\right)^2 = \frac{1}{\sqrt{5}}\left(\frac{6+2\sqrt{5}}{4}\right) - \frac{1}{\sqrt{5}}\left(\frac{6-2\sqrt{5}}{4}\right)$

$\qquad = \frac{6}{4\sqrt{5}} + \frac{1}{2} - \frac{6}{4\sqrt{5}} + \frac{1}{2} = 1$.

Similarly, $a_3 = 2$, $a_4 = 3$, $a_5 = 5$, $a_6 = 8$, $a_7 = 13$, and $a_8 = 21$.

**61** (a) Since the amount of chlorine decreases by a factor of 0.20 each day {retain 80%}, $a_n = 0.8a_{n-1}$, where $a_0$ is the initial amount of chlorine in the pool.

(b) Let $a_0 = 7$ and $a_n = 0.8a_{n-1}$.

| Day ($n$) | 0 | 1 | 2 | 3 | 4 | 5 |
|---|---|---|---|---|---|---|
| Chlorine ($a_n$) | 7.00 | 5.60 | 4.48 | 3.58 | 2.87 | 2.29 |

The chlorine level will drop below 3 ppm during the fourth day.

**62** (a) $a_0 = 2$, $a_1 = 0.8a_0 + 0.5 = 2.1$, $a_2 = 0.8a_1 + 0.5 = 2.18$, $a_3 = 0.8a_2 + 0.5 = 2.244$,

$a_4 = 0.8a_3 + 0.5 = 2.2952$. In general, the next value can be calculated by multiplying the previous value by

0.8 and adding 0.5. Thus, $a_n = 0.8a_{n-1} + 0.5$.

(b) Using the table, $a_{15} \approx 2.482$. By continuing to calculate $a_n$ for larger and larger $n$, we see that the amount of

chlorine appears to level off at 2.5 ppm.

| $n$ | $a_n$ | | $n$ | $a_n$ | | $n$ | $a_n$ |
|---|---|---|---|---|---|---|---|
| 1 | 2.100 | | 6 | 2.369 | | 11 | 2.457 |
| 2 | 2.180 | | 7 | 2.395 | | 12 | 2.466 |
| 3 | 2.244 | | 8 | 2.416 | | 13 | 2.473 |
| 4 | 2.295 | | 9 | 2.433 | | 14 | 2.478 |
| 5 | 2.336 | | 10 | 2.446 | | 15 | 2.482 |

(c) Since we are retaining 80% each day, we are replacing 20%. Because the target amount is 1.5 ppm, we must

replace 20% of 1.5 ppm, or equivalently, 0.3 ppm.

**Note:** You could also solve this part by trial and error—from part (b) we know 0.5 is too large, so decrease

that amount until you arrive at 0.3.

**63** If $1 \le n \le 4$, then $C(n) = 89.95n$. If $5 \le n \le 9$, then $C(n) = 87.95n$—there are no changes in prices; that is,

you don't pay \$89.95 for the first 4 and then \$87.95 for the next one. If $n \ge 10$, then $C(n) = 85.95n$.

Summarizing in a piecewise-defined function gives us $C(n) = \begin{cases} 89.95n & \text{if } 1 \le n \le 4 \\ 87.95n & \text{if } 5 \le n \le 9 \\ 85.95n & \text{if } n \ge 10 \end{cases}$

*Figure 63*

*Figure 64*

**64** Note that in this case the price changes for the DVD players over 4 units—that is, you pay \$20 for the first 4 and

then \$17 for all units over 4. $C(n) = \begin{cases} 20n & \text{if } 1 \le n \le 4 \\ 80 + 17(n-4) & \text{if } n \ge 5 \end{cases}$

**65** $N = 5$ and $x_1 = \frac{5}{2}$ $\Rightarrow$ $x_2 = \frac{1}{2}\left(x_1 + \frac{N}{x_1}\right) = \frac{1}{2}\left(2.5 + \frac{5}{2.5}\right) = 2.25$ $\Rightarrow$

$x_3 = \frac{1}{2}\left(2.25 + \frac{5}{2.25}\right) \approx 2.236111$ $\Rightarrow$ $x_4 \approx 2.236068$ $\Rightarrow$ $x_5 \approx 2.236068$. Thus, $\sqrt{5} \approx 2.236068$.

**Note:** TI users—see the key sequence at the end of the solution to Exercise 69.

**66** $N = 18$ and $x_1 = \frac{18}{2} = 9$ $\Rightarrow$ $x_2 = \frac{1}{2}\left(x_1 + \frac{N}{x_1}\right) = \frac{1}{2}\left(9 + \frac{18}{9}\right) = 5.5$ $\Rightarrow$ $x_3 \approx 4.386364$ $\Rightarrow$

$x_4 \approx 4.244995$ $\Rightarrow$ $x_5 \approx 4.242641$ $\Rightarrow$ $x_6 \approx 4.242641$. Thus, $\sqrt{18} \approx 4.242641$.

**67** $x_1 = 2$ and $x_2 = \frac{1}{3}\sqrt[3]{x_1} + 2$ $\Rightarrow$ $x_2 \approx 2.419974$ $\Rightarrow$ $x_3 \approx 2.447523$ $\Rightarrow$ $x_4 \approx 2.449215$ $\Rightarrow$

$x_5 \approx 2.449319$ $\Rightarrow$ $x_6 \approx 2.449325$. The root is approximately $2.4493$.

**Note:** TI users—see the key sequence at the end of the solution to Exercise 69.

**68** $2x + \dfrac{1}{x^4 + x + 2} = 0$ $\Rightarrow$ $x = -\dfrac{1}{2(x^4 + x + 2)}$ $\Rightarrow$ $x_2 = -\dfrac{1}{2(x_1^4 + x_1 + 2)}$.

$x_1 = 0$ $\Rightarrow$ $x_2 = -0.25$ $\Rightarrow$ $x_3 \approx -0.285078$ $\Rightarrow$ $x_4 \approx -0.290440$ $\Rightarrow$ $x_5 \approx -0.291261$ $\Rightarrow$

$x_6 \approx -0.291386$ $\Rightarrow$ $x_7 \approx -0.291405$. The root is approximately $-0.2914$.

**69** (a) $f(1) = (1 - 2 + \log 1) = (1 - 2 + 0) = -1 < 0$ and $f(2) = (2 - 2 + \log 2) = \log 2 \approx 0.30 > 0$.

Thus, $f$ assumes both positive and negative values on $[1, 2]$.

(b) Solving $x - 2 + \log x = 0$ for $x$ in terms of $x$ gives us $x = 2 - \log x$.

$x_1 = 1.5$ $\Rightarrow$ $x_2 = 2 - \log x_1 = 2 - \log 1.5 \approx 1.823909$ $\Rightarrow$ $x_3 \approx 1.738997$ $\Rightarrow$ $x_4 \approx 1.759701$ $\Rightarrow$

$x_5 \approx 1.754561$ $\Rightarrow$ $x_6 \approx 1.755832$ $\Rightarrow$ $x_7 \approx 1.755517$. The zero is approximately $1.76$.

**Note:** If you are using a TI-8x, type 1.5 and press the ENTER key to store 1.5 in the memory location ANS.

Now type $2 - $ LOG ANS and then successively press the ENTER key to obtain the approximations for $x_1$, $x_2$,

and so on. (See the display below.)

| 1 | . | 5 | ENTER | 2 | $-$ | LOG | ANS | ENTER | ENTER | ...

Similar key sequences for Exercises 65 and 67, respectively, are:

| 2 | . | 5 | ENTER | . | 5 | ( | ANS | + | 5 | $\div$ | ANS | ) | ENTER | ENTER | ...

| 2 | ENTER | MATH | 4 | ANS | $\div$ | 3 | + | 2 | ENTER | ENTER | ...

Alternatively, we can use the memory location X instead of ANS by using the | STO ▷ | key, as shown in the figure.

Figure 69

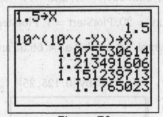

Figure 70

**70** (a) $f(1) = -0.1 < 0$ and $f(2) \approx 0.29 > 0$. Thus, $f$ assumes both positive and negative values on $[1, 2]$.

(b) $\log x - 10^{-x} = 0$ $\Rightarrow$ $\log x = 10^{-x}$ $\Rightarrow$ $x = (10)^{10^{-x}}$. $x_1 = 1.5$, $x_2 = (10)^{10^{-x_1}} = (10)^{10^{-1.5}} \approx 1.075531$,

$x_3 \approx 1.213492$, $x_4 \approx 1.151240$, $x_5 \approx 1.176502$, $x_6 \approx 1.165745$, $x_7 \approx 1.170237$.

The zero is approximately $1.17$.

**71** Graph $y = \left(1 + \dfrac{1}{x} + \dfrac{1}{2x^2}\right)^x$ on the interval $[1, 100]$. The graph approaches the horizontal asymptote

$y \approx 2.718 \approx e$. For increasing values of $n$, the terms of the sequence appear to approximate $e$.

$[1, 100, 10]$ by $[0, 3]$               $[1, 100, 10]$ by $[0, 3]$

*Figure 71*                   *Figure 72*

**72** Graph $y = x^{1/x}$ on the interval $[1, 100]$. The graph approaches the horizontal asymptote $y \approx 1$ from above.

For increasing values of $n$, the terms of the sequence appear to approximate 1.

**73** Graph $y = (1/x)^{1/x}$ on the interval $[1, 100]$. The graph approaches the horizontal asymptote $y \approx 1$ from below.

For increasing values of $n$, the terms of the sequence appear to approximate 1.

$[1, 100, 10]$ by $[0, 3]$               $[1, 100, 20]$ by $[0, 5]$

*Figure 73*                   *Figure 74*

**74** Graph $y = (2.1^x + 1)^{1/x}$ on the interval $[1, 100]$. The graph approaches the horizontal asymptote $y \approx 2.1$.

For increasing values of $n$, the terms of the sequence appear to approximate 2.1.

**75** ***Note to TI-83/4 users:*** Under MODE, make sure you are in Seq mode. Under Y =, let $n$Min = 1, u($n$Min) = .25, and u($n$) = 1.7u($n - 1$) + .5. { u is ⎡2nd⎤ ⎡7⎤ and $n$ is ⎡X, T, $\theta$, $n$⎤ }. Under WINDOW, let $n$Min = 1, $n$Max = 20, PlotStart = 1, PlotStep = 1, and the rest of the window parameters as shown in the figure. By tracing the graph we see that $a_9 \approx 66.55$ and $a_{10} \approx 113.64$. Thus, $k = 10$.

$[0, 20, 5]$ by $[0, 125, 25]$           $[0, 20, 5]$ by $[0, 125, 25]$

*Figure 75*                   *Figure 76*

**76** $a_1 = 6$, $a_k = 1.05a_{k-1} + 4$ • By tracing the graph we see that $a_{16} \approx 98.79$ and $a_{17} \approx 107.73$. Thus, $k = 17$.

[77] $a_1 = 7.25$, $a_k = 0.1a_{k-1}^2 + 2$ • By tracing the graph we see that $a_{18} \approx 50.39$ and $a_{19} \approx 255.96$. Thus, $k = 19$.

$[0, 20, 5]$ by $[0, 300, 50]$          $[0, 20, 5]$ by $[0, 375, 50]$

*Figure 77*

*Figure 78*

[78] $a_1 = 1$, $a_k = 0.2a_{k-1}^2 + 1.5$ • By tracing the graph we see that $a_{14} \approx 42.12$ and $a_{15} \approx 356.37$. Thus, $k = 15$.

[79] (a) $a_{k+1} = ca_k(1 - a_k)$ • $c = 0.5$ $\Rightarrow$ $a_{k+1} = 0.5a_k(1 - a_k)$.

Then, $a_1 = 0.25$, $a_2 = 0.5a_1(1 - a_1) = 0.5(0.25)(1 - 0.25) = 0.09375$. In a similar manner, $a_3 \approx 0.04248$, $a_4 \approx 0.02034, \ldots$ , $a_{10} \approx 0.00031$, $a_{11} \approx 0.00015$, $a_{12} \approx 0.00008$. The insect population is initially $1000a_1 = 1000(0.25) = 250$. It then becomes approximately 94, 42, 20, and so on, until the population decreases to zero.

(b) The sequence determined is $a_1 = 0.25$, $a_2 \approx 0.28125$, $a_3 \approx 0.30322$, $a_4 \approx 0.31692, \ldots$ , $a_{18} \approx 0.33333$, $a_{19} \approx 0.33333$, $a_{20} \approx 0.33333$. The insect population is initially 250. It then becomes approximately 281, 303, 317, and so on, until the population stabilizes at 333.

(c) The sequence determined is $a_1 = 0.25$, $a_2 \approx 0.51563$, $a_3 \approx 0.68683$, $a_4 \approx 0.59151, \ldots$ , $a_{40} \approx 0.63636$, $a_{41} \approx 0.63636$, $a_{42} \approx 0.63636$. The insect population is initially 250. It then becomes approximately 516, 687, 592, and so on, until the population stabilizes at 636.

[80] (a) One conjecture is that the insect population will decrease to zero as in part (a) of the previous exercise.

(b) Whenever $0 < c < 1$, the insect population decreases to zero.

## 9.2 Exercises

[1] To show that the given sequence, $-6, -2, 2, \ldots, 4n - 10, \ldots$, is arithmetic, we must show that $a_{k+1} - a_k$ is equal to some constant, which is the common difference.

$$a_n = 4n - 10 \quad \Rightarrow \quad a_{k+1} - a_k = [4(k+1) - 10] - [4(k) - 10] = 4k + 4 - 10 - 4k + 10 = 4$$

[2] $53, 48, 43, \ldots, 58 - 5n, \ldots$ • $a_n = 58 - 5n \quad \Rightarrow$

$$a_{k+1} - a_k = [58 - 5(k+1)] - [58 - 5k] = 58 - 5k - 5 - 58 + 5k = -5$$

***Note:*** For Exercises 3–14, we find the $n$th term first, and then use that term to find $a_5$ and $a_{10}$.

[3] The common difference can be found by subtracting any term from its successor.
$d = 6 - 2 = 4$; $a_n = a_1 + (n - 1)d = 2 + (n - 1)(4) = 2 + 4n - 4 = 4n - 2$;

$$a_5 = 4(5) - 2 = 18; a_{10} = 4(10) - 2 = 38$$

[4] $d = 7 - 1 = 6$; $a_n = a_1 + (n - 1)d = 1 + (n - 1)(6) = 1 + 6n - 6 = 6n - 5$;

$$a_5 = 6(5) - 5 = 25; a_{10} = 6(10) - 5 = 55$$

**5**   $d = 13 - 16 = -3; a_n = a_1 + (n-1)d = 16 + (n-1)(-3) = 16 - 3n + 3 = -3n + 19;$

$$a_5 = -3(5) + 19 = 4; a_{10} = -3(10) + 19 = -11$$

**6**   $d = 27 - 32 = -5; a_n = a_1 + (n-1)d = 32 + (n-1)(-5) = 32 - 5n + 5 = -5n + 37;$

$$a_5 = -5(5) + 37 = 12; a_{10} = -5(10) + 37 = -13$$

**7**   $d = 2.7 - 3 = -0.3; a_n = a_1 + (n-1)d = 3 + (n-1)(-0.3) = 3 - 0.3n + 0.3 = -0.3n + 3.3;$

$$a_5 = -0.3(5) + 3.3 = 1.8; a_{10} = -0.3(10) + 3.3 = 0.3$$

**8**   $d = -4.5 - (-6) = 1.5; a_n = a_1 + (n-1)d = -6 + (n-1)(1.5) = -6 + 1.5n - 1.5 = 1.5n - 7.5;$

$$a_5 = 1.5(5) - 7.5 = 0; a_{10} = 1.5(10) - 7.5 = 7.5$$

**9**   $d = -3.9 - (-7) = 3.1; a_n = a_1 + (n-1)d = -7 + (n-1)(3.1) = -7 + 3.1n - 3.1 = 3.1n - 10.1;$

$$a_5 = 3.1(5) - 10.1 = 5.4; a_{10} = 3.1(10) - 10.1 = 20.9$$

**10**   $d = 1.5 - 4.2 = -2.7; a_n = a_1 + (n-1)d = 4.2 + (n-1)(-2.7) = 4.2 - 2.7n + 2.7 = -2.7n + 6.9;$

$$a_5 = -2.7(5) + 6.9 = -6.6; a_{10} = -2.7(10) + 6.9 = -20.1$$

**11**   $d = (-6x + 9) - (-8x + 12) = 2x - 3;$

      $a_n = a_1 + (n-1)d = (-8x + 12) + (n-1)(2x - 3)$

         $= -8x + 12 + n(2x - 3) - 2x + 3 = -10x + 15 + n(2x - 3),$ or $(2n - 10)x + 15 - 3n;$

      $a_5 = -10x + 15 + (5)(2x - 3) = -10x + 15 + 10x - 15 = 0;$

      $a_{10} = -10x + 15 + (10)(2x - 3) = -10x + 15 + 20x - 30 = 10x - 15$

**12**   $d = (x - 3) - (x - 8) = 5; a_n = a_1 + (n-1)d = x - 8 + (n-1)(5) = x + 5n - 13;$

$$a_5 = x + 5(5) - 13 = x + 12; a_{10} = x + 5(10) - 13 = x + 37$$

**13**   $\ln 3, \ln 9, \ln 27, \ln 81, \ldots$   •   An equivalent sequence is $\ln 3, \ln 3^2, \ln 3^3, \ln 3^4, \ldots,$ which is also equivalent to the

      sequence $\ln 3, 2\ln 3, 3\ln 3, 4\ln 3, \ldots; d = 2\ln 3 - \ln 3 = \ln 3;$

         $a_n = a_1 + (n-1)d = \ln 3 + (n-1)(\ln 3) = n\ln 3$ or $\ln 3^n; a_5 = 5\ln 3$ or $\ln 3^5; a_{10} = 10\ln 3$ or $\ln 3^{10}$

**14**   $\log 1000, \log 100, \log 10, \log 1, \ldots$   •

      An equivalent sequence is $3, 2, 1, 0, \ldots; d = 2 - 3 = -1; a_n = a_1 + (n-1)d = 3 + (n-1)(-1) = -n + 4;$

$$a_5 = -(5) + 4 = -1; a_{10} = -(10) + 4 = -6$$

**15**   $a_6 = a_1 + 5d$ and $a_2 = a_1 + d \Rightarrow a_6 - a_2 = (a_1 + 5d) - (a_1 + d) = 4d.$

               But $a_6 - a_2 = -11 - 21 = -32.$ Hence, $4d = -32$ and $d = -8.$

**16**   $a_{11} = a_1 + 10d$ and $a_4 = a_1 + 3d \Rightarrow a_{11} - a_4 = 7d.$

               But $a_{11} - a_4 = 35 - 14 = 21.$ Hence, $7d = 21$ and $d = 3.$

**17**   Given $a_1$ and $a_2$, we can find the difference $d$. $d = a_2 - a_1 = 7.5 - 9.1 = -1.6.$

         The twelfth term is equal to the first term plus eleven differences. $a_{12} = 9.1 + (11)(-1.6) = -8.5.$

**18**   $d = 1 - \sqrt{2}; a_{11} = \left(2 + \sqrt{2}\right) + (10)\left(1 - \sqrt{2}\right) = 12 - 9\sqrt{2}$

**19**   $d = a_7 - a_6 = 5.2 - 2.7 = 2.5; a_6 = a_1 + 5d \Rightarrow 2.7 = a_1 + 5(2.5) \Rightarrow a_1 = -9.8$

**20**   $a_9 = 53$ and $a_8 = 47 \Rightarrow d = 6. a_8 = a_1 + 7d \Rightarrow 47 = a_1 + 7(6) \Rightarrow a_1 = 5$

**21** $a_3 = a_1 + 2d$ and $a_{20} = a_1 + 19d$ $\Rightarrow$ $a_{20} - a_3 = (a_1 + 19d) - (a_1 + 2d) = 17d$.

$a_3 = 7$ and $a_{20} = 43$ $\Rightarrow$ $17d = 43 - 7$ $\Rightarrow$ $d = \frac{36}{17}$. $a_{15} = a_3 + 12d = 7 + 12\left(\frac{36}{17}\right) = \frac{551}{17}$.

**22** $a_2 = 1$ and $a_{18} = 49$ $\Rightarrow$ $(18 - 2)d = 49 - 1$ $\Rightarrow$ $d = \frac{48}{16} = 3$. $a_{10} = a_2 + 8d = 1 + 8(3) = 25$.

**23** $a_8 = 201$ and $a_{317} = 2364$ $\Rightarrow$ $(317 - 8)d = 2364 - 201$ $\Rightarrow$ $d = \frac{2163}{309} = 7$.

$a_{410} = a_8 + 402d = 201 + 402(7) = 3015$.

**24** $a_9 = -253$ and $a_{412} = 2971$ $\Rightarrow$ $(412 - 9)d = 2971 - (-253)$ $\Rightarrow$ $d = \frac{3224}{403} = 8$.

$a_{500} = a_9 + 491d = -253 + 491(8) = 3675$.

**Note:** To find the sums in Exercises 25–36, we use the sum formulas

$$\text{(1) } S_n = \frac{n}{2}[2a_1 + (n-1)d] \quad \text{and} \quad \text{(2) } S_n = \frac{n}{2}(a_1 + a_n).$$

**25** $a_1 = 40, d = -3, n = 30$ • Using sum formula **(1)**, we get $S_{30} = \frac{30}{2}[2(40) + (29)(-3)] = -105$.

**26** $a_1 = 5, d = 0.1, n = 40$ • Using sum formula **(1)**, we get $S_{40} = \frac{40}{2}[2(5) + (39)(0.1)] = 278$.

**27** $a_1 = -9, a_{10} = 15, n = 10$ • Using sum formula **(2)**, we get $S_{10} = \frac{10}{2}(-9 + 15) = 30$.

**28** $a_1 = 5, a_{20} = 9, n = 20$ • Using sum formula **(2)**, we get $S_{20} = \frac{20}{2}(5 + 9) = 140$.

**29** $a_7 = a_1 + 6d$ $\Rightarrow$ $\frac{7}{3} = a_1 + 6\left(-\frac{2}{3}\right)$ $\Rightarrow$ $a_1 = \frac{19}{3}$. $S_{15} = \frac{15}{2}\left[2\left(\frac{19}{3}\right) + (14)\left(-\frac{2}{3}\right)\right] = 25$

**30** $a_6 = a_1 + 5d$ $\Rightarrow$ $-2 = a_1 + 5\left(-\frac{3}{4}\right)$ $\Rightarrow$ $a_1 = \frac{7}{4}$. $S_{40} = \frac{40}{2}\left[2\left(\frac{7}{4}\right) + (39)\left(-\frac{3}{4}\right)\right] = -515$

**31** $\sum_{k=1}^{20} (3k - 5)$ • Using **(2)** with $n = 20$, $a_1 = 3(1) - 5 = -2$, and $a_{20} = 3(20) - 5 = 55$,

we obtain $S_{20} = \frac{20}{2}(-2 + 55) = 530$.

**32** $\sum_{k=1}^{12} (7 - 4k)$ • $a_1 = 3$ and $a_{12} = -41$ $\Rightarrow$ $S_{12} = \frac{12}{2}[3 + (-41)] = -228$.

**33** $\sum_{k=1}^{18} \left(\frac{1}{2}k + 7\right)$ • $a_1 = \frac{15}{2}, a_{18} = 16, n = 18$ $\Rightarrow$ $S_{18} = \frac{18}{2}\left(\frac{15}{2} + 16\right) = \frac{423}{2}$.

**34** $\sum_{k=1}^{10} \left(\frac{1}{4}k + 3\right)$ • $a_1 = \frac{13}{4}$ and $a_{10} = \frac{11}{2}$ $\Rightarrow$ $S_{10} = \frac{10}{2}\left(\frac{13}{4} + \frac{11}{2}\right) = \frac{175}{4}$.

**35** $\sum_{k=126}^{592} (5k + 2j) = \sum_{k=126}^{592} 5k + \sum_{k=126}^{592} 2j = 5\sum_{k=126}^{592} k + 2\sum_{k=126}^{592} j = 5(\text{SUM1}) + 2(\text{SUM2})$.

The number of terms is $n = 592 - 126 + 1 = 467$. To evaluate SUM1, we use (1) with $a_1 = 126$, $d = 1$, and $n = 467$ to get

$$S_{467} = \frac{467}{2}[2(126) + (466)(1)] = \frac{467}{2}[718] = 167,653.$$

SUM2 is just $467 \cdot j$ because $j$ is a constant ($k$ is the index).

Thus, $5(\text{SUM1}) + 2(\text{SUM2}) = 5(167,653) + 2(467j) = 838,265 + 934j$.

**36** $\sum_{k=88}^{371} (3j - 2k) = \sum_{k=88}^{371} 3j - \sum_{k=88}^{371} 2k = 3\sum_{k=88}^{371} j - 2\sum_{k=88}^{371} k = 3(\text{SUM1}) - 2(\text{SUM2})$.

The number of terms is $n = 371 - 88 + 1 = 284$. SUM1 is just $284 \cdot j$ because $j$ is a constant ($k$ is the index).

To evaluate SUM2, we use (1) with $a_1 = 88$, $d = 1$, and $n = 284$ to get

$$S_{284} = \frac{284}{2}[2(88) + (283)(1)] = \frac{284}{2}[459] = 65,178.$$

Thus, $3(\text{SUM1}) - 2(\text{SUM2}) = 3(284j) - 2(65,178) = 852j - 130,356$.

**37** $4 + 11 + 18 + 25 + 32$  •  The number of terms is $n = 5$. The difference in terms is $d = 11 - 4 = 7$.

The general term is $a_n = a_1 + (n-1)d = 4 + (n-1)7 = 4 + 7n - 7 = 7n - 3$.

We can represent the sum in terms of summation notation as $\sum\limits_{n=1}^{5} a_n = \sum\limits_{n=1}^{5} (7n - 3)$.

Sometimes it is easier to use $\sum\limits_{n=0}^{4} a_{n+1}$ than $\sum\limits_{n=1}^{5} a_n$. In this case, $a_{n+1} = a_1 + nd = 4 + n \cdot 7$, so an alternate form of

the summation notation is $\sum\limits_{n=0}^{4} (4 + 7n)$.

**38** $3 + 8 + 13 + 18 + 23$  •  $n = 5, d = 5, a_n = a_1 + (n-1)d = 3 + (n-1)5 = 5n - 2$.

The sum in terms of summation notation is $\sum\limits_{n=1}^{5} a_n = \sum\limits_{n=1}^{5} (5n - 2)$ or $\sum\limits_{n=0}^{4} (3 + 5n)$.

**39** $4 + 11 + 18 + \cdots + 466$  •  From Exercise 37, the general term is $7n - 3$ with $n$ starting at 1.

To find the largest value of $n$, set the general term equal to the largest value of the sum and solve for $n$.

$7n - 3 = 466 \Rightarrow 7n = 469 \Rightarrow n = 67$. Thus, we have $\sum\limits_{n=1}^{67} (7n - 3)$ or $\sum\limits_{n=0}^{66} (4 + 7n)$.

**40** $3 + 8 + 13 + \cdots + 463$  •  From Exercise 38, the general term is $5n - 2$ with $n$ starting at 1.

$5n - 2 = 463 \Rightarrow n = 93$, the largest value of $n$. $\sum\limits_{n=1}^{93} (5n - 2)$ or $\sum\limits_{n=0}^{92} (3 + 5n)$

**41** $\dfrac{3}{7} + \dfrac{6}{11} + \dfrac{9}{15} + \dfrac{12}{19} + \dfrac{15}{23} + \dfrac{18}{27}$  •  The numerators increase by 3, the denominators increase by 4.

The general terms are $3 + (n-1)3 = 3n$ and $7 + (n-1)4 = 4n + 3$. $\qquad\qquad \sum\limits_{n=1}^{6} \dfrac{3n}{4n+3}$

**42** $\dfrac{5}{13} + \dfrac{10}{11} + \dfrac{15}{9} + \dfrac{20}{7}$  •  The numerators increase by 5, the denominators decrease by 2.

The general terms are $5 + (n-1)5 = 5n$ and $13 + (n-1)(-2) = 15 - 2n$. $\qquad\qquad \sum\limits_{n=1}^{4} \dfrac{5n}{15-2n}$

**43** $8 + 19 + 30 + \cdots + 16{,}805$  •  $d = 19 - 8 = 11$ and $a_n = a_1 + (n-1)d = 8 + (n-1)11 = 11n - 3$.

Find the largest value of $n$: $11n - 3 = 16{,}805 \Rightarrow 11n = 16{,}808 \Rightarrow n = 1528$.

Thus, the summation notation is $\sum\limits_{n=1}^{1528} (11n - 3)$. Now find the sum: $S_{1528} = \frac{1528}{2}(8 + 16{,}805) = 12{,}845{,}132$.

**44** $2 + 11 + 20 + \cdots + 16{,}058$  •  $d = 11 - 2 = 9$ and $a_n = a_1 + (n-1)d = 2 + (n-1)9 = 9n - 7$.

Find the largest value of $n$: $9n - 7 = 16{,}058 \Rightarrow 9n = 16{,}065 \Rightarrow n = 1785$.

Thus, the summation notation is $\sum\limits_{n=1}^{1785} (9n - 7)$. Now find the sum: $S_{1785} = \frac{1785}{2}(2 + 16{,}058) = 14{,}333{,}550$.

**45** $a_1 = 5$, last term $= 11$, $S = 224$, and $S_n = \dfrac{n}{2}(a_1 + a_n) \Rightarrow 224 = \dfrac{n}{2}(5 + 11) \Rightarrow 448 = n(16) \Rightarrow$
$$n = 28.$$

**46** $a_1 = 3$, last term $= 17$, $S = 420$, and $S_n = \dfrac{n}{2}(a_1 + a_n) \Rightarrow 420 = \dfrac{n}{2}(3 + 17) \Rightarrow 840 = n(20) \Rightarrow$
$$n = 42.$$

**47** $a_1 = -2$, $d = \dfrac{1}{4}$, $S = 21$, and $S_n = \dfrac{n}{2}[2a_1 + (n-1)(d)] \Rightarrow 21 = \dfrac{n}{2}\left[2(-2) + (n-1)\left(\dfrac{1}{4}\right)\right] \Rightarrow$

$42 = n\left(\frac{1}{4}n - \frac{17}{4}\right) \Rightarrow 168 = n^2 - 17n \Rightarrow n^2 - 17n - 168 = 0 \Rightarrow (n-24)(n+7) = 0 \Rightarrow$
$$n = 24, -7. \text{ Since } n \text{ cannot be negative, } n = 24.$$

**48** $a_1 = -1$, $d = \frac{1}{5}$, $S = 21$, and $S_n = \frac{n}{2}[2a_1 + (n-1)(d)]$ $\Rightarrow$ $21 = \frac{n}{2}\left[2(-1) + (n-1)\left(\frac{1}{5}\right)\right]$ $\Rightarrow$

$42 = n\left(\frac{1}{5}n - \frac{11}{5}\right)$ $\Rightarrow$ $210 = n^2 - 11n$ $\Rightarrow$ $n^2 - 11n - 210 = 0$ $\Rightarrow$ $(n-21)(n+10) = 0$ $\Rightarrow$

$\qquad\qquad\qquad\qquad\qquad\qquad\qquad\qquad\qquad$ $n = 21, -10$. Since $n$ cannot be negative, $n = 21$.

**49** $S_n = \frac{n}{2}[2a_1 + (n-1)(d)]$ $\Rightarrow$ $-36 = \frac{n}{2}\left[2\left(-\frac{29}{6}\right) + (n-1)\left(\frac{1}{3}\right)\right]$ $\Rightarrow$

$-72 = n\left(-\frac{29}{3} + \frac{1}{3}n - \frac{1}{3}\right)$ $\Rightarrow$ $-216 = n(n-30)$ $\Rightarrow$ $n^2 - 30n + 216 = 0$ $\Rightarrow$

$(n-12)(n-18) = 0$ $\Rightarrow$ $n = 12, 18$. $\qquad\qquad$ There are two sequences that satisfy the given conditions.

**50** $a_6 = a_1 + 5d$ $\Rightarrow$ $-3 = a_1 + 1$ $\Rightarrow$ $a_1 = -4$; $S_n = \frac{n}{2}[2a_1 + (n-1)(d)]$ $\Rightarrow$

$-33 = \frac{n}{2}[2(-4) + (n-1)(0.2)]$ $\Rightarrow$ $-66 = n(0.2n - 8.2)$ $\Rightarrow$ $2n^2 - 82n + 660 = 0$ $\Rightarrow$

$n^2 - 41n + 330 = 0$ $\Rightarrow$ $(n-11)(n-30) = 0$ $\Rightarrow$ $n = 11, 30$.

$\qquad\qquad\qquad\qquad\qquad\qquad\qquad\qquad$ There are two sequences that satisfy the given conditions.

**51** If we insert five arithmetic means between 2 and 10, there will be 6 differences that span the distance from 2 to 10.

Hence, $6d = 10 - 2$ $\Rightarrow$ $d = \frac{8}{6} = \frac{4}{3}$. $\qquad\qquad\qquad\qquad$ The terms are $2, \frac{10}{3}, \frac{14}{3}, 6, \frac{22}{3}, \frac{26}{3}, 10$.

**52** If we insert three arithmetic means between 3 and $-5$, there will be 4 differences that span the distance from 3 to

$-5$. Hence, $4d = -5 - 3$ $\Rightarrow$ $d = \frac{-8}{4} = -2$. $\qquad\qquad\qquad$ The terms are $3, 1, -1, -3, -5$.

**53** If we insert three arithmetic means between 52 and $-56$, there will be 4 differences that span the distance from 52

to $-56$. Hence, $4d = -56 - 52$ $\Rightarrow$ $d = \frac{-108}{4} = -27$. $\qquad\qquad$ The terms are $52, 25, -2, -29, -56$.

**54** If we insert four arithmetic means between 22 and 108, there will be 5 differences that span the distance from 22 to

108. Hence, $5d = 108 - 22$ $\Rightarrow$ $d = \frac{86}{5} = 17.2$. $\qquad\qquad$ The terms are $22, 39.2, 56.4, 73.6, 90.8, 108$.

**55** (a) The first integer greater than 32 that is divisible by 6 is 36 $\{6 \cdot 6\}$ and the last integer less than 395 that is

divisible by 6 is 390 $\{65 \cdot 6\}$. $\qquad\qquad\qquad$ The number of terms is then $65 - 6 + 1 = 60$.

(b) The sum is $S_{60} = \frac{60}{2}(36 + 390) = 12{,}780$.

**56** (a) The first integer greater than $-500$ that is divisible by 33 is $-495$ $\{-15 \cdot 33\}$.

$\qquad\qquad\qquad$ There are 15 negative integers greater than $-500$ that are divisible by 33.

(b) The sum is $S_{15} = \frac{15}{2}[-495 + (-33)] = -3960$.

**57** There are $(24 - 10 + 1) = 15$ layers.

$\qquad\qquad$ Model this problem as an arithmetic sequence with $a_1 = 10$ and $a_{15} = 24$. $S_{15} = \frac{15}{2}(10 + 24) = 255$.

**58** Model this problem as an arithmetic sequence with $a_1 = 30$ and $d = 2$. $S_{10} = \frac{10}{2}[2(30) + (10-1)(2)] = 390$.

$\qquad\qquad$ The last ten rows $\{$11th to 20th$\}$ each have $10(50) = 500$ seats so that the total is 890 seats.

**59** This is similar to inserting 9 arithmetic means between 4 and 24. $10d = 20$ $\Rightarrow$ $d = 2$.

The circumference of each ring is $\pi D$ with $D = 4, 6, 8, \ldots, 24$.

$\qquad\qquad\qquad\qquad\qquad$ $a_1 = 4\pi$ and $a_{11} = 24\pi$ $\Rightarrow$ $S_{11} = \frac{11}{2}(4\pi + 24\pi) = 154\pi$ ft.

**60** The sequence of feet traveled each second is $4, 9, 14, \ldots$. $\qquad$ $S_{11} = \frac{11}{2}[2(4) + (11-1)(5)] = 319$ ft.

**61** $n = 5$, $S_5 = 5000$, $d = -100$ $\Rightarrow$ $5000 = \frac{5}{2}[2a_1 + 4(-100)]$ $\Rightarrow$ $2000 = 2a_1 - 400$ $\Rightarrow$ $a_1 = \$1200$

**62** $n = 10$, $S_{10} = 46{,}000$, $a_1 = 1000$ $\Rightarrow$ $46{,}000 = \frac{10}{2}[2(1000) + 9d]$ $\Rightarrow$ $7200 = 9d$ $\Rightarrow$ $d = 800$.

The bonuses {from 10th to 1st} are: $1000, $1800, $2600, $3400, $4200, $5000, $5800, $6600, $7400, and $8200.

**63** The sequence $16, 48, 80, 112, \dots$, is an arithmetic sequence with $a_1 = 16$ and $d = 48 - 16 = 32$.

The total distance traveled in $n$ seconds is

$$a_1 + a_2 + \cdots + a_n = \frac{n}{2}[2a_1 + (n-1)d] = \frac{n}{2}[2(16) + (n-1)(32)] = \frac{n}{2}(32n) = 16n^2.$$

**64** Let $f$ be the linear function $f(n) = a(n) + b$. The difference between the $(n+1)$st term and the $n$th term is

$$f(n+1) - f(n) = [a(n+1) + b] - [a(n) + b] = an + a + b - an - b = a.$$

$\therefore$ successive terms differ by the same real number and the sequence is arithmetic.

**65** If the $n$th term is $\dfrac{1}{x_n}$ and $x_{n+1} = \dfrac{x_n}{1 + x_n}$, then the $(n+1)$st term is

$$\frac{1}{x_{n+1}} = \frac{1}{\dfrac{x_n}{1 + x_n}} = \frac{1 + x_n}{x_n} = \frac{1}{x_n} + \frac{x_n}{x_n} = 1 + \frac{1}{x_n},$$

which is 1 greater than the $n$th term and therefore the sequence is arithmetic.

**66** The sequence of the lengths is $2 \times 1$-inch lengths, $2 \times 2$-in, $2 \times 3$ in, $\dots$, $2 \times 16$ in.

This sequence is the same as $2, 4, 6, \dots, 32$, and has sum $S_{16} = \frac{16}{2}(2 + 32) = 272$ in.

If the width is 32, then the sequence is $2, 4, 6, \dots, 64$, and the sum is $S_{32} = \frac{32}{2}(2 + 64) = 1056$ in.

**67** (a) $T_8 = 1 + 2 + \cdots + 8 = 36$. $A_k = \dfrac{n - k + 1}{T_n}$ $\Rightarrow$ $A_1 = \dfrac{8 - 1 + 1}{36} = \dfrac{8}{36}$.

$$A_2 = \tfrac{7}{36}, A_3 = \tfrac{6}{36}, A_4 = \tfrac{5}{36}, A_5 = \tfrac{4}{36}, A_6 = \tfrac{3}{36}, A_7 = \tfrac{2}{36}, A_8 = \tfrac{1}{36}.$$

(b) $d = A_{k+1} - A_k = -\frac{1}{36}$ for $k = 1, 2, \dots, 7$. $S_8 = \sum\limits_{k=1}^{8} A_k = \frac{8}{36} + \frac{7}{36} + \cdots + \frac{1}{36} = 1$.

(c) $1000\left(\frac{8}{36} + \frac{7}{36} + \frac{6}{36} + \frac{5}{36}\right) \approx $722.22$

**68** (a) $A_1 = \dfrac{n - 1 + 1}{T_n} = \dfrac{n}{T_n}$. $A_2, A_3, \dots, A_n = \dfrac{n-1}{T_n}, \dfrac{n-2}{T_n}, \dots, \dfrac{1}{T_n}$.

(b) $d = A_{k+1} - A_k = \dfrac{n - (k+1) + 1}{T_n} - \dfrac{n - k + 1}{T_n} = -\dfrac{1}{T_n}$.

$$S_n = \sum_{k=1}^{n} A_k = \frac{1}{T_n} + \frac{2}{T_n} + \cdots + \frac{n}{T_n} = \frac{1 + 2 + \cdots + n}{T_n} = \frac{1 + 2 + \cdots + n}{1 + 2 + \cdots + n} = 1.$$

## 9.3 Exercises

**1** To show that the given sequence, $5, -\frac{5}{4}, \frac{5}{16}, \dots, 5\left(-\frac{1}{4}\right)^{n-1}, \dots$, is geometric,

we must show that $\dfrac{a_{k+1}}{a_k}$ is equal to some constant, which is the common ratio.

$$a_n = a_1 r^{n-1} = 5\left(-\tfrac{1}{4}\right)^{n-1} \Rightarrow \frac{a_{k+1}}{a_k} = \frac{5\left(-\frac{1}{4}\right)^{(k+1)-1}}{5\left(-\frac{1}{4}\right)^{k-1}} = -\frac{1}{4}$$

**2** $\frac{1}{7}, \frac{3}{7}, \frac{9}{7}, \dots, \frac{1}{7}(3)^{n-1}, \dots$ • $a_n = \frac{1}{7}(3)^{n-1}$ $\Rightarrow$ $\dfrac{a_{k+1}}{a_k} = \dfrac{\frac{1}{7}(3)^{(k+1)-1}}{\frac{1}{7}(3)^{k-1}} = 3$

**Note:** For Exercises 3–14, we will find the $n$th term first and then use that term to find $a_5$ and $a_8$.

**3** The common ratio can be found by *dividing* any term by its successor. $r = \frac{4}{8} = \frac{1}{2}$;
$a_n = a_1 r^{n-1} = 8\left(\frac{1}{2}\right)^{n-1} = 2^3 (2^{-1})^{n-1} = 2^3 \, 2^{1-n} = 2^{4-n}$; $a_5 = 2^{4-5} = 2^{-1} = \frac{1}{2}$; $a_8 = 2^{4-8} = 2^{-4} = \frac{1}{16}$

**4** $r = \frac{1.2}{4} = 0.3$; $a_n = 4(0.3)^{n-1}$; $a_5 = 4(0.3)^4 = 0.0324$; $a_8 = 4(0.3)^7 = 0.0008748$

**5** $r = \frac{-30}{300} = -0.1$; $a_n = a_1 r^{n-1} = 300(-0.1)^{n-1}$; $a_5 = 300(-0.1)^4 = 0.03$; $a_8 = 300(-0.1)^7 = -0.00003$

**6** $r = \frac{-\sqrt{3}}{1} = -\sqrt{3}$; $a_n = 1\left(-\sqrt{3}\right)^{n-1}$; $a_5 = \left(-\sqrt{3}\right)^4 = 9$; $a_8 = \left(-\sqrt{3}\right)^7 = -27\sqrt{3}$

**7** $r = \frac{25}{5} = 5$; $a_n = 5(5)^{n-1} = 5^n$; $a_5 = 5^5 = 3125$; $a_8 = 5^8 = 390{,}625$

**8** $r = \frac{6}{2} = 3$; $a_n = 2(3)^{n-1}$; $a_5 = 2 \cdot 3^4 = 162$; $a_8 = 2 \cdot 3^7 = 4374$

**9** $r = \frac{-6}{4} = -1.5$; $a_n = 4(-1.5)^{n-1}$; $a_5 = 4(-1.5)^4 = 20.25$; $a_8 = 4(-1.5)^7 = -68.34375$

**10** $r = \frac{-54}{162} = -\frac{1}{3}$; $a_n = 162\left(-\frac{1}{3}\right)^{n-1}$; $a_5 = 162\left(-\frac{1}{3}\right)^4 = 2$; $a_8 = 162\left(-\frac{1}{3}\right)^7 = -\frac{2}{27}$

**11** $r = \frac{-x^2}{1} = -x^2$; $a_n = a_1 r^{n-1} = 1\left(-x^2\right)^{n-1} = (-1)^{n-1} x^{2n-2}$; $a_5 = (-1)^4 x^{10-2} = x^8$; $a_8 = (-1)^7 x^{16-2} = -x^{14}$

**12** $r = \dfrac{-\frac{x}{3}}{1} = -\frac{x}{3}$; $a_n = 1\left(-\frac{x}{3}\right)^{n-1} = (-1)^{n-1}\left(\frac{x}{3}\right)^{n-1}$; $a_5 = \frac{x^4}{81}$; $a_8 = -\frac{x^7}{2187}$

**13** $r = \frac{2^{x+1}}{2} = 2^x$; $a_n = 2(2^x)^{n-1} = 2^{[x(n-1)]} \cdot 2^1 = 2^{(n-1)x+1}$; $a_5 = 2^{4x+1}$; $a_8 = 2^{7x+1}$

**14** $r = \frac{10^{2x-1}}{10} = 10^{2x-2}$; $a_n = 10\left(10^{2x-2}\right)^{n-1} = 10^{2(n-1)x+(3-2n)}$; $a_5 = 10^{8x-7}$; $a_8 = 10^{14x-13}$

**15** $\frac{a_6}{a_3} = \frac{56}{7} = 8$ and $\frac{a_6}{a_3} = \frac{a_1 r^5}{a_1 r^2} = r^3$. Hence, $r^3 = 8$ and $r = 2$.

**16** $\frac{a_7}{a_4} = \frac{-27}{1} = -27$ and $\frac{a_7}{a_4} = \frac{a_1 r^6}{a_1 r^3} = r^3$. Hence, $r^3 = -27$ and $r = -3$.

**17** $\frac{a_6}{a_4} = \frac{9}{3} = 3$ and $\frac{a_6}{a_4} = \frac{a_1 r^5}{a_1 r^3} = r^2$. Hence, $r^2 = 3$ and $r = \pm\sqrt{3}$.

**18** $\frac{a_7}{a_3} = \frac{1/4}{4} = \frac{1}{16}$ and $\frac{a_7}{a_3} = \frac{a_1 r^6}{a_1 r^2} = r^4$. Hence, $r^4 = \frac{1}{16}$ and $r = \pm\frac{1}{2}$.

**19** $r = \frac{a_2}{a_1} = \frac{6}{4} = \frac{3}{2}$; $a_6 = a_1 r^{6-1} = 4\left(\frac{3}{2}\right)^5 = \frac{243}{8}$

**20** $r = \frac{a_3}{a_2} = \frac{-\sqrt{3}}{3} = -\frac{1}{\sqrt{3}}$; $a_7 = a_2 r^{7-2} = 3\left(-\frac{1}{\sqrt{3}}\right)^5 = 3\left(-\frac{1}{9\sqrt{3}}\right) = -\frac{1}{3\sqrt{3}}$, or $-\frac{\sqrt{3}}{9}$

**21** $r = \frac{a_3}{a_2} = \frac{-\sqrt{2}}{3}$; $a_6 = a_2 r^{6-2} = 3\left(-\frac{\sqrt{2}}{3}\right)^4 = 3\left(\frac{4}{3^4}\right) = \frac{4}{27}$

**22** $r = \frac{a_2}{a_1} = \frac{7}{4}$; $a_5 = a_1 r^{5-1} = 4\left(\frac{7}{4}\right)^4 = 4\left(\frac{7^4}{4^4}\right) = \frac{7^4}{4^3} = \frac{2401}{64}$

**23** $\frac{a_7}{a_4} = \frac{12}{4} = 3$ and $\frac{a_7}{a_4} = \frac{a_1 r^6}{a_1 r^3} = r^3$. Hence, $r^3 = 3$ and $r = \sqrt[3]{3}$. Since the tenth term can be obtained by multiplying the seventh term by the common ratio three times, $a_{10} = a_7 r^3 = 12(3) = 36$.

**24** $a_2 = 3$ and $a_5 = -81$ $\Rightarrow$ $r^3 = \frac{-81}{3} = -27$ $\Rightarrow$ $r = -3$. $a_9 = a_5 r^4 = (-81)(-3)^4 = -6561$.

**25** $a_1 = -4$ and $a_3 = -1$ $\Rightarrow$ $r^2 = \frac{-1}{-4} = \frac{1}{4}$ $\Rightarrow$ $r = \pm\frac{1}{2}$. $a_7 = a_1 r^6 = (-4)\left(\pm\frac{1}{2}\right)^6 = (-4)\left(\frac{1}{64}\right) = -\frac{1}{16}$.

**26** $a_2 = 3$ and $a_4 = 6$ $\Rightarrow$ $r^2 = \frac{6}{3} = 2$ $\Rightarrow$ $r = \pm\sqrt{2}$. $a_8 = a_2 r^6 = (3)\left(\pm\sqrt{2}\right)^6 = 3(8) = 24$.

**27** $a_1 = \frac{3}{16}$, $r = 2$, $n = 9$, and $S_n = a_1 \cdot \frac{1-r^n}{1-r}$ $\Rightarrow$ $S_9 = \frac{3}{16} \cdot \frac{1-2^9}{1-2} = \frac{3}{16} \cdot \frac{-511}{-1} = \frac{3}{16} \cdot \frac{-511}{-1} = \frac{1533}{16}$.

**28** $a_1 = \frac{17}{16}$, $r = 3$, $n = 8$, and $S_n = a_1 \cdot \frac{1-r^n}{1-r}$ $\Rightarrow$ $S_8 = \frac{17}{16} \cdot \frac{1-3^8}{1-3} = \frac{17}{16} \cdot \frac{-6560}{-2} = 3485$.

**29** $a_4 = a_1 r^{4-1}$ $\Rightarrow$ $27 = a_1\left(\frac{1}{3}\right)^3$ $\Rightarrow$ $a_1 = 729$. $S_7 = 729 \cdot \frac{1-\left(\frac{1}{3}\right)^7}{1-\frac{1}{3}} = 729 \cdot \frac{\frac{2186}{2187}}{\frac{2}{3}} = 1093$.

**30** $a_4 = a_1 r^{4-1}$ $\Rightarrow$ $\frac{4}{13} = a_1\left(\frac{1}{4}\right)^3$ $\Rightarrow$ $a_1 = \frac{256}{13}$. $S_6 = \frac{256}{13} \cdot \frac{1-\left(\frac{1}{4}\right)^6}{1-\frac{1}{4}} = \frac{256}{13} \cdot \frac{\frac{4095}{4096}}{\frac{3}{4}} = \frac{105}{4}$.

**31** Using the formula for $S_n$, $S_n = a_1 \cdot \frac{1-r^n}{1-r}$, with $n = 10$, $r = 3$, and $a_1 = 3^1 = 3$, we get

$$\sum_{k=1}^{10} 3^k = 3 \cdot \frac{1-3^{10}}{1-3} = 3 \cdot \frac{-59{,}048}{-2} = 88{,}572.$$

**32** $\sum_{k=1}^{9} \left(-\sqrt{5}\right)^k = -\sqrt{5} \cdot \frac{1-\left(-\sqrt{5}\right)^9}{1-\left(-\sqrt{5}\right)} = \frac{\left(-\sqrt{5}\right)\left(1+625\sqrt{5}\right)}{1+\sqrt{5}} \cdot \frac{1-\sqrt{5}}{1-\sqrt{5}} = \frac{3124\sqrt{5}-3120}{-4} = 780 - 781\sqrt{5}$

**33** $\sum_{k=0}^{9} \left(-\frac{1}{2}\right)^{k+1} = \sum_{k=1}^{10} \left(-\frac{1}{2}\right)^k = -\frac{1}{2} \cdot \frac{1-\left(-\frac{1}{2}\right)^{10}}{1-\left(-\frac{1}{2}\right)} = -\frac{1}{2} \cdot \frac{\frac{1023}{1024}}{\frac{3}{2}} = -\frac{1023}{3072} = -\frac{341}{1024}$

**34** $\sum_{k=1}^{7} \left(3^{-k}\right) = \sum_{k=1}^{7} \left(\frac{1}{3}\right)^k = \frac{1}{3} \cdot \frac{1-\left(\frac{1}{3}\right)^7}{1-\frac{1}{3}} = \frac{1}{3} \cdot \frac{\frac{2186}{2187}}{\frac{2}{3}} = \frac{1093}{2187}$

**35** $\sum_{k=16}^{26} \left(2^{k-14} + 5j\right) = \sum_{k=16}^{26} 2^{k-14} + 5\sum_{k=16}^{26} j = \text{SUM1} + 5(\text{SUM2})$. To evaluate SUM1, we use $a_1 = 2^{16-14} = 4$, $r = 2$, and $n = 26 - 16 + 1 = 11$ to get $S_{11} = 4 \cdot \frac{1-2^{11}}{1-2} = 4 \cdot \frac{-2047}{-1} = 8188$.

SUM2 is just $11 \cdot j$ because $j$ is a constant ($k$ is the index).

Thus, $\text{SUM1} + 5(\text{SUM2}) = 8188 + 5(11j) = 8188 + 55j$.

**36** $\sum_{k=8}^{14} \left(3^{k-7} + 2j^2\right) = \sum_{k=8}^{14} 3^{k-7} + 2\sum_{k=8}^{14} j^2 = \text{SUM1} + 2(\text{SUM2})$. To evaluate SUM1, we use $a_1 = 3^{8-7} = 3$, $r = 3$, and $n = 14 - 8 + 1 = 7$ to get $S_7 = 3 \cdot \frac{1-3^7}{1-3} = 3 \cdot \frac{-2186}{-2} = 3279$.

SUM2 is just $7 \cdot j^2$ because $j$ is a constant ($k$ is the index).

Thus, $\text{SUM1} + 2(\text{SUM2}) = 3279 + 2(7j^2) = 3279 + 14j^2$.

**37** $2 + 4 + 8 + 16 + 32 + 64 + 128 = 2^1 + 2^2 + 2^3 + 2^4 + 2^5 + 2^6 + 2^7 = \sum_{n=1}^{7} 2^n$

**38** $2 - 4 + 8 - 16 + 32 - 64 = 2^1 - 2^2 + 2^3 - 2^4 + 2^5 - 2^6$.

The terms have alternating signs and are doubling. $\sum_{n=1}^{6} (-1)^{n+1}(2)^n$

**39** $\frac{1}{4} - \frac{1}{12} + \frac{1}{36} - \frac{1}{108} = \frac{1}{4} - \frac{1}{4} \cdot \frac{1}{3^1} + \frac{1}{4} \cdot \frac{1}{3^2} - \frac{1}{4} \cdot \frac{1}{3^3} = \sum_{n=1}^{4} (-1)^{n+1} \frac{1}{4}\left(\frac{1}{3}\right)^{n-1}$

**40** $3 + \frac{3}{5} + \frac{3}{25} + \frac{3}{125} + \frac{3}{625} = 3 + 3\left(\frac{1}{5}\right)^1 + 3\left(\frac{1}{5}\right)^2 + 3\left(\frac{1}{5}\right)^3 + 3\left(\frac{1}{5}\right)^4 = \sum_{n=1}^{5} 3\left(\frac{1}{5}\right)^{n-1}$

**41** $1 - \frac{1}{2} + \frac{1}{4} - \frac{1}{8} + \cdots$ • $\qquad a_1 = 1, r = -\frac{1}{2}; S = \frac{a}{1-r} = \frac{1}{1-\left(-\frac{1}{2}\right)} = \frac{1}{\frac{3}{2}} = \frac{2}{3}$

**42** $2 + \frac{2}{3} + \frac{2}{9} + \frac{2}{27} + \cdots$ • $\qquad a_1 = 2, r = \frac{1}{3}, S = \frac{a}{1-r} = \frac{2}{1-\frac{1}{3}} = 3$

**43** $1.5 + 0.015 + 0.00015 + \cdots$ • $\quad a_1 = 1.5, r = \frac{0.015}{1.5} = 0.01, S = \frac{a}{1-r} = \frac{1.5}{1-0.01} = \frac{1.5}{0.99} = \frac{150}{99} = \frac{50}{33}$

**44** $1 - 0.1 + 0.01 - 0.001 + \cdots$ • $\qquad a_1 = 1, r = -0.1, S = \frac{a}{1-r} = \frac{1}{1+0.1} = \frac{10}{11}$

**45** $\sqrt{2} - 2 + \sqrt{8} - 4 + \cdots$ • $\quad$ The ratio $r = \frac{-2}{\sqrt{2}} = -\sqrt{2}$, but since $|r| = \sqrt{2} > 1$, the sum *does not exist*.

**46** $1 + \frac{3}{2} + \frac{9}{4} + \frac{27}{8} + \cdots$ • $\qquad \bigstar$ Since $|r| = \frac{3}{2} > 1$, the sum *does not exist*.

**47** $256 + 192 + 144 + 108 + \cdots$ • $\qquad a_1 = 256, r = \frac{192}{256} = \frac{3}{4}, S = \frac{a}{1-r} = \frac{256}{1-\frac{3}{4}} = 1024$

**48** $250 - 100 + 40 - 16 + \cdots$ • $\qquad a_1 = 250, r = -\frac{2}{5}, S = \frac{a}{1-r} = \frac{250}{1+\frac{2}{5}} = \frac{1250}{7}$

**49** $\frac{x}{3} + \frac{x^2}{9} + \frac{x^3}{27} + \cdots, |x| < 3$ •

$a_1 = \frac{x}{3}$ and $r = \frac{\frac{x^2}{9}}{\frac{x}{3}} = \frac{x}{3}$. Since $|x| < 3$, $|r| < 1$, and $S = \frac{a}{1-r} = \frac{\frac{x}{3}}{1-\frac{x}{3}} = \frac{\frac{x}{3}}{\frac{3-x}{3}} = \frac{x}{3-x}$.

**50** $2x + 4x^2 + 8x^3 + \cdots, |x| < \frac{1}{2}$ •

$a_1 = 2x$ and $r = \frac{4x^2}{2x} = 2x$. Since $|x| < \frac{1}{2}, |r| < 1$, and $S = \frac{a}{1-r} = \frac{2x}{1-2x}$.

**51** $0.\overline{23}$ • If we write $0.\overline{23}$ as $\frac{23}{100} + \frac{23}{10,000} + \cdots$, we see that the first term is $\frac{23}{100}$ and the common ratio is $\frac{1}{100}$.

$a_1 = 0.23, r = 0.01, S = \frac{a}{1-r} = \frac{0.23}{1-0.01} = \frac{23}{99}$

**52** $0.\overline{071}$ • $a_1 = 0.071, r = 0.01, S = \frac{0.071}{1-0.01} = \frac{71}{990}$

**53** $2.4\overline{17} = 2.4171717\ldots = 2.4 + \frac{17}{1000} + \frac{17}{1000} \cdot \frac{1}{100} + \frac{17}{1000} \cdot \left(\frac{1}{100}\right)^2 + \cdots$.

$a_1 = \frac{17}{1000}$ and $r = \frac{1}{100}$ $\Rightarrow$ $S = \frac{\frac{17}{1000}}{1-\frac{1}{100}} = \frac{\frac{17}{1000}}{\frac{99}{100}} = \frac{17}{990}$, so $2.4\overline{17} = 2.4 + \frac{17}{990} = \frac{2376}{990} + \frac{17}{990} = \frac{2393}{990}$.

**54** $10.\overline{5}$ • $a_1 = 0.5, r = 0.1, S = \frac{0.5}{1-0.1} = \frac{5}{9}$; $10.\overline{5} = 10 + \frac{5}{9} = \frac{95}{9}$

**55** $5.\overline{146}$ • In this problem, we work only with $0.\overline{146}$ and add its rational number representation to 5.

$a_1 = 0.146, r = 0.001, S = \frac{0.146}{1-0.001} = \frac{146}{999}$; $5.\overline{146} = 5 + \frac{146}{999} = \frac{5141}{999}$

**56** $3.2\overline{394}$ • $\qquad a_1 = 0.0394, r = 0.001, S = \frac{0.0394}{1-0.001} = \frac{394}{9990}$; $3.2\overline{394} = 3.2 + \frac{394}{9990} = \frac{32,362}{9990} = \frac{16,181}{4995}$

**57** $1.\overline{6124}$ • $\qquad a_1 = 0.6124, r = 0.0001, S = \frac{0.6124}{1-0.0001} = \frac{6124}{9999}$; $1.\overline{6124} = 1 + \frac{6124}{9999} = \frac{16,123}{9999}$

**58** $123.61\overline{83}$ • $a_1 = 0.0083, r = 0.01, S = \frac{0.0083}{1-0.01} = \frac{83}{9900}$;

$\qquad\qquad 123.61\overline{83} = 123.61 + \frac{83}{9900} = \frac{1,223,822}{9900} = \frac{611,911}{4950}$

**59** The geometric mean of 12 and 48 is $\sqrt{12 \cdot 48} = \sqrt{576} = 24$.

**60** The geometric mean of 20 and 25 is $\sqrt{20 \cdot 25} = \sqrt{500} = 10\sqrt{5}$.

**61** Inserting two geometric means results in a sequence that looks like 4, $x$, $y$, 500. Now $4r = x$, $4r^2 = y$, and $4r^3 = 500$. Thus, $4r^3 = 500 \Rightarrow r^3 = \frac{500}{4} = 125 \Rightarrow r = 5$. The terms are 4, 20, 100, and 500.

**62** 3 geometric means $\Rightarrow 2 \cdot r^{3+1} = 512 \Rightarrow r^4 = \frac{512}{2} = 256 \Rightarrow r = 4 \{r > 0\}$.

The terms are 2, 8, 32, 128, and 512.

**63** Let $a_1 = x$ {the original amount of air in the container} and $r = \frac{1}{2}$.
$$a_{11} = x\left(\frac{1}{2}\right)^{10} = \frac{1}{1024}x.$$ This is $\left(\frac{1}{1024} \cdot 100\right)\%$ or $\frac{25}{256}\%$ or approximately 0.1% of $x$.

**64** Let $a_1 = 20{,}000$ and $r = 1 - \frac{1}{4} = \frac{3}{4}$ {since the value at the end of the year is 75%

of its value at the beginning of the year}. $a_7 = 20{,}000\left(\frac{3}{4}\right)^6 \approx \$3559.57$

**65** Let $a_1 = 10{,}000$ and $r = 1.2$, i.e., 120% every hour.

(a) $N(1) = a_2 = 10{,}000(1.2)^1$, $N(2) = a_3 = 10{,}000(1.2)^2, \ldots, N(t) = a_{t+1} = 10{,}000(1.2)^t$

(b) $N(10) = a_{11} = 10{,}000(1.2)^{10} \approx 61{,}917$.

**66** The sequence of terms is $P, P + P \cdot \dfrac{r}{4} = P\left(1 + \dfrac{r}{4}\right)^1$,
$$P\left(1 + \frac{r}{4}\right) + P\left(1 + \frac{r}{4}\right) \cdot \frac{r}{4} = P\left(1 + \frac{r}{4}\right)\left(1 + \frac{r}{4}\right) = P\left(1 + \frac{r}{4}\right)^2, \ldots.$$

In $n$ years, there will be $4n$ compounding periods. $a_{4n} = P\left(1 + \dfrac{r}{4}\right)^{4n}$

**67** $\text{Distance}_{\text{total}} = \text{Distance}_{\text{down}} + \text{Distance}_{\text{up}} = 60 + 2 \cdot \text{Distance}_{\text{up}} = 60 + 2\left[60\left(\frac{2}{3}\right) + 60\left(\frac{2}{3}\right)^2 + \cdots\right]$
$$= 60 + 2 \cdot \frac{60(2/3)}{1 - (2/3)} = 60 + 2(120) = 300 \text{ ft.}$$

**68** The pendulum travels $24 + 24\left(\frac{5}{6}\right) + 24\left(\frac{5}{6}\right)^2 + \cdots = \dfrac{24}{1 - \frac{5}{6}} = 144$ cm.

**69** Total amount of local spending $= 2{,}000{,}000(0.60) + 2{,}000{,}000(0.60)^2 + \cdots$. We have
$$a_1 = 2{,}000{,}000(0.60) = 1{,}200{,}000 \text{ and } r = 0.60, \text{ so } S = = \frac{1{,}200{,}000}{1 - 0.60} = \$3{,}000{,}000.$$

**70** (a) The number of flies after $n$ days for one group of flies is $a_n = N(0.9)^{n-1}$. Since $N$ flies are released each day,
the number of flies on the $n$th day is $\sum_{k=1}^{n} a_k = \sum_{k=1}^{n} N(0.9)^{k-1} = N + (0.9)N + (0.9)^2 N + \cdots + (0.9)^{n-1}N$.

(b) $r = 0.9 < 1$. For a long-range goal, the sum of an infinite geometric series may be used with $S = 20{,}000$ and
$a_1 = N$. $S = \dfrac{a_1}{1 - r} \Rightarrow 20{,}000 = \dfrac{N}{1 - 0.9} \Rightarrow N = 2000$ flies per day.

Alternatively, since 10% of the flies *do not* survive a given day, we need to replace 10% of 20,000, or

2000 flies per day.

**71** (a) A half-life of 2 hours means there will be $\frac{1}{2}\left(\frac{1}{2}D\right) = \frac{1}{4}D$ after 4 hours. The amount remaining after $n$ doses
{not hours} for a given dose is $a_n = D\left(\frac{1}{4}\right)^{n-1}$. Since $D$ mg are administered every 4 hours, the amount of the
drug in the bloodstream after $n$ doses is $\sum_{k=1}^{n} a_k = \sum_{k=1}^{n} D\left(\frac{1}{4}\right)^{k-1} = D + \frac{1}{4}D + \cdots + \left(\frac{1}{4}\right)^{n-1}D$.

Since $r = \frac{1}{4} < 1$, $S_n$ may be approximated by $S = \dfrac{a_1}{1 - r}$ for large $n$. $S = \dfrac{D}{1 - \frac{1}{4}} = \frac{4}{3}D$.

(b) Since the amount of the drug in the bloodstream is given by $\frac{4}{3}D$, and this amount must be less than or equal to 500 mg, we have $\frac{4}{3}D \leq 500$ mg, or, equivalently, $D \leq 375$ mg.

**72** From the figure we see that 2 prior generations yields 4 grandparents, 3 prior generations yields 8 grandparents, and in general $n$ prior generations yields $2^n$ grandparents for $n \geq 2$. Going back 10 generations, there would be $2^{10}$ {1024} grandparents and the total would be $\sum_{k=2}^{10} 2^k = \sum_{k=1}^{9} 2^{k+1} = 4 \cdot \frac{1-2^9}{1-2} = 2044$.

**73** (a) From the figure on the right, we see that
$$\left(\tfrac{1}{4}a_k\right)^2 + \left(\tfrac{3}{4}a_k\right)^2 = (a_{k+1})^2 \quad \Rightarrow \quad \tfrac{10}{16}a_k^2 = a_{k+1}^2 \quad \Rightarrow \quad a_{k+1} = \tfrac{1}{4}\sqrt{10}\, a_k.$$

(b) From part (a), the common ratio $r = \dfrac{a_{k+1}}{a_k} = \tfrac{1}{4}\sqrt{10}$, so $a_n = a_1 r^{n-1} = a_1\left(\tfrac{1}{4}\sqrt{10}\right)^{n-1}$.

For the square $S_{k+1}$, the area $A_{k+1} = a_{k+1}^2$. But from part (a), $a_{k+1}^2 = \tfrac{10}{16}a_k^2$. Since $a_k^2$ is the area $A_k$ of square $S_k$, we have $A_{k+1} = \tfrac{5}{8}A_k$, and hence $A_n = \left(\tfrac{5}{8}\right)^{n-1}A_1$. Similarly, for the perimeter of the square $S_k$, $P_{k+1} = 4a_{k+1} = 4 \cdot \tfrac{1}{4}\sqrt{10}\, a_k = \sqrt{10}\, a_k = \sqrt{10}\left(\tfrac{1}{4}P_k\right)$, and hence $P_n = \left(\tfrac{1}{4}\sqrt{10}\right)^{n-1}P_1$.

(c) $\sum_{n=1}^{\infty} P_n$ is an infinite geometric series with first term $P_1$ and $r = \tfrac{1}{4}\sqrt{10}$.
$$S = \frac{P_1}{1 - \tfrac{1}{4}\sqrt{10}} \cdot \frac{4}{4} = \frac{4P_1}{4 - \sqrt{10}} = \frac{16a_1}{4 - \sqrt{10}}.$$

**74** (a) Let $s_n$ denote the length of a side of the $n$th square and $\tfrac{1}{2}s_n$ the length of the radius of the inscribed circle. Now $C_n = \pi\left(\tfrac{1}{2}s_n\right)^2 = \tfrac{\pi}{4}s_n^2 = \tfrac{\pi}{4}S_n$, i.e., $S_n = \dfrac{4}{\pi}C_n$. Let $r_n$ be the radius of the $n$th circle. The inscribed square will have a side of length $s_{n+1} = \sqrt{r_n^2 + r_n^2} = \sqrt{2}\, r_n$.
$$\text{Thus, } C_n = \pi r_n^2 \text{ and } S_{n+1} = s_{n+1}^2 = 2r_n^2 \quad \Rightarrow \quad C_n = \tfrac{\pi}{2}S_{n+1}.$$

(b) The shaded region has area
$$(S_1 - C_1) + (S_2 - C_2) + (S_3 - C_3) + \cdots = \sum_{n=1}^{\infty} S_n - \sum_{n=1}^{\infty} C_n = \sum_{n=1}^{\infty} S_n - \sum_{n=1}^{\infty} \tfrac{\pi}{4}S_n = \frac{4-\pi}{4}\sum_{n=1}^{\infty} S_n.$$

From part (a), $S_{n+1} = \tfrac{2}{\pi}\left(\tfrac{\pi}{4}S_n\right) = \tfrac{1}{2}S_n$. Hence, $\sum_{n=1}^{\infty} S_n = S_1 + \tfrac{1}{2}S_1 + \tfrac{1}{4}S_1 + \cdots = \dfrac{S_1}{1 - \tfrac{1}{2}} = 2S_1$.
$$\text{Thus, the area is } \frac{4-\pi}{4}(2S_1) = \frac{4-\pi}{2}S_1 \text{ or approximately } 43\% \text{ of } S_1.$$

**75** (a) The sequence is $1, 3, 9, 27, 81, \ldots$. Thus, $a_k = 3^{k-1}$ for $k = 1, 2, 3, \ldots$.

(b) $a_{15} = 3^{14} = 4{,}782{,}969$

(c) The area of the triangle removed first is $\tfrac{1}{4}$. During the next step, 3 triangles with an area of $\tfrac{1}{16}$ are removed. Then, 9 triangles with an area of $\tfrac{1}{64}$ are removed. At each step the number of triangles increase by a factor of 3, while the area of each triangle decreases by a factor of 4. Thus, $b_k = \dfrac{3^{k-1}}{4^k} = \dfrac{1}{4}\left(\dfrac{3}{4}\right)^{k-1}$.

(d) $b_7 = \tfrac{1}{4}\left(\tfrac{3}{4}\right)^6 = \dfrac{729}{16{,}384} \approx 0.0445 = 4.45\%$.

**76** (a) From the previous exercise, $\sum_{k=1}^{n} a_k = \sum_{k=1}^{n} 3^{k-1}$.

(b) $\sum_{k=1}^{12} 3^{k-1} = 3^0 + 3^1 + 3^2 + 3^3 + \cdots + 3^{11} = 1 \cdot \dfrac{1 - 3^{12}}{1 - 3} = 265{,}720$

(c) From the previous exercise, $\sum_{k=1}^{n} b_k = \sum_{k=1}^{n} \tfrac{1}{4}\left(\tfrac{3}{4}\right)^{k-1}$.

(d) $\sum_{k=1}^{12} \frac{1}{4}\left(\frac{3}{4}\right)^{k-1} = \frac{1}{4} + \frac{1}{4}\left(\frac{3}{4}\right) + \frac{1}{4}\left(\frac{3}{4}\right)^2 + \frac{1}{4}\left(\frac{3}{4}\right)^3 + \cdots + \frac{1}{4}\left(\frac{3}{4}\right)^{11} = \left(\frac{1}{4}\right)\dfrac{1-\left(\frac{3}{4}\right)^{12}}{1-\frac{3}{4}} \approx 0.96832 \approx 97\%$

**77** Let $a_k = 100\left(1 + \dfrac{0.06}{12}\right)^k = 100(1.005)^k$, where $k$ represents the number of compounding periods for each deposit. For the first deposit, $k = 18 \cdot 12 = 216$. For the last deposit, $k = 1$.

$S_{216} = a_1 + a_2 + \cdots + a_{216} = 100(1.005)^1 + 100(1.005)^2 + \cdots + 100(1.005)^{216}$

$= 100(1.005)\left(\dfrac{1-(1.005)^{216}}{1-(1.005)}\right) \approx \$38{,}929.00$

**78** $A = P\left(1 + \dfrac{r}{12}\right)^1 + P\left(1 + \dfrac{r}{12}\right)^2 + \cdots + P\left(1 + \dfrac{r}{12}\right)^n$

$= P\left(1 + \dfrac{r}{12}\right)\left[\dfrac{1-\left(1+\frac{r}{12}\right)^n}{1-\left(1+\frac{r}{12}\right)}\right] = P\left(1 + \dfrac{r}{12}\right)\left[\dfrac{1-\left(1+\frac{r}{12}\right)^n}{-\frac{r}{12}}\right] = P\left(\dfrac{12}{r} + 1\right)\left[\left(1+\dfrac{r}{12}\right)^n - 1\right]$

**79** Use $A = P\left(\dfrac{12}{r} + 1\right)\left[\left(1 + \dfrac{r}{12}\right)^n - 1\right]$ with $P = 100$, $r = 0.08$, and $n = 60$ to get

$A = 100\left(\tfrac{12}{0.08} + 1\right)\left[\left(1 + \tfrac{0.08}{12}\right)^{60} - 1\right] \approx \$7396.67.$

**80** First, solve for $n$. $A = P\left(\dfrac{12}{r} + 1\right)\left[\left(1 + \dfrac{r}{12}\right)^n - 1\right] \Rightarrow \left(1 + \dfrac{r}{12}\right)^n - 1 = \dfrac{Ar}{P(12+r)} \Rightarrow$

$\left(1 + \dfrac{r}{12}\right)^n = \dfrac{Ar}{P(12+r)} + 1 \Rightarrow n\ln\left(1 + \dfrac{r}{12}\right) = \ln\left(\dfrac{Ar}{P(12+r)} + 1\right) \Rightarrow n = \dfrac{\ln\left(\frac{Ar}{P(12+r)} + 1\right)}{\ln\left(1+\frac{r}{12}\right)}$

(a) $A = 100{,}000$, $r = 0.10$, and $P = 100 \Rightarrow n \approx 268.25$ mo, or, 22.35 yr.

(b) $A = 100{,}000$, $r = 0.10$, and $P = 200 \Rightarrow n \approx 197.08$ mo, or, 16.42 yr.

**81** (a) $A_1 = \frac{2}{5}\left(1 - \frac{2}{5}\right)^{1-1} = \frac{2}{5}\left(\frac{3}{5}\right)^0 = \frac{2}{5}.$

$A_2 = \frac{2}{5}\left(\frac{3}{5}\right)^1 = \frac{6}{25}, A_3 = \frac{2}{5}\left(\frac{3}{5}\right)^2 = \frac{18}{125}, A_4 = \frac{2}{5}\left(\frac{3}{5}\right)^3 = \frac{54}{625}, A_5 = \frac{2}{5}\left(\frac{3}{5}\right)^4 = \frac{162}{3125}.$

(b) $r = A_{k+1}/A_k = \frac{3}{5}$ for $k = 1, 2, 3, 4$.

$S_5 = \sum_{k=1}^{5} A_k = A_1 + A_2 + A_3 + A_4 + A_5 = \frac{2}{5} \cdot \dfrac{1-\left(\frac{3}{5}\right)^5}{1-\frac{3}{5}} = 1 - \left(\frac{3}{5}\right)^5 = \frac{2882}{3125} = 0.92224.$

(c) $\$25{,}000\left(\frac{2}{5} + \frac{6}{25}\right) = \$25{,}000\left(\frac{16}{25}\right) = \$16{,}000$

**82** (a) $A_1 = \frac{2}{n}\left(1 - \frac{2}{n}\right)^{1-1} = \frac{2}{n}\left(1 - \frac{2}{n}\right)^0 = \frac{2}{n}.$

$A_2, A_3, \ldots, A_n = \frac{2}{n}\left(1 - \frac{2}{n}\right)^1, \frac{2}{n}\left(1 - \frac{2}{n}\right)^2, \ldots, \frac{2}{n}\left(1 - \frac{2}{n}\right)^{n-1}.$

(b) $r = \dfrac{A_{k+1}}{A_k} = \dfrac{\frac{2}{n}\left(1 - \frac{2}{n}\right)^{(k+1)-1}}{\frac{2}{n}\left(1 - \frac{2}{n}\right)^{k-1}} = \left(1 - \frac{2}{n}\right)^{k-(k-1)} = 1 - \frac{2}{n}.$

$S_n = \sum_{k=1}^{n} A_k = A_1\dfrac{1-r^n}{1-r} = \dfrac{2}{n} \cdot \dfrac{1 - \left(1 - \frac{2}{n}\right)^n}{1 - \left(1 - \frac{2}{n}\right)} = 1 - \left(1 - \frac{2}{n}\right)^n.$

## 9.4 Exercises

**1** (1) $P_1$ is true, since $2(1) = 1(1 + 1) = 2$.

(2) Assume $P_k$ is true: $2 + 4 + 6 + \cdots + 2k = k(k+1)$. Hence,

$$2 + 4 + 6 + \cdots + 2k + 2(k+1) = k(k+1) + 2(k+1) = (k+1)(k+2) = (k+1)(k+1+1).$$

Thus, $P_{k+1}$ is true, and the proof is complete.

**2** (1) $P_1$ is true, since $4(1) = 2(1+1) = 4$.

(2) Assume $P_k$ is true: $4 + 8 + 12 + \cdots + 4k = 2k(k+1)$. Hence,

$$4 + 8 + 12 + \cdots + 4k + 4(k+1) = 2k(k+1) + 4(k+1) = (k+1)(2k+4) = 2(k+1)(k+1+1).$$

Thus, $P_{k+1}$ is true, and the proof is complete.

**3** (1) $P_1$ is true, since $2(1) - 1 = (1)^2 = 1$.

(2) Assume $P_k$ is true: $1 + 3 + 5 + \cdots + (2k-1) = k^2$. Hence,

$$1 + 3 + 5 + \cdots + (2k-1) + 2(k+1) - 1 = k^2 + 2(k+1) - 1 = k^2 + 2k + 1 = (k+1)^2.$$

Thus, $P_{k+1}$ is true, and the proof is complete.

**4** (1) $P_1$ is true, since $6(1) - 3 = 3(1)^2 = 3$.

(2) Assume $P_k$ is true: $3 + 9 + 15 + \cdots + (6k-3) = 3k^2$. Hence,

$$3 + 9 + 15 + \cdots + (6k-3) + 6(k+1) - 3 = 3k^2 + 6(k+1) - 3 = 3k^2 + 6k + 3$$
$$= 3(k^2 + 2k + 1) = 3(k+1)^2.$$

Thus, $P_{k+1}$ is true, and the proof is complete.

**5** (1) $P_1$ is true, since $5(1) - 3 = \frac{1}{2}(1)[5(1) - 1] = 2$.

(2) Assume $P_k$ is true: $2 + 7 + 12 + \cdots + (5k-3) = \frac{1}{2}k(5k-1)$. Hence,

$$2 + 7 + 12 + \cdots + (5k-3) + 5(k+1) - 3 = \frac{1}{2}k(5k-1) + 5(k+1) - 3$$
$$= \frac{5}{2}k^2 + \frac{9}{2}k + 2$$
$$= \frac{1}{2}(5k^2 + 9k + 4)$$
$$= \frac{1}{2}(k+1)(5k+4)$$
$$= \frac{1}{2}(k+1)[5(k+1) - 1].$$

Thus, $P_{k+1}$ is true, and the proof is complete.

**6** (1) $P_1$ is true, since $3(1) - 2 = \frac{1}{2}(1)[3(1) - 1] = 1$.

(2) Assume $P_k$ is true: $1 + 4 + 7 + \cdots + (3k-2) = \frac{1}{2}k(3k-1)$. Hence,

$$1 + 4 + 7 + \cdots + (3k-2) + 3(k+1) - 2 = \frac{1}{2}k(3k-1) + 3(k+1) - 2$$
$$= \frac{3}{2}k^2 + \frac{5}{2}k + 1$$
$$= \frac{1}{2}(3k^2 + 5k + 2)$$
$$= \frac{1}{2}(k+1)(3k+2)$$
$$= \frac{1}{2}(k+1)[3(k+1) - 1].$$

Thus, $P_{k+1}$ is true, and the proof is complete.

**7** (1) $P_1$ is true, since $2 \cdot 3^{1-1} = 3^1 - 1 = 2$.

(2) Assume $P_k$ is true: $2 + 6 + 18 + \cdots + 2 \cdot 3^{k-1} = 3^k - 1$. Hence,

$$2 + 6 + 18 + \cdots + 2 \cdot 3^{k-1} + 2 \cdot 3^k = 3^k - 1 + 2 \cdot 3^k = 1 \cdot 3^k + 2 \cdot 3^k - 1 = 3^1 \cdot 3^k - 1 = 3^{k+1} - 1.$$

Thus, $P_{k+1}$ is true, and the proof is complete.

**8** (1) $P_1$ is true, since $3 \cdot 4^{1-1} = 4^1 - 1 = 3$.

   (2) Assume $P_k$ is true: $3 + 12 + 48 + \cdots + 3 \cdot 4^{k-1} = 4^k - 1$. Hence,

$$3 + 12 + 48 + \cdots + 3 \cdot 4^{k-1} + 3 \cdot 4^k = 4^k - 1 + 3 \cdot 4^k = 1 \cdot 4^k + 3 \cdot 4^k - 1 = 4^1 \cdot 4^k - 1 = 4^{k+1} - 1.$$

Thus, $P_{k+1}$ is true, and the proof is complete.

**9** (1) $P_1$ is true, since $1 \cdot 2^{1-1} = 1 + (1 - 1) \cdot 2^1 = 1$.

   (2) Assume $P_k$ is true: $1 + 2 \cdot 2 + 3 \cdot 2^2 + \cdots + k \cdot 2^{k-1} = 1 + (k - 1) \cdot 2^k$. Hence,

$$1 + 2 \cdot 2 + 3 \cdot 2^2 + \cdots + k \cdot 2^{k-1} + (k + 1) \cdot 2^k = 1 + (k - 1) \cdot 2^k + (k + 1) \cdot 2^k$$
$$= 1 + k \cdot 2^k - 2^k + k \cdot 2^k + 2^k = 1 + k \cdot 2^1 \cdot 2^k$$
$$= 1 + [(k + 1) - 1] \cdot 2^{k+1}.$$

Thus, $P_{k+1}$ is true, and the proof is complete.

**10** (1) $P_1$ is true, since $(-1)^1 = \dfrac{(-1)^1 - 1}{2} = -1$.

   (2) Assume $P_k$ is true: $(-1)^1 + (-1)^2 + (-1)^3 + \cdots + (-1)^k = \dfrac{(-1)^k - 1}{2}$. Hence,

$$(-1)^1 + (-1)^2 + (-1)^3 + \cdots + (-1)^k + (-1)^{k+1} = \frac{(-1)^k - 1}{2} + (-1)^{k+1} = \frac{1(-1)^k}{2} - \frac{1}{2} - \frac{2(-1)^k}{2}$$
$$= \frac{(-1)^k \cdot (-1) - 1}{2} = \frac{(-1)^{k+1} - 1}{2}.$$

Thus, $P_{k+1}$ is true, and the proof is complete.

**11** (1) $P_1$ is true, since $(1)^1 = \dfrac{1(1 + 1)[2(1) + 1]}{6} = 1$.

   (2) Assume $P_k$ is true: $1^2 + 2^2 + 3^2 + \cdots + k^2 = \dfrac{k(k + 1)(2k + 1)}{6}$. Hence,

$$1^2 + 2^2 + 3^2 + \cdots + k^2 + (k + 1)^2 = \frac{k(k + 1)(2k + 1)}{6} + (k + 1)^2 = (k + 1)\left[\frac{k(2k + 1)}{6} + \frac{6(k + 1)}{6}\right]$$
$$= \frac{(k + 1)(2k^2 + 7k + 6)}{6} = \frac{(k + 1)(k + 2)(2k + 3)}{6}.$$

Thus, $P_{k+1}$ is true, and the proof is complete.

**12** (1) $P_1$ is true, since $(1)^3 = \left[\dfrac{1(1 + 1)}{2}\right]^2 = 1$.

   (2) Assume $P_k$ is true: $1^3 + 2^3 + 3^3 + \cdots + k^3 = \left[\dfrac{k(k + 1)}{2}\right]^2$. Hence,

$$1^3 + 2^3 + 3^3 + \cdots + k^3 + (k + 1)^3 = \left[\frac{k(k + 1)}{2}\right]^2 + (k + 1)^3 = \frac{(k + 1)^2}{2^2}[k^2 + 4(k + 1)]$$
$$= \frac{(k + 1)^2}{2^2}(k + 2)^2 = \left[\frac{(k + 1)[(k + 1) + 1]}{2}\right]^2.$$

Thus, $P_{k+1}$ is true, and the proof is complete.

**13** (1) $P_1$ is true, since $\dfrac{1}{1(1 + 1)} = \dfrac{1}{1 + 1} = \dfrac{1}{2}$.

   (2) Assume $P_k$ is true: $\dfrac{1}{1 \cdot 2} + \dfrac{1}{2 \cdot 3} + \dfrac{1}{3 \cdot 4} + \cdots + \dfrac{1}{k(k + 1)} = \dfrac{k}{k + 1}$. Hence,

$$\frac{1}{1\cdot 2}+\frac{1}{2\cdot 3}+\frac{1}{3\cdot 4}+\cdots+\frac{1}{k(k+1)}+\frac{1}{(k+1)(k+2)}=\frac{k}{k+1}+\frac{1}{(k+1)(k+2)}$$

$$=\frac{k}{k+1}+\frac{1}{(k+1)(k+2)}=\frac{k(k+2)+1}{(k+1)(k+2)}$$

$$=\frac{k^2+2k+1}{(k+1)(k+2)}=\frac{k+1}{(k+1)+1}.$$

Thus, $P_{k+1}$ is true, and the proof is complete.

**14** (1) $P_1$ is true, since $\dfrac{1}{1(1+1)(1+2)}=\dfrac{1(1+3)}{4(1+1)(1+2)}=\dfrac{1}{6}$.

(2) Assume $P_k$ is true: $\dfrac{1}{1\cdot 2\cdot 3}+\dfrac{1}{2\cdot 3\cdot 4}+\dfrac{1}{3\cdot 4\cdot 5}+\cdots+\dfrac{1}{k(k+1)(k+2)}=\dfrac{k(k+3)}{4(k+1)(k+2)}$. Hence,

$$\frac{1}{1\cdot 2\cdot 3}+\frac{1}{2\cdot 3\cdot 4}+\frac{1}{3\cdot 4\cdot 5}+\cdots+\frac{1}{k(k+1)(k+2)}+\frac{1}{(k+1)(k+2)(k+3)}$$

$$=\frac{k(k+3)}{4(k+1)(k+2)}+\frac{1}{(k+1)(k+2)(k+3)}=\frac{k(k+3)^2+4}{4(k+1)(k+2)(k+3)}$$

$$=\frac{k(k^2+6k+9)+4}{4(k+1)(k+2)(k+3)}=\frac{k^3+6k^2+9k+4}{4(k+1)(k+2)(k+3)}=\frac{(k+1)(k^2+5k+4)}{4(k+1)(k+2)(k+3)}$$

$$=\frac{(k+1)(k+4)}{4(k+2)(k+3)}.$$

Thus, $P_{k+1}$ is true, and the proof is complete.

**15** (1) $P_1$ is true, since $3^1=\frac{3}{2}(3^1-1)=3$.

(2) Assume $P_k$ is true: $3+3^2+3^3+\cdots+3^k=\frac{3}{2}(3^k-1)$. Hence,

$$3+3^2+3^3+\cdots+3^k+3^{k+1}=\frac{3}{2}(3^k-1)+3^{k+1}=\frac{3}{2}\cdot 3^k-\frac{3}{2}+3\cdot 3^k=\frac{9}{2}\cdot 3^k-\frac{3}{2}=\frac{3}{2}(3\cdot 3^k-1)$$

$$=\frac{3}{2}(3^{k+1}-1).$$

Thus, $P_{k+1}$ is true, and the proof is complete.

**16** (1) $P_1$ is true, since $[2(1)-1]^3=(1)^2(2\cdot 1^2-1)=1$.

(2) Assume $P_k$ is true: $1^3+3^3+5^3+\cdots+(2k-1)^3=k^2(2k^2-1)$. Hence,

$$1^3+3^3+5^3+\cdots+(2k-1)^3+[2(k+1)-1]^3=k^2(2k^2-1)+[2(k+1)-1]^3$$

$$=k^2(2k^2-1)+[2(k+1)-1]^3=2k^4-k^2+(2k+1)^3=2k^4+8k^3+11k^2+6k+1$$

$$=(k+1)^2(2k^2+4k+1)=(k+1)^2[2(k+1)^2-1].$$

Thus, $P_{k+1}$ is true, and the proof is complete.

**17** (1) $P_1$ is true, since $1<2^1$.

(2) Assume $P_k$ is true: $k<2^k$. Now $k+1<k+k=2(k)$ for $k>1$.

From $P_k$, we see that $2(k)<2(2^k)=2^{k+1}$ and conclude that $k+1<2^{k+1}$.

Thus, $P_{k+1}$ is true, and the proof is complete.

**18** (1) $P_1$ is true, since $1+2(1)\le 3^1$.

(2) Assume $P_k$ is true: $1+2k\le 3^k$.

$1+2(k+1)=2k+3<6k+3$ which is $3(1+2k)$.

From $P_k$, we see that $3(1+2k)<3(3^k)=3^{k+1}$ and conclude that $1+2(k+1)\le 3^{k+1}$.

Thus, $P_{k+1}$ is true, and the proof is complete.

**19** (1) $P_1$ is true, since $1 < \frac{1}{8}[2(1)+1]^2 = \frac{9}{8}$.

(2) Assume $P_k$ is true: $1 + 2 + 3 + \cdots + k < \frac{1}{8}(2k+1)^2$. Hence,

$$1 + 2 + 3 + \cdots + k + (k+1) < \frac{1}{8}(2k+1)^2 + (k+1)$$
$$= \frac{1}{2}k^2 + \frac{3}{2}k + \frac{9}{8} = \frac{1}{8}(4k^2 + 12k + 9) = \frac{1}{8}(2k+3)^2$$
$$= \frac{1}{8}[2(k+1)+1]^2.$$

Thus, $P_{k+1}$ is true, and the proof is complete.

**20** (1) If $0 < a < b$, then $a^2b < ab^2$ {multiply by $ab$} and $\frac{a^2}{b^2} < \frac{a}{b}$ {divide by $b^3$}. This is $P_1$: $\left(\frac{a}{b}\right)^2 < \left(\frac{a}{b}\right)^1$.

(2) Assume $P_k$ is true: $\left(\frac{a}{b}\right)^{k+1} < \left(\frac{a}{b}\right)^k$. Hence, $a^{k+1}b^k < a^kb^{k+1}$ $\Rightarrow$

$a^{k+2}b^{k+1} < a^{k+1}b^{k+2}$ {multiply by $ab$} $\Rightarrow$ $\frac{a^{k+2}}{b^{k+2}} < \frac{a^{k+1}}{b^{k+1}}$ {divide by $b^{2k+3}$}.

The last inequality is $P_{k+1}$: $\left(\frac{a}{b}\right)^{k+2} < \left(\frac{a}{b}\right)^{k+1}$.

Thus, $P_{k+1}$ is true, and the proof is complete.

**21** (1) For $n = 1$, $n^3 - n + 3 = 3$ and 3 is a factor of 3.

(2) Assume 3 is a factor of $k^3 - k + 3$. The $(k+1)$st term is

$(k+1)^3 - (k+1) + 3 = k^3 + 3k^2 + 2k + 3 = (k^3 - k + 3) + 3k^2 + 3k = (k^3 - k + 3) + 3(k^2 + k)$.

By the induction hypothesis, 3 is a factor of $k^3 - k + 3$ and 3 is a factor of $3(k^2 + k)$, so 3 is a factor of the $(k+1)$st term.

Thus, $P_{k+1}$ is true, and the proof is complete.

**22** (1) For $n = 1$, $n^2 + n = 2$ and 2 is a factor of 2.

(2) Assume 2 is a factor of $k^2 + k$. The $(k+1)$st term is

$(k+1)^2 + (k+1) = k^2 + 3k + 2 = (k^2 + k) + 2k + 2 = (k^2 + k) + 2(k+1)$.

By the induction hypothesis, 2 is a factor of $k^2 + k$ and 2 is a factor of $2(k+1)$, so 2 is a factor of the $(k+1)$st term.

Thus, $P_{k+1}$ is true, and the proof is complete.

**23** (1) For $n = 1$, $5^n - 1 = 4$ and 4 is a factor of 4.

(2) Assume 4 is a factor of $5^k - 1$. The $(k+1)$st term is $5^{k+1} - 1 = 5 \cdot 5^k - 1 = 5 \cdot 5^k - 5 + 4 = 5(5^k - 1) + 4$.

By the induction hypothesis, 4 is a factor of $5^k - 1$ and 4 is a factor of 4, so 4 is a factor of the $(k+1)$st term.

Thus, $P_{k+1}$ is true, and the proof is complete.

**24** (1) For $n = 1$, $10^{n+1} + 3 \cdot 10^n + 5 = 135$ and 9 is a factor of 135.

(2) Assume 9 is a factor of $10^{k+1} + 3 \cdot 10^k + 5$. The $(k+1)$st term is

$10^{k+2} + 3 \cdot 10^{k+1} + 5 = 10 \cdot 10^{k+1} + 10 \cdot 3 \cdot 10^k + 5 = 10^{k+1} + 9 \cdot 10^{k+1} + 3 \cdot 10^k + 9 \cdot 3 \cdot 10^k + 5$
$$= (10^{k+1} + 3 \cdot 10^k + 5) + 9(10^{k+1} + 3 \cdot 10^k).$$

By the induction hypothesis, 9 is a factor of $10^{k+1} + 3 \cdot 10^k + 5$ and 9 is a factor of $9(10^{k+1} + 3 \cdot 10^k)$, so 9 is a factor of the $(k+1)$st term.

Thus, $P_{k+1}$ is true and the proof is complete.

**25** (1) If $a > 1$, then $a^1 = a > 1$, so $P_1$ is true.

(2) Assume $P_k$ is true: $a^k > 1$. Multiply both sides by $a$ to obtain $a^{k+1} > a$, but since $a > 1$, we have $a^{k+1} > 1$.

Thus, $P_{k+1}$ is true, and the proof is complete.

**26** (1) For $n = 1$, $ar^{1-1} = a$ and $\dfrac{a(1 - r^1)}{1 - r} = a$, so $P_1$ is true.

(2) Assume $P_k$ is true: $a + ar + ar^2 + \cdots + ar^{k-1} = \dfrac{a(1 - r^k)}{1 - r}$. Hence,

$$a + ar + ar^2 + \cdots + ar^{k-1} + ar^k = \dfrac{a(1 - r^k)}{1 - r} + ar^k = a\left[\dfrac{1 - r^k}{1 - r} + \dfrac{r^k(1 - r)}{1 - r}\right]$$
$$= a\left(\dfrac{1 - r^k + r^k - r^{k+1}}{1 - r}\right) = \dfrac{a(1 - r^{k+1})}{1 - r}.$$

Thus, $P_{k+1}$ is true, and the proof is complete.

**27** (1) For $n = 1$, $a - b$ is a factor of $a^1 - b^1$.

(2) Assume $a - b$ is a factor of $a^k - b^k$. Following the hint for the $(k + 1)$st term,
$$a^{k+1} - b^{k+1} = a^k \cdot a - b \cdot a^k + b \cdot a^k - b^k \cdot b = a^k(a - b) + (a^k - b^k)b.$$
Since $(a - b)$ is a factor of $a^k(a - b)$ and since by the induction hypothesis $a - b$ is a factor of $(a^k - b^k)$, it follows that $a - b$ is a factor of the $(k + 1)$st term.

Thus, $P_{k+1}$ is true, and the proof is complete.

**28** (1) For $n = 1$, $a + b$ is a factor of $a^{2(1)-1} + b^{2(1)-1} = a + b$.

(2) Assume $a + b$ is a factor of $a^{2k-1} + b^{2k-1}$. The $(k + 1)$st term is
$$a^{2k+1} + b^{2k+1} = a^{2k-1} \cdot a^2 - a^{2k-1} \cdot b^2 + a^{2k-1} \cdot b^2 + b^{2k-1} \cdot b^2 = a^{2k-1}(a^2 - b^2) + b^2(a^{2k-1} + b^{2k-1}).$$
Since $(a + b)$ is a factor of $a^{2k-1}(a^2 - b^2)$ $\{a^2 - b^2 = (a + b)(a - b)\}$ and since by the induction hypothesis, $a + b$ is a factor of $b^2(a^{2k-1} + b^{2k-1})$, it follows that $a + b$ is a factor of the $(k + 1)$st term.

Thus, $P_{k+1}$ is true, and the proof is complete.

**Note:** For Exercises 29–34 in this section and Exercises 53–54 in the Chapter Review, there are several ways to find $j$. Possibilities include: solve the inequality, sketch the graphs of functions representing each side, and trial and error. Trial and error may be the easiest to use.

**29** $n + 12 \le n^2$ • For $j$: $n^2 \ge n + 12 \Rightarrow n^2 - n - 12 \ge 0 \Rightarrow (n - 4)(n + 3) \ge 0 \Rightarrow n \ge 4 \{n > 0\}$

(1) $P_4$ is true, since $4 + 12 \le 4^2$.

(2) Assume $P_k$ is true: $k + 12 \le k^2$. Hence, $(k + 1) + 12 = (k + 12) + 1 \le (k^2) + 1 < k^2 + 2k + 1 = (k + 1)^2$.

Thus, $P_{k+1}$ is true, and the proof is complete.

**30** $n^2 + 18 \le n^3$ • For $j$: By trial and error, $j = 3$.

(1) $P_3$ is true, since $3^2 + 18 \le 3^3$.

(2) Assume $P_k$ is true: $k^2 + 18 \le k^3$. Hence,
$$(k + 1)^2 + 18 = (k^2 + 18) + 2k + 1 \le (k^3) + 2k + 1 < k^3 + 3k^2 + 3k + 1 = (k + 1)^3.$$

Thus, $P_{k+1}$ is true, and the proof is complete.

**31** $5 + \log_2 n \le n$  •  For $j$: By sketching $y = 5 + \log_2 x$ and $y = x$, we see that the solution for $x > 1$ must be larger than 5. By trial and error, $j = 8$.

(1) $P_8$ is true, since $5 + \log_2 8 \le 8$.

(2) Assume $P_k$ is true: $5 + \log_2 k \le k$. Hence,
$$5 + \log_2(k + 1) < 5 + \log_2(k + k) = 5 + \log_2 2k = 5 + \log_2 2 + \log_2 k = (5 + \log_2 k) + 1 \le k + 1.$$

Thus, $P_{k+1}$ is true, and the proof is complete.

Figure 31

Figure 32

**32** $n^2 \le 2^n$  •  For $j$: By sketching $y = x^2$ and $y = 2^x$, we see that there are three intersection points, the largest being 4. Discussion Exercise 5 in Chapter 4 also dealt with this type of problem.

(1) $P_4$ is true, since $4^2 \le 2^4$.

(2) Assume $P_k$ is true: $k^2 \le 2^k$. Hence,
$$(k + 1)^2 = k^2 + 2k + 1 = k\left(k + 2 + \frac{1}{k}\right) < k(k + k) = 2k^2 \le 2 \cdot 2^k = 2^{k+1}.$$

Thus, $P_{k+1}$ is true, and the proof is complete.

**33** $2n + 2 \le 2^n$  •  For $j$: By sketching $y = 2x + 2$ and $y = 2^x$, we see there is one positive solution. By trial and error, $j = 3$.

(1) $P_3$ is true, since $2(3) + 2 \le 2^3$.

(2) Assume $P_k$ is true: $2k + 2 \le 2^k$. Hence, $2(k + 1) + 2 = (2k + 2) + 2 \le 2^k + 2^k = 2 \cdot 2^k = 2^{k+1}$.

Thus, $P_{k+1}$ is true, and the proof is complete.

Figure 33

Figure 34

**34** $n \log_2 n + 20 \le n^2$  •  For $j$: Since $n^2 < 20$ if $n = 4$, a reasonable first guess would be $j = 5$. By trial and error, $j = 6$.

(1) $P_6$ is true, since $6 \log_2 6 + 20 \le 6^2$.

(2) Assume $P_k$ is true: $k \log_2 k + 20 \le k^2$. Hence,

$$(k + 1) \log_2(k + 1) + 20 = k \log_2(k + 1) + \log_2(k + 1) + 20$$
$$< k \log_2 2k + \log_2 2k + 20 = k \log_2 k + k + 1 + \log_2 k + 20$$
$$\le k^2 + k + 1 + \log_2 k < k^2 + 2k + 1 = (k + 1)^2.$$

Thus, $P_{k+1}$ is true, and the proof is complete.

**35** $\displaystyle\sum_{k=1}^{n}(k + 2) = \sum_{k=1}^{n} k + \sum_{k=1}^{n} 2 = \left[\frac{n(n + 1)}{2}\right] + 2n = \frac{n^2 + n}{2} + \frac{4n}{2} = \frac{n^2 + 5n}{2}$

**36** $\displaystyle\sum_{k=1}^{n}(k - 3) = \sum_{k=1}^{n} k - \sum_{k=1}^{n} 3 = \left[\frac{n(n + 1)}{2}\right] - 3n = \frac{n^2 + n}{2} - \frac{6n}{2} = \frac{n^2 - 5n}{2}$

**37** $\displaystyle\sum_{k=1}^{n}(k^2 + 3k + 5) = \sum_{k=1}^{n} k^2 + 3\sum_{k=1}^{n} k + \sum_{k=1}^{n} 5 = \frac{n(n + 1)(2n + 1)}{6} + 3\left[\frac{n(n + 1)}{2}\right] + 5n$

$$= \frac{n(n + 1)(2n + 1) + 9n(n + 1) + 30n}{6} = \frac{(2n^3 + 3n^2 + n) + (9n^2 + 9n) + 30n}{6}$$

$$= \frac{2n^3 + 12n^2 + 40n}{6} = \frac{n^3 + 6n^2 + 20n}{3}$$

**38** $\displaystyle\sum_{k=1}^{n}(3k^2 - 2k + 1) = 3\sum_{k=1}^{n} k^2 - 2\sum_{k=1}^{n} k + \sum_{k=1}^{n} 1 = 3\left[\frac{n(n + 1)(2n + 1)}{6}\right] - 2\left[\frac{n(n + 1)}{2}\right] + 1n$

$$= \frac{n(n + 1)(2n + 1) - 2n(n + 1) + 2n}{2} = \frac{(2n^3 + 3n^2 + n) - (2n^2 + 2n) + 2n}{6}$$

$$= \frac{2n^3 + n^2 + n}{2}$$

**39** $\displaystyle\sum_{k=1}^{n}(4k^3 + 2k - 1) = 4\sum_{k=1}^{n} k^3 + 2\sum_{k=1}^{n} k - \sum_{k=1}^{n} 1 = 4\left[\frac{n(n + 1)}{2}\right]^2 + 2\left[\frac{n(n + 1)}{2}\right] - 1n$

$$= n^2(n + 1)^2 + n(n + 1) - n = n^2(n^2 + 2n + 1) + n^2 + n - n$$

$$= (n^4 + 2n^3 + n^2) + n^2 = n^4 + 2n^3 + 2n^2$$

**40** $\displaystyle\sum_{k=1}^{n}(k^3 + 2k^2 - k + 4) = \sum_{k=1}^{n} k^3 + 2\sum_{k=1}^{n} k^2 - \sum_{k=1}^{n} k + \sum_{k=1}^{n} 4$

$$= \left[\frac{n(n + 1)}{2}\right]^2 + 2\left[\frac{n(n + 1)(2n + 1)}{6}\right] - \left[\frac{n(n + 1)}{2}\right] + 4n$$

$$= \frac{3n^2(n + 1)^2 + 4n(n + 1)(2n + 1) - 6n(n + 1) + 48n}{12}$$

$$= \frac{(3n^4 + 6n^3 + 3n^2) + (8n^3 + 12n^2 + 4n) - (6n^2 + 6n) + 48n}{12}$$

$$= \frac{3n^4 + 14n^3 + 9n^2 + 46n}{12}$$

**41** (a) $n = 1 \Rightarrow a(1)^3 + b(1)^2 + c(1) = 1^2 \Rightarrow a + b + c = 1$

$n = 2 \Rightarrow a(2)^3 + b(2)^2 + c(2) = 1^2 + 2^2 \Rightarrow 8a + 4b + 2c = 5$

$n = 3 \Rightarrow a(3)^3 + b(3)^2 + c(3) = 1^2 + 2^2 + 3^2 \Rightarrow 27a + 9b + 3c = 14$

$$AX = B \Rightarrow \begin{bmatrix} 1 & 1 & 1 \\ 8 & 4 & 2 \\ 27 & 9 & 3 \end{bmatrix}\begin{bmatrix} a \\ b \\ c \end{bmatrix} = \begin{bmatrix} 1 \\ 5 \\ 14 \end{bmatrix} \Rightarrow X = A^{-1}B = \begin{bmatrix} \frac{1}{3} \\ \frac{1}{2} \\ \frac{1}{6} \end{bmatrix}.$$

(b) $a = \frac{1}{3}$, $b = \frac{1}{2}$, $c = \frac{1}{6}$ $\Rightarrow$ $1^2 + 2^2 + 3^2 + \cdots + n^2 = \frac{1}{3}n^3 + \frac{1}{2}n^2 + \frac{1}{6}n = \dfrac{n(n+1)(2n+1)}{6}$, which is the

formula found in Exercise 11. This method does not verify the formula for all $n$ but only for $n = 1, 2, 3$.
Mathematical induction should be used to verify the formula for all $n$ as in Exercise 11.

**42** (a) $n = 1$ $\Rightarrow$ $a(1)^4 + b(1)^3 + c(1)^2 + d(1) = 1^3$ $\Rightarrow$ $a + b + c + d = 1$

$n = 2$ $\Rightarrow$ $a(2)^4 + b(2)^3 + c(2)^2 + d(2) = 1^3 + 2^3$ $\Rightarrow$ $16a + 8b + 4c + 2d = 9$

$n = 3$ $\Rightarrow$ $a(3)^4 + b(3)^3 + c(3)^2 + d(3) = 1^3 + 2^3 + 3^3$ $\Rightarrow$ $81a + 27b + 9c + 3d = 36$

$n = 4$ $\Rightarrow$ $a(4)^4 + b(4)^3 + c(4)^2 + d(4) = 1^3 + 2^3 + 3^3 + 4^3$ $\Rightarrow$ $256a + 64b + 16c + 4d = 100$

$$AX = B \Rightarrow \begin{bmatrix} 1 & 1 & 1 & 1 \\ 16 & 8 & 4 & 2 \\ 81 & 27 & 9 & 3 \\ 256 & 64 & 16 & 4 \end{bmatrix} \begin{bmatrix} a \\ b \\ c \\ d \end{bmatrix} = \begin{bmatrix} 1 \\ 9 \\ 36 \\ 100 \end{bmatrix} \Rightarrow X = A^{-1}B = \begin{bmatrix} \frac{1}{4} \\ \frac{1}{2} \\ \frac{1}{4} \\ 0 \end{bmatrix}$$

(b) $a = \frac{1}{4}$, $b = \frac{1}{2}$, $c = \frac{1}{4}$, $d = 0$ $\Rightarrow$ $1^3 + 2^3 + 3^3 + \cdots + n^3 = \frac{1}{4}n^4 + \frac{1}{2}n^3 + \frac{1}{4}n^2 = \left[\dfrac{n(n+1)}{2}\right]^2$, which is the

formula found in Exercise 12. This method does not verify the formula for all $n$ but only for $n = 1, 2, 3, 4$.
Mathematical induction should be used to verify the formula for all $n$ as in Exercise 12.

**43** (1) For $n = 1$, $\sin(\theta + 1\pi) = \sin\theta\cos\pi + \cos\theta\sin\pi = -\sin\theta = (-1)^1\sin\theta$.

(2) Assume $P_k$ is true: $\sin(\theta + k\pi) = (-1)^k\sin\theta$. Hence,

$\sin[\theta + (k+1)\pi] = \sin[(\theta + k\pi) + \pi] = \sin(\theta + k\pi)\cos\pi + \cos(\theta + k\pi)\sin\pi$

$\qquad = \left[(-1)^k\sin\theta\right]\cdot(-1) + \cos(\theta + k\pi)\cdot(0) = (-1)^{k+1}\sin\theta$.

Thus, $P_{k+1}$ is true, and the proof is complete.

**44** (1) For $n = 1$, $\cos(\theta + 1\pi) = \cos\theta\cos\pi - \sin\theta\sin\pi = -\cos\theta = (-1)^1\cos\theta$.

(2) Assume $P_k$ is true: $\cos(\theta + k\pi) = (-1)^k\cos\theta$. Hence,

$\cos[\theta + (k+1)\pi] = \cos[(\theta + k\pi) + \pi] = \cos(\theta + k\pi)\cos\pi - \sin(\theta + k\pi)\sin\pi$

$\qquad = \left[(-1)^k\cos\theta\right]\cdot(-1) - \sin(\theta + k\pi)\cdot(0) = (-1)^{k+1}\cos\theta$.

Thus, $P_{k+1}$ is true, and the proof is complete.

**45** (1) For $n = 1$, $[r(\cos\theta + i\sin\theta)]^1 = r^1[\cos(1\theta) + i\sin(1\theta)]$.

(2) Assume $P_k$ is true: $[r(\cos\theta + i\sin\theta)]^k = r^k(\cos k\theta + i\sin k\theta)$. Hence,

$[r(\cos\theta + i\sin\theta)]^{k+1} = [r(\cos\theta + i\sin\theta)]^k[r(\cos\theta + i\sin\theta)] = r^k[\cos k\theta + i\sin k\theta][r(\cos\theta + i\sin\theta)]$

$\qquad = r^{k+1}[(\cos k\theta\cos\theta - \sin k\theta\sin\theta) + i(\sin k\theta\cos\theta + \cos k\theta\sin\theta)]$

$\qquad\qquad\qquad\qquad\qquad$ {Use the addition formulas for the sine and cosine.}

$\qquad = r^{k+1}[\cos(k+1)\theta + i\sin(k+1)\theta]$.

Thus, $P_{k+1}$ is true, and the proof is complete.

**46** (1) For $n = 3$, $(n-2)\cdot 180° = 180°$, which is true for any triangle.

(2) Assume the sum of the interior angles of a polygon of $k$ sides is $(k-2)\cdot 180°$. Now any $(k+1)$-sided polygon can be dissected into a $k$-sided polygon and a triangle by drawing a line from vertex $i$ to vertex $(i+2)$. Its angles add up to the sum of $(k-2)\cdot 180°$ {since it is $k$-sided, by hypothesis} and $180°$ {for the triangle}, which is $(k-1)\cdot 180°$.

Thus, $P_{k+1}$ is true, and the proof is complete.

## 9.5 Exercises

**1** $6!\,0! = (6 \cdot 5 \cdot 4 \cdot 3 \cdot 2 \cdot 1) \cdot (1)$ {Remember that $0! = 1$.} $= 720$

**2** $8!\,0! = (8 \cdot 7 \cdot 6 \cdot 5 \cdot 4 \cdot 3 \cdot 2 \cdot 1) \cdot (1)$ {Remember that $0! = 1$.} $= 40{,}320$

**3** $3!\,5! = (3 \cdot 2 \cdot 1) \cdot (5 \cdot 4 \cdot 3 \cdot 2 \cdot 1) = 6 \cdot 120 = 720$

**4** $4!\,7! = (4 \cdot 3 \cdot 2 \cdot 1) \cdot (7 \cdot 6 \cdot 5 \cdot 4 \cdot 3 \cdot 2 \cdot 1) = 24 \cdot 5040 = 120{,}960$

**5** $\dfrac{8!}{5!} = \dfrac{8 \cdot 7 \cdot 6 \cdot 5!}{5!}$ {cancel $5!$} $= 8 \cdot 7 \cdot 6 = 336$

**6** $\dfrac{6!}{3!} = \dfrac{6 \cdot 5 \cdot 4 \cdot 3!}{3!}$ {cancel $3!$} $= 6 \cdot 5 \cdot 4 = 120$

**7** $\dbinom{8}{0} = \dfrac{8!}{0!\,8!}$ {cancel $8!$} $= \dfrac{1}{0!} = \dfrac{1}{1} = 1$

**8** $\dbinom{9}{9} = \dfrac{9!}{9!\,0!}$ {cancel $9!$} $= \dfrac{1}{0!} = \dfrac{1}{1} = 1$

**9** $\dbinom{7}{5} = \dfrac{7!}{5!\,2!}$ {cancel $5!$} $= \dfrac{7 \cdot 6}{2} = 21$

**10** $\dbinom{8}{4} = \dfrac{8!}{4!\,4!}$ {cancel $4!$} $= \dfrac{8 \cdot 7 \cdot 6 \cdot 5}{4 \cdot 3 \cdot 2} = 70$

**11** $\dbinom{52}{5} = \dfrac{52!}{5!\,47!}$ {cancel $47!$} $= \dfrac{52 \cdot 51 \cdot 50 \cdot 49 \cdot 48}{5 \cdot 4 \cdot 3 \cdot 2} = 2{,}598{,}960$

**12** $\dbinom{52}{2} = \dfrac{52!}{2!\,50!}$ {cancel $50!$} $= \dfrac{52 \cdot 51}{2} = 1326$

**13** $\dfrac{n!}{(n-2)!} = \dfrac{n(n-1)(n-2)!}{(n-2)!}$ {cancel $(n-2)!$} $= n(n-1)$

**14** $\dfrac{(n+1)!}{(n-1)!} = \dfrac{(n+1)(n)(n-1)!}{(n-1)!}$ {cancel $(n-1)!$} $= (n+1)n$

**15** $\dfrac{(2n+2)!}{(2n)!} = \dfrac{(2n+2)(2n+1)(2n)!}{(2n)!}$ {cancel $(2n)!$} $= (2n+2)(2n+1)$

**16** $\dfrac{(3n+1)!}{(3n-1)!} = \dfrac{(3n+1)(3n)(3n-1)!}{(3n-1)!}$ {cancel $(3n-1)!$} $= (3n+1)(3n)$

**17** $\dfrac{[(n+1)!]^2}{(n!)^2} = \dfrac{(n+1)!\,(n+1)!}{(n!)\,(n!)}$ {cancel $(n!)$ twice} $= \dfrac{(n+1)(n+1)}{1 \cdot 1} = (n+1)^2$

**18** $\dfrac{[(2n+2)!]^2}{[(2n)!]^2} = \dfrac{(2n+2)!\,(2n+2)!}{(2n)!\,(2n)!}$ {cancel $(2n)!$ twice} $= \dfrac{(2n+2)(2n+1)\,(2n+2)(2n+1)}{1 \cdot 1}$

$$= (2n+2)^2(2n+1)^2$$

**19** We use the binomial theorem formula with $a = 4x$, $b = -y$, and $n = 3$.

$$(4x - y)^3 = \dbinom{3}{0}(4x)^3(-y)^0 + \dbinom{3}{1}(4x)^2(-y)^1 + \dbinom{3}{2}(4x)^1(-y)^2 + \dbinom{3}{3}(4x)^0(-y)^3$$

$$= (1)(64x^3)(1) + (3)(16x^2)(-y) + (3)(4x)(y^2) + (1)(1)(-y^3) = 64x^3 - 48x^2y + 12xy^2 - y^3$$

**20** $(x^2 + 2y)^3 = \dbinom{3}{0}(x^2)^3(2y)^0 + \dbinom{3}{1}(x^2)^2(2y)^1 + \dbinom{3}{2}(x^2)^1(2y)^2 + \dbinom{3}{3}(x^2)^0(2y)^3$

$$= (1)(x^6)(1) + (3)(x^4)(2y) + (3)(x^2)(4y^2) + (1)(1)(8y^3) = x^6 + 6x^4y + 12x^2y^2 + 8y^3$$

**21** We use the binomial theorem formula with $a = x$, $b = y$, and $n = 6$.

$$(x + y)^6 = \binom{6}{0}x^6 + \binom{6}{1}x^5y^1 + \binom{6}{2}x^4y^2 + \binom{6}{3}x^3y^3 + \binom{6}{4}x^2y^4 + \binom{6}{5}x^1y^5 + \binom{6}{6}y^6$$
$$= x^6 + 6x^5y + 15x^4y^2 + 20x^3y^3 + 15x^2y^4 + 6xy^5 + y^6$$

**22** $(x + y)^4 = \binom{4}{0}x^4y^0 + \binom{4}{1}x^3y^1 + \binom{4}{2}x^2y^2 + \binom{4}{3}x^1y^3 + \binom{4}{4}x^0y^4$
$$= x^4 + 4x^3y + 6x^2y^2 + 4xy^3 + y^4$$

**23** We use the binomial theorem formula with $a = x$, $b = -y$, and $n = 7$.

$$(x - y)^7 = x^7 + \binom{7}{1}x^6(-y)^1 + \binom{7}{2}x^5(-y)^2 + \binom{7}{3}x^4(-y)^3 + \binom{7}{4}x^3(-y)^4 + \binom{7}{5}x^2(-y)^5 + \binom{7}{6}x^1(-y)^6 + (-y)^7$$
$$= x^7 - 7x^6y + 21x^5y^2 - 35x^4y^3 + 35x^3y^4 - 21x^2y^5 + 7xy^6 - y^7$$

**24** $(x - y)^6 = \binom{6}{0}x^6 + \binom{6}{1}x^5(-y)^1 + \binom{6}{2}x^4(-y)^2 + \binom{6}{3}x^3(-y)^3 + \binom{6}{4}x^2(-y)^4 + \binom{6}{5}x^1(-y)^5 + \binom{6}{6}(-y)^6$
$$= x^6 - 6x^5y + 15x^4y^2 - 20x^3y^3 + 15x^2y^4 - 6xy^5 + y^6$$

**25** We use the binomial theorem formula with $a = 3t$, $b = -5s$, and $n = 4$.

$$(3t - 5s)^4 = \binom{4}{0}(3t)^4(-5s)^0 + \binom{4}{1}(3t)^3(-5s)^1 + \binom{4}{2}(3t)^2(-5s)^2 + \binom{4}{3}(3t)^1(-5s)^3 + \binom{4}{4}(3t)^0(-5s)^4$$
$$= (1)(81t^4)(1) + (4)(27t^3)(-5s) + (6)(9t^2)(25s^2) + (4)(3t)(-125s^3) + (1)(1)(625s^4)$$
$$= 81t^4 - 540t^3s + 1350t^2s^2 - 1500ts^3 + 625s^4$$

**26** $(2t - s)^5$

$$= \binom{5}{0}(2t)^5(-s)^0 + \binom{5}{1}(2t)^4(-s)^1 + \binom{5}{2}(2t)^3(-s)^2 + \binom{5}{3}(2t)^2(-s)^3 + \binom{5}{4}(2t)^1(-s)^4 + \binom{5}{5}(2t)^0(-s)^5$$
$$= (1)(32t^5)(1) + (5)(16t^4)(-s) + (10)(8t^3)(s^2) + (10)(4t^2)(-s^3) + (5)(2t)(s^4) + (1)(1)(-s^5)$$
$$= 32t^5 - 80t^4s + 80t^3s^2 - 40t^2s^3 + 10ts^4 - s^5$$

**27** We use the binomial theorem formula with $a = \frac{1}{3}x$, $b = y^2$, and $n = 5$.

$$\left(\tfrac{1}{3}x + y^2\right)^5$$
$$= \binom{5}{0}\left(\tfrac{1}{3}x\right)^5(y^2)^0 + \binom{5}{1}\left(\tfrac{1}{3}x\right)^4(y^2)^1 + \binom{5}{2}\left(\tfrac{1}{3}x\right)^3(y^2)^2 + \binom{5}{3}\left(\tfrac{1}{3}x\right)^2(y^2)^3 + \binom{5}{4}\left(\tfrac{1}{3}x\right)^1(y^2)^4 + \binom{5}{5}\left(\tfrac{1}{3}x\right)^0(y^2)^5$$
$$= (1)\left(\tfrac{1}{243}x^5\right)(1) + (5)\left(\tfrac{1}{81}x^4\right)(y^2) + (10)\left(\tfrac{1}{27}x^3\right)(y^4) + (10)\left(\tfrac{1}{9}x^2\right)(y^6) + (5)\left(\tfrac{1}{3}x\right)(y^8) + (1)(1)(y^{10})$$
$$= \tfrac{1}{243}x^5 + \tfrac{5}{81}x^4y^2 + \tfrac{10}{27}x^3y^4 + \tfrac{10}{9}x^2y^6 + \tfrac{5}{3}xy^8 + y^{10}$$

**28** $\left(\tfrac{1}{2}x + y^3\right)^4 = \binom{4}{0}\left(\tfrac{1}{2}x\right)^4(y^3)^0 + \binom{4}{1}\left(\tfrac{1}{2}x\right)^3(y^3)^1 + \binom{4}{2}\left(\tfrac{1}{2}x\right)^2(y^3)^2 + \binom{4}{3}\left(\tfrac{1}{2}x\right)^1(y^3)^3 + \binom{4}{4}\left(\tfrac{1}{2}x\right)^0(y^3)^4$
$$= (1)\left(\tfrac{1}{16}x^4\right)(1) + (4)\left(\tfrac{1}{8}x^3\right)(y^3) + (6)\left(\tfrac{1}{4}x^2\right)(y^6) + (4)\left(\tfrac{1}{2}x\right)(y^9) + (1)(1)(y^{12})$$
$$= \tfrac{1}{16}x^4 + \tfrac{1}{2}x^3y^3 + \tfrac{3}{2}x^2y^6 + 2xy^9 + y^{12}$$

**29** We use the binomial theorem formula with $a = x^{-2}$, $b = 3x$, and $n = 6$.

$$\left(\frac{1}{x^2} + 3x\right)^6 = (x^{-2} + 3x)^6$$

$$= \binom{6}{0}(x^{-2})^6(3x)^0 + \binom{6}{1}(x^{-2})^5(3x)^1 + \binom{6}{2}(x^{-2})^4(3x)^2 + \binom{6}{3}(x^{-2})^3(3x)^3 +$$
$$\binom{6}{4}(x^{-2})^2(3x)^4 + \binom{6}{5}(x^{-2})^1(3x)^5 + \binom{6}{6}(x^{-2})^0(3x)^6$$

$$= (1)(x^{-12})(1) + (6)(x^{-10})(3x^1) + (15)(x^{-8})(9x^2) + (20)(x^{-6})(27x^3) +$$
$$(15)(x^{-4})(81x^4) + (6)(x^{-2})(243x^5) + (1)(1)(729x^6)$$

$$= x^{-12} + 18x^{-9} + 135x^{-6} + 540x^{-3} + 1215 + 1458x^3 + 729x^6$$

**30** $\left(\dfrac{1}{x^3} - 2x\right)^5 = \left(x^{-3} - 2x\right)^5$

$$= \binom{5}{0}(x^{-3})^5(-2x)^0 + \binom{5}{1}(x^{-3})^4(-2x)^1 + \binom{5}{2}(x^{-3})^3(-2x)^2 +$$
$$\binom{5}{3}(x^{-3})^2(-2x)^3 + \binom{5}{4}(x^{-3})^1(-2x)^4 + \binom{5}{5}(x^{-3})^0(-2x)^5$$
$$= (1)(x^{-15})(1) + (5)(x^{-12})(-2x) + (10)(x^{-9})(4x^2) +$$
$$(10)(x^{-6})(-8x^3) + (5)(x^{-3})(16x^4) + (1)(1)(-32x^5)$$
$$= x^{-15} - 10x^{-11} + 40x^{-7} - 80x^{-3} + 80x - 32x^5$$

**31** We use the binomial theorem formula with $a = x^{1/2}$, $b = -x^{-1/2}$, and $n = 5$.

$$\left(\sqrt{x} - \dfrac{1}{\sqrt{x}}\right)^5 = \left(x^{1/2} - x^{-1/2}\right)^5$$
$$= \binom{5}{0}(x^{1/2})^5(-x^{-1/2})^0 + \binom{5}{1}(x^{1/2})^4(-x^{-1/2})^1 + \binom{5}{2}(x^{1/2})^3(-x^{-1/2})^2 +$$
$$\binom{5}{3}(x^{1/2})^2(-x^{-1/2})^3 + \binom{5}{4}(x^{1/2})^1(-x^{-1/2})^4 + \binom{5}{5}(x^{1/2})^0(-x^{-1/2})^5$$
$$= (1)(x^{5/2})(1) + (5)(x^2)(-x^{-1/2}) + (10)(x^{3/2})(x^{-1}) +$$
$$(10)(x^1)(-x^{-3/2}) + (5)(x^{1/2})(x^{-2}) + (1)(1)(-x^{-5/2})$$
$$= x^{5/2} - 5x^{3/2} + 10x^{1/2} - 10x^{-1/2} + 5x^{-3/2} - x^{-5/2}$$

**32** $\left(\sqrt{x} + \dfrac{1}{\sqrt{x}}\right)^5 = \left(x^{1/2} + x^{-1/2}\right)^5$

$$= \binom{5}{0}(x^{1/2})^5(x^{-1/2})^0 + \binom{5}{1}(x^{1/2})^4(x^{-1/2})^1 + \binom{5}{2}(x^{1/2})^3(x^{-1/2})^2 +$$
$$\binom{5}{3}(x^{1/2})^2(x^{-1/2})^3 + \binom{5}{4}(x^{1/2})^1(x^{-1/2})^4 + \binom{5}{5}(x^{1/2})^0(x^{-1/2})^5$$
$$= (1)(x^{5/2})(1) + (5)(x^2)(x^{-1/2}) + (10)(x^{3/2})(x^{-1}) +$$
$$(10)(x^1)(x^{-3/2}) + (5)(x^{1/2})(x^{-2}) + (1)(1)(x^{-5/2})$$
$$= x^{5/2} + x^{3/2} + 10x^{1/2} + 10x^{-1/2} + 5x^{-3/2} + x^{-5/2}$$

**33** For the binomial expression $(x^3 - 2x^{-2})^8$, the first two terms are

$$\sum_{k=0}^{1} \binom{8}{k}(x^3)^{8-k}(-2x^{-2})^k = \binom{8}{0}(x^3)^8(-2x^{-2})^0 + \binom{8}{1}(x^3)^7(-2x^{-2})^1$$
$$= (1)(x^{24})(1) + (8)(x^{21})(-2x^{-2}) = x^{24} - 16x^{19}$$

**34** For the binomial expression $(2x^4 + 3x^{-2})^6$, the first two terms are

$$\sum_{k=0}^{1} \binom{6}{k}(2x^4)^{6-k}(3x^{-2})^k = \binom{6}{0}(2x^4)^6(3x^{-2})^0 + \binom{6}{1}(2x^4)^5(3x^{-2})^1$$
$$= (1)(64x^{24})(1) + (6)(32x^{20})(3x^{-2}) = 64x^{24} + 576x^{18}$$

**35** For the binomial expression $(3c^{2/5} + c^{4/5})^{25}$, the first three terms are

$$\sum_{k=0}^{2} \binom{25}{k}(3c^{2/5})^{25-k}(c^{4/5})^k = \binom{25}{0}(3c^{2/5})^{25}(c^{4/5})^0 + \binom{25}{1}(3c^{2/5})^{24}(c^{4/5})^1 + \binom{25}{2}(3c^{2/5})^{23}(c^{4/5})^2$$
$$= (1)(3^{25}c^{10})(1) + (25)(3^{24}c^{48/5})(c^{4/5}) + (300)(3^{23}c^{46/5})(c^{8/5})$$
$$= 3^{25}c^{10} + 25 \cdot 3^{24}c^{52/5} + 300 \cdot 3^{23}c^{54/5}$$

**36** For the binomial expression $(x^3 + 5x^{-2})^{20}$, the first three terms are

$$\sum_{k=0}^{2} \binom{20}{k}(x^3)^{20-k}(5x^{-2})^k = \binom{20}{0}(x^3)^{20}(5x^{-2})^0 + \binom{20}{1}(x^3)^{19}(5x^{-2})^1 + \binom{20}{2}(x^3)^{18}(5x^{-2})^2$$

$$= (1)(x^{60})(1) + (20)(x^{57})(5x^{-2}) + (190)(x^{54})(25x^{-4})$$

$$= x^{60} + 100x^{55} + 4750x^{50}$$

**37** For the binomial expression $(4z^{-1} - 3z)^{15}$, the last three terms are

$$\sum_{k=13}^{15} \binom{15}{k}(4z^{-1})^{15-k}(-3z)^k = \binom{15}{13}(4z^{-1})^2(-3z)^{13} + \binom{15}{14}(4z^{-1})^1(-3z)^{14} + \binom{15}{15}(4z^{-1})^0(-3z)^{15}$$

$$= (105)(16z^{-2})(-3^{13}z^{13}) + (15)(4z^{-1})(3^{14}z^{14}) + (1)(1)(-3^{15}z^{15})$$

$$= -1680 \cdot 3^{13}z^{11} + 60 \cdot 3^{14}z^{13} - 3^{15}z^{15}$$

**38** $(s - 2t^3)^{12}$; last three terms are $\sum_{k=10}^{12} \binom{12}{k}(s)^{12-k}(-2t^3)^k = 67{,}584s^2t^{30} - 24{,}576st^{33} + 4096t^{36}$

**Note:** For the following exercises, the general formula for the $(k+1)$st term of the expansion of $(a+b)^n$ is

$$\boxed{\binom{n}{k}(a)^{n-k}(b)^k.}$$

**39** $\left(\dfrac{3}{c} + \dfrac{c^2}{4}\right)^7$; sixth term $\{k = 5\}$ is $\binom{7}{5}\left(\dfrac{3}{c}\right)^2\left(\dfrac{c^2}{4}\right)^5 = 21\left(\dfrac{9}{c^2}\right)\left(\dfrac{c^{10}}{1024}\right) = \dfrac{189}{1024}c^8$

**40** $(3x^2 - \sqrt{y})^9$; fifth term is $\binom{9}{4}(3x^2)^5(-\sqrt{y})^4 = 126(243x^{10})(y^2) = 30{,}618x^{10}y^2$

**41** $\left(\tfrac{1}{3}u + 4v\right)^8$; seventh term $\{k = 6\}$ is $\binom{8}{6}\left(\tfrac{1}{3}u\right)^2(4v)^6 = 28\left(\tfrac{1}{9}u^2\right)(4096v^6) = \dfrac{114{,}688}{9}u^2v^6$

**42** $(3x^2 - y^3)^{10}$; fourth term is $\binom{10}{3}(3x^2)^7(-y^3)^3 = 120(3^7x^{14})(-y^9) = -120 \cdot 3^7 x^{14}y^9$

**43** Since there are 9 terms, the middle term is the fifth term $\left\{\tfrac{9+1}{2} = 5\right\}$.

Using the formula in the note above, we obtain the fifth term of $(x^{1/2} + y^{1/2})^8$, $\binom{8}{4}(x^{1/2})^4(y^{1/2})^4 = 70x^2y^2$.

**44** $(rs^2 + t)^7$; two middle terms $\{$4th and 5th terms$\}$ are $\binom{7}{3}(rs^2)^4(t)^3 = 35r^4s^8t^3$ and $\binom{7}{4}(rs^2)^3(t)^4 = 35r^3s^6t^4$

**45** $(2y + x^2)^8$; term that contains $x^{10}$ • Consider only the variable $x$ in the expansion.

$$(x^2)^k = x^{10} \Rightarrow x^{2k} = x^{10} \Rightarrow 2k = 10 \Rightarrow k = 5; \text{ sixth term is } \binom{8}{5}(2y)^3(x^2)^5 = 448y^3x^{10}$$

**46** $(x^2 - 2y^3)^5$; term that contains $y^6$ • Consider only the variable $y$ in the expansion.

$$(y^3)^k = y^6 \Rightarrow y^{3k} = y^6 \Rightarrow 3k = 6 \Rightarrow k = 2; \text{ third term is } \binom{5}{2}(x^2)^3(-2y^3)^2 = 40x^6y^6$$

**47** $(3y^3 - 2x^2)^4$; term that contains $y^9$ • Consider only the variable $y$ in the expansion.

$$(y^3)^{4-k} = y^9 \Rightarrow y^{12-3k} = y^9 \Rightarrow 12 - 3k = 9 \Rightarrow k = 1; \text{ second term is } \binom{4}{1}(3y^3)^3(-2x^2)^1 = -216y^9x^2$$

**48** $\left(\sqrt{c} + \sqrt{d}\right)^8$; term that contains $c^2$ • Consider only the variable $c$ in the expansion. $(c^{1/2})^{8-k} = c^2 \Rightarrow$

$$c^{4-(1/2)k} = c^2 \Rightarrow 4 - \tfrac{1}{2}k = 2 \Rightarrow 2 = \tfrac{1}{2}k \Rightarrow k = 4; \text{ fifth term is } \binom{8}{4}(\sqrt{c})^4(\sqrt{d})^4 = 70c^2d^2$$

**49** $\left(3x - \dfrac{1}{4x}\right)^6$; term that does not contain $x$ • Consider only the variable $x$ in the expansion.

$$x^{6-k}(x^{-1})^k = x^0 \Rightarrow x^{6-k}(x^{-k}) = x^0 \Rightarrow x^{6-2k} = x^0 \Rightarrow 6 - 2k = 0 \Rightarrow 6 = 2k \Rightarrow k = 3;$$

$$\text{fourth term is } \binom{6}{3}(3x)^3\left(-\dfrac{1}{4x}\right)^3 = -\dfrac{135}{16}$$

**50** $(xy - 3y^{-3})^8$; term that does not contain $y$ • Consider only the variable $y$ in the expansion.

$$y^{8-k}(y^{-3})^k = y^0 \implies y^{8-k}(y^{-3k}) = y^0 \implies y^{8-4k} = y^0 \implies 8 - 4k = 0 \implies 8 = 4k \implies k = 2;$$

$$\text{third term is } \binom{8}{2}(xy)^6(-3y^{-3})^2 = 252x^6$$

**51** The first three terms in the expansion of $(1 + 0.2)^{10}$ are

$$\sum_{k=0}^{2} \binom{10}{k}(1)^{10-k}(0.2)^k = \binom{10}{0}(1)^{10}(0.2)^0 + \binom{10}{1}(1)^9(0.2)^1 + \binom{10}{2}(1)^8(0.2)^2$$

$$= (1)(1)(1) + (10)(1)(0.2) + (45)(1)(0.04) = 1 + 2 + 1.8 = 4.8.$$

The calculator result for $(1.2)^{10}$ is approximately 6.19.

**52** $\sum_{k=0}^{2} \binom{4}{k}(1)^{4-k}(-0.1)^k = 1 - 0.4 + 0.06 = 0.66$; calculator result for $(0.9)^4 = 0.6561$

**53** $\dfrac{(x+h)^4 - x^4}{h} = \dfrac{(x^4 + 4x^3h + 6x^2h^2 + 4xh^3 + h^4) - x^4}{h} = \dfrac{h(4x^3 + 6x^2h + 4xh^2 + h^3)}{h}$

$$= 4x^3 + 6x^2h + 4xh^2 + h^3$$

**54** $\dfrac{(x+h)^5 - x^5}{h} = \dfrac{(x^5 + 5x^4h + 10x^3h^2 + 10x^2h^3 + 5xh^4 + h^5) - x^5}{h}$

$$= \dfrac{h(5x^4 + 10x^3h + 10x^2h^2 + 5xh^3 + h^4)}{h} = 5x^4 + 10x^3h + 10x^2h^2 + 5xh^3 + h^4$$

**55** $\binom{n}{1} = \dfrac{n!}{(n-1)!\,1!} = n$ and $\binom{n}{n-1} = \dfrac{n!}{[n-(n-1)]!(n-1)!} = \dfrac{n!}{1!(n-1)!} = n$

**56** $\binom{n}{0} = \dfrac{n!}{(n-0)!\,0!} = \dfrac{n!}{n!} = 1$ and $\binom{n}{n} = \dfrac{n!}{(n-n)!\,n!} = \dfrac{n!}{0!\,n!} = 1$

## 9.6 Exercises

**1** $P(17, 1) = \dfrac{17!}{(17-1)!} = \dfrac{17!}{16!} = \dfrac{17 \cdot 16!}{16!}$ {cancel 16!} $= 17$

**2** $P(20, 1) = \dfrac{20!}{(20-1)!} = \dfrac{20!}{19!} = \dfrac{20 \cdot 19!}{19!}$ {cancel 19!} $= 20$

**3** $P(9, 6) = \dfrac{9!}{(9-6)!} = \dfrac{9!}{3!} = \dfrac{9 \cdot 8 \cdot 7 \cdot 6 \cdot 5 \cdot 4 \cdot 3!}{3!}$ {cancel 3!} $= 9 \cdot 8 \cdot 7 \cdot 6 \cdot 5 \cdot 4 = 60{,}480$

**4** $P(5, 3) = \dfrac{5!}{(5-3)!} = \dfrac{5!}{2!} = \dfrac{5 \cdot 4 \cdot 3 \cdot 2!}{2!}$ {cancel 2!} $= 5 \cdot 4 \cdot 3 = 60$

**5** $P(5, 5) = \dfrac{5!}{(5-5)!} = \dfrac{5!}{0!} = \dfrac{5 \cdot 4 \cdot 3 \cdot 2 \cdot 1}{1} = 120$

**6** $P(4, 4) = \dfrac{4!}{(4-4)!} = \dfrac{4!}{0!} = \dfrac{4 \cdot 3 \cdot 2 \cdot 1}{1} = 24$

**7** $P(6, 5) = \dfrac{6!}{(6-5)!} = \dfrac{6!}{1!} = \dfrac{6 \cdot 5 \cdot 4 \cdot 3 \cdot 2 \cdot 1}{1} = 720$

**8** $P(7, 6) = \dfrac{7!}{(7-6)!} = \dfrac{7!}{1!} = \dfrac{7 \cdot 6 \cdot 5 \cdot 4 \cdot 3 \cdot 2 \cdot 1}{1} = 5040$

**9** $P(52, 5) = \dfrac{52!}{(52-5)!} = \dfrac{52!}{47!} = \dfrac{52 \cdot 51 \cdot 50 \cdot 49 \cdot 48 \cdot 47!}{47!}$ {cancel 47!} $= 52 \cdot 51 \cdot 50 \cdot 49 \cdot 48 = 311{,}875{,}200$

**10** $P(52, 2) = \dfrac{52!}{(52-2)!} = \dfrac{52!}{50!} = \dfrac{52 \cdot 51 \cdot 50!}{50!}$ {cancel 50!} $= 52 \cdot 51 = 2652$

**11**  $P(n, 0) = \dfrac{n!}{(n - 0)!} = \dfrac{n!}{n!} = 1$

**12**  $P(n, 1) = \dfrac{n!}{(n - 1)!} = \dfrac{n(n - 1)!}{(n - 1)!} = n$

**13**  $P(n, n - 1) = \dfrac{n!}{[n - (n - 1)]!} = \dfrac{n!}{1!} = \dfrac{n!}{1} = n!$

**14**  $P(n, 2) = \dfrac{n!}{(n - 2)!} = \dfrac{n(n - 1)(n - 2)!}{(n - 2)!} = n(n - 1)$

**15**  (a)  We can think of the three-digit numbers as filling 3 slots. There are 5 digits to pick from for filling the first slot. There are 4 remaining digits to pick from to fill the second slot. There are 3 remaining digits to pick from to fill the third slot. By the fundamental counting principle, there are a total of $5 \cdot 4 \cdot 3 = 60$ three-digit numbers.

(b)  The difference between parts (a) and (b) is that we can use any of the 5 digits for all 3 slots. Hence, there are a total of $5 \cdot 5 \cdot 5 = 125$ three-digit numbers if repetitions are allowed.

**16**  (a)  $5 \cdot 4 \cdot 3 \cdot 2 = 120$                              (b)  $5 \cdot 5 \cdot 5 \cdot 5 = 625$

**17**  There are 4 one digit numbers, $4 \cdot 3 = 12$ two digit numbers, $4 \cdot 3 \cdot 2 = 24$ three digit numbers, and
$4 \cdot 3 \cdot 2 \cdot 1 = 24$ four digit numbers. The total number of numbers is $4 + 12 + 24 + 24 = 64$.

**18**  There are 4 one digit numbers, $4 \cdot 4 = 4^2$ two digit numbers, $4 \cdot 4 \cdot 4 = 4^3$ three digit numbers, and
$4 \cdot 4 \cdot 4 \cdot 4 = 4^4$ four digit numbers. The total number of numbers is $4 + 16 + 64 + 256 = 340$.

**19**  We want eight teams taken three at a time.  $P(8, 3) = \dfrac{8!}{(8 - 3)!} = \dfrac{8!}{5!} = 8 \cdot 7 \cdot 6 = 336$

**20**  We want 12 teams taken three at a time.  $P(12, 3) = \dfrac{12!}{(12 - 3)!} = \dfrac{12!}{9!} = 12 \cdot 11 \cdot 10 = 1320$

**21**  By the fundamental counting principle, $4 \cdot 6 = 24$.

**22**  By the fundamental counting principle, $4 \cdot 6 \cdot 3 = 72$.

**23**  (a)  By the fundamental counting principle, $26 \cdot 9 \cdot 10^4 = 2,340,000$.

(b)  By the fundamental counting principle, $24 \cdot 9 \cdot 10^4 = 2,160,000$.

**24**  By the fundamental counting principle, the dice can fall $6 \cdot 6 = 36$ ways.

(a)  2 & 1 or 1 & 2; 2 ways to equal 3                    (b)  4 & 1 twice, 3 & 2 twice; 4 ways to equal 5

(c)  6 & 1 twice, 5 & 2 twice, 4 & 3 twice; 6 ways to equal 7

(d)  5 & 4 twice, 6 & 3 twice; 4 ways to equal 9          (e)  6 & 5 twice; 2 ways to equal 11

**25**  (a)  $P(10, 6) = \dfrac{10!}{(10 - 6)!} = \dfrac{10!}{4!} = 10 \cdot 9 \cdot 8 \cdot 7 \cdot 6 \cdot 5 = 151,200$

(b)  $\boxed{\text{Boy}} - \text{Girl}$  seatings:  $\boxed{6} \cdot 4 \cdot \boxed{5} \cdot 3 \cdot \boxed{4} \cdot 2 = 2880$.

 $\text{Girl} - \boxed{\text{Boy}}$  seatings:  $4 \cdot \boxed{6} \cdot 3 \cdot \boxed{5} \cdot 2 \cdot \boxed{4} = 2880$.

The total number of seatings is $2880 + 2880 = 5760$.

**26** Picking (in order) the <u>M</u>ath, <u>E</u>nglish, and <u>H</u>istory classes, we obtain:

<u>M</u> @ 8, E-9, H-11, 2, 3;        E-10, H-11, 2, 3;        E-1, H-11, 2, 3;        E-2, H-11, 3.

{3 + 3 + 3 + 2 = 11 ways to pick with Math at 8.}

<u>M</u> @ 10, E-9, H-8, 11, 2, 3;        E-1, H-8, 11, 2, 3;        E-2, H-8, 11, 3.

{4 + 4 + 3 = 11 ways to pick with Math at 10.}

<u>M</u> @ 11, E-9, H-8, 2, 3;        E-10, H-8, 2, 3;        E-1, H-8, 2, 3;        E-2, H-8, 3.

{3 + 3 + 3 + 2 = 11 ways to pick with Math at 11.}

<u>M</u> @ 2, E-9, H-8, 11, 3;        E-10, H-8, 11, 3;        E-1, H-8, 11, 3.

{3 + 3 + 3 = 9 ways to pick with Math at 2. Thus, there are 11 + 11 + 11 + 9 = 42 total ways.}

**27** There are 2 choices for each of the 10 questions. 2 times itself 10 times = $2^{10} = 1024$

**28** There are 5 choices for each of the 6 questions. 5 times itself 6 times = $5^6 = 15,625$

**29** We want 8 people taken 8 at a time. $P(8,8) = \dfrac{8!}{(8-8)!} = \dfrac{8!}{0!} = 8! = 40,320$

**30** We want 10 books taken 10 at a time. $P(10,10) = \dfrac{10!}{(10-10)!} = \dfrac{10!}{0!} = 10! = 3,628,800$

**31** We want 6 flags taken 3 at a time. $P(6,3) = \dfrac{6!}{(6-3)!} = \dfrac{6!}{3!} = 6 \cdot 5 \cdot 4 = 120$

**32** We want 12 books taken 5 at a time. $P(12,5) = \dfrac{12!}{(12-5)!} = \dfrac{12!}{7!} = 12 \cdot 11 \cdot 10 \cdot 9 \cdot 8 = 95,040$

**33** (a) The number of choices for each letter are: $2 \cdot \underline{25} \cdot \underline{24} \cdot \underline{23} = 27,600$

(b) The number of choices for each letter are: $2 \cdot \underline{26} \cdot \underline{26} \cdot \underline{26} = 35,152$

**34** (a) $P(24,3) = \dfrac{24!}{21!} = 24 \cdot 23 \cdot 22 = 12,144$        (b) $24 \cdot 24 \cdot 24 = 13,824$

**35** We have a choice of 9 digits for the first number and a choice of 10 digits for the other numbers.

By the fundamental counting principle, $9 \cdot 10^9 = 9,000,000,000.$

**36** There are $9 - 2 = 7$ spots to fill. $P(7,7) = \dfrac{7!}{0!} = 7! = 5040$

**37** $P(4,4) = \dfrac{4!}{(4-4)!} = \dfrac{4!}{0!} = 4! = 24$

**38** Suppose the "2" is repeated. There are 4! ways to arrange $2_a, 2_b, 7,$ and 9.

Since $2_a, 2_b, 7, 9$ and $2_b, 2_a, 7, 9$ are not distinguishable permutations, we divide 4! by 2.

Since there are 3 numbers to repeat, the total number of trials is $3 \cdot \frac{4!}{2} = 36.$

**39** We have 60 numbers and want 3 of them, which gives us $P(60,3) = 205,320$ possibilities. Each one takes 8 seconds, so it would take $8(205,320) = 1,642,560$ seconds, or $1,642,560/60^2 \approx 456$ hours.

**40** There are 10 choices for each of the 6 dials, so we get $10 \cdot 10 \cdot 10 \cdot 10 \cdot 10 \cdot 10 = 10^6$ possible combinations. Each one takes 3 seconds, so it would take $3(10^6)$ seconds, or $3(10^6)/60^2 = 833\frac{1}{3}$ hours.

**41** There are 3! ways to choose the ordering of the couples and 2 ways for each couple to sit.

By the fundamental counting principle, $3! \cdot 2^3 = 48.$

**42** We want 10 horses taken 3 at a time. $P(10,3) = \dfrac{10!}{(10-3)!} = \dfrac{10!}{7!} = 10 \cdot 9 \cdot 8 = 720$

**43** There are 16 "fixins" and each one can be "on" or "off" your sandwich (or hot dog or salad). With just the "fixins," we have $\underbrace{2 \cdot 2 \cdot 2 \cdot \cdots \cdot 2}_{\text{sixteen 2's}} = 2^{16}$, but we subtract 1 because that would be the one choice that would have no "fixins."

Now we have 17 sandwiches, hot dogs, or salads that can be combined with any of the choices of "fixins," so we use the fundamental counting principle to obtain $(2^{16} - 1) \cdot 17 = 1{,}114{,}095$ different lunches.

**44** (a) $52 \cdot 51 \cdot 50 \cdot \cdots \cdot 3 \cdot 2 \cdot 1 = 52! \approx 8.07 \times 10^{67}$

(b) The aces can be arranged in 4! ways and the other 48 cards can be arranged in 48! ways.

Total number of arrangements $= 4! \cdot 48! \approx 2.98 \times 10^{62}$

**45** (a) There are 9 choices for the first digit {can't have 0}, 10 for the second, 10 for the third, and 1 for the fourth and fifth.

$9 \cdot 10 \cdot 10 \cdot 1 \cdot 1 = 900$

(b) If $n$ is even, we need to select the first $\frac{n}{2}$ digits. There are 9 choices for the first digit and 10 choices for each of the next $\left(\frac{n}{2} - 1\right)$ digits, so the total number of even $n$-digit palindromes is $9 \cdot 10^{(n/2)-1}$.

If $n$ is odd, we need to select the first $\left(\frac{n}{2} + \frac{1}{2}\right)$ digits. There are 9 choices for the first digit and 10 choices for each of the next $\left(\frac{n}{2} + \frac{1}{2} - 1\right) = \left(\frac{n}{2} - \frac{1}{2}\right) = \frac{n-1}{2}$ digits, so the total number of odd $n$-digit palindromes is $9 \cdot 10^{(n-1)/2}$.

**46** There are 10 choices for the first square and 9 choices for each successive square.

The number of ways of coloring the strip is $10 \cdot 9^5 = 590{,}490$.

**47** (a) There is a horizontal asymptote of $y = 1$.

(b) $\dfrac{n! \, e^n}{n^n \sqrt{2\pi n}} \approx 1 \;\Rightarrow\; n! \approx \dfrac{n^n \sqrt{2\pi n}}{e^n}$.

Example: $50! \approx \dfrac{50^{50} \sqrt{2\pi(50)}}{e^{50}} \approx 3.0363 \times 10^{64}$.

The actual value is closer to $3.0414 \times 10^{64}$.

**48** (a) Calculators such as the TI-83/4 Plus give an error message since they can only deal with numbers the size of $10^n$, where $n$ is a 2-digit number. Looking ahead to part (b), we see that there is a 3-digit number in the exponent. Calculators such as the TI-86 fail to calculate $P(800, 400)$, which is about $1.2 \times 10^{1108}$.

(b) $\log n! \approx \dfrac{n \ln n - n}{\ln 10}$  •  $P(150, 50) = 10^r \;\Rightarrow\; \dfrac{150!}{(150-50)!} = 10^r \;\Rightarrow\; r = \log \dfrac{150!}{100!} \;\Rightarrow$

$r = \log 150! - \log 100! \;\Rightarrow\; r \approx \dfrac{150 \ln 150 - 150}{\ln 10} - \dfrac{100 \ln 100 - 100}{\ln 10} \approx 104.7$.

Thus, $P(150, 50) \approx 10^{104.7}$.

## 9.7 Exercises

**1** $C(17, 1) = \dfrac{17!}{(17-1)! \, 1!} = \dfrac{17!}{16! \, 1!} = \dfrac{17 \cdot 16!}{16! \cdot 1}$ {cancel 16!} $= 17$

**2** $C(20, 1) = \dfrac{20!}{(20-1)! \, 1!} = \dfrac{20!}{19! \, 1!} = \dfrac{20 \cdot 19!}{19! \cdot 1} \; \{\text{cancel } 19!\} = 20$

**3** $C(9, 6) = \dfrac{9!}{(9-6)! \, 6!} = \dfrac{9!}{3! \, 6!} = \dfrac{9 \cdot 8 \cdot 7 \cdot 6!}{3 \cdot 2 \cdot 1 \cdot 6!} \; \{\text{cancel } 6!\} = \dfrac{9 \cdot 8 \cdot 7}{3 \cdot 2} = 84$

**4** $C(5, 3) = \dfrac{5!}{(5-3)! \, 3!} = \dfrac{5!}{2! \, 3!} = \dfrac{5 \cdot 4 \cdot 3!}{2 \cdot 1 \cdot 3!} \; \{\text{cancel } 3!\} = \dfrac{5 \cdot 4}{2} = 10$

**5** $C(5, 5) = \dfrac{5!}{(5-5)! \, 5!} = \dfrac{5!}{0! \, 5!} \; \{\text{cancel } 5!\} = \dfrac{1}{0!} = \dfrac{1}{1} = 1$

**6** $C(4, 4) = \dfrac{4!}{(4-4)! \, 4!} = \dfrac{4!}{0! \, 4!} \; \{\text{cancel } 4!\} = \dfrac{1}{0!} = \dfrac{1}{1} = 1$

**7** $C(6, 5) = \dfrac{6!}{(6-5)! \, 5!} = \dfrac{6!}{1! \, 5!} = \dfrac{6 \cdot 5!}{1 \cdot 5!} \; \{\text{cancel } 5!\} = \dfrac{6}{1} = 6$

**8** $C(7, 6) = \dfrac{7!}{(7-6)! \, 6!} = \dfrac{7!}{1! \, 6!} = \dfrac{7 \cdot 6!}{1 \cdot 6!} \; \{\text{cancel } 6!\} = \dfrac{7}{1} = 7$

**9** $C(52, 5) = \dfrac{52!}{(52-5)! \, 5!} = \dfrac{52!}{47! \, 5!} \; \{\text{cancel } 47!\} = \dfrac{52 \cdot 51 \cdot 50 \cdot 49 \cdot 48}{5 \cdot 4 \cdot 3 \cdot 2 \cdot 1} = 2{,}598{,}960$

**10** $C(52, 2) = \dfrac{52!}{(52-2)! \, 2!} = \dfrac{52!}{50! \, 2!} \; \{\text{cancel } 50!\} = \dfrac{52 \cdot 51}{2 \cdot 1} = 1326$

**11** $C(n, 0) = \dfrac{n!}{(n-0)! \, 0!} = \dfrac{n!}{n! \, 0!} \; \{\text{cancel } n!\} = \dfrac{1}{0!} = \dfrac{1}{1} = 1$

**12** $C(n, 1) = \dfrac{n!}{(n-1)! \, 1!} = \dfrac{n \cdot (n-1)!}{(n-1)! \cdot 1} \; \{\text{cancel } (n-1)!\} = \dfrac{n}{1} = n$

**13** $C(n, n-1) = \dfrac{n!}{[n-(n-1)]! \, (n-1)!} = \dfrac{n!}{1! \, (n-1)!} = \dfrac{n \cdot (n-1)!}{1 \cdot (n-1)!} \; \{\text{cancel } (n-1)!\} = \dfrac{n}{1} = n$

**14** $C(n, 2) = \dfrac{n!}{(n-2)! \, 2!} = \dfrac{n \cdot (n-1) \cdot (n-2)!}{(n-2)! \cdot 2} \; \{\text{cancel } (n-2)!\} = \dfrac{n \cdot (n-1)}{2}, \text{ or } \dfrac{1}{2}n(n-1)$

**15** There are 12! total permutations. We want the number of *distinguishable* permutations of the 12 disks.

Using the second theorem on distinguishable permutations, we have $\dfrac{(5+3+2+2)!}{5! \, 3! \, 2! \, 2!} = \dfrac{12!}{5! \, 3! \, 2! \, 2!} = 166{,}320.$

**16** There are 12! total permutations. We want the number of *distinguishable* permutations of the 12 disks.

Using the second theorem on distinguishable permutations, we have $\dfrac{(3+3+3+3)!}{3! \, 3! \, 3! \, 3!} = \dfrac{12!}{(3!)^4} = 369{,}600.$

**17** In the 10-letter word *bookkeeper*, there are 3 e's, 2 o's, and 2 k's.

Using the second theorem on distinguishable permutations, we have $\dfrac{10!}{3! \, 2! \, 2! \, 1! \, 1! \, 1!} = 151{,}200.$

**18** In the 4-letter word *moon*, there are 2 o's, 1 m, and 1 n.

Using the second theorem on distinguishable permutations, we have $\dfrac{4!}{2! \, 1! \, 1!} = 12.$

**19** There are $C(10, 5) = \dfrac{10!}{(10-5)! \, 5!} = \dfrac{10!}{5! \, 5!} = \dfrac{10 \cdot 9 \cdot 8 \cdot 7 \cdot 6 \cdot 5!}{5 \cdot 4 \cdot 3 \cdot 2 \cdot 1 \cdot 5!} \; \{\text{cancel } 5!\} = \dfrac{10 \cdot 9 \cdot 8 \cdot 7 \cdot 6}{5 \cdot 4 \cdot 3 \cdot 2} = 252$ ways to

pick the first team. The second team is determined once the first team is selected.

**20** (a) $C(10, 6) = \dfrac{10!}{(10-6)! \, 6!} = \dfrac{10!}{4! \, 6!} = 210$

(b) The student needs to answer 4 of the last 8. $C(8, 4) = \dfrac{8!}{(8-4)! \, 4!} = \dfrac{8!}{4! \, 4!} = 70$

**21** Two points determine a unique line. $C(8, 2) = \dfrac{8!}{(8-2)!\, 2!} = \dfrac{8!}{6!\, 2!} = 28$

**22** Three points determine a unique triangle. $C(8, 3) = \dfrac{8!}{(8-3)!\, 3!} = \dfrac{8!}{5!\, 3!} = 56$

**23** There are 3! ways to order the categories. $(5! \cdot 4! \cdot 8!) \cdot 3! = 696{,}729{,}600$

**24** (a) $C(12, 5) = \dfrac{12!}{7!\, 5!} = 792$     (b) $C(2, 1) \cdot C(10, 4) = 2 \cdot 210 = 420$

**25** Pick the center, $C(3, 1)$; two guards, $C(10, 2)$; two tackles from the 8 remaining linemen, $C(8, 2)$;

two ends, $C(4, 2)$; two halfbacks, $C(6, 2)$; the quarterback, $C(3, 1)$; and the fullback, $C(4, 1)$.

The total number of different ways that a team can be selected from the squad is

$$3 \cdot C(10, 2) \cdot C(8, 2) \cdot C(4, 2) \cdot C(6, 2) \cdot 3 \cdot 4 = 3 \cdot 45 \cdot 28 \cdot 6 \cdot 15 \cdot 3 \cdot 4 = 4{,}082{,}400.$$

**26** There would be 7! orderings if the keys were in a row. Since the keys are on a ring, any unique ordering can be shifted to 7 different positions and would be counted as only 1 ordering. $\frac{7!}{7} = 6! = 720$

**27** There are $C(12, 3) = 220$ ways to pick the men and $C(8, 2) = 28$ ways to pick the women.

By the fundamental counting principle, the total number of ways to pick the committee is $220 \cdot 28 = 6160$.

**28** If we thought of 6 positions for birth order, the girls could be selected $C(6, 3)$ ways to be put in those positions and the boys would fill the remaining positions.                          $C(6, 3) = 20$

**29** We need 3 U's out of 8 moves. $C(8, 3) = \dfrac{8!}{(8-3)!\, 3!} = \dfrac{8!}{5!\, 3!} = 56$

**30** We need 6 U's out of 15 moves. $C(15, 6) = \dfrac{15!}{(15-6)!\, 6!} = \dfrac{15!}{9!\, 6!} = 5005$

**31** (a) We want 6 of the 49 numbers and order is not important. $C(49, 6) = \dfrac{49!}{43!\, 6!} = 13{,}983{,}816$

(b) There are 24 even numbers from 1 to 49. $C(24, 6) = \dfrac{24!}{18!\, 6!} = 134{,}596$

**32** There are $C(10, 2) = 45$ ways to pick the two faculty members to share an office.

There are 9! ways to pick the offices. $C(10, 2) \cdot 9! = 16{,}329{,}600$

**33** Let $n$ denote the number of players. A match consists of 2 players. $C(n, 2) = 45 \;\Rightarrow\; \dfrac{n!}{(n-2)!\, 2!} = 45 \;\Rightarrow$

$\dfrac{n \cdot (n-1) \cdot (n-2)!}{(n-2)! \cdot 2} = 45 \;\Rightarrow\; n(n-1) = 90 \;\Rightarrow\; n^2 - n - 90 = 0 \;\Rightarrow\; (n-10)(n+9) = 0 \;\Rightarrow$

$n = 10 \ \{\text{since } n > 0\}$

**34** (a) There are 2 answers for each question. $2^{20} = 1{,}048{,}576$

(b) Select the 10 questions to be answered correctly. $C(20, 10) = 184{,}756$

**35** Each team must win 3 of the first 6 games for the series to be extended to a 7th game. $C(6, 3) = \dfrac{6!}{3!\, 3!} = 20$

**36** (a) Select 3 of the 8 vertices to form a triangle. $C(8, 3) = 56$

(b) Select 4 of the 8 vertices to form a quadrilateral. $C(8, 4) = 70$

**37** They may have computed $C(31, 3)$, which is 4495.

**38** Consider each condiment as either being *on* or *off*. Hence, there are 2 choices for each condiment and $2^8 = 256$ possible combinations. Alternatively, we could calculate $\sum_{k=0}^{8} \binom{8}{k}$, which is also 256.

**39** (a) The amounts received are the same, so the order of selection *is not* important, and we use a combination.
$$C(1000, 30) = \frac{1000!}{970!\, 30!} \approx 2.43 \times 10^{57}$$

(b) The amounts received are different, so the order of selection *is* important, and we use a permutation.
$$P(1000, 30) = \frac{1000!}{970!} \approx 6.44 \times 10^{89}$$

**40** (a) The order of selection *is not* important, so we have $C(12, 4) = 495$.

(b) The order of selection is important, so we have $P(12, 4) = 11{,}880$.

**41** We want to select 3 of the 4 kings and 2 of the remaining 48 cards. The order of selection is not important, so we use combinations. Any of the groups of 3 kings can be selected with any pair of the remaining 48 cards, so by the fundamental counting principle the total number of hands is $C(4, 3) \cdot C(48, 2) = 4 \cdot 1128 = 4512$.

**42** We want 7 of the 13 spades and 6 of the remaining 39 cards.
$$C(13, 7) \cdot C(39, 6) = 1716 \cdot 3{,}262{,}623 = 5{,}598{,}661{,}068$$

**43** (a) $S_1 = \binom{1}{1} + \binom{1}{3} + \binom{1}{5} + \cdots = 1 + 0 + 0 + \cdots = 1$.
$S_2 = \binom{2}{1} + \binom{2}{3} + \binom{2}{5} + \cdots = 2 + 0 + 0 + \cdots = 2$.
$S_3 = 3 + 1 + 0 + \cdots = 4$. $S_4 = 4 + 4 + 0 + \cdots = 8$.
$$S_5 = 16, \ S_6 = 32, \ S_7 = 64, \ S_8 = 128, \ S_9 = 256, \ S_{10} = 512.$$

(b) It appears that $S_n = 2^{n-1}$.

**44** (a) $S_1 = 1$ and $S_n = 0$ for $n = 2, 3, 4, \ldots, 10$.        (b) $S_1 = 1$ and $S_n = 0$ for $n > 1$.

**45** (a) Graph the values of $C(10, 1), C(10, 2), C(10, 3), \ldots, C(10, 10)$.

(b) The maximum value of $C(10, r)$ is 252 and occurs at $r = 5$.

[0, 10] by [0, 300, 50]          [0, 13] by [0, 2000, 500]

*Figure 45*                    *Figure 46*

**46** (a) Graph the values of $C(13, 1), C(13, 2), C(13, 3), \ldots, C(13, 13)$.

(b) The maximum value of $C(13, r)$ is 1716 and occurs at $r = 6, 7$.

**47** (a) Graph the values of $C(19, 1), C(19, 2), C(19, 3), \ldots, C(19, 19)$.

    (b) The maximum value of $C(19, r)$ is 92,378 and occurs at $r = 9, 10$.

            [0, 19] by [0, $10^5$, $10^4$]                          [0, 20] by [0, 2E5, 5E4]

                    *Figure 47*                                  *Figure 48*

**48** (a) Graph the values of $C(20, 1), C(20, 2), C(20, 3), \ldots, C(20, 20)$.

    (b) The maximum value of $C(20, r)$ is 184,756 and occurs at $r = 10$.

**49** $C(n, r - 1) + C(n, r) = \dfrac{n!}{[n - (r - 1)]!(r - 1)!} + \dfrac{n!}{(n - r)!\, r!}$

$$= \frac{n!}{(n - r + 1)!(r - 1)!} + \frac{n!}{(n - r)!\, r!}$$

$$= \frac{n!}{(n - r + 1)(n - r)!(r - 1)!} + \frac{n!}{(n - r)!\, r(r - 1)!} = \frac{n!\, r + n!(n - r + 1)}{(n - r + 1)(n - r)!\, r(r - 1)!}$$

$$= \frac{n![r + (n - r + 1)]}{(n - r + 1)!\, r!} = \frac{n!(n + 1)}{(n - r + 1)!\, r!} = \frac{(n + 1)!}{(n - r + 1)!\, r!} = \frac{(n + 1)!}{r![(n + 1) - r]!}$$

$$= C(n + 1, r)$$

## 9.8 Exercises

**1** (a) The sample space is the 52-card deck, so $n(S) = 52$. Let $E$ be the event of drawing a king.

    There are 4 kings, so the probability is $P(E) = \dfrac{n(E)}{n(S)} = \dfrac{4}{52} = \dfrac{1}{13}$.

    There are $52 - 4 = 48$ ways for $E'$ to occur. The odds are $n(E)$ to $n(E')$, which are 4 to 48, or 1 to 12.

    (b) There are 4 queens. $P(E) = \frac{4}{52} + \frac{4}{52} = \frac{8}{52} = \frac{2}{13}$; $O(E)$ are 8 to 44, or 2 to 11

    (c) There are 4 jacks. $P(E) = \frac{4}{52} + \frac{4}{52} + \frac{4}{52} = \frac{12}{52} = \frac{3}{13}$; $O(E)$ are 12 to 40, or 3 to 10

**2** (a) Let $E$ be the event of drawing a heart. There are 13 hearts. $P(E) = \frac{13}{52} = \frac{1}{4}$; $O(E)$ are 13 to 39, or 1 to 3

    (b) There are 13 diamonds. $P(E) = \frac{13}{52} + \frac{13}{52} = \frac{26}{52} = \frac{1}{2}$; $O(E)$ are 26 to 26, or 1 to 1

    (c) There are 13 clubs. $P(E) = \frac{13}{52} + \frac{13}{52} + \frac{13}{52} = \frac{39}{52} = \frac{3}{4}$; $O(E)$ are 39 to 13, or 3 to 1

**3** The sample space is $S = \{1, 2, 3, 4, 5, 6\}$, so $n(S) = 6$.

    (a) $P(\text{rolling a } 4) = \frac{1}{6}$. There's 1 way to get a 4 and 5 ways to not get a 4, so $O(E)$ are 1 to 5.

    (b) $P(\text{rolling a } 6) = \frac{1}{6}$; $O(E)$ are 1 to 5.

    (c) $P(\text{rolling a 4 or 6}) = \frac{1}{6} + \frac{1}{6} = \frac{2}{6} = \frac{1}{3}$; $O(E)$ are 2 to 4, or 1 to 2.

**4** (a) $P(\text{rolling an even number } (2, 4, \text{or } 6)) = \frac{3}{6}$; $O(E)$ are 3 to 3, or 1 to 1

    (b) $P(\text{rolling a } 5) = \frac{1}{6}$; $O(E)$ are 1 to 5

(c) $P(\text{rolling an even number or a 5}) = \frac{3}{6} + \frac{1}{6} = \frac{4}{6} = \frac{2}{3}$; $O(E)$ are 4 to 2, or 2 to 1

**5** $n(S) = 5 + 6 + 4 = 15$

(a) $P(\text{drawing a red ball}) = \frac{5}{15} = \frac{1}{3}$; $O(E)$ are 5 to 10, or 1 to 2.

(b) $P(\text{drawing a green ball}) = \frac{6}{15} = \frac{2}{5}$; $O(E)$ are 6 to 9, or 2 to 3.

(c) $P(\text{drawing a red or white ball}) = \frac{5}{15} + \frac{4}{15} = \frac{9}{15} = \frac{3}{5}$; $O(E)$ are 9 to 6, or 3 to 2

**6** $n(S) = 5 + 6 + 4 = 15$

(a) $P(\text{drawing a white ball}) = \frac{4}{15}$; $O(E)$ are 4 to 11

(b) $P(\text{drawing a green or white ball}) = \frac{6}{15} + \frac{4}{15} = \frac{10}{15} = \frac{2}{3}$; $O(E)$ are 10 to 5, or 2 to 1

(c) $P(\text{drawing a "not green" ball}) = 1 - \frac{6}{15} = \frac{9}{15} = \frac{3}{5}$; $O(E)$ are 9 to 6, or 3 to 2

**7** The following table summarizes the results for the sum of two dice being tossed.

Notice the symmetry in the second row about the sum of 7.

| Sum of two dice | 2 | 3 | 4 | 5 | 6 | 7 | 8 | 9 | 10 | 11 | 12 |
|---|---|---|---|---|---|---|---|---|---|---|---|
| Number of ways possible | 1 | 2 | 3 | 4 | 5 | 6 | 5 | 4 | 3 | 2 | 1 |

(a) $P(\text{sum is 11}) = \frac{2}{36} = \frac{1}{18}$; $O(E)$ are 2 to 34, or 1 to 17

(b) $P(\text{sum is 8}) = \frac{5}{36}$; $O(E)$ are 5 to 31

(c) $P(\text{sum is 11 or 8}) = \frac{2}{36} + \frac{5}{36} = \frac{7}{36}$; $O(E)$ are 7 to 29

**8** (a) $P(10) + P(11) + P(12) = \frac{3}{36} + \frac{2}{36} + \frac{1}{36} = \frac{6}{36} = \frac{1}{6}$; $O(E)$ are 6 to 30, or 1 to 5

(b) $P(3) + P(5) + P(7) + P(9) + P(11) = \frac{2}{36} + \frac{4}{36} + \frac{6}{36} + \frac{4}{36} + \frac{2}{36} = \frac{18}{36} = \frac{1}{2}$; $O(E)$ are 18 to 18, or 1 to 1

**9** $n(S) = 6 \times 6 \times 6 = 216$. There are 6 ways to make a sum of 5 (3 with 1, 1, 3 and 3 with 1, 2, 2).

$$P(\text{sum is 5}) = \frac{6}{216} = \frac{1}{36}.$$

**10** We must have a 6, not a 6, and not a 6. There are $3(1 \cdot 5 \cdot 5) = 75$ ways this can occur.

$$P(\text{a 6 turns up on exactly one die}) = \frac{75}{216} = \frac{25}{72}.$$

**11** There are 2 choices for each of the 3 coins, so $n(S) = 2 \cdot 2 \cdot 2 = 8$. Getting two heads to turn up is the same as getting one tail to turn up. There are 3 ways to get one tail: THH, HTH, HHT. The probability is $\frac{3}{2^3} = \frac{3}{8}$.

**12** There are 2 choices for each of the 4 coins, so $n(S) = 2 \cdot 2 \cdot 2 \cdot 2 = 16$. There are $C(4, 2)$ ways to obtain two heads from 4 coins. The probability is $\frac{C(4, 2)}{2^4} = \frac{6}{16} = \frac{3}{8}$.

**13** If $P(E) = \frac{5}{7}$, then $O(E)$ are 5 to 2 and $O(E') $ are 2 to 5.

**14** If $P(E) = 0.4 = \frac{4}{10} = \frac{2}{5}$, then $O(E)$ are 2 to 3 and $O(E')$ are 3 to 2.

**15** If $O(E)$ are 9 to 5, then $O(E')$ are 5 to 9 and $P(E) = \frac{9}{5 + 9} = \frac{9}{14}$.

**16** If $O(E')$ are 7 to 3, then $O(E)$ are 3 to 7 and $P(E) = \frac{3}{3 + 7} = \frac{3}{10}$.

**17** $P(E) \approx 0.659 = \frac{659}{1000}$, so $n(E) = 659$ and $n(E') = 1000 - 659 = 341$ and $O(E)$ are 659 to 341.

Divide both numbers by 341 to get odds of 1.93 to 1.

18 $P(E) \approx 0.822 = \frac{822}{1000}$, so $n(E) = 822$ and $n(E') = 1000 - 822 = 178$ and $O(E)$ are 822 to 178.

Divide both numbers by 178 to get odds of 4.62 to 1.

**Note:** For Exercises 19–24, there are $C(52, 5) = 2,598,960$ ways to draw 5 cards.

19 There are 13 denominations (or ranks) to pick from and any one of them (2, 3, 4, 5, 6, 7, 8, 9, 10, J, Q, K, A) could be combined with any one of the remaining 48 cards. $\frac{48 \cdot 13}{C(52, 5)} = \frac{624}{2,598,960} = \frac{1}{4165} \approx 0.00024$

20 Pick the 3 aces from 4, $C(4, 3)$, and the 2 kings from 4, $C(4, 2)$. $\frac{C(4, 3) \cdot C(4, 2)}{C(52, 5)} = \frac{1}{108,290} \approx 0.00000923$

21 Pick 4 of the 13 diamonds and 1 of the 13 spades. $\frac{C(13, 4) \cdot C(13, 1)}{C(52, 5)} = \frac{715 \cdot 13}{2,598,960} = \frac{143}{39,984} \approx 0.00358$

22 Pick 5 of the 12 face cards. $\frac{C(12, 5)}{C(52, 5)} = \frac{792}{2,598,960} = \frac{33}{108,290} \approx 0.000305$

23 Pick 5 of the 13 cards in one suit. There are 4 suits. $\frac{C(13, 5) \cdot 4}{C(52, 5)} = \frac{1287 \cdot 4}{2,598,960} = \frac{33}{16,660} \approx 0.00198$

24 There are 4 of these hands, one in each suit. $\frac{4}{C(52, 5)} = \frac{1}{649,740} \approx 0.00000154$

25 Let $E_1$ be the event that the number is odd, $E_2$ that the number is prime. $E_1 = \{1, 3, 5\}$ and $E_2 = \{2, 3, 5\}$.

$$P(E_1 \cup E_2) = P(E_1) + P(E_2) - P(E_1 \cap E_2) = \frac{3}{6} + \frac{3}{6} - \frac{2}{6} = \frac{4}{6} = \frac{2}{3}.$$

26 Let $E_1$ be the event that the card is red, $E_2$ that the card is a face card.

$$P(E_1 \cup E_2) = P(E_1) + P(E_2) - P(E_1 \cap E_2) = \frac{26}{52} + \frac{12}{52} - \frac{6}{52} = \frac{32}{52} = \frac{8}{13}.$$

27 The probability that the player does *not* get a hit is $1 - 0.326 = 0.674$. The probability that the player does not get a hit four times in a row is $(0.674) \cdot (0.674) \cdot (0.674) \cdot (0.674) = (0.674)^4 \approx 0.2064$.

28 $P(\text{at least } 1) = 1 - P(\text{none}) = 1 - (0.1)^2 = 0.99$

29 (a) $P(E_2) = P(2) + P(3) + P(4) = 0.10 + 0.15 + 0.20 = 0.45$

(b) $P(E_1 \cap E_2) = P(2) = 0.10$

(c) $P(E_1 \cup E_2) = P(E_1) + P(E_2) - P(E_1 \cap E_2) = 0.35 + 0.45 - 0.10 = 0.70$

(d) $P(E_2 \cup E_3') = P(E_2) + P(E_3') - P(E_2 \cap E_3')$. $E_3' = \{1, 2, 3, 5\}$ and $E_2 \cap E_3' = \{2, 3\}$ $\Rightarrow$

$$P(E_2 \cup E_3') = 0.45 + 0.75 - 0.25 = 0.95.$$

30 (a) $P(E_2) = P(3) + P(4) = 0.15 + 0.20 = 0.35$      (b) $P(E_1 \cap E_2) = P(3) = 0.15$

(c) $P(E_1 \cup E_2) = P(E_1) + P(E_2) - P(E_1 \cap E_2) = 0.55 + 0.35 - 0.15 = 0.75$

(d) $P(E_2 \cup E_3') = P(E_2) + P(E_3') - P(E_2 \cap E_3')$. $E_3' = \{1, 2, 3\}$ and $E_2 \cap E_3' = \{3\}$ $\Rightarrow$

$$P(E_2 \cup E_3') = 0.35 + 0.50 - 0.15 = 0.70.$$

**Note:** For Exercises 31–32, there are $C(60, 5) = 5,461,512$ ways to draw 5 chips.

31 (a) We want 5 blue and 0 non-blue. There are 20 blue and 40 non-blue chips in the box.

$$P(5 \text{ blue}) = \frac{C(20, 5) \cdot C(40, 0)}{C(60, 5)} = \frac{15,504 \cdot 1}{5,461,512} = \frac{34}{11,977} \approx 0.0028.$$

(b) $P(\text{at least 1 green}) = 1 - P(\text{no green})$

$$= 1 - \frac{C(30,0) \cdot C(30,5)}{C(60,5)} = 1 - \frac{1 \cdot 142{,}506}{5{,}461{,}512} = 1 - \frac{117}{4484} = \frac{4367}{4484} \approx 0.9739.$$

(c) $P(\text{at most 1 red}) = P(0 \text{ red}) + P(1 \text{ red})$

$$= \frac{C(10,0) \cdot C(50,5)}{C(60,5)} + \frac{C(10,1) \cdot C(50,4)}{C(60,5)}$$

$$= \frac{1 \cdot 2{,}118{,}760}{5{,}461{,}512} + \frac{10 \cdot 230{,}300}{5{,}461{,}512} = \frac{4{,}421{,}760}{5{,}461{,}512} = \frac{26{,}320}{32{,}509} \approx 0.8096.$$

**32** (a) We want 4 green and 1 non-green. $P(4 \text{ green}) = \dfrac{C(30,4) \cdot C(30,1)}{C(60,5)} = \dfrac{27{,}405 \cdot 30}{5{,}461{,}512} = \dfrac{675}{4484} \approx 0.1505.$

(b) This event is the complement of part (c) in the previous exercise.

$$P(\text{at least 2 red}) = 1 - P(\text{at most 1 red}) \approx 1 - 0.8096 = 0.1904.$$

(c) $P(\text{at most 2 blue}) = P(0 \text{ blue}) + P(1 \text{ blue}) + P(2 \text{ blue})$

$$= \frac{C(20,0) \cdot C(40,5)}{C(60,5)} + \frac{C(20,1) \cdot C(40,4)}{C(60,5)} + \frac{C(20,2) \cdot C(40,3)}{C(60,5)}$$

$$= \frac{1 \cdot 658{,}008}{5{,}461{,}512} + \frac{20 \cdot 91{,}390}{5{,}461{,}512} + \frac{190 \cdot 9880}{5{,}461{,}512} = \frac{4{,}363{,}008}{5{,}461{,}512} = \frac{181{,}792}{227{,}563} \approx 0.7989.$$

**33** (a) We want 8 correct of a possible 8 questions. $\dfrac{C(8,8)}{2^8} = \dfrac{1}{256} \approx 0.00391$

(b) We want 7 correct of a possible 8 questions. $\dfrac{C(8,7)}{2^8} = \dfrac{8}{256} = \dfrac{1}{32} = 0.03125$

(c) We want 6 correct of a possible 8 questions. $\dfrac{C(8,6)}{2^8} = \dfrac{28}{256} = \dfrac{7}{64} = 0.109375$

(d) $P(\text{at least six}) = P(6, 7, \text{or } 8) = \dfrac{C(8,6) + C(8,7) + C(8,8)}{2^8} = \dfrac{28 + 8 + 1}{256} = \dfrac{37}{256} \approx 0.14453$

**34** $P(3 \text{ men and 3 women}) = \dfrac{C(8,3) \cdot C(14,3)}{C(22,6)} = \dfrac{56 \cdot 364}{74{,}613} = \dfrac{2912}{10{,}659} \approx 0.2732$

**35** $P(\text{obtaining at least one ace}) = 1 - P(\text{no aces})$

$$= 1 - \frac{C(4,0) \cdot C(48,5)}{C(52,5)} = 1 - \frac{1 \cdot 1{,}712{,}304}{2{,}598{,}960} = 1 - \frac{35{,}673}{54{,}145} = \frac{18{,}472}{54{,}145} \approx 0.34116$$

**36** $P(\text{at least 1 heart}) = 1 - P(\text{no hearts})$

$$= 1 - \frac{C(13,0) \cdot C(39,5)}{C(52,5)} = 1 - \frac{1 \cdot 575{,}757}{2{,}598{,}960} = 1 - \frac{2109}{9520} = \frac{7411}{9520} \approx 0.7785$$

**37** (a) We may use ordered pairs to represent the outcomes of the sample space $S$ of the experiment. A representative outcome is (nine of clubs, 3). The number of outcomes in the sample space $S$ is $n(S) = 52 \cdot 6 = 312$.

(b) For each integer $k$, where $2 \le k \le 6$, there are 4 ways to obtain an outcome of the form $(k, k)$ since there are 4 suits. Because there are 5 values of $k$, $n(E_1) = 5 \cdot 4 = 20$. $n(E_1') = n(S) - n(E_1) = 312 - 20 = 292$.

$$P(E_1) = \frac{n(E_1)}{n(S)} = \frac{20}{312} = \frac{5}{78}.$$

(c) No, if $E_2$ or $E_3$ occurs, then the other event may occur. Yes, the occurrence of either $E_2$ or $E_3$ has no effect on the other event. $P(E_2) = \dfrac{n(E_2)}{n(S)} = \dfrac{12 \cdot 6}{312} = \dfrac{72}{312} = \dfrac{3}{13}$ and $P(E_3) = \dfrac{n(E_3)}{n(S)} = \dfrac{52 \cdot 3}{312} = \dfrac{156}{312} = \dfrac{1}{2}$.

Since $E_2$ and $E_3$ are independent, $P(E_2 \cap E_3) = P(E_2) \cdot P(E_3) = \frac{3}{13} \cdot \frac{1}{2} = \frac{3}{26} = \frac{36}{312}$.

$P(E_2 \cup E_3) = P(E_2) + P(E_3) - P(E_2 \cap E_3) = \frac{72}{312} + \frac{156}{312} - \frac{36}{312} = \frac{192}{312} = \frac{8}{13}$.

(d) Yes, if $E_1$ or $E_2$ occurs, then the other event cannot occur. No, the occurrence of either $E_1$ or $E_2$ influences the occurrence of the other event. Remember, (non-empty) *mutually exclusive events **cannot** be independent events*. Since $E_1$ and $E_2$ are mutually exclusive, $P(E_1 \cap E_2) = 0$ and

$$P(E_1 \cup E_2) = P(E_1) + P(E_2) = \tfrac{20}{312} + \tfrac{72}{312} = \tfrac{92}{312} = \tfrac{23}{78}.$$

**38** (a) A representative outcome of the sample space $S$ of the experiment is C7.

The number of outcomes in the sample space $S$ is $n(S) = 26 \cdot 10 = 260$.

(b) The digits 1, 2, 3, 4, 5, and 6 can be matched with 3 letters each. For example, A1, K1, and U1 are the outcomes with 1 as the selected digit. The digits $7, 8, 9,$ and 0 can be matched with 2 letters each. Thus, $n(E_1) = 6 \cdot 3 + 4 \cdot 2 = 26$. This answer makes sense because each letter can be paired with exactly one digit. $n(E_1') = n(S) - n(E_1) = 260 - 26 = 234.$   $\qquad P(E_1) = \dfrac{n(E_1)}{n(S)} = \dfrac{26}{260} = \dfrac{1}{10}.$

(c) No, if $E_2$ or $E_3$ occurs, then the other event may occur.

Yes, the occurrence of either $E_2$ or $E_3$ has no effect on the other event.
$$P(E_2) = \dfrac{n(E_2)}{n(S)} = \dfrac{5 \cdot 10}{260} = \dfrac{50}{260} = \dfrac{5}{26} \text{ and } P(E_3) = \dfrac{n(E_3)}{n(S)} = \dfrac{26 \cdot 4}{260} = \dfrac{104}{260} = \dfrac{2}{5}.$$
Since $E_2$ and $E_3$ are independent, $P(E_2 \cap E_3) = P(E_2) \cdot P(E_3) = \tfrac{5}{26} \cdot \tfrac{2}{5} = \tfrac{1}{13} = \tfrac{20}{260}.$
$$P(E_2 \cup E_3) = P(E_2) + P(E_3) - P(E_2 \cap E_3) = \tfrac{50}{260} + \tfrac{104}{260} - \tfrac{20}{260} = \tfrac{134}{260} = \tfrac{67}{130}.$$

(d) The numerical values of the five vowels are: A-1, E-5, I-9, O-15, U-21. Since if $E_2$ or $E_4$ occurs, the other event cannot occur, the events are mutually exclusive.

No, the occurrence of either $E_2$ or $E_4$ influences the occurrence of the other event. Remember, (non-empty) *mutually exclusive events **cannot** be independent events*.

Since $E_2$ and $E_4$ are mutually exclusive, $P(E_2 \cap E_4) = 0$. $P(E_4) = \dfrac{n(E_4)}{n(S)} = \dfrac{13 \cdot 10}{260} = \dfrac{130}{260} = \dfrac{1}{2}.$

Since $E_2$ and $E_4$ are mutually exclusive, $P(E_2 \cup E_4) = P(E_2) + P(E_4) = \tfrac{50}{260} + \tfrac{130}{260} = \tfrac{180}{260} = \tfrac{9}{13}.$

**39** $P(\text{sum} > 5) = 1 - P(\text{sum} \le 5) = 1 - P(\text{sum is } 2, 3, 4, \text{ or } 5) = 1 - \left( \tfrac{1}{36} + \tfrac{2}{36} + \tfrac{3}{36} + \tfrac{4}{36} \right) = 1 - \tfrac{10}{36} = \tfrac{26}{36} = \tfrac{13}{18}.$

**40** There is 1 way to obtain a sum of 18 $(6, 6, 6)$, 3 ways for a sum of 17 $(6, 6, 5; \ 6, 5, 6; \ 5, 6, 6)$, and 6 ways for a sum of 16 (3 with $6, 5, 5$ and 3 with $6, 6, 4$).

$$P(\text{sum} < 16) = 1 - P(\text{sum} \ge 16) = 1 - \left( \tfrac{6}{216} + \tfrac{3}{216} + \tfrac{1}{216} \right) = 1 - \tfrac{10}{216} = \tfrac{206}{216} = \tfrac{103}{108} \approx 0.9537.$$

**41** (a) Each birth is independent of the others and the probability of having a boy is $\tfrac{1}{2}$.

$$P(\text{all boys}) = \tfrac{1}{2} \cdot \tfrac{1}{2} \cdot \tfrac{1}{2} \cdot \tfrac{1}{2} \cdot \tfrac{1}{2} = \tfrac{1}{32} = 0.03125.$$

(b) $P(\text{at least one girl}) = 1 - P(\text{all boys}) = 1 - \tfrac{1}{32} = \tfrac{31}{32} = 0.96875.$

**42** $P(\text{bell and bell and bell}) = \tfrac{5}{20} \cdot \tfrac{4}{20} \cdot \tfrac{2}{20} = \tfrac{40}{8000} = \tfrac{1}{200} = 0.005$

**43** There are 4! ways to place the cards, so $n(S) = 4!$.

(a) $\dfrac{C(4, 4)}{4!} = \dfrac{1}{24} \approx 0.04167$ \qquad\qquad (b) $\dfrac{C(4, 2)}{4!} = \dfrac{6}{24} = \dfrac{1}{4} = 0.25$

**44** (a) There is 1 chance in 216 that all three dice show the same value and there are six different values.

$$6 \cdot \tfrac{1}{216} = \tfrac{6}{216} = \tfrac{1}{36} = 0.02\overline{7}$$

(b) After the first value is chosen, the second value could be one of 5 others, and third could be one of 4 others.

$$\dfrac{P(6, 3)}{6^3} = \dfrac{120}{216} = \dfrac{5}{9} = 0.\overline{5}$$

(c)  Same number of dots: $6\left(\dfrac{1}{6^n}\right) = \dfrac{1}{6^{n-1}}$ for $n \geq 1$.  Dots all different: $\dfrac{P(6, n)}{6^n}$ for $n \leq 6$ and 0 for $n > 6$

**45** (a)  The 3, 4, or 5 on the left die would need to combine with a 4, 3, or 2 on the right die to sum to 7,

   but the right die only has 1, 5, or 6.  The probability is 0.

(b)  To obtain 8, we would need a 3 on the left die and a 5 on the right.     $\dfrac{1}{3} \cdot \dfrac{1}{3} = \dfrac{1}{9} = 0.\overline{1}$

**46** There is 1 way to obtain a sum of 3, 3 ways for a sum of 4 (1, 1, 2; 1, 2, 1; 2, 1, 1), 6 ways for a sum of 5 (three with

   1, 1, 3 and three with 1, 2, 2), and 10 ways for a sum of 6 (three with 1, 1, 4; six with 1, 2, 3; one with 2, 2, 2).

   $$\frac{1}{729} + \frac{3}{729} + \frac{6}{729} + \frac{10}{729} = \frac{20}{729} \approx 0.0274$$

**47** There are 40,025 smoking-related deaths that are not in any of the 3 categories.

(a)  $P(\text{cardiovascular disease or cancer}) = \dfrac{148,605 + 155,761}{442,398} = \dfrac{304,366}{442,398} \approx 0.688$

(b)  $P(not \text{ respiratory}) = 1 - P(\text{respiratory}) = \dfrac{442,398 - 98,007}{442,398} = \dfrac{344,391}{442,398} \approx 0.778$

**48** (a)  $P(\text{between 6 A.M. and midnight}) = \dfrac{60.4 + 18.3}{8.2 + 60.4 + 18.3} = \dfrac{78.7}{86.9} \approx 0.906$

(b)  $P(\text{between midnight and 6 A.M.}) = \frac{8.2}{86.9} \approx 0.094$, or by using the complement of part (a), $1 - 0.906 = 0.094$.

**49** Start the tree diagram by making branches for those with cancer ($C$, 2%) and those without cancer ($C'$, 98%).

   On the $C$ branch, make a branch for those exposed to high levels of arsenic ($E$, 70%) and a branch for those not

   exposed ($E'$, 30%).  On the $C'$ branch, make a branch for those exposed to high levels of arsenic ($E$, 10%) and a

   branch for those not exposed ($E'$, 90%).  Find the products: $0.02 \cdot 0.70 = \mathbf{0.014}$,  $0.02 \cdot 0.30 = \mathbf{0.006}$,

   $0.98 \cdot 0.10 = \mathbf{0.098}$, and $0.98 \cdot 0.90 = \mathbf{0.882}$.  Note that the sum of the boldface numbers equals 1.

   The fraction of people that have been exposed to high levels of arsenic and have cancer is

   $$\frac{\text{exposed and have cancer}}{\text{all those exposed}} = \frac{C \text{ and } E}{C \text{ and } E + C' \text{ and } E} = \frac{0.014}{0.014 + 0.098} = \frac{0.014}{0.112} = 0.125, \text{ a percentage of 12.5\%.}$$

*Figure 49*

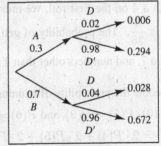

*Figure 50*

**50** From the figure, the fraction of defective chips that are from supplier $B$ is

   $$\frac{\text{from } B \text{ and defective}}{\text{all defective chips}} = \frac{B \text{ and } D}{A \text{ and } D + B \text{ and } D} = \frac{0.028}{0.006 + 0.028} = \frac{0.028}{0.034} \approx 0.824,$$

so the percentage is about 82.4%.

**51** (a)  The ball must take 4 "lefts".  $P(4 \text{ lefts}) = \dfrac{1}{2} \cdot \dfrac{1}{2} \cdot \dfrac{1}{2} \cdot \dfrac{1}{2} = \dfrac{1}{16} = 0.0625 \left\{ \text{or use } \dfrac{C(4,4)}{2^4} \right\}$

(b)  We need two "lefts".  $P(2 \text{ lefts}) = \dfrac{C(4,2)}{2^4} = \dfrac{6}{16} = \dfrac{3}{8} = 0.375$

**52** (a)  There are 18 black slots.  $P(\text{ball lands in a black slot}) = \dfrac{18}{38} = \dfrac{9}{19} \approx 0.4737$

(b)  $P(\text{ball lands in a black slot twice in succession}) = \dfrac{18}{38} \cdot \dfrac{18}{38} = \dfrac{9}{19} \cdot \dfrac{9}{19} = \dfrac{81}{361} \approx 0.2244$

**53** For one ticket, $P(E) = \dfrac{n(E)}{n(S)} = \dfrac{C(6,6)}{C(54,6)} = \dfrac{1}{25,827,165}$.

For two tickets, $P(E) = \dfrac{2 \times 1}{25,827,165}$, or about 1 chance in 13 million.

**54** $P(\text{match } 5) = \dfrac{C(6,5) \times C(48,1)}{C(54,6)} = \dfrac{6 \times 48}{25,827,165} = \dfrac{288}{25,827,165}$.

$P(\text{match } 4) = \dfrac{C(6,4) \times C(48,2)}{C(54,6)} = \dfrac{15 \times 1128}{25,827,165} = \dfrac{16,920}{25,827,165}$.

$P(\text{win}) = P(\text{match } 4, 5, \text{ or } 6) = \dfrac{288}{25,827,165} + \dfrac{16,920}{25,827,165} + \dfrac{1}{25,827,165} = \dfrac{17,209}{25,827,165} \approx 0.000666$

(about 1 chance in 1500).

**55** The probability that the first bulb is not defective is $\frac{195}{200}$ since 195 of the 200 bulbs are not defective. If the first bulb is not replaced and not defective, then there are 199 bulbs left, and 194 of them are not defective. The probability that the second bulb is not defective is then $\frac{194}{199}$. Thus, the probability that both bulbs are not defective is $\frac{195}{200} \times \frac{194}{199} = \frac{37,830}{39,800} \approx 0.9505$. The event that either light bulb is defective is the complement of the event that neither bulb is defective. The probability that the sample will be rejected is $1 - \frac{37,830}{39,800} = \frac{1970}{39,800} \approx 0.0495$.

**56** (a) Let $E_1$ denote the event that the man is alive 10 years from now and $E_2$ that the woman is alive in 10 years. Since their life expectancies are unrelated, they are independent events. Thus,
$$P(E_1 \cap E_2) = P(E_1) \cdot P(E_2) = 0.74 \times 0.94 = 0.6956.$$

(b) The probability that the man will be dead in 10 years is $1 - 0.74 = 0.26$ and the probability for the woman is $1 - 0.94 = 0.06$. Since their life expectancies are independent events, the probability that both of them will be dead in 10 years is $0.26 \times 0.06 = 0.0156$.

(c) Using the complement of part (b), we have $1 - 0.0156 = 0.9844$.

**57** (a) $P(7 \text{ or } 11) = P(7) + P(11) = \frac{6}{36} + \frac{2}{36} = \frac{8}{36}$

(b) To win with a 4 on the first roll, we must first get a 4, and then get another 4 before a 7. The probability of getting a 4 is $\dfrac{3}{36}$. The probability of getting another 4 before a 7 is $\dfrac{3}{3+6}$ since there are 3 ways to get a 4, 6 ways to get a 7, and numbers other than 4 and 7 are immaterial. Thus, $P(\text{winning with } 4) = \dfrac{3}{36} \cdot \dfrac{3}{3+6} = \dfrac{1}{36}$.

(c) Let $P(k)$ denote the probability of winning a pass line bet with the number $k$. We first note that $P(4) = P(10)$, $P(5) = P(9)$, and $P(6) = P(8)$.

$P(\text{winning}) = 2 \cdot P(4) + 2 \cdot P(5) + 2 \cdot P(6) + P(7) + P(11)$

$= 2 \cdot \dfrac{3}{36} \cdot \dfrac{3}{3+6} + 2 \cdot \dfrac{4}{36} \cdot \dfrac{4}{4+6} + 2 \cdot \dfrac{5}{36} \cdot \dfrac{5}{5+6} + \dfrac{6}{36} + \dfrac{2}{36}$

$= 2 \cdot \dfrac{1}{36} + 2 \cdot \dfrac{2}{45} + 2 \cdot \dfrac{25}{396} + \dfrac{1}{6} + \dfrac{1}{18} = \dfrac{488}{990} = \dfrac{244}{495} \approx 0.4929$

**58** (a) Using the same notation as in Exercise 57, and the additional facts that $P(2) = P(12)$ and $P(3) = P(11)$,

$P(\text{winning}) = 2 \cdot P(2) + 2 \cdot P(3) + 2 \cdot P(4) + 2 \cdot P(5) + 2 \cdot P(6) + P(7)$

$= 2 \cdot \dfrac{1}{36} \cdot \dfrac{1}{1+6} + 2 \cdot \dfrac{2}{36} \cdot \dfrac{2}{2+6} + 2 \cdot \dfrac{3}{36} \cdot \dfrac{3}{3+6} + 2 \cdot \dfrac{4}{36} \cdot \dfrac{4}{4+6} + 2 \cdot \dfrac{5}{36} \cdot \dfrac{5}{5+6} + \dfrac{6}{36}$

$= \dfrac{2}{36}\left(\dfrac{1}{7} + \dfrac{4}{8} + \dfrac{9}{9} + \dfrac{16}{10} + \dfrac{25}{11} + 3\right) = \dfrac{1}{18} \cdot \dfrac{6557}{770} = \dfrac{6557}{13,860} \approx 0.4731$.

Note that this probability is almost 2% less than the one for the game of craps.

**59** $\left(\frac{199}{200}\right)^n = 0.40 \quad \Rightarrow \quad \ln\left(\frac{199}{200}\right)^n = \ln 0.40 \quad \Rightarrow \quad n \ln \frac{199}{200} = \ln 0.40 \quad \Rightarrow \quad n = 183$

**60** $\left(\frac{99}{100}\right)^n = 0.40 \quad \Rightarrow \quad \ln\left(\frac{99}{100}\right)^n = \ln 0.40 \quad \Rightarrow \quad n \ln \frac{99}{100} = \ln 0.40 \quad \Rightarrow \quad n = 91$

**61** $\left(\frac{17}{20}\right)^n = 0.20 \quad \Rightarrow \quad \ln\left(\frac{17}{20}\right)^n = \ln 0.20 \quad \Rightarrow \quad n \ln \frac{17}{20} = \ln 0.20 \quad \Rightarrow \quad n = 10$

**62** $\left(\frac{22}{24}\right)^n = 0.10 \quad \Rightarrow \quad n = 26$ (27 for *at least* a 90% chance)

**63** (a) $p = P((S_1 \cap S_2) \cup (S_3 \cap S_4))$

$= P(S_1 \cap S_2) + P(S_3 \cap S_4) - P((S_1 \cap S_2) \cap (S_3 \cap S_4))$

$= P(S_1) \cdot P(S_2) + P(S_3) \cdot P(S_4) - P(S_1 \cap S_2) \cdot P(S_3 \cap S_4)$

$= P(S_1) \cdot P(S_2) + P(S_3) \cdot P(S_4) - P(S_1) \cdot P(S_2) \cdot P(S_3) \cdot P(S_4)$

Let $P(S_k) = x$. Then $p = x \cdot x + x \cdot x - x \cdot x \cdot x \cdot x = -x^4 + 2x^2$. $x = 0.9 \quad \Rightarrow \quad p = 0.9639$.

(b) $p = 0.99 \quad \Rightarrow \quad -x^4 + 2x^2 = 0.99$. The graph of $y = -x^4 + 2x^2 - 0.99$ is shown in the first figure. The region near $x = 1$ is enlarged in the second figure to show that the graph is above the $x$-axis for some values of $x$. The approximate $x$-intercepts are $\pm 0.95, \pm 1.05$. Since $0 \le P(S_k) \le 1$, $P(S_k) = 0.95$.

$[-2.25, 2.25, 0.5]$ by $[-2, 1, 0.5]$

$[0.96, 1.05, 0.5]$ by $[-0.03, 0.04, 0.5]$

**64** (a) $p = P((S_1 \cup S_2) \cup (S_3 \cap S_4)) = P(S_1 \cup S_2) + P(S_3 \cap S_4) - P((S_1 \cup S_2) \cap (S_3 \cap S_4))$

$= P(S_1 \cup S_2) + P(S_3 \cap S_4) - P(S_1 \cup S_2) \cdot P(S_3 \cap S_4)$

Let $P(S_k) = x$. Then

$P(S_1 \cup S_2) = P(S_1) + P(S_2) - P(S_1 \cap S_2) = P(S_1) + P(S_2) - P(S_1) \cdot P(S_2) = x + x - x \cdot x = 2x - x^2$.

Also, $P(S_3 \cap S_4) = P(S_3) \cdot P(S_4) = x \cdot x = x^2$.

Thus, $p = (2x - x^2) + x^2 - (2x - x^2)x^2 = x^4 - 2x^3 + 2x$. $x = 0.9 \quad \Rightarrow \quad p = 0.9981$.

(b) $p = 0.99 \quad \Rightarrow \quad x^4 - 2x^3 + 2x = 0.99$. Graph

$y = x^4 - 2x^3 + 2x - 0.99$. The approximate $x$-intercepts are $-1.00$ and $0.82$. Since $0 \le P(S_k) \le 1$, $P(S_k) = 0.82$. Note that lowering the individual probability from $0.90$ to approximately $0.82$ *only* lowers the system probability from $0.9981$ to approximately $0.99$.

$[-4.5, 4.5]$ by $[-3, 3]$

**65** (a) The number of ways that $n$ people can all have a different birthday is $P(365, n)$. The number of outcomes in the sample space is $365^n$. Thus, $p = \dfrac{P(365, n)}{365^n} = \dfrac{365!}{365^n (365 - n)!}$.

(b) $n = 32 \quad \Rightarrow \quad p = \dfrac{365!}{365^{32}\, 333!} \quad \Rightarrow \quad \ln p = \ln \dfrac{365!}{365^{32}\, 333!} \quad \Rightarrow$

$\ln p = \ln 365! - \ln 365^{32} - \ln 333! \approx (365 \ln 365 - 365) - (32 \ln 365) - (333 \ln 333 - 333) \approx -1.45$.

Thus, $p \approx e^{-1.45} \approx 0.24$. The probability that two or more people have the same birthday is $1 - p \approx 0.76$.

**66** *Using the hint*: The first person can "pick" any day, the second person can pick 1 of 364 remaining days, the third person can pick 1 of 363 remaining days, and so on.

This gives us the probability $p = \dfrac{365}{365} \cdot \dfrac{364}{365} \cdot \dfrac{363}{365} \cdots \cdots \dfrac{365 - n + 1}{365}$, which can be written $\dfrac{365!}{365^n (365 - n)!}$.

Use a calculator to multiply the probabilities. We find that if $n = 23$, the probability of everyone having a different birthday is less than $\frac{1}{2}$.

*Another way:* $p = \dfrac{365!}{365^n (365 - n)!} \;\Rightarrow\; \ln p = \ln 365! - n \ln 365 - \ln(365 - n)! \;\Rightarrow\;$

$\ln p \approx (365 \ln 365 - 365) - n \ln 365 - [(365 - n) \ln(365 - n) - (365 - n)].$

To find the value of $n$ such that $\ln p = \ln 0.5$, we graph

$y = (365 \ln 365 - 365) - x \ln 365 -$

$\qquad\qquad [(365 - x) \ln(365 - x) - (365 - x)] - \ln 0.5$

and estimate the positive $x$-intercept. From the graph, we see that this occurs at $x \approx 22.26$. Thus, if $n = 23$, the probability of everyone having a different birthday is less than $\frac{1}{2}$. The following $(n, p)$ pairs may be of interest: $(30, 0.294)$, $(40, 0.109)$, $(50, 0.030)$, $(60, 0.006)$.

$[0, 50, 10]$ by $[-1, 1, 0.5]$

**67** From Exercise 57(c), the payoff amount of \$2 has a probability of $\frac{244}{495}$. Hence, $EV = 2 \cdot \frac{244}{495} = \frac{488}{495} \approx \$0.986$, or about \$0.99. Of course, after paying \$1 to play, you can expect to lose about \$7 for every 495 one-dollar pass line bets.

**68** From Exercise 52(a), the payoff amount of \$2 has a probability of $\frac{18}{38}$. Hence, $EV = 2 \cdot \frac{18}{38} = \frac{18}{19} \approx \$0.947$,

$\qquad\qquad\qquad\qquad\qquad\qquad\qquad\qquad\qquad\qquad\qquad\qquad\qquad\qquad$ or about \$0.95.

**69** $EV = 1{,}000{,}000 \cdot \dfrac{1}{20{,}000{,}000} + 100{,}000 \cdot \dfrac{10}{20{,}000{,}000} + 10{,}000 \cdot \dfrac{100}{20{,}000{,}000} + 1000 \cdot \dfrac{1000}{20{,}000{,}000}$

$\qquad = \$0.20 \text{ \{less than the cost of a first class stamp\}}$

**70** $EV = 1000 \cdot \frac{1}{80} + 500 \cdot \frac{1}{80} + 300 \cdot \frac{1}{80} + 200 \cdot \frac{1}{80} + 100 \cdot 6 \cdot \frac{1}{80} = \$32.50$

## Chapter 9 Review Exercises

**1** $a_n = \dfrac{5n}{3 - 2n^2}$ • $a_1 = \dfrac{5(1)}{3 - 2(1)^2} = \dfrac{5}{1} = 5$, $\quad a_2 = \dfrac{5(2)}{3 - 2(2)^2} = \dfrac{10}{-5} = -2$, $\quad a_3 = \dfrac{5(3)}{3 - 2(3)^2} = \dfrac{15}{-15} = -1$,

$a_4 = \dfrac{5(4)}{3 - 2(4)^2} = \dfrac{20}{-29} = -\dfrac{20}{29}$, $\quad a_7 = \dfrac{5(7)}{3 - 2(7)^2} = \dfrac{35}{-95} = -\dfrac{7}{19}$. $\qquad\qquad$ ★ $5, -2, -1, -\frac{20}{29}; -\frac{7}{19}$

**2** $a_n = (-1)^{n+1} - (0.1)^n$ • $a_1 = (-1)^2 - (0.1)^1 = 1 - 0.1 = 0.9$, $\quad a_2 = -1 - 0.01 = -1.01$,

$a_3 = 1 - 0.001 = 0.999$, $\quad a_4 = -1 - 0.0001 = -1.0001$, $\quad a_7 = 1 - 0.0000001 = 0.9999999$.

$\qquad\qquad\qquad\qquad\qquad\qquad\qquad\qquad\qquad\qquad\qquad$ ★ $0.9, -1.01, 0.999, -1.0001; 0.9999999$

**3** $a_n = 1 + \left(-\frac{1}{2}\right)^{n-1}$ • $a_1 = 1 + \left(-\frac{1}{2}\right)^0 = 1 + 1 = 2$, $\quad a_2 = 1 + \left(-\frac{1}{2}\right)^1 = 1 - \frac{1}{2} = \frac{1}{2}$,

$a_3 = 1 + \left(-\frac{1}{2}\right)^2 = 1 + \frac{1}{4} = \frac{5}{4}$, $\quad a_4 = 1 + \left(-\frac{1}{2}\right)^3 = 1 - \frac{1}{8} = \frac{7}{8}$, $\quad a_7 = 1 + \left(-\frac{1}{2}\right)^6 = 1 + \frac{1}{64} = \frac{65}{64}$.

$\qquad\qquad\qquad\qquad\qquad\qquad\qquad\qquad\qquad\qquad\qquad\qquad\qquad$ ★ $2, \frac{1}{2}, \frac{5}{4}, \frac{7}{8}; \frac{65}{64}$

**4** $a_n = \dfrac{2^n}{(n+1)(n+2)(n+3)}$ • $a_1 = \dfrac{2^1}{(2)(3)(4)} = \dfrac{1}{(3)(4)} = \dfrac{1}{12}$, $a_2 = \dfrac{2^2}{(3)(4)(5)} = \dfrac{1}{(3)(5)} = \dfrac{1}{15}$,

$a_3 = \dfrac{2^3}{(4)(5)(6)} = \dfrac{2}{(5)(6)} = \dfrac{1}{15}$, $a_4 = \dfrac{2^4}{(5)(6)(7)} = \dfrac{2^3}{(5)(3)(7)} = \dfrac{8}{105}$, $a_7 = \dfrac{2^7}{(8)(9)(10)} = \dfrac{2^3}{(9)(5)} = \dfrac{8}{45}$.

★ $\dfrac{1}{12}, \dfrac{1}{15}, \dfrac{1}{15}, \dfrac{8}{105}; \dfrac{8}{45}$

**5** $a_1 = 10$, $a_{k+1} = 1 + (1/a_k)$ • $a_2 = a_{1+1} \{k = 1\} = 1 + 1/a_1 = 1 + 1/10 = \dfrac{10}{10} + \dfrac{1}{10} = \dfrac{11}{10}$

$a_3 = a_{2+1} = 1 + 1/a_2 = 1 + \dfrac{1}{11/10} = 1 + \dfrac{10}{11} = \dfrac{11}{11} + \dfrac{10}{11} = \dfrac{21}{11}$

$a_4 = a_{3+1} = 1 + 1/a_3 = 1 + \dfrac{1}{21/11} = 1 + \dfrac{11}{21} = \dfrac{21}{21} + \dfrac{11}{21} = \dfrac{32}{21}$

$a_5 = a_{4+1} = 1 + 1/a_4 = 1 + \dfrac{1}{32/21} = 1 + \dfrac{21}{32} = \dfrac{32}{32} + \dfrac{21}{32} = \dfrac{53}{32}$.

★ $10, \dfrac{11}{10}, \dfrac{21}{11}, \dfrac{32}{21}, \dfrac{53}{32}$

**6** $a_1 = 2$, $a_{k+1} = a_k!$ • $a_2 = a_1! = 2! = 2$, $a_3 = a_2! = 2! = 2$, $a_4 = a_3! = 2! = 2$, $a_5 = a_4! = 2! = 2$.

★ $2, 2, 2, 2, 2$

**7** $a_1 = 9$, $a_{k+1} = \sqrt{a_k}$ • $a_2 = a_{1+1} \{k = 1\} = \sqrt{a_1} = \sqrt{9} = 3$, $a_3 = a_{2+1} = \sqrt{a_2} = \sqrt{3}$,

$a_4 = a_{3+1} = \sqrt{a_3} = \sqrt{\sqrt{3}} = \sqrt[4]{3}$, $a_5 = a_{4+1} = \sqrt{a_4} = \sqrt{\sqrt[4]{3}} = \sqrt[8]{3}$.

★ $9, 3, \sqrt{3}, \sqrt[4]{3}, \sqrt[8]{3}$

**8** $a_1 = 1$, $a_{k+1} = (1 + a_k)^{-1}$ • $a_2 = (1 + a_1)^{-1} = (1 + 1)^{-1} = (2)^{-1} = \dfrac{1}{2}$,

$a_3 = (1 + a_2)^{-1} = \left(1 + \dfrac{1}{2}\right)^{-1} = \left(\dfrac{3}{2}\right)^{-1} = \dfrac{2}{3}$, $a_4 = (1 + a_3)^{-1} = \left(1 + \dfrac{2}{3}\right)^{-1} = \left(\dfrac{5}{3}\right)^{-1} = \dfrac{3}{5}$,

$a_5 = (1 + a_4)^{-1} = \left(1 + \dfrac{3}{5}\right)^{-1} = \left(\dfrac{8}{5}\right)^{-1} = \dfrac{5}{8}$.

★ $1, \dfrac{1}{2}, \dfrac{2}{3}, \dfrac{3}{5}, \dfrac{5}{8}$

**9** $\displaystyle\sum_{k=1}^{5}(k^2 + 4) = (1^2 + 4) + (2^2 + 4) + (3^2 + 4) + (4^2 + 4) + (5^2 + 4) = 5 + 8 + 13 + 20 + 29 = 75$

**10** $\displaystyle\sum_{k=2}^{6}\dfrac{2k - 8}{k - 1} = (-4) + (-1) + 0 + \dfrac{1}{2} + \dfrac{4}{5} = -\dfrac{37}{10}$

**11** $\displaystyle\sum_{k=7}^{100} 10 = (100 - 7 + 1)(10) = 94(10) = 940$

**12** $\displaystyle\sum_{k=1}^{4}(2^k - 10) = (-8) + (-6) + (-2) + 6 = -10$

**13** $\displaystyle\sum_{k=5}^{72}(3x^2) = (72 - 5 + 1)(3x^2) = 68(3x^2) = 204x^2$

**14** $\displaystyle\sum_{k=0}^{100}\left(\dfrac{\pi}{2} - \sqrt{2}\right) = (100 - 0 + 1)\left(\dfrac{\pi}{2} - \sqrt{2}\right) = 101\left(\dfrac{\pi}{2} - \sqrt{2}\right) = \dfrac{101}{2}\pi - 101\sqrt{2}$

**15** $3 + 6 + 9 + 12 + 15 = 3(1) + 3(2) + 3(3) + 3(4) + 3(5) = \displaystyle\sum_{n=1}^{5}(3n)$

**16** We first note that $4 + 2 + 1 + \dfrac{1}{2} + \dfrac{1}{4} + \dfrac{1}{8}$ is the sum of six terms of a geometric sequence with first term 4 and ratio $\dfrac{1}{2}$—that is, $a_n = a_1 r^{n-1} = 4\left(\dfrac{1}{2}\right)^{n-1}$.

$$4 + 2 + 1 + \dfrac{1}{2} + \dfrac{1}{4} + \dfrac{1}{8} = \sum_{n=1}^{6} 4\left(\dfrac{1}{2}\right)^{n-1} = \sum_{n=1}^{6} 2^2(2^{-1})^{n-1} = \sum_{n=1}^{6} 2^2 \, 2^{1-n} = \sum_{n=1}^{6} 2^{3-n}$$

**17** $\dfrac{1}{1 \cdot 2} + \dfrac{1}{2 \cdot 3} + \dfrac{1}{3 \cdot 4} + \cdots + \dfrac{1}{99 \cdot 100} = \displaystyle\sum_{n=1}^{99}\dfrac{1}{n(n+1)}$

**18** $\dfrac{1}{1 \cdot 2 \cdot 3} + \dfrac{1}{2 \cdot 3 \cdot 4} + \dfrac{1}{3 \cdot 4 \cdot 5} + \cdots + \dfrac{1}{98 \cdot 99 \cdot 100} = \displaystyle\sum_{n=1}^{98}\dfrac{1}{n(n+1)(n+2)}$

**19** $\frac{1}{2} + \frac{2}{5} + \frac{3}{8} + \frac{4}{11}$ • The numerators are just the positive integers, so we'll use the summation notation with $n$ having values from 1 to 4. The denominators increase by 3, so it must be of the form $3n + k$. When $n = 1$, $3n + k = 3(1) + k = 3 + k$ and $3 + k$ must equal 2 (the first denominator).

Thus, $3 + k = 2 \Rightarrow k = -1$, so the denominator is $3n - 1$ and the summation notation is $\sum\limits_{n=1}^{4} \dfrac{n}{3n - 1}$.

**20** $\frac{1}{4} + \frac{2}{9} + \frac{3}{14} + \frac{4}{19}$. The numerators increase by 1, the denominators by 5. $\sum\limits_{n=1}^{4} \dfrac{n}{5n - 1}$

**21** $100 - 95 + 90 - 85 + 80$ • The terms have alternating signs and decrease by 5 in magnitude.

For $n = 1$, we subtract 5 from 105 to get 100. $\sum\limits_{n=1}^{5} (-1)^{n+1}(105 - 5n)$

**22** $1 - \frac{1}{2} + \frac{1}{3} - \frac{1}{4} + \frac{1}{5} - \frac{1}{6} + \frac{1}{7}$ •

The terms have alternating signs, the numerator is 1, and the denominators increase by 1. $\sum\limits_{n=1}^{7} (-1)^{n-1} \dfrac{1}{n}$

**23** $a_0 + a_1 x^4 + a_2 x^8 + \cdots + a_{25} x^{100}$ {the exponents are multiples of 4} $= \sum\limits_{n=0}^{25} a_n x^{4n}$

**24** $a_0 + a_1 x^3 + a_2 x^6 + \cdots + a_{20} x^{60} = \sum\limits_{n=0}^{20} a_n x^{3n}$

**25** $1 - \dfrac{x^2}{2} + \dfrac{x^4}{4} - \dfrac{x^6}{6} + \cdots + (-1)^n \dfrac{x^{2n}}{2n}$ • The pattern begins with the second term and the general term is listed.

$1 + \sum\limits_{k=1}^{n} (-1)^k \dfrac{x^{2k}}{2k}$

**26** $1 + x + \dfrac{x^2}{2} + \dfrac{x^3}{3} + \cdots + \dfrac{x^n}{n}$. The pattern begins with the second term and the general term is listed. $1 + \sum\limits_{k=1}^{n} \dfrac{x^k}{k}$

**27** $a_1 = 4, a_2 = 5, a_{k+1} = 2a_k + a_{k-1}$ for $k \geq 2$ {given formula} ★ 14, 33
$a_3 = 2a_2 + a_1 = 2(5) + 4 = 14$ {$k = 2$}
$a_4 = 2a_3 + a_2 = 2(14) + 5 = 33$ {$k = 3$}

**28** $d = a_2 - a_1 = 3 - \left(4 + \sqrt{3}\right) = -1 - \sqrt{3}$.

$a_n = a_1 + (n - 1)d \Rightarrow a_{10} = \left(4 + \sqrt{3}\right) + (9)\left(-1 - \sqrt{3}\right) = -5 - 8\sqrt{3}$.

$S_n = \frac{n}{2}(a_1 + a_n) \Rightarrow S_{10} = \frac{10}{2}\left[\left(4 + \sqrt{3}\right) + \left(-5 - 8\sqrt{3}\right)\right] = 5\left(-1 - 7\sqrt{3}\right) = -5 - 35\sqrt{3}$.

**29** $a_4 = a_1 + 3d \Rightarrow 9 = a_1 - 15 \Rightarrow a_1 = 24$.

$S_n = \frac{n}{2}[2a_1 + (n - 1)(d)] \Rightarrow S_8 = \frac{8}{2}[2(24) + (8 - 1)(-5)] = 4(48 - 35) = 52$.

**30** $a_5 = a_1 + 4d = 5$ and $a_{13} = a_1 + 12d = 77$.

$a_{13} - a_5 = (a_1 + 12d) - (a_1 + 4d) = 8d$ and $a_{13} - a_5 = 77 - 5 = 72 \Rightarrow 8d = 72 \Rightarrow d = 9$.

Thus, $a_5 = a_1 + 4d \Rightarrow 5 = a_1 + 36 \Rightarrow a_1 = -31$ and $a_{10} = -31 + 9(9) = 50$.

**31** $S_n = \frac{n}{2}[2a_1 + (n - 1)(d)] \Rightarrow 342 = \frac{n}{2}[2(1) + (n - 1)(5)] \Rightarrow 684 = n(5n - 3) \Rightarrow$

$684 = 5n^2 - 3n \Rightarrow 0 = 5n^2 - 3n - 684 \Rightarrow (n - 12)(5n + 57) = 0 \Rightarrow n = 12 \{n > 0\}$

**32** If we insert four arithmetic means between 20 and $-10$, there will be 5 differences that span the distance from 20 to $-10$. Hence, $5d = -10 - 20 \Rightarrow d = \frac{-30}{5} = -6$.     The terms are $20, 14, 8, 2, -4,$ and $-10$.

**33** $r = \dfrac{\frac{1}{4}}{\frac{1}{8}} = 2; a_n = \dfrac{1}{8}(2)^{n-1} = 2^{-3} \cdot 2^{n-1} = 2^{n-4} \Rightarrow a_{10} = 2^6 = 64$

**34** We can divide the fourth term by the third term to obtain the common ratio, $r = \frac{-0.3}{3} = -0.1$.

If we multiply the third term by $r$ five times, we will get the eighth term. $a_8 = a_3 r^5 = 3(-0.1)^5 = -0.00003$.

**35** $a_7 = a_3 r^4 \Rightarrow 625 = 16r^4 \Rightarrow r^4 = \frac{625}{16} \Rightarrow r^2 = \frac{25}{4} \Rightarrow r = \pm\frac{5}{2}$.

Since $a_8 = a_7 r$, $a_8 = 625\left(\pm\frac{5}{2}\right) = \pm 1562.5$.

**36** The geometric mean of 4 and 8 is $\sqrt{4 \cdot 8} = \sqrt{32} = 4\sqrt{2}$.

**37** $a_8 = a_1 r^7 \Rightarrow 100 = a_1\left(-\frac{3}{2}\right)^7 \Rightarrow a_1 = 100\left(-\frac{2}{3}\right)^7 = -\frac{12,800}{2187}$

**38** Inserting two geometric means results in a sequence that looks like 7, $x$, $y$, 354,571. Now $7r = x$, $7r^2 = y$, and $7r^3 = 354{,}571$. Thus, $7r^3 = 354{,}571 \Rightarrow r^3 = \frac{354{,}571}{7} = 50{,}653 \Rightarrow r = 37$. The terms are 7, 259, 9583, and 354,571.

**39** $S_{12} = \frac{12}{2}(a_1 + a_{12}) \Rightarrow 402 = 6(a_1 + 50) \Rightarrow 67 = a_1 + 50 \Rightarrow a_1 = 17$.

$a_{12} = a_1 + 11d \Rightarrow 50 = 17 + 11d \Rightarrow 33 = 11d \Rightarrow d = 3$.

**40** $a_5 = a_1 r^4 \Rightarrow \frac{1}{16} = a_1\left(\frac{3}{2}\right)^4 \Rightarrow a_1 = \frac{1}{16} \cdot \frac{16}{81} = \frac{1}{81}$.

$$S_5 = \frac{1}{81} \cdot \frac{1 - \left(\frac{3}{2}\right)^5}{1 - \frac{3}{2}} = \frac{1}{81} \cdot \frac{1 - \frac{243}{32}}{-\frac{1}{2}} = \frac{1}{81} \cdot \frac{-\frac{211}{32}}{-\frac{1}{2}} = \frac{211}{1296}.$$

**41** $\displaystyle\sum_{k=1}^{15}(5k - 2)$ • The sequence of terms is arithmetic.

$a_1 = 5(1) - 2 = 3$ and $a_{15} = 5(15) - 2 = 73$, so $S_{15} = \frac{15}{2}(3 + 73) = 570$.

**42** $\displaystyle\sum_{k=1}^{10}\left(6 - \frac{1}{2}k\right)$ • The sequence of terms is arithmetic.

$a_1 = 6 - \frac{1}{2}(1) = 5.5$ and $a_{10} = 6 - \frac{1}{2}(10) = 1$, so $S_{10} = \frac{10}{2}(5.5 + 1) = 32.5$.

**43** This sum can be written as a sum of a geometric sequence and an arithmetic sequence.

$$\sum_{k=1}^{10}\left(2^k - \frac{1}{2}\right) = \sum_{k=1}^{10} 2^k - \sum_{k=1}^{10}\frac{1}{2} = 2 \cdot \frac{1 - 2^{10}}{1 - 2} - 10\left(\frac{1}{2}\right) = 2046 - 5 = 2041$$

**44** This sum can be written as a sum of an arithmetic sequence and a geometric sequence.

$$\sum_{k=1}^{8}\left(\frac{1}{2} - 2^k\right) = \sum_{k=1}^{8}\frac{1}{2} - \sum_{k=1}^{8} 2^k = 8\left(\frac{1}{2}\right) - 2 \cdot \frac{1 - 2^8}{1 - 2} = 4 - 510 = -506$$

**45** $1 - \frac{2}{5} + \frac{4}{25} - \frac{8}{125} + \cdots$ • $a_1 = 1$, $r = -\frac{2}{5} \Rightarrow S = \dfrac{a}{1 - r} = \dfrac{1}{1 - \left(-\frac{2}{5}\right)} = \dfrac{1}{\frac{7}{5}} = \dfrac{5}{7}$.

**46** $6.\overline{274}$ • $a_1 = 0.274$, $r = 0.001 \Rightarrow S = \dfrac{a}{1 - r} = \dfrac{0.274}{1 - 0.001} = \dfrac{274}{999}$. Thus, $6.\overline{274} = 6 + \dfrac{274}{999} = \dfrac{6268}{999}$.

**47** (1) $P_1$ is true, since $3(1) - 1 = \dfrac{1[3(1) + 1]}{2} = 2$.

(2) Assume $P_k$ is true: $2 + 5 + 8 + \cdots + (3k - 1) = \dfrac{k(3k + 1)}{2}$. Hence,

$$2 + 5 + 8 + \cdots + (3k - 1) + 3(k + 1) - 1 = \frac{k(3k + 1)}{2} + 3(k + 1) - 1 = \frac{3k^2 + k + 6k + 4}{2}$$

$$= \frac{3k^2 + 7k + 4}{2} = \frac{(k + 1)(3k + 4)}{2} = \frac{(k + 1)[3(k + 1) + 1]}{2}.$$

Thus, $P_{k+1}$ is true, and the proof is complete.

**48** (1) $P_1$ is true, since $[2(1)]^2 = \dfrac{[2(1)]\,[2(1)+1]\,[1+1]}{3} = 4.$

(2) Assume $P_k$ is true: $2^2 + 4^2 + 6^2 + \cdots + (2k)^2 = \dfrac{(2k)(2k+1)(k+1)}{3}$. Hence,

$$2^2 + 4^2 + 6^2 + \cdots + (2k)^2 + [2(k+1)]^2 = \dfrac{(2k)(2k+1)(k+1)}{3} + [2(k+1)]^2$$

$$= (k+1)\left[\dfrac{4k^2 + 2k}{3} + \dfrac{12(k+1)}{3}\right]$$

$$= \dfrac{(k+1)(4k^2 + 14k + 12)}{3}$$

$$= \dfrac{2(k+1)(2k+3)(k+2)}{3}.$$

Thus, $P_{k+1}$ is true, and the proof is complete.

**49** (1) $P_1$ is true, since $\dfrac{1}{[2(1)-1][2(1)+1]} = \dfrac{1}{2(1)+1} = \dfrac{1}{3}.$

(2) Assume $P_k$ is true: $\dfrac{1}{1\cdot 3} + \dfrac{1}{3\cdot 5} + \dfrac{1}{5\cdot 7} + \cdots + \dfrac{1}{(2k-1)(2k+1)} = \dfrac{k}{2k+1}$. Hence,

$$\dfrac{1}{1\cdot 3} + \dfrac{1}{3\cdot 5} + \dfrac{1}{5\cdot 7} + \cdots + \dfrac{1}{(2k-1)(2k+1)} + \dfrac{1}{(2k+1)(2k+3)} = \dfrac{k}{2k+1} + \dfrac{1}{(2k+1)(2k+3)}$$

$$= \dfrac{k(2k+3)+1}{(2k+1)(2k+3)} = \dfrac{2k^2 + 3k + 1}{(2k+1)(2k+3)} = \dfrac{(2k+1)(k+1)}{(2k+1)(2k+3)} = \dfrac{k+1}{2(k+1)+1}.$$

Thus, $P_{k+1}$ is true, and the proof is complete.

**50** (1) $P_1$ is true, since $1(1+1) = \dfrac{(1)\,(1+1)\,(1+2)}{3} = 2.$

(2) Assume $P_k$ is true: $1\cdot 2 + 2\cdot 3 + 3\cdot 4 + \cdots + k(k+1) = \dfrac{k(k+1)(k+2)}{3}$. Hence,

$$1\cdot 2 + 2\cdot 3 + 3\cdot 4 + \cdots + k(k+1) + (k+1)(k+2) = \dfrac{k(k+1)(k+2)}{3} + (k+1)(k+2)$$

$$= (k+1)(k+2)\left(\dfrac{k}{3} + 1\right) = \dfrac{(k+1)(k+2)(k+3)}{3}.$$

Thus, $P_{k+1}$ is true, and the proof is complete.

**51** (1) For $n = 1$, $n^3 + 2n = 3$ and 3 is a factor of 3.

(2) Assume 3 is a factor of $k^3 + 2k$. The $(k+1)$st term is

$$(k+1)^3 + 2(k+1) = k^3 + 3k^2 + 5k + 3 = (k^3 + 2k) + (3k^2 + 3k + 3) = (k^3 + 2k) + 3(k^2 + k + 1).$$

By the induction hypothesis, 3 is a factor of $k^3 + 2k$ and 3 is a factor of $3(k^2 + k + 1)$, so 3 is a factor of the $(k+1)$st term.

Thus, $P_{k+1}$ is true, and the proof is complete.

**52** (1) $P_5$ is true, since $5^2 + 3 < 2^5.$

(2) Assume $P_k$ is true: $k^2 + 3 < 2^k$. Hence,

$$(k+1)^2 + 3 = k^2 + 2k + 4 = (k^2 + 3) + (k+1) < 2^k + (k+1) < 2^k + 2^k = 2\cdot 2^k = 2^{k+1}.$$

Thus, $P_{k+1}$ is true, and the proof is complete.

**53** For $j$: Examining the pattern formed by letting $n = 1, 2, 3, 4$ leads us to the conclusion that $j = 4$.

(1) $P_4$ is true, since $2^4 \le 4!.$

(2) Assume $P_k$ is true: $2^k \le k!$. Hence, $2^{k+1} = 2\cdot 2^k \le 2\cdot k! < (k+1)\cdot k! = (k+1)!.$

Thus, $P_{k+1}$ is true, and the proof is complete.

**54** For $j$: $10^n \le n^n \Rightarrow \left(\frac{n}{10}\right)^n \ge 1$. This is true if $\frac{n}{10} \ge 1$ or $n \ge 10$. Thus, $j = 10$.

(1) $P_{10}$ is true, since $10^{10} \le 10^{10}$.

(2) Assume $P_k$ is true: $10^k \le k^k$. Hence,
$$10^{k+1} = 10 \cdot 10^k \le 10 \cdot k^k < (k+1) \cdot k^k < (k+1) \cdot (k+1)^k = (k+1)^{k+1}.$$

Thus, $P_{k+1}$ is true, and the proof is complete.

**55** We use the binomial theorem formula with $a = x^2$, $b = -3y$, and $n = 6$.
$$(x^2 - 3y)^6 = \binom{6}{0}(x^2)^6 + \binom{6}{1}(x^2)^5(-3y)^1 + \binom{6}{2}(x^2)^4(-3y)^2 + \binom{6}{3}(x^2)^3(-3y)^3$$
$$+ \binom{6}{4}(x^2)^2(-3y)^4 + \binom{6}{5}(x^2)^1(-3y)^5 + \binom{6}{6}(-3y)^6$$
$$= x^{12} - 6 \cdot 3x^{10}y + 15 \cdot 9x^8y^2 - 20 \cdot 27x^6y^3 + 15 \cdot 81x^4y^4 - 6 \cdot 243x^2y^5 + 729y^6$$
$$= x^{12} - 18x^{10}y + 135x^8y^2 - 540x^6y^3 + 1215x^4y^4 - 1458x^2y^5 + 729y^6$$

**56** $(2x + y^3)^4 = \binom{4}{0}(2x)^4(y^3)^0 + \binom{4}{1}(2x)^3(y^3)^1 + \binom{4}{2}(2x)^2(y^3)^2 + \binom{4}{3}(2x)^1(y^3)^3 + \binom{4}{4}(2x)^0(y^3)^4$
$$= (1)(16x^4)(1) + (4)(8x^3)(y^3) + (6)(4x^2)(y^6) + (4)(2x)(y^9) + (1)(1)(y^{12})$$
$$= 16x^4 + 32x^3y^3 + 24x^2y^6 + 8xy^9 + y^{12}$$

**57** $(x^{2/5} + 2x^{-3/5})^{20}$; first three terms  •  The first three terms are
$$\binom{20}{0}(x^{2/5})^{20}(2x^{-3/5})^0 + \binom{20}{1}(x^{2/5})^{19}(2x^{-3/5})^1 + \binom{20}{2}(x^{2/5})^{18}(2x^{-3/5})^2$$
$$= 1 \cdot x^8 \cdot 1 + 20 \cdot x^{38/5} \cdot 2x^{-3/5} + 190 \cdot x^{36/5} \cdot 4x^{-6/5} = x^8 + 40 \cdot x^{35/5} + 760 \cdot x^{30/5} = x^8 + 40x^7 + 760x^6$$

**58** $(y^3 - \frac{1}{2}c^2)^9$; sixth term $\{k = 5\} = \binom{9}{5}(y^3)^4(-\frac{1}{2}c^2)^5 = -\frac{63}{16}y^{12}c^{10}$

**59** $(4x^2 - y)^7$; term that contains $x^{10}$  •  Consider only the variable $x$ in the expansion.
$$(x^2)^{7-k} = x^{10} \Rightarrow x^{14-2k} = x^{10} \Rightarrow 14 - 2k = 10 \Rightarrow 4 = 2k \Rightarrow k = 2.$$
$$(k+1)\text{st term} = 3\text{rd term} = \binom{7}{2}(4x^2)^5(-y)^2 = (21)(1024x^{10})(y^2) = 21{,}504x^{10}y^2$$

**60** $(2c^3 + 5c^{-2})^{10}$; term that does not contain $c$  •  The exponent on $c$ must be zero.
$$(c^3)^{10-k}(c^{-2})^k = c^0 \Rightarrow c^{30-3k-2k} = c^0 \Rightarrow 30 - 3k - 2k = 0 \Rightarrow 30 = 5k \Rightarrow k = 6;$$
$$(k+1)\text{st term} = 7\text{th term} = \binom{10}{6}(2c^3)^4(5c^{-2})^6 = 210 \cdot 16c^{12} \cdot 15{,}625c^{-12} = 52{,}500{,}000$$

**61** (a) $S_5 = 10 \Rightarrow 10 = \frac{5}{2}(2a_1 + 4d) \Rightarrow 4 = 2a_1 + 4d \Rightarrow 4d = 4 - 2a_1 \Rightarrow d = 1 - \frac{1}{2}a_1$.

Since $a_1$ is positive, $1 - \frac{1}{2}a_1$ is less than 1 ft.

(b) $a_1 = \frac{1}{2} \Rightarrow d = 1 - \frac{1}{2}(\frac{1}{2}) = \frac{3}{4}$. The lengths of the other four pieces are $1\frac{1}{4}$, $2$, $2\frac{3}{4}$, and $3\frac{1}{2}$ ft.

**62** $n = 16 \Rightarrow a_{16} = a_1 + 15d \Rightarrow 16 = 20 + 15d \Rightarrow d = -\frac{4}{15}$.
$$S_{16} = \frac{16}{2}[2(20) + 15(-\frac{4}{15})] = 8(40 - 4) = 288 \text{ in. or 24 ft.}$$

**63** If $s_1 = 1$, then $s_2 = f$, $s_3 = f^2, \ldots$ . There are two of each of the $s_k$'s. Since $0 < f < 1$, and $f$ is the common ratio, we can sum the infinite sequence. The sum of the $s_k$'s is $2(1 + f + f^2 + \cdots) = 2\left(\frac{1}{1-f}\right) = \frac{2}{1-f}$.

**64** Two ways to sum these integers are $1 + 2 + 3 + 4 + 5 + 6 + 7 + 8 + 9 + 10$ and
$$2 + 1 + 4 + 3 + 6 + 5 + 8 + 7 + 10 + 9. \quad P(10, 10) = \frac{10!}{(10-10)!} = \frac{10!}{0!} = 10! = 3{,}628{,}800$$

**65** (a) We want 13 of the 52 cards. Order is important, so we use a permutation. $P(52, 13) \approx 3.954 \times 10^{21}$

(b) $P(13, 5) \cdot P(13, 3) \cdot P(13, 3) \cdot P(13, 2) \approx 7.094 \times 10^{13}$

**66** (a) We want 6 digits taken 4 at a time. Order is important, so we use a permutation.
$$P(6,4) = \frac{6!}{(6-4)!} = \frac{6 \cdot 5 \cdot 4 \cdot 3 \cdot 2!}{2!} = 6 \cdot 5 \cdot 4 \cdot 3 = 360$$

(b) Since repetitions are allowed, we can use any of the 6 digits for each choice: $6 \cdot 6 \cdot 6 \cdot 6 = 6^4 = 1296$

**67** (a) We want 8 of the 12 questions. Order is not important, so we use a combination.
$$C(12,8) = \frac{12!}{(12-8)!\,8!} = \frac{12 \cdot 11 \cdot 10 \cdot 9 \cdot 8!}{4 \cdot 3 \cdot 2 \cdot 8!} = 495$$

(b) We now want 5 of the remaining 9 questions. $C(9,5) = 126$

**68** $\dfrac{(6+5+4+2)!}{6!\,5!\,4!\,2!} = \dfrac{17!}{6!\,5!\,4!\,2!} = 85{,}765{,}680$

**69** If $O(E)$ are 8 to 5, then $O(E')$ are 5 to 8 and $P(E) = \dfrac{8}{5+8} = \dfrac{8}{13}$.

**70** There is one way to get all heads and one way to get all tails, so there are only two ways to get the coins to match.

(a) With two boys, $n(S) = 2 \cdot 2 = 4$, so the probability of a match is $\frac{2}{4} = \frac{1}{2}$.

(b) With three boys, $n(S) = 2 \cdot 2 \cdot 2 = 8$, so the probability of a match is $\frac{2}{8} = \frac{1}{4}$.

**71** (a) We need 4 of the 26 cards of one color. There are 2 colors. $\dfrac{P(26,4) \cdot 2}{P(52,4)} = \dfrac{92}{833} \approx 0.1104$

(b) We need R-B-R-B. $\dfrac{26^2 \cdot 25^2}{P(52,4)}$ or $\dfrac{26}{52} \cdot \dfrac{26}{51} \cdot \dfrac{25}{50} \cdot \dfrac{25}{49} = \dfrac{325}{4998} \approx 0.0650$

**72** (a) $P(\text{winning with 1 ticket}) = \frac{1}{1000}$ (b) $\frac{10}{1000} = \frac{1}{100}$ (c) $\frac{50}{1000} = \frac{1}{20}$

**73** $P(1 \text{ head}) = \dfrac{C(4,1)}{2^4} = \dfrac{4}{16} = \dfrac{1}{4} = 0.25$. Odds are 4 to 12, or 1 to 3.

**74** (a) $P(\text{passing}) = P(4, 5, \text{or } 6 \text{ correct}) = \dfrac{C(6,4) + C(6,5) + C(6,6)}{2^6} = \dfrac{15+6+1}{64} = \dfrac{22}{64} = \dfrac{11}{32}$

(b) $P(\text{failing}) = 1 - P(\text{passing}) = 1 - \frac{22}{64} = \frac{42}{64}$

**75** (a) $P(\text{tossing a 6 } and \text{ drawing the king of hearts}) = \frac{1}{6} \cdot \frac{1}{52} = \frac{1}{312} \approx 0.0032$

(b) $P(\text{tossing a 6 } or \text{ drawing the king of hearts}) = \frac{1}{6} + \frac{1}{52} - \frac{1}{312} = \frac{52+6-1}{312} = \frac{57}{312} = \frac{19}{104} \approx 0.1827$

**76** Let $O$ denote the event that the individual is over 60 and $F$ denote the event that the individual is female.
$$P(O \cup F) = P(O) + P(F) - P(O \cap F) = \frac{1000}{5000} + \frac{2000}{5000} - \frac{0.40(2000)}{5000} = \frac{2200}{5000} = 0.44$$

**77** There are 2 ways to obtain 10 (6, 4 and 4, 6), 2 ways for 11 (6, 5 and 5, 6),
1 way for 12, 16, 20, and 24 (double 3's, 4's, 5's, and 6's). $\dfrac{2+2+1+1+1+1}{36} = \dfrac{8}{36} = \dfrac{2}{9} = 0.\overline{2}$

**78** $\left(\frac{51}{52}\right)^n = 0.25 \;\Rightarrow\; \ln\left(\frac{51}{52}\right)^n = \ln 0.25 \;\Rightarrow\; n \ln \frac{51}{52} = \ln 0.25 \;\Rightarrow\; n = 71$

**79** The two teams, A and B, can play as few as 4 games or as many as 7 games.
Since the two teams are equally matched, the probability that either team wins any particular game is $\frac{1}{2}$.
$P(\text{team A wins in 4 games}) = \frac{1}{2} \cdot \frac{1}{2} \cdot \frac{1}{2} \cdot \frac{1}{2} = \left(\frac{1}{2}\right)^4 = \frac{1}{16} = 0.0625$
$P(\text{team A wins in 5 games}) = P(\text{team A wins 3 of the first 4 games \{losing 1 game\} } and \text{ then wins game 5})$
$$= \binom{4}{3}\left(\tfrac{1}{2}\right)^3 \cdot \left(\tfrac{1}{2}\right)^1 \cdot \tfrac{1}{2} = \binom{4}{3}\left(\tfrac{1}{2}\right)^5 = \tfrac{4}{32} = 0.125.$$

In a similar fashion,

$P(\text{team A wins in 6 games}) = \binom{5}{3}\left(\frac{1}{2}\right)^6 = \frac{10}{64} = \frac{5}{32} = 0.15625$ and

$P(\text{team A wins in 7 games}) = \binom{6}{3}\left(\frac{1}{2}\right)^7 = \frac{20}{128} = \frac{5}{32} = 0.15625$.

Thus, the probability that team A wins the series is $0.0625 + 0.125 + 0.15625 + 0.15625 = 0.5$, which agrees with our common sense. Since the probabilities for team B winning the series are the same, the expected number of games is $4\left(2 \cdot \frac{1}{16}\right) + 5\left(2 \cdot \frac{4}{32}\right) + 6\left(2 \cdot \frac{5}{32}\right) + 7\left(2 \cdot \frac{5}{32}\right) = 5\frac{13}{16} = 5.8125$.

**80** The probability that the first card is an ace is $\frac{4}{52}$ and the probability that the second card is an ace is $\frac{3}{51}$. We can multiply these to get $\frac{12}{2652} = \frac{1}{221}$. Another approach using combinations is to think of the deck as consisting of aces and non-aces. We want 2 of the 4 aces, and 0 of the 48 non-aces. The probability is

$$\frac{C(4,2) \cdot C(48,0)}{C(52,2)} = \frac{6 \cdot 1}{1326} = \frac{1}{221}.$$

## Chapter 9 Discussion Exercises

**1** Probably the easiest way to describe this sequence is by using a piecewise-defined function. If $1 \le n \le 4$, then $2n$ describes the sequence $2, 4, 6, 8$. For $n = 5$, we need to obtain $a$ as the general term—one way to symbolize this is $(n-4)a$. Hence, one possibility is $a_n = \begin{cases} 2n & \text{if } 1 \le n \le 4 \\ (n-4)a & \text{if } n \ge 5 \end{cases}$

A more sophisticated (and complicated) approach is to add a term to $2n$—call this term $k$—so that $k$ is 0 for $n = 1$, 2, 3, and 4, but equal to $a - 10$ for $n = 5$ {the *minus* 10 is needed to compensate for the *plus* 10 from the $2n$ term}. We can do this by starting with the expression $(n-1)(n-2)(n-3)(n-4)$, which is zero for $n = 1, 2, 3,$ and 4. For $n = 5$, this expression is $4 \cdot 3 \cdot 2 \cdot 1 = 24$, so we will divide it by 24 and multiply it by $a - 10$ to obtain $a - 10$. Thus, another possibility is $a_n = 2n + \dfrac{(n-1)(n-2)(n-3)(n-4)(a-10)}{24}$.

**2** Examining the graphs of $y_1 = x$ and $y_2 = (\ln x)^3$, we see that $y_1 = y_2 \Rightarrow x \approx 6.4$ or $93.35$.

For large values of $x$, $y_1 \boxed{\ge} y_2$. The value of $j$ is 94.

**3** (a) Following the pattern from Exercises 41 and 42 in Section 9.4, write

$1^4 + 2^4 + 3^4 + \cdots + n^4 = an^5 + bn^4 + cn^3 + dn^2 + en$. Then, it follows that:

$n = 1 \Rightarrow a(1)^5 + b(1)^4 + c(1)^3 + d(1)^2 + e(1) = 1^4 \Rightarrow a + b + c + d + e = 1,$

$n = 2 \Rightarrow a(2)^5 + b(2)^4 + c(2)^3 + d(2)^2 + e(2) = 1^4 + 2^4 \Rightarrow 32a + 16b + 8c + 4d + 2e = 17,$

$n = 3 \Rightarrow a(3)^5 + b(3)^4 + c(3)^3 + d(3)^2 + e(3) = 1^4 + 2^4 + 3^4 \Rightarrow$

$243a + 81b + 27c + 9d + 3e = 98,$

$n = 4 \Rightarrow a(4)^5 + b(4)^4 + c(4)^3 + d(4)^2 + e(4) = 1^4 + 2^4 + 3^4 + 4^4 \Rightarrow$

$1024a + 256b + 64c + 16d + 4e = 354,$

$n = 5 \Rightarrow a(5)^5 + b(5)^4 + c(5)^3 + d(5)^2 + e(5) = 1^4 + 2^4 + 3^4 + 4^4 + 5^4 \Rightarrow$

$3125a + 625b + 125c + 25d + 5e = 979.$

$$AX = B \Rightarrow \begin{bmatrix} 1 & 1 & 1 & 1 & 1 \\ 32 & 16 & 8 & 4 & 2 \\ 243 & 81 & 27 & 9 & 3 \\ 1024 & 256 & 64 & 16 & 4 \\ 3125 & 625 & 125 & 25 & 5 \end{bmatrix} \begin{bmatrix} a \\ b \\ c \\ d \\ e \end{bmatrix} = \begin{bmatrix} 1 \\ 17 \\ 98 \\ 354 \\ 979 \end{bmatrix} \Rightarrow X = A^{-1}B = \begin{bmatrix} \frac{1}{5} \\ \frac{1}{2} \\ \frac{1}{3} \\ 0 \\ -\frac{1}{30} \end{bmatrix}$$

Thus, $1^4 + 2^4 + 3^4 + \cdots + n^4 = \frac{1}{5}n^5 + \frac{1}{2}n^4 + \frac{1}{3}n^3 - \frac{1}{30}n$. This formula must be verified.

(b) Let $P_n$ be the statement that $1^4 + 2^4 + 3^4 + \cdots + n^4 = \frac{1}{5}n^5 + \frac{1}{2}n^4 + \frac{1}{3}n^3 - \frac{1}{30}n$.

(1) $1^4 = \frac{1}{5} + \frac{1}{2} + \frac{1}{3} - \frac{1}{30} = 1$ and $P_1$ is true.

(2) Assume that $P_k$ is true. We must show that $P_{k+1}$ is true. $P_k \Rightarrow$

$$1^4 + 2^4 + 3^4 + \cdots + k^4 = \frac{1}{5}k^5 + \frac{1}{2}k^4 + \frac{1}{3}k^3 - \frac{1}{30}k \Rightarrow$$

$$1^4 + 2^4 + 3^4 + \cdots + k^4 + (k+1)^4 = \frac{1}{5}k^5 + \frac{1}{2}k^4 + \frac{1}{3}k^3 - \frac{1}{30}k + (k+1)^4 \Rightarrow$$

$$1^4 + 2^4 + 3^4 + \cdots + k^4 + (k+1)^4 = \frac{1}{5}k^5 + \frac{1}{2}k^4 + \frac{1}{3}k^3 - \frac{1}{30}k + \left(k^4 + 4k^3 + 6k^2 + 4k + 1\right) \Rightarrow$$

$$1^4 + 2^4 + 3^4 + \cdots + k^4 + (k+1)^4 = \frac{1}{5}k^5 + \frac{3}{2}k^4 + \frac{13}{3}k^3 + 6k^2 + \frac{119}{30}k + 1. \; P_{k+1} \Rightarrow$$

$$1^4 + 2^4 + 3^4 + \cdots + k^4 + (k+1)^4 = \frac{1}{5}(k+1)^5 + \frac{1}{2}(k+1)^4 + \frac{1}{3}(k+1)^3 - \frac{1}{30}(k+1)$$

$$= \frac{1}{5}\left(k^5 + 5k^4 + 10k^3 + 10k^2 + 5k + 1\right) +$$

$$\frac{1}{2}\left(k^4 + 4k^3 + 6k^2 + 4k + 1\right) + \frac{1}{3}(k^3 + 3k^2 + 3k + 1) - \frac{1}{30}(k+1)$$

$$= \frac{1}{5}k^5 + \frac{3}{2}k^4 + \frac{13}{3}k^3 + 6k^2 + \frac{119}{30}k + 1.$$

Thus, the formula is true for all $n$.

$\boxed{4}$ (a) Following the pattern of setting the sum equal to a polynomial of degree one higher than the power in the exercise we write $2^3 + 4^3 + 6^3 + \cdots + (2n)^3 = an^4 + bn^3 + cn^2 + dn$. Then, it follows that:

$$n = 1 \Rightarrow a(1)^4 + b(1)^3 + c(1)^2 + d(1) = 2^3 \Rightarrow a + b + c + d = 8$$

$$n = 2 \Rightarrow a(2)^4 + b(2)^3 + c(2)^2 + d(2) = 2^3 + 4^3 \Rightarrow 16a + 8b + 4c + 2d = 72$$

$$n = 3 \Rightarrow a(3)^4 + b(3)^3 + c(3)^2 + d(3) = 2^3 + 4^3 + 6^3 \Rightarrow 81a + 27b + 9c + 3d = 288$$

$$n = 4 \Rightarrow a(4)^4 + b(4)^3 + c(4)^2 + d(4) = 2^3 + 4^3 + 6^3 + 8^3 \Rightarrow 256a + 64b + 16c + 4d = 800$$

$$AX = B \Rightarrow \begin{bmatrix} 1 & 1 & 1 & 1 \\ 16 & 8 & 4 & 2 \\ 81 & 27 & 9 & 3 \\ 256 & 64 & 16 & 4 \end{bmatrix} \begin{bmatrix} a \\ b \\ c \\ d \end{bmatrix} = \begin{bmatrix} 8 \\ 72 \\ 288 \\ 800 \end{bmatrix} \Rightarrow X = A^{-1}B = \begin{bmatrix} 2 \\ 4 \\ 2 \\ 0 \end{bmatrix}$$

$$a = 2, b = 4, c = 2, d = 0 \Rightarrow 2^3 + 4^3 + 6^3 + \cdots + (2n)^3 = 2n^4 + 4n^3 + 2n^2.$$

(b) Let $P_n$ be the statement that $2^3 + 4^3 + 6^3 + \cdots + (2n)^3 = 2n^4 + 4n^3 + 2n^2$

(1) $2^3 = 2 + 4 + 2 = 8$ and $P_1$ is true.

(2) Assume that $P_k$ is true. We must show that $P_{k+1}$ is true.

$$P_k \Rightarrow 2^3 + 4^3 + 6^3 + \cdots + (2k)^3 = 2k^4 + 4k^3 + 2k^2 \Rightarrow$$

$$2^3 + 4^3 + 6^3 + \cdots + (2k)^3 + (2k+2)^3 = 2k^4 + 4k^3 + 2k^2 + (2k+2)^3 = 2k^4 + 12k^3 + 26k^2 + 24k + 8$$

$$P_{k+1} \Rightarrow 2^3 + 4^3 + 6^3 + \cdots + (2k)^3 + (2k+2)^3 = 2(k+1)^4 + 4(k+1)^3 + 2(k+1)^2$$

$$= 2\left(k^4 + 4k^3 + 6k^2 + 4k + 1\right) + 4\left(k^3 + 3k^2 + 3k + 1\right) + 2\left(k^2 + 2k + 1\right)$$

$$= 2k^4 + 12k^3 + 26k^2 + 24k + 8.$$

Thus, the formula is true for all $n$.

$\boxed{5}$ Examine the number of digits in the exponent of the value in scientific notation. The TI-82/3/4 can compute 69!, but not 70!, because the exponent of 70! has more than two digits. The TI-85/6 can compute 449!, but not 450!, because the exponent of 450! has more than three digits.

$\boxed{6}$ The $(k+1)$st coefficient $(k = 0, 1, 2, \ldots, n)$ of the expansion of $(a+b)^n$, namely $\binom{n}{k}$, is the same as the number of $k$-element subsets of an $n$-element set.

[7] $\text{Time}_{\text{total}} = \text{Time}_{\text{down}} + \text{Time}_{\text{up}}$ {note $h = 10$ and $d = 10 \cdot \frac{1}{2}$ for the first rebound}

$$= \left[ \frac{\sqrt{10}}{4} + \frac{\sqrt{10 \cdot \frac{1}{2}}}{4} + \frac{\sqrt{10 \cdot \left(\frac{1}{2}\right)^2}}{4} + \cdots \right] + \left[ \frac{\sqrt{10 \cdot \frac{1}{2}}}{4} + \frac{\sqrt{10 \cdot \left(\frac{1}{2}\right)^2}}{4} + \cdots \right]$$

$$= \frac{\sqrt{10}}{4} + 2 \left[ \frac{\sqrt{10 \cdot \frac{1}{2}}}{4} + \frac{\sqrt{10 \cdot \left(\frac{1}{2}\right)^2}}{4} + \cdots \right]$$

The ratio of this geometric sequence is $\sqrt{\frac{1}{2}}$ and its absolute value is less than 1, so we can find its infinite sum using

$S = a_1/(1 - r)$. Thus, the total time is $\dfrac{\sqrt{10}}{4} + 2 \cdot \dfrac{\frac{\sqrt{5}}{4}}{1 - \sqrt{\frac{1}{2}}} \approx 4.61$ seconds.

[8] There are $8 \times 36 = 288$ contestants daily and $288 \times 30 = 8640$ contestants for the month. The probability that a contestant wins any particular prize for the daily tournament and the monthly tournament is $p_1 = \frac{1}{288}$ and $p_2 = \frac{1}{8640}$, respectively. If the game is to be fair, then the total expected value should equal the entry fee.

$EV_1(\text{daily}) = 250p_1 + 100p_1 + 50p_1 = 400p_1$.

$EV_2(\text{month}) = 4000p_2 + 2000p_2 + 1500p_2 + 1000p_2 + 800p_2 + 600p_2 + 500p_2 + 400p_2 + 300p_2 + 200p_2 +$
$$100(40p_2) + 75(50p_2) + 50(200p_2) + 25(200p_2)$$
$$= 34{,}050p_2.$$

Thus, $EV_{\text{total}} = EV_1 + EV_2 = 400p_1 + 34{,}050p_2 = 400 \cdot \frac{1}{288} + 34{,}050 \cdot \frac{1}{8640} = \frac{46{,}050}{8640} = \frac{1535}{288} \approx \$5.33$.

[9] To the nearest penny with $r = 1.1008163$ (found by trial and error), we have the places 1st–10th:

| | | | | | | | | | | |
|---|---|---|---|---|---|---|---|---|---|---|
| $0.01: | 237.37 | 215.63 | 195.89 | 177.95 | 161.65 | 146.85 | 133.40 | 121.18 | 110.08 | 100 |
| $1.00: | 237.00 | 216.00 | 196.00 | 178.00 | 162.00 | 147.00 | 133.00 | 121.00 | 110.00 | 100 |
| $5.00: | 240.00 | 215.00 | 195.00 | 180.00 | 160.00 | 145.00 | 135.00 | 120.00 | 110.00 | 100 |
| $10.00: | 240.00 | 220.00 | 200.00 | 180.00 | 160.00 | 140.00 | 130.00 | 120.00 | 110.00 | 100 |

If the amounts are to be realistic, the amounts may not be rounded to the nearest amount—i.e, \$134 may be rounded to \$140 rather than \$130.

[10] Since we can have 0 to 5 toppings on a pizza, the number of ways to order one pizza is $\sum_{k=0}^{5} \binom{n}{k}$. Because there are

two pizzas, we have $\left[ \sum_{k=0}^{5} \binom{n}{k} \right]^2 = 1{,}048{,}576 \;\Rightarrow\; \sum_{k=0}^{5} \binom{n}{k} = 1024$. By trial and error, we find that $n = 11$.

On the TI graphing calculators, store 11 in N and use "sum(seq(N nCr R, R, 0, 5, 1))" to obtain 1024.

[11] First, calculate the probabilities for all prizes: $n(S) = C(55, 5) \cdot 42 = 146{,}107{,}962$

$$\begin{array}{llll}
n(5W, 1R) = C(5,5) \cdot C(50,0) \cdot 1 & \Rightarrow & P(5W, 1R) = & 1/146{,}107{,}962 & (p_1) \\
n(5W, 0R) = C(5,5) \cdot C(50,0) \cdot 41 & \Rightarrow & P(5W, 0R) = & 41/146{,}107{,}962 & (p_2) \\
n(4W, 1R) = C(5,4) \cdot C(50,1) \cdot 1 & \Rightarrow & P(4W, 1R) = & 250/146{,}107{,}962 & (p_3) \\
n(4W, 0R) = C(5,4) \cdot C(50,1) \cdot 41 & \Rightarrow & P(4W, 0R) = & 10{,}250/146{,}107{,}962 & (p_4) \\
n(3W, 1R) = C(5,3) \cdot C(50,2) \cdot 1 & \Rightarrow & P(3W, 1R) = & 12{,}250/146{,}107{,}962 & (p_5) \\
n(3W, 0R) = C(5,3) \cdot C(50,2) \cdot 41 & \Rightarrow & P(3W, 0R) = & 502{,}250/146{,}107{,}962 & (p_6) \\
n(2W, 1R) = C(5,2) \cdot C(50,3) \cdot 1 & \Rightarrow & P(2W, 1R) = & 196{,}000/146{,}107{,}962 & (p_7) \\
n(1W, 1R) = C(5,1) \cdot C(50,4) \cdot 1 & \Rightarrow & P(1W, 1R) = & 1{,}151{,}500/146{,}107{,}962 & (p_8) \\
n(0W, 1R) = C(5,0) \cdot C(50,5) \cdot 1 & \Rightarrow & P(0W, 1R) = & 2{,}118{,}760/146{,}107{,}962 & (p_9)
\end{array}$$

(a) The probability of winning the jackpot is $\frac{1}{146{,}107{,}962}$.

(b) The probability of winning any prize is the sum of all the probabilities, that is, $\frac{3,991,302}{146,107,962}$. This gives us odds of 142,116,660 to 3,991,302 (or about 35.6 to 1) for not winning any prize.

(c) The expected value of the game without the jackpot is

$$\sum_{k=2}^{9} a_k p_k = (\$200,000)p_2 + (\$10,000)p_3 + (\$100)p_4 + (\$100)p_5 + (\$7)p_6 + (\$7)p_7 + (\$4)p_8 + (\$3)p_9$$

$$= \frac{28,800,030}{146,107,962} \approx 0.20$$

(d) Assuming that one ticket costs \$1, we must have an expected value of 1 to be a fair game. Since the probability of winning the jackpot is $\frac{1}{146,107,962}$, we must multiply that probability by \$117,307,932 {146,107,962 − 28,800,030} so that the numerator of the expected value in part (c) is equal to the denominator.

**12** $P(M) = 0.20 = \frac{1}{5}$, so $O(M)$ are 1 to 4. Since the odds are three times more favorable for a female applicant, $O(F)$ are 3 to 4. Hence, $P(F) = \frac{3}{7} \approx 0.43$.

**13** We are given that $(a+b)^n = \sum_{k=0}^{n} \binom{n}{k}(a)^{n-k}(b)^k$. Thus,

$$(0+1)^n = \sum_{k=0}^{n} \binom{n}{k}(0)^{n-k}(1)^k \qquad \text{let } a = 0 \text{ and } b = 1$$

$$1^n = 0^n \cdot 1^0 + 0^{n-1} \cdot 1^1 + \cdots + 0^0 \cdot 1^n \qquad \text{expand}$$

$$1 = 0 + 0 + \cdots + 0^0 \qquad \text{simplify}$$

$$1 = 0^0 \qquad \text{simplify}$$

So we can use the result $0^0 = 1$, which is consistent with results in mathematics courses at a higher level.

**14** $S = \sum_{n=0}^{\infty} (-1)^n \frac{3^{3/2}}{2^{3n+2}} \left( \frac{2}{3n+1} + \frac{1}{3n+2} \right)$

| $n$ | $a_n$ | $s_n$ |
|---|---|---|
| 0 | 3.247 595 264 191 | 3.247 595 264 |
| 1 | −0.113 665 834 247 | 3.133 929 430 |
| 2 | 0.008 336 461 058 | 3.142 265 891 |
| 3 | −0.000 738 089 833 | 3.141 527 801 |
| 4 | 0.000 071 445 423 | 3.141 599 247 |
| 5 | −0.000 007 287 408 | 3.141 591 959 |
| 6 | 0.000 000 769 397 | 3.141 592 729 |
| 7 | −0.000 000 083 244 | 3.141 592 645 |
| 8 | 0.000 000 009 172 | 3.141 592 655 |
| 9 | −0.000 000 000 103 | 3.141 592 653 |
| 10 | 0.000 000 000 116 | 3.141 592 654 |

As $n \to \infty$, $s_n \to \pi$. The infinite sum, $S$, is equal to $\pi$ (not approximately equal to $\pi$).

**15** (a) The pattern has a 1 in the denominator, an $n$ in the numerator, and the next terms of any row of Pascal's triangle oscillate between denominator and numerator. The signs are in pairs (two positive, two negative, etc.) The power of $\tan x$ increases one with each term. Thus,

$$\tan 5x = \frac{5\tan x - 10\tan^3 x + \tan^5 x}{1 - 10\tan^2 x + 5\tan^4 x}.$$

(b) The coefficients listed in the text are in the form 1–2–1. The next identities are:

$$\cos 3x = 1\cos^3 x \quad - \quad 3\cos x \sin^2 x$$
$$\sin 3x = \quad 3\cos^2 x \sin x \quad - \quad 1\sin^3 x$$
$$\cos 4x = 1\cos^4 x \quad - \quad 6\cos^2 x\sin^2 x \quad + \quad 1\sin^4 x$$
$$\sin 4x = \quad 4\cos^3 x \sin x \quad - \quad 4\cos x \sin^3 x$$

Notice the pattern of coefficients: for $\cos 3x$ and $\sin 3x$ we have 1-3-3-1; for $\cos 4x$ and $\sin 4x$ we have 1-4-6-4-1. Since these are rows in Pascal's triangle, we predict the pattern 1-5-10-10-5-1 for $\cos 5x$ and $\sin 5x$:

$$\cos 5x = 1\cos^5 x \quad - \quad 10\cos^3 x\sin^2 x \quad + \quad 5\cos x\sin^4 x$$
$$\sin 5x = \quad 5\cos^4 x \sin x \quad - \quad 10\cos^2 x\sin^3 x \quad + \quad 1\sin^5 x$$

## Chapter 9 Test

**1** $\{3 + 1/n\}$ • The fourth term is $3\frac{1}{4}$. The eighth term is $3\frac{1}{8}$. The sum is $3\frac{1}{4} + 3\frac{1}{8} = 6\frac{3}{8}$.

**2** $a_1 = 6$, $a_2 = 2$, $a_{k+2} = 4a_{k+1} - 3a_k$ for $k \geq 1$     {given formula}      ★ $-10, -46$
$$a_3 = 4a_2 - 3a_1 = 4(2) - 3(6) = 8 - 18 = -10 \quad \{k = 1\}$$
$$a_4 = 4a_3 - 3a_2 = 4(-10) - 3(2) = -40 - 6 = -46 \quad \{k = 2\}$$

**3** By (2) of the theorem on the sum of a constant, $\sum\limits_{k=189}^{652} \frac{3}{29} = (652 - 189 + 1)(\frac{3}{29}) = 464(\frac{3}{29}) = 48$.

**4** $\sum\limits_{k=0}^{8}(2j - 7) = (8 - 0 + 1)(2j - 7) = 9(2j - 7) = 18j - 63$ { note that $k$, not $j$, is the summation variable }

**5** $d = 18 - 25 = -7$; $a_n = 25 + (n - 1)(-7) = -7n + 32$, so a formula for the $n$th term is $a_n = -7n + 32$.

**6** $a_{12} = 109$ and $a_{347} = 2119$ $\Rightarrow$ $(347 - 12)d = 2119 - 109$ $\Rightarrow$ $d = \frac{2010}{335} = 6$.
$$a_{856} = a_{12} + (856 - 12)d = 109 + 844(6) = 5173.$$

**7** $6 + 17 + 28 + \cdots + 25{,}460$ • $d = 17 - 6 = 11$ and $a_n = a_1 + (n - 1)d = 6 + (n - 1)11 = 11n - 5$.

Find the largest value of $n$: $11n - 5 = 25{,}460$ $\Rightarrow$ $11n = 25{,}465$ $\Rightarrow$ $n = 2315$.

Thus, the summation notation is $\sum\limits_{n=1}^{2315}(11n - 5)$. Now find the sum: $S_{2315} = \frac{2315}{2}(6 + 25{,}460) = 29{,}476{,}895$.

**8** $5217 + 4d = 8789$ $\Rightarrow$ $4d = 3572$ $\Rightarrow$ $d = 893$. The means are $5217 + 893 = 6110$, $6110 + 893 = 7003$, and $7003 + 893 = 7896$.      ★ $6110, 7003, 7896$

**9** $1 + 6d = 3.8$ $\Rightarrow$ $6d = 2.8$ $\Rightarrow$ $d = \frac{2.8}{6} = \frac{7}{15} = 0.4\overline{6}$. The settings are $1$, $1.4\overline{6}$, $1.9\overline{3}$, $2.4$, $2.8\overline{6}$, $3.\overline{3}$, and $3.8$. The settings between 2.5 and 3.5, to the nearest 0.01 inch, are 2.87 and 3.33 inches.

**10** $36, 12, 4, \ldots$ • $r = \frac{12}{36} = \frac{1}{3}$, so a formula for the $n$th term is $a_n = 36(\frac{1}{3})^{n-1}$.

**11** $a_2 = \frac{1}{2}$ and $a_5 = -32$ $\Rightarrow$ $r^3 = \frac{-32}{1/2} = -64$ $\Rightarrow$ $r = -4$. $a_9 = a_5 r^4 = (-32)(-4)^4 = -8192$.

**12** $\sum\limits_{k=1}^{8} \frac{3}{8}(3)^{k-1} = \frac{3}{8} \cdot \frac{1 - 3^8}{1 - 3} = \frac{3}{8} \cdot \frac{-6560}{-2} = 1230$

**13** $2125 - 1275 + 765 - \cdots$ • $r = \frac{-1275}{2125} = -0.6$, so $S = \frac{a_1}{1 - r} = \frac{2125}{1 - (-0.6)} = 1328.125$.

**14** For $1.\overline{47} = 1 + 0.\overline{47}$, $a_1 = 0.47$, $r = 0.01$, so $S = 1 + \frac{0.47}{1 - 0.01} = 1 + \frac{47}{99} = \frac{99}{99} + \frac{47}{99} = \frac{146}{99}$.

**15** The geometric mean of 40 and 250 is $\sqrt{40 \cdot 250} = \sqrt{10{,}000} = 100$.

**16** 8% growth means that the ratio of the second year to the first year is 1.08. A formula for the $n$th term of a geometric sequence is $a_n = a_1 r^{n-1} = (1)(1.08)^{n-1}$, or $a_n = (1.08)^{n-1}$. Thus, $a_{15} = (1.08)^{14} \approx 2.94$, which means that after 14 years of 8% growth, any amount invested would be worth about 2.94 times its original amount.

**17** (1) $P_1$ is true, since $6(1) - 4 = 2$ and $3(1)^2 - 1 = 2$.

    (2) Assume $P_k$ is true: $2 + 8 + 14 + \cdots + (6k - 4) = 3k^2 - k$. Hence,

$$2 + 8 + 14 + \cdots + (6k - 4) + [6(k+1) - 4] = 3k^2 - k + [6(k+1) - 4]$$
$$= 3k^2 - k + 6k + 2$$
$$= 3k^2 + 6k + 3 - (k+1)$$
$$= 3(k^2 + 2k + 1) - (k+1)$$
$$= 3(k+1)^2 - (k+1)$$

Thus, $P_{k+1}$ is true, and the proof is complete.

**18** $(2x - 5y^2)^3 = \binom{3}{0}(2x)^3(-5y^2)^0 + \binom{3}{1}(2x)^2(-5y^2)^1 + \binom{3}{2}(2x)^1(-5y^2)^2 + \binom{3}{3}(2x)^0(-5y^2)^3$
$$= (1)(8x^3)(1) - (3)(4x^2)(5y^2) + (3)(2x)(25y^4) - (1)(1)(125y^6)$$
$$= 8x^3 - 60x^2y^2 + 150xy^4 - 125y^6$$

**19** $(2x^2 - x^{-1})^{18}$ • 14th term $= \binom{18}{13}(2x^2)^5 (-x^{-1})^{13} = 8568(32x^{10})(-x^{-13}) = -274{,}176x^{-3}$

**20** $(x^4 - 3x^{-2})^{12}$ • first two terms $= \binom{12}{0}(x^4)^{12} (-3x^{-2})^0 + \binom{12}{1}(x^4)^{11} (-3x^{-2})^1$
$$= (1)(x^{48})(1) + (12)(x^{44})(-3x^{-2})$$
$$= x^{48} - 36x^{42}$$

**21** $P(150, 50) = \dfrac{150!}{100!}$ and $C(150, 50) = \dfrac{150!}{100!\,50!}$, so $P(150, 50)$ is 50! times $C(150, 50)$. Note that $P(150, 50)$ is too large to be calculated by most calculators.

**22** There are 10 digits, so the number of 9 digit social security numbers is $10^9 = 1$ billion.

    1 billion $-$ 300 million $=$ 700 million unused numbers.

**23** By the fundamental counting principle, $26 \cdot 25 \cdot 10 \cdot 10 = 65{,}000$.

**24** We need to pick 17 teams from a group of 30 teams and the order of selection is important, so this is a permutation. $P(30, 17) \approx 4.3 \times 10^{22}$

**25** There are 2 choices for each game, which gives us $2^8 = 256$ ways to list the winners (or losers).

**26** There are 13! ways to order the spades and 39! ways to order the other cards. By the fundamental counting principle, there are $13! \times 39! \approx 1.27 \times 10^{56}$ ways to shuffle the deck.

**27** There are $C(10, 3)$ ways to pick the men and $C(12, 4)$ ways to pick the women. There are $C(22, 7)$ ways to pick the committee, so the desired probability is $\dfrac{C(10, 3) \cdot C(12, 4)}{C(22, 7)} = \dfrac{120 \cdot 495}{170{,}544} = \dfrac{59{,}400}{170{,}544} \approx 0.3483$.

**28** The amounts received are the same, so the order of selection *is not* important, and we use a combination.
$$C(5000, 5) = \frac{5000!}{4995!\,5!} \approx 2.6 \times 10^{16}$$

**29** $P(7 \text{ heads in 10 flips}) = \dfrac{C(10, 7)}{2^{10}} = \dfrac{120}{1024} \approx 11.7\%$

**30** $P(B \cup F) = P(B) + P(F) - P(B \cap F) = \frac{26}{52} + \frac{12}{52} - \frac{6}{52} = \frac{32}{52}$

**31** There are 3 ways for the event to occur and 8 ways for the event to *not* occur. Thus, the odds of the event occurring are 3 to 8.

**32** $P(E) = 0.63 = \frac{63}{100}$, so $O(E)$ is 63 to 37, or 1.70 to 1.

**33** The probability of rolling a six is $\frac{1}{6}$ and of not rolling a six is $\frac{5}{6}$. The probability of not rolling a six in 4 rolls is $\left(\frac{5}{6}\right)^4 = \frac{625}{1296}$.

**34** The probability of rolling a six is $\frac{1}{6}$ and of not rolling a six is $\frac{5}{6}$. We want to know how many rolls it takes to give us a 10% chance of *not* rolling a six. $\left(\frac{5}{6}\right)^n = 0.10 \quad \Rightarrow \quad \ln\left(\frac{5}{6}\right)^n = \ln 0.10 \quad \Rightarrow \quad n \ln \frac{5}{6} = \ln 0.10 \quad \Rightarrow \quad n = 13$

**35** Use M for million.
$$EV = 1\,\text{M} \cdot \frac{1}{20\,\text{M}} + 0.1\,\text{M} \cdot \frac{10}{20\,\text{M}} + 5000 \cdot \frac{50}{20\,\text{M}}$$
$$= \frac{1}{20\,\text{M}}(1\,\text{M} + 0.1\,\text{M} \cdot 10 + 5000 \cdot 50)$$
$$= \frac{1}{20\,\text{M}}(2{,}250{,}000) = \$0.1125$$

30. $P(A \cup B) = P(A) + P(B) - P(A \cap B) = \frac{6}{13} + \frac{1}{13} - \frac{2}{13} = \frac{5}{13}$

31. There are 3 ways for the event to occur and 5 ways for the event to not occur. Thus, the odds of the event occurring are 3 to 5.

32. $P(E) = \frac{30}{100} = 0.3$, so $O(E)$ is 30 to 70, or 3 to 7.

33. The probability of rolling a six is $\frac{1}{6}$ and of not rolling a six in 4 rolls is $\left(\frac{5}{6}\right)^4 = \frac{625}{1296}$

34. The probability of rolling a six is $\frac{1}{6}$ and of not rolling a six is $\frac{5}{6}$. We want to know how many rolls to give us a 90% chance of not rolling a six. $\left(\frac{5}{6}\right)^n = 0.10 \implies \ln\left(\frac{5}{6}\right)^n = \ln 0.10 \implies n\ln\frac{5}{6} = \ln 0.10 \implies n = \frac{\ln 0.10}{\ln\frac{5}{6}} \approx 13$

35. Use M formation. $EV = 1 \cdot M - \frac{1}{20}M + 0.1 M \cdot \frac{1}{20}M - 5000 \cdot \frac{10}{20}M - \frac{30}{20}M$
$= \frac{1}{20}M(1 M + 0.1 M \cdot 10 - 5000 - 60)$
$= \frac{1}{20}M(2,260,000) = \$0.1125$

### 10.1 Exercises

**Note:** For Exercises 1–12, we will put each parabola equation in one of the forms listed on page 719—either

$$(x - h)^2 = 4p(y - k) \quad \text{or} \quad (y - k)^2 = 4p(x - h).$$

Once in one of those forms, the information concerning the vertex, focus, and directrix is easily obtainable and illustrated in the chart in the text. Let $V$, $F$, and $l$ denote the vertex, focus, and directrix, respectively.

$\boxed{1}$ $8y = x^2 \Rightarrow y = \frac{1}{8}x^2 \Rightarrow p = \frac{1}{4a} = \frac{1}{4\left(\frac{1}{8}\right)} = \frac{1}{\frac{1}{2}} = 2.$ We know that the parabola opens either upward or downward since the variable "$x$" is squared. Since $p$ is positive, we know that the parabola opens upward and that the focus is 2 units above the vertex. The directrix is 2 units below the vertex. $\quad V(0,0); F(0,2); l: y = -2$

Figure 1

Figure 2

$\boxed{2}$ $x^2 = -3y \Rightarrow (x - 0)^2 = -3(y - 0) \Rightarrow 4p = -3 \Rightarrow p = -\frac{3}{4}; V(0,0); F\left(0, -\frac{3}{4}\right); l: y = \frac{3}{4}$

$\boxed{3}$ $2y^2 = -3x \Rightarrow (y - 0)^2 = -\frac{3}{2}(x - 0) \Rightarrow 4p = -\frac{3}{2} \Rightarrow p = -\frac{3}{8}.$ We know that the parabola opens either right or left since the variable "$y$" is squared. Since $p$ is negative, we know that the parabola opens left and that the focus is $\frac{3}{8}$ unit to the left of the vertex. The directrix is $\frac{3}{8}$ unit to the right of the vertex.

$$V(0,0); F\left(-\frac{3}{8}, 0\right); l: x = \frac{3}{8}$$

Figure 3

Figure 4

$\boxed{4}$ $20x = y^2 \Rightarrow x = \frac{1}{20}y^2 \Rightarrow p = \frac{1}{4\left(\frac{1}{20}\right)} = 5; V(0,0); F(5,0); l: x = -5$

**581**

**5** $(x+2)^2 = -8(y-1) \Rightarrow 4p = -8 \Rightarrow p = -2$. The $(x+2)$ and $(y-1)$ factors indicate that we need to shift the vertex of the parabola having equation $x^2 = -8y$, 2 units left and 1 unit up—that is, move it from $(0,0)$ to $(-2,1)$.

$$V(-2,1); \ F(-2,-1); \ l: y = 3$$

*Figure 5*

*Figure 6*

**6** $(x-3)^2 = \frac{1}{2}(y+1) \Rightarrow 4p = \frac{1}{2} \Rightarrow p = \frac{1}{8}; \ V(3,-1); \ F\left(3,-\frac{7}{8}\right); \ l: y = -\frac{9}{8}$

**7** $(y-2)^2 = \frac{1}{4}(x-3) \Rightarrow 4p = \frac{1}{4} \Rightarrow p = \frac{1}{16}$. "$y$" squared and $p$ positive imply that the parabola opens to the right and the focus is to the right of the vertex. The $(x-3)$ and $(y-2)$ factors indicate that we need to shift the vertex 3 units right and 2 units up from $(0,0)$ to $(3,2)$.

$$V(3,2); \ F\left(\tfrac{49}{16},2\right); \ l: x = \tfrac{47}{16}$$

*Figure 7*

*Figure 8*

**8** $(y+1)^2 = -12(x+2) \Rightarrow 4p = -12 \Rightarrow p = -3; \ V(-2,-1); \ F(-5,-1); \ l: x = 1$

**9** For this exercise, we need to "complete the square" in order to get the equation in proper form. The term we need to add is $\left[\frac{1}{2}(\text{coefficient of } x)\right]^2$. In this case, that value is $\left[\frac{1}{2}(-4)\right]^2 = 4$. Notice that we add and subtract the value 4 from the same side of the equation as opposed to adding 4 to both sides of the equation.

$y = x^2 - 4x + 2 \Rightarrow y = (x^2 - 4x + \underline{4}) + 2 - \underline{4} \Rightarrow y = (x-2)^2 - 2 \Rightarrow (y+2) = 1(x-2)^2 \Rightarrow$
$4p = 1 \Rightarrow p = \frac{1}{4}$.

$$V(2,-2); \ F\left(2,-\tfrac{7}{4}\right); \ l: y = -\tfrac{9}{4}$$

*Figure 9*

*Figure 10*

**10** $x^2 + 20y = 10 \Rightarrow x^2 = -20y + 10 \Rightarrow (x-0)^2 = -20\left(y - \frac{1}{2}\right) \Rightarrow 4p = -20 \Rightarrow p = -5$.

$$V\left(0,\tfrac{1}{2}\right); \ F\left(0,-\tfrac{9}{2}\right); \ l: y = \tfrac{11}{2}$$

**11**   $y^2 + 14y + 4x + 45 = 0 \Rightarrow -4x = (y^2 + 14y + \underline{49}) + 45 - \underline{49} \Rightarrow -4x + 4 = (y + 7)^2 \Rightarrow$

$\qquad (y + 7)^2 = -4(x - 1) \Rightarrow 4p = -4 \Rightarrow p = -1; V(1, -7); F(0, -7); l: x = 2$

*Figure 11*

*Figure 12*

**12**   $y^2 - 4y - 2x - 4 = 0 \Rightarrow 2x = (y^2 - 4y + \underline{4}) - 4 - \underline{4} \Rightarrow 2(x + 4) = (y - 2)^2 \Rightarrow 4p = 2 \Rightarrow$

$\qquad p = \frac{1}{2}; V(-4, 2); F\left(-\frac{7}{2}, 2\right); l: x = -\frac{9}{2}$

**13**   Since the vertex is at $(1, 0)$ and the parabola has a horizontal axis, the standard equation has the form $(y - 0)^2 = 4p(x - 1)$. The distance from the focus $F(6, 0)$ to the vertex $V(1, 0)$ is $6 - 1 = 5$, which is the value of $p$. Hence, an equation of the parabola is $y^2 = 20(x - 1)$.

**14**   $V(0, -2) \Rightarrow x^2 = 4p(y + 2). \ F(0, 1) \Rightarrow x^2 = 4[1 - (-2)](y + 2) \Rightarrow x^2 = 12(y + 2).$

**15**   An equation of a parabola with vertex $V(-2, 3)$ is $(x + 2)^2 = 4p(y - 3)$. Since the point $P(2, 2)$ is on the graph, we'll substitute 2 for $x$ and 2 for $y$ and then find $p$. $x = 2, y = 2 \Rightarrow (2 + 2)^2 = 4p(2 - 3) \Rightarrow$

$\qquad 16 = 4p(-1) \Rightarrow p = -4$, so an equation is $(x + 2)^2 = -16(y - 3)$.

**16**   $V(3, -2) \Rightarrow (y + 2)^2 = 4p(x - 3). \ x = 1, y = 0 \Rightarrow 4 = 4p(-2) \Rightarrow p = -\frac{1}{2}. \ (y + 2)^2 = -2(x - 3).$

**17**   The distance from the focus $F(3, 2)$ to the directrix $l: y = -1$ is $2 - (-1) = 3$ units. The vertex $V$ is the point $\left(3, \frac{1}{2}\right)$ {halfway between $F$ and $l$}, so the form of an equation of the parabola is $(x - 3)^2 = 4p\left(y - \frac{1}{2}\right)$.

The value of $p$ is the difference in the $y$-values; that is, $p = 2 - \frac{1}{2} = \frac{3}{2}$.

Thus, the equation is $(x - 3)^2 = 4\left(\frac{3}{2}\right)\left(y - \frac{1}{2}\right)$, or, equivalently, $(x - 3)^2 = 6\left(y - \frac{1}{2}\right)$.

**18**   The distance from the focus $F(2, -2)$ to the directrix $l: y = 4$ is $4 - (-2) = 6$ units. The vertex $V$ is the point $(2, 1)$ {halfway between $F$ and $l$}, so the form of an equation of the parabola is $(x - 2)^2 = 4p(y - 1)$.

The value of $p$ is the difference in the $y$-values; that is, $p = -2 - 1 = -3$.

Thus, the equation is $(x - 2)^2 = 4(-3)(y - 1)$, or, equivalently, $(x - 2)^2 = -12(y - 1)$.

**19**   The distance from the focus $F(-1, -3)$ to the directrix $l: x = -2$ is $-1 - (-2) = 1$ unit.

The vertex $V$ is the point $\left(-\frac{3}{2}, -3\right)$ {halfway between $F$ and $l$}.

$V\left(-\frac{3}{2}, -3\right) \Rightarrow (y + 3)^2 = 4p\left(x + \frac{3}{2}\right)$.

$F(-1, -3) \Rightarrow (y + 3)^2 = 4\left[-1 - \left(-\frac{3}{2}\right)\right]\left(x + \frac{3}{2}\right) \Rightarrow (y + 3)^2 = 2\left(x + \frac{3}{2}\right)$.

**20**   The distance from the focus $F(-2, 1)$ to the directrix $l: x = 3$ is $3 - (-2) = 5$ units.

The vertex $V$ is the point $\left(\frac{1}{2}, 1\right)$ {halfway between $F$ and $l$}.

$V\left(\frac{1}{2}, 1\right) \Rightarrow (y - 1)^2 = 4p\left(x - \frac{1}{2}\right)$.

$F(-2, 1) \Rightarrow (y - 1)^2 = 4\left[-2 - \frac{1}{2}\right]\left(x - \frac{1}{2}\right) \Rightarrow (y - 1)^2 = -10\left(x - \frac{1}{2}\right)$.

**21** The distance from the directrix $x = -2$ to the focus $F(2, 0)$ is $2 - (-2) = 4$ units.

The vertex $V(0, 0)$ is halfway between the directrix and the focus—that is, 2 units from either one.

Since the focus is 2 units to the right of the vertex, $p$ is 2. Using one of the forms of an equation of a parabola with vertex at $(h, k)$, we have $(y - 0)^2 = 4p(x - 0)$, or, equivalently, $y^2 = 8x$.

**22** $F(-4, 0)$ and $l: x = 4 \Rightarrow p = -4$ and $V(0, 0)$. $(y - 0)^2 = 4p(x - 0) \Rightarrow y^2 = -16x$.

**23** $F(6, 4)$ and $l: y = -2 \Rightarrow 2p = 4 - (-2) \Rightarrow 2p = 6 \Rightarrow p = 3$ and $V(6, 1)$.
$$(x - 6)^2 = 4p(y - 1) \Rightarrow (x - 6)^2 = 12(y - 1).$$

**24** $F(-3, -2)$ and $l: y = 1 \Rightarrow 2p = -2 - 1 \Rightarrow 2p = -3 \Rightarrow p = -\frac{3}{2}$ and $V\left(-3, -\frac{1}{2}\right)$.
$$(x + 3)^2 = 4p\left(y + \tfrac{1}{2}\right) \Rightarrow (x + 3)^2 = -6\left(y + \tfrac{1}{2}\right).$$

**25** $V(3, -5)$ and $l: x = 2 \Rightarrow p = 3 - 2 = 1$. $(y + 5)^2 = 4p(x - 3) \Rightarrow (y + 5)^2 = 4(x - 3)$.

**26** $V(-2, 3)$ and $l: x = 1 \Rightarrow p = -2 - 1 = -3$. $(y - 3)^2 = 4p(x + 2) \Rightarrow (y - 3)^2 = -12(x + 2)$.

**27** $V(-2, 3)$ and $l: y = 5 \Rightarrow p = 3 - 5 = -2$. $(x + 2)^2 = 4p(y - 3) \Rightarrow (x + 2)^2 = -8(y - 3)$.

**28** $V(4, 2)$ and $l: y = -6 \Rightarrow p = 2 - (-6) = 8$. $(x - 4)^2 = 4p(y - 2) \Rightarrow (x - 4)^2 = 32(y - 2)$.

**29** $V(-1, 0)$ and $F(-4, 0) \Rightarrow p = -4 - (-1) = -3$. $(y - 0)^2 = 4p(x + 1) \Rightarrow y^2 = -12(x + 1)$.

**30** $V(-2, 1)$ and $F(2, 1) \Rightarrow p = 2 - (-2) = 4$. $(y - 1)^2 = 4p(x + 2) \Rightarrow (y - 1)^2 = 16(x + 2)$.

**31** $V(1, -2)$ and $F(1, 0) \Rightarrow p = 0 - (-2) = 2$. $(x - 1)^2 = 4p(y + 2) \Rightarrow (x - 1)^2 = 8(y + 2)$.

**32** $V(4, 7)$ and $F(4, 2) \Rightarrow p = 2 - 7 = -5$. $(x - 4)^2 = 4p(y - 7) \Rightarrow (x - 4)^2 = -20(y - 7)$.

**33** The vertex at the origin and symmetric to the $y$-axis imply that the equation is of the form $y = ax^2$.

Substituting $x = 2$ and $y = -3$ into that equation yields $-3 = a \cdot 4 \Rightarrow a = -\frac{3}{4}$.

Thus, an equation is $y = -\frac{3}{4}x^2$, or $3x^2 = -4y$.

**34** $y = ax^2 \Rightarrow 3 = a(6)^2 \Rightarrow a = \frac{1}{12}$. $y = \frac{1}{12}x^2$, or $12y = x^2$.

**35** The vertex at $(-3, 5)$ and axis parallel to the $x$-axis imply that the equation is of the form $(y - 5)^2 = 4p(x + 3)$.

Substituting $x = 5$ and $y = 9$ into that equation yields $16 = 4p \cdot 8 \Rightarrow p = \frac{1}{2}$.

Thus, an equation is $(y - 5)^2 = 2(x + 3)$.

**36** $(y + 2)^2 = 4p(x - 3) \Rightarrow (1 + 2)^2 = 4p(0 - 3) \Rightarrow -\frac{9}{12} = p \Rightarrow (y + 2)^2 = -3(x - 3)$

**37** Refer to the definition of a parabola. The point $P(0, 5)$ is the fixed point (focus) and the line $l: y = -3$ is the fixed line (directrix). The vertex is halfway between the focus and the directrix—that is, at $V(0, 1)$. An equation is of the form $(x - h)^2 = 4p(y - k) \Rightarrow (x - 0)^2 = 4p(y - 1)$. The distance from the vertex to the focus is $p = 5 - 1 = 4$. Thus, an equation is $(x - 0)^2 = 4(4)(y - 1) \Rightarrow x^2 = 16(y - 1)$.

**38** $P(7, 0)$ and $l: x = 1 \Rightarrow V(4, 0)$. $p = 7 - 4 = 3 \Rightarrow y^2 = 4p(x - 4) \Rightarrow y^2 = 12(x - 4)$.

**39** The point $P(-6, 3)$ is the fixed point (focus) and the line $l: x = -2$ is the fixed line (directrix). The vertex is halfway between the focus and the directrix—that is, at $V(-4, 3)$. An equation is of the form $(y - 3)^2 = 4p(x + 4)$. The distance from the vertex to the focus is $p = -6 - (-4) = -2$.

Thus, an equation is $(y - 3)^2 = -8(x + 4)$.

**40** $P(5, -2)$ and $l$: $y = 4$ $\Rightarrow$ $V(5, 1)$.
$$p = -2 - 1 = -3 \Rightarrow (x - 5)^2 = 4p(y - 1) \Rightarrow (x - 5)^2 = -12(y - 1).$$

**Note:** To find an equation for a lower or upper half, we need to solve for $y$ (use $-$ or $+$ respectively). For the left or right half, solve for $x$ (use $-$ or $+$ respectively).

**41** Lower half of $(y + 1)^2 = x + 3$ $\Rightarrow$ $y + 1 = \pm\sqrt{x + 3}$ $\Rightarrow$ $y = -\sqrt{x + 3} - 1$

**42** Upper half of $(y - 2)^2 = x - 4$ $\Rightarrow$ $y - 2 = \pm\sqrt{x - 4}$ $\Rightarrow$ $y = \sqrt{x - 4} + 2$

**43** Right half of $(x + 1)^2 = y - 4$ $\Rightarrow$ $x + 1 = \pm\sqrt{y - 4}$ $\Rightarrow$ $x = \sqrt{y - 4} - 1$

**44** Left half of $(x + 3)^2 = y + 2$ $\Rightarrow$ $x + 3 = \pm\sqrt{y + 2}$ $\Rightarrow$ $x = -\sqrt{y + 2} - 3$

**45** Upper half of $(y - 5)^2 = x + 2$ $\Rightarrow$ $y - 5 = \pm\sqrt{x + 2}$ $\Rightarrow$ $y = \sqrt{x + 2} + 5$

**46** Lower half of $(y + 4)^2 = x - 3$ $\Rightarrow$ $y + 4 = \pm\sqrt{x - 3}$ $\Rightarrow$ $y = -\sqrt{x - 3} - 4$

**47** Left half of $(x - 2)^2 = y + 1$ $\Rightarrow$ $x - 2 = \pm\sqrt{y + 1}$ $\Rightarrow$ $x = -\sqrt{y + 1} + 2$

**48** Right half of $(x - 4)^2 = y - 5$ $\Rightarrow$ $x - 4 = \pm\sqrt{y - 5}$ $\Rightarrow$ $x = \sqrt{y - 5} + 4$

**49** $y = \sqrt{x - 6} - 2$ $\Rightarrow$ $y + 2 = \sqrt{x - 6}$ $\Rightarrow$ $(y + 2)^2 = x - 6$.

Since $y \geq -2$ in the original equation, the graph is the *upper half* of the parabola $(y + 2)^2 = x - 6$.

**50** $y = -\sqrt{x + 3} + 4$ $\Rightarrow$ $y - 4 = -\sqrt{x + 3}$ $\Rightarrow$ $(y - 4)^2 = x + 3$.

Since $y \leq 4$ in the original equation, the graph is the *lower half* of the parabola $(y - 4)^2 = x + 3$.

**51** $x = -\sqrt{y + 7} - 3$ $\Rightarrow$ $x + 3 = -\sqrt{y + 7}$ $\Rightarrow$ $(x + 3)^2 = y + 7$.

Since $x \leq -3$ in the original equation, the graph is the *left half* of the parabola $(x + 3)^2 = y + 7$.

**52** $x = \sqrt{y - 4} + 8$ $\Rightarrow$ $x - 8 = \sqrt{y - 4}$ $\Rightarrow$ $(x - 8)^2 = y - 4$.

Since $x \geq 8$ in the original equation, the graph is the *right half* of the parabola $(x - 8)^2 = y - 4$.

**53** The parabola has an equation of the form $y = ax^2 + bx + c$. Substituting the $x$- and $y$-values of

$P(2, 5)$, $Q(-2, -3)$, and $R(1, 6)$ into this equation yields:
$$\begin{cases} 4a + 2b + c = 5 & P & (E_1) \\ 4a - 2b + c = -3 & Q & (E_2) \\ a + b + c = 6 & R & (E_3) \end{cases}$$

Solving $E_3$ for $c$ $\{c = 6 - a - b\}$ and substituting into $E_1$ and $E_2$ yields: $\begin{cases} 3a + b = -1 & (E_4) \\ 3a - 3b = -9 & (E_5) \end{cases}$

$E_4 - E_5$ $\Rightarrow$ $4b = 8$ $\Rightarrow$ $b = 2$; $a = -1$; $c = 5$. The equation is $y = -x^2 + 2x + 5$.

**54** The parabola has an equation of the form $y = ax^2 + bx + c$. Substituting the $x$- and $y$-values of

$P(3, -1)$, $Q(1, -7)$, and $R(-2, 14)$ into this equation yields: $\begin{cases} 9a + 3b + 3c = -1 & P & (E_1) \\ a + b + c = -7 & Q & (E_2) \\ 4a - 2b + c = 14 & R & (E_3) \end{cases}$

Solving $E_2$ for $c$ $\{c = -7 - a - b\}$ and substituting into $E_1$ and $E_3$ yields:
$\begin{cases} 8a + 2b = 6 & (E_4) \\ 3a - 3b = 21 & (E_5) \end{cases}$ $\Rightarrow$ $\begin{cases} 4a + b = 3 & (E_6) \\ a - b = 7 & (E_7) \end{cases}$

$E_6 + E_7$ $\Rightarrow$ $5a = 10$ $\Rightarrow$ $a = 2$; $b = -5$; $c = -4$. The equation is $y = 2x^2 - 5x - 4$.

**55** The parabola has an equation of the form $x = ay^2 + by + c$. Substituting the $x$- and $y$-values of

$P(-1, 1)$, $Q(11, -2)$, and $R(5, -1)$ into this equation yields: $\begin{cases} a + b + c = -1 & P & (E_1) \\ 4a - 2b + c = 11 & Q & (E_2) \\ a - b + c = 5 & R & (E_3) \end{cases}$

Solving $E_3$ for $c$ $\{c = 5 - a + b\}$ and substituting into $E_1$ and $E_2$ yields: $\begin{cases} 2b = -6 & (E_4) \\ 3a - b = 6 & (E_5) \end{cases}$

$E_4 \Rightarrow b = -3; a = 1; c = 1$. The equation is $x = y^2 - 3y + 1$.

**56** The parabola has an equation of the form $x = ay^2 + by + c$. Substituting the $x$ and $y$ values of

$P(2, 1)$, $Q(6, 2)$, and $R(12, -1)$ into this equation yields: $\begin{cases} a + b + c = 2 & P & (E_1) \\ 4a + 2b + c = 6 & Q & (E_2) \\ a - b + c = 12 & R & (E_3) \end{cases}$

Solving $E_3$ for $c$ $\{c = 12 - a + b\}$ and substituting into $E_1$ and $E_2$ yields: $\begin{cases} 2b = -10 & (E_4) \\ 3a + 3b = -6 & (E_5) \end{cases}$

$E_4 \Rightarrow b = -5; a = 3; c = 4$. The equation is $x = 3y^2 - 5y + 4$.

**57** A cross-section of the mirror is a parabola with $V(0, 0)$ and passing through $P(4, 1)$. The incoming light will collect at the focus $F$. A general equation of this form of a parabola is $y = ax^2$. Substituting $x = 4$ and $y = 1$ gives us $1 = a(4)^2 \Rightarrow a = \frac{1}{16}$. $p = 1/(4a) = 1/\left(\frac{1}{4}\right) = 4$.

The light will collect 4 inches from the center of the mirror.

**58** $y = ax^2 \Rightarrow 3 = a(5)^2 \Rightarrow a = \frac{3}{25}$. $p = \frac{1}{4a} = \frac{1}{12/25} = \frac{25}{12}$ ft.

**59** If we set up a coordinate system with a parabola opening upward and the vertex at the origin, then the phrase "3 feet across at the opening and 1 foot deep" implies that the points $\left(\pm\frac{3}{2}, 1\right)$ are on the parabola.

$y = ax^2 \Rightarrow 1 = a\left(\frac{3}{2}\right)^2 \Rightarrow a = \frac{4}{9}$. $p = \frac{1}{4a} = \frac{1}{16/9} = \frac{9}{16}$ ft from center of paraboloid.

**60** $y = ax^2 \Rightarrow \frac{3}{4} = a(2)^2 \Rightarrow a = \frac{3}{16}$. $p = \frac{1}{4a} = \frac{1}{3/4} = \frac{4}{3}$ in. from center of mirror

**61** $p = 5 \Rightarrow a = \frac{1}{4p} = \frac{1}{4 \cdot 5} = \frac{1}{20}$. $y = ax^2$ $\{y = 2 \text{ ft} = 24 \text{ inches}\} \Rightarrow 24 = \frac{1}{20}x^2 \Rightarrow x^2 = 480 \Rightarrow$ $x = \sqrt{480}$. The width is twice the value of $x$. Width $= 2\sqrt{480} \approx 43.82$ in.

**62** $a = \frac{1}{4p} = \frac{1}{4 \cdot 9} = \frac{1}{36}$. $24 = \frac{1}{36}x^2 \Rightarrow x = \sqrt{864}$. Width $= 2\sqrt{864} \approx 58.79$ in.

**63** (a) Let the parabola have the equation $x^2 = 4py$. Since the point $(r, h)$ is on the parabola, we can substitute $r$ for $x$ and $h$ for $y$, giving us $r^2 = 4ph$. Solving for $p$ we have $p = \dfrac{r^2}{4h}$.

(b) $p = 10$ and $h = 5 \Rightarrow 10 = \dfrac{r^2}{4(5)} \Rightarrow r^2 = (10)(20) \Rightarrow r = \sqrt{200} = 10\sqrt{2}$.

**64** Note that the value of $p$ completely determines the parabola. If $(x_1, y_1)$ is on the parabola, then

$y_1^2 = 4p(x_1 + p) \Rightarrow 4p^2 + 4x_1 p - y_1^2 = 0 \Rightarrow p = \dfrac{-4x_1 \pm \sqrt{16x_1^2 + 16y_1^2}}{8} = \dfrac{-x_1 \pm \sqrt{x_1^2 + y_1^2}}{2}$.

If $y_1 \neq 0$, then there are exactly two values for $p$ and hence, exactly two parabolas.

**65** With $a = 125$ and $p = 75$, $S = \dfrac{8\pi p^2}{3}\left[\left(1 + \dfrac{a^2}{4p^2}\right)^{3/2} - 1\right] \approx 56{,}816 \text{ ft}^2 \approx 57{,}000 \text{ ft}^2$.

**66** (a) From the figure we can see that the distance between Mars and the origin should be 58,000 miles.

Thus, $p = 58{,}000$. $x = \dfrac{1}{4p}y^2 \Rightarrow x = \dfrac{1}{232{,}000}y^2$.

(b) Since $v = \sqrt{\dfrac{2k}{r}}$, the velocity of the satellite will be maximum when the distance $r$ between the satellite and Mars is minimum. The minimum value of $r$ is 58,000 miles, when the satellite is located at the vertex. First, convert $r$ to meters. $58{,}000 \text{ mi} \times 1610 \text{ m/mi} \approx 9.34 \times 10^7$ m.

$$\text{Thus, } v = \sqrt{\frac{2k}{r}} = \sqrt{\frac{2 \times 4.28 \times 10^{13}}{9.34 \times 10^7}} \approx 957 \text{ m/sec.}$$

(c) From part (a), $x = \dfrac{1}{232{,}000}\, y^2$. $y = 100{,}000 \;\Rightarrow\; x = \dfrac{100{,}000^2}{232{,}000} \approx 43{,}100$.

If the satellite is located at the point $(43{,}100, 100{,}000)$ and Mars is located at the point $(58{,}000, 0)$, then

$$r = \sqrt{(58{,}000 - 43{,}100)^2 + (100{,}000 - 0)^2} \approx 101{,}100 \text{ mi} \approx 1.63 \times 10^8 \text{ m.}$$

$$\text{Thus, } v = \sqrt{\frac{2k}{r}} = \sqrt{\frac{2 \times 4.28 \times 10^{13}}{1.63 \times 10^8}} \approx 725 \text{ m/sec.}$$

**67** Depending on the type of calculator or software used, we may need to solve for $y$ in terms of $x$. $x = -y^2 + 2y + 5 \;\Rightarrow\; y^2 - 2y + (x - 5) = 0$. This is a quadratic equation in $y$. Using the quadratic formula to solve for $y$ yields

$$y = \frac{-(-2) \pm \sqrt{(-2)^2 - 4(1)(x-5)}}{2(1)} = \frac{2 \pm \sqrt{24 - 4x}}{2} = \frac{2 \pm \sqrt{4}\sqrt{6-x}}{2} = 1 \pm \sqrt{6-x}.$$

$[-11, 10, 2]$ by $[-7, 7]$        $[-11, 10]$ by $[-7, 7]$

*Figure 67*           *Figure 68*

**68** $x = 2y^2 + 3y - 7 \;\Rightarrow\; 0 = 2y^2 + 3y - (x+7) \;\Rightarrow\; y = \dfrac{-3 \pm \sqrt{3^2 + 4(2)(x+7)}}{2(2)} = -\dfrac{3}{4} \pm \dfrac{1}{4}\sqrt{8x+65}$

**69** $y = x^2 - 2.1x - 1;\; x = y^2 + 1 \;\Rightarrow\; y = \pm\sqrt{x-1}$. From the graph, we can see that there are 2 points of intersection. Their coordinates are approximately $(2.08, -1.04)$ and $(2.92, 1.38)$.

$[-2, 4]$ by $[-3, 3]$        $[-4, 4]$ by $[-5, 3]$

*Figure 69*           *Figure 70*

**70** $y = -2.1x^2 + 0.1x + 1.2;\; x = 0.6y^2 + 1.7y - 1.1 \;\Rightarrow$

$$y = \frac{-1.7 \pm \sqrt{(1.7)^2 + 4(0.6)(x+1.1)}}{2(0.6)} = \frac{-1.7 \pm \sqrt{2.4x + 5.53}}{1.2}.$$

From the graph, we can see that there are 4 points of intersection.

Their coordinates are approximately $(-1.34, -2.69)$, $(-0.65, 0.24)$, $(0.49, 0.74)$, and $(1.59, -3.97)$.

## *10.2 Exercises*

**Note:** Let $C$, $V$, $F$, and $M$ denote the center, the vertices, the foci, and the endpoints of the minor axis, respectively.

    Let $c$ denote the distance from the center of the ellipse to a focus.

[1]   $\dfrac{x^2}{9} + \dfrac{y^2}{4} = 1$   •   The $x$-intercepts are $\pm\sqrt{9} = \pm 3$. The $y$-intercepts are $\pm\sqrt{4} = \pm 2$. The major axis {the longer

of the two axes} is the horizontal axis and has length $2(3) = 6$. The minor axis {the shorter} is the vertical axis and

has length $2(2) = 4$.

To find the foci, it is helpful to remember the relationship $\left[\frac{1}{2}(\text{minor axis})\right]^2 + \left[c\right]^2 = \left[\frac{1}{2}(\text{major axis})\right]^2$.

Using the values from above we have $\left[\frac{1}{2}(4)\right]^2 + c^2 = \left[\frac{1}{2}(6)\right]^2 \;\Rightarrow\; 4 + c^2 = 9 \;\Rightarrow\; c^2 = 5 \;\Rightarrow\; c = \pm\sqrt{5}$.

Simply put, $c^2$ is equal to difference of the denominators.      $V(\pm 3, 0);\, F\left(\pm\sqrt{5}, 0\right);\, M(0, \pm 2)$

*Figure 1*                             *Figure 2*

[2]   $\dfrac{x^2}{25} + \dfrac{y^2}{16} = 1$   •   $c^2 = 25 - 16 \;\Rightarrow\; c = \pm 3;\, V(\pm 5, 0);\, F(\pm 3, 0);\, M(0, \pm 4)$

[3]   $\dfrac{x^2}{15} + \dfrac{y^2}{16} = 1$   •   Since the 16 in the denominator of the term with the variable $y$ is larger than the 15 in the

denominator of the term with the variable $x$, the vertices and foci are on the $y$-axis and the major axis is the vertical

axis. $c^2 = 16 - 15 \;\Rightarrow\; c = \pm 1$.      $V(0, \pm 4);\, F(0, \pm 1);\, M\left(\pm\sqrt{15}, 0\right)$

*Figure 3*                             *Figure 4*

[4]   $\dfrac{x^2}{45} + \dfrac{y^2}{49} = 1$   •   $c^2 = 49 - 45 \;\Rightarrow\; c = \pm 2;\, V(0, \pm 7);\, F(0, \pm 2);\, M\left(\pm\sqrt{45}, 0\right)$

[5]   We first divide by 16 to obtain the "1" on the right side of the equation. $4x^2 + y^2 = 16 \;\Rightarrow\; \dfrac{x^2}{4} + \dfrac{y^2}{16} = 1$. Since

the 16 in the denominator of the term with the variable $y$ is larger than the 4 in the denominator of the term with the

variable $x$, the vertices and foci are on the $y$-axis and the major axis is the vertical axis.

         $4 + c^2 = 16 \;\Rightarrow\; c^2 = 16 - 4 \;\Rightarrow\; c = \pm\sqrt{12} = \pm 2\sqrt{3}.\; V(0, \pm 4);\, F\left(0, \pm 2\sqrt{3}\right);\, M(\pm 2, 0)$

*Figure 5*

*Figure 6*

**6** $y^2 + 9x^2 = 9 \Rightarrow \dfrac{x^2}{1} + \dfrac{y^2}{9} = 1; c^2 = 9 - 1 \Rightarrow c = \pm 2\sqrt{2}; V(0, \pm 3); F\left(0, \pm 2\sqrt{2}\right); M(\pm 1, 0)$

**7** First write $4x^2 + 25y^2 = 1$ in standard form: $\dfrac{x^2}{\frac{1}{4}} + \dfrac{y^2}{\frac{1}{25}} = 1$. $\dfrac{1}{25} + c^2 = \dfrac{1}{4} \Rightarrow c^2 = \dfrac{1}{4} - \dfrac{1}{25} = \dfrac{21}{100} \Rightarrow$

$$c = \pm \dfrac{1}{10}\sqrt{21}. \; V\left(\pm \tfrac{1}{2}, 0\right); F\left(\pm \tfrac{1}{10}\sqrt{21}, 0\right); M\left(0, \pm \tfrac{1}{5}\right)$$

*Figure 7*

*Figure 8*

**8** $10y^2 + x^2 = 5 \Rightarrow \dfrac{x^2}{5} + \dfrac{y^2}{\frac{1}{2}} = 1; c^2 = 5 - \dfrac{1}{2} = \dfrac{9}{2} \Rightarrow c = \pm \dfrac{3}{2}\sqrt{2};$

$$V\left(\pm\sqrt{5}, 0\right); F\left(\pm \tfrac{3}{2}\sqrt{2}, 0\right); M\left(0, \pm \tfrac{1}{2}\sqrt{2}\right)$$

**9** $\dfrac{(x-3)^2}{16} + \dfrac{(y+4)^2}{9} = 1$ • The effect of the factors $(x - 3)$ and $(y + 4)$ is to shift the center of the ellipse from $(0, 0)$ to $(3, -4)$. Since the larger denominator, 16, is in the term with $x$, the major axis will be horizontal. The endpoints are 4 units in either direction of the center. Their coordinates are the points $(3 \pm 4, -4)$, or, equivalently, $(7, -4)$ and $(-1, -4)$. The minor axis will be vertical with endpoints $(3, -4 \pm 3)$, or, equivalently, $(3, -1)$ and $(3, -7)$. $9 + c^2 = 16 \Rightarrow c^2 = 16 - 9 \Rightarrow c = \pm\sqrt{7}$. Remember that $c$ is the distance from the center to a focus. Hence, the coordinates of the foci are $\left(3 \pm \sqrt{7}, -4\right)$.

$$C(3, -4); V(3 \pm 4, -4); F\left(3 \pm \sqrt{7}, -4\right); M(3, -4 \pm 3)$$

*Figure 9*

*Figure 10*

**10** $\dfrac{(x+2)^2}{25} + \dfrac{(y-3)^2}{4} = 1$  •  $c^2 = 25 - 4 \implies c = \pm\sqrt{21};$

$$C(-2,3); V(-2 \pm 5, 3); F\left(-2 \pm \sqrt{21}, 3\right); M(-2, 3 \pm 2)$$

**11** $4x^2 + 9y^2 - 32x - 36y + 64 = 0 \implies (4x^2 - 32x) + (9y^2 - 36y) = -64 \implies$

{first group the $x$ terms and the $y$ terms}                    $4(x^2 - 8x) + 9(y^2 - 4y) = -64 \implies$

{factor out the coefficients of $x^2$ and $y^2$}        $4(x^2 - 8x + \underline{16}) + 9(y^2 - 4y + \underline{4}) = -64 + \underline{64} + \underline{36} \implies$

{Complete the squares—remember that we have added $\underline{4}$(16) and $\underline{9}$(4), not 16 and 4. Thus, we add 64 and 36 to

the right side of the equation.}                $4(x-4)^2 + 9(y-2)^2 = 36 \implies \dfrac{(x-4)^2}{9} + \dfrac{(y-2)^2}{4} = 1.$

$$c^2 = 9 - 4 \implies c = \pm\sqrt{5}. \, C(4,2); V(4 \pm 3, 2); F\left(4 \pm \sqrt{5}, 2\right); M(4, 2 \pm 2)$$

*Figure 11*

*Figure 12*

**12** $x^2 + 2y^2 + 2x - 20y + 43 = 0 \implies (x^2 + 2x + \underline{1}) + 2(y^2 - 10y + \underline{25}) = -43 + \underline{1} + \underline{50} \implies$

$(x+1)^2 + 2(y-5)^2 = 8 \implies \dfrac{(x+1)^2}{8} + \dfrac{(y-5)^2}{4} = 1; c^2 = 8 - 4 \implies c = \pm 2;$

$$C(-1,5); V\left(-1 \pm 2\sqrt{2}, 5\right); F(-1 \pm 2, 5); M(-1, 5 \pm 2)$$

**13** $25x^2 + 4y^2 - 250x - 16y + 541 = 0 \implies 25(x^2 - 10x + \underline{25}) + 4(y^2 - 4y + \underline{4}) = -541 + \underline{625} + \underline{16} \implies$

$25(x-5)^2 + 4(y-2)^2 = 100 \implies \dfrac{(x-5)^2}{4} + \dfrac{(y-2)^2}{25} = 1. \, c^2 = 25 - 4 \implies c = \pm\sqrt{21}.$

$$C(5,2); V(5, 2 \pm 5); F\left(5, 2 \pm \sqrt{21}\right); M(5 \pm 2, 2)$$

*Figure 13*

*Figure 14*

**14** $4x^2 + y^2 = 2y \implies 4x^2 + y^2 - 2y + \underline{1} = \underline{1} \implies \dfrac{x^2}{\frac{1}{4}} + \dfrac{(y-1)^2}{1} = 1; c^2 = 1 - \frac{1}{4} \implies c = \pm\frac{1}{2}\sqrt{3};$

$$C(0,1); V(0, 1 \pm 1); F\left(0, 1 \pm \frac{1}{2}\sqrt{3}\right); M\left(0 \pm \frac{1}{2}, 1\right)$$

**Note:** Let $a$ denote the distance equal to $\frac{1}{2}$(major axis length) and $b$ the distance equal to $\frac{1}{2}$(minor axis length).

**15** $M(2,0)$ and $V(0,6)$ $\Rightarrow$ $b = 2$ and $a = 6$ $\Rightarrow$ $\dfrac{x^2}{b^2} + \dfrac{y^2}{a^2} = 1$ is $\dfrac{x^2}{4} + \dfrac{y^2}{36} = 1$.

**16** $M(0,3)$ and $V(4,0)$ $\Rightarrow$ $b = 3$ and $a = 4$ $\Rightarrow$ $\dfrac{x^2}{a^2} + \dfrac{y^2}{b^2} = 1$ is $\dfrac{x^2}{16} + \dfrac{y^2}{9} = 1$.

**17** The center of the ellipse is $(-2, 1)$. $M(-2, 3)$ and $V(3, 1)$ $\Rightarrow$
$$b = 3 - 1 = 2 \text{ and } a = 3 - (-2) = 5 \quad \Rightarrow \quad \dfrac{(x-h)^2}{a^2} + \dfrac{(y-k)^2}{b^2} = 1 \text{ is } \dfrac{(x+2)^2}{25} + \dfrac{(y-1)^2}{4} = 1.$$

**18** The center of the ellipse is $(1, -2)$. $M(3, -2)$ and $V(1, 2)$ $\Rightarrow$
$$a = 2 - (-2) = 4 \text{ and } b = 3 - 1 = 2 \quad \Rightarrow \quad \dfrac{(x-h)^2}{b^2} + \dfrac{(y-k)^2}{a^2} = 1 \text{ is } \dfrac{(x-1)^2}{4} + \dfrac{(y+2)^2}{16} = 1.$$

**19** Since the vertices are at $V(\pm 8, 0)$, $\frac{1}{2}$(major axis) $= 8$. Since the foci are at $F(\pm 5, 0)$, $c = 5$.

Using the relationship $\left[ \frac{1}{2}(\text{minor axis}) \right]^2 + [c]^2 = \left[ \frac{1}{2}(\text{major axis}) \right]^2$, we have $\left[ \frac{1}{2}(\text{minor axis}) \right]^2 + 5^2 = 8^2$ $\Rightarrow$

$\left[ \frac{1}{2}(\text{minor axis}) \right]^2 = 64 - 25 = 39$. An equation is $\dfrac{x^2}{64} + \dfrac{y^2}{39} = 1$.

**20** $V(0, \pm 7)$ and $F(0, \pm 2)$ $\Rightarrow$ $b^2 = 7^2 - 2^2 = 45$. An equation is $\dfrac{x^2}{45} + \dfrac{y^2}{49} = 1$.

**21** If the length of the minor axis is 3, then $b = \frac{1}{2}(3) = \frac{3}{2}$.

The vertices are $V(0, \pm 5)$, so an equation is $\dfrac{x^2}{\left(\frac{3}{2}\right)^2} + \dfrac{y^2}{5^2} = 1$, or, equivalently, $\dfrac{4x^2}{9} + \dfrac{y^2}{25} = 1$.

**22** If the length of the minor axis is 5, then $b = \frac{1}{2}(5) = \frac{5}{2}$.

The vertices are $V(\pm 7, 0)$, so an equation is $\dfrac{x^2}{7^2} + \dfrac{y^2}{\left(\frac{5}{2}\right)^2} = 1$, or, equivalently, $\dfrac{x^2}{49} + \dfrac{4y^2}{25} = 1$.

**23** If the length of the minor axis is 2, then $b = \frac{1}{2}(2) = 1$. The foci are $F(\pm 3, 0)$, so $c = 3$. $a^2 = 3^2 + 1^2 = 10$.

An equation is $\dfrac{x^2}{10} + \dfrac{y^2}{1^2} = 1$, or, equivalently, $\dfrac{x^2}{10} + y^2 = 1$.

**24** If the length of the minor axis is 4, then $b = \frac{1}{2}(4) = 2$. The foci are $F(0, \pm 4)$, so $c = 4$. $a^2 = 4^2 + 2^2 = 20$.

An equation is $\dfrac{x^2}{2^2} + \dfrac{y^2}{20} = 1$, or, equivalently, $\dfrac{x^2}{4} + \dfrac{y^2}{20} = 1$.

**25** With the vertices at $V(0, \pm 6)$, an equation of the ellipse is $\dfrac{x^2}{b^2} + \dfrac{y^2}{6^2} = 1$.

Substituting $x = 3$ and $y = 2$ and solving for $b^2$ yields $\dfrac{9}{b^2} + \dfrac{4}{36} = 1$ $\Rightarrow$ $\dfrac{9}{b^2} = \dfrac{8}{9}$ $\Rightarrow$ $b^2 = \dfrac{81}{8}$.

An equation is $\dfrac{x^2}{\frac{81}{8}} + \dfrac{y^2}{36} = 1$, or, equivalently, $\dfrac{8x^2}{81} + \dfrac{y^2}{36} = 1$.

**26** With the vertices at $V(\pm 13, 0)$, an equation of the ellipse is $\dfrac{x^2}{13^2} + \dfrac{y^2}{b^2} = 1$.

Substituting $x = 5$ and $y = 6$ and solving for $b^2$ yields $\dfrac{25}{169} + \dfrac{36}{b^2} = 1$ $\Rightarrow$ $\dfrac{36}{b^2} = \dfrac{144}{169}$ $\Rightarrow$ $b^2 = \dfrac{169}{4}$.

An equation is $\dfrac{x^2}{169} + \dfrac{y^2}{\frac{169}{4}} = 1$, or, equivalently, $\dfrac{x^2}{169} + \dfrac{4y^2}{169} = 1$.

**27** Substituting the $x$ and $y$ values for $(2, 3)$ and $(6, 1)$ into $\dfrac{x^2}{a^2} + \dfrac{y^2}{b^2} = 1$ yields the equations $\dfrac{4}{a^2} + \dfrac{9}{b^2} = 1$ {$E_1$} and $\dfrac{36}{a^2} + \dfrac{1}{b^2} = 1$ {$E_2$}, respectively. Solving, $E_2 - 9E_1 \Rightarrow -\dfrac{80}{b^2} = -8 \Rightarrow b^2 = 10$ and $E_1 - 9E_2 \Rightarrow$
$$-\dfrac{320}{a^2} = -8 \Rightarrow a^2 = 40. \text{ An equation is } \dfrac{x^2}{40} + \dfrac{y^2}{10} = 1.$$

**28** Substituting the $x$ and $y$ values for $(2, 8)$ and $(4, 4)$ into $\dfrac{x^2}{a^2} + \dfrac{y^2}{b^2} = 1$ yields the equations $\dfrac{4}{a^2} + \dfrac{64}{b^2} = 1$ {$E_1$} and $\dfrac{16}{a^2} + \dfrac{16}{b^2} = 1$ {$E_2$}, respectively. Solving, $E_2 - 4E_1 \Rightarrow -\dfrac{240}{b^2} = -3 \Rightarrow b^2 = 80$ and $E_1 - 4E_2 \Rightarrow$
$$-\dfrac{60}{a^2} = -3 \Rightarrow a^2 = 20. \text{ An equation is } \dfrac{x^2}{20} + \dfrac{y^2}{80} = 1.$$

**29** With vertices $V(0, \pm 4)$, an equation of the ellipse is $\dfrac{x^2}{b^2} + \dfrac{y^2}{16} = 1$. Remember the formula for the eccentricity:

$$\boxed{\text{eccentricity } e = \dfrac{\text{distance from center to focus}}{\text{distance from center to vertex}} = \dfrac{c}{a} = \dfrac{\sqrt{a^2 - b^2}}{a}}$$

Hence, $e = \dfrac{c}{a} = \dfrac{3}{4}$ and $a = 4 \Rightarrow c = 3$. Thus, $b^2 + c^2 = a^2 \Rightarrow b^2 = a^2 - c^2 = 4^2 - 3^2 = 16 - 9 = 7.$
$$\text{An equation is } \dfrac{x^2}{7} + \dfrac{y^2}{16} = 1.$$

**30** With vertices $V(\pm 7, 0)$, an equation of the ellipse is $\dfrac{x^2}{49} + \dfrac{y^2}{b^2} = 1$. Now $e = \dfrac{c}{a} = \dfrac{4}{7}$ and $a = 7 \Rightarrow c = 4.$

Thus, $b^2 + c^2 = a^2 \Rightarrow b^2 = a^2 - c^2 = 7^2 - 4^2 = 49 - 16 = 33.$ An equation is $\dfrac{x^2}{49} + \dfrac{y^2}{33} = 1.$

**31** An equation of the ellipse with vertices on the $x$-axis is $\dfrac{x^2}{a^2} + \dfrac{y^2}{b^2} = 1$. $(1, 3)$ on the ellipse $\Rightarrow$
$$\dfrac{1}{a^2} + \dfrac{9}{b^2} = 1 \Rightarrow b^2 = \dfrac{9a^2}{a^2 - 1}. \; e = \dfrac{c}{a} = \dfrac{1}{2} \Rightarrow c = \dfrac{1}{2}a. \; b^2 = a^2 - c^2 = a^2 - \dfrac{1}{4}a^2 = \dfrac{3}{4}a^2.$$
$$\text{Thus, } \dfrac{9a^2}{a^2 - 1} = \dfrac{3}{4}a^2 \Rightarrow 9\left(\dfrac{4}{3}\right) = a^2 - 1 \Rightarrow a^2 = 13 \text{ and } b^2 = \dfrac{39}{4}. \text{ An equation is } \dfrac{x^2}{13} + \dfrac{4y^2}{39} = 1.$$

**32** An equation of the ellipse with vertices on the $y$-axis is $\dfrac{x^2}{b^2} + \dfrac{y^2}{a^2} = 1$. $(1, 4)$ on the ellipse $\Rightarrow$
$$\dfrac{1}{b^2} + \dfrac{16}{a^2} = 1 \Rightarrow \dfrac{1}{b^2} = 1 - \dfrac{16}{a^2} \Rightarrow b^2 = \dfrac{a^2}{a^2 - 16}. \; e = \dfrac{c}{a} = \dfrac{2}{3} \Rightarrow c = \dfrac{2}{3}a \Rightarrow c^2 = \dfrac{4}{9}a^2.$$
$$b^2 + c^2 = a^2 \Rightarrow \dfrac{a^2}{a^2 - 16} + \dfrac{4}{9}a^2 = a^2 \Rightarrow \dfrac{1}{a^2 - 16} = 1 - \dfrac{4}{9} \Rightarrow a^2 - 16 = \dfrac{9}{5} \Rightarrow a^2 = \dfrac{89}{5} \text{ and }$$
$$b^2 = \dfrac{89}{9}. \text{ An equation is } \dfrac{x^2}{\frac{89}{9}} + \dfrac{y^2}{\frac{89}{5}} = 1, \text{ or, equivalently, } \dfrac{9x^2}{89} + \dfrac{5y^2}{89} = 1.$$

**33** $x$-intercepts $= \pm 2$ and $y$-intercepts $= \pm \dfrac{1}{3} \Rightarrow \dfrac{x^2}{2^2} + \dfrac{y^2}{\left(\frac{1}{3}\right)^2} = 1 \Rightarrow \dfrac{x^2}{4} + \dfrac{y^2}{\frac{1}{9}} = 1 \Rightarrow \dfrac{x^2}{4} + 9y^2 = 1.$

**34** $x$-intercepts $= \pm \dfrac{1}{2}$ and $y$-intercepts $= \pm 4 \Rightarrow \dfrac{x^2}{\left(\frac{1}{2}\right)^2} + \dfrac{y^2}{4^2} = 1 \Rightarrow \dfrac{x^2}{\frac{1}{4}} + \dfrac{y^2}{16} = 1 \Rightarrow 4x^2 + \dfrac{y^2}{16} = 1.$

**35** Remember to divide the lengths of the major and minor axes by 2.
$$\dfrac{x^2}{\left(\frac{1}{2} \cdot 8\right)^2} + \dfrac{y^2}{\left(\frac{1}{2} \cdot 5\right)^2} = 1 \Rightarrow \dfrac{x^2}{4^2} + \dfrac{y^2}{\left(\frac{5}{2}\right)^2} = 1 \Rightarrow \dfrac{x^2}{16} + \dfrac{4y^2}{25} = 1.$$

**36** Remember to divide the lengths of the major and minor axes by 2.
$$\dfrac{x^2}{\left(\frac{1}{2} \cdot 6\right)^2} + \dfrac{y^2}{\left(\frac{1}{2} \cdot 7\right)^2} = 1 \Rightarrow \dfrac{x^2}{3^2} + \dfrac{y^2}{\left(\frac{7}{2}\right)^2} = 1 \Rightarrow \dfrac{x^2}{9} + \dfrac{4y^2}{49} = 1.$$

**37** The graph of $x^2 + 4y^2 = 20$, or, equivalently, $\dfrac{x^2}{20} + \dfrac{y^2}{5} = 1$, is that of an ellipse with $x$-intercepts at $\pm\sqrt{20}$ and

$y$-intercepts $\pm\sqrt{5}$. The graph of $x + 2y = 6$, or, equivalently, $y = -\frac{1}{2}x + 3$, is that of a line with $y$-intercept 3 and

slope $-\frac{1}{2}$. Substituting $x = 6 - 2y$ into $x^2 + 4y^2 = 20$ yields $(6 - 2y)^2 + 4y^2 = 20 \Rightarrow$

$8y^2 - 24y + 16 = 0 \Rightarrow 8(y^2 - 3y + 2) = 0 \Rightarrow 8(y - 1)(y - 2) = 0 \Rightarrow y = 1, 2; x = 4, 2.$

The two points of intersection are $(2, 2)$ and $(4, 1)$.

Figure 37

Figure 38

**38** $3x + y = 7 \Rightarrow y = 7 - 3x$. Now substitute $7 - 3x$ for $y$ in $5x^2 + y^2 = 189$ to get $5x^2 + (7 - 3x)^2 = 189 \Rightarrow$

$14x^2 - 42x - 140 = 0 \Rightarrow x^2 - 3x - 10 = 0 \Rightarrow (x - 5)(x + 2) = 0 \Rightarrow x = 5, -2; y = -8, 13.$

The two points of intersection are $(5, -8)$ and $(-2, 13)$.

**39** $E_2 - E_1 \Rightarrow (3x^2 + y^2 = 43) - (x^2 + y^2 = 25) \Rightarrow 2x^2 = 18 \Rightarrow x^2 = 9; y^2 = 16.$

The *four* points of intersection are $(\pm 3, \pm 4)$.

Figure 39

Figure 40

**40** $E_1 - E_2 \Rightarrow (x^2 + 4y^2 = 36) - (x^2 + y^2 = 12) \Rightarrow 3y^2 = 24 \Rightarrow y^2 = 8; x^2 = 4.$

The *four* points of intersection are $\left(\pm 2, \pm 2\sqrt{2}\right)$.

**41** Refer to the definition of an ellipse. As in the discussion on page 725, we will let the positive constant, $k$, equal $2a$.

$k = 10 \Rightarrow 2a = 10 \Rightarrow a = 5.$ $F(3, 0)$ and $F'(-3, 0) \Rightarrow c = 3.$

$b^2 = a^2 - c^2 = 25 - 9 = 16.$ An equation is $\dfrac{x^2}{25} + \dfrac{y^2}{16} = 1.$

**42** $k = 2a = 26 \Rightarrow a = 13.$ $F(12, 0)$ and $F'(-12, 0) \Rightarrow c = 12.$

$b^2 = a^2 - c^2 = 169 - 144 = 25.$ An equation is $\dfrac{x^2}{169} + \dfrac{y^2}{25} = 1.$

**43** $k = 34 \Rightarrow 2a = 34 \Rightarrow a = 17.$ $F(0, 15)$ and $F'(0, -15) \Rightarrow c = 15.$

$b^2 = a^2 - c^2 = 289 - 225 = 64.$ An equation is $\dfrac{x^2}{64} + \dfrac{y^2}{289} = 1.$

**44** $k = 2a = 20 \;\Rightarrow\; a = 10.$ $F(0,8)$ and $F'(0,-8) \;\Rightarrow\; c = 8.$

$$b^2 = a^2 - c^2 = 100 - 64 = 36. \text{ An equation is } \frac{x^2}{36} + \frac{y^2}{100} = 1.$$

**45** $k = 2a = 7 + 3 = 10 \;\Rightarrow\; a = 5.$ $F(4,0)$ and $F'(-4,0) \;\Rightarrow\; c = 4.$

$$b^2 = a^2 - c^2 = 25 - 16 = 9. \text{ An equation is } \frac{x^2}{25} + \frac{y^2}{9} = 1.$$

Figure 45

Figure 46

**46** $k = 2a = 5 + 15 = 20 \;\Rightarrow\; a = 10.$ $F(0,6)$ and $F'(0,-6) \;\Rightarrow\; c = 6.$

$$b^2 = a^2 - c^2 = 100 - 36 = 64. \text{ An equation is } \frac{x^2}{64} + \frac{y^2}{100} = 1.$$

**47** Left half of $\dfrac{x^2}{36} + \dfrac{y^2}{25} = 1 \;\Rightarrow\; \dfrac{x^2}{36} = 1 - \dfrac{y^2}{25} \;\Rightarrow\; \dfrac{x^2}{36} = \dfrac{25 - y^2}{25} \;\Rightarrow\; x^2 = \dfrac{36}{25}\left(25 - y^2\right) \;\Rightarrow$

$$x = -\tfrac{6}{5}\sqrt{25 - y^2}$$

**48** Right half of $\dfrac{x^2}{9} + \dfrac{y^2}{121} = 1 \;\Rightarrow\; \dfrac{x^2}{9} = 1 - \dfrac{y^2}{121} \;\Rightarrow\; \dfrac{x^2}{9} = \dfrac{121 - y^2}{121} \;\Rightarrow\; x^2 = \dfrac{9}{121}\left(121 - y^2\right) \;\Rightarrow$

$$x = \tfrac{3}{11}\sqrt{121 - y^2}$$

**49** Upper half of $x^2 + 3y^2 = 17 \;\Rightarrow\; 3y^2 = 17 - x^2 \;\Rightarrow\; y^2 = \dfrac{17 - x^2}{3} \;\Rightarrow\; y = \sqrt{\dfrac{17 - x^2}{3}}$

**50** Lower half of $2x^2 + 5y^2 = 12 \;\Rightarrow\; 5y^2 = 12 - 2x^2 \;\Rightarrow\; y^2 = \dfrac{12 - 2x^2}{5} \;\Rightarrow\; y = -\sqrt{\dfrac{12 - 2x^2}{5}}$

**51** $y = 11\sqrt{1 - \dfrac{x^2}{49}} \;\Rightarrow\; \dfrac{y}{11} = \sqrt{1 - \dfrac{x^2}{49}} \;\Rightarrow\; \dfrac{x^2}{49} + \dfrac{y^2}{121} = 1.$

Since $y \geq 0$ in the original equation, its graph is the upper half of the ellipse.

**52** $y = -6\sqrt{1 - \dfrac{x^2}{25}} \;\Rightarrow\; \dfrac{y}{-6} = \sqrt{1 - \dfrac{x^2}{25}} \;\Rightarrow\; \dfrac{x^2}{25} + \dfrac{y^2}{36} = 1;$ lower half

**53** $x = -\tfrac{1}{3}\sqrt{9 - y^2} \;\Rightarrow\; -3x = \sqrt{9 - y^2} \;\Rightarrow\; 9x^2 = 9 - y^2 \;\Rightarrow\; x^2 + \dfrac{y^2}{9} = 1.$

Since $x \leq 0$ in the original equation, its graph is the left half of the ellipse.

**54** $x = \tfrac{4}{5}\sqrt{25 - y^2} \;\Rightarrow\; \tfrac{5}{4}x = \sqrt{25 - y^2} \;\Rightarrow\; \dfrac{25}{16}x^2 = 25 - y^2 \;\Rightarrow\; \dfrac{x^2}{16} + \dfrac{y^2}{25} = 1;$ right half

**55** $x = 1 + 2\sqrt{1 - \dfrac{(y+2)^2}{9}} \;\Rightarrow\; \dfrac{x - 1}{2} = \sqrt{1 - \dfrac{(y+2)^2}{9}} \;\Rightarrow\; \dfrac{(x-1)^2}{4} + \dfrac{(y+2)^2}{9} = 1.$

Since $x \geq 1$ in the original equation, its graph is the right half of the ellipse.

**56** $x = -2 - 5\sqrt{1 - \dfrac{(y-1)^2}{16}} \;\Rightarrow\; \dfrac{x + 2}{-5} = \sqrt{1 - \dfrac{(y-1)^2}{16}} \;\Rightarrow\; \dfrac{(x+2)^2}{25} + \dfrac{(y-1)^2}{16} = 1;$ left half

**57** $y = 2 - 7\sqrt{1 - \dfrac{(x+1)^2}{9}}$ $\Rightarrow$ $\dfrac{y-2}{-7} = \sqrt{1 - \dfrac{(x+1)^2}{9}}$ $\Rightarrow$ $\dfrac{(x+1)^2}{9} + \dfrac{(y-2)^2}{49} = 1.$

Since $y \le 2$ in the original equation, its graph is the lower half of the ellipse.

**58** $y = -1 + \sqrt{1 - \dfrac{(x-3)^2}{16}}$ $\Rightarrow$ $y + 1 = \sqrt{1 - \dfrac{(x-3)^2}{16}}$ $\Rightarrow$ $\dfrac{(x-3)^2}{16} + (y+1)^2 = 1;$ upper half

**59** Model this problem as an ellipse with $V(\pm 15, 0)$ and $M(0, \pm 10)$. Substituting $x = 6$ into $\dfrac{x^2}{15^2} + \dfrac{y^2}{10^2} = 1$ yields $\dfrac{y^2}{100} = \dfrac{189}{225}$ $\Rightarrow$ $y^2 = 84.$ The desired height is $\sqrt{84} = 2\sqrt{21} \approx 9.165$ ft.

**60** (a) This problem can be modeled as an ellipse with $V(\pm 100, 0)$ and passing through the point $(25, 30)$. Substituting $x = 25$ and $y = 30$ into $\dfrac{x^2}{100^2} + \dfrac{y^2}{b^2} = 1$ yields $\dfrac{30^2}{b^2} = \dfrac{15}{16}$ $\Rightarrow$ $b^2 = 960.$ An equation for the ellipse is $\dfrac{x^2}{10,000} + \dfrac{y^2}{960} = 1.$ An equation for the top half of the ellipse is $y = \sqrt{960\left(1 - \dfrac{x^2}{10,000}\right)}.$

(b) The height in the middle of the bridge is $\sqrt{960} = 8\sqrt{15} \approx 31$ ft.

**61** $e = \dfrac{c}{a} = 0.017$ $\Rightarrow$ $c = 0.017a = 0.017(93,000,000) = 1,581,000.$

The maximum and minimum distances are $a + c = 94,581,000$ miles and $a - c = 91,419,000$ miles.

**62** $e = \dfrac{c}{a}$ $\Rightarrow$ $c = ae = \left(\tfrac{1}{2} \cdot 0.774\right)(0.206) = (0.387)(0.206) \approx 0.080.$ As in Example 7, the maximum and minimum distances are $a + c \approx 0.387 + 0.080 = 0.467$ AU and $a - c \approx 0.387 - 0.080 = 0.307$ AU, respectively.

**63** (a) Let $c$ denote the distance from the center of the hemi-ellipsoid to $F$.
Hence, $\left(\tfrac{1}{2}k\right)^2 + c^2 = h^2$ $\Rightarrow$ $c^2 = h^2 - \tfrac{1}{4}k^2$ $\Rightarrow$ $c = \sqrt{h^2 - \tfrac{1}{4}k^2}.$
$d = d(V, F) = h - c$ $\Rightarrow$ $d = h - \sqrt{h^2 - \tfrac{1}{4}k^2}$ and $d' = d(V, F') = h + c$ $\Rightarrow$ $d' = h + \sqrt{h^2 - \tfrac{1}{4}k^2}.$

(b) From part (a), $d' = h + c$ $\Rightarrow$ $c = d' - h = 32 - 17 = 15.$ $c = \sqrt{h^2 - \tfrac{1}{4}k^2}$ $\Rightarrow$ $15 = \sqrt{17^2 - \tfrac{1}{4}k^2}$ $\Rightarrow$ $225 = 289 - \tfrac{1}{4}k^2$ $\Rightarrow$ $\tfrac{1}{4}k^2 = 64$ $\Rightarrow$ $k^2 = 256$ $\Rightarrow$ $k = 16$ cm. $d = h - c = 17 - 15 = 2$ $\Rightarrow$ $F$ should be located 2 cm from $V$.

**64** (a) From the previous exercise, $c = \sqrt{h^2 - \tfrac{1}{4}k^2} = \sqrt{15^2 - \tfrac{1}{4}(18)^2} = 12.$

The focus $F$ should be located $d = h - c = 15 - 12 = 3$ cm from $V$.

(b) The kidney stone should be located $d' = h + c = 15 + 12 = 27$ cm from $V$.

**65** $c^2 = \left(\tfrac{1}{2} \cdot 50\right)^2 - 15^2 = 625 - 225 = 400$ $\Rightarrow$ $c = 20.$ Their feet should be $25 - 20 = 5$ ft from the vertices.

**66** $c^2 + \left(\tfrac{1}{2} \cdot 24\right)^2 = \left(\tfrac{1}{2} \cdot 60\right)^2$ $\Rightarrow$ $c = \sqrt{30^2 - 12^2} = \sqrt{756} \approx 27.5.$ The top of the door is $\tfrac{1}{2} \cdot 80 = 40$ inches from the center of the door, so insert the pushpins $40 - 27.5 = 12.5$ inches from each end.

The string should be $2 \cdot 30 = 60$ inches long.

**67** First determine an equation of the ellipse for the orbit of Earth. $e = \dfrac{c}{a}$ $\Rightarrow$ $c = ae = 0.093 \times 149.6 = 13.9128.$ $b^2 = a^2 - c^2 = 149.6^2 - 13.9128^2$ $\Rightarrow$ $b \approx 148.95 \approx 149.0.$ An approximate equation for the orbit of Earth is $\dfrac{x^2}{149.6^2} + \dfrac{y^2}{149.0^2} = 1.$ Solving for $y$ gives us $\dfrac{y^2}{149^2} = 1 - \dfrac{x^2}{149.6^2}$ $\Rightarrow$ $y^2 = 149^2\left(1 - \dfrac{x^2}{149.6^2}\right)$ $\Rightarrow$ $y = \pm 149\sqrt{1 - \dfrac{x^2}{149.6^2}}.$ Graph $Y_1 = 149\sqrt{1 - \dfrac{x^2}{149.6^2}}$ and $Y_2 = -Y_1.$

The sun is at $(\pm 13.9128, 0)$. Plot the point $(13.9128, 0)$ for the sun. See *Figure 67*.

$[-300, 300, 100]$ by $[-200, 200, 100]$    $[-9000, 9000, 1000]$ by $[-6000, 6000, 1000]$

Figure 67    Figure 68

**68** First determine an equation of the ellipse for the orbit of Pluto. $e = \frac{c}{a} \Rightarrow c = ae = 0.249 \times 5913 = 1472.337$.
$b^2 = a^2 - c^2 = 5913^2 - 1472.337^2 \Rightarrow b \approx 5726.76 \approx 5727$. An equation for the orbit of Pluto is
$\dfrac{x^2}{5913^2} + \dfrac{y^2}{5727^2} = 1$. Graph $Y_1 = 5727\sqrt{1 - (x^2/5913^2)}$ and $Y_2 = -Y_1$.

The sun is at $(\pm 1472.337, 0)$. Plot the point $(1472.337, 0)$ for the sun.

**69** $\dfrac{x^2}{2.9} + \dfrac{y^2}{2.1} = 1 \Rightarrow \dfrac{y^2}{2.1} = 1 - \dfrac{x^2}{2.9} \Rightarrow y^2 = 2.1\left(1 - \dfrac{x^2}{2.9}\right) \Rightarrow y = \pm\sqrt{2.1\left(1 - \dfrac{x^2}{2.9}\right)}$.
$\dfrac{x^2}{4.3} + \dfrac{(y - 2.1)^2}{4.9} = 1 \Rightarrow \dfrac{(y - 2.1)^2}{4.9} = 1 - \dfrac{x^2}{4.3} \Rightarrow (y - 2.1)^2 = 4.9\left(1 - \dfrac{x^2}{4.3}\right) \Rightarrow$
$y - 2.1 = \pm\sqrt{4.9(1 - x^2/4.3)} \Rightarrow y = 2.1 \pm \sqrt{4.9(1 - x^2/4.3)}$.

From the graph, the points of intersection are approximately $(\pm 1.540, 0.618)$.

$[-6, 6]$ by $[-2, 6]$    $[-6, 6]$ by $[-4, 4]$

Figure 69    Figure 70

**70** $\dfrac{x^2}{3.9} + \dfrac{y^2}{2.4} = 1 \Rightarrow \dfrac{y^2}{2.4} = 1 - \dfrac{x^2}{3.9} \Rightarrow y^2 = 2.4\left(1 - \dfrac{x^2}{3.9}\right) \Rightarrow y = \pm\sqrt{2.4\left(1 - \dfrac{x^2}{3.9}\right)}$.
$\dfrac{(x + 1.9)^2}{4.1} + \dfrac{y^2}{2.5} = 1 \Rightarrow \dfrac{y^2}{2.5} = 1 - \dfrac{(x + 1.9)^2}{4.1} \Rightarrow y^2 = 2.5\left[1 - \dfrac{(x + 1.9)^2}{4.1}\right] \Rightarrow$
$y = \pm\sqrt{2.5\left[1 - (x + 1.9)^2/4.1\right]}$. From the graph, the points of intersection are approximately $(-0.905, \pm 1.377)$.

**71** $\dfrac{(x + 0.1)^2}{1.7} + \dfrac{y^2}{0.9} = 1 \Rightarrow \dfrac{y^2}{0.9} = 1 - \dfrac{(x + 0.1)^2}{1.7} \Rightarrow y^2 = 0.9\left[1 - \dfrac{(x + 0.1)^2}{1.7}\right] \Rightarrow$
$y = \pm\sqrt{0.9\left[1 - (x + 0.1)^2/1.7\right]}$.
$\dfrac{x^2}{0.9} + \dfrac{(y - 0.25)^2}{1.8} = 1 \Rightarrow \dfrac{(y - 0.25)^2}{1.8} = 1 - \dfrac{x^2}{0.9} \Rightarrow (y - 0.25)^2 = 1.8\left(1 - \dfrac{x^2}{0.9}\right) \Rightarrow$
$y - 0.25 = \pm\sqrt{1.8(1 - x^2/0.9)} \Rightarrow y = 0.25 \pm \sqrt{1.8(1 - x^2/0.9)}$.

From the graph, the points of intersection are approximately $(-0.88, 0.76)$, $(-0.48, -0.91)$, $(0.58, -0.81)$, and
$(0.92, 0.59)$.

[−3, 3] by [−2, 2]

*Figure 71*

[−4.5, 4.5] by [−3, 3]

*Figure 72*

**72** $\dfrac{x^2}{3.1} + \dfrac{(y-0.2)^2}{2.8} = 1 \;\Rightarrow\; y = 0.2 \pm \sqrt{2.8\left(1 - \dfrac{x^2}{3.1}\right)}$.

$\dfrac{(x+0.23)^2}{1.8} + \dfrac{y^2}{4.2} = 1 \;\Rightarrow\; y = \pm\sqrt{4.2\left[1 - \dfrac{(x+0.23)^2}{1.8}\right]}$. From the graph, the points of intersection are

approximately $(-1.49, -0.68)$, $(-1.19, 1.44)$, $(0.36, 1.84)$, and $(0.82, -1.28)$.

## 10.3 Exercises

***Note:*** Let $C$, $V$, $F$, and $W$ denote the center, the vertices, the foci, and the endpoints of the conjugate axis, respectively. Let $c$ denote the distance from the center of the hyperbola to a focus.

**1** $\dfrac{x^2}{9} - \dfrac{y^2}{4} = 1$ • The hyperbola will have a right branch and a left branch since the term containing $x$ is positive. The vertices will be on the horizontal transverse axis, $\pm\sqrt{9} = \pm 3$ units from the center. The endpoints of the vertical conjugate axis are $\left(0, \pm\sqrt{4}\right) = (0, \pm 2)$. The asymptotes have equations

$$y = \pm\left[\dfrac{\sqrt{\text{constant under } y^2}}{\sqrt{\text{constant under } x^2}}\right](x) \quad \text{or} \quad y = \pm\left[\dfrac{\frac{1}{2}(\text{vertical axis length})}{\frac{1}{2}(\text{horizontal axis length})}\right](x).$$

Note that the terms are "vertical" and "horizontal" and not transverse and conjugate since the latter can be either vertical or horizontal. In this case, we have $y = \pm\dfrac{\sqrt{4}}{\sqrt{9}}(x) = \pm\dfrac{2}{3}x$. The positive sign corresponds to the asymptote with positive slope and the negative sign corresponds to the asymptote with negative slope.

To find the foci, it is helpful to remember the relationship

$$\left[\tfrac{1}{2}(\text{transverse axis})\right]^2 + \left[\tfrac{1}{2}(\text{conjugate axis})\right]^2 = [c]^2,$$

which is the same as $c^2 = (\text{constant under } x^2) + (\text{constant under } y^2)$. Thus, $c^2 = 9 + 4 \;\Rightarrow\; c = \pm\sqrt{13}$.

$$V(\pm 3, 0); \; F\left(\pm\sqrt{13}, 0\right); \; W(0, \pm 2); \; y = \pm\tfrac{2}{3}x$$

*Figure 1*

*Figure 2*

**2** $\dfrac{y^2}{49} - \dfrac{x^2}{16} = 1$ • $c^2 = 49 + 16 \;\Rightarrow\; c = \pm\sqrt{65}; \; V(0, \pm 7); \; F\left(0, \pm\sqrt{65}\right); \; W(\pm 4, 0); \; y = \pm\tfrac{7}{4}x$

$\boxed{3}$   $\dfrac{y^2}{9} - \dfrac{x^2}{4} = 1$   •   The hyperbola will have an upper branch and a lower branch since the term containing $y$ is positive. The vertices will be on the vertical transverse axis, $\pm\sqrt{9} = \pm 3$ units from the center. The endpoints of the horizontal conjugate axis are $\left(\pm\sqrt{4}, 0\right) = (\pm 2, 0)$. The asymptotes have equations $y = \pm\dfrac{\sqrt{9}}{\sqrt{4}}(x) = \pm\dfrac{3}{2}x$.

Using the foci relationship given in Exercise 1, we have $c^2 = 9 + 4 \;\Rightarrow\; c = \pm\sqrt{13}$.

$$V(0, \pm 3); \; F\left(0, \pm\sqrt{13}\right); \; W(\pm 2, 0); \; y = \pm\tfrac{3}{2}x$$

*Figure 3*

*Figure 4*

$\boxed{4}$   $\dfrac{x^2}{49} - \dfrac{y^2}{16} = 1$   •   $c^2 = 49 + 16 \;\Rightarrow\; c = \pm\sqrt{65}; \; V(\pm 7, 0); \; F\left(\pm\sqrt{65}, 0\right); \; W(0, \pm 4); \; y = \pm\tfrac{4}{7}x$

$\boxed{5}$   $x^2 - \dfrac{y^2}{24} = 1 \;\Leftrightarrow\; \dfrac{x^2}{1} - \dfrac{y^2}{24} = 1$   •   The asymptotes have equations $y = \pm\dfrac{\sqrt{24}}{\sqrt{1}}(x) = \pm\sqrt{24}\,x$.

For the foci: $c^2 = 1 + 24 \;\Rightarrow\; c = \pm 5. \; V(\pm 1, 0); \; F(\pm 5, 0); \; W\left(0, \pm\sqrt{24}\right); \; y = \pm\sqrt{24}\,x$

*Figure 5*

*Figure 6*

$\boxed{6}$   $y^2 - \dfrac{x^2}{15} = 1$   •   $c^2 = 1 + 15 \;\Rightarrow\; c = \pm 4; \; V(0, \pm 1); \; F(0, \pm 4); \; W\left(\pm\sqrt{15}, 0\right); \; y = \pm\dfrac{1}{\sqrt{15}}x$

$\boxed{7}$   $y^2 - 4x^2 = 16$ {divide by 16} $\;\Rightarrow\; \dfrac{y^2}{16} - \dfrac{x^2}{4} = 1$   •   The vertices will be $\pm\sqrt{16} = \pm 4$ units from the center on the vertical transverse axis. The endpoints of the horizontal conjugate axis are $\left(\pm\sqrt{4}, 0\right) = (\pm 2, 0)$.

The asymptotes have equations $y = \pm\dfrac{\sqrt{16}}{\sqrt{4}}(x) = \pm\dfrac{4}{2}x = \pm 2x$. For the foci: $c^2 = 4 + 16 \;\Rightarrow\; c^2 = 20 \;\Rightarrow\;$
$c = \pm\sqrt{20} \;\Rightarrow\; c = \pm 2\sqrt{5}$.

$$V(0, \pm 4); \; F\left(0, \pm 2\sqrt{5}\right); \; W(\pm 2, 0); \; y = \pm 2x$$

*Figure 7*

*Figure 8*

**8** $x^2 - 2y^2 = 8 \Rightarrow \frac{x^2}{8} - \frac{y^2}{4} = 1; c^2 = 8 + 4 \Rightarrow c = \pm 2\sqrt{3};$

$$V\left(\pm 2\sqrt{2}, 0\right); F\left(\pm 2\sqrt{3}, 0\right); W(0, \pm 2); y = \pm \frac{1}{2}\sqrt{2}\, x$$

**9** $16x^2 - 36y^2 = 1$ {rewrite in standard form} $\Rightarrow \frac{x^2}{\frac{1}{16}} - \frac{y^2}{\frac{1}{36}} = 1.$

The asymptotes have equations $y = \pm \frac{\sqrt{\frac{1}{36}}}{\sqrt{\frac{1}{16}}}(x) = \pm \frac{\frac{1}{6}}{\frac{1}{4}}(x) = \pm \frac{4}{6}(x) = \pm \frac{2}{3}x.$

For the foci: $c^2 = \frac{1}{16} + \frac{1}{36} \Rightarrow c^2 = \frac{9}{144} + \frac{4}{144} \Rightarrow c^2 = \frac{13}{144} \Rightarrow c = \pm \frac{1}{12}\sqrt{13}.$

$$V\left(\pm \frac{1}{4}, 0\right); F\left(\pm \frac{1}{12}\sqrt{13}, 0\right); W\left(0, \pm \frac{1}{6}\right); y = \pm \frac{2}{3}x$$

Note that the branches of the hyperbola almost coincide with the asymptotes.

*Figure 9*

*Figure 10*

**10** $y^2 - 16x^2 = 1 \Rightarrow \frac{y^2}{1} - \frac{x^2}{\frac{1}{16}} = 1; c^2 = 1 + \frac{1}{16} \Rightarrow c = \pm \frac{1}{4}\sqrt{17};$

$$V(0, \pm 1); F\left(0, \pm \frac{1}{4}\sqrt{17}\right); W\left(\pm \frac{1}{4}, 0\right); y = \pm 4x$$

**11** $\frac{(y+2)^2}{9} - \frac{(x+2)^2}{4} = 1$ • The effect of the factors $(x+2)$ and $(y+2)$ is to shift the center of the hyperbola from $(0,0)$ to $(-2, -2)$. Since the term involving $y$ is positive, the transverse axis will be vertical.

The vertices are 3 units in either direction of the center. Their coordinates are $(-2, -2 \pm 3)$ or equivalently, $(-2, 1)$ and $(-2, -5)$. The conjugate axis will be horizontal with endpoints $(-2 \pm 2, -2)$, or, equivalently, $(0, -2)$ and $(-4, -2)$. Remember that $c$ is the distance *from the center* to a focus. $c^2 = 9 + 4 \Rightarrow c = \pm\sqrt{13}.$

Hence, the coordinates of the foci are $\left(-2, -2 \pm \sqrt{13}\right)$. If the center of the hyperbola was at the origin, we would have asymptote equations $y = \pm \frac{3}{2}x.$ Since the center of the hyperbola has been shifted by distances $y + 2$ and $x + 2$, we can shift the asymptote equations using the same distances. Hence, these equations are $(y+2) = \pm \frac{3}{2}(x+2).$ $C(-2, -2); V(-2, -2 \pm 3); F\left(-2, -2 \pm \sqrt{13}\right); W(-2 \pm 2, -2)$

*Figure 11*

*Figure 12*

**12** $\frac{(x-3)^2}{25} - \frac{(y-1)^2}{4} = 1; c^2 = 25 + 4 \Rightarrow c = \pm\sqrt{29};$

$$C(3, 1); V(3 \pm 5, 1); F\left(3 \pm \sqrt{29}, 1\right); W(3, 1 \pm 2); (y-1) = \pm \frac{2}{5}(x-3)$$

**13** $144x^2 - 25y^2 + 864x - 100y - 2404 = 0 \Rightarrow$

$144(x^2 + 6x + \underline{9}) - 25(y^2 + 4y + \underline{4}) = 2404 + \underline{1296} - \underline{100} \Rightarrow$

$144(x + 3)^2 - 25(y + 2)^2 = 3600 \Rightarrow \dfrac{(x+3)^2}{25} - \dfrac{(y+2)^2}{144} = 1. \ c^2 = 25 + 144 \Rightarrow c = \pm 13.$

$C(-3, -2); V(-3 \pm 5, -2); F(-3 \pm 13, -2); W(-3, -2 \pm 12); (y + 2) = \pm\frac{12}{5}(x + 3)$

*Figure 13*

*Figure 14*

**14** $y^2 - 4x^2 - 12y - 16x + 16 = 0 \Rightarrow (y^2 - 12y + \underline{36}) - 4(x^2 + 4x + \underline{4}) = -16 + \underline{36} - \underline{16} \Rightarrow$

$(y - 6)^2 - 4(x + 2)^2 = 4 \Rightarrow \dfrac{(y-6)^2}{4} - \dfrac{(x+2)^2}{1} = 1; c^2 = 4 + 1 \Rightarrow c = \pm\sqrt{5};$

$C(-2, 6); V(-2, 6 \pm 2); F\left(-2, 6 \pm \sqrt{5}\right); W(-2 \pm 1, 6); (y - 6) = \pm 2(x + 2)$

**15** $4y^2 - x^2 + 40y - 4x + 60 = 0 \Rightarrow 4(y^2 + 10y + \underline{25}) - 1(x^2 + 4x + \underline{4}) = -60 + \underline{100} - \underline{4} \Rightarrow$

$4(y + 5)^2 - (x + 2)^2 = 36 \Rightarrow \dfrac{(y+5)^2}{9} - \dfrac{(x+2)^2}{36} = 1. \ c^2 = 9 + 36 \Rightarrow c = \pm 3\sqrt{5}.$

$C(-2, -5); V(-2, -5 \pm 3); F\left(-2, -5 \pm 3\sqrt{5}\right); W(-2 \pm 6, -5); (y + 5) = \pm\frac{1}{2}(x + 2)$

*Figure 15*

*Figure 16*

**16** $25x^2 - 9y^2 + 100x - 54y + 10 = 0 \Rightarrow 25(x^2 + 4x + \underline{4}) - 9(y^2 + 6y + \underline{9}) = -10 + \underline{100} - \underline{81} \Rightarrow$

$25(x + 2)^2 - 9(y + 3)^2 = 9 \Rightarrow \dfrac{(x+2)^2}{\frac{9}{25}} - \dfrac{(y+3)^2}{1} = 1; c^2 = \frac{9}{25} + 1 \Rightarrow c = \pm\frac{1}{5}\sqrt{34};$

$C(-2, -3); V\left(-2 \pm \frac{3}{5}, -3\right); F\left(-2 \pm \frac{1}{5}\sqrt{34}, -3\right); W(-2, -3 \pm 1); (y + 3) = \pm\frac{5}{3}(x + 2)$

**Note:** Let $a$ denote the distance equal to $\frac{1}{2}$(transverse axis length) and $b$ the distance equal to $\frac{1}{2}$(conjugate axis length).

**17** $V(3, 0)$ and $F(5, 0) \Rightarrow a = 3$ and $c = 5 \Rightarrow b^2 = c^2 - a^2 = 16. \ \dfrac{x^2}{a^2} - \dfrac{y^2}{b^2} = 1$ is then $\dfrac{x^2}{9} - \dfrac{y^2}{16} = 1.$

**18** $V(0, 4)$ and $F(0, 6) \Rightarrow a = 4$ and $c = 6 \Rightarrow b^2 = c^2 - a^2 = 20. \ \dfrac{y^2}{a^2} - \dfrac{x^2}{b^2} = 1$ is then $\dfrac{y^2}{16} - \dfrac{x^2}{20} = 1.$

**19** The center of the hyperbola is $(-2, -3)$. $V(-2, -2)$ and $F(-2, -1) \Rightarrow a = 1$ and $c = 2 \Rightarrow$

$b^2 = 2^2 - 1^2 = 3$ and an equation is $\dfrac{(y+3)^2}{1^2} - \dfrac{(x+2)^2}{3} = 1$, or, equivalently, $(y + 3)^2 - \dfrac{(x+2)^2}{3} = 1.$

**20** The center of the hyperbola is $(1, 2)$. $V(2, 2)$ and $F(4, 2)$ $\Rightarrow$ $a = 1$ and $c = 3$ $\Rightarrow$

$b^2 = 3^2 - 1^2 = 8$ and an equation is $\dfrac{(x - 1)^2}{1^2} - \dfrac{(y - 2)^2}{8} = 1$, or, equivalently, $(x - 1)^2 - \dfrac{(y - 2)^2}{8} = 1$.

**21** $F(0, \pm 4)$ $\Rightarrow$ $c = 4$. $V(0, \pm 1)$ $\Rightarrow$ $a = 1$. $a^2 + b^2 = c^2$ $\Rightarrow$ $b^2 = 4^2 - 1^2 = 15$.

Since the vertices are on the $y$-axis, the "$1^2$" is associated with the $y^2$ term. An equation is $\dfrac{y^2}{1} - \dfrac{x^2}{15} = 1$.

**22** $F(\pm 8, 0)$ and $V(\pm 5, 0)$ $\Rightarrow$ $b^2 = c^2 - a^2 = 8^2 - 5^2 = 39$ $\Rightarrow$ $W\left(0, \pm\sqrt{39}\right)$. An equation is $\dfrac{x^2}{25} - \dfrac{y^2}{39} = 1$.

**23** $F(\pm 5, 0)$ and $V(\pm 3, 0)$ $\Rightarrow$ $b^2 = c^2 - a^2 = 5^2 - 3^2 = 16$ $\Rightarrow$ $W(0, \pm 4)$. An equation is $\dfrac{x^2}{9} - \dfrac{y^2}{16} = 1$.

**24** $F(0, \pm 3)$ and $V(0, \pm 2)$ $\Rightarrow$ $b^2 = c^2 - a^2 = 3^2 - 2^2 = 5$ $\Rightarrow$ $W\left(\pm\sqrt{5}, 0\right)$. An equation is $\dfrac{y^2}{4} - \dfrac{x^2}{5} = 1$.

**25** Conjugate axis of length 4 implies that $b = 2$. $F(0, \pm 5)$ $\Rightarrow$ $c = 5$.

$$a^2 + b^2 = c^2 \Rightarrow a^2 = 5^2 - 2^2 = 21. \text{ An equation is } \dfrac{y^2}{21} - \dfrac{x^2}{4} = 1.$$

**26** Conjugate axis of length 8 implies that $b = 4$. $F(\pm 7, 0)$ $\Rightarrow$ $c = 7$.

$$a^2 + b^2 = c^2 \Rightarrow a^2 = 7^2 - 4^2 = 33. \text{ An equation is } \dfrac{x^2}{33} - \dfrac{y^2}{16} = 1.$$

**27** An equation of a hyperbola with vertices at $(\pm 4, 0)$ is $\dfrac{x^2}{16} - \dfrac{y^2}{b^2} = 1$. Substituting $x = 8$ and $y = 2$ yields

$$4 - \dfrac{4}{b^2} = 1 \Rightarrow \dfrac{4}{b^2} = 3 \Rightarrow b^2 = \dfrac{4}{3}. \text{ An equation is } \dfrac{x^2}{16} - \dfrac{3y^2}{4} = 1.$$

**28** An equation of a hyperbola with vertices at $(0, \pm 12)$ is $\dfrac{y^2}{144} - \dfrac{x^2}{b^2} = 1$. Substituting $x = 5$ and $y = 13$ yields

$$\dfrac{169}{144} - \dfrac{25}{b^2} = 1 \Rightarrow \dfrac{25}{b^2} = \dfrac{25}{144} \Rightarrow b^2 = 144. \text{ An equation is } \dfrac{y^2}{144} - \dfrac{x^2}{144} = 1.$$

**29** Since the asymptote equations are $y = \pm 2x$ and we know that the point $(3, 0)$ is on the hyperbola, we conclude that the upper right corner of the rectangle formed by the transverse and conjugate axes has coordinates $(3, 6)$ {substitute $x = 3$ in $y = 2x$ to obtain the 6}. Thus we have endpoints of the conjugate axis at $(0, \pm 6)$.

$$\text{An equation is } \dfrac{x^2}{3^2} - \dfrac{y^2}{6^2} = 1, \text{ or } \dfrac{x^2}{9} - \dfrac{y^2}{36} = 1.$$

**30** Since the asymptote equations are $y = \pm 3x$ and we know that the point $(0, 6)$ is on the hyperbola, we conclude that the upper right corner of the rectangle formed by the transverse and conjugate axes has coordinates $(2, 6)$ {substitute $y = 6$ in $y = 3x$ to obtain the 2}. Thus we have endpoints of the conjugate axis at $(\pm 2, 0)$.

$$\text{An equation is } \dfrac{y^2}{6^2} - \dfrac{x^2}{2^2} = 1, \text{ or } \dfrac{y^2}{36} - \dfrac{x^2}{4} = 1.$$

**31** Let the $y$ value of $V$ equal $a$ and the $x$ value of $W$ equal $b$. Now $a = \frac{1}{3}b$ {from the asymptote equation $y = \pm\frac{1}{3}x$} and $a^2 + b^2 = 10^2$ {from the foci} $\Rightarrow$ $\left(\frac{1}{3}b\right)^2 + b^2 = 10^2$ $\Rightarrow$ $\frac{10}{9}b^2 = 100$ $\Rightarrow$ $b^2 = 90$ and $a^2 = 10$.

$$\text{An equation is } \dfrac{y^2}{10} - \dfrac{x^2}{90} = 1.$$

**32** Let the $x$ value of $V$ equal $a$ and the $y$ value of $W$ equal $b$. Now $b = \frac{3}{5}a$ {from the asymptote equation $y = \pm\frac{3}{5}x$} and $a^2 + b^2 = 34^2$ {from the foci} $\Rightarrow$ $a^2 + \left(\frac{3}{5}a\right)^2 = 34^2$ $\Rightarrow$ $\frac{34}{25}a^2 = 34^2$ $\Rightarrow$ $a^2 = 850$ and $b^2 = 306$.

$$\text{An equation is } \dfrac{x^2}{850} - \dfrac{y^2}{306} = 1.$$

**33** $x$-intercepts $\pm 5$, asymptotes $y = \pm 2x$ $\bullet$ $a = 5$, $b = 2(5) = 10$. $\dfrac{x^2}{5^2} - \dfrac{y^2}{10^2} = 1$ $\Rightarrow$ $\dfrac{x^2}{25} - \dfrac{y^2}{100} = 1$.

**34** $y$-intercepts $\pm 2$, asymptotes $y = \pm\frac{1}{4}x$ • $a = 2, 2 = \frac{1}{4}(b)$ $\Rightarrow$ $b = 8.$ $\dfrac{y^2}{2^2} - \dfrac{x^2}{8^2} = 1$ $\Rightarrow$ $\dfrac{y^2}{4} - \dfrac{x^2}{64} = 1.$

**35** Since the transverse axis is vertical, the $y^2$ term will be positive.

An equation is $\dfrac{y^2}{\left(\frac{1}{2}\cdot 10\right)^2} - \dfrac{x^2}{\left(\frac{1}{2}\cdot 14\right)^2} = 1$, or $\dfrac{y^2}{25} - \dfrac{x^2}{49} = 1.$

**36** Since the transverse axis is horizontal, the $x^2$ term will be positive.

An equation is $\dfrac{x^2}{\left(\frac{1}{2}\cdot 6\right)^2} - \dfrac{y^2}{\left(\frac{1}{2}\cdot 2\right)^2} = 1$, or $\dfrac{x^2}{9} - \dfrac{y^2}{1} = 1.$

**37** $\frac{1}{3}(x+2) = y^2$ •

We have a first degree $x$-term and a second degree $y$-term, so this is a parabola with a horizontal axis.

**38** $y^2 = \frac{14}{3} - x^2$ $\Leftrightarrow$ $x^2 + y^2 = \frac{14}{3}$, a circle with center at the origin and radius $\sqrt{\frac{14}{3}}$.

**39** $x^2 + 6x - y^2 = 7$ • The coefficient of $x^2$ is positive and the coefficient of $y^2$ is negative, so this is a hyperbola.

**40** $x^2 + 4x + 4y^2 - 24y = -36$ • The coefficients of $x^2$ and $y^2$ are positive, so this is an ellipse.

**41** $-x^2 = y^2 - 25$ $\Leftrightarrow$ $x^2 + y^2 = 25$, a circle with center at the origin and radius 5.

**42** $x = 2x^2 - y + 4$ •

We have a first degree $y$-term and a second degree $x$-term, so this is a parabola with a vertical axis.

**43** $4x^2 - 16x + 9y^2 + 36y = -16$ • The coefficients of $x^2$ and $y^2$ are positive, so this is an ellipse.

**44** $x + 4 = y^2 + y$ •

We have a first degree $x$-term and a second degree $y$-term, so this is a parabola with a horizontal axis.

**45** $x^2 + 3x = 3y - 6$ •

We have a first degree $y$-term and a second degree $x$-term, so this is a parabola with a vertical axis.

**46** $9x^2 - y^2 = 10 - 2y$ • The coefficient of $x^2$ is positive and the coefficient of $y^2$ is negative, so this is a hyperbola.

**47** The graph of $y^2 - 4x^2 = 16$, or, equivalently, $\dfrac{y^2}{16} - \dfrac{x^2}{4} = 1$, is that of a hyperbola with $y$-intercepts $\pm 4$. The graph of $y - x = 4$, or, equivalently, $y = x + 4$, is that of a line with $y$-intercept 4 and slope 1. Substituting $y = x + 4$ into $y^2 - 4x^2 = 16$ yields $(x+4)^2 - 4x^2 = 16$ $\Rightarrow$ $3x^2 - 8x = 0$ $\Rightarrow$ $x(3x - 8) = 0$ $\Rightarrow$ $x = 0, \frac{8}{3};\ y = 4, \frac{20}{3}.$ The two points of intersection are $(0, 4)$ and $\left(\frac{8}{3}, \frac{20}{3}\right)$.

*Figure 47*                    *Figure 48*

**48** Adding the two equations yields $x^2 - 3x = 4$ $\Rightarrow$ $x^2 - 3x - 4 = 0$ $\Rightarrow$ $(x-4)(x+1) = 0$ $\Rightarrow$ $x = 4, -1.$ Substituting these values in the second equation, we find that for $x = 4$, $y = \pm 2\sqrt{3}$, and for $x = -1$, there are no real solutions for $y$. The two points of intersection are $\left(4, \pm 2\sqrt{3}\right)$.

**49** $E_2 - E_1 \Rightarrow (x^2 + 4y^2 = 32) - (x^2 - 3y^2 = 4) \Rightarrow 7y^2 = 28 \Rightarrow y^2 = 4; x^2 = 16.$

The *four* points of intersection are $(\pm 4, \pm 2)$.

*Figure 49*

*Figure 50*

**50** $E_2 - E_1 \Rightarrow (x^2 + y^2 = 106) - (y^2 - 3x^2 = 6) \Rightarrow 4x^2 = 100 \Rightarrow x^2 = 25; y^2 = 81.$

The *four* points of intersection are $(\pm 5, \pm 9)$.

**51** Refer to the definition of a hyperbola. As in the discussion on page 738 of the text, we will let the positive constant, $k$, equal $2a$. $k = 24 \Rightarrow 2a = 24 \Rightarrow a = 12$. $F(13, 0)$ and $F'(-13, 0) \Rightarrow c = 13.$

$$b^2 = c^2 - a^2 = 13^2 - 12^2 = 169 - 144 = 25. \text{ An equation is } \frac{x^2}{144} - \frac{y^2}{25} = 1.$$

**52** $k = 2a = 8 \Rightarrow a = 4$. $F(5, 0)$ and $F'(-5, 0) \Rightarrow c = 5.$

$$b^2 = c^2 - a^2 = 25 - 16 = 9. \text{ An equation is } \frac{x^2}{16} - \frac{y^2}{9} = 1.$$

**53** $k = 16 \Rightarrow 2a = 16 \Rightarrow a = 8$. $F(0, 10)$ and $F'(0, -10) \Rightarrow c = 10.$

$$b^2 = c^2 - a^2 = 10^2 - 8^2 = 100 - 64 = 36. \text{ An equation is } \frac{y^2}{64} - \frac{x^2}{36} = 1.$$

**54** $k = 2a = 30 \Rightarrow a = 15$. $F(0, 17)$ and $F'(0, -17) \Rightarrow c = 17.$

$$b^2 = c^2 - a^2 = 289 - 225 = 64. \text{ An equation is } \frac{y^2}{225} - \frac{x^2}{64} = 1.$$

**55** $k = 2a = 11 - 3 = 8 \Rightarrow a = 4$. $F(0, 5)$ and $F'(0, -5) \Rightarrow c = 5.$

$$b^2 = c^2 - a^2 = 25 - 16 = 9. \text{ An equation is } \frac{y^2}{16} - \frac{x^2}{9} = 1.$$

*Figure 55*

*Figure 56*

**56** $k = 2a = 29 - 5 = 24 \Rightarrow a = 12$. $F(13, 0)$ and $F'(-13, 0) \Rightarrow c = 13.$

$$b^2 = c^2 - a^2 = 169 - 144 = 25. \text{ An equation is } \frac{x^2}{144} - \frac{y^2}{25} = 1.$$

**57** Lower branch of $\dfrac{y^2}{25} - \dfrac{x^2}{36} = 1 \begin{Bmatrix} Solve \\ for\ y < 0 \end{Bmatrix} \Rightarrow \dfrac{y^2}{25} = 1 + \dfrac{x^2}{36} \Rightarrow y^2 = 25\left(\dfrac{36 + x^2}{36}\right) \Rightarrow$

$$y = -\tfrac{5}{6}\sqrt{x^2 + 36}$$

**58** Upper branch of $\dfrac{y^2}{49} - \dfrac{x^2}{25} = 1 \left\{ \begin{array}{c} \textit{Solve} \\ \textit{for } y > 0 \end{array} \right\}$ $\Rightarrow$ $\dfrac{y^2}{49} = 1 + \dfrac{x^2}{25}$ $\Rightarrow$ $y^2 = 49\left(\dfrac{25 + x^2}{25}\right)$ $\Rightarrow$

$$y = \tfrac{7}{5}\sqrt{x^2 + 25}$$

**59** Left branch of $\dfrac{x^2}{4} - \dfrac{y^2}{16} = 1 \left\{ \begin{array}{c} \textit{Solve} \\ \textit{for } x < 0 \end{array} \right\}$ $\Rightarrow$ $\dfrac{x^2}{4} = 1 + \dfrac{y^2}{16}$ $\Rightarrow$ $x^2 = 4\left(\dfrac{16 + y^2}{16}\right)$ $\Rightarrow$

$$x = -\tfrac{1}{2}\sqrt{y^2 + 16}$$

**60** Right branch of $\dfrac{x^2}{16} - \dfrac{y^2}{4} = 1 \left\{ \begin{array}{c} \textit{Solve} \\ \textit{for } x > 0 \end{array} \right\}$ $\Rightarrow$ $\dfrac{x^2}{16} = 1 + \dfrac{y^2}{4}$ $\Rightarrow$ $x^2 = 16\left(\dfrac{4 + y^2}{4}\right)$ $\Rightarrow$

$$x = 2\sqrt{y^2 + 4}$$

**61** Right halves of the branches of $\dfrac{y^2}{4} - \dfrac{x^2}{81} = 1 \left\{ \begin{array}{c} \textit{Solve} \\ \textit{for } x \geq 0 \end{array} \right\}$ $\Rightarrow$ $\dfrac{y^2}{4} - 1 = \dfrac{x^2}{81}$ $\Rightarrow$ $x^2 = 81\left(\dfrac{y^2 - 4}{4}\right)$ $\Rightarrow$

$$x = \tfrac{9}{2}\sqrt{y^2 - 4}$$

**62** Left halves of the branches of $\dfrac{y^2}{36} - \dfrac{x^2}{16} = 1 \left\{ \begin{array}{c} \textit{Solve} \\ \textit{for } x \leq 0 \end{array} \right\}$ $\Rightarrow$ $\dfrac{y^2}{36} - 1 = \dfrac{x^2}{16}$ $\Rightarrow$ $x^2 = 16\left(\dfrac{y^2 - 36}{36}\right)$ $\Rightarrow$

$$x = -\tfrac{2}{3}\sqrt{y^2 - 36}$$

**63** Upper halves of the branches of $\dfrac{x^2}{9} - \dfrac{y^2}{36} = 1 \left\{ \begin{array}{c} \textit{Solve} \\ \textit{for } y \geq 0 \end{array} \right\}$ $\Rightarrow$ $\dfrac{x^2}{9} - 1 = \dfrac{y^2}{36}$ $\Rightarrow$ $y^2 = 36\left(\dfrac{x^2 - 9}{9}\right)$ $\Rightarrow$

$$y = 2\sqrt{x^2 - 9}$$

**64** Lower halves of the branches of $\dfrac{x^2}{9} - \dfrac{y^2}{49} = 1 \left\{ \begin{array}{c} \textit{Solve} \\ \textit{for } y \leq 0 \end{array} \right\}$ $\Rightarrow$ $\dfrac{x^2}{9} - 1 = \dfrac{y^2}{49}$ $\Rightarrow$ $y^2 = 49\left(\dfrac{x^2 - 9}{9}\right)$ $\Rightarrow$

$$y = -\tfrac{7}{3}\sqrt{x^2 - 9}$$

**65** $x = \tfrac{5}{4}\sqrt{y^2 + 16}$ $\Rightarrow$ $\tfrac{4}{5}x = \sqrt{y^2 + 16}$ $\Rightarrow$ $\tfrac{16}{25}x^2 = y^2 + 16$ $\Rightarrow$ $\tfrac{16}{25}x^2 - y^2 = 16$ $\Rightarrow$ $\dfrac{x^2}{25} - \dfrac{y^2}{16} = 1$,

which is an equation of a hyperbola with right and left branches.

        Since $x > 0$ in the original equation, its graph is the *right* branch of the hyperbola.

**66** $x = -\tfrac{5}{4}\sqrt{y^2 + 16}$ $\Rightarrow$ $-\tfrac{4}{5}x = \sqrt{y^2 + 16}$ $\Rightarrow$ $\tfrac{16}{25}x^2 = y^2 + 16$ $\Rightarrow$ $\tfrac{16}{25}x^2 - y^2 = 16$ $\Rightarrow$ $\dfrac{x^2}{25} - \dfrac{y^2}{16} = 1$.

        Since $x < 0$ in the original equation, its graph is the *left* branch of the hyperbola.

**67** $y = \tfrac{3}{7}\sqrt{x^2 + 49}$ $\Rightarrow$ $\tfrac{7}{3}y = \sqrt{x^2 + 49}$ $\Rightarrow$ $\tfrac{49}{9}y^2 = x^2 + 49$ $\Rightarrow$ $\tfrac{49}{9}y^2 - x^2 = 49$ $\Rightarrow$ $\dfrac{y^2}{9} - \dfrac{x^2}{49} = 1$.

        Since $y > 0$ in the original equation, its graph is the *upper* branch of the hyperbola.

**68** $y = -\tfrac{3}{7}\sqrt{x^2 + 49}$ $\Rightarrow$ $-\tfrac{7}{3}y = \sqrt{x^2 + 49}$ $\Rightarrow$ $\tfrac{49}{9}y^2 = x^2 + 49$ $\Rightarrow$ $\tfrac{49}{9}y^2 - x^2 = 49$ $\Rightarrow$ $\dfrac{y^2}{9} - \dfrac{x^2}{49} = 1$.

        Since $y < 0$ in the original equation, its graph is the *lower* branch of the hyperbola.

**69** $y = -\tfrac{9}{4}\sqrt{x^2 - 16}$ $\Rightarrow$ $-\tfrac{4}{9}y = \sqrt{x^2 - 16}$ $\Rightarrow$ $\tfrac{16}{81}y^2 = x^2 - 16$ $\Rightarrow$ $16 = x^2 - \tfrac{16}{81}y^2$ $\Rightarrow$ $\dfrac{x^2}{16} - \dfrac{y^2}{81} = 1$.

    Since $y \leq 0$ in the original equation, its graph is the *lower halves* of the branches of the hyperbola.

**70** $y = \tfrac{9}{4}\sqrt{x^2 - 16}$ $\Rightarrow$ $\tfrac{4}{9}y = \sqrt{x^2 - 16}$ $\Rightarrow$ $\tfrac{16}{81}y^2 = x^2 - 16$ $\Rightarrow$ $16 = x^2 - \tfrac{16}{81}y^2$ $\Rightarrow$ $\dfrac{x^2}{16} - \dfrac{y^2}{81} = 1$.

    Since $y \geq 0$ in the original equation, its graph is the *upper halves* of the branches of the hyperbola.

**71** $x = -\frac{2}{3}\sqrt{y^2 - 36} \Rightarrow -\frac{3}{2}x = \sqrt{y^2 - 36} \Rightarrow \frac{9}{4}x^2 = y^2 - 36 \Rightarrow 36 = y^2 - \frac{9}{4}x^2 \Rightarrow \frac{y^2}{36} - \frac{x^2}{16} = 1.$

Since $x \leq 0$ in the original equation, its graph is the *left halves* of the branches of the hyperbola.

**72** $x = \frac{2}{3}\sqrt{y^2 - 36} \Rightarrow \frac{3}{2}x = \sqrt{y^2 - 36} \Rightarrow \frac{9}{4}x^2 = y^2 - 36 \Rightarrow 36 = y^2 - \frac{9}{4}x^2 \Rightarrow \frac{y^2}{36} - \frac{x^2}{16} = 1.$

Since $x \geq 0$ in the original equation, its graph is the *right halves* of the branches of the hyperbola.

**73** Their equations are $\frac{x^2}{25} - \frac{y^2}{9} = 1$ and $\frac{x^2}{25} - \frac{y^2}{9} = -1$, or, equivalently, $\frac{y^2}{9} - \frac{x^2}{25} = 1$. Conjugate hyperbolas have

the same asymptotes and exchange transverse and conjugate axes.

Figure 73

Figure 75

**74** The center is $C(h, k)$ with $W(h, k \pm b)$. An equation is $\dfrac{(x-h)^2}{a^2} - \dfrac{(y-k)^2}{b^2} = 1.$

**75** See the above figure modeling the given information. The hyperbolic branch can be modeled with the equation

$\dfrac{x^2}{24^2} - \dfrac{y^2}{b^2} = 1.$ Let $x = 50$ and $y = -84$ to get $\dfrac{50^2}{24^2} - 1 = \dfrac{(-84)^2}{b^2} \Rightarrow \dfrac{50^2 - 24^2}{24^2} = \dfrac{84^2}{b^2} \Rightarrow$

$b^2 = \dfrac{84^2 \cdot 24^2}{1924}.$ Now let $x = d$ and $y = 36$ to get $\dfrac{d^2}{24^2} - \dfrac{36^2 \cdot 1924}{84^2 \cdot 24^2} = 1 \Rightarrow$

$d^2 \approx 929.388 \Rightarrow d \approx 30.486$ and $2d \approx 60.97$ meters.

**76** Let $A$ and $P$ be the points $(3, 0)$ and $(x, y)$, respectively.

$S = [d(A, P)]^2 = (x - 3)^2 + (y - 0)^2 = x^2 - 6x + 9 + y^2$

$\qquad = x^2 - 6x + 9 + \left(\frac{1}{2}x^2 + 4\right)$ {from $2y^2 - x^2 = 8$} $= \frac{3}{2}x^2 - 6x + 13.$

Since $S$ is a quadratic function, its minimum occurs at $x = -\dfrac{b}{2a} = -\dfrac{-6}{2\left(\frac{3}{2}\right)} = 2.$

If $x = 2$, $S = 7$, and the plane comes within $\sqrt{7}$ miles of $A$.

**77** Set up a coordinate system like the one in Example 6. Let the origin be located on the shoreline halfway between $A$

and $B$ and let $P(x, y)$ denote the coordinates of the ship. The coordinates of $A$ and $B$ (which can be thought of as

the foci of the hyperbola) are $(-100, 0)$ and $(100, 0)$, respectively. Hence, $c = 100$.

As in Exercise 51, the difference in distances is a constant—that is,

$$d(P, A) - d(P, B) = 2a \Rightarrow 160 = 2a \Rightarrow a = 80.$$

$b^2 = c^2 - a^2 = 100^2 - 80^2 \Rightarrow b = 60.$ An equation of the hyperbola is $\dfrac{x^2}{80^2} - \dfrac{y^2}{60^2} = 1.$

Now, $y = 100 \Rightarrow \dfrac{x^2}{80^2} = 1 + \dfrac{100^2}{60^2} \Rightarrow x^2 = 80^2 \cdot \dfrac{13,600}{60^2} \Rightarrow x = 80 \cdot \dfrac{10}{60}\sqrt{136} = \dfrac{80}{3}\sqrt{34}.$

The ship's coordinates are $\left(\dfrac{80}{3}\sqrt{34}, 100\right) \approx (155.5, 100).$

**78** By the reflective property of parabolic mirrors (see page 721 of the text) parallel rays striking the parabolic mirror will be reflected toward $F_1$. By the reflective property of hyperbolic mirrors (see page 745 of the text), these rays will be reflected toward the exterior focus of the hyperbolic mirror, which is located below the parabolic mirror in the figure.

**79** $\dfrac{(y-0.1)^2}{1.6} - \dfrac{(x+0.2)^2}{0.5} = 1 \;\Rightarrow\; \dfrac{(y-0.1)^2}{1.6} = 1 + \dfrac{(x+0.2)^2}{0.5} \;\Rightarrow$

$(y-0.1)^2 = 1.6\left[1 + \dfrac{(x+0.2)^2}{0.5}\right] \;\Rightarrow\; y - 0.1 = \pm\sqrt{1.6\left[1 + \dfrac{(x+0.2)^2}{0.5}\right]} \;\Rightarrow$

$$y = 0.1 \pm \sqrt{1.6\left[1 + \dfrac{(x+0.2)^2}{0.5}\right]}.$$

$\dfrac{(y-0.5)^2}{2.7} - \dfrac{(x-0.1)^2}{5.3} = 1 \;\Rightarrow\; \dfrac{(y-0.5)^2}{2.7} = 1 + \dfrac{(x-0.1)^2}{5.3} \;\Rightarrow$

$(y-0.5)^2 = 2.7\left[1 + \dfrac{(x-0.1)^2}{5.3}\right] \;\Rightarrow\; y - 0.5 = \pm\sqrt{2.7\left[1 + \dfrac{(x-0.1)^2}{5.3}\right]} \;\Rightarrow$

$$y = 0.5 \pm \sqrt{2.7\left[1 + \dfrac{(x-0.1)^2}{5.3}\right]}.$$

From the graph, the point of intersection in the first quadrant is approximately $(0.741, 2.206)$.

$[-15, 15]$ by $[-10, 10]$

*Figure 79*

$[-4.5, 4.5]$ by $[-3, 3]$

*Figure 80*

**80** $\dfrac{(x-0.1)^2}{0.12} - \dfrac{y^2}{0.1} = 1 \;\Rightarrow\; 0.1(x-0.1)^2 - 0.12y^2 = 0.012 \;\Rightarrow\; y = \pm\sqrt{\frac{1}{0.12}\left[0.1(x-0.1)^2 - 0.012\right]}.$

$\dfrac{x^2}{0.9} - \dfrac{(y-0.3)^2}{2.1} = 1 \;\Rightarrow\; 2.1x^2 - 0.9(y-0.3)^2 = 1.89 \;\Rightarrow\; y = 0.3 \pm \sqrt{\frac{1}{0.9}[2.1x^2 - 1.89]}.$

From the graph, the point of intersection in the first quadrant is approximately $(0.994, 0.752)$.

**81** $\dfrac{(x-0.3)^2}{1.3} - \dfrac{y^2}{2.7} = 1 \;\Rightarrow\; \dfrac{(x-0.3)^2}{1.3} - 1 = \dfrac{y^2}{2.7} \;\Rightarrow\; y^2 = 2.7\left[-1 + \dfrac{(x-0.3)^2}{1.3}\right] \;\Rightarrow$

$$y = \pm\sqrt{2.7\left[-1 + \dfrac{(x-0.3)^2}{1.3}\right]}.$$

$\dfrac{y^2}{2.8} - \dfrac{(x-0.2)^2}{1.2} = 1 \;\Rightarrow\; \dfrac{y^2}{2.8} = 1 + \dfrac{(x-0.2)^2}{1.2} \;\Rightarrow\; y^2 = 2.8\left[1 + \dfrac{(x-0.2)^2}{1.2}\right] \;\Rightarrow$

$$y = \pm\sqrt{2.8\left[1 + \dfrac{(x-0.2)^2}{1.2}\right]}.$$

The two graphs nearly intersect in the second and fourth quadrants, but there are no points of intersection.

$[-15, 15, 2]$ by $[-10, 10, 2]$

**Figure 81**

$[-25, 25, 5]$ by $[-25, 25, 5]$

**Figure 82**

**82** $\dfrac{(x+0.2)^2}{1.75} - \dfrac{(y-0.5)^2}{1.6} = 1 \;\Rightarrow\; y = 0.5 \pm \sqrt{1.6\left[-1 + \dfrac{(x+0.2)^2}{1.75}\right]}.$

$\dfrac{(x-0.6)^2}{2.2} - \dfrac{(y+0.4)^2}{2.35} = 1 \;\Rightarrow\; y = -0.4 \pm \sqrt{2.35\left[-1 + \dfrac{(x-0.6)^2}{2.2}\right]}.$

From the graph, we can see that there are two points of intersection.

One is in the first quadrant, near the point $(23, 23)$, and the other is in the fourth quadrant, near the point $(3, -2)$.

**83** (a) The comet's path is hyperbolic with $a^2 = 26 \times 10^{14}$ and $b^2 = 18 \times 10^{14}$.

$c^2 = a^2 + b^2 = 26 \times 10^{14} + 18 \times 10^{14} = 44 \times 10^{14} \;\Rightarrow\; c \approx 6.63 \times 10^7.$

The coordinates of the sun are approximately $\left(6.63 \times 10^7, 0\right)$.

(b) The minimum distance between the comet and the sun will be

$$c - a = \sqrt{44 \times 10^{14}} - \sqrt{26 \times 10^{14}} = 1.53 \times 10^7 \text{ mi}.$$

Since $r$ must be in meters, $1.53 \times 10^7 \text{ mi} \times 1610 \text{ m/mi} \approx 2.47 \times 10^{10} \text{ m}.$

At this distance, $v$ must be greater than $\sqrt{\dfrac{2k}{r}} \approx \sqrt{\dfrac{2(1.325 \times 10^{20})}{2.47 \times 10^{10}}} \approx 103{,}600 \text{ m/sec}.$

## 10.4 Exercises

**1** For this exercise (and others), we solve for $t$ in terms of $x$, and then substitute that expression for $t$ in the equation that relates $y$ and $t$. $x = t - 2 \;\Rightarrow\; t = x + 2.$ $y = 2t + 3 = 2(x+2) + 3 = 2x + 7.$

As $t$ varies from 0 to 5, $(x, y)$ varies from $(-2, 3)$ to $(3, 13)$.

**Figure 1**

**Figure 2**

**2** $y = 1 + t \;\Rightarrow\; t = y - 1.$ $x = 1 - 2t = 1 - 2(y-1) = -2y + 3.$

As $t$ varies from $-1$ to 4, $(x, y)$ varies from $(3, 0)$ to $(-7, 5)$.

**3.** $x = t^2 + 1 \;\Rightarrow\; t^2 = x - 1.$  $y = t^2 - 1 = x - 2.$

As $t$ varies from $-2$ to $2$, $(x, y)$ varies from $(5, 3)$ to $(1, -1)$ {when $t = 0$} and back to $(5, 3)$.

*Figure 3*

*Figure 4*

**4.** $x = t^3 + 1 \;\Rightarrow\; t^3 = x - 1.$  $y = t^3 - 1 = x - 2.$ As $t$ varies from $-2$ to $2$, $(x, y)$ varies from $(-7, -9)$ to $(9, 7)$.

**5.** Since $y$ is linear in $t$, it is easier to solve the second equation for $t$ than it is to solve the first equation for $t$.

Hence, we solve for $t$ in terms of $y$, and then substitute that expression for $t$ in the equation that relates $x$ and $t$.

$y = 2t + 3 \;\Rightarrow\; t = \frac{1}{2}(y - 3).$  $x = 4\left[\frac{1}{2}(y - 3)\right]^2 - 5 \;\Rightarrow\; (y - 3)^2 = x + 5.$ This is a parabola with vertex at $(-5, 3)$. Since $t$ takes on all real values, so does $y$, and the curve $C$ is the entire parabola.

*Figure 5*

*Figure 6*

**6.** $y = 3t + 1 \;\Rightarrow\; 3t = y - 1 \;\Rightarrow\; (3t)^2 = (y - 1)^2.$

$x = 1 - 9t^2 = 1 - (y - 1)^2 = 1 - (y^2 - 2y + 1) = 2y - y^2.$ This is a parabola with vertex at $(1, 1)$. Since $t$ takes on all real values, so does $y$, and the curve $C$ is the entire parabola.

**7.** $y = t^3;\, t \geq -1 \;\Rightarrow\; y^2 = t^6.$  $x = t^6 - 5 = y^2 - 5.$ As $t$ varies from $-1$ to $\infty$, $y$ varies from $-1$ to $\infty$, and $x$ varies from $-4$ to $-5$ and then increases without bound. The graph is the portion of the parabola shown in the figure.

*Figure 7*

*Figure 8*

**8.** $x = \sqrt{t} \;\Rightarrow\; t = x^2.$  $y = 3t + 4 = 3x^2 + 4.$ As $t$ varies from $0$ to $\infty$,

$x$ varies from $0$ to $\infty$ and the graph is the right half of the parabola.

**9** $x = 4\cos t + 1$, $y = 3\sin t$; $0 \le t \le 2\pi$ $\Rightarrow$ $\dfrac{x-1}{4} = \cos t$ and $\dfrac{y}{3} = \sin t$ $\Rightarrow$

$\dfrac{(x-1)^2}{4^2} + \dfrac{y^2}{3^2} = \cos^2 t + \sin^2 t$ $\Rightarrow$ $\dfrac{(x-1)^2}{16} + \dfrac{y^2}{9} = 1$. This is an ellipse with center $(1,0)$, horizontal major

axis of length $2(4) = 8$, and vertical minor axis of length $2(3) = 6$. As $t$ varies from $0$ to $2\pi$, $(x, y)$ traces the

ellipse from $(5, 0)$ in a counterclockwise direction back to $(5, 0)$.

Figure 9

Figure 10

**10** $x = 2\sin t$, $y = 3\cos t$; $0 \le t \le 2\pi$ $\Rightarrow$ $\dfrac{x}{2} = \sin t$ and $\dfrac{y}{3} = \cos t$ $\Rightarrow$ $\dfrac{x^2}{4} + \dfrac{y^2}{9} = \sin^2 t + \cos^2 t = 1$.

As $t$ varies from $0$ to $2\pi$, $(x, y)$ traces the ellipse from $(0, 3)$ in a clockwise direction back to $(0, 3)$.

**11** $x = 2 - 3\sin t$, $y = -1 - 3\cos t$; $0 \le t \le 2\pi$ $\Rightarrow$ $\dfrac{x-2}{-3} = \sin t$ and $\dfrac{y+1}{-3} = \cos t$ $\Rightarrow$

$\dfrac{(x-2)^2}{(-3)^2} + \dfrac{(y+1)^2}{(-3)^2} = \sin^2 t + \cos^2 t$ $\Rightarrow$ $\dfrac{(x-2)^2}{9} + \dfrac{(y+1)^2}{9} = 1$ $\Rightarrow$ $(x-2)^2 + (y+1)^2 = 9$.

This is a circle with center $(2, -1)$ and radius $3$. As $t$ varies from $0$ to $2\pi$, $(x, y)$ traces the circle from $(2, -4)$ in a

clockwise direction back to $(2, -4)$.

Figure 11

Figure 12

**12** $x = \cos t - 2$, $y = \sin t + 3$; $0 \le t \le 2\pi$ $\Rightarrow$ $x + 2 = \cos t$ and $y - 3 = \sin t$ $\Rightarrow$

$(x+2)^2 + (y-3)^2 = \cos^2 t + \sin^2 t = 1$. As $t$ varies from $0$ to $2\pi$,

$(x, y)$ traces the circle from $(-1, 3)$ in a counterclockwise direction back to $(-1, 3)$.

**13** $x = \sec t$ and $y = \tan t$ $\Rightarrow$ $x^2 - y^2 = \sec^2 t - \tan^2 t = 1$. As $t$ varies from $-\frac{\pi}{2}$ to $\frac{\pi}{2}$, $(x, y)$ traces the right branch of the hyperbola along the asymptote $y = -x$ to $(1, 0)$ and then along the asymptote $y = x$.

Figure 13

Figure 14

**14** $x = \csc t$ and $y = \cot t$ $\Rightarrow$ $x^2 - y^2 = \csc^2 t - \cot^2 t = 1$. As $t$ varies from $-\pi$ to $0$, $(x, y)$ traces the left branch of the hyperbola along the asymptote $y = -x$ to $(-1, 0)$ and then along the asymptote $y = x$.

**15** $x = \cos 2t = 1 - 2\sin^2 t = 1 - 2y^2$. As $t$ varies from $-\pi$ to $\pi$, $(x, y)$ varies from $(1, 0)$ {the vertex} down to $(-1, -1)$ {when $t = -\frac{\pi}{2}$}, back to the vertex when $t = 0$, up to $(-1, 1)$ {when $t = \frac{\pi}{2}$}, and finally back to the vertex.

Figure 15

Figure 16

**16** $y = \cos 2t = 1 - 2\sin^2 t = 1 - 2(1 - \cos^2 t) = 2\cos^2 t - 1 = 2x^2 - 1$. As $t$ varies from $-\pi$ to $\pi$, $(x, y)$ varies from $(-1, 1)$ {when $t = -\pi$}, down to $(0, -1)$ {the vertex}, up to $(1, 1)$ {when $t = 0$}, back to the vertex when $t = \frac{\pi}{2}$, and finally back to $(-1, 1)$.

**17** $y = 2\ln t = \ln t^2$ {since $t > 0$} $= \ln x$. As $t$ varies from $0$ to $\infty$, so does $x$, and $y$ varies from $-\infty$ to $\infty$.

Figure 17

Figure 18

**18** $x = \cos^3 t$ and $y = \sin^3 t$ $\Rightarrow$ $x^{2/3} = \cos^2 t$ and $y^{2/3} = \sin^2 t$ $\Rightarrow$ $x^{2/3} + y^{2/3} = 1$ or $y = \pm\left(1 - x^{2/3}\right)^{3/2}$. As $t$ varies from $0$ to $2\pi$, $(x, y)$ traces the astroid from $(1, 0)$ in a counterclockwise direction back to $(1, 0)$.

**19** $y = \csc t = \dfrac{1}{\sin t} = \dfrac{1}{x}$. As $t$ varies from $0$ to $\frac{\pi}{2}$, $(x, y)$ varies asymptotically from the positive $y$-axis to $(1, 1)$.

*Figure 19*

*Figure 20*

**20** $y = e^{-t} = (e^t)^{-1} = x^{-1} = \dfrac{1}{x}$.

As $t$ varies from $-\infty$ to $\infty$, $(x, y)$ varies asymptotically from the positive $y$-axis to the positive $x$-axis.

**21** $x = t$ and $y = \sqrt{t^2 - 1}$ $\Rightarrow$ $y = \sqrt{x^2 - 1}$ $\Rightarrow$ $x^2 - y^2 = 1$.

Since $y$ is nonnegative, the graph is the top half of both branches of the hyperbola.

*Figure 21*

*Figure 22*

**22** $x = -\sqrt{t^2 - 1}$ and $y = t$; $|t| \geq 1$ $\Rightarrow$ $x = -\sqrt{y^2 - 1}$ $\Rightarrow$ $x^2 = y^2 - 1$ $\Rightarrow$ $y^2 - x^2 = 1$.

Since $x$ is nonpositive, the graph is the left half of both branches of the hyperbola.

**23** $y = t$ and $x = -2\sqrt{1 - t^2}$ $\Rightarrow$ $x = -2\sqrt{1 - y^2}$ $\Rightarrow$ $x^2 = 4 - 4y^2$ $\Rightarrow$ $x^2 + 4y^2 = 4$.

As $t$ varies from $-1$ to $1$, $(x, y)$ traces the ellipse from $(0, -1)$ to $(0, 1)$.

*Figure 23*

*Figure 24*

**24** $y = t$ and $x = \dfrac{6}{5}\sqrt{25 - t^2}$ $\Rightarrow$ $x = \dfrac{6}{5}\sqrt{25 - y^2}$ $\Rightarrow$ $x^2 = \dfrac{36}{25}(25 - y^2)$ $\Rightarrow$ $\dfrac{25x^2}{36} = 25 - y^2$ $\Rightarrow$

$\dfrac{25x^2}{36} + y^2 = 25$ $\Rightarrow$ $\dfrac{x^2}{36} + \dfrac{y^2}{25} = 1$. As $t$ varies from $-5$ to $5$, $(x, y)$ traces the ellipse from $(0, -5)$ to $(0, 5)$.

**25** $x = t$ and $y = \sqrt{t^2 - 2t + 1}$ $\Rightarrow$ $y = \sqrt{x^2 - 2x + 1} = \sqrt{(x-1)^2} = |x - 1|$.

As $t$ varies from 0 to 4, $(x, y)$ traces $y = |x - 1|$ from $(0, 1)$ to $(4, 3)$.

Figure 25

Figure 26

**26** $y = 8t^3 = (2t)^3 = x^3$. As $t$ varies from $-1$ to 1, $(x, y)$ varies from $(-2, -8)$ to $(2, 8)$.

**27** $x = (t + 1)^3$ $\Rightarrow$ $t = x^{1/3} - 1$. $y = (t + 2)^2 = (x^{1/3} + 1)^2$. This is probably an unfamiliar graph. The graph of $y = x^{1/3}$ is similar to the graph of $y = x^{1/2}$ $\{y = \sqrt{x}\}$ but is symmetric with respect to the origin. The "+1" shifts $y = x^{1/3}$ up 1 unit and the "squaring" makes all $y$ values nonnegative. Since we have restrictions on the variable $t$, we only have a portion of this graph. As $t$ varies from 0 to 2, $(x, y)$ varies from $(1, 4)$ to $(27, 16)$.

Figure 27

Figure 28

**28** $x = t^3$ $\Rightarrow$ $t = \sqrt[3]{x}$. $y = t^2 = x^{2/3}$. $x$ takes on all real values.

**29** $y = e^{-2t} = (e^t)^{-2} = x^{-2} = 1/x^2$. This is a rational function.

Only the first quadrant portion is used and as $t$ varies from $-\infty$ to $\infty$, $x$ varies from 0 to $\infty$, excluding 0.

Figure 29

Figure 30

**30** As $t$ varies from $-\frac{\pi}{2}$ to $\frac{\pi}{2}$, $x$ varies from $-\infty$ to $\infty$. $y$ is always 1 so we have the graph of $y = 1$.

**31** (a) $x = 3 + 2\sin t$, $y = -2 + 2\cos t$; $0 \le t \le 2\pi$. We'll make use of the identity $\sin^2 t + \cos^2 t = 1$.

$x - 3 = 2\sin t$, $y + 2 = 2\cos t$ $\Rightarrow$ $(x - 3)^2 = 4\sin^2 t$, $(y + 2)^2 = 4\cos^2 t$ $\Rightarrow$

$(x - 3)^2 + (y + 2)^2 = 4\sin^2 t + 4\cos^2 t$ $\Rightarrow$ $(x - 3)^2 + (y + 2)^2 = 4(\sin^2 t + \cos^2 t)$ $\Rightarrow$

$(x - 3)^2 + (y + 2)^2 = 4$. So the curve $C$ is a circle with center $(3, -2)$ and radius $\sqrt{4} = 2$.

As $t$ varies from $0$ to $2\pi$, $(x, y)$ traces the circle from $(3, 0)$ in a clockwise direction back to $(3, 0)$.

(b) $x = 3 - 2\sin t$, $y = -2 + 2\cos t$; $0 \le t \le 2\pi$. The orientation changes to counterclockwise.

(c) $x = 3 - 2\sin t$, $y = -2 - 2\cos t$; $0 \le t \le 2\pi$. The starting and ending point changes to $(3, -4)$.

**32** (a) $x = -2 + 3\sin t$, $y = 3 - 3\cos t$; $0 \le t \le 2\pi$. We'll make use of the identity $\sin^2 t + \cos^2 t = 1$.

$x + 2 = 3\sin t$, $y - 3 = -3\cos t$ $\Rightarrow$ $(x + 2)^2 = 9\sin^2 t$, $(y - 3)^2 = 9\cos^2 t$ $\Rightarrow$

$(x + 2)^2 + (y - 3)^2 = 9\sin^2 t + 9\cos^2 t$ $\Rightarrow$ $(x + 2)^2 + (y - 3)^2 = 9(\sin^2 t + \cos^2 t)$ $\Rightarrow$

$(x + 2)^2 + (y - 3)^2 = 9$. So the curve $C$ is a circle with center $(-2, 3)$ and radius $\sqrt{9} = 3$.

As $t$ varies from $0$ to $2\pi$, $(x, y)$ traces the circle from $(-2, 0)$ in a counterclockwise direction back to $(-2, 0)$.

(b) $x = -2 - 3\sin t$, $y = 3 + 3\cos t$; $0 \le t \le 2\pi$. The starting and ending point changes to $(-2, 6)$.

(c) $x = -2 + 3\sin t$, $y = 3 + 3\cos t$; $0 \le t \le 2\pi$.

           The starting and ending point changes to $(-2, 6)$ and the orientation changes to clockwise.

**33** All of the curves are a portion of the parabola $x = y^2$.

$C_1$: $x = t^2 = y^2$. $y$ takes on all real values and we have the entire parabola.

$C_2$: $x = t^4 = (t^2)^2 = y^2$. $C_2$ is only the top half since $y = t^2$ is nonnegative. As $t$ varies from $-\infty$ to $\infty$, the top portion is traced twice.

$C_3$: $x = \sin^2 t = (\sin t)^2 = y^2$. $C_3$ is the portion of the curve from $(1, -1)$ to $(1, 1)$. The point $(1, 1)$ is reached at $t = \frac{\pi}{2} + 2\pi n$ and the point $(1, -1)$ when $t = \frac{3\pi}{2} + 2\pi n$.

$C_4$: $x = e^{2t} = (e^t)^2 = (-e^t)^2 = y^2$. $C_4$ is the bottom half of the parabola since $y$ is negative. As $t$ approaches $-\infty$, the parabola approaches the origin.

**34** All of the curves are a portion of the line $x + y = 1$.

$C_1$: $x + y = t + (1 - t) = 1$.
$C_1$ is the entire line since $x$ takes on all real values.

$C_2$: $x + y = (1 - t^2) + t^2 = 1$. $C_2$ is the portion of the line where $y \geq 0$ since $y = t^2$.

$C_3$: $x + y = \cos^2 t + \sin^2 t = 1$.
$C_3$ is only the portion from $(0, 1)$ to $(1, 0)$ since $\sin^2 t$ and $\cos^2 t$ are bounded by 0 and 1.

$C_4$: $x + y = (\ln t - t) + (1 + t - \ln t) = 1$.
$C_4$ is defined when $t > 0$.
When $t = 1$, $(x, y) = (-1, 2)$.
As $t$ approaches 0 or $\infty$, $x$ approaches $-\infty$.

**35** In each part, the motion is on the unit circle since $x^2 + y^2 = 1$.

(a) For $0 \leq t \leq \pi$, $x$ {$\cos t$} varies from 1 to $-1$ and $y$ {$\sin t$} is nonnegative.

$P(x, y)$ moves from $(1, 0)$ counterclockwise to $(-1, 0)$.

(b) For $0 \leq t \leq \pi$, $y$ {$\cos t$} varies from 1 to $-1$ and $x$ {$\sin t$} is nonnegative.

$P(x, y)$ moves from $(0, 1)$ clockwise to $(0, -1)$.

(c) For $-1 \leq t \leq 1$, $x$ {$t$} varies from $-1$ to 1 and $y$ {$\sqrt{1 - t^2}$} is nonnegative.

$P(x, y)$ moves from $(-1, 0)$ clockwise to $(1, 0)$.

*Figure 35(a)*

*Figure 35(b)*

*Figure 35(c)*

**36** In each part, the motion is on a line since $x + y = 1$.

(a) $x = t^2, y = 1 - t^2; 0 \le t \le 1$ • $P(x, y)$ moves from $(0, 1)$ to $(1, 0)$.

(b) $x = 1 - \ln t, y = \ln t; 1 \le t \le e$ • $P(x, y)$ moves from $(1, 0)$ to $(0, 1)$.

(c) $x = \cos^2 t, y = \sin^2 t; 0 \le t \le 2\pi$ • $P(x, y)$ moves from $(1, 0)$ to $(0, 1)$ twice in each direction.

*Figure 36(a)*

*Figure 36(b)*

*Figure 36(c)*

**37** $x = a \cos t + h$ and $y = b \sin t + k; 0 \le t \le 2\pi$ $\Rightarrow$

$\dfrac{x - h}{a} = \cos t$ and $\dfrac{y - k}{b} = \sin t$ $\Rightarrow$ $\dfrac{(x - h)^2}{a^2} + \dfrac{(y - k)^2}{b^2} = \cos^2 t + \sin^2 t = 1.$

This is the equation of an ellipse with center $(h, k)$ and semiaxes of lengths $a$ and $b$ (axes of lengths $2a$ and $2b$).

**38** $x = a \sec t + h$ and $y = b \tan t + k; -\frac{\pi}{2} < t < \frac{3\pi}{2}$ and $t \ne \frac{\pi}{2}$ $\Rightarrow$

$\dfrac{x - h}{a} = \sec t$ and $\dfrac{y - k}{b} = \tan t$ $\Rightarrow$ $\dfrac{(x - h)^2}{a^2} - \dfrac{(y - k)^2}{b^2} = \sec^2 t - \tan^2 t = 1.$

This is an equation of a hyperbola with center $(h, k)$, vertices $V(h \pm a, k)$ and $W(h, k \pm b)$. The transverse axis has length $2a$ and the conjugate axis has length $2b$. The right branch corresponds to $-\frac{\pi}{2} < t < \frac{\pi}{2}$ and the left branch corresponds to $\frac{\pi}{2} < t < \frac{3\pi}{2}$.

**39** Some choices for parts (a) and (b) are given—there are an infinite number of choices.

(a) (1) $y = x^2$ • $x = t, y = t^2; t \in \mathbb{R}$. Letting $x$ equal $t$ is usually the simplest choice we can make.

(2) $x = \tan t, y = \tan^2 t; -\frac{\pi}{2} < t < \frac{\pi}{2}$

(3) $x = t^3, y = t^6; t \in \mathbb{R}$

(b) (1) $x = e^t, y = e^{2t}; t \in \mathbb{R}$. This choice gives only $x > 0$ since $e^t$ is always positive for $t \in \mathbb{R}$.

(2) $x = \sin t, y = \sin^2 t; t \in \mathbb{R}$. This choice gives only $-1 \le x \le 1$ since $-1 \le \sin t \le 1$ for $t \in \mathbb{R}$.

(3) $x = \tan^{-1} t, y = (\tan^{-1} t)^2; t \in \mathbb{R}$. This choice gives only $-\frac{\pi}{2} < x < \frac{\pi}{2}$ since $-\frac{\pi}{2} < \tan^{-1} t < \frac{\pi}{2}$ for $t \in \mathbb{R}$.

**40** (a) (1) $y = \ln x$ • $x = t, y = \ln t; t > 0$

(2) $x = e^t, y = t; t \in \mathbb{R}$

(3) $x = t^2, y = 2 \ln t; t > 0$

(b) (1) $x = \sec t, y = \ln \sec t; -\frac{\pi}{2} < t < \frac{\pi}{2}$ (gives only $x \ge 1$)

(2) $x = \sin t, y = \ln \sin t; 0 < t < \pi$ (gives only $0 < x \le 1$)

(3) $x = \tan^{-1} t, y = \ln \tan^{-1} t; t > 0$ (gives only $0 < x < \frac{\pi}{2}$)

**41** We use $x(t) = (s\cos\alpha)t$ and $y(t) = -\frac{1}{2}gt^2 + (s\sin\alpha)t + h$ with $s = 256\sqrt{3}$, $\alpha = 60°$, and $h = 400$ to give us $x = 256\sqrt{3}\left(\frac{1}{2}\right)t$ and $y = -\frac{1}{2}(32)t^2 + 256\sqrt{3}\left(\frac{\sqrt{3}}{2}\right)t + 400$ $\Rightarrow$ $x = 128\sqrt{3}t$ and $y = -16t^2 + 384t + 400$.

To find the range, we let $y = 0$ $\Rightarrow$ $-16t^2 + 384t + 400 = 0$ $\Rightarrow$ $t^2 - 24t - 25 = 0$ {divide by $-16$} $\Rightarrow$ $(t - 25)(t + 1) = 0$ $\Rightarrow$ $t = 25$ seconds, and then substitute 25 for $t$ in the equation for $x$.

$$x = 128\sqrt{3}(25) = 3200\sqrt{3} \approx 5542.56 \text{ feet.}$$

To find the maximum altitude, we'll determine the values of $t$ for which the height is 400, and then use the symmetry property of a parabola to find the vertex. $y = 400$ $\Rightarrow$ $-16t^2 + 384t + 400 = 400$ $\Rightarrow$ $-16t^2 + 384t = 0$ $\Rightarrow$ $-16t(t - 24) = 0$ $\Rightarrow$ $t = 0, 24$. Thus, the maximum altitude occurs when $t = \frac{1}{2}(24) = 12$. This value of $h$ is $y = -16(12)^2 + 384(12) + 400 = 2704$ feet.

**42** $x = 512\sqrt{2}\left(\frac{\sqrt{2}}{2}\right)t$ and $y = -\frac{1}{2}(32)t^2 + 512\sqrt{2}\left(\frac{\sqrt{2}}{2}\right)t + 1088$ $\Rightarrow$ $x = 512t$ and $y = -16t^2 + 512t + 1088$.

$y = 0$ $\Rightarrow$ $-16t^2 + 512t + 1088 = 0$ $\Rightarrow$ $t^2 - 32t - 68 = 0$ $\Rightarrow$ $(t - 34)(t + 2) = 0$ $\Rightarrow$ $t = 34$ seconds. $x = 512(34) = 17,408$ feet.

$y = 1088$ $\Rightarrow$ $-16t^2 + 512t + 1088 = 1088$ $\Rightarrow$ $-16t^2 + 512t = 0$ $\Rightarrow$ $-16t(t - 32) = 0$ $\Rightarrow$ $t = 0, 32$. The maximum altitude occurs when $t = \frac{1}{2}(32) = 16$ and has value

$$y = -16(16)^2 + 512(16) + 1088 = 5184 \text{ feet.}$$

**43** $x = 704\left(\frac{\sqrt{2}}{2}\right)t$ and $y = -\frac{1}{2}(32)t^2 + 704\left(\frac{\sqrt{2}}{2}\right)t + 0$ $\Rightarrow$ $x = 352\sqrt{2}t$ and $y = -16t^2 + 352\sqrt{2}t$.

$y = 0$ $\Rightarrow$ $-16t^2 + 352\sqrt{2}t = 0$ $\Rightarrow$ $-16t\left(t - 22\sqrt{2}\right) = 0$ $\Rightarrow$ $t = 22\sqrt{2}$ seconds.

$$x = 352\sqrt{2}\left(22\sqrt{2}\right) = 15,488 \text{ feet.}$$

The maximum altitude occurs when $t = \frac{1}{2}\left(22\sqrt{2}\right) = 11\sqrt{2}$ and has value

$$y = -16\left(11\sqrt{2}\right)^2 + 352\sqrt{2}\left(11\sqrt{2}\right) = 3872 \text{ feet.}$$

**44** $x = 2448\left(\frac{\sqrt{3}}{2}\right)t$ and $y = -\frac{1}{2}(32)t^2 + 2448\left(\frac{1}{2}\right)t + 0$ $\Rightarrow$ $x = 1224\sqrt{3}t$ and $y = -16t^2 + 1224t$.

$y = 0$ $\Rightarrow$ $-16t^2 + 1224t = 0$ $\Rightarrow$ $-8t(2t - 153) = 0$ $\Rightarrow$ $t = 76.5$ seconds.

$$x = 1224\sqrt{3}(76.5) = 93,636\sqrt{3} \approx 162,182.31 \text{ feet.}$$

The maximum altitude occurs when $t = \frac{1}{2}(76.5) = 38.25$ and has value

$$y = -16(38.25)^2 + 1224(38.25) = 23,409 \text{ feet.}$$

**45** (a) $x = a\sin\omega t$ and $y = b\cos\omega t$ $\Rightarrow$ $\frac{x}{a} = \sin\omega t$ and $\frac{y}{b} = \cos\omega t$ $\Rightarrow$ $\frac{x^2}{a^2} + \frac{y^2}{b^2} = 1$.

The figure is an ellipse with center $(0, 0)$ and axes of lengths $2a$ and $2b$.

(b) $f(t + p) = a\sin[\omega_1(t + p)] = a\sin(\omega_1 t + \omega_1 p) = a\sin(\omega_1 t + 2\pi n) = a\sin\omega_1 t = f(t)$.

$g(t + p) = b\cos[\omega_2(t + p)] = b\cos\left(\omega_2 t + \frac{\omega_2}{\omega_1}2\pi n\right) = b\cos\left(\omega_2 t + \frac{m}{n}2\pi n\right) = b\cos(\omega_2 t + 2\pi m)$

$= b\cos\omega_2 t = g(t)$.

Since $f$ and $g$ are periodic with period $p$, the curve retraces itself every $p$ units of time.

**46** Since $x = 2\sin 3t$ has period $\frac{2\pi}{3}$ and $y = 3\sin(1.5t)$ has period $\frac{4\pi}{3}$, the curve repeats itself every $\frac{4\pi}{3}$ units of time.

**47** (a) Let $x = 3\sin(240\pi t)$ and $y = 4\sin(240\pi t)$ for $0 \le t \le 0.01$.

(b) From the graph, $y_{int} = 0$ and $y_{max} = 4$. Thus, the phase difference is $\phi = \sin^{-1}\dfrac{y_{int}}{y_{max}} = \sin^{-1}\dfrac{0}{4} = 0°$.

$[-9,9]$ by $[-6,6]$   $[-9,9]$ by $[-6,6]$

*Figure 47*       *Figure 48*

**48** (a) Let $x = 6\sin(120\pi t)$ and $y = 5\cos(120\pi t)$ for $0 \le t \le 0.02$. **Note:** $5\cos(120\pi t) = 5\sin\left(120\pi t + \frac{\pi}{2}\right)$

(b) From the graph, $y_{int} = 5$ and $y_{max} = 5$. Thus, the phase difference is $\phi = \sin^{-1}\dfrac{y_{int}}{y_{max}} = \sin^{-1}\dfrac{5}{5} = 90°$.

**49** (a) Let $x = 80\sin(60\pi t)$ and $y = 70\cos\left(60\pi t - \frac{\pi}{3}\right)$ for $0 \le t \le 0.035$.

(b) See the figure. From the graph, $y_{int} = 35$ and $y_{max} = 70$.

Thus, the phase difference is $\phi = \sin^{-1}\dfrac{y_{int}}{y_{max}} = \sin^{-1}\dfrac{35}{70} = 30°$.

**Note:** Tstep must be sufficiently small to obtain the maximum of 70 on the graph.

$$70\cos\left(60\pi t - \tfrac{\pi}{3}\right) = 70\sin\left(60\pi t + \tfrac{\pi}{6}\right)$$

$[-120,120,10]$ by $[-80,80,10]$    $[-300,300,100]$ by $[-200,200,100]$

*Figure 49*       *Figure 50*

**50** (a) Let $x = 163\sin(120\pi t)$ and $y = 163\sin\left(120\pi t + \frac{\pi}{4}\right)$ for $0 \le t \le 0.02$.

(b) From the graph, $y_{int} \approx 115.26$ and $y_{max} = 163$. Thus, the phase difference is $\phi = \sin^{-1}\dfrac{y_{int}}{y_{max}} = \sin^{-1}\dfrac{115}{163} \approx 45°$.

**51** $x(t) = \sin(6\pi t)$, $y(t) = \cos(5\pi t)$ for $0 \le t \le 2$

$[-1,1,0.5]$ by $[-1,1,0.5]$    $[-1,1,0.5]$ by $[-1,1,0.5]$

*Figure 51*       *Figure 52*

**52** $x(t) = \sin(4t)$, $y(t) = \sin\left(3t + \frac{\pi}{6}\right)$ for $0 \le t \le 6.5$

**53** Let $\theta = \angle FDP$ and $\alpha = \angle GDP = \angle EDP$. Then $\angle ODG = \left(\frac{\pi}{2} - t\right)$ and $\alpha = \theta - \left(\frac{\pi}{2} - t\right) = \theta + t - \frac{\pi}{2}$. Arcs $AF$ and $PF$ are equal in length since each is the distance rolled. Thus, $at = b\theta$, or $\theta = \frac{a}{b}t$ and $\alpha = \frac{a+b}{b}t - \frac{\pi}{2}$.

Note that $\cos\alpha = \sin\left(\frac{a+b}{b}t\right)$ and $\sin\alpha = -\cos\left(\frac{a+b}{b}t\right)$.

For the location of the points as illustrated, the coordinates of $P$ are:

$x = d(O, G) + d(G, B) = d(O, G) + d(E, P) = (a + b)\cos t + b\sin\alpha$

$\quad = (a + b)\cos t - b\cos\left(\frac{a+b}{b}t\right)$,

$y = d(B, P) = d(G, D) - d(D, E) = (a + b)\sin t - b\cos\alpha$

$\quad = (a + b)\sin t - b\sin\left(\frac{a+b}{b}t\right)$.

It can be verified that these equations are valid for all locations of the points.

**54** (a) The line from $O$ to $C$, the center of the smaller circle, must also pass through $B$, the common point of tangency as the smaller circle rolls inside the larger. Note that:

    (1) $t = \alpha$ by the properties of parallel lines

    (2) $\overline{OB} = \overline{OA} = a$                       (3) $\overline{CB} = \overline{CP} = b$

    (4) $\overline{OC} = \overline{OB} - \overline{CB} = a - b$

    (5) $\angle CPD = \beta$ by the properties of parallel lines

    (6) $\angle BCP = \alpha + \beta = t + \beta$              (7) in $\triangle OCE$, $\overline{OE} = \overline{OC}\cos t$ and $\overline{EC} = \overline{OC}\sin t$

    (8) in $\triangle DCP$, $\overline{DP} = \overline{CP}\cos\angle CPD$ and $\overline{DC} = \overline{CP}\sin\angle CPD$         (9) $\overline{DP} = \overline{EF}$

    (10) in the smaller circle, arc $BP$ has length $b(\angle BCP)$

    (11) in the larger circle, arc $BA$ has length $a(\angle BOA)$

    (12) since arc $BP$ is the same length as arc $BA$ (each is the distance rolled),

        $b(\angle BCP) = at \quad \Rightarrow \quad \angle BCP = \frac{a}{b}t$

Now, $x = \overline{OE} + \overline{EF} = \overline{OC}\cos t + \overline{CP}\cos\angle CPD = (a - b)\cos t + b\cos\beta$

$\quad = (a - b)\cos t + b\cos(\angle BCP - \alpha) = (a - b)\cos t + b\cos\left(\frac{a}{b}t - t\right) = (a - b)\cos t + b\cos\left(\frac{a-b}{b}t\right)$.

Similarly, $y = \overline{EC} - \overline{DC} = \overline{OC}\sin t - \overline{CP}\sin\angle CPD = (a - b)\sin t - b\sin\beta$

$\quad = (a - b)\sin t - b\sin(\angle BCP - \alpha) = (a - b)\sin t - b\sin\left(\frac{a}{b}t - t\right) = (a - b)\sin t - b\sin\left(\frac{a-b}{b}t\right)$.

(b) If $b = \frac{1}{4}a$, then

$x = \left(a - \frac{1}{4}a\right)\cos t + \frac{1}{4}a\cos\left(\dfrac{a - \frac{1}{4}a}{\frac{1}{4}a}t\right) = \frac{3}{4}a\cos t + \frac{1}{4}a\cos 3t$

$\quad = \frac{3}{4}a\cos t + \frac{1}{4}a(4\cos^3 t - 3\cos t) = a\cos^3 t$.

Also,

$y = \left(a - \frac{1}{4}a\right)\sin t - \frac{1}{4}a\sin\left(\dfrac{a - \frac{1}{4}a}{\frac{1}{4}a}t\right) = \frac{3}{4}a\sin t - \frac{1}{4}a\sin 3t$

$\quad = \frac{3}{4}a\sin t - \frac{1}{4}a(3\sin t - 4\sin^3 t) = a\sin^3 t$.

The identities used for $\cos 3t$ and $\sin 3t$ can be derived by applying the addition, double angle, and fundamental identities.

**55** $b = \frac{1}{3}a \implies a = 3b$. Substituting into the equations from Exercise 53 yields:

$$x = (3b + b)\cos t - b\cos\left(\frac{3b+b}{b} t\right) = 4b\cos t - b\cos 4t \qquad y = (3b + b)\sin t - b\sin\left(\frac{3b+b}{b} t\right) = 4b\sin t - b\sin 4t$$

As an aid in graphing, to determine where the path of the smaller circle will intersect the path of the larger circle (for the original starting point of intersection at $A(a, 0)$), we can solve $x^2 + y^2 = a^2$ for $t$.

$$x^2 + y^2 = 16b^2\cos^2 t - 8b^2\cos t\cos 4t + b^2\cos^2 4t + 16b^2\sin^2 t - 8b^2\sin t\sin 4t + b^2\sin^2 4t$$
$$= 17b^2 - 8b^2\cos t\cos 4t + \sin t\sin 4t = 17b^2 - 8b^2[\cos(t - 4t)] = 17b^2 - 8b^2\cos 3t.$$

Thus, $x^2 + y^2 = a^2 \implies 17b^2 - 8b^2\cos 3t = a^2 = 9b^2 \implies 8b^2 = 8b^2\cos 3t \implies 1 = \cos 3t \implies$
$3t = 2\pi n \implies t = \frac{2\pi}{3}n$. It follows that the intersection points are at $t = \frac{2\pi}{3}, \frac{4\pi}{3}$, and $2\pi$.

*Figure 55*

*Figure 56*

**56** Let $C'(h, k)$ be the center of the circle $C$ (in the figure) and $a = 3b$. Its coordinates are always $x = 4b\cos t$ and $y = 4b\sin t$ since it can be thought of as being on a circle of radius $4b$. Since the equations given in Exercise 55 are for a point $P$ relative to the origin, we can see that the coordinates of $P$ relative to $C'$ are $P(x', y') = P(-b\cos 4t, -b\sin 4t)$. At the starting point $A$, the coordinates of $P$ relative to $C'$ are $(-b, 0)$. Each time $P$ has these relative coordinates, it will have made one revolution.

Setting the coordinates equal to each other and solving for $t$ we have:

$-b\cos 4t = -b \implies \cos 4t = 1 \implies 4t = 2\pi n \implies t = \frac{\pi}{2}n$
and also $-b\sin 4t = 0 \implies \sin 4t = 0 \implies 4t = \pi n \implies t = \frac{\pi}{4}n$.

These results indicate that $C$ will make one revolution every $\frac{\pi}{2}$ units, or 4 revolutions in $2\pi$ units.

**57** Change "Param" from "Function" under $\boxed{\text{MODE}}$. Make the assignments $3(\sin T)^5$ to $X_{1T}$, $3(\cos T)^5$ to $Y_{1T}$,

0 to Tmin, 6.28 to Tmax, and 0.105 to Tstep. Algebraically, we have $x = 3\sin^5 t$ and $y = 3\cos^5 t \implies$

$$\frac{x}{3} = \sin^5 t \text{ and } \frac{y}{3} = \cos^5 t \implies \left(\frac{x}{3}\right)^{2/5} + \left(\frac{y}{3}\right)^{2/5} = \sin^2 t + \cos^2 t = 1. \text{ The graph traces an astroid.}$$

$[-6, 6]$ by $[-4, 4]$

*Figure 57*

$[-15, 15]$ by $[-10, 10]$

*Figure 58*

**58** The graph traces an epicycloid. See Exercise 53 with $a = 6$ and $b = 2$.

**59** The graph traces a curtate cycloid.

$[-30, 30, 5]$ by $[-20, 20, 5]$

*Figure 59*

$[-15, 15]$ by $[-10, 10]$

*Figure 60*

**60** The graph traces a prolate cycloid.

**61** The figure is a mask with a mouth, nose, and eyes. This graph may be obtained with a graphing utility that has the capability to graph five sets of parametric equations.

*Figure 61*

*Figure 62*

**62** $C_1: x = \frac{3}{2}\cos t + 1$ and $y = \sin t - 1 \Rightarrow \frac{2}{3}(x - 1) = \cos t$ and $(y + 1) = \sin t \Rightarrow$
$\dfrac{(x - 1)^2}{\frac{9}{4}} + (y + 1)^2 = 1$. This curve is part of an ellipse with center $(1, -1)$ and endpoints $(1, -2)$ and $(1, 0)$.

Similarly, $C_2$ is part of an ellipse with center $(1, 1)$ and endpoints $(1, 0)$ and $(1, 2)$. $C_3$ is a vertical line, $x = 1$, with endpoints $(1, -2)$ and $(1, 2)$. The figure is the letter B.

**63** $C_1$ is the line $y = 3x$ from $(0, 0)$ to $(1, 3)$. For $C_2$, $x - 1 = \tan t$ and $1 - \frac{1}{3}y = \tan t \Rightarrow x - 1 = 1 - \frac{1}{3}y \Rightarrow$
$y = -3x + 6$. This line is sketched from $(1, 3)$ to $(2, 0)$. $C_3$ is the horizontal line $y = \frac{3}{2}$ from $\left(\frac{1}{2}, \frac{3}{2}\right)$ to $\left(\frac{3}{2}, \frac{3}{2}\right)$.
The figure is the letter A.

*Figure 63*

*Figure 64*

**64** $C_1$ is the circle $(x - 1)^2 + (y - 1)^2 = 1$ from $\left(\frac{3}{2}, 1 + \frac{1}{2}\sqrt{3}\right)$ to $(2, 1)$. $C_2$ is the horizontal line $y = 1$ from $(1, 1)$
to $(2, 1)$. The figure is the letter G.

## 10.5 Exercises

**Note:** For the following exercises, the substitutions $y = r\sin\theta$, $x = r\cos\theta$, $r^2 = x^2 + y^2$, and $\tan\theta = \dfrac{y}{x}$ are used without mention. We have found it helpful to find the "pole" values {when the graph intersects the pole} to determine which values of $\theta$ should be used in the construction of an $r$-$\theta$ chart. The numbers listed on each line of the $r$-$\theta$ chart correspond to the numbers labeled on the figures.

[1] (a) Since $\frac{7\pi}{3}$ is coterminal with $\frac{\pi}{3}$, $\left(3, \frac{7\pi}{3}\right)$ represents the same point as $\left(3, \frac{\pi}{3}\right)$.

   (b) The point $\left(3, -\frac{\pi}{3}\right)$ is in QIV, not QI. The point $\left(3, \frac{\pi}{3}\right)$ is in QI.

   (c) The angle $\frac{4\pi}{3}$ is $\pi$ radians larger than $\frac{\pi}{3}$, so its terminal side is on the same line as the terminal side of the angle $\frac{\pi}{3}$. $r = -3$ in the $\frac{4\pi}{3}$ direction is equivalent to $r = 3$ in the $\frac{\pi}{3}$ direction, so $\left(-3, \frac{4\pi}{3}\right)$ represents the same point as $\left(3, \frac{\pi}{3}\right)$.

   (d) The point $\left(3, -\frac{2\pi}{3}\right)$ is diametrically opposite the point $\left(3, \frac{\pi}{3}\right)$.

   (e) From part (d), we deduce that the point $\left(-3, -\frac{2\pi}{3}\right)$ would represent the same point as $\left(3, \frac{\pi}{3}\right)$.

   (f) The point $\left(-3, -\frac{\pi}{3}\right)$ is in QII, not QI.

Thus, choices (a), (c), and (e) represent the same point as $\left(3, \frac{\pi}{3}\right)$.

[2] Choices (b) $\left(4, \frac{7\pi}{2}\right)$, (d) $\left(4, -\frac{5\pi}{2}\right)$, (e) $\left(-4, -\frac{3\pi}{2}\right)$, and (f) $\left(-4, \frac{\pi}{2}\right)$ represent the same point as $\left(4, -\frac{\pi}{2}\right)$.

[3] Use (1) in the "relationship between rectangular and polar coordinates."

   (a) $x = r\cos\theta = 3\cos\frac{\pi}{4} = 3\left(\frac{\sqrt{2}}{2}\right) = \frac{3}{2}\sqrt{2}$. $y = r\sin\theta = 3\sin\frac{\pi}{4} = 3\left(\frac{\sqrt{2}}{2}\right) = \frac{3}{2}\sqrt{2}$.

                          Hence, rectangular coordinates for $\left(3, \frac{\pi}{4}\right)$ are $\left(\frac{3}{2}\sqrt{2}, \frac{3}{2}\sqrt{2}\right)$.

   (b) $x = -1\cos\frac{2\pi}{3} = -1\left(-\frac{1}{2}\right) = \frac{1}{2}$. $y = -1\sin\frac{2\pi}{3} = -1\left(\frac{\sqrt{3}}{2}\right) = -\frac{1}{2}\sqrt{3}$. $\left(\frac{1}{2}, -\frac{1}{2}\sqrt{3}\right)$

[4] (a) $x = 5\cos\frac{5\pi}{6} = 5\left(-\frac{\sqrt{3}}{2}\right) = -\frac{5}{2}\sqrt{3}$. $y = 5\sin\frac{5\pi}{6} = 5\left(\frac{1}{2}\right) = \frac{5}{2}$. $\left(-\frac{5}{2}\sqrt{3}, \frac{5}{2}\right)$

   (b) $x = -6\cos\frac{7\pi}{3} = -6\left(\frac{1}{2}\right) = -3$. $y = -6\sin\frac{7\pi}{3} = -6\left(\frac{\sqrt{3}}{2}\right) = -3\sqrt{3}$. $\left(-3, -3\sqrt{3}\right)$

[5] (a) $x = 8\cos\left(-\frac{2\pi}{3}\right) = 8\left(-\frac{1}{2}\right) = -4$. $y = 8\sin\left(-\frac{2\pi}{3}\right) = 8\left(-\frac{\sqrt{3}}{2}\right) = -4\sqrt{3}$. $\left(-4, -4\sqrt{3}\right)$

   (b) $x = -3\cos\frac{5\pi}{3} = -3\left(\frac{1}{2}\right) = -\frac{3}{2}$. $y = -3\sin\frac{5\pi}{3} = -3\left(-\frac{\sqrt{3}}{2}\right) = \frac{3}{2}\sqrt{3}$. $\left(-\frac{3}{2}, \frac{3}{2}\sqrt{3}\right)$

[6] (a) $x = 4\cos\left(-\frac{\pi}{4}\right) = 4\left(\frac{\sqrt{2}}{2}\right) = 2\sqrt{2}$. $y = 4\sin\left(-\frac{\pi}{4}\right) = 4\left(-\frac{\sqrt{2}}{2}\right) = -2\sqrt{2}$. $\left(2\sqrt{2}, -2\sqrt{2}\right)$

   (b) $x = -2\cos\frac{7\pi}{6} = -2\left(-\frac{\sqrt{3}}{2}\right) = \sqrt{3}$. $y = -2\sin\frac{7\pi}{6} = -2\left(-\frac{1}{2}\right) = 1$. $\left(\sqrt{3}, 1\right)$

[7] Let $\theta = \arctan\frac{3}{4}$. Then we have $\cos\theta = \frac{4}{5}$ and $\sin\theta = \frac{3}{5}$.

                          $x = 6\cos\theta = 6\left(\frac{4}{5}\right) = \frac{24}{5}$. $y = 6\sin\theta = 6\left(\frac{3}{5}\right) = \frac{18}{5}$. $\left(\frac{24}{5}, \frac{18}{5}\right)$

[8] Let $\theta = \arccos\left(-\frac{1}{3}\right)$. $x = 10\cos\theta = 10\left(-\frac{1}{3}\right) = -\frac{10}{3}$. $y = 10\sin\theta = 10\left(\frac{\sqrt{8}}{3}\right) = \frac{10}{3}\sqrt{8} = \frac{20}{3}\sqrt{2}$. $\left(-\frac{10}{3}, \frac{20}{3}\sqrt{2}\right)$

## 10.5 EXERCISES

**9** Use (2) in the "relationship between rectangular and polar coordinates."

(a) $r^2 = x^2 + y^2 = (-1)^2 + (1)^2 = 2 \implies r = \sqrt{2}$ {since we want $r > 0$}.

$$\tan\theta = \frac{y}{x} = \frac{1}{-1} = -1 \implies \theta = \frac{3\pi}{4} \ \{\theta \text{ in QII}\}. \ \left(\sqrt{2}, \frac{3\pi}{4}\right)$$

(b) $r^2 = \left(-2\sqrt{3}\right)^2 + (-2)^2 = 16 \implies r = \sqrt{16} = 4. \ \tan\theta = \frac{-2}{-2\sqrt{3}} = \frac{1}{\sqrt{3}} \implies \theta = \frac{7\pi}{6} \ \{\theta \text{ in QIII}\}. \ \left(4, \frac{7\pi}{6}\right)$

**10** (a) $r^2 = \left(3\sqrt{3}\right)^2 + 3^2 = 36 \implies r = 6. \ \tan\theta = \frac{3}{3\sqrt{3}} = \frac{1}{\sqrt{3}} \implies \theta = \frac{\pi}{6} \ \{\theta \text{ in QI}\}. \ \left(6, \frac{\pi}{6}\right)$

(b) $r^2 = 2^2 + (-2)^2 = 8 \implies r = 2\sqrt{2}. \ \tan\theta = \frac{-2}{2} = -1 \implies \theta = \frac{7\pi}{4} \ \{\theta \text{ in QIV}\}. \ \left(2\sqrt{2}, \frac{7\pi}{4}\right)$

**11** (a) $r^2 = 7^2 + \left(-7\sqrt{3}\right)^2 = 196 \implies r = \sqrt{196} = 14.$

$$\tan\theta = \frac{-7\sqrt{3}}{7} = -\sqrt{3} \implies \theta = \frac{5\pi}{3} \ \{\theta \text{ in QIV}\}. \ \left(14, \frac{5\pi}{3}\right)$$

(b) $r^2 = 5^2 + 5^2 = 50 \implies r = \sqrt{50} = 5\sqrt{2}. \ \tan\theta = \frac{5}{5} = 1 \implies \theta = \frac{\pi}{4} \ \{\theta \text{ in QI}\}. \ \left(5\sqrt{2}, \frac{\pi}{4}\right)$

**12** (a) $r^2 = \left(-2\sqrt{2}\right)^2 + \left(-2\sqrt{2}\right)^2 = 16 \implies r = 4. \ \tan\theta = \frac{-2\sqrt{2}}{-2\sqrt{2}} = 1 \implies \theta = \frac{5\pi}{4} \ \{\theta \text{ in QIII}\}. \ \left(4, \frac{5\pi}{4}\right)$

(b) $r^2 = (-4)^2 + \left(4\sqrt{3}\right)^2 = 64 \implies r = 8. \ \tan\theta = \frac{4\sqrt{3}}{-4} = -\sqrt{3} \implies \theta = \frac{2\pi}{3} \ \{\theta \text{ in QII}\}. \ \left(8, \frac{2\pi}{3}\right)$

**13** $x = -3 \implies r\cos\theta = -3 \implies r = \dfrac{-3}{\cos\theta} \implies r = -3\sec\theta$

**14** $y = 2 \implies r\sin\theta = 2 \implies r = \dfrac{2}{\sin\theta} \implies r = 2\csc\theta$

**15** $y = -4 \implies r\sin\theta = -4 \implies r = \dfrac{-4}{\sin\theta} \implies r = -4\csc\theta$

**16** $x = 5 \implies r\cos\theta = 5 \implies r = \dfrac{5}{\cos\theta} \implies r = 5\sec\theta$

**17** $x^2 + y^2 = 16 \implies r^2 = 16 \implies r = \pm 4$ {both are circles with radius 4}.

**18** $x^2 + y^2 = 2 \implies r^2 = 2 \implies r = \pm\sqrt{2}$ {both are circles with radius $\sqrt{2}$}.

**19** $y^2 = 6x \implies r^2\sin^2\theta = 6r\cos\theta \implies r^2\sin^2\theta - 6r\cos\theta = 0 \implies r(r\sin^2\theta - 6\cos\theta) = 0 \implies$

$r\sin^2\theta - 6\cos\theta = 0 \implies r\sin^2\theta = 6\cos\theta \implies r = \dfrac{6\cos\theta}{\sin^2\theta} = 6 \cdot \dfrac{\cos\theta}{\sin\theta} \cdot \dfrac{1}{\sin\theta} = 6\cot\theta\csc\theta.$

Note that $r = 0$ {the pole} is included in the graph of $r = 6\cot\theta\csc\theta$.

**20** $x^2 = 8y \implies r^2\cos^2\theta = 8r\sin\theta \implies r^2\cos^2\theta - 8r\sin\theta = 0 \implies r(r\cos^2\theta - 8\sin\theta) = 0 \implies$

$r\cos^2\theta - 8\sin\theta = 0 \implies r\cos^2\theta = 8\sin\theta \implies r = \dfrac{8\sin\theta}{\cos^2\theta} = 8 \cdot \dfrac{\sin\theta}{\cos\theta} \cdot \dfrac{1}{\cos\theta} = 8\tan\theta\sec\theta.$

Note that $r = 0$ {the pole} is included in the graph of $r = 8\tan\theta\sec\theta$.

**21** $x^2 = 5y \implies r^2\cos^2\theta = 5r\sin\theta \implies r^2\cos^2\theta - 5r\sin\theta = 0 \implies r(r\cos^2\theta - 5\sin\theta) = 0 \implies$

$r\cos^2\theta - 5\sin\theta = 0 \implies r\cos^2\theta = 5\sin\theta \implies r = \dfrac{5\sin\theta}{\cos^2\theta} = 5 \cdot \dfrac{\sin\theta}{\cos\theta} \cdot \dfrac{1}{\cos\theta} = 5\tan\theta\sec\theta.$

Note that $r = 0$ {the pole} is included in the graph of $r = 5\tan\theta\sec\theta$.

**22** $y^2 = 3x \implies r^2\sin^2\theta = 3r\cos\theta \implies r^2\sin^2\theta - 3r\cos\theta = 0 \implies r(r\sin^2\theta - 3\cos\theta) = 0 \implies$

$r\sin^2\theta - 3\cos\theta = 0 \implies r\sin^2\theta = 3\cos\theta \implies r = \dfrac{3\cos\theta}{\sin^2\theta} = 3 \cdot \dfrac{\cos\theta}{\sin\theta} \cdot \dfrac{1}{\sin\theta} = 3\cot\theta\csc\theta.$

Note that $r = 0$ {the pole} is included in the graph of $r = 3\cot\theta\csc\theta$.

**23** $x + y = 3 \Rightarrow r\cos\theta + r\sin\theta = 3 \Rightarrow r(\cos\theta + \sin\theta) = 3 \Rightarrow r = \dfrac{3}{\cos\theta + \sin\theta}$

**24** $2y = -x + 4 \Rightarrow 2r\sin\theta = -r\cos\theta + 4 \Rightarrow 2r\sin\theta + r\cos\theta = 4 \Rightarrow r(2\sin\theta + \cos\theta) = 4 \Rightarrow$
$$r = \dfrac{4}{2\sin\theta + \cos\theta}$$

**25** $2y = -x \Rightarrow \dfrac{y}{x} = -\dfrac{1}{2} \Rightarrow \tan\theta = -\dfrac{1}{2} \Rightarrow \theta = \tan^{-1}\left(-\dfrac{1}{2}\right)$

**26** $y = 6x \Rightarrow \dfrac{y}{x} = 6 \Rightarrow \tan\theta = 6 \Rightarrow \theta = \tan^{-1}6 \ \{\approx 1.41 \text{ or } 80.54°\}$

**27** $y^2 - x^2 = 4 \Rightarrow r^2\sin^2\theta - r^2\cos^2\theta = 4 \Rightarrow -r^2(\cos^2\theta - \sin^2\theta) = 4 \Rightarrow$
$$-r^2\cos 2\theta = 4 \Rightarrow r^2 = \dfrac{-4}{\cos 2\theta} \Rightarrow r^2 = -4\sec 2\theta$$

**28** $xy = 8 \Rightarrow (r\cos\theta)(r\sin\theta) = 8 \Rightarrow r^2\left(\dfrac{1}{2}\right)(2\sin\theta\cos\theta) = 8 \Rightarrow$
$$r^2\sin 2\theta = 16 \Rightarrow r^2 = \dfrac{16}{\sin 2\theta} \Rightarrow r^2 = 16\csc 2\theta$$

**29** $xy = -3 \Rightarrow (r\cos\theta)(r\sin\theta) = -3 \Rightarrow r^2\left(\dfrac{1}{2}\right)(2\sin\theta\cos\theta) = -3 \Rightarrow$
$$r^2\sin 2\theta = -6 \Rightarrow r^2 = \dfrac{-6}{\sin 2\theta} \Rightarrow r^2 = -6\csc 2\theta$$

**30** $x^2 - y^2 = 9 \Rightarrow r^2\cos^2\theta - r^2\sin^2\theta = 9 \Rightarrow r^2(\cos^2\theta - \sin^2\theta) = 9 \Rightarrow$
$$r^2\cos 2\theta = 9 \Rightarrow r^2 = \dfrac{9}{\cos 2\theta} \Rightarrow r^2 = 9\sec 2\theta$$

**31** $(x-1)^2 + y^2 = 1 \Rightarrow x^2 - 2x + 1 + y^2 = 1 \Rightarrow x^2 + y^2 = 2x \Rightarrow r^2 = 2r\cos\theta \Rightarrow r = 2\cos\theta$

**32** $(x+2)^2 + y^2 = 4 \Rightarrow x^2 + 4x + 4 + y^2 = 4 \Rightarrow x^2 + y^2 = -4x \Rightarrow r^2 = -4r\cos\theta \Rightarrow r = -4\cos\theta$

**33** $x^2 + (y+3)^2 = 9 \Rightarrow x^2 + y^2 + 6y + 9 = 9 \Rightarrow x^2 + y^2 = -6y \Rightarrow r^2 = -6r\sin\theta \Rightarrow r = -6\sin\theta$

**34** $x^2 + (y-1)^2 = 1 \Rightarrow x^2 + y^2 - 2y + 1 = 1 \Rightarrow x^2 + y^2 = 2y \Rightarrow r^2 = 2r\sin\theta \Rightarrow r = 2\sin\theta$

**35** $(x+2)^2 + (y-3)^2 = 13 \Rightarrow x^2 + 4x + 4 + y^2 - 6y + 9 = 13 \Rightarrow x^2 + y^2 = 6y - 4x \Rightarrow$
$$r^2 = 6r\sin\theta - 4r\cos\theta \Rightarrow r = 6\sin\theta - 4\cos\theta$$

**36** $(x-3)^2 + (y+4)^2 = 25 \Rightarrow x^2 - 6x + 9 + y^2 + 8y + 16 = 25 \Rightarrow x^2 + y^2 = 6x - 8y \Rightarrow$
$$r^2 = 6r\cos\theta - 8r\sin\theta \Rightarrow r = 6\cos\theta - 8\sin\theta$$

**37** $r\cos\theta = 5 \Rightarrow x = 5$. This is a vertical line with $x$-intercept $(5, 0)$.

*Figure 37*

*Figure 38*

**38** $r\sin\theta = -2 \Rightarrow y = -2$

**39** $r = -3\csc\theta \;\Rightarrow\; r\sin\theta = -3 \;\Rightarrow\; y = -3$

Figure 39

Figure 40

**40** $r = 4\sec\theta \;\Rightarrow\; r\cos\theta = 4 \;\Rightarrow\; x = 4.$ $\theta$ is undefined at $\frac{\pi}{2} + \pi n$.

**41** $r = -5 \;\Rightarrow\; r^2 = 25 \;\Rightarrow\; x^2 + y^2 = 25$

Figure 41

Figure 42

**42** $r = 2 \;\Rightarrow\; r^2 = 4 \;\Rightarrow\; x^2 + y^2 = 4$

**43** $r - 6\sin\theta = 0 \;\Rightarrow\; r^2 = 6r\sin\theta \;\Rightarrow\; x^2 + y^2 = 6y \;\Rightarrow\; x^2 + y^2 - 6y + \underline{9} = \underline{9} \;\Rightarrow\; x^2 + (y-3)^2 = 9$

Figure 43

Figure 44

**44** $r - 6\cos\theta = 0 \;\Rightarrow\; r^2 = 6r\cos\theta \;\Rightarrow\; x^2 + y^2 = 6x \;\Rightarrow\; x^2 - 6x + \underline{9} + y^2 = \underline{9} \;\Rightarrow\; (x-3)^2 + y^2 = 9$

**45** $\theta = \dfrac{\pi}{4} \;\Rightarrow\; \tan\theta = \tan\dfrac{\pi}{4} \;\Rightarrow\; \dfrac{y}{x} = 1 \;\Rightarrow\; y = x$

Figure 45

Figure 46

**46** $\theta = \dfrac{2\pi}{3} \;\Rightarrow\; \tan\theta = \tan\dfrac{2\pi}{3} \;\Rightarrow\; \dfrac{y}{x} = -\sqrt{3} \;\Rightarrow\; y = -\sqrt{3}x$

**47** $r^2(4\sin^2\theta - 9\cos^2\theta) = 36 \quad \Rightarrow \quad 4r^2\sin^2\theta - 9r^2\cos^2\theta = 36 \quad \Rightarrow \quad 4y^2 - 9x^2 = 36 \quad \Rightarrow \quad \dfrac{y^2}{9} - \dfrac{x^2}{4} = 1$

*Figure 47*

*Figure 48*

**48** $r^2(\cos^2\theta + 4\sin^2\theta) = 16 \quad \Rightarrow \quad r^2\cos^2\theta + 4r^2\sin^2\theta = 16 \quad \Rightarrow \quad x^2 + 4y^2 = 16 \quad \Rightarrow \quad \dfrac{x^2}{16} + \dfrac{y^2}{4} = 1$

**49** $r^2\sin 2\theta = 4 \quad \Rightarrow \quad r^2(2\sin\theta\cos\theta) = 4 \quad \Rightarrow \quad (r\sin\theta)(r\cos\theta) = 2 \quad \Rightarrow \quad xy = 2$

*Figure 49*

*Figure 50*

**50** $r^2\sin 2\theta = -10 \quad \Rightarrow \quad r^2(2\sin\theta\cos\theta) = -10 \quad \Rightarrow \quad (r\sin\theta)(r\cos\theta) = -5 \quad \Rightarrow \quad xy = -5$

**51** $r^2\cos 2\theta = 1 \quad \Rightarrow \quad r^2(\cos^2\theta - \sin^2\theta) = 1 \quad \Rightarrow \quad r^2\cos^2\theta - r^2\sin^2\theta = 1 \quad \Rightarrow \quad x^2 - y^2 = 1$

*Figure 51*

*Figure 52*

**52** $r^2\cos 2\theta = -9 \quad \Rightarrow \quad r^2(\cos^2\theta - \sin^2\theta) = -9 \quad \Rightarrow \quad r^2\cos^2\theta - r^2\sin^2\theta = -9 \quad \Rightarrow$
$$x^2 - y^2 = -9 \quad \Rightarrow \quad y^2 - x^2 = 9$$

**53** $r(\sin\theta - 2\cos\theta) = 6 \quad \Rightarrow \quad r\sin\theta - 2r\cos\theta = 6 \quad \Rightarrow \quad y - 2x = 6$

*Figure 53*

*Figure 54*

**54** $r(3\cos\theta - 4\sin\theta) = 12 \quad \Rightarrow \quad 3r\cos\theta - 4r\sin\theta = 12 \quad \Rightarrow \quad 3x - 4y = 12$

**55** $r(\sin\theta + r\cos^2\theta) = 1 \quad\Rightarrow\quad r\sin\theta + r^2\cos^2\theta = 1 \quad\Rightarrow\quad y + x^2 = 1 \quad\Rightarrow\quad y = -x^2 + 1$

*Figure 55*

*Figure 56*

**56** $r(r\sin^2\theta - \cos\theta) = 3 \quad\Rightarrow\quad r^2\sin^2\theta - r\cos\theta = 3 \quad\Rightarrow\quad y^2 - x = 3 \quad\Rightarrow\quad x = y^2 - 3$

**57** $r = 8\sin\theta - 2\cos\theta \quad\Rightarrow\quad r^2 = 8r\sin\theta - 2r\cos\theta \quad\Rightarrow\quad x^2 + y^2 = 8y - 2x \quad\Rightarrow$

$$x^2 + 2x + \underline{1} + y^2 - 8y + \underline{16} = \underline{1} + \underline{16} \quad\Rightarrow\quad (x+1)^2 + (y-4)^2 = 17$$

*Figure 57*

*Figure 58*

**58** $r = 2\cos\theta - 4\sin\theta \quad\Rightarrow\quad r^2 = 2r\cos\theta - 4r\sin\theta \quad\Rightarrow\quad x^2 + y^2 = 2x - 4y \quad\Rightarrow$

$$x^2 - 2x + \underline{1} + y^2 + 4y + \underline{4} = \underline{1} + \underline{4} \quad\Rightarrow\quad (x-1)^2 + (y+2)^2 = 5$$

**59** $r = \tan\theta \quad\Rightarrow\quad r^2 = \tan^2\theta \quad\Rightarrow\quad x^2 + y^2 = \dfrac{y^2}{x^2} \quad\Rightarrow\quad x^4 + x^2 y^2 = y^2 \quad\Rightarrow\quad y^2 - x^2 y^2 = x^4 \quad\Rightarrow$

$y^2(1 - x^2) = x^4 \quad\Rightarrow\quad y^2 = \dfrac{x^4}{1 - x^2}$. This is a tough one even after getting the equation in $x$ and $y$. Since we have

solved for $y^2$, the right side must be positive. Since $x^4$ is always nonnegative, we must have $1 - x^2 > 0$, or

equivalently, $|x| < 1$. We have vertical asymptotes at $x = \pm 1$, that is, when the denominator is 0.

*Figure 59*

*Figure 60*

**60** $r = 6\cot\theta \quad\Rightarrow\quad r^2 = 36\cot^2\theta \quad\Rightarrow\quad x^2 + y^2 = 36\left(\dfrac{x^2}{y^2}\right) \quad\Rightarrow\quad x^2 y^2 + y^4 = 36x^2 \quad\Rightarrow$

$$36x^2 - x^2 y^2 = y^4 \quad\Rightarrow\quad x^2(36 - y^2) = y^4 \quad\Rightarrow\quad x^2 = \dfrac{y^4}{36 - y^2}$$

**61** $r = 5$ $\Rightarrow$ $r^2 = 25$ $\Rightarrow$ $x^2 + y^2 = 25$, a circle centered at the origin with radius 5.

*Figure 61*

*Figure 62*

**62** $r = -2$ $\Rightarrow$ $r^2 = 4$ $\Rightarrow$ $x^2 + y^2 = 4$, a circle centered at the origin with radius 2.

**63** $\theta = -\dfrac{\pi}{6}$ $\Rightarrow$ $\tan\theta = \tan\left(-\dfrac{\pi}{6}\right)$ $\Rightarrow$ $\dfrac{y}{x} = -\dfrac{1}{\sqrt{3}}$ $\Rightarrow$ $y = -\dfrac{1}{3}\sqrt{3}\,x$.

This is a line through the origin with slope $-\dfrac{1}{3}\sqrt{3}$.

*Figure 63*

*Figure 64*

**64** $\theta = \frac{\pi}{4}$ and $r \in \mathbb{R}$. The line is $y = (\tan\theta)x$, or $y = x$.

**65** $r = 3\cos\theta$ $\Rightarrow$ {multiply by $r$ to obtain $r^2$} $r^2 = 3r\cos\theta$ $\Rightarrow$
$x^2 + y^2 = 3x$ $\Rightarrow$ {recognize this as an equation of a circle and complete
the square} $\left(x^2 - 3x + \dfrac{9}{4}\right) + y^2 = \dfrac{9}{4}$ $\Rightarrow$ $\left(x - \dfrac{3}{2}\right)^2 + y^2 = \dfrac{9}{4}$.

This is a circle with center $\left(\dfrac{3}{2}, 0\right)$ and radius $\sqrt{\dfrac{9}{4}} = \dfrac{3}{2}$. From the table, we see

that as $\theta$ varies from 0 to $\dfrac{\pi}{2}$, $r$ will vary from 3 to 0. This corresponds to the

portion of the circle in the first quadrant. As $\theta$ varies from $\dfrac{\pi}{2}$ to $\pi$, $r$ varies

from 0 to $-3$. Remember that $-3$ in the $\pi$ direction is the same as 3 in the 0

direction. This corresponds to the portion of the circle in the fourth quadrant.

| | Variation of $\theta$ | Variation of $r$ |
|---|---|---|
| 1) | $0 \to \frac{\pi}{2}$ | $3 \to 0$ |
| 2) | $\frac{\pi}{2} \to \pi$ | $0 \to -3$ |

**66** $r = -2\sin\theta$ $\Rightarrow$ $r^2 = -2r\sin\theta$ $\Rightarrow$ $x^2 + y^2 = -2y$ $\Rightarrow$
$x^2 + y^2 + 2y + \underline{1} = \underline{1}$ $\Rightarrow$ $x^2 + (y+1)^2 = 1$.

| | Variation of $\theta$ | Variation of $r$ |
|---|---|---|
| 1) | $0 \to \frac{\pi}{2}$ | $0 \to -2$ |
| 2) | $\frac{\pi}{2} \to \pi$ | $-2 \to 0$ |

**67** $r = 4\cos\theta + 2\sin\theta \;\Rightarrow\; r^2 = 4r\cos\theta + 2r\sin\theta \;\Rightarrow$
$x^2 + y^2 = 4x + 2y \;\Rightarrow\; x^2 - 4x + \underline{4} + y^2 - 2y + \underline{1} = \underline{4} + \underline{1} \;\Rightarrow$
$(x-2)^2 + (y-1)^2 = 5.$

| | Variation of $\theta$ | Variation of $r$ |
|---|---|---|
| 1) | $0 \to \frac{\pi}{2}$ | $4 \to 2$ |
| 2) | $\frac{\pi}{2} \to \pi$ | $2 \to -4$ |

**68** $r = 6\cos\theta - 2\sin\theta \;\Rightarrow\; r^2 = 6r\cos\theta - 2r\sin\theta \;\Rightarrow$
$x^2 + y^2 = 6x - 2y \;\Rightarrow\; x^2 - 6x + \underline{9} + y^2 + 2y + \underline{1} = \underline{9} + \underline{1} \;\Rightarrow$
$(x-3)^2 + (y+1)^2 = 10.$

| | Variation of $\theta$ | Variation of $r$ |
|---|---|---|
| 1) | $0 \to \frac{\pi}{2}$ | $6 \to -2$ |
| 2) | $\frac{\pi}{2} \to \pi$ | $-2 \to -6$ |

**69** $r = 4(1 - \sin\theta)$ is a cardioid since the coefficient of $\sin\theta$ has the same magnitude as the constant term.

$0 = 4(1 - \sin\theta) \;\Rightarrow\; \sin\theta = 1 \;\Rightarrow\; \theta = \frac{\pi}{2} + 2\pi n.$

The V in the heart-shaped curve corresponds to the pole value $\frac{\pi}{2}$.

| | Variation of $\theta$ | Variation of $r$ |
|---|---|---|
| 1) | $0 \to \frac{\pi}{2}$ | $4 \to 0$ |
| 2) | $\frac{\pi}{2} \to \pi$ | $0 \to 4$ |
| 3) | $\pi \to \frac{3\pi}{2}$ | $4 \to 8$ |
| 4) | $\frac{3\pi}{2} \to 2\pi$ | $8 \to 4$ |

**70** $r = 3(1 + \cos\theta)$ is a cardioid. $0 = 3(1 + \cos\theta) \;\Rightarrow$
$\cos\theta = -1 \;\Rightarrow\; \theta = \pi + 2\pi n.$

| | Variation of $\theta$ | Variation of $r$ |
|---|---|---|
| 1) | $0 \to \frac{\pi}{2}$ | $6 \to 3$ |
| 2) | $\frac{\pi}{2} \to \pi$ | $3 \to 0$ |
| 3) | $\pi \to \frac{3\pi}{2}$ | $0 \to 3$ |
| 4) | $\frac{3\pi}{2} \to 2\pi$ | $3 \to 6$ |

**71** $r = -6(1 + \cos\theta)$ is a cardioid.

$0 = -6(1 + \cos\theta) \;\Rightarrow\; \cos\theta = -1 \;\Rightarrow\; \theta = \pi + 2\pi n.$

The V in the heart-shaped curve corresponds to the pole value $\pi$.

| | Variation of $\theta$ | Variation of $r$ |
|---|---|---|
| 1) | $0 \to \frac{\pi}{2}$ | $-12 \to -6$ |
| 2) | $\frac{\pi}{2} \to \pi$ | $-6 \to 0$ |
| 3) | $\pi \to \frac{3\pi}{2}$ | $0 \to -6$ |
| 4) | $\frac{3\pi}{2} \to 2\pi$ | $-6 \to -12$ |

**72** $r = 2(1 + \sin\theta)$ is a cardioid.

$0 = 2(1 + \sin\theta) \Rightarrow \sin\theta = -1 \Rightarrow \theta = \frac{3\pi}{2} + 2\pi n.$

|  | Variation of $\theta$ | Variation of $r$ |
|---|---|---|
| 1) | $0 \to \frac{\pi}{2}$ | $2 \to 4$ |
| 2) | $\frac{\pi}{2} \to \pi$ | $4 \to 2$ |
| 3) | $\pi \to \frac{3\pi}{2}$ | $2 \to 0$ |
| 4) | $\frac{3\pi}{2} \to 2\pi$ | $0 \to 2$ |

**73** $r = 2 + 4\sin\theta$ is a limaçon with a loop since the constant term has a smaller magnitude than the coefficient of $\sin\theta$.

$0 = 2 + 4\sin\theta \Rightarrow \sin\theta = -\frac{1}{2} \Rightarrow \theta = \frac{7\pi}{6} + 2\pi n, \frac{11\pi}{6} + 2\pi n.$ Trace through the table and the figure to make sure you understand what values of $\theta$ form the loop.

|  | Variation of $\theta$ | Variation of $r$ |
|---|---|---|
| 1) | $0 \to \frac{\pi}{2}$ | $2 \to 6$ |
| 2) | $\frac{\pi}{2} \to \pi$ | $6 \to 2$ |
| 3) | $\pi \to \frac{7\pi}{6}$ | $2 \to 0$ |
| 4) | $\frac{7\pi}{6} \to \frac{3\pi}{2}$ | $0 \to -2$ |
| 5) | $\frac{3\pi}{2} \to \frac{11\pi}{6}$ | $-2 \to 0$ |
| 6) | $\frac{11\pi}{6} \to 2\pi$ | $0 \to 2$ |

**74** $r = 1 + 2\cos\theta$ is a limaçon with a loop. $0 = 1 + 2\cos\theta \Rightarrow \cos\theta = -\frac{1}{2} \Rightarrow \theta = \frac{2\pi}{3} + 2\pi n, \frac{4\pi}{3} + 2\pi n.$

|  | Variation of $\theta$ | Variation of $r$ |
|---|---|---|
| 1) | $0 \to \frac{\pi}{2}$ | $3 \to 1$ |
| 2) | $\frac{\pi}{2} \to \frac{2\pi}{3}$ | $1 \to 0$ |
| 3) | $\frac{2\pi}{3} \to \pi$ | $0 \to -1$ |
| 4) | $\pi \to \frac{4\pi}{3}$ | $-1 \to 0$ |
| 5) | $\frac{4\pi}{3} \to \frac{3\pi}{2}$ | $0 \to 1$ |
| 6) | $\frac{3\pi}{2} \to 2\pi$ | $1 \to 3$ |

**75** $r = \sqrt{3} - 2\sin\theta$ is a limaçon with a loop. $0 = \sqrt{3} - 2\sin\theta \Rightarrow \sin\theta = \sqrt{3}/2 \Rightarrow \theta = \frac{\pi}{3} + 2\pi n, \frac{2\pi}{3} + 2\pi n.$

Let $a = \sqrt{3} - 2 \approx -0.27$ and $b = \sqrt{3} + 2 \approx 3.73$.

|  | Variation of $\theta$ | Variation of $r$ |
|---|---|---|
| 1) | $0 \to \frac{\pi}{3}$ | $\sqrt{3} \to 0$ |
| 2) | $\frac{\pi}{3} \to \frac{\pi}{2}$ | $0 \to a$ |
| 3) | $\frac{\pi}{2} \to \frac{2\pi}{3}$ | $a \to 0$ |
| 4) | $\frac{2\pi}{3} \to \pi$ | $0 \to \sqrt{3}$ |
| 5) | $\pi \to \frac{3\pi}{2}$ | $\sqrt{3} \to b$ |
| 6) | $\frac{3\pi}{2} \to 2\pi$ | $b \to \sqrt{3}$ |

**76** $r = 2\sqrt{3} - 4\cos\theta$ is a limaçon with a loop. $0 = 2\sqrt{3} - 4\cos\theta \;\Rightarrow\; \cos\theta = \frac{\sqrt{3}}{2} \;\Rightarrow\;$
$\theta = \frac{\pi}{6} + 2\pi n, \frac{11\pi}{6} + 2\pi n$. Let $a = 2\sqrt{3} - 4 \approx -0.54$ and $b = 2\sqrt{3} + 4 \approx 7.46$.

| | Variation of $\theta$ | Variation of $r$ |
|---|---|---|
| 1) | $0 \to \frac{\pi}{6}$ | $a \to 0$ |
| 2) | $\frac{\pi}{6} \to \frac{\pi}{2}$ | $0 \to 2\sqrt{3}$ |
| 3) | $\frac{\pi}{2} \to \pi$ | $2\sqrt{3} \to b$ |
| 4) | $\pi \to \frac{3\pi}{2}$ | $b \to 2\sqrt{3}$ |
| 5) | $\frac{3\pi}{2} \to \frac{11\pi}{6}$ | $2\sqrt{3} \to 0$ |
| 6) | $\frac{11\pi}{6} \to 2\pi$ | $0 \to a$ |

**77** $r = 2 - \cos\theta$ • $0 = 2 - \cos\theta \;\Rightarrow\; \cos\theta = 2 \;\Rightarrow\;$ no pole values.

| | Variation of $\theta$ | Variation of $r$ |
|---|---|---|
| 1) | $0 \to \frac{\pi}{2}$ | $1 \to 2$ |
| 2) | $\frac{\pi}{2} \to \pi$ | $2 \to 3$ |
| 3) | $\pi \to \frac{3\pi}{2}$ | $3 \to 2$ |
| 4) | $\frac{3\pi}{2} \to 2\pi$ | $2 \to 1$ |

**78** $r = 5 + 3\sin\theta$ • $0 = 5 + 3\sin\theta \;\Rightarrow\; \sin\theta = -\frac{5}{3} \;\Rightarrow\;$ no pole values.

| | Variation of $\theta$ | Variation of $r$ |
|---|---|---|
| 1) | $0 \to \frac{\pi}{2}$ | $5 \to 8$ |
| 2) | $\frac{\pi}{2} \to \pi$ | $8 \to 5$ |
| 3) | $\pi \to \frac{3\pi}{2}$ | $5 \to 2$ |
| 4) | $\frac{3\pi}{2} \to 2\pi$ | $2 \to 5$ |

**79** $r = 4\csc\theta \;\Rightarrow\; r\sin\theta = 4 \;\Rightarrow\; y = 4$. $r$ is undefined at $\theta = \pi n$. This is a horizontal line with $y$-intercept $(0, 4)$.

*Figure 79*

*Figure 80*

**80** $r = -3\sec\theta \;\Rightarrow\; r\cos\theta = -3 \;\Rightarrow\; x = -3$. $r$ is undefined at $\theta = \frac{\pi}{2} + \pi n$.

**81** $r = 8\cos 3\theta$ is a 3-leafed rose since 3 is odd.

$$0 = 8\cos 3\theta \quad \Rightarrow \quad \cos 3\theta = 0 \quad \Rightarrow \quad 3\theta = \frac{\pi}{2} + \pi n \quad \Rightarrow \quad \theta = \frac{\pi}{6} + \frac{\pi}{3} n.$$

| | Variation of $\theta$ | Variation of $r$ |
|---|---|---|
| 1) | $0 \to \frac{\pi}{6}$ | $8 \to 0$ |
| 2) | $\frac{\pi}{6} \to \frac{\pi}{3}$ | $0 \to -8$ |
| 3) | $\frac{\pi}{3} \to \frac{\pi}{2}$ | $-8 \to 0$ |
| 4) | $\frac{\pi}{2} \to \frac{2\pi}{3}$ | $0 \to 8$ |
| 5) | $\frac{2\pi}{3} \to \frac{5\pi}{6}$ | $8 \to 0$ |
| 6) | $\frac{5\pi}{6} \to \pi$ | $0 \to -8$ |

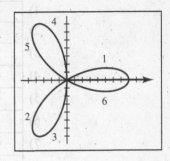

**82** $r = 2\sin 4\theta$ is an 8-leafed rose since 4 is even. $0 = 2\sin 4\theta \quad \Rightarrow \quad \sin 4\theta = 0 \quad \Rightarrow \quad 4\theta = \pi n \quad \Rightarrow \quad \theta = \frac{\pi}{4} n.$

Steps 9 through 16 follow a similar pattern to steps 1 through 8 and are labeled in the correct order.

| | Variation of $\theta$ | Variation of $r$ |
|---|---|---|
| 1) | $0 \to \frac{\pi}{8}$ | $0 \to 2$ |
| 2) | $\frac{\pi}{8} \to \frac{\pi}{4}$ | $2 \to 0$ |
| 3) | $\frac{\pi}{4} \to \frac{3\pi}{8}$ | $0 \to -2$ |
| 4) | $\frac{3\pi}{8} \to \frac{\pi}{2}$ | $-2 \to 0$ |
| 5) | $\frac{\pi}{2} \to \frac{5\pi}{8}$ | $0 \to 2$ |
| 6) | $\frac{5\pi}{8} \to \frac{3\pi}{4}$ | $2 \to 0$ |
| 7) | $\frac{3\pi}{4} \to \frac{7\pi}{8}$ | $0 \to -2$ |
| 8) | $\frac{7\pi}{8} \to \pi$ | $-2 \to 0$ |

**83** $r = 3\sin 2\theta$ is a 4-leafed rose. $0 = 3\sin 2\theta \quad \Rightarrow \quad \sin 2\theta = 0 \quad \Rightarrow \quad 2\theta = \pi n \quad \Rightarrow \quad \theta = \frac{\pi}{2} n.$

| | Variation of $\theta$ | Variation of $r$ |
|---|---|---|
| 1) | $0 \to \frac{\pi}{4}$ | $0 \to 3$ |
| 2) | $\frac{\pi}{4} \to \frac{\pi}{2}$ | $3 \to 0$ |
| 3) | $\frac{\pi}{2} \to \frac{3\pi}{4}$ | $0 \to -3$ |
| 4) | $\frac{3\pi}{4} \to \pi$ | $-3 \to 0$ |
| 5) | $\pi \to \frac{5\pi}{2}$ | $0 \to 3$ |
| 6) | $\frac{5\pi}{4} \to \frac{3\pi}{2}$ | $3 \to 0$ |
| 7) | $\frac{3\pi}{2} \to \frac{7\pi}{4}$ | $0 \to -3$ |
| 8) | $\frac{7\pi}{4} \to 2\pi$ | $-3 \to 0$ |

**84** $r = 8\cos 5\theta$ is a 5-leafed rose.     $0 = 8\cos 5\theta \;\Rightarrow\; \cos 5\theta = 0 \;\Rightarrow\; 5\theta = \frac{\pi}{2} + \pi n \;\Rightarrow\; \theta = \frac{\pi}{10} + \frac{\pi}{5}n.$

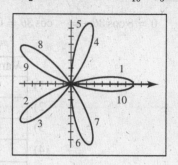

| | Variation of $\theta$ | Variation of $r$ |
|---|---|---|
| 1) | $0 \to \frac{\pi}{10}$ | $8 \to 0$ |
| 2) | $\frac{\pi}{10} \to \frac{\pi}{5}$ | $0 \to -8$ |
| 3) | $\frac{\pi}{5} \to \frac{3\pi}{10}$ | $-8 \to 0$ |
| 4) | $\frac{3\pi}{10} \to \frac{2\pi}{5}$ | $0 \to 8$ |
| 5) | $\frac{2\pi}{5} \to \frac{\pi}{2}$ | $8 \to 0$ |
| 6) | $\frac{\pi}{2} \to \frac{3\pi}{5}$ | $0 \to -8$ |
| 7) | $\frac{3\pi}{5} \to \frac{7\pi}{10}$ | $-8 \to 0$ |
| 8) | $\frac{7\pi}{10} \to \frac{4\pi}{5}$ | $0 \to 8$ |
| 9) | $\frac{4\pi}{5} \to \frac{9\pi}{10}$ | $8 \to 0$ |
| 10) | $\frac{9\pi}{10} \to \pi$ | $0 \to -8$ |

**85** $r^2 = 4\cos 2\theta$ (lemniscate)  •  $0 = 4\cos 2\theta \;\Rightarrow\; \cos 2\theta = 0 \;\Rightarrow\; 2\theta = \frac{\pi}{2} + \pi n \;\Rightarrow\; \theta = \frac{\pi}{4} + \frac{\pi}{2}n.$

Note that as $\theta$ varies from 0 to $\frac{\pi}{4}$, we have $r^2 = 4$ or $r = \pm 2$ to $r^2 = 0$—both parts labeled "1" are traced with this range of $\theta$. When $\theta$ varies from $\frac{\pi}{4}$ to $\frac{3\pi}{4}$, $2\theta$ varies from $\frac{\pi}{2}$ to $\frac{3\pi}{2}$, and $\cos 2\theta$ is negative. Since $r^2$ can't equal a negative value, no portion of the graph is traced for these values of $\theta$.

| | Variation of $\theta$ | Variation of $r$ |
|---|---|---|
| 1) | $0 \to \frac{\pi}{4}$ | $\pm 2 \to 0$ |
| 2) | $\frac{\pi}{4} \to \frac{\pi}{2}$ | undefined |
| 3) | $\frac{\pi}{2} \to \frac{3\pi}{4}$ | undefined |
| 4) | $\frac{3\pi}{4} \to \pi$ | $0 \to \pm 2$ |

**86** $r^2 = -16\sin 2\theta$  •  $0 = -16\sin 2\theta \;\Rightarrow\;$
$\sin 2\theta = 0 \;\Rightarrow\; 2\theta = \pi n \;\Rightarrow\; \theta = \frac{\pi}{2}n.$

| | Variation of $\theta$ | Variation of $r$ |
|---|---|---|
| 1) | $0 \to \frac{\pi}{4}$ | undefined |
| 2) | $\frac{\pi}{4} \to \frac{\pi}{2}$ | undefined |
| 3) | $\frac{\pi}{2} \to \frac{3\pi}{4}$ | $0 \to \pm 4$ |
| 4) | $\frac{3\pi}{4} \to \pi$ | $\pm 4 \to 0$ |

**87** $r = 2^{\theta}, \theta \geq 0$ (spiral)  •

| | Variation of $\theta$ | Variation of $r$ |
|---|---|---|
| 1) | $0 \to \frac{\pi}{2}$ | $1 \to 2.97$ |
| 2) | $\frac{\pi}{2} \to \pi$ | $2.97 \to 8.82$ |
| 3) | $\pi \to \frac{3\pi}{2}$ | $8.82 \to 26.22$ |
| 4) | $\frac{3\pi}{2} \to 2\pi$ | $26.22 \to 77.88$ |

**88** The values in the table are listed to emphasize the exponential growth.

Note that $e^{2\theta} = (e^2)^\theta$.

| | Variation of $\theta$ | Variation of $r$ |
|---|---|---|
| 1) | $0 \to \frac{\pi}{2}$ | $1 \to 23.14$ |
| 2) | $\frac{\pi}{2} \to \pi$ | $23.14 \to 535$ |
| 3) | $\pi \to \frac{3\pi}{2}$ | $535 \to 12{,}392$ |
| 4) | $\frac{3\pi}{2} \to 2\pi$ | $12{,}392 \to 286{,}751$ |

**89** $r = 2\theta, \theta \geq 0$ •

| | Variation of $\theta$ | Variation of $r$ |
|---|---|---|
| 1) | $0 \to \frac{\pi}{2}$ | $0 \to \pi$ |
| 2) | $\frac{\pi}{2} \to \pi$ | $\pi \to 2\pi$ |
| 3) | $\pi \to \frac{3\pi}{2}$ | $2\pi \to 3\pi$ |

**90** $r\theta = 1, \theta > 0$ (spiral) • $r\theta = 1 \Rightarrow r = 1/\theta$. $r$ is undefined at $\theta = 0$.

| | Variation of $\theta$ | Variation of $r$ |
|---|---|---|
| 1) | $0 \to \frac{\pi}{2}$ | $\infty \to 0.64$ |
| 2) | $\frac{\pi}{2} \to \pi$ | $0.64 \to 0.32$ |
| 3) | $\pi \to \frac{3\pi}{2}$ | $0.32 \to 0.21$ |
| 4) | $\frac{3\pi}{2} \to 2\pi$ | $0.21 \to 0.16$ |

**91** To simplify $\sin^2\left(\frac{\theta}{2}\right)$, recall the half-angle identity for the sine.

$r = 6\sin^2\left(\frac{\theta}{2}\right) = 6\left(\frac{1 - \cos\theta}{2}\right) = 3(1 - \cos\theta)$ is a cardioid.

$0 = 3(1 - \cos\theta) \Rightarrow \cos\theta = 1 \Rightarrow \theta = 2\pi n.$

| | Variation of $\theta$ | Variation of $r$ |
|---|---|---|
| 1) | $0 \to \frac{\pi}{2}$ | $0 \to 3$ |
| 2) | $\frac{\pi}{2} \to \pi$ | $3 \to 6$ |
| 3) | $\pi \to \frac{3\pi}{2}$ | $6 \to 3$ |
| 4) | $\frac{3\pi}{2} \to 2\pi$ | $3 \to 0$ |

**92** $r = -4\cos^2\left(\frac{\theta}{2}\right) = -4\left(\frac{1 + \cos\theta}{2}\right) = -2(1 + \cos\theta)$ is a cardioid.

$0 = -2(1 + \cos\theta) \Rightarrow \cos\theta = -1 \Rightarrow \theta = \pi + 2\pi n.$

| | Variation of $\theta$ | Variation of $r$ |
|---|---|---|
| 1) | $0 \to \frac{\pi}{2}$ | $-4 \to -2$ |
| 2) | $\frac{\pi}{2} \to \pi$ | $-2 \to 0$ |
| 3) | $\pi \to \frac{3\pi}{2}$ | $0 \to -2$ |
| 4) | $\frac{3\pi}{2} \to 2\pi$ | $-2 \to -4$ |

**93** Note that $r = 2\sec\theta$ is equivalent to $x = 2$. If $0 < \theta < \frac{\pi}{2}$ or $\frac{3\pi}{2} < \theta < 2\pi$,

then $\sec\theta > 0$ and the graph of $r = 2 + 2\sec\theta$ is to the right of $x = 2$.

If $\frac{\pi}{2} < \theta < \frac{3\pi}{2}$, $\sec\theta < 0$ and $r = 2 + 2\sec\theta$ is to the left of $x = 2$.

$r$ is undefined at $\theta = \frac{\pi}{2} + \pi n$.

$0 = 2 + 2\sec\theta \ \Rightarrow \ \sec\theta = -1 \ \Rightarrow \ \theta = \pi + 2\pi n$.

| | Variation of $\theta$ | Variation of $r$ |
|---|---|---|
| 1) | $0 \to \frac{\pi}{2}$ | $4 \to \infty$ |
| 2) | $\frac{\pi}{2} \to \pi$ | $-\infty \to 0$ |
| 3) | $\pi \to \frac{3\pi}{2}$ | $0 \to -\infty$ |
| 4) | $\frac{3\pi}{2} \to 2\pi$ | $\infty \to 4$ |

**94** Note that $r = -\csc\theta$ is equivalent to $y = -1$. If $0 < \theta < \pi$, then $\csc\theta > 0$

and the graph of $r = 1 - \csc\theta$ is above $y = -1$. If $\pi < \theta < 2\pi$, $\csc\theta < 0$

and $r = 1 - \csc\theta$ is below $y = -1$.  $r$ is undefined at $\theta = \pi n$.

$0 = 1 - \csc\theta \ \Rightarrow \ \csc\theta = 1 \ \Rightarrow \ \theta = \frac{\pi}{2} + 2\pi n$.

| | Variation of $\theta$ | Variation of $r$ |
|---|---|---|
| 1) | $0 \to \frac{\pi}{2}$ | $-\infty \to 0$ |
| 2) | $\frac{\pi}{2} \to \pi$ | $0 \to -\infty$ |
| 3) | $\pi \to \frac{3\pi}{2}$ | $\infty \to 2$ |
| 4) | $\frac{3\pi}{2} \to 2\pi$ | $2 \to \infty$ |

**95** Let $P_1(r_1, \theta_1)$ and $P_2(r_2, \theta_2)$ be points in an $r\theta$-plane. Let $a = r_1$, $b = r_2$,

$c = d(P_1, P_2)$, and $\gamma = \theta_2 - \theta_1$.   Substituting into the law of cosines,

$c^2 = a^2 + b^2 - 2ab\cos\gamma$, gives us the formula.

$$[d(P_1, P_2)]^2 = r_1^2 + r_2^2 - 2r_1 r_2 \cos(\theta_2 - \theta_1)$$

**96** (a) $r = a\sin\theta \ \Rightarrow \ r^2 = ar\sin\theta \ \Rightarrow \ x^2 + y^2 - ay = 0 \ \Rightarrow$

$\qquad x^2 + y^2 - ay + \frac{1}{4}a^2 = \frac{1}{4}a^2 \ \Rightarrow \ x^2 + \left(y - \frac{1}{2}a\right)^2 = \frac{1}{4}a^2$. $C\left(0, \frac{1}{2}a\right)$; $r = \frac{1}{2}|a|$

(b) $r = b\cos\theta \ \Rightarrow \ r^2 = br\cos\theta \ \Rightarrow \ x^2 + y^2 - bx = 0 \ \Rightarrow$

$\qquad x^2 + y^2 - bx + \frac{1}{4}b^2 = \frac{1}{4}b^2 \ \Rightarrow \ \left(x - \frac{1}{2}b\right)^2 + y^2 = \frac{1}{4}b^2$. $C\left(\frac{1}{2}b, 0\right)$; $r = \frac{1}{2}|b|$

(c) $r = a\sin\theta + b\cos\theta \ \Rightarrow \ r^2 = ar\sin\theta + br\cos\theta \ \Rightarrow \ x^2 - bx + y^2 - ay = 0 \ \Rightarrow$

$\qquad \left(x - \frac{1}{2}b\right)^2 + \left(y - \frac{1}{2}a\right)^2 = \frac{1}{4}b^2 + \frac{1}{4}a^2$. $C\left(\frac{1}{2}b, \frac{1}{2}a\right)$; $r = \frac{1}{2}\sqrt{b^2 + a^2}$

**97** (a) $I = \frac{1}{2}I_0[1 + \cos(\pi \sin \theta)] \Rightarrow r = 2.5[1 + \cos(\pi \sin \theta)]$ for $\theta \in [0, 2\pi]$.

(b) The signal is maximum in an east–west direction and minimum in a north-south direction.

$[-9, 9]$ by $[-6, 6]$        $[-9, 9]$ by $[-6, 6]$

*Figure 97*           *Figure 98*

**98** (a) $I = \frac{1}{2}I_0[1 + \cos(\pi \sin 2\theta)] \Rightarrow r = 2.5[1 + \cos(\pi \sin 2\theta)]$ for $\theta \in [0, 2\pi]$.

(b) The signal is maximum in the east, west, north, and south directions. It is minimum in northwest, southeast, northeast, and southwest directions.

**99** Change to "Pol" mode under ☐ MODE ☐, assign $2(\sin \theta)^2 (\tan \theta)^2$ to r1 under ☐ Y = ☐, and $-\frac{\pi}{3}$ to $\theta$min, $\frac{\pi}{3}$ to $\theta$max, and 0.04 to $\theta$step under ☐ WINDOW ☐. The graph is symmetric with respect to the polar axis.

$[-9, 9]$ by $[-6, 6]$        $[-9, 9]$ by $[-6, 6]$

*Figure 99*           *Figure 100*

**100** Assign $4/(1 + (\sin \theta)^2)$ to r1, 0 to $\theta$min, $2\pi$ to $\theta$max, and $\frac{\pi}{30}$ to $\theta$step. The graph is symmetric with respect to the polar axis, the line $\theta = \frac{\pi}{2}$, and the pole.

**101** Assign $8\cos(3\theta)$ to r1, $4 - 2.5\cos \theta$ to r2, 0 to $\theta$min, $2\pi$ to $\theta$max, and $\frac{\pi}{30}$ to $\theta$step. From the graph, there are six points of intersection. The approximate polar coordinates are $(1.75, \pm 0.45)$, $(4.49, \pm 1.77)$, and $(5.76, \pm 2.35)$.

$[-12, 12]$ by $[-9, 9]$        $[-3, 3]$ by $[-2, 2]$

*Figure 101*           *Figure 102*

**102** Assign $2(\sin \theta)^2$ to r1, $0.75(\theta + (\cos \theta)^2)$ to r2, $-\pi$ to $\theta$min, $\pi$ to $\theta$max, and $\frac{\pi}{30}$ to $\theta$step. Be sure to plot r2 for both positive and negative values of $\theta$. From the graph, there are five points of intersection. The approximate polar coordinates are $(0, 0)$, $(0.32, -0.41)$, $(0.96, 0.77)$, $(1.39, 0.99)$, and $(1.64, 2.01)$.

## 10.6 Exercises

**Note:** (1)  For an ellipse, the major axis is vertical if the denominator contains $\sin\theta$, horizontal if the denominator contains $\cos\theta$.

(2)  For a hyperbola, the transverse axis is vertical if the denominator contains $\sin\theta$, horizontal if the denominator contains $\cos\theta$. The focus at the pole is called $F$ and $V$ is the vertex associated with (or closest to) $F$. $d(V, F)$ denotes the distance from the vertex to the focus. The foci are not asked for in the directions, but are listed.

(3)  For a parabola, the directrix is on the right, left, top, or bottom of the focus depending on the term "$+\cos$", "$-\cos$", "$+\sin$", or "$-\sin$", respectively, appearing in the denominator.

$\boxed{1}$  Divide the numerator and denominator by the constant term in the denominator, i.e., 6. $r = \dfrac{12}{6 + 2\sin\theta} = \dfrac{2}{1 + \frac{1}{3}\sin\theta} \;\Rightarrow\; e = \frac{1}{3} < 1$, ellipse. From the note above, we see that the denominator has "$+\sin\theta$" and we have vertices when $\theta = \frac{\pi}{2}$ and $\frac{3\pi}{2}$. They are $V\left(\frac{3}{2}, \frac{\pi}{2}\right)$ and $V'\left(3, \frac{3\pi}{2}\right)$. The distance from the focus at the pole to the vertex $V$ is $\frac{3}{2}$. The distance from $V'$ to $F'$ must also be $\frac{3}{2}$ and we see that $F' = \left(\frac{3}{2}, \frac{3\pi}{2}\right)$. We will use the following notation to summarize this in future problems: $d(V, F) = \frac{3}{2} \;\Rightarrow\; F' = \left(\frac{3}{2}, \frac{3\pi}{2}\right)$.

*Figure 1*

*Figure 2*

$\boxed{2}$  $r = \dfrac{12}{6 - 2\sin\theta} = \dfrac{2}{1 - \frac{1}{3}\sin\theta} \;\Rightarrow\; e = \frac{1}{3} < 1$, ellipse.

$V\left(\frac{3}{2}, \frac{3\pi}{2}\right)$ and $V'\left(3, \frac{\pi}{2}\right)$. $d(V, F) = \frac{3}{2} \;\Rightarrow\; F' = \left(\frac{3}{2}, \frac{\pi}{2}\right)$.

$\boxed{3}$  Divide both the numerator and the denominator by 2 to obtain the "1" in the standard form. $r = \dfrac{12}{2 - 6\cos\theta} = \dfrac{6}{1 - 3\cos\theta} \;\Rightarrow\; e = 3 > 1$, hyperbola.

$V\left(\frac{3}{2}, \pi\right)$ and $V'(-3, 0)$. $d(V, F) = \frac{3}{2} \;\Rightarrow\; F' = \left(-\frac{9}{2}, 0\right)$.

*Figure 3*

*Figure 4*

$\boxed{4}$  $r = \dfrac{12}{2 + 6\cos\theta} = \dfrac{6}{1 + 3\cos\theta} \;\Rightarrow\; e = 3 > 1$, hyperbola.

$V\left(\frac{3}{2}, 0\right)$ and $V'(-3, \pi)$. $d(V, F) = \frac{3}{2} \;\Rightarrow\; F' = \left(-\frac{9}{2}, \pi\right)$.

**5** $r = \dfrac{3}{2 + 2\cos\theta} = \dfrac{\frac{3}{2}}{1 + 1\cos\theta}$ $\Rightarrow$ $e = 1$, parabola.

Note that the expression is undefined in the $\theta = \pi$ direction. The vertex is in the $\theta = 0$ direction, $V\left(\frac{3}{4}, 0\right)$.

*Figure 5*

*Figure 6*

**6** $r = \dfrac{3}{2 - 2\sin\theta} = \dfrac{\frac{3}{2}}{1 - 1\sin\theta}$ $\Rightarrow$ $e = 1$, parabola. The vertex is in the $\theta = \frac{3\pi}{2}$ direction, $V\left(\frac{3}{4}, \frac{3\pi}{2}\right)$.

**7** $r = \dfrac{4}{\cos\theta - 2} = \dfrac{-2}{1 - \frac{1}{2}\cos\theta}$ $\Rightarrow$ $e = \frac{1}{2} < 1$, ellipse.

$V\left(-\frac{4}{3}, \pi\right)$ and $V'(-4, 0)$. $d(V, F) = \frac{4}{3}$ $\Rightarrow$ $F' = \left(-\frac{8}{3}, 0\right)$

*Figure 7*

*Figure 8*

**8** $r = \dfrac{4\sec\theta}{2\sec\theta - 1} \cdot \dfrac{\cos\theta}{\cos\theta} = \dfrac{4}{2 - 1\cos\theta} = \dfrac{2}{1 - \frac{1}{2}\cos\theta}$ $\Rightarrow$ $e = \frac{1}{2} < 1$, ellipse.

$V\left(\frac{4}{3}, \pi\right)$ and $V'(4, 0)$. $d(V, F) = \frac{4}{3}$ $\Rightarrow$ $F' = \left(\frac{8}{3}, 0\right)$. Since the original equation is undefined when $\sec\theta$ is undefined, the points $\left(2, \frac{\pi}{2}\right)$ and $\left(2, \frac{3\pi}{2}\right)$ are excluded from the graph.

**9** We multiply by $\dfrac{\sin\theta}{\sin\theta}$ to obtain the standard form of a conic.

$r = \dfrac{6\csc\theta}{2\csc\theta + 3} \cdot \dfrac{\sin\theta}{\sin\theta} = \dfrac{6}{2 + 3\sin\theta} = \dfrac{3}{1 + \frac{3}{2}\sin\theta}$ $\Rightarrow$ $e = \frac{3}{2} > 1$, hyperbola. $V\left(\frac{6}{5}, \frac{\pi}{2}\right)$ and $V'\left(-6, \frac{3\pi}{2}\right)$.

$d(V, F) = \frac{6}{5}$ $\Rightarrow$ $F' = \left(-\frac{36}{5}, \frac{3\pi}{2}\right)$. Since the original equation is undefined when $\csc\theta$ is undefined {which is when $\theta = \pi n$}, the points $(3, 0)$ and $(3, \pi)$ are excluded from the graph.

*Figure 9*

*Figure 10*

**10** $r = \dfrac{8\csc\theta}{2\csc\theta - 5} \cdot \dfrac{\sin\theta}{\sin\theta} = \dfrac{8}{2 - 5\sin\theta} = \dfrac{4}{1 - \frac{5}{2}\sin\theta}$ $\Rightarrow$ $e = \frac{5}{2} > 1$, hyperbola.

$V\left(\frac{8}{7}, \frac{3\pi}{2}\right)$ and $V'\left(-\frac{8}{3}, \frac{\pi}{2}\right)$. $d(V, F) = \frac{8}{7}$ $\Rightarrow$ $F' = \left(-\frac{80}{21}, \frac{\pi}{2}\right)$. Since the original equation is undefined when $\csc\theta$ is undefined, the points $(4, 0)$ and $(4, \pi)$ are excluded from the graph.

**11** $r = \dfrac{4\csc\theta}{1+\csc\theta} \cdot \dfrac{\sin\theta}{\sin\theta} = \dfrac{4}{1+1\sin\theta}$ $\Rightarrow$ $e = 1$, parabola. The vertex is in the $\theta = \frac{\pi}{2}$ direction, $V\left(2, \frac{\pi}{2}\right)$. Since

the original equation is undefined when $\csc\theta$ is undefined, the points $(4,0)$ and $(4,\pi)$ are excluded from the graph.

Figure 11

Figure 12

**12** $r = \csc\theta\,(\csc\theta - \cot\theta) = \dfrac{1}{\sin\theta}\left(\dfrac{1-\cos\theta}{\sin\theta}\right) = \dfrac{1-\cos\theta}{1-\cos^2\theta} = \dfrac{1}{1+1\cos\theta}$ $\Rightarrow$ $e = 1$, parabola.

The vertex is in the $\theta = 0$ direction, $V\left(\frac{1}{2}, 0\right)$. Since the original equation is undefined when $\csc\theta$ is undefined,

the point $\left(\frac{1}{2}, 0\right)$ is excluded from the graph.

**13** $r = \dfrac{12}{6+2\sin\theta}$ $\Rightarrow$ $6r + 2r\sin\theta = 12$ $\Rightarrow$ $6r + 2y = 12$ $\Rightarrow$ {Isolate the term with the "$r$" so that by

squaring both sides of the equation, we can make the substitution $r^2 = x^2 + y^2$.} $3r = 6 - y$ $\Rightarrow$

$\qquad 9r^2 = 36 - 12y + y^2$ $\Rightarrow$ $9(x^2 + y^2) = 36 - 12y + y^2$ $\Rightarrow$ $9x^2 + 8y^2 + 12y - 36 = 0$

**14** $r = \dfrac{12}{6-2\sin\theta}$ $\Rightarrow$ $6r - 2y = 12$ $\Rightarrow$ $3r = y + 6$ $\Rightarrow$ $9r^2 = y^2 + 12y + 36$ $\Rightarrow$

$\qquad\qquad\qquad\qquad\qquad\qquad\qquad\qquad\qquad\qquad\qquad\qquad\qquad 9x^2 + 8y^2 - 12y - 36 = 0$

**Note:** In the following solutions, the substitutions $x = r\cos\theta$, $y = r\sin\theta$, and $r^2 = x^2 + y^2$ are made without mention.

**15** $r = \dfrac{12}{2-6\cos\theta}$ $\Rightarrow$ $2r - 6x = 12$ $\Rightarrow$ $r = 3x + 6$ $\Rightarrow$ $r^2 = 9x^2 + 36x + 36$ $\Rightarrow$

$\qquad\qquad\qquad\qquad\qquad\qquad\qquad\qquad\qquad\qquad\qquad\qquad 8x^2 - y^2 + 36x + 36 = 0$

**16** $r = \dfrac{12}{2+6\cos\theta}$ $\Rightarrow$ $2r + 6x = 12$ $\Rightarrow$ $r = 6 - 3x$ $\Rightarrow$ $r^2 = 36 - 36x + 9x^2$ $\Rightarrow$

$\qquad\qquad\qquad\qquad\qquad\qquad\qquad\qquad\qquad\qquad\qquad\qquad 8x^2 - y^2 - 36x + 36 = 0$

**17** $r = \dfrac{3}{2+2\cos\theta}$ $\Rightarrow$ $2r + 2x = 3$ $\Rightarrow$ $2r = 3 - 2x$ $\Rightarrow$ $4r^2 = 4x^2 - 12x + 9$ $\Rightarrow$ $4y^2 + 12x - 9 = 0$

**18** $r = \dfrac{3}{2-2\sin\theta}$ $\Rightarrow$ $2r - 2y = 3$ $\Rightarrow$ $2r = 2y + 3$ $\Rightarrow$ $4r^2 = 4y^2 + 12y + 9$ $\Rightarrow$ $4x^2 - 12y - 9 = 0$

**19** $r = \dfrac{4}{\cos\theta - 2}$ $\Rightarrow$ $x - 2r = 4$ $\Rightarrow$ $x - 4 = 2r$ $\Rightarrow$ $x^2 - 8x + 16 = 4r^2$ $\Rightarrow$ $3x^2 + 4y^2 + 8x - 16 = 0$

**20** $r = \dfrac{4\sec\theta}{2\sec\theta - 1} \cdot \dfrac{\cos\theta}{\cos\theta} = \dfrac{4}{2-1\cos\theta}$ $\Rightarrow$ $2r - x = 4$ $\Rightarrow$ $2r = x + 4$ $\Rightarrow$ $4r^2 = x^2 + 8x + 16$ $\Rightarrow$

$\qquad\qquad\qquad\qquad\qquad\qquad\qquad\qquad\qquad\qquad\qquad\qquad 3x^2 + 4y^2 - 8x - 16 = 0.$

$r$ is undefined when $\theta = \frac{\pi}{2}$ or $\frac{3\pi}{2}$. For the rectangular equation, these points correspond to $x = 0$ (or $r\cos\theta = 0$).

Substituting $x = 0$ into the above rectangular equation yields $4y^2 = 16$, or $y = \pm 2$. $\therefore$ *exclude* $(0, \pm 2)$

**21** $r = \dfrac{6 \csc \theta}{2 \csc \theta + 3} \cdot \dfrac{\sin \theta}{\sin \theta} = \dfrac{6}{2 + 3 \sin \theta}$ $\Rightarrow$ $2r + 3y = 6$ $\Rightarrow$ $2r = 6 - 3y$ $\Rightarrow$

$4r^2 = 36 - 36y + 9y^2$ $\Rightarrow$ $4x^2 - 5y^2 + 36y - 36 = 0$. $r$ is undefined when $\theta = 0$ or $\pi$. For the rectangular

equation, these points correspond to $y = 0$ (or $r \sin \theta = 0$). Substituting $y = 0$ into the above rectangular equation

yields $4x^2 = 36$, or $x = \pm 3$. $\therefore$ *exclude* $(\pm 3, 0)$

**22** $r = \dfrac{8 \csc \theta}{2 \csc \theta - 5} \cdot \dfrac{\sin \theta}{\sin \theta} = \dfrac{8}{2 - 5 \sin \theta}$ $\Rightarrow$ $2r - 5y = 8$ $\Rightarrow$ $2r = 5y + 8$ $\Rightarrow$

$4r^2 = 25y^2 + 80y + 64$ $\Rightarrow$ $4x^2 - 21y^2 - 80y - 64 = 0$. $r$ is undefined when $\theta = 0$ or $\pi$. For the rectangular

equation, these points correspond to $y = 0$ (or $r \sin \theta = 0$). Substituting $y = 0$ into the above rectangular equation

yields $4x^2 = 64$, or $x = \pm 4$. $\therefore$ *exclude* $(\pm 4, 0)$

**23** $r = \dfrac{4 \csc \theta}{1 + \csc \theta} \cdot \dfrac{\sin \theta}{\sin \theta} = \dfrac{4}{1 + 1 \sin \theta}$ $\Rightarrow$ $r + y = 4$ $\Rightarrow$ $r = 4 - y$ $\Rightarrow$ $r^2 = y^2 - 8y + 16$ $\Rightarrow$

$x^2 + 8y - 16 = 0$. $r$ is undefined when $\theta = 0$ or $\pi$. For the rectangular equation, these points correspond to $y = 0$

(or $r \sin \theta = 0$). Substituting $y = 0$ into the above rectangular equation yields $x^2 = 16$, or $x = \pm 4$. $\therefore$ *exclude*

$(\pm 4, 0)$

**24** $r = \csc \theta (\csc \theta - \cot \theta) = \dfrac{1}{\sin \theta} \left( \dfrac{1 - \cos \theta}{\sin \theta} \right) = \dfrac{1 - \cos \theta}{1 - \cos^2 \theta} = \dfrac{1}{1 + \cos \theta}$ $\Rightarrow$ $r + x = 1$ $\Rightarrow$

$r = 1 - x$ $\Rightarrow$ $r^2 = 1 - 2x + x^2$ $\Rightarrow$ $y^2 + 2x - 1 = 0$. $r$ is undefined when $\theta = 0$ or $\pi$. For the rectangular

equation, this point corresponds to $y = 0$ (or $r \sin \theta = 0$). Substituting $y = 0$ into the above rectangular equation

yields $2x - 1 = 0$, or $x = \frac{1}{2}$. $\therefore$ *exclude* $\left( \frac{1}{2}, 0 \right)$

**25** $r = 2 \sec \theta$ $\Rightarrow$ $r \cos \theta = 2$ $\Rightarrow$ $x = 2$. Remember that $d$ is the distance from the focus at the pole to the

directrix. Thus, $d = 2$ and since the directrix is on the right of the focus at the pole, we use "$+ \cos \theta$".

$$r = \frac{de}{1 + e \cos \theta} = \frac{2\left(\frac{1}{3}\right)}{1 + \frac{1}{3} \cos \theta} \cdot \frac{3}{3} = \frac{2}{3 + \cos \theta}.$$

**26** $r \cos \theta = 5$ $\Rightarrow$ $x = 5$. Thus, $d = 5$ and since the directrix is on the right of the focus at the pole,

$$\text{we use "} + \cos \theta\text{".} \quad r = \frac{de}{1 + e \cos \theta} = \frac{5(1)}{1 + 1 \cos \theta} = \frac{5}{1 + \cos \theta}.$$

**27** $r \cos \theta = -3$ $\Rightarrow$ $x = -3$. Thus, $d = 3$ and since the directrix is on the left of the focus at the pole,

$$\text{we use "} - \cos \theta\text{".} \quad r = \frac{de}{1 - e \cos \theta} = \frac{3\left(\frac{4}{3}\right)}{1 - \frac{4}{3} \cos \theta} \cdot \frac{3}{3} = \frac{12}{3 - 4 \cos \theta}.$$

**28** $r = -4 \sec \theta$ $\Rightarrow$ $r \cos \theta = -4$ $\Rightarrow$ $x = -4$. Thus, $d = 4$ and since the directrix is on the left of the focus at

$$\text{the pole, we use "} - \cos \theta\text{".} \quad r = \frac{de}{1 - e \cos \theta} = \frac{4(3)}{1 - 3 \cos \theta} = \frac{12}{1 - 3 \cos \theta}.$$

**29** $r \sin \theta = -2$ $\Rightarrow$ $y = -2$. Thus, $d = 2$ and since the directrix is below the focus at the pole, we use "$- \sin \theta$".

$$r = \frac{de}{1 - e \sin \theta} = \frac{2(1)}{1 - 1 \sin \theta} = \frac{2}{1 - \sin \theta}.$$

**30** $r = -3 \csc \theta$ $\Rightarrow$ $r \sin \theta = -3$ $\Rightarrow$ $y = -3$. Thus, $d = 3$ and since the directrix is below the focus at the pole,

$$\text{we use "} - \sin \theta\text{".} \quad r = \frac{de}{1 - e \sin \theta} = \frac{3(4)}{1 - 4 \sin \theta} = \frac{12}{1 - 4 \sin \theta}.$$

**31** $r = 4 \csc \theta$ $\Rightarrow$ $r \sin \theta = 4$ $\Rightarrow$ $y = 4$. Thus, $d = 4$ and since the directrix is above the focus at the pole,

$$\text{we use "} + \sin \theta\text{".} \quad r = \frac{de}{1 + e \sin \theta} = \frac{4\left(\frac{2}{5}\right)}{1 + \frac{2}{5} \sin \theta} \cdot \frac{5}{5} = \frac{8}{5 + 2 \sin \theta}.$$

**32** $r\sin\theta = 5 \Rightarrow y = 5$. Thus, $d = 5$ and since the directrix is above the focus at the pole, we use "$+\sin\theta$".

$$r = \frac{de}{1 + e\sin\theta} = \frac{5\left(\frac{3}{4}\right)}{1 + \frac{3}{4}\sin\theta} \cdot \frac{4}{4} = \frac{15}{4 + 3\sin\theta}.$$

**33** $V\left(4, \frac{\pi}{2}\right)$ • For a parabola, $e = 1$. The vertex is 4 units above the focus at the pole,

so $d = 2(4)$ and we should use "$+\sin\theta$" in the denominator. $r = \dfrac{8}{1 + \sin\theta}$

**34** $V(5,0)$ • For a parabola, $e = 1$. The vertex is 5 units to the right of the focus at the pole,

so $d = 2(5)$ and we should use "$+\cos\theta$" in the denominator. $r = \dfrac{10}{1 + \cos\theta}$

**35** (a) $e = \dfrac{c}{a} = \dfrac{d(C,F)}{d(C,V)} = \dfrac{3}{4}$.

(b) Since the vertex is below the focus at the pole, use "$-\sin\theta$".

$r = \dfrac{d\left(\frac{3}{4}\right)}{1 - \frac{3}{4}\sin\theta}$ and $r = 1$ when $\theta = \frac{3\pi}{2}$ $\Rightarrow$

$1 = \dfrac{d\left(\frac{3}{4}\right)}{1 - \frac{3}{4}(-1)} \Rightarrow 1 = \dfrac{\frac{3}{4}d}{\frac{7}{4}} \Rightarrow d = \frac{7}{3}$.

Thus, $r = \dfrac{\left(\frac{7}{3}\right)\left(\frac{3}{4}\right)}{1 - \frac{3}{4}\sin\theta} \cdot \dfrac{4}{4} = \dfrac{7}{4 - 3\sin\theta}$.

An equivalent rectangular equation is $\dfrac{x^2}{7} + \dfrac{(y-3)^2}{16} = 1$.

**36** (a) $e = \dfrac{c}{a} = \dfrac{d(C,F)}{d(C,V)} = \dfrac{2}{3}$.

(b) The vertex is to the right of the focus at the pole, so use "$+\cos\theta$".

$r = \dfrac{d\left(\frac{2}{3}\right)}{1 + \frac{2}{3}\cos\theta}$ and $r = 1$ when $\theta = 0$ $\Rightarrow$ $1 = \dfrac{d\left(\frac{2}{3}\right)}{1 + \frac{2}{3}(1)}$ $\Rightarrow$

$1 = \dfrac{\frac{2}{3}d}{\frac{5}{3}} \Rightarrow d = \frac{5}{2}$. Thus, $r = \dfrac{\left(\frac{5}{2}\right)\left(\frac{2}{3}\right)}{1 + \frac{2}{3}\cos\theta} \cdot \dfrac{3}{3} = \dfrac{5}{3 + 2\cos\theta}$.

An equivalent rectangular equation is $\dfrac{(x+2)^2}{9} + \dfrac{y^2}{5} = 1$.

**37** (a) Let $V$ and $C$ denote the vertex closest to the sun and the center of the ellipse, respectively.

Let $s$ denote the distance from $V$ to the directrix to the left of $V$.

$d(O,V) = d(C,V) - d(C,O) = a - c = a - ea = a(1 - e)$.

Also, by the first theorem in Section 10.6, $\dfrac{d(O,V)}{s} = e \Rightarrow s = \dfrac{d(O,V)}{e} = \dfrac{a(1-e)}{e}$.

Now, $d = s + d(O,V) = \dfrac{a(1-e)}{e} + a(1-e) = \dfrac{a(1-e^2)}{e}$ and $de = a(1 - e^2)$.

Thus, the equation of the orbit is $r = \dfrac{(1 - e^2)a}{1 - e\cos\theta}$.

(b) The minimum distance occurs when $\theta = \pi$. $r_{per} = \dfrac{(1-e^2)a}{1 - e(-1)} = a(1 - e)$.

The maximum distance occurs when $\theta = 0$. $r_{aph} = \dfrac{(1-e^2)a}{1 - e(1)} = a(1 + e)$.

**38** $r = \dfrac{(1-e^2)a}{1 - e\cos\theta} = \dfrac{(1+e)[(1-e)a]}{1 - e\cos\theta} = \dfrac{(1+0.249)(29.62)}{1 - 0.249\cos\theta}$ {since $r_{per} = a(1-e)$} $\approx \dfrac{37.00}{1 - 0.249\cos\theta}$ is an

equation of Pluto's orbit. $r_{aph} = a(1 + e) = \left(\dfrac{r_{per}}{1 - e}\right)(1 + e) = \left(\dfrac{29.62}{1 - 0.249}\right)(1 + 0.249) \approx 49.26$ AU.

**39** (a)  Since $e = 0.9673 < 1$, the orbit of Halley's Comet is elliptical.

(b)  The polar equation for the orbit of Saturn is $r = \dfrac{9.006(1 + 0.056)}{1 - 0.056 \cos\theta}$.

The polar equation for Halley's comet is $r = \dfrac{0.5871(1 + 0.9673)}{1 - 0.9673 \cos\theta}$.

$[-36, 36, 3]$ by $[-24, 24, 3]$               $[-18, 18, 3]$ by $[-12, 12, 3]$

*Figure 39*

*Figure 40*

**40** (a)  Since $e = 0.8499 < 1$, the orbit of Encke's Comet is elliptical.

(b)  The polar equation for Encke's comet is $r = \dfrac{0.3317(1 + 0.8499)}{1 - 0.8499 \cos\theta}$.

**41** (a)  Since $e = 1.003 > 1$, the orbit of Comet 1959 III is hyperbolic.

(b)  The polar equation for Comet 1959 III is $r = \dfrac{1.251(1 + 1.003)}{1 - 1.003 \cos\theta}$.

$[-18, 18, 3]$ by $[-12, 12, 3]$               $[-18, 18, 3]$ by $[-12, 12, 3]$

*Figure 41*

*Figure 42*

**42** (a)  Since $e = 1.000$, the orbit of Comet 1973.99 is parabolic.

(b)  The polar equation for Comet 1973.99 is $r = \dfrac{0.142(1 + 1.000)}{1 - 1.000 \cos\theta}$.

**43** From Exercise 37, $r_{aph} = a(1 + e) = a + ae$ and $r_{per} = a(1 - e) = a - ae$.

Adding the two equations gives us $r_{aph} + r_{per} = 2a \;\Rightarrow\; a = \dfrac{r_{aph} + r_{per}}{2}$.

Subtracting the two equations gives us $r_{aph} - r_{per} = 2ae \;\Rightarrow\; e = \dfrac{r_{aph} - r_{per}}{2a} = \dfrac{r_{aph} - r_{per}}{2 \cdot \dfrac{r_{aph} + r_{per}}{2}} = \dfrac{r_{aph} - r_{per}}{r_{aph} + r_{per}}$.

**Note:** The notation used here is the same as in Sections 10.1–10.3.

$\boxed{1}$   $y^2 = 64x \;\;\Rightarrow\;\; x = \frac{1}{64}y^2 \;\;\Rightarrow\;\; a = \frac{1}{64}. \; p = \dfrac{1}{4\left(\frac{1}{64}\right)} = 16. \; V(0,0); \; F(16,0); \; l: x = -16$

Figure 1

Figure 2

$\boxed{2}$   $y = 8x^2 + 32x + 33 \;\;\Rightarrow\;\; a = 8. \; p = \frac{1}{4(8)} = \frac{1}{32}. \; V(-2,1); \; F\left(-2, \frac{33}{32}\right); \; l: y = \frac{31}{32}$

$\boxed{3}$   $9y^2 = 144 - 16x^2 \;\;\Rightarrow\;\; 16x^2 + 9y^2 = 144 \;\;\Rightarrow\;\; \dfrac{16x^2}{144} + \dfrac{9y^2}{144} = \dfrac{144}{144} \;\;\Rightarrow\;\; \dfrac{x^2}{9} + \dfrac{y^2}{16} = 1.$
$c^2 = 16 - 9 \;\;\Rightarrow\;\; c = \pm\sqrt{7}.$
$$V(0,\pm 4); \; F\left(0, \pm\sqrt{7}\right); \; M(\pm 3, 0)$$

Figure 3

Figure 4

$\boxed{4}$   $9y^2 = 144 + 16x^2 \;\;\Rightarrow\;\; \dfrac{y^2}{16} - \dfrac{x^2}{9} = 1. \; c^2 = 16 + 9 \;\;\Rightarrow\;\; c = \pm 5. \; V(0,\pm 4); \; F(0,\pm 5); \; W(\pm 3, 0); \; y = \pm\frac{4}{3}x$

$\boxed{5}$   $x^2 - y^2 - 4 = 0 \;\;\Rightarrow\;\; \dfrac{x^2}{4} - \dfrac{y^2}{4} = 1. \; c^2 = 4 + 4 \;\;\Rightarrow\;\; c = \pm\sqrt{8} \;\;\Rightarrow\;\; c = \pm 2\sqrt{2}.$
$$V(\pm 2, 0); \; F\left(\pm 2\sqrt{2}, 0\right); \; W(0, \pm 2); \; y = \pm x$$

Figure 5

Figure 6

$\boxed{6}$   $25x^2 + 36y^2 = 1 \;\;\Rightarrow\;\; \dfrac{x^2}{\frac{1}{25}} + \dfrac{y^2}{\frac{1}{36}} = 1. \; c^2 = \frac{1}{25} - \frac{1}{36} = \frac{11}{900} \;\;\Rightarrow\;\; c = \pm\frac{1}{30}\sqrt{11}.$
$$V\left(\pm\tfrac{1}{5}, 0\right); \; F\left(\pm\tfrac{1}{30}\sqrt{11}, 0\right); \; M\left(0, \pm\tfrac{1}{6}\right)$$

$\boxed{7}$   $25y = 100 - x^2 \;\Rightarrow\; y = 4 - \frac{1}{25}x^2 \;\Rightarrow\; \cdot a = -\frac{1}{25}.\; p = \dfrac{1}{4\left(-\frac{1}{25}\right)} = -\frac{25}{4}.$

The vertex is at $(0, 4)$ and the focus is $\frac{25}{4}$ units below the vertex. $4 - \frac{25}{4} = -\frac{9}{4}$.

The directrix is $\frac{25}{4}$ units above the vertex. $4 + \frac{25}{4} = \frac{41}{4}$.      $V(0, 4);\; F\left(0, -\frac{9}{4}\right);\; l: y = \frac{41}{4}$

Figure 7

Figure 8

$\boxed{8}$   $3x^2 + 4y^2 - 18x + 8y + 19 = 0 \;\Rightarrow\; 3(x^2 - 6x + \underline{9}) + 4(y^2 + 2y + \underline{1}) = -19 + \underline{27} + \underline{4} \;\Rightarrow$

$3(x-3)^2 + 4(y+1)^2 = 12 \;\Rightarrow\; \dfrac{(x-3)^2}{4} + \dfrac{(y+1)^2}{3} = 1.\; c^2 = 4 - 3 \;\Rightarrow\; c = \pm 1.$

$$C(3, -1);\; V(3 \pm 2, -1);\; F(3 \pm 1, -1);\; M\left(3, -1 \pm \sqrt{3}\right)$$

$\boxed{9}$   $x^2 - 9y^2 + 8x + 90y - 210 = 0 \;\Rightarrow\; (x^2 + 8x + \underline{16}) - 9(y^2 - 10y + \underline{25}) = 210 + \underline{16} - \underline{225} \;\Rightarrow$

$(x+4)^2 - 9(y-5)^2 = 1 \;\Rightarrow\; \dfrac{(x+4)^2}{1} - \dfrac{(y-5)^2}{\frac{1}{9}} = 1.\; c^2 = 1 + \frac{1}{9} \;\Rightarrow\; c = \pm\frac{1}{3}\sqrt{10}.$

$$C(-4, 5);\; V(-4 \pm 1, 5);\; F\left(-4 \pm \tfrac{1}{3}\sqrt{10}, 5\right);\; W\left(-4, 5 \pm \tfrac{1}{3}\right);\; (y-5) = \pm\tfrac{1}{3}(x+4)$$

Figure 9

Figure 10

$\boxed{10}$   $x = 2y^2 + 8y + 3 \;\Rightarrow\; a = 2.\; p = \frac{1}{4(2)} = \frac{1}{8}.\; V(-5, -2);\; F\left(-\frac{39}{8}, -2\right);\; l: x = -\frac{41}{8}$

[11] $4x^2 + 9y^2 + 24x - 36y + 36 = 0 \Rightarrow 4(x^2 + 6x + \underline{9}) + 9(y^2 - 4y + \underline{4}) = -36 + \underline{36} + \underline{36} \Rightarrow$

$4(x+3)^2 + 9(y-2)^2 = 36 \Rightarrow \dfrac{(x+3)^2}{9} + \dfrac{(y-2)^2}{4} = 1.\ c^2 = 9 - 4 \Rightarrow c = \pm\sqrt{5}.$

$C(-3, 2);\ V(-3 \pm 3, 2);\ F\left(-3 \pm \sqrt{5}, 2\right);\ M(-3, 2 \pm 2)$

*Figure 11*

*Figure 12*

[12] $4x^2 - y^2 - 40x - 8y + 88 = 0 \Rightarrow 4(x^2 - 10x + \underline{25}) - (y^2 + 8y + \underline{16}) = -88 + \underline{100} - \underline{16} \Rightarrow$

$4(x-5)^2 - (y+4)^2 = -4 \Rightarrow \dfrac{(y+4)^2}{4} - \dfrac{(x-5)^2}{1} = 1.\ c^2 = 4 + 1 \Rightarrow c = \pm\sqrt{5}.$

$C(5, -4);\ V(5, -4 \pm 2);\ F\left(5, -4 \pm \sqrt{5}\right);\ W(5 \pm 1, -4);\ (y+4) = \pm 2(x-5)$

[13] $y^2 - 8x + 8y + 32 = 0 \Rightarrow x = \tfrac{1}{8}y^2 + y + 4 \Rightarrow a = \tfrac{1}{8}.\ p = \dfrac{1}{4\left(\frac{1}{8}\right)} = 2.\ V(2, -4);\ F(4, -4);\ l: x = 0$

*Figure 13*

*Figure 14*

[14] $4x^2 + y^2 - 24x + 4y + 36 = 0 \Rightarrow 4(x^2 - 6x + \underline{9}) + (y^2 + 4y + \underline{4}) = -36 + \underline{36} + \underline{4} \Rightarrow$

$4(x-3)^2 + (y+2)^2 = 4 \Rightarrow \dfrac{(x-3)^2}{1} + \dfrac{(y+2)^2}{4} = 1.\ c^2 = 4 - 1 \Rightarrow c = \pm\sqrt{3}.$

$C(3, -2);\ V(3, -2 \pm 2);\ F\left(3, -2 \pm \sqrt{3}\right);\ M(3 \pm 1, -2)$

[15] $x^2 - 9y^2 + 8x + 7 = 0 \Rightarrow (x^2 + 8x + \underline{16}) - 9(y^2) = -7 + \underline{16} \Rightarrow (x+4)^2 - 9(y^2) = 9 \Rightarrow$

$\dfrac{(x+4)^2}{9} - \dfrac{y^2}{1} = 1.\ c^2 = 9 + 1 \Rightarrow c = \pm\sqrt{10}.$

$C(-4, 0);\ V(-4 \pm 3, 0);\ F\left(-4 \pm \sqrt{10}, 0\right);\ W(-4, 0 \pm 1);\ y = \pm\tfrac{1}{3}(x+4)$

*Figure 15*

*Figure 16*

**16** $y^2 - 2x^2 + 6y + 8x - 3 = 0 \Rightarrow (y^2 + 6y + \underline{9}) - 2(x^2 - 4x + \underline{4}) = 3 + \underline{9} - \underline{8} \Rightarrow$

$(y+3)^2 - 2(x-2)^2 = 4 \Rightarrow \dfrac{(y+3)^2}{4} - \dfrac{(x-2)^2}{2} = 1. \ c^2 = 4 + 2 \Rightarrow c = \pm\sqrt{6}.$

$C(2, -3); \ V(2, -3 \pm 2); \ F\left(2, -3 \pm \sqrt{6}\right); \ W\left(2 \pm \sqrt{2}, -3\right); \ (y+3) = \pm\sqrt{2}(x - 2)$

**17** The vertex is halfway between the $x$-intercepts of $-10$ and $-4$, so it is of the form $V(-7, k)$.

$y = a(x+10)(x+4)$ and $x = 0, y = 80$ {$y$-intercept $80$} $\Rightarrow 80 = a(10)(4) \Rightarrow a = 2$.

$x = -7 \Rightarrow y = 2(3)(-3) = -18$. Hence, $y = 2(x+7)^2 - 18$.

**18** The vertex is halfway between the $x$-intercepts of $-11$ and $3$, so it is of the form $V(-4, k)$.

$y = a(x+11)(x-3)$ and $x = 2, y = 39$ {passing through $(2, 80)$} $\Rightarrow 39 = a(13)(-1) \Rightarrow a = -3$.

$x = -4 \Rightarrow y = -3(7)(-7) = 147$. Hence, $y = -3(x+4)^2 + 147$.

**19** An equation of a hyperbola with vertices $V(0, \pm 7)$ and endpoints of the conjugate axis $(\pm 3, 0)$ is

$$\dfrac{y^2}{7^2} - \dfrac{x^2}{3^2} = 1 \text{ or } \dfrac{y^2}{49} - \dfrac{x^2}{9} = 1.$$

**20** $F(-4, 0)$ and $l : x = 4 \Rightarrow p = -4$ and $V(0, 0)$. An equation is $(y - 0)^2 = [4(-4)](x - 0)$, or $y^2 = -16x$.

**21** $F(0, -10)$ and $l : y = 10 \Rightarrow p = -10$ and $V(0, 0)$. An equation is $(x - 0)^2 = [4(-10)](y - 0)$, or $x^2 = -40y$.

**22** The general equation of a parabola that is symmetric to the $x$-axis and has its vertex at the origin is $x = ay^2$.

Substituting $x = 5$ and $y = -1$ into that equation yields $a = 5$. An equation is $x = 5y^2$.

**23** Ellipse with $V(0, \pm 10)$ and $F(0, \pm 5) \Rightarrow b^2 = 10^2 - 5^2 = 100 - 25 = 75$.

$$\text{An equation is } \dfrac{x^2}{75} + \dfrac{y^2}{10^2} = 1 \text{ or } \dfrac{x^2}{75} + \dfrac{y^2}{100} = 1.$$

**24** Hyperbola with $F(\pm 10, 0)$ and $V(\pm 5, 0) \Rightarrow b^2 = 10^2 - 5^2 = 100 - 25 = 75$.

$$\text{An equation is } \dfrac{x^2}{5^2} - \dfrac{y^2}{75} = 1 \text{ or } \dfrac{x^2}{25} - \dfrac{y^2}{75} = 1.$$

**25** Hyperbola, with vertices $V(0, \pm 6)$ and asymptotes $y = \pm 9x$ • The equations of the asymptotes are

$y = \pm\dfrac{a}{b}x$ and $a = 6$, so $9 = \dfrac{6}{b} \Rightarrow b = \dfrac{6}{9} = \dfrac{2}{3}$. An equation is $\dfrac{y^2}{6^2} - \dfrac{x^2}{\left(\frac{2}{3}\right)^2} = 1$ or $\dfrac{y^2}{36} - \dfrac{x^2}{\frac{4}{9}} = 1$.

**26** Ellipse with $F(\pm 2, 0) \Rightarrow c^2 = 4$. Now $\dfrac{x^2}{a^2} + \dfrac{y^2}{b^2} = 1$ can be written as $\dfrac{x^2}{a^2} + \dfrac{y^2}{a^2 - 4} = 1$ since $b^2 = a^2 - c^2$.

Substituting $x = 2$ and $y = \sqrt{2}$ into that equation yields $\dfrac{4}{a^2} + \dfrac{2}{a^2 - 4} = 1 \Rightarrow 4a^2 - 16 + 2a^2 = a^4 - 4a^2 \Rightarrow$

$a^4 - 10a^2 + 16 = 0 \Rightarrow (a^2 - 2)(a^2 - 8) = 0 \Rightarrow a^2 = 2, 8$. Since $a > c$, $a^2$ must be 8 and $b^2$ is equal to 4.

$$\text{An equation is } \dfrac{x^2}{8} + \dfrac{y^2}{4} = 1.$$

**27** Ellipse with $M(\pm 5, 0) \;\Rightarrow\; b = 5$. $e = \dfrac{c}{a} = \dfrac{\sqrt{a^2 - b^2}}{a} = \dfrac{\sqrt{a^2 - 25}}{a} = \dfrac{2}{3} \;\Rightarrow\; \frac{2}{3}a = \sqrt{a^2 - 25} \;\Rightarrow\;$

$\frac{4}{9}a^2 = a^2 - 25 \;\Rightarrow\; \frac{5}{9}a^2 = 25 \;\Rightarrow\; a^2 = 45$. An equation is $\dfrac{x^2}{25} + \dfrac{y^2}{45} = 1$.

**28** Ellipse with $F(\pm 12, 0) \;\Rightarrow\; c = 12$. $e = \dfrac{c}{a} = \dfrac{12}{a} = \dfrac{3}{4} \;\Rightarrow\; a = 16$.

$b^2 = a^2 - c^2 = 16^2 - 12^2 = 112$. An equation is $\dfrac{x^2}{256} + \dfrac{y^2}{112} = 1$.

**29** Right half of $(x - 2)^2 = 4(y + 3) \left\{ \substack{Solve \\ for\ x \ge 2} \right\} \;\Rightarrow\; x - 2 = +2\sqrt{y + 3} \;\Rightarrow\; x = 2 + 2\sqrt{y + 3}$

**30** Lower half of $(y + 3)^2 = \frac{1}{4}(x - 5) \left\{ \substack{Solve \\ for\ y \le -3} \right\} \;\Rightarrow\; y + 3 = -\frac{1}{2}\sqrt{x - 5} \;\Rightarrow\; y = -3 - \frac{1}{2}\sqrt{x - 5}$

**31** Left half of $\dfrac{x^2}{25} + \dfrac{y^2}{64} = 1 \left\{ \substack{Solve \\ for\ x \le 0} \right\} \;\Rightarrow\; \dfrac{x^2}{25} = 1 - \dfrac{y^2}{64} \;\Rightarrow\; x^2 = 25\left(\dfrac{64 - y^2}{64}\right) \;\Rightarrow\;$

$x = -\frac{5}{8}\sqrt{64 - y^2}$

**32** Upper half of $x^2 + 4y^2 = 16 \left\{ \substack{Solve \\ for\ y \ge 0} \right\} \;\Rightarrow\; 4y^2 = 16 - x^2 \;\Rightarrow\; y^2 = \frac{1}{4}(16 - x^2) \;\Rightarrow\; y = \frac{1}{2}\sqrt{16 - x^2}$

**33** Right branch of $9x^2 - 4y^2 = 64 \left\{ \substack{Solve \\ for\ x > 0} \right\} \;\Rightarrow\; 9x^2 = 64 + 4y^2 \;\Rightarrow\; x^2 = \frac{4}{9}(16 + y^2) \;\Rightarrow\; x = \frac{2}{3}\sqrt{y^2 + 16}$

**34** Lower branch of $\dfrac{y^2}{16} - \dfrac{x^2}{100} = 1 \left\{ \substack{Solve \\ for\ y < 0} \right\} \;\Rightarrow\; \dfrac{y^2}{16} = 1 + \dfrac{x^2}{100} \;\Rightarrow\; y^2 = 16\left(\dfrac{100 + x^2}{100}\right) \;\Rightarrow\;$

$y = -\frac{2}{5}\sqrt{x^2 + 100}$

**35** (a) Substituting $x = 2$ and $y = -3$ in $Ax^2 + 2y^2 = 4 \;\Rightarrow\; A(2)^2 + 2(-3)^2 = 4 \;\Rightarrow\; A = -\frac{7}{2}$

(b) The equation is $-\dfrac{7}{2}x^2 + 2y^2 = 4 \;\Rightarrow\; -\dfrac{7}{8}x^2 + \dfrac{2}{4}y^2 = 1 \;\Rightarrow\; \dfrac{y^2}{2} - \dfrac{7x^2}{8} = 1$, a hyperbola.

**36** The vertex of the square in the first quadrant has coordinates $(x, x)$. The vertex is on the ellipse, so

$\dfrac{x^2}{a^2} + \dfrac{y^2}{b^2} = 1 \;\Rightarrow\; b^2 x^2 + a^2 x^2 = a^2 b^2 \;\Rightarrow\; x^2 (b^2 + a^2) = a^2 b^2 \;\Rightarrow\; x^2 = \dfrac{a^2 b^2}{a^2 + b^2}$. Since $x^2$ is one-quarter

of the area of the square, the area is $A = \dfrac{4a^2 b^2}{a^2 + b^2}$.

**37** The focus of the parabola $y = \frac{1}{8}x^2$ is a distance of $p = \dfrac{1}{4a} = \dfrac{1}{4 \cdot \frac{1}{8}} = \dfrac{1}{\frac{1}{2}} = 2$ units from the origin.

So the center of the circle is $(0, 2)$ and since the circle passes through the origin, the radius of the circle must be 2.

An equation of the circle is $(x - 0)^2 + (y - 2)^2 = 2^2$, or $x^2 + (y - 2)^2 = 4$.

**38** $y = f(x) = \frac{1}{64}\omega^2 x^2 + k$ can be written in the form $x^2 = 4p(y - k)$ as $x^2 = \dfrac{64}{\omega^2}(y - k)$,

so $4p = \dfrac{64}{\omega^2} \;\Rightarrow\; p = \dfrac{16}{\omega^2}$. Now $p = 2 \;\Rightarrow\; \omega^2 = 8 \;\Rightarrow\; \omega = 2\sqrt{2}$ rad/sec $\approx 0.45$ rev/sec.

**39** Since $a = p + c$, $b^2 = a^2 - c^2 = (p + c)^2 - c^2 = p^2 + 2pc = p(p + 2c)$. Thus, the ellipse has the equation

$\dfrac{[x - (p + c)]^2}{(p + c)^2} + \dfrac{y^2}{p(p + 2c)} = 1 \;\Rightarrow\; y^2 = p(p + 2c)\left[1 - \dfrac{(x - p - c)^2}{(p + c)^2}\right] = \dfrac{p(p + 2c)(2xp + 2xc - x^2)}{(p + c)^2}$.

Consider the expression to be a rational function of $c$ with $4px$ as the coefficient of $c^2$ in the numerator and 1 as the coefficient of $c^2$ in the denominator. Hence, as $c \to \infty$, $y^2 \to 4px$.

**40** With $V(\pm 3, 0)$ and $y = \frac{1}{2}x$, we must have the endpoints of the conjugate axis at $W\left(0, \pm \frac{3}{2}\right)$. The path is a

hyperbola with $V(\pm 3, 0)$ and $W\left(0, \pm \frac{3}{2}\right)$. An equation is $\dfrac{x^2}{(3)^2} - \dfrac{y^2}{\left(\frac{3}{2}\right)^2} = 1$ or equivalently, $x^2 - 4y^2 = 9$. If only

the right branch is considered, then $x = \sqrt{9 + 4y^2}$ is an equation of the path.

**41** $y = t - 1 \;\Rightarrow\; t = y + 1$. $x = 3 + 4t = 3 + 4(y + 1) = 4y + 7$.

As $t$ varies from $-2$ to $2$, $(x, y)$ varies from $(-5, -3)$ to $(11, 1)$.

*Figure 41*

*Figure 42*

**42** $x = \sqrt{-t} \;\Rightarrow\; t = -x^2$. $y = t^2 - 4 = x^4 - 4$.

As $t$ varies from $-\infty$ to $0$, $x$ varies from $\infty$ to $0$ and the graph is the right half of the quartic.

**43** $x = \cos^2 t - 2 \;\Rightarrow\; x + 2 = \cos^2 t$; $y = \sin t + 1 \;\Rightarrow\; (y - 1)^2 = \sin^2 t$.

$\sin^2 t + \cos^2 t = 1 = x + 2 + (y - 1)^2 \;\Rightarrow\; (y - 1)^2 = -(x + 1)$. This is a parabola with vertex at $(-1, 1)$ and

opening to the left. $t = 0$ corresponds to the vertex and as $t$ varies from $0$ to $2\pi$, the point $(x, y)$ moves to $(-2, 2)$

at $t = \frac{\pi}{2}$, back to the vertex at $t = \pi$, down to $(-2, 0)$ at $t = \frac{3\pi}{2}$, and finishes at the vertex at $t = 2\pi$.

*Figure 43*

*Figure 44*

*Figure 45*

**44** $x = \sqrt{t} \;\Rightarrow\; x^2 = t$ and $y = 2^{-x^2}$. The graph is a bell-shaped curve with a maximum point at $t = 0$, or $(0, 1)$.

As $t$ increases, $x$ increases, and $y$ gets close to $0$.

**45** $x = \dfrac{1}{t} + 1 \;\Rightarrow\; x - 1 = \dfrac{1}{t} \;\Rightarrow\; t = \dfrac{1}{x - 1}$ and

$$y = \frac{2}{t} - t = 2(x - 1) - \left(\frac{1}{x - 1}\right) = \frac{2(x^2 - 2x + 1) - 1}{x - 1} = \frac{2x^2 - 4x + 1}{x - 1}.$$

This is a rational function with a vertical asymptote at $x = 1$ and an oblique asymptote of $y = 2x - 2$. The graph

has a minimum point at $\left(\frac{5}{4}, -\frac{7}{2}\right)$ when $t = 4$ and then approaches the oblique asymptote as $t$ approaches $0$.

**46** All of the curves are a portion of the circle $x^2 + y^2 = 16$.

$C_1$: $y = \sqrt{16 - t^2} = \sqrt{16 - x^2}$.

Since $y = \sqrt{16 - t^2}$, $y$ must be nonnegative and we have the top half of the circle.

$C_2$: $x = -\sqrt{16 - t} = -\sqrt{16 - \left(-\sqrt{t}\right)^2}$
$= -\sqrt{16 - y^2}$.

This is the left half of the circle. Since $y = -\sqrt{t}$, $y$ can only be nonpositive. Hence we have only the third quadrant portion of the circle.

$C_3$: $x = 4\cos t$, $y = 4\sin t$ $\Rightarrow$ $\dfrac{x}{4} = \cos t$,

$\dfrac{y}{4} = \sin t$ $\Rightarrow$ $\dfrac{x^2}{16} = \cos^2 t$, $\dfrac{y^2}{16} = \sin^2 t$ $\Rightarrow$

$\dfrac{x^2}{16} + \dfrac{y^2}{16} = \cos^2 t + \sin^2 t = 1$ $\Rightarrow$

$x^2 + y^2 = 16$. This is the entire circle.

$C_4$: $y = -\sqrt{16 - e^{2t}} = -\sqrt{16 - (e^t)^2}$
$= -\sqrt{16 - x^2}$.

This is the bottom half of the circle. Since $e^t$ is positive, $x$ takes on all positive real values.

Note that $(0, -4)$ is *not* included on the graph since $x \neq 0$.

**47** $x = 1024\left(\frac{\sqrt{3}}{2}\right)t$ and $y = -\frac{1}{2}(32)t^2 + 1024\left(\frac{1}{2}\right)t + 5120$ $\Rightarrow$ $x = 512\sqrt{3}\,t$ and $y = -16t^2 + 512t + 5120$.

$y = 0$ $\Rightarrow$ $-16t^2 + 512t + 5120 = 0$ $\Rightarrow$ $t^2 - 32t - 320 = 0$ $\Rightarrow$ $(t - 40)(t + 8) = 0$ $\Rightarrow$
$\qquad t = 40$ seconds. $x = 512\sqrt{3}(40) = 20{,}480\sqrt{3} \approx 35{,}472.40$ feet.

$y = 5120$ $\Rightarrow$ $-16t^2 + 512t + 5120 = 5120$ $\Rightarrow$ $-16t^2 + 512t = 0$ $\Rightarrow$ $-16t(t - 32) = 0$ $\Rightarrow$
$t = 0, 32$. The maximum altitude occurs when $t = \frac{1}{2}(32) = 16$ and has value
$$y = -16(16)^2 + 512(16) + 5120 = 9216 \text{ feet.}$$

**48** Two polar coordinate points that represent the same point as $\left(2, \frac{\pi}{4}\right)$ are $\left(-2, \frac{5\pi}{4}\right)$ {negative $r$ and opposite direction} and $\left(2, \frac{9\pi}{4}\right)$ {same $r$ with $\theta$ increased by $2\pi$}.

**49** $x = r\cos\theta = 5\cos\frac{7\pi}{4} = 5\left(\frac{\sqrt{2}}{2}\right) = \frac{5}{2}\sqrt{2}$. $y = r\sin\theta = 5\sin\frac{7\pi}{4} = 5\left(-\frac{\sqrt{2}}{2}\right) = -\frac{5}{2}\sqrt{2}$. $\left(\frac{5}{2}\sqrt{2}, -\frac{5}{2}\sqrt{2}\right)$

**50** $r^2 = x^2 + y^2 = \left(2\sqrt{3}\right)^2 + (-2)^2 = 16$ $\Rightarrow$ $r = 4$. $\tan\theta = \frac{y}{x} = \frac{-2}{2\sqrt{3}} = -\frac{1}{\sqrt{3}}$ $\Rightarrow$ $\theta = \frac{11\pi}{6}$ {$\theta$ in QIV}.

**51** $y^2 = 4x$ $\Rightarrow$ $r^2\sin^2\theta = 4r\cos\theta$ $\Rightarrow$ $r = \dfrac{4r\cos\theta}{r\sin^2\theta} = 4 \cdot \dfrac{\cos\theta}{\sin\theta} \cdot \dfrac{1}{\sin\theta}$ $\Rightarrow$ $r = 4\cot\theta\csc\theta$.

**52** $x^2 + y^2 - 3x + 4y = 0 \Rightarrow r^2 - 3r\cos\theta + 4r\sin\theta = 0 \Rightarrow r - 3\cos\theta + 4\sin\theta = 0 \Rightarrow$

$$r = 3\cos\theta - 4\sin\theta.$$

**53** $2x - 3y = 8 \Rightarrow 2r\cos\theta - 3r\sin\theta = 8 \Rightarrow r(2\cos\theta - 3\sin\theta) = 8.$

**54** $x^2 + y^2 = 2xy \Rightarrow r^2 = 2r^2\cos\theta\sin\theta \Rightarrow 1 = 2\sin\theta\cos\theta \Rightarrow \sin 2\theta = 1 \Rightarrow$

$$2\theta = \tfrac{\pi}{2} + 2\pi n \Rightarrow \theta = \tfrac{\pi}{4}, \tfrac{5\pi}{4} \text{ on } [0, 2\pi), \text{ which are the same lines.}$$

In rectangular coordinates:

$$x^2 + y^2 = 2xy \Rightarrow x^2 - 2xy + y^2 = 0 \Rightarrow (x - y)^2 = 0 \Rightarrow x - y = 0, \text{ or } y = x.$$

**55** $r^2 = \tan\theta \Rightarrow x^2 + y^2 = \dfrac{y}{x} \Rightarrow x^3 + xy^2 = y.$

**56** $r = 2\cos\theta + 3\sin\theta \Rightarrow r^2 = 2r\cos\theta + 3r\sin\theta \Rightarrow x^2 + y^2 = 2x + 3y.$

**57** $r^2 = 4\sin 2\theta \Rightarrow r^2 = 4(2\sin\theta\cos\theta) \Rightarrow r^2 = 8\sin\theta\cos\theta \Rightarrow r^2 \cdot r^2 = 8(r\sin\theta)(r\cos\theta) \Rightarrow$

$$\left(x^2 + y^2\right)^2 = 8xy.$$

**58** $\theta = \sqrt{3} \Rightarrow \tan^{-1}\left(\dfrac{y}{x}\right) = \sqrt{3} \Rightarrow \dfrac{y}{x} = \tan\sqrt{3} \Rightarrow y = \left(\tan\sqrt{3}\right)x.$

Note that $\tan\sqrt{3} \approx -6.15$. This is a line through the origin making an angle of

approximately $99.24°$ with the positive $x$-axis. The line is *not* $y = \tfrac{\pi}{3}x$.

**59** $r = 5\sec\theta + 3r\sec\theta \Rightarrow r\cos\theta = 5 + 3r \Rightarrow x - 5 = 3r \Rightarrow x^2 - 10x + 25 = 9r^2 \Rightarrow$

$$x^2 - 10x + 25 = 9x^2 + 9y^2 \Rightarrow 8x^2 + 9y^2 + 10x - 25 = 0$$

**60** $r^2\sin\theta = 6\csc\theta + r\cot\theta \Rightarrow r^2\sin^2\theta = 6 + r\cos\theta \text{ \{multiply by } \sin\theta \text{ to get } r^2\sin^2\theta\} \Rightarrow y^2 = 6 + x$

**61** $r = -4\sin\theta \Rightarrow r^2 = -4r\sin\theta \Rightarrow x^2 + y^2 = -4y \Rightarrow x^2 + y^2 + 4y + \underline{4} = \underline{4} \Rightarrow$

$$x^2 + (y + 2)^2 = 4.$$

Figure 61

Figure 62

Figure 63

**62** $r = 8\sec\theta \Rightarrow r\cos\theta = 8 \Rightarrow x = 8.$

**63** $r = 3\sin 5\theta$ is a 5-leafed rose. $0 = 3\sin 5\theta \Rightarrow \sin 5\theta = 0 \Rightarrow 5\theta = \pi n \Rightarrow \theta = \tfrac{\pi}{5}n.$

The numbers 1–10 correspond to $\theta$ ranging from 0 to $\pi$ in $\tfrac{\pi}{10}$ increments.

One leaf is centered on the line $\theta = \tfrac{\pi}{2}$ and the others are equally spaced apart $\left(\tfrac{360°}{5} = 72°\right)$.

**64** $r = 6 - 3\cos\theta$ • $0 = 6 - 3\cos\theta \Rightarrow \cos\theta = 2 \Rightarrow$ no pole values.

| | Variation of $\theta$ | Variation of $r$ |
|---|---|---|
| 1) | $0 \to \frac{\pi}{2}$ | $3 \to 6$ |
| 2) | $\frac{\pi}{2} \to \pi$ | $6 \to 9$ |
| 3) | $\pi \to \frac{3\pi}{2}$ | $9 \to 6$ |
| 4) | $\frac{3\pi}{2} \to 2\pi$ | $6 \to 3$ |

**65** $r = 3 - 3\sin\theta$ is a cardioid since the coefficient of $\sin\theta$ has the same

magnitude as the constant term.

$0 = 3 - 3\sin\theta \Rightarrow \sin\theta = 1 \Rightarrow \theta = \frac{\pi}{2} + 2\pi n$.

| | Variation of $\theta$ | Variation of $r$ |
|---|---|---|
| 1) | $0 \to \frac{\pi}{2}$ | $3 \to 0$ |
| 2) | $\frac{\pi}{2} \to \pi$ | $0 \to 3$ |
| 3) | $\pi \to \frac{3\pi}{2}$ | $3 \to 6$ |
| 4) | $\frac{3\pi}{2} \to 2\pi$ | $6 \to 3$ |

**66** $r = 2 + 4\cos\theta$ is a limaçon with a loop.

$0 = 2 + 4\cos\theta \Rightarrow \cos\theta = -\frac{1}{2} \Rightarrow \theta = \frac{2\pi}{3} + 2\pi n, \frac{4\pi}{3} + 2\pi n$.

| | Variation of $\theta$ | Variation of $r$ |
|---|---|---|
| 1) | $0 \to \frac{\pi}{2}$ | $6 \to 2$ |
| 2) | $\frac{\pi}{2} \to \frac{2\pi}{3}$ | $2 \to 0$ |
| 3) | $\frac{2\pi}{3} \to \pi$ | $0 \to -2$ |
| 4) | $\pi \to \frac{4\pi}{3}$ | $-2 \to 0$ |
| 5) | $\frac{4\pi}{3} \to \frac{3\pi}{2}$ | $0 \to 2$ |
| 4) | $\frac{3\pi}{2} \to 2\pi$ | $2 \to 6$ |

**67** $r^2 = 9\sin 2\theta$ • $0 = 9\sin 2\theta \Rightarrow \sin 2\theta = 0 \Rightarrow 2\theta = \pi n \Rightarrow$
$\theta = \frac{\pi}{2}n$.

| | Variation of $\theta$ | Variation of $r$ |
|---|---|---|
| 1) | $0 \to \frac{\pi}{4}$ | $0 \to \pm 3$ |
| 2) | $\frac{\pi}{4} \to \frac{\pi}{2}$ | $\pm 3 \to 0$ |
| 3) | $\frac{\pi}{2} \to \frac{3\pi}{4}$ | undefined |
| 4) | $\frac{3\pi}{4} \to \pi$ | undefined |

**68** $2r = \theta \Rightarrow r = \frac{1}{2}\theta$. Positive values of $\theta$ yield the "counterclockwise spiral" while the "clockwise spiral" is obtained from the negative values of $\theta$.

| Figure 68 | Figure 69 | Figure 70 |

**69** $r = \dfrac{8}{1 - 3\sin\theta} \Rightarrow e = 3 > 1$, hyperbola. See §10.6 for more details on this problem.

$$V\left(2, \tfrac{3\pi}{2}\right) \text{ and } V'\left(-4, \tfrac{\pi}{2}\right). \quad d(V, F) = 2 \Rightarrow F'\left(-6, \tfrac{\pi}{2}\right).$$

**70** $r = 6 - r\cos\theta \Rightarrow r + r\cos\theta = 6 \Rightarrow r(1 + \cos\theta) = 6 \Rightarrow r = \dfrac{6}{1 + 1\cos\theta} \Rightarrow e = 1$, parabola.

$$\text{The vertex is in the } \theta = 0 \text{ direction. It is } V(3, 0).$$

**71** $r = \dfrac{6}{3 + 2\cos\theta} = \dfrac{2}{1 + \frac{2}{3}\cos\theta} \Rightarrow e = \frac{2}{3} < 1$, ellipse.

$$V\left(\tfrac{6}{5}, 0\right) \text{ and } V'(6, \pi). \quad d(V, F) = \tfrac{6}{5} \Rightarrow F' = \left(\tfrac{24}{5}, \pi\right).$$

| Figure 71 | Figure 72 |

**72** $r = \dfrac{-6\csc\theta}{1 - 2\csc\theta} \cdot \dfrac{-\sin\theta}{-\sin\theta} = \dfrac{6}{2 - \sin\theta} = \dfrac{3}{1 - \frac{1}{2}\sin\theta} \Rightarrow e = \frac{1}{2} < 1$, ellipse.

$V\left(2, \tfrac{3\pi}{2}\right)$ and $V'\left(6, \tfrac{\pi}{2}\right)$. $d(V, F) = 2 \Rightarrow F' = \left(4, \tfrac{\pi}{2}\right)$. Since the original equation is undefined when $\csc\theta$ is undefined, the points $(3, 0)$ and $(3, \pi)$ are excluded from the graph.

## Chapter 10 Discussion Exercises

**1** For $y = ax^2$, the horizontal line through the focus is $y = p$. Since $a = \dfrac{1}{4p}$, we have $p = \dfrac{1}{4p}x^2 \Rightarrow$

$x^2 = 4p^2 \Rightarrow x = 2|p|$. Doubling this value for the width gives us $w = 4|p|$.

**2** The circle goes through both foci and all four vertices of the auxiliary rectangle.

**3** Refer to Figure 2 and the derivation on page 726 of the text.

**4** Refer to Figure 1 and the derivation on page 738 of the text.

**5** $P(x, y)$ is a distance of $(2 + d)$ from $(0, 0)$ and a distance of $d$ from $(4, 0)$. The difference of these distances is $(2 + d) - d = 2$, a *positive constant*. By the definition of a hyperbola, $P(x, y)$ lies on the right branch of the hyperbola with foci $(0, 0)$ and $(4, 0)$. The center of the hyperbola is halfway between the foci, that is, $(2, 0)$. The vertex is halfway from $(2, 0)$ to $(4, 0)$ since the distance from the circle to $P$ equals the distance from $P$ to $(4, 0)$.

Thus, the vertex is $(3, 0)$ and $a = 1$. $b^2 = c^2 - a^2 = 2^2 - 1^2 = 3$ and an equation of the right branch of the hyperbola is $\dfrac{(x - 2)^2}{1} - \dfrac{y^2}{3} = 1$, $x \geq 3$

or $x = 2 + \sqrt{1 + \dfrac{y^2}{3}}$.

**6** $y = \dfrac{a}{b}\sqrt{x^2 + b^2} \;\Rightarrow\; y^2 = \dfrac{a^2}{b^2}(x^2 + b^2) \;\Rightarrow\; b^2 y^2 = a^2 x^2 + a^2 b^2 \;\Rightarrow\; b^2 y^2 - a^2 x^2 = a^2 b^2 \;\Rightarrow\;$
$\dfrac{b^2 y^2}{a^2 b^2} - \dfrac{a^2 x^2}{a^2 b^2} = 1 \;\Rightarrow\; \dfrac{y^2}{a^2} - \dfrac{x^2}{b^2} = 1$. This is an equation of a hyperbola with one focus at $c = \sqrt{a^2 + b^2}$.
The equation of the parabola is $y = dx^2$, so its focus is at $p = 1/(4d)$ and we have

$$d = \frac{1}{4p} = \frac{1}{4\sqrt{a^2 + b^2}} \quad \{\text{since } p = c\}.$$

**7** Solve $y = -16t^2 + 1024(\sin\alpha)t + 2304$ for $t$ when $y = 0$. This gives $t_1 = 32\sin\alpha + 4\sqrt{64\sin^2\alpha + 9}$. The range $r$ is given by $r = 1024(\cos\alpha)t_1$. Table $r$ as a function of $\alpha$ to find that the maximum value of $r$ occurs when

$$\alpha \approx 0.752528 \text{ radians, or about } 43.12°.$$

**8** (a) The projectile strikes the ground when $y = 0 \;\Rightarrow\; -\frac{1}{2}gt^2 + (s\sin\alpha)t = 0 \;\Rightarrow\;$
$t\left(-\frac{1}{2}gt + s\sin\alpha\right) = 0 \;\Rightarrow\; t = 0$ or $-\frac{1}{2}gt + s\sin\alpha = 0$, which gives us $t = \dfrac{2s\sin\alpha}{g}$.

(b) Use the answer from part (a) to get $x = (s\cos\alpha)t = (s\cos\alpha)\dfrac{2s\sin\alpha}{g} = \dfrac{s^2(2\cos\alpha\sin\alpha)}{g}$, so $r = \dfrac{s^2\sin 2\alpha}{g}$.

(c) From part (b), $r = \dfrac{s^2\sin 2\alpha}{g}$ is a maximum when $\sin 2\alpha$ is a maximum; that is, when $\sin 2\alpha = 1 \;\Rightarrow\;$

$$2\alpha = 90° \;\Rightarrow\; \alpha = 45°.$$

(d) $x = (s\cos\alpha)t \;\Rightarrow\; t = \dfrac{x}{s\cos\alpha}$, so $y = -\dfrac{1}{2}g\left(\dfrac{x}{s\cos\alpha}\right)^2 + (s\sin\alpha)\left(\dfrac{x}{s\cos\alpha}\right)$, or

$$y = -\frac{g}{2s^2\cos^2\alpha}x^2 + (\tan\alpha)x.$$

(e) The time at which the maximum height is reached is one-half the time needed for the range; that is, one-half of the answer in part (a). So $t = \dfrac{1}{2}\left(\dfrac{2s\sin\alpha}{g}\right) = \dfrac{s\sin\alpha}{g}$.

(f) Substitute the answer from part (e) for $t$ in

$$y = -\frac{1}{2}gt^2 + (s\sin\alpha)t = -\frac{1}{2}g\left(\frac{s\sin\alpha}{g}\right)^2 + (s\sin\alpha)\left(\frac{s\sin\alpha}{g}\right) = -\frac{1}{2}g\left(\frac{s^2\sin^2\alpha}{g^2}\right) + \frac{s^2\sin^2\alpha}{g}$$

$$= -\frac{1}{2}\left(\frac{s^2\sin^2\alpha}{g}\right) + \frac{s^2\sin^2\alpha}{g} = \frac{s^2\sin^2\alpha}{2g}.$$

| | | |
|---|---|---|
| **9** | $x = \sin 2t$ | {given} |
| | $x = 2\sin t \cos t$ | {double-angle formula} |
| | $x^2 = 4\sin^2 t \cos^2 t$ | {square both sides} |
| | $x^2 = 4(1 - \cos^2 t)\cos^2 t$ | {Pythagorean identity} |
| | $x^2 = 4(1 - y^2)y^2$ | {$y = \cos t$} |
| | $4y^4 - 4y^2 + x^2 = 0$ | {equivalent equation} |
| | $y^2 = \dfrac{4 \pm \sqrt{16 - 16x^2}}{8}$ | {use the quadratic formula to solve for $y^2$} |
| | $y^2 = \dfrac{1 \pm \sqrt{1 - x^2}}{2}$ | {simplify} |
| | $y = \pm\sqrt{\dfrac{1 \pm \sqrt{1 - x^2}}{2}}$ | {take square roots} |

These complicated equations should indicate the advantage of expressing the curve in parametric form.

**10** The graph of $r = f(\theta - \alpha)$ is the graph of $r = f(\theta)$ rotated counterclockwise through an angle $\alpha$, whereas the graph $r = f(\theta + \alpha)$ is rotated clockwise.

**11** $n$ **even:** There are $2n$ leaves, each having a leaf angle of $(180/n)°$. There is no open space between the leaves.

$n$ **odd:** There are $n$ leaves, each having a leaf angle of $(180/n)°$. There is 180° of open space—each space is $(180/n)°$, equispaced between the leaves. If $n = 4k - 1$, where $k$ is a natural number, there is a leaf centered on the $\theta = 3\pi/2$ axis; and if $n = 4k + 1$, there is a leaf centered on the $\theta = \frac{\pi}{2}$ axis.

For $r = \sin n\theta$, the pole values start at 0° and occur every $(180/n)°$. For $r = \cos n\theta$, the pole values start at $(90/n)°$ and occur every $(180/n)°$.

**12** $r = 4\sin\theta$ and $r = 4\cos\theta$ $\Rightarrow$ $\sin\theta = \cos\theta$ $\Rightarrow$ $\dfrac{\sin\theta}{\cos\theta} = \tan\theta = 1$ $\Rightarrow$ $\theta = \frac{\pi}{4} + \pi n$.

So this gives us the solution $\theta = \frac{\pi}{4}$, but not the solution at the pole. Changing to rectangular equations, we have $r = 4\sin\theta$ $\Rightarrow$ $r^2 = 4r\sin\theta$ $\Rightarrow$ $x^2 + y^2 = 4y$ $\Rightarrow$ $x^2 + y^2 - 4y = 0$ $\Rightarrow$ $x^2 + y^2 - 4y + 4 = 4$ $\Rightarrow$ $x^2 + (y - 2)^2 = 4$ and similarly, $r = 4\cos\theta$ $\Leftrightarrow$ $(x - 2)^2 + y^2 = 4$. Solving for $y$ we get $y = 2 \pm \sqrt{4 - x^2}$ and $y = \pm\sqrt{4 - (x - 2)^2}$. Referring to Figure 17 in Section 10.5 of the text, we'll determine the values of $x$ and $y$ for which the lower semicircle {in red} intersects the upper semicircle {in blue}.

| | |
|---|---|
| $2 - \sqrt{4 - x^2} = \sqrt{4 - (x - 2)^2}$ | {lower red = upper blue} |
| $4 - 4\sqrt{4 - x^2} + 4 - x^2 = 4 - (x - 2)^2$ | {square both sides} |
| $4 - 4\sqrt{4 - x^2} + 4 - x^2 = 4 - (x^2 - 4x + 4)$ | {expand} |
| $8 - 4x = 4\sqrt{4 - x^2}$ | {simplify} |
| $2 - x = \sqrt{4 - x^2}$ | {divide by 4} |
| $4 - 4x + x^2 = 4 - x^2$ | {square both sides} |
| $2x^2 - 4x = 0$ | {set one side equal to zero} |
| $2x(x - 2) = 0$ | {factor} |
| $2x = 0, \quad x - 2 = 0$ | {set each factor equal to 0} |
| $x = 0, \quad\quad x = 2$ | {solve for $x$} |

Substituting 0 and 2 for $x$ in $y = 2 - \sqrt{4 - x^2}$ gives us $y = 0$ and $y = 2$; that is, the points $(0, 0)$ and $(2, 2)$, as expected. The point $(x, y) = (2, 2)$ corresponds to $(r, \theta) = \left(2\sqrt{2}, \frac{\pi}{4}\right)$ on both graphs. The point $(x, y) = (0, 0)$ corresponds to $(r, \theta) = (0, 0)$ on $r = 4\sin\theta$, but it corresponds to $(r, \theta) = \left(0, \frac{\pi}{2}\right)$ on $r = 4\cos\theta$, and that's why the answer to the first system did not reveal the solution at the pole. Graph the polar equations in simultaneous mode to see the *collision point* (same values of $r$ and $\theta$) at $\left(2\sqrt{2}, \frac{\pi}{4}\right)$.

## Chapter 10 Test

**1**   $(x+3)^2 = -6(y-2) \;\Rightarrow\; 4p = -6 \;\Rightarrow\; p = -\frac{3}{2};$
    $V(-3,2);\; F(-3, \frac{1}{2});\; l:\, y = \frac{7}{2}$

**2**   $V(5,-1) \;\Rightarrow\; (y+1)^2 = 4p(x-5).\; x = 0,\, y = -3 \;\Rightarrow\; 4 = 4p(-5) \;\Rightarrow\; p = -\frac{1}{5}.$
$$(y+1)^2 = -\tfrac{4}{5}(x-5).$$

**3**   $V(-2,1)$ and $l:\, y = 0$ {the $x$-axis} $\;\Rightarrow\; p = 1.\; (x+2)^2 = 4p(y-1) \;\Rightarrow\; (x+2)^2 = 4(y-1).$

**4**   $(y-4)^2 = x+2 \;\Rightarrow\; y - 4 = \pm\sqrt{x+2} \;\Rightarrow\; y = -\sqrt{x+2} + 4$ {choose $-$ for *lower* half}

**5**   The parabola has an equation of the form $x = ay^2 + by + c$. Substituting the $x$ and $y$ values of

$P(4,1)$, $Q(5,2)$, and $R(8,-1)$ into this equation yields: $\begin{cases} a + b + c = 4 & P & (E_1) \\ 4a + 2b + c = 5 & Q & (E_2) \\ a - b + c = 8 & R & (E_3) \end{cases}$

    Solving $E_3$ for $c$, $c = 8 - a + b$, and substituting into $E_1$ and $E_2$ yields: $\begin{cases} 2b = -4 & (E_4) \\ 3a + 3b = -3 & (E_5) \end{cases}$

$E_4 \;\Rightarrow\; b = -2;\; a = 1;\; c = 5.$ The equation is $x = y^2 - 2y + 5.$

**6**   $y = ax^2 \;\Rightarrow\; 7 = a\left(\frac{40}{2}\right)^2 \;\Rightarrow\; a = \frac{7}{400}.\; p = 1/(4a) = 1/\left(\frac{7}{100}\right) = \frac{100}{7}$ inches from the center of the paraboloid.

**7**   $\dfrac{(x-1)^2}{36} + \dfrac{y^2}{9} = 1 \;\bullet\; c^2 = 36 - 9 \;\Rightarrow\; c = \pm\sqrt{27} \approx 5.2;$
    $C(1,0);\; V(1\pm6, 0);\; F(1\pm\sqrt{27}, 0);\; M(1, 0\pm3)$

**8**   Ellipse with $V(\pm9, 0)$ and $F(\pm3, 0) \;\Rightarrow\; b^2 = 9^2 - 3^2 = 81 - 9 = 72.$

An equation is $\dfrac{x^2}{9^2} + \dfrac{y^2}{72} = 1$ or $\dfrac{x^2}{81} + \dfrac{y^2}{72} = 1.$

**9**   Ellipse with $V(\pm7, 0)$ and minor axis length 8 $\;\bullet\; c^2 = a^2 - b^2 = 7^2 - \left(\frac{1}{2}\cdot 8\right)^2 = 49 - 16 = 33 \;\Rightarrow\; c = \sqrt{33}.$
The eccentricity of the ellipse is $e = \frac{c}{a} = \frac{\sqrt{33}}{7}.$

**10**   $k = 2a = 20 \;\Rightarrow\; a = 10.\; F(5,0)$ and $F'(-5,0) \;\Rightarrow\; c = 5.\; b^2 = a^2 - c^2 = 10^2 - 5^2 = 75.$

An equation is $\dfrac{x^2}{100} + \dfrac{y^2}{75} = 1.$

**11** Left half of $\dfrac{x^2}{64} + \dfrac{y^2}{16} = 1 \left\{ \begin{array}{c} Solve \\ for\ x \le 0 \end{array} \right\} \Rightarrow \dfrac{x^2}{64} = 1 - \dfrac{y^2}{16} \Rightarrow \dfrac{x^2}{64} = \dfrac{16 - y^2}{16} \Rightarrow$

$$x^2 = \dfrac{64}{16}(16 - y^2) \Rightarrow x = -2\sqrt{16 - y^2}$$

**12** Model this problem as an ellipse with $V(\pm 20, 0)$ and $M(0, \pm 12)$. Substituting $x = 8$ into

$$\dfrac{x^2}{20^2} + \dfrac{y^2}{12^2} = 1 \text{ yields } \dfrac{y^2}{144} = \dfrac{336}{400} \Rightarrow y^2 = \dfrac{3024}{25}. \text{ The desired height is } \sqrt{\dfrac{3024}{25}} \approx 11.0 \text{ ft.}$$

**13** $9y^2 - 4x^2 = 36 \Rightarrow \dfrac{y^2}{4} - \dfrac{x^2}{9} = 1;$

$c^2 = 4 + 9 \Rightarrow c = \pm\sqrt{13} \approx 3.6;$

$V(0, \pm 2); F(0, \pm\sqrt{13}); W(\pm 3, 0); y = \pm\frac{2}{3}x$

**14** Hyperbola with $V(\pm 4, 0)$ and $F(\pm 9, 0) \Rightarrow c^2 = a^2 + b^2 \Rightarrow 9^2 = 4^2 + b^2 \Rightarrow b^2 = 81 - 16 = 65.$

An equation of the hyperbola is $\dfrac{x^2}{16} - \dfrac{y^2}{65} = 1$, and equations of the asymptotes are $y = \pm\dfrac{\sqrt{65}}{4}x.$

**15** Conjugate axis of length 6 and $F(\pm 7, 0) \Rightarrow W(0, \pm 3)$ and $V(\pm\sqrt{40}, 0)$. An equation is $\dfrac{x^2}{40} - \dfrac{y^2}{9} = 1.$

**16** $\dfrac{x^2}{121} - \dfrac{y^2}{49} = 1 \Rightarrow \dfrac{x^2}{121} = 1 + \dfrac{y^2}{49} \Rightarrow x^2 = \dfrac{121}{49}(49 + y^2),$

so an equation for the left branch of the hyperbola is $x = -\frac{11}{7}\sqrt{49 + y^2}.$

**17** $x = 2\cos t + 3, y = 5\sin t; 0 \le t \le 2\pi \Rightarrow \dfrac{x - 3}{2} = \cos t$ and $\dfrac{y}{5} = \sin t \Rightarrow$

$\dfrac{(x-3)^2}{2^2} + \dfrac{y^2}{5^2} = \cos^2 t + \sin^2 t \Rightarrow \dfrac{(x-3)^2}{4} + \dfrac{y^2}{25} = 1.$ This is an ellipse with center $(3, 0)$, horizontal minor

axis of length $2(2) = 4$, and vertical major axis of length $2(5) = 10$. As $t$ varies from 0 to $2\pi$, $(x, y)$ traces the

ellipse from $(5, 0)$ in a counterclockwise direction back to $(5, 0)$.

**18** $y = 3t + 5 \Rightarrow t = \frac{1}{3}(y - 5).$

$x = 9\left[\frac{1}{3}(y-5)\right]^2 + 3 \Rightarrow (y - 5)^2 = x - 3.$

This is a horizontal parabola with vertex at $(3, 5)$.

Since $t$ takes on all real values, so does $y$,

and the curve $C$ is the entire parabola.

**19** $y^2 - x^2 = 4 \Rightarrow y = \pm\sqrt{x^2 + 4}$, so $y = -\sqrt{x^2 + 4}$ is an equation for the bottom branch of the hyperbola.

A parametrization is $x = t, y = -\sqrt{t^2 + 4}; t$ in $\mathbb{R}.$

**20** $x = 4 + 3\sin t, y = -1 + 3\cos t; 0 \le t \le \pi/2.$ $(x - 4)^2 = 9\sin^2 t, (y + 1)^2 = 9\cos^2 t \Rightarrow$

$(x - 4)^2 + (y + 1)^2 = 9\sin^2 t + 9\cos^2 t \Rightarrow (x - 4)^2 + (y + 1)^2 = 9(\sin^2 t + \cos^2 t) \Rightarrow$

$(x - 4)^2 + (y + 1)^2 = 9.$ This represents a circle with center $(4, -1)$ and radius $\sqrt{9} = 3.$ As $t$ varies from

0 to $\pi/2$, $(x, y)$ traces the circle from $(4, 2)$ in a clockwise direction to $(7, -1)$, so the curve $C$ is a quarter-circle.

**21** We use $x(t) = (s \cos \alpha)t$ and $y(t) = -\frac{1}{2}gt^2 + (s \sin \alpha)t + h$ with $s = 544$, $\alpha = 30°$, and $h = 960$:

$x = 544(\sqrt{3}/2)t$ and $y = -\frac{1}{2}(32)t^2 + 544(\frac{1}{2})t + 960$ $\Rightarrow$ $x = 272\sqrt{3}t$ and $y = -16t^2 + 272t + 960$.

To find the range, we let $y = 0$ $\Rightarrow$ $-16t^2 + 272t + 960 = 0$ $\Rightarrow$ $t^2 - 17t - 60 = 0$ { divide by $-16$ } $\Rightarrow$

$(t - 20)(t + 3) = 0$ $\Rightarrow$ $t = 20$ seconds, and then substitute 20 for $t$ in the equation for $x$.

$$x = 272\sqrt{3}\,(20) = 5440\sqrt{3} \approx 9422.4 \text{ feet.}$$

**22** $r^2 = (2\sqrt{3})^2 + (-2)^2 = 16$ $\Rightarrow$ $r = \pm 4$. $\tan\theta = \frac{-2}{2\sqrt{3}} = -\frac{1}{\sqrt{3}}$ $\Rightarrow$ $\theta = \frac{11\pi}{6}$ { $\theta$ in QIV }.

To have $r < 0$, we can use $\theta = \frac{11\pi}{6} - \pi = \frac{5\pi}{6}$, and use the coordinates $(-4, \frac{5\pi}{6})$ to satisfy the requirements.

**23** $x^2 - y^2 = 7$ $\Rightarrow$ $r^2\cos^2\theta - r^2\sin^2\theta = 7$ $\Rightarrow$ $r^2(\cos^2\theta - \sin^2\theta) = 7$ $\Rightarrow$ $r^2\cos 2\theta = 7$ $\Rightarrow$

$$r^2 = \frac{7}{\cos 2\theta} \quad \Rightarrow \quad r^2 = 7\sec 2\theta$$

**24** $r - 4\sin\theta = 0$ $\Rightarrow$ $r^2 = 4r\sin\theta$ $\Rightarrow$ $x^2 + y^2 = 4y$ $\Rightarrow$ $x^2 + y^2 - 4y + \underline{4} = \underline{4}$ $\Rightarrow$

$$x^2 + (y-2)^2 = 4.$$

**25** $r = \sqrt{3} - 2\cos\theta$ is a limaçon with a loop.

$0 = \sqrt{3} - 2\cos\theta$ $\Rightarrow$ $\cos\theta = \sqrt{3}/2$ $\Rightarrow$

$\theta = \frac{\pi}{6} + 2\pi n, \frac{11\pi}{6} + 2\pi n$.

The pole values are $\frac{\pi}{6}$ and $\frac{11\pi}{6}$ for $0 \le \theta \le 2\pi$.

**26** $r = 5\sin 2\theta$ is a 4-leafed rose. $0 = 5\sin 2\theta$ $\Rightarrow$

$\sin 2\theta = 0$ $\Rightarrow$ $2\theta = \pi n$ $\Rightarrow$ $\theta = \frac{\pi}{2}n$.

The pole values are $0, \frac{\pi}{2}, \pi, \frac{3\pi}{2}$, and $2\pi$.

**27** $r = \dfrac{8}{4 - 6\cos\theta} = \dfrac{2}{1 - \frac{3}{2}\cos\theta}$ $\Rightarrow$

$e = \frac{3}{2} > 1$, hyperbola. $V(\frac{4}{5}, \pi)$ and $V'(-4, 0)$.

$d(V, F) = \frac{4}{5}$ $\Rightarrow$ $F' = (-\frac{24}{5}, 0)$.

**28** $r = \dfrac{8}{4 - 6\cos\theta}$ $\Rightarrow$ $4r - 6x = 8$ $\Rightarrow$ $4r = 6x + 8$ $\Rightarrow$ $16r^2 = 36x^2 + 96x + 64$ $\Rightarrow$

$$16(x^2 + y^2) = 36x^2 + 96x + 64 \quad \Rightarrow \quad 16y^2 = 20x^2 + 96x + 64.$$

**29** $r = 4\sec\theta$ $\Rightarrow$ $r\cos\theta = 4$ $\Rightarrow$ $x = 4$. Thus, $d = 4$ and since the directrix is on the right of the focus at the

pole, we use "$+\cos\theta$". $r = \dfrac{4(\frac{1}{2})}{1 + \frac{1}{2}\cos\theta} \cdot \dfrac{2}{2} = \dfrac{4}{2 + \cos\theta}$.